PRESCHOOL PERIOD (3 to 6 years)	MIDDLE CHILDHOOD (6 to 12 years)	

PRESCHOOL PERIOD (3 to 6 years)

- Height and weight continue to increase rapidly.
- The body becomes less rounded, more muscular.
- The brain grows larger, neural interconnections continue to develop, and lateralization emerges.
- Gross and fine motor skills advance quickly. Children can throw and catch balls, run, use forks and spoons, and tie shoelaces.
- Children begin to develop handedness.

MIDDLE CHILDHOOD (6 to 12 years)

- Growth becomes slow and steady. Muscles develop, and "baby fat" is lost.
- Gross motor skills (biking, swimming, skating, ball handling) and fine motor skills (writing, typing, fastening buttons) continue to improve.

- Children show egocentric thinking (viewing world from their own perspective) and "centration," a focus on only one aspect of a stimulus.
- Memory, attention span, and symbolic thinking improve, and intuitive thought begins.
- Language (sentence length, vocabulary, syntax, and grammar) improves rapidly.

- Children apply logical operations to problems.
- Understanding of conservation (that changes in shape do not necessarily affect quantity) and transformation (that objects can go through many states without changing) emerge.
- Children can "decenter"—take multiple perspectives into account.
- Memory encoding, storage, and retrieval improve, and control strategies (meta-memory) develop.
- Language pragmatics (social conventions) and metalinguistic awareness (self-monitoring) improve.

- Children develop self-concepts, which may be exaggerated.
- A sense of gender and racial identity emerges.
- Children begin to see peers as individuals and form friendships based on trust and shared interests.
- Morality is rule-based and focused on rewards and punishments.
- Play becomes more constructive and cooperative, and social skills become important.

- Children refer to psychological traits to define themselves. Sense of self becomes differentiated.
- Social comparison is used to understand one's standing and identity.
- Self-esteem grows differentiated, and a sense of self-efficacy (an appraisal of what one can and cannot do) develops.
- Children approach moral problems intent on maintaining social respect and accepting what society defines as right.
- Friendship patterns of boys and girls differ. Boys mostly interact with boys in groups, and girls tend to interact singly or in pairs with other girls.

Preoperational stage	Concrete operational stage	
Initiative-versus-guilt stage	Industry-versus-inferiority stage	
Phallic stage	Latency period	
Preconventional morality level	Conventional morality level	

Development Across the Life Span

FIFTH EDITION

ROBERT S. FELDMAN
University of Massachusetts at Amherst

PEARSON

Prentice
Hall

Upper Saddle River, NJ 07458

Library of Congress Cataloging-in-Publication Data

Feldman, Robert S. (Robert Stephen)

   Development across the life span / Robert S. Feldman.— 5th ed.

     p. cm.

Includes bibliographical references and index.

ISBN 0-13-601610-3

1. Developmental psychology—Textbooks. I. Title.

BF713.F45 2008

155—dc22   2007030310

To Alex

Editorial Director: Leah Jewell
Executive Editor: Jeff Marshall
Project Manager, Editorial: LeeAnn Doherty
Editorial Assistant: Aaron Talwar
Director of Marketing: Brandy Dawson
Senior Marketing Manager: Jeanette Koskinas
Marketing Assistant: Laura Kennedy
Associate Managing Editor: Maureen Richardson
Project Manager, Production: Shelly Kupperman
Permissions Project Manager: Peggy Davis
Senior Operations Supervisor: Sherry Lewis
Senior Art Director: Nancy Wells

Interior Designer: Robert Aleman
Cover Designer: Ximena Tamvakopoulos
Manager, Visual Research: Beth Brenzel
Cover Image Specialist: Karen Sanatar
Image Permissions Coordinator: Michelina
   Vicusi/Cynthia Vincenti
AV Project Manager: Maria Piper
Interior Art: Precision Graphics
Cover Image: Masterfile Royalty Free Division
Composition/Full-Service Project Management:
   S4Carlisle Publishing Services-Emily Bush
Printer/Binder: Courier Companies, Inc.
Cover Printer: Phoenix Color Corp.

Credits and acknowledgments borrowed from other sources and reproduced, with permission, in this textbook appear on pages 732–734.

Pearson Education LTD., London
Pearson Education Singapore, Pte., Ltd.
Pearson Education Canada, Ltd., Toronto
Pearson Education—Japan
Pearson Education Australia PTY, Limited

Pearson Education North Asia Ltd.
Pearson Educacion de Mexico, S.A. de C.V
Pearson Education Malaysia, Pte., Ltd.
Pearson Education, Upper Saddle River, New Jersey

10 9 8 7 6 5 4 3 2

ISBN-13: 978-0-13-601610-6
ISBN-10:   0-13-601610-3

Brief Contents

PART 1   BEGINNINGS

   1 An Introduction to Lifespan Development ... 2
   2 The Start of Life: Prenatal Development ... 46
   3 Birth and the Newborn Infant ... 84

PART 2   INFANCY: FORMING THE FOUNDATIONS OF LIFE

   4 Physical Development in Infancy ... 114
   5 Cognitive Development in Infancy ... 148
   6 Social and Personality Development in Infancy ... 180

PART 3   THE PRESCHOOL YEARS

   7 Physical and Cognitive Development in the Preschool Years ... 210
   8 Social and Personality Development in the Preschool Years ... 250

PART 4   THE MIDDLE CHILDHOOD YEARS

   9 Physical and Cognitive Development in Middle Childhood ... 284
   10 Social and Personality Development in Middle Childhood ... 330

PART 5   ADOLESCENCE

   11 Physical and Cognitive Development in Adolescence ... 370
   12 Social and Personality Development in Adolescence ... 406

PART 6   EARLY ADULTHOOD

   13 Physical and Cognitive Development in Early Adulthood ... 440
   14 Social and Personality Development in Early Adulthood ... 476

PART 7   MIDDLE ADULTHOOD

   15 Physical and Cognitive Development in Middle Adulthood ... 510
   16 Social and Personality Development in Middle Adulthood ... 540

PART 8   LATE ADULTHOOD

   17 Physical and Cognitive Development in Late Adulthood ... 570
   18 Social and Personality Development in Late Adulthood ... 602

PART 9   ENDINGS

   19 Death and Dying ... 636

Contents

Preface   xxviii
About the Author   xxxvii

PART 1 BEGINNINGS

1 An Introduction to Lifespan Development   **2**

Prologue: New Conceptions   3
Looking Ahead   5

An Orientation to Lifespan Development   5
Characterizing Lifespan Development: The Scope of the Field   6
Topical Areas in Lifespan Development   6
Age Ranges and Individual Differences   6
The Links Between Topics and Ages   8

■ Developmental Diversity—How Culture, Ethnicity, and Race
Influence Development   8
Cohort and Other Influences on Development: Developing
with Others in a Social World   9

**Key Issues and Questions: Determining
the Nature—and Nurture—of Lifespan Development   10**
Continuous Change Versus Discontinuous Change   11
Critical and Sensitive Periods: Gauging the Impact of Environmental Events   11
Lifespan Approaches Versus a Focus on Particular Periods   12
The Relative Influence of Nature and Nurture on Development   12

Review and Apply   14

Theoretical Perspectives   14
The Psychodymanic Perspective: Focusing on the Inner Person   15
    Freud's Psychoanalytic Theory   15
    Erikson's Psychosocial Theory   17
    Assessing the Psychodynamic Perspective   17
The Behavioral Perspective: Focusing on Observable Behavior   18
    Classical Conditioning: Stimulus Substitution   18
    Operant Conditioning   18
    Social-Cognitive Learning Theory: Learning Through Imitation   19
    Assessing the Behavioral Perspective   19
The Cognitive Perspective: Examining the Roots of Understanding   20
    Piaget's Theory of Cognitive Development   20
    Information Processing Approaches   21
    Cognitive Neuroscience Approaches   22
The Humanistic Perspective: Concentrating on the Unique
    Qualities of Human Beings   22
    Assessing the Humanististic Perspective   23
The Contextual Perspective: Taking a Broad Approach to Development   23

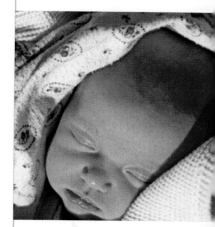

The Bioecological Approach to Development   23

    Vygotsky's Sociocultural Theory   25

    Assessing Vygotsky's Theory   26

Evolutionary Perspectives: Our Ancestors' Contributions to Behavior   26

    Assessing the Evolutionary Perspective   27

Why "Which Approach Is Right?" Is the Wrong Question   27

Review and Apply   28

Research Methods   29

Theories and Hypotheses: Posing Developmental Questions   30

Choosing a Research Strategy: Answering Questions   31

Correlational Studies   31

    The Correlation Coefficient   32

    Types of Correlational Studies   33

    Psychophysiological Methods   34

Experiments: Determining Cause and Effect   34

    Independent and Dependent Variables   35

    Choosing a Research Setting   36

Theoretical and Applied Research: Complementary Approaches   36

Measuring Developmental Change   37

    Longitudinal Studies: Measuring Individual Change   37

■ **From Research to Practice**—*Using Developmental Research to Improve Public Policy*   37

    Cross-Sectional Studies   38

    Sequential Studies   39

Ethics and Research   39

■ Becoming an Informed Consumer of Development—**Thinking Critically About "Expert" Advice**   40

Review and Apply   42

Epilogue   43

Looking Back   43

Key Terms and Concepts   44

2 The Start of Life: Prenatal Development   46

Prologue: The Future Is Now   47

Looking Ahead   48

Earliest Development   48

Genes and Chromosomes: The Code of Life   48

Multiple Births: Two—or More—for the Genetic Price of One   49

    Boy or Girl? Establishing the Sex of the Child   50

The Basics of Genetics: The Mixing and Matching of Traits   50

Transmission of Genetic Information   51

    Polygenic Traits   52

The Human Genome and Behavioral Genetics: Cracking the Genetic Code   53

Inherited and Genetic Disorders: When Development Deviates from the Norm   54

Genetic Counseling: Predicting the Future from the Genes of the Present   56

Prenatal Testing   56

Screening for Future Problems   57

■ **From Research to Practice**—*Are "Designer Babies" in Our Future?* 59

Review and Apply   59

The Interaction of Heredity and Environment   60

The Role of Environment in Determining the Expression of Genes: From Genotypes to Phenotypes   60

Interaction of Factors   61

Studying Development: How Much Is Nature? How Much Is Nurture?   62

Nonhuman Animal Studies: Controlling Both Genetics and Environment   62

Contrasting Relatedness and Behavior: Adoption, Twin, and Family Studies   62

Physical Traits: Family Resemblances   63

Intelligence: More Research, More Controversy   64

Genetic and Environmental Influences on Personality: Born to Be Outgoing?   65

■ Developmental Diversity—**Cultural Differences In Physical Arousal: Might a Culture's Philosophical Outlook Be Determined by Genetics?   66**

Psychological Disorders: The Role of Genetics and Environment   68

Can Genes Influence the Environment?   69

Review and Apply   69

Prenatal Growth and Change   70

Fertilization: The Moment of Conception   70

The Stages of the Prenatal Period: The Onset of Development   71

The Germinal Stage: Fertilization to 2 Weeks   71

The Embryonic Stage: 2 Weeks to 8 Weeks   72

The Fetal Stage: 8 Weeks to Birth   72

Pregnancy Problems   74

Infertility   74

Ethical Issues   75

Miscarriage and Abortion   75

The Prenatal Environment: Threats to Development   76

Mother's Diet   76

Mother's Age   77

Mother's Prenatal Support   78

Mother's Health   78

Mother's Drug Use   78

Mother's Use of Alcohol and Tobacco   79

Do Fathers Affect the Prenatal Environment?   80

■ Becoming an Informed Consumer of Development—**Optimizing the Prenatal Environment   81**

Review and Apply   82

Epilogue 82
Looking Back 83
Key Terms and Concepts 83

3 Birth and the Newborn Infant 84
Prologue: A 22-Ounce Miracle 85
Looking Ahead 86

Birth 86
Labor: The Process of Birth Begins 86
Birth: From Fetus to Neonate 88
    The Apgar Scale 88
    Physical Appearance and Initial Encounters 89
Approaches to Childbirth: Where Medicine and Attitudes Meet 90
    Alternative Birthing Procedures 91
    Childbirth Attendants: Who Delivers? 92
    Pain and Childbirth 92
    Use of Anesthesia and Pain-Reducing Drugs 93
    Postdelivery Hospital Stay: Deliver, Then Depart? 93
    Newborn Medical Screening 94

■ Becoming an Informed Consumer of Development—Dealing with Labor 94
Review and Apply 95

Birth Complications 95
Preterm Infants: Too Soon, Too Small 95
    Very-Low-Birthweight Infants: The Smallest of the Small 97
    What Causes Preterm and Low-Birthweight Deliveries? 97
Postmature Babies: Too Late, Too Large 98

■ **Careers in Lifespan Development**—Diana Hegger, Neonatal Nurse and Educator 99

Cesarean Delivery: Intervening in the Process of Birth 99
Infant Mortality and Stillbirth: The Tragedy of Premature Death 100

■ Developmental Diversity—Overcoming Racial and Cultural Differences in Infant Mortality 101

Postpartum Depression: Moving from the Heights of Joy to the Depths of Despair 103
Review and Apply 104

The Competent Newborn 105
Physical Competence: Meeting the Demands of a New Environment 105
Sensory Capabilities: Experiencing the World 106
Early Learning Capabilities 107
    Classical Conditioning 107

■ **From Research to Practice**—Circumcision of Newborn Male Infants: The Unkindest Cut? 108

    Operant Conditioning 109
    Habituation 109
Social Competence: Responding to Others 110
Review and Apply 111

Epilogue 112
Looking Back 112
Key Terms and Concepts 113

PART 2 INFANCY: FORMING THE FOUNDATIONS OF LIFE

4 Physical Development in Infancy 114
Prologue: First Steps 115
Looking Ahead 116

Growth and Stability 116
Physical Growth: The Rapid Advances of Infancy 116
   Four Principles of Growth 117
The Nervous System and Brain: The Foundations of Development 118
   Synaptic Pruning 119
   Environmental Influences on Brain Development 120
Integrating the Bodily Systems: The Life Cycles of Infancy 121
   Rhythms and States 121
   Sleep: Perchance to Dream? 121
SIDS: The Unanticipated Killer 124

Review and Apply 125

Motor Development 126
Reflexes: Our Inborn Physical Skills 126
   The Basic Reflexes 126
   Ethnic and Cultural Differences and Similarities in Reflexes 128
Motor Development in Infancy: Landmarks of Physical Achievement 128
   Gross Motor Skills 128
   Fine Motor Skills 129
   Dynamic Systems Theory: How Motor Development Is Coordinated 130
   Developmental Norms: Comparing the Individual to the Group 131

  ■ Developmental Diversity—**The Cultural Dimensions
of Motor Development 131**

Nutrition in Infancy: Fueling Motor Development 132
   Malnutrition 133
   Obesity 134

  ■ **From Research to Practice**—*Fast-Food Babies* 135

Breast or Bottle? 135
   Social Patterns in Breastfeeding 137
Introducing Solid Foods: When and What? 138

Review and Apply 138

The Development of the Senses 139
Visual Perception: Seeing the World 139
Auditory Perception: The World of Sound 140
Smell and Taste 142

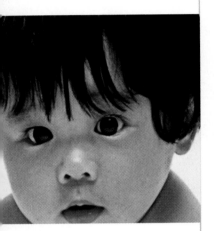

Sensitivity to Pain and Touch 142

    Contemporary Views on Infant Pain 143

    Responding to Touch 143

    Multimodal Perception: Combining Individual Sensory Inputs 144

■ Becoming an Informed Consumer of Development—Exercising Your Infant's Body and Senses 145

Review and Apply 145

Epilogue 146

Looking Back 147

Key Terms and Concepts 147

5 Cognitive Development in Infancy 148

Prologue: The Electric Nanny 149

Looking Ahead 150

Piaget's Approach to Cognitive Development 150

Key Elements of Piaget's Theory 151

The Sensorimotor Period: The Earliest Stage of Cognitive Growth 152

    Substage 1: Simple Reflexes 153

    Substage 2: First Habits and Primary Circular Reactions 153

    Substage 3: Secondary Circular Reactions 153

    Substage 4: Coordination of Secondary Circular Reactions 154

    Substage 5: Tertiary Circular Reactions 155

■ **Careers in Lifespan Development**—*Linda G. Miller, Toy Consultant 155*

    Substage 6: Beginnings of Thought 156

Appraising Piaget: Support and Challenges 156

Review and Apply 158

Information Processing Approaches to Cognitive Development 158

Encoding, Storage, and Retrieval: The Foundations of Information Processing 159

    Automatization 159

Memory During Infancy: They Must Remember This . . . 160

    Memory Capabilities in Infancy 161

    The Duration of Memories 161

    The Cognitive Neuroscience of Memories 162

Individual Differences in Intelligence: Is One Infant Smarter than Another? 162

    What Is Infant Intelligence? 163

    Developmental Scales 163

    Information Processing Approaches to Individual Differences 164

    Assessing Information Processing Approaches 165

■ **From Research to Practice**—*Do Educational Media for Infants Enhance Their Cognitive Development?: Taking the Einstein Out of Baby Einstein 166*

Review and Apply 167

The Roots of Language 167

The Fundamentals of Language: From Sounds to Symbols   167
  Early Sounds and Communication   169
  First Words   170
  First Sentences   170
The Origins of Language Development   172
  Learning Theory Approaches: Language as a Learned Skill   172
  Nativist Approaches: Language as an Innate Skill   173
  The Interactionist Approaches   173
Speaking to Children: The Language of Infant-Directed Speech   175
  Infant-Directed Speech   174
  ■ Developmental Diversity—Is Infant-Directed Speech Similar in All Cultures?   175
  Gender Differences   176
  ■ Becoming an Informed Consumer of Development—What Can You Do to Promote Infants' Cognitive Development?   176

Review and Apply 177

Epilogue   178
Looking Back   178
Key Terms and Concepts   179

6 Social and Personality Development in Infancy   180
Prologue: The Velcro Chronicles   181
Looking Ahead   182

Developing the Roots of Sociability 182

Emotions in Infancy: Do Infants Experience Emotional Highs and Lows?   182
  Experiencing Emotions   184
  Stranger Anxiety and Separation Anxiety   184
  Smiling   185
  Decoding Others' Facial and Vocal Expressions   186
Social Referencing: Feeling What Others Feel   186
Facial Expressions
  Two Explanations of Social Referencing   187
The Development of Self: Do Infants Know Who They Are?   187
Theory of Mind: Infants' Perspectives on the Mental Lives of Others—and Themselves   189

Review and Apply 189

Forming Relationships 190

Attachment: Forming Social Bonds   190
  The Ainsworth Strange Situation and Patterns of Attachment   191
Producing Attachment: The Roles of the Mother and Father   193
  Mothers and Attachment   193
  Fathers and Attachment   194
  Are There Differences in Attachment to Mothers and Fathers?   194

■ Developmental Diversity—Does Attachment Differ Across Cultures?   195

Infant Interactions: Developing a Working Relationship   196

Infants' Sociability with Their Peers: Infant–Infant Interaction   198

Review and Apply   199

Differences Among Infants   199

Personality Development: The Characteristics That Make Infants Unique   199

Temperament: Stabilities in Infant Behavior   200

    Categorizing Temperament: Easy, Difficult, and Slow-to-Warm Babies   201

    The Consequences of Temperament: Does Temperament Matter?   201

    The Biological Basis of Temperament   202

Gender: Boys in Blue, Girls in Pink   202

    Gender Differences   203

    Gender Roles   203

Family Life in the 21st Century   204

■ Becoming an Informed Consumer of Development—**Choosing the Right Infant Care Provider   205**

■ **From Research to Practice**—*How Does Infant Child Care Affect Later Development?   206*

Review and Apply   207

Epilogue   208
Looking Back   208
Key Terms and Concepts   209

PART 3   THE PRESCHOOL YEARS

7   Physical and Cognitive Development in the Preschool Years   **210**

Prologue: Aaron   211
Looking Ahead   212

Physical Growth   212

The Growing Body   213

    Individual Differences in Height and Weight   213

    Changes in Body Shape and Structure   213

    Nutrition: Eating the Right Foods   213

    Health and Illness   214

    Injuries During the Preschool Year: Playing It Safe   214

    The Silent Danger: Lead Poisoning in Young Children   215

The Growing Brain   216

    Brain Lateralization   216

    The Links Between Brain Growth and Cognitive Development   217

Motor Development   218

    Gross Motor Skills   218

    Potty Wars: When—and How—Should Children Be Toilet Trained?   219

    Fine Motor Skills   220

    Handedness   220

■ Becoming an Informed Consumer of Development—**Keeping Preschoolers Healthy** 221

Review and Apply **222**

Intellectual Development **223**

Piaget's Stage of Preoperational Thinking   223

    The Relation Between Language and Thought   224

    Centration: What You See Is What You Think   224

    Conservation: Learning That Appearances Are Deceiving   225

    Incomplete Understanding of Transformation   225

    Egocentrism: The Inability to Take Others' Perspectives   226

    The Emergence of Intuitive Thought   227

    Evaluating Piaget's Approach to Cognitive Development   228

Information Processing Approaches to Cognitive Development   228

    Preschoolers' Understanding of Numbers   229

    Memory: Recalling the Past   229

    Children's Eyewitness Testimony: Memory on Trial   230

    Information Processing in Perspective   231

Vygotsky's View of Cognitive Development: Taking Culture into Account   232

    The Zone of Proximal Development and Scaffolding: Foundations of Cognitive Development   233

    Evaluating Vygotsky's Contributions   234

Review and Apply **235**

The Growth of Language and Learning **236**

Language Development   236

    Private Speech and Social Speech   237

    Poverty and Language Development   238

Learning from the Media: Television and the Internet   239

    Television: Controlling Exposure   240

    Sesame Street: A Teacher in Every Home?   241

Early Childhood Education: Taking the "Pre" Out of the Preschool Period   241

    The Varieties of Early Education   242

    The Effectiveness of Child Care   243

    The Quality of Child Care   243

■ Developmental Diversity—**Preschools Around the World: Why Does the United States Lag Behind?** **244**

    Preparing Preschoolers for Academic Pursuits: Does Head Start Truly Provide a Head Start?   245

    Are We Pushing Children Too Hard and Too Fast?   245

■ **From Research to Practice**—*The Montessori Approach: Is It Effective?* *246*

Review and Apply **247**

Epilogue   248
Looking Back   248
Key Terms and Concepts   249

8 Social and Personality Development in the Preschool Years 250

Prologue: Feeling His Mother's Pain 251
Looking Ahead 252

Forming a Sense of Self 252
Psychosocial Development: Resolving the Conflicts 252
Self-Concept in the Preschool Years: Thinking About the Self 253

■ Developmental Diversity—Developing Racial and Ethnic Awareness 254
Gender Identity: Developing Femaleness and Maleness 254
  Biological Perspectives on Gender 255
  Psychoanalytic Perspectives 256
  Social Learning Approaches 257
  Cognitive Approaches 257
Review and Apply **259**

Friends and Family: Preschoolers' Social Lives 259
The Development of Friendships 259
Playing by the Rules: The Work of Play 260
  Categorizing Play 260
  The Social Aspects of Play 260
Preschoolers' Theory of Mind: Understanding What Others Are Thinking 262
  The Emergence of Theory of Mind 263
Preschoolers' Family Lives 264
Effective Parenting: Teaching Desired Behavior 264
  Cultural Differences in Child-Rearing Practices 266

■ **From Research to Practice**—*Parenting Coaches: Teaching Parents to Teach Their Children 267*
Child Abuse and Psychological Maltreatment: The Grim Side of Family Life 267
  Physical Abuse 267
  Psychological Maltreatment 269
Resilience: Overcoming the Odds 270

■ **Careers in Lifespan Development**—*Debra A. Littler 271*
■ Becoming an Informed Consumer of Development—Disciplining Children 272
Review and Apply **272**

Moral Development and Aggression 273
Developing Morality: Following Society's Rights and Wrongs 273
  Piaget's View of Moral Development 273
  Evaluating Piaget's Approach to Moral Development 274
  Social Learning Approaches to Morality 274
  Empathy and Moral Behavior 275
Aggression and Violence in Preschoolers: Sources and Consequences 275
  The Roots of Aggression 276
  Social Learning Approaches to Aggression 277
  Viewing Violence on TV: Does It Matter? 278
  Cognitive Approaches to Aggression: The Thoughts Behind Violence 279

■ Becoming an Informed Consumer of Development—Increasing Moral Behavior and Reducing Aggression in Preschool-Age Children 280

Review and Apply **281**
Epilogue 282
Looking Back 282
Key Terms and Concepts 283

PART 4 THE MIDDLE CHILDHOOD YEARS

9 Physical and Cognitive Development in Middle Childhood **284**
Prologue: La-Toya Pankey and The Witches 285
Looking Ahead 286

Physical Development **286**
The Growing Body 287
    Height and Weight Changes 287
    Cultural Patterns of Growth 287
    Promoting Growth with Hormones: Should Short Children Be Made to Grow? 287
    Nutrition 288
    Childhood Obesity 289
Motor Development 290
    Gross Motor Skills 291
    Fine Motor Skills 292
Health During Middle Childhood 292
    Asthma 292
    Accidents 293
    Safety in Cyberspace 293
Psychological Disorders 294
Children with Special Needs 295
    Sensory Difficulties: Visual, Auditory, and Speech Problems 295
    Learning Disabilities: Discrepancies Between Achievement and Capacity
        to Learn 296
Attention-Deficit Hyperactivity Disorder 297

■ Becoming an Informed Consumer of Development—Keeping Children Fit 298
Review and Apply **299**

Intellectual Development **299**
Piagetian Approaches to Cognitive Development 300
    The Rise of Concrete Operational Thought 300
    Piaget in Perspective: Piaget Was Right, Piaget Was Wrong 300
Information Processing in Middle Childhood 302
    Memory 302
    Improving Memory 303
Vygotsky's Approach to Cognitive Development and Classroom Instruction 303
Language Development: What Words Mean 304
    Mastering the Mechanics of Language 304
    Metalinguistic Awareness 305

How Language Promotes Self-Control 306

Bilingualism: Speaking in Many Tongues 306

Review and Apply 308

Schooling: The Three Rs (and More) of Middle Childhood 308

Schooling Around the World and Across Genders: Who Gets Educated? 309

Reading: Learning to Decode the Meaning Behind Words 309

Reading Stages 309

■ **From Research to Practice**—*Making the Grade: Are We Pushing Too Hard? 311*

How Should We Teach Reading? 311

Educational Trends: Beyond the Three Rs 312

■ Developmental Diversity—**Multicultural Education 313**

Cultural Assimilation or Pluralistic Society? 313

Fostering a Bicultural Identity 314

Intelligence: Determining Individual Strengths 314

Intelligence Benchmarks: Differentiating the Intelligent from the Unintelligent 315

Binet's Test 315

Measuring IQ: Present-Day Approaches to Intelligence 317

What IQ Tests Don't Tell: Alternative Conceptions of Intelligence 319

Group Differences in IQ 321

Explaining Racial Differences in IQ 321

The Bell Curve Controversy 322

Below and Above Intelligence Norms: Mental Retardation and the Intellectually Gifted 323

Ending Segregation by Intelligence Levels: The Benefits of Mainstreaming 324

Below the Norm: Mental Retardation 324

Above the Norm: The Gifted and Talented 325

■ **Careers in Lifespan Development**—*Vikas M. Darji, Special Education Teacher 326*

Educating the Gifted and Talented 327

Review and Apply 327

Epilogue 328
Looking Back 328
Key Terms and Concepts 329

10 Social and Personality Development in Middle Childhood 330

Prologue: Play Time 331
Looking Ahead 332

The Developing Self 332

Psychosocial Development in Middle Childhood: Industry Versus Inferiority 332

Understanding One's Self: A New Response to "Who Am I?" 333

The Shift in Self-Understanding from the Physical to the Psychological 333

Social Comparison 333

Self-Esteem: Developing a Positive—or Negative—View of the Self 335

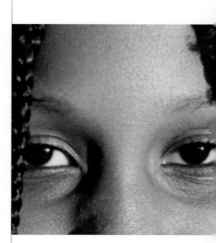

Change and Stability in Self-Esteem 335

Race and Self-Esteem 336

■ Developmental Diversity——Are Children of Immigrant Families
Well Adjusted? 337

Moral Development 338

Moral Development in Girls 340

Review and Apply **342**

Relationships: Building Friendship In Middle Childhood **342**

Stages of Friendship: Changing Views of Friends 343

Stage 1: Basing Friendship or Others' Behavior 343

Stage 2: Basing Friendship on Trust 344

Stage 3: Basing Friendship on Psychological Closeness 344

Individual Differences in Friendship: What Makes a Child Popular? 344

Status Among School-Age Children: Establishing One's Position 344

What Personal Characteristics Lead to Popularity? 345

Social Problem-Solving Abilities 346

Teaching Social Competence 347

Bullying: Schoolyard and Online Victimization 348

Gender and Friendships: The Sex Segregation of Middle Childhood 348

Cross-Race Friendships: Integration In and Out of the Classroom 350

■ Becoming an Informed Consumer of Development——Increasing Children's Social
Competence 350

Review and Apply **351**

**Family and School: Shaping Children's Behavior
in Middle Childhood** **351**

Family: The Changing Home Environment 352

Family Life 352

■ **From Research to Practice**—*Learning to Get Along: How Children
Are Influenced by Their Siblings* *353*

When Both Parents Work Outside the Home: How Do Children Fare? 353

Home and Alone: What Do Children Do? 354

Divorce 355

Single-Parent Families 356

Multigenerational Families 357

Living in Blended Families 357

Families with Gay and Lesbian Parents 358

Race and Family Life 358

Poverty and Family Life 359

Group Care: Orphanages in the 21st Century 359

School: The Academic Environment 361

How Children Explain Academic Success and Failure 361

Cultural Comparisons: Individual Differences in Attribution 361

■ Developmental Diversity——Explaining Asian Academic Success 362

Expectation Effects: How Others' Expectancies Influence Children's Behavior 363

Beyond the 3Rs: Should Schools Teach Emotional Intelligence? 365

Review and Apply **367**

Epilogue 368
Looking Back 368
Key Terms and Concepts 369

PART 5 ADOLESCENCE

11 Physical and Cognitive Development in Adolescence 370

Prologue: A Teenager's Day 371
Looking Ahead 372

Physical Maturation **372**

Growth During Adolescence: The Rapid Pace of Physical and Sexual Maturation 373

Puberty: The Start of Sexual Maturation 373

Puberty in Girls 374

Puberty in Boys 375

Body Image: Reactions to Physical Changes in Adolescence 376

The Timing of Puberty: The Consequences of Early and Late Maturation 376

Nutrition, Food, and Eating Disorders: Fueling the Growth of Adolescence 378

Obesity 378

Anorexia Nervosa and Bulimia 379

Brain Development and Thought: Paving the Way for Cognitive Growth 380

■ **From Research to Practice**—*The Immature Brain Argument: Too Young for the Death Penalty?* *382*

Sleep Deprivation 382

Review and Apply **383**

Cognitive Development and Schooling **383**

Piagetian Approaches to Cognitive Development: Using Formal Operations 383

Using Formal Operations to Solve Problems 384

The Consequences of Adolescents' Use of Formal Operations 386

Evaluating Piaget's Approach 386

Information Processing Perspectives: Gradual Transformations in Abilities 387

Egocentrism in Thinking: Adolescents' Self-Absorption 388

School Performance 389

Socioeconomic Status and School Performance: Individual Differences in Achievement 391

Ethnic and Racial Differences in School Achievement 391

Cyberspace: Adolescents Online 392

Dropping Out of School 393

Review and Apply **394**

Threats To Adolescents' Well-Being **394**

Illegal Drugs 395

■ **Careers in Lifespan Development**—*Daniel W. Prior, Counselor*   *396*

Alcohol: Use and Abuse   397

■ Becoming an Informed Consumer of Development—Hooked on Drugs or Alcohol?   398

Tobacco: The Dangers of Smoking   399

■ Developmental Diversity—Selling Death: Pushing Smoking to the Less Advantaged   399

Sexually Transmitted Infections   400

AIDS   400

Other Sexually Transmitted Infections   401

Avoiding STIs   402

Review and Apply   403

Epilogue   404
Looking Back   404
Key Terms and Concepts   405

12 Social and Personality Development in Adolescence   406

Prologue: Adolescent Trio   407
Looking Ahead   408

Identity: Asking "Who Am I?"   408

Self-Concept: What Am I Like?   409

Self-Esteem: How Do I Like Myself?   409

Gender Differences in Self-Esteem   410

Socioeconomic Status and Race Differences in Self-Esteem   410

Identity Formation: Change or Crisis?   411

Societal Pressures and Reliance on Friends and Peers   412

Psychological Moratorium   412

Limitations of Erikson's Theory   413

Marcia's Approach to Identity Development: Updating Erikson   413

Identity, Race, and Ethnicity   415

Depression and Suicide: Psychological Difficulties in Adolescence   416

Adolescent Depression   416

Adolescent Suicide   417

■ Becoming an Informed Consumer of Development—Preventing Adolescent Suicide   419

Review and Apply   419

Relationships: Family and Friends   420

Family Ties: Changing Relations with Relations   420

The Quest for Autonomy   420

The Myth of the Generation Gap   422

Conflicts with Parents   423

Cultural Differences in Parent–Child Conflicts During Adolescence   424

Relationships with Peers: The Importance of Belonging   425

Social Comparison   425

Reference Groups   425

Cliques and Crowds: Belonging to a Group   425

Gender Relations   426

■ Developmental Diversity——Race Segregation: The Great Divide of Adolescence   427

Popularity and Rejection   428

Conformity: Peer Pressure in Adolescence   429

Juvenile Delinquency: The Crimes of Adolescence   430

■ **From Research to Practice**—*Know When to Fold 'Em: The Growing Problem of Online Gambling*   431

Review and Apply   432

Dating, Sexual Behavior, and Teenage Pregnancy   432

Dating: Close Relationships in the 21st Century   432

The Functions of Dating   433

Dating, Race, and Ethnicity   433

Sexual Relationships   433

Masturbation   433

Sexual Intercourse   434

Sexual Orientation: Heterosexuality, Homosexuality, and Bisexuality   435

What Determines Sexual Orientation?   436

Teenage Pregnancies   436

Review and Apply   437

Epilogue   438
Looking Back   438
Key Terms and Concepts   439

PART 6   EARLY ADULTHOOD

13 Physical and Cognitive Development in Early Adulthood   **440**
Prologue: A Tale of Two Students   441
Looking Ahead   442

Physical Development   442

Physical Development and the Senses   443

Motor Functioning, Fitness, and Health: Staying Well   443

Physical Fitness   443

Health   444

■ Developmental Diversity——How Cultural Beliefs Influence Health and Health Care   446

Eating, Nutrition, and Obesity: A Weighty Concern   447

Good Nutrition   447

Obesity   447

■ **Careers in Lifespan Development**—*Martin Binks, Behavioral Health Clinician*   448

Physical Disabilities: Coping with Physical Challenge   449

Stress and Coping: Dealing with Life's Challenges   449

The Origins of Stress   450

The Consequences of Stress   451

Coping with Stress   452

Hardiness, Resilience, and Coping   453

■ Becoming an Informed Consumer of Development—Coping with Stress   454

Review and Apply   455

Cognitive Development   456

Intellectual Growth in Early Adulthood   456

Postformal Thought   456

Perry's Approach to Postformal Thinking   457

Schaie's Stages of Development   457

Intelligence: What Matters in Early Adulthood?   459

Practical and Emotional Intelligence   460

Creativity: Novel Thought   460

Life Events and Cognitive Development   462

Review and Apply   463

College: Pursuing Higher Education   463

The Demographics of Higher Education   464

The Gender Gap in College Attendance   465

■ **From Research to Practice**—*Does a Racially Diverse College Campus Make for a Richer Learning Environment?   466*

The Changing College Student: Never Too Late to Go to College?   466

College Adjustment: Reacting to the Demands of College Life   467

■ Becoming an Informed Consumer of Development—When Do College Students Need Professional Help with Their Problems?   468

Gender and College Performance   468

Benevolent Sexism: When Being Nice Is Not So Nice   470

Stereotype Threat and Disidentification with School   470

Dropping Out of College   473

Review and Apply   473

Epilogue   474

Looking Back   474

Key Terms and Concepts   475

14 Social and Personality Development in Early Adulthood   476

Prologue: Love Without Borders   476

Looking Ahead   479

Forging Relationships: Intimacy, Liking, and Loving During Early Adulthood   479

The Components of Happiness: Fulfillment of Psychological Needs   479

The Social Clocks of Adulthood   480

Women's Social Clocks   480

Seeking Intimacy: Erikson's View of Young Adulthood   481

Friendship   481

Falling in Love: When Liking Turns to Loving   482

Passionate and Companionate Love: The Two Faces of Love 483

Sternberg's Triangular Theory: The Three Faces of Love 484

Choosing a Partner: Recognizing Mr. or Ms. Right 485

Seeking a Spouse: Is Love the Only Thing That Matters? 485

Filtering Models: Sifting Out a Spouse 487

Attachment Styles and Romantic Relationships: Do Adult Loving Styles Reflect Attachment in Infancy? 589

■ Developmental Diversity—Gay and Lesbian Relationships: Men with Men and Women with Women 490

Review and Apply **491**

The Course of Relationships **491**

Marriage, POSSLQ, and Other Relationship Choices: Sorting Out the Options of Early Adulthood 492

What Makes Marriage Work? 493

Early Marital Conflict 494

Parenthood: Choosing to Have Children 495

Family Size 496

Dual-Earner Couples 496

The Transition to Parenthood: Two's a Couple, Three's a Crowd? 497

Gay and Lesbian Parents 498

Staying Single: I Want to Be Alone 499

■ **From Research to Practice**—*A Majority of American Women Are Living Without a Spouse* 499

Review and Apply **500**

Work: Choosing and Embarking on a Career **500**

Identity During Young Adulthood: The Role of Work 500

Picking an Occupation: Choosing Life's Work 501

Ginzberg's Career Choice Theory 501

Holland's Personality Type Theory 502

Gender and Career Choices: Women's Work 502

Why Do People Work? More Than Earning a Living 504

Intrinsic and Extrinsic Motivation 504

Satisfaction on the Job 505

■ Becoming an Informed Consumer of Development—Choosing a Career 506

Review and Apply **507**

Epilogue 508
Looking Back 508
Key Terms and Concepts 509

PART 7 MIDDLE ADULTHOOD

15 Physical and Cognitive Development in Middle Adulthood **510**

Prologue: Fit for Life 511
Looking Ahead 512

Physical Development   **512**

Physical Transitions: The Gradual Change in the Body's Capabilities   512

Height, Weight, and Strength: The Benchmarks of Change   513

The Senses: The Sights and Sounds of Middle Age   514

    Vision   514

    Hearing   514

Reaction Time: Not-so-Slowing Down   515

Sex in Middle Adulthood: The Ongoing Sexuality of Middle Age   516

    The Female Climacteric and Menopause   517

    The Psychological Consequences of Menopause   518

    The Male Climacteric   518

■ **From Research to Practice**—*The Dilemma of Hormone Therapy: No Easy Answer*   *519*

Review and Apply   **520**

Health   **520**

Wellness and Illness: The Ups and Downs of Middle Adulthood   521

■ Developmental Diversity—**Individual Variation in Health: Ethnic and Gender Differences**   **523**

Stress in Middle Adulthood   524

The A's and B's of Coronary Heart Disease: Linking Health and Personality   525

    Risk Factors for Heart Disease   525

    Type A's and Type B's   526

The Threat of Cancer   527

    Routine Mammograms: At What Age Should Women Start?   527

    Psychological Factors Relating to Cancer: Mind over Tumor?   528

Review and Apply   **530**

Cognitive Development   **530**

Does Intelligence Decline in Adulthood?   531

    The Difficulties in Answering the Question   531

    Crystallized and Fluid Intelligence   532

    Reframing the Issue: What Is the Source of Competence During Middle Adulthood?   533

The Development of Expertise: Separating Experts from Novices   534

Memory: You Must Remember This   535

    Types of Memory   535

    Memory Schemas   536

■ Becoming an Informed Consumer of Development—**Effective Strategies for Remembering**   **536**

Review and Apply   **537**

Epilogue   538
Looking Back   538
Key Terms and Concepts   539

16 Social and Personality Development in Middle Adulthood **540**

Prologue: From Boxer to Poetry Professor 541

Looking Ahead 542

Personality Development 542

Two Perspectives on Adult Personality Development: Normative-Crisis
Versus Life Events 542

Erikson's Stage of Generativity Versus Stagnation 543

Building on Erikson's Views: Valliant, Gould, and Levinson 543

The Midlife Crisis: Reality or Myth? 545

■ Developmental Diversity—Middle Age: In Some Cultures It Doesn't Exist 546

Stability Versus Change in Personality 547

Stability and Change in the "Big Five" Personality Traits 547

Happiness Across the Life Span 548

Review and Apply 549

Relationships: Family In Middle Age 549

Marriage 550

The Ups and Downs of Marriage 551

■ **From Research to Practice**—*After the Vows: Changes in Marital
Satisfaction over Time 552*

Divorce 552

Remarriage 553

Family Evolutions: From Full House to Empty Nest 554

Boomerang Children: Refilling the Empty Nest 555

The Sandwich Generation: Between Children and Parents 555

Becoming a Grandparent: Who, Me? 556

Family Violence: The Hidden Epidemic 557

The Prevalence of Spousal Abuse 557

The Cycle of Violence 558

■ Becoming an Informed Consumer of Development—Dealing with
Spousal Abuse 559

Spousal Abuse and Society: The Cultural Roots of Violence 559

Review and Apply 560

Work and Leisure 560

Work and Careers: Jobs at Midlife 561

Challenges of Work: On-the-Job Dissatisfaction 561

Burnout 561

Unemployment: The Dashing of the Dream 562

Switching—and Starting—Careers at Midlife 563

■ Developmental Diversity—Immigrants on the Job: Making It
in America 564

■ **Careers in Lifespan Development**—*Cathy Goodwin, Career
Counselor 565*

Leisure Time: Life Beyond Work 565

Review and Apply   566

Epilogue   568
Looking Back   568
Key Terms and Concepts   569

PART 8   LATE ADULTHOOD

17   Physical and Cognitive Development in Late Adulthood   **570**
Prologue: Cycling Through Late Adulthood   571
Looking Ahead   572

Physical Development in Late Adulthood   572
Aging: Myth and Reality   573
    The Demographics of Late Adulthood   573
    Ageism: Confronting the Stereotypes of Late Adulthood   573
Physical Transitions in Older People   574
    Outward Signs of Aging   575
    Internal Aging   576
Slowing Reaction Time   578
The Senses: Sight, Sound, Taste, and Smell   579
    Vision   579
    Hearing   579
    Taste and Smell   580

Review and Apply   581

Health and Wellness in Late Adulthood   581
Health Problems in Older People: Physical and Psychological
    Disorders   582
    Common Physical Disorders   582
    Psychological and Mental Disorders   582
    Alzheimer's Disease   583

■ Becoming an Informed Consumer of Development—Caring for People with
    Alzheimer's Disease   585
Wellness in Late Adulthood: The Relationship Between
    Aging and Illness   585
Promoting Good Health   586
Sexuality in Old Age: Use It or Lose It   587
Approaches to Aging: Why Is Death Inevitable?   588
    Genetic Programming Theories of Aging   588
    Wear-and-Tear Theories of Aging   588
    Reconciling the Theories of Aging   589
    Life Expectancy: How Long Have I Got?   589
Postponing Aging: Can Scientists Find the Fountain of Youth?   590

■ Developmental Diversity—Gender, Race, and Ethnic Differences
    in Average Life Expectancy: Separate Lives, Separate
    Deaths   591

Review and Apply   593

Cognitive Development in Late Adulthood 593

Intelligence in Older People 593

Recent Conclusions About the Nature of Intelligence in Older People 594

Memory: Remembrance of Things Past—and Present 595

■ **From Research to Practice**—*Exercising the Aging Brain* 596

Autobiographical Memory: Recalling the Days of Our Lives 597

Explaining Memory Changes in Old Age 597

Learning in Later Life: Never Too Late to Learn 598

Review and Apply 599

Epilogue 600
Looking Back 600
Key Terms and Concepts 601

18 Social and Personality Development in Late Adulthood 602

Prologue: Late Love 603
Looking Ahead 604

Personality Development and Successful Aging 604

Continuity and Change in Personality During Late Adulthood 604

Ego Integrity Versus Despair: Erikson's Final Stage 605

Peck's Developmental Tasks 605

Levinson's Final Season: The Winter of Life 606

Coping with Aging: Neugarten's Study 607

Life Review and Reminiscence: The Common Theme of Personality Development 607

Age Stratification Approaches to Late Adulthood 609

■ Developmental Diversity—**How Culture Shapes the Way We Treat People in Late Adulthood** 609

Does Age Bring Wisdom? 610

Successful Aging: What Is the Secret? 611

Disengagement Theory: Gradual Retreat 612

Activity Theory: Continued Involvement 613

Continuity Theory: A Compromise Position 614

Selective Optimization with Compensation: A General Model of Successful Aging 614

Review and Apply 615

The Daily Life of Late Adulthood 616

Living Arrangements: The Places and Spaces of Their Lives 616

Living at Home 616

Specialized Living Environments 616

Institutionalism and Learned Helplessness 617

Financial Issues: The Economics of Late Adulthood 618

Work and Retirement in Late Adulthood 619

Older Workers: Combating Age Discrimination 620

■ **From Research to Practice**—*Retirement: Looking Back and Looking Forward* 620

Retirement: Filling a Life of Leisure 621

■ Becoming an Informed Consumer of Development—Planning for—and Living— a Good Retirement   622

Review and Apply   623

Relationships: Old and New   623

Marriage in the Later Years: Together, Then Alone   624

Dealing with Retirement: Too Much Togetherness?   625

Caring for an Aging Spouse   625

The Death of a Spouse: Becoming Widowed   626

The Social Networks of Late Adulthood   628

Friendship: Why Friends Matter in Late Adulthood   628

Social Support: The Significance of Others   629

Family Relationships: The Ties That Bind   629

Children   630

Grandchildren and Great-Grandchildren   631

Elder Abuse: Relationships Gone Wrong   632

Review and Apply   633

Epilogue   633
Looking Back   634
Key Terms and Concepts   635

PART 9   ENDINGS

19   Endings: Death and Dying   636

Prologue: Choosing Death   637
Looking Ahead   638

Dying and Death Across the Life Span   638

Defining Death: Determining the Point at Which Life Ends   638

Death Across the Life Span: Causes and Reactions   639

Death in Infancy and Childhood   639

Death in Adolescence   641

Death in Young Adulthood   641

Death in Middle Adulthood   642

Death in Late Adulthood   642

■ Developmental Diversity—Differing Conceptions of Death   643

Can Death Education Prepare Us for the Inevitable?   644

Review and Apply   645

Confronting Death   646

Understanding the Process of Dying: Are There Steps Toward Death?   646

Denial   647

Anger   647

Bargaining   647

Depression   648

Acceptance   648

Evaluating Kübler-Ross's Theory   648

Choosing the Nature of Death: Is DNR the Way to Go?   649
   Living Wills   650
   Euthanasia and Assisted Suicide   650
Caring for the Terminally Ill: The Place of Death   653
■ **Careers in Lifespan Development**—*Dina C. Bianga, Hospice Nurse*   654

Review and Apply   **654**

Grief and Bereavement   **655**
Mourning and Funerals: Final Rites   655
   Cultural Differences in Grieving   656
Bereavement and Grief: Adjusting to the Death of a Loved One   656
   Differentiating Unhealthy Grief from Normal Grief   657
■ **From Research to Practice**—*Moving On: Surviving the Loss of a Long-Time Spouse   658*
   The Consequences of Grief and Bereavement   658

■ Becoming an Informed Consumer of Development—Helping a Child Cope with Grief   659
Review and Apply   660

Epilogue   660
Looking Back   661
Key Terms and Concepts   661

References   662
Glossary   724
Credits   732
Name Index   736
Subject Index   746

Preface

This book tells a story: the story of our lives, and our parents' lives, and the lives of our children. It is the story of human beings and how they get to be the way they are.

Unlike any other area of study, lifespan development speaks to us in a very personal sense. It covers the range of human existence from its beginnings at conception to its inevitable ending at death. It is a discipline that deals with ideas and concepts and theories, but one that above all has at its heart people—our fathers and mothers, our friends and acquaintances, our very selves.

Development Across the Life Span seeks to capture the discipline in a way that sparks, nurtures, and shapes readers' interest. It is meant to excite students about the field, to draw them into its way of looking at the world, and to build their understanding of developmental issues. By exposing readers to both the current content and the promise inherent in lifespan development, the text is designed to keep interest in the discipline alive long after students' formal study of the field has ended.

Overview of the Fifth Edition

Development Across the Life Span, Fifth Edition—like its predecessors—provides a broad overview of the field of human development. It covers the entire range of the human life, from the moment of conception through death. The text furnishes a broad, comprehensive introduction to the field, covering basic theories and research findings as well as highlighting current applications outside the laboratory. It covers the life span chronologically, encompassing the prenatal period, infancy and toddlerhood, the preschool years, middle childhood, adolescence, early and middle adulthood, and late adulthood. Within these periods, it focuses on physical, cognitive, and social and personality development.

The book seeks to accomplish the following four major goals:

- First and foremost, the book is designed to provide a broad, balanced overview of the field of lifespan development. It introduces readers to the theories, research, and applications that constitute the discipline, examining both the traditional areas of the field as well as more recent innovations. It pays particular attention to the applications developed by lifespan development specialists, demonstrating how lifespan developmentalists use theory, research, and applications to help solve significant social problems.

- The second goal of the text is to explicitly tie development to students' lives. Findings from the study of lifespan development have a significant degree of relevance to students, and this text illustrates how these findings can be applied in a meaningful, practical sense. Applications are presented in a contemporaneous framework, including current news items, timely world events, and contemporary uses of lifespan development that draw readers into the field. Numerous descriptive scenarios and vignettes reflect everyday situations in people's lives, explaining how they relate to the field.

- The third goal is to highlight both the commonalities and diversity of today's multicultural society. Consequently, the book incorporates material relevant to diversity in all its forms—racial, ethnic, gender, sexual orientation, religion, and cultural diversity—throughout every chapter. In addition, every chapter has at least one "Developmental Diversity" section. These features explicitly consider how cultural factors relevant to development both unite and diversify our contemporary, global society.

- Finally, the fourth goal is one that is implicit in the other three: making the field of lifespan development engaging, accessible, and interesting to students. Lifespan development is a joy both to study and teach, because so much of it has direct, immediate meaning to our lives. Because all of us are involved in our own developmental paths, we are tied in very personal ways to the content areas covered by the book. ***Development Across the Life Span,*** then, is meant to engage and nurture this interest, planting a seed that will develop and flourish throughout readers' lifetimes.

In accomplishing these goals, the book strives to be user-friendly. Written in a direct, conversational voice, it replicates as much as possible a dialogue between author and student. The text is meant to be understood and mastered on its own by students of every level of interest and motivation. To that end, it includes a variety of pedagogical features that promote mastery of the material and encourage critical thinking.

In short, the book blends and integrates theory, research, and applications, focusing on the breadth of human development. Furthermore, rather than attempting to provide a detailed historical record of the field, it focuses on the here-and-now, drawing on the past where appropriate, but with a view toward delineating the field as it now stands and the directions toward which it is evolving. Similarly, while providing descriptions of classic studies, the emphasis is more on current research findings and trends.

Development Across the Life Span is meant to be a book that readers will want to keep in their own personal libraries, one that they will take off the shelf when considering problems related to that most intriguing of questions: How do people come to be the way they are?

What's New in the Fifth Edition?

The fifth edition of ***Development Across the Life Span*** has been extensively revised in response to the comments of dozens of reviewers. Among the major changes are the following:

Additions of New and Updated Material

The revision incorporates a significant amount of new and updated information. For instance, advances in such areas as behavioral genetics, brain development, evolutionary perspectives, and cross-cultural approaches to development receive expanded and new coverage. Overall, more than a thousand new citations have been added, with most of those from articles and books published in the last 3 years.

New topics were added to every chapter. The following sample of new and revised topics featured in this edition provides a good indication of the currency of the revision:

Chapter 1
Critical thinking and evaluating research
Cohort effects and terrorism
Cognitive neuroscience perspective
Contextual perspective
Replication
Meta-analysis
Psychophysiological methods
Electroencephalogram (EEG)
Computerized axial tomography (CAT) scan
Functional magnetic resonance imaging
    (fMRI) scan

Chapter 2
"Designer babies"
Prenatal vitamins and folic acid
Prenatal testing

Chapter 3
Bradley birthing method
Hypnobirthing
Circumcision of newborn male infants
Side effects to use of birthing drugs, including
    Ransjö-Arvidson article
Postpartum depression
Newborn medical screening

Chapter 4
Gender, ethnic, and racial differences in
    weight/height norms
Overweight infants
Connection between reflexes and evolutionary
    perspective
Shaken baby syndrome
Infant discrimination of rhythm

Chapter 5
Exposing infants to educational material
Infant-directed speech material
Importance of reading to infants
Distinction between implicit and explicit
    memory
New evidence for nativist position on language

Chapter 6
Cultural differences in self-recognition
New findings from NICHD Study of Early Child
    Care and Youth Development on increased
    disruptiveness of children in child care
Mirror neurons and their link to imitation
    and autism
Conceptual definition of emotion
Adaptive value of emotions

(continued on page xxxii)

Special Features

Prologue: A 22-Ounce Miracle

She looked like a little old man," says Elizabeth Thatcher of her daughter, Hattie, who was born at 25 weeks, weighing 1 pound 6 ounces. "She wasn't plump like a baby should be. She was skin and bones."

Hattie, Elizabeth and husband Brad's firstborn, faced tough odds, but the Montclair, N.J., couple held out hope. A friend's baby born at 23 weeks was doing fine—so, too, the Thatchers prayed, would their little girl. . . .

The Thatchers visited Hattie every day, singing and talking to her. Preemies can't handle much stimulation, so instead of holding her, they lovingly cupped her head and body with their hands.

A fighter from the start, today Hattie, 6, is an outgoing little girl who loves pretending to be a lion. She's eagerly looking forward to Valentine's Day, busy making paper hearts for everyone in her family and "all my neighbors."

Hattie plays soccer every Monday. "I like kicking the ball," she says.

At a recent five-year reunion for NICU [Neonatal Intensive Care Unit] babies from Roosevelt Hospital, Hattie bounced around the room, happily hugging her former nurses.

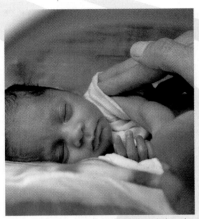

Despite their tiny size, preterm babies have an increasingly good chance of survival.

CHAPTER-OPENING PROLOGUES

Each chapter begins with a short vignette, describing an individual or situation that is relevant to the basic developmental.

Issues being addressed in the chapter. For instance, the chapter on birth describes a premature birth; one of the chapters on adolescence provides accounts of three teenagers; and a chapter on late adulthood discusses turning 100.

LOOKING AHEAD SECTIONS

These opening sections orient readers to the topics to be covered, bridging the opening prologue with the remainder of the chapter and providing orienting questions.

Looking Ahead

We next examine some of the possible complications of birth. Problems that can occur range from premature births to infant mortality. Finally, we consider the extraordinary range of capabilities of newborns. We'll look not only at their physical and perceptual abilities, but at the way they enter the world with the ability to learn and with skills that help form the foundations of their future relationships with others.

After reading this chapter, you will be able to answer these questions:

- What is the normal process of labor?
- What complications can occur at birth, and what are their causes, effects, and treatments?
- What capabilities does the newborn have?

From Research to Practice

Fast-Food Babies

At 20 pounds and 27 inches long, Zachary Miller was a happy and healthy, but not especially active, baby. "The pediatrician told me, 'The big ones don't like to move,'" says Zach's mom, Ellie. "She told me to put him on the floor and on his tummy as often as possible. He hates that. But it does get him to push up on his arms and roll over."

At 7 months, Zach was already overweight. (Sachs, 2006, p. 112)

Childhood obesity is on the rise, and as Zachary Miller's story suggests, the problem sometimes begins at a very early age. Children of overweight parents are particularly at risk of becoming overweight themselves, but heredity seems to be only part of the explanation. At issue is what children are eating in their first years of life.

were being fed adult diets. About a quarter of infants and toddlers between 7 and 24 months were eating no vegetables and about the same proportion were eating no fruits. Even among the children who were eating vegetables, french fries topped the list for toddlers over 18 months—and it was in the top three vegetables for infants between 9 and 12 months. By 8 months, nearly half of infants were already consuming desserts or sweetened drinks. By 24 months, a majority of toddlers were eating pastries and nearly half were drinking sweetened drinks (Fox et al., 2004).

These findings reveal a problem with how we are feeding our children in the critical early years, when they are developing food preferences and eating habits that will likely remain with them

FROM RESEARCH TO PRACTICE

Each chapter includes a section that describes current developmental research or research issues, applied to everyday problems. For instance, these sections include discussions of the use spanking, stereotypes and academic performance of women and African-Americans, and comforting the dying.

DEVELOPMENTAL DIVERSITY

Every chapter has at least one "Developmental Diversity" section incorporated into the text. These sections highlight issues relevant to today's multicultural society. Examples of these sections include discussions of preschools around the world, gay and lesbian relationships, the marketing of cigarettes to the less advantaged, and race, gender, and ethnic differences in life expectancy.

Developmental Diversity

The Cultural Dimensions of Motor Development

Among the Ache people, who live in the rain forest of South America, infants face an early life of physical restriction. Because the Ache lead a nomadic existence, living in a series of tiny camps in the rain forest, open space is at a premium. Consequently, for the first few years of life, infants spend nearly all their time in direct physical contact with their mothers. Even when they are not physically touching their mothers, they are permitted to venture no more than a few feet away.

***

Infants among the Kipsigis people, who live in a more open environment in rural Kenya, Africa, lead quite a different existence. Their lives are filled with activity and exercise. Parents seek to teach their children to sit up, stand, and walk from the earliest

Becoming an Informed Consumer of Development

Exercising Your Infant's Body and Senses

Recall how cultural expectations and environments affect the age at which various physical milestones, such as the first step, occur. While most experts feel attempts to accelerate physical and sensory-perceptual development yield little advantage, parents should ensure that their infants receive sufficient physical and sensory stimulation. There are several specific ways to accomplish this goal:

- Carry a baby in different positions—in a backpack, in a frontpack, or in a football hold with the infant's head in the palm of your hand and its feet lying on your arm. This lets the infant view the world from several perspectives.

BECOMING AN INFORMED CONSUMER OF DEVELOPMENT

Every chapter includes information on specific uses that can be derived from research conducted by developmental investigators. For instance, the text provides concrete information on how to encourage children to become more physically active, help troubled adolescents who might be contemplating suicide, and planning and living a good retirement.

CAREERS IN LIFESPAN DEVELOPMENT

Many chapters include an interview with a person working in a field that uses the findings of lifespan development. Among those interviewed are a toy designer, career advisor, and hospice nurse.

Careers in Lifespan Development

**Linda G. Miller,
Toy Consultant**

Education: BS in Education, Auburn University at Montgomery, Alabama; MA in Education, Auburn University, PhD, Education, Auburn University.

Position: Author, with Mary Jo Gibbs, *Making Toys for Infants and Toddlers: Using Ordinary Stuff for Extraordinary Play*. Adjunct Professor of Education, Auburn University at Montgomery, Alabama.

Home: Wetumpka, Alabama

"Infants are exploring their environments at all times," Miller noted, "and initially they explore with their mouths. It is also important not to have toys appropriate for older children in a younger child's environment."

Miller added that it is also important to introduce enough new toys to retain interest, but to retain enough of the older ones to maintain familiarity. "You wouldn't want to change cuddle toys every week," she added.

A major component in the development of an infant's cognitive abilities is to develop a connection with a familiar adult, and toys can be one way of achieving this.

"With a connection to a familiar adult young children feel safe and connected in the world and that feeling can sustain them

Review and Apply

Review

- In the first stage of labor, contractions increase in frequency, duration, and intensity until the baby's head is able to pass through the cervix. In the second stage, the baby moves through the cervix and birth canal and leaves the mother's body. In the third stage, the umbilical cord and placenta emerge.
- Immediately after birth, birthing attendants usually examine the neonate using a measurement system such as the Apgar scale.

REVIEW AND APPLY SECTIONS

Interspersed throughout each chapter are three short recaps of the chapters' main points, followed by questions designed to provoke critical thinking.

RUNNING GLOSSARY

Key terms are defined in the margins of the page on which the term is presented.

bonding close physical and emotional contact between parent and child during the period immediately following birth, argued by some to affect later relationship strength.

Epilogue

This chapter has covered the amazing and intense processes of labor and birth. A number of birthing options are available to parents, and these options need to be weighed in light of possible complications that can arise during the birthing process. In addition to considering the remarkable progress that has been made regarding the various treatments and interventions available for babies that are too early or too late, we examined the grim topics of stillbirth and infant mortality. We concluded with a discussion of the surprising capabilities of newborns and their early development of social competence.

Before we move on to a more detailed discussion of infants' physical development, return for a moment to the case of the premature birth of Hattie Thatcher, discussed in the prologue. Using your understanding of the issues discussed in this chapter, answer the following questions.

1. Hattie was born more than 3 months early. Why was the fact that she was born alive so surprising? Can you discuss her birth in terms of "the age of viability"?

2. What procedures and activities were most likely set into motion immediately after her birth?

3. What dangers was Hattie subject to immediately after birth because of her high degree of prematurity? What dangers would be likely to continue into her childhood?

4. What ethical considerations affect the decision of whether the high costs of medical interventions for highly premature babies are justifiable? Who should pay those costs?

END-OF-CHAPTER MATERIAL

Each chapter ends with an Epilogue that refers back to the opening Prologue, a numbered summary, and a list of key terms and concepts. This material is designed to help students study and retain the information in the chapter.

Reactive attachment disorder
Darwin and evolutionary perspective within discussion of infants' facial expressions

Chapter 7
Montessori schools
Brain development (e.g., cerebellum development)
Computer use by preschoolers
Reggio Emilia preschools
Baron-Cohen theory of autism (extreme male brain)
Forensic developmental psychology

Chapter 8
Table on types of play
Age differences in targets of abuse
Parent coaching
Role of genetics in influence on child-rearing practices
Prevalence of physical discipline in other cultures

Chapter 9
Increasing school pressure
Decline in life expectancy due to childhood obesity
School lunches as a cause of obesity
Elimination of recess and obesity
Fetal alcohol syndrome
Familial retardation
Stanford-Binet, 5th ed. (SB5)
ADHD behavioral treatment
Contemporary calculation of IQ scores
Importance of good diet to staying fit
Connection between ADHD and diet

Chapter 10
How children are influenced by their siblings
Online bullying
Multigenerational families
Family life and poverty

Chapter 11
Adolescence and brain development
Sleep deprivation
Cyberspace dangers
Internet gambling
Intellectual/academic development due to prefrontal cortex development
STI avoidance
STD terminology changed to STI
HPV and HPV vaccine
Leptin hypothesis regarding obesity and early onset of puberty

Chapter 12
Online gambling
Identity development and cognitive gains
Relationship of clique/crowds membership and cognitive development

Cultural and gender differences in the development of autonomy

Chapter 13
Advantages of a racially diverse college campus
Continued neurological pruning and myelination during middle adulthood
Racial diversity of college and cognition
Hardiness
Resilience

Chapter 14
Women living without a spouse
Filtering model
Transition to parenthood
Cultural differences in the transition to parenthood
Co-parenting team models
Women living alone

Chapter 15
Hormone replacement therapy controversy
Type D behavior
Role of hostility in Type A behavior
Findings/recommendations regarding hormone replacement therapy and the Women's Health Initiative

Chapter 16
Trends in marital satisfaction over time
Violence against women worldwide
Multigenerational families
Divorce statistics
Consequences of divorce in middle adulthood

Chapter 17
Exercising the aging brain
Telomeres
Neural growth possible throughout lifespan
Link between physical exercise and neural growth
Macular degeneration
Link between mental exercise and reduction of cognitive declines
Link between hearing loss and cognitive declines
Sirtuins family of genes that promote longevity

Chapter 18
Retirement
Cultural views of aging
Nursing home programs that encourage intergenerational interaction, such as through day-care centers
Poverty in the elderly
Peck's stages

Chapter 19
Surviving the death of a long-term spouse
Terry Schaivo case
Living wills
Assisted suicide
Cultural differences in mourning
Marital relationships and grief

Ancillaries

Development Across the Life Span, **Fifth Edition** is accompanied by a superb set of teaching and learning materials.

Print and Media Supplements for the Instructor

- **Instructor's Resource Manual.** Updated by Karen Paiva, Ph.D. of West Chester University, the Instructor's Resource Manual includes learning objectives, key terms and concepts, self-contained lecture suggestions and class activities for each chapter with handouts, supplemental reading suggestions, and an annotated list of additional multimedia resources. The Instructor's Resource Manual will be available as a print item, or for download via the Prentice Hall Instructor's Resource Center or the MyDevelopmentLab® platform.

- **PowerPoint Lecture Slides.** The lecture slides have been wholly reworked and completely revised by Pauline D. Zeece of the University of Nebraska—Lincoln, and feature prominent figures and tables from the text. The PowerPoint Lecture Slides are available for download via the Prentice Hall Instructor's Resource Center or the MyDevelopmentLab platform.

- **Classroom Response System PowerPoint Slides.** These slides are not only intended to be the basis for class lectures, but also for class discussions. The incorporation of the CRS questions into each chapter slideshow facilitates the use of 'clickers'—small hardware devices similar to remote-controls, which process student responses to questions, and interpret and display results in real time. CRS questions are a great means to engage students in learning and precipitate contemplation of text concepts. The slides were also created by Pauline D. Zeece of the University of Nebraska—Lincoln, and will be available for download via the Prentice Hall Instructor's Resource Center or the MyDevelopmentLab platform.

- **Test Item File with TestGen Software.** Completely revised and rewritten for the fifth edition text, the Test Item File to accompany "Development Across the Life Span" boasts more applied-type questions than ever before. Designed to better measure student comprehension of important concepts, the Test Item File was diligently prepared by Richard Cavasina, Ed.D. of California University of Pennsylvania, with applied-learning as the focus. Together with the compatible TestGen software the Test Item File helps to ensure all text topics are covered, and takes the measure of student understanding to the next level. The Test Item File will be available as a print item and the TestGen as a CD software package; both supplements will also be available for download via the Prentice Hall Instructor's Resource Center or the MyDevelopmentLab platform.

- **Virtual Child Software.** *The Virtual Child* is an interactive, web-based simulation that allows students to act as a parent and raise their own "child." By making decisions about specific scenarios, students can raise their children from birth to age 17 and learn first-hand how their own decisions and other parenting-actions affect their child over time. At each age, students are given feedback about the various milestones their child has attained; key stages of the child's development will include personalized feedback. As in real life, certain "unplanned" events may occur randomly. Access codes are needed for the Virtual Child, and can be obtained by purchase via the Prentice Hall website. Existing users can login to the site at http://www.prenhall.com/virtualchild.

- **Instructor's Resource CD-ROM.** Contains electronic versions of all available supplements. Resources are also available for download from the Prentice Hall Instructor's Resource Center or the MyDevelopmentLab® platform.

- **Developmental Psychology Overhead Transparencies.** Developed by Sheree Watson of the University of Southern Mississippi, this set of over 100 full-color transparencies are designed to be used in large lecture settings and includes illustrations from the text as well as images from a variety of other sources. The Developmental Psychology Overhead Transparencies are available in acetate form, or for download via the Prentice Hall Instructor's Resource Center or the MyDevelopmentLab platform.

- **MyDevelopmentLab®.** This new course management platform promises to revolutionize the way in which instructors teach and students learn. Developed by an elite team of Prentice Hall publishing and technology experts, the MyDevelopmentLab® platform is inspired by the higher education "outcomes assessment" revolution of the new millennium. This robust course management platform enables instructors to assign tests, quizzes, and projects online, and view the results of those assignments as a class aggregate, or as focused as on a student-by-student, text section-by-text section basis. Based upon these assignment results, instructors are presented with a detailed teaching plan to bolster student comprehension of any topic areas not well understood, and to supplement all other chapter sections.

  Krista D. Forrest, Ph.D. of The University of Nebraska—Kearney, oversaw the creation of all diagnostic test content for this exciting new platform, and many others contributed to the creation of a diversified collection of study content and activities encompassing *LivePsych!* animations, the *Observations* videos accompanying the text, the American Psychological Association (APA) reader *Current Directions in Developmental* Psychology, websites, and more.

- **Blackboard and WebCT®.** These course management platforms enable instructors to assign tests, quizzes, and projects online. Access to these platforms will be open, with password-protected links to MyDevelopmentLab for all, and the full set of supplementary materials for instructors.

Video Resources for Instructors

Prentice Hall is proud to present you with the following video packages, available exclusively to qualified adopters of *Development Across the Life Span,* Fifth Edition.

- **Prentice Hall Lecture Launcher Video for Developmental Psychology.** Adopters can receive this new video that includes short clips covering all major topics in introductory psychology. The videos have been carefully selected from the Films for Humanities and Sciences library and edited to provide brief and compelling video content for enhancing your lectures. Contact your local representative for a full list of video clips on this tape.

Print and Media Supplements for the Student

- **SafariX WebBook.** This new *Pearson Choice* offers students an online subscription to *Development Across the Life Span,* Fourth Edition online at a 50% savings. With the SafariX WebBook, students can search the text, make notes online, print out reading assignments that incorporate lecture notes, and bookmark important passages. Ask your Prentice Hall representative for details, or visit www.safarix.com.

- **Observations in Developmental Psychology.** These videos bring to life more than 30 key concepts discussed in the narrative of the text, indicated by a marginal icon, and offers additional extended videos that coincide with each part in the text to allow students see real children in action. Students get to view each video twice: once with an introduction to the concept being illustrated and again with commentary describing what is taking place at crucial points in the video. Whether your course has an observation component or not, these videos provide your students the opportunity to see children in action. The videos can be accessed through MyPsychLab by purchasing the supplementary CD-ROM on prenhall.com.

- **Study Guide.** Revised by Sachi Horback of Bucks County Community College, the Study Guide helps students to master the core concepts presented in each chapter. Each chapter includes learning objectives, a brief chapter summary, outline of the text chapter, three different practice tests, and a closing recap and review of important concepts.

- **Companion Website.** This online study tool allows students to review each chapter's material, take practice tests, research topics for course projects, and more! The Companion Website for the text includes: chapter objectives, online flashcards, researcher biographies, author-selected web links, and a diversified Study Guide providing immediate feedback. Access to the web site is free and unrestricted to all students.

- **MyDevelopmentLab.** With this exciting new tool students are able to self-assess using embedded diagnostic tests and instantly view results along with a customized study plan.

The customized study plan will focus on the student's strengths and weaknesses, based upon the results of the diagnostic testing, and present a list of activities and resources for review and remediation, organized by chapter section. Some study resources intended for use with portable electronic devices are made available exclusively through the MyDevelopmentLab, such as key terms flashcards and optimized *Observations* video clips. Students will be able to quickly and easily analyze their own comprehension level of the course material, and study more efficiently, leading to exceptional exam results!

Supplementary Texts

Contact your Prentice Hall representative to package any of these supplementary texts with *Development Across the Life Span,* Fifth Edition.

* ***Current Directions in Developmental Psychology.*** Readings from the American Psychological Society. This new and exciting reader includes over 20 articles that have been carefully selected for the undergraduate audience, and taken from the very accessible Current Directions in Psychological Science journal. These timely, cutting-edge articles allow instructors to bring their students real-world perspective about today's most current and pressing issues in psychology. Discounted when packaged with this text for college adoptions.

* ***Twenty Studies That Revolutionized Child Psychology by Wallace E. Dixon, Jr.*** Presenting the seminal research studies that have shaped modern developmental psychology, this brief text provides an overview of the environment that gave rise to each study, its experimental design, its findings, and its impact on current thinking in the discipline.

* ***Human Development in Multicultural Context: A Book of Readings.*** Written by Michele A. Paludi, this compilation of readings highlights cultural influences in developmental psychology.

* ***The Psychology Major: Careers and Strategies for Success.*** Written by Eric Landrum (Idaho State University), Stephen Davis (Emporia State University), and Terri Landrum (Idaho State University), this 160-page paperback provides valuable information on career options available to psychology majors, tips for improving academic performance, and a guide to the APA style of research reporting.

Acknowledgments

I am grateful to the following reviewers who provided a wealth of comments, constructive criticism, and encouragement:

Amy Boland, Columbus State Community College
Ginny Boyum, Rochester Community and Technical College
Krista Forrest, University of Nebraska at Kearney
John Gambon, Ozarks Technical College
Tim Killian, University of Arkansas
Peter Matsos, Riverside City College
Troy Schiedenhelm, Rowan-Cabarrus Community College
Charles Shairs, Bunker Hill Community College
Deirdre Slavik, NorthWest Arkansas Community College
Cassandra George Sturges, Washtenaw Community College
Rachelle Tannenbaum, Anne Arundel Community College
Lois Willoughby, Miami Dade College

I am grateful to the following reviewers of the fourth-edition text:

Nancy Ashton, R. Stockton College; Dana Davidson, University of Hawaii at Manoa; Margaret Dombrowski, Harrisburg Area Community College; Bailey Drechsler, Cuesta College; Jennifer Farell, University of North Carolina-Greensboro; Carol Flaugher, University at Buffalo; Rebecca Glover, University of North Texas; R.J.Grisham, Indian River Community College; Martha Kuehn, Central Lakes College; Heather Nash, University of Alaska Southeast; Sadie Oates, Pitt Community College; Patricia Sawyer, Middlesex Community College; Barbara Simon, Midlands Technical College; Archana Singh, Utah State University; Joan Thomas-Spiegel, Los Angeles Harbor College; Linda Veltri, University of Portland.

Many others deserve a great deal of thanks. I am indebted to the numerous people who provided me with a superb education, first at Wesleyan University and later at the University of Wisconsin. Specifically, Karl Scheibe played a pivotal role in my undergraduate education, and the late Vernon Allen acted as mentor and guide through my graduate years. It was in graduate school that I learned about development, being exposed to such experts as Ross Parke, John Balling, Joel Levin, Herb Klausmeier, and many others. My education continued when I became a professor. I am especially grateful to my colleagues at the University of Massachusetts, who make the university such a wonderful place in which to teach and do research.

Several people played central roles in the development of this book. John Bickford and Christopher Poirier provided important research and editorial input, and I am thankful for their help. Most of all, John Graiff was essential in juggling and coordinating the multiple aspects of writing a book, and I am very grateful for the substantial role he played.

I am also grateful to the superb Prentice Hall team that was instrumental in the inception and development of this book. Jeff Marshall, Executive Editor, has brought creativity and a wealth of good ideas to this edition and is a pleasure to work with. Leah Jewell stood behind the project. I am grateful for their support. On the production end of things, Maureen Richardson, the production update supervisor, and, Michelina Vicusi and Cynthia Vincenti photo editors, helped in giving the book its distinctive look. Finally, I'd like to thank (in advance) marketing manager Jeanette Kosinkas, on whose skills I'm counting.

I also wish to acknowledge the members of my family, who play such an essential role in my life. My brother, Michael, my sisters-in-law and brother-in-law, my nieces and nephews—all make up an important part of my life. In addition, I am always indebted to the older generation of my family, who led the way in a manner I can only hope to emulate. I will always be obligated to Harry Brochstein and the late Mary Vorwerk and Ethel Radler. Most of all, the list is headed by my father, the late Saul Feldman, and my mother, Leah Brochstein.

In the end, it is my immediate family who deserve the greatest thanks. My terrific kids, Jonathan (and his wife, Leigh), Joshua, and Sarah not only are nice, smart, and good-looking, but my pride and joy. My grandson Alex has brought immense happiness from the moment of his birth. And ultimately my wife, Katherine Vorwerk, provides the love and grounding that makes everything worthwhile. I thank them, with all my love.

Robert S. Feldman
University of Massachusetts at Amherst

About the Author

Robert S. Feldman is Professor of Psychology and Associate Dean of the College of Social and Behavioral Sciences at the University of Massachusetts at Amherst. A recipient of the College Distinguished Teacher Award, he teaches psychology classes ranging in size from 15 to nearly 500 students. During the course of more than two decades as a college instructor, he has taught both undergraduate and graduate courses at Mount Holyoke College, Wesleyan University, and Virginia Commonwealth University in addition to the University of Massachusetts.

Professor Feldman, who initiated the Minority Mentoring Program at the University of Massachusetts, also has served as a Hewlett Teaching Fellow and Senior Online Teaching Fellow. He initiated distance learning courses in psychology at the University of Massachusetts.

A Fellow of both the American Psychological Association and the Association for Psychological Science, Professor Feldman received a B.A. with High Honors from Wesleyan University and an MS and PhD from the University of Wisconsin-Madison. He is a winner of a Fulbright Senior Research Scholar and Lecturer award, and he has written more than 100 books, book chapters, and scientific articles. He has edited *Development of Nonverbal Behavior in Children* (Springer-Verlag) and *Applications of Nonverbal Behavioral Theory and Research* (Erlbaum), and co-edited *Fundamentals of Nonverbal Behavior* (Cambridge University Press). He is also author of *Child Development, Understanding Psychology* and *P.O.W.E.R. Learning: Strategies for Success in College and Life.* His books have been translated into a number of languages, including Spanish, French, Portuguese, Dutch, Chinese, and Japanese. His research interests include honesty and deception in everyday life and the use of nonverbal behavior in impression management, and his research has been supported by grants from the National Institute of Mental Health and the National Institute on Disabilities and Rehabilitation Research.

Professor Feldman loves music, is an enthusiastic pianist, and enjoys cooking and traveling. He has three children, a young grandson, and he and his wife, a psychologist, live in western Massachusetts, in a home overlooking the Holyoke mountain range.

1 An Introduction to Lifespan Development

Chapter Overview

AN ORIENTATION TO LIFESPAN DEVELOPMENT

Characterizing Lifespan Development: The Scope of the Field

Development

Cohort and Other Influences on Development: Developing with Others in a Social World

KEY ISSUES AND QUESTIONS: DETERMINING THE NATURE— AND NURTURE—OF LIFESPAN DEVELOPMENT

Continuous Change Versus Discontinuous Change

Critical and Sensitive Periods: Gauging the Impact of Environmental Events

Lifespan Approaches Versus a Focus on Particular Periods

The Relative Influence of Nature and Nurture on Development

THEORETICAL PERSPECTIVES ON LIFESPAN DEVELOPMENT

The Psychodynamic Perspective: Focusing on the Inner Person

The Behavioral Perspective: Focusing on Observable Behavior

The Cognitive Perspective: Examining the Roots of Understanding

The Humanistic Perspective: Concentrating on the Unique Qualities of Human Beings

The Contextual Perspective: Taking a Broad Approach to Development

Evolutionary Perspectives: Our Ancestors' Contributions to Behavior

Why "Which Approach Is Right?" Is the Wrong Question

RESEARCH METHODS

Theories and Hypotheses: Posing Developmental Questions

Choosing a Research Strategy: Answering Questions

Correlational Studies

Experiments: Determining Cause and Effect

Theoretical and Applied Research: Complementary Approaches

Measuring Developmental Change

Ethics and Research

Prologue: New Conceptions

What if, for your entire life, the image that others held of you was colored by the way in which you were conceived?

In some ways, that's what it has been like for Louise Brown, who was the world's first "test tube baby," born by *in vitro fertilization (IVF)*, a procedure in which fertilization of a mother's egg by a father's sperm takes place outside of the mother's body.

Louise was a preschooler when her parents told her about how she was conceived, and throughout her childhood she was bombarded with questions. It became routine to explain to her classmates that she, in fact, was not born in a laboratory.

As a child, Louise sometimes felt completely alone. "I thought it was something peculiar to me," she recalled.

In fact, today Louise is hardly isolated. More than 1.5 million babies have been born using the procedure, which has become almost routine. And at the age of 28, Louise became a mother herself, giving birth to a baby boy named Cameron— conceived, by the way, in the old-fashioned way (Moreton, 2007).

Louise Brown (center front) celebrates with hundreds of other guests, all of whom have been conceived by *in vitro* fertilization.

Louise Brown's conception may have been novel, but her development, from infancy, through childhood and adolescence, and to her marriage and the birth of her baby, has followed a predictable pattern. Though the specifics of our development vary—some encounter economic deprivation or live in war-torn territories; others contend with genetic or family issues such as divorce and stepparents—the broad strokes of the development set in motion in that test tube 28 years ago are remarkably similar for all of us. Shaquille O'Neal, Donald Trump, the Queen of England, and each and every one of us are traversing the territory known as lifespan development.

Louise Brown's conception in the lab is just one of the brave new worlds of the 21st century. Issues ranging from cloning to the consequences of poverty on development to the prevention of AIDS raise significant concerns about factors that affect human development. Underlying these are even more fundamental issues: How do we develop physically? How does our understanding of the world grow and change throughout our lives? And how do our personalities and our social relationships develop as we move from birth through the entire span of our lives?

Each of these questions, and many others we'll encounter throughout this book, is central to the field of lifespan development. As a field, lifespan development encompasses not only a broad span of time—from before birth to death—but also a wide range of areas of development. Consider, for example, the range of interests that different specialists in lifespan development focus on when considering the life of Louise Brown:

- Lifespan development researchers who investigate behavior at the level of biological processes might determine if Louise's functioning prior to birth was affected by her conception outside the womb.

- Specialists in lifespan development who study genetics might examine how the genetic endowment from Louise's parents affects her later behavior.

- For lifespan development specialists who investigate the ways that thinking changes over the course of life, Louise's life might be examined in terms of how her understanding of the nature of her conception changed as she grew older.

- Other researchers in lifespan development, who focus on physical growth, might consider whether her growth rate differed from children conceived more traditionally.

- Lifespan development experts who specialize in the social world and social relationships might look at the ways that Louise interacted with others and the kinds of friendships she developed.

Although their interests take many forms, these specialists in lifespan development share one concern: understanding the growth and change that occur during the course of life. Taking many differing approaches, developmentalists study how both our biological inheritance from our parents and the environment in which we live jointly affect our behavior.

Some developmentalists focus on explaining how our genetic background can determine not only how we look but also how we behave and relate to others in a consistent manner—that is, matters of personality. They explore ways to identify how much of our potential as human beings is provided—or limited—by heredity. Other lifespan development specialists look to the environment, exploring ways in which our lives are shaped by the world that we encounter. They investigate the extent to which we are shaped by our early environments, and how our current circumstances influence our behavior in both subtle and evident ways.

Whether they focus on heredity or environment, all developmental specialists acknowledge that neither heredity nor environment alone can account for the full range of human development and change. Instead, our understanding of people's development requires that we look at the joint effects of the interaction of heredity and environment, attempting to grasp how both, in the end, underlie human behavior.

In this chapter, we orient ourselves to the field of lifespan development. We begin with a discussion of the scope of the discipline, illustrating the wide array of topics it covers and the full range of ages it examines. We also survey the key issues and controversies of the field and consider the broad perspectives that developmentalists take. Finally, we discuss the ways developmentalists use research to ask and answer questions.

After reading this chapter, you will be able to answer these questions:

- **What is lifespan development, and what are some of the basic influences on human development?**

- **What are the key issues in the field of development?**

- **Which theoretical perspectives have guided lifespan development?**

- **What role do theories and hypotheses play in the study of development?**

- **How are developmental research studies conducted?**

Looking Ahead

An Orientation to Lifespan Development

Have you ever wondered how it is possible that an infant tightly grips your finger with tiny, perfectly formed hands? Or marveled at how a preschooler methodically draws a picture? Or at the way an adolescent can make involved decisions about whom to invite to a party or the ethics of downloading music files? Or the way a middle-aged politician can deliver a long, flawless speech from memory? Or wondered what it is that makes a grandfather at 80 so similar to the father he was when he was 40?

If you've ever wondered about such things, you are asking the kinds of questions that scientists in the field of lifespan development pose. **Lifespan development** is the field of study that examines patterns of growth, change, and stability in behavior that occur throughout the entire lifespan.

Although the definition of the field seems straightforward, the simplicity is somewhat misleading. In order to understand what development is actually about, we need to look underneath the various parts of the definition.

In its study of growth, change, and stability, lifespan development takes a *scientific* approach. Like members of other scientific disciplines, researchers in lifespan development test their assumptions about the nature and course of human development by applying scientific methods. As we'll see later in the chapter, they develop theories about development, and they use methodical, scientific techniques to validate the accuracy of their assumptions systematically.

Lifespan development focuses on *human* development. Although there are developmentalists who study the course of development in nonhuman species, the vast majority examine growth and change in people. Some seek to understand universal principles of development, while others focus on how cultural, racial, and ethnic differences affect the course of development. Still others aim to understand the unique aspects of individuals, looking at the traits and characteristics that differentiate one person from another. Regardless of approach, however, all developmentalists view development as a continuing process throughout the lifespan.

As developmental specialists focus on the ways people change and grow during their lives, they also consider stability in people's lives. They ask in which areas, and in what periods, people show change and growth, and when and how their behavior reveals consistency and continuity with prior behavior.

lifespan development the field of study that examines patterns of growth, change, and stability in behavior that occur throughout the entire life span.

How people grow and change over the course of their lives is the focus of lifespan development.

physical development development involving the body's physical makeup, including the brain, nervous system, muscles, and senses, and the need for food, drink, and sleep.

cognitive development development involving the ways that growth and change in intellectual capabilities influence a person's behavior.

personality development development involving the ways that the enduring characteristics that differentiate one person from another change over the life span.

social development the way in which individuals' interactions with others and their social relationships grow, change, and remain stable over the course of life.

Finally, developmentalists assume that the process of development persists throughout every part of people's lives, beginning with the moment of conception and continuing until death. Developmental specialists assume that in some ways people continue to grow and change right up to the end of their lives, while in other respects their behavior remains stable. At the same time, developmentalists believe that no particular, single period of life governs all development. Instead, they believe that every period of life contains the potential for both growth and decline in abilities, and that individuals maintain the capacity for substantial growth and change throughout their lives.

Characterizing Lifespan Development: The Scope of the Field

Clearly, the definition of lifespan development is broad and the scope of the field is extensive. Consequently, lifespan development specialists cover several quite diverse areas, and a typical developmentalist will choose to specialize in both a topical area and an age range.

Topical Areas in Lifespan Development. Some developmentalists focus on **physical development,** examining the ways in which the body's makeup—the brain, nervous system, muscles, and senses, and the need for food, drink, and sleep—helps determine behavior. For example, one specialist in physical development might examine the effects of malnutrition on the pace of growth in children, while another might look at how athletes' physical performance declines during adulthood.

Other developmental specialists examine **cognitive development,** seeking to understand how growth and change in intellectual capabilities influence a person's behavior. Cognitive developmentalists examine learning, memory, problem-solving skills, and intelligence. For example, specialists in cognitive development might want to see how problem-solving skills change over the course of life, or if cultural differences exist in the way people explain their academic successes and failures. They would also be interested in how a person who experiences significant or traumatic events early in life would remember them later in life.

Finally, some developmental specialists focus on personality and social development. **Personality development** is the study of stability and change in the enduring characteristics that differentiate one person from another over the lifespan. **Social development** is the way in which individuals' interactions with others and their social relationships grow, change, and remain stable over the course of life. A developmentalist interested in personality development might ask whether there are stable, enduring personality traits throughout the lifespan, while a specialist in social development might examine the effects of racism or poverty or divorce on development. These four major topic areas—physical, cognitive, social, and personality development—are summarized in Table 1-1.

Age Ranges and Individual Differences. In addition to choosing to specialize in a particular topical area, developmentalists also typically look at a particular age range. The lifespan is usually divided into broad age ranges: the prenatal period (the period from conception to birth); infancy and toddlerhood (birth to age 3); the preschool period (ages 3 to 6); middle childhood (ages 6 to 12); adolescence (ages 12 to 20); young adulthood (ages 20 to 40); middle adulthood (ages 40 to 65); and late adulthood (age 65 to death).

It's important to keep in mind that these broad periods—which are largely accepted by lifespan developmentalists—are social constructions. A *social construction* is a shared notion of reality, one that is widely accepted but is a function of society and culture at a given time. Consequently, the age ranges within a period—and even the periods themselves—are in many ways arbitrary and often culturally derived. For example, we'll discuss later how the concept of childhood as a special period did not even exist during the 17th century—at that time, children were seen simply as miniature adults. Furthermore, while some periods have a clear-cut

Table 1-1	Approaches to Lifespan Development	
Orientation	**Defining Characteristics**	**Examples of Question Asked***
Physical development	Emphasizes how brain, nervous system, muscles, sensory capabilities, needs for food, drink, and sleep affect behavior	• What determines the sex of a child? (2) • What are the long-term results of premature birth? (3) • What are the benefits of breast milk? (4) • What are the consequences of early or late sexual maturation? (1) • What leads to obesity in adulthood? (13) • How do adults cope with stress? (15) • What are the outward and internal signs of aging? (17) • How do we define death? (19)
Cognitive development	Emphasizes intellectual abilities, including learning, memory, problem solving, and intelligence	• What are the earliest memories that can be recalled from infancy? (5) • What are the intellectual consequences of watching television? (7) • Do spatial reasoning skills relate to music practice? (7) • Are there benefits to bilingualism? (9) • How does an adolescent's egocentrism affect his or her view of the world? (11) • Are there ethnic and racial differences in intelligence? (9) • How does creativity relate to intelligence? (13) • Does intelligence decline in late adulthood? (17)
Personality and social development	Emphasizes enduring characteristics that differentiate one person from another, and how interactions with others and social relationships grow and change over the lifetime	• Do newborns respond differently to their mothers than to others? (3) • What is the best procedure for disciplining children? (8) • When does a sense of gender identity develop? (8) • How can we promote cross-race friendships? (10) • What are the causes of adolescent suicide? (12) • How do we choose a romantic partner? (14) • Do the effects of parental divorce last into old age? (18) • Do people withdraw from others in late adulthood? (18) • What are the emotions involved in confronting death? (19)

*Numbers in parentheses indicate in which chapter the question is addressed.

boundary (infancy begins with birth, the preschool period ends with entry into public school, and adolescence starts with sexual maturity), others don't.

For instance, consider the period of young adulthood, which at least in Western cultures is typically assumed to begin at age 20. That age, however, is notable only because it marks the end of the teenage period. In fact, for many people, such as those enrolled in higher education, the age change from 19 to 20 has little special significance, coming as it does in the middle of the college years. For them, more substantial changes may occur when they leave college and enter the workforce, which is more likely to happen around age 22. Furthermore, in some non-Western cultures, adulthood may be considered to start much earlier, when children whose educational opportunities are limited begin full-time work.

This wedding of two children in India is an example of how environmental factors can play a significant role in determining the age when a particular event is likely to occur.

In short, there are substantial *individual differences* in the timing of events in people's lives. In part, this is a biological fact of life: People mature at different rates and reach developmental milestones at different points. However, environmental factors also play a significant role in determining the age at which a particular event is likely to occur. For example, the typical age of marriage varies substantially from one culture to another, depending in part on the functions that marriage plays in a given culture.

It is important to keep in mind, then, that when developmental specialists discuss age ranges, they are talking about averages—the times when people, on average, reach particular milestones. Some people will reach the milestone earlier, some later, and many will reach it around the time of the average. Such variation becomes noteworthy only when children show substantial deviation from the average. For example, parents whose child begins to speak at a much later age than average might decide to have their son or daughter evaluated by a speech therapist.

The Links Between Topics and Ages.   Each of the broad topical areas of lifespan development—physical, cognitive, social, and personality development—plays a role throughout the lifespan. Consequently, some developmental experts focus on physical development during the prenatal period, and others during adolescence. Some might specialize in social development during the preschool years, while others look at social relationships in late adulthood. And still others might take a broader approach, looking at cognitive development through every period of life.

In this book, we'll take a comprehensive approach, proceeding chronologically from the prenatal period through late adulthood and death. Within each period, we'll look at different topical areas: physical, cognitive, social, and personality. Furthermore, we'll also be considering the impact of culture on development, as we discuss next.

Developmental Diversity

How Culture, Ethnicity, and Race Influence Development

Mayan mothers in Central America are certain that almost constant contact between themselves and their infant children is necessary for good parenting, and they are physically upset if contact is not possible. They are shocked when they see a North American mother lay her infant down, and they attribute the baby's crying to the poor parenting of the North American. (Morelli et al., 1992)

What are we to make of the two views of parenting expressed in this passage? Is one right and the other wrong? Probably not, if we take into consideration the cultural context in which the mothers are operating. In fact, different cultures and subcultures have their own views of appropriate and inappropriate childrearing, just as they have different developmental goals for children (Greenfield, 1997; Haight, 2002; Tolchinsky, 2003; Feldman & Masalha, 2007).

It has become clear that in order to understand development, developmentalists must take into consideration broad cultural factors, such as an orientation toward individualism or collectivism. They must also take into account finer ethnic, racial, socioeconomic, and gender differences if they are to achieve an understanding of how people change and grow throughout the lifespan. If developmentalists succeed in doing so, not only can they achieve a better understanding of human development, but they may be able to derive more precise applications for improving the human social condition.

Although the field of lifespan development is increasingly concerned with issues of human diversity, its actual progress in this domain has been slow, and in some ways it has actually regressed. For instance, between 1970 and 1989, only 4.6% of the articles published in *Developmental Psychology*, the premier journal of the discipline, focused on African American participants. Moreover, the number of published studies involving African American participants actually declined over that 20-year period (Graham, 1992; MacPhee, Kreutzer, & Fritz, 1994).

Furthermore, members of the research community—as well as society at large—have sometimes used terms such as *race* and *ethnic group* in inappropriate ways. *Race* is a biological concept, which should be employed to refer to classifications based on physical and structural characteristics of species. In contrast, *ethnic group* and *ethnicity* are broader terms, referring to cultural background, nationality, religion, and language.

The concept of race has proven particularly problematic. Although it formally refers to biological factors, race has taken on substantially more meanings—many of them inappropriate—that range from skin color to religion to culture. Moreover, the concept of race is exceedingly imprecise; depending on how it is defined, there are between 3 and 300 races, and no race is genetically distinct. The fact that 99.9% of humans' genetic makeup is identical in all humans makes the question of race seem comparatively insignificant (Bamshad & Olson, 2003; Helms, Jernigan, & Mascher, 2005; Smedley & Smedley, 2005).

In addition, there is little agreement about which names best reflect different races and ethnic groups. Should the term *African American*—which has geographical and cultural implications—be preferred over *black,* which focuses primarily on race and skin color? Is *Native American* preferable to *Indian?* Is *Hispanic* more appropriate than *Latino?* And how can researchers accurately categorize people with multiracial backgrounds?

The choice of category has important implications for the validity (and usefulness) of research. The choice even has political implications. For example, the decision to permit people to identify themselves as "multiracial" on U.S. government forms and in the U.S. Census was highly controversial. In short, although race has little biological significance, it does have social and cultural importance because of the meaning that people give to it (Perlmann & Waters, 2002).

In order to fully understand development, then, we need to take the complex issues associated with human diversity into account. In fact, it is only by looking for similarities and differences among various ethnic, cultural, and racial groups that developmental researchers can distinguish principles of development that are universal from ones that are culturally determined. In the years ahead, then, it is likely that lifespan development will move from a discipline that primarily focuses on North American and European development to one that encompasses development around the globe (Bamshad & Olson, 2003; Fowers & Davidov, 2006; Matsumoto & Yoo, 2006).

Cohort and Other Influences on Development: Developing with Others in a Social World

Bob, born in 1947, is a baby boomer; he was born soon after the end of World War II, when an enormous bulge in the birth rate occurred as soldiers returned to the United States from overseas. He was an adolescent at the height of the civil rights movement and the beginning of protests against the Vietnam War. His mother, Leah, was born in 1922; she is part of the generation that passed its childhood and teenage years in the shadow of the Great Depression. Bob's son, Jon, was born in 1975. Now building a career after graduating from college and starting his own family, he is a member of what has been called Generation X. Jon's younger sister, Sarah, who was born in 1982, is part of the next generation, which sociologists have called the Millennial Generation.

These people are in part products of the social times in which they live. Each belongs to a particular **cohort,** a group of people born at around the same time in the same place. Such major social events as wars, economic upturns and depressions, famines, and epidemics (like the one due to the AIDS virus) work similar influences on members of a particular cohort (Mitchell, 2002; Dittmann, 2005).

Cohort effects provide an example of *history-graded influences,* which are biological and environmental influences associated with a particular historical moment. For instance, people who lived in New York City during the 9/11 terrorist attack on the World Trade Center experienced shared biological and environmental challenges due to the attack (Bonanno et al., 2006; Laugharne, Janca, & Widiger, 2007). In fact, the specter of terrorism is a history-graded influence that is common to people living in the United States today.

In contrast, *age-graded influences* are biological and environmental influences that are similar for individuals in a particular age group, regardless of when or where they are raised. For example, biological events such as puberty and menopause are universal events that occur at relatively the same time throughout all societies. Similarly, a sociocultural event such as entry into formal education can be considered an age-graded influence because it occurs in most cultures around age 6.

Development is also affected by *sociocultural-graded influences,* the social and cultural factors present at a particular time for a particular individual, depending on such variables as ethnicity, social class, and subcultural membership. For example, sociocultural-graded influences will be considerably different for children who are white and affluent than for children who are members of a minority group and living in poverty (Rose et al., 2003).

Finally, *non-normative life events* are specific, atypical events that occur in a particular person's life at a time when such events do not happen to most people. For example, a child whose parents die in an automobile accident when she is 6 years old has experienced a significant non-normative life event.

Key Issues and Questions: Determining the Nature—and Nurture— of Lifespan Development

Lifespan development is a decades-long journey. Though there are some shared markers along the way—such as learning to speak, going to school, and finding a job—there are, as we have just seen, many individual routes with twists and turns along the way that also influence this journey.

For developmentalists working in the field, the range and variation in lifespan development raises a number of issues and questions. What are the best ways to think about the enormous changes that a person undergoes from before birth to death? How important is chronological age? Is there a clear timetable for development? How can one begin to find common threads and patterns?

These questions have been debated since lifespan development first became established as a separate field in the late 19th and early 20th centuries, though a fascination with the nature and course of human development can be traced back to the ancient Egyptians and Greeks. We will look at some of these issues, which are summarized in Table 1-2.

Table 1-2	Major Issues in Lifespan Development	

Continuous Change

- Change is gradual.
- Achievements at one level build on previous level.
- Underlying developmental processes remain the same over the lifespan.

Discontinuous Change

- Change occurs in distinct steps or stages.
- Behavior and processes are qualitatively different at different stages.

Critical Periods

- Certain environmental stimuli are necessary for normal development.
- Emphasized by early developmentalists.

Sensitive Periods

- People are susceptible to certain environmental stimuli, but consequences of absent stimuli are reversible.
- Current emphasis in lifespan development.

Lifespan Approach

- Current theories emphasize growth and change throughout life, relatedness of different periods.

Focus on Particular Periods

- Infancy and adolescence emphasized by early developmentalists as most important periods.

Nature (Genetic Factors)

- Emphasis is on discovering inherited genetic traits and abilities.

Nurture (Environmental Factors)

- Emphasis is on environmental influences that affect a person's development.

Continuous Change Versus Discontinuous Change

One of the primary issues challenging developmentalists is whether development proceeds in a continuous or discontinuous fashion. In **continuous change,** development is gradual, with achievements at one level building on those of previous levels. Continuous change is quantitative in nature; the basic underlying developmental processes that drive change remain the same over the course of the life span. Continuous change, then, produces changes that are a matter of degree, not of kind. Changes in height prior to adulthood, for example, are continuous. Similarly, as we'll see later in the chapter, some theorists suggest that changes in people's thinking capabilities are also continuous, showing gradual quantitative improvements rather than developing entirely new cognitive processing capabilities.

In contrast, one can view development as made up of primarily **discontinuous change,** occurring in distinct stages. Each stage or change brings about behavior that is assumed to be qualitatively different from behavior at earlier stages. Consider the example of cognitive development again. We'll see later in the chapter that some cognitive developmentalists suggest that our thinking changes in fundamental ways as we develop, and that such development is not just a matter of quantitative change but of qualitative change.

Most developmentalists agree that taking an either/or position on the continuous–discontinuous issue is inappropriate. While many types of developmental change are continuous, others are clearly discontinuous (Flavell, 1994; Heimann, 2003).

Critical and Sensitive Periods: Gauging the Impact of Environmental Events

If a woman comes down with a case of rubella (German measles) in the 11th week of pregnancy, the consequences for the child she is carrying are likely to be devastating: They include the potential for blindness, deafness, and heart defects. However, if she comes down with the exact same strain of rubella in the 30th week of pregnancy, damage to the child is unlikely.

The differing outcomes of the disease in the two periods demonstrate the concept of critical periods. A **critical period** is a specific time during development when a particular event has

continuous change gradual development in which achievements at one level build on those of previous levels.

discontinuous change development that occurs in distinct steps or stages, with each stage bringing about behavior that is assumed to be qualitatively different from behavior at earlier stages.

critical period a specific time during development when a particular event has its greatest consequences and the presence of certain kinds of environmental stimuli is necessary for development to proceed normally.

sensitive period a point in development when organisms are particularly susceptible to certain kinds of stimuli in their environments, but the absence of those stimuli does not always produce irreversible consequences.

its greatest consequences. Critical periods occur when the presence of certain kinds of environmental stimuli is necessary for development to proceed normally (Uylings, 2006).

Although early specialists in lifespan development placed great emphasis on the importance of critical periods, more recent thinking suggests that in many realms individuals are more malleable than was first thought, particularly in the domain of personality and social development. For instance, rather than suffering permanent damage from a lack of certain kinds of early social experiences, there is increasing evidence that people can use later experiences to their benefit, to help them overcome earlier deficits. Consequently, developmentalists are now more likely to speak of **sensitive periods** rather than critical periods. In a sensitive period, organisms are particularly susceptible to certain kinds of stimuli in their environments. In contrast to a critical period, however, the absence of those stimuli during a sensitive period does not always produce irreversible consequences (Barinaga, 2000; Thompson & Nelson, 2001; Beauchaine, 2003).

Lifespan Approaches Versus a Focus on Particular Periods

On which part of the life span should developmentalists focus their attention? For early developmentalists, the answers tended to be infancy and adolescence. Most attention was clearly concentrated on those two periods, largely to the exclusion of other parts of the life span.

Today, however, the story is different. Developmentalists now believe the entire life span is important, for several reasons. One is the discovery that developmental growth and change continue during every part of life—as we'll discuss throughout this book.

Furthermore, an important part of every person's environment is the other people around him or her, the person's social environment. To fully understand the social influences on people of a given age, we need to understand the people who are in large measure providing those influences. For instance, to understand development in infants, we need to unravel the effects of their parents' ages on their social environments. A 15-year-old first-time mother will provide parental influences of a very different sort from those provided by an experienced 37-year-old mother. Consequently, infant development is in part an outgrowth consequence of adult development.

Additionally, as lifespan developmentalist Paul Baltes points out, development across the lifespan involves both gains and losses. With age, certain capabilities become more refined and sophisticated, while others involve loss of skill and capacity. For example, vocabulary tends to grow throughout childhood and continues this growth through most of adulthood. At the same time, certain physical abilities, like reaction time, improve until early and middle adulthood, when they begin to decline (Baltes, Staudinger, & Lindenberger, 1999; Baltes, 2003).

People also shift in how they invest their resources (in terms of motivation, energy, and time) at different points during the life span. Early in life, more of one's personal resources are devoted to activities involving growth, such as studying or learning new skills. As one grows older, more resources are devoted to dealing with the losses people face during late adulthood (Staudinger & Leipold, 2003).

The Relative Influence of Nature and Nurture on Development

One of the enduring questions of development involves how much of people's behavior is due to their genetically determined nature and how much is due to nurture, the influences of the physical and social environment in which a child is raised. This issue, which has deep philosophical and historical roots, has dominated much work in lifespan development (Wexler, 2006).

In this context, *nature* refers to traits, abilities, and capacities that are inherited from one's parents. It encompasses any factor that is produced by the predetermined unfolding of genetic information—a process known as **maturation.** These genetic, inherited influences are at work as we move from the one-cell organism that is created at the moment of conception to the billions of cells that make up a fully formed human. Nature influences whether our eyes are blue or brown, whether we have thick hair throughout life or eventually go bald, and how good we are at athletics. Nature allows our brains to develop in such a way that we can read the words on this page.

In contrast, *nurture* refers to the environmental influences that shape behavior. Some of these influences may be biological, such as the impact of a pregnant mother's use of cocaine on her unborn child or the amount and kind of food available to children. Other environmental influences are more social, such as the ways parents discipline their children and the effects of peer pressure on an adolescent. Finally, some influences are a result of larger, societal-level factors, such as the socioeconomic circumstances in which people find themselves.

The Later Action of Nature and Nurture.　If our traits and behavior were determined solely by either nature or nurture, there would probably be little debate regarding the issue. However, for most critical behaviors this is hardly the case. Take, for instance, one of the most controversial areas: intelligence. As we'll consider in detail in Chapter 9, the question of whether intelligence is determined primarily by inherited, genetic factors—nature—or is shaped by environmental factors—nurture—has caused lively and often bitter arguments that have spilled out of the scientific arena and into the realm of politics and social policy.

Consider the implications of the issue: If the extent of one's intelligence is primarily determined by heredity and consequently is largely fixed at birth, then efforts to improve intellectual performance later in life may be doomed to failure. In contrast, if intelligence is primarily a result of environmental factors, such as the amount and quality of schooling and stimulation to which one is exposed, then we would expect that an improvement in social conditions could bring about an increase in intelligence.

The extent of social policy affected by ideas about the origins of intelligence illustrates the significance of issues that involve the nature–nurture question. As we address it in relation to several topical areas throughout this book, we should keep in mind that developmentalists reject the notion that behavior is the result solely of either nature *or* nurture. Instead, the question is one of degree—and the specifics of that, too, are hotly debated.

Furthermore, the interaction of genetic and environmental factors is complex, in part because certain genetically determined traits have not only a direct influence on children's behavior, but an indirect influence in shaping children's *environments* as well. For example, a child who is consistently cranky and who cries a great deal—a trait that may be produced by genetic factors—may influence his or her environment by making his or her parents so highly responsive to the insistent crying that they rush to comfort the child whenever he or she cries. Their responsivity to the child's genetically determined behavior consequently becomes an environmental influence on his or her subsequent development.

Similarly, although our genetic background orients us toward particular behaviors, those behaviors will not necessarily occur without an appropriate environment. People with similar genetic backgrounds (such as identical twins) may behave in very different ways; and people with highly dissimilar genetic backgrounds can behave quite similarly to one another in certain areas (Morange, 2002).

In sum, the question of how much of a given behavior is due to nature, and how much to nurture, is a challenging one. Ultimately, we should consider the two sides of the nature–nurture issue as opposite ends of a continuum, with particular behaviors falling somewhere between the two ends. We can say something similar about the other controversies that we have considered. For instance, continuous versus discontinuous development is not an either/or proposition; some forms of development fall toward the continuous end of the continuum, while others lie closer to the discontinuous end. In short, few statements about development involve either/or absolutes (Rutter, 2006; Deater-Deckard & Cahill, 2007).

maturation the predetermined unfolding of genetic information.

Review and Apply

Review

- Lifespan development, a scientific approach to understanding human growth and change throughout life, encompasses physical, cognitive, social, and personality development.
- Culture and ethnicity also play an important role in development, both broad culture and aspects of culture, such as race, ethnicity, and socioeconomic status.
- Membership in a cohort, based on age and place of birth, subjects people to influences based on historical events (history-graded influences). People are also subject to age-graded influences, sociocultural-graded influences, and non-normative life events.
- Four important issues in lifespan development are continuity versus discontinuity in development, the importance of critical periods, whether to focus on certain periods or on the entire life span, and the nature–nurture controversy.

Applying Lifespan Development

- What are some examples of the ways culture (either broad culture or aspects of culture) affects human development?
- *From an educator's perspective:* How would a student's cohort membership affect his or her readiness for school? For example, what would be the benefits and drawbacks of coming from a cohort in which Internet use was routine, compared with earlier cohorts prior to the appearance of the Internet?

Theoretical Perspectives on Lifespan Development

In Europe, there was no concept of "childhood" until the 17th century. Instead, children were simply thought of as miniature adults. They were assumed to be subject to the same needs and desires as adults, to have the same vices and virtues as adults, and to warrant no more privileges than adults. They were dressed the same as adults, and their work hours were the same as adults'. Children also received the same punishments for misdeeds. If they stole, they were hanged; if they did well, they could achieve prosperity, at least so far as their station in life or social class would allow.

This view of childhood seems wrong-headed now, but at the time it is what passed for lifespan development. From this perspective, there were no differences due to age; except for size, people were assumed to be virtually unchanging, at least on a psychological level, throughout most of the life span (Ariès, 1962; Acocella, 2003; Hutton, 2004; Wines, 2006).

Although, looking back over several centuries, it is easy to reject the medieval view of childhood, it is less clear how to formulate a contemporary substitute. Should our view of development focus on the biological aspects of change, growth, and stability over the life span? The cognitive or social aspects? Or some other factors?

In fact, people who study lifespan development approach the field from a number of different perspectives. Each broad perspective encompasses one or more **theories,** broad, organized explanations and predictions concerning phenomena of interest. A theory provides

theories   explanations and predictions concerning phenomena of interest, providing a framework for understanding the relationships among an organized set of facts or principles.

a framework for understanding the relationships among a seemingly unorganized set of facts or principles.

We all develop theories about development, based on our experience, folklore, and articles in magazines and newspapers. However, theories in lifespan development are different. Whereas our own personal theories are built on unverified observations that are developed haphazardly, developmentalists' theories are more formal, based on a systematic integration of prior findings and theorizing. These theories allow developmentalists to summarize and organize prior observations, and they allow them to move beyond existing observations to draw deductions that may not be immediately apparent. In addition, these theories are then subject to rigorous testing in the form of research. By contrast, the developmental theories of individuals are not subject to such testing and may never be questioned at all (Thomas, 2001).

We will consider six major theoretical perspectives used in lifespan development: the psychodynamic, behavioral, cognitive, humanistic, contextual, and evolutionary perspectives. Each emphasizes somewhat different aspects of development and steers developmentalists in particular directions. Furthermore, each perspective continues to evolve and change, as befits a growing and dynamic discipline.

Society's view of childhood, and what is appropriate to ask of children, has changed through the ages. These children worked full-time in mines in the early 1900s.

The Psychodynamic Perspective: Focusing on the Inner Person

When Marisol was 6 months old, she was involved in a bloody automobile accident—or so her parents tell her, since she has no conscious recollection of it. Now, however, at age 24, she is having difficulty maintaining relationships, and her therapist is seeking to determine whether her current problems are a result of the earlier accident.

Looking for such a link might seem a bit far-fetched, but to proponents of the **psychodynamic perspective,** it is not so improbable. Advocates of the psychodynamic perspective believe that much of behavior is motivated by inner forces, memories, and conflicts of which a person has little awareness or control. The inner forces, which may stem from one's childhood, continually influence behavior throughout the life span.

Freud's Psychoanalytic Theory.   The psychodynamic perspective is most closely associated with a single person and theory: Sigmund Freud and his psychoanalytic theory. Freud, who lived from 1856 to 1939, was a Viennese physician whose revolutionary ideas ultimately had a profound effect not only on the fields of psychology and psychiatry, but on Western thought in general (Masling & Bornstein, 1996).

Freud's **psychoanalytic theory** suggests that unconscious forces act to determine personality and behavior. To Freud, the *unconscious* is a part of the personality about which a person is unaware. It contains infantile wishes, desires, demands, and needs that are hidden, because of their disturbing nature, from conscious awareness. Freud suggested that the unconscious is responsible for a good part of our everyday behavior.

Sigmund Freud

According to Freud, everyone's personality has three aspects: id, ego, and superego. The *id* is the raw, unorganized, inborn part of personality that is present at birth. It represents primitive drives related to hunger, sex, aggression, and irrational impulses. The id operates according to the *pleasure principle*, in which the goal is to maximize satisfaction and reduce tension.

The *ego* is the part of personality that is rational and reasonable. The ego acts as a buffer between the real world outside of us and the primitive id. The ego operates on the *reality principle*, in which instinctual energy is restrained in order to maintain the safety of the individual and help integrate the person into society.

Finally, Freud proposed that the *superego* represents a person's conscience, incorporating distinctions between right and wrong. It begins to develop around age 5 or 6 and is learned from an individual's parents, teachers, and other significant figures.

psychodynamic perspective   the approach stating that behavior is motivated by inner forces, memories, and conflicts that are generally beyond people's awareness and control.

psychoanalytic theory   the theory proposed by Freud that suggests that unconscious forces act to determine personality and behavior.

In addition to providing an account of the various parts of the personality, Freud also suggested the ways in which personality developed during childhood. He argued that **psychosexual development** occurs as children pass through a series of stages in which pleasure, or gratification, is focused on a particular biological function and body part. As illustrated in Table 1-3, he suggested that pleasure shifts from the mouth (the *oral stage*) to the anus (the *anal stage*) and eventually to the genitals (the *phallic stage* and the *genital stage*).

Table 1-3   Freud's and Erikson's Theories

Approximate Age	Freud's Stages of Psychosexual Development	Major Characteristics of Freud's Stages	Erikson's Stages of Psychosocial Development	Positive and Negative Outcomes of Erikson's Stages
Birth to 12–18 months	Oral	Interest in oral gratification from sucking, eating, mouthing, biting	Trust vs. mistrust	*Positive:* Feelings of trust from environmental support *Negative:* Fear and concern regarding others
12–18 months to 3 years	Anal	Gratification from expelling and withholding feces; coming to terms with society's controls relating to toilet training	Autonomy vs. shame and doubt	*Positive:* Self-sufficiency if exploration is encouraged *Negative:* Doubts about self, lack of independence
3 to 5–6 years	Phallic	Interest in the genitals; coming to terms with Oedipal conflict, leading to identification with same sex parent	Initiative vs. guilt	*Positive:* Discovery of ways to initiate actions *Negative:* Guilt from actions and thoughts
5–6 years to adolescence	Latency	Sexual concerns largely unimportant	Industry vs. inferiority	*Positive:* Development of sense of competence *Negative:* Feelings of inferiority, no sense of mastery
Adolescence to adulthood (Freud) Adolescence (Erikson)	Genital	Reemergence of sexual interests and establishment of mature sexual relationships	Identity vs. role diffusion	*Positive:* Awareness of uniqueness of self, knowledge of role to be followed *Negative:* Inability to identify appropriate roles in life
Early adulthood (Erikson)			Intimacy vs. isolation	*Positive:* Development of loving, sexual relationships and close friendships *Negative:* Fear of relationships with others
Middle adulthood (Erikson)			Generativity vs. stagnation	*Positive:* Sense of contribution to continuity of life *Negative:* Trivialization of one's activities
Late adulthood (Erikson)			Ego-integrity vs. despair	*Positive:* Sense of unity in life's accomplishments *Negative:* Regret over lost opportunities of life

According to Freud, if children are unable to gratify themselves sufficiently during a particular stage, or conversely, if they receive too much gratification, fixation may occur. *Fixation* is behavior reflecting an earlier stage of development due to an unresolved conflict. For instance, fixation at the oral stage might produce an adult unusually absorbed in oral activities—eating, talking, or chewing gum. Freud also argued that fixation is represented through symbolic sorts of oral activities, such as the use of "biting" sarcasm.

Erikson's Psychosocial Theory.   Psychoanalyst Erik Erikson, who lived from 1902 to 1994, provided an alternative psychodynamic view in his theory of psychosocial development, which emphasizes our social interaction with other people. In Erikson's view, society and culture both challenge and shape us. **Psychosocial development** encompasses changes in our interactions with and understandings of one another as well as in our knowledge and understanding of us as members of society (Erikson, 1963).

Erikson's theory suggests that developmental change occurs throughout our lives in eight distinct stages (see Table 1-3). The stages emerge in a fixed pattern and are similar for all people. Erikson argued that each stage presents a crisis or conflict that the individual must resolve. Although no crisis is ever fully resolved, making life increasingly complicated, the individual must at least address the crisis of each stage sufficiently to deal with demands made during the next stage of development.

Unlike Freud, who regarded development as relatively complete by adolescence, Erikson suggested that growth and change continue throughout the life span. For instance, as we'll discuss further in Chapter 16, he suggested that during middle adulthood, people pass through the *generativity versus stagnation stage*, in which their contributions to family, community, and society can produce either positive feelings about the continuity of life or a sense of stagnation and disappointment about what they are passing on to future generations (de St. Aubin, McAdams, & Kim, 2004).

Assessing the Psychodynamic Perspective.   It is hard for us to grasp the full significance of psychodynamic theories represented by Freud's psychoanalytic theory and Erikson's theory of psychosocial development. Freud's introduction of the notion that unconscious influences affect behavior was a monumental accomplishment, and that it seems at all reasonable to us shows how extensively the idea of the unconscious has pervaded thinking in Western cultures. In fact, work by contemporary researchers studying memory and learning suggests that we carry with us memories—of which we are not consciously aware—that have a significant impact on our behavior. The example of Marisol, who was in a car accident when she was a baby, shows one application of psychodynamically based thinking and research.

Some of the most basic principles of Freud's psychoanalytic theory have been called into question, however, because they have not been validated by subsequent research. In particular, the notion that people pass through stages in childhood that determine their adult personalities has little definitive research support. In addition, because much of Freud's theory was based on a limited population of upper-middle-class Austrians living during a strict, puritanical era, its application to broad, multicultural populations is questionable. Finally, because Freud's theory focuses primarily on male development, it has been criticized as sexist and may be interpreted as devaluing women. For such reasons, many developmentalists question Freud's theory (Crews, 1993; Guterl, 2002; Messer & McWilliams, 2003).

Erikson's view that development continues throughout the lifespan is highly important—and has received considerable support. However, the theory also has its drawbacks. Like Freud's theory, it focuses more on men's than women's development. It is also vague in some respects, making it difficult for researchers to test rigorously. And, as is the case with psychodynamic theories in general, it is difficult to make definitive predictions about a given individual's behavior using the theory. In sum, then, the psychodynamic perspective provides good descriptions of past behavior, but imprecise predictions of future behavior (Whitbourne et al., 1992; Zauszniewski & Martin, 1999; de St. Aubin & McAdams, 2004).

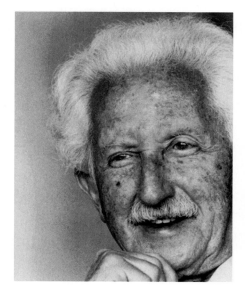

Erik Erikson

psychosocial development the approach that encompasses changes in our interactions with and understandings of one another, as well as in our knowledge and understanding of ourselves as members of society.

behavioral perspective the approach suggesting that the keys to understanding development are observable behavior and outside stimuli in the environment.

classical conditioning a type of learning in which an organism responds in a particular way to a neutral stimulus that normally does not bring about that type of response.

operant conditioning a form of learning in which a voluntary response is strengthened or weakened by its association with positive or negative consequences.

The Behavioral Perspective: Focusing on Observable Behavior

When Elissa Sheehan was 3, a large brown dog bit her, and she needed dozens of stitches and several operations. From the time she was bitten, she broke into a sweat whenever she saw a dog, and in fact never enjoyed being around any pet.

To a lifespan development specialist using the behavioral perspective, the explanation for Elissa's behavior is straightforward: She has a learned fear of dogs. Rather than looking inside the organism at unconscious processes, the **behavioral perspective** suggests that the keys to understanding development are observable behavior and outside stimuli in the environment. If we know the stimuli, we can predict the behavior. In this respect, the behavioral perspective reflects the view that nurture is more important to development than nature.

Behavioral theories reject the notion that people universally pass through a series of stages. Instead, people are assumed to be affected by the environmental stimuli to which they happen to be exposed. Developmental patterns, then, are personal, reflecting a particular set of environmental stimuli, and behavior is the result of continuing exposure to specific factors in the environment. Furthermore, developmental change is viewed in quantitative, rather than qualitative, terms. For instance, behavioral theories hold that advances in problem-solving capabilities as children age are largely a result of greater mental *capacities*, rather than changes in the *kind* of thinking that children are able to bring to bear on a problem.

Classical Conditioning: Stimulus Substitution

> Give me a dozen healthy infants, well-formed, and my own specified world to bring them up in and I'll guarantee to take any one at random and train him to become any type of specialist I might select—doctor, lawyer, artist, merchant-chief, and yes, even beggar-man and thief, regardless of his talents, penchants, tendencies, abilities. . . . (Watson, 1925)

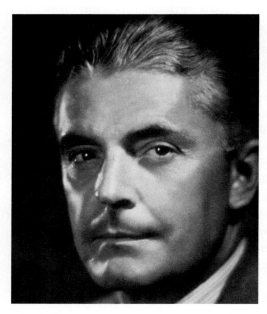

John B. Watson

With these words, John B. Watson, one of the first American psychologists to advocate a behavioral approach, summed up the behavioral perspective. Watson, who lived from 1878 to 1958, believed strongly that we could gain a full understanding of development by carefully studying the stimuli that composed the environment. In fact, he argued that by effectively controlling a person's environment, it was possible to produce virtually any behavior.

As we'll consider further in Chapter 5, **classical conditioning** occurs when an organism learns to respond in a particular way to a neutral stimulus that normally does not evoke that type of response. For instance, if a dog is repeatedly exposed to the pairing of the sound of a bell and the presentation of meat, it may learn to react to the bell alone in the same way it reacts to the meat—by salivating and wagging its tail with excitement. Dogs don't typically respond to bells in this way; the behavior is a result of conditioning, a form of learning in which the response associated with one stimulus (food) comes to be connected to another—in this case, the bell.

The same process of classical conditioning explains how we learn emotional responses. In the case of dog-bite victim Elissa Sheehan, for instance, Watson would say that one stimulus has been substituted for another: Elissa's unpleasant experience with a particular dog (the initial stimulus) has been transferred to other dogs and to pets in general.

Operant Conditioning.　In addition to classical conditioning, other types of learning also derive from the behavioral perspective. In fact, the learning approach that probably has had the greatest influence is operant conditioning. **Operant conditioning** is a form of learning in which a voluntary response is strengthened or weakened by its association with positive or negative consequences. It differs from classical conditioning in that the response being conditioned is voluntary and purposeful rather than automatic (such as salivating).

In operant conditioning, formulated and championed by psychologist B. F. Skinner (1904–1990), individuals learn to act deliberately on their environments in order to bring about desired consequences (Skinner, 1975). In a sense, then, people *operate* on their environments to bring about a desired state of affairs.

Whether or not children and adults will seek to repeat a behavior depends on whether it is followed by reinforcement. *Reinforcement* is the process by which a stimulus is provided that increases the probability that a preceding behavior will be repeated. Hence, a student is apt to work harder in school if he or she receives good grades; workers are likely to labor harder at their jobs if their efforts are tied to pay increases; and people are more apt to buy lottery tickets if they are reinforced by winning occasionally. In addition, *punishment*, the introduction of an unpleasant or painful stimulus or the removal of a desirable stimulus, will decrease the probability that a preceding behavior will occur in the future.

Behavior that is reinforced, then, is more likely to be repeated in the future, while behavior that receives no reinforcement or is punished is likely to be discontinued, or in the language of operant conditioning, *extinguished*. Principles of operant conditioning are used in **behavior modification,** a formal technique for promoting the frequency of desirable behaviors and decreasing the incidence of unwanted ones. Behavior modification has been used in a variety of situations, ranging from teaching severely retarded people the rudiments of language to helping people stick to diets (Katz, 2001; Christophersen & Mortweet, 2003; Hoek & Gendall, 2006).

behavior modification   a formal technique for promoting the frequency of desirable behaviors and decreasing the incidence of unwanted ones.

social-cognitive learning theory   learning by observing the behavior of another person, called a model.

Social-Cognitive Learning Theory: Learning Through Imitation. A 5-year-old boy seriously injures his 22-month-old cousin while imitating a violent wrestling move he had seen on television. Although the infant sustained spinal cord injuries, he improved and was discharged 5 weeks after his hospital admission (Reuters Health eLine, 2002).

Cause and effect? We can't know for sure, but it certainly seems possible, especially looking at the situation from the perspective of social-cognitive learning theory. According to developmental psychologist Albert Bandura and colleagues, a significant amount of learning is explained by **social-cognitve learning theory,** an approach that emphasizes learning by observing the behavior of another person, called a *model* (Bandura, 1977, 1994, 2002).

Rather than learning being a matter of trial and error, as it is with operant conditioning, according to social-cognitive learning theory, behavior is learned through observation. We don't need to experience the consequences of a behavior ourselves to learn it. Social-cognitive learning theory holds that when we see the behavior of a model being rewarded, we are likely to imitate that behavior. For instance, in one classic experiment, children who were afraid of dogs were exposed to a model, nicknamed the "Fearless Peer," who was seen playing happily with a dog (Bandura, Grusec, & Menlove, 1967). After exposure, the children who previously had been afraid were more likely to approach a strange dog than children who had not seen the model.

Bandura suggests that social-cognitive learning proceeds in four steps (Bandura, 1986). First, an observer must pay attention and perceive the most critical features of a model's behavior. Second, the observer must successfully recall the behavior. Third, the observer must reproduce the behavior accurately. Finally, the observer must be motivated to learn and carry out the behavior.

On the reality show *Survivor*, contestants often must learn new survival skills in order to be successful. What form of learning is prevalent?

Assessing the Behavioral Perspective.   Research using the behavioral perspective has made significant contributions, ranging from techniques for educating children with severe mental retardation to identifying procedures for curbing aggression. At the same time, there are controversies regarding the behavioral perspective. For example, although they are part of the same general behavioral perspective, classical and operant conditioning and social learning theory disagree in some basic ways. Both classical and operant conditioning consider learning

cognitive perspective the approach that focuses on the processes that allow people to know, understand, and think about the world.

in terms of external stimuli and responses, in which the only important factors are the observable features of the environment. In such an analysis, people and other organisms are like inanimate "black boxes"; nothing that occurs inside the box is understood—nor much cared about, for that matter.

To social learning theorists, such an analysis is an oversimplification. They argue that what makes people different from rats and pigeons is the occurrence of mental activity, in the form of thoughts and expectations. A full understanding of people's development, they maintain, cannot occur without moving beyond external stimuli and responses.

In many ways, social learning theory has come to predominate in recent decades over classical and operant conditioning theories. In fact, another perspective that focuses explicitly on internal mental activity has become enormously influential. This is the cognitive approach, which we consider next.

The Cognitive Perspective: Examining the Roots of Understanding

When 3-year-old Jake is asked why it sometimes rains, he answers "so the flowers can grow." When his 11-year-old sister Lila is asked the same question, she responds "because of evaporation from the surface of the Earth." And when their cousin Ajima, who is studying meteorology in graduate school, considers the same question, her extended answer includes a discussion of cumulo-nimbus clouds, the coriolis effect, and synoptic charts.

To a developmental theorist using the cognitive perspective, the difference in the sophistication of the answers is evidence of a different degree of knowledge and understanding, or cognition. The **cognitive perspective** focuses on the processes that allow people to know, understand, and think about the world.

The cognitive perspective emphasizes how people internally represent and think about the world. By using this perspective, developmental researchers hope to understand how children and adults process information and how their ways of thinking and understanding affect their behavior. They also seek to learn how cognitive abilities change as people develop, the degree to which cognitive development represents quantitative and qualitative growth in intellectual abilities, and how different cognitive abilities are related to one another.

Piaget's Theory of Cognitive Development. No single person has had a greater impact on the study of cognitive development than Jean Piaget. A Swiss psychologist who lived from 1896 to 1980, Piaget proposed that all people pass in a fixed sequence through a series of universal stages of cognitive development. He suggested that not only does the quantity of information increase in each stage, but the quality of knowledge and understanding changes as well. His focus was on the change in cognition that occurs as children move from one stage to the next (Piaget, 1952, 1962, 1983).

Although we'll consider Piaget's theory in detail beginning in Chapter 5, we can get a broad sense of it now. Piaget suggested that human thinking is arranged into *schemes*, organized mental patterns that represent behaviors and actions. In infants, such schemes represent concrete behavior—a scheme for sucking, for reaching, and for each separate behavior. In older children, the schemes become more sophisticated and abstract, such as the set of skills involved in riding a bike or playing an interactive video game. Schemes are like intellectual computer software programs that direct and determine how data from the world are looked at and dealt with.

Piaget suggests that the growth in children's understanding of the world can be explained by the two basic principles of assimilation and accommodation. *Assimilation* is the process in which people understand an experience in terms of their current stage of cognitive development and way of thinking. Assimilation occurs when people use their current ways of thinking about and understanding the world to perceive and understand a new experience. In contrast, *accommodation* refers to changes in existing ways of thinking in response to encounters with new stimuli or events. Assimilation and accommodation work in tandem to bring about cognitive development.

Assessing Piaget's Theory. Piaget has profoundly influenced our understanding of cognitive development and is one of the towering figures in lifespan development. He provided masterful descriptions of how intellectual growth proceeds during childhood—descriptions that have stood the test of literally thousands of investigations. By and large, then, Piaget's broad view of the sequence of cognitive development is accurate.

However, the specifics of the theory, particularly in terms of change in cognitive capabilities over time, have been called into question. For instance, some cognitive skills clearly emerge earlier than Piaget suggested. Furthermore, the universality of Piaget's stages has been disputed. A growing amount of evidence suggests that the emergence of particular cognitive skills occurs according to a different timetable in non-Western cultures. And in every culture, some people never seem to reach Piaget's highest level of cognitive sophistication: formal, logical thought (Rogoff & Chavajay, 1995; McDonald & Stuart-Hamilton, 2003; Genovese, 2006).

Ultimately, the greatest criticism leveled at the Piagetian perspective is that cognitive development is not necessarily as discontinuous as Piaget's stage theory suggests. Remember that Piaget argued that growth proceeds in four distinct stages in which the quality of cognition differs from one stage to the next. However, many developmental researchers argue that growth is considerably more continuous. These critics have suggested an alternative perspective, known as the information processing approach, that focuses on the processes that underlie learning, memory, and thinking throughout the life span.

Information Processing Approaches.   Information processing approaches have become an important alternative to Piagetian approaches. **Information processing approaches** to cognitive development seek to identify the ways individuals take in, use, and store information.

Information processing approaches grew out of developments in the electronic processing of information, particularly as carried out by computers. They assume that even complex behavior such as learning, remembering, categorizing, and thinking can be broken down into a series of individual, specific steps.

Like computers, children are assumed by information processing approaches to have limited capacity for processing information. As they develop, though, they employ increasingly sophisticated strategies that allow them to process information more efficiently.

In stark contrast to Piaget's view that thinking undergoes qualitative advances as children age, information processing approaches assume that development is marked more by quantitative advances. Our capacity to handle information changes with age, as does our processing speed and efficiency. Furthermore, information processing approaches suggest that as we age, we are better able to control the nature of processing and that we can change in the strategies we use to process information.

An information processing approach that builds on Piaget's research is known as neo-Piagetian theory. In contrast to Piaget's original work, which viewed cognition as a single system of increasingly sophisticated general cognitive abilities, *neo-Piagetian theory* considers cognition as made up of different types of individual skills. Using the terminology of information processing approaches, neo-Piagetian theory suggests that cognitive development proceeds quickly in certain areas and more slowly in others. For example, reading ability and the skills needed to recall stories may progress sooner than the sorts of abstract computational abilities used in algebra or trigonometry. Furthermore, neo-Piagetian theorists believe that experience plays a greater role in advancing cognitive development than traditional Piagetian approaches claim (Case, 1999; Case, Demetriou, & Platsidou, 2001; Yan & Fischer, 2002).

Assessing Information Processing Approaches. As we'll see in future chapters, information processing approaches have become a central part of our understanding of development. At the same time, they do not offer a complete explanation for behavior. For example, information

information processing approaches models that seek to identify the ways individuals take in, use, and store information.

processing approaches have paid little attention to behavior such as creativity, in which the most profound ideas often are developed in a seemingly nonlogical, nonlinear manner. In addition, they do not take into account the social context in which development takes place. That's one of the reasons that theories that emphasize the social and cultural aspects of development have become increasingly popular—as we'll discuss next.

Cognitive Neuroscience Approaches.   One of the most recent additions to the array of approaches taken by lifespan developmentalists, **cognitive neuroscience approaches** look at cognitive development through the lens of brain processes. Like other cognitive perspectives, cognitive neuroscience approaches consider internal, mental processes, but they focus specifically on the neurological activity that underlies thinking, problem solving, and other cognitive behavior.

Cognitive neuroscientists seek to identify actual locations and functions within the brain that are related to different types of cognitive activity, rather than simply assuming that there are hypothetical or theoretical cognitive structures related to thinking. For example, using sophisticated brain scanning techniques, cognitive neuroscientists have demonstrated that thinking about the meaning of a word activates different areas of the brain than thinking about how the word sounds when spoken.

Work of cognitive neuroscientists is also providing clues to the cause of *autism*, a major developmental disability that can produce profound language deficits and self-injurious behavior in young children. For example, neuroscientists have found that the brains of children with the disorder show explosive, dramatic growth in the first year of life, making their heads significantly larger than those of children without the disorder (see Figure 1-1). By identifying children with the disorder very early in their lives, health-care providers can provide crucial early intervention (Courchesne, Carper, & Akshoomoff, 2003; Herbert et al., 2005; Akshoomoff, 2006).

Cognitive neuroscience approaches are also on the forefront of cutting-edge research that has identified specific genes that are associated with disorders ranging from physical problems such as breast cancer to psychological disorders such as schizophrenia (DeLisi & Fleischhaker, 2007). Identifying the genes that make one vulnerable to such disorders is the first step in genetic engineering in which gene therapy can reduce or even prevent the disorder from occurring.

The Humanistic Perspective: Concentrating on the Unique Qualities of Human Beings

The unique qualities of humans are the central focus of the humanistic perspective, the fourth of the major theories used by lifespan developmentalists. Rejecting the notion that our behavior is largely determined by unconscious processes, by learning from our environment, or by rational cognitive processing, the **humanistic perspective** contends that people have a natural capacity to make decisions about their lives and to control their behavior. According to this approach, each individual has the ability and motivation to reach more advanced levels of maturity, and people naturally seek to reach their full potential.

The humanistic perspective emphasizes *free will*, the ability of humans to make choices and come to decisions about their lives. Instead of relying on societal standards, then, people are assumed to be motivated to make their own decisions about what they do with their lives.

Carl Rogers, one of the major proponents of the humanistic perspective, suggested that all people have a need for positive regard that results from an underlying wish to be loved and respected. Because it is other people who provide this positive regard, we become dependent upon them. Consequently, our view of ourselves and our self-worth is a reflection of how we think others view us (Rogers, 1971; Motschnig & Nykl, 2003). Rogers, along with another key figure in the humanistic perspective, Abraham Maslow, suggests that self-actualization is a primary goal in life. *Self-actualization* is a state of self-fulfillment in which people achieve their highest potential in their own unique way. Although the concept initially was deemed to apply

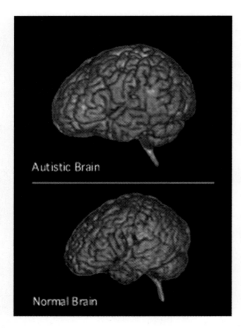

Autistic Brain

Normal Brain

FIGURE 1-1 **THE AUTISTIC BRAIN**
Neuroscientists have found that the brain of an individual with autism is larger than those of individuals without autism. This finding might help determine the disorder early so proper health care can be provided.
(*Source:* Courchesne website at http://www.courchesneautismlab.org/mri.html.)

to only a few select, famous people, such as Eleanor Roosevelt, Abraham Lincoln, and Albert Einstein, later theorists expanded the concept to apply to any person who realizes his or her own potential and possibilities (Maslow, 1970; Jones & Crandall, 1991; Sheldon, Joiner, & Pettit, 2003).

Assessing the Humanistic Perspective.   Despite its emphasis on important and unique human qualities, the humanistic perspective has not had a major impact on the field of lifespan development. Its lack of influence is primarily due to its inability to identify any sort of broad developmental change that is the result of increasing age or experience. Still, some of the concepts drawn from the humanistic perspective, such as self-actualization, have helped describe important aspects of human behavior and are widely discussed in areas ranging from health care to business (Neher, 1991; Dorer & Mahoney, 2006; Laas, 2006; Zalenski & Raspa, 2006).

The Contextual Perspective: Taking a Broad Approach to Development

Although lifespan developmentalists often consider the course of development in terms of physical, cognitive, personality, and social factors separately, such a categorization has one serious drawback: In the real world, none of these broad influences occurs in isolation from any other. Instead, there is a constant, ongoing interaction between the different types of influence.

The **contextual perspective** considers the relationship between individuals and their physical, cognitive, personality, and social worlds. It suggests that a person's unique development cannot be properly viewed without seeing how that person is enmeshed within a rich social and cultural context. We'll consider two major theories that fall under this category, Bronfenbrenner's bioecological approach and Vygotsky's sociocultural theory.

The Bioecological Approach to Development.   In acknowledging the problem with traditional approaches to lifespan development, psychologist Urie Bronfenbrenner (1989, 2000, 2002) has proposed an alternative perspective, called the bioecological approach. The **bioecological approach** suggests there are four levels of the environment that simultaneously influence individuals. Bronfenbrenner suggests that we cannot fully understand development without considering how a person is influenced by each of these levels (illustrated in Figure 1-2).

- The *microsystem* is the everyday, immediate environment in which children lead their daily lives. Homes, caregivers, friends, and teachers all are influences that are part of the microsystem. But the child is not just a passive recipient of these influences. Instead, children actively help construct the microsystem, shaping the immediate world in which they live. The microsystem is the level at which most traditional work in child development has been directed.

- The *mesosystem* provides connections between the various aspects of the microsystem. Like links in a chain, the mesosystem binds children to parents, students to teachers, employees to bosses, friends to friends. It acknowledges the direct and indirect influences that bind us to one another, such as those that affect a mother or father who has a bad day at the office and then is short-tempered with her or his son or daughter at home.

- The *exosystem* represents broader influences, encompassing societal institutions such as local government, the community, schools, places of worship, and the local media. Each of these larger institutions of society can have an immediate, and major, impact on personal development, and each affects how the microsystem and mesosystem operate. For example, the quality of a school will affect a child's cognitive development and potentially can have long-term consequences.

- The *macrosystem* represents the larger cultural influences on an individual. Society in general, types of governments, religious and political value systems, and other broad,

contextual perspective   the theory that considers the relationship between individuals and their physical, cognitive, personality, and social worlds.

bioecological approach   the perspective suggesting that different levels of the environment simultaneously influence individuals.

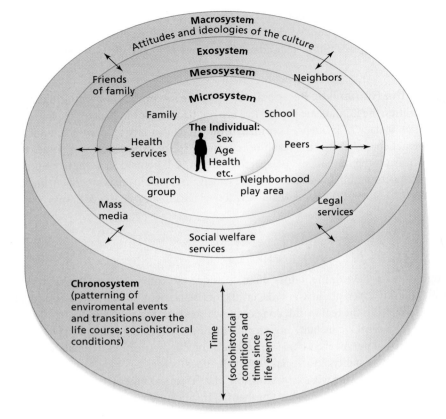

FIGURE 1-2   BRONFENBRENNER'S APPROACH TO DEVELOPMENT

Urie Bronfenbrenner's bioecological approach to development offers four levels of the environment that simultaneously influence individuals: the macrosystem, exosystem, mesosystem, and microsystem.

(*Source:* Bronfenbrenner, 1979.)

encompassing factors are parts of the macrosystem. For example, the value a culture or society places on education or the family will affect the values of the people who live in that society. Children are part of both a broader culture (such as Western culture) as well as being influenced by their membership in a particular subculture (for instance, being part of the Mexican-American subculture).

- Finally, the *chronosystem* underlies each of the previous systems. It involves the way the passage of time, including historical events (such as the terrorist attacks in September of 2001) and more gradual historical changes (such as changes in the number of women who work outside of the home) affect children's development.

The bioecological approach emphasizes the *interconnectedness of the influences on development*. Because the various levels are related to one another, a change in one part of the system affects other parts of the system. For instance, a parent's loss of a job (involving the mesosystem) has an impact upon a child's microsystem.

Conversely, changes on one environmental level may make little difference if other levels are not also changed. For instance, improving the school environment may have a negligible effect on academic performance if children receive little support for academic success at home. Similarly, the bioecological approach illustrates that the influences among different family members are multidirectional. Parents don't just influence their child's behavior—the child also influences the parents' behavior.

Finally, the bioecological approach stresses the importance of broad cultural factors that affect development. Researchers in lifespan development increasingly look at how membership in cultural and subcultural groups influences behavior.

Consider, for instance, whether you agree that children should be taught that their class-mates' assistance is indispensable to getting good grades in school, or that they should definitely plan to continue their fathers' businesses, or that children should follow their parents'

The bioecological approach to development focuses on the vast differences in environments in which children develop.

advice in determining their career plans. If you have been raised in the most widespread North American culture, you would likely disagree with all three statements, since they violate the premises of *individualism,* the dominant Western philosophy that emphasizes personal identity, uniqueness, freedom, and the worth of the individual.

On the other hand, if you were raised in a traditional Asian culture, your agreement with the three statements would be considerably more likely. The reason? The statements reflect the value orientation known as collectivism. *Collectivism* is the notion that the well-being of the group is more important than that of the individual. People raised in collectivistic cultures tend to emphasize the welfare of the groups to which they belong, sometimes even at the expense of their own personal well-being.

The individualism–collectivism spectrum is one of several dimensions along which cultures differ, and it illustrates differences in the cultural contexts in which people operate. As we'll see in Chapter 12, such broad cultural values play an important role in shaping the ways people view the world and behave (Choi, 2002; Sedikides, Gaertner, & Toguchi, 2003; Leung, 2005).

Assessing the Bioecological Approach. Although Bronfenbrenner considers biological influences as an important component of the bioecological approach, ecological influences are central to the theory. In fact, some critics argue that the perspective pays insufficient attention to biological factors. Still, the bioecological approach is of considerable importance to child development, suggesting as it does the multiple levels at which the environment affects children's development.

Vygotsky's Sociocultural Theory.   To Russian developmentalist Lev Semenovich Vygotsky, a full understanding of development was impossible without taking into account the culture in which people develop. Vygotsky's **sociocultural theory** emphasizes how cognitive development proceeds as a result of social interactions between members of a cultures (Vygotsky, 1926/1997, 1979; Beilin, 1996; Winsler, 2003; Edwards, 2005).

Vygotsky, who lived a brief life from 1896 to 1934, argued that children's understanding of the world is acquired through their problem-solving interactions with adults and other children. As children play and cooperate with others, they learn what is important in their society and, at the same time, advance cognitively in their understanding of the world. Consequently, to understand the course of development, we must consider what is meaningful to members of a given culture.

More than most other theories, sociocultural theory emphasizes that development is a *reciprocal transaction* between the people in a child's environment and the child. Vygotsky believed that people and settings influence the child, who in turn influences the people and

According to Vygotsky, children can develop cognitively in their understanding of the world, and learn what is important in society, through play and cooperation with others.

sociocultural theory   the approach that emphasizes how cognitive development proceeds as a result of social interactions between members of a culture.

settings. This pattern continues in an endless loop, with children being both recipients of socialization influences and sources of influence. For example, a child raised with his or her extended family nearby will grow up with a different sense of family life than a child whose relatives live a considerable distance away. Those relatives, too, are affected by that situation and that child, depending on how close and frequent their contact is with the child.

Assessing Vygotsky's Theory. Sociocultural theory has become increasingly influential, despite Vygotsky's death almost eight decades ago. The reason is the growing acknowledgment of the central importance of cultural factors in development. Children do not develop in a cultural vacuum. Instead, their attention is directed by society to certain areas, and as a consequence, they develop particular kinds of skills that are an outcome of their cultural environment. Vygotsky was one of the first developmentalists to recognize and acknowledge the importance of culture, and—as today's society becomes increasingly multicultural—sociocultural theory is helping us to understand the rich and varied influences that shape development (Reis, Collins, & Berscheid, 2000; Matusov & Hayes, 2000; Fowers & Davidov, 2006).

Sociocultural theory is not without its critics, however. Some suggest that Vygotsky's strong emphasis on the role of culture and social experience led him to ignore the effects of biological factors on development. In addition, his perspective seems to minimize the role that individuals can play in shaping their own environment. In fact, as we can see from the emphasis of the humanistic perspective—described in a moment—each individual can play a central role in determining the course of his or her own development.

Evolutionary Perspectives: Our Ancestors' Contributions to Behavior

One increasingly influential approach is the evolutionary perspective, the sixth and final developmental perspective that we will consider. The **evolutionary perspective** seeks to identify behavior that is the result of our genetic inheritance from our ancestors (Buss & Kern, 2003; Bjorklund, 2005; Goetz & Shackelford, 2006).

Evolutionary approaches grow out of the groundbreaking work of Charles Darwin. In 1859, Darwin argued in his book *On the Origin of Species* that a process of natural selection creates traits in a species that are adaptive to its environment. Using Darwin's arguments, evolutionary approaches contend that our genetic inheritance not only determines such physical traits as skin and eye color, but certain personality traits and social behaviors as well. For instance, some evolutionary developmentalists suggest that behaviors such as shyness and jealousy are produced in part by genetic causes, presumably because they helped in increasing survival rates of humans' ancient relatives (Plomin & McClearn, 1993; Buss, 2003a).

The evolutionary perspective draws heavily on the field of *ethology*, which examines the ways in which our biological makeup influences our behavior. A primary proponent of ethology was Konrad Lorenz (1903–1989), who discovered that newborn geese are genetically preprogrammed to become attached to the first moving object they see after birth. His work, which demonstrated the importance of biological determinants in influencing behavior patterns, ultimately led developmentalists to consider the ways in which human behavior might reflect inborn genetic patterns.

As we'll consider further in Chapter 2, the evolutionary perspective encompasses one of the fastest growing areas within the field of lifespan development: behavioral genetics. *Behavioral genetics* studies the effects of heredity on behavior. Behavioral geneticists seek to understand how we might inherit certain behavioral traits and how the environment influences whether we actually display such traits. It also considers how genetic factors may produce psychological disorders such as schizophrenia (Gottlieb, 2003; Eley, Lichtenstein, & Moffitt, 2003; Li, 2003; Bjorklund & Ellis, 2005).

evolutionary perspective   the theory that seeks to identify behavior that is a result of our genetic inheritance from our ancestors.

Assessing the Evolutionary Perspective. There is little argument among lifespan developmentalists that Darwin's evolutionary theory provides an accurate description of basic genetic processes, and the evolutionary perspective is increasingly visible in the field of lifespan development. However, applications of the evolutionary perspective have been subjected to considerable criticism.

Some developmentalists are concerned that because of its focus on genetic and biological aspects of behavior, the evolutionary perspective pays insufficient attention to the environmental and social factors involved in producing children's and adults' behavior. Other critics argue that there is no good way to experimentally test theories derived from the evolutionary approach because they all happened so long ago. For example, it is one thing to say that jealousy helped individuals to survive more effectively and another thing to prove it. Still, the evolutionary approach has stimulated a significant amount of research on how our biological inheritance influences at least partially our traits and behaviors (Buss & Reeve, 2003; Quartz, 2003; Scher & Rauscher, 2003).

Konrad Lorenz, seen here with geese who from their birth have followed him, considered the ways in which behavior reflects inborn genetic patterns.

Why "Which Approach Is Right?" Is the Wrong Question

We have considered the six major perspectives on development: psychodynamic, behavioral, cognitive, humanistic, contextual, and evolutionary—summarized in Table 1-4 and applied to a case of a young adult who is overweight. It would be natural to wonder which of the six provides the most accurate account of human development.

For several reasons, this is not an entirely appropriate question. For one thing, each perspective emphasizes somewhat different aspects of development. For instance, the psychodynamic approach emphasizes emotions, motivational conflicts, and unconscious determinants of behavior. In contrast, behavioral perspectives emphasize overt behavior, paying far more attention to what people *do* than to what goes on inside their heads, which is deemed largely irrelevant. The cognitive and humanistic perspectives take quite the opposite tack, looking more at what people *think* than at what they do. Finally, the evolutionary perspective focuses on how inherited biological factors underlie development.

For example, a developmentalist using the psychodynamic approach might consider how the 9/11 terrorist attacks on the World Trade Center and Pentagon might affect children, unconsciously, for their entire life span. A cognitive approach might focus on how children perceived and came to interpret and understand terrorism, while a contextual approach might consider what personality and social factors led the perpetrators to adopt terrorist tactics.

Clearly, each perspective is based on its own premises and focuses on different aspects of development. Furthermore, the same developmental phenomenon can be looked at from a number of perspectives simultaneously. In fact, some lifespan developmentalists use an *eclectic* approach, drawing on several perspectives simultaneously.

We can think of the different perspectives as analogous to a set of maps of the same general geographical area. One map may contain detailed depictions of roads; another map may show geographical features; another may show political subdivisions, such as cities, towns, and counties; and still another may highlight particular points of interest, such as scenic areas and historical landmarks. Each of the maps is accurate, but each provides a different point of view and way of thinking. No one map is "complete," but by considering them together, we can come to a fuller understanding of the area. In the same way, the various theoretical perspectives provide different ways of looking at development. Considering them together paints a fuller portrait of the myriad ways human beings change and grow over the course of their lives. However, not all theories and claims derived from the various perspectives are accurate. How do we choose among competing explanations? The answer is *research*, which we consider in the final part of this chapter.

Table 1-4   Major Perspectives on Lifespan Development

Perspective	Key Ideas About Human Behavior and Development	Major Proponents	Example
Psychodynamic	Behavior throughout life is motivated by inner, unconscious forces, stemming from childhood, over which we have little control.	Sigmund Freud, Erik Erikson	This view might suggest that a young adult who is overweight has a fixation in the oral stage of development.
Behavioral	Development can be understood through studying observable behavior and environmental stimuli.	John B. Watson, B. F. Skinner, Albert Bandura	In this perspective, a young adult who is overweight might be seen as not being rewarded for good nutritional and exercise habits.
Cognitive	Emphasis on how changes or growth in the ways people know, understand, and think about the world affect behavior.	Jean Piaget	This view might suggest that a young adult who is overweight hasn't learned effective ways to stay at a healthy weight and doesn't value good nutrition.
Humanistic	Behavior is chosen through *free will* and motivated by our natural capacity to strive to reach our full potential.	Carl Rogers, Abraham Maslow	In this view, a young adult who is overweight may eventually choose to seek an optimal weight as part of an overall pattern of individual growth.
Contextual	Development should be viewed in terms of the interrelationship of a person's physical, cognitive, personality, and social worlds.	Urie Bronfenbrenner, Lev Vygotsky	In this perspective, being overweight is caused by a number of interrelated factors in that person's physical, cognitive, personality, and social worlds.
Evolutionary	Behavior is the result of genetic inheritance from our ancestors; traits and behavior that are adaptive for promoting the survival of our species have been inherited through natural selection.	Influenced by early work of Charles Darwin, Konrad Lorenz	This view might suggest that a young adult might have a genetic tendency toward obesity because extra fat helped his or her ancestors to survive in times of famine.

Review and Apply

Review

- The psychodynamic perspective looks primarily at the influence of internal, unconscious forces on development.
- The behavioral perspective focuses on external, observable behaviors as the key to development.
- The cognitive perspective focuses on mental activity.
- The humanistic perspective concentrates on the theory that each individual has the ability and motivation to reach more advanced levels of maturity and that people naturally seek to reach their full potential.
- The contextual perspective focuses on the relationship between individuals and the social context in which they lead their lives.
- Finally, the evolutionary perspective seeks to identify behavior that is a result of our genetic inheritance from our ancestors.

The diversity of America is reflected in these children's faces. The various perspectives on development all seek to improve the human condition by explaining the course of human development over the lifespan.

Applying Lifespan Development

● What examples of human behavior have you seen that seem as though they may have been inherited from our ancestors because they helped individuals survive and adapt more effectively? Why do you think they are inherited?

● *From a social worker's perspective:* How do the concepts of social learning and modeling relate to the mass media, and how might exposure to mass media influence a child's family life?

Research Methods

The Egyptians had long believed that they were the most ancient race on earth, and Psamtik [King of Egypt in the 7th century B.C.], driven by intellectual curiosity, wanted to prove that flattering belief. Like a good researcher, he began with a hypothesis: If children had no opportunity to learn a language from older people around them, they would spontaneously speak the primal, inborn language of humankind—the natural language of its most ancient people—which, he expected to show, was Egyptian.

To test his hypothesis, Psamtik commandeered two infants of a lower-class mother and turned them over to a herdsman to bring up in a remote area. They were to be kept in a sequestered cottage, properly fed and cared for, but were never to hear anyone speak so much as a word. The Greek historian Herodotus, who tracked the story down and learned what he calls "the real facts" from priests of Hephaestus in Memphis, says that Psamtik's goal "was to know, after the indistinct babblings of infancy were over, what word they would first articulate."

The experiment, he tells us, worked. One day, when the children were two years old, they ran up to the herdsman as he opened the door of their cottage and cried out "Becos!" Since this meant nothing to him, he paid no attention, but when it happened repeatedly, he sent word to Psamtik, who at once ordered the children brought to him. When he too heard them say it, Psamtik made inquiries and learned that becos was the Phrygian word for bread. He concluded that, disappointingly, the Phrygians were an older race than the Egyptians. (Hunt, 1993, pp. 1–2)

With the perspective of several thousand years, we can easily see the shortcomings—both scientific and ethical—in Psamtik's approach. Yet his procedure represents an improvement over mere speculation, and as such is sometimes looked upon as the first developmental experiment in recorded history (Hunt, 1993).

Theories and Hypotheses: Posing Developmental Questions

Questions such as those raised by Psamtik drive the study of development. In fact, develomentalists are still studying how children learn language. Others are trying to find answers to such questions as, What are the effects of malnutrition on later intellectual performance? How do infants form relationships with their parents, and does participation in day care disrupt such relationships? Why are adolescents particularly susceptible to peer pressure? Can mentally challenging activities reduce the declines in intellectual abilities related to aging? Do any mental faculties improve with age?

To answer such questions, developmentalists, like all psychologists and other scientists, rely on the scientific method. The **scientific method** is the process of posing and answering questions using careful, controlled techniques that include systematic, orderly observation and the collection of data. The scientific method involves three major steps: (1) identifying questions of interest, (2) formulating an explanation, and (3) carrying out research that either lends support to the explanation or refutes it.

The scientific method involves the formulation of *theories*, broad explanations, and predictions about phenomena of interest. For instance, many people theorize that there is a crucial bonding period between parent and child immediately after birth, which is a necessary ingredient in forming a lasting parent–child relationship. Without such a bonding period, they assume, the parent–child relationship will be forever compromised (Furnham & Weir, 1996).

Developmental researchers use theories to form hypotheses. A **hypothesis** is a prediction stated in a way that permits it to be tested. For instance, someone who subscribes to the general theory that bonding is a crucial ingredient in the parent–child relationship might derive the more specific hypothesis that adopted children whose adoptive parents never had the chance to bond with them immediately after birth may ultimately have less secure relationships with their adoptive parents. Others might derive other hypotheses, such as that effective bonding occurs only if it lasts for a certain length of time, or that bonding affects the mother–child relationship, but not the father–child relationship. (In case you're wondering: As we'll discuss in Chapter 3, these particular hypotheses have *not* been upheld; there are no long-term reactions to the separation of parent and child immediately after birth, even if the separation lasts several days.)

- - - - - - - - - - - - - - - - - - -

scientific method   the process of posing and answering questions using careful, controlled techniques that include systematic, orderly observation and the collection of data.

hypothesis   a prediction stated in a way that permits it to be tested.

Choosing a Research Strategy: Answering Questions

Once researchers have formed a hypothesis, they must develop a research strategy for testing its validity. There are two major categories of research: correlational research and experimental research. **Correlational research** seeks to identify whether an association or relationship between two factors exists. As we'll see, correlational research cannot be used to determine whether one factor *causes* changes in the other. For instance, correlational research could tell us if there is an association between the number of minutes a mother and her newborn child are together immediately after birth and the quality of the mother–child relationship when the child reaches 2 years of age. Such correlational research indicates whether the two factors are *associated* or *related* to one another, but not whether the initial contact caused the relationship to develop in a particular way (Schutt, 2001).

In contrast, **experimental research** is designed to discover *causal* relationships between various factors. In experimental research, researchers deliberately introduce a change in a carefully structured situation in order to see the consequences of that change. For instance, a researcher conducting an experiment might vary the number of minutes that mothers and children interact immediately following birth, in an attempt to see whether the amount of bonding time affects the mother–child relationship.

Because experimental research is able to answer questions of causality, it is fundamental to finding answers to various developmental hypotheses. However, some research questions cannot be answered through experiments, for either technical or ethical reasons (for example, it would be unethical to design an experiment in which a group of infants was offered no chance to bond with a caregiver at all). In fact, a great deal of pioneering developmental research—such as that conducted by Piaget and Vygotsky—employed correlational techniques. Consequently, correlational research remains an important tool in the developmental researcher's toolbox.

correlational research research that seeks to identify whether an association or relationship between two factors exists.

experimental research research designed to discover causal relationships between various factors.

In experimental research, one uses controlled conditions to attempt to discover causal relationships between various factors.

Correlational Studies

As we've noted, correlational research examines the relationship between two variables to determine whether they are associated, or *correlated*. For instance, researchers interested in the relationship between televised aggression and subsequent behavior have found that children who watch a good deal of aggression on television—murders, crime shows, shootings, and the like—tend to be more aggressive than those who watch only a little. In other words, as we'll discuss in greater detail in Chapter 15, viewing of aggression and actual aggression are strongly associated, or correlated, with one another (Center for Communication & Social Policy, 1998; Singer & Singer, 2000).

But does this mean we can conclude that the viewing of televised aggression *causes* the more aggressive behavior of the viewers? Not at all. Consider some of the other possibilities: It might be that being aggressive in the first place makes children more likely to choose to watch violent programs. In such a case, then, it is the aggressive tendency that causes the viewing behavior, and not the other way around.

Or consider another possibility. Suppose that children who are raised in poverty are more likely to behave aggressively *and* to watch higher levels of aggressive television than those raised in more affluent settings. In this case, it is a third variable—low socioeconomic status—that causes *both* the aggressive behavior and the television viewing. The various possibilities are illustrated in Figure 1-3.

In short, finding that two variables are correlated proves nothing about causality. Although it is possible that the variables are linked causally, this is not necessarily the case.

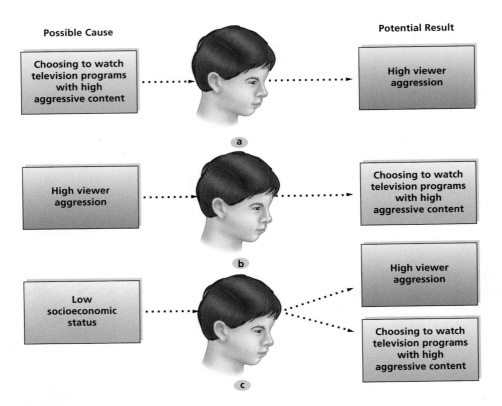

Possible Cause

Potential Result

Choosing to watch television programs with high aggressive content

High viewer aggression

a

High viewer aggression

Choosing to watch television programs with high aggressive content

b

Low socioeconomic status

High viewer aggression

Choosing to watch television programs with high aggressive content

c

FIGURE 1-3   FINDING A CORRELATION

Finding a correlation between two factors does not imply that one factor *causes* the other factor to vary. For instance, suppose a study found that viewing television shows with high levels of aggression is correlated with actual aggression in children. The correlation may reflect at least three possibilities: (a) watching television programs containing high levels of aggression causes aggression in viewers; (b) children who behave aggressively choose to watch TV programs with high levels of aggression; or (c) some third factor, such as a child's socioeconomic status, leads both to high viewer aggression and to choosing to watch television programs with high levels of aggression. What other factors, besides socioeconomic status, might be plausible third factors?

Correlational studies do provide important information, however. For instance, as we'll see in later chapters, we know from correlational studies that the closer the genetic link between two people, the more highly associated is their intelligence. We have learned that the more parents speak to their young children, the more extensive are the children's vocabularies. And we know from correlational studies that the better the nutrition that infants receive, the fewer the cognitive and social problems they experience later (Plomin, 1994b; Hart, 2004; Colom, Lluis-Font, & Andrés-Pueyo, 2005).

The Correlation Coefficient.   The strength and direction of a relationship between two factors is represented by a mathematical score, called a *correlation coefficient*, that ranges from +1.0 to −1.0. A positive correlation indicates that as the value of one factor increases, it can be predicted that the value of the other will also increase. For instance, if we find that the more money people make in their first job after college, the higher their scores on a survey of job satisfaction, and that people who make less money have lower scores when surveyed about their job satisfaction, we have found a positive correlation. (Higher values of the factor "salary" are associated with higher values of the factor "job satisfaction," and lower values of "salary" are associated with lower values of "job satisfaction.") The correlation coefficient, then, would be indicated by a positive number, and the stronger the association between salary and job satisfaction, the closer the number would be to +1.0.

In contrast, a correlation coefficient with a negative value informs us that as the value of one factor increases, the value of the other factor declines. For example, suppose we found that the greater the number of hours adolescents spend using instant messaging on their computers, the worse their academic performance is. Such a finding would result in a negative correlation, ranging between 0 and −1. More instant messaging is associated with lower performance, and less instant messaging is associated with better performance. The stronger the association between instant messaging and school performance, the closer the correlation coefficient will be to −1.0.

Finally, it is possible that two factors are unrelated to one another. For example, it is unlikely that we would find a correlation between school performance and shoe size. In this case, the lack of a relationship would be indicated by a correlation coefficient close to 0.

It is important to reiterate what we noted earlier: Even if the correlation coefficient involving two variables is very strong, there is no way we can know whether one factor *causes* another factor to vary. It simply means that the two factors are associated with one another in a predictable way.

Types of Correlational Studies. There are several types of correlational studies. **Naturalistic observation** is the observation of a naturally occurring behavior without intervention in the situation. For instance, an investigator who wishes to learn how often preschool children share toys with one another might observe a classroom over a 3-week period, recording how often the preschoolers spontaneously share with one another. The key point about naturalistic observation is that the investigator simply observes the children, without interfering with the situation whatsoever (e.g., Beach, 2003; Prezbindowski & Lederberg, 2003).

Though naturalistic observation has the advantage of identifying what children do in their "natural habitat," there is an important drawback to the method: Researchers are unable to exert control over factors of interest. For instance, in some cases researchers might find so few naturally occurring instances of the behavior of interest that they are unable to draw any conclusions at all. In addition, children who know they are being watched may modify their behavior as a result of the observation. Consequently, their behavior may not be representative of how they would behave if they were not being watched.

Ethnography. Increasingly, naturalistic observation employs *ethnography,* a method borrowed from the field of anthropology and used to investigate cultural questions. In ethnography, a researcher's goal is to understand a culture's values and attitudes through careful, extended examination. Typically, researchers using ethnography act as participant observers, living for a period of weeks, months, or even years in another culture. By carefully observing everyday life and conducting in-depth interviews, researchers are able to obtain a deep understanding of the nature of life within another culture (Fetterman, 1998; Dyson, 2003).

Although ethnographic studies provide a fine-grained view of everyday behavior in another culture, they suffer from several drawbacks. As mentioned, the presence of a participant observer may influence the behavior of the individuals being studied. Furthermore, because only a small number of individuals are studied, it may be hard to generalize the findings to people in other cultures. Finally, ethnographers may misinterpret and misconceive what they are observing, particularly in cultures that are very different from their own (Polkinghome, 2005).

Case studies involve extensive, in-depth interviews with a particular individual or small group of individuals. They often are used not just to learn about the individual being interviewed, but to derive broader principles or draw tentative conclusions that might apply to others. For example, case studies have been conducted on children who display unusual

naturalistic observation a type of correlational study in which some naturally occurring behavior is observed without intervention in the situation.

case studies studies that involve extensive, in-depth interviews with a particular individual or small group of individuals.

survey research   a type of study where a group of people chosen to represent some larger population are asked questions about their attitudes, behavior, or thinking on a given topic.

psychophysiological methods   research that focuses on the relationship between physiological processes and behavior.

experiment   a process in which an investigator, called an experimenter, devises two different experiences for participants.

genius and on children who have spent their early years in the wild, apparently without human contact. These case studies have provided important information to researchers, and have suggested hypotheses for future investigation (Lane, 1976; Goldsmith, 2000; Cohen & Cashon, 2003).

Using *diaries*, participants are asked to keep a record of their behavior on a regular basis. For example, a group of adolescents may be asked to record each time they interact with friends for more than 5 minutes, thereby providing a way to track their social behavior.

Surveys represent another sort of correlational research. In **survey research,** a group of people chosen to represent some larger population are asked questions about their attitudes, behavior, or thinking on a given topic. For instance, surveys have been conducted about parents' use of punishment on their children and on attitudes toward breastfeeding. From the responses, inferences are drawn regarding the larger population represented by the individuals being surveyed.

Psychophysiological Methods.   Some developmental researchers, particularly those using a cognitive neuroscience approach, make use of psychophysiological methods. **Psychophysiological methods** focus on the relationship between physiological processes and behavior. For instance, a researcher might examine the relationship between blood flow within the brain and problem-solving capabilities. Similarly, some studies use infants' heart rate as a measure of their interest in stimuli to which they are exposed.

Among the most frequently used psychophysiological measures:

- *Electroencephalogram (EEG).* The EEG reports electrical activity within the brain recorded by electrodes placed on the outside of the skull. That brain activity is transformed into a pictorial representation of the brain, permitting the representation of brain wave patterns and diagnosis of disorders such as epilepsy and learning disabilities.

- *Computerized axial tomography (CAT) scan.* In a CAT scan, a computer constructs an image of the brain by combining thousands of individual x-rays taken at slightly different angles. Although it does not show brain activity, it does illuminate the structure of the brain.

- *Functional magnetic resonance imaging (fMRI) scan.* An fMRI provides a detailed, three-dimensional computer-generated image of brain activity by aiming a powerful magnetic field at the brain. It offers one of the best ways of learning about the operation of the brain, down to the level of individual nerves.

Experiments: Determining Cause and Effect

In an **experiment,** an investigator or experimenter typically devises two different conditions (or *treatments*) and then studies and compares the outcomes of the participants exposed to those two different conditions in order to see how behavior is affected. One group, the *treatment* or *experimental group,* is exposed to the treatment variable being studied; the other, the *control group,* is not.

Although the terminology may seem daunting at first, there is an underlying logic to it that helps sort it out. Think in terms of a medical experiment in which the aim is to test the effectiveness of a new drug. In testing the drug, we wish to see if the drug successfully *treats* the disease. Consequently, the group that receives the drug would be called the *treatment* group. In comparison, another group of participants would not receive the drug treatment. Instead, they would be part of the no-treatment *control* group.

Similarly, suppose you want to see if exposure to movie violence makes viewers more aggressive. You might take a group of adolescents and show them a series of movies that contain a great deal of violent imagery. You would then measure their subsequent aggression. This group would constitute the treatment group. For the control group you might take a second group of adolescents, show them movies that contain no aggressive imagery, and then measure their subsequent aggression. By comparing the amount of aggression displayed by members of the treatment and control groups, you would be able to determine if exposure to violent imagery produces aggression in viewers. And this is just what a group of researchers at the University of Louvain in Belgium found: Running an experiment of this very sort, psychologist Jacques-Philippe Leyens and colleagues (Leyens et al., 1975) found that the level of aggression rose significantly for the adolescents who had seen the movies containing violence.

The central feature of this experiment—and all experiments—is the comparison of the consequences of different treatments. The use of both treatment and control groups allows researchers to rule out the possibility that something other than the experimental manipulation produced the results found in the experiment. For instance, if a control group was not used, experimenters could not be certain that some other factor, such as the time of day the movies were shown, the need to sit still during the movie, or even the mere passage of time, produced the changes that were observed. By using a control group, then, experimenters can draw accurate conclusions about causes and effects.

Independent and Dependent Variables. The **independent variable** is the variable that researchers manipulate in the experiment (in our example, it is the type of movie participants saw—violent or nonviolent). In contrast, the **dependent variable** is the variable that researchers measure in an experiment and expect to change as a result of the experimental manipulation. In our example, the degree of aggressive behavior shown by the participants after viewing violent or nonviolent films is the dependent variable. (One way to remember the difference: A hypothesis predicts how a dependent variable *depends* on the manipulation of the independent variable.) In an experiment studying the effects of taking a drug, for instance, manipulating whether participants receive or don't receive a drug is the independent variable. Measurement of the effectiveness of the drug or no-drug treatment is the dependent variable. Every experiment has an independent and dependent variable.

Experimenters need to make sure their studies are not influenced by factors other than those they are manipulating. For this reason, they take great care to make sure that the participants in both the treatment and control groups are not aware of the purpose of the experiment (which could affect their responses or behavior) and that the experimenters do not have any influence over who is chosen for the control and treatment groups. The procedure that is used is known as random assignment. In *random assignment*, participants are assigned to different experimental groups or "conditions" on the basis of chance and chance alone. By using this technique, the laws of statistics ensure that personal characteristics that might affect the outcome of the experiment are divided proportionally among the participants in the different groups, making groups equivalent. Equivalent groups achieved by random assignment allow an experimenter to draw conclusions with confidence.

Given the advantage of experimental research—that it provides a means of determining causality—why aren't experiments always used? The answer is that there are some situations that a researcher, no matter how ingenious, simply cannot control. And there are some situations in which control would be unethical, even if it were possible. For instance, no researcher would be able to assign different groups of infants to parents of high and low socioeconomic status in order to learn the effects of such status on subsequent development. Similarly, we cannot control what a group of children watch on television throughout their childhood years in order to learn if childhood exposure to televised aggression leads to aggressive behavior later in life. Consequently, in situations in which experiments are logistically or ethically impossible, developmentalists employ correlational research.

independent variable the variable that researchers manipulate in an experiment.

dependent variable the variable that researchers measure in an experiment and expect to change as a result of the experimental manipulation.

Naturalistic observation is utilized to examine a situation in its natural habitat without interference of any sort. What are some disadvantages of naturalistic observation?

sample the group of participants chosen for the experiment.

field study a research investigation carried out in a naturally occurring setting.

laboratory study a research investigation conducted in a controlled setting explicitly designed to hold events constant.

theoretical research research designed specifically to test some developmental explanation and expand scientific knowledge.

applied research research meant to provide practical solutions to immediate problems.

Furthermore, it's also important to keep in mind that a single experiment is insufficient to answer a research question definitively. Instead, before complete confidence can be placed in a conclusion, research must be *replicated*, or repeated, sometimes using other procedures and techniques with other participants. Sometimes developmentalists use a procedure called *meta-analysis*, which permits the combination of results of many studies into one overall conclusion (Peterson & Brown, 2005).

Choosing a Research Setting. Deciding *where* to conduct a study may be as important as determining *what* to do. In the Belgian experiment on the influence of exposure to media aggression, the researchers used a real-world setting—a group home for boys who had been convicted of juvenile delinquency. They chose this **sample,** the group of participants chosen for the experiment, because it was useful to have adolescents whose normal level of aggression was relatively high, and because they could incorporate showing the films into the everyday life of the home with minimal disruption.

Using a real-world setting like the one in the aggression experiment is the hallmark of a field study. A **field study** is a research investigation carried out in a naturally occurring setting. Field studies may be carried out in preschool classrooms, at community playgrounds, on school buses, or on street corners. Field studies capture behavior in real-life settings, and research participants may behave more naturally than they would if they were brought into a laboratory.

Field studies may be used in both correlational studies and experiments. Field studies typically employ naturalistic observation, the technique we discussed earlier in which researchers observe some naturally occurring behavior without intervening or making changes in the situation. For instance, a researcher might examine behavior in a child-care center, view the groupings of adolescents in high school corridors, or observe elderly adults in a senior center.

However, it often is difficult to run an experiment in real-world settings, where it is hard to exert control over the situation and environment. Consequently, field studies are more typical of correlational designs than experimental designs, and most developmental research experiments are conducted in laboratory settings. A **laboratory study** is a research investigation conducted in a controlled setting explicitly designed to hold events constant. The laboratory may be a room or building designed for research, as in a university's psychology department. Their ability to control the settings in laboratory studies enables researchers to learn more clearly how their treatments affect participants.

Theoretical and Applied Research: Complementary Approaches

Developmental researchers typically focus on one of two approaches to research, carrying out either theoretical research or applied research. **Theoretical research** is designed specifically to test some developmental explanation and expand scientific knowledge, while **applied research** is meant to provide practical solutions to immediate problems. For instance, if we were interested in the processes of cognitive change during childhood, we might carry out a study of how many digits children of various ages can remember after one exposure to multidigit numbers—a theoretical approach. Alternatively, we might focus on how children learn by examining ways in which elementary school instructors can teach children to remember information more easily. Such a study would represent applied research, because the findings are applied to a particular setting and problem.

There is not always a clear-cut distinction between theoretical and applied research. For instance, is a study that examines the consequences of ear infections in infancy on later hearing loss theoretical or applied research? Because such a study may help illuminate the basic processes involved in hearing, it can be considered theoretical. But to the extent that the study helps us to understand how to prevent hearing loss in children and how various medicines may ease the consequences of the infection, it may be considered applied research (Lerner, Fisher, & Weinberg, 2000).

In short, even the most applied research can help advance our theoretical understanding of a particular topical area, and theoretical research can provide concrete solutions to a range of practical problems. In fact, as we discuss in the accompanying *From Research to Practice* box, research of both a theoretical and applied nature has played a significant role in shaping and resolving a variety of public policy questions.

Measuring Developmental Change

How people grow and change through the life span is central to the work of all developmental researchers. Consequently, one of the thorniest research issues they face concerns the measurement of change and differences over age and time. To solve this problem, researchers have developed three major research strategies: longitudinal research, cross-sectional research, and sequential research.

Longitudinal Studies: Measuring Individual Change. If you were interested in learning how a child's moral development changes between the ages of 3 and 5, the most

---

From Research to Practice

Using Developmental Research to Improve Public Policy

Is national legislation designed to "leave no child behind" effective in improving the lives of children?

Does research support the legalization of marijuana?

What are the effects of gay marriage on children in such unions?

Should preschoolers diagnosed with attention deficit hyperactivity disorder receive drugs to treat their condition?

Is DARE—the national program designed to curb drug abuse in schoolchildren—effective?

Each of these questions represents a national policy issue that can be answered only by considering the results of relevant research studies. By conducting controlled studies, developmental researchers have made a number of important contributions affecting education, family life, and health on a national scale. Consider, for instance, the variety of ways that public policy issues have been informed by various types of research findings (Brooks-Gunn, 2003; Maton et al., 2004; Mervis, 2004; Aber et al., 2007):

- *Research findings can provide policymakers a means of determining what questions to ask in the first place.* For example, studies of children's caregivers (some of which we'll consider in Chapter 10) have led policymakers to question whether the benefits of infant day care are outweighed by possible deterioration in parent–child bonds.

- *Research findings and the testimony of researchers are often part of the process by which laws are drafted.* A good deal of legislation has been passed based on findings from developmental researchers. For example, research revealed that children with developmental disabilities benefit from exposure to children without special needs, ultimately leading to passage of national legislation mandating that children with disabilities be placed in regular school classes as much as possible.

- *Policymakers and other professionals use research findings to determine how best to implement programs.* Research has shaped programs designed to reduce the incidence of unsafe sex among teenagers, to increase the level of prenatal care for pregnant mothers, to raise class attendance rates in school-age children, and to promote flu shots for older adults. The common thread among such programs is that many of the details of the programs are built upon basic research findings.

- *Research techniques are used to evaluate the effectiveness of existing programs and policies.* Once a public policy has been implemented, it is necessary to determine whether it has been effective and successful in accomplishing its goals. To do this, researchers employ formal evaluation techniques, developed from basic research procedures. For instance, researchers have continually scrutinized the Head Start preschool program, which has received massive federal funding, to ensure that it really does what it is supposed to do—improve children's academic performance.

Similarly, careful studies of DARE, a highly popular program meant to reduce children's use of drugs, began to find that it was ineffective. Using the research findings of developmentalists, DARE instigated new techniques, and preliminary findings suggest the revised program is more effective (Rhule, 2005; University of Akron, 2006).

By building upon research findings, developmentalists have worked hand-in-hand with policymakers, and research has a substantial impact on public policies that can benefit us all.

- *What are some policy issues affecting children and adolescents that are currently being debated nationally?*

- *Despite the existence of research data that might inform policy about development, politicians rarely discuss such data in their speeches. Why do you think that is the case?*

longitudinal research   research in which the behavior of one or more participants in a study is measured as they age.

cross-sectional research   research in which people of different ages are compared at the same point in time.

direct approach would be to take a group of 3-year-olds and follow them until they were 5, testing them periodically.

Such a strategy illustrates longitudinal research. In **longitudinal research**, the behavior of one or more study participants is measured as they age. Longitudinal research measures change over time. By following many individuals over time, researchers can understand the general course of change across some period of life.

The granddaddy of longitudinal studies, which has become a classic, is a study of gifted children begun by Lewis Terman about 80 years ago. In the study—which has yet to be concluded—a group of 1,500 children with high IQs were tested about every 5 years. Now in their 80s, the participants—who call themselves "Termites"—have provided information on everything from intellectual accomplishment to personality and longevity (Terman & Oden, 1959; Feldhusen, 2003; McCullough, Tsang, & Brion, 2003).

Longitudinal research has also provided great insight into language development. For instance, by tracing how children's vocabularies increase on a day-by-day basis, researchers have been able to understand the processes that underlie the human ability to become competent in using language.

Longitudinal studies can provide a wealth of information about change over time. However, they have several drawbacks. For one thing, they require a tremendous investment of time, because researchers must wait for participants to become older. Furthermore, participants often drop out over the course of the research. Participants may drop out of a study, move away, or become ill or even die as the research proceeds.

Finally, participants who are observed or tested repeatedly may become "test-wise" and perform better each time they are assessed as they become more familiar with the procedure. Even if the observations of participants in a study are not terribly intrusive (such as simply recording, over a lengthy period of time, vocabulary increases in infants and preschoolers), experimental participants may be affected by the repeated presence of an experimenter or observer.

Consequently, despite the benefits of longitudinal research, particularly its ability to look at change within individuals, developmental researchers often turn to other methods in conducting research. The alternative they choose most often is the cross-sectional study.

Cross-Sectional Studies.   Suppose again that you want to consider how children's moral development, their sense of right and wrong, changes from ages 3 to 5. Instead of using a longitudinal approach and following the same children over several years, we might conduct the study by simultaneously looking at three groups of children: 3-year-olds, 4-year-olds, and 5-year-olds, perhaps presenting each group with the same problem, and then seeing how they respond to it and explain their choices.

Such an approach typifies cross-sectional research. In **cross-sectional research,** people of different ages are compared at the same point in time. Cross-sectional studies provide information about differences in development between different age groups.

Cross-sectional research is considerably more economical in terms of time than longitudinal research: Participants are tested at just one point in time. For instance, Terman's study conceivably might have been completed 75 years ago if Terman had simply looked at a group of gifted 15-year-olds, 20-year-olds, 25-year-olds, and so forth, all the way through a group of 80-year-olds. Because the participants would not be periodically tested, there would be no chance that they would become test-wise, and problems of participant attrition would not occur. Why, then, would anyone choose to use a procedure other than cross-sectional research?

The answer is that cross-sectional research brings its own set of difficulties. Recall that every person belongs to a particular *cohort*, the group of people born at around the same time in the same place. If we find that people of different ages vary along some dimension, it may be due to differences in cohort membership, not age per se.

Cross-sectional research allows researchers to compare representatives of different age groups at the same time.

Consider a concrete example: If we find in a correlational study that people who are 25 years old perform better on a test of intelligence than those who are 75 years old, there are several explanations. Although the finding may be due to decreased intelligence in older people, it may also be attributable to cohort differences. The group of 75-year-olds may have had less formal education than the 25-year-olds, because members of the older cohort were less likely to finish high school and attend college than members of the younger one. Or perhaps the older group performed less well because as infants they received less adequate nutrition than members of the younger group. In short, we cannot fully rule out the possibility that differences we find between people of different age groups in cross-sectional studies are due to cohort differences.

Cross-sectional studies also may suffer from *selective dropout*, in which participants in some age groups are more likely to quit participating in a study than others. For example, suppose a study of cognitive development in preschoolers includes a lengthy assessment of cognitive abilities. It is possible that young preschoolers would find the task more difficult and demanding than older preschoolers. As a result, the younger children would be more likely to discontinue participation in the study than the older preschoolers. If the least competent young preschoolers are the ones who drop out, then the remaining sample of participants in the study will consist of the more competent young preschoolers—together with a broader and more representative sample of older preschoolers. The results of such a study would be questionable (Miller, 1998).

Finally, cross-sectional studies have an additional, and more basic, disadvantage: They are unable to inform us about changes in individuals or groups. If longitudinal studies are like videos taken of a person at various ages, cross-sectional studies are like snapshots of entirely different groups. Although we can establish differences related to age, we cannot fully determine if such differences are related to change over time.

Sequential Studies. Because both longitudinal and cross-sectional studies have drawbacks, researchers have turned to some compromise techniques. Among the most frequently employed are sequential studies, which are essentially a combination of longitudinal and cross-sectional studies.

In **sequential studies,** researchers examine a number of different age groups at several points in time. For instance, an investigator interested in children's moral behavior might begin a sequential study by examining the behavior of three groups of children, who are either 3 years old, 4 years old, or 5 years old at the time the study begins. (This is no different from the way a cross-sectional study would be done.)

However, the study wouldn't stop there, but would continue for the next several years. During this period, each of the research participants would be tested annually. Thus, the 3-year-olds would be tested at ages 3, 4, and 5; the 4-year-olds at ages 4, 5, and 6; and the 5-year-olds at ages 5, 6, and 7. Such an approach combines the advantages of longitudinal and cross-sectional research, and it permits developmental researchers to tease out the consequences of age *change* versus age *difference*. The major research techniques for studying development are summarized in Figure 1-4.

Ethics and Research

In the "study" conducted by Egyptian King Psamtik, two children were removed from their mothers and held in isolation in an effort to learn about the roots of language. If you found yourself thinking this was extraordinarily cruel, you are in good company. Clearly, such an experiment raises blatant ethical concerns, and nothing like it would ever be done today.

But sometimes ethical issues are more subtle. For instance, in seeking to understand the roots of aggressive behavior, U.S. government researchers proposed holding a conference to examine possible genetic roots of aggression. Based on work conducted by neuroscientists and geneticists, some researchers had begun to raise the possibility that genetic markers might be found that would allow the identification of children as being particularly violence-prone. In

sequential studies research in which researchers examine a number of different age groups over several points in time.

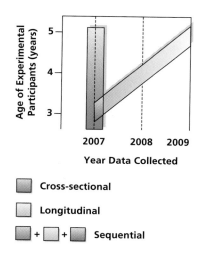

FIGURE 1-4 RESEARCH TECHNIQUES FOR STUDYING DEVELOPMENT

In a *cross-sectional study*, 3-, 4-, and 5-year-olds are compared at a similar point in time (in 2007). In *longitudinal research*, a set of participants who are 3 years old in 2007 are studied when they are 4 years old (in 2008) and when they are 5 years old (in 2009). Finally, a *sequential study* combines cross-sectional and longitudinal techniques; here, a group of 3-year-olds would be compared initially in 2007 with 4- and 5-year-olds, but would also be studied 1 and 2 years later, when they themselves were 4 and 5 years old. Although the graph does not illustrate this, researchers carrying out this sequential study might also choose to retest the children who were 4 and 5 in 2007 for the next 2 years. What advantages do the three kinds of studies offer?

such cases, it might be possible to track these violence-prone children and provide interventions that might reduce the likelihood of later violence.

Critics objected strenuously, however. They argued that such identification might lead to a self-fulfilling prophecy. Children labeled as violence-prone might be treated in a way that would actually *cause* them to be more aggressive than if they hadn't been so labeled. Ultimately, under intense political pressure, the conference was canceled (Wright, 1995).

In order to help researchers deal with such ethical problems, the major organizations of developmentalists, including the Society for Research in Child Development and the American Psychological Association, have developed comprehensive ethical guidelines for researchers. Among the basic principles that must be followed are those involving freedom from harm, informed consent, the use of deception, and maintenance of participants' privacy (Sales & Folkman, 2000; American Psychological Association, 1992, 2002; Fisher, 2003, 2004, 2005):

- *Researchers must protect participants from physical and psychological harm.* Their welfare, interests, and rights come before those of researchers. In research, participants' rights always come first (Sieber, 2000; Fisher, 2004).

- *Researchers must obtain informed consent from participants before their involvement in a study.* If they are over the age of 7, participants must voluntarily agree to be in a study. For those under 18, their parents or guardians must also provide consent.

  The requirement for informed consent raises some difficult issues. Suppose, for instance, researchers want to study the psychological effects of abortion on adolescents. Although they may be able to obtain the consent of an adolescent who has had an abortion, the researchers may need to get her parents' permission as well, because she is a minor. But if the adolescent hasn't told her parents about the abortion, the mere request for permission from the parents would violate her privacy—leading to a breach of ethics.

- *The use of deception in research must be justified and cause no harm.* Although deception to disguise the true purpose of an experiment is permissible, any experiment that uses deception must undergo careful scrutiny by an independent panel before it is conducted. Suppose, for example, we want to know the reaction of participants to success and failure. It is ethical to tell participants that they will be playing a game when the true purpose is actually to observe how they respond to doing well or poorly on the task. However, such a procedure is ethical only if it causes no harm to participants, has been approved by a review panel, and ultimately includes a full debriefing, or explanation, for participants when the study is over (Underwood, 2005).

- *Participants' privacy must be maintained.* If participants are videotaped during the course of a study, for example, they must give their permission for the videotapes to be viewed. Furthermore, access to the tapes must be carefully restricted.

Becoming an Informed Consumer of Development

Thinking Critically About "Expert" Advice

If you immediately comfort crying babies, you'll spoil them.
If you let babies cry without comforting them, they'll be untrusting and clingy as adults.

. . . .

Spanking is one of the best ways to discipline your child.
Never hit your child.

. . . .

If a marriage is unhappy, children are better off if their parents divorce than if they stay together.
No matter how difficult a marriage is, parents should avoid divorce for the sake of their children.

There is no lack of advice on the best way to raise a child or, more generally, to lead one's life. From best-sellers such as *Men Are from Mars, Women Are from Venus* to magazine and newspaper columns that provide advice on every imaginable topic, each of us is exposed to tremendous amounts of information.

Yet not all advice is equally valid. The mere fact that something is in print or on television does not make it legitimate or accurate. Fortunately, some guidelines can help distinguish when recommendations and suggestions are reasonable and when they are not:

- Consider the source of the advice. Information from established, respected organizations such as the American Medical Association, the American Psychological Association, and the American Academy of Pediatrics is likely to be the result of years of study, and its accuracy is probably high. If you don't know the organization, investigate further to find out more about its goals and philosophy.

- Evaluate the credentials of the person providing advice. Information coming from established, acknowledged researchers and experts in a field is likely to be more accurate than that coming from a person whose credentials are obscure. Consider where the author is employed and whether he or she has a particular political or personal agenda.

- Understand the difference between anecdotal evidence and scientific evidence. Anecdotal evidence is based on one or two instances of a phenomenon, haphazardly discovered or encountered; scientific evidence is based on careful, systematic procedures. If an aunt tells you that all her children slept through the night by 2 months of age and therefore so can your child, that is quite different from reading a report that 75% of children sleep through the night by 9 months. Of course, even with such a report, it would be a good idea to find out how large the study was or how this number was arrived at.

- If advice is based on research findings, there should be a clear, transparent description of the studies on which the conclusion is based. Who were the participants in the study? What were the methods used? What do the results show? Think critically about the way in which the findings were obtained before accepting them.

- Do not overlook the cultural context of the information. Although an assertion may be valid in some contexts, it may not be true in all situations. For example, it is typically assumed that providing infants the freedom to move about and exercise their limbs facilitates their muscular development and mobility. Yet in some cultures, infants spend most of their time closely bound to their mothers—with no apparent long-term damage (Kaplan & Dove, 1987; Tronick, 1995).

Don't assume that because many people believe something, it is necessarily true. Scientific evaluation has often proved that some of the most basic presumptions about the effectiveness of various techniques are invalid.

In short, the key to evaluating information relating to human development is to maintain a healthy dose of skepticism. No source of information is invariably, unfailingly accurate. By keeping a critical eye on the statements you encounter, you'll be in a better position to determine the very real contributions made by developmentalists to understanding how humans develop over the course of the life span.

Review and Apply

Review

- Theories in development are systematically derived explanations of facts or phenomena. Theories suggest hypotheses, which are predictions that can be tested.

- Correlational studies examine relationships between factors without demonstrating causality. Naturalistic observation, case studies, and survey research are types of correlational studies.

- Experimental research seeks to discover cause-and-effect relationships by the use of a treatment group and a control group. By manipulating the independent variable and observing changes in the dependent variable, researchers find evidence of causal links between variables.

- Research studies may be conducted in field settings, where participants are subject to natural conditions, or in laboratories, where conditions can be controlled.

- Researchers measure age-related change through longitudinal studies, cross-sectional studies, and sequential studies.

Applying Lifespan Development

- Formulate a theory about one aspect of human development and a hypothesis that relates to it.

- *From the perspective of a healthcare provider:* Do you think there are some special circumstances involving adolescents, who are not legally adults, that would justify allowing them to participate in a study without obtaining their parents' permission? What might such circumstances involve?

Epilogue

As we've seen, the scope of lifespan development is broad, touching on a wide range of topics that address how people grow and change through the course of life. We've also found that there are a variety of techniques by which developmentalists seek to answer questions of interest.

Before proceeding to the next chapter, take a few minutes to reconsider the prologue of this chapter—about the Louise Brown, the first child to be born through in vitro fertilization. Based on what you now know about lifespan development, answer the following questions:

1. What are some of the potential benefits, and the costs, of the type of conception—in vitro fertilization—that was carried out for Louise's parents?

2. What are some questions that developmentalists who study either physical, cognitive, or personality and social development might ask about the effects on Louise of being conceived via in vitro fertilization?

3. Louise reported feeling lonely and isolated as a child. Why do you think this occurred, and what effects might it have on her as an adult?

4. Louise's own son was conceived in the traditional manner. How do you think his development will differ from that of his mother Louise, and why?

Looking Back

■ **What is lifespan development, and what are some of the basic influences on human development?**

- Lifespan development is a scientific approach to questions about growth, change, and stability in the physical, cognitive, social, and personality characteristics at all ages from conception to death.

- Culture—both broad and narrow—is an important issue in lifespan development. Many aspects of development are influenced not only by broad cultural differences, but by ethnic, racial, and socioeconomic differences within a particular culture.

- Each individual is subject to normative history-graded influences, normative age-graded influences, normative sociocultural-graded influences, and non-normative life events.

■ **What are the key issues in the field of development?**

- Four key issues in lifespan development are (1) whether developmental change is continuous or discontinuous; (2) whether development is largely governed by critical periods during which certain influences or experiences must occur for development to be normal; (3) whether to focus on certain particularly important periods in human development or on the entire life span; and (4) the nature–nurture controversy, which focuses on the relative importance of genetic versus environmental influences.

■ **Which theoretical perspectives have guided lifespan development?**

- Six major theoretical perspectives currently dominate lifespan development: the psychodynamic perspective (which focuses on inner, largely unconscious forces), the behavioral perspective (which focuses on external, observable actions), the cognitive perspective (which focuses on intellectual, cognitive processes), the humanistic perspective (which focuses on the unique qualities of human beings), the contextual perspective (which focuses on the relationship between individuals and their physical, cognitive, personality, and social worlds), and the evolutionary perspective (which focuses on our genetic inheritance).

- The psychodynamic perspective is exemplified by the psychoanalytic theory of Freud and the psychosocial theory of Erikson. Freud focused attention on the unconscious and on stages through which children must pass successfully to avoid harmful fixations. Erikson identified eight distinct stages of development, each characterized by a conflict, or crisis, to work out.

- The behavioral perspective typically concerns stimulus–response learning, exemplified by classical conditioning, the operant conditioning of Skinner, and Bandura's social-cognitive learning theory.

- Within the cognitive perspective, the most notable theorist is Piaget, who identified developmental stages through which all children are assumed to pass. Each stage involves qualitative differences in thinking. In contrast, information processing approaches attribute cognitive growth to quantitative changes in mental processes and capacities, and cognitive neuroscience approaches focus on biological brain processes.

- The humanistic perspective contends that people have a natural capacity to make decisions about their lives and control their behavior. The humanistic perspective emphasizes free will and the natural desire of humans to reach their full potential.

- The contextual perspective considers the relationship between individuals and their physical, cognitive, personality, and social worlds. The bioecological approach stresses the interrelatedness of developmental areas and the importance of broad cultural factors in human development. Vygotsky's sociocultural theory emphasizes the central influence on cognitive development exerted by social interactions between members of a culture.

- The evolutionary perspective attributes behavior to genetic inheritance from our ancestors, contending that genes determine not only traits such as skin and eye color, but certain personality traits and social behaviors as well.

■ What role do theories and hypotheses play in the study of development?

- Theories are broad explanations of facts or phenomena of interest, based on a systematic integration of prior findings and theories. Hypotheses are theory-based predictions that can be tested. The process of posing and answering questions systematically is called the scientific method.

- Researchers test hypotheses by correlational research (to determine if two factors are associated) and experimental research (to discover cause-and-effect relationships).

■ How are developmental research studies conducted?

- Correlational studies use naturalistic observation, case studies, and survey research to investigate whether certain characteristics of interest are associated with other characteristics. Correlational studies lead to no direct conclusions about cause and effect.

- Typically, experimental research studies are conducted on participants in a treatment group who receive the experimental treatment and participants in a control group who do not. Following the treatment, differences between the two groups can help the experimenter to determine the effects of the treatment. Experiments may be conducted in a laboratory or in a real-world setting.

- To measure change across human ages, researchers use longitudinal studies of the same participants over time, cross-sectional studies of different-age participants conducted at one time, and sequential studies of different-age participants at several points in time.

- Ethical guidelines for research include the protection of participants from harm, informed consent of participants, limits on the use of deception, and the maintenance of privacy.

Key Terms and Concepts

lifespan development (p. 5)
physical development (p. 6)
cognitive development (p. 6)
personality development (p. 6)
social development (p. 6)
cohort (p. 10)
continuous change (p. 11)
discontinuous change (p. 11)
critical period (p. 11)
sensitive period (p. 12)

maturation (p. 13)
theories (p. 14)
psychodynamic perspective (p. 15)
psychoanalytic theory (p. 15)
psychosexual development (p. 16)
psychosocial development (p. 17)
behavioral perspective (p. 18)
classical conditioning (p. 18)

operant conditioning (p. 18)
behavior modification (p. 19)
social-cognitive learning theory (p. 19)
cognitive perspective (p. 20)
information processing approaches (p. 21)
cognitive neuroscience approaches (p. 22)
humanistic perspective (p. 22)

contextual perspective
(p. 23)
bioecological perspective
(p. 23)
sociocultural theory (p. 25)
evolutionary perspective
(p. 26)
scientific method (p. 30)
hypothesis (p. 30)
correlational research (p. 31)

experimental research
(p. 31)
naturalistic observation
(p. 33)
case studies (p. 33)
survey research (p. 34)
psychophysiological
methods (p. 34)
experiment (p. 34)
independent variable (p. 35)

dependent variable (p. 35)
sample (p. 36)
field study (p. 36)
laboratory study (p. 36)
theoretical research (p. 36)
applied research (p. 36)
longitudinal research (p. 38)
cross-sectional research
(p. 38)
sequential studies (p. 39)

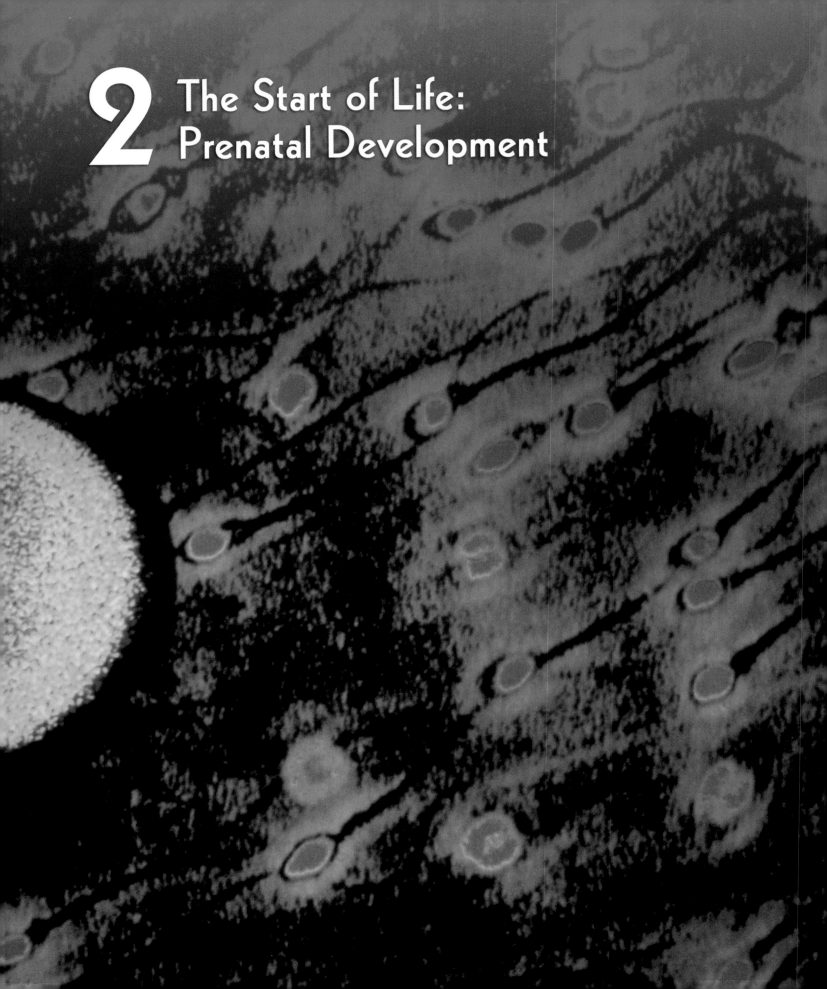

2 The Start of Life: Prenatal Development

Chapter Overview

EARLIEST DEVELOPMENT

Genes and Chromosomes: The Code of Life

Multiple Births: Two—or More—for the Genetic Price of One

The Basics of Genetics: The Mixing and Matching of Traits

Transmission of Genetic Information

The Human Genome and Behavioral Genetics: Cracking the Genetic Code

Inherited and Genetic Disorders: When Development Deviates from the Norm

Genetic Counseling: Predicting the Future from the Genes of the Present

THE INTERACTION OF HEREDITY AND ENVIRONMENT

The Role of the Environment in Determining the Expression of Genes: From Genotypes to Phenotypes

Studying Development: How Much Is Nature? How Much Is Nurture?

Physical Traits: Family Resemblances

Intelligence: More Research, More Controversy

Genetic and Environmental Influences on Personality: Born to Be Outgoing?

Psychological Disorders: The Role of Genetics and Environment

Can Genes Influence the Environment?

PRENATAL GROWTH AND CHANGE

Fertilization: The Moment of Conception

The Stages of the Prenatal Period: The Onset of Development

Pregnancy Problems

The Prenatal Environment: Threats to Development

Prologue: The Future Is Now

It came out of the blue: Jana and Tom Monaco's seemingly healthy 3-year-old son Stephen developed a life-threatening stomach virus that led to severe brain damage. His diagnosis: a rare but treatable disease called isovaleric acidemia (IVA), marked by the body's inability to metabolize an amino acid found in dietary protein. Jana and Tom were unknowing carriers of the disease. . . The Monacos had no warning whatsoever.

Not so when Jana got pregnant again. Her daughter, Caroline, was tested by amniocentesis while still in the womb. Knowing Caroline had the mutation, doctors were able to administer medication the day she was born—and the Monacos were prepared to monitor her diet immediately to keep her healthy. Today Stephen, 9, is unable to walk, talk, or feed himself. Caroline, meanwhile, is an active, healthy 4-year-old. Genetic testing, says Jana, "gives Caroline the future that Stephen didn't get to have" (Kalb, 2006, p. 52).

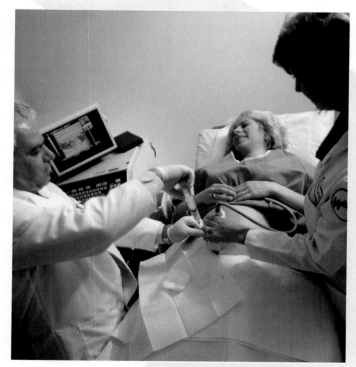

Prenatal tests have become increasingly sophisticated.

A hidden genetic disorder robbed Jana and Tom Monaco's first child of a normal, healthy life. Their second child was spared the same fate by advances in genetic testing, which gave the Monacos a chance to intervene before the damage was done. They were able to stop Caroline's inherited disorder from doing the same damage by controlling aspects of her environment.

In this chapter, we'll examine what developmental researchers and other scientists have learned about ways that heredity and the environment work in tandem to create and shape human beings, and how that knowledge is being used to improve people's lives. We begin with the basics of heredity, the genetic transmission of characteristics from biological parents to their children, by examining how we receive our genetic endowment. We'll consider an area of study, behavioral genetics, that specializes in the consequences of heredity on behavior. We'll also discuss what happens when genetic factors cause development to go off track, and how such problems are dealt with through genetic counseling and gene therapy.

But genes are only one part of the story of prenatal development. We'll also consider the ways in which a child's genetic heritage interacts with the environment in which he or she grows up—how one's family, socioeconomic status, and life events can affect a variety of characteristics, including physical traits, intelligence, and even personality.

Finally, we'll focus on the very first stage of development, tracing prenatal growth and change. We'll review some of the alternatives available to couples who find it difficult to conceive. We'll also talk about the stages of the prenatal period and how the prenatal environment offers both threats to—and the promise of—future growth.

After reading this chapter, you will be able to answer these questions:

■ **What is our basic genetic endowment, and how can human development go off track?**

■ **How do the environment and genetics work together to determine human characteristics?**

■ **Which human characteristics are significantly influenced by heredity?**

■ **What happens during the prenatal stages of development?**

■ **What are the threats to the fetal environment, and what can be done about them?**

Looking Ahead

mydevelopmentlab

VIDEO CLIP

PRENATAL DEVELOPMENT

- - - - - - - - - - - - - - - - - -

zygote   the new cell formed by the process of fertilization.

genes   the basic unit of genetic information.

DNA (deoxyribonucleic acid) molecules   the substance that genes are composed of that determines the nature of every cell in the body and how it will function.

chromosomes   rod-shaped portions of DNA that are organized in 23 pairs.

Earliest Development

We humans begin the course of our lives simply. Like individuals from tens of thousands of other species, we start as a single cell, a tiny speck probably weighing no more than a 20-millionth of an ounce. But from this humble beginning, in a matter of just several months if all goes well, a living, breathing individual infant is born. This first cell is created when a male reproductive cell, a *sperm,* pushes through the membrane of the *ovum,* the female reproductive cell. These *gametes,* as the male and female reproductive cells also are known, each contain huge amounts of genetic information. About an hour or so after the sperm enters the ovum, the two gametes suddenly fuse, becoming one cell, a **zygote.** The resulting combination of their genetic instructions—over two billion chemically coded messages—is sufficient to begin creating a whole person.

Genes and Chromosomes: The Code of Life

The blueprints for creating a person are stored and communicated in our **genes,** the basic units of genetic information. The roughly 25,000 human genes are the biological equivalent of "software" that programs the future development of all parts of the body's "hardware."

All genes are composed of specific sequences of **DNA (deoxyribonucleic acid) molecules.** The genes are arranged in specific locations and in a specific order along 46 **chromosomes,** rod-shaped portions of DNA that are organized in 23 pairs. Only sex cells—the ova and the sperm—contain half this number, so that a child's mother and father each provide one of the two chromosomes in each of the 23 pairs. The 46 chromosomes (in 23 pairs) in the new zygote contain the genetic blueprint that will guide cell activity for the rest of the individual's life (Pennisi, 2000; International Human Genome Sequencing Consortium, 2001; see Figure 2-1). Through a process called *mitosis*, which accounts for the replication of most types of cells, nearly all the cells of the body will contain the same 46 chromosomes as the zygote.

Specific genes in precise locations on the chain of chromosomes determine the nature and function of every cell in the body. For instance, genes determine which cells will ultimately become part of the heart and which will become part of the muscles of the leg. Genes also establish how different parts of the body will function—how rapidly the heart will beat, for example, or how much strength a muscle will have.

If each parent provides just 23 chromosomes, where does the potential for the vast diversity of human beings come from? The answer resides primarily in the nature of the processes that underlie the cell division of the gametes. When gametes—the sex cells, sperm and ova—are formed in the adult human body in a process called *meiosis*, each gamete receives one of the two chromosomes that make up each of the 23 pairs. Because for each of the 23 pairs it is largely a matter of chance which member of the pair is contributed, there are 2^{23}, or some eight million, different combinations possible. Furthermore, other processes, such as random transformations of particular genes, add to the variability of the genetic brew. The ultimate outcome: tens of *trillions* of possible genetic combinations.

With so many possible genetic mixtures provided by heredity, there is no likelihood that someday you'll bump into a genetic duplicate of yourself—with one exception: an identical twin.

monozygotic twins   twins who are genetically identical.

dizygotic twins   twins who are produced when two separate ova are fertilized by two separate sperm at roughly the same time.

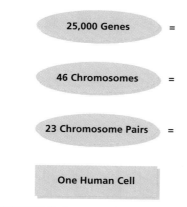

FIGURE 2-1   THE CONTENTS OF A SINGLE HUMAN CELL

At the moment of conception, humans receive about 25,000 genes, contained on 46 chromosomes in 23 pairs.

Multiple Births: Two—or More— for the Genetic Price of One

Although it doesn't seem surprising when dogs and cats give birth to several offspring at one time, in humans multiple births are cause for comment. They should be: Less than 3% of all pregnancies produce twins, and the odds are even slimmer for three or more children.

Why do multiple births occur? Some occur when a cluster of cells in the ovum splits off within the first 2 weeks after fertilization. The result is two genetically identical zygotes, which, because they come from the same original zygote, are called monozygotic. **Monozygotic twins** are twins who are genetically identical. Any differences in their future development can be attributed only to environmental factors, since genetically they are exactly the same.

There is a second, and actually more common, mechanism that produces multiple births. In these cases, two separate ova are fertilized by two separate sperm at roughly the same time. Twins produced in this fashion are known as **dizygotic twins.** Because they are the result of two separate ovum-sperm combinations, they are no more genetically similar than two siblings born at different times.

Of course, not all multiple births produce only two babies. Triplets, quadruplets, and even more births are produced by either (or both) of the mechanisms that yield twins. Thus, triplets may be some combination of monozygotic, dizygotic, or trizygotic.

Although the chances of having a multiple birth are typically slim, the odds rise considerably when couples use fertility drugs to improve the probability they will conceive a child. For example, 1 in 10 couples using fertility drugs have dizygotic twins, compared to an overall figure of 1 in 86 for Caucasian couples in the United States. Older women, too, are more likely to have multiple births, and multiple births are also more common in some families than in others. The increased use of fertility drugs and rising average age of mothers giving birth has

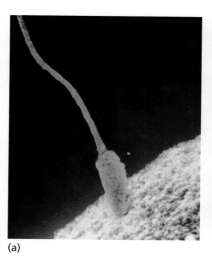

(a)

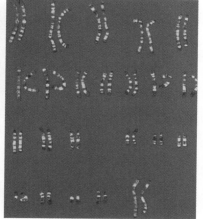

(b)

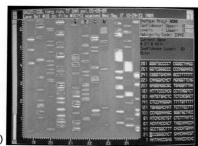

(c)

At the moment of conception (a), humans receive 23 pairs of chromosomes (b), half from the mother and half from the father. These chromosomes contain thousands of genes, shown in the computer-generated map (c).

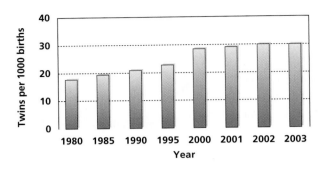

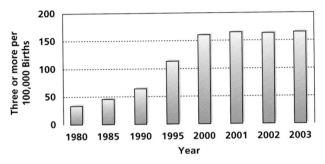

FIGURE 2-2 **RISING MULTIPLES**

Multiple births have increased significantly over the last 25 years. What are some of the reasons for this phenomenon?

(*Source:* Martin et al., 2005.)

meant that multiple births have increased in the last 25 years (see Figure 2-2; Martin et al., 2005).

There are also racial, ethnic, and national differences in the rate of multiple births, probably due to inherited differences in the likelihood that more than one ovum will be released at a time. One out of 70 African American couples have dizygotic births, compared with 1 out of 86 for white American couples (Vaughan, McKay, & Behrman, 1979; Wood, 1997).

Mothers carrying multiple children run a higher-than-average risk of premature delivery and birth complications. Consequently, these mothers must be particularly concerned about their prenatal care.

Boy or Girl? Establishing the Sex of the Child. Recall that there are 23 matched pairs of chromosomes. In 22 of these pairs, each chromosome is similar to the other member of its pair. The one exception is the 23rd pair, which is the one that determines the sex of the child. In females, the 23rd pair consists of two matching, relatively large, X-shaped chromosomes, appropriately identified as XX. In males, on the other hand, the members of the pair are dissimilar. One consists of an X-shaped chromosome, but the other is a shorter, smaller, Y-shaped chromosome. This pair is identified as XY.

As we discussed earlier, each gamete carries one chromosome from each of the parent's 23 pairs of chromosomes. Since a female's 23rd pair of chromosomes are both Xs, an ovum will always carry an X chromosome, no matter which chromosome of the 23rd pair it gets. A male's 23rd pair is XY, so each sperm could carry either an X or a Y chromosome.

If the sperm contributes an X chromosome when it meets an ovum (which, remember, will always contribute an X chromosome), the child will have an XX pairing on the 23rd chromosome—and will be a female. If the sperm contributes a Y chromosome, the result will be an XY pairing—a male (see Figure 2-3).

It is clear from this process that the father's sperm determines the gender of the child. This fact is leading to the development of techniques that will allow parents to increase the chances of specifying the gender of their child. In one new technique, lasers measure the DNA in sperm. By discarding sperm that harbor the unwanted sex chromosome, the chances of having a child of the desired sex increase dramatically (Hayden, 1998; Belkin, 1999; Van Balen, 2005).

Of course, procedures for choosing a child's sex raise ethical and practical issues. For example, in cultures that value one gender over the other, might there be a kind of gender discrimination prior to birth? Furthermore, a shortage of children of the less-preferred sex might ultimately emerge. Many questions remain, then, before sex selection becomes routine (Liao, 2005).

The Basics of Genetics: The Mixing and Matching of Traits

What determined the color of your hair? Why are you tall or short? What made you susceptible to hay fever? And why do you have so many freckles? To answer these questions, we need to consider the basic mechanisms involved in the way that the genes we inherit from our parents transmit information.

We can start by examining the discoveries of an Austrian monk, Gregor Mendel, in the mid-1800s. In a series of simple yet convincing experiments, Mendel cross-pollinated pea plants that always produced yellow seeds with pea plants that always produced green seeds. The result was not, as one might guess, a plant with a combination of yellow and green seeds. Instead, all of the resulting plants had yellow seeds. At first it appeared that the green-seeded plants had no influence on the resulting plants.

However, additional research on Mendel's part proved this was not true. He bred together plants from the new, yellow-seeded generation that had resulted from his original cross-breeding of the green-seeded and yellow-seeded plants. The consistent result was a ratio of three-quarters yellow seeds to one-quarter green seeds.

Why did this 2-to-1 ratio of yellow to green seeds appear so consistently? It was Mendel's genius to provide an answer. Based on his experiments with pea plants, he argued that when two competing traits, such as a green or yellow coloring of seeds, were both present, only one could be expressed. The one that was expressed was called a **dominant trait.** Meanwhile, the other trait remained present in the organism, although it was not expressed (displayed). This was called a **recessive trait.** In the case of Mendel's original pea plants, the offspring plants received genetic information from both the green-seeded and yellow-seeded parents. However, the yellow trait was dominant, and consequently the recessive green trait did not assert itself.

Keep in mind, however, that genetic material relating to both parent plants is present in the offspring, even though it cannot be seen. The genetic information is known as the organism's genotype. A **genotype** is the underlying combination of genetic material present (but outwardly invisible) in an organism. In contrast, a **phenotype** is the observable trait, the trait that actually is seen.

Although the offspring of the yellow-seeded and green-seeded pea plants all have yellow seeds (i.e., they have a yellow-seeded phenotype), the genotype consists of genetic information relating to both parents.

And what is the nature of the information in the genotype? To answer that question, let's turn from peas to people. In fact, the principles are the same not just for plants and humans, but for the majority of species.

Recall that parents transmit genetic information to their offspring via the chromosomes they contribute through the gamete they provide during fertilization. Some of the genes form pairs called *alleles*, genes governing traits that may take alternate forms, such as hair or eye color. For example, brown eye color is a dominant trait (B); blue eyes are recessive (b). A child's allele may contain similar or dissimilar genes from each parent. If the child receives similar genes, he or she is said to be **homozygous** for the trait. On the other hand, if the child receives different forms of the gene from its parents, he or she is said to be **heterozygous.** In the case of heterozygous alleles (Bb), the dominant characteristic, brown eyes, is expressed. However, if the child happens to receive a recessive allele from each of its parents, and therefore lacks a dominant characteristic (bb), it will display the recessive characteristic, such as blue eyes.

Transmission of Genetic Information

We can see this process at work in humans by considering the transmission of *phenylketonuria (PKU)*, an inherited disorder in which a child is unable to make use of phenylalanine, an essential amino acid present in proteins found in milk and other foods. If left untreated, PKU allows phenylalanine to build up to toxic levels, causing brain damage and mental retardation.

PKU is produced by a single allele, or pair of genes. As shown in Figure 2-4, we can label each gene of the pair with a *P* if it carries a dominant gene, which causes the normal production of phenylalanine, or a *p* if it carries the recessive gene that produces PKU. In cases in which neither parent is a PKU carrier, both the mother's and the father's pairs of genes are the dominant form, symbolized as *PP*. Consequently, no matter which member of the pair is contributed by the mother and father, the resulting pair of genes in the child will be *PP*, and the child will not have PKU.

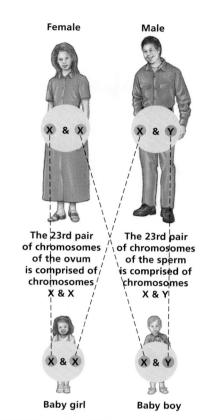

FIGURE 2-3 DETERMINING SEX

When an ovum and sperm meet at the moment of fertilization, the ovum is certain to provide an X chromosome, while the sperm will provide either an X or a Y chromosome. If the sperm contributes its X chromosome, the child will have an XX pairing on the 23rd chromosome and will be a girl. If the sperm contributes a Y chromosome, the result will be an XY pairing—a boy. Does this mean that girls are more likely to be conceived than boys?

dominant trait the one trait that is expressed when two competing traits are present.

recessive trait a trait within an organism that is present, but is not expressed.

genotype the underlying combination of genetic material present (but not outwardly visible) in an organism.

phenotype an observable trait; the trait that actually is seen.

homozygous inheriting from parents similar genes for a given trait.

heterozygous inheriting from parents different forms of a gene for a given trait.

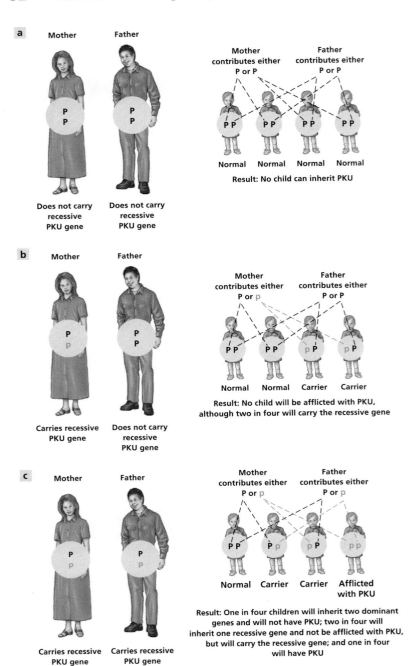

FIGURE 2-4 PKU PROBABILITIES

PKU, a disease that causes brain damage and mental retardation, is produced by a single pair of genes inherited from one's mother and father. If neither parent carries a gene for the disease (a), a child cannot develop PKU. Even if one parent carries the recessive gene, but the other doesn't (b), the child cannot inherit the disease. However, if both parents carry the recessive gene (c), there is a one in four chance that the child will have PKU.

However, consider what happens if one of the parents has a recessive *p* gene. In this case, which we can symbolize as *Pp*, the parent will not have PKU, since the normal *P* gene is dominant. But the recessive gene can be passed down to the child. This is not so bad: If the child has only one recessive gene, it will not suffer from PKU. But what if both parents carry a recessive *p* gene? In this case, although neither parent has the disorder, it is possible for the child to receive a recessive gene from both parents. The child's genotype for PKU then will be *pp*, and he or she will have the disorder.

Remember, though, that even children whose parents both have the recessive gene for PKU have only a 25% chance of inheriting the disorder. Due to the laws of probability, 25% of children with *Pp* parents will receive the dominant gene from each parent (these children's genotype would be *PP*), and 50% will receive the dominant gene from one parent and the recessive gene from the other (their genotypes would be either *Pp* or *pP*). Only the unlucky 25% who receive the recessive gene from each parent and end up with the genotype *pp* will suffer from PKU.

Polygenic Traits. The transmission of PKU is a good way of illustrating the basic principles of how genetic information passes from parent to child, although the case of PKU is simpler than most cases of genetic transmission. Relatively few traits are governed by a single pair of genes. Instead, most traits are the result of polygenic inheritance. In **polygenic inheritance**, a combination of multiple gene pairs is responsible for the production of a particular trait.

Furthermore, some genes come in several alternate forms, and still others act to modify the way that particular genetic traits (produced by other alleles) are displayed. Genes also vary in terms of their *reaction range*, the potential degree of variability in the actual expression of a trait due to environmental conditions. And some traits, such as blood type, are produced by genes in which neither member of a pair of genes can be classified as purely dominant or recessive. Instead, the trait is expressed in terms of a combination of the two genes—such as type AB blood.

A number of recessive genes, called **X-linked genes**, are located only on the X chromosome. Recall that in females, the 23rd pair of chromosomes is an XX pair, while in males it is an XY pair. One result is that males have a higher risk for a variety of X-linked disorders, since males lack a second X chromosome that can counteract the genetic information that produces the disorder. For example, males are significantly more apt to have red-green color blindness, a disorder produced by a set of genes on the X chromosome.

Similarly, *hemophilia*, a blood disorder, is produced by X-linked genes. Hemophilia has been a recurrent problem in the royal families of Europe, as illustrated in Figure 2-5, which shows the inheritance of hemophilia in the descendants of Queen Victoria of Great Britain.

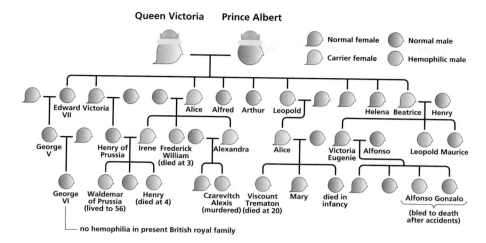

Queen Victoria   **Prince Albert**

Normal female   Normal male
Carrier female   Hemophilic male

Edward Victoria   Alice   Alfred   Arthur   Leopold   Helena Beatrice   Henry
VII

George   Henry of   Irene Frederick   Alexandra   Alice   Victoria Alfonso   Leopold Maurice
V   Prussia   William   Eugenie
                   (died at 3)

George   Waldemar   Henry   Czarevitch   Viscount   Mary   died in   Alfonso Gonzalo
VI   of Prussia   (died at 4)   Alexis   Trematon   infancy
      (lived to 56)   (murdered) (died at 20)   (bled to death
                                               after accidents)

no hemophilia in present British royal family

FIGURE 2-5   **INHERITING HEMOPHILIA**

Hemophilia, a blood-clotting disorder, has been an inherited problem throughout the royal families of Europe, as illustrated by the descendants of Queen Victoria of Britain. (*Source:* Adapted from Kimball, 1983.)

The Human Genome and Behavioral Genetics: Cracking the Genetic Code

Mendel's achievements in recognizing the basics of genetic transmission of traits were trailblazing. However, they mark only the beginning of our understanding of the ways those particular sorts of characteristics are passed on from one generation to the next.

The most recent milestone in understanding genetics was reached in early 2001, when molecular geneticists succeeded in mapping the specific sequence of genes on each chromosome. This accomplishment stands as one of the most important moments in the history of genetics, and, for that matter, all of biology (International Human Genome Sequencing Consortium, 2001).

Already, the mapping of the gene sequence has provided important advances in our understanding of genetics. For instance, the number of human genes, long thought to be 100,000, has been revised downward to 25,000—not many more than organisms that are far less complex (see Figure 2-6). Furthermore, scientists have discovered that 99.9% of the gene sequence is shared by all humans. What this means is that we humans are far more similar to one another than we are different. It also indicates that many of the differences that seemingly separate people—such as race—are, literally, only skin-deep. Mapping of the human genome will also help in the identification of particular disorders to which a given individual is susceptible (International Human Genome Sequencing Consortium, 2001; Human Genome Program, 2003; Gee, 2004; DeLisi & Fleischhaker, 2007; Gupta & State, 2007).

The mapping of the human gene sequence is supporting the field of behavioral genetics. As the name implies, **behavioral genetics** studies the effects of heredity on behavior and psychological characteristics. Rather than simply examining stable, unchanging characteristics such as hair or eye color, behavioral genetics takes a broader approach, considering how our personality and behavioral habits are affected by genetic factors (Dick & Rose, 2002; Eley, Lichtenstein, & Moffitt, 2003; Li, 2003). Personality traits such as shyness or sociability, moodiness, and assertiveness are among the areas being studied. Other behavior geneticists study psychological disorders, such as depression, attention deficit hyperactivity disorder, and schizophrenia, looking for possible genetic links (Conklin & Iacono, 2002; see Table 2-1).

The promise of behavioral genetics is substantial. For one thing, researchers working within the field have gained a better understanding of the specifics of the genetic code that underlies human behavior and development.

Even more important, researchers are seeking to identify how genetic defects may be remedied (Plomin & Rutter, 1998; Peltonen & McKusick, 2001). To understand how that possibility might come about, we need to consider the ways in which genetic factors, which normally cause development to proceed so smoothly, may falter.

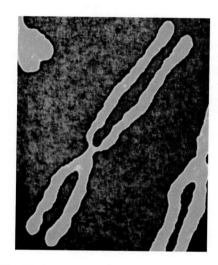

The X chromosome is not only important in determining gender, but is also the site of genes controlling other aspects of development.

polygenic inheritance inheritance in which a combination of multiple gene pairs is responsible for the production of a particular trait.

X-linked genes genes that are considered recessive and located only on the X chromosome.

behavioral genetics the study of the effects of heredity on behavior and psychological characteristics.

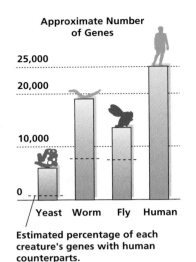

Approximate Number of Genes

FIGURE 2-6 **UNIQUELY HUMAN?**

Humans have about 25,000 genes, making them not much more genetically complex than some primitive species.

(*Source:* Celera Genomics: International Human Genome Sequencing Consortium, 2001.)

Table 2-1	Current Understanding of the Genetic Basis of Selected Behavioral Disorders and Traits
Behavioral Trait	**Current Ideas of Genetic Basis**
Huntington's disease	Huntington gene identified.
Early onset (familial) Alzheimer's disease	Three distinct genes have been identified.
Fragile X mental retardation	Two genes have been identified.
Late onset Alzheimer's disease	One set of genes has been associated with increased risk.
Attention deficit hyperactivity disorder	Three locations related to the genetics involved with the neurotransmitter dopamine may contribute.
Dyslexia	Relationships to two locations, on chromosomes 6 and 15, have been suggested.
Schizophrenia	There is no consensus, but links to numerous chromosomes, including 1, 5, 6, 10, 13, 15, and 22 have been reported.

(*Source:* Adapted from McGuffin, Riley, & Plomin, 2001.)

Inherited and Genetic Disorders: When Development Deviates from the Norm

PKU is just one of several disorders that may be inherited. Like a bomb that is harmless until its fuse is lit, a recessive gene responsible for a disorder may be passed on unknowingly from one generation to the next, revealing itself only when, by chance, it is paired with another recessive gene. It is only when two recessive genes come together like a match and a fuse that the gene will express itself and a child will inherit the genetic disorder.

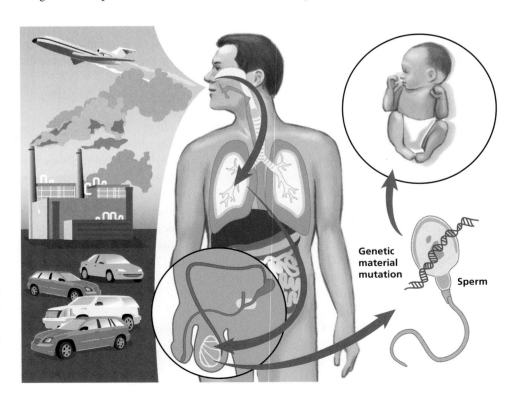

FIGURE 2-7 **INHALED AIR AND GENETIC MUTATIONS**

Inhalation of unhealthy, polluted air may lead to mutations in genetic material in sperm. These mutations may be passed on, damaging the fetus and affecting future generations.

(*Source:* Based on Samet, DeMarini, & Malling, 2004, p. 971.)

But there is another way that genes are a source of concern: In some cases, genes become physically damaged. For instance, genes may break down due to wear and tear or chance events occurring during the cell division processes of meiosis and mitosis. Sometimes genes, for no known reason, spontaneously change their form, a process called *spontaneous mutation.*

Alternatively, certain environmental factors, such as exposure to x-rays or even highly polluted air, may produce a malformation of genetic material (see Figure 2-7). When such damaged genes are passed on to a child, the results can be disastrous in terms of future physical and cognitive development (Samet, DeMarini, & Malling, 2004).

In addition to PKU, which occurs once in 10,000 to 20,000 births, other inherited and genetic disorders include:

Sickle-cell anemia, named for the presence of misshapen red blood cells, is carried in the genes of 1 in 10 African Americans.

- *Down syndrome.* As noted earlier, most people have 46 chromosomes, arranged in 23 pairs. One exception is individuals with **Down syndrome,** a disorder produced by the presence of an extra chromosome on the 21st pair. Once referred to as mongolism, Down syndrome is the most frequent cause of mental retardation. It occurs in about 1 out of 500 births, although the risk is much greater in mothers who are unusually young or old (Crane & Morris, 2006).

- *Fragile X syndrome.* **Fragile X syndrome** occurs when a particular gene is injured on the X chromosome. The result is mild to moderate mental retardation.

- *Sickle-cell anemia.* Around one-tenth of people of African descent carry genes that produce sickle-cell anemia, and 1 in 400 actually has the disease. **Sickle-cell anemia** is a blood disorder that gets its name from the shape of the red blood cells in those who have it. Symptoms include poor appetite, stunted growth, swollen stomach, and yellowish eyes. People afflicted with the most severe form of the disease rarely live beyond childhood. However, for those with less severe cases, medical advances have produced significant increases in life expectancy.

- *Tay-Sachs disease.* Occurring mainly in Jews of Eastern European ancestry and in French-Canadians, **Tay-Sachs disease** usually causes death before its victims reach school age. There is no treatment for the disorder, which produces blindness and muscle degeneration prior to death.

- *Klinefelter's syndrome.* One male out of every 400 is born with **Klinefelter's syndrome,** the presence of an extra X chromosome. The resulting XXY complement produces underdeveloped genitals, extreme height, and enlarged breasts. Klinefelter's syndrome is one of a number of genetic abnormalities that result from receiving the improper number of sex chromosomes. For instance, there are disorders produced by an extra Y chromosome (XYY), a missing second chromosome (X0, called *Turner syndrome*), and three X chromosomes (XXX). Such disorders are typically characterized by problems relating to sexual characteristics and by intellectual deficits (Sorenson, 1992; Sotos, 1997).

It is important to keep in mind that the mere fact that a disorder has genetic roots does not mean that environmental factors do not also play a role (Moldin & Gottesman, 1997). Consider, for instance, sickle-cell anemia, which primarily afflicts people of African descent. Because the disease can be fatal in childhood, we'd expect that those who suffer from it would be unlikely to live long enough to pass it on. And this does seem to be true, at least in the United States: Compared with parts of West Africa, the incidence in the United States is much lower.

But why shouldn't the incidence of sickle-cell anemia also be gradually reduced for people in West Africa? This question proved puzzling for many years, until scientists determined that carrying the sickle-cell gene raises immunity to malaria, which is a common disease in West Africa. This heightened immunity meant that people with the sickle-cell gene had a genetic advantage (in terms of resistance to malaria) that offset, to some degree, the disadvantage of being a carrier of the sickle-cell gene.

The lesson of sickle-cell anemia is that genetic factors are intertwined with environmental considerations and can't be looked at in isolation. Furthermore, we need to remember that although we've been focusing on inherited factors that can go awry, in the vast majority of cases

Down syndrome   a disorder produced by the presence of an extra chromosome on the 21st pair; once referred to as mongolism.

fragile X syndrome   a disorder produced by injury to a gene on the X chromosome, producing mild to moderate mental retardation.

sickle-cell anemia   a blood disorder that gets its name from the shape of the red blood cells in those who have it.

Tay-Sachs disease   a disorder that produces blindness and muscle degeneration prior to death; there is no treatment.

Klinefelter's syndrome   a disorder resulting from the presence of an extra X chromosome that produces underdeveloped genitals, extreme height, and enlarged breasts.

the genetic mechanisms with which we are endowed work quite well. Overall, 95% of children born in the United States are healthy and normal. For the some 250,000 who are born each year with some sort of physical or mental disorder, appropriate intervention often can help treat and, in some cases, cure the problem.

Moreover, due to advances in behavioral genetics, genetic difficulties increasingly can be forecast, anticipated, and planned for before a child's birth, enabling parents to take steps before the child is born to reduce the severity of certain genetic conditions. In fact, as scientists' knowledge regarding the specific location of particular genes expands, predictions of what the genetic future may hold are becoming increasingly exact, as we discuss next (Plomin & Rutter, 1998).

Genetic Counseling: Predicting the Future from the Genes of the Present

If you knew that your mother and grandmother had died of Huntington's disease—a devastating, always fatal inherited disorder marked by tremors and intellectual deterioration—to whom could you turn to learn your own chances of coming down with the disease? The best person to turn to would be a member of a field that, just a few decades ago, was nonexistent: genetic counseling. **Genetic counseling** focuses on helping people deal with issues relating to inherited disorders.

Genetic counselors use a variety of data in their work. For instance, couples contemplating having a child may seek to determine the risks involved in a future pregnancy. In such a case, a counselor will take a thorough family history, seeking any familial incidence of birth defects that might indicate a pattern of recessive or X-linked genes. In addition, the counselor will take into account factors such as the age of the mother and father and any previous abnormalities in other children they may have already had (Fransen, Meertens, & Schrander-Stumpel, 2006; Resta et al., 2006).

Typically, genetic counselors suggest a thorough physical examination. Such an exam may identify physical abnormalities that potential parents may have and not be aware of. In addition, samples of blood, skin, and urine may be used to isolate and examine specific chromosomes. Possible genetic defects, such as the presence of an extra sex chromosome, can be identified by assembling a *karyotype*, a chart containing enlarged photos of each of the chromosomes.

Prenatal Testing.   If the woman is already pregnant, there are a variety of techniques to assess the health of her unborn child (see Table 2-2 for a list of currently available tests). The earliest test is a *first-trimester screen*, which combines a blood test and ultrasound sonography in the 11th to 13th week of pregnancy and can identify chromosomal abnormalities and other disorders, such as heart problems. In **ultrasound sonography,** high-frequency sound waves bombard the mother's womb. These waves produce a rather indistinct, but useful, image of the unborn baby, whose size and shape can then be assessed. Repeated use of ultrasound sonography can reveal developmental patterns. Although the accuracy of blood tests and ultrasound in identifying abnormalities is not high early in pregnancy, it becomes more accurate later in pregnancy as the developing child becomes more differentiated.

A more invasive test, **chorionic villus sampling (CVS),** can be employed in the 10th to 13th week of the first trimester if blood tests and ultrasound have identified a potential problem or if there is a family history of inherited disorders. CVS involves inserting a thin needle into the fetus and taking small samples of hairlike material that surrounds the embryo. The test can be done between the 8th and 11th week of pregnancy. However, it produces a risk of miscarriage of 1 in 100 to 1 in 200. Because of the risk, its use is relatively infrequent.

In **amniocentesis,** a small sample of fetal cells is drawn by a tiny needle inserted into the amniotic fluid surrounding the unborn fetus. Carried out 15 to 20 weeks into the pregnancy, amniocentesis allows the analysis of the fetal cells that can identify a variety of genetic defects with nearly 100% accuracy. In addition, the sex of the child can be determined. Although there is always a danger to the fetus in an invasive procedure such as amniocentesis, it is generally safe.

genetic counseling   the discipline that focuses on helping people deal with issues relating to inherited disorders.

ultrasound sonography   a process in which high-frequency sound waves scan the mother's womb to produce an image of the unborn baby, whose size and shape can then be assessed.

chorionic villus sampling (CVS)   a test used to find genetic defects that involves taking samples of hairlike material that surrounds the embryo.

amniocentesis   the process of identifying genetic defects by examining a small sample of fetal cells drawn by a needle inserted into the amniotic fluid surrounding the unborn fetus.

Table 2-2 Fetal Development Monitoring Techniques

Technique	Description
Amniocentesis	Done between the 15th and 20th week of pregnancy, this procedure examines a sample of the amniotic fluid, which contains fetal cells. Recommended if either parent carries Tay-Sachs, spina bifida, sickle-cell, Down syndrome, muscular dystrophy, or Rh disease.
Chorionic villus sampling (CVS)	Done at 8 to 11 weeks, either transabdominally or transcervically, depending on where the placenta is located. Involves inserting a needle (abdominally) or a catheter (cervically) into the substance of the placenta but staying outside the amniotic sac and removing 10 to 15 milligrams of tissue. This tissue is manually cleaned of maternal uterine tissue and then grown in culture, and a karyotype is made, as with amniocentesis.
Embryoscopy	Examines the embryo or fetus during the first 12 weeks of pregnancy by means of a fiber-optic endoscope inserted through the cervix. Can be performed as early as week 5. Access to the fetal circulation may be obtained through the instrument, and direct visualization of the embryo permits the diagnosis of malformations.
Fetal blood sampling (FBS)	Performed after 18 weeks of pregnancy by collecting a small amount of blood from the umbilical cord for testing. Used to detect Down syndrome and most other chromosome abnormalities in the fetuses of couples who are at increased risk of having an affected child. Many other diseases can be diagnosed using this technique.
Sonoembryology	Used to detect abnormalities in the first trimester of pregnancy. Involves high-frequency transvaginal probes and digital image processing. In combination with ultrasound, can detect more than 80% of all malformations during the second trimester.
Sonogram	Uses ultrasound to produce a visual image of the uterus, fetus, and placenta.
Ultrasound sonography	Uses very high frequency sound waves to detect structural abnormalities or multiple pregnancies, measure fetal growth, judge gestational age, and evaluate uterine abnormalities. Also used as an adjunct to other procedures such as amniocentesis.

After the various tests are complete (see Table 2-2) and all possible information is available, the couple will meet with the genetic counselor again. Typically, counselors avoid giving specific recommendations. Instead, they lay out the facts and present various options, ranging from doing nothing to taking more drastic steps, such as terminating the pregnancy through abortion. Ultimately, it is the parents who must decide what course of action to follow.

Screening for Future Problems.   The newest role of genetic counselors involves testing people to identify whether they themselves, rather than their children, are susceptible to future disorders because of genetic abnormalities. For instance, Huntington's disease typically does not appear until people reach their 40s. However, genetic testing can identify much earlier whether a person carries the flawed gene that produces Huntington's disease. Presumably, people's knowledge that they carry the gene can help them prepare themselves for the future (van't Spijker & ten Kroode, 1997; Ensenauer, Michels, & Reinke, 2005).

In addition to Huntington's disease, more than a thousand disorders can be predicted on the basis of genetic testing (see Table 2-3). Although such testing may bring welcome relief from future worries—if the results are negative—positive results may produce just the opposite effect. In fact, genetic testing raises difficult practical and ethical questions (Johannes, 2003; Human Genome Project, 2006; Twomey, 2006).

Suppose, for instance, a woman who thought she was susceptible to Huntington's disease was tested in her 20s and found that she did not carry the defective gene. Obviously, she would experience tremendous relief. But suppose she found that she did carry the flawed gene and was therefore going to get the disease. In this case, she might well experience depression and remorse. In fact, some studies show that 10%

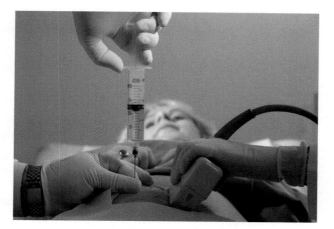

In amniocentesis, a sample of fetal cells is withdrawn from the amniotic sac and used to identify a number of genetic defects.

Table 2-3   Some Currently Available DNA-Based Gene Tests

Disease	Description
Adult polycystic kidney disease	Kidney failure and liver disease
Alpha-1-antitrypsin deficiency	Emphysema and liver disease
Alzheimer's disease	Late-onset variety of senile dementia
Amyotrophic lateral sclerosis (Lou Gehrig's disease)	Progressive motor function loss leading to paralysis and death
Ataxia telangiectasia	Progressive brain disorder resulting in loss of muscle control and cancers
Breast and ovarian cancer (inherited)	Early-onset tumors of breasts and ovaries
Charcot-Marie-Tooth	Loss of feeling in ends of limbs
Congenital adrenal hyperplasia	Hormone deficiency, ambiguous genitalia and male pseudohermaphroditism
Cystic fibrosis	Thick mucus accumulations in lungs and chronic infections in lungs and pancreas
Duchenne muscular dystrophy (Becker muscular dystrophy)	Severe to mild muscle wasting, deterioration, weakness
Dystonia	Muscle rigidity, repetitive twisting movements
Factor V-Leiden	Blood-clotting disorder
Fanconi anemia, group	Anemia, leukemia, skeletal deformities
Fragile X syndrome	Mental retardation
Gaucher disease	Enlarged liver and spleen, bone degeneration
Hemophilia A and B	Bleeding disorders
Hereditary nonpolyposis colon cancer[a]	Early-onset tumors of colon and sometimes other organs
Huntington's disease	Progressive neurological degeneration, usually beginning in midlife
Myotonic dystrophy	Progressive muscle weakness
Neurofibromatosis, type 1	Multiple benign nervous system tumors that can be disfiguring; cancers
Phenylketonuria	Progressive mental retardation due to missing enzyme; correctable by diet
Prader Willi/Angelman syndromes	Decreased motor skills, cognitive impairment, early death
Sickle-cell disease	Blood cell disorder chronic pain and infections
Spinal muscular atrophy	Severe, usually lethal progressive muscle-wasting disorder in children
Spinocerebellar ataxia, type 1	Involuntary muscle movements, reflex disorders, explosive speech
Tay-Sachs disease	Seizures, paralysis, fatal neurological disease of early childhood
Thalassemias	Anemias

[a] These are susceptibility tests that provide only an estimated risk for developing the disorder.

(*Source:* Human Genome Project, 2006, http://www.ornl.gov/sci/techresources/Human_Genome/medicine/genetest.shtml.)

of people who find they have the flawed gene that leads to Huntington's disease never recover fully on an emotional level (Groopman, 1998; Myers, 2004; Wahlin, 2007).

Genetic testing clearly is a complicated issue. It rarely provides a simple yes or no answer as to whether an individual will be susceptible to a disorder. Instead, typically it presents a range of probabilities. In some cases, the likelihood of actually becoming ill depends on the type of environmental stressors to which a person is exposed. Personal differences also affect a given person's susceptibility to a disorder (Holtzman et al., 1997; Patenaude, Guttmacher, & Collins, 2002; Bonke et al., 2005).

As our understanding of genetics continues to grow, researchers and medical practitioners have moved beyond testing and counseling to actively working to change flawed genes. The possibilities for genetic intervention and manipulation increasingly border on what once was science fiction—as we consider in the accompanying *From Research to Practice* box about preimplantation genetic diagnosis.

From Research to Practice

Are "Designer Babies" in Our Future?

Adam Nash was born to save his older sister Molly's life—literally. Molly was suffering from a rare disorder called Fanconi anemia, which meant that her bone marrow was failing to produce blood cells. This disease can have devastating effects on young children, including birth defects and certain cancers. Many don't survive to adulthood. Molly's best hope for overcoming this disease was to grow healthy bone marrow by receiving a transplant of immature blood cells from the placenta of a newborn sibling. But not just any sibling would do—it had to be one with compatible cells that would not be rejected by Molly's immune system. So Molly's parents turned to a new and risky technique that had the potential to save Molly by using cells from her unborn brother.

Molly's parents were the first to use a genetic screening technique called *preimplantation genetic diagnosis* (PGD) to ensure that their next child would be free of Fanconi anemia. With PGD, a newly fertilized embryo can be screened for a variety of genetic diseases before it is implanted in the mother's uterus to develop. Doctors fertilized several of Molly's mother's eggs with her husband's sperm in a test tube. They then examined the embryos to ensure that they would only implant the embryo that PGD revealed to be both genetically healthy and a match for Molly. When Adam was born 9 months later, Molly got a new lease on life, too: the transplant was a success, and Molly was cured of her disease.

Molly's parents were understandably focused on saving their seriously ill daughter's life, but they and their doctors also opened a controversial new chapter in genetic engineering involving the use of advances in reproductive medicine that give parents a degree of prenatal control over the traits of their children. Another procedure that makes this level of genetic control possible is *germ line therapy*, in which cells are taken from an embryo and then replaced after the defective genes they contain have been repaired.

While PGD and germ line therapy have important uses in the prevention and treatment of serious genetic disorders, concerns have been raised over whether such scientific advances can lead to the development of "designer babies"—infants that have been genetically manipulated to have traits their parents wish for. The question is whether these procedures can and should be used not only to correct undesirable genetic defects, but also to breed infants for specific purposes or to "improve" future generations on a genetic level.

The ethical concerns are numerous: Is it right to tailor babies to serve a specific purpose, however noble? Does this kind of genetic control pose any dangers to the human gene pool? Would unfair advantages be conferred on the offspring of those who are wealthy or privileged enough to have access to these procedures (Frankel & Chapman, 2000; Sheldon & Wilkinson, 2004)?

Designer babies aren't with us yet; scientists do not yet understand enough about the human genome to identify the genes that control most traits, much less to make genetic modifications to control how those traits will be expressed. Moreover, the term itself is a bit misleading. For one thing, babies aren't being genetically engineered; PGD merely entails selecting an embryo that already has the desired genetic makeup. For another thing, it's a difficult and expensive procedure that does not lend itself to casual use. Still, as Adam Nash's case reveals, we are inching closer to a day when it is possible for parents to decide what genes their children will and will not have.

- *How might the circumstances of Adam's birth affect the relationship between him and Molly as they grow up?*

- *How might Adam feel when he learns that he was selected to be born in order to save his sister?*

- *What if our understanding of the human genome develops to the point that it becomes possible to use PGD to control the future intelligence, attractiveness, or sexuality of one's children? Where should we draw the line on parents' ability to dictate what traits their children will have?*

Review and Apply

Review

- In humans, the male sex cell (the sperm) and the female sex cell (the ovum) provide the developing baby with 23 chromosomes each.

- A genotype is the underlying combination of genetic material present in an organism, but invisible; a phenotype is the visible trait, the expression of the genotype.

- The field of behavioral genetics, a combination of psychology and genetics, studies the effects of genetics on behavior and psychological characteristics.

- Several inherited and genetic disorders are due to damaged or mutated genes.
- Genetic counselors use a variety of data and techniques to advise future parents of possible genetic risks to their unborn children.

Applying Child Development

- How can the study of identical twins who were separated at birth help researchers determine the effects of genetic and environmental factors on human development?

- *From the perspective of a health-care provider:* What are some ethical and philosophical questions that surround the issue of genetic counseling? Might it sometimes be unwise to know ahead of time about possible genetically linked disorders that might afflict your child or yourself?

The Interaction of Heredity and Environment

Like many other parents, Jared's mother, Leesha, and his father, Jamal, tried to figure out which one of them their new baby resembled the most. He seemed to have Leesha's big, wide eyes and Jamal's generous smile. As he grew, Jared grew to resemble his mother and father even more. His hair grew in with a hairline just like Leesha's, and his teeth, when they came, made his smile resemble Jamal's even more. He also seemed to act like his parents. For example, he was a charming little baby, always ready to smile at people who visited the house—just like his friendly, jovial dad. He seemed to sleep like his mom, which was lucky since Jamal was an extremely light sleeper who could do with as little as 4 hours a night, while Leesha liked a regular 7 or 8 hours.

Were Jared's ready smile and regular sleeping habits something he just luckily inherited from his parents? Or did Jamal and Leesha provide a happy and stable home that encouraged these welcome traits? What causes our behavior? Nature or nurture? Is behavior produced by inherited, genetic influences, or is it triggered by factors in the environment?

The simple answer is: There is no simple answer.

The Role of the Environment in Determining the Expression of Genes: From Genotypes to Phenotypes

As developmental research accumulates, it is becoming increasingly clear that to view behavior as due to *either* genetic *or* environmental factors is inappropriate. A given behavior is not caused just by genetic factors; nor is it caused solely by environmental forces. Instead, as we first discussed in Chapter 1, the behavior is the product of some combination of the two.

For instance, consider **temperament,** patterns of arousal and emotionality that represent consistent and enduring characteristics in an individual. Suppose we found—as increasing evidence suggests is the case—that a small percentage of children are born with temperaments that produce an unusual degree of physiological reactivity. Having a tendency to shrink from anything unusual, such infants react to novel stimuli with a rapid increase in heartbeat and unusual excitability of the limbic system of the brain. Such heightened reactivity to stimuli at the start of life, which seems to be linked to inherited factors, is also likely to cause children, by the time they are 4 or 5, to be considered shy by their parents and teachers. But not always—some

temperament patterns of arousal and emotionality that represent consistent and enduring characteristics in an individual.

of them behave indistinguishably from their peers at the same age (Kagan & Snidman, 1991; McCrae et al., 2000).

What makes the difference? The answer seems to be the environment in which the children are raised. Children whose parents encourage them to be outgoing by arranging new opportunities for them may overcome their shyness. In contrast, children raised in a stressful environment marked by marital discord or a prolonged illness may be more likely to retain their shyness later in life (Kagan, Arcus, & Snidman, 1993; Joseph, 1999; Propper & Moore, 2006). Jared, described earlier, may have been born with an easy temperament, which was easily reinforced by his caring parents.

Interaction of Factors.   Such findings illustrate that many traits reflect **multifactorial transmission,** meaning that they are determined by a combination of both genetic and environmental factors. In multifactorial transmission, a genotype provides a particular range within which a phenotype may achieve expression. For instance, people with a genotype that permits them to gain weight easily may never be slim, no matter how much they diet. They may be *relatively* slim, given their genetic heritage, but they may never be able to get beyond a certain degree of thinness (Faith, Johnson, & Allison, 1997). In many cases, then, it is the environment that determines the way in which a particular genotype will be expressed as a phenotype (Plomin, 1994a; Wachs, 1992, 1993, 1996).

On the other hand, certain genotypes are relatively unaffected by environmental factors. In such cases, development follows a preordained pattern, relatively independent of the specific environment in which a person is raised. For instance, research on pregnant women who were severely malnourished during famines caused by World War II found that their children were, on average, unaffected physically or intellectually as adults (Stein et al., 1975). Similarly, no matter how much health food people eat, they are not going to grow beyond certain genetically imposed limitations in height. Little Jared's hairline was probably affected very little by any actions on the part of his parents.

Ultimately, of course, it is the unique interaction of inherited and environmental factors that determines people's patterns of development.

The more appropriate question, then, is *how much* of the behavior is caused by genetic factors, and *how much* by environmental factors? (See, for example, the range of possibilities for the determinants of intelligence, illustrated in Figure 2-8.) At one extreme is the idea that opportunities in the environment are solely responsible for intelligence; on the other, that in-

multifactorial transmission   the determination of traits by a combination of both genetic and environmental factors in which a genotype provides a range within which a phenotype may be expressed.

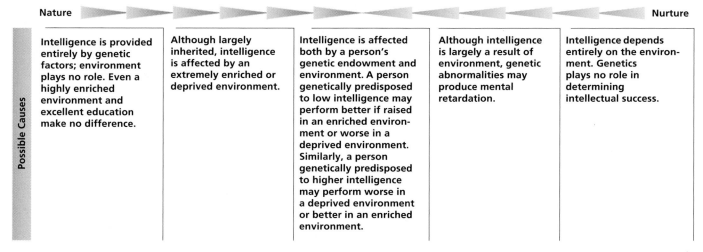

FIGURE 2-8   POSSIBLE SOURCES OF INTELLIGENCE

Intelligence may be explained by a range of differing possible sources, spanning the nature–nurture continuum. Which of these explanations do you find most convincing, given the evidence discussed in the chapter?

telligence is purely genetic—you either have it or you don't. The usefulness of such extremes seems to be to point us toward the middle ground—that intelligence is the result of some combination of natural mental ability and environmental opportunity.

Studying Development: How Much Is Nature? How Much Is Nurture?

Developmental researchers use several strategies to try to resolve the question of the degree to which traits, characteristics, and behavior are produced by genetic or environmental factors. Their studies involve both nonhuman species and humans.

Nonhuman Animal Studies: Controlling Both Genetics and Environment. It is relatively simple to develop breeds of animals that are genetically similar to one another in terms of specific traits. The people who raise Butterball turkeys for Thanksgiving do it all the time, producing turkeys that grow especially rapidly so that they can be brought to market inexpensively. Similarly, strains of laboratory animals can be bred to share similar genetic backgrounds.

By observing animals with similar genetic backgrounds in different environments, scientists can determine, with reasonable precision, the effects of specific kinds of environmental stimulation. For example, animals can be raised in unusually stimulating environments, with lots of items to climb over or through, or they can be raised in relatively barren environments, to determine the results of living in such different settings. Conversely, researchers can examine groups of animals that have been bred to have significantly *different* genetic backgrounds on particular traits. Then, by exposing such animals to identical environments, they can determine the role that genetic background plays.

Of course, the drawback to using nonhumans as research subjects is that we can't be sure how well the findings we obtain can be generalized to people. Still, the opportunities that animal research offers are substantial.

Contrasting Relatedness and Behavior: Adoption, Twin, and Family Studies. Obviously, researchers can't control either the genetic backgrounds or the environments of humans in the way they can with nonhumans. However, nature conveniently has provided the potential to carry out various kinds of "natural experiments"—in the form of twins.

"The title of my science project is 'My Little Brother: Nature or Nurture.'"

Recall that identical, monozygotic twins are also identical genetically. Because their inherited backgrounds are precisely the same, any variations in their behavior must be due entirely to environmental factors.

It would be rather simple for researchers to make use of identical twins to draw unequivocal conclusions about the roles of nature and nurture. For instance, by separating identical twins at birth and placing them in totally different environments, researchers could assess the impact of environment unambiguously. Of course, ethical considerations make this impossible. What researchers can—and do—study, however, are cases in which identical twins have been put up for adoption at birth and are raised in substantially different environments. Such instances allow us to draw fairly confident conclusions about the relative contributions of genetics and environment (Bouchard & Pederson, 1999; Bailey et al., 2000; Richardson & Norgate, 2007).

The data from such studies of identical twins raised in different environments are not always without bias. Adoption agencies typically take the characteristics (and wishes) of birth mothers into account when they place babies in adoptive homes. For instance, children tend to be placed with families of the same race and religion. Consequently, even when monozygotic twins are placed in different adoptive homes, there are often similarities between the two home environments. As a result, researchers can't always be certain that differences in behavior are due to differences in the environment.

Studies of nonidentical dizygotic twins also present opportunities to learn about the relative contributions of nature and nurture. Recall that dizygotic twins are genetically no more similar than siblings in a family born at different times. By comparing behavior within pairs of dizygotic twins with that of pairs of monozygotic twins (who are genetically identical), researchers can determine if monozygotic twins are more similar on a particular trait, on average, than dizygotic twins. If so, they can assume that genetics plays an important role in determining the expression of that trait.

Still another approach is to study people who are totally unrelated to one another and who therefore have dissimilar genetic backgrounds, but who share an environmental background. For instance, a family that adopts, at the same time, two very young unrelated children probably will provide them with quite similar environments throughout their childhood. In this case, similarities in the children's characteristics and behavior can be attributed with some confidence to environmental influences (Segal, 1993, 2000).

Finally, developmental researchers have examined groups of people in light of their degree of genetic similarity. For instance, if we find a high association on a particular trait between biological parents and their children, but a weaker association between adoptive parents and their children, we have evidence for the importance of genetics in determining the expression of that trait. On the other hand, if there is a stronger association on a trait between adoptive parents and their children than between biological parents and their children, we have evidence for the importance of the environment in determining that trait. If a particular trait tends to occur at similar levels among genetically similar individuals, but occurs at different levels among genetically more distant individuals, signs point to the fact that genetics plays an important role in the development of that trait (Rowe, 1994).

Developmental researchers have used all these approaches, and more, to study the relative impact of genetic and environmental factors. What have they found?

Before turning to specific findings, here's the general conclusion resulting from decades of research. Virtually all traits, characteristics, and behaviors are the joint result of the combination and interaction of nature and nurture. Genetic and environmental factors work in tandem, each affecting and being affected by the other, creating the unique individual that each of us is and will become (Robinson, 2004; Waterland & Jirtle, 2004).

Physical Traits: Family Resemblances

When patients entered the examining room of Dr. Cyril Marcus, they didn't realize that sometimes they were actually being treated by his identical twin brother, Dr. Stewart Marcus. So similar in appearance and manner were the twins that even long-time patients were fooled by this admittedly unethical behavior, which occurred in a bizarre case made famous in the film *Dead Ringers.*

Monozygotic twins are merely the most extreme example of the fact that the more genetically similar two people are, the more likely they are to share physical characteristics. Tall parents tend to have tall children, and short ones tend to have short children. Obesity, which is defined as being more than 20% above the average weight for a given height, also has a strong genetic component. For example, in one study, pairs of identical twins were put on diets that contained an extra 1,000 calories a day—and ordered not to exercise. Over a 3-month period, the twins gained almost identical amounts of weight. Moreover, different pairs of twins varied substantially in how much weight they gained, with some pairs gaining almost three times as much weight as other pairs (Bouchard et al., 1990).

Other, less obvious physical characteristics also show strong genetic influences. For instance, blood pressure, respiration rates, and even the age at which life ends are more similar in closely related individuals than in those who are less genetically alike (Jost & Sontag, 1944; Sorensen et al., 1988; Price & Gottesman, 1991).

Intelligence: More Research, More Controversy

No other issue involving the relative influence of heredity and environment has generated more research than the topic of intelligence. Why? The main reason is that intelligence, generally measured in terms of an IQ score, is a central human characteristic that differentiates humans from other species. In addition, intelligence is strongly related to success in scholastic endeavors and, somewhat less strongly, to other types of achievement.

Genetics plays a significant role in intelligence. In studies of both overall or general intelligence and of specific subcomponents of intelligence (such as spatial skills, verbal skills, and memory), as can be seen in Figure 2-9, the closer the genetic link between two individuals, the greater the correspondence of their overall IQ scores.

Not only is genetics an important influence on intelligence, but the impact increases with age. For instance, as fraternal (i.e., dizygotic) twins move from infancy to adolescence, their IQ scores become less similar. In contrast, the IQ scores of identical (monozygotic) twins become increasingly similar over the course of time. These opposite patterns suggest the intensifying influence of inherited factors with increasing age (Brody, 1993; McGue et al., 1993).

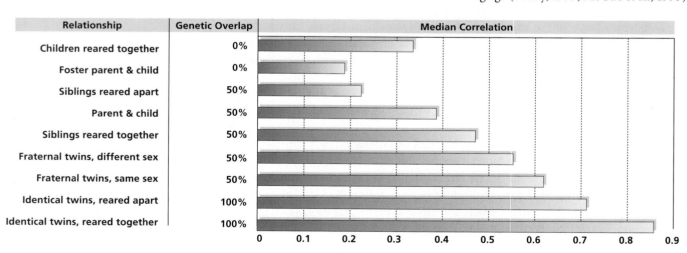

FIGURE 2-9 **GENETICS AND IQ**

The closer the genetic link between two individuals, the greater the correspondence between their IQ scores. Why do you think there is a sex difference in the fraternal twins' figures? Might there be other sex differences in other sets of twins or siblings, not shown on this chart?
(*Source:* Bouchard & McGue, 1981.)

Although it is clear that heredity plays an important role in intelligence, investigators are much more divided on the question of the degree to which it is inherited. Perhaps the most extreme view is held by psychologist Arthur Jensen (2003), who argued that as much as 80% of intelligence is a result of heredity. Others have suggested more modest figures, ranging from 50% to 70%. It is critical to keep in mind that such figures are averages across large groups of people, and any particular individual's degree of inheritance cannot be predicted from these averages (e.g., Herrnstein & Murray, 1994; Devlin, Daniels, & Roeder, 1997).

It is important to keep in mind that although heredity clearly plays an important role in intelligence, environmental factors such as exposure to books, good educational experiences, and intelligent peers are profoundly influential. Even those like Jensen who make the most extreme estimates of the role of genetics still allow for environmental factors to play a significant role. In fact, in terms of public policy, environmental influences are the focus of efforts geared toward maximizing people's intellectual success. As developmental psychologist Sandra Scarr suggests, we should be asking what can be done to maximize the intellectual development of each individual (Scarr & Carter-Saltzman, 1982; Storfer, 1990; Bouchard, 1997).

Monozygotic and dizygotic twins present opportunities to learn about the relative contributions of heredity and situational factors. What kinds of things can psychologists learn from studying twins?

Genetic and Environmental Influences on Personality: Born to Be Outgoing?

Do we inherit our personality? At least in part. There's increasing research evidence suggesting that some of our most basic personality traits have genetic roots. For example, two of the key "Big Five" personality traits, neuroticism and extroversion, have been linked to genetic factors. *Neuroticism*, as used by personality researchers, is the degree of emotional stability an individual characteristically displays. *Extroversion* is the degree to which a person seeks to be with others, to behave in an outgoing manner, and generally to be sociable. For instance, Jared, the baby described earlier in this chapter, may have inherited a tendency to be outgoing from his extroverted father, Jamal (Plomin & Caspi, 1998; Benjamin, Ebstein, & Belmaker, 2002; Zuckerman, 2003).

How do we know which personality traits reflect genetics? Some evidence comes from direct examination of genes themselves. For instance, it appears that a specific gene is very influential in determining risk-taking behavior. This novelty-seeking gene affects the production of the brain chemical dopamine, making some people more prone than others to seek out novel situations and to take risks (Ebstein et al., 1996; Gillespie et al., 2003).

Other evidence for the role of genetics in the determination of personality traits comes from studies of twins. For instance, in one major study, researchers looked at the personality traits of hundreds of pairs of twins. Because a good number of the twins were genetically identical but had been raised apart, it was possible to determine with some confidence the influence of genetic factors (Tellegen et al., 1988). The researchers found that certain traits reflected the contribution of genetics considerably more than others. As you can see in Figure 2-10, social potency (the tendency to be a masterful, forceful leader who enjoys being the center of attention) and traditionalism (strict endorsement of rules and authority) are strongly associated with genetic factors (Harris, Vernon, & Jang, 2007).

Even less-basic personality traits are linked to genetics. For example, political attitudes, religious interests and values, and even attitudes toward human sexuality have genetic components (Eley, Bolton, & O'Connor, 2003; Bouchard, 2004; Koenig et al., 2005).

Clearly, genetic factors play a role in determining personality. At the same time, the environment in which a child is raised also affects personality development. For example, some

Although genetic factors clearly play a significant role in the development of intelligence, the level of environmental enrichment is also crucial.

Social potency		61%

A person high in this trait is masterful, a forceful leader who likes to be the center of attention.

Traditionalism		60%

Follows rules and authority, endorses high moral standards and strict discipline.

Stress reaction		55%

Feels vulnerable and sensitive and is given to worries and is easily upset.

Absorption		55%

Has a vivid imagination readily captured by rich experience; relinquishes sense of reality.

Alienation		55%

Feels mistreated and used, that "the world is out to get me."

Well-being		54%

Has a cheerful disposition, feels confident and optimistic.

Harm avoidance		50%

Shuns the excitement of risk and danger, prefers the safe route even if it is tedious.

Aggression		48%

Is physically aggressive and vindictive, has taste for violence and is "out to get the world."

Achievement		46%

Works hard, strives for mastery, and puts work and accomplishment ahead of other things.

Control		43%

Is cautious and plodding, rational and sensible, likes carefully planned events.

Social closeness		33%

Prefers emotional intimacy and close ties, turns to others for comfort and help.

FIGURE 2-10   INHERITING TRAITS

These traits are among the personality factors that are related most closely to genetic factors. The higher the percentage, the greater the degree to which the trait reflects the influence of heredity. Do these figures mean that "leaders are born, not made"? Why or why not?

(*Source:* Adapted from Tellegen et al., 1988.)

parents encourage high activity levels, seeing activity as a manifestation of independence and intelligence. Other parents may encourage lower levels of activity on the part of their children, feeling that more passive children will get along better in society. Part of these parental attitudes are culturally determined; parents in the United States may encourage higher activity levels, while parents in Asian cultures may encourage greater passivity. In both cases, children's personalities will be shaped in part by their parents' attitudes.

Because both genetic and environmental factors have consequences for a child's personality, personality development is a perfect example of a central fact of child development: nature and nurture are closely intertwined. Furthermore, the way in which nature and nurture interact can be reflected not just in the behavior of individuals, but in the very foundations of a culture, as we see next.

Developmental Diversity

Cultural Differences in Physical Arousal: Might a Culture's Philosophical Outlook Be Determined by Genetics?

The Buddhist philosophy, an inherent part of many Asian cultures, emphasizes harmony and peacefulness. In contrast, some traditional Western philosophies, such as those of Martin Luther and John Calvin, accentuate the importance of controlling the anxiety, fear, and guilt that they assume to be basic parts of the human condition.

Could such philosophical approaches reflect, in part, genetic factors? That is the controversial suggestion made by developmental psychologist Jerome Kagan and his colleagues. They speculate that the underlying temperament of a given society, determined genetically, may predispose people in that society toward a particular philosophy (Kagan, Arcus, & Snidman, 1993; Kagan, 2003a).

Kagan bases his admittedly speculative suggestion on well-confirmed findings that show clear differences in temperament between Caucasian and Asian children. For instance, one study that compared 4-month-old infants in China, Ireland, and the United States found

Table 2-4	Mean Behavioral Scores for Caucasian American, Irish, and Chinese 4-Month-Old Infants		
Behavior	**American**	**Irish**	**Chinese**
Motor activity	48.6	36.7	11.2
Crying (in seconds)	7.0	2.9	1.1
Fretting (% trials)	10.0	6.0	1.9
Vocalizing (% trials)	31.4	31.1	8.1
Smiling (% trials)	4.1	2.6	3.6
(*Source:* Kagan, Arcus, & Snidman, 1993.)			

several relevant differences. In comparison to the Caucasian American babies and the Irish babies, the Chinese babies had significantly lower motor activity, irritability, and vocalization (see Table 2-4).

Kagan suggests that the Chinese, who enter the world temperamentally calmer, may find Buddhist philosophical notions of serenity more in tune with their natural inclinations. In contrast, Westerners, who are emotionally more volatile and tense, and who report higher levels of guilt, are more likely to be attracted to philosophies that articulate the necessity of controlling the unpleasant feelings that they are more apt to encounter in their everyday experience (Kagan et al., 1994; Kagan, 2003).

It is important to note that this does not mean that one philosophical approach is necessarily better or worse than the other. Nor does it mean that either of the temperaments from which the philosophies are thought to spring is superior or inferior to the other. Similarly, we must keep in mind that any single individual within a culture can be more or less temperamentally volatile and that the range of temperaments found even within a particular culture is vast. Finally, as noted in our initial discussion of temperament, environmental conditions can have a significant effect on the portion of a person's temperament that is not genetically determined. But what Kagan and his colleagues' speculation does attempt to address is the back-and-forth-interchange between culture and temperament. As religion may help mold temperament, so may temperament make certain religious ideals more attractive.

The notion that the very basis of culture—its philosophical traditions—may be affected by genetic factors is intriguing. More research is necessary to determine just how the unique interaction of heredity and environment within a given culture may produce a framework for viewing and understanding the world.

The Buddhist philosophy emphasizes harmony and peacefulness. Could this decidedly non-Western philosophy be a reflection, in part, of genetic causes?

Psychological Disorders: The Role of Genetics and Environment

Lori Schiller began to hear voices when she was a teenager in summer camp. Without warning, the voices screamed "You must die! Die! Die!" She ran from her bunk into the darkness, where she thought she could get away. Camp counselors found her screaming as she jumped wildly on a trampoline. "I thought I was possessed," she said later. (Bennett, 1992)

In a sense, she was possessed: possessed with schizophrenia, one of the severest types of psychological disorders. Normal and happy through childhood, Schiller's world took a tumble during adolescence as she increasingly lost her hold on reality. For the next two decades, she would be in and out of institutions, struggling to ward off the ravages of the disorder.

What was the cause of Schiller's mental disorder? Increasing evidence suggests that schizophrenia is brought about by genetic factors. The disorder runs in families, with some families showing an unusually high incidence. Moreover, the closer the genetic links between someone with schizophrenia and another family member, the more likely it is that the other person will also develop schizophrenia. For instance, a monozygotic twin has close to a 50% risk of developing schizophrenia when the other twin develops the disorder (see Figure 2-11). On the other hand, a niece or nephew of a person with schizophrenia has less than a 5% chance of developing the disorder (Prescott & Gottesman, 1993; Hanson & Gottesman, 2005).

However, these data also illustrate that genetics alone does not influence the development of the disorder. If genetics were the sole cause, the risk for an identical twin would be 100%. Consequently, other factors account for the disorder, ranging from structural abnormalities in the brain to a biochemical imbalance (e.g., Lyons et al., 2002; Hietala, Cannon, & van Erp, 2003).

It also seems that even if individuals harbor a genetic predisposition toward schizophrenia, they are not destined to develop the disorder. Instead, they may inherit an unusual sensitivity to stress in the environment. If stress is low, schizophrenia will not occur. But if stress is sufficiently strong, it will lead to schizophrenia. On the other hand, for someone with a strong genetic predisposition toward the disorder, even relatively weak environmental stressors may lead to schizophrenia (Paris, 1999; Norman & Malla, 2001).

Several other psychological disorders have been shown to be related, at least in part, to genetic factors. For instance, major depression, alcoholism, autism, and attention-deficit hyperactivity disorder have significant inherited components (Gallagher et al., 2003; Prescott et al., 2005; Dick, Rose, & Kaprio, 2006).

The example of schizophrenia and other genetically related psychological disorders also illustrates a fundamental principle regarding the relationship between heredity and environment, one that underlies much of our previous discussion. Specifically, the role of genetics is often to produce tendency toward a future course of development. When and whether a certain behavioral characteristic will actually be displayed depends on the nature of the environment. Thus, although a predisposition for schizophrenia may be present at birth, typically people do not show the disorder until adolescence—if at all.

Similarly, certain other kinds of traits are more likely to be displayed as the influence of parents and other socializing factors

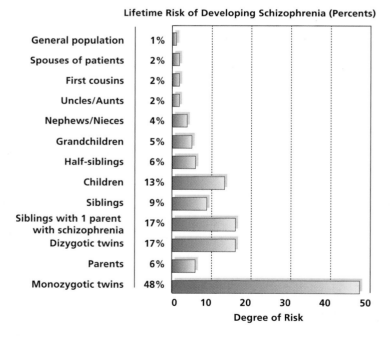

Lifetime Risk of Developing Schizophrenia (Percents)

General population	1%
Spouses of patients	2%
First cousins	2%
Uncles/Aunts	2%
Nephews/Nieces	4%
Grandchildren	5%
Half-siblings	6%
Children	13%
Siblings	9%
Siblings with 1 parent with schizophrenia	17%
Dizygotic twins	17%
Parents	6%
Monozygotic twins	48%

Degree of Risk

FIGURE 2-11   THE GENETICS OF SCHIZOPHRENIA

The psychological disorder of schizophrenia has clear genetic components. The closer the genetic links between someone with schizophrenia and another family member, the more likely it is that the other person will also develop schizophrenia.

(*Source:* Gottesman, 1991.)

declines. For example, adopted children may, early in their lives, display traits that are relatively similar to their adoptive parents' traits, given the overwhelming influence of the environment on young children. As they get older and their parents' day-to-day influence declines, genetically influenced traits may begin to manifest themselves as unseen genetic factors begin to play a greater role (Caspi & Moffitt, 1993; Arsenault et al., 2003; Poulton & Caspi, 2005).

Can Genes Influence the Environment?

According to developmental psychologist Sandra Scarr (1993, 1998), the genetic endowment provided to children by their parents not only determines their genetic characteristics, but also actively influences their environment. Scarr suggests three ways a child's genetic predisposition might influence his or her environment.

Children tend to actively focus on those aspects of their environment that are most connected with their genetically determined abilities. For example, an active, more aggressive child will gravitate toward sports, while a more reserved child will be more engaged by academics or solitary pursuits such as computer games or drawing. They also pay less attention to those aspects of the environment that are less compatible with their genetic endowment. For instance, two girls may be reading the same school bulletin board. One may notice the sign advertising tryouts for Little League baseball, while her less coordinated but more musically endowed friend might be more apt to spot the notice recruiting students for an after-school chorus. In each case, the child is attending to those aspects of the environment in which her genetically determined abilities can flourish.

In some cases, the gene–environment influence is more passive and less direct. For example, a particularly sports-oriented parent, who has genes that promote good physical coordination, may provide many opportunities for a child to play sports.

Finally, the genetically driven temperament of a child may *evoke* certain environmental influences. For instance, an infant's demanding behavior may cause parents to be more attentive to the infant's needs than they would be if the infant were less demanding. Or, for instance, a child who is genetically inclined to be well coordinated may play ball with anything in the house so often that her parents notice. They may then decide that she should have some sports equipment.

In sum, determining whether behavior is primarily attributable to nature or nurture is a bit like shooting at a moving target. Not only are behaviors and traits a joint outcome of genetic and environmental factors, but the relative influence of genes and environment for specific characteristics shifts over the course of people's lives. Although the pool of genes we inherit at birth sets the stage for our future development, the constantly shifting scenery and the other characters in our lives determine just how our development eventually plays out. The environment both influences our experiences and is molded by the choices we are temperamentally inclined to make.

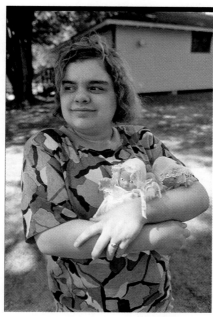

This person suffers from schizophrenia, a major psychological disorder, which is the result of both genetic and environmental causes.

Review and Apply

Review

- Human characteristics and behavior are a joint outcome of genetic and environmental factors.

- Genetic influences have been identified in physical characteristics, intelligence, personality traits and behaviors, and psychological disorders.

- There is some speculation that entire cultures may be predisposed genetically toward certain types of philosophical viewpoints and attitudes.

Applying Child Development

- How might an environment different from the one you experienced have affected the development of personality characteristics that you believe you inherited from one or both of your parents?

- *From an educator's perspective:* Some people have used the proven genetic basis of intelligence to argue against strenuous educational efforts on behalf of individuals with below-average IQs. Does this viewpoint make sense based on what you have learned about heredity and environment? Why or why not?

Prenatal Growth and Change

Robert accompanied Lisa to her first appointment with the midwife. The midwife checked the results of tests done to confirm the couple's own positive home pregnancy test. "Yep, you're going to have a baby," she confirmed, speaking to Lisa. "You'll need to set up monthly visits for the next 6 months, then more frequently as your due date approaches. You can get this prescription for prenatal vitamins filled at any pharmacy, and here are some guidelines about diet and exercise. You don't smoke, do you? That's good." Then she turned to Robert. "How about you? Do you smoke?" After giving lots of instructions and advice, she left the couple feeling slightly dazed, but ready to do whatever they could to have a healthy baby.

From the moment of conception, development proceeds relentlessly. As we've seen, many aspects are guided by the complex set of genetic guidelines inherited from the parents. Of course, prenatal growth, like all development, is also influenced from the start by environmental factors (Leavitt & Goldson, 1996). As we'll see, both parents, like Lisa and Robert, can take part in providing a good prenatal environment.

Fertilization: The Moment of Conception

When most of us think about the facts of life, we tend to focus on the events that cause a male's sperm cells to begin their journey toward a female's ovum. Yet the act of sex that brings about the potential for conception is both the consequence and the start of a long string of events that precede and follow **fertilization,** or conception: the joining of sperm and ovum to create the single-celled zygote from which each of us began our lives.

Both the male's sperm and the female's ovum come with a history of their own. Females are born with around 400,000 ova located in the two ovaries (see Figure 2-12 for the basic anatomy of the female reproductive organs). However, the ova do not mature until the female reaches puberty. From that point until she reaches menopause, the female will ovulate about every 28 days. During ovulation, an egg is released from one of the ovaries and pushed by minute hair cells through the fallopian tube toward the uterus. If the ovum meets a sperm in the fallopian tube, fertilization takes place (Aitken, 1995).

fertilization the process by which a sperm and an ovum—the male and female gametes, respectively—join to form a single new cell.

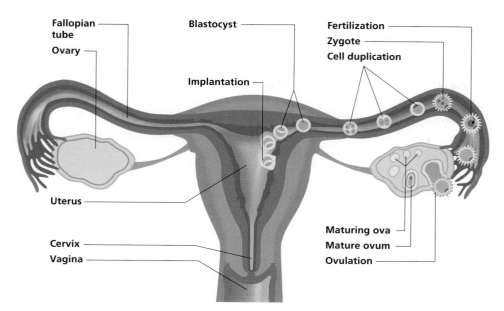

Fallopian tube
Ovary
Blastocyst
Implantation
Fertilization
Zygote
Cell duplication
Uterus
Cervix
Vagina
Maturing ova
Mature ovum
Ovulation

FIGURE 2-12   ANATOMY OF THE FEMALE REPRODUCTIVE ORGANS

The basic anatomy of the female reproductive organs is illustrated in this cutaway view. (*Source:* Moore & Persaud, 2003.)

Sperm, which look a little like microscopic tadpoles, have a shorter life span. They are created by the testicles at a rapid rate: An adult male typically produces several hundred million sperm a day. Consequently, the sperm ejaculated during sexual intercourse are of considerably more recent origin than the ovum to which they are heading.

When sperm enter the vagina, they begin a winding journey that takes them through the cervix, the opening into the uterus, and into the fallopian tube, where fertilization may take place. However, only a tiny fraction of the 300 million cells that are typically ejaculated during sexual intercourse ultimately survive the arduous journey. That's usually okay, though: It takes only one sperm to fertilize an ovum, and each sperm and ovum contains all the genetic data necessary to produce a new human.

The Stages of the Prenatal Period: The Onset of Development

The prenatal period consists of three phases: the germinal, embryonic, and fetal stages. They are summarized in Table 2-5.

The Germinal Stage: Fertilization to 2 Weeks.   In the **germinal stage,** the first—and shortest—stage of the prenatal period, the zygote begins to divide and grow in complexity during the first 2 weeks following conception. During the germinal stage, the fertilized egg (now called a *blastocyst*) travels toward the *uterus*, where it becomes implanted in the uterus's wall, which is rich in nutrients. The germinal stage is characterized by methodical cell division, which gets off to a quick start: Three days after fertilization, the organism consists of some 32 cells, and by the next day the number doubles. Within a week, it is made up of 100 to 150 cells, and the number rises with increasing rapidity.

In addition to increasing in number, the cells of the organism become increasingly specialized. For instance, some cells form a protective layer around the mass of cells, while others begin to establish the rudiments of a placenta and umbilical cord. When fully developed,

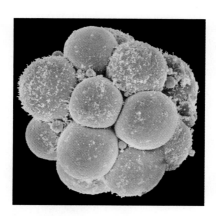

The germinal stage of the prenatal period gets off to a fast start. Here, the embryo has divided into 16 cells only days after fertilization.

germinal stage   the first—and shortest—stage of the prenatal period, which takes place during the first 2 weeks following conception.

Table 2-5   Stages of the Prenatal Period

GERMINAL	EMBRYONIC	FETAL
Fertilization to 2 Weeks	**2 Weeks to 8 Weeks**	**8 Weeks to Birth**
The germinal stage is the first and shortest, characterized by methodical cell division and the attachment of the organism to the wall of the uterus. Three days after fertilization, the zygote consists of 32 cells, a number that doubles by the next day. Within a week, the zygote multiplies to 100 to 150 cells. The cells become specialized, with some forming a protective layer around the zygote.	The zygote is now designated an embryo. The embryo develops three layers, which ultimately form a different set of structures as development proceeds. The layers are as follows: Ectoderm: Skin, sense organs, brain, spinal cord Endoderm: Digestive system, liver, respiratory system Mesoderm: Muscles, blood, circulatory system At 8 weeks, the embryo is 1 inch long.	The fetal stage formally starts when the differentiation of the major organs has occurred. Now called a fetus, the individual grows rapidly as length increases 20 times. At 4 months, the fetus weighs an average of 4 ounces; at 7 months, 3 pounds; and at the time of birth, the average child weighs just over 7 pounds.

placenta   a conduit between the mother and fetus, providing nourishment and oxygen via the umbilical cord.

embryonic stage   the period from 2 to 8 weeks following fertilization during which significant growth occurs in the major organs and body systems.

fetal stage   the stage that begins at about 8 weeks after conception and continues until birth.

fetus   a developing child, from 8 weeks after conception until birth.

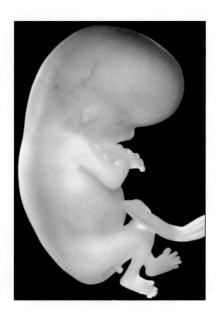

The fetal stage begins at 8 weeks following conception.

the **placenta** serves as a conduit between the mother and fetus, providing nourishment and oxygen via the *umbilical cord*. In addition, waste materials from the developing child are removed through the umbilical cord.

The Embryonic Stage: 2 Weeks to 8 Weeks.   By the end of the germinal period—just 2 weeks after conception—the organism is firmly secured to the wall of the mother's uterus. At this point, the child is called an *embryo*. The **embryonic stage** is the period from 2 to 8 weeks following fertilization. One of the highlights of this stage is the development of the major organs and basic anatomy.

At the beginning of the embryonic stage, the developing child has three distinct layers, each of which will ultimately form a different set of structures as development proceeds. The outer layer of the embryo, the *ectoderm*, will form skin, hair, teeth, sense organs, and the brain and spinal cord. The *endoderm*, the inner layer, produces the digestive system, liver, pancreas, and respiratory system. Sandwiched between the ectoderm and endoderm is the *mesoderm*, from which the muscles, bones, blood, and circulatory system are forged. Every part of the body is formed from these three layers.

If you were looking at an embryo at the end of the embryonic stage, you might be hard-pressed to identify it as human. Only an inch long, an 8-week-old embryo has what appear to be gills and a tail-like structure. On the other hand, a closer look reveals several familiar features. Rudimentary eyes, nose, lips, and even teeth can be recognized, and the embryo has stubby bulges that will form arms and legs.

The head and brain undergo rapid growth during the embryonic period. The head begins to represent a significant proportion of the embryo's size, encompassing about 50% of its total length. The growth of nerve cells, called *neurons*, is astonishing: As many as 100,000 neurons are produced every minute during the second month of life! The nervous system begins to function around the 5th week, and weak brain waves begin to be produced as the nervous system starts to function (Lauter, 1998; Nelson & Bosquet, 2000).

The Fetal Stage: 8 Weeks to Birth.   It is not until the final period of prenatal development, the fetal stage, that the developing child becomes easily recognizable. The **fetal stage** starts at about 8 weeks after conception and continues until birth. The fetal stage formally starts when the differentiation of the major organs has occurred.

Now called a **fetus**, the developing child undergoes astoundingly rapid change during the fetal stage. For instance, it increases in length some 20 times, and its proportions change dramatically. At 2 months, around half the fetus is what will ultimately be its head; by 5 months, the head accounts for just over a quarter of its total size (see Figure 2-13). The fetus also substantially increases in weight. At 4 months, the fetus weighs an average of about 4 ounces; at 7 months, it weighs about 3 pounds; and at the time of birth the average child weighs just over 7 pounds.

At the same time, the developing child is rapidly becoming more complex. Organs become more differentiated and start to work. By 3 months, for example, the fetus swallows and urinates. In addition, the interconnections between the different parts of the body become more complex and integrated. Arms develop hands; hands develop fingers; fingers develop nails.

As this is happening, the fetus makes itself known to the outside world. In the earliest stages of pregnancy, mothers may be unaware that they are, in fact, pregnant. As the fetus becomes increasingly active, however, most mothers certainly take notice. By 4 months, a mother can feel the movement of her child, and several months later others can feel the baby's kicks through the mother's skin. In addition to the kicks that alert its mother to its presence, the fetus can turn, do somersaults, cry, hiccup, clench its fist, open and close its eyes, and suck its thumb.

The brain becomes increasingly sophisticated during the fetal stage. The two symmetrical left and right halves of the brain, known as *hemispheres*, grow rapidly, and the interconnections between neurons become more complex. The neurons become coated with an insulating material called *myelin* that helps speed the transmission of messages from the brain to the rest of the body.

By the end of the fetal period, brain waves are produced that indicate the fetus passes through different stages of sleep and wakefulness. The fetus is also able to hear (and feel the vibrations of) sounds to which it is exposed. For instance, researchers Anthony DeCasper and Melanie Spence (1986) asked a group of pregnant mothers to read aloud the Dr. Seuss story *The Cat in the Hat* two times a day during the later months of pregnancy. Three days after the babies were born, they appeared to recognize the story they had heard, responding more to it than to another story that had a different rhythm.

In weeks 8 to 24 following conception, hormones are released that lead to the increasing differentiation of male and female fetuses. For example, high levels of androgen are produced in males that affect the size of brain cells and the growth of neural connections, which, some scientists speculate, ultimately may lead to differences in male and female brain structure and even later variations in gender-related behavior (Berenbaum & Bailey, 2003; Reiner & Gearhart, 2004; Knickmeyer & Baron-Cohen, 2006).

Just as no two adults are alike, no two fetuses are the same. Although development during the prenatal period follows the broad patterns outlined here, there are significant differences in the specific nature of individual fetuses' behavior. Some fetuses are exceedingly active, while others are more sedentary. (The more active fetuses will probably be more active after birth.) Some have relatively quick heart rates, while others' heart rates are slower, with the typical range varying between 120 and 160 beats per minute (DiPietro et al., 2002; Niederhofer, 2004; Tongsong et al., 2005).

Such differences in fetal behavior are due in part to genetic characteristics inherited at the moment of fertilization. Other kinds of differences, though, are brought about by the nature of the environment in which the child spends its first 9 months of life. As we will see, there are numerous ways in which the prenatal environment of infants affects their development—in good ways and bad.

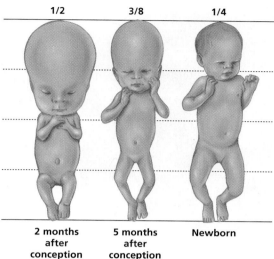

1/2   3/8   1/4

2 months after conception   5 months after conception   Newborn

FIGURE 2-13 BODY PROPORTIONS

During the fetal period, the proportions of the body change dramatically. At 2 months, the head represents about half the fetus, but by the time of birth, it is one-quarter of its total size.

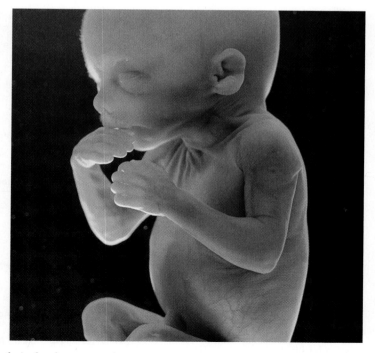

This fetus, shown at around 5 months after conception, looks distinctly human.

As with adults, there are broad differences in the nature of fetuses. Some are very active while others are more reserved, characteristics that they can carry over after birth.

Pregnancy Problems

For some couples, conception presents a major challenge. Let's consider some of the challenges—both physical and ethical—that relate to pregnancy.

Infertility. Some 15% of couples suffer from **infertility,** the inability to conceive after 12 to 18 months of trying to become pregnant. Infertility is negatively correlated with age. The older the parents, the more likely infertility will occur; see Figure 2-14.

In men, infertility is typically a result of producing too few sperm. Use of illicit drugs or cigarettes and previous bouts of sexually transmitted diseases also increase infertility. For women, the most common cause of infertility is failure to release an egg through ovulation. This may occur because of a hormone imbalance, a damaged fallopian tube or uterus, stress, or abuse of alcohol or drugs (Gibbs, 2002; Pasqualotto et al., 2005; Lewis, Legato, & Fisch, 2006).

Several treatments for infertility exist. Some difficulties can be corrected through the use of drugs or surgery. Another option may be **artificial insemination,** a procedure in which a man's sperm is placed directly into a woman's vagina by a physician. In some situations, the woman's husband provides the sperm, while in others it is an anonymous donor from a sperm bank.

In other cases, fertilization takes place outside of the mother's body. **In vitro fertilization (IVF)** is a procedure in which a woman's ova are removed from her ovaries, and a man's sperm are used to fertilize the ova in a laboratory. The fertilized egg is then implanted in a woman's uterus. Similarly, *gamete intrafallopian transfer (GIFT)* and *zygote intrafallopian transfer (ZIFT)* are procedures in which an egg and sperm or fertilized egg are implanted in a woman's fallopian tubes. In IVF, GIFT, and ZIFT, implantation is done either in the woman who provided the donor eggs or, in rarer instances, in a *surrogate mother,* a woman who agrees to carry the child to term. Surrogate mothers may also be used in cases in which the mother is unable to conceive; the surrogate mother is artificially inseminated by the biological father, and she agrees to give up rights to the infant (Frazier et al., 2004; Kolata, 2004).

infertility the inability to conceive after 12 to 18 months of trying to become pregnant.

artificial insemination a process of fertilization in which a man's sperm is placed directly into a woman's vagina by a physician.

in vitro fertilization (IVF) a procedure in which a woman's ova are removed from her ovaries, and a man's sperm are used to fertilize the ova in a laboratory.

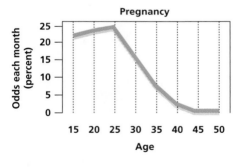

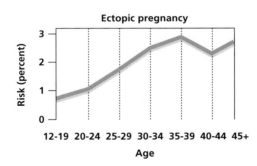

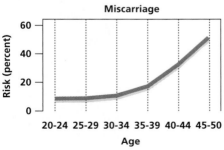

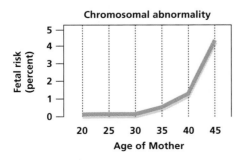

FIGURE 2-14   OLDER WOMEN AND RISKS OF PREGNANCY

Not only does the rate of infertility increase as women get older, but the risk of chromosomal abnormality increases as well.

(*Source:* Reproductive Medicine Associates of New Jersey, 2002.)

In vitro fertilization is increasingly successful, with success rates of as high as 33% for younger women (but with lower rates for older women). Furthermore, reproductive technologies are becoming increasingly sophisticated, permitting parents to choose the sex of their baby. One technique is to separate sperm carrying the X and Y chromosome and later implanting the desired type into a woman's uterus. In another technique, eggs are removed from a woman and fertilized with sperm using in vitro fertilization. Three days after fertilization, the embryos are tested to determine their sex. If they are the desired gender, they are then implanted into the mother (Duenwald, 2003, 2004; Kalb, 2004).

Ethical Issues. The use of surrogate mothers, in vitro fertilization, and sex selection techniques present a web of ethical and legal issues, as well as many emotional concerns. In some cases, surrogate mothers have refused to give up the child after its birth, while in others the surrogate mother has sought to have a role in the child's life. In such cases, the rights of the mother, the father, the surrogate mother, and ultimately the baby are in conflict. Even more troubling are concerns raised by sex selection techniques.

"I'm their real child, and you're just a frozen embryo thingy they bought from some laboratory."

Is it ethical to terminate the life of an embryo based on its sex? Do cultural pressures that may favor boys over girls make it permissible to seek medical intervention to produce male offspring? And—even more disturbing—if it is permissible to intervene in the reproductive process to obtain a favored sex, what about other characteristics determined by genetics that it may be possible in the future to preselect for? For instance, assuming the technology advances, would it be ethical to select for a favored eye or hair color, a certain level of intelligence, or a particular kind of personality? That's not feasible now, but it is not beyond the realm of possibility in the future.

For the moment, many of these ethical issues remain unresolved. But we can answer one question: How do children conceived using emerging reproductive technologies such as in vitro fertilization fare?

Research shows that they do quite well. In fact, some studies find that the quality of family life for those who have used such techniques may be superior to that in families with naturally conceived children. Furthermore, the later psychological adjustment of children conceived using in vitro fertilization and artificial insemination is no different from that of children conceived using natural techniques (Hahn & DiPietro, 2001; Golumbok et al., 2004; DiPietro, Costigan, & Gurewitsch, 2005; Hjelmstedt, Widström, & Collins, 2006).

On the other hand, the increasing use of IVF techniques by older individuals (who might be quite elderly when their children reach adolescence) may change these positive findings. Because widespread use of IVF is only recent, we just don't know yet what will happen with aging parents (Colpin & Soenen, 2004).

Miscarriage and Abortion. A *miscarriage*—known as a spontaneous abortion—occurs when pregnancy ends before the developing child is able to survive outside the mother's womb. The embryo detaches from the wall of the uterus and is expelled.

Some 15% to 20% of all pregnancies end in miscarriage, usually in the first several months of pregnancy. Many occur so early that the mother is not even aware she was pregnant and may not even know she has suffered a miscarriage. Typically, miscarriages are attributable to some sort of genetic abnormality.

In *abortion*, a mother voluntarily chooses to terminate pregnancy. Involving a complex set of physical, psychological, legal, and ethical issues, abortion is a difficult choice for every woman. A task force of the American Psychological Association, which looked at the after-effects of abortion, found that, following an abortion, most women experienced a combination of relief over terminating an unwanted pregnancy and regret and guilt. However, in most cases, the negative

teratogen a factor that produces a birth defect.

psychological after-effects did not last, except for a small proportion of women who already had serious emotional problems (APA Reproductive Choice Working Group, 2000).

Other research finds that abortion may be associated with an increased risk of future psychological problems, however, the findings are mixed, and there are significant individual differences in how women respond to the experience of abortion. What is clear is that in all cases, abortion is a difficult decision (Fergusson, Horwood, & Ridder, 2006).

The Prenatal Environment: Threats to Development

According to the Siriono people of South America, if a pregnant woman eats the meat of certain kinds of animals, she runs the risk of having a child who may act and look like those animals. According to opinions offered on daytime television talk shows, a pregnant mother should avoid getting angry in order to spare her child from entering the world with anger (Cole, 1992).

Such views are largely the stuff of folklore, although there is some evidence that a mother's anxiety during pregnancy may affect the sleeping patterns of the fetus prior to birth. There are certain aspects of a mother's and father's behavior, both before and after conception, that can produce lifelong consequences for the child. Some consequences show up immediately, but half the possible problems aren't apparent before birth. Other problems, more insidious, may not appear until years after birth (Groome et al., 1995; Couzin, 2002). Some of the most profound consequences are brought about by teratogenic agents. A **teratogen** is an environmental agent such as a drug, chemical, virus, or other factor that produces a birth defect. Although it is the job of the placenta to keep teratogens from reaching the fetus, the placenta is not entirely successful at this, and probably every fetus is exposed to some teratogens.

The timing and quantity of exposure to a teratogen are crucial. At some phases of prenatal development, a certain teratogen may have only a minimal impact. At other periods, however, the same teratogen may have profound consequences. Generally, teratogens have their largest effects during periods of especially rapid prenatal development. Sensitivity to specific teratogens is also related to racial and cultural background. For example, Native American fetuses are more susceptible to the effects of alcohol than those of European American descent (Kinney et al., 2003; Winger & Woods, 2004).

Furthermore, different organ systems are vulnerable to teratogens at different times during development. For example, the brain is most susceptible 15 to 25 days after conception, while the heart is most vulnerable 20 to 40 days following conception (see Figure 2-15; Needleman & Bellinger, 1994; Bookstein et al., 1996; Pakjrt et al., 2004).

When considering the findings relating to specific teratogens, as we'll do next, we need to keep in mind the broader social and cultural context in which teratogen exposure occurs. For example, living in poverty increases the chances of exposure to teratogens. Mothers who are poor may not be able to afford adequate diets, and they may not be able to afford adequate medical care, making them more susceptible to illnesses that can damage a developing fetus. They are more likely to be exposed to pollution. Consequently, it is important to consider the social factors that permit exposure to teratogens.

Mother's Diet.   Most of our knowledge of the environmental factors that affect the developing fetus comes from the study of the mother. For instance, as the midwife pointed out in the example of Lisa and Robert, a mother's diet clearly plays an important role in bolstering the development of the fetus. A mother who eats a varied diet high in nutrients is apt to have fewer complications during pregnancy, an easier labor, and a generally healthier baby than a mother whose diet is restricted in nutrients (Kaiser & Allen, 2002; Guerrini, Thomson, & Gurling, 2007).

The problem of diet is of immense global concern, with 800 million hungry people in the world. Even worse, the number of people vulnerable to hunger is close to one *billion*. Clearly, restrictions in diet that bring about hunger on such a massive scale affect millions of children born to women living in those conditions (United Nations, 2004).

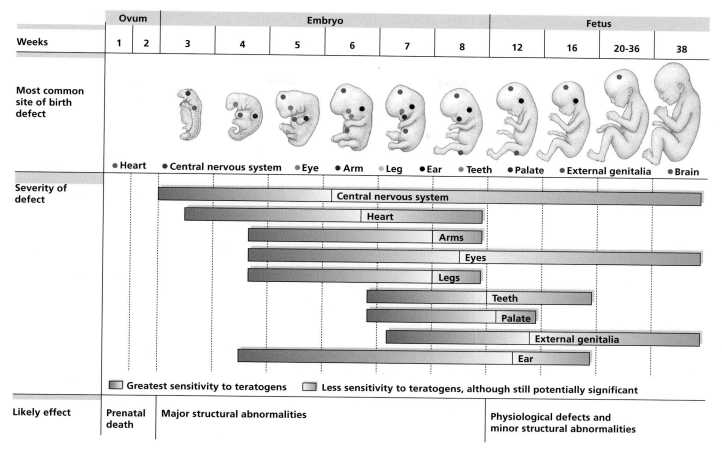

	Ovum		Embryo						Fetus			
Weeks	1	2	3	4	5	6	7	8	12	16	20-36	38

Most common site of birth defect

● Heart   ● Central nervous system   ● Eye   ● Arm   ● Leg   ● Ear   ● Teeth   ● Palate   ● External genitalia   ● Brain

Severity of defect

Central nervous system
Heart
Arms
Eyes
Legs
Teeth
Palate
External genitalia
Ear

■ Greatest sensitivity to teratogens   □ Less sensitivity to teratogens, although still potentially significant

Likely effect | Prenatal death | Major structural abnormalities | Physiological defects and minor structural abnormalities

FIGURE 2-15   TERATOGEN SENSITIVITY

Depending on their state of development, some parts of the body vary in their sensitivity to teratogens. (*Source:* Moore, 1974.)

Fortunately, there are ways to counteract the types of maternal malnourishment that affect prenatal development. Dietary supplements given to mothers can reverse some of the problems produced by a poor diet. Furthermore, research shows that babies who were malnourished as fetuses, but who are subsequently raised in enriched environments, can overcome some of the effects of their early malnourishment. However, the reality is that few of the world's children whose mothers were malnourished *before* their birth are apt to find themselves in enriched environments after birth (Grantham-McGregor et al., 1994; Karmer, 2003; Olness, 2003).

Mother's Age.   More women are giving birth later in life than was true just two or three decades ago. The cause for this change is largely due to transformations in society, as more women choose to continue their education with advanced degrees and to start careers prior to giving birth to their first child (Gibbs, 2002; Wildberger, 2003; Bornstein et al., 2006).

Consequently, the number of women who give birth in their 30s and 40s has grown considerably since the 1970s. However, this delay in childbirth has potential consequences for both mothers' and children's health. Women who give birth when over the age of 30 are at greater risk for a variety of pregnancy and birth complications than younger ones. For instance, they are more apt to give birth prematurely, and their children are more likely to have low birth weights. This occurs in part because of a decline in the condition of a woman's eggs. For example, by the time they are 42 years old, 90% of a woman's eggs are no longer normal

(Cnattingius, Berendes, & Forman, 1993; Gibbs, 2002). Older mothers are also considerably more likely to give birth to children with Down syndrome, a form of mental retardation. About one out of 100 babies born to mothers over 40 has Down syndrome; for mothers over 50, the incidence increases to 25%, or one in four (Gaulden, 1992). On the other hand, some research shows that older mothers are not automatically at risk for more pregnancy problems. For instance, one study found that when women in their 40s who had not experienced health difficulties were considered, they were no more likely to have prenatal problems than those in their 20s (Ales, Druzin, & Santini, 1990; Dildy et al., 1996).

The risks involved in pregnancy are greater not only for older mothers, but for atypically young women as well. Women who become pregnant during adolescence—and such pregnancies actually encompass 20% of all pregnancies—are more likely to have premature deliveries. Furthermore, the mortality rate of infants born to adolescent mothers is double that for mothers in their 20s (Kirchengast & Hartmann, 2003).

Mother's Prenatal Support.   Keep in mind, though, that the higher mortality rate for babies of adolescent mothers reflects more than just physiological problems related to the mothers' young age. Young mothers often face adverse social and economic factors that can affect infant health. Many teenage mothers do not have enough money or social support, a situation that prevents them from getting good prenatal care and parenting support after the baby is born. Poverty or social circumstances, such as a lack of parental involvement or supervision, may even have set the stage for the adolescent to become pregnant in the first place (DiPietro, 2004; Huizink, Mulder, & Buitelaar, 2004).

Mother's Health.   Depending on when it strikes, an illness in a pregnant woman can have devastating consequences. For instance, the onset of *rubella* (German measles) in the mother prior to the 11th week of pregnancy is likely to cause serious consequences in the baby, including blindness, deafness, heart defects, or brain damage. In later stages of a pregnancy, however, adverse consequences of rubella become increasingly less likely.

Several other diseases may affect a developing fetus, again depending on when the illness is contracted. For instance, *chicken pox* may produce birth defects, while *mumps* may increase the risk of miscarriage.

Some sexually transmitted diseases, such as *syphilis*, can be transmitted directly to the fetus, who will be born suffering from the disease. In some cases, sexually transmitted diseases such as *gonorrhea* are communicated to the child as it passes through the birth canal to be born.

AIDS (acquired immune deficiency syndrome) is the newest of the diseases to affect a newborn. Mothers who have the disease or who merely are carriers of the virus may pass it on to their fetuses through the blood that reaches the placenta. However, if mothers with AIDS are treated with antiviral drugs such as AZT during pregnancy, less than 5% of infants are born with the disease. Those infants who are born with AIDS must remain on antiviral drugs their entire lives (Nesheim et al., 2004).

Mother's Drug Use.   Mother's use of many kinds of drugs—both legal and illegal—poses serious risks to the unborn child. Even over-the-counter remedies for common ailments can have surprisingly injurious consequences. For instance, aspirin taken for a headache can lead to fetal bleeding and growth impairments (Griffith, Azuma, & Chasnoff, 1994).

Even drugs prescribed by medical professionals have sometimes had disastrous consequences. In the 1950s, many women who were told to take *thalidomide* for morning sickness during their pregnancies gave birth to children with stumps instead of arms and legs. Although the physicians who prescribed the drug did not know it, thalidomide inhibited the growth of limbs that normally would have occurred during the first 3 months of pregnancy.

Some drugs taken by mothers cause difficulties in their children literally decades after they were taken. As recently as the 1970s, the artificial hormone *DES (diethylstilbestrol)* was frequently prescribed to prevent miscarriage. Only later was it found that the daughters of mothers who took DES stood a much higher-than-normal chance of developing a rare form of vaginal or cervical cancer and had more difficulties during their pregnancies. Sons of the mothers who had taken DES had their own problems, including a higher-than-average rate of reproductive difficulties (Adams Hillard, 2001; Schecter, Finkelstein, & Koren, 2005).

Birth control or fertility pills taken by pregnant women before they are aware of their pregnancy can also cause fetal damage. Such medicines contain sex hormones that affect developing brain structures in the fetus. These hormones, which when produced naturally are related to sexual differentiation in the fetus and gender differences after birth, can cause significant damage (Miller, 1998; Brown, Hines, & Fane, 2002).

Illicit drugs may pose equally great, and sometimes even greater, risks for the environments of prenatal children. For one thing, the purity of drugs purchased illegally varies significantly, so drug users can never be quite sure what specifically they are ingesting. Furthermore, the effects of some commonly used illicit drugs can be particularly devastating (H. E. Jones, 2006).

Consider, for instance, the use of *marijuana*. Certainly one of the most commonly used illegal drugs—millions of people in the United States have admitted trying it—marijuana used during pregnancy can restrict the oxygen that reaches the fetus. Its use can lead to infants who are irritable, nervous, and easily disturbed. Children exposed to marijuana prenatally show learning and memory deficits at the age of 10 (Richardson et al., 2002; Porath & Fried, 2005; Huizink & Mulder, 2006).

During the early 1990s, *cocaine* use by pregnant women led to an epidemic of thousands of so-called "crack babies." Cocaine produces an intense restriction of the arteries leading to the fetus, causing a significant reduction in the flow of blood and oxygen, increasing the risks of fetal death and a number of birth defects and disabilities.

Children whose mothers were addicted to cocaine may themselves be born addicted to the drug and may have to suffer through the pain of withdrawal. Even if not addicted, they may be born with significant problems. They are often shorter and weigh less than average, and they may have serious respiratory problems, visible birth defects, or seizures. They behave quite differently from other infants: Their reactions to stimulation are muted, but once they start to cry, it may be hard to soothe them (Singer et al., 2000; Myers, Dawson, & Britt, 2003; Eiden, Foote, & Schuetze, 2007).

It is difficult to determine the long-term effects of mothers' cocaine use in isolation, because such drug use is often accompanied by poor prenatal care and impaired nurturing following birth. In fact, in many cases it is the poor caregiving by mothers who use cocaine that results in children's problems, and not exposure to the drug. Treatment of children exposed to cocaine consequently requires not only that the child's mother stop using the drug, but an improvement in the level of care the mother or other caregivers provide to the infant (Mayes & Lombroso, 2003; Brown et al., 2004; H. E. Jones, 2006).

Mother's Use of Alcohol and Tobacco. A pregnant woman who reasons that having a drink every once in a while or smoking an occasional cigarette has no appreciable effect on her unborn child is kidding herself: Increasing evidence suggests that even small amounts of alcohol and nicotine can disrupt the development of the fetus.

Mothers' use of alcohol can have profound consequences for the unborn child. The children of alcoholics, who consume substantial quantities of alcohol during pregnancy, are at the greatest risk. Approximately 1 out of every 750 infants is born with **fetal alcohol syndrome (FAS)**, a disorder that may include below-average intelligence and sometimes mental retardation, delayed growth, and facial deformities. FAS is now the primary preventable cause of mental retardation (Steinhausen & Spohr, 1998; Burd et al., 2003; Calhoun & Warren, 2007).

Pregnant women who use tobacco place their unborn children at significant risk.

fetal alcohol syndrome (FAS) a disorder caused by the pregnant mother consuming substantial quantities of alcohol during pregnancy, potentially resulting in mental retardation and delayed growth in the child.

fetal alcohol effects (FAE) a condition in which children display some, although not all, of the problems of fetal alcohol syndrome due to the mother's consumption of alcohol during pregnancy.

Even mothers who use smaller amounts of alcohol during pregnancy place their children at risk. **Fetal alcohol effects (FAE)** is a condition in which children display some, although not all, of the problems of FAS due to their mother's consumption of alcohol during pregnancy (Streissguth, 1997; Baer, Sampson, & Barr, 2003).

Children who do not have FAE may still be affected by their mothers' use of alcohol. Studies have found that maternal consumption of an average of just two alcoholic drinks a day during pregnancy is associated with lower intelligence in their offspring at age 7. Other research concurs, suggesting that relatively small quantities of alcohol taken during pregnancy can have future adverse effects on children's behavior and psychological functioning. Furthermore, the consequences of alcohol ingestion during pregnancy are long-lasting. For example, one study found that 14-year-olds' success on a test involving spatial and visual reasoning was related to their mothers' alcohol consumption during pregnancy. The more the mothers reported drinking, the less accurately their children responded (Johnson et al., 2001; Lynch et al., 2003; Mattson, Calarco, & Lang, 2006).

Because of the risks associated with alcohol, physicians today counsel pregnant women (and even those who are trying to become pregnant) to avoid drinking any alcoholic beverages. In addition, they caution against another practice proven to have an adverse effect on an unborn child: smoking.

Smoking produces several consequences, none good. For starters, smoking reduces the oxygen content and increases the carbon monoxide of the mother's blood, which quickly reduces the oxygen available to the fetus. In addition, the nicotine and other toxins in cigarettes slow the respiration rate of the fetus and speed up its heart.

The ultimate result is an increased possibility of miscarriage and a higher likelihood of death during infancy. In fact, estimates suggest that smoking by pregnant women leads to more than 100,000 miscarriages and the deaths of 5,600 babies in the United States alone each year (Mills, 1999; Ness et al., 1999; Haslam & Lawrence, 2004).

Smokers are two times as likely as nonsmokers to have babies with an abnormally low birth weight, and smokers' babies are shorter, on average, than those of nonsmokers. Furthermore, women who smoke during pregnancy are 50% more likely to have mentally retarded children. Finally, mothers who smoke are more likely to have children who exhibit disruptive behavior during childhood (Fried & Watkinson, 1990; Drews et al., 1996; Dejin-Karlsson et al., 1998; Wakschalg et al., 2006).

Do Fathers Affect the Prenatal Environment? It would be easy to reason that once the father has done his part in the sequence of events leading to conception, he would have no role in the *prenatal* environment of the fetus. In fact, developmental researchers have in the past generally shared this view, and there is relatively little research investigating fathers' influence on the prenatal environment.

However, it is becoming increasingly clear that fathers' behavior may well influence the prenatal environment. Consequently, as the example of Lisa and Robert's visit to the midwife, earlier in the chapter, showed, health practitioners are applying the research to suggest ways fathers can support healthy prenatal development.

For instance, fathers-to-be should avoid smoking. Secondhand smoke from a father's cigarettes may affect the mother's health, which in turn influences her unborn child. The greater the level of a father's smoking, the lower the birth weight of his children (Hyssaelae, Rautava, & Helenius, 1995; Tomblin, Hammer, & Zhang, 1998).

Similarly, a father's use of alcohol and illegal drugs can have significant effects on the fetus. Alcohol and drug use impairs sperm and may lead to chromosomal damage that may affect the fetus at conception. In addition, alcohol and drug use during pregnancy may also affect the prenatal environment by creating stress in the mother and generally producing an unhealthy environment. A father's exposure to environmental toxins in the workplace, such as lead or mercury, may cause the toxins to bind themselves to sperm and cause birth defects (Wakefield et al., 1998; Dare et al., 2002; Choy et al., 2002).

Finally, fathers who are physically or emotionally abusive to their pregnant wives can damage their unborn children. By increasing the level of maternal stress, or actually causing physical damage, abusive fathers increase the risk of harm to their unborn children. In fact, 4% to 8% of women face physical abuse during pregnancy (Gilliland & Verny, 1999; Gazmarian et al., 2000; Bacchus, Mezey, & Bewley, 2006; Martin et al., 2006).

Becoming an Informed Consumer of Development

Optimizing the Prenatal Environment

If you are contemplating ever having a child, you may be overwhelmed, at this point in the chapter, by the number of things that can go wrong. Don't be. Although both genetics and the environment pose their share of risks, in the vast majority of cases, pregnancy and birth proceed without mishap. Moreover, there are several things that women can do—both before and during pregnancy—to optimize the probability that pregnancy will progress smoothly. Among them:

- For women who are planning to become pregnant, several precautions are in order. First, women should have nonemergency x-rays only during the first 2 weeks after their menstrual periods. Second, women should be vaccinated against rubella (German measles) at least 3, and preferably 6, months before getting pregnant. Finally, women who are planning to become pregnant should avoid the use of birth control pills at least 3 months before trying to conceive, because of disruptions to hormonal production caused by the pills.

- Eat well, both before and during (and after, for that matter!) pregnancy. Pregnant mothers are, as the old saying goes, eating for two. This means that it is more essential than ever to eat regular, well-balanced meals. In addition, physicians typically recommend taking prenatal vitamins that include folic acids, which can decrease the likelihood of birth defects (Amitai et al., 2004).

- Don't use alcohol and other drugs. The evidence is clear that many drugs pass directly to the fetus and may cause birth defects. It is also clear that the more one drinks, the greater the risk to the fetus. The best advice, whether you are already pregnant or planning to have a child: Don't use *any* drug unless directed by a physician. If you are planning to get pregnant, encourage your partner to avoid using alcohol or other drugs too (O'Connor & Whaley, 2006).

- Monitor caffeine intake. Although it is still unclear whether caffeine produces birth defects, it is known that the caffeine found in coffee, tea, and chocolate can pass to the fetus, acting as a stimulant. Because of this, you probably shouldn't drink more than a few cups of coffee a day (Wisborg et al., 2003).

- Whether pregnant or not, don't smoke. This holds true for mothers, fathers, and anyone else in the vicinity of the pregnant mother, since research suggests that smoke in the fetal environment can affect birth weight.

- Exercise regularly. In most cases, women can continue to exercise, particularly exercise involving low-impact routines. On the other hand, extreme exercise should be avoided, especially on very hot or very cold days. "No pain, no gain" isn't applicable during pregnancy (O'Toole, Sawicki, & Artal, 2003; Paisley, Joy, & Price, 2003; Schmidt et al., 2006).

Review and Apply

Review

- Fertilization joins the sperm and ovum to start the journey of prenatal development. Some couples, however, need medical help to help them conceive. Among the alternate routes to conception are artificial insemination and in vitro fertilization (IVF).

- The prenatal period consists of three stages: germinal, embryonic, and fetal.

- The prenatal environment significantly influences the development of the baby. The diet, age, prenatal support, and illnesses of mothers can affect their babies' health and growth.

- Mothers' use of drugs, alcohol, tobacco, and caffeine can adversely affect the health and development of the unborn child. Fathers' and others' behaviors (e.g., smoking) can also affect the health of the unborn child.

Applying Child Development

- Studies show that "crack babies" who are now entering school have significant difficulty dealing with multiple stimuli and forming close attachments. How might both genetic and environmental influences have combined to produce these results?

- *From a healthcare provider's perspective:* In addition to avoiding smoking, what other sorts of things might fathers-to-be do to help their unborn children develop normally in the womb?

Epilogue

In this chapter, we have discussed the basics of heredity and genetics, including the way in which the code of life is transmitted across generations through DNA. We have also seen how genetic transmission can go wrong, and we have discussed ways in which genetic disorders can be treated—and perhaps prevented—through new interventions such as genetic counseling and gene therapy.

One important theme in this chapter has been the interaction between hereditary and environmental factors in the determination of a number of human traits. While we have encountered a number of surprising instances in which heredity plays a part—including in the development of personality traits and even personal preferences and tastes—we have also seen that heredity is virtually never the sole factor in any complex trait. Environment nearly always plays an important role.

Finally, we reviewed the main stages of prenatal growth—germinal, embryonic, and fetal—and examined threats to the prenatal environment and ways to optimize that environment for the fetus.

Before moving on, return to the prologue of this chapter—about the Monaco children and IVA—and answer the following questions based on your understanding of genetics and prenatal development.

1. How could Jana and Tom Monaco have passed on a rare genetic disease to their children without knowing that they were carriers of it?

2. From the Monacos' story, would you guess that IVA is an X-linked trait or not?

3. What evidence is there in the story of the Monacos' children that the debilitating effects of IVA are determined by a combination of both genetic and environmental factors?

4. Could the Monacos have learned that they were carriers of IVA before their son Stephen was born? How?

Looking Back

What is our basic genetic endowment, and how can human development go off track?

- A child receives 23 chromosomes from each parent. These 46 chromosomes provide the genetic blueprint that will guide cell activity for the rest of the individual's life.

- Gregor Mendel discovered an important genetic mechanism that governs the interactions of dominant and recessive genes and their expression in alleles. Traits such as hair and eye color and the presence of phenylketonuria (PKU) are alleles and follow this pattern.

- Genes may become physically damaged or may spontaneously mutate. If damaged genes are passed on to the child, the result can be a genetic disorder.

- Behavioral genetics, which studies the genetic basis of human behavior, focuses on personality characteristics and behaviors, and on psychological disorders such as schizophrenia. Researchers are now discovering how to remedy certain genetic defects through gene therapy.

- Genetic counselors use data from tests and other sources to identify potential genetic abnormalities in women and men who plan to have children. Recently, they have begun testing individuals for genetically based disorders that may eventually appear in the individuals themselves.

How do the environment and genetics work together to determine human characteristics?

- Behavioral characteristics are often determined by a combination of genetics and environment. Genetically based traits represent a potential, called the genotype, which may be affected by the environment and is ultimately expressed in the phenotype.

- To work out the different influences of heredity and environment, researchers use nonhuman studies and human studies, particularly of twins.

Which human characteristics are significantly influenced by heredity?

- Virtually all human traits, characteristics, and behaviors are the result of the combination and interaction of nature and nurture. Many physical characteristics show strong genetic influences. Intelligence contains a strong genetic component, but can be significantly influenced by environmental factors.

- Some personality traits, including neuroticism and extroversion, have been linked to genetic factors, and even attitudes, values, and interests have a genetic component. Some personal behaviors may be genetically influenced through the mediation of inherited personality traits.

- The interaction between genetic and environmental effects has been classified into three types: active genotype–environment influences, passive genotype–environment influences, and evocative genotype–environment influences.

What happens during the prenatal stages of development?

- The union of a sperm and ovum at the moment of fertilization, which begins the process of prenatal development, can be difficult for some couples. Infertility, which occurs in some 15% of couples, can be treated by drugs, surgery, artificial insemination, and in vitro fertilization.

- The germinal stage (fertilization to 2 weeks) is marked by rapid cell division and specialization, and the attachment of the zygote to the wall of the uterus. During the embryonic stage (2 to 8 weeks), the ectoderm, the mesoderm, and the endoderm begin to grow and specialize. The fetal stage (8 weeks to birth) is characterized by a rapid increase in complexity and differentiation of the organs. The fetus becomes active and most of its systems become operational.

What are the threats to the fetal environment, and what can be done about them?

- Factors in the mother that may affect the unborn child include diet, age, illnesses, and drug, alcohol, and tobacco use. The behaviors of fathers and others in the environment may also affect the health and development of the unborn child.

KeyTerms and Concepts

zygote (p. 48)
genes (p. 48)
DNA (deoxyribonucleic acid) molecules (p. 48)
chromosomes (p. 48)
monozygotic twins (p. 49)
dizygotic twins (p. 49)
dominant trait (p. 51)
recessive trait (p. 51)
genotype (p. 51)
phenotype (p. 51)
homozygous (p. 51)

heterozygous (p. 51)
polygenic inheritance (p. 52)
X-linked genes (p. 52)
behavioral genetics (p. 53)
Down syndrome (p. 55)
fragile X syndrome (p. 55)
sickle-cell anemia (p. 55)
Tay-Sachs disease (p. 55)
Klinefelter's syndrome (p. 55)
genetic counseling (p. 56)
ultrasound sonography (p. 56)

chorionic villus sampling (CVS) (p. 56)
amniocentesis (p. 56)
temperament (p. 60)
multifactorial transmission (p. 61)
fertilization (p. 70)
germinal stage (p. 71)
placenta (p. 72)
embryonic stage (p. 72)
fetal stage (p. 72)

fetus (p. 72)
infertility (p. 74)
artificial insemination (p. 74)
in vitro fertilization (IVF) (p. 74)
teratogen (p. 76)
fetal alcohol syndrome (FAS) (p. 79)
fetal alcohol effects (FAE) (p. 80)

3 Birth and the Newborn Infant

Chapter Overview

BIRTH

Labor: The Process of Birth Begins

Birth: From Fetus to Neonate

Approaches to Childbirth: Where Medicine and Attitudes Meet

BIRTH COMPLICATIONS

Preterm infants: Too Soon, Too Small

Postmature Babies: Too Late, Too Large

Cesarean Delivery: Intervening in the Process of Birth

Mortality and Stillbirth: The Tragedy of Premature Death

Postpartum Depression: Moving from the Heights of Joy to the Depths of Despair

THE COMPETENT NEWBORN

Physical Competence: Meeting the Demands of a New Environment

Sensory Capabilities: Experiencing the World

Early Learning Capabilities

Social Competence: Responding to Others

Prologue: A 22-Ounce Miracle

She looked like a little old man," says Elizabeth Thatcher of her daughter, Hattie, who was born at 25 weeks, weighing 1 pound 6 ounces. "She wasn't plump like a baby should be. She was skin and bones."

Hattie, Elizabeth and husband Brad's firstborn, faced tough odds, but the Montclair, N.J., couple held out hope. A friend's baby born at 23 weeks was doing fine—so, too, the Thatchers prayed, would their little girl. . . .

The Thatchers visited Hattie every day, singing and talking to her. Preemies can't handle much stimulation, so instead of holding her, they lovingly cupped her head and body with their hands.

A fighter from the start, today Hattie, 6, is an outgoing little girl who loves pretending to be a lion. She's eagerly looking forward to Valentine's Day, busy making paper hearts for everyone in her family and "all my neighbors."

Hattie plays soccer every Monday. "I like kicking the ball," she says.

At a recent five-year reunion for NICU [Neonatal Intensive Care Unit] babies from Roosevelt Hospital, Hattie bounced around the room, happily hugging her former nurses.

Some children came in wheelchairs. "It made us realize how lucky we really are," says Brad gratefully. (Kelly, 2006, p. 26)

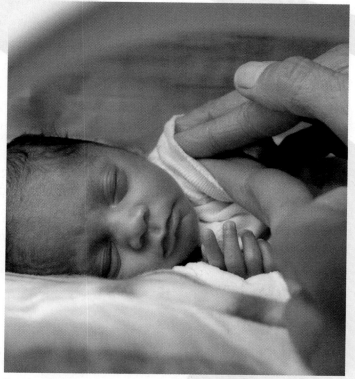

Despite their tiny size, preterm babies have an increasingly good chance of survival.

Infants were not meant to be born as early as Hattie. Yet, for a variety of reasons, more than 10% of all babies today are born early, and the outlook for them to lead a normal life is improving dramatically.

All births, even those that reach full term, are tinged with a combination of excitement and some degree of anxiety. In the vast majority of cases delivery goes smoothly, and it is an amazing and joyous moment when a new being enters the world. The excitement of birth is soon replaced by wonder at the extraordinary nature of newborns themselves. Babies enter the world with a surprising array of capabilities, ready from the first moments of life outside the womb to respond to the world and the people in it.

In this chapter we'll examine the events that lead to the delivery and birth of a child, and take an initial look at the newborn. We first consider labor and delivery, exploring how the process usually proceeds as well as several alternative approaches.

We next examine some of the possible complications of birth. Problems that can occur range from premature births to infant mortality. Finally, we consider the extraordinary range of capabilities of newborns. We'll look not only at their physical and perceptual abilities, but at the way they enter the world with the ability to learn and with skills that help form the foundations of their future relationships with others.

After reading this chapter, you will be able to answer these questions:

- **What is the normal process of labor?**
- **What complications can occur at birth, and what are their causes, effects, and treatments?**
- **What capabilities does the newborn have?**

Looking Ahead

Birth

Her head was cone-shaped at the top. Although I knew this was due to the normal movement of the head bones as she came through the birth canal and that this would change in a few days, I was still startled. She also had some blood on the top of her head and was damp, a result of the amniotic fluid in which she had spent the last nine months. There was some white, cheesy substance over her body, which the nurse wiped off just before she placed her in my arms. I could see a bit of downy hair on her ears, but I knew this, too, would disappear before long. Her nose looked a little as if she had been on the losing end of a fistfight: It was squashed into her face, flattened by its trip through the birth canal. But as she seemed to fix her eyes on me and grasped my finger, it was clear that she was nothing short of perfect. (Adapted from Brazelton, 1969)

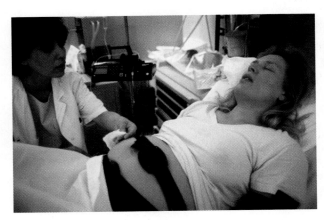

Labor can be exhausting and seem never ending, but support, communication, and a willingness to try different techniques can all be helpful.

For those of us accustomed to thinking of newborns in the images of baby food commercials, this portrait of a typical newborn may be surprising. Yet most **neonates**—the term used for newborns—are born resembling this one. Make no mistake, however: Despite their temporary blemishes, babies are a welcome sight to their parents from the moment of their birth.

The neonate's outward appearance is caused by a variety of factors in its journey from the mother's uterus, down the birth canal, and out into the world. We can trace its passage, beginning with the release of the chemicals that initiate the process of labor.

Labor: The Process of Birth Begins

About 266 days after conception, a protein called *corticotropin-releasing hormone* (CRH) triggers (for some still unknown reason) the release of various hormones, and the process that leads to birth begins. One critical hormone is *oxytocin,* which is released by the mother's

neonates   the term used for newborns.

pituitary gland. When the concentration of oxytocin becomes high enough, the mother's uterus begins periodic contractions (Smith, 1999; Herterelendy & Zakar, 2004).

During the prenatal period, the uterus, which is composed of muscle tissue, slowly expands as the fetus grows. Although for most of the pregnancy it is inactive, after the fourth month it occasionally contracts in order to ready itself for the eventual delivery. These contractions, called *Braxton-Hicks contractions*, are sometimes called "false labor," because while they can fool eager and anxious expectant parents, they do not signify that the baby will be born soon.

When birth is actually imminent, the uterus begins to contract intermittently. Its increasingly intense contractions act as if it were a vise, opening and closing to force the head of the fetus against the *cervix*, the neck of the uterus that separates it from the vagina. Eventually, the force of the contractions becomes strong enough to propel the fetus slowly down the birth canal until it enters the world as a newborn (Mittendorf, et al., 1990). It is this exertion and the narrow birth passageway that often gives newborns the battered, conehead appearance described in the chapter prologue.

Labor proceeds in three stages (see Figure 3-1). In the *first stage of labor*, the uterine contractions initially occur around every 8 to 10 minutes and last about 30 seconds. As labor proceeds, the contractions occur more frequently and last longer. Toward the end of labor, the contractions may occur every 2 minutes and last almost 2 minutes. During the final part of the first stage of labor, the contractions increase to their greatest intensity, a period known as *transition*. The mother's cervix fully opens, eventually expanding enough (usually to around 10 cm) to allow the baby's head (the widest part of the body) to pass through.

This first stage of labor is the longest. Its duration varies significantly, depending on the mother's age, race, ethnicity, number of prior pregnancies, and a variety of other factors involving both the fetus and the mother. Typically, labor takes 16 to 24 hours for firstborn children, but there are wide variations. Births of subsequent children usually involve shorter periods of labor.

During the *second stage of labor*, which typically lasts around 90 minutes, the baby's head emerges further from the mother with each contraction, increasing the size of the vaginal opening. Because the area between the vagina and rectum must stretch a good deal, an incision called an **episiotomy** is sometimes made to increase the size of the opening of the vagina.

episiotomy an incision sometimes made to increase the size of the opening of the vagina to allow the baby to pass.

Stage 1

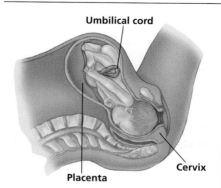

Uterine contractions initially occur every 8 to 10 minutes and last 30 seconds. Toward the end of labor, contractions may occur every 2 minutes and last as long as 2 minutes. As the contractions increase, the cervix, which separates the uterus from the vagina, becomes wider, eventually expanding to allow the baby's head to pass through.

Stage 2

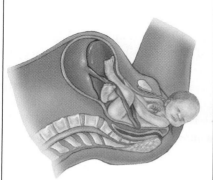

The baby's head starts to move through the cervix and birth canal. Typically lasting around 90 minutes, the second stage ends when the baby has completely left the mother's body.

Stage 3

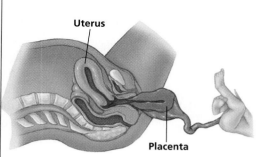

The child's umbilical cord (still attached to the neonate) and the placenta are expelled from the mother. This stage is the quickest and easiest, taking just a few minutes.

FIGURE 3-1 THE THREE STAGES OF LABOR

However, this practice has been increasingly criticized in recent years as potentially causing more harm than good, and the number of episiotomies has fallen drastically in the last decade (Goldberg et al., 2002; Graham et al., 2005).

The second stage of labor ends when the baby has completely left the mother's body. Finally, the *third stage of labor* occurs when the child's umbilical cord (still attached to the neonate) and the placenta are expelled from the mother. This stage is the quickest and easiest, taking just a few minutes.

The nature of a woman's reactions to labor reflect, in part, cultural factors. Although there is no evidence that the physiological aspects of labor differ among women of different cultures, expectations about labor and interpretations of its pain do vary significantly from one culture to another (Scopesi, Zanobini, & Carossino, 1997; Callister et al., 2003).

For instance, there is a kernel of truth to popular stories of pregnant women in certain societies putting down the tools with which they are tilling their fields, stepping aside and giving birth, and immediately returning to work with their neonates wrapped and bundled on their backs. Accounts of the !Kung people in Africa describe the woman in labor sitting calmly beside a tree and without much ado—or assistance—successfully giving birth to a child and quickly recovering. On the other hand, many societies regard childbirth as dangerous, and some even view it in terms befitting an illness. Such cultural perspectives color the way that people in a given society view the experience of childbirth.

Birth: From Fetus to Neonate

The exact moment of birth occurs when the fetus, having left the uterus through the cervix, passes through the vagina to emerge fully from its mother's body. In most cases, babies automatically make the transition from taking in oxygen via the placenta to using their lungs to breathe air. Consequently, as soon as they are outside the mother's body, most newborns spontaneously cry. This helps them clear their lungs and breathe on their own.

What happens next varies from situation to situation and from culture to culture. In Western cultures, health-care workers are almost always on hand to assist with the birth. In the United States, 99% of births are attended by professional health-care workers, but worldwide only about 50% of births have professional health-care workers in attendance (United Nations, 1990).

The Apgar Scale.   In most cases, the newborn infant first undergoes a quick visual inspection. Parents may be counting fingers and toes, but trained health-care workers look for something more. Typically, they employ the **Apgar scale,** a standard measurement system that looks for a variety of indications of good health (see Table 3-1). Developed by physician Virginia Apgar, the scale directs attention to five basic qualities, recalled most easily by using Apgar's name as a guide: *a*ppearance (color), *p*ulse (heart rate), *g*rimace (reflex irritability), *a*ctivity (muscle tone), and *r*espiration (respiratory effort).

Using the scale, health-care workers assign the newborn a score ranging from 0 to 2 on each of the five qualities, producing an overall score that can range from 0 to 10. The vast majority of children score 7 or above. The 10% of neonates who score under 7 require help to start breathing. Newborns who score under 4 need immediate, life-saving intervention.

Although low Apgar scores may indicate problems or birth defects that were already present in the fetus, the process of birth itself may sometimes cause difficulties. Among the most profound are those relating to a temporary deprivation of oxygen.

At various junctures during labor, the fetus may not get sufficient oxygen. This can happen for any of a number of reasons. For instance, the umbilical cord may get wrapped around the neck of the fetus. The cord can also be pinched during a prolonged contraction, thereby cutting off the supply of oxygen that flows through it.

Lack of oxygen for a few seconds is not harmful to the fetus, but deprivation for any longer time may cause serious harm. A restriction of oxygen, or **anoxia,** lasting a few minutes can

Apgar scale   a standard measurement system that looks for a variety of indications of good health in newborns.

anoxia   a restriction of oxygen to the baby, lasting a few minutes during the birth process, that can produce brain damage.

Table 3-1 Apgar Scale

A score is given for each sign at 1 minute and 5 minutes after the birth. If there are problems with the baby, an additional score is given at 10 minutes. A score of 7–10 is considered normal, whereas 4–7 might require some resuscitative measures, and a baby with an Apgar score under 4 requires immediate resuscitation.

	Sign	0 Points	1 Point	2 Points
A	Appearance (skin color)	Blue-gray, pale all over	Normal, except for extremities	Normal over entire body
P	Pulse	Absent	Below 100 bpm	Above 100 bpm
G	Grimace (reflex irritability)	No response	Grimace	Sneezes, coughs, pulls away
A	Activity (muscle tone)	Absent	Arms and legs flexed	Active movement
R	Respiration	Absent	Slow, irregular	Good, crying

(*Source:* Apgar, 1953.)

produce cognitive deficits such as language delays and even mental retardation due to brain cell death (Hopkins-Golightly, Raz, & Sander, 2003).

Physical Appearance and Initial Encounters.   After assessing the newborn's health, health-care workers next deal with the remnants of the child's passage through the birth canal. You'll recall the description of the thick, greasy substance (like cottage cheese) that covers the newborn. This material, called *vernix,* smoothes the passage through the birth canal; it is no longer needed once the child is born and is quickly cleaned away. Newborns' bodies are also covered with a fine, dark fuzz known as *lanugo;* this soon disappears. The newborn's eyelids may be puffy due to an accumulation of fluids during labor, and the newborn may have blood or other fluids on parts of its body.

After being cleansed, the newborn is usually returned to the mother and the father, if he is present. The everyday and universal occurrence of childbirth makes it no less miraculous to parents, and most cherish this time to make their first acquaintance with their child.

The importance of this initial encounter between parent and child has become a matter of considerable controversy. Some psychologists and physicians argued in the 1970s and early 1980s that **bonding,** the close physical and emotional contact between parent and child during the period immediately following birth, was a crucial ingredient for forming a lasting relationship between parent and child. Their arguments were based in part on research conducted on nonhuman species such as ducklings. This work showed that there was a critical period just after birth when organisms showed a particular readiness to learn, or *imprint,* from other members of their species who happened to be present (Lorenz, 1957).

According to the concept of bonding applied to humans, a critical period begins just after birth and lasts only a few hours. During this period actual skin-to-skin contact between mother and child supposedly leads to deep, emotional bonding. The corollary to this assumption is that if circumstances prevent such contact, the bond between mother and child will forever be lacking in some way. Because so many babies were taken from their mothers and placed in incubators or in the hospital nursery, medical practices prevalent at the time often left little opportunity for sustained mother and child physical contact immediately after birth (deChateau, 1980; Eyer, 1992).

There was just one problem: Scientific evidence for the notion was lacking. When developmental researchers carefully reviewed the research literature, they found little support for the idea. Although it does appear that mothers who have early physical contact with their babies

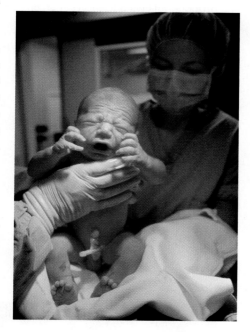

The image of newborns portrayed in commercials differs dramatically from reality.

bonding close physical and emotional contact between parent and child during the period immediately following birth, argued by some to affect later relationship strength.

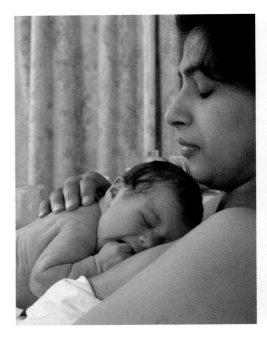

Although observation of nonhuman animals highlights the importance of contact between mother and offspring following birth, research on humans suggests that immediate physical contact is less critical.

are more responsive to them than those who don't have such contact, the difference lasts only a few days. Furthermore, although parents may experience concern, anxiety, and even disappointment, there are no lingering reactions to separations immediately following birth, even for those that extend for several days.

Such news is reassuring to parents whose children must receive immediate, intensive medical attention just after birth, such as in the case of Hattie Thatcher, described in the chapter prologue. It is also comforting to parents who adopt children and are not present at all at their births (Redshaw, 1997; Else-Quest, Hyde, & Clark, 2003; Weinberg, 2004; Miles et al., 2006).

Although mother–child bonding does not seem critical, it is important for newborns to be gently touched and massaged soon after birth. The physical stimulation they receive stimulates the production of chemicals in the brain that instigate growth (Field, 2001).

Approaches to Childbirth: Where Medicine and Attitudes Meet

Ester Iverem knew herself well enough to know that she didn't like the interaction she had with medical doctors. So she opted for a nurse-midwife at Manhattan's Maternity Center where she was free to use a birthing stool and to have her husband, Nick Chiles, by her side. When contractions began, Iverem and Chiles went for a walk, stopping periodically to rock— a motion, she says, "similar to the way children dance when they first learn how, shifting from foot to foot." That helped her work through the really powerful contractions.

"I sat on the birthing chair [a Western version of the traditional African stool, which lies low to the ground and has an opening in the middle for the baby to come through] and Nick was sitting right behind me. When the midwife said 'Push!' the baby's head just went 'pop!,' and out he came." Their son, Mazi (which means "Sir" in Ibo) Iverem Chiles, was placed on Ester's breast while the midwives went to prepare for his routine examination. (Knight, 1994, p. 122)

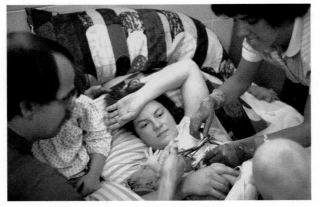

A midwife helps in this home delivery.

Parents in the Western world have developed a variety of strategies—and some very strong opinions—to help them deal with something as natural as giving birth, which occurs apparently without much thought throughout the nonhuman animal world. Today parents need to decide, should the birth take place in a hospital or in the home? Should a physician, a nurse, or a midwife assist? Is the father's presence desirable? Should siblings and other family members be on hand to participate in the birth?

Most of these questions cannot be answered definitively, primarily because the choice of childbirth techniques often comes down to a matter of values and opinions. No single procedure will be effective for all mothers and fathers, and no conclusive research evidence has proven that one procedure is significantly more effective than another. As we'll see, there is a wide variety of different issues and options involved, and certainly one's culture plays a role in choices of birthing procedures.

The abundance of choices is largely due to a reaction to traditional medical practices that had been common in the United States until the early 1970s. Before that time, the typical birth went something like this: A woman in labor was placed in a room with many other women, all of whom were in various stages of childbirth, and some of whom were screaming in pain. Fathers and other family members were not allowed to be present. Just before delivery, the woman was rolled into a delivery room, where the birth took place. Often she was so drugged that she was not aware of the birth at all.

Physicians argued that such procedures were necessary to ensure the health of the newborn and the mother. However, critics charged that alternatives were available that not only would maximize the medical well-being of the participants in the birth, but would represent an emotional and psychological improvement as well (Pascoe, 1993).

Alternative Birthing Procedures.   Not all mothers give birth in hospitals, and not all births follow a traditional course. Among the major alternatives to traditional birthing practices are the following:

- *Lamaze birthing techniques.* The Lamaze method has achieved widespread popularity in the United States. Based on the writings of Dr. Fernand Lamaze, the method makes use of breathing techniques and relaxation training (Lamaze, 1970). Typically, mothers-to-be participate in a series of weekly training sessions in which they learn exercises that help them relax various parts of the body on command. A "coach," most typically the father, is trained along with the future mother. The training allows women to cope with painful contractions by concentrating on their breathing and producing relaxation response, rather than by tensing up, which can make the pain more acute. Women learn to focus on a relaxing stimulus, such as a tranquil scene in a picture. The goal is to learn how to deal positively with pain and to relax at the onset of a contraction.

  Does the procedure work? Most mothers, as well as fathers, report that a Lamaze birth is a very positive experience. They enjoy the sense of mastery that they gain over the process of labor, a feeling of being able to exert some control over what can be a formidable experience. On the other hand, we can't be sure that parents who choose the Lamaze method aren't already more highly motivated about the experience of childbirth than parents who do not choose the technique. It is therefore possible that the accolades they express after Lamaze births are due to their initial enthusiasm, and not to the Lamaze procedures themselves (Larsen et al., 2001; Mackey, 1990).

  Participation in Lamaze procedures—as well as other natural childbirth techniques in which the emphasis is on educating the parents about the process of birth and minimizing the use of drugs—is relatively rare among members of lower-income groups, including many members of ethnic minorities. Parents in these groups may not have the transportation, time, or financial resources to attend childbirth preparation classes. The result is that women in lower-income groups tend to be less prepared for the events of labor and consequently may suffer more pain during childbirth (Brueggemann, 1999; Lu et al., 2003).

- *Bradley Method.* The Bradley Method, which is sometimes known as "husband-coached childbirth," is based on the principle that childbirth should be as natural as possible and involve no medication or medical interventions. Women are taught to "tune into" their bodies in order to deal with the pain of childbirth.

  To prepare for childbirth, mothers-to-be are taught muscle relaxation techniques, similar to Lamaze procedures, and good nutrition and exercise during pregnancy are seen as important to prepare for delivery. Parents are urged to take responsibility for childbirth, and the use of physicians is viewed as unnecessary and sometimes even dangerous. As you might

In Lamaze classes, parents are taught relaxation techniques to prepare for childbirth and to reduce the need for anesthetics.

expect, the discouragement of traditional medical interventions is quite controversial (McCutcheon-Rosegg, Ingraham, & Bradley, 1996).

- *Hypnobirthing.* Hypnobirthing is a new, but increasingly popular, technique. It involves a form of self-hypnosis during delivery that produces a sense of peace and calm, thereby reducing pain. The basic concept is to produce a state of focused concentration in which a mother relaxes her body while focusing inward. Increasing research evidence shows the technique can be effective in reducing pain (Mongan, 2005; Cyna, Andrew, & McAuliffe, 2006; Olson, 2006).

Childbirth Attendants: Who Delivers?   Traditionally, *obstetricians*, physicians who specialize in delivering babies, have been the childbirth attendants of choice. In the last few decades, more mothers have chosen to use a *midwife*, a childbirth attendant who stays with the mother throughout labor and delivery. Midwives—most often nurses specializing in childbirth—are used primarily for pregnancies in which no complications are expected. The use of midwives has increased steadily in the United States—there are now 7,000 of them— and they are employed in 10% of births. Midwives help deliver some 80% of babies in other parts of the world, often at home. Home birth is common in countries at all levels of economic development. For instance, a third of all births in the Netherlands occur at home (Ayoub, 2005).

The newest trend in childbirth assistance is also one of the oldest: the doula (pronounced doo-lah). A *doula* is trained to provide emotional, psychological, and educational support during birth. A doula does not replace an obstetrician or midwife, and does not do medical exams. Instead, doulas, who are often well-versed in birthing alternatives, provide the mother with support and makes sure parents are aware of alternatives and possibilities regarding the birth process.

Although the use of doulas is new in the United States, they represent a return to an older tradition that has existed for centuries in other cultures. Although they may not be called "doulas," supportive, experienced older women have helped mothers as they give birth in non-Western cultures for centuries.

A growing body of research indicates that the presence of a doula is beneficial to the birth process, speeding deliveries and reducing reliance on drugs. Yet concerns remain about their use. Unlike certified midwives, who are nurses and receive an additional year or two of training, doulas do not need to be certified or have any particular level of education (Stein, Kennell, & Fulcher, 2003; Carmichael, 2004; Breedlove, 2005; Ballen & Fulcher, 2006).

Pain and Childbirth.   Any woman who has delivered a baby will agree that childbirth is painful. But how painful, exactly, is it?

Such a question is largely unanswerable. One reason is that pain is a subjective, psychological phenomenon, one that cannot be easily measured. No one is able to answer the question of whether their pain is "greater" or "worse" than someone else's pain, although some studies have tried to quantify it. For instance, in one survey women were asked to rate the pain they experienced during labor on a 1-to-5 scale, with 5 being the most painful (Yarrow, 1992). Nearly half (44%) said "5," and an additional one-quarter said "4."

Because pain is usually a sign that something is wrong in one's body, we have learned to react to pain with fear and concern. Yet during childbirth, pain is actually a signal that the body is working appropriately—that the contractions that are meant to propel the baby through the birth canal are doing their job. Consequently, the experience of pain during labor is difficult for women in labor to interpret, thereby potentially increasing their anxiety and making the contractions seem even more painful. Ultimately, every woman's delivery depends on such variables as how much preparation and support she has before and during delivery, her culture's view of pregnancy and delivery, and the specific nature of the delivery itself (DiMatteo & Kahn, 1997; Walker & O'Brien, 1999; Abushaikha, 2007).

Use of Anesthesia and Pain-Reducing Drugs.   Among the greatest advances of modern medicine is the ongoing discovery of drugs that reduce pain. However, the use of medication during childbirth is a practice that holds both benefits and pitfalls (Shute, 1997).

About a third of women who receive anesthesia do so in the form of *epidural anesthesia*, which produces numbness from the waist down. Traditional epidurals produce an inability to walk and in some cases prevent women from helping to push the baby out during delivery. However, a newer form of epidural, known as a *walking epidural* or *dual spinal-epidural*, uses smaller needles and a system for administering continuous doses of anesthetic. It permits women to move about more freely during labor and has fewer side effects than traditional epidural anesthesia.

It is clear that drugs hold the promise of greatly reducing, and even eliminating, pain associated with labor, which can be extreme and exhausting. However, pain reduction comes at a cost: Drugs administered during labor reach not just the mother but the fetus as well. The stronger the drug, the greater its effects on the fetus and neonate. Because of the small size of the fetus relative to the mother, drug doses that might have only a minimal effect on the mother can have a magnified effect on the fetus.

Anesthetics may temporarily depress the flow of oxygen to the fetus and slow labor. In addition, newborns whose mothers have been anesthetized are less physiologically responsive, show poorer motor control during the first days of life after birth, cry more, and may have more difficulty in initiating breastfeeding (Walker & O'Brien, 1999; Ransjö-Arvidson et al., 2001; Torvaldsen et al., 2006).

However, most research suggests that drugs, as they are currently employed during labor, produce only minimal risks to the fetus and neonate. Guidelines issued by the American College of Obstetricians and Gynecologists suggest that a woman's request for pain relief at any stage of labor should be honored, and that the proper use of minimal amounts of drugs for pain relief is reasonable and has no significant effect on a child's later well-being (Shute, 1997; ACOG, 2002; Albers et al., 2007).

Postdelivery Hospital Stay: Deliver, Then Depart?   When New Jersey mother Diane Mensch was sent home from the hospital just a day after the birth of her third child, she still felt exhausted. But her insurance company insisted that 24 hours was sufficient time to recover, and it refused to pay for more. Three days later, her newborn was back in the hospital, suffering from jaundice. Mensch is convinced the problem would have been discovered and treated sooner had she and her newborn been allowed to remain in the hospital longer (Begley, 1995).

Mensch's experience is not unusual. In the 1970s the average hospital stay for a normal birth was 3.9 days. By the 1990s, it was 2 days. These changes were prompted in large part by medical insurance companies, who advocated hospital stays of only 24 hours following birth in order to reduce costs.

Medical care providers have fought against this trend, believing that there are definite risks involved, both for mothers and for their newborns. For instance, mothers may begin to bleed if they tear tissue injured during childbirth. It is also riskier for newborns to be discharged prematurely from the intensive medical care that hospitals can provide. Furthermore, mothers are better rested and more satisfied with their medical care when they stay longer (Finkelstein, Harper, & Rosenthal, 1998; see Figure 3-2).

In accordance with these views, the American Academy of Pediatrics states that women should stay in the hospital no less than 48 hours after giving birth, and the U.S. Congress has passed legislation mandating a minimum insurance coverage of 48 hours for childbirth (American Academy of Pediatrics, 1995).

Mothers who spend more time in the hospital following the birth of a child do better than those discharged after a shorter period.

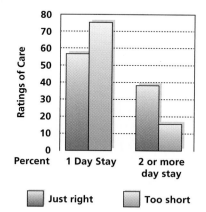

FIGURE 3-2   LONGER IS BETTER

Clearly, mothers are most satisfied with their medical care if they stay longer following a birth than if they are discharged after only one day. However, some medical insurance companies prefer for a reduction to a stay of only 24 hours following a birth. Do you think such a reduction is justified?

(*Source:* Finkelstein, Harper, & Rosenthal, 1998.)

Newborn Medical Screening.   Just after birth, newborns typically are tested for a variety of diseases and genetic conditions. The American College of Medical Genetics recommends that all newborns be screened for 29 disorders, ranging from hearing difficulties and sickle-cell anemia to extremely rare conditions such as isovaleric acidemia, a disorder involving metabolism. These disorders can be detected from a tiny quantity of blood drawn from an infant's heel (American College of Medical Genetics, 2006).

The advantage of newborn screening is that it permits early treatment of problems that might go undetected for years. In some cases, devastating conditions can be prevented through early treatment of the disorder, such as the implementation of a particular kind of diet (Goldfarb, 2005; Kayton, 2007).

The exact number of tests that a newborn experiences varies drastically from state to state. In some states, only three tests are mandated, while in others over 30 are required. In jurisdictions with only a few tests, many disorders go undiagnosed. In fact, each year around 1,000 infants in the United States suffer from disorders that could have been detected at birth if appropriate screening had been conducted (American Academy of Pediatrics, 2005).

Becoming an Informed Consumer of Development

Dealing with Labor

Every woman who is soon to give birth has some fear of labor. Most have heard gripping tales of extended, 48-hour labors or vivid descriptions of the pain that accompanies labor. Still, few mothers would dispute the notion that the rewards of giving birth are worth the effort.

There is no single right or wrong way to deal with labor. However, several strategies can help make the process as positive as possible:

- **Be flexible.** Although you may have carefully worked out what to do during labor, don't feel an obligation to follow through exactly. If a strategy is ineffective, turn to another one.
- **Communicate with your health-care providers.** Let them know what you are experiencing. They may be able to suggest ways to deal with what you are encountering. As your labor progresses, they may also be able to give you a fairly clear idea of how much longer you will be in labor. Knowing the worst of the pain is going to last only another 20 minutes or so, you may feel you can handle it.
- **Remember that labor is . . . laborious.** Expect that you may become fatigued, but realize that as the final stages of labor occur, you may well get a second wind.
- **Accept your partner's support.** If a spouse or other partner is present, allow that person to make you comfortable and provide support. Research has shown that women who are supported by a spouse or partner have a more comfortable birth experience (Bader, 1995; Kennell, 2002).
- **Be realistic and honest about your reactions to pain.** Even if you had planned an unmedicated delivery, realize that you may find the pain difficult to tolerate. At that point, consider the use of drugs. Above all, don't feel that asking for pain medication is a sign of failure. It isn't.
- **Focus on the big picture.** Keep in mind that labor is part of a process that ultimately leads to an event unmatched in the joy it can bring.

Review and Apply

Review

- In the first stage of labor, contractions increase in frequency, duration, and intensity until the baby's head is able to pass through the cervix. In the second stage, the baby moves through the cervix and birth canal and leaves the mother's body. In the third stage, the umbilical cord and placenta emerge.

- Immediately after birth, birthing attendants usually examine the neonate using a measurement system such as the Apgar scale.

- Many birthing options are available to parents today. They may weigh the advantages and disadvantages of anesthetic drugs during birth, and they may choose alternatives to traditional hospital birthing, including the Lamaze method, the use of a birthing center, and the use of a midwife.

Applying Lifespan Development

- Why might cultural differences exist in expectations and interpretations of labor?

- *From a healthcare worker's perspective:* While 99% of U.S. births are attended by professional medical workers or birthing attendants, this is the case in only about half of births worldwide. What do you think are some reasons for this, and what are the implications of this statistic?

Birth Complications

In addition to the usual complimentary baby supplies that most hospitals bestow on new mothers, the maternity nurses at Greater Southeast Hospital have become practiced in handing out "grief baskets."

Inside are items memorializing one of [Washington, D.C.'s] grimmest statistics—an infant mortality rate that's more than twice the national average. The baskets contain a photograph of the dead newborn, a snip of its hair, the tiny cap it wore, and a yellow rose. (Thomas, 1994, p. A14)

The infant mortality rate in Washington, D.C., capital of the richest country in the world, is 12.2 deaths per 1,000 births, exceeding the rate of countries such as Hungary, Cuba, Kuwait, and Costa Rica. Overall, the United States ranks 22nd among industrialized countries, with 6.37 deaths for every 1,000 live births (Singh & Yu, 1995; *Washington Post*, 2007; The World Factbook, 2007; see Figure 3-3).

Why is infant survival less likely in the United States than in other, less developed countries? To answer this question, we need to consider the nature of the problems that can occur during labor and delivery.

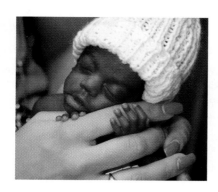

Preterm infants stand a much greater chance of survival today than they did even a decade ago.

Preterm Infants: Too Soon, Too Small

Like Hattie Thatcher, whose birth was described in the chapter prologue, 11% of infants are born earlier than normal. **Preterm infants,** or premature infants, are born prior to 38 weeks after conception. Because they have not had time to develop fully as fetuses, preterm infants are at high risk for illness and death (Jeng, Yau, & Teng, 1998).

The extent of danger faced by preterm babies largely depends on the child's weight at birth, which has great significance as an indicator of the extent of the baby's development. Although

preterm infants infants who are born prior to 38 weeks after conception (also known as premature infants).

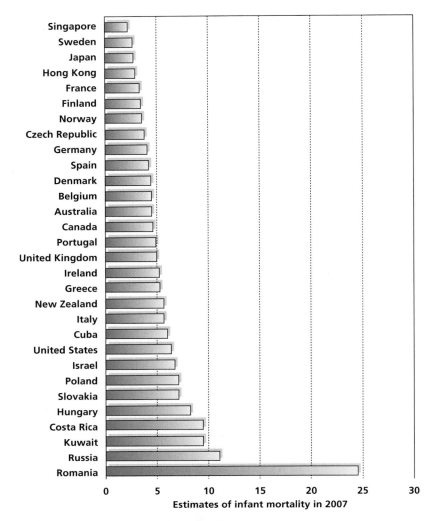

Estimates of infant mortality in 2007

FIGURE 3-3   INTERNATIONAL INFANT MORTALITY

While the United States has greatly reduced its infant mortality rate in the past 25 years, it ranks only 22nd among industrialized countries as of 2007. What are some of the reasons for this?

(*Source:* The World Factbook, 2007.)

low-birthweight infants infants who weigh less than 2,500 grams (around 5 1/2 pounds) at birth.

small-for-gestational-age infants infants who, because of delayed fetal growth, weigh 90% (or less) of the average weight of infants of the same gestational age.

the average newborn weighs around 3,400 grams (about 7 1/2 pounds), **low-birthweight infants** weigh less than 2,500 grams (around 5 1/2 pounds). Although only 7% of all newborns in the United States fall into the low-birthweight category, they account for the majority of newborn deaths (Gross, Spiker, & Haynes, 1997).

Although most low-birthweight infants are preterm, some are small-for-gestational-age babies. **Small-for-gestational-age infants** are infants who, because of delayed fetal growth, weigh 90% (or less) of the average weight of infants of the same gestational age. Small-for-gestational-age infants are sometimes also preterm, but may not be (Meisels & Plunket, 1988; Shiono & Behrman, 1995).

If the degree of prematurity is not too great and weight at birth is not extremely low, the threat to the child's well-being is relatively minor. In such cases, the main treatment may be to keep the baby in the hospital to gain weight. Additional weight is critical because fat layers help prevent chilling in neonates, who are not particularly efficient at regulating body temperature.

Newborns who are born more prematurely and who have birthweights significantly below average face a tougher road. For them, simply staying alive is a major task. For instance, low-birthweight infants are highly vulnerable to infection and because their lungs have not had sufficient time to develop completely, they have problems taking in sufficient oxygen. As a consequence, they may experience *respiratory distress syndrome (RDS)*, with potentially fatal consequences.

To deal with respiratory distress syndrome, low-birthweight infants are often placed in incubators, enclosures in which temperature and oxygen content are controlled. The exact amount of oxygen is carefully monitored. Too low a concentration of oxygen will not provide relief, and too high a concentration can damage the delicate retinas of the eyes, leading to permanent blindness.

The immature development of preterm neonates makes them unusually sensitive to stimuli in their environment. They can easily be overwhelmed by the sights, sounds, and sensations they experience, and their breathing may be interrupted or their heart rates may slow. They are often unable to move smoothly; their arm and leg movements are uncoordinated, causing them to jerk about and appear startled. Such behavior is quite disconcerting to parents (Doussard-Roosevelt et al., 1997; Miles et al., 2006).

Despite the difficulties they experience at birth, the majority of preterm infants eventually develop normally in the long run. However, the tempo of development often proceeds more slowly for preterm children compared to children born at full term, and more subtle problems sometimes emerge later. For example, by the end of their first year, only 10% of prematurely born infants display significant problems, and only 5% are seriously disabled. By the age of 6, however, approximately 38% have mild problems that call for special educational interventions. For instance, some preterm children show learning disabilities, behavior disorders, or lower-than-average IQ scores. Others have difficulties with physical coordination. Still, around 60% of preterm infants are free of even minor problems (Nadeau et al., 2001; Arseneault, Moffit, & Caspi, 2003; Dombrowski, Noonan, & Martin, 2007).

Very-Low-Birthweight Infants: The Smallest of the Small. The story is less positive for the most extreme cases of prematurity—very-low-birthweight infants. **Very-low-birthweight infants** weigh less than 1,250 grams (around 2 1/4 pounds) or, regardless of weight, have been in the womb less than 30 weeks.

Very-low-birthweight infants not only are tiny—some, like little Hattie Thatcher, fitting easily in the palm of the hand at birth—they hardly seem to belong to the same species as full-term newborns. Their eyes may be fused shut and their earlobes may look like flaps of skin on the sides of their heads. Their skin is a darkened red color, whatever their race.

Very-low-birthweight babies are in grave danger from the moment they are born, due to the immaturity of their organ systems. Before the mid-1980s, these babies would not have survived outside their mothers' wombs. However, medical advances have led to a higher chance of survival, pushing the *age of viability*, the point at which an infant can survive prematurely, to about 22 weeks—some 4 months earlier than the term of a normal delivery. Of course, the longer the period of development beyond conception, the higher are a newborn's chances of survival. A baby born earlier than 25 weeks has less than a 50–50 chance of survival (see Figure 3-4).

The physical and cognitive problems experienced by low-birthweight and preterm babies are even more pronounced in very-low-birthweight infants, with astonishing financial consequences. A 3-month stay in an incubator in an intensive care unit can run hundreds of thousands of dollars, and about half of these newborns ultimately die, despite massive medical intervention (Taylor et al., 2000).

Even if a very-low-birthweight preterm infant survives, the medical costs can continue to mount. For instance, one estimate suggests that the average monthly cost of medical care for such infants during the first 3 years of life may be between 3 and 50 times higher than the medical costs for a full-term child. Such astronomical costs have raised ethical debates about the expenditure of substantial financial and human resources in cases in which a positive outcome may be unlikely (Prince, 2000; Doyle, 2004a; Petrou, 2006).

As medical capabilities progress and developmental researchers come up with new strategies for dealing with preterm infants and improving their lives, the age of viability is likely to be pushed even earlier. Emerging evidence suggests that high-quality care can provide protection from some of the risks associated with prematurity, and that in fact by the time they reach adulthood, premature babies may be little different from other adults (Hack et al., 2002).

Research also shows that preterm infants who receive more responsive, stimulating, and organized care are apt to show more positive outcomes than those children whose care is not as good. Some of these interventions are quite simple. For example, "Kangaroo Care," in which infants are held skin-to-skin against their parents' chests, appears to be effective in helping preterm infants develop. Massaging preterm infants several times a day triggers the release of hormones that promote weight gain, muscle development, and abilities to cope with stress (Field, 2001; Burkhammer, Anderson, & Chiu, 2004; Feldman et al., 2003; Tallandini & Scalembra, 2006).

What Causes Preterm and Low-Birthweight Deliveries?

About half of preterm and low-birthweight births are unexplained, but several known causes account for the remainder. In some cases, premature labor results from difficulties relating to the mother's reproductive system. For instance, mothers carrying twins have unusual stress placed on them, which can lead to early labor. In fact, most multiple births are preterm to some degree (Paneth, 1995; Cooperstock et al., 1998; Tan et al., 2004).

In other cases, preterm and low-birthweight babies are a result of the immaturity of the mother's reproductive system. Young mothers—under the age of 15—are more prone to deliver prematurely than older ones. In addition, a woman who becomes pregnant within 6 months of her previous pregnancy and delivery is more likely to deliver a preterm or low-birthweight infant than a woman whose reproductive system has had a chance to recover from a prior delivery. The father's age matters, too: Wives of older fathers are more likely to have preterm deliveries (Smith et al., 2003; Zhu & Weiss, 2005; Branum, 2006).

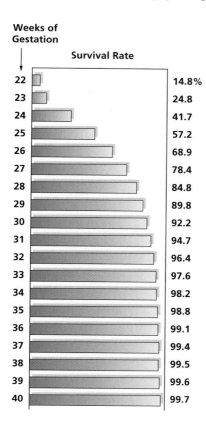

Weeks of Gestation	Survival Rate
22	14.8%
23	24.8
24	41.7
25	57.2
26	68.9
27	78.4
28	84.8
29	89.8
30	92.2
31	94.7
32	96.4
33	97.6
34	98.2
35	98.8
36	99.1
37	99.4
38	99.5
39	99.6
40	99.7

FIGURE 3-4 SURVIVAL AND GESTATIONAL AGE

Chances of a fetus surviving greatly improve after 28 to 32 weeks. Rates shown are the percentages of babies born in the United States after specified lengths of gestation who survive the first year of life.

(*Source:* National Center for Health Statistics, 1997.)

very-low-birthweight infants infants who weigh less than 1,250 grams (around 2.25 pounds) or, regardless of weight, have been in the womb less than 30 weeks.

Table 3-2 Factors Associated with Increased Risk of Low Birthweight

I. Demographic Risks
   A. Age (less than 17; over 34)
   B. Race (minority)
   C. Low socioeconomic status
   D. Unmarried
   E. Low level of education

II. Medical Risks Predating Pregnancy
   A. Number of previous pregnancies (0 or more than 4)
   B. Low weight for height
   C. Genitourinary anomalies/surgery
   D. Selected diseases such as diabetes, chronic hypertension
   E. Nonimmune status for selected infections such as rubella
   F. Poor obstetric history, including previous low-birthweight infant, multiple spontaneous abortions
   G. Maternal genetic factors (such as low maternal weight at own birth)

III. Medical Risks in Current Pregnancy
   A. Multiple pregnancy
   B. Poor weight gain
   C. Short interpregnancy interval
   D. Low blood pressure
   E. Hypertension/preeclampsia/toxemia
   F. Selected infections such as asymptomatic bacteriuria, rubella, and cytomegalovirus
   G. First or second trimester bleeding

   H. Placental problems such as placenta previa, abruptio placentae
   I. Severe morning sickness
   J. Anemia/abnormal hemoglobin
   K. Severe anemia in a developing baby
   L. Fetal anomalies
   M. Incompetent cervix
   N. Spontaneous premature rupture of membrane

IV. Behavioral and Environmental Risks
   A. Smoking
   B. Poor nutritional status
   C. Alcohol and other substance abuse
   D. DES exposure and other toxic exposure, including occupational hazards
   E. High altitude

V. Health-Care Risks
   A. Absent or inadequate prenatal care
   B. Iatrogenic prematurity

VI. Evolving Concepts of Risks
   A. Stress, physical and psychosocial
   B. Uterine irritability
   C. Events triggering uterine contractions
   D. Cervical changes detected before onset of labor
   E. Selected infections such as mycoplasma and chlamydia trachomatis
   F. Inadequate plasma volume expansion
   G. Progesterone deficiency

(*Source:* Adapted from Committee to Study the Prevention of Low Birthweight, 1985.)

Finally, factors that affect the general health of the mother, such as nutrition, level of medical care, amount of stress in the environment, and economic support, all are related to prematurity and low birthweight. Rates of preterm births differ between racial groups, not because of race per se, but because members of racial minorities have disproportionately lower incomes and higher stress as a result. For instance, the percentage of low-birthweight infants born to African American mothers is double that for Caucasian American mothers. (A summary of the factors associated with increased risk of low birthweight is shown in Table 3-2; Carlson & Hoem, 1999; Stein, Lu, & Gelberg, 2000; Field, Diego, & Hernandez-Reif, 2006.) (Also see the *Careers in Lifespan Development* interview with a nurse who cares for preterm and low-birthweight babies.)

Postmature Babies: Too Late, Too Large

One might imagine that a baby who spends extra time in the womb might have some advantages, given the opportunity to continue growth undisturbed by the outside world. Yet **postmature infants**—those still unborn 2 weeks after the mother's due date—face several risks.

For example, the blood supply from the placenta may become insufficient to nourish the still-growing fetus adequately. Consequently, the blood supply to the brain may be decreased, leading to the potential of brain damage. Similarly, labor becomes riskier (for both the child and the mother) as a fetus who may be equivalent in size to a 1-month-old infant has to make its way through the birth canal (Shea, Wilcox, & Little, 1998; Fok et al., 2006).

Difficulties involving postmature infants are more easily prevented than those involving preterm babies, since medical practitioners can induce labor artificially if the pregnancy continues too long. Not only can certain drugs bring on labor, but physicians also have the option of performing Cesarean deliveries, a form of delivery we consider next.

postmature infants infants still unborn 2 weeks after the mother's due date.

Careers in Lifespan Development

Diana Hegger, RN, BSN

Education: BSN, San Diego State University, San Diego, California

Position: Neonatal Nurse and Educator at Children's Healthcare of Atlanta hospital

Home: Ryoston, GA

The care and treatment of preterm infants as young as 23 weeks not only calls for the most sophisticated use of modern medicine, but for dedicated and skilled professionals such as Diana Hegger.

Hegger, a neonatal nurse and educator at Children's Healthcare of Atlanta hospital, says that the treatment of preterm newborns begins immediately upon birth, right in the delivery room.

"Because their breathing capacity is not well developed, we immediately put them on a ventilator and give them a medication so that their lungs do not stick together," she noted.

"We also put them in an isolete [incubator], which provides an environment close to body temperature. This is because they are constantly trying to keep warm, and in the process they are using precious calories and require more oxygen," Hegger noted.

These are just two of the many vital signs that are monitored in the preterm infant, according to Hegger.

"We also have to think about maintaining blood pressure, and because the skin is not developed there is water loss. Since they cannot eat, everything has to be provided intravenously," she said. "The blood-brain barrier is very fragile, and if you have a fluctuation in blood pressure, it can result in bleeding in the head which can lead to mental retardation and cerebral palsy."

Only a quarter of those born at 23 weeks survive, and a substantial number are subject to a variety of ailments that range from blindness to cerebral palsy. Because of the magnitude of the problems, Hegger and her colleagues pay almost as much attention to parents as to their children.

"We pride ourselves in reaching and meeting with parents," Hegger said. "Before a child is born, and if we have prior knowledge of a known disease, counseling is provided," she said. "After the child is born, we have what we call Heart-to-Heart groups where parents can meet with social workers, lactation consultants, as well as clergy."

"We also do baby showers, and follow-ups if a baby has died. We also provide Memory Boxes that contain a lock of the child's hair and other mementos. Some parents do not want them, but we keep them and have found that sometimes a year later they will ask for them. The strength of the human parent still amazes me," Hegger said.

Cesarean Delivery: Intervening in the Process of Birth

As Elena entered her 18th hour of labor, the obstetrician who was monitoring her progress began to look concerned. She told Elena and her husband, Pablo, that the fetal monitor revealed that the fetus's heart rate had begun to repeatedly fall after each contraction. After trying some simple remedies, such as repositioning Elena on her side, the obstetrician came to the conclusion that the fetus was in distress. She told them that the baby should be delivered immediately, and to accomplish that, she would have to carry out a Cesarean delivery.

Elena became one of the more than one million mothers in the United States who have a Cesarean delivery each year. In a **Cesarean delivery** (sometimes known as a *c-section*), the baby is surgically removed from the uterus, rather than traveling through the birth canal.

Cesarean deliveries occur most frequently when the fetus shows distress of some sort. For instance, if the fetus appears to be in danger, as indicated by a sudden rise in its heart rate or if blood is seen coming from the mother's vagina during labor, a Cesarean may be performed. In addition, older mothers, over the age of 40, are more likely to have Cesarean deliveries than younger ones (Dulitzki et al., 1998; Gilbert, Nesbitt, & Danielsen, 1999; Tang, et al., 2006).

Cesarean deliveries are also used in some cases of *breech position*, in which the baby is positioned feet first in the birth canal. Breech position births, which occur in about 1 out of 25 births, place the baby at risk, because the umbilical cord is more likely to be compressed, depriving the baby of oxygen. Cesarean deliveries are also more likely in *transverse position* births, in which the baby lies crosswise in the uterus, or when the baby's head is so large it has trouble moving through the birth canal.

The routine use of **fetal monitors,** devices that measure the baby's heartbeat during labor, has contributed to a soaring rate of Cesarean deliveries. Some 25% of all children in the United

Cesarean delivery a birth in which the baby is surgically removed from the uterus, rather than traveling through the birth canal.

fetal monitor a device that measures the baby's heartbeat during labor.

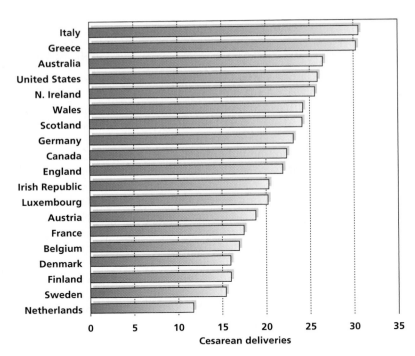

FIGURE 3-5   CESAREAN DELIVERIES

The rate at which Cesarean deliveries are performed varies substantially from one country to another. Why do you think the United States has one of the highest rates?

(*Source:* International Cesarean Awareness Network, 2004.)

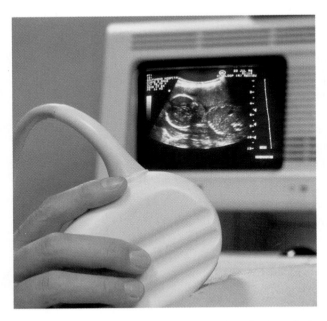

The use of fetal monitoring has contributed to a sharp increase of Cesarean deliveries in spite of evidence showing few benefits from the procedure.

• • • • • • • • • • • • • • • • • • • •

stillbirth   the delivery of a child who is not alive, occurring in less than 1 delivery in 100.

infant mortality   death within the first year of life.

States are born in this way, up some 500% from the early 1970s (National Center for Health Statistics, 2003).

Are Cesareans an effective medical intervention? Other countries have substantially lower rates of Cesarean deliveries (see Figure 3-5), and there is no association between successful birth consequences and the rate of Cesarean deliveries. In addition, Cesarean deliveries carry dangers. Cesarean delivery represents major surgery, and the mother's recovery can be relatively lengthy, particularly when compared to a normal delivery. In addition, the risk of maternal infection is higher with Cesarean deliveries (Fisher, Astbury, & Smith, 1997; Koroukian, Trisel, & Rimm, 1998).

Finally, a Cesarean delivery presents some risks for the baby. Because Cesarean babies are spared the stresses of passing through the birth canal, their relatively easy passage into the world may deter the normal release of certain stress-related hormones, such as catecholamines, into the newborn's bloodstream. These hormones help prepare the neonate to deal with the stress of the world outside the womb, and their absence may be detrimental to the newborn child. In fact, research indicates that babies born by Cesarean delivery who have not experienced labor are more likely to experience breathing problems upon birth than those who experience at least some labor prior to being born via a Cesarean delivery. Finally, mothers who deliver by Cesarean are less satisfied with the birth experience, although their dissatisfaction does not influence the quality of mother–child interactions (Hales, Morgan & Thurnau, 1993; Durik, Hyde, & Clark, 2000).

Because the increase in Cesarean deliveries is, as we have said, connected to the use of fetal monitors, medical authorities now currently recommend that they not be used routinely. There is evidence that outcomes are no better for newborns who have been monitored than for those who have not been monitored. In addition, monitors tend to indicate fetal distress when there is none—false alarms—with disquieting regularity (Levano et al., 1986; Albers & Krulewitch, 1993). Monitors do, however, play a critical role in high-risk pregnancies and in cases of preterm and postmature babies.

Mortality and Stillbirth: The Tragedy of Premature Death

The joy that accompanies the birth of a child is completely reversed when a newborn dies. The relative rarity of their occurrence makes infant deaths even harder for parents to bear.

Sometimes a child does not even live beyond its passage through the birth canal. **Stillbirth,** the delivery of a child who is not alive, occurs in less than 1 delivery out of 100. Sometimes the death is detected before labor begins. In this case, labor is typically induced, or physicians may carry out a Cesarean delivery in order to remove the body from the mother as soon as possible. In other cases of stillbirth, the baby dies during its travels through the birth canal.

The overall rate of **infant mortality** (defined as death within the first year of life) is 7 deaths per 1,000 live births. Infant mortality generally has been declining since the 1960s (MacDorman et al., 2005).

Whether the death is a stillbirth or occurs after the child is born, the loss of a baby is tragic, and the impact on parents is enormous. The loss and grief parents feel, and their passage through it, is similar to that experienced when an older loved one dies (discussed in Chapter 19). In fact, the juxtaposition of the first dawning of life and an unnaturally early death may make the death particularly difficult to accept and deal with. Depression is common (Finkbeiner, 1996; McGreal, Evans, & Burrows, 1997; Murray et al., 2000).

Developmental Diversity

Overcoming Racial and Cultural Differences in Infant Mortality

Even though there has been a general decline in the infant mortality rate in the United States over the past several decades, African American babies are more than twice as likely to die before the age of 1 than white babies. This difference is largely the result of socioeconomic factors: African American women are significantly more likely to be living in poverty than Caucasian women and to receive less prenatal care. As a result, their babies are more likely to be of low birthweight—the factor most closely linked to infant mortality—than infants of mothers of other racial groups (see Figure 3-6; Stolberg, 1999; Duncan & Brooks-Gunn, 2000).

But it is not just members of particular racial groups in the United States who suffer from poor mortality rates. As mentioned earlier, the rate of infant mortality in the United States is higher than the rate in many other countries. For example, the mortality rate in the United States is almost double that of Japan.

Why does the United States fare so poorly in terms of newborn survival? One answer is that the United States has a higher rate of low-birthweight and preterm deliveries than many other countries. In fact, when U.S. infants are compared to infants of the same weight who are born in other countries, the differences in mortality rates disappear (Paneth, 1995; Wilcox et al., 1995).

Another reason for the higher U.S. mortality rate relates to economic diversity. The United States has a higher proportion of people living in poverty than many other countries. Because people in lower economic categories are less likely to have adequate medical care and tend to

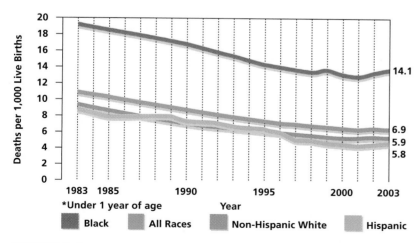

FIGURE 3-6   RACE AND INFANT MORTALITY

Although infant mortality is dropping for both African American and white children, the death rate is still more than twice as high for African American children. These figures show the number of deaths in the first year of life for every 1,000 live births.

(*Source:* Child Health USA, 2005.)

be less healthy, the relatively high proportion of economically deprived individuals in the United States has an impact on the overall mortality rate (Terry, 2000; Bremner & Fogel, 2004; MacDorman et al., 2005).

Many countries do a significantly better job than the United States in providing prenatal care to mothers-to-be. For instance, low-cost and even free care, both before and after delivery, is often available in other countries. Furthermore, paid maternity leave is frequently provided to pregnant women, lasting in some cases as long as 51 weeks (see Table 3-3). The opportunity to take an extended maternity leave can be important: Mothers who spend more time on maternity leave may have better mental health and higher-quality interactions with their infants (Hyde et al., 1995; Clark et al., 1997; Waldfogel, 2001).

Table 3-3	Childbirth-Related Leave Policies in the United States and 10 Peer Nations		
Country	**Type of Leave Provided**	**Total Duration (in months)**	**Payment Rate**
United States	12 weeks of family leave	2.8	Unpaid
Canada	17 weeks maternity leave 10 weeks parental leave	6.2	15 weeks at 55% of prior earnings 55% of prior earnings
Denmark	28 weeks maternity leave 1 year parental leave	18.5	60% of prior earnings 90% of unemployment benefit rate
Finland	18 weeks maternity leave 26 weeks parental leave Child rearing leave until child is 3	36.0	70% of prior earnings 70% of prior earnings Flat rate
Norway	52 weeks parental leave 2 years child rearing leave	36.0	80% of prior earnings Flat rate
Sweden	18 months parental leave	18.0	12 months at 80% of prior earnings, 3 months flat rate, 3 months unpaid
Austria	16 weeks maternity leave 2 years parental leave	27.7	100% of prior earnings 18 months of unemployment benefit rate, 6 months unpaid
France	16 weeks maternity leave Parental leave until child is 3	36.0	100% of prior earnings Unpaid for one child; paid at flat rate (income is tested) for two or more
Germany	14 weeks maternity leave 3 years parental leave	39.2	100% of prior earnings Flat rate (income-tested) for 2 years, unpaid for third year
Italy	5 months maternity leave 6 months parental leave	11.0	80% of prior earnings 30% of prior earnings
United Kingdom	18 weeks maternity leave 13 weeks parental leave	7.2	90% for 6 weeks and flat rate for 12 weeks, if sufficient work history; otherwise, flat rate

(*Source:* "From Maternity to Parental Leave Policies: Women's Health, Employment, and Child and Family Well-Being," by S. B. Kamerman, 2000 (Spring), *The Journal of the American Women's Medical Association*, p. 55, table 1; "Parental Leave Policies: An Essential Ingredient in Early Childhood Education and Care Policies," by S. B. Kamerman, 2000, *Social Policy Report*, p. 14, Table 1.0.)

Better health care is only part of the story. In certain European countries, in addition to a comprehensive package of services involving general practitioner, obstetrician, and midwife, pregnant women receive many privileges, such as transportation benefits for visits to healthcare providers. In Norway, pregnant women may be given living expenses for up to 10 days so they can be close to a hospital when it is time to give birth. And when their babies are born, new moth-

Good prenatal care leads to a significantly lower mortality rate.

ers receive, for just a small payment, the assistance of trained home helpers (Morice, 1998; DeVries, 2005).

In the United States, the story is very different. The lack of national healthcare insurance or a national health policy means that prenatal care is often haphazardly provided to the poor. About one out of every six pregnant women has insufficient prenatal care. Some 20% of white women and close to 40% of African American women receive no prenatal care early in their pregnancies. Five percent of white mothers and 11% of African American mothers do not see a healthcare provider until the last 3 months of pregnancy; some never see a healthcare provider at all (Johnson, Primas, & Coe, 1994; Mikhail, 2000; Laditka, Laditka, & Probst, 2006).

Ultimately, the lack of prenatal services results in a higher mortality rate. Yet this situation can be changed if greater support is provided. A start would be to ensure that all economically disadvantaged pregnant women have access to free or inexpensive high-quality medical care from the very beginning of pregnancy. Furthermore, barriers that prevent poor women from receiving such care should be reduced. For instance, programs can be developed that help pay for transportation to a health facility or for the care of older children while the mother is making a healthcare visit. The cost of these programs is likely to be offset by the savings they make possible—healthy babies cost less than infants with chronic problems as a result of poor nutrition and prenatal care (Carnegie Task Force on Meeting the Needs of Young Children, 1994; Fangman et al., 1994; Kronenfeld, 2002).

Postpartum Depression: Moving from the Heights of Joy to the Depths of Despair

Renata had been overjoyed when she found out that she was pregnant and had spent the months of her pregnancy happily preparing for her baby's arrival. The birth was routine, the baby a healthy, pink-cheeked boy. But a few days after her son's birth, she sank into the depths of depression. Constantly crying, confused, and feeling incapable of caring for her child, she was experiencing unshakable despair.

The diagnosis: a classic case of postpartum depression. *Postpartum depression*, a period of deep depression following the birth of a child, affects some 10% of all new mothers. Although it takes several forms, its main symptom is an enduring, deep feeling of sadness and unhappiness, lasting in some cases for months or even years. In about 1 in 500 cases, the symptoms are even worse, evolving into a total break with reality. In extremely rare instances, postpartum depression may turn deadly. For example, Andrea Yates, a mother in Texas who was charged with drowning all five of her children in a bathtub, said that postpartum depression led to her actions (Yardley, 2001; Oretti et al., 2003).

For mothers who suffer from postpartum depression, the symptoms are often bewildering. The onset of depression usually comes as a complete surprise. Certain mothers do seem more likely to become depressed, such as those who have been clinically depressed at some point in the past or who have depressed family members. Furthermore, women who are unprepared for the range of emotions that follow the birth of a child—some positive, some negative—may be more prone to depression.

Finally, postpartum depression may be triggered by the pronounced swings in hormone production that occur after birth. During pregnancy, the production of the female hormones of estrogen and progesterone increase significantly. However, within the first 24 hours following birth, they plunge to normal levels. This rapid change may result in depression (Honey, Bennett, & Morgan, 2003; Verkerk, Pop, & Van Son, 2003; Klier et al., 2007).

Whatever the cause, maternal depression leaves its marks on the infant. As we'll see later in the chapter, babies are born with impressive social capacities, and they are highly attuned to the moods of their mothers. When depressed mothers interact with their infants, they are likely to display little emotion and to act detached and withdrawn. This lack of responsiveness leads infants to display fewer positive emotions and to withdraw from contact not only with their mothers but with other adults as well. In addition, children of depressed mothers are more prone to antisocial activities such as violence (Weinberg & Tronick, 1996a; Hay, Pawlby, & Angold, 2003; Nylen et al., 2006).

Review and Apply

Review

- Largely because of low birthweight, preterm infants may have substantial difficulties after birth and later in life.
- Very-low-birthweight infants are in special danger because of the immaturity of their organ systems.
- Preterm and low-birthweight deliveries can be caused by health, age, and pregnancy-related factors in the mother. Income (and, because of its relationship with income, race) is also an important factor.
- Cesarean deliveries are performed with postmature babies or when the fetus is in distress, in the wrong position, or unable to progress through the birth canal.
- Infant mortality rates can be affected by the availability of inexpensive health care and good education programs for mothers-to-be.
- Postpartum depression affects about 10% of new mothers.

Applying Lifespan Development

- What are some ethical considerations relating to providing intensive medical care to very-low-birthweight babies? Do you think such interventions should be routine practice? Why or why not?
- *From an educator's perspective:* Why do you think the United States lacks educational and healthcare policies that could reduce infant mortality rates overall and among poorer people? What arguments would you make to change this situation?

The Competent Newborn

Relatives gathered around the infant car seat and its occupant, Kaita Castro. Born just 2 days ago, this is Kaita's first day home from the hospital with her mother. Kaita's nearest cousin, 4-year-old Tabor, seems uninterested in the new arrival. "Babies can't do anything fun. They can't even do anything at all," he says.

Kaita's cousin Tabor is partly right. There are many things babies cannot do. Neonates arrive in the world quite incapable of successfully caring for themselves, for example. Why are human infants born so dependent, while members of other species seem to arrive much better equipped for their lives?

One reason is that, in one sense, humans are born too soon. The brain of the average newborn is just one-quarter of what it will be at adulthood. In comparison, the brain of the macaque monkey, which is born after just 24 weeks of gestation, is 65% of its adult size. Because of the relative puniness of the infant human brain, some observers have suggested that we are propelled out of the womb some 6 to 12 months sooner than we ought to be.

In reality, evolution probably knew what it was doing: If we stayed inside our mothers' bodies an additional half-year to a year, our heads would be so large that we'd never manage to get through the birth canal (Schultz, 1969; Gould, 1977; Kotre & Hall, 1990).

The relatively underdeveloped brain of the human newborn helps explain the infant's apparent helplessness. Because of this, the earliest views of newborns focused on the things that they could not do, comparing them rather unfavorably to older members of the human species.

Today, however, such beliefs have taken a backseat to more favorable views of the neonate. As developmental researchers have begun to understand more about the nature of newborns, they have come to realize that infants enter this world with an astounding array of capabilities in all domains of development: physical, cognitive, and social.

Physical Competence: Meeting the Demands of a New Environment

The world faced by a neonate is remarkably different from the one it experienced in the womb. Consider, for instance, the significant changes in functioning that Kaita Castro encountered as she began the first moments of life in her new environment (summarized in Table 3-4).

Table 3-4 Kaita Castro's First Encounters upon Birth

1. As soon as she is through the birth canal, Kaita automatically begins to breathe on her own despite no longer being attached to the umbilical cord that provided precious air in the womb.

2. Reflexes—unlearned, organized involuntary responses that occur in the presence of stimuli—begin to take over. Sucking and swallowing reflexes permit Kaita immediately to ingest food.

3. The rooting reflex, which involves turning in the direction of a source of stimulation, guides Kaita toward potential sources of food that are near her mouth, such as her mother's nipple.

4. Kaita begins to cough, sneeze, and blink—reflexes that help her avoid stimuli that are potentially bothersome or hazardous.

5. Her senses of smell and taste are highly developed. Physical activities and sucking increase when she smells peppermint. Her lips pucker when a sour taste is placed on her lips.

6. Objects with colors of blue and green seem to catch Kaita's attention more than other colors, and she reacts sharply to loud, sudden noises. She will also continue to cry if she hears other newborns cry, but will stop if she hears a recording of her own voice crying.

The sucking and swallowing reflexes allow newborns to begin to ingest food immediately after birth.

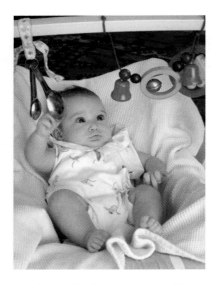

Starting at birth, infants are able to distinguish colors and even show preferences for particular ones.

Kaita's most immediate task was to bring sufficient air into her body. Inside her mother, air was delivered through the umbilical cord, which also provided a means for taking away carbon dioxide. The realities of the outside world are different: Once the umbilical cord was cut, Kaita's respiratory system needed to begin its lifetime's work.

For Kaita, the task was automatic. As we noted earlier, most newborn babies begin to breathe on their own as soon as they are exposed to air. The ability to breathe immediately is a good indication that the respiratory system of the normal neonate is reasonably well developed, despite its lack of rehearsal in the womb.

Neonates emerge from the uterus more practiced in other types of physical activities. For example, newborns such as Kaita show several **reflexes**—unlearned, organized involuntary responses that occur automatically in the presence of certain stimuli. Some of these reflexes are well rehearsed, having been present for several months before birth. The *sucking reflex* and the *swallowing reflex* permit Kaita to begin right away to ingest food. The *rooting reflex,* which involves turning in the direction of a source of stimulation (such as a light touch) near the mouth, is also related to eating. It guides the infant toward potential sources of food that are near its mouth, such as a mother's nipple.

Not all of the reflexes that are present at birth lead the newborn to seek out desired stimuli such as food. For instance, Kaita can cough, sneeze, and blink—reflexes that help her to avoid stimuli that are potentially bothersome or hazardous. (We'll discuss more reflexes in Chapter 4.) Kaita's sucking and swallowing reflexes, which help her to consume her mother's milk, are coupled with the newfound ability to digest nutriments. The newborn's digestive system initially produces feces in the form of *meconium,* a greenish-black material that is a remnant of the neonate's days as a fetus.

Because the liver, a critical component of the digestive system, does not always work effectively at first, almost half of all newborns develop a distinctly yellowish tinge to their bodies and eyes. This change in color is a symptom of *neonatal jaundice.* It is most likely to occur in preterm and low-weight neonates, and it is typically not dangerous. Treatment most often consists of placing the baby under fluorescent lights or administering medicine.

Sensory Capabilities: Experiencing the World

Just after Kaita was born, her father was certain that she looked directly at him. Did she, in fact, see him?

This is a hard question to answer for several reasons. For one thing, when sensory experts talk of "seeing," they mean both a sensory reaction due to the stimulation of the visual sensory organs and an interpretation of that stimulation (the distinction, as you might recall from an introductory psychology class, between sensation and perception). Furthermore, as we'll discuss further when we consider sensory capabilities during infancy in Chapter 4, it is tricky, to say the least, to pinpoint the specific sensory skills of newborns who lack the ability to explain what they are experiencing.

Still, we do have some answers to the question of what newborns are capable of seeing and, for that matter, questions about their other sensory capabilities. For example, it is clear that neonates such as Kaita can see to some extent. Although their visual acuity is not fully developed, newborns actively pay attention to certain types of information in their environment.

For instance, neonates pay closest attention to portions of scenes in their field of vision that are highest in information, such as objects that sharply contrast with the rest of their environment. Furthermore, infants can discriminate different levels of brightness. There is even evidence suggesting that newborns have a sense of size constancy. They seem aware that objects stay the same size even though the size of the image on the retina varies with distance (Slater, Mattock, & Brown, 1990; Slater & Johnson, 1998; Chien et al., 2006).

In addition, not only can newborn babies distinguish different colors, they seem to prefer particular ones. For example, they are able to distinguish between red, green, yellow, and blue, and they take more time staring at blue and green objects—suggesting a partiality for those colors (Adams, Mauer, & Davis, 1986; Dobson, 2000; Alexander & Hines, 2002).

Newborns are also clearly capable of hearing. They react to certain kinds of sounds, showing startle reactions to loud, sudden noises, for instance. The also exhibit familiarity with certain sounds. For example, a crying newborn will continue to cry when he or she hears other newborns crying. If the baby hears a recording of its own crying, on the other hand, he or she is more likely to stop crying, as if recognizing the familiar sound (Dondi, Simion, & Caltran, 1999; Fernald, 2001).

As with vision, however, the degree of auditory acuity is not as great as it will be later. The auditory system is not completely developed. Moreover, amniotic fluid, which is initially trapped in the middle ear, must drain out before the newborn can fully hear.

In addition to sight and hearing, the other senses also function quite adequately in the newborn. It is obvious that newborns are sensitive to touch. For instance, they respond to stimuli such as the hairs of a brush, and they are aware of puffs of air so weak that adults cannot notice them. In fact, the newborn's sensitivity to touch—and to pain—is part of the controversy surrounding circumcision of male infants, as we consider in the *From Research to Practice* box.

The senses of smell and taste are also well developed. Newborns suck and increase other physical activity when the odor of peppermint is placed near the nose. They also pucker their lips when a sour taste is placed on them, and respond with suitable facial expressions to other tastes as well. Such findings clearly indicate that the senses of touch, smell, and taste are not only present at birth, but are reasonably sophisticated (Marlier, Schaal, & Soussignan, 1998; Cohen & Cashon, 2003).

In one sense, the sophistication of the sensory systems of newborns such as Kaita is not surprising. After all, the typical neonate has had 9 months to prepare for his or her encounter with the outside world. As we discussed in Chapter 2, human sensory systems begin their development well before birth. Furthermore, the passage through the birth canal may place babies in a state of heightened sensory awareness, preparing them for the world that they are about to encounter for the first time.

Early Learning Capabilities

One-month-old Michael Samedi was on a car ride with his family when a thunderstorm suddenly began. The storm rapidly became violent, and flashes of lightning were quickly followed by loud thunderclaps. Michael was clearly disturbed and began to sob. With each new thunderclap, the pitch and fervor of his crying increased. Unfortunately, before very long it wasn't just the sound of the thunder that would raise Michael's anxiety; the sight of the lightning alone was enough to make him cry out in fear. In fact, even as an adult, Michael feels his chest tighten and his stomach churn at the mere sight of lightning.

Classical Conditioning.   The source of Michael's fear is classical conditioning, a basic type of learning first identified by Ivan Pavlov (and discussed in Chapter 1). In **classical conditioning** an organism learns to respond in a particular way to a neutral stimulus that normally does not bring about that type of response.

Pavlov discovered that by repeatedly pairing two stimuli, such as the sound of a bell and the arrival of meat, he could make hungry dogs learn to respond (in this case by salivating) not only when the meat was presented, but even when the bell was sounded without the presence of meat (Pavlov, 1927).

The key feature of classical conditioning is stimulus substitution, in which a stimulus that doesn't naturally bring about a particular response is paired with a stimulus that does evoke that response. Repeatedly presenting the two stimuli together results in the second stimulus taking on the properties of the first. In effect, the second stimulus is substituted for the first.

One of the earliest examples of the power of classical conditioning in shaping human emotions was demonstrated in the case of an 11-month-old infant known by researchers as "Little Albert" (Watson & Rayner, 1920). Although he initially adored furry animals and showed no

classical conditioning   a type of learning in which an organism responds in a particular way to a neutral stimulus that normally does not bring about that type of response.

From Research to Practice

Circumcision of Newborn Male Infants: The Unkindest Cut?

Throughout much of her pregnancy, Sandi Levine and her husband Jim were worried about the health of their unborn son. Genetic testing and other diagnostic procedures revealed no genetic disorders, and the birth of Adam Levine was uneventful. Yet they were barely out of the delivery room before Jim and Sandi were confronted with a difficult decision they had been avoiding.

"I don't see the problem," Jim argued. "It's just tradition. Millions of boys are circumcised and they grow up just fine."

"Tradition or not, Adam's our son," countered Sandi. "I feel like we're forcing our will on him. I just don't know if one of his first experiences in life should be a painful, irreversible surgical procedure. I mean, tradition aside, what's the point?"

The Levines' dilemma is not an unusual one. More than a million male newborn infants—over 57%—are circumcised every year in the United States. *Circumcision* is the surgical removal of part or all of the foreskin from the penis. Although the procedure may be performed on males of any age, it is most commonly performed shortly after birth (National Center for Health Statistics, 2006).

Until recently, the arguments in favor of circumcision have sounded a lot like Jim Levine's. Parents usually choose to have their newborn sons circumcised for a combination of health, religious, cultural, or traditional reasons. But although it is one of the most commonly performed surgical procedures in the United States, national medical associations such as the American Medical Association, the American Academy of Pediatrics, and the American Academy of Family Physicians have long maintained that circumcision is not medically necessary and do not recommend that it be performed routinely (American Academy of Pediatrics, 1999; American Academy of Family Physicians, 2002).

But emerging research findings have added a new twist to the controversy: Circumcision provides protection against future sexually transmitted diseases. A number of studies conducted in Africa (where HIV infection rates are high) have found that circumcised men are less likely to become infected with HIV, even when other factors such as hygiene are controlled. In fact, large experimental studies being conducted in Kenya and Uganda were stopped early when the researchers found compelling evidence that circumcision of healthy adult males cut their risk of subsequent HIV infection approximately in half (the studies were stopped early to allow the uncircumcised men in the control groups to get circumcised for the same protective benefits; American Academy of Family Physicians, 2002; Meier, Bukusi, & Cohen, 2006; Mills & Seigfried, 2006; National Institutes of Health, 2006).

Circumcision may produce other medical benefits as well. The risk of urinary tract infections is reduced in circumcised males, especially during the first year of life. The benefit is small, however, given that this risk is already low in uncircumcised males. The risk of penile cancer is about three times higher in uncircumcised men than in men who were circumcised at birth, but again, the overall risk is already very low even for uncircumcised men (Frisch et al., 1995; American Academy of Pediatrics, 1999).

Circumcision opponents nevertheless raise some important concerns. Estimates range widely on the rate at which complications arise from circumcision, but the most common ones are bleeding and infection, both of which are usually minor and easily treated. More serious complications, such as failure to remove enough of the foreskin or inflammation of the urinary opening, occur more rarely. Furthermore, as we'll discuss in the next chapter, the procedure is also painful and stressful to the infant, as it is typically done without general anesthesia. Some experts believe that circumcision reduces sensation and sexual pleasure later in life, while others argue that the overriding concern is the ethicality of removing a healthy, intact part of a person's body without his own consent when there is no medical need to do so (American Academy of Pediatrics, 1999; American Academy of Family Physicians, 2002).

One thing is clear: Circumcision is a controversial practice that evokes strong emotions on both sides of the debate. The decision to circumcise a newborn son or not is a complex one that may ultimately come down to personal preferences and values (Goldman, 2004).

- *Do you agree that tradition alone is enough of a reason to circumcise a male infant? Why or why not?*

- *Considering that men can be circumcised at any age, is protection against HIV infection enough of a medical reason to circumcise a male infant? Why or why not?*

---

fear of rats, Little Albert learned to fear them when, during a laboratory demonstration, a loud noise was sounded every time he played with a cute and harmless white rat. In fact, the fear generalized to other furry objects, including rabbits and even a Santa Claus mask. (By the way, such a demonstration would be considered unethical today, and it would never be conducted.)

Infants are capable of learning very early through classical conditioning. For instance, 1- and 2-day-old newborns who are stroked on the head just before being given a drop of a sweet-tasting liquid soon learn to turn their heads and suck at the head-stroking alone. Clearly, classical conditioning is in operation from the time of birth (Blass, Ganchrow, & Steiner, 1984; Dominguez, Lopez, & Molina, 1999).

Operant Conditioning.   But classical conditioning is not the only mechanism through which infants learn; they also respond to operant conditioning. As we noted in Chapter 1, **operant conditioning** is a form of learning in which a *voluntary* response is strengthened or weakened, depending on its association with positive or negative consequences. In operant conditioning, infants learn to act deliberately on their environments in order to bring about some desired consequence. An infant who learns that crying in a certain way is apt to bring her parents' immediate attention is displaying operant conditioning.

Like classical conditioning, operant conditioning functions from the earliest days of life. For instance, researchers have found that even newborns readily learn through operant conditioning to keep sucking on a nipple when it permits them to continue hearing their mothers read a story or to listen to music (DeCasper & Fifer, 1980; Lipsitt, 1986a).

Habituation.   Probably the most primitive form of learning is demonstrated by the phenomenon of habituation. **Habituation** is the decrease in the response to a stimulus that occurs after repeated presentations of the same stimulus.

Habituation in infants relies on the fact that when newborns are presented with a new stimulus, they produce an *orienting response*, in which they become quiet, attentive, and experience a slowed heart rate as they take in the novel stimulus. When the novelty wears off due to repeated exposure to the stimulus, the infant no longer reacts with this orienting response. If a new and different stimulus is presented, the infant once again reacts with an orienting response. When this happens, we can say that the infant has learned to recognize the original stimulus and to distinguish it from others.

Habituation occurs in every sensory system, and researchers have studied it in several ways. One is to examine changes in sucking, which stops temporarily when a new stimulus is presented. This reaction is not unlike that of an adult who temporarily puts down her knife and fork when a dinner companion makes an interesting statement to which she wishes to pay particular attention. Other measures of habituation include changes in heart rate, respiration rate, and the length of time an infant looks at a particular stimulus.

The development of habituation is linked to physical and cognitive maturation. It is present at birth and becomes more pronounced over the first 12 weeks of infancy. Difficulties involving habituation represent a signal of developmental problems such as mental retardation (Moon, 2002). The three basic processes of learning that we've considered—classical conditioning, operant conditioning, and habituation—are summarized in Table 3-5.

operant conditioning a form of learning in which a voluntary response is strengthened or weakened, depending on its association with positive or negative consequences.

habituation the decrease in the response to a stimulus that occurs after repeated presentations of the same stimulus.

VIDEO CLIP
HABITUATION/ DISHABITUATION

Table 3-5	Three Basic Processes of Learning	
Type	**Description**	**Example**
Classical Conditioning	A situation in which an organism learns to respond in a particular way to a neutral stimulus that normally does not bring about that type of response.	A hungry baby stops crying when her mother picks her up because she has learned to associate being picked up with subsequent feeding.
Operant Conditioning	A form of learning in which a voluntary response is strengthened or weakened, depending on its positive or negative consequences.	An infant who learns that smiling at his or her parents brings positive attention may smile more often.
Habituation	The decrease in the response to a stimulus that occurs after repeated presentations of the same stimulus.	A baby who showed interest and surprise at first seeing a novel toy may show no interest after seeing the same toy several times.

This infant is imitating the happy expressions of the adult. Why is this important?

Social Competence: Responding to Others

Soon after Kaita was born, her older brother looked down at her in her crib and opened his mouth wide, pretending to be surprised. Kaita's mother, looking on, was amazed when it appeared that Kaita imitated his expression, opening her mouth as if *she* were surprised.

Researchers registered surprise of their own when they first found that newborns did indeed have the capability to imitate others' behavior. Although infants were known to have all the muscles in place to produce facial expressions related to basic emotions, the actual appearance of such expressions was assumed to be largely random.

However, research beginning in the late 1970s began to suggest a different conclusion. For instance, developmental researchers found that when exposed to an adult modeling a behavior that the infant already performed spontaneously, such as opening the mouth or sticking out the tongue, the newborn appeared to imitate the behavior (Meltzoff & Moore, 1977, 2002; Nagy, 2006).

Even more exciting were findings from a series of studies conducted by developmental psychologist Tiffany Field and her colleagues (Field, 1982; Field & Walden, 1982; Field et al., 1984). They initially showed that infants could discriminate between such basic facial expressions as happiness, sadness, and surprise. They then exposed newborns to an adult model with a happy, sad, or surprised facial expression. The results suggested that newborns produced a reasonably accurate imitation of the adult's expression.

However, subsequent research seemed to point to a different conclusion, as other investigators found consistent evidence only for a single imitative movement: sticking out the tongue. And even that response seemed to disappear around the age of 2 months. Since it seems unlikely that imitation would be limited to a single gesture and only appear for a few months, some researchers began to question the earlier findings. In fact, some researchers suggested that even sticking out the tongue was not imitation, but merely an exploratory behavior (Anisfeld, 1996; Bjorklund, 1997a; S. Jones, 2006).

The jury is still out on exactly when true imitation begins, although it seems clear that some forms of imitation begin very early in life. Such imitative skills are important, because effective social interaction with others relies in part on the ability to react to other people in an appropriate manner and to understand the meaning of others' emotional states. Consequently, newborns' ability to imitate provides them with an important foundation for social interaction later in life (Heimann, 2001; Meltzoff, 2002; Rogers & Williams, 2006; Zeedyk & Heimann, 2006).

Several other aspects of newborns' behavior also act as forerunners for more formal types of social interaction that they will develop as they grow. As shown in Table 3-6, certain characteristics of neonates mesh with parental behavior to help produce a social relationship between child and parent, as well as social relationships with others (Eckerman & Oehler, 1992).

For example, newborns cycle through various **states of arousal,** different degrees of sleep and wakefulness, that range from deep sleep to great agitation. Caregivers become involved in

states of arousal   different degrees of sleep and wakefulness through which newborns cycle, ranging from deep sleep to great agitation.

Table 3-6   Factors That Encourage Social Interaction Between Full-Term Newborns and Their Parents

Full-Term Newborn	Parent
Has organized states	Helps regulate infant's states
Attends selectively to certain stimuli	Provides these stimuli
Behaves in ways interpretable as specific communicative intent	Searches for communicative intent
Responds systematically to parent's acts	Wants to influence newborn, feel effective
Acts in temporally predictable ways	Adjusts actions to newborn's temporal rhythms
Learns from, adapts to parent's behavior	Acts repetitively and predictably

(*Source:* Eckerman & Oehler, 1992.)

trying to help ease the baby through transitions from one state to another. For instance, a father who rhythmically rocks his crying daughter in an effort to calm her is engaged in a joint activity that is a prelude to future social interactions of different sorts. Similarly, newborns tend to pay particular attention to their mothers' voices, in part because they have become quite familiar after months in the womb. In turn, parents and others modify their speech when talking to infants to gain their attention and encourage interaction, using a different pitch and tempo than they use with older children and adults (DeCasper & Fifer, 1980; Trainor, Austin, & Desjardins, 2000; Kisilevsky et al., 2003; Newman & Hussain, 2006).

The ultimate outcome of the social interactive capabilities of the newborn infant, and the responses such behavior brings about from parents, is to pave the way for future social interactions. Just as the neonate shows remarkable skills on a physical and perceptual level, then, its social capabilities are no less sophisticated.

Review and Apply

Review

- Neonates are in many ways helpless, but studies of what they *can* do, rather than what they *can't* do, have revealed some surprising capabilities.

- Newborns' respiratory and digestive systems begin to function at birth. They have an array of reflexes to help them eat, swallow, find food, and avoid unpleasant stimuli.

- Newborns' sensory competence includes the ability to distinguish objects in the visual field and to see color differences, the ability to hear and to discern familiar sounds, and sensitivity to touch, odors, and tastes.

- The processes of classical conditioning, operant conditioning, and habituation demonstrate infants' learning capabilities.

- Infants develop the foundations of social competence early in life.

Applying Lifespan Development

- Can you think of examples of the use of classical conditioning on adults in everyday life, in such areas as entertainment, advertising, or politics?

- *From a childcare worker's perspective:* Developmental researchers no longer view the neonate as a helpless, incompetent creature, but rather as a remarkably competent, developing human being. What do you think are some implications of this change in viewpoint for methods of child rearing and child care?

Epilogue

This chapter has covered the amazing and intense processes of labor and birth. A number of birthing options are available to parents, and these options need to be weighed in light of possible complications that can arise during the birthing process. In addition to considering the remarkable progress that has been made regarding the various treatments and interventions available for babies that are too early or too late, we examined the grim topics of stillbirth and infant mortality. We concluded with a discussion of the surprising capabilities of newborns and their early development of social competence.

Before we move on to a more detailed discussion of infants' physical development, return for a moment to the case of the premature birth of Hattie Thatcher, discussed in the prologue. Using your understanding of the issues discussed in this chapter, answer the following questions.

1. Hattie was born more than 3 months early. Why was the fact that she was born alive so surprising? Can you discuss her birth in terms of "the age of viability"?

2. What procedures and activities were most likely set into motion immediately after her birth?

3. What dangers was Hattie subject to immediately after birth because of her high degree of prematurity? What dangers would be likely to continue into her childhood?

4. What ethical considerations affect the decision of whether the high costs of medical interventions for highly premature babies are justifiable? Who should pay those costs?

Looking Back

■ **What is the normal process of labor?**

• In the first stage of labor contractions occur about every 8 to 10 minutes, increasing in frequency, duration, and intensity until the mother's cervix expands. In the second stage of labor, which lasts about 90 minutes, the baby begins to move through the cervix and birth canal and ultimately leaves the mother's body. In the third stage of labor, which lasts only a few minutes, the umbilical cord and placenta are expelled from the mother.

• After it emerges, the newborn, or neonate, is usually inspected for irregularities, cleaned, and returned to its mother and father.

• Parents-to-be have a variety of choices regarding the setting for the birth, medical attendants, and whether or not to use pain-reducing medication. Sometimes, medical intervention, such as Cesarean birth, becomes necessary.

■ **What complications can occur at birth, and what are their causes, effects, and treatments?**

• Preterm, or premature, infants, born less than 38 weeks following conception, generally have low birthweight, which can cause chilling, vulnerability to infection, respiratory distress syndrome, and hypersensitivity to environmental stimuli. They may even show adverse effects later in life, including slowed development, learning disabilities, behavior disorders, below-average IQ scores, and problems with physical coordination.

• Very-low-birthweight infants are in special danger because of the immaturity of their organ systems. However, medical advances have pushed the age of viability of the infant back to about 24 weeks following conception.

• Postmature babies, who spend extra time in their mothers' wombs, are also at risk. However, physicians can artificially induce labor or perform a Cesarean delivery to address this situation. Cesarean deliveries are performed when the fetus is in distress, in the wrong position, or unable to progress through the birth canal.

• The infant mortality rate in the United States is higher than the rate in many other countries, and higher for low-income families than higher-income families.

• Postpartum depression, an enduring, deep feeling of sadness, affects about 10% of new mothers. In severe cases, its effects can be harmful to the mother and the child, and aggressive treatment may be employed.

■ **What capabilities does the newborn have?**

• Human newborns quickly master breathing through the lungs, and they are equipped with reflexes to help them eat, swallow, find food, and avoid unpleasant stimuli. Their sensory capabilities are also sophisticated.

• From birth, infants learn through habituation, classical conditioning, and operant conditioning. Newborns are able to imitate the behavior of others, a capability that helps them form social relationships and facilitates the development of social competence.

Key Terms and Concepts

neonate (p. 86)
episiotomy (p. 87)
Apgar scale (p. 88)
anoxia (p. 88)
bonding (p. 89)
preterm infants (p. 95)
low-birthweight infants
(p. 96)

small-for-gestational-age
infants (p. 96)
very-low-birthweight
infants (p. 97)
postmature infants (p. 98)
Cesarean delivery (p. 99)
fetal monitor (p. 99)
stillbirth (p. 100)

infant mortality (p. 100)
reflexes (p. 106)
classical conditioning
(p. 107)
operant conditioning
(p. 109)
habituation (p. 109)
states of arousal (p. 110)

4 Physical Development in Infancy

Chapter Overview

GROWTH AND STABILITY

Physical Growth: The Rapid Advances of Infancy

The Nervous System and Brain: The Foundations of Development

Integrating the Bodily Systems: The Life Cycles of Infancy

SIDS: The Unanticipated Killer

MOTOR DEVELOPMENT

Reflexes: Our Inborn Physical Skills

Motor Development in Infancy: Landmarks of Physical Achievement

Nutrition in Infancy: Fueling Motor Development

Breast or Bottle?

Introducing Solid Foods: When and What?

THE DEVELOPMENT OF THE SENSES

Visual Perception: Seeing the World

Auditory Perception: The World of Sound

Smell and Taste

Sensitivity to Pain and Touch

Multimodal Perception: Combining Individual Sensory Inputs

Prologue: First Steps

We had intimations that his first steps would not be too far in the future. Josh had previously dragged himself up, and, clutching the side of chairs and tables, managed to progress slowly around our living room. For the last few weeks, he'd even been able to stand, unmoving, for several moments without holding on.

But walking? It seemed too early: Josh was only 10 months old, and the books we read told us that most children would not take their first steps on their own until they were a year old. And our older son, Jon, hadn't walked until he was 14 months of age.

So, when Josh suddenly lurched forward, taking one awkward step after another away from the safety of the furniture and moved toward the center of the room, we were astounded. Despite the appearance that he was about to keel over at any second, he moved one, then two, then three steps forward, until our awe at his accomplishment overtook our ability to count each step.

Josh tottered all the way across the room, until he reached the other side. Not quite knowing how to stop, he toppled over, landing in a happy heap. It was a moment of pure glory.

Infants' physical accomplishments proceed at a rapid pace during their first year of life.

Josh's first steps at the age of 10 months was just one of the succession of milestones that characterize the dramatic physical attainments during infancy. In this chapter we consider the nature of physical development during infancy, a period that starts at birth and continues until the second birthday. We begin by discussing the pace of growth during infancy, noting obvious changes in height and weight as well as less apparent changes in the nervous system. We also consider how infants quickly develop increasingly stable patterns in such basic activities as sleeping, eating, and attending to the world.

Our discussion then turns to infants' thrilling gains in motor development as skills emerge that eventually will allow an infant to roll over, take the first step, and pick up a cookie crumb from the floor—skills that ultimately form the basis of later, even more complex behaviors. We start with basic, genetically determined reflexes and consider how even these may be modified through experience. We also discuss the nature and timing of the development of particular physical skills, look at whether their emergence can be speeded up, and consider the importance of early nutrition to their development.

Finally, we explore how infants' senses develop. We investigate how sensory systems like hearing and vision operate, and how infants sort through the raw data from their sense organs and transform it into meaningful information.

After reading this chapter, you will be able to answer these questions:

■ **How do the human body and nervous system develop?**

■ **Does the environment affect the pattern of development?**

■ **What developmental tasks must infants accomplish in this period?**

■ **What is the role of nutrition in physical development?**

■ **What sensory capabilities do infants possess?**

Looking Ahead

Growth and Stability

The average newborn weighs just over 7 pounds, which is less than the weight of the average Thanksgiving turkey. Its length is about 20 inches, shorter than a loaf of French bread. It is helpless; if left to fend for itself, it could not survive.

Yet after just a few years, the story is very different. Babies become much larger, they are mobile, and they become increasingly independent. How does this growth happen? We can answer this question first by describing the changes in weight and height that occur over the first 2 years of life, and then by examining some of the principles that underlie and direct that growth.

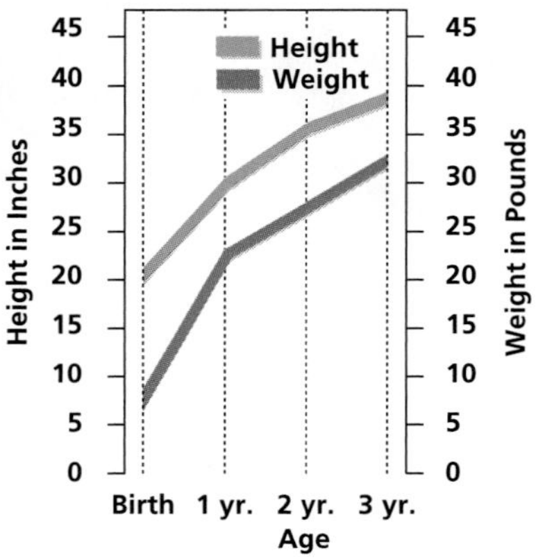

Physical Growth: The Rapid Advances of Infancy

Infants grow at a rapid pace over the first 2 years of their lives (see Figure 4-1). By the age of 5 months, the average infant's birthweight has doubled to around 15 pounds. By the first birthday, the baby's weight has tripled to about 22 pounds. Although the pace of weight gain slows during the second year, it still continues to increase. By the end of his or her second year, the average child weighs around four times as much as he or she did at birth. Of course, there is a good deal of variation among infants. Height and weight measurements, which are taken regularly at physician's visits during a baby's first year, provide a way to spot problems in development.

The weight gains of infancy are matched by increased length. By the end of the first year, the typical baby grows almost a foot and is about 30 inches tall. By their second birthdays, children average a height of 3 feet.

Not all parts of an infant's body grow at the same rate. For instance, as we saw first in Chapter 2, at birth the head accounts for one-quarter of the newborn's entire body size. During the first 2 years of life, the rest of the body begins to catch up. By the age of 2 the baby's head is only one-fifth of body length, and by adulthood it is only one-eighth (see Figure 4-2).

FIGURE 4-1   HEIGHT AND WEIGHT GROWTH

Although the greatest increase in height and weight occurs during the first year of life, children continue to grow throughout infancy and toddlerhood.

(*Source:* Cratty, 1979.)

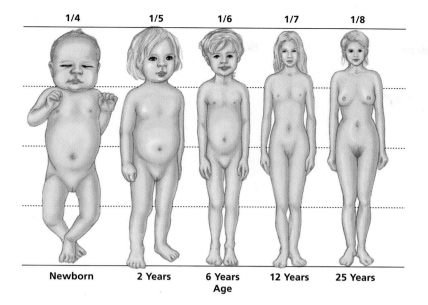

1/4   1/5   1/6   1/7   1/8

Newborn   2 Years   6 Years   12 Years   25 Years
Age

FIGURE 4-2 DECREASING PROPORTIONS

At birth, the head represents one-quarter of the neonate's body. By adulthood, the head is only one-eighth the size of the body. Why is the neonate's head so large?

There also are gender and ethnic differences in weight and length. Girls generally are slightly shorter and weigh slightly less than boys, and these differences remain throughout childhood (and, as we will see later in the book, the disparities become considerably greater during adolescence). Furthermore, Asian infants tend to be slightly smaller than North American Caucasian infants, and African American infants tend to be slightly bigger than North American Caucasian infants.

Four Principles of Growth.   The disproportionately large size of infants' heads at birth is an example of one of four major principles that govern growth. The **cephalocaudal principle** states that growth follows a direction and pattern that begins with the head and upper body parts and then proceeds to the rest of the body. The word *cephalocaudal* is derived Greek and Latin roots meaning "head-to-tail." The cephalocaudal growth principle means that we develop visual abilities (located in the head) well before we master the ability to walk (closer to the end of the body). The cephalocaudal principle operates both prenatally and after birth.

Three other principles (summarized in Table 4-1) help explain the patterns by which growth occurs. The **proximodistal principle** states that development proceeds from the center of the body outward. Based on the Latin words for "near" and "far," the proximodistal principle means that the trunk of the body grows before the extremities of the arms and legs. Similarly, it is only after growth has occurred in the arms and legs that the fingers and toes can grow. Furthermore, the development of the ability to use various parts of the body also follows the proximodistal principle. For instance, the effective use of the arms precedes the ability to use the hands.

cephalocaudal principle the principle that growth follows a pattern that begins with the head and upper body parts and then proceeds down to the rest of the body.

proximodistal principle the principle that development proceeds from the center of the body outward.

Table 4-1 The Major Principles Governing Growth			
Cephalocaudal Principle	**Proximodistal Principle**	**Principle of Hierarchical Integration**	**Principle of the Independence of Systems**
Growth follows a pattern that begins with the head and upper body parts and then proceeds to the rest of the body. Based on Greek and Latin roots meaning "head-to-tail."	Development proceeds from the center of the body outward. Based on the Latin words for "near" and "far."	Simple skills typically develop separately and independently. Later they are integrated into more complex skills.	Different body systems grow at different rates.

FIGURE 4-3 **MATURATION RATES**

Different body systems mature at different rates. For instance, the nervous system is highly developed during infancy, while body size is considerably less developed. The development of sexual characteristics lags even more, maturing at adolescence. Do you think this pattern is universal among all species, or is it unique to humans?

(*Source:* Bornstein & Lamb, 1992.)

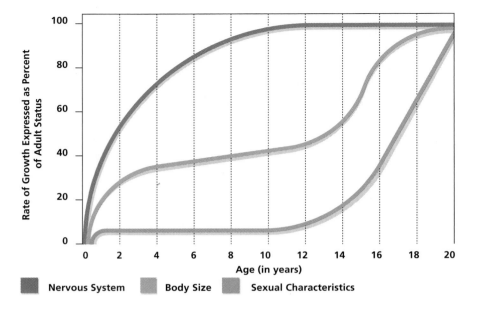

Related to this is the way complex skills build upon simpler ones. The **principle of hierarchical integration** states that simple skills typically develop separately and independently. Later, however, these simple skills are integrated into more complex ones. Thus, the relatively complex skill of grasping something in the hand cannot be mastered until the developing infant learns how to control—and integrate—the movements of the individual fingers.

Finally, the fourth and last major principle of growth is the **principle of the independence of systems,** which suggests that different body systems grow at different rates. This principle means that growth in one system does not necessarily imply that growth is occurring in others. For instance, Figure 4-3 illustrates the patterns of growth for three very different systems: body size, which we've already discussed, the nervous system, and sexual characteristics. As you can see, both the rate and timing of these different aspects of growth are independent.

The Nervous System and Brain: The Foundations of Development

When Rina was born, she was the first baby among her parents' circle of friends. These young adults marveled at the infant, oohing and aahing at every sneeze and smile and whimper, trying to guess at their meaning. Whatever feelings, movements, and thoughts Rina was experiencing, they were all brought about by the same complex network: the infant's nervous system. The *nervous system* is comprised of the brain and the nerves that extend throughout the body.

Neurons are the basic cells of the nervous system. Figure 4-4 shows the structure of an adult neuron. Like all cells in the body, neurons have a cell body containing a nucleus. But unlike other cells, neurons have a distinctive ability: They can communicate with other cells, using a cluster of fibers called *dendrites* at one end. Dendrites receive messages from other cells. At their opposite end, neurons have a long extension called an *axon,* the part of the neuron that carries messages destined for other neurons. Neurons do not actually touch one another. Rather, they communicate with other neurons by means of chemical messengers, *neurotransmitters,* that travel across the small gaps, known as **synapses,** between neurons.

Although estimates vary, infants are born with between 100 and 200 billion neurons. In order to reach this number, neurons multiply at an amazing rate prior to birth. In fact, at some points in prenatal development, cell division creates some 250,000 additional neurons every minute.

At birth, most neurons in an infant's brain have relatively few connections to other neurons. During the first 2 years of life, however, a baby's brain will establish billions of new connections

principle of hierarchical integration the principle that simple skills typically develop separately and independently but are later integrated into more complex skills.

principle of the independence of systems the principle that different body systems grow at different rates.

neuron the basic nerve cell of the nervous system.

synapse the gap at the connection between neurons, through which neurons chemically communicate with one another.

between neurons. Furthermore, the network of neurons becomes increasingly complex, as illustrated in Figure 4-5. The intricacy of neural connections continues to increase throughout life. In fact, in adulthood a single neuron is likely to have a minimum of 5,000 connections to other neurons or other body parts.

Synaptic Pruning. Babies are actually born with many more neurons than they need. In addition, although synapses are formed throughout life, based on our changing experiences, the billions of new synapses infants form during the first 2 years are more numerous than necessary. What happens to the extra neurons and synaptic connections?

Like a farmer who, in order to strengthen the vitality of a fruit tree, prunes away unnecessary branches, brain development enhances certain capabilities in part by a "pruning down" of unnecessary neurons. Neurons that do not become interconnected with other neurons as the infant's experience of the world increases become unnecessary. They eventually die out, increasing the efficiency of the nervous system.

As unnecessary neurons are being reduced, connections between remaining neurons are expanded or eliminated as a result of their use or disuse during the baby's experiences. If a baby's experiences do not stimulate certain nerve connections, these, like unused neurons, are eliminated—a process called **synaptic pruning.** The result of synaptic pruning is to allow established neurons to build more elaborate communication networks with other neurons. Unlike most other aspects of growth, then, the development of the nervous system proceeds most effectively through the loss of cells (Johnson, 1998; Mimura, Kimoto, & Okada, 2003; Iglesias et al., 2005).

After birth, neurons continue to increase in size. In addition to growth in dendrites, the axons of neurons become coated with **myelin,** a fatty substance that, like the insulation on an electric wire, provides protection and speeds the transmission of nerve impulses. So, even though many neurons are lost, the increasing size and complexity of the remaining ones contribute to impressive brain growth. A baby's brain triples its weight during his or her first 2 years of life, and it reaches more than three-quarters of its adult weight and size by the age of 2.

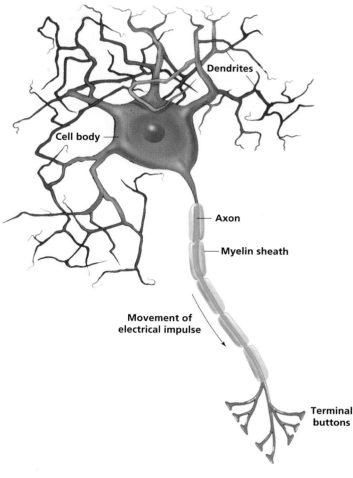

FIGURE 4-4   THE NEURON

The basic element of the nervous system, the neuron, is comprised of a number of components.

(*Source:* Van de Graaff, 2000.)

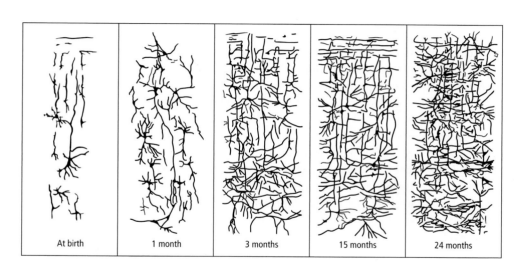

| At birth | 1 month | 3 months | 15 months | 24 months |

FIGURE 4-5   NEURON NETWORKS

Over the first 2 years of life, networks of neurons become increasingly complex and interconnected. Why are these connections important?

(*Source:* Conel, 1930/1963.)

synaptic pruning   the elimination of neurons as the result of nonuse or lack of stimulation.

myelin   a fatty substance that helps insulate neurons and speeds the transmission of nerve impulses.

As they grow, the neurons also reposition themselves, becoming arranged by function. Some move into the **cerebral cortex,** the upper layer of the brain, while others move to *subcortical levels,* which are below the cerebral cortex. The subcortical levels, which regulate such fundamental activities as breathing and heart rate, are the most fully developed at birth. As time passes, however, the cells in the cerebral cortex, which are responsible for higher-order processes such as thinking and reasoning, become more developed and interconnected.

Although the brain is protected by the bones of the skull, it is highly sensitive to some forms of injury. One particularly devastating injury comes from a form of child abuse called *shaken baby syndrome* in which an infant is shaken by a caretaker or parent, usually out of frustration or anger due to a baby's crying. Shaking can lead the brain to rotate within the skull, causing blood vessels to tear and destroying the intricate connections between neurons. The results can be devastating, leading to severe medical problems, long-term physical and learning disabilities, and often death (Miehl, 2005; Gerber & Coffman, 2007; Jayawant & Parr, 2007).

Environmental Influences on Brain Development.   Brain development, much of which unfolds automatically because of genetically predetermined patterns, is also strongly susceptible to environmental influences. In fact, the brain's **plasticity,** the degree to which a developing structure or behavior is modifiable due to experience, is relatively great for the brain. For instance, as we've seen, an infant's sensory experience affects both the size of individual neurons and the structure of their interconnections. Consequently, compared with those brought up in more enriched environments, infants raised in severely restricted settings are likely to show differences in brain structure and weight (Cicchetti, 2003; Cirulli, Berry, & Alleva, 2003; Couperus & Nelson, 2006).

Work with nonhumans has helped reveal the nature of the brain's plasticity. Studies have compared rats raised in an unusually visually stimulating environment to those raised in more typical, and less interesting, cages. Results of such research show that areas of the brain associated with vision are both thicker and heavier for the rats reared in enriched settings (Black & Greenough, 1986; Cynader, 2000; Degroot, Wolff, & Nomikos, 2005).

On the other hand, environments that are unusually barren or in some way restricted may impede the brain's development. Again, work with nonhumans provides some intriguing data. In one study, young kittens were fitted with goggles that restricted their vision so that they could view only vertical lines (Hirsch & Spinelli, 1970). When the cats grew up and had their goggles removed, they were unable to see horizontal lines, although they saw vertical lines perfectly well. Analogously, kittens whose goggles restricted their vision of vertical lines early in life were effectively blind to vertical lines during their adulthood—although their vision of horizontal lines was accurate.

In contrast, when goggles are placed on older cats that have lived relatively normal lives as kittens, such results are not seen after the goggles are removed. The conclusion is that there is a sensitive period for the development of vision. As we noted in Chapter 1, a **sensitive period** is a specific, but limited, time, usually early in an organism's life, during which the organism is particularly susceptible to environmental influences relating to some particular facet of development. A sensitive period may be associated with a behavior—such as the development of full vision—or with the development of a structure of the body, such as the configuration of the brain (Uylings, 2006).

The existence of sensitive periods raises several important issues. For one thing, it suggests that unless an infant receives a certain level of early environmental stimulation during a sensitive period, the infant may suffer damage or fail to develop capabilities that can never be fully remedied. If this is true, providing successful later intervention for such children may prove to be particularly challenging (Gottlieb & Blair, 2004).

The opposite question also arises: Does an unusually high level of stimulation during sensitive periods produce developmental gains beyond what a more commonplace level of stimulation would provide?

cerebral cortex   the upper layer of the brain.

plasticity   the degree to which a developing structure or behavior is modifiable due to experience.

sensitive period   a specific, but limited, time, usually early in an organism's life, during which the organism is particularly susceptible to environmental influences relating to some particular facet of development.

Such questions have no simple answers. Determining how unusually impoverished or enriched environments affect later development is one of the major questions addressed by developmental researchers as they try to find ways to maximize opportunities for developing children. In the meantime, many developmentalists suggest that there are many simple ways parents and caregivers can provide a stimulating environment that will encourage healthy brain growth. Cuddling, talking and singing to, and playing with babies all help enrich their environment. In addition, holding children and reading to them is important, as it simultaneously engages multiple senses, including vision, hearing, and touch (Lafuente et al., 1997; Garlick, 2003).

Integrating the Bodily Systems: The Life Cycles of Infancy

If you happen to overhear new parents discuss their newborns, chances are one or several bodily functions will be the subject. In the first days of life, infants' body rhythms—waking, eating, sleeping, and going to the bathroom—govern the infant's behavior, often at seemingly random times.

These most basic activities are controlled by a variety of bodily systems. Although each of these individual behavioral patterns probably is functioning quite effectively, it takes some time and effort for infants to integrate the separate behaviors. In fact, one of the neonate's major missions is to make its individual behaviors work in harmony, helping it, for example, to sleep through the night (Ingersoll & Thoman, 1999; Waterhouse & DeCoursey, 2004).

Rhythms and States.   One of the most important ways that behavior becomes integrated is through the development of various **rhythms,** which are repetitive, cyclical patterns of behavior. Some rhythms are immediately obvious, such as the change from wakefulness to sleep. Others are more subtle, but still easily noticeable, such as breathing and sucking patterns. Still other rhythms may require careful observation to be noticed. For instance, newborns may go through periods in which they jerk their legs in a regular pattern every minute or so. Although some of these rhythms are apparent just after birth, others emerge slowly over the first year as the neurons of the nervous system become increasingly integrated (Groome et al., 1997; Thelen & Bates, 2003).

One of the major body rhythms is that of an infant's **state,** the degree of awareness it displays to both internal and external stimulation. As can be seen in Table 4-2, such states include various levels of wakeful behaviors, such as alertness, fussing, and crying, and different levels of sleep as well. Each change in state brings about an alteration in the amount of stimulation required to get the infant's attention (Balaban, Snidman, & Kagan, 1997; Diambra & Menna-Barreto, 2004).

Some of the different states that infants experience produce changes in electrical activity in the brain. These changes are reflected in different patterns of electrical *brain waves*, which can be measured by a device called an *electroencephalogram*, or *EEG*. Starting at 3 months before birth, these brain wave patterns are relatively irregular. However, by the time an infant reaches the age of 3 months, a more mature pattern emerges and the brain waves become more regular (Burdjalov, Baumgart, & Spitzer, 2003; Thordstein et al., 2006).

Sleep: Perchance to Dream?   At the beginning of infancy, the major state that occupies a baby's time is sleep—much to the relief of exhausted parents, who often regard sleep as a welcome respite from caregiving responsibilities. On average, newborn infants sleep some 16 to 17 hours a day. However, there are wide variations. Some sleep more than 20 hours, while others sleep as little as 10 hours a day (Peirano, Algarin, & Uauy, 2003; Buysse, 2005).

Infants sleep a lot, but you probably shouldn't ever wish to "sleep like a baby." The sleep of infants comes in fits and starts. Rather than covering one long stretch, sleep initially comes in spurts of around 2 hours, followed by periods of wakefulness. Because of this, infants—and their sleep-deprived parents—are "out of sync" with the rest of the world, for whom sleep

rhythms repetitive, cyclical patterns of behavior.

state the degree of awareness an infant displays to both internal and external stimulation.

Table 4-2 Primary Behavioral States

States	Characteristics	Percentage of Time When Alone in State
Awake States		
Alert	Attentive or scanning, the infant's eyes are open, bright, and shining.	6.7
Nonalert waking	Eyes are usually open, but dull and unfocused. Varied, but typically high motor activity.	2.8
Fuss	Fussing is continuous or intermittent, at low levels.	1.8
Cry	Intense vocalizations occurring singly or in succession.	1.7
Transition States Between Sleep and Waking		
Drowse	Infant's eyes are heavy-lidded, but opening and closing slowly. Low level of motor activity.	4.4
Daze	Open, but glassy and immobile eyes. State occurs between episodes of Alert and Drowse. Low level of activity.	1.0
Sleep-wake transition	Behaviors of both wakefulness and sleep are evident. Generalized motor activity; eyes may be closed, or they open and close rapidly. State occurs when baby is awakening.	1.3
Sleep States		
Active sleep	Eyes closed; uneven respiration; intermittent rapid eye movements. Other behaviors: smiles, frowns, grimaces, mouthing, sucking, sighs, and sigh-sobs.	50.3
Quiet sleep	Eyes are closed and respiration is slow and regular. Motor activity limited to occasional startles, sigh-sobs, or rhythmic mouthing.	28.1
Transitional Sleep States		
Active-quiet transition sleep	During this state, which occurs between periods of Active Sleep and Quiet Sleep, the eyes are closed and there is little motor activity. Infant shows mixed behavioral signs of Active Sleep and Quiet Sleep.	1.9

(*Source:* Adapted from Thoman & Whitney, 1990.)

comes at night and wakefulness during the day (Groome et al., 1997; Burnham et al., 2002). Most babies do not sleep through the night for several months. Parents' sleep is interrupted, sometimes several times a night, by the infant's cries for food and physical contact.

Luckily for their parents, infants gradually settle into a more adultlike pattern. After a week, babies sleep a bit more at night and are awake for slightly longer periods during the day. Typically, by the age of 16 weeks infants begin to sleep as much as 6 continuous hours at night, and daytime sleep falls into regular naplike patterns. Most infants sleep through the night by the end of the first year, and the total amount of sleep they need each day is down to about 15 hours (Thoman & Whitney, 1989; Mao, 2004).

Hidden beneath the supposedly tranquil sleep of infants is another cyclic pattern. During periods of sleep, infants' heart rates increase and become irregular, their blood pressure rises, and they begin to breathe more rapidly (Montgomery-Downs & Thomas, 1998). Sometimes, although not always, their closed eyes begin to move in a back-and-forth pattern, as if they were viewing an action-packed scene. This period of active sleep is similar, although not identical, to the **rapid eye movement,** or **REM, sleep** that is found in older children and adults and is associated with dreaming.

rapid eye movement (REM) sleep   the period of sleep that is found in older children and adults and is associated with dreaming.

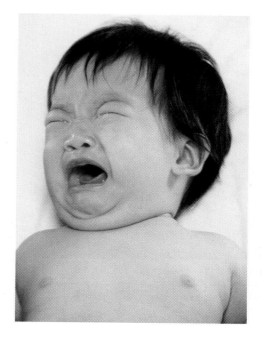
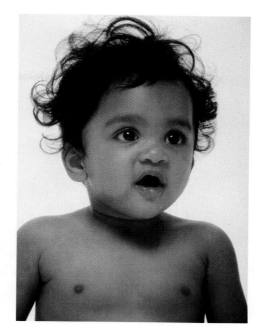

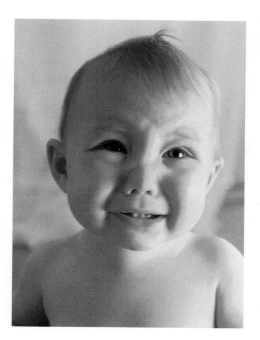

Infants cycle through various states, including crying and alertness. These states are integrated through bodily rhythms.

At first, this active, REM-like sleep takes up around one-half of an infant's sleep, compared with just 20% of an adult's sleep (see Figure 4-6). However, the quantity of active sleep quickly declines, and by the age of 6 months, amounts to just one-third of total sleep time (Coons & Guilleminault, 1982; Burnham et al., 2002; Staunton, 2005).

The appearance of active sleep periods that are similar to REM sleep in adults raises the intriguing question of whether infants dream during those periods. No one knows the answer, although it seems unlikely. First of all, young infants do not have much to dream about, given their relatively limited experiences. Furthermore, the brain waves of sleeping infants appear to be qualitatively different from those of adults who are dreaming. It is not until the baby reaches 3 or 4 months of age that the wave patterns become similar to those of dreaming adults,

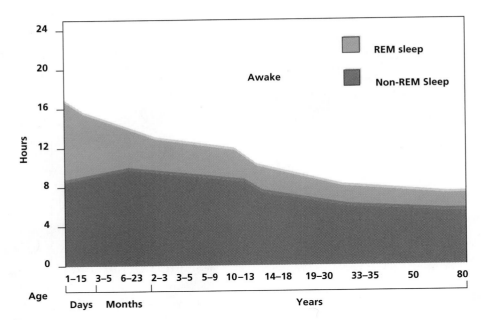

FIGURE 4-6 REM SLEEP THROUGH THE LIFE SPAN

As we age, the proportion of REM sleep increases as the proportion of non-REM sleep declines. In addition, the total amount of sleep falls as we get older.

(*Source:* Adapted from Roffwarg, Muzio, & Dement, 1966.)

Infants sleep in spurts, often making them out of sync with the rest of the world.

suggesting that young infants are not dreaming during active sleep—or at least are not doing so in the same way as adults do (McCall, 1979; Parmelee & Sigman, 1983; Zampi, Fagidi, & Salzarulo, 2002).

Then what is the function of REM sleep in infants? Although we don't know for certain, some researchers think it provides a means for the brain to stimulate itself—a process called *autostimulation* (Roffwarg, Muzio, & Dement, 1966). Stimulation of the nervous system would be particularly important in infants, who spend so much time sleeping and relatively little in alert states.

Infants' sleep cycles seem largely preprogrammed by genetic factors, but environmental influences also play a part. For instance, both long- and short-term stressors in infants' environments (such as a heat wave) can affect their sleep patterns. When environmental circumstances keep babies awake, sleep, when at last it comes, is apt to be less active (and quieter) than usual (Halpern, MacLean, & Baumeister, 1995; Goodlin-Jones, Burnham, & Anders, 2000).

Cultural practices also affect infants' sleep patterns. For example, among the Kipsigis of Africa, infants sleep with their mothers at night and are allowed to nurse whenever they wake. In the daytime, they accompany their mothers during daily chores, often napping while strapped to their mothers' backs. Because they are often out and on the go, Kipsigis infants do not sleep through the night until much later than babies in Western societies, and for the first 8 months of life, they seldom sleep longer than 3 hours at a stretch. In comparison, 8-month-old infants in the United States may sleep as long as 8 hours at a time (Super & Harkness, 1982; Anders & Taylor, 1994; Gerard, Harris, & Thach, 2002).

SIDS: The Unanticipated Killer

For a tiny percentage of infants, the rhythm of sleep is interrupted by a deadly affliction: sudden infant death syndrome, or SIDS. **Sudden infant death syndrome (SIDS)** is a disorder in which seemingly healthy infants die in their sleep. Put to bed for a nap or for the night, an infant simply never wakes up.

SIDS strikes about 1 in 1,000 infants in the United States each year. Although it seems to occur when the normal patterns of breathing during sleep are interrupted, scientists have been unable to discover why that might happen. It is clear that infants don't smother or choke; they die a peaceful death, simply ceasing to breathe.

sudden infant death syndrome (SIDS) the unexplained death of a seemingly healthy baby.

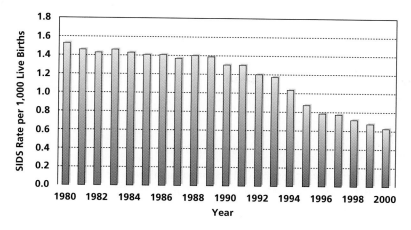

FIGURE 4-7 DECLINING RATES OF SIDS

In the United States, SIDS rates have dropped dramatically as parents have become more informed and put babies to sleep on their backs instead of their stomachs.

(*Source:* American SIDS Institute, based on data from the Center for Disease Control and the National Center for Health Statistics, 2004.)

While no reliable means for preventing the syndrome has been found, the American Academy of Pediatrics now suggests that babies sleep on their backs rather than on their sides or stomachs—called the *back-to-sleep* guideline. In addition, they suggest that parents consider giving their babies a pacifier during naps and bedtime (Task Force on Sudden Infant Death Syndrome, 2005).

The number of deaths from SIDS has decreased significantly since these guidelines were developed (see Figure 4-7). Still, SIDS is the leading cause of death in children under the age of 1 year (Eastman, 2003; Daley, 2004).

Some infants are more at risk for SIDS than others. For instance, boys and African Americans are at greater risk. In addition, low birthweight and low Apgar scores found at birth are associated with SIDS, as is having a mother who smokes during pregnancy. Some evidence also suggests that a brain defect that affects breathing may produce SIDS. In a small number of cases, child abuse may be the actual cause. Still, there is no clear-cut factor that explains why some infants die from the syndrome. SIDS is found in children of every race and socioeconomic group and in children who have had no apparent health problems (Muhuri, MacDorman, & Ezzati-Rice, 2004; Anderson, Johns, & Batal, 2005; Fleming, Tsogt, & Blair, 2006; Paterson et al., 2006).

Many hypotheses have been suggested to explain why infants die from SIDS. These include such problems as undiagnosed sleep disorders, suffocation, nutritional deficiencies, problems with reflexes, and undiagnosed illness. Still, the actual cause of SIDS remains elusive (Lipsitt, 2003; Hunt & Hauck, 2006).

Because parents are unprepared for the death of an infant from SIDS, the event is particularly devastating. Parents often feel guilt, fearing that they were neglectful or somehow contributed to their child's death. Such guilt is unwarranted, since nothing has been identified so far that can invariably prevent SIDS (Krueger, 2006).

Review and Apply

Review

- The major principles of growth are the cephalocaudal principle, the proximodistal principle, the principle of hierarchical integration, and the principle of the independence of systems.

- The development of the nervous system first entails the development of billions of neurons and interconnections among them. Later, the numbers of both neurons and connections decrease as a result of the infant's experiences.

- Brain plasticity, the susceptibility of a developing organism to environmental influences, is relatively high.

● Researchers have identified sensitive periods during the development of body systems and behaviors—limited periods when the organism is particularly susceptible to environmental influences.

● Babies integrate their individual behaviors by developing rhythms—repetitive, cyclical patterns of behavior. A major rhythm relates to the infant's state—the awareness it displays to internal and external stimulation.

Applying Lifespan Development

● What evolutionary advantage could there be for infants to be born with more nerve cells than they actually need or use? How might our understanding of synaptic "pruning" affect the way we treat infants?

● *From a social worker's perspective:* What are some cultural or subcultural influences that might affect parents' child-rearing practices?

Motor Development

Suppose you were hired by a genetic engineering firm to redesign newborns and were charged with replacing the current version with a new, more mobile one. The first change you'd probably consider in carrying out this (luckily fictitious) job would be in the conformation and composition of the baby's body.

The shape and proportions of newborn babies are simply not conducive to easy mobility. Their heads are so large and heavy that young infants lack the strength to raise them. Because their limbs are short in relation to the rest of the body, their movements are further impeded. Furthermore, their bodies are mainly fat, with a limited amount of muscle; the result is that they lack strength.

Fortunately, it doesn't take too long before infants begin to develop a remarkable amount of mobility. In fact, even at birth they have an extensive repertoire of behavioral possibilities brought about by innate reflexes, and their range of motor skills grows rapidly during the first 2 years of life.

Reflexes: Our Inborn Physical Skills

When her father pressed 3-day-old Christina's palm with his finger, she responded by tightly winding her small fist around his finger and grasping it. When he moved his finger upward, she held on so tightly that it seemed he might be able to lift her completely off her crib floor.

The Basic Reflexes.   In fact, her father was right: Christina probably could have been lifted in this way. The reason for her resolute grip was activation of one of the dozens of reflexes with which infants are born. **Reflexes** are unlearned, organized, involuntary responses that occur automatically in the presence of certain stimuli. Newborns enter the world with a repertoire of reflexive behavioral patterns that help them adapt to their new surroundings and serve to protect them.

As we can see from the list of reflexes in Table 4-3, many reflexes clearly represent behavior that has survival value, helping to ensure the well-being of the infant. For instance, the *swimming reflex* makes a baby who is lying face down in a body of water paddle and kick in a sort of swimming motion. The obvious consequence of such behavior is to help the baby move from danger and survive until a caregiver can come to its rescue. Similarly, the *eye-blink reflex* seems designed to protect the eye from too much direct light, which might damage the retina.

reflexes unlearned, organized, involuntary responses that occur automatically in the presence of certain stimuli.

Table 4-3 Some Basic Reflexes in Infants

Reflex	Approximate Age of Disappearance	Description	Possible Function
Rooting reflex	3 weeks	Neonate's tendency to turn its head toward things that touch its cheek.	Food intake
Stepping reflex	2 months	Movement of legs when held upright with feet touching the floor.	Prepares infants for independent locomotion
Swimming reflex	4–6 months	Infant's tendency to paddle and kick in a sort of swimming motion when lying face down in a body of water.	Avoidance of danger
Moro reflex	6 months	Activated when support for the neck and head is suddenly removed. The arms of the infant are thrust outward and then appear to grasp onto something.	Similar to primates' protection from falling
Babinski reflex	8–12 months	An infant fans out its toes in response to a stroke on the outside of its foot.	Unknown
Startle reflex	Remains in different form	An infant, in response to a sudden noise, flings out its arms, arches its back, and spreads its fingers.	Protection
Eye-blink reflex	Remains	Rapid shutting and opening of eye on exposure to direct light.	Protection of eye from direct light
Sucking reflex	Remains	Infant's tendency to suck at things that touch its lips.	Food intake
Gag reflex	Remains	An infant's reflex to clear its throat.	Prevents choking

Given the protective value of many reflexes, it might seem beneficial for them to remain with us for our entire lives. In fact, some do: The eye-blink reflex remains functional throughout the full life span. On the other hand, quite a few reflexes, such as the swimming reflex, disappear after a few months. Why should this be the case?

Researchers who focus on evolutionary explanations of development attribute the gradual disappearance of reflexes to the increase in voluntary control over behavior that occurs as infants become more able to control their muscles. In addition, it may be that reflexes form the foundation for future, more complex behaviors. As these more intricate behaviors become well learned, they encompass the earlier reflexes (Myklebust & Gottlieb, 1993; Lipsitt, 2003).

It may be that reflexes stimulate parts of the brain responsible for more complex behaviors, helping them develop. For example, some researchers argue that exercise of the stepping reflex helps the brain's cortex later develop the ability to walk. As evidence, developmental psychologist Philip R. Zelazo and his colleagues conducted a study in which they provided 2-week-old infants practice in walking for four sessions of 3 minutes each over a 6-week period. The results showed that the children who had the walking practice actually began to walk unaided several months earlier than those who had no such practice. Zelazo suggests that the training produced stimulation of the stepping reflex, which in turn led to stimulation of the brain's cortex, readying the infant earlier for independent locomotion (Zelazo et al., 1993; Zelazo, 1998).

Do these findings suggest that parents should make out-of-the-ordinary efforts to stimulate their infant's reflexes? Probably not. Although the evidence shows that intensive practice may produce an earlier appearance of certain motor activities, there is no evidence that the activities are performed qualitatively any better in practiced infants than in unpracticed infants. Furthermore, even when early gains are found, they do not seem to produce an adult who is more proficient in motor skills.

(a)

(b)

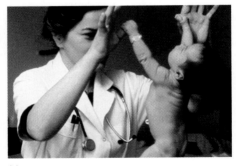

(c)

Infants showing (a) the rooting reflex, (b) the startle reflex, and (c) the Babinski reflex.

In fact, structured exercise may do more harm than good. According to the American Academy of Pediatrics, structured exercise for infants may lead to muscle strain, fractured bones, and dislocated limbs, consequences that far outweigh the unproven benefits that may come from the practice (American Academy of Pediatrics, 1988).

Ethnic and Cultural Differences and Similarities in Reflexes.   Although reflexes are, by definition, genetically determined and universal throughout all infants, there are actually some cultural variations in the ways they are displayed. For instance, consider the *Moro reflex* (often called the *startle response*), which is activated when support for the neck and head is suddenly removed. The Moro reflex consists of the infant's arms thrusting outward and then appearing to seek to grasp onto something. Most scientists feel that the Moro reflex represents a leftover response that we humans have inherited from our nonhuman ancestors. The Moro reflex is an extremely useful behavior for monkey babies, who travel about by clinging to their mothers' backs. If they lose their grip, they fall down unless they are able to grasp quickly onto their mother's fur—using a Moro-like reflex (Prechtl, 1982; Zafeiriou, 2004).

The Moro reflex is found in all humans, but it appears with significantly different vigor in different children. Some differences reflect cultural and ethnic variations (Freedman, 1979). For instance, Caucasian infants show a pronounced response to situations that produce the Moro reflex. Not only do they fling out their arms, but they also cry and respond in a generally agitated manner. In contrast, Navajo babies react to the same situation much more calmly. Their arms do not flail out as much, and they cry only rarely.

In some cases, reflexes can serve as helpful diagnostic tools for pediatricians. Because reflexes emerge and disappear on a regular timetable, their absence—or presence—at a given point of infancy can provide a clue that something may be amiss in an infant's development. (Even for adults, physicians include reflexes in their diagnostic bags of tricks, as anyone knows who has had his or her knee tapped with a rubber mallet to see if the lower leg jerks forward.)

Reflexes evolved because they had, at one point in humankind's history, survival value. For example, the sucking reflex automatically helps infants obtain nourishment, and the rooting reflex helps them search for the presence of a nipple. In addition, some reflexes also serve a social function, promoting caregiving and nurturance. For instance, Christina's father, who found his daughter gripping his finger tightly when he pressed her palm, probably cares little that she is simply responding with an innate reflex. Instead, he will more likely view his daughter's action as responsiveness to him, a signal perhaps of increasing interest and affection on her part. As we will see in Chapter 6, when we discuss the social and personality development of infants, such apparent responsiveness can help cement the growing social relationship between an infant and its caregivers.

Motor Development in Infancy: Landmarks of Physical Achievement

Probably no physical changes are more obvious—and more eagerly anticipated—than the increasing array of motor skills that babies acquire during infancy. Most parents can remember their child's first steps with a sense of pride and awe at how quickly she or he changed from a helpless infant, unable even to roll over, into a person who could navigate quite effectively in the world.

This 5-month-old girl demonstrates her gross motor skills.

Gross Motor Skills.   Even though the motor skills of newborn infants are not terribly sophisticated, at least compared with attainments that will soon appear, young infants still are able to accomplish some kinds of movement. For instance, when placed on their stomachs they wiggle their arms and legs and may try to lift their heavy heads. As their strength increases, they are able to push hard enough against the surface on which they are resting to propel their bodies in different directions. They often end up moving backward rather than forward, but by the

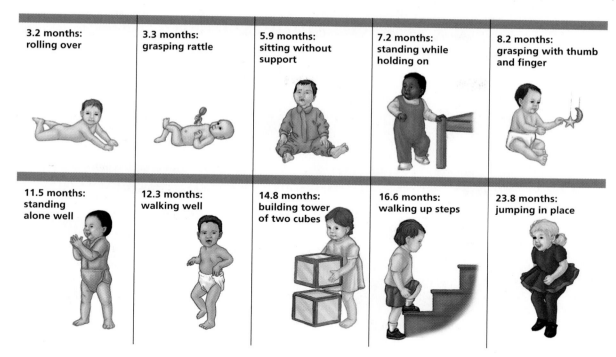

FIGURE 4-8 MILESTONES OF MOTOR DEVELOPMENT

Fifty percent of children are able to perform each skill at the month indicated in the figure. However, the specific timing at which each skill appears varies widely. For example, one-quarter of children are able to walk well at 11.1 months; by 14.9 months, 90% of children are walking well. Is knowledge of such average benchmarks helpful or harmful to parents?

(*Source:* Adapted from Frankenburg et al., 1992.)

age of 6 months they become rather accomplished at moving themselves in particular directions. These initial efforts are the forerunners of crawling, in which babies coordinate the motions of their arms and legs and propel themselves forward. Crawling appears typically between 8 and 10 months. Figure 4-8 provides a summary of some of the milestones of normal motor development.

Walking comes later. At around the age of 9 months, most infants are able to walk by supporting themselves on furniture, and half of all infants can walk well by the end of their first year of life.

At the same time infants are learning to move around, they are perfecting the ability to remain in a stationary sitting position. At first, babies cannot remain seated upright without support. But they quickly master this ability, and most are able to sit without support by the age of 6 months.

Fine Motor Skills. As infants are perfecting their gross motor skills, such as sitting upright and walking, they are also making advances in their fine motor skills (see Table 4-4). For instance, by the age of 3 months, infants show some ability to coordinate the movements of their limbs.

Furthermore, although infants are born with a rudimentary ability to reach toward an object, this ability is neither very sophisticated nor very accurate, and it disappears around the age of 4 weeks. A different, more precise form of reaching reappears at 4 months. It takes some time for infants to coordinate successful grasping after they reach out, but in fairly short order they are able to reach out and hold onto an object of interest (Claxton, Keen, & McCarty, 2003).

Table 4-4	Milestones of Fine Motor Development
Age (months)	**Skill**
3	Opens hand prominently
3	Grasps rattle
8	Grasps with thumb and finger
11	Holds crayon adaptively
14	Builds tower of two cubes
16	Places pegs in board
24	Imitates strokes on paper
33	Copies circle

(*Source:* Adapted from Frankenburg et al., 1992.)

The sophistication of fine motor skills continues to grow. By the age of 11 months, infants are able to pick up off the ground objects as small as marbles—something caregivers need to be concerned about, since the next place such objects often go is the mouth. By the time they are 2 years old, children can carefully hold a cup, bring it to their lips, and take a drink without spilling a drop.

Grasping, like other motor advances, follows a sequential developmental pattern in which simple skills are combined into more sophisticated ones. For example, infants first begin picking things up with their whole hand. As they get older, they use a *pincer grasp*, where thumb and index finger meet to form a circle. The pincer grasp allows for considerably more precise motor control.

Dynamic Systems Theory: How Motor Development Is Coordinated.   Although it is easy to think about motor development in terms of a series of individual motoric achievements, the reality is that each of these skills does not develop in a vacuum. Each skill (such as a baby's ability to pick up a spoon and guide it to her lips) advances in the context of other motor abilities (such as the ability to reach out and lift the spoon in the first place). Furthermore, as motor skills are developing, so also are nonmotoric skills such as visual capabilities.

Developmentalist Esther Thelen has created an innovative theory to explain how motor skills develop and are coordinated. **Dynamic systems theory** describes how motor behaviors are assembled. By "assembled," Thelen means the coordination of a variety of skills that develop in a child, ranging from the development of an infant's muscles, its perceptual abilities and nervous system, as well as its motivation to carry out particular motor activities, and support from the environment (Thelen, 2002; Thelen & Bates, 2003; Thelen & Smith, 2006).

According to dynamic systems theory, motor development in a particular sphere, such as beginning to crawl, is not just dependent on the brain initiating a "crawling program" that permits the muscles to propel the baby forward. Instead, crawling requires the coordination of muscles, perception, cognition, and motivation. The theory emphasizes how children's exploratory activities, which produce new challenges as they interact with their environment, lead them to advancements in motor skills.

Dynamic systems theory is noteworthy for its emphasis on a child's own motivation (a cognitive state) in advancing important aspects of motor development. For example, infants need to be motivated to touch something out of their reach in order to develop the skills they need to crawl to it. The theory also may help explain individual differences in the emergence of motor abilities in different children, which we consider next.

dynamic systems theory   a theory of how motor skills develop and are coordinated.

Developmental Norms: Comparing the Individual to the Group. Keep in mind that the timing of the milestones in motor development that we have been discussing is based on norms. **Norms** represent the average performance of a large sample of children of a given age. They permit comparisons between a particular child's performance on a particular behavior and the average performance of the children in the norm sample.

For instance, one of the most widely used techniques to determine infants' normative standing is the **Brazelton Neonatal Behavior Assessment Scale (NBAS),** a measure designed to determine infants' neurological and behavioral responses to their environment.

The NBAS provides a supplement to the traditional Apgar test (discussed in Chapter 3) that is given immediately following birth. Taking about 30 minutes to administer, the NBAS includes 27 separate categories of responses that constitute four general aspects of infants' behavior: interactions with others (such as alertness and cuddliness), motor behavior, physiological control (such as the ability to be soothed after being upset), and responses to stress (Brazelton, 1973, 1990; Davis & Emory, 1995; Canals, Fernandez-Ballart, & Espuro, 2003).

Although the norms provided by scales such as the NBAS are useful in making broad generalizations about the timing of various behaviors and skills, they must be interpreted with caution. Because norms are averages, they mask substantial individual differences in the times when children attain various achievements. For example, some children, like Josh, whose first steps were described earlier, may be ahead of the norm. Other perfectly normal children may be a bit behind. Norms also may hide the fact that the sequence in which various behaviors are achieved may differ somewhat from one child to another.

Norms are useful only to the extent that they are based on data from a large, heterogeneous, culturally diverse sample of children. Unfortunately, many of the norms on which developmental researchers have traditionally relied have been based on groups of infants who are predominantly Caucasian and from the middle and upper socioeconomic strata (e.g., Gesell, 1946). The reason: much of the research was conducted on college campuses, using the children of graduate students and faculty.

This limitation would not be critical if no differences existed in the timing of development in children from different cultural, racial, and social groups. But they do. For example, as a group, African American babies show more rapid motor development than Caucasian babies throughout infancy. Moreover, there are significant variations related to cultural factors, as we discuss next (Werner, 1972; Keefer et al., 1991; Gartstein, Slobodskaya, & Kinsht, 2003; de Onis et al., 2007).

norms the average performance of a large sample of children of a given age.

Brazelton Neonatal Behavioral Assessment Scale (NBAS) a measure designed to determine infants' neurological and behavioral responses to their environment.

Developmental Diversity

The Cultural Dimensions of Motor Development

Among the Ache people, who live in the rain forest of South America, infants face an early life of physical restriction. Because the Ache lead a nomadic existence, living in a series of tiny camps in the rain forest, open space is at a premium. Consequently, for the first few years of life, infants spend nearly all their time in direct physical contact with their mothers. Even when they are not physically touching their mothers, they are permitted to venture no more than a few feet away.

***

Infants among the Kipsigis people, who live in a more open environment in rural Kenya, Africa, lead quite a different existence. Their lives are filled with activity and exercise. Parents seek to teach their children to sit up, stand, and walk from the earliest days of infancy. For example, very young infants are placed in shallow holes in the ground designed to keep them in an upright position. Parents begin to teach their children to walk starting at the eighth week of life. The infants are held with their feet touching the ground, and they are pushed forward.

Cultural influences affect the rate of the development of motor skills.

clearly, the infants in these two societies lead very different lives (Super, 1976; Kaplan & Dove, 1987). But do the relative lack of early motor stimulation for Ache infants and the efforts of the Kipsigis to encourage motor development really make a difference?

The answer is both yes and no. It's yes, in that Ache infants tend to show delayed motor development, relative both to Kipsigis infants and to children raised in Western societies. Although their social abilities are no different, Ache children tend to begin walking at around 23 months, about a year later than the typical child in the United States. In contrast, Kipsigis children, who are encouraged in their motor development, learn to sit up and walk several weeks earlier, on average, than U.S. children.

In the long run, however, the differences between Ache, Kipsigis, and Western children disappear. By late childhood, about age 6, there is no evidence of differences in general, overall motor skills among Ache, Kipsigis, and Western children.

As we see with the Ache and Kipsigis babies, variations in the timing of motor skills seem to depend in part on parental expectations of what is the "appropriate" schedule for the emergence of specific skills. For instance, one study examined the motor skills of infants who lived in a single city in England, but whose mothers varied in ethnic origin. In the research, English, Jamaican, and Indian mothers' expectations were first assessed regarding several markers of their infants' motor skills. The Jamaican mothers expected their infants to sit and walk significantly earlier than the English and Indian mothers, and the actual emergence of these activities was in line with their expectations. The source of the Jamaican infants' earlier mastery seemed to lie in the treatment of the children by their parents. For instance, Jamaican mothers gave their children practice in stepping quite early in infancy (Hopkins & Westra, 1989, 1990).

In sum, cultural factors help determine the time at which specific motor skills appear. Activities that are an intrinsic part of a culture are more apt to be purposely taught to infants in that culture, leading to the potential of their earlier emergence (Nugent, Lester, & Brazelton, 1989).

It is not all that surprising that children in a given culture who are expected by their parents to master a particular skill, and who are taught components of that skill from an early age, are more likely to be proficient in that skill earlier than children from other cultures with no such expectations and no such training. The larger question, however, is whether the earlier emergence of a basic motor behavior in a given culture has lasting consequences for specific motor skills and for achievements in other domains. On this issue, the jury is still out.

One thing that is clear, however, is that there are certain limitations on how early a skill can emerge. It is physically impossible for 1-month-old infants to stand and walk, regardless of the encouragement and practice they may get within their culture. Parents who are eager to accelerate their infants' motor development, then, should be cautioned not to hold overly ambitious goals. In fact, they might well ask themselves whether it matters if an infant acquires a motor skill a few weeks earlier than his or her peers.

The most reasonable answer is "no." Although some parents may take pride in a child who walks earlier than other babies (just as some parents may be concerned over a delay of a few weeks), in the long run the timing of this activity will probably make no difference.

Nutrition in Infancy: Fueling Motor Development

Rosa sighed as she sat down to nurse the baby—again. She had fed 4-week-old Juan about every hour today, and he still seemed hungry. Some days, it seemed like all she did was breast-feed her baby. "Well, he must be going through a growth spurt," she decided, as she settled into her favorite rocking chair and put the baby to her nipple.

The rapid physical growth that occurs during infancy is fueled by the nutrients that infants receive. Without proper nutrition, infants cannot reach their physical potential, and they may suffer cognitive and social consequences as well (Tanner & Finn-Stevenson, 2002; Costello, Compton, & Keeler, 2003; Gregory, 2005).

Although there are vast individual differences in what constitutes appropriate nutrition—infants differ in terms of growth rates, body composition, metabolism, and activity levels—some broad guidelines do hold. In general, infants should consume about 50 calories per day for each pound they weigh—an allotment that is twice the suggested caloric intake for adults (Dietz & Stern, 1999; Skinner et al., 2004).

Typically, though, it's not necessary to count calories for infants. Most infants regulate their caloric intake quite effectively on their own. If they are allowed to consume as much as they seem to want, and not pressured to eat more, they will do fine.

Malnutrition.   *Malnutrition*, the condition of having an improper amount and balance of nutrients, produces several results, none good. For instance, malnutrition is more common among children living in many developing countries than among children who live in more industrialized, affluent countries. Malnourished children in these countries begin to show a slower growth rate by the age of 6 months. By the time they reach the age of 2 years, their height and weight are only 95% of the height and weight of children in more industrialized countries.

Children who have been chronically malnourished during infancy later score lower on IQ tests and tend to do less well in school. These effects may linger even after the children's diet has improved substantially (Grantham-McGregor, Ani, & Fernald, 2001; Ratanachu-Ek, 2003).

The problem of malnutrition is greatest in underdeveloped countries, where overall 10% of infants are severely malnourished. In some countries the problem is especially severe. For example, 60% of North Korean children aged 6 months to 7 years are suffering moderate to severe malnutrition (United Nations World Food Programme, 2004; see Figure 4-9). Problems of malnourishment are not restricted to developing countries, however. In the United States, some 12 million children live in poverty, which puts them at risk for malnutrition. In fact, although overall poverty rates are no worse than they were 20 years ago, the poverty rate for children under the age of 3 has *increased*. Some one-quarter of families who have children 2 years old and younger live in poverty. And, as we can see in Figure 4-10, the rates are even higher for African American and Hispanic families as well as for single-parent families (Einbinder, 1992; Carnegie Task Force on Meeting the Needs of Young Children, 1994; Duncan & Brooks-Gunn, 2000).

Social service programs mean that these children rarely become severely malnourished, but such children remain susceptible to *undernutrition*, in which there is some deficiency in diet. In fact, some surveys find that as many as a quarter of 1- to 5-year-old children in the United States have diets that fall below the minimum caloric intake recommended by nutritional experts. Although the consequences are not as severe as those of malnutrition, undernutrition also has long-term costs. For instance, cognitive development later in childhood is affected by even mild to moderate undernutrition (Sigman, 1995; Pollitt et al., 1996; Tanner & Finn-Stevenson, 2002).

Malnourishment at an early age can lower IQ scores, even if diet improves later. How might this deficit be overcome?

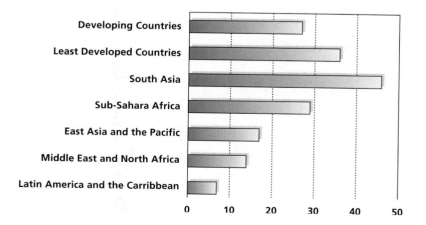

FIGURE 4-9   UNDERWEIGHT CHILDREN

The percentage of children under 5 years who are moderately and severely underweight.

(*Source:* UNICEF, The State of the World's Children, 2005.)

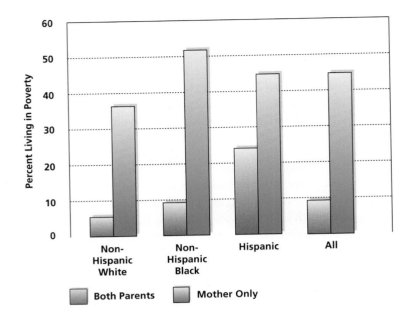

FIGURE 4-10 CHILDREN LIVING IN POVERTY

The incidence of poverty among children under the age of 3 is particularly high in minority and single-parent households. (Figures are shown only for single mothers, and not fathers, because 97% of all children under 3 who live with a single parent live with their mothers; only 3% live with their fathers.)

(*Source:* National Center for Children in Poverty at the Joseph L. Mailman School of Public Health of Columbia University. Analysis based on U.S. Bureau of the Census, 2000 Current Population Survey.)

Severe malnutrition during infancy may lead to several disorders. Malnutrition during the first year can produce *marasmus,* a disease in which infants stop growing. Marasmus, attributable to a severe deficiency in proteins and calories, causes the body to waste away and ultimately results in death. Older children are susceptible to *kwashiorkor,* a disease in which a child's stomach, limbs, and face swell with water. To a casual observer, it appears that a child with kwashiorkor is actually chubby. However, this is an illusion: The child's body is in fact struggling to make use of the few nutrients that are available.

In some cases, infants who receive sufficient nutrition act as though they have been deprived of food. Looking as though they suffer from marasmus, they are underdeveloped, listless, and apathetic. The real cause, though, is emotional: They lack sufficient love and emotional support. In such cases, known as **nonorganic failure to thrive,** children stop growing not for biological reasons but due to a lack of stimulation and attention from their parents. Usually occurring by the age of 18 months, nonorganic failure to thrive can be reversed through intensive parent training or by placing children in a foster home where they can receive emotional support.

Obesity. It is clear that malnourishment during infancy has potentially disastrous consequences for an infant. Less clear, however, are the effects of *obesity,* defined as weight greater than 20% above the average for a given height. While there is no clear correlation between obesity during infancy and obesity at the age of 16 years, some research suggests that overfeeding during infancy may lead to the creation of an excess of fat cells, which remain in the body throughout life and may predispose a person to be overweight. In fact, weight gains during infancy are associated with weight at age 6. Other research shows an association between obesity after the age of 6 and adult obesity, suggesting that obesity in babies ultimately may be found to be associated with adult weight problems. A clear link between overweight babies and overweight adults, however, has not yet been found (Gunnarsdottir & Thorsdottir, 2003; Toschke et al., 2004; Dennison et al., 2006).

Although the evidence linking infant obesity to adult obesity is inconclusive, it's plain that the societal view that "a fat baby is a healthy baby" is not necessarily correct. Parents should concentrate less on their baby's weight and more on providing appropriate nutrition, as discussed in the *From Research to Practice* box. But just what constitutes proper nutrition? Probably the biggest question revolves around whether infants should be breastfed or given a formula of commercially processed cow's milk with vitamin additives, as we consider next.

nonorganic failure to thrive a disorder in which infants stop growing due to a lack of stimulation and attention as the result of inadequate parenting.

From Research to Practice

Fast-Food Babies

At 20 pounds and 27 inches long, Zachary Miller was a happy and healthy, but not especially active, baby. "The pediatrician told me, 'The big ones don't like to move,'" says Zach's mom, Ellie. "She told me to put him on the floor and on his tummy as often as possible. He hates that. But it does get him to push up on his arms and roll over." At 7 months, Zach was already overweight. (Sachs, 2006, p. 112)

Childhood obesity is on the rise, and as Zachary Miller's story suggests, the problem sometimes begins at a very early age. Children of overweight parents are particularly at risk of becoming overweight themselves, but heredity seems to be only part of the explanation. At issue is what children are eating in their first years of life—or rather, what their parents are feeding them (Breen, Plomin, & Wardle, 2006; Flegal, Tabak, & Ogden, 2006; Mennella, Kennedy, & Beauchamp, 2006).

Research shows that children's food preferences are determined early on. One study that tracked children's eating habits over a period of 6 years found that the strongest predictor of preferred foods at age 8 was preferred foods at age 4, and moreover that children were more likely to accept new foods before age 4 than after that time. In other words, children develop their taste for certain foods at an early age and then tend to stick with those foods as they get older (Skinner et al., 2002).

But the real issue is what children are developing a taste for: the same study also found that children tended to like foods that their mothers liked, which is unsurprising—the mothers tended not to offer foods that they themselves did not like (Skinner et al., 2002).

So what kinds of foods are parents feeding their young children? Another study examined the foods actually eaten over the course of a day by 3,000 infants and toddlers aged 4 to 24 months. Some of the findings were startling: infants as young as 7 months were being fed adult diets. About a quarter of infants and toddlers between 7 and 24 months were eating no vegetables and about the same proportion were eating no fruits. Even among the children who were eating vegetables, french fries topped the list for toddlers over 18 months—and it was in the top three vegetables for infants between 9 and 12 months. By 8 months, nearly half of infants were already consuming desserts or sweetened drinks. By 24 months, a majority of toddlers were eating pastries and nearly half were drinking sweetened drinks (Fox et al., 2004).

These findings reveal a problem with how we are feeding our children in the critical early years, when they are developing food preferences and eating habits that will likely remain with them through adulthood. Convenience foods that are high in sugar and fat but low in nutrients may be a significant component of parents' diets, but if parents provide these same foods to their young children, they may be paving the way to a lifetime of unhealthful dietary habits. Experts recommend that such foods be offered to infants and toddlers sparingly, if at all. Better options include fruits, vegetables, or grains in place of snack foods and water, milk, or pure fruit juices in place of sweetened drinks. Providing these foods may take extra planning and effort on the part of parents—especially when they are foods that parents don't particularly like themselves—but experts agree that doing so is essential to stem the growing problem of childhood obesity (Fox et al., 2004; O'Dea and Wilson, 2006; Linsday et al., 2006).

- *If you were to advise new parents on the right and wrong foods to offer their newborn child, what would you tell them?*

- *Why might parents be inclined to serve their young children unhealthful adult foods? Why might they not be serving the children more fruits and vegetables instead?*

Breast or Bottle?

Fifty years ago, if a mother asked her pediatrician whether breastfeeding or bottle-feeding was better, she would have received a simple and clear-cut answer: Bottle-feeding was the preferred method. Starting around the 1940s, the general belief among child-care experts was that breastfeeding was an obsolete method that put children unnecessarily at risk.

With bottle-feeding, the argument went, parents could keep track of the amount of milk their baby was receiving and could thereby ensure that the child was taking in sufficient nutrients. In contrast, mothers who breastfed their babies could never be certain just how much milk their infants were getting. Use of the bottle was also supposed to help mothers keep their feedings to a rigid schedule of one bottle every 4 hours, the recommended procedure at that time.

Today, however, a mother would get a very different answer to the same question. Child-care authorities agree: For the first 12 months of life, there is no better food for an infant than breast milk. Breast milk not only contains all the nutrients necessary for growth, but it also seems to offer some degree of immunity to a variety of childhood diseases, such as respiratory illnesses, ear infections, diarrhea, and allergies. Breast milk is more easily digested than cow's milk or formula, and it is sterile, warm, and convenient for the mother to dispense. There is even some evidence

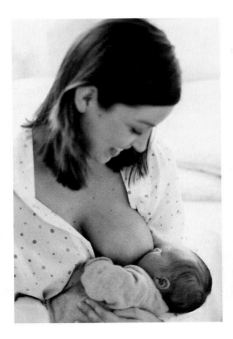

Breast or bottle? Although infants receive adequate nourishment from breast- or bottle-feeding, most authorities agree "breast is best."

that breast milk may enhance cognitive growth, leading to high adult intelligence (Feldman & Eidelman, 2003; American Academy of Pediatrics, 2005; Der, Batty, & Deary, 2006).

Breastfeeding also offers significant emotional advantages for both mother and child. Most mothers report that the experience of breastfeeding brings about feelings of well-being and intimacy with their infants, perhaps because of the production of endorphins in mothers' brains. Breastfed infants are also more responsive to their mothers' touch and their mothers' gaze during feeding, and they are calmed and soothed by the experience. As we'll see in Chapter 6, this mutual responsiveness may lead to healthy social development (Gerrish & Mennella, 2000; Zenardo et al., 2001).

Breastfeeding may even be advantageous to mothers' health. For instance, research suggests that women who breastfeed may have lower rates of ovarian cancer and breast cancer prior to menopause. Furthermore, the hormones produced during breastfeeding help shrink the

"I forgot to say I was breast-fed."

uteruses of women following birth, enabling their bodies to return more quickly to a prepregnancy state. These hormones also may inhibit ovulation, reducing (but not eliminating!) the chance of becoming pregnant, and thereby helping to space the birth of additional children (Altemus et al., 1995; Ma et al., 2006; Kim et al., 2007).

Breastfeeding is not a cure-all for infant nutrition and health, and the millions of individuals who have been raised on formula should not be concerned that they have suffered irreparable harm. (In fact, recent research suggests that infants fed enriched formula show better cognitive development than those using traditional formula.) But it does continue to be clear that the popular slogan used by groups advocating the use of breastfeeding is right on target: "Breast Is Best" (Birch et al., 2000; Avestad et al., 2003; Rabin, 2006).

Social Patterns in Breastfeeding.

Although it has several advantages, only about 70% of all new mothers in the United States employ breastfeeding. Issues of age, social status, and race influence the decision of whether to breastfeed. The rates of breastfeeding are highest among women who are older, have better education, are of higher socioeconomic status, and have social or cultural support. Connected to these factors, breastfeeding among Caucasian mothers in the United States occurs at a significantly higher rate than for African American mothers. Globally, countries in which there is significant social and governmental support for breastfeeding have higher rates of breastfeeding than in the United States. For example, almost all mothers in the Scandinavian countries of Norway, Denmark, and Sweden breastfeed (Forste, Weiss, & Lippincott, 2001; Greve, 2003; Merewood, 2006; see Figure 4-11).

If authorities are in agreement about the benefits of breastfeeding, why in so many cases do women not breastfeed? In some cases, they can't. Some women have difficulties producing milk, while others are taking some type of medicine or have an infectious disease such as AIDS that could be passed on to their infants through breast milk. Sometimes infants are too ill to nurse successfully. And in many cases of adoption, where the birth mother is unavailable after giving birth, the adoptive mother has no choice but to bottle-feed.

For some women, the decision not to breastfeed is based on practical considerations. Women who hold jobs outside the home may not have sufficiently flexible schedules to breastfeed their infants. This problem is particularly true with less affluent women who may have less control over their schedules. Such problems may account for the lower rate of breastfeeding among mothers of lower socioeconomic status, who may lack social support for breastfeeding (Arlotti, Cottrell, & Hughes, 1998; Cardala et al., 2003).

Education is also an issue: Some women simply do not receive adequate information and advice regarding the advantages of breastfeeding, and choose to use formula because they think it is the best choice. Indeed, some hospitals may inadvertently encourage the use of formula by including it in the gift packets new mothers receive as they leave the hospital.

In developing countries, the use of formula is particularly problematic. Because formula often comes in powdered form that must be mixed with water, pollution of the local water supply can make using formula particularly dangerous. Poverty-stricken parents may dilute

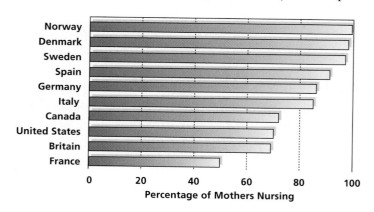

FIGURE 4-11 NURSING MOTHERS

Norway and other European countries lead the way in the percentage of mothers who breastfeed their newborns. What social changes in the United States might encourage more mothers to breastfeed?

(*Source:* LaLeche League International, 2003.)

Infants generally start solid foods at around 4 to 6 months, gradually working their way up to a variety of different foods.

formula too much because they can't afford to buy the proper amounts, leading to problems with infant malnutrition or undernutrition.

Educational, social, and cultural support for breastfeeding is particularly important. Women need to be educated about the health advantages of breastfeeding and given specific information on just how to do it. Although breastfeeding is a natural act, mothers require a bit of practice to learn how to hold the baby properly and position the nipple correctly, so he or she can "latch on." They may also need help dealing with such potential problems as sore nipples.

Introducing Solid Foods: When and What?

Although pediatricians agree that breast milk is the ideal initial food, at some point infants require more nutriments than breast milk alone can provide. The American Academy of Pediatrics and the American Academy of Family Physicians suggest that babies can start solids at around 6 months, although they aren't needed until 9 to 12 months of age (American Academy of Pediatrics, 1997; American Academy of Family Physicians, 1997).

Solid foods are introduced into an infant's diet gradually, one at a time, in order to be able to be aware of preferences and allergies. Most often cereal comes first, followed by strained fruits. Vegetables and other foods typically are introduced next, although the order varies significantly from one infant to another.

The timing of *weaning*, the gradual cessation of breast- or bottle-feeding, varies greatly. In developed countries such as the United States, weaning frequently occurs as early as 3 or 4 months. On the other hand, some mothers continue breastfeeding for 2 or 3 years. The American Academy of Pediatrics recommends that infants be fed breast milk for the first 12 months (American Academy of Pediatrics, 1997).

Review and Apply

Review

- Reflexes are universal, genetically acquired physical behaviors.
- During infancy children reach a series of milestones in their physical development on a fairly consistent schedule, with some individual and cultural variations.
- Training and cultural expectations affect the timing of the development of motor skills.
- Nutrition strongly affects physical development. Malnutrition can slow growth, affect intellectual performance, and cause diseases such as marasmus and kwashiorkor. The victims of undernutrition also suffer negative effects.
- The advantages of breastfeeding are numerous, including nutritional, immunological, emotional, and physical benefits for the infant, and physical and emotional benefits for the mother as well.

Applying Lifespan Development

- What advice might you give a friend who is concerned that her infant is still not walking at 14 months, when every other baby she knows started walking by the first birthday?
- *From an educator's perspective:* What might be some of the reasons that malnourishment, which slows physical growth, also harms IQ scores and school performance? How might malnourishment affect education in third-world countries?

The Development of the Senses

William James, one of the founding fathers of psychology, believed the world of the infant is a "blooming, buzzing confusion" (James, 1890/1950). Was he right?

In this case, James's wisdom failed him. The newborn's sensory world does lack the clarity and stability that we can distinguish as adults, but day by day the world grows increasingly comprehensible as the infant's ability to sense and perceive the environment develops. In fact, babies appear to thrive in an environment enriched by pleasing sensations.

The processes that underlie infants' understanding of the world around them are sensation and perception. **Sensation** is the physical stimulation of the sense organs, and **perception** is the mental process of sorting out, interpreting, analyzing, and integrating stimuli from the sense organs and brain.

The study of infants' capabilities in the realm of sensation and perception challenges the ingenuity of investigators. As we'll see, researchers have developed a number of procedures for understanding sensation and perception in different realms.

Visual Perception: Seeing the World

From the time of Lee Eng's birth, everyone who met him felt that he gazed at them intently. His eyes seemed to meet those of visitors. They seemed to bore deeply and knowingly into the faces of people who looked at him.

How good, in fact, was Lee's vision, and what, precisely, could he make out of his environment? Quite a bit, at least up close. According to some estimates, a newborn's distance vision ranges from 20/200 to 20/600, which means that an infant can only see with accuracy visual material up to 20 feet that an adult with normal vision is able to see with similar accuracy from a distance of between 200 and 600 feet (Haith, 1991).

These figures indicate that infants' distance vision is one-tenth to one-third that of the average adult's. This isn't so bad, actually: The vision of newborns provides the same degree of distance acuity as the uncorrected vision of many adults who wear eyeglasses or contact lenses. (If you wear glasses or contact lenses, remove them to get a sense of what an infant can see of the world.) Furthermore, infants' distance vision grows increasingly acute. By 6 months of age, the average infant's vision is already 20/20—in other words, identical to that of adults (Aslin, 1987; Cavallini, Fazzi, & Viviani, 2002).

Other visual abilities grow rapidly. For instance, *binocular vision*, the ability to combine the images coming to each eye to see depth and motion, is achieved at around 14 weeks. Before then, infants do not integrate the information from each eye.

Depth perception is a particularly useful ability, helping babies acknowledge heights and avoid falls. In a classic study by developmental psychologists Eleanor Gibson and Richard Walk (1960) infants were placed on a sheet of heavy glass. A checkered pattern appeared under one-half of the glass sheet, making it seem that the infant was on a stable floor. However, in the middle of the glass sheet, the pattern dropped down several feet, forming an apparent "visual cliff." The question Gibson and Walk asked was whether infants would willingly crawl across the cliff when called by their mothers (see Figure 4-12).

The results were unambiguous. Most of the infants in the study, who ranged in age from 6 to 14 months, could not be coaxed over the apparent cliff. Clearly the ability to perceive depth had already developed in most of them by that age. On the other hand, the experiment did not pinpoint when depth perception emerged, since only infants who had already learned to crawl could be tested. But other experiments, in which infants of 2 and 3 months were placed on their stomachs above the apparent floor and above the visual cliff, revealed differences in heart rate between the two positions (Campos, Langer, & Krowitz, 1970).

Still, it is important to keep in mind that such findings do not permit us to know whether infants are responding to depth itself or merely to the *change* in visual stimuli that occurs when they are moved from a lack of depth to depth.

While an infant's distant vision is 10 to 30 times poorer than the average adult's, the vision of newborns provides the same degree of distance acuity as the uncorrected vision of many adults who wear eyeglasses or contact lenses.

sensation   the physical stimulation of the sense organs.

perception   the sorting out, interpretation, analysis, and integration of stimuli involving the sense organs and brain.

FIGURE 4-12   VISUAL CLIFF

The "visual cliff" experiment examines the depth perception of infants. Most infants in the age range of 6 to 14 months cannot be coaxed to cross the cliff, apparently responding to the fact that the patterned area drops several feet.

Infants also show clear visual preferences, preferences that are present from birth. Given a choice, infants reliably prefer to look at stimuli that include patterns than to look at simpler stimuli (see Figure 4-13). How do we know? Developmental psychologist Robert Fantz (1963) created a classic test. He built a chamber in which babies could lie on their backs and see pairs of visual stimuli above them. Fantz could determine which of the stimuli the infants were looking at by observing the reflections of the stimuli in their eyes.

Fantz's work was the impetus for a great deal of research on the preferences of infants, most of which points to a critical conclusion: Infants are genetically preprogrammed to prefer particular kinds of stimuli. For instance, just minutes after birth they show preferences for certain colors, shapes, and configurations of various stimuli. They prefer curved over straight lines, three-dimensional figures to two-dimensional ones, and human faces to nonfaces. Such capabilities may be a reflection of the existence of highly specialized cells in the brain that react to stimuli of a particular pattern, orientation, shape, and direction of movement (Rubenstein, Kalakanis, & Langlois, 1999; Hubel & Wiesel, 1979, 2004; Kellman & Arterberry, 2006).

However, genetics is not the sole determinant of infant visual preferences. Just a few hours after birth, infants have already learned to prefer their own mother's face to other faces. Similarly, between the ages of 6 and 9 months, infants become more adept at distinguishing between the faces of humans, while they become less able to distinguish faces of members of other species (see Figure 4-14). They also distinguish between male and female faces. Such findings provide another clear piece of evidence of how heredity and environmental experiences are woven together to determine an infant's capabilities (Mondloch et al., 1999; Pascalis, deHaan, & Nelson, 2002; Turati et al., 2006; Ramsey-Rennels & Langlois, 2006).

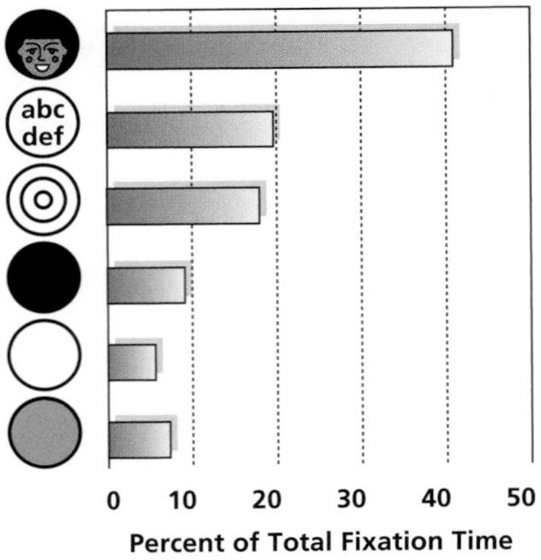

Auditory Perception: The World of Sound

What is it about a mother's lullaby that helps soothe a crying, fussy baby? Some clues emerge when we look at the capabilities of infants in the realm of auditory sensation and perception.

0   10   20   30   40   50
Percent of Total Fixation Time

FIGURE 4-13   PREFERRING COMPLEXITY

In a classic experiment, researcher Robert Fantz found that 2- and 3-month-old infants preferred to look at more complex stimuli than simple ones.

(*Source:* Adapted from Fantz, 1961.)

Infants hear from the time of birth—and even before. As noted in Chapter 2, the ability to hear begins prenatally. Even in the womb, the fetus responds to sounds outside of its mother. Furthermore, infants are born with preferences for particular sound combinations (Schellenberg & Trehub, 1996; Trehub, 2003).

Because they have had some practice in hearing before birth, it is not surprising that infants have reasonably good auditory perception after they are born. In fact, infants actually are more sensitive to certain very high and very low frequencies than adults—a sensitivity that seems to increase during the first 2 years of life. On the other hand, infants are initially less sensitive than adults to middle-range frequencies. Eventually, however, their capabilities within the middle range improve (Fenwick & Morongiello, 1991; Werner & Marean, 1996; Fernald, 2001).

It is not fully clear what leads to the improvement during infancy in sensitivity to mid-frequency sounds, although it may be related to the maturation of the nervous system. More puzzling is why, after infancy, children's ability to hear very high and low frequencies gradually declines. One explanation may be that exposure to high levels of noise may diminish capacities at the extreme ranges (Trehub et al., 1988, 1989; Stewart, Scherer, & Lehman, 2003).

In addition to the ability to detect sound, infants need several other abilities in order to hear effectively. For instance, *sound localization* permits us to pinpoint the direction from which a sound is emanating. Compared to adults, infants have a slight handicap in this task because effective sound localization requires the use of the slight difference in the times at which a sound reaches our two ears. Sound that we hear first in the right ear tells us that the source of the sound is to our right. Because infants' heads are smaller than those of adults, the difference in timing of the arrival of sound at the two ears is less than it is in adults, so they have difficulty determining from which direction sound is coming.

However, despite the potential limitation brought about by their smaller heads, infants' sound localization abilities are actually fairly good even at birth, and they reach adult levels of success by the age of 1 year. Interestingly, their improvement is not steady: Although we don't know why, studies show that the accuracy of sound localization actually declines between birth and 2 months of age, but then begins to increase (Clifton, 1992; Litovsky & Ashmead, 1997; Fenwick & Morrongiello, 1998).

Infants can discriminate groups of different sounds, in terms of their patterns and other acoustical characteristics, quite well. For instance, infants as young as 6 months old can detect the change of a single note in a six-tone melody. They also react to changes in musical key and rhythm. In sum, they listen with a keen ear to the melodies of lullabies sung to them by their mothers and fathers (Trehub, 2003; Phillips-Silver & Trainor, 2005; Masataka, 2006).

Even more important to their ultimate success in the world, young infants are capable of making the fine discriminations that their future understanding of language will require (Bijeljac-Babic, Bertoncini, & Mehler, 1993). For instance, in one classic study, a group of 1- to 4-month-old infants sucked on nipples that activated a recording of a person saying "ba" every time they sucked (Eimas et al., 1971). At first, their interest in the sound made them suck vigorously. Soon, though, they became acclimated to the sound (through a process called *habituation*, discussed in Chapter 3) and sucked with less energy. On the other hand, when the experimenters changed the sound to "pa," the infants immediately showed new interest and sucked with greater vigor once again. The clear conclusion: Infants as young as 1 month old could make the distinction between the two similar sounds (Eimas et al., 1971; Goodman & Nusbaum, 1994; Miller & Eimas, 1995).

Even more intriguing, young infants are able to discriminate one language from another. By the age of 4 1/2 months, infants are able to discriminate their own names from other, similar-sounding words. By the age of 5 months, they can distinguish the difference between English and Spanish passages, even when the two are similar in meter, number of syllables, and speed of recitation. In fact, some evidence suggests that even 2-day-olds show preferences for the language spoken by those around them over other languages (Mandel, Jusczyk, & Pisoni, 1995; Rivera-Gaxiola, Silva-Pereyra, & Kuhl, 2005; Kuhl, 2006).

FIGURE 4-14   DISTINGUISHING FACES

Examples of faces used in a study found that 6-month-old infants distinguished human or monkey faces equally well, whereas 9-month-olds were less adept at distinguishing monkey faces as compared to human faces. (*Source:* Pascalis, de Haan, & Nelson, 2002, p. 1322.)

By the age of 4 months infants are able to discriminate their own names from other, similar sounding, words. What are some ways an infant is able to discriminate his or her name from other words?

Infants' sense of smell is so well developed they can distinguish their mothers on the basis of smell alone.

Given their ability to discriminate a difference in speech as slight as the difference between two consonants, it is not surprising that infants can distinguish different people on the basis of voice. In fact, from an early age they show clear preferences for some voices over others. For instance, in one experiment newborns were allowed to suck a nipple that turned on a recording of a human voice reading a story. The infants sucked significantly longer when the voice was that of their mother than when the voice was that of a stranger (DeCasper & Fifer, 1980; Fifer, 1987).

How do such preferences arise? One hypothesis is that prenatal exposure to the mother's voice is the key. As support for this conjecture, researchers point to the fact that newborns do not show a preference for their fathers' voices over other male voices. Furthermore, newborns prefer listening to melodies sung by their mothers before they were born to melodies that were not sung before birth. It seems, then, that the prenatal exposure to their mothers' voices—although muffled by the liquid environment of the womb—helps shape infants' listening preferences (DeCasper & Prescott, 1984; Kisilevsky et al., 2003; Saffran, Werker, & Werner, 2006).

Smell and Taste

What do infants do when they smell a rotten egg? Pretty much what adults do—crinkle their noses and generally look unhappy. On the other hand, the scents of bananas and butter both produce a pleasant reaction on the part of infants (Steiner, 1979; Pomares, Schirrer, & Abadie, 2002).

The sense of smell is so well developed, even among very young infants, that at least some 12- to 18-day-old babies can distinguish their mothers on the basis of smell alone. For instance, in one experiment infants were exposed to the smell of gauze pads worn under the arms of adults the previous evening. Infants who were being breastfed were able to distinguish their mothers' scent from those of other adults. However, not all infants could do this: Those who were being bottle-fed were unable to make the distinction. Moreover, both breastfed and bottle-fed infants were unable to distinguish their fathers on the basis of odor (Porter, Bologh, & Malkin, 1988; Soussignan et al., 1997; Mizuno & Ueda, 2004).

Infants seem to have an innate sweet tooth (even before they have teeth!), and they show facial expressions of disgust when they taste something bitter. Very young infants smile when a sweet-tasting liquid is placed on their tongues. They also suck harder at a bottle if it is sweetened. Since breast milk has a sweet taste, it is possible that this preference may be part of our evolutionary heritage, retained because it offered a survival advantage. Infants who preferred sweet tastes may have been more likely to ingest sufficient nutrients and to survive than those who did not (Steiner, 1979; Rosenstein & Oster, 1988; Porges, Lipsitt, & Lewis, 1993).

Infants also develop taste preferences based on what their mothers drank while they were in the womb. For instance, one study found that women who drank carrot juice while pregnant had children who had a preference for the taste of carrots during infancy (Mennella, 2000).

Sensitivity to Pain and Touch

When Eli Rosenblatt was 8 days old, he participated in the ancient Jewish ritual of circumcision (which we discussed in Chapter 3). As he lay nestled in his father's arms, the foreskin of his penis was removed. Although Eli shrieked in what seemed to his anxious parents as pain, he soon settled down and went back to sleep. Others who had watched the ceremony assured his parents that at Eli's age babies don't really experience pain, at least not in the same way that adults do.

Were Eli's relatives accurate in saying that young infants don't experience pain? In the past, many medical practitioners would have agreed. In fact, because they assumed that infants didn't experience pain in truly bothersome ways, many physicians routinely carried out medical procedures, and even some forms of surgery, without the use of painkillers or anesthesia.

Their argument was that the risks from the use of anesthesia outweighed the potential pain that the young infants experienced.

Contemporary Views on Infant Pain.   Today, however, it is widely acknowledged that infants are born with the capacity to experience pain. Obviously, no one can be sure if the experience of pain in children is identical to that in adults, any more than we can tell if an adult friend who complains of a headache is experiencing pain that is more or less severe than our own pain when we have a headache.

What we do know is that pain produces distress in infants. Their heartbeat increases, they sweat, show facial expressions of discomfort, and change the intensity and tone of crying when they are hurt (Simons et al., 2003; Warnock & Sandrin, 2004).

There appears to be a developmental progression in reactions to pain. For example, a newborn infant who has her heel pricked for a blood test responds with distress, but it takes her several seconds to show the response. In contrast, only a few months later, the same procedure brings a much more immediate response. It is possible that the delayed reaction in infants is produced by the relatively slower transmission of information within the newborn's less-developed nervous system (Anand & Hickey, 1992; Axia, Bonichini, & Benini, 1995; Puchalsi & Hummel, 2002).

Research with rats suggests that exposure to pain in infancy may lead to a permanent rewiring of the nervous system resulting in greater sensitivity to pain during adulthood. Such findings indicate that infants who must undergo extensive, painful medical treatments and tests may be unusually sensitive to pain when older (Ruda et al., 2000; Taddio et al., 2002).

In response to increasing support for the notion that infants experience pain and that its effects may be long-lasting, medical experts now endorse the use of anesthesia and painkillers during surgery for even the youngest infants. According to the American Academy of Pediatrics, painkilling drugs are appropriate in most types of surgery—including circumcision.

Responding to Touch.   It clearly does not take the sting of pain to get an infant's attention. Even the youngest infants respond to gentle touches, such as a soothing caress, which can calm a crying, fussy infant (Hertenstein & Campos, 2001; Hertenstein, 2002).

In fact, touch is one of the most highly developed sensory systems in a newborn, and it is also one of the first to develop; there is evidence that by 32 weeks after conception, the entire body is sensitive to touch. Furthermore, several of the basic reflexes present at birth, such as the rooting reflex, require touch sensitivity to operate: An infant must sense a touch near the mouth in order to seek automatically a nipple to suck (Haith, 1986).

Infants' abilities in the realm of touch are particularly helpful in their efforts to explore the world. Several theorists have suggested that one of the ways children gain information about the world is through touching. As mentioned earlier, at the age of 6 months, infants are apt to place almost any object in their mouths, apparently taking in data about its configuration from their sensory responses to the feel of it in their mouths (Ruff, 1989).

In addition, as we first discussed in Chapter 3, touch plays an important role in an organism's future development, for it triggers a complex chemical reaction that assists infants in their efforts to survive. For example, gentle massage stimulates the production of certain chemicals in an infant's brain that instigate growth. Periodic massage is also helpful in treating several kinds of medical conditions, including premature delivery and the effects of prenatal exposure to AIDS or cocaine. Furthermore, massage is beneficial for infants and even older children whose mothers are depressed and for those who suffer from burns, cancer, asthma, and a variety of other medical conditions (Hernandez-Reif et al., 1999; Dieter et al., 2003a; Field, Diego & Hernandez-Reif, 2006; Field, Hernandez-Reif, & Diego, 2006).

In one study that illustrates the benefits of massage, a group of preterm infants who were massaged for 15 minutes three times a day gained weight some 50% faster than a group of preterm infants of the same age who were not stroked (see Figure 4-15). The massaged infants also were more active and responsive to stimuli. Ultimately, the preterm infants who

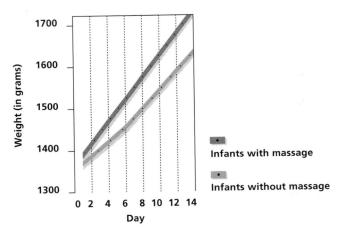

FIGURE 4-15 EFFECT OF MASSAGE ON WEIGHT GAIN

The weight gain of premature infants who were systematically massaged is greater than those who did not receive the massage. How can this phenomenon be explained?

(*Source:* T. M. Field, 1988.)

• • • • • • • • • • • • • • • • • •

multimodal approach to perception the approach that considers how information that is collected by various individual sensory systems is integrated and coordinated.

were massaged were discharged earlier from the hospital, and the costs of their medical care were significantly lower than for infants in the unmassaged group (Field, 1988a, 1995).

Multimodal Perception: Combining Individual Sensory Inputs

When Eric Pettigrew was 7 months old, his grandparents presented him with a squeaky rubber doll. As soon as he saw it, he reached out for it, grasped it in his hand, and listened as it squeaked. He seemed delighted with the gift.

One way of considering Eric's sensory reaction to the doll is to focus on each of the senses individually: what the doll looked like to Eric, how it felt in his hand, and what it sounded like. In fact, this approach has dominated the study of sensation and perception in infancy.

However, let's consider another approach: We might examine how the various sensory responses are integrated with one another. Instead of looking at each individual sensory response, we could consider how the responses work together and are combined to produce Eric's ultimate reaction. The **multimodal approach to perception** considers how information that is collected by various individual sensory systems is integrated and coordinated.

Although the multimodal approach is a relatively recent innovation in the study of how infants understand their sensory world, it raises some fundamental issues about the development of sensation and perception. For instance, some researchers argue that sensations are initially integrated with one another in the infant, while others maintain that the infant's sensory systems are initially separate and that brain development leads to increasing integration (De Gelder, 2000; Lickliter & Bahrick, 2000; Lewkowicz, 2002).

We do not know yet which view is correct. However, it does appear that by an early age infants are able to relate what they have learned about an object through one sensory channel to what they have learned about it through another. For instance, even 1-month-old infants are able to recognize by sight objects that they have previously held in their mouths but never seen (Meltzoff, 1981; Steri & Spelke, 1988). Clearly, some cross-talk between various sensory channels is already possible a month after birth.

The senses of sight and touch are integrated by infants through multimodal perception.

Infants' abilities at multimodal perception showcase the sophisticated perceptual abilities of infants, which continue to grow throughout the period of infancy. Such perceptual growth is aided by infants' discovery of **affordances,** the options that a given situation or stimulus provides. For example, infants learn that they might potentially fall when walking down a steep ramp—that is, the ramp *affords* the possibility of falling. Such knowledge is crucial as infants make the transition from crawling to walking. Similarly, infants learn that an object shaped in a certain way can slip out of their hands if not grasped correctly. For example, Eric is learning that his toy has several affordances: He can grab it and squeeze it, listen to it squeak, and even chew comfortably on it if he is teething (Adolph, 1997; McCarty & Ashmead, 1999; Flom & Bahrick, 2007; Wilcox et al., 2007).

> **affordances** options that a given situation or stimulus provides.

Becoming an Informed Consumer of Development

Exercising Your Infant's Body and Senses

Recall how cultural expectations and environments affect the age at which various physical milestones, such as the first step, occur. While most experts feel attempts to accelerate physical and sensory-perceptual development yield little advantage, parents should ensure that their infants receive sufficient physical and sensory stimulation. There are several specific ways to accomplish this goal:

- Carry a baby in different positions—in a backpack, in a frontpack, or in a football hold with the infant's head in the palm of your hand and its feet lying on your arm. This lets the infant view the world from several perspectives.

- Let infants explore their environment. Don't contain them too long in a barren environment. Let them crawl or wander around—after first making the environment "childproof" by removing dangerous objects.

- Engage in "rough-and-tumble" play. Wrestling, dancing, and rolling around on the floor—if not violent—are activities that are fun and that stimulate older infants' motor and sensory systems.

- Let babies touch their food and even play with it. Infancy is too early to start teaching table manners.

- Provide toys that stimulate the senses, particularly toys that can stimulate more than one sense at a time. For example, brightly colored, textured toys with movable parts are enjoyable and help sharpen infants' senses.

Review and Apply

Review

- Sensation refers to the activation of the sense organs by external stimuli. Perception is the analysis, interpretation, and integration of sensations.

- Infants' sensory abilities are surprisingly well developed at or shortly after birth. Their perceptions help them explore and begin to make sense of the world.

- Very early, infants can see depth and motion, distinguish colors and patterns, localize and discriminate sounds, and recognize the sound and smell of their mothers.

- Infants are sensitive to pain and touch, and most medical authorities now subscribe to procedures, including anesthesia, that minimize infants' pain.
- Infants also have a keen ability to integrate information from more than one sense.

Applying Lifespan Development

- What might be the advantages and disadvantages of swaddling, a practice in which a baby is snuggly wrapped in a blanket and that usually calms an infant?

- *From healthcare worker's perspective:* Persons who are born without the use of one sense often develop unusual abilities in one or more other senses. What can health-care professionals do to help infants who are lacking in a particular sense?

Epilogue

In this chapter, we discussed the nature and pace of infants' physical growth and the pace of less obvious growth in the brain and nervous system and in the regularity of infants' patterns and states.

We next looked at motor development, the development and uses of reflexes, the role of environmental influences on the pace and shape of motor development, and the importance of nutrition.

We closed the chapter with a look at the senses, and the infant's ability to combine data from multiple sensory sources.

Turn back for a moment to the prologue of this chapter, about a baby's first steps, and answer these questions.

1. Which principle or principles of growth (i.e., cephalocaudal, proximodistal, hierarchical integration, independence of systems) account for the progression of physical activities that precedes Josh's first steps?

2. What conclusions about Josh's future physical development can be drawn based on the fact that his first steps occurred approximately 2 months early? Can conclusions be drawn about his future cognitive development? Why?

3. In walking at 10 months of age, Josh outpaced his brother Jon by 4 months. Does this fact have any implications for the comparative physical or cognitive abilities of the two brothers? Why?

4. Do you think anything changed in the environment between the time Jon and Josh were born that might account for their different "first step" schedules? If you were researching this question, what environmental factors would you look for?

5. Why were Josh's parents so pleased and proud about his accomplishment, which is, after all, a routine and universal occurrence? What cultural factors exist in U.S. culture that make the "first steps" milestone so significant?

Looking Back

■ **How do the human body and nervous system develop?**

- Human babies grow rapidly in height and weight, especially during the first 2 years of life.

- Major principles that govern human growth include the cephalocaudal principle, the proximodistal principle, the principle of hierarchical integration, and the principle of the independence of systems.

- The nervous system contains a huge number of neurons, more than will be needed as an adult. For neurons to survive and become useful, they must form interconnections with other neurons based on the infant's experience of the world. "Extra" connections and neurons that are not used are eliminated as an infant develops.

■ **Does the environment affect the pattern of development?**

- Brain development, largely predetermined genetically, also contains a strong element of plasticity—a susceptibility to environmental influences.

- Many aspects of development occur during sensitive periods when the organism is particularly susceptible to environmental influences.

■ **What developmental tasks must infants undertake in this period?**

- One of the primary tasks of the infant is the development of rhythms—cyclical patterns that integrate individual behaviors. An important rhythm pertains to the infant's state—the degree of awareness it displays to stimulation.

- Reflexes are unlearned, automatic responses to stimuli that help newborns survive and protect themselves. Some reflexes also have value as the foundation for future, more conscious behaviors.

- The development of gross and fine motor skills proceeds along a generally consistent timetable in normal children, with substantial individual and cultural variations.

■ **What is the role of nutrition in physical development?**

- Adequate nutrition is essential for physical development. Malnutrition and undernutrition affect physical aspects of growth and also may affect IQ and school performance.

- Breastfeeding has distinct advantages over bottle-feeding, including the nutritional completeness of breast milk, its provision of a degree of immunity to certain childhood diseases, and its easy digestibility. In addition, breastfeeding offers significant physical and emotional benefits to both child and mother.

■ **What sensory capabilities do infants possess?**

- Sensation, the stimulation of the sense organs, differs from perception, the interpretation and integration of sensed stimuli.

- Infants' visual and auditory perception are rather well developed, as are the senses of smell and taste. Infants use their highly developed sense of touch to explore and experience the world. In addition, touch plays an important role in the individual's future development, which is only now being understood.

Key Terms and Concepts

cephalocaudal principle (p. 117)
proximodistal principle (p. 117)
principle of hierarchical integration (p. 118)
principle of the independence of systems (p. 118)
neuron (p. 118)
synapse (p. 118)
synaptic pruning (p. 119)
myelin (p. 119)

cerebral cortex (p. 120)
plasticity (p. 120)
sensitive period (p. 120)
rhythms (p. 121)
state (p. 121)
rapid eye movement (REM) sleep (p. 122)
sudden infant death syndrome (SIDS) (p. 124)
reflexes (p. 126)
dynamic systems theory (p. 130)
norms (p. 131)

Brazelton Neonatal Behavioral Assessment Scale (NBAS) (p. 131)
nonorganic failure to thrive (p. 134)
sensation (p. 139)
perception (p. 139)
multimodal approach to perception (p. 144)
affordances (p. 145)

5 Cognitive Development in Infancy

Chapter Overview

PIAGET'S APPROACH TO COGNITIVE DEVELOPMENT

Key Elements of Piaget's Theory

The Sensorimotor Period: The Earliest Stage of Cognitive Growth

Appraising Piaget: Support and Challenges

INFORMATION PROCESSING APPROACHES TO COGNITIVE DEVELOPMENT

Encoding, Storage, and Retrieval: The Foundations of Information Processing

Memory During Infancy: They Must Remember This . . .

Individual Differences in Intelligence: Is One Infant Smarter Than Another?

THE ROOTS OF LANGUAGE

The Fundamentals of Language: From Sounds to Symbols

The Origins of Language Development

Speaking to Children: The Language of Infant-Directed Speech

Prologue: The Electric Nanny

Thomas Bausman, 2, and his brother Jake, 10 months, are typical American babies. Every day, Thomas settles down to watch two hours of television, while Jake sits in front of the set for an hour, the national average for their respective ages. Their favorite thing to watch, by far? *Baby Einstein*. Anita Bausman could not be more pleased with her children's preference. Jake, she reports, learned colors, numbers, and his love of robots from the popular videos, which are filled with puppets, animals and moving objects, often set to classical music. "It's not just turning on Nickelodeon," Bausman says. "It's educational and beneficial. I know he's happy watching, and I can pop in and point out something onscreen, then go deal with the laundry." (Paul, 2006, p. 104)

Does viewing television benefit infants' cognitive development?

Can infants really become miniature Einsteins by watching educational media? What concepts are babies as young as 10-month-old Jake Bausman actually grasping, and what intellectual abilities remain undeveloped at that age? Can an infant's cognitive development really be accelerated through intellectual stimulation, or does the process unfold on its own timetable despite the best efforts of parents to hasten it?

We address these and related questions in this chapter as we consider cognitive development during the first years of life. Our examination focuses on the work of developmental researchers who seek to understand how infants develop their knowledge and understanding of the world. We first discuss the work of Swiss psychologist Jean Piaget, whose theory of developmental stages served as a highly influential impetus for a considerable amount of work on cognitive development. We look at both the limitations and the contributions of this important developmental specialist.

We then cover more contemporary views of cognitive development, examining information processing approaches that seek to explain how cognitive growth occurs. After considering how learning takes place, we examine memory in infants and the ways in which infants process, store, and retrieve information. We discuss the controversial issue of the recollection of events that occurred during infancy. We also address individual differences in intelligence.

Finally, we consider language, the cognitive skill that permits infants to communicate with others. We look at the roots of language in prelinguistic speech and trace the milestones indicating the development of language skills in the progression from baby's first words to phrases and sentences. We also look at the characteristics of adults' communication addressed to infants, characteristics that are surprisingly similar across different cultures.

After reading this chapter, you will be able to answer these questions:

- **What are the fundamental features of Piaget's theories of cognitive development?**
- **How do infants process information?**
- **How is infant intelligence measured?**
- **By what processes do children learn to use language?**
- **How do children influence adults' language?**

Looking Ahead

Piaget's Approach to Cognitive Development

Olivia's dad is wiping up the mess around the base of her high chair—for the third time today! It seems to him that 14-month-old Olivia takes great delight in dropping food from the high chair. She also drops toys, spoons, anything it seems, just to watch how it hits the floor. She almost appears to be experimenting to see what kind of noise or what size of splatter is created by each different thing she drops.

Swiss psychologist Jean Piaget (1896–1980) probably would have said that Olivia's dad is right in theorizing that Olivia is conducting her own series of experiments to learn more about the workings of her world. Piaget's views of the ways infants learn could be summed in a simple equation: *Action = Knowledge.*

Piaget argued that infants do not acquire knowledge from facts communicated by others, nor through sensation and perception. Instead, Piaget suggested that knowledge is the product of direct motor behavior. Although many of his basic explanations and propositions have been challenged by subsequent research, as we'll discuss later, the view that in significant ways infants learn by doing remains unquestioned (Piaget, 1952, 1962, 1983; Bullinger, 1997).

Swiss psychologist Jean Piaget.

Key Elements of Piaget's Theory

As first noted in Chapter 1, Piaget's theory is based on a stage approach to development. He assumed that all children pass through a series of four universal stages in a fixed order from birth through adolescence: sensorimotor, preoperational, concrete operational, and formal operational. He also suggested that movement from one stage to the next occurs when a child reaches an appropriate level of physical maturation *and* is exposed to relevant experiences. Without such experience, children are assumed to be incapable of reaching their cognitive potential. Some approaches to cognition focus on changes in the *content* of children's knowledge about the world, but Piaget argued that it was critical to also consider the changes in the *quality* of children's knowledge and understanding as they move from one stage to another.

For instance, as they develop cognitively, infants experience changes in their understanding about what can and cannot occur in the world. Consider a baby who participates in an experiment during which she is exposed to three identical versions of her mother all at the same time, thanks to some well-placed mirrors. A 3-month-old infant will interact happily with each of these images of mother. However, by 5 months of age, the child becomes quite agitated at the sight of multiple mothers. Apparently by this time the child has figured out that she has but one mother, and viewing three at a time is thoroughly alarming (Bower, 1977). To Piaget, such reactions suggest that a baby is beginning to master principles regarding the way the world operates, indicating that she has begun to construct a mental sense of the world that she didn't have 2 months earlier.

According to Piaget, a baby will use a sensorimotor *scheme*, such as mouthing or banging, to understand a new object.

Piaget believed that the basic building blocks of the way we understand the world are mental structures called **schemes,** organized patterns of functioning that adapt and change with mental development. At first, schemes are related to physical, or sensorimotor, activity, such as picking up or reaching for toys. As children develop, their schemes move to a mental level, reflecting thought. Schemes are similar to computer software: They direct and determine how data from the world, such as new events or objects, are considered and dealt with (Achenbach, 1992; Rakison & Oakes, 2003).

If you give a baby a new cloth book, for example, he or she will touch it, mouth it, and perhaps try to tear it or bang it on the floor. To Piaget, each of these actions may represent a scheme, and they are the infant's way of gaining knowledge and understanding of this new object. Adults, on the other hand, would use a different scheme upon encountering the book. Rather than picking it up and putting it in their mouths or banging it on the floor, they would probably be drawn to the letters on the page, seeking to understand the book through the meaning of the printed words—a very different approach.

Piaget suggested that two principles underlie the growth in children's schemes: assimilation and accommodation. **Assimilation** is the process by which people understand an experience in terms of their current stage of cognitive development and way of thinking. Assimilation occurs, then, when a stimulus or event is acted upon, perceived, and understood in accordance with existing patterns of thought. For example, an infant who tries to suck on any toy in the same way is assimilating the objects to her existing sucking scheme. Similarly, a child who encounters a flying squirrel at a zoo and calls it a "bird" is assimilating the squirrel to his existing scheme of bird.

In contrast, when we change our existing ways of thinking, understanding, or behaving in response to encounters with new stimuli or events, **accommodation** takes place. For instance, when a child sees a flying squirrel and calls it "a bird with a tail," he is beginning to *accommodate* new knowledge, modifying his scheme of bird.

Piaget believed that the earliest schemes are primarily limited to the reflexes with which we are all born, such as sucking and rooting. Infants start to modify these simple early schemes almost immediately, through the processes of assimilation and accommodation, in response to their exploration of the environment. Schemes quickly become more sophisticated as infants become more advanced in their motor capabilities—to Piaget, a signal of the potential for more

scheme an organized pattern of sensorimotor functioning.

assimilation the process in which people understand an experience in terms of their current stage of cognitive development and way of thinking.

accommodation changes in existing ways of thinking that occur in response to encounters with new stimuli or events.

sensorimotor stage (of cognitive development) Piaget's initial major stage of cognitive development, which can be broken down into six substages.

advanced cognitive development. Because Piaget's sensorimotor stage of development begins at birth and continues until the child is about 2 years old, we consider it here in detail. (In future chapters, we'll discuss development during the later stages.)

The Sensorimotor Period: The Earliest Stage of Cognitive Growth

Piaget suggests that the **sensorimotor stage**, the initial major stage of cognitive development, can be broken down into six substages. These are summarized in Table 5-1. It is important to keep in mind that although the specific substages of the sensorimotor period may at first appear to unfold with great regularity, as though infants reach a particular age and smoothly proceed into the next substage, the reality of cognitive development is somewhat different. First, the ages at which infants actually reach a particular stage vary a good deal among different children. The exact timing of a stage reflects an interaction between the infant's level of physical maturation

Table 5-1   Piaget's Six Substages of the Sensorimotor Stage

Substage	Age	Description	Example
Substage 1: Simple reflexes	First month of life	During this period, the various reflexes that determine the infant's interactions with the world are at the center of its cognitive life.	The sucking reflex causes the infant to suck at anything placed in its lips.
Substage 2: First habits and primary circular reactions	From 1 to 4 months	At this age infants begin to coordinate what were separate actions into single, integrated activities.	An infant might combine grasping an object with sucking on it, or staring at something with touching it.
Substage 3: Secondary circular reactions	From 4 to 8 months	During this period, infants take major strides in shifting their cognitive horizons beyond themselves and begin to act on the outside world.	A child who repeatedly picks up a rattle in her crib and shakes it in different ways to see how the sound changes is demonstrating her ability to modify her cognitive scheme about shaking rattles.
Substage 4: Coordination of secondary circular reactions	From 8 to 12 months	In this stage infants begin to use more calculated approaches to producing events, coordinating several schemes to generate a single act. They achieve object performance during this stage.	An infant will push one toy out of the way to reach another toy that is lying, partially exposed, under it.
Substage 5: Tertiary circular reactions	From 12 to 18 months	At this age infants develop what Piaget regards as the deliberate variation of actions that bring desirable consequences. Rather than just repeating enjoyable activities, infants appear to carry out miniature experiments to observe the consequences.	A child will drop a toy repeatedly, varying the position from which he drops it, carefully observing each time to see where it falls.
Substage 6: Beginnings of thought	From 18 months to 2 years	The major achievement of Substage 6 is the capacity for mental representation or symbolic thought. Piaget argued that only at this stage can infants imagine where objects that they cannot see might be.	Children can even plot in their heads unseen trajectories of objects, so that if a ball rolls under a piece of furniture, they can figure out where it is likely to emerge on the other side.

and the nature of the social environment in which the child is being raised. Consequently, although Piaget contended that the order of the substages does not change from one child to the next, he admitted that the timing can and does vary to some degree.

Piaget viewed development as a more gradual process than the notion of different stages might seem to imply. Infants do not go to sleep one night in one substage and wake up the next morning in the next one. Instead, there is a rather gradual and steady shifting of behavior as a child moves toward the next stage of cognitive development. Infants also pass through periods of transition, in which some aspects of their behavior reflect the next higher stage, while other aspects indicate their current stage (see Figure 5-1).

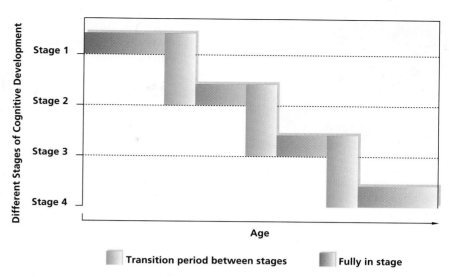

FIGURE 5-1 TRANSITIONS

Infants do not suddenly shift from one stage of cognitive development to the next. Instead, Piaget argues that there is a period of transition in which some behavior reflects one stage, while other behavior reflects the more advanced stage. Does this gradualism argue against Piaget's interpretation of stages?

Substage 1: Simple Reflexes.

The first substage of the sensorimotor period is *Substage 1: Simple reflexes*, encompassing the first month of life. During this time, the various inborn reflexes, described in Chapters 3 and 4, are at the center of a baby's physical and cognitive life, determining the nature of his or her interactions with the world. At the same time, some of the reflexes begin to accommodate the infant's experience with the nature of the world. For instance, an infant who is being breastfed, but who also receives supplemental bottles, may start to change the way he or she sucks, depending on whether a nipple is on a breast or a bottle.

Substage 2: First Habits and Primary Circular Reactions.

Substage 2: First habits and primary circular reactions, the second substage of the sensorimotor period, occurs from 1 to 4 months of age. In this period, infants begin to coordinate what were separate actions into single, integrated activities. For instance, an infant might combine grasping an object with sucking on it, or staring at something while touching it.

If an activity engages a baby's interests, he or she may repeat it over and over, simply for the sake of continuing to experience it. This repetition of a chance motor event helps the baby start building cognitive schemes through a process known as a *circular reaction. Primary circular reactions* are schemes reflecting an infant's repetition of interesting or enjoyable actions, just for the enjoyment of doing them, which focus on the infant's own body. Thus, when an infant first puts his thumb in his mouth and begins to suck, it is a mere chance event. However, when he repeatedly sucks his thumb in the future, it represents a primary circular reaction, which he is repeating because the sensation of sucking is pleasurable.

Substage 3: Secondary Circular Reactions.

In *Substage 3: Secondary circular reactions*, the infant's actions are more purposeful. According to Piaget, this third stage of cognitive development in infancy occurs from 4 to 8 months of age. During this period, a child begins to act upon the outside world. For instance, infants now seek to repeat enjoyable events in their environments if they happen to produce them through chance activities. A child who repeatedly picks up a rattle in her crib and shakes it in different ways to see how the sound changes is demonstrating her ability to modify her cognitive scheme about shaking rattles. She is engaging in what Piaget calls *secondary circular reactions*, which are schemes regarding repeated actions that bring about a desirable consequence. The major difference between primary circular reactions and secondary circular reactions is whether the infant's activity is focused on the infant and his or her own body (primary circular reactions), or involves actions relating to the world outside (secondary circular reactions).

Infants in substage 4 can coordinate their secondary circular reactions, displaying an ability to plan or calculate how to produce a desired outcome.

Substage 4: Coordination of Secondary Circular Reactions.   Some major leaps forward occur in *Substage 4: Coordination of secondary circular reactions,* which lasts from around 8 months to 12 months. In Substage 4, infants begin to employ *goal-directed behavior,* in which several schemes are combined and coordinated to generate a single act to solve a problem. For instance, they will push one toy out of the way to reach another toy that is lying, partially exposed, under it. They also begin to anticipate upcoming events.

Infants' newfound purposefulness, their ability to use means to attain particular ends, and their skill in anticipating future circumstances owe their appearance in part to the developmental achievement of object permanence that emerges in Substage 4. **Object permanence** is the realization that people and objects exist even when they cannot be seen. It is a simple principle, but its mastery has profound consequences.

Consider, for instance, 7-month-old Chu, who has yet to learn the idea of object permanence. Chu's mother shakes a rattle in front of him, then takes the rattle and places it under a blanket. To Chu, who has not mastered the concept of object permanence, the rattle no longer exists. He will make no effort to look for it.

Several months later, when he reaches Substage 4, the story is quite different (see Figure 5-2). This time, as soon as his mother places the rattle under the blanket, Chu tries to toss the cover aside, eagerly searching for the rattle. Chu clearly has learned that the object continues to exist even when it cannot be seen. For the infant who achieves an understanding of object permanence, then, out of sight is decidedly not out of mind.

The attainment of object permanence extends not only to inanimate objects, but to people, too. It gives Chu the security that his father and mother still exist even when they have left the room. This awareness is likely a key element in the development of social attachments, which we consider in Chapter 6. The recognition of object permanence also feeds infants' growing assertiveness: As they realize that an object taken away from them doesn't just cease to exist, but is merely somewhere else, their only-too-human reaction may be to want it back—and quickly.

Although the understanding of object permanence emerges in Substage 4, it is only a rudimentary understanding. It takes several months for the concept to be fully comprehended, and infants continue for several months to make certain kinds of errors relating to object permanence. For instance, they often are fooled when a toy is hidden first under one blanket and then

Before Object Permanence

After Object Permanence

FIGURE 5-2   OBJECT PERMANENCE

Before an infant has understood the idea of object permanence, he will not search for an object that has been hidden right before his eyes. But several months later, he will search for it, illustrating that he has attained object permanence. Why is the concept of object permanence important?

object permanence   the realization that people and objects exist even when they cannot be seen.

under a second blanket. In seeking out the toy, Substage 4 infants most often turn to the first hiding place, ignoring the second blanket under which the toy is currently located—even if the hiding was done in plain view. (For more on the role of play and toys from a toy designer's perspective, see the *Careers in Development* interview.)

Substage 5: Tertiary Circular Reactions.   *Substage 5: Tertiary circular reactions* is reached at around the age of 12 months and extends to 18 months. As the name of the stage indicates, during this period infants develop tertiary circular reactions, which are schemes regarding the deliberate variation of actions that bring desirable consequences. Rather than just repeating enjoyable activities, as they do with secondary circular reactions, infants appear to carry out miniature experiments to observe the consequences.

For example, Piaget observed his son Laurent dropping a toy swan repeatedly, varying the position from which he dropped it, carefully observing each time to see where it fell. Instead of just repeating the action each time (as in a secondary circular reaction), Laurent made modifications in the situation to learn about their consequences. As you may recall from our discussion of research methods in Chapter 1, this behavior represents the essence of the scientific method: An experimenter varies a situation in a laboratory to learn the effects of the variation. To infants in Substage 5, the world is their laboratory, and they spend their days leisurely carrying out one miniature experiment after another. Olivia, the baby described earlier who enjoyed dropping different things from her high chair, is a little scientist in action.

Careers in Lifespan Development

**Linda G. Miller,
Toy Consultant**

Education: BS in Education, Auburn University at Montgomery, Alabama; MA in Education, Auburn University, PhD, Education, Auburn University.

Position: Author, with Mary Jo Gibbs, *Making Toys for Infants and Toddlers: Using Ordinary Stuff for Extraordinary Play.* Adjunct Professor of Education, Auburn University at Montgomery, Alabama.

Home: Wetumpka, Alabama

When watching an infant play, one might think the child is randomly swatting various toys and objects, but research has found that children as young as infants not only interact with toys, but are developing cognitively at the same time.

According to educator and author Linda Miller, the young infant is very aware and sensitive of his or her background.

"Young children enjoy high-contrast colors, but brighter colors tend to overstimulate all children, not just infants," Miller said. "From research we have found that background colors such as beige are best."

"It's important to have the color in the activity instead of the environment. You don't want to have bright red walls, but rather have a red carpet where activity takes place," she added.

While toys can be in a variety of shapes, safety issues are of extreme importance when providing an infant with any toy.

"Infants are exploring their environments at all times," Miller noted, "and initially they explore with their mouths. It is also important not to have toys appropriate for older children in a younger child's environment."

Miller added that it is also important to introduce enough new toys to retain interest, but to retain enough of the older ones to maintain familiarity. "You wouldn't want to change cuddle toys every week," she added.

A major component in the development of an infant's cognitive abilities is to develop a connection with a familiar adult, and toys can be one way of achieving this.

"With a connection to a familiar adult young children feel safe and connected in the world and that feeling can sustain them into adulthood," Miller said. "Triangulation can be used to interact with a child, in which the adult interacts with the new toy and then introduces it to the child. The child then plays with the toy and the adult."

Dramatic play with items such as cuddle toys, dolls, and even hats can help in developing the child's connectedness with a familiar adult.

Miller also notes the importance of literacy in infant development. "It is very important to have books for young children and model that behavior," she explained. "Literacy begins at a very young age. The rhythm of the way sentences begin and end and the visual things associated with books are important."

"Songs and rhymes have also been found to be important," Miller added. "Some research has suggested that reading difficulties later in life can be linked to the absence of these songs and rhymes."

mental representation an internal image of a past event or object.

deffered imitation an act in which a person who is no longer present is imitated by children who have witnessed a similar act.

Substage 6: Beginnings of Thought. The final stage of the sensorimotor period is *Substage 6: Beginnings of thought*, which lasts from around 18 months to 2 years. The major achievement of Substage 6 is the capacity for mental representation, or symbolic thought. A **mental representation** is an internal image of a past event or object. Piaget argued that by this stage infants can imagine where objects might be that they cannot see. They can even plot in their heads unseen trajectories of objects, so if a ball rolls under a piece of furniture, they can figure out where it is likely to emerge on the other side.

Because of children's new abilities to create mental representations of objects, their understanding of causality also becomes more sophisticated. The attainment of mental representation also permits another important development: the ability to pretend. Using the skill of what Piaget refers to as **deferred imitation,** in which a person who is no longer present is imitated later, children are able to pretend that they are driving a car, feeding a doll, or cooking dinner long after they have witnessed such scenes played out in reality. To Piaget, deferred imitation provided clear evidence that children form internal mental representations.

Appraising Piaget: Support and Challenges

Most developmental researchers would probably agree that in many significant ways, Piaget's descriptions of how cognitive development proceeds during infancy are quite accurate (Harris, 1983, 1987; Marcovitch, Zelazo, & Schmuckler, 2003). Yet, there is substantial disagreement over the validity of the theory and many of its specific predictions.

With the attainment of the cognitive skill of deferred imitation, children are able to imitate people and scenes they have witnessed in the past.

Let's start with what is clearly accurate about the Piagetian approach. Piaget was a masterful reporter of children's behavior, and his descriptions of growth during infancy remain a monument to his powers of observation. Furthermore, literally thousands of studies have supported Piaget's view that children learn much about the world by acting on objects in their environment. Finally, the broad outlines sketched out by Piaget of the sequence of cognitive development and the increasing cognitive accomplishments that occur during infancy are generally accurate (Gratch & Schatz, 1987; Kail, 2004).

On the other hand, specific aspects of the theory have come under increasing scrutiny—and criticism—in the decades since Piaget carried out his pioneering work. For example, some researchers question the stage conception that forms the basis of Piaget's theory. Although, as noted earlier, even Piaget acknowledged that children's transitions between stages are gradual, critics contend that development proceeds in a much more continuous fashion. Rather than showing major leaps of competence at the end of one stage and the beginning of the next, improvement comes in more gradual increments, growing step-by-step in a skill-by-skill manner.

For instance, developmental researcher Robert Siegler suggests that cognitive development proceeds not in stages but in "waves." According to Siegler, children don't one day drop a mode of thinking and the next take up a new form. Instead, there is an ebb and flow of cognitive approaches that children use to understand the world. One day children may use one form of cognitive strategy, while another day they may choose a less advanced strategy—moving back and forth over a period of time. Although one strategy may be used most frequently at a given age, children still may have access to alternative ways of thinking. Siegler thus sees cognitive development as in constant flux (Siegler, 1995, 2003; Lavelli & Fogel, 2005).

Other critics dispute Piaget's notion that cognitive development is grounded in motor activities. They charge that Piaget overlooked the importance of the sensory and perceptual systems that are present from a very early age in infancy—systems about which Piaget knew little, since so much of the research illustrating how sophisticated they are even in infancy was done relatively recently. Studies of children born without arms and legs (due to their mothers' unwitting use of teratogenic drugs during pregnancy, as described in Chapter 2) show that such children display normal cognitive development, despite their lack of practice with motor activities—further evidence that the connection Piaget made between motor development and cognitive development was exaggerated (Decarrie, 1969; Butterworth, 1994).

To bolster their views, Piaget's critics also point to more recent studies that cast doubt on Piaget's view that infants are incapable of mastering the concept of object permanence until they are close to a year old. For instance, some work suggests that younger infants did not appear to understand object permanence because the techniques used to test their abilities were not sensitive enough to their true capabilities (Aguiar & Baillargeon, 2002; Baillargeon, 2004; Krojgaard, 2005).

It may be that a 4-month-old doesn't search for a rattle hidden under a blanket because she hasn't learned the motor skills necessary to do the searching—not because she doesn't understand that the rattle still exists. Similarly, the apparent inability of young infants to comprehend object permanence may reflect more about their memory deficits than their lack of understanding of the concept: The memories of young infants may be poor enough that they simply do not recall the earlier concealment of the toy. In fact, when more age-appropriate tasks were employed, some researchers found indications of object permanence in children as young as 3 1/2 months (Aguiar & Baillargeon, 2002; Wang, Baillargeon, & Paterson, 2005; Ruffman, Slade, & Redman, 2006).

Other types of behavior likewise seem to emerge earlier than Piaget suggested. For instance, recall the ability of neonates to imitate basic facial expressions of adults just hours after birth, as discussed in Chapter 3. The presence of this skill at such an early age contradicts Piaget's view that initially infants are able to imitate only behavior that they see in others, using parts of their own body that they can plainly view—such as their hands and feet. In fact, facial imitation suggests that humans are born with a basic, innate capability for imitating others' actions, a capability that depends on certain kinds of environmental experiences, but one that Piaget believed develops later in infancy (Meltzoff & Moore, 1989, 2002; Nagy, 2006).

Piaget's work also seems to describe children from developed, Western countries better than those in non-Western cultures. For instance, some evidence suggests that cognitive skills emerge on a different timetable for children in non-Western cultures than for children living in Europe and the United States. Infants raised in the Ivory Coast of Africa, for example, reach the various substages of the sensorimotor period at an earlier age than infants reared in France (Dasen et al., 1978). This is not altogether surprising, since parents in the Ivory Coast tend to emphasize motor skills more heavily than parents in Western societies, thereby providing greater opportunity for practice of those skills (Dasen et al., 1978; Rogoff & Chavajay, 1995; Mistry & Saraswathi, 2003).

Despite these problems regarding Piaget's view of the sensorimotor period, even his most passionate critics concede that he has provided us with a masterful description of the broad outlines of cognitive development during infancy. His failings seem to be in underestimating the capabilities of younger infants and in his claims that sensorimotor skills develop in a consistent, fixed pattern. Still, his influence has been enormous, and although the focus of many contemporary developmental researchers has shifted to newer information processing approaches that we discuss next, Piaget remains a towering and pioneering figure in the field of development (Fischer & Hencke, 1996; Roth, Slone, & Dar, 2000; Kail, 2004).

Appraising Piaget: Research on babies in non-Western cultures suggests that Piaget's stages are not universal, but are to some degree culturally derived.

Review and Apply

Review

- Jean Piaget's theory of human cognitive development involves a succession of stages through which children progress from birth to adolescence.

- As humans move from one stage to another, the way they understand the world changes.

- The sensorimotor stage, from birth to about 2 years, involves a gradual progression through simple reflexes, single coordinated activities, interest in the outside world, purposeful combinations of activities, manipulation of actions to produce desired outcomes, and symbolic thought. The sensorimotor stage has six substages.

- Piaget is respected as a careful observer of children's behavior and a generally accurate interpreter of the way human cognitive development proceeds, though subsequent research on his theory does suggest several limitations.

Applying Lifespan Development

- Think of a common young children's toy with which you are familiar. How might its use be affected by the principles of assimilation and accommodation?

- *From a caregiver's perspective:* In general, what are some implications for child-rearing practices of Piaget's observations about the ways children gain an understanding of the world? Would you use the same approaches in child rearing for a child growing up in a non-Western culture? Why or why not?

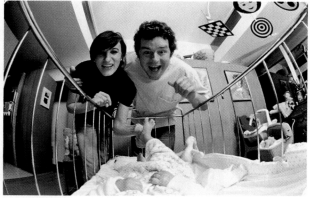

Because infants and children, like all people, are exposed to massive amounts of information, they are able to encode selectively, choosing what they will pay attention to without being overwhelmed.

information processing approaches   the model that seeks to identify the way that individuals take in, use, and store information.

Information Processing Approaches to Cognitive Development

Amber Nordstrom, 3 months old, breaks into a smile as her brother Marcus stands over her crib, picks up a doll, and makes a whistling noise through his teeth. In fact, Amber never seems to tire of Marcus's efforts at making her smile, and soon whenever Marcus appears and simply picks up the doll, her lips begin to curl into a smile.

Clearly, Amber remembers Marcus and his humorous ways. But how does she remember him? And how much else can Amber remember?

To answer questions such as these, we need to diverge from the road that Piaget laid out for us. Rather than seeking to identify the universal, broad milestones in cognitive development through which all infants pass, as Piaget tried to do, we must consider the specific processes by which individual babies acquire and use the information to which they are exposed. We need, then, to focus less on the qualitative changes in infants' mental lives and consider more closely their quantitative capabilities.

Information processing approaches to cognitive development seek to identify the way that individuals take in, use, and store information. According to this approach, the quantitative changes in infants' abilities to organize and manipulate information represent the hallmarks of cognitive development.

Taking this perspective, cognitive growth is characterized by increasing sophistication, speed, and capacity in information processing. Earlier, we compared Piaget's idea of schemes to computer software, which directs the computer in how to deal with data from the world. We might compare the information processing perspective on cognitive growth to the improvements that come from the use of more efficient programs that lead to increased speed and sophistication in the processing of information. Information processing approaches, then, focus on the types of "mental programs" that people use when they seek to solve problems (Reyna, 1997; Siegler, 1998; Cohen & Cashon, 2003).

Encoding, Storage, and Retrieval: The Foundations of Information Processing

Information processing has three basic aspects: encoding, storage, and retrieval (see Figure 5-3). *Encoding* is the process by which information is initially recorded in a form usable to memory. Infants and children—indeed, all people—are exposed to a massive amount of information; if they tried to process it all, they would be overwhelmed. Consequently, they encode selectively, picking and choosing the information to which they will pay attention.

Even if someone has been exposed to the information initially and has encoded it in an appropriate way, there is still no guarantee that he or she will be able to use it in the future. Information must also have been stored in memory adequately. *Storage* refers to the placement of material into memory. Finally, success in using the material in the future depends on retrieval processes. *Retrieval* is the process by which material in memory storage is located, brought into awareness, and used.

We can use our comparison to computers again here. Information processing approaches suggest that the processes of encoding, storage, and retrieval are analogous to different parts of a computer. Encoding can be thought of as a computer's keyboard, through which one inputs information; storage is the computer's hard drive, where information is stored; and retrieval is analogous to software that accesses the information for display on the screen. Only when all three processes are operating—encoding, storage, and retrieval—can information be processed.

Automatization.   In some cases, encoding, storage, and retrieval are relatively automatic, while in other cases they are deliberate. *Automatization* is the degree to which an activity requires attention. Processes that require relatively little attention are automatic; processes that require relatively large amounts of attention are controlled. For example, some activities such as walking, eating with a fork, or reading may be automatic for you, but at first they required your full attention.

Automatic mental processes help children in their initial encounters with the world by enabling them to easily and "automatically" process information in particular ways. For instance, by the age of 5, children automatically encode information in terms of frequency. Without a lot of attention to counting or tallying, they become aware, for example, of how often they have encountered various people, permitting them to differentiate familiar from unfamiliar people (Hasher & Zacks, 1984).

Furthermore, without intending to and without being aware of it, infants and children develop a sense of how often different stimuli are found together simultaneously. This permits them to develop an understanding of *concepts*, categorizations of objects, events, or people that share common properties. For example, by encoding the information that four legs, a wagging tail, and

FIGURE 5-3   INFORMATION PROCESSING

The process by which information is encoded, stored, and retrieved.

FIGURE 5-4   MICKEY MOUSE MATH

Researcher Dr. Karen Wynn found that 5-month-olds like Michelle Follet, pictured here, reacted differently according to whether the number of Mickey Mouse statuettes they saw represented correct or incorrect addition. Do you think this ability is unique to humans? How would you find out?

barking are often found together, we learn very early in life to understand the concept of "dog." Children—as well as adults—are rarely aware of how they learn such concepts, and they are often unable to articulate the features that distinguish one concept (such as a dog) from another (such as cat). Instead, learning tends to occur automatically.

Some of the things we learn automatically are unexpectedly complex. For example, infants have the ability to learn subtle statistical patterns and relationships; these results are consistent with a growing body of research showing that the mathematical skills of infants are surprisingly good. Infants as young as 5 months are able to calculate the outcome of simple addition and subtraction problems. In a study by developmental psychologist Karen Wynn, infants first were shown an object—a 4-inch-high Mickey Mouse statuette (see Figure 5-4). A screen was then raised, hiding the statuette. Next, the experimenter showed the infants a second, identical Mickey Mouse, and then placed it behind the same screen (Wynn, 1992, 1995, 2000).

Finally, depending on the experimental condition, one of two outcomes occurred. In the "correct addition" condition, the screen dropped, revealing the two statuettes (analogous to $1 + 1 = 2$). But in the "incorrect addition" condition, the screen dropped to reveal just one statuette (analogous to the incorrect $1 + 1 = 1$).

Because infants look longer at unexpected occurrences than at expected ones, the researchers examined the pattern of infants' gazes in the different conditions. In support of the notion that infants can distinguish between correct and incorrect addition, the infants in the experiment gazed longer at the incorrect result than at the correct one, indicating they expected a different number of statuettes. In a similar procedure, infants also looked longer at incorrect subtraction problems than at correct ones. The conclusion: Infants have rudimentary mathematical skills that enable them to understand whether a quantity is accurate or not.

The results of this research suggest that infants have an innate grasp of certain basic mathematical functions and statistical patterns. This inborn proficiency is likely to form the basis for learning more complex mathematics and statistical relationships later in life (Gelman & Gallistel, 2004; McCrink & Wynn, 2004; vanMarle & Wynn, 2006).

We turn now to several aspects of information processing, focusing on memory and individual differences in intelligence.

Memory During Infancy: They Must Remember This . . .

Simona Young spent her infancy with virtually no human contact. For up to 20 hours each day, she was left alone in a crib in a squalid Romanian orphanage. Cold bottles of milk were propped above her small body, which she clutched to get nourishment. She rocked back and forth, rarely feeling any soothing touch or hearing words of comfort. Alone in her bleak surroundings, she rocked back and forth for hours on end.

Simona's story, however, has a happy ending. After being adopted by a Canadian couple when she was two, Simona's life is now filled with the usual activities of childhood involving friends, classmates, and above all, a loving family. In fact, now, at age six, she can remember almost nothing of her miserable life in the orphanage. It is as if she has entirely forgotten the past. (Blakeslee, 1995, p. C1)

How likely is it that Simona truly remembers nothing of her infancy? And if she ever does recall her first 2 years of life, how accurate will her memories be? To answer these questions, we need to consider the qualities of memory that exist during infancy.

Memory Capabilities in Infancy. Certainly, infants have **memory** capabilities, defined as the process by which information is initially recorded, stored, and retrieved. As we've seen, infants can distinguish new stimuli from old, and this implies that some memory of the old must be present. Unless the infants had some memory of an original stimulus, it would be impossible for them to recognize that a new stimulus differed from the earlier one (Newcombe, Drummey, & Lie, 1995).

However, infants' capability to recognize new stimuli from old tells us little about how age brings about changes in the capacities of memory and in its fundamental nature. Do infants' memory capabilities increase as they get older? The answer is clearly affirmative. In one study, infants were taught that they could move a mobile hanging over the crib by kicking their legs (see photo). It took only a few days for 2-month-old infants to forget their training, but 6-month-old infants still remembered for as long as 3 weeks (Rovee-Collier, 1993, 1999).

Furthermore, infants who were later prompted to recall the association between kicking and moving the mobile showed evidence that the memory continued to exist even longer. Infants who had received just two training sessions lasting 9 minutes each still recalled the association about a week later, as illustrated by the fact that they began to kick when placed in the crib with the mobile. Two weeks later, however, they made no effort to kick, suggesting that they had forgotten entirely.

But they hadn't: When the babies saw a reminder—a moving mobile—their memories were apparently reactivated. In fact, the infants could remember the association, following prompting, for as long as an additional month (Sullivan, Rovee-Collier, & Tynes, 1979). Other evidence confirms these results, suggesting that hints can reactivate memories that at first seem lost, and that the older the infant, the more effective such prompting is (Rovee-Collier, Hayne, & Columbo, 2001; Hildreth, Sweeney, & Rovee-Collier, 2003; Bearce & Rovee-Collier, 2006).

Is infant memory qualitatively different from that in older children and adults? Researchers generally believe that information is processed similarly throughout the life span, even though the kind of information being processed changes and different parts of the brain may be used. According to memory expert Carolyn Rovee-Collier, people, regardless of their age, gradually lose memories, although, just like babies, they may regain them if reminders are provided. Moreover, the more times a memory is retrieved, the more enduring the memory becomes (Rovee-Collier, 1999; Barr, Marrott, & Rovee-Collier, 2003; Barr et al., 2007).

The Duration of Memories. Although the processes that underlie memory retention and recall seem similar throughout the life span, the quantity of information stored and recalled does differ markedly as infants develop. Older infants can retrieve information more rapidly and they can remember it longer. But just how long? Can memories from infancy be recalled, for example, after babies grow up?

Researchers disagree on the age from which memories can be retrieved. Although early research supported the notion of **infantile amnesia**, the lack of memory for experiences occurring prior to 3 years of age, more recent research shows that infants do retain memories. For example, Nancy Myers and her colleagues exposed a group of 6-month-old children to an unusual series of events in a laboratory, such as intermittent periods of light and dark and unusual sounds. When the children were later tested at the age of 1 1/2 years or 2 1/2 years, they demonstrated clear evidence that they had some memory of their participation in the earlier experience. Other research shows that infants show memory for behavior and situations that they have seen only once (Myers, Clifton, & Clarkson, 1987; Howe, Courage, & Edison, 2004; Neisser, 2004).

Such findings are consistent with evidence that the physical trace of a memory in the brain appears to be relatively permanent, suggesting that memories, even from infancy, may be enduring. However, memories may not be easily, or accurately, retrieved. For example, memories are susceptible to interference from other, newer information, which may displace or block out the older information, thereby preventing its recall.

One reason why infants appear to remember less may be because language plays a key role in determining the way in which memories from early in life can be recalled: Older children and

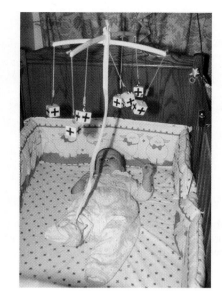

Infants who have learned the association between a moving mobile and kicking showed surprising recall ability if they were exposed to a reminder.

memory the process by which information is initially recorded, stored, and retrieved.

infantile amnesia the lack of memory for experiences that occurred prior to 3 years of age.

Though researchers disagree as to the age from which memories can be retrieved, people generally cannot remember events or experiences that occurred before the age of 3.

adults may only be able to report memories using the vocabulary that they had available at the time of the initial event, when the memories were stored. Because their vocabulary at the time of initial storage may have been quite limited, they are unable to describe the event later in life, even though it is actually in their memories (Bauer et al., 2000; Simcock & Hayne, 2002; Heimann et al., 2006).

The question of how well memories formed during infancy are retained in adulthood remains not fully answered. Although infants' memories may be highly detailed and can be enduring if the infants experience repeated reminders, it is still not clear how accurate those memories remain over the course of the life span. In fact, early memories are susceptible to mis-recollection if people are exposed to related, and contradictory, information following the initial formation of the memory. Not only does such new information potentially impair recall of the original material, but the new material may be inadvertently incorporated into the original memory, thereby corrupting its accuracy (Bauer, 1996; DuBreuil, Garry, & Loftus, 1998; Cordón et al., 2004).

In sum, the data suggest that although it is at least theoretically possible for memories to remain intact from a very young age—if subsequent experiences do not interfere with their recollection—in most cases memories of personal experiences in infancy do not last into adulthood. Current findings suggest that memories of personal experience seem not to become accurate before age 18 to 24 months (Howe, 2003; Howe et al., 2004).

The Cognitive Neuroscience of Memory. Some of the most exciting research on the development of memory is coming from studies of the neurological basis of memory. Advances in brain scan technology, as well as studies of adults with brain damage, suggest that there are two separate systems involved with long-term memory. These two systems, called explicit memory and implicit memory, retain different sorts of information.

Explicit memory is memory that is conscious and can be recalled intentionally. When we try to recall a name or phone number, we're using explicit memory. In comparison, *implicit memory* consists of memories of which we are not consciously aware, but that affect performance and behavior. Implicit memory consists of motor skills, habits, and activities that can be remembered without conscious cognitive effort, such as how to ride a bike or climb a stairway.

Explicit and implicit memories emerge at different rates and involve different parts of the brain. The earliest memories seem to be implicit, and they involve the cerebellum and brain stem. The forerunner of explicit memory involves the hippocampus, but true explicit memory doesn't emerge until the second half of the first year. When explicit memory does emerge, it involves an increasing number of areas of the cortex of the brain (Vargha-Khadem et al., 1997; Bauer et al., 2003; Bauer, 2004; Squire & Knowlton, 2005).

Individual Differences in Intelligence: Is One Infant Smarter Than Another?

Maddy Rodriguez is a bundle of curiosity and energy. At 6 months of age, she cries heartily if she can't reach a toy, and when she sees a reflection of herself in a mirror, she gurgles and seems, in general, to find the situation quite amusing.

Jared Lynch, at 6 months, is a good deal more inhibited than Maddy. He doesn't seem to care much when a ball rolls out of his reach, losing interest in it rapidly. And, unlike Maddy, when he sees himself in a mirror, he pretty much ignores the reflection.

As anyone who has spent any time at all observing more than one baby can tell you, not all infants are alike. Some are full of energy and life, apparently displaying a natural-born curiosity, while others seem, by comparison, somewhat less interested in the world around them. Does this mean that such infants differ in intelligence?

Answering questions about how and to what degree infants vary in their underlying intelligence is not easy. Although it is clear that different infants show significant variations in their behavior, the issue of just what types of behavior may be related to cognitive ability is complicated. Interestingly, the examination of individual differences between infants was the initial approach taken by developmental specialists to understand cognitive development, and such issues still represent an important focus within the field.

What is intelligence? Is it doing well on standardized tests or the ability to navigate the sea without modern equipment?

What Is Infant Intelligence?   Before we can address whether and how infants may differ in intelligence, we need to consider what is meant by the term "intelligence." Educators, psychologists, and other experts on development have yet to agree upon a general definition of intelligent behavior, even among adults. Is it the ability to do well in scholastic endeavors? Proficiency in business negotiations? Competence in navigating across treacherous seas, such as that shown by peoples of the South Pacific who have no knowledge of Western navigational techniques?

It is even more difficult to define and measure intelligence in infants than it is in adults. Do we base it on the speed with which a new task is learned through classical or operant conditioning? How fast a baby becomes habituated to a new stimulus? The age at which an infant learns to crawl or walk? Even if we are able to identify particular behaviors that seem to differentiate one infant from another in terms of intelligence during infancy, we need to address a further, and probably more important, issue: How well do measures of infant intelligence relate to eventual adult intelligence?

Clearly, such questions are not simple, and no simple answers have been found. However, developmental specialists have devised several approaches (summarized in Table 5-2) to illuminate the nature of individual differences in intelligence during infancy.

Developmental Scales.   Developmental psychologist Arnold Gesell formulated the earliest measure of infant development, which was designed to distinguish between normally developing and atypically developing babies (Gesell, 1946). Gesell based his scale on examinations of hundreds of babies. He compared their performance at different ages to learn what behaviors were most common at a particular age. If an infant varied significantly from the norms of a given age, he or she was considered to be developmentally delayed or advanced.

Following the lead of researchers who sought to quantify intelligence through a specific score (known as an intelligence quotient, or IQ, score), Gesell developed a developmental quotient, or DQ. The **developmental quotient** is an overall developmental score that relates to performance in four domains: motor skills (for example, balance and sitting), language use, adaptive behavior (such as alertness and exploration), and personal-social behaviors.

developmental quotient   an overall developmental score that relates to performance in four domains: motor skills, language use, adaptive behavior, and personal-social.

Table 5-2	Approaches Used to Detect Differences in Intelligence During Infancy
Developmental quotient	Formulated by Arnold Gesell, the developmental quotient is an overall development score that relates to performance in four domains: motor skills (balance and sitting), language use, adaptive behavior (alertness and exploration), and personal-social behavior.
Bayley Scales of Infant Development	Developed by Nancy Bayley, the Bayley Scales of Infant Development evaluate an infant's development from 2 to 42 months. The Bayley Scales focus on two areas: mental (senses, perception, memory, learning, problem solving, and language) and motor abilities (fine and gross motor skills).
Visual-recognition memory measurement	Measures of visual-recognition memory, the memory of and recognition of a stimulus that has been previously seen, also relate to intelligence. The more quickly an infant can retrieve a representation of a stimulus from memory, the more efficient, presumably, is that infant's information processing.

Table 5-3	Sample Items from the Bayley Scales of Infant Development

Age	Mental Scale	Motor Scale
2 months	Turns head to sound	Holds head erect/steady for 15 seconds
	Reacts to disappearance of face	Sits with support
6 months	Lifts cup by handle	Sits alone for 30 seconds
	Looks at pictures in book	Grasps foot with hands
12 months	Builds tower of 2 cubes	Walks with help
	Turns pages of book	Grasps pencil in middle
17–19 months	Imitates crayon stroke	Stands alone on right foot
	Identifies objects in photo	Walks up stairs with help
23–25 months	Matches pictures	Laces 3 beads
	Imitates a 2-word sentence	Jumps distance of 4 inches
38–42 months	Names 4 colors	Copies circle
	Uses past tense	Hops twice on 1 foot
	Identifies gender	Walks down stairs, alternating feet

(*Source:* Bayley, N.7 1993. *Bayley scales of infant development* [BSID-II] 2nd ed., San Antonio, IX: The Psychological Corporation.

Later researchers have created other developmental scales. For instance, Nancy Bayley developed one of the most widely used measures for infants. The **Bayley Scales of Infant Development** evaluate an infant's development from 2 to 42 months. The Bayley Scales focus on two areas: mental and motor abilities. The mental scale focuses on the senses, perception, memory, learning, problem solving, and language, while the motor scale evaluates fine and gross motor skills (see Table 5-3). Like Gesell's approach, the Bayley yields a developmental quotient (DQ). A child who scores at an average level—meaning average performance for other children at the same age—receives a score of 100 (Bayley, 1969; Black & Matula, 1999; Gagnon & Nagle, 2000).

The virtue of approaches such as those taken by Gesell and Bayley is that they provide a good snapshot of an infant's current developmental level. Using these scales, we can tell in an objective manner whether a particular infant falls behind or is ahead of his or her same-age peers. They are particularly useful in identifying infants who are substantially behind their peers, and who therefore need immediate special attention (Culbertson & Gyurke, 1990; Aylward, & Verhulst, 2000).

What such scales are not useful for is predicting a child's future course of development. A child whose development is identified by these measures as relatively slow at the age of 1 year will not necessarily display slow development at age 5, or 12, or 25. The association between most measures of behavior during infancy and adult intelligence, then, is minimal (Siegel, 1989; DiLalla et al., 1990; Molfese & Acheson, 1997).

Because of the difficulties in using developmental scales to obtain measures of infant intelligence that are related to later intelligence, investigators have turned in the last decade to other techniques that may help assess intelligence in a meaningful way. Some have proven to be quite useful.

Information Processing Approaches to Individual Differences in Intelligence. When we speak of intelligence in everyday parlance, we often differentiate between "quick" individuals and those who are "slow." Actually, according to research on the speed of information processing, such terms hold some truth. Contemporary approaches to infant intelligence suggest that the speed with which infants process information may correlate most strongly with later intelligence, as measured by IQ tests administered during adulthood (Rose & Feldman, 1997; Sigman, Cohen, & Beckwith, 1997).

How can we tell if a baby is processing information quickly or not? Most researchers use habituation tests. Infants who process information efficiently ought to be able to learn about stimuli more quickly. Consequently, we would expect that they would turn their attention away from a given stimulus more rapidly than those who are less efficient at information processing, leading to the phenomenon of habituation. Similarly, measures of *visual-recognition memory,*

Bayley Scales of Infant Development a measure that evaluates an infant's development from 2 to 42 months.

the memory and recognition of a stimulus that has been previously seen, also relate to IQ. The more quickly an infant can retrieve a representation of a stimulus from memory, the more efficient, presumably, is that infant's information processing (Tamis-Lemonda & Bornstein, 1993; Canfield et al., 1997; Rose, Jankowski, & Feldman, 2002; Robinson & Pascalis, 2005).

Research using an information processing framework clearly suggests a relationship between information processing efficiency and cognitive abilities: Measures of how quickly infants lose interest in stimuli that they have previously seen, as well as their responsiveness to new stimuli, correlate moderately well with later measures of intelligence. Infants who are more efficient information processors during the 6 months following birth tend to have higher intelligence scores between 2 and 12 years of age, as well as higher scores on other measures of cognitive competence (Sigman, Cohen, & Beckwith, 2000; Rose, Feldman, & Jankowski, 2004).

Other research suggests that abilities related to the *multimodal approach to perception,* which we considered in Chapter 4, may offer clues about later intelligence. For instance, the ability to identify a stimulus that previously has been experienced through only one sense by using another sense (called *cross-modal transference*) is associated with intelligence. A baby who is able to recognize by sight a screwdriver that she has previously only touched, but not seen, is displaying cross-modal transference. Research has found that the degree of cross-modal transference displayed by an infant at age 1—which requires a high level of abstract thinking—is associated with intelligence scores several years later (Spelke, 1987; Rose et al., 1991; Rose, Feldman, & Jankowski, 1999, 2004).

Although information processing efficiency and cross-modal transference abilities during infancy relate moderately well to later IQ scores, we need to keep in mind two qualifications. First, even though there is an association between early information processing capabilities and later measures of IQ, the correlation is only moderate in strength. Other factors, such as the degree of environmental stimulation, also play a crucial role in helping to determine adult intelligence. Consequently, we should not assume that intelligence is somehow permanently fixed in infancy.

Second, and perhaps even more important, intelligence measured by traditional IQ tests relates to a particular type of intelligence, one that emphasizes abilities that lead to academic, and certainly not artistic or professional, success. Consequently, predicting that a child may do well on IQ tests later in life is not the same as predicting that the child will be successful later in life.

Despite these qualifications, the relatively recent finding that an association exists between efficiency of information processing and later IQ scores does suggest some consistency of cognitive development across the life span. Whereas the earlier reliance on scales such as the Bayley led to the misconception that little continuity existed, the more recent information processing approaches suggest that cognitive development unfolds in a more orderly, continuous manner from infancy to the later stages of life.

Assessing Information Processing Approaches.   The information processing perspective on cognitive development during infancy is very different from Piaget's. Rather than focusing on broad explanations of the *qualitative* changes that occur in infants' capabilities, as Piaget does, information processing looks at *quantitative* change. Piaget sees cognitive growth occurring in fairly sudden spurts; information processing sees more gradual, step-by-step growth. (Think of the difference between a track-and-field runner leaping hurdles versus a slow-but-steady marathon racer.)

Because information processing researchers consider cognitive development in terms of a collection of individual skills, they are often able to use more precise measures of cognitive ability, such as processing speed and memory recall, than proponents of Piaget's approach. Still, the very precision of these individual measures makes it harder to get an overall sense of the nature of cognitive development, something at which Piaget was a master. It's as if information processing approaches focus more on the individual pieces of the puzzle of cognitive development, while Piagetian approaches focus more on the whole puzzle.

Ultimately, both Piagetian and information processing approaches are critical in providing an account of cognitive development in infancy. Coupled with advances in the biochemistry of the brain and theories that consider the effects of social factors on learning and cognition (which we'll discuss in Chapter 6), the two help us paint a full picture of cognitive development. (Also see the *From Research to Practice* box.)

From Research to Practice

Do Educational Media for Infants Enhance Their Cognitive Development?: Taking the Einstein Out of Baby Einstein

Jetta is 11 months old, with big eyes, a few pearly teeth—and a tiny index finger that can already operate electronic entertainment devices.

"We own everything electronic that's educational—LeapFrog, Baby Einstein, everything," said her mother, Naira Soibatian. "She has an HP laptop, bigger than mine. I know one leading baby book says, very simply, it's a waste of money. But there's only one thing better than having a baby, and that's having a smart baby. And at the end of the day, what can it hurt? She learns things, and she loves them." (Lewin, 2005, p. A1)

Naira Soibatian's philosophy captures the sentiments of many parents who believe that exposing infants to educational media like the Baby Einstein series of videos may be beneficial to their cognitive growth. For instance, one survey found that about half the parents agreed that educational media are "very important" contributors to their children's intellectual development. And there is certainly a wide variety of products to try, ranging from DVDs to computer games and electronic devices, that are marketed with claims of having educational value. But one important question for parents is whether their infant children are really deriving any benefit from these products— and if they are not, is it truly a safe assumption that such products are completely harmless (Wartella et al., 2004)?

A report from the Kaiser Family Foundation reveals that the marketing of educational media for infants is far outpacing the research on its effectiveness. In fact, practically no such research evidence exists. One part of the reason is the difficulty in conducting such research experimentally; much of the limited evidence is based on correlational studies that cannot rule out such factors as natural intelligence or parental education—or even discern true benefits of the media exposure from normal cognitive development over time (Garrison & Christakis, 2005).

Another part of the reason for the lack of research on the effectiveness of electronic media is that companies producing such products are reluctant to test the claims that their products are of value. Although they do conduct research on whether children can understand the media well enough to use it, their research on actual beneficial outcomes is very limited. Quite simply, they find that outcome research doesn't affect their sales nearly as much as the entertainment value of their products does. And they seem to have a point, because parents are buying and using their products despite the lack of scientific evidence. For example, another Kaiser Family Foundation report revealed that babies as young as 6 months are spending over 1½ hours a day on average with television, video, and other on-screen media (Rideout et al., 2003).

But there may be reason to think that an overreliance on educational media products can actually be harmful. Consider the research of language expert Patricia Kuhl, who helped establish the unique language learning abilities of infants. Kuhl has found that infants don't learn language from rote repetition, such as on an audiotape. Nine-month-old American infants who interacted with Mandarin-speaking adults acquired a sensitivity to the sounds of the Mandarin language—but not so for infants who were exposed to the language through audio and video media. Social interaction seems to be a critical part of language learning. Without social context, the language lessons were little more than meaningless noise to the infants. Other research also shows that very young children learn better from live demonstrations than they do from videotapes (Kuhl, Tsao, & Liu, 2003; Anderson & Pempek, 2005).

What constitutes appropriate use of educational media for infants? Developmentalists agree that such materials are no replacement for learning that comes from social interaction, and they caution against allowing educational media use to supplant other activities such as free play and interaction with caregivers. On the other hand, if educational media are replacing other passive media-based activities used to keep a child entertained— such as television programs lacking an educational component—then their use may be reasonable. In addition, education media products often have at least one advantage over run-of-the-mill educational television: They typically include printed inserts, parent guides, and other resources to facilitate the kind of parent–child interaction that is known to benefit infants' cognitive development (Garrison & Christakis, 2005; Arnold & Colburn, 2007).

- *Do you think that educational media for infants is worth a try, despite the lack of scientific research supporting its use? Why? Under what conditions might its use actually have undesirable consequences?*

- *Why do you think parents generally do not seem to be concerned about the lack of scientific evidence for the effectiveness of educational media for infants?*

Review and Apply

Review

- Information processing approaches consider quantitative changes in children's abilities to organize and use information. Cognitive growth is regarded as the increasing sophistication of encoding, storage, and retrieval.

- Infants clearly have memory capabilities from a very early age, although the duration and accuracy of such memories are unresolved questions.

- Traditional measures of infant intelligence focus on behavioral attainments, which can help identify developmental delays or advances but are not strongly related to measures of adult intelligence.

- Information processing approaches to assessing intelligence rely on variations in the speed and quality with which infants process information.

Applying Lifespan Development

- What information from this chapter could you use to refute the claims of books or educational programs that promise to help parents increase their babies' intelligence or instill advanced intellectual skills in infants? Based on valid research, what approaches would you use for intellectual development of infants?

- *From a nurse's perspective:* In what ways is the use of such developmental scales as Gesell's or Bayley's helpful? In what ways is it dangerous? How would you maximize the helpfulness and minimize the danger if you were advising a parent?

The Roots of Language

Vicki and Dominic were engaged in a friendly competition over whose name would be the first word their baby, Maura, said. "Say 'mama,'" Vicki would coo, before handing Maura over to Dominic for a diaper change. Grinning, he would take her and coax, "No, say 'daddy.'" Both parents ended up losing—and winning—when Maura's first word sounded more like "baba," and seemed to refer to her bottle.

Mama. No. Cookie. Dad. Jo. Most parents can remember their baby's first word, and no wonder. It's an exciting moment, this emergence of a skill that is, arguably, unique to human beings.

But those initial words are just the first and most obvious manifestations of language. Many months earlier, infants began to understand the language used by others to make sense of the world around them. How does this linguistic ability develop? What is the pattern and sequence of language development? And how does the use of language transform the cognitive world of infants and their parents? We consider these questions, and others, as we address the development of language during the first years of life.

The Fundamentals of Language: From Sounds to Symbols

Language, the systematic, meaningful arrangement of symbols, provides the basis for communication. But it does more than this: It is closely tied to the way we think and how we understand the world. It enables us to reflect on people and objects and to convey our thoughts to others.

language the systematic, meaningful arrangement of symbols, which provides the basis for communication.

Although we tend to think of language in terms of the production of words and then groups of words, infants can begin to communicate linguistically well before they say their first word.

Language has several formal characteristics that must be mastered as linguistic competence is developed. They include:

- **Phonology.** Phonology refers to the basic sounds of language, called *phonemes*, that can be combined to produce words and sentences. For instance, the "a" in "mat" and the "a" in "mate" represent two different phonemes in English. Although English employs just 40 phonemes to create every word in the language, other languages have as many as 85 phonemes—and some as few as 15 (Akmajian, Demers, & Harnish, 1984).

- **Morphemes.** A morpheme is the smallest language unit that has meaning. Some morphemes are complete words, while others add information necessary for interpreting a word, such as the endings "-s" for plural and "-ed" for past tense.

- **Semantics.** Semantics are the rules that govern the meaning of words and sentences. As their knowledge of semantics develops, children are able to understand the subtle distinction between "Ellie was hit by a ball" (an answer to the question of why Ellie doesn't want to play catch) and "A ball hit Ellie" (used to announce the current situation).

In considering the development of language, we need to distinguish between linguistic *comprehension*, the understanding of speech, and linguistic *production*, the use of language to communicate. One principle underlies the relationship between the two: Comprehension precedes production. An 18-month-old may be able to understand a complex series of directions ("Pick up your coat from the floor and put it on the chair by the fireplace.") but may not yet have strung more than two words together when speaking for herself. Throughout infancy comprehension also outpaces production. For instance, during infancy, comprehension of words expands at a rate of 22 new words a month, while production of words increases at a rate of about 9 new words a month, once talking begins (Benedict, 1979; Tincoff & Jusczyk, 1999; Rescorla, Alley, & Christine, 2001; see Figure 5-5).

**FIGURE 5-5
COMPREHENSION
PRECEDES
PRODUCTION**

Throughout infancy, the comprehension of speech precedes the production of speech.

(*Source:* Adapted from Bornstein & Lamb, 1992.)

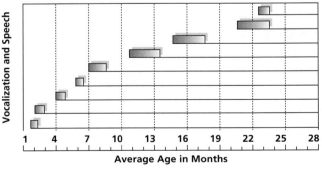

Vocalization and Speech — Average Age in Months

Uses first pronoun, phrase, sentence
Uses two words in combination
Says five words or more
Says first word
Two syllables with repetition of first: "ma-ma," "da-da"
Clear vocalization of several syllables
Babbling
Cooing
One syllable

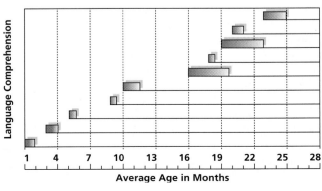

Language Comprehension — Average Age in Months

Understands two prepositions: "in," "under"
Repeats things said
Names a picture in a book: "dog"
Understands a simple question
Understands a prohibition
Responds to simple commands
Understands gestures and responds to "bye-bye"
Discriminates between friendly and angry talking
Vocalizes to social stimulation
Responds and attends to speaking voice

Early Sounds and Communication.   Spend 24 hours with even a very young infant and you will hear a variety of sounds: cooing, crying, gurgling, murmuring, and assorted types of other noises. These sounds, although not meaningful in themselves, play an important role in linguistic development, paving the way for true language (Bloom, 1993; O'Grady & Aitchison, 2005).

Prelinguistic communication is communication through sounds, facial expressions, gestures, imitation, and other nonlinguistic means. When a father responds to his daughter's "ah" with an "ah" of his own, and then the daughter repeats the sound, and the father responds once again, they are engaged in prelinguistic communication. Clearly, the "ah" sound has no particular meaning. However, its repetition, which mimics the give-and-take of conversation, teaches the infant something about turn-taking and the back-and-forth of communication (Reddy, 1999).

The most obvious manifestation of prelinguistic communication is babbling. **Babbling**, making speechlike but meaningless sounds, starts at the age of 2 or 3 months and continues until around the age of 1 year. When they babble, infants repeat the same vowel sound over and over, changing the pitch from high to low (as in "ee-ee-ee," repeated at different pitches). After the age of 5 months, the sounds of babbling begin to expand, reflecting the addition of consonants (such as "bee-bee-bee-bee").

Babbling is a universal phenomenon, accomplished in the same way throughout all cultures. While they are babbling, infants spontaneously produce all of the sounds found in every language, not just the language they hear people around them speaking.

In fact, even deaf children display their own form of babbling: Infants who cannot hear and who are exposed to sign language babble with their hands instead of their voices. Their gestural babbling thus is analogous to the verbal babbling of children who can hear (see photo). Furthermore, as shown in Figure 5-6, the areas of the brain activated during the production of hand gestures are similar to the areas activated during speech production, suggesting that spoken language may have evolved from gestural language (Holowaka & Petitto, 2002; Senghas, Petitto, Holowka, & Sergio, 2004; Kita, & Özyürek, 2004; Gentilucci & Corballis, 2006).

Babbling typically follows a progression from simple to more complex sounds. Although exposure to the sounds of a particular language does not seem to influence babbling initially, eventually experience does make a difference. By the age of 6 months, babbling reflects the sounds of the language to which infants are exposed (Blake & Boysson-Bardies, 1992). The difference is so noticeable that even untrained listeners can distinguish between babbling infants who have been raised in cultures in which French, Arabic, or Cantonese languages are spoken. Furthermore, the speed at which infants begin homing in on their own language is related to the speed of later language development (Oller et al., 1997; Tsao, Liu, & Kuhl, 2004).

babbling   making speechlike but meaningless sounds.

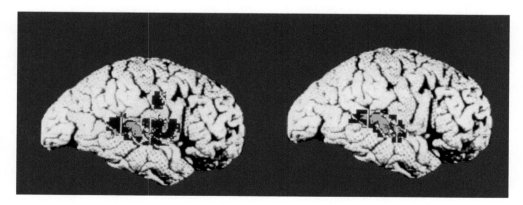

FIGURE 5-6   BROCA'S AREA

Areas of the brain that are activated during speech are similar to the areas activated during the production of hand gestures.

(*Source:* Krantz, 1999.)

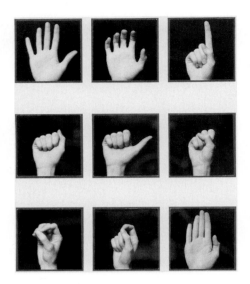

Deaf infants who are exposed to sign language do their own type of babbling, related to the use of signs.

There are other indications of prelinguistic speech. For instance, consider 5-month-old Marta, who spies her red ball just beyond her reach. After reaching for it and finding that she is unable to get to it, she makes a cry of anger that alerts her parents that something is amiss, and her mother hands it to her. Communication has occurred.

Four months later, when Marta faces the same situation, she no longer bothers to reach for the ball and doesn't respond in anger. Instead, she holds out her arm in the direction of the ball, and with great purpose, seeks to catch her mother's eye. When her mother sees the behavior, she knows just what Marta wants. Clearly, Marta's communicative skills—although still prelinguistic—have taken a leap forward.

Even these prelinguistic skills are supplanted in just a few months, when the gesture gives way to a new communicative skill: producing an actual word. Marta's parents clearly hear her say "ball."

First Words. When a mother and father first hear their child say "Mama" or "Dada," or even "baba," as in the case of Maura, the baby described earlier in this section, it is hard to be anything but delighted. But their initial enthusiasm may be dampened a bit when they find that the same sound is used to ask for a cookie, a doll, and a ratty old blanket.

First words generally are spoken somewhere around the age of 10 to 14 months, but may occur as early as 9 months. Linguists differ on just how to recognize that a first word has actually been uttered. Some say it is when an infant clearly understands words and can produce a sound that is close to a word spoken by adults, such as a child who uses "mama" for any request she may have. Other linguists use a stricter criterion for the first word; they restrict "first word" to cases in which children give a clear, consistent name to a person, event, or object. In this view, "mama" counts as a first word only if it is consistently applied to the same person, seen in a variety of situations and doing a variety of things, and is not used to label other people (Hollich et al., 2000; Masataka, 2003).

Although there is disagreement over when we can say a first word has been uttered, no one disputes that once an infant starts to produce words, vocabulary increases at a rapid rate. By the age of 15 months, the average child has a vocabulary of 10 words and methodically expands until the one-word stage of language development ends at around 18 months. Once that happens, a sudden spurt in vocabulary occurs. In just a short period—a few weeks somewhere between 16 and 24 months of age—there is an explosion of language, in which a child's vocabulary typically increases from 50 to 400 words (Gleitman & Landau, 1994; Fernald et al., 1989; Nazzi & Bertoncini, 2003).

As you can see from the list in Table 5-4, the first words in children's early vocabularies typically regard objects and things, both animate and inanimate. Most often they refer to people or objects who constantly appear and disappear ("Mama"), to animals ("kitty"), or to temporary states ("wet"). These first words are often **holophrases**, one-word utterances that stand for a whole phrase, whose meaning depends on the particular context in which they are used. For instance, a youngster may use the phrase "ma" to mean, depending on the context, "I want to be picked up by Mom" or "I want something to eat, Mom" or "Where's Mom?" (Dromi, 1987; O'Grady & Aitchison, 2005).

Culture has an effect on the type of first words spoken. For example, unlike North American English-speaking infants, who are more apt to use nouns initially, Chinese Mandarin-speaking infants use more verbs than nouns. On the other hand, by the age of 20 months, there are remarkable cross-cultural similarities in the types of words spoken. For example, a comparison of 20-month-olds in Argentina, Belgium, France, Israel, Italy, and the Republic of Korea found that children's vocabularies in every culture contained greater proportions of nouns than other classes of words (Tardif, 1996; Bornstein, Cole, & Maital, 2004).

holophrases one-word utterances that stand for a whole phrase, whose meaning depends on the particular context in which they are used.

First Sentences. When Aaron was 19 months old, he heard his mother coming up the back steps, as she did every day just before dinner. Aaron turned to his father and distinctly said, "Ma come." In stringing those two words together, Aaron took a giant step in his language development.

Table 5-4 The Top 50: The First Words Children Understand and Speak	Comprehension Percentage	Production Percentage
1. *Nominals (Words referring to "things")*	56	61
Specific (people, animals, objects)	17	11
General (words referring to all members of a category)	39	50
Animate (objects)	9	13
Inanimate (objects)	30	37
Pronouns (e.g., this, that, they)	1	2
2. *Action words*	36	19
Social action games (e.g., peek-a-boo)	15	11
Events (e.g., "eat")	1	NA
Locatives (locating or putting something in specific location)	5	1
General action and inhibitors (e.g., "don't touch")	15	6
3. *Modifiers*	3	10
Status (e.g., "all gone")	2	4
Attributes (e.g., "big")	1	3
Locatives (e.g., "outside")	0	2
Possessives (e.g., "mine")	1	1
4. *Personal-social*	5	10
Assertions (e.g., "yes")	2	9
Social expressive (e.g., "bye-bye")	4	1

Note: Percentage refers to percentage of children who include this type of word among their first 50 words.
(*Source:* Adapted from Benedict, 1979.)

The increase in vocabulary that comes at around 18 months is accompanied by another accomplishment: the linking together of individual words into sentences that convey a single thought. Although there is a good deal of variability in the time at which children first create two-word phrases, it is generally around 8 to 12 months after they say their first word.

The linguistic advance represented by two-word combinations is important because the linkage not only provides labels for things in the world but also indicates the relations between them. For instance, the combination may declare something about possession ("Mama key") or recurrent events ("Dog bark"). Interestingly, most early sentences don't represent demands or even necessarily require a response. Instead, they are often merely comments and observations about events occurring in the child's world (Halliday, 1975; O'Grady & Aichison, 2005).

Two-year-olds using two-word combinations tend to employ particular sequences that are similar to the ways in which adult sentences are constructed. For instance, sentences in English typically follow a pattern in which the subject of the sentence comes first, followed by the verb, and then the object ("Josh threw the ball"). Children's speech most often uses a similar order, although not all the words are initially included. Consequently, a child might say "Josh threw" or "Josh ball" to indicate the same thought. What is significant is that the order is typically not "threw Josh" or "ball Josh," but rather the usual order of English, which makes the utterance much easier for an English speaker to comprehend (Brown, 1973; Hirsh-Pasek & Michnick-Golinkoff, 1995; Masataka, 2003).

Although the creation of two-word sentences represents an advance, the language used by children still is by no means adultlike. As we've just seen, 2-year-olds tend to leave out words that aren't critical to the message, similar to the way we might write a telegram for which we were paying by the word. For that reason, their talk is often called **telegraphic speech**. Rather than saying, "I showed you the book," a child using telegraphic speech might say, "I show book." "I am drawing a dog" might become "Drawing dog" (see Table 5-5).

By the age of two, most children use two-word phrases, such as "ball play."

telegraphic speech speech in which words not critical to the message are left out.

Table 5-5	Children's Imitation of Sentences Showing Decline of Telegraphic Speech					
	Eve, 25.5 Months	**Adam, 28.5 Months**	**Helen, 30 Months**	**Ian, 31.5 Months**	**Jimmy, 32 Months**	**June, 35.5 Months**
I showed you the book.	I show book.	(I show) book.	C	I show you the book.	C	Show you the book.
I am very tall.	(My) tall.	I (very) tall.	I very tall.	I'm very tall.	Very tall.	I very tall.
It goes in a big box.	Big box.	Big box.	In big box.	It goes in the box.	C	C
I am drawing a dog.	Drawing dog.	I draw dog.	I drawing dog.	Dog.	C	C
I will read the book.	Read book.	I will read book.	I read the book.	I read the book.	C	C
I can see a cow.	See cow.	I want see cow.	C	Cow.	C	C
I will not do that again.	Do-again.	I will that again.	I do that.	I again.	C	C

C = correct imitation.

(*Source:* Adapted from R. Brown & C. Fraser, 1963.)

Early language has other characteristics that differentiate it from the language used by adults. For instance, consider Sarah, who refers to the blanket she sleeps with as "blankie." When her Aunt Ethel gives her a new blanket, Sarah refuses to call the new one a "blankie," restricting the word to her original blanket.

Sarah's inability to generalize the label of "blankie" to blankets in general is an example of **underextension**, using words too restrictively, which is common among children just mastering spoken language. Underextension occurs when language novices think that a word refers to a specific instance of a concept, instead of to all examples of the concept (Caplan & Barr, 1989; Masataka, 2003).

As infants like Sarah grow more adept with language, the opposite phenomenon sometimes occurs. In **overextension**, words are used too broadly, overgeneralizing their meaning. For example, when Sarah refers to buses, trucks, and tractors as "cars," she is guilty of overextension, making the assumption that any object with wheels must be a car. Although overextension reflects speech errors, it also shows that advances are occurring in the child's thought processes: The child is beginning to develop general mental categories and concepts (Johnson & Eilers, 1998; McDonough, 2002).

Infants also show individual differences in the style of language they use. For example, some use a **referential style**, in which language is used primarily to label objects. Others tend to use an **expressive style**, in which language is used primarily to express feelings and needs about oneself and others (Bates et al., 1994; Nelson, 1996). Language styles reflect, in part, cultural factors. For example, mothers in the United States label objects more frequently than do Japanese mothers, encouraging a more referential style of speech. In contrast, mothers in Japan are more apt to speak about social interactions, encouraging a more expressive style of speech (Fernald & Morikawa, 1993).

The Origins of Language Development

The immense strides in language development during the preschool years raise a fundamental question: How does proficiency in language come about? Linguists are deeply divided on how to answer this question.

Learning Theory Approaches: Language as a Learned Skill.   One view of language development emphasizes the basic principles of learning. According to the **learning theory approach**, language acquisition follows the basic laws of reinforcement and conditioning

underextension   the overly restrictive use of words; common among children just mastering spoken language.

overextension   the overly broad use of words, overgeneralizing their meaning.

referential style   a style of language use in which language is used primarily to label objects.

expressive style   a style of language use in which language is used primarily to express feelings and needs about oneself and others.

learning theory approach   the theory that language acquisition follows the basic laws of reinforcement and conditioning.

discussed in Chapter 1 (Skinner, 1957). For instance, a child who articulates the word "da" may be hugged and praised by her father, who jumps to the conclusion that she is referring to him. This reaction reinforces the child, who is more likely to repeat the word. In sum, the learning theory perspective on language acquisition suggests that children learn to speak by being rewarded for making sounds that approximate speech. Through the process of *shaping*, language becomes more and more similar to adult speech.

There's a problem, though, with the learning theory approach. It doesn't seem to adequately explain how children acquire the rules of language as readily as they do. For instance, young children are reinforced when they make errors. Parents are apt to be just as responsive if their child says, "Why the dog won't eat?" as they are if the child phrases the question more correctly ("Why won't the dog eat?"). Both forms of the question are understood correctly, and both elicit the same response; reinforcement is provided for both correct and incorrect language usage. Under such circumstances, learning theory is hard-put to explain how children learn to speak properly.

Children are also able to move beyond specific utterances they have heard and produce novel phrases, sentences, and constructions, an ability that also cannot be explained by learning theory. Furthermore, children can apply linguistic rules to nonsense words. In one study, 4-year-old children heard the nonsense verb "to pilk" in the sentence "the bear is pilking the horse." Later, when asked what was happening to the horse, they responded by placing the nonsense verb in the correct tense and voice: "He's getting pilked by the bear."

Nativist Approaches: Language as an Innate Skill.

Such conceptual difficulties with the learning theory approach have led to the development of an alternative, championed by linguist Noam Chomsky and known as the nativist approach (1968, 1978, 1991, 1999, 2005). The **nativist approach** argues that there is a genetically determined, innate mechanism that directs the development of language. According to Chomsky, people are born with an innate capacity to use language, which emerges, more or less automatically, due to maturation.

Chomsky's analysis of different languages suggests that all the world's languages share a similar underlying structure, which he calls **universal grammar**. In this view, the human brain is wired with a neural system called the **language-acquisition device,** or LAD, that both permits the understanding of language structure and provides a set of strategies and techniques for learning the particular characteristics of the language to which a child is exposed. In this view, language is uniquely human, made possible by a genetic predisposition to both comprehend and produce words and sentences (Nowak, Komarova, & Niyogi, 2001, 2002; Hauser, Chomsky, & Fitch, 2002; Lidz & Gleitman, 2004).

Support for Chomsky's nativist approach comes from recent findings identifying a specific gene related to speech production. Further support comes from research showing that language processing in infants involves brain structures similar to those in adult speech processing, suggesting an evolutionary basis for language (see Figure 5-7; Wade, 2001; Monaco, 2005; Dehaene-Lambertz, Hertz-Pannier, & Dubois, 2006).

On the other hand, the view that language is an innate ability unique to humans also has its critics. For instance, some researchers argue that certain primates are able to learn at least the basics of language, an ability that calls into question the uniqueness of the human linguistic capacity. Others point out that although humans may be genetically primed to use language, its use still requires significant social experience in order for it to be used effectively (MacWhinney, 1991; Savage-Rumbaugh et al., 1993; Goldberg, 2004).

The Interactionist Approaches.

Neither the learning theory nor the nativist perspective fully explains language acquisition. As a result, some theorists have turned to a theory that

nativist approach the theory that a genetically determined, innate mechanism directs language development.

universal grammar Noam Chomsky's theory that all the world's languages share a similar underlying structure.

language-acquisition device (LAD) a neural system of the brain hypothesized to permit understanding of language.

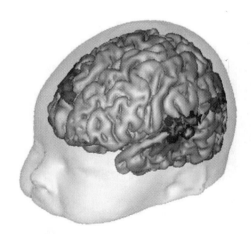

FIGURE 5-7 INFANT'S SPEECH PROCESSING

This fMRI scan of a 3-month-old infant shows speech processing activity similar to that of an adult, suggesting there may be an evolutionary basis to language.

(*Source:* Dehaene-Lambertz, Hertz-Pannier, & Dubois, 2006.)

infant-directed speech a type of speech directed toward infants; characterized by short, simple sentences.

combines both schools of thought. The *interactionist perspective* suggests that language development is produced through a combination of genetically determined predispositions and environmental circumstances that help teach language.

The interactionist perspective accepts that innate factors shape the broad outlines of language development. However, interactionists also argue that the specific course of language development is determined by the language to which children are exposed and the reinforcement they receive for using language in particular ways. Social factors are considered to be key to development, since the motivation provided by one's membership in a society and culture and one's interactions with others leads to the use of language and the growth of language skills (Dixon, 2004; Yang, 2006).

Just as there is support for some aspects of learning theory and nativist positions, the interactionist perspective has also received some support. We don't know, at the moment, which of these positions will ultimately provide the best explanation. It is more likely that different factors play different roles at different times during childhood. The full explanation for language acquisition, then, remains to be found.

Speaking to Children: The Language of Infant-Directed Speech

Say the following sentence aloud: Do you like the applesauce?

Now pretend that you are going to ask the same question of an infant, and speak it as you would for a young child's ears.

Chances are several things happened when you translated the phrase for the infant. First of all, the wording probably changed, and you may have said something like, "Does baby like the applesauce?" At the same time, the pitch of your voice probably rose, your general intonation most likely had a singsong quality, and you probably separated your words carefully.

Infant-Directed Speech. The shift in your language was due to your use of **infant-directed speech**, a style of speech that characterizes much of the verbal communication directed toward infants. This type of speech pattern used to be called *motherese*, because it was assumed that it applied only to mothers. However, that assumption was wrong, and the gender-neutral term *infant-directed speech* is now used more frequently.

Motherese, or, more precisely, infant-directed speech, includes the use of short, simple sentences and is said in a pitch that is higher than that used with older children and adults.

Infant-directed speech is characterized by short, simple sentences. Pitch becomes higher, the range of frequencies increases, and intonation is more varied. There is also repetition of words, and topics are restricted to items that are assumed to be comprehensible to infants, such as concrete objects in the baby's environment.

Sometimes infant-directed speech includes amusing sounds that are not even words, imitating the prelinguistic speech of infants. In other cases, it has little formal structure, but is similar to the kind of telegraphic speech that infants use as they develop their own language skills.

Infant-directed speech changes as children become older. Around the end of the first year, infant-directed speech takes on more adultlike qualities. Sentences become longer and more complex, although individual words are still spoken slowly and deliberately. Pitch is also used to focus attention on particularly important words.

Infant-directed speech plays an important role in infants' acquisition of language. As discussed next, infant-directed speech occurs all over the world, though there are cultural variations. Newborns prefer such speech to regular language, a fact that suggests that they may be particularly receptive to it. Furthermore, some research suggests that babies who are exposed to a great deal of infant-directed speech early in life seem to begin to use words and exhibit other forms of linguistic competence earlier (Liu, Kuhl, & Tsao, 2003; Thiessen, Hill, & Saffran, 2005; Englund & Behne, 2006; Werker et al., 2007).

Developmental Diversity

Is Infant-Directed Speech Similar in All Cultures?

Do mothers in the United States, Sweden, and Russia speak the same way to their infants? In some respects, they clearly do. Although the words themselves differ across languages, the way the words are spoken to infants is quite similar. According to a growing body of research, there are basic similarities across cultures in the nature of infant-directed speech (Papousek & Papousek, 1991; Rabain-Jamin & Sabeau-Jouannet, 1997; Werker et al., 2007).

For example, 6 of the 10 most frequent major characteristics of speech directed at infants used by native speakers of English and Spanish are common to both languages: exaggerated intonation, high pitch, lengthened vowels, repetition, lower volume, and heavy stress on certain key words (such as emphasizing the word "ball" in the sentence, "No, that's a *ball*") (Blount, 1982). Similarly, mothers in the United States, Sweden, and Russia all exaggerate and elongate the pronunciation of the three vowel sounds of "ee," "ah," and "oh" when speaking to infants in similar ways, despite differences in the languages in which the sounds are used (Kuhl et al., 1997).

Even deaf mothers use a form of infant-directed speech: When communicating with their infants, deaf mothers use sign language at a significantly slower tempo than when communicating with adults, and they frequently repeat the signs (Swanson, Leonard, & Gandour, 1992; Masataka, 1996, 1998, 2000).

The cross-cultural similarities in infant-directed speech are so great, in fact, that they appear in some facets of language specific to particular types of interactions. For instance, evidence comparing American English, German, and Mandarin Chinese speakers shows that in each of the languages, pitch rises when a mother is attempting to get an infant's attention or produce a response, while pitch falls when she is trying to calm an infant (Papousek & Papousek, 1991).

Why do we find such similarities across very different languages? One hypothesis is that the characteristics of infant-directed speech activate innate responses in infants. As we have noted, infants seem to prefer infant-directed speech over adult-directed speech, suggesting that their perceptual systems may be more responsive to such characteristics. Another explanation is that

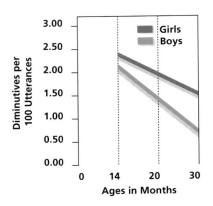

FIGURE 5-8 **DIMINISHING DIMINUTIVES**

Though the use of diminutives toward both male and female infants declines with age, they are consistently used more often in speech directed at females. What do you think is the cultural significance of this?

(*Source:* Gleason et al., 1991.)

infant-directed speech facilitates language development, providing cues as to the meaning of speech before infants have developed the capacity to understand the meaning of words (Kuhl et al., 1997; Trainor & Desjardins, 2002; Falk, 2004).

Despite the similarities in the style of infant-directed speech across diverse cultures, there are some important cultural differences in the *quantity* of speech that infants hear from their parents. For example, although the Gusii of Kenya care for their infants in an extremely close, physical way, they speak to them less than American parents do (LeVine, 1994).

There are also some stylistic differences related to cultural factors in the United States. A major factor, it seems, might be gender.

Gender Differences

To a girl, a bird is a birdie, a blanket a blankie, and a dog a doggy. To a boy, a bird is a bird, a blanket a blanket, and a dog a dog.

At least that's what parents of boys and girls appear to think, as illustrated by the language they use toward their sons and daughters. Virtually from the time of birth, the language parents employ with their children differs depending on the child's sex, according to research conducted by developmental psychologist Jean Berko Gleason (Gleason et al., 1994; Gleason & Ely, 2002).

Gleason found that by the age of 32 months, girls hear twice as many diminutives (words such as "kitty" or "dolly" instead of "cat" or "doll") as boys hear. Although the use of diminutives declines with increasing age, their use consistently remains higher in speech directed at girls than in that directed at boys (see Figure 5-8).

Parents also are more apt to respond differently to children's requests depending on the child's gender. For instance, when turning down a child's request, mothers are likely to respond with a firm "no" to a male child, but to soften the blow to a female child by providing a diversionary response ("Why don't you do this instead?") or by somehow making the refusal less direct. Consequently, boys tend to hear firmer, clearer language, while girls are exposed to warmer phrases, often referring to inner emotional states (Perlmann & Gleason, 1990).

Do such differences in language directed at boys and girls during infancy affect their behavior as adults? There is no direct evidence that plainly supports such an association, but men and women do use different sorts of language as adults. For instance, as adults, women tend to use more tentative, less assertive language, such as "Maybe we should try to go to a movie," than men ("I know, let's go to a movie!"). Though we don't know if these differences are a reflection of early linguistic experiences, such findings are certainly intriguing (Matlin, 1987; Tannen, 1991; Leaper, Anderson, & Sanders, 1998; Peterson & Roberts, 2003; Tenenbaum & Leaper, 2003).

Becoming an Informed Consumer of Development

What Can You Do to Promote Infants' Cognitive Development?

All parents want their children to reach their full cognitive potential, but sometimes efforts to reach this goal take a bizarre path. For instance, some parents spend hundreds of dollars enrolling in workshops with titles such as "How to Multiply Your Baby's Intelligence" and buying books with titles such as *How to Teach Your Baby to Read* (Doman & Doman, 2002).

Do such efforts ever succeed? Although some parents swear they do, there is no scientific support for the effectiveness of such programs. For example, despite the many cognitive skills of infants, no infant can actually read. Furthermore, "multiplying" a baby's intelligence is impossible, and such organizations as the American Academy of Pediatrics and the American Academy of Neurology have denounced programs that claim to do so.

On the other hand, certain things can be done to promote cognitive development in infants. The following suggestions, based upon findings of developmental researchers, offer a starting point (Schulman, 1991; Gopnik, Meltzoff, & Kuhl, 2000):

- *Provide infants the opportunity to explore the world.* As Piaget suggests, children learn by doing, and they need the opportunity to explore and probe their environment. Make sure the environment contains a variety of toys, books, and other sources of stimulation. (Also see the *Careers in Lifespan Development* box.)

- *Be responsive to infants on both a verbal and a nonverbal level.* Try to speak *with* babies, as opposed to *at* them. Ask questions, listen to their responses, and provide further communication.

- *Read to your infants.* Although they may not understand the meaning of your words, they will respond to your tone of voice and the intimacy provided by the activity. Reading together also is associated with later literacy skills and begins to create a lifelong reading habit. In fact, the American Academy of Pediatrics recommends daily reading to children starting at the age of 6 months (American Academy of Pediatrics, 1997; Reutzel, Fawson, & Smith, 2006; Weigel, Martin, & Bennett, 2006).

- *Keep in mind that you don't have to be with an infant 24 hours a day.* Just as infants need time to explore their world on their own, parents and other caregivers need time off from child-care activities.

- *Don't push infants and don't expect too much too soon.* Your goal should not be to create a genius; it should be to provide a warm, nurturing environment that will allow an infant to reach his or her potential.

Even if they don't understand the meaning of the words, infants still benefit from being read to.

Review and Apply

Review

- Before they speak, infants understand many adult utterances and engage in several forms of prelinguistic communication, including the use of facial expressions, gestures, and babbling.

- Children typically produce their first words between 10 and 14 months, and rapidly increase their vocabularies from that point on, especially during a spurt at about 18 months.

- Children's language development proceeds through a pattern of holophrases, two-word combinations, and telegraphic speech.

- Learning theorists believe that basic learning processes account for language development, whereas nativists like Noam Chomsky and his followers argue that humans have an innate language capacity. The interactionists suggest that language is a consequence of both environmental and innate factors.

- When talking to infants, adults of all cultures tend to use infant-directed speech.

Applying Lifespan Development

- What are some ways in which children's linguistic development reflects their acquisition of new ways of interpreting and dealing with their world?

- *From an educator's perspective:* What are some implications of differences in the ways adults speak to boys and girls? How might such speech differences contribute to later differences not only in speech, but also in attitudes?

Epilogue

In this chapter we looked at infants' cognitive development from perspectives ranging from Piaget to information processing theory. We examined infant learning, memory, and intelligence, and we concluded the chapter with a look at language.

Before we proceed to social and personality development in the next chapter, turn back to the prologue of this chapter, about Jake Bausman's apparent eagerness to view Baby Einstein and other education media, and answer the following questions.

1. Is Anita Bausman correct to assume that her infant son Jake is "happy watching" educational videos just because he eagerly spends time in front of the television?

2. If a certain minimum amount of stimulation is necessary for an infant's cognitive development, does that necessarily mean that extra stimulation will accelerate the process?

3. In what ways might Anita Bausman unwittingly be limiting Jake's cognitive development if she relies too heavily on Baby Einstein videos to keep him occupied?

4. Do Anita Bausman's claims about the benefits to Jake of Baby Einstein videos ring true, or do they seem exaggerated? How might Jake's true intellectual capacity be more accurately assessed?

Looking
Back

■ **What are the fundamental features of Piaget's theories of cognitive development?**

- Jean Piaget's stage theory asserts that children pass through stages of cognitive development in a fixed order. The stages represent changes not only in the quantity of infants' knowledge, but in the quality of that knowledge as well.

- According to Piaget, all children pass gradually through the four major stages of cognitive development (sensorimotor, preoperational, concrete operational, and formal operational) and their various substages when they are at an appropriate level of maturation and are exposed to relevant types of experiences.

- In the Piagetian view, children's understanding grows through assimilation of their experiences into their current way of thinking or through accommodation of their current way of thinking to their experiences.

- During the sensorimotor period (birth to about 2 years) with its six substages, infants progress from the use of simple reflexes, through the development of repeated and integrated actions that gradually increase in complexity, to the ability to generate purposeful effects from their actions. By the end of the sixth substage of the sensorimotor period, infants are beginning to engage in symbolic thought.

■ **How do infants process information?**

- Information processing approaches to the study of cognitive development seek to learn how individuals receive, organize, store, and retrieve information. Such approaches differ from Piaget's by considering quantitative changes in children's abilities to process information.

- Infants have memory capabilities from their earliest days, although the accuracy of infant memories is a matter of debate.

■ **How is infant intelligence measured?**

- Traditional measures of infant intelligence, such as Gesell's developmental quotient and the Bayley Scales of Infant Development, focus on average behavior observed at particular ages in large numbers of children.

- Information processing approaches to assessing intelligence rely on variations in the speed and quality with which infants process information.

■ **By what processes do children learn to use language?**

- Prelinguistic communication involves the use of sounds, gestures, facial expressions, imitation, and other nonlinguistic means to express thoughts and states. Prelinguistic communication prepares the infant for speech.

- Infants typically produce their first words between the ages of 10 and 14 months. At around 18 months, children typically begin to link words together into primitive sentences that express single thoughts. Beginning speech is characterized by the use of holophrases, telegraphic speech, underextension, and overextension.

- The learning theory approach to language acquisition assumes that adults and children use basic behavioral processes—such as conditioning, reinforcement, and shaping—in language learning. A different approach proposed by Chomsky holds that humans are genetically endowed with a language-acquisition device, which permits them to detect and use the principles of universal grammar that underlie all languages.

■ **How do children influence adults' language?**

- Adult language is influenced by the children to whom it is addressed. Infant-directed speech takes on characteristics, surprisingly invariant across cultures, that make it appealing to infants and that probably encourage language development.

- Adult language also exhibits differences based on the gender of the child to whom it is directed, which may have effects that emerge later in life.

Key Terms and Concepts

scheme (p. 151)
assimilation (p. 151)
accommodation (p. 151)
sensorimotor stage (of cognitive development) (p. 152)
object permanence (p. 154)
information processing approaches (p. 158)
memory (p. 161)
infantile amnesia (p. 161)

developmental quotient (p. 163)
Bayley Scales of Infant Development (p. 164)
language (p. 167)
babbling (p. 169)
holophrases (p. 170)
telegraphic speech (p. 171)
underextension (p. 172)
overextension (p. 172)

referential style (p. 172)
expressive style (p. 172)
learning theory approach (p. 172)
nativist approach (p. 173)
universal grammar (p. 173)
language-acquisition device (LAD) (p. 173)
infant-directed speech (p. 174)

6 Social and Personality Development in Infancy

Chapter Overview

DEVELOPING THE ROOTS OF SOCIABILITY

Emotions in Infancy: Do Infants Experience Emotional Highs and Lows?

Social Referencing: Feeling What Others Feel

The Development of Self: Do Infants Know Who They Are?

Theory of Mind: Infants' Perspectives on the Mental Lives of Others—and Themselves

FORMING RELATIONSHIPS

Attachment: Forming Social Bonds

Producing Attachment: The Roles of the Mother and Father

Infant Interactions: Developing a Working Relationship

Infants' Sociability with Their Peers: Infant–Infant Interaction

DIFFERENCES AMONG INFANTS

Personality Development: The Characteristics That Make Infants Unique

Temperament: Stabilities in Infant Behavior

Gender: Boys in Blue, Girls in Pink

Family Life in the 21st Century

Prologue: The Velcro Chronicles

It was during the windy days of March that the problem in the child-care center first arose. Its source: 10-month-old Russell Ruud. Otherwise a model of decorum, Russell had somehow learned how to unzip the Velcro chin strap to his winter hat. He would remove the hat whenever he got the urge, seemingly oblivious to the potential health problems that might follow.

But that was just the start of the real difficulty. To the chagrin of the teachers in the child-care center, not to speak of the children's parents, soon other children were following his lead, removing their own caps at will.

Russell's mother, made aware of the anarchy at the child-care center—and the other parents' distress over Russell's behavior—pleaded innocent. "I never showed Russell how to unzip the Velcro," claimed his mother, Judith Ruud, an economist with the Congressional Budget Office in Washington, D.C. "He learned by trial and error, and the other kids saw him do it one day when they were getting dressed for an outing." (Goleman, 1993, C10)

By then, though, it was too late for excuses: Russell, it seems, was an excellent teacher. Keeping the children's hats on their heads proved to be no easy task. Even more ominous was the thought that if the infants could master the Velcro straps on their hats, would they soon be unfastening the Velcro straps on their shoes and removing *them?*

Infants not only learn desirable behaviors, but less positive ones (like shoe removal techniques), through observation of their more "expert" peers.

As babies like Russell show us, children are sociable from a very early age. This anecdote also demonstrates one of the side benefits of infants' participation in child care, and something research has begun to suggest: Through their social interactions, babies acquire new skills and abilities from more "expert" peers. Infants, as we will see, have an amazing capacity to learn from other children, and their interactions with others can play a central role in their developing social and emotional worlds.

In this chapter we consider social and personality development in infancy. We begin by examining the emotional lives of infants, considering which emotions they feel and how well they can read others' emotions. We also look at how others' responses shape infants' own reactions, and how babies view their own and others' mental lives.

We then turn to infants' social relationships. We look at how they forge bonds of attachment and the ways they interact with family members and peers.

Finally, we cover the characteristics that differentiate one infant from another and discuss differences in the way children are treated depending on their gender. We'll consider the nature of family life and discuss how it differs from earlier eras. The chapter closes with a look at the advantages and disadvantages of infant child care outside the home, a child-care option that today's families increasingly employ.

After reading this chapter, you will be able to answer these questions:

- Do infants experience emotions?
- What sort of mental lives do infants have?
- What is attachment in infancy and how does it affect a person's future social competence?
- What roles do other people play in infants' social development?
- What individual differences distinguish one infant from another?
- How does nonparental child care impact infants?

Looking Ahead

Developing the Roots of Sociability

Germaine smiles when he catches a glimpse of his mother. Tawanda looks angry when her mother takes away the spoon that she is playing with. Sydney scowls when a loud plane flies overhead.

A smile. A look of anger. A scowl. The emotions of infancy are written all over a baby's face. Yet do infants experience emotions in the same way that adults do? When do they become capable of understanding what others are experiencing emotionally? And how do they use others' emotional states to make sense of their environment? We consider some of these questions as we seek to understand how infants develop emotionally and socially.

Emotions in Infancy: Do Infants Experience Emotional Highs and Lows?

Anyone who spends any time at all around infants knows they display facial expressions that seem indicative of their emotional states. In situations in which we expect them to be happy, they seem to smile; when we might assume they are frustrated, they show anger; and when we might expect them to be unhappy, they look sad.

In fact, these basic facial expressions are remarkably similar across the most diverse cultures. Whether we look at babies in India, the United States, or the jungles of New Guinea, the expression of basic emotions is the same (see Figure 6-1). Furthermore, the nonverbal expression of emotion, called *nonverbal encoding,* is fairly consistent among people of all ages. These consistencies have led researchers to conclude that we are born with the capacity to display basic emotions (Scharfe, 2000; Sullivan & Lewis, 2003; Ackerman & Izard, 2004).

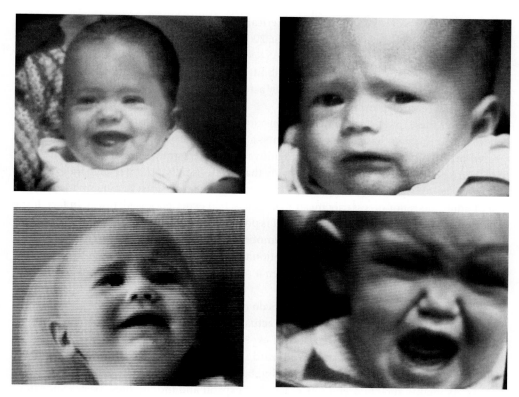

FIGURE 6-1 UNIVERSALS IN FACIAL EXPRESSIONS

Across every culture, infants show similar facial expressions relating to basic emotions. Do you think such expressions are similar in nonhuman animals?

Infants display a fairly wide range of emotional expressions. According to research on what mothers see in their children's nonverbal behavior, almost all think that by the age of 1 month, their babies have expressed interest and joy. In addition, 84% of mothers think their infants have expressed anger, 75% surprise, 58% fear, and 34% sadness. Research using the *Maximally Discriminative Facial Movement Coding System (MAX)*, developed by developmental psychologist Carroll Izard, also finds that interest, distress, and disgust are present at birth, and that other emotions emerge over the next few months (see Figure 6-2). Such findings are consistent with the work of the famous naturalist Charles Darwin, whose 1872 book *The Expression of the Emotions in Man and Animals* argued that humans and primates have an inborn, universal set of emotional expressions—a view consistent with today's evolutionary approach to development (Izard, 1982; Sroufe, 1996; Benson, 2003).

Although infants display similar *kinds* of emotions, the *degree* of emotional expressivity varies among infants. Children in different cultures show reliable differences in emotional expressiveness, even during infancy. For example, by the age of 11 months, Chinese infants are

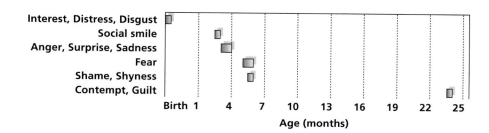

FIGURE 6-2 EMERGENCE OF EMOTIONAL EXPRESSIONS

Emotional expressions emerge at roughly these times. Keep in mind that expressions in the first few weeks after birth do not necessarily reflect particular inner feelings.

generally less expressive than European, American, and Japanese infants (Camras et al., 1998; Eisenberg et al., 2000; Camras, Meng, & Ujiie, 2002).

Experiencing Emotions.　Does the capability of infants to express emotions nonverbally in a consistent, reliable manner mean that they actually *experience* emotions, and—if they do—is the experience similar to that of adults?

To answer these questions, we need to consider just what emotions are. Developmentalists believe a true *emotion* has three components: a biological arousal component (such as increased breathing rate or heartbeat), a cognitive component (awareness of feeling anger or fear), and a behavioral component (displaying that one feels unhappy by crying, for example).

Consequently, the fact that children display nonverbal expressions in a manner similar to that of adults does not necessarily mean that their actual experience is identical. In fact, if the nature of such displays is innate, or inborn, it is possible that facial expressions can occur without any accompanying awareness of their emotional experience (the cognitive component). Nonverbal expressions, then, might be emotionless in young infants, in much the same way that your knee reflexively jerks forward when a physician taps it, without the involvement of emotions (Soussignan et al., 1997).

However, most developmental researchers do not think this is the case: They argue that the nonverbal expressions of infants represent actual emotional experiences. In fact, emotional expressions may not only reflect emotional experiences, but also help regulate the emotion itself. Developmental psychologist Carroll Izard suggests that infants are born with an innate repertoire of emotional expressions, reflecting basic emotional states such as happiness and sadness. As infants and children grow older, they expand and modify these basic expressions and become more adept at controlling their nonverbal behavioral expressions. For example, they eventually may learn that by smiling at the right time, they can increase the chances of getting their own way. Emotional expressions thus have an adaptive function, permitting infants to express their needs nonverbally to caretakers before they have developed linguistic skills.

In sum, infants do appear to experience emotions, although the range of emotions at birth is fairly restricted. However, as they get older, infants both display and experience a wider range of increasingly complex emotions. Furthermore, in addition to *expressing* a wider variety of emotions, as children develop they also *experience* a wider array of emotions (Camras, Malatesta, & Izard, 1991; Buss & Goldsmith, 1998; Izard et al., 2003; Buss & Kiel, 2004).

The advances in infants' emotional life are made possible by the increasing sophistication of their brains. Initially, the differentiation of emotions occurs as the cerebral cortex becomes operative in the first 3 months of life. By the age of 9 or 10 months, the structures that make up the limbic system (the site of emotional reactions) begin to grow. The limbic system starts to work in tandem with the frontal lobes, allowing for an increased range of emotions (Sroufe, 1996; Davidson, 2003; Schore, 2003).

Stranger Anxiety and Separation Anxiety.　"She used to be such a friendly baby," thought Erika's mother. "No matter whom she encountered, she had a big smile. But almost the day she turned 7 months old, she began to react to strangers as if she were seeing a ghost. Her face crinkles up with a frown, and she either turns away or stares at them with suspicion. And she doesn't want to be left with anyone she doesn't already know. It's as if she has undergone a personality transplant."

What happened to Erika is, in fact, quite typical. By the end of the first year, infants often develop both stranger anxiety and separation anxiety. **Stranger anxiety** is the caution and wariness displayed by infants when encountering an unfamiliar person. Such anxiety typically appears in the second half of the first year.

What brings on stranger anxiety? Here, too, brain development, and the increased cognitive abilities of infants, plays a role. As infants' memory develops, they are able to separate the people they know from the people they don't. The same cognitive advances that allow them to

mydevelopmentlab

VIDEO CLIP
STRANGER ANXIETY

. . . .
stranger anxiety　the caution and wariness displayed by infants when encountering an unfamiliar person.

respond so positively to those people with whom they are familiar also give them the ability to recognize people who are unfamiliar. Furthermore, between 6 and 9 months, infants begin trying to make sense of their world, trying to anticipate and predict events. When something happens that they don't expect—such as with the appearance of an unknown person—they experience fear. It's as if an infant has a question but is unable to answer it (Ainsworth, 1973; Kagan, Kearsley, & Zelazo, 1978).

Although stranger anxiety is common after the age of 6 months, significant differences exist between children. Some infants, particularly those who have a lot of experience with strangers, tend to show less anxiety than those whose experience with strangers is limited. Furthermore, not all strangers evoke the same reaction. For instance, infants tend to show less anxiety with female strangers than with male strangers. In addition, they react more positively to strangers who are children than to strangers who are adults, perhaps because their size is less intimidating (Brooks & Lewis, 1976; Thompson & Limber, 1990; Murray et al., 2007).

Separation anxiety is the distress displayed by infants when a customary care provider departs. Separation anxiety, which is also universal across cultures, usually begins at about 7 or 8 months (see Figure 6-3). It peaks around 14 months, and then decreases. Separation anxiety is largely attributable to the same reasons as stranger anxiety. Infants' growing cognitive skills allow them to ask reasonable questions, but they may be questions that they are too young to understand the answer to: "Why is my mother leaving?" "Where is she going?" and "Will she come back?"

Stranger anxiety and separation anxiety represent important social progress. They reflect both cognitive advances and the growing emotional and social bonds between infants and their caregivers—bonds that we'll consider later in the chapter when we discuss infants' social relationships.

Smiling. As Luz lay sleeping in her crib, her mother and father caught a glimpse of the most beautiful smile crossing her face. Her parents were sure that Luz was having a pleasant dream. Were they right?

Probably not. The earliest smiles expressed during sleep probably have little meaning, although no one can be absolutely sure. By 6 to 9 weeks babies begin to smile reliably at the sight of stimuli that please them, including toys, mobiles, and—to the delight of parents—people. The first smiles tend to be relatively indiscriminate, as infants first begin to smile at the sight of almost anything they find amusing. However, as they get older, they become more selective in their smiles.

A baby's smile in response to another person, rather than to nonhuman stimuli, is considered a **social smile.** As babies get older, their social smiles become directed toward particular

separation anxiety   the distress displayed by infants when a customary care provider departs.

social smile   smiling in response to other individuals.

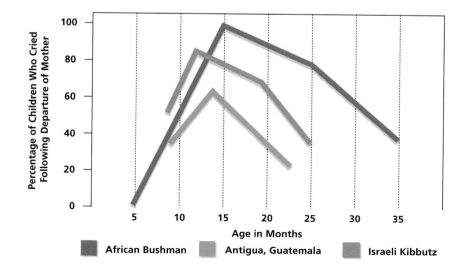

FIGURE 6-3   SEPARATION ANXIETY

Separation anxiety, the distress displayed by infants when their usual care provider leaves their presence, is a universal phenomenon beginning at around the age of 7 or 8 months. It peaks at around the age of 14 months and then begins to decline. Does separation anxiety have survival value for humans?

(*Source:* Kagan, Kearsley, & Zelazo, 1978.)

When infants smile at a person, rather than a nonhuman stimulus, they are displaying a social smile.

individuals, not just anyone. By the age of 18 months, social smiling, directed more toward mothers and other caregivers, becomes more frequent than smiling directed toward nonhuman objects. Moreover, if an adult is unresponsive to a child, the amount of smiling decreases. In short, by the end of the second year children are quite purposefully using smiling to communicate their positive emotions, and they are sensitive to the emotional expressions of others (Carvajal & Iglesias, 2000; Messinger, 2002; Carver, Dawson, & Panagiotides, 2003; Bigelow & Rochat, 2006; Fogel et al., 2006).

Decoding Others' Facial and Vocal Expressions. In Chapter 3, we discussed the possibility that neonates can imitate adults' facial expressions even minutes after birth. Although their imitative abilities certainly do not imply that they can understand the meaning of others' facial expressions, such imitation does pave the way for *nonverbal decoding* abilities, which begin to emerge fairly soon. Using these abilities, infants can interpret others' facial and vocal expressions that carry emotional meaning. For example, they can tell when a caregiver is happy to see them and pick up on worry or fear in the faces of others (Bornstein & Arterberry, 2003; Hernandez-Reif et al., 2006; Striano & Vaish, 2006).

Infants seem to be able to discriminate vocal expressions of emotion at a slightly earlier age than they discriminate facial expressions. Although relatively little attention has been given to infants' perception of vocal expressions, it does appear that they are able to discriminate happy and sad vocal expressions at the age of 5 months (Soken & Pick, 1999; Montague & Walker-Andrews, 2002).

Scientists know more about the *sequence* in which nonverbal facial decoding ability progresses. In the first 6 to 8 weeks, infants' visual precision is sufficiently limited that they cannot pay much attention to others' facial expressions. But they soon begin to discriminate among different facial expressions of emotion and even seem to be able to respond to differences in emotional intensity conveyed by facial expressions. They also respond to unusual facial expressions. For instance, they show distress when their mothers pose bland, unresponsive, neutral facial expressions (Nelson, 1987; Adamson & Frick, 2003; Bertin & Striano, 2006).

By the time they reach the age of 4 months, infants may already have begun to understand the emotions that lie behind the facial and vocal expressions of others. How do we know this? One important clue comes from a study in which 7-month-old infants were shown a pair of facial expressions relating to joy and sadness, and simultaneously heard a vocalization representing either joy (a rising tone of voice) or sadness (a falling tone of voice). When the facial expression matched the tone, infants paid more attention, suggesting that they had at least a rudimentary understanding of the emotional meaning of facial expressions and voice tones (Walker & Andrews, 1997; Soken & Pick, 1999; Kahana-Kalman & Walker-Andrews, 2001; Kochanska & Aksan, 2004; Grossmann, Striano, & Friederici, 2006).

In sum, infants learn early both to produce and to decode emotions, and they begin to learn the effect of their own emotions on others. Such abilities play an important role not only in helping them experience their own emotions, but—as we see next—in using others' emotions to understand the meaning of ambiguous social situations (Buss & Kiel, 2004).

Social Referencing: Feeling What Others Feel

Twenty-three-month-old Stephania watches as her older brother Eric and his friend Chen argue loudly with each other and begin to wrestle. Uncertain of what is happening, Stephania glances at her mother. Her mother, though, wears a smile, knowing that Eric and Chen are just playing. On seeing her mother's reaction, Stephania smiles too, mimicking her mother's facial expression.

mydevelopmentlab

VIDEO CLIP

SOCIAL REFERENCING

Like Stephania, most of us have been in situations in which we feel uncertain. In such cases, we sometimes turn to others to see how they are reacting. This reliance on others, known as social referencing, helps us decide what an appropriate response ought to be.

Social referencing is the intentional search for information about others' feelings to help explain the meaning of uncertain circumstances and events. Like Stephania, we use social referencing to clarify the meaning of a situation and thus reduce our uncertainty about what is occurring.

Social referencing first occurs around the age of 8 or 9 months. It is a fairly sophisticated social ability: Infants need it not only to understand the significance of others' behavior, by using such cues as their facial expressions, but also understand the meaning of those behaviors within the context of a specific situation (Mumme & Fernald, 2003; de Rosnay et al., 2006; Carver & Vaccaro, 2007).

Infants make particular use of facial expressions in their social referencing, the way Stephania did when she noticed her mother's smile. For instance, in one study infants were given an unusual toy to play with. The amount of time they played with it depended on their mothers' facial expressions. When their mothers displayed disgust, they played with it significantly less than when their mothers appeared pleased. Furthermore, when given the opportunity to play with the same toy later, the infants remained reluctant to play with it, despite the mothers' now neutral-appearing facial reactions, suggesting that parental attitudes may have lasting consequences (Hornik & Gunnar, 1988; Hertenstein & Campos, 2004).

Two Explanations of Social Referencing.   Although it is clear that social referencing begins fairly early in life, researchers are still not certain *how* it operates. It may be that observing someone else's facial expression brings about the emotion the expression represents. That is, an infant who views someone looking sad may come to feel sad herself, and her behavior may be affected. On the other hand, it may be the case that viewing another's facial expression simply provides information. In this case, the infant does not experience the particular emotion represented by another's facial expression; she simply uses the display as data to guide her own behavior.

Both explanations for social referencing have received some support in research studies, and so we still don't know which is correct. What we do know is that social referencing is most likely to occur when a situation breeds uncertainty and ambiguity. Furthermore, infants who reach the age when they are able to use social referencing become quite upset if they receive conflicting nonverbal messages from their mothers and fathers. For example, if a mother shows with her facial expressions that she is annoyed with her son for knocking over a carton of milk, while his grandmother sees it as cute and smiles, the child receives two contradictory messages. Such mixed messages can be a real source of stress for an infant (Hirshberg & Svejda, 1990; Stenberg, 2003; Vaish & Striano, 2004).

The Development of Self: Do Infants Know Who They Are?

Elysa, 8 months old, crawls past the full-length mirror that hangs on a door in her parents' bedroom. She barely pays any attention to her reflection as she moves by. On the other hand, her cousin Brianna, who is almost 2 years old, stares at herself in the mirror as she passes and laughs as she notices, and then rubs off, a smear of jelly on her forehead.

Perhaps you have had the experience of catching a glimpse of yourself in a mirror and noticing a hair out of place. You probably reacted by attempting to push the unruly hair back into place. Your reaction shows more than that you care about how you look. It implies that you have a sense of yourself, the awareness and knowledge that you are an independent social entity to which others react, and which you attempt to present to the world in ways that reflect favorably upon you.

However, we are not born with the knowledge that we exist independently from others and the larger world. Very young infants do not have a sense of themselves as individuals;

social referencing   the intentional search for information about others' feelings to help explain the meaning of uncertain circumstances and events.

Research suggests that this 18-month-old is exhibiting a clearly developed sense of self.

they do not recognize themselves in photos or mirrors. However, the roots of **self-awareness,** knowledge of oneself, begin to grow at around the age of 12 months. We know this from a simple but ingenious experimental technique. An infant's nose is secretly colored with a dab of red powder, and the infant is seated in front of a mirror. If infants touch their noses or attempt to wipe off the rouge, we have evidence that they have at least some knowledge of their physical characteristics. For them, this awareness is one step in developing an understanding of themselves as independent objects. For instance, Brianna, in the example at the beginning of this section, showed her awareness of her independence when she tried to rub the jam off her forehead (Gallup, 1977; Asendorpf, Warkentin, & Baudonniere, 1996; Rochat, 2004).

Although some infants as young as 12 months seem startled on seeing the rouge spot, for most a reaction does not occur until between 17 and 24 months of age. It is also around this age that children begin to show awareness of their own capabilities. For instance, infants who participate in experiments when they are between the ages of 23 and 25 months sometimes begin to cry if the experimenter asks them to imitate a complicated sequence of behaviors involving toys, although they readily accomplish simpler sequences. Their reaction suggests that they are conscious that they lack the ability to carry out difficult tasks and are unhappy about it—a reaction that provides a clear indication of self-awareness (Kagan, 1981; Legerstee et al., 1998; Asendorpf, 2002).

Children's cultural upbringing also impacts the development of self-recognition. For instance, Greek children—who experience parenting practices that emphasize autonomy and separation—show self-recognition at an earlier age than children from Cameroon in Africa. In the Cameroonian culture, parenting practices emphasize body contact and warmth, leading to more interdependence between infants and parents, and ultimately later development of self-recognition (Keller et al., 2004; Keller, Voelker, & Yovsi, 2005).

In general, by the age of 18 to 24 months, infants in Western cultures have developed at least an awareness of their own physical characteristics and capabilities, and they understand that their appearance is stable over time. Although it is not clear how far this awareness extends, it is becoming increasingly evident that, as we discuss next, infants have not only a basic understanding of themselves, but also the beginnings of an understanding of how the mind operates—what has come to be called a "theory of mind" (Forrester, 2001; Fogel, de Koeyer, & Bellagamba, 2002; Nielsen, Dissanayake, & Kashima, 2003; Lewis & Ramsay, 2004).

self-awareness knowledge of oneself.

Theory of Mind: Infants' Perspectives on the Mental Lives of Others—and Themselves

What are infants' thoughts about thinking? According to developmental psychologist John Flavell, infants begin to understand certain things about their own and others' mental processes at quite an early age. Flavell has investigated children's **theory of mind,** their knowledge and beliefs about how the mind works and how it influences behavior. Theories of mind are the explanations that children use to explain how others think.

For instance, cognitive advances during infancy that we discussed in Chapter 5 permit older infants to see people in a very different way from other objects. They learn to see other people as *compliant agents,* beings similar to themselves who behave under their own power and who have the capacity to respond to infants' requests. Eighteen-month-old Chris, for example, has come to realize that he can ask his father to get him more juice (Flavell, Green, & Flavell, 1995; Poulin-Dubois, 1999; Rochat, 1999, 2004).

In addition, children's capacity to understand intentionality and causality grows during infancy. They begin to understand that others' behaviors have some meaning and that the behaviors they see people enacting are designed to accomplish particular goals, in contrast to the "behaviors" of inanimate objects. For example, a child comes to understand that his father has a specific goal when he is in the kitchen making sandwiches. In contrast, his father's car is simply parked in the driveway, having no mental life or goal (Golinkoff, 1993; Ahn, Gelman, & Amsterlaw, 2000).

Another piece of evidence for infants' growing sense of mental activity is that by the age of 2, infants begin to demonstrate the rudiments of empathy. **Empathy** is an emotional response that corresponds to the feelings of another person. At 24 months of age, infants sometimes comfort others or show concern for them. In order to do this, they need to be aware of the emotional states of others. For example, as noted in Chapter 5, 1-year-olds are able to pick up emotional cues by observing the behavior of an actress on television (Gauthier, 2003; Mumme & Fernald, 2003).

Further, during their second year, infants begin to use deception, both in games of "pretend" and in outright attempts to fool others. A child who plays "pretend" and who uses falsehoods must be aware that others hold beliefs about the world—beliefs that can be manipulated. In short, by the end of infancy children have developed the rudiments of their own personal theory of mind. It helps them understand the actions of others and it affects their own behavior (Zahn-Waxler, Robinson, & Emde, 1992; Lee & Homer, 1999; van der Mark et al., 2002).

theory of mind knowledge and beliefs about how the mind works and how it affects behavior.

empathy an emotional response that corresponds to the feelings of another person.

VIDEO CLIP

THEORY OF MIND

Review and Apply

Review

- Infants appear to express and to experience emotions, and their emotions broaden in range to reflect increasingly complex emotional states.

- Infants from all cultures use similar facial expressions to express basic emotional states.

- As they develop cognitively and begin to distinguish familiar from unfamiliar people, infants begin to experience stranger anxiety at about 6 months and separation anxiety at around 8 months of age.

- The ability to decode the nonverbal facial and vocal expressions of others develops early in infants. The use of nonverbal decoding to clarify situations of uncertainty and determine appropriate responses is called *social referencing.*

- Infants develop self-awareness, the knowledge that they exist separately from the rest of the world, after about 12 months of age.

- By the age of 2, children have developed the rudiments of a theory of mind.

attachment the positive emotional bond that develops between a child and a particular individual.

Applying Lifespan Development

- Why would the sad or flat emotional expressiveness of a depressed parent be hard on an infant? How might it be counteracted?

- *From a social worker's perspective:* In what situations do adults rely on social referencing to work out appropriate responses? How might social referencing be used to influence parents' behavior toward their children?

Forming Relationships

Louis Moore became the center of attention on the way home [from the hospital]. His father brought Martha, aged 5, and Tom, aged 3, to the hospital with him when Louis and his mother were discharged. Martha rushed to see "her" new baby and ignored her mother. Tom clung to his mother's knees in the reception hall of the hospital.

A hospital nurse carried Louis to the car. . . . The two older children immediately climbed over the seat and swamped mother and baby with their attention. Both children stuck their faces into his, smacked at him, and talked to him. They soon began to fight over him with loud voices. The loud argument and the jostling of his mother upset Louis, and he started to cry. He let out a wail that came like a shotgun blast into the noisy car. The children quieted immediately and looked with awe at this new infant. His insistent wails drowned out their bickering. He had already asserted himself in their eyes. Martha's lip quivered as she watched her mother attempt to comfort Louis, and she added her own soft cooing in imitation of her mother. Tom squeezed even closer to his mother, put his thumb in his mouth, and closed his eyes to shut out the commotion. (Brazelton, 1983, p. 48)

The arrival of a newborn brings a dramatic change to a family's dynamics. No matter how welcome a baby's birth, it causes a fundamental shift in the roles that people play within the family. Mothers and fathers must start to build a relationship with their infant, and older children must adjust to the presence of a new member of the family and build their own alliance with their infant brother or sister.

Although the process of social development during infancy is neither simple nor automatic, it is crucial: The bonds that grow between infants and their parents, siblings, family, and others provide the foundation for a lifetime's worth of social relationships.

The foundations of empathy, emotional responses that correspond to the feelings of another person, are formed in the early years of life.

Attachment: Forming Social Bonds

The most important aspect of social development that takes place during infancy is the formation of attachment. **Attachment** is the positive emotional bond that develops between a child and a particular, special individual. When children experience attachment to a given person, they feel pleasure when they are with them and feel comforted by their presence at times of distress. As we'll see when we consider social development in early adulthood (Chapter 14), the nature of our attachment during infancy affects how we relate to others throughout the rest of our lives (Fraley, 2002; Grossmann, Grossuan, & Waters, 2005; Hofer, 2006).

To understand attachment, the earliest researchers turned to the bonds that form between parents and children in the nonhuman animal kingdom. For instance, ethologist Konrad Lorenz (1965) observed newborn goslings, who have an innate tendency to follow their mother, the first moving object to which they typically are exposed after birth. Lorenz found that goslings whose eggs were raised in an incubator and who viewed him just after hatching would follow his every movement, as if he were their mother. As discussed in Chapter 3, he labeled this process *imprinting*: behavior that takes place during a critical period and involves attachment to the first moving object that is observed.

Lorenz's findings suggested that attachment was based on biologically determined factors, and other theorists agreed. For instance, Freud suggested that attachment grew out of a mother's ability to satisfy a child's oral needs.

It turns out, however, that the ability to provide food and other physiological needs may not be as crucial as Freud and other theorists first thought. In a classic study, psychologist Harry Harlow gave infant monkeys the choice of cuddling a wire "monkey" that provided food or a soft, terry cloth monkey that was warm but did not provide food (see Figure 6-4). Their preference was clear: Baby monkeys spent most of their time clinging to the cloth monkey, although they made occasional expeditions to the wire monkey to nurse. Harlow suggested that the preference for the warm cloth monkey provided *contact comfort* (Harlow & Zimmerman, 1959; Blum, 2002).

Harlow's work illustrates that food alone is not the basis for attachment. Given that the monkeys' preference for the soft cloth "mothers" developed some time after birth, these findings are consistent with the research discussed in Chapter 3, showing little support for the existence of a critical period for bonding between human mothers and infants immediately following birth.

The earliest work on human attachment, which is still highly influential, was carried out by British psychiatrist John Bowlby (1951). In Bowlby's view, attachment is based primarily on infants' needs for safety and security—their genetically determined motivation to avoid predators. As they develop, infants come to learn that their safety is best provided by a particular individual. This realization ultimately leads to the development of a special relationship with that individual, who is typically the mother. Bowlby suggested that this single relationship with the primary caregiver is qualitatively different from the bonds formed with others, including the father—a suggestion that, as we'll see later, has been a source of some disagreement.

According to Bowlby, attachment provides a type of home base. As children become more independent, they can progressively roam further away from their secure base.

The Ainsworth Strange Situation and Patterns of Attachment.

Developmental psychologist Mary Ainsworth built on Bowlby's theorizing to develop a widely used experimental technique to measure attachment (Ainsworth et al., 1978). The **Ainsworth Strange Situation** consists of a sequence of staged episodes that illustrate the strength of attachment between a child and (typically) his or her mother. The "strange situation" follows this general eight-step pattern: (1) The mother and baby enter an unfamiliar room; (2) the mother sits down, leaving the baby free to explore; (3) an adult stranger enters the room and converses first with the mother and then with the baby; (4) the mother exits the room, leaving the baby alone with the stranger; (5) the mother returns, greeting and comforting the baby, and the stranger leaves; (6) the mother departs again, leaving the baby alone; (7) the stranger returns; and (8) the mother returns and the stranger leaves (Ainsworth et al., 1978).

Infants' reactions to the various aspects of the Strange Situation vary considerably, depending on the nature of their attachment to their mothers. One-year-olds typically show one of four major patterns—secure, avoidant, ambivalent, and disorganized-disoriented (summarized in Table 6-1). Children who have a **secure attachment pattern** use the mother as the type of home base that Bowlby described. These children seem at ease in the Strange Situation as long as their mothers are present. They explore independently, returning to her occasionally. Although they may or may not appear upset when she leaves, securely attached children immediately go to her when she returns and seek contact. Most North American children—about two-thirds—fall into the securely attached category.

FIGURE 6-4 MONKEY MOTHERS MATTER

Harlow's research showed that monkeys preferred the warm, soft "mother" over the wire "monkey" that provided food.

Mary Ainsworth, who devised the Strange Situation to measure infant attachment.

Ainsworth Strange Situation a sequence of staged episodes that illustrates the strength of attachment between a child and (typically) his or her mother.

secure attachment pattern a style of attachment in which children use the mother as a kind of home base and are at ease when she is present; when she leaves, they become upset and go to her as soon as she returns.

Table 6-1 Classifications of Infant Attachment

	CLASSIFICATION CRITERIA			
Label	**Seeking Proximity with Caregiver**	**Maintaining Contact with Caregiver**	**Avoiding Proximity with Caregiver**	**Resisting Contact with Caregiver**
Avoidant	Low	Low	High	Low
Secure	High	High (if distressed)	Low	Low
Ambivalent	High	High (often pre-separation)	Low	High
Disorganized-disoriented	Inconsistent	Inconsistent	Inconsistent	Inconsistent

avoidant attachment pattern a style of attachment in which children do not seek proximity to the mother; after the mother has left, they seem to avoid her when she returns as if they are angered by her behavior.

ambivalent attachment pattern a style of attachment in which children display a combination of positive and negative reactions to their mothers; they show great distress when the mother leaves, but upon her return they may simultaneously seek close contact but also hit and kick her.

disorganized-disoriented attachment pattern a style of attachment in which children show inconsistent, often contradictory behavior, such as approaching the mother when she returns but not looking at her; they may be the least securely attached children of all.

In contrast, children with an **avoidant attachment pattern** do not seek proximity to the mother, and after she has left, they typically do not seem distressed. Furthermore, they seem to avoid her when she returns. It is as if they are indifferent to her behavior. Some 20% of 1-year-old children are in the avoidant category.

Children with an **ambivalent attachment pattern** display a combination of positive and negative reactions to their mothers. Initially, ambivalent children are in such close contact with the mother that they hardly explore their environment. They appear anxious even before the mother leaves, and when she does leave, they show great distress. But upon her return, they show ambivalent reactions, seeking to be close to her but also hitting and kicking, apparently in anger. About 10% to 15% of 1-year-olds fall into the ambivalent classification (Cassidy & Berlin, 1994).

Although Ainsworth identified only three categories, a more recent expansion of her work finds that there is a fourth category: disorganized-disoriented. Children who have a **disorganized-disoriented attachment pattern** show inconsistent, contradictory, and confused behavior. They may run to the mother when she returns but not look at her, or seem initially calm and then suddenly break into angry weeping. Their confusion suggests that they may be the least securely attached children of all. About 5% to 10% of all children fall into this category (Mayseless, 1996; Cole, 2005).

A child's attachment style would be of only minor consequence were it not for the fact that the quality of attachment between infants and their mothers has significant consequences for relationships at later stages of life. For example, boys who are securely attached at the age of 1 year show fewer psychological difficulties at older ages than do avoidant or ambivalent children. Similarly, children who are securely attached as infants tend to be more socially and emotionally competent later, and others view them more positively. Adult romantic relationships are associated with the kind of attachment style developed during infancy (Waters et al., 2000; Schneider, Atkinson, & Tardif, 2001; Aviezer, Sagi, & Resnick, 2002; Mikulincer & Shaver, 2005; Simpson et al., 2007).

On the other hand, we cannot say that children who do not have a secure attachment style during infancy invariably experience difficulties later in life, nor that those with a secure attachment at age 1 always have good adjustment later on. In fact, some evidence suggests that children with avoidant and ambivalent attachment—as measured by the Strange Situation— do quite well (Lewis, Feiring, & Rosenthal, 2000; Weinfeld, Sroufe, & Egeland, 2000; Fraley & Spieker, 2003).

In cases in which the development of attachment has been severely disrupted, children may suffer from *reactive attachment disorder,* a psychological problem characterized by extreme problems in forming attachments to others. In young children, it can be displayed in feeding difficulties, unresponsiveness to social overtures from others, and a general failure to thrive. Reactive attachment disorder is rare and typically the result of abuse or neglect (Hanson & Spratt, 2000; Hardy, 2007).

Producing Attachment: The Roles of the Mother and Father

As 5-month-old Annie cries passionately, her mother comes into the room and gently lifts her from her crib. After just a few moments, as her mother rocks Annie and speaks softly, Annie's cries cease, and she cuddles in her mother's arms. But the moment her mother places her back in the crib, Annie begins to wail again, leading her mother to pick her up once again.

The pattern is familiar to most parents. The infant cries, the parent reacts, and the child responds in turn. Such seemingly insignificant sequences as these, repeatedly occurring in the lives of infants and parents, help pave the way for the development of relationships between children, their parents, and the rest of the social world. We'll consider how each of the major caregivers and the infant play a role in the development of attachment.

In this illustration of the strange situation, the infant first explores the playroom on his own, as long as his mother is present. But when she leaves, he begins to cry. On her return, however, he is immediately comforted and stops crying. The conclusion: he is securely attached.

Mothers and Attachment. Sensitivity to their infants' needs and desires is the hallmark of mothers of securely attached infants. Such a mother tends to be aware of her child's moods, and she takes into account her child's feelings as they interact. She is also responsive during face-to-face interactions, provides feeding "on demand," and is warm and affectionate to her infant (Ainsworth, 1993; Thompson, Easterbrooks, & Padilla-Walker, 2003; McElwain & Booth-LaForce, 2006).

It is not only a matter of responding in *any* fashion to their infants' signals that separates mothers of securely attached and insecurely attached children. Mothers of secure infants tend to provide the appropriate level of response. In fact, research has shown that overly responsive mothers are just as likely to have insecurely attached children as underresponsive mothers. In contrast, mothers whose communication involves *interactional synchrony,* in which caregivers respond to infants appropriately and both caregiver and child match emotional states, are more likely to produce secure attachment (Belsky, Rovine, & Taylor, 1984; Kochanskya, 1998; Hane, Feldstein, & Dernetz, 2003).

The research showing the correspondence between mothers' sensitivity to their infants and the security of the infants' attachment is consistent with Ainsworth's arguments that attachment depends on how mothers react to their infants' emotional cues. Ainsworth suggests that mothers of securely attached infants respond rapidly and positively to their infants. For example, Annie's mother responds quickly to her cries by cuddling and comforting her. In contrast, the way for mothers to produce insecurely attached infants, according to Ainsworth, is to ignore their behavioral cues, to behave inconsistently with them, and to ignore or reject their social efforts. For example, picture a child who repeatedly and unsuccessfully tries to gain her mother's attention by calling or turning and gesturing from her stroller while her mother, engaged in conversation, ignores her. This baby is likely to be less securely attached than a child whose mother acknowledges her child more quickly and consistently.

But how do mothers learn how to respond to their infants? One way is from their own mothers. Mothers typically respond to their infants based on their own attachment styles. As a

A growing body of research highlights the importance of a father's demonstration of love for his children. In fact, certain disorders such as depression and substance abuse have been found to be more related to fathers' than to mothers' behavior.

result, there is substantial similarity in attachment patterns from one generation to the next (Benoit & Parker, 1994; Peck, 2003).

It is important to realize that a mother's (and others') behavior toward infants is at least in part a reaction to the child's ability to provide effective cues. A mother may not be able to respond effectively to a child whose own behavior is unrevealing, misleading, or ambiguous. For instance, children who clearly display their anger or fear or unhappiness will be easier to read—and respond to effectively—than children whose behavior is ambiguous. Consequently, the kind of signals an infant sends may in part determine how successful the mother will be in responding.

Fathers and Attachment. Up to now, we've barely touched upon one of the key players involved in the upbringing of a child: the father. In fact, if you looked at the early theorizing and research on attachment, you'd find little mention of the father and his potential contributions to the life of the infant (Russell & Radojevic, 1992; Tamis-LeMonda & Cabrera, 1999).

There are at least two reasons for this absence. First, John Bowlby, who provided the initial theory of attachment, suggested that there was something unique about the mother–child relationship. He believed the mother was uniquely equipped, biologically, to provide sustenance for the child, and he concluded that this capability led to the development of a special relationship between mothers and children. Second, the early work on attachment was influenced by the traditional social views of the time, which considered it "natural" for the mother to be the primary caregiver, while the father's role was to work outside the home to provide a living for his family.

Several factors led to the demise of this view. One was that societal norms changed, and fathers began to take a more active role in child-rearing activities. More important, it became increasingly clear from research findings that—despite societal norms that relegated fathers to secondary child-rearing roles—some infants formed their primary initial relationship with their fathers (Volling & Belsky, 1992; Lewis & Lamb, 2003).

In addition, a growing body of research has showed that fathers' expressions of nurturance, warmth, affection, support, and concern are extremely important to their children's emotional and social well-being. In fact, certain kinds of psychological disorders, such as substance abuse and depression, have been found to be related more to fathers' than mothers' behavior (Tamis-LeMonda & Cabrera, 1999, 2002; Veneziano, 2003; Parke, 2004; Roelofs et al., 2006).

Infants' social bonds extend beyond their parents, especially as they grow older. For example, one study found that although most infants formed their first primary relationship with one person, around one-third had multiple relationships, and it was difficult to determine which attachment was primary. Furthermore, by the time the infants were 18 months old, most had formed multiple relationships. In sum, infants may develop attachments not only to their mothers, but to a variety of others as well (Rosen & Burke, 1999; Silverstein & Auerbach, 1999; Booth, Kelly, & Spieker, 2003).

Are There Differences in Attachment to Mothers and Fathers? Although infants are fully capable of forming attachments to both mother and father—as well as other individuals—the nature of attachment between infants and mothers, on the one hand, and infants and fathers, on the other hand, is not identical. For example, when they are in unusually stressful circumstances, most infants prefer to be soothed by their mother rather than by their father (Pipp, Easterbrooks, & Brown, 1993; Thompson et al., 2003; Schoppe-Sullivan et al., 2006).

One reason for qualitative differences in attachment involves the differences in what fathers and mothers do with their children. Mothers spend a greater proportion of their time feeding and directly nurturing their children. In contrast, fathers spend more time, proportionally, playing with infants. Almost all fathers do contribute to child care: Surveys show that 95% say they do some childcare chores every day. But on average they still do less than mothers. For instance, 30% of fathers with wives who work do 3 or more hours of daily child care.

In comparison, 74% of employed married mothers spend that amount of time every day in childcare activities (Grych & Clark, 1999; Kazura, 2000; Whelan & Lally, 2002).

Furthermore, the nature of fathers' play with their babies is often quite different from that of mothers. Fathers engage in more physical, rough-and-tumble activities with their children. In contrast, mothers play traditional games such as peek-a-boo and games with more verbal elements (Parke, 1996; Paquette, Carbonneau, & Dubeau, 2003).

These differences in the ways that fathers and mothers play with their children occur even in the minority of families in the United States in which the father is the primary caregiver. Moreover, the differences occur in very diverse cultures: Fathers in Australia, Israel, India, Japan, Mexico, and even in the Aka Pygmy tribe in central Africa all engage more in play than in caregiving, although the amount of time they spend with their infants varies widely. For instance, Aka fathers spend more time caring for their infants than members of any other known culture, holding and cuddling their babies at a rate some five times higher than anywhere else in the world (Roopnarine, 1992; Bronstein, 1999; DeLoache & Gottlieb, 2000; Hewlett & Lamb, 2002).

These similarities and differences in child-rearing practices across different societies raise an important question: How does culture affect attachment?

The difference in the ways that fathers and mothers play with their children occurs even in families in which the father is the primary caregiver. Based on this observation, how does culture affect attachment?

Developmental Diversity

Does Attachment Differ Across Cultures?

John Bowlby's observations of the biologically motivated efforts of the young of other species to seek safety and security were the basis for his views on attachment and his reason for suggesting that seeking attachment was biologically universal, a trait that we should find not only in other species, but among humans of all cultures as well.

However, research has shown that human attachment is not as culturally universal as Bowlby predicted. Certain attachment patterns seem more likely among infants of particular cultures. For example, one study of German infants showed that most fell into the avoidant category. Other studies, conducted in Israel and Japan, have found a smaller proportion of infants who were securely attached than in the United States. Finally, comparisons of Chinese and Canadian children show that Chinese children are more inhibited than Canadians in the Strange Situation (Grossmann et al., 1982; Takahashi, 1986; Chen et al., 1998; Rothbaum et al., 2000). Do such findings suggest that we should abandon the notion that attachment is a universal biological tendency?

Not necessarily. Though it is possible that Bowlby's claim that the desire for attachment is universal was too strongly stated, most of the data on attachment have been obtained by using the Ainsworth Strange Situation, which may not be the most appropriate measure in non-Western cultures. For example, Japanese parents seek to avoid separation and stress during infancy, and they don't strive to foster independence to the same degree as parents in many Western societies. Because of their relative lack of prior experience in separation, then, infants placed in the Strange Situation may experience unusual stress—producing the appearance of less secure attachment in Japanese children. If a different measure of attachment were used, one that might be administered later in infancy, more Japanese infants could likely be classified as secure (Nakagawa, Lamb, & Miyaki, 1992; Vereijken et al., 1997; Dennis, Cole, & Zahn-Waxler, 2002).

Japanese parents seek to avoid separation and stress during infancy and do not foster independence. As a result, Japanese children often have the appearance of being less securely attached according to the Strange Situation, but using other measurement techniques they may well score higher in attachment.

Attachment is now viewed as susceptible to cultural norms and expectations. Cross-cultural and within-cultural differences in attachment reflect the nature of the measure employed and the expectations of various cultures. Some developmental specialists suggest that attachment should be viewed as a general tendency, but one that varies in the way it is expressed according to how actively caregivers in a society seek to instill independence in their children. Secure attachment, as defined by the Western-oriented Strange Situation, may be seen earliest in cultures that promote independence, but may be delayed in societies in which independence is a less important cultural value (Harwood, Miller, & Irizarry, 1995; Rothbaum et al., 2000; Rothbaum, Rosen, & Ujiie, 2002).

Infant Interactions: Developing a Working Relationship

Research on attachment is clear in showing that infants may develop multiple attachment relationships, and that over the course of time the specific individuals with whom the infant is primarily attached may change. These variations in attachment highlight the fact that the development of relationships is an ongoing process, not only during infancy, but throughout our lifetimes.

Which processes underlie the development of relationships during infancy? One answer comes from studies that examine how parents interact with their children. For instance, across almost all cultures, mothers behave in typical ways with their infants. They tend to exaggerate their facial and vocal expressions—the nonverbal equivalent of the infant-directed speech that they use when they speak to infants (as discussed in Chapter 5). Similarly, they often imitate their infants' behavior, responding to distinctive sounds and movements by repeating them. There are even types of games, such as peek-a-boo, itsy-bitsy spider, and pat-a-cake, that are nearly universal (Field, 1990; Kochanska, 1997, 2002; Harrist & Waugh, 2002).

According to the **mutual regulation model,** it is through these sorts of interactions that infants and parents learn to communicate emotional states to one another and to respond appropriately. For instance, in pat-a-cake, both infant and parent act jointly to regulate turn-taking behavior, with one individual waiting until the other completes a behavioral act before starting another. Consequently, at the age of 3 months, infants and their mothers have about the same influence on each other's behavior. Interestingly, by the age of 6 months, infants have

mutual regulation model the model in which infants and parents learn to communicate emotional states to one another and to respond appropriately.

more control over turn-taking, although by the age of 9 months both partners once again become roughly equivalent in terms of mutual influence (Tronick, 1998, 2003).

One of the ways infants and parents signal each other when they interact is through facial expressions. As we saw earlier in this chapter, even quite young infants are able to read, or decode, the facial expressions of their caregivers, and they react to those expressions.

For example, an infant whose mother, during an experiment, displays a stony, immobile facial expression reacts by making a variety of sounds, gestures, and facial expressions of her own in response to such a puzzling situation—and possibly to elicit some new response from her mother. Infants also show more happiness themselves when their mothers appear happy, and they look at their mothers longer. On the other hand, infants are apt to respond with sad looks and to turn away when their mothers display unhappy expressions (Termin & Izard, 1988; Crockenberg & Leerkes, 2003; Reissland & Shepherd, 2006).

In short, the development of attachment in infants does not merely represent a reaction to the behavior of the people around them. Instead, there is a process of **reciprocal socialization,** in which infants' behaviors invite further responses from parents and other caregivers. In turn, the caregivers' behaviors bring about a reaction from the child, continuing the cycle. Recall, for instance, Annie, the baby who kept crying to be picked up when her mother put her in her crib. Ultimately, the actions and reactions of parents and child lead to an increase in attachment, forging and strengthening bonds between infants and caregivers as babies and caregivers communicate their needs and responses to each other. Figure 6-5 summarizes the sequence of infant–caregiver interaction (Bell & Ainsworth, 1972; Ainsworth & Bowlby, 1991; Bradley & Caldwell, 1995; Kochanska & Aksan, 2004).

reciprocal socialization   a process in which infants' behaviors invite further responses from parents and other caregivers, which in turn bring about further responses from the infants.

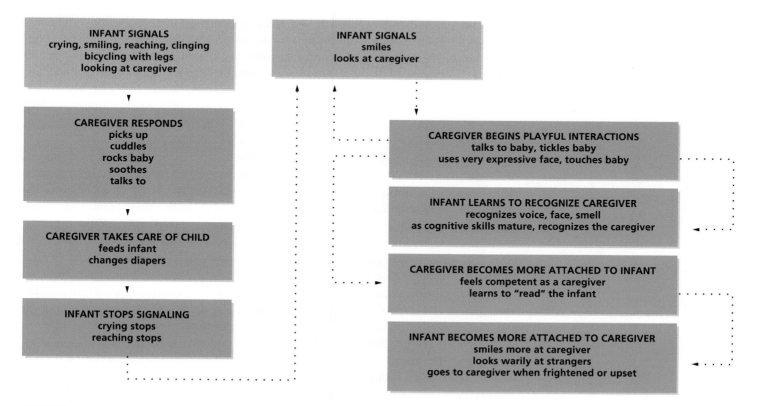

FIGURE 6-5   SEQUENCE OF INFANT–CAREGIVER INTERACTION

The actions and reactions of caregivers and infants influence each other in complex ways. Do you think a similar pattern shows up in adult–adult interactions?

(Adapted from Bell & Ainsworth, 1972; Tomlinson-Keasey, 1985.)

Infants' Sociability with Their Peers: Infant–Infant Interaction

How sociable are infants with other children? Although it is clear that they do not form "friendships" in the traditional sense, babies do react positively to the presence of peers from early in life, and they engage in rudimentary forms of social interaction.

Infants' sociability is expressed in several ways. From the earliest months of life, they smile, laugh, and vocalize while looking at their peers. They show more interest in peers than in inanimate objects and pay greater attention to other infants than they do to a mirror image of themselves. They also begin to show preferences for peers with whom they are familiar compared with those they do not know. For example, studies of identical twins show that twins exhibit a higher level of social behavior toward each other than toward an unfamiliar infant (Field, 1990; Legerstee et al., 1998).

Infants' level of sociability generally rises with age. Nine- to 12-month-olds mutually present and accept toys, particularly if they know each other. They also play social games, such as peek-a-boo or crawl-and-chase. Such behavior is important, as it serves as a foundation for future social exchanges in which children will try to elicit responses from others and then offer reactions to those responses. These kinds of exchanges are important to learn, since they continue even into adulthood. For example, someone who says, "Hi, what's up?" may be trying to elicit a response to which he or she can then reply (Endo, 1992; Eckerman & Peterman, 2001).

Finally, as infants age, they begin to imitate each other (Russon & Waite, 1991). For instance, 14-month-old infants who are familiar with one another sometimes reproduce each other's behavior (Mueller & Vandell, 1979). Such imitation serves a social function and can also be a powerful teaching tool. For example, recall the story of 10-month-old Russell Ruud in the chapter prologue, who showed the other children in his child-care center how he could remove his hat by unfastening its Velcro straps, and soon had others following his lead.

According to Andrew Meltzoff, a developmental psychologist at the University of Washington, Russell's ability to impart this information is only one example of how so-called "expert" babies are able to teach skills and information to other infants. According to the research of Meltzoff and his colleagues, the abilities learned from the "experts" are retained and later utilized to a remarkable degree. Learning by exposure starts early in life. Recent evidence shows that even 6-week-old infants can perform delayed imitation of a novel stimulus to which they have earlier been exposed, such as an adult sticking the tongue out the side of the mouth (Meltzoff & Moore, 1994, 1999; Barr & Hayne, 1999; Meltzoff, 2002).

To some developmentalists, the capacity of young children to engage in imitation suggests that imitation may be inborn. In support of this view, research has identified a class of neurons in the brain that seems related to an innate ability to imitate. *Mirror neurons* are neurons that fire not only when an individual enacts a particular behavior, but also when the individual simply observes *another* organism carrying out the same behavior (Falck-Ytter, 2006).

For example, research on brain functioning shows activation of the inferior frontal gyrus both when an individual carries out a particular task and also when observing another individual carrying out the same task. Mirror neurons may help infants to understand others' actions and to develop a theory of mind. Dysfunction of mirror neurons may be related to the development of disorders involving children's theory of mind as well as autism, a psychological disorder involving significant emotional and linguistic problems (Dapretto et al., 2006; Kilner, Friston, & Frith, 2007).

The idea that through exposure to other children, infants learn new behaviors, skills, and abilities has several implications. For one thing, it suggests that interactions between infants provide more than social benefits; they may have an impact on children's future cognitive development as well. Even more important, these findings illustrate that infants may benefit from participation in child-care centers (which we consider later in this chapter). Although we don't know for sure, the opportunity to learn from their peers may prove to be a lasting advantage for infants in group child-care settings.

Review and Apply

Review

- Attachment, the positive emotional bond between an infant and a significant individual, affects a person's later social competence as an adult.

- By the amount of emotion they display nonverbally, infants help determine the nature and quality of their caregivers' responses to them.

- Infants and the persons with whom they interact engage in reciprocal socialization as they mutually adjust to one another's interactions.

- Infants react differently to other children than to inanimate objects, and gradually they engage in increasing amounts of peer social interaction.

Applying Lifespan Development

- In what sort of society might an avoidant attachment style be encouraged by cultural attitudes toward child rearing? In such a society, would characterizing the infant's consistent avoidance of its mother as anger be an accurate interpretation?

- *From a social worker's perspective:* What might a social worker seeking to find a good home for a foster child look for when evaluating potential foster parents?

Differences Among Infants

Lincoln was a difficult baby, his parents both agreed. For one thing, it seemed like they could never get him to sleep at night. He cried at the slightest noise, a problem since his crib was near the windows facing a busy street. Worse yet, once he started crying, it seemed to take forever to calm him down again. One day his mother, Aisha, was telling her mother-in-law, Mary, about the challenges of being Lincoln's mom. Mary recalled that her own son, Lincoln's father Malcom, had been much the same way. "He was my first child, and I thought this was how all babies acted. So, we just kept trying different ways until we found out how he worked. I remember, we put his crib all over the apartment until we finally found out where he could sleep, and it ended up being in the hallway for a long time. Then his sister, Maleah, came along, and she was so quiet and easy, I didn't know what to do with my extra time!"

As the story of Lincoln's family shows, babies are not all alike, and neither are their families. In fact, as we'll see, some of the differences among people seem to be present from the moment we are born. The differences among infants include overall personality and temperament, and differences in the lives they lead—differences based on their gender, the nature of their families, and the ways in which they are cared for.

Personality Development: The Characteristics That Make Infants Unique

The origins of **personality,** the sum total of the enduring characteristics that differentiate one individual from another, stem from infancy. From birth onward, infants begin to show unique, stable traits and behaviors that ultimately lead to their development as distinct, special individuals (Caspi, 2000; Kagan, 2000; Shiner, Masten, & Roberts, 2003).

According to psychologist Erik Erikson, whose approach to personality development we first discussed in Chapter 1, infants' early experiences are responsible for shaping one of the key aspects of their personalities: whether they will be basically trusting or mistrustful.

personality the sum total of the enduring characteristics that differentiate one individual from another.

Erikson's theory of psychosocial development   the theory that considers how individuals come to understand themselves and the meaning of others'—and their own—behavior.

trust-versus-mistrust stage   according to Erikson, the period during which infants develop a sense of trust or mistrust, largely depending on how well their needs are met by their caregivers.

autonomy-versus-shame-and-doubt stage   the period during which, according to Erikson, toddlers (aged 18 months to 3 years) develop independence and autonomy if they are allowed the freedom to explore, or shame and self-doubt if they are restricted and overprotected.

temperament   patterns of arousal and emotionality that are consistent and enduring characteristics of an individual.

Erikson's theory of psychosocial development considers how individuals come to understand themselves and the meaning of others'—and their own—behavior (Erikson, 1963). The theory suggests that developmental change occurs throughout people's lives in eight distinct stages, the first of which occurs in infancy.

According to Erikson, during the first 18 months of life, we pass through the **trust-versus-mistrust stage.** During this period, infants develop a sense of trust or mistrust, largely depending on how well their needs are met by their caregivers. Mary's attention to Malcom's needs, in the previous example, probably helped him develop a basic sense of trust in the world. Erikson suggests that if infants are able to develop trust, they experience a sense of hope, which permits them to feel as if they can fulfill their needs successfully. On the other hand, feelings of mistrust lead infants to see the world as harsh and unfriendly, and they may have later difficulties in forming close bonds with others.

During the end of infancy, children enter the **autonomy-versus-shame-and-doubt stage,** which lasts from around 18 months to 3 years. During this period, children develop independence and autonomy if parents encourage exploration and freedom within safe boundaries. However, if children are restricted and overly protected, they feel shame, self-doubt, and unhappiness.

Erikson argues that personality is primarily shaped by infants' experiences. However, as we discuss next, other developmentalists concentrate on consistencies of behavior that are present at birth, even before the experiences of infancy. These consistencies are viewed as largely genetically determined and as providing the raw material of personality.

Temperament: Stabilities in Infant Behavior

Sarah's parents thought there must be something wrong. Unlike her older brother Josh, who had been so active as an infant that he seemed never to be still, Sarah was much more placid. She took long naps and was easily soothed on those relatively rare occasions when she became agitated. What could be producing her extreme calmness?

The most likely answer: The difference between Sarah and Josh reflected differences in temperament. As we first discussed in Chapter 2, **temperament** encompasses patterns of arousal and emotionality that are consistent and enduring characteristics of an individual (Rothbart, Ahadi, & Evans, 2000; Kochanska, & Aksan, 2004).

Temperament refers to *how* children behave, as opposed to *what* they do or *why* they do it. Infants show temperamental differences in general disposition from the time of birth, largely due initially to genetic factors, and temperament tends to be fairly stable well into adolescence. On the other hand, temperament is not fixed and unchangeable: Child-rearing practices can modify temperament significantly. In fact, some children show little consistency in temperament from one age to another (McCrae et al., 2000; Rothbart, Derryberry, & Hershey, 2000; Rothbart & Derryberry, 2002).

Temperament is reflected in several dimensions of behavior. One central dimension is *activity level,* which reflects the degree of overall movement. Some babies (like Sarah and Maleah, in the earlier examples) are relatively placid, and their movements are slow and almost leisurely. In contrast, the activity level of other infants (like Josh) is quite high, with strong, restless movements of the arms and legs.

According to Erikson, children from 18 months to 3 years develop independence and autonomy if parents encourage exploration and freedom, within safe boundaries. What does Erikson theorize if children are restricted and overly protected at this stage?

Another important dimension of temperament is the nature and quality of an infant's mood, and in particular a child's *irritability.* Like Lincoln, who was described in the example at the beginning of this section, some infants are easily disturbed and cry easily, while others are relatively easygoing. Irritable infants fuss a great deal, and they are easily upset. They are also difficult to soothe when they do begin to cry. Such irritability is relatively stable: Infants who are irritable at birth remain irritable at the age of 1, and even at age 2 they are still more easily upset than infants who were not irritable just after birth (Worobey & Bajda, 1989). (Other aspects of temperament are listed in Table 6-2).

Table 6-2	Dimensions of Temperament	
Dimension	**Definition**
Activity level	Proportion of active time periods to inactive time periods
Approach-withdrawal	The response to a new person or object, based on whether the child accepts the new situation or withdraws from it
Adaptability	How easily the child is able to adapt to changes in his or her environment
Quality of mood	The contrast of the amount of friendly, joyful, and pleasant behavior with unpleasant, unfriendly behavior
Attention span and persistence	The amount of time the child devotes to an activity and the effect of distraction on that activity
Distractibility	The degree to which stimuli in the environment alter behavior
Rhythmicity (regularity)	The regularity of basic functions such as hunger, excretion, sleep, and wakefulness
Intensity of reaction	The energy level or reaction of the child's response
Threshold of responsiveness	The intensity of stimulation needed to elicit a response

(*Source:* Thomas, Chess, & Birch, 1968.)

Categorizing Temperament: Easy, Difficult, and Slow-to-Warm Babies. Because temperament can be viewed along so many dimensions, some researchers have asked whether there are broader categories that can be used to describe children's overall behavior. According to Alexander Thomas and Stella Chess, who carried out a large-scale study of a group of infants that has come to be known as the *New York Longitudinal Study* (Thomas & Chess, 1980), babies can be described according to one of several profiles:

- *Easy babies.* **Easy babies** have a positive disposition. Their body functions operate regularly, and they are adaptable. They are generally positive, showing curiosity about new situations, and their emotions are moderate or low in intensity. This category applies to about 40% (the largest number) of infants.

- *Difficult babies.* **Difficult babies** have more negative moods and are slow to adapt to new situations. When confronted with a new situation, they tend to withdraw. About 10% of infants belong in this category.

- *Slow-to-warm babies.* **Slow-to-warm babies** are inactive, showing relatively calm reactions to their environment. Their moods are generally negative, and they withdraw from new situations, adapting slowly. Approximately 15% of infants are slow-to-warm.

As for the remaining 35%, they cannot be consistently categorized. These children show a variety of combinations of characteristics. For instance, one infant may have relatively sunny moods, but react negatively to new situations, or another may show little stability of any sort in terms of general temperament.

The Consequences of Temperament: Does Temperament Matter? One obvious question to emerge from the findings of the relative stability of temperament is whether a particular kind of temperament is beneficial. The answer seems to be that no single type of temperament is invariably good or bad. Instead, children's long-term adjustment depends on

easy babies babies who have a positive disposition; their body functions operate regularly, and they are adaptable.

difficult babies babies who have negative moods and are slow to adapt to new situations; when confronted with a new situation, they tend to withdraw.

slow-to-warm babies babies who are inactive, showing relatively calm reactions to their environment; their moods are generally negative, and they withdraw from new situations, adapting slowly.

goodness-of-fit   the notion that development is dependent on the degree of match between children's temperament and the nature and demands of the environment in which they are being raised.

the **goodness-of-fit** of their particular temperament and the nature and demands of the environment in which they find themselves. For instance, children with a low activity level and low irritability may do particularly well in an environment in which they are left to explore on their own and are allowed largely to direct their own behavior. In contrast, high-activity-level, highly irritable children may do best with greater direction, which permits them to channel their energy in particular directions (Thomas & Chess, 1977, 1980; Strelau, 1998; Schoppe-Sullivan et al., 2007). Mary, the grandmother in the earlier example, found ways to adjust the environment for her son, Malcom. Malcom and Aisha may need to do the same for their own son, Lincoln.

Some research does suggest that certain temperaments are, in general, more adaptive than others. For instance, difficult children, in general, are more likely to show behavior problems by school age than those classified in infancy as easy children. But not all difficult children experience problems. The key determinant seems to be the way parents react to their infants' difficult behavior. If they react by showing anger and inconsistency—responses that their child's difficult, demanding behavior readily evokes—then the child is ultimately more likely to experience behavior problems. On the other hand, parents who display more warmth and consistency in their responses are more likely to have children who avoid later problems (Thomas, Chess, & Birch, 1968; Teerikangas et al., 1998; Pauli-Pott, Mertesacker, & Bade, 2003).

Furthermore, temperament seems to be at least weakly related to infants' attachment to their adult caregivers. For example, infants vary considerably in how much emotion they display nonverbally. Some are "poker-faced," showing little expressivity, while others' reactions tend to be much more easily decoded. More expressive infants may provide more easily discernible cues to others, thereby easing the way for caregivers to be more successful in responding to their needs and facilitating attachment (Feldman & Rimé, 1991; Seifer, Schiller, & Sameroff, 1996; Meritesacker, Bade, & Haverkock, 2004).

Cultural differences also have a major influence on the consequences of a particular temperament. For instance, children who would be described as "difficult" in Western cultures actually seem to have an advantage in the East African Masai culture. The reason? Mothers offer their breast to their infants only when they fuss and cry; therefore, the irritable, more difficult infants are apt to receive more nourishment than the more placid, easy infants. Particularly when environmental conditions are bad, such as during a drought, difficult babies may have an advantage (deVries, 1984).

The Biological Basis of Temperament.   Recent approaches to temperament grow out of the framework of behavioral genetics discussed in Chapter 2. From this perspective, temperamental characteristics are seen as inherited traits that are fairly stable during childhood and across the entire life span. These traits are viewed as making up the core of personality and playing a substantial role in future development.

Consider, for example, the trait of physiological reactivity, a characteristic of temperament that relates to how a high degree of physiological reactivity to novel stimulus. This high reactivity, which has been termed *inhibtion to the unfamiliar,* is exhibited as shyness.

There is a clear biological basis underlying inhibition to the unfamiliar, in which any novel stimulus produces a rapid increase in heartbeat, blood pressure, and pupil dilation, as well as high excitability of the brain's limbic system. For example, people who were categorized as inhibited at 2 years of age show high reactivity in their brain's amygdala in adulthood when viewing unfamiliar faces. The shyness associated with this physiological pattern seems to continue through childhood and even into adulthood (McCrae et al., 2000; Arcus, 2001; Propper & Moore, 2006).

Gender: Boys in Blue, Girls in Pink

"It's a boy." "It's a girl."

One of these two statements, or some variant, is probably the first announcement made after the birth of a child. From the moment of birth, girls and boys are treated differently. Their parents send out different kinds of birth announcements. They are dressed in different clothes and wrapped in different-colored blankets. They are given different toys (Bridges, 1993; Coltrane & Adams, 1997; Serbin, Poulin-Dubois, & Colburne, 2001).

Parents play with boy and girl babies differently: From birth on, fathers tend to interact more with sons than daughters, while mothers interact more with daughters. Because, as noted earlier in the chapter, mothers and fathers play in different ways (with fathers typically engaging in more physical, rough-and-tumble activities and mothers in traditional games such as peek-a-boo), male and female infants are clearly exposed to different styles of activity and interaction from their parents (Parke, 1996; Laflamme, Pomerleau, & Malcuit, 2002; Clearfield & Nelson, 2006).

The behavior exhibited by girls and boys is interpreted in very different ways by adults. For instance, when researchers showed adults a video of an infant whose name was given as either "John" or "Mary," adults perceived "John" as adventurous and inquisitive, while "Mary" was fearful and anxious, although it was the same baby performing a single set of behaviors (Condry & Condry, 1976). Clearly, adults view the behavior of children through the lens of gender. **Gender** refers to our sense of being male or female. The term "gender" is often used to mean the same thing as "sex," but they are not actually the same. *Sex* typically refers to sexual anatomy and sexual behavior, whereas gender refers to the social perceptions of maleness or femaleness. All cultures prescribe *gender roles* for males and females, but these roles differ greatly from one culture to another.

gender the sense of being male or female.

Gender Differences.   There is a considerable amount of disagreement over both the extent and causes of such gender differences, even though most agree that boys and girls do experience at least partially different worlds based on gender. Some gender differences are fairly clear from the time of birth. For example, male infants tend to be more active and fussier than female infants. Boys' sleep tends to be more disturbed than that of girls. Boys grimace more, although no gender difference exists in the overall amount of crying. There is also some evidence that male newborns are more irritable than female newborns, although the findings are inconsistent (Phillips, King, & DuBois, 1978; Eaton & Enns, 1986).

Differences between male and female infants, however, are generally minor. In fact, in most ways infants seem so similar that usually adults cannot discern whether a baby is a boy or girl, as the "John" and "Mary" video research shows. Furthermore, it is important to keep in mind that there are much larger differences among individual boys and among individual girls than there are, on average, between boys and girls (Crawford & Unger, 2004).

Gender Roles.   Gender differences emerge more clearly as children age—and become increasingly influenced by the gender roles that society sets out for them. For instance, by the age of 1 year, infants are able to distinguish between males and females. Girls at this age prefer to play with dolls or stuffed animals, while boys seek out blocks and trucks. Often, of course, these are the only options available to them, due to the choices their parents and other adults have made in the toys they provide (Caldera & Sciaraffa, 1998; Serbin et al., 2001; Cherney, Kelly-Vance, & Glover, 2003).

Children's preferences for certain kinds of toys are reinforced by their parents. In general, however, parents of boys are more apt to be concerned about their child's choices than are parents of girls. Boys receive more reinforcement for playing with toys that society deems appropriate for boys and this reinforcement increases with age. On the other hand, a girl playing with a truck is viewed with considerably less concern than a boy playing with a doll might be. Girls who play with toys seen by society as "masculine" are less discouraged for their behavior than boys who play with toys seen as "feminine" (Leaper, 2002; Martin, Ruble, & Szkrybalo, 2002; Schmalz & Kerstetter, 2006; Hill & Flom, 2007).

Parents of girls who play with toys related to activities associated with boys are apt to be less concerned than parents of boys who play with toys associated with girls.

The number of single-parent families has increased dramatically over the past 20 years. If the current trend continues, 60 percent of all children will live at some time with a single parent.

By the time they reach the age of 2, boys behave more independently and less compliantly than girls. Much of this behavior can be traced to parental reactions to earlier behavior. For instance, when a child takes his or her first steps, parents tend to react differently, depending on the child's gender: Boys are encouraged more to go off and explore the world, while girls are hugged and kept close. It is hardly surprising, then, that by the age of 2, girls tend to show less independence and greater compliance (Kuczynski & Kochanska, 1990; Poulin-Dubois, Serbin, & Eichstedt, 2002).

Societal encouragement and reinforcement do not, however, completely explain differences in behavior between boys and girls. For example, as we'll discuss further in Chapter 8, one study examined girls who were exposed before birth to abnormally high levels of *androgen*, a male hormone, because their mothers unwittingly took a drug containing the hormone while pregnant. Later, these girls were more likely to play with toys stereotypically preferred by boys (such as cars) and less likely to play with toys stereotypically associated with girls (such as dolls). Although there are many alternative explanations for these results—you can probably think of several yourself—one possibility is that exposure to male hormones affected the brain development of the girls, leading them to favor toys that involve certain kinds of preferred skills (Levine et al., 1999; Mealey, 2000; Servin et al., 2003).

In sum, differences in behavior between boys and girls begin in infancy, and—as we will see in future chapters—continue throughout childhood (and beyond). Although gender differences have complex causes, representing some combination of innate, biologically related factors and environmental factors, they play a profound role in the social and emotional development of infants.

Family Life in the 21st Century

A look back at television shows of the 1950s finds a world of families portrayed in a way that today seems oddly old-fashioned and quaint: mothers and fathers, married for years, and their good-looking children making their way in a world that seems to have few, if any, serious problems.

As discussed in Chapter 1, even in the 1950s such a view of family life was overly romantic and unrealistic. Today, however, it is broadly inaccurate, representing only a minority of families in the United States. A quick review tells the story:

- The number of single-parent families has increased dramatically in the last two decades, as the number of two-parent households has declined. Just under one-third of all families with children are headed by single parents. Twenty-three percent of children live with only their mothers, 5% live with only their fathers, and 4% live with neither of their parents. Sixty-five percent of African American children and 37% of Hispanic children live in single-parent households (U.S. Bureau of the Census, 1998; ChildStats.gov, 2005).

- The average size of families is shrinking. Today, on average, there are 2.6 persons per household, compared to 2.8 in 1980. The number of people living in nonfamily households (without any relatives) is close to 30 million.

- Although the number of adolescents giving birth has declined substantially over the last 5 years, there are still half a million births to teenage women, the vast majority of whom are unmarried.

- Close to 50% of children under the age of 3 are cared for by other adults while their parents work, and more than half of mothers of infants work outside the home.

- One in three children lives in low-income households in the United States. The rates are even higher for African American and Hispanic families, and for single-parent families of young children. More children under 3 live in poverty than do older children, adults, or the elderly. Furthermore, the proportion of children living in low-income families began rising in 2000, reversing a decade of decline (Federal Interagency Forum on Child and Family Statistics, 2003; National Center for Children in Poverty, 2005).

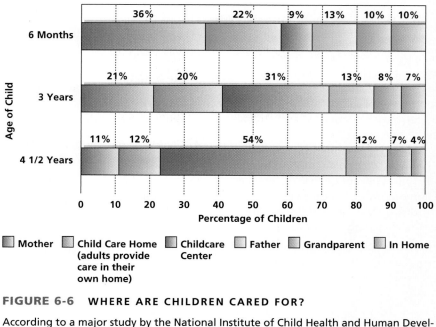

FIGURE 6-6 **WHERE ARE CHILDREN CARED FOR?**

According to a major study by the National Institute of Child Health and Human Development (NICHD), children spend more time in some kind of child care outside the home or family as they get older.

(*Source:* NICHD Early Child Care Research Network, 2006.)

Review and Apply

Review

- According to Erikson, during infancy individuals move from the trust-versus-mistrust stage of psychosocial development to the autonomy-versus-shame-and-guilt stage.

- Temperament encompasses enduring levels of arousal and emotionality that are characteristic of an individual.

- Gender differences become more pronounced as infants age.

- Child care outside of the home can have neutral, positive, or negative effects on the social development of children, depending largely on its quality.

- Research on the effects of child care must take into account the varying quality of different child-care settings and the social characteristics of the parents who tend to use child care.

Applying Lifespan Development

- If you were introducing a bill in Congress regarding the minimum licensing requirements for child-care centers, what would you emphasize?

- *From a social worker's perspective:* Imagine you are a social worker visiting a foster home. It is 11 AM. You find the breakfast dishes in the sink and books and toys all over the floor. The infant you have placed in the home is happily pounding on pots and pans as his foster mother claps time. The kitchen floor is gooey under the baby's high chair. What is your assessment?

Epilogue

The road infants travel as they develop as social individuals is a long and winding one. We saw in this chapter that infants begin decoding and encoding emotions early, using social referencing and eventually developing a "theory of mind." We also considered how the attachment patterns that infants display can have long-term effects, influencing even what kind of parent the child eventually becomes. In addition to examining Erik Erikson's theory of psychosocial development, we also discussed temperament and explored the nature and causes of gender differences. We concluded with a discussion of infant childcare options.

Return to the prologue of this chapter, about Russell Ruud's Velcro discovery, and answer the following questions.

1. Is this episode evidence of self-awareness on the part of Russell or his childcare companions? Why or why not?

2. What role do you think social referencing might have played in this scenario? If Russell's care providers had reacted negatively, would this have stopped the other children from imitating Russell?

3. How does this story relate to the sociability of infants?

4. Can we form any opinion about Russell's personality based on this event? Why or why not?

5. Do you think Russell's actions might have brought a different response from his adult care providers if he had been a girl? Would the response from his peers have been different? Why or why not?

Looking Back

■ **Do infants experience emotions?**

- Infants display a variety of facial expressions, which are similar across cultures and appear to reflect basic emotional states.

- By the end of the first year, infants often develop both stranger anxiety, wariness around an unknown person, and separation anxiety, distress displayed when a customary care provider departs.

- Early in life, infants develop the capability of nonverbal decoding: determining the emotional states of others based on their facial and vocal expressions.

- Through social referencing, infants from the age of 8 or 9 months use the expressions of others to clarify ambiguous situations and learn appropriate reactions to them.

■ **What sort of mental lives do infants have?**

- Infants begin to develop self-awareness at about the age of 12 months.

- They also begin to develop a theory of mind at this time: knowledge and beliefs about how they and others think.

■ **What is attachment in infancy, and how does it affect a person's future social competence?**

- Attachment, a strong, positive emotional bond that forms between an infant and one or more significant persons, is a crucial factor in enabling individuals to develop social relationships.

- Infants display one of four major attachment patterns: securely attached, avoidant, ambivalent, and disorganized-disoriented. Research suggests an association between an infant's attachment pattern and his or her social and emotional competence as an adult.

■ **What roles do other people play in infants' social development?**

- Mothers' interactions with their babies are particularly important for social development. Mothers who respond effectively to their babies' social overtures appear to contribute to the babies' ability to become securely attached.

- Through a process of reciprocal socialization, infants and caregivers interact and affect one another's behavior, which strengthens their mutual relationship.

- From an early age, infants engage in rudimentary forms of social interaction with other children, and their level of sociability rises as they age.

■ **What individual differences distinguish one infant from another?**

- The origins of personality, the sum total of the enduring characteristics that differentiate one individual from another, arise during infancy.

- Temperament encompasses enduring levels of arousal and emotionality that are characteristic of an individual. Temperamental differences underlie the broad classification of infants into easy, difficult, and slow-to-warm categories.

- As infants age, gender differences become more pronounced, mostly due to environmental influences. Differences are accentuated by parental expectations and behavior.

■ **How does nonparental child care impact infants?**

- Child care, a societal response to the changing nature of the family, can be beneficial to the social development of children, fostering social interaction and cooperation, if it is of high quality.

Key Terms and Concepts

stranger anxiety (p. 184)
separation anxiety (p. 185)
social smile (p. 185)
social referencing
  (p. 187)
self-awareness (p. 188)
theory of mind (p. 189)
empathy (p. 189)
attachment (p. 190)
Ainsworth Strange
  Situation (p. 191)
secure attachment pattern
  (p. 191)

avoidant attachment
  pattern (p. 192)
ambivalent
  attachment pattern
  (p. 192)
disorganized-disoriented
  attachment pattern
  (p. 192)
mutual regulation model
  (p. 196)
reciprocal socialization
  (p. 197)
personality (p. 199)

Erikson's theory of
  psychosocial development
  (p. 200)
trust-versus-mistrust stage
  (p. 200)
autonomy-versus-shame-
  and-doubt stage (p. 200)
temperament (p. 200)
easy babies (p. 201)
difficult babies (p. 201)
slow-to-warm babies (p. 201)
goodness-of-fit (p. 202)
gender (p. 203)

7 Physical and Cognitive Development in the Preschool Years

Chapter Overview

PHYSICAL GROWTH

The Growing Body

The Growing Brain

Motor Development

INTELLECTUAL DEVELOPMENT

Piaget's Stage of Preoperational Thinking

Information Processing Approaches to Cognitive Development

Vygotsky's View of Cognitive Development: Taking Culture into Account

THE GROWTH OF LANGUAGE AND LEARNING

Language Development

Learning from the Media: Television and the Internet

Early Childhood Education: Taking the "Pre" Out of the Preschool Period

Prologue: Aaron

aron, a wildly energetic preschooler who has just turned 3, was trying to stretch far enough to reach the jar of cookies that he spied sitting on the kitchen counter. Because the jar was just beyond his grasp, he pushed a chair from the kitchen table over to the counter and climbed up.

He still couldn't reach the cookies from the chair, so Aaron climbed onto the kitchen counter and crawled over to the cookie jar. He pried the lid off the jar, thrust his hand in, pulled out a cookie, and began to munch on it.

But not for long. His curiosity getting the better of him, he grabbed another cookie and began to work his body along the counter toward the sink. He climbed in, twisted the cold water faucet to the "on" position, and happily splashed in the cold water.

Aaron's father, who had left the room for only a moment, returned to find Aaron sitting in the sink, soaked, with a contented smile on his face.

If he reaches the forbidden cookie, will this preschooler feel guilty?

Three years ago, Aaron could not even lift his head. Now he can move with confidence—pushing furniture, opening jars, turning knobs, and climbing on chairs. These advances in mobility are challenging to parents, who must rise to a whole new level of vigilance in order to prevent injuries, the greatest threat to preschoolers' physical well-being. (Think what would have happened if Aaron had turned on the hot water, rather than the cold, when he reached the sink.)

The preschool period is an exciting time in children's lives. In one sense, the preschool years mark a time of preparation: a period spent anticipating and getting ready for the start of a child's formal education, through which society will begin the process of passing on its intellectual tools to a new generation.

But it is a mistake to take the label "preschool" too literally. The years between 3 and 6 are hardly a mere waystation in life, an interval spent waiting for the next, more important period to start. Instead, the preschool years are a time of tremendous change and growth, where physical, intellectual, and social development proceeds at a rapid pace.

In this chapter, we focus on the physical, cognitive, and linguistic growth that occurs during the preschool years. We begin by considering the physical changes children undergo during those years. We discuss weight and height, nutrition, and health and wellness. The brain and its neural pathways change too, and we will touch on some intriguing findings relating to gender differences in the way that the brain functions. We also look at how both gross and fine motor skills change over the preschool years.

Intellectual development is the focus of much of the remainder of the chapter. We examine the major approaches to cognitive development, including the next stages of Piaget's theory, information processing approaches, and a view of cognitive development as heavily influenced by culture.

Finally, the chapter considers the important advances in language development that occur during the preschool years. We end with a discussion of several factors that influence cognitive development, including exposure to television and participation in child-care and preschool programs.

After reading this chapter, you will be able to answer these questions:

■ **What is the state of children's bodies and overall health during the preschool years?**

■ **How do preschool children's brains and physical skills develop?**

■ **How does Piaget interpret cognitive development during the preschool years?**

■ **How do other views of cognitive development differ from Piaget's?**

■ **How does children's language develop in the preschool years?**

■ **What effects does television have on preschoolers?**

■ **What kinds of preschool educational programs are available?**

Looking
Ahead

Physical Growth

It is an unseasonably warm spring day at the Cushman Hill Preschool, one of the first nice days after a long winter. The children in Mary Scott's class have happily left their winter coats in the classroom for the first time this spring, and they are excitedly playing outside. Jessie plays a game of catch with Germaine, while Illya and Molly climb on the jungle gym. Craig and Marta chase one another, while Jordan and Bernstein try, with gales of giggles, to play leap-frog. Virginia and Ollie sit across from each other on the teeter-totter, successively bumping it so hard into the ground that they both are in danger of being knocked off. Erik, Jim, Scott, and Marek race around the perimeter of the playground, running for the sheer joy of it.

These same children, now so active and mobile, were unable even to crawl just a few years earlier. The advances in their physical abilities that have occurred in such a short time are nothing short of astounding. Just how far they have developed is apparent when we look at the specific changes they have undergone in their size, shape, and physical abilities.

The Growing Body

By age 2, the average child in the United States weighs around 25 to 30 pounds and is close to 36 inches tall—around half the height of the average adult. Children grow steadily during the preschool period, and by the time they are 6 years old, they weigh, on average, about 46 pounds and stand 46 inches tall (see Figure 7-1).

Individual Differences in Height and Weight.   These averages mask great individual differences in height and weight. For instance, 10% of 6-year-olds weigh 55 pounds or more, and 10% weigh 36 pounds or less. Furthermore, average differences in height and weight between boys and girls increase during the preschool years. Although at age 2 the differences are relatively small, during the preschool years boys start becoming taller and heavier, on average, than girls.

Global economics also affect these averages. There are profound differences in height and weight between children in economically developed countries and those in developing countries. The better nutrition and health care received by children in developed countries translates into significant differences in growth. For instance, the average Swedish 4-year-old is as tall as the average 6-year-old in Bangladesh (United Nations, 1991; Leathers & Foster, 2004).

Differences in height and weight reflect economic factors within the United States, as well. For instance, children in families whose incomes are below the poverty level are far more likely to be unusually short than children raised in more affluent homes (Barrett & Frank, 1987; Ogden et al., 2002).

Changes in Body Shape and Structure.   If we compare the bodies of a 2-year-old and a 6-year-old, we find that the bodies vary not only in height and weight, but also in shape. During the preschool years, boys and girls begin to burn off some of the fat they have carried from their infancy, and they no longer have a pot-bellied appearance. They become less round and chubby and more slender. Moreover, their arms and legs lengthen, and the size relationship between the head and the rest of the body becomes more adultlike. In fact, by the time children reach 6 years of age, their proportions are quite similar to those of adults.

Other physical changes are occurring internally. Muscle size increases, and children grow stronger. Bones become sturdier. The sense organs continue to develop. For instance, the *eustachian tube* in the ear, which carries sounds from the external part of the ear to the internal part, moves from a position that is almost parallel to the ground at birth to a more angular position. This change sometimes leads to an increase in the frequency of earaches during the preschool years.

Nutrition: Eating the Right Foods.   Because the rate of growth during this period is slower than during infancy, preschoolers need less food to maintain their growth. The change in food consumption may be so noticeable that parents sometimes worry that their preschooler

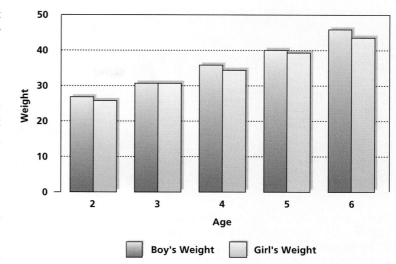

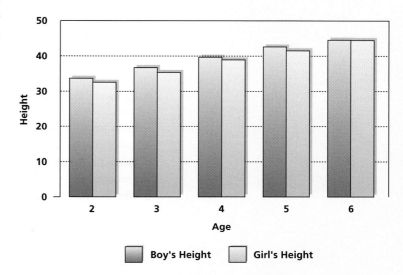

FIGURE 7-1   GAINING HEIGHT AND WEIGHT

The preschool years are marked by steady increases in height and weight. The figures show the median point for boys and girls at each age, in which 50% of children in each category are above this height or weight level and 50% are below.

(*Source:* National Center for Health Statistics in collaboration with the National Center for Chronic Disease Prevention and Health Promotion, 2000.)

Encouraging children to eat more than they seem to want naturally may lead them to increase their food intake beyond an appropriate level.

is not eating enough. However, children tend to be quite adept at maintaining an appropriate intake of food, if provided with nutritious meals. In fact, anxiously encouraging children to eat more than they seem to want naturally may lead them to increase their food intake beyond an appropriate level.

Ultimately, some children's food consumption can become so high as to lead to **obesity,** which is defined as a body weight more than 20% higher than the average weight for a person of a given age and height. The prevalence of obesity among older preschoolers has increased significantly over the last 20 years. (We'll discuss the causes of obesity in Chapter 9.)

How do parents ensure that their children have good nutrition without turning mealtimes into a tense, adversarial situation? In most cases, the best strategy is to make sure that a variety of foods, low in fat and high in nutritional content, is available. Foods that have a relatively high iron content are particularly important: Iron-deficiency anemia, which causes constant fatigue, is one of the prevalent nutritional problems in developed countries such as the United States. High-iron foods include dark green vegetables (such as broccoli), whole grains, and some kinds of meat such as lean hamburger (Ranade, 1993).

Because preschool children, like adults, will not find all foods equally appealing, children should be given the opportunity to develop their own natural preferences. As long as their overall diet is adequate, no single food is indispensable. Exposing children to a wide variety of foods by encouraging them to take just one bite of new foods is a relatively low-stress way of expanding children's diets (Shapiro, 1997).

Health and Illness.   The average preschooler has 7 to 10 colds and other minor respiratory illnesses in each of the years from age 3 to 5. In the United States, a runny nose due to the common cold is the most frequent—and happily, the least severe—kind of health problem during the preschool years. In fact, the majority of children in the United States are reasonably healthy during this period (Kalb, 1997).

Although the sniffles and coughs that are the symptoms of such illnesses are certainly distressing to children, the unpleasantness is usually not too severe and the illnesses usually last only a few days.

Actually, such minor illnesses may offer some unexpected benefits: Not only may they help children build up immunity to more severe illnesses to which they may be exposed in the future, but they also may provide some emotional benefits. Specifically, some researchers argue that minor illness permits children to understand their bodies better. It also may permit them to learn coping skills that will help them deal more effectively with future, more severe diseases. Furthermore, it gives them the ability to understand better what others who are sick are going through. This ability to put oneself in another's shoes, known as empathy, may teach children to be more sympathetic and better caretakers (Notaro, Gelman, & Zimmerman, 2002; Raman & Winer, 2002; Williams & Binnie, 2002).

Although physical illness is typically a minor problem during the preschool years, an increasing number of children are being treated with drugs for emotional disorders such as depression. In fact, the use of drugs such as antidepressants and stimulants has grown significantly (see Figure 7-2). Although it is not clear why the increase has occurred, some experts believe that parents and preschool teachers may be seeking a quick fix for behavior problems that may, in fact, represent normal difficulties (Pear, 2000; Zito et al., 2000; Colino, 2002; Zito, 2002).

Injuries During the Preschool Years: Playing It Safe.   The greatest risk that preschoolers face comes from neither illness nor nutritional problems but from accidents: Before the age of 10, children have twice the likelihood of dying from an injury than from an illness. In fact, children in the United States have a one in three chance every year of receiving an injury that requires medical attention (National Safety Council, 1989; Field & Behrman, 2003).

obesity   body weight more than 20% higher than the average weight for a person of a given age and height.

The danger of injuries during the preschool years is in part a result of the children's high levels of physical activity. A 3-year-old might think that it is perfectly reasonable to climb on an unsteady chair to get something that is out of reach, and a 4-year-old might enjoy holding on to a low tree branch and swinging her legs up and down. It is this physical activity, in combination with the curiosity and lack of judgment that also characterize this age group, that makes preschoolers so accident-prone.

Furthermore, some children are more apt to take risks than others, and such preschoolers are more likely to be injured than their more cautious peers. Boys, who are more active than girls and tend to take more risks, have a higher rate of injuries. Ethnic differences, probably due to differences in cultural norms about how closely children need to be supervised, can also be seen in accident rates. Asian American children in the United States, who tend to be supervised particularly strictly by their parents, have one of the lowest accident rates for children. Economic factors also play a role. Children raised under conditions of poverty in urban areas, whose inner-city neighborhoods may contain more hazards than more affluent areas, are two times more likely to die of injuries than children living in affluence (Morrongiello, Midgett, & Stanton, 2000; Morrongiello & Hogg, 2004; Morrongiello et al., 2006).

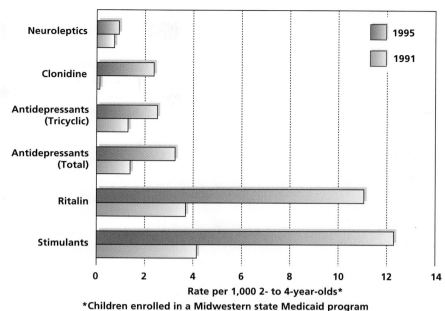

FIGURE 7-2   NUMBERS OF PRESCHOOL CHILDREN TAKING MEDICATION FOR BEHAVIORAL PROBLEMS

Although there is no clear explanation as to why the use of stimulants and antidepressants has increased among children, some experts believe that medication is a quick-fix solution for behavior problems that are actually be normal difficulties.
(*Source:* Zito et al., 2000.)

The range of dangers that preschoolers face is wide. Injuries come from falls, burns from stoves and fires, drowning in bathtubs indoors and standing water outdoors, and suffocation in places such as abandoned refrigerators. Auto accidents also account for a large number of injuries. Finally, children face injuries from poisonous substances, such as household cleaners.

Parents and caregivers of preschoolers can take several precautions to prevent injuries, although, as we've seen, none of these measures eliminates the need for close supervision. Caregivers can start by "childproofing" preschoolers' homes and classrooms, placing covers on electrical outlets and child locks on cabinets where poisons are kept, for example. Child car seats and bike helmets can help prevent injuries in case of accidents. Parents and teachers also need to be aware of the dangers from long-term hazards, such as lead poisoning.

The Silent Danger: Lead Poisoning in Young Children.

At the age of 3, Tory couldn't sit still. He was unable to watch a television show for more than 5 minutes, and sitting still while his mother read to him seemed to be an impossibility. He was often irritable, and he impulsively took risks when he was playing with other children.

When his behavior reached a point where his parents thought there was something seriously wrong with him, they took him to a pediatrician for a thorough physical examination. After testing Tory's blood, the pediatrician found that his parents were right: Tory was suffering from lead poisoning.

Some 14 million children are at risk for lead poisoning due to exposure to potentially toxic levels of lead, according to the Centers for Disease Control. Although there are now stringent legal restrictions on the amount of lead in paint and gasoline, lead is still found on painted walls and window frames—particularly in older homes, and in gasoline, ceramics, lead-soldered pipes, and even dust and water. People who live in areas of substantial air pollution due to automobile and truck traffic may also be exposed to high levels of lead. The U.S. Department of Health and

The danger of injuries during the preschool years is in part a result of children's high levels of physical activity. It is important to take protective measures to reduce the hazards.

The urban environment in which poor children often live make them especially susceptible to lead poisoning.

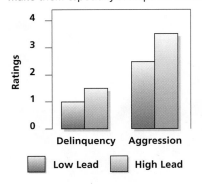

FIGURE 7-3 THE CONSEQUENCE OF LEAD POISONING

High levels of lead have been linked to higher levels of antisocial behavior, including aggression and delinquency, in school-age children.

(*Source:* Needleman et al., 1996.)

lateralization the process in which certain cognitive functions are located more in one hemisphere of the brain than in the other.

Human Services has called lead poisoning the most hazardous health threat to children under the age of 6 (Duncan & Brooks-Gunn, 2000; Ripple & Zigler, 2003; Hubbs-Tait et al., 2005).

Even tiny amounts of lead can permanently harm children. Exposure to lead has been linked to lower intelligence, problems in verbal and auditory processing, and—as in the case of Tory—hyperactivity and distractibility. High lead levels have also been linked to higher levels of antisocial behavior, including aggression and delinquency, in school-age children (see Figure 7-3). At yet higher levels of exposure, lead poisoning results in illness and death (Wasserman, Factor-Litvak, & Liu, 2003; Fraser, Muckle, & Després, 2006; Kincl, Dietrich, & Bhattacharya, 2006).

Poor children are particularly susceptible to lead poisoning, and the results of poisoning tend to be worse for them than for children from more affluent families. Children living in poverty are more apt to reside in housing that contains peeling and chipping lead paint, or to live near heavily trafficked urban areas with high levels of air pollution. At the same time, many families living in poverty may be less stable and unable to provide consistent opportunities for intellectual stimulation that might serve to offset some of the cognitive problems caused by the poisoning. Consequently, lead poisoning is especially harmful to poorer children (Duncan & Brooks-Gunn, 2000; Dilworth-Bart & Moore, 2006; Polivka, 2006).

The Growing Brain

The brain grows at a faster rate than any other part of the body. Two-year-olds have brains that are about three-quarters of the size and weight of an adult brain. By age 5, children's brains weigh 90% of average adult brain weight. In comparison, the average 5-year-old's total body weight is just 30% of average adult body weight (Schuster & Ashburn, 1986; Lowrey, 1986; Nihart, 1993).

Why does the brain grow so rapidly? One reason is an increase in the number of interconnections among cells, as we saw in Chapter 4. These interconnections allow for more complex communication between neurons, and they permit the rapid growth of cognitive skills that we'll discuss later in the chapter. In addition, the amount of myelin—protective insulation that surrounds parts of neurons—increases, which speeds the transmission of electrical impulses along brain cells but also adds to brain weight.

By the end of the preschool period, some parts of the brain have undergone particularly significant growth. For example, the *corpus callosum,* a bundle of nerve fibers that connects the two hemispheres of the brain, becomes considerably thicker, developing as many as 800 million individual fibers that help coordinate brain functioning between the two hemispheres.

Brain Lateralization. The two halves of the brain also begin to become increasingly differentiated and specialized. **Lateralization,** the process in which certain functions are located more in one hemisphere than the other, becomes more pronounced during the preschool years.

For most people, the left hemisphere is primarily involved with tasks that necessitate verbal competence, such as speaking, reading, thinking, and reasoning. The right hemisphere develops its own strengths, especially in nonverbal areas such as comprehension of spatial relationships, recognition of patterns and drawings, music, and emotional expression (McAuliffe & Knowlton, 2001; Koivisto & Revonsuo, 2003; Pollak, Holt, & Wismer Fries, 2004; see Figure 7-4).

Each of the two hemispheres also begins to process information in a slightly different manner. The left hemisphere processes information sequentially, one piece of data at a time. The right hemisphere processes information in a more global manner, reflecting on it as a whole (Gazzaniga, 1983; Springer & Deutsch, 1989; Leonard et al., 1996).

Though there is some specialization of the hemispheres, in most respects the two hemispheres act in tandem. They are interdependent, and the differences between the two are minor.

Even the hemispheric specialization in certain tasks is not absolute. In fact, each hemisphere can perform most of the tasks of the other. For example, the right hemisphere does some language processing and plays an important role in language comprehension (Corballis, 2003; Hutchinson, Whitman, & Abeare, 2003; Szaflarski et al., 2006).

There are also individual and cultural differences in lateralization. For example, many of the 10% of people who are left-handed or ambidextrous (able to use both hands interchangeably) have language centered in their right hemispheres or have no specific language center (Banich & Nicholas, 1998; Compton & Weissman, 2002).

Even more intriguing are differences in lateralization related to gender and culture. For instance, starting during the first year of life and continuing in the preschool years, boys and girls show some hemispheric differences associated with lower body reflexes and the processing of auditory information. Boys also clearly tend to show greater lateralization of language in the left hemisphere; among females, language is more evenly divided between the two hemispheres. Such differences may help explain why—as we'll see later in the chapter—girls' language development proceeds at a more rapid pace during the preschool years than boys' language development (Gur et al., 1982; Grattan et al., 1992; Bourne & Todd, 2004).

According to psychologist Simon Baron-Cohen, the differences between male and female brains may help explain the puzzling riddle of autism, the profound developmental disability that produces language deficits and great difficulty in interacting with others. Baron-Cohen argues that children with autism (who are predominately male) have what he calls an "extreme male brain." The extreme male brain, while relatively good at systematically sorting out the world, is poor at understanding the emotions of others and experiencing empathy for others' feelings. To Baron-Cohen, individuals with an extreme male brain have traits associated with the normal male brain, but display the traits to such an extent that their behavior is viewed as autistic (Baron-Cohen, 2003, 2005; Ashwin et al., 2007).

Although Baron-Cohen's theory is quite controversial, it is clear that some kind of gender differences exist in lateralization. But we still don't know the extent of the differences, and why they occur. One explanation is genetic: that female and male brains are predisposed to function in slightly different ways. Such a view is supported by data suggesting that there are minor structural differences between males' and females' brains. For instance, a section of the corpus callosum is proportionally larger in women than in men. Furthermore, studies conducted among other species, such as primates, rats, and hamsters, have found size and structural differences in the brains of males and females (Witelson, 1989; Highley et al., 1999; Matsumoto, 1999).

Before we accept a genetic explanation for the differences between female and male brains, we need to consider an equally plausible alternative: It may be that verbal abilities emerge earlier in girls because girls receive greater encouragement for verbal skills than boys do. For instance, even as infants, girls are spoken to more than boys (Beal, 1994). Such higher levels of verbal stimulation may produce growth in particular areas of the brain that does not occur in boys. Consequently, environmental factors rather than genetic ones may lead to the gender differences we find in brain lateralization. Most likely, a combination of genetics and environment is at work, as it is with many of our other human characteristics. Once again, we find that teasing out the relative impact of heredity and environment is a challenging task.

The Links Between Brain Growth and Cognitive Development.   Neuroscientists are just beginning to understand the ways in which brain development is related to cognitive development. For example, it appears that there are periods during childhood in which the brain shows unusual growth spurts, and these periods are linked to advances in cognitive abilities. One study that measured electrical activity in the brain across the life span found unusual spurts at between 1½ and 2 years, a time when language abilities increase rapidly. Other spurts occurred around other ages when cognitive advances are particularly intense (see Figure 7-5; Fischer & Rose, 1995; Mabbott et al., 2006; Westermann et al., 2007).

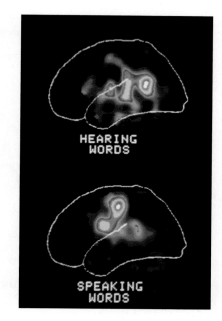

HEARING
WORDS

SPEAKING
WORDS

FIGURE 7-4   LOOKING INTO THE BRAIN

This series of PET brain scans illustrates that activity in the right or left hemisphere of the brain differs according to the task in which a person is engaged. How might educators use this finding in their approach to teaching?

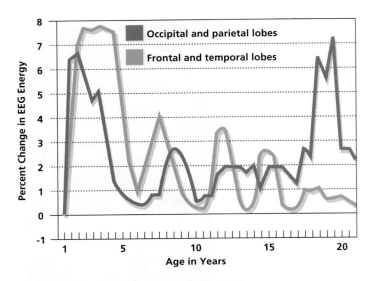

FIGURE 7-5   **BRAIN GROWTH SPURT**

According to one study, electrical activity in the brain has been linked to advances in cognitive abilities at various stages across the life span. In this graph activity increases dramatically between 1½ and 2 years of age, a period during which language rapidly develops.

(*Source:* Fischer & Rose, 1995.)

Other research has suggested that increases in **myelin,** the protective insulation that surrounds parts of neurons, may be related to preschoolers' growing cognitive capabilities. For example, myelination of the *reticular formation,* an area of the brain associated with attention and concentration, is completed by the time children are about 5. This may be associated with children's growing attention spans as they approach school age. The improvement in memory that occurs during the preschool years may also be associated with myelination: During the preschool years, myelination is completed in the hippocampus, an area associated with memory (Rolls, 2000).

In addition, there is significant growth in the nerves connecting the *cerebellum,* the part of the brain that controls balance and movement, to the *cerebral cortex,* the structure responsible for sophisticated information processing. The growth in these nerve fibers is related to the significant advances in motor skills that occur during the preschool years, as well as to advances in cognitive processing (Carson, 2005; Gordon, 2007).

We do not yet know the direction of causality (does brain development produce cognitive advances, or do cognitive accomplishments fuel brain development?). However, it is clear that increases in our understanding of the physiological aspects of the brain will eventually have important implications for parents and teachers.

Motor Development

> *Anya sat in the sandbox at the park, chatting with the other parents and playing with her two children, 5-year-old Nicholai and 13-month old Smetna. While she chatted, she kept a close eye on Smetna, who would still put sand in her mouth sometimes if she wasn't stopped. Today, however, Smetna seemed content to run the sand through her hands and try to put it into a bucket. Nicholai, meanwhile, was busy with two other boys, rapidly filling and emptying the other sand buckets to build an elaborate sand city, which they would then destroy with toy trucks.*

When children of different ages gather at a playground, it's easy to see that preschool children have come a long way in their motor development since infancy. Both their gross and fine motor skills have become increasingly fine-tuned. Smetna, for example, is still mastering putting sand into a bucket, while her brother Nicholai uses that skill easily as part of his larger goal of building a sand city.

Gross Motor Skills.   By the time they are 3, children have mastered a variety of skills: jumping, hopping on one foot, skipping, and running. By 4 and 5, their skills have become more refined as they have gained increasing control over their muscles. For instance, at 4 they can throw a ball with enough accuracy that a friend can catch it, and by age 5 they can toss a ring and have it land on a peg 5 feet away. Five-year-olds can learn to ride bikes, climb ladders, and ski downhill—activities that all require considerable coordination (Clark & Humphrey, 1985). (Table 7-1 summarizes major gross motor skills that emerge during the preschool years.)

These achievements may be related to brain development and myelination of neurons in areas of the brain related to balance and coordination. Another reason that motor skills develop at such a rapid clip during the preschool years is that children spend a great deal of time practicing them. During this period, the general level of activity is extraordinarily high: Preschoolers seem to be perpetually in motion. In fact, the activity level is higher at age 3 than at any other point in the entire life span (Eaton & Yu, 1989; Poest et al., 1990).

myelin   protective insulation that surrounds parts of neurons.

Table 7-1	Major Gross Motor Skills in Early Childhood	
3-Year-Olds	**4-Year-Olds**	**5-Year-Olds**
Cannot turn or stop suddenly or quickly	Have more effective control of stopping, starting, and turning	Start, turn, and stop effectively in games
Jump a distance of 15 to 24 inches	Jump a distance of 24 to 33 inches	Can make a running jump of 28 to 36 inches
Ascend a stairway unaided, alternating the feet	Descend a long stairway alternating the feet, if supported	Descend a long stairway alternating the feet
Can hop, using largely an irregular series of jumps with some variations added	Hop 4 to 6 steps on one foot	Easily hop a distance of 16 feet

(*Source:* Corbin, 1973.)

During the preschool years, children grow in both gross and fine motor skills.

Girls and boys differ in certain aspects of gross motor coordination, in part because of differences in muscle strength, which is somewhat greater in boys than in girls. For instance, boys can typically throw a ball better and jump higher, and a boy's overall activity level tends to be greater than a girl's (Eaton & Yu, 1989). On the other hand, girls generally surpass boys in tasks that involve the coordination of limbs. For instance, at the age of 5, girls are better than boys at jumping jacks and balancing on one foot (Cratty, 1979).

Another aspect of muscular skills—one that parents of toddlers often find most problematic—is bowel and bladder control, as we discuss next.

Potty Wars: When—and How—Should Children Be Toilet Trained?

Ann Wright, of University Park, Maryland, woke up on a sweltering night in June at 3 AM, her head spinning as she reenacted the previous day's parenting trauma: She and her husband, Oliver, had told their 4-year-old daughter, Elizabeth, on Thursday night that it was time for her to stop using her pull-up training pants. For the next 18 hours, the girl had withheld her urine, refusing to use the toilet.

"We had been talking to her for months about saying goodbye to the pull-ups, and she seemed ready," says Wright. "But on the day of the big break she refused to sit on the toilet. Two hours before she finally went, she was crying and constantly moving, clearly uncomfortable."

Eventually the child wet herself. (Gerhardt, 1999, p. C1)

Few childcare issues raise so much concern among parents as toilet training. And on few issues are there so many opposing opinions from experts and laypersons. Often, the various viewpoints are played out in the media and even take on political overtones. For instance, well-known pediatrician T. Berry Brazelton suggests a flexible approach to toilet training, advocating that it be put off until the child shows signs of readiness (Brazelton, 1997; Brazelton et al., 1999). On the other hand, psychologist John Rosemond, known primarily for his media advocacy of a conservative,

Among the signs that children are ready to give up diapers is evidence that they are able to follow directions and can get to the bathroom and undress on their own.

traditional stance to child rearing, argues for a more rigid approach, saying that toilet training should be done early and quickly.

What is clear is that the age at which toilet training takes place has been rising over the last few decades. For example, in 1957, 92% of children were toilet trained by the age of 18 months. In 1999, only 25% were toilet trained at that age, and just 60% of 36-month-olds were toilet trained. Some 2% were still not toilet trained at the age of 4 years (Goode, 1999).

Current guidelines of the American Academy of Pediatrics echo Brazelton's position, suggesting that there is no single time to begin toilet training and that training should begin only when children show that they are ready The signs of readiness include staying dry at least 2 hours at a time during the day or waking up dry after naps; regular and predictable bowel movements; an indication, through facial expressions or words, that urination or a bowel movement is about to occur; the ability to follow simple directions; the ability to get to the bathroom and undress alone; discomfort with soiled diapers; asking to use the toilet or potty chair; and the desire to wear underwear.

Furthermore, children must be ready not only physically, but emotionally, and if they show strong signs of resistance to toilet training, like Elizabeth in the previous example, toilet training should be put off. Children younger than 12 months have no bladder or bowel control, and only slight control for 6 months longer. Although some children show signs of readiness for toilet training between 18 and 24 months, some are not ready until 30 months or older (American Academy of Pediatrics, 1999; Fritz & Rockney, 2004; Connell-Carrick, 2006).

Even after children are toilet trained during the day, it often takes months or years before they are able to achieve control at night. Around three-quarters of boys and most girls are able to stay dry after the age of 5 years.

Complete toilet training eventually occurs in almost all children as they mature and attain greater control over their muscles. However, delayed toilet training can be a cause for concern if a child is upset about it or if it makes the child a target of ridicule from siblings or peers. In such cases, several types of treatments have proven effective. In particular, treatments in which children are rewarded for staying dry or are awakened by a battery device that senses when they have wet the bed are often effective (American Psychiatric Association, 1994; Nawaz, Griffiths, & Tappin, 2002; Houts, 2003).

Fine Motor Skills.   At the same time gross motor skills are developing, children are progressing in their ability to use fine motor skills, which involve more delicate, smaller body movements such as using a fork and spoon, cutting with scissors, tying one's shoelaces, and playing the piano.

The skills involved in fine motor movements require a good deal of practice, as anyone who has watched a 4-year-old struggling painstakingly to copy letters of the alphabet knows. The emergence of these fine motor skills shows clear developmental patterns. At the age of 3, children are already able to draw a circle and square with a crayon, and they can undo their clothes when they go to the bathroom. They can put a simple jigsaw puzzle together, and they can fit blocks of different shapes into matching holes. However, they do not show much precision and polish in accomplishing such tasks. For instance, they may try to force puzzle pieces into place.

By the age of 4, their fine motor skills are considerably better. They can draw a person that looks like a person, and they can fold paper into triangular designs. And by the time they are 5, they are able to hold and manipulate a thin pencil properly.

Handedness.   How do preschoolers decide which hand to hold the pencil in as they work on their copying and other fine motor skills? For many, their choice was established soon after birth.

Beginning in early infancy, many children show signs of a preference for the use of one hand over another—the development of **handedness.** For instance, young infants may show a preference for one side of their bodies over another. By the age of 7 months, some infants seem to favor one hand by grabbing more with it than the other (Michel, 1981; Hinojosa, Sheu, & Michel, 2003).

Most children display a clear-cut tendency to use one hand over the other by the end of the preschool years. Some 90% are right-handed and 10% are left-handed. Furthermore, there is a gender difference: More boys than girls are left-handed.

Much speculation has been devoted to the meaning of handedness, fueled in part by long-standing myths about the sinister nature of left-handedness. (In fact, the word "sinister" itself is derived from the Latin word meaning "on the left.") In Islamic cultures, for instance, the left hand is generally used in going to the toilet, and it is considered uncivilized to serve food with that hand. Many artistic portrayals of the devil show him as left-handed.

Not only is there no scientific basis for myths that suggest that there is something wrong with being left-handed, left-handedness may be associated with certain advantages. For example, a study of 100,000 students who took the SAT college entry exam showed that 20% in the highest-scoring category were left-handed, double the proportion of left-handed people in the general population. Moreover, such individuals as Michelangelo, Leonardo da Vinci, Benjamin Franklin, and Pablo Picasso were left-handed (Bower, 1985).

Although some educators of the past tried to force left-handed children to use the right hand, particularly when learning to write, thinking has changed. Most teachers now encourage children to use the hand they prefer. Still, most left-handed people will agree that the design of desks, scissors, and most other everyday objects favors those who are right-handed. In fact, the world is so "right-biased" that it may prove to be a dangerous place for those who are left-handed: Some research suggests that left-handed people have a higher mortality rate than right-handed people, perhaps due to an elevated accident rate for left-handed individuals (Ellis & Engh, 2000; Mackenzie & Peters, 2000; Martin & Freitas, 2002).

handedness   the preference of using one hand over another.

Becoming an Informed Consumer of Development

Keeping Preschoolers Healthy

There is no way around it: Even the healthiest preschooler occasionally gets sick. Social interaction with others ensures that illnesses will be passed from one child to another. However, some diseases are preventable, and others can be minimized if simple precautions are taken:

- Preschoolers should eat a well-balanced diet containing the proper nutrients, particularly foods containing sufficient protein. (The recommended energy intake for children at age 24 months is about 1,300 calories a day, and for those aged 4 to 6, it is around 1,700 calories a day.) Although some fruit juice, such as a glass of orange juice with breakfast, is fine, generally juice has so much sugar that it should be avoided. In addition, keep offering healthy foods, even if children initially reject them; they may grow to like them.

- Encourage preschoolers to exercise. Children who exercise are less likely to become obese than those who are sedentary.

- Children should get as much sleep as they wish. Being run-down from lack of either nutrition or sleep makes children more susceptible to illness.

- Children should avoid contact with others who are ill. Parents should make sure that children wash their hands after playing with other kids who are obviously sick (as well as emphasizing the importance of hand-washing generally).

- Ensure that children follow an appropriate schedule of immunizations. As illustrated in Table 7-2, current recommendations state that a child should have received nine different vaccines and other preventive medicines in five to seven separate visits to the doctor.
- Finally, if a child does get ill, remember this: Minor illnesses during childhood sometimes provide immunity to more serious illnesses later on.

Table 7-2	Vaccination Schedule

Vaccines are listed under routinely recommended ages. **Bars** indicate range of recommended ages for immunization. Any dose not given at the recommended age should be given as a "catch-up" immunization at any subsequent visit when indicated and feasible. **Ovals** indicate vaccines to be given if previously recommended doses were missed or given earlier than the recommended minimum age.

Age ▶ / Vaccine ▼	Birth	1 mo	2 mos	4 mos	6 mos	12 mos	15 mos	18 mos	24 mos	4–6 yrs	11–12 yrs	14–18 yrs
Hepatitis B		Hep B #1	Hep B #1	Hep B #2	Hep B #2	Hep B #3	Hep B #3	Hep B #3			Hep B	
Diphtheria, Tetanus, Pertussis			DTaP	DTaP	DTaP		DTaP	DTaP		DTaP	Td	
H. influenzae type b			Hib	Hib	Hib	Hib	Hib					
Inactivated Polio			IPV	IPV	IPV	IPV	IPV	IPV		IPV		
Pneumococcal Conjugate			PCV	PCV	PCV	PCV	PCV					
Measles, Mumps, Rubella						MMR	MMR			MMR	MMR	
Varicella						Var	Var	Var			Var	
Hepatitis A										Hep A-in selected areas		

Approved by the Advisory Committee on Immunization Practices (ACIP), the American Academy of Pediatrics (AAP), and the American Academy of Family Physicians (AAFP).

For additional information about the vaccines listed above, please visit the National Immunization Program Home Page at www.cdc.gov/nipor call the National Immunization Hotline at 800-232-2522 (English) or 800-232-0233 (Spanish). (*Source:* American Academy of Pediatrics, 2000.)

Review and Apply

Review

- The preschool period is marked by steady physical growth.
- Preschoolers tend to eat less than they did as babies, but generally regulate their food intake appropriately, given nutritious options and the freedom to develop their own choices and controls.
- Brain growth is rapid during the preschool years. In addition, the brain develops lateralization, a tendency of the two hemispheres to adopt specialized tasks.
- The preschool period is generally the healthiest time of life, with only minor illnesses threatening children. Accidents and environmental hazards are the greatest threats to preschoolers' health. Parents and caregivers need to be aware of steps they can take to keep preschoolers healthy and prevent injuries.
- Gross and fine motor development also advances rapidly during the preschool years. Boys' and girls' gross motor skills begin to diverge, and children develop handedness.

Applying Lifespan Development

- What are some ways that increased understanding of issues relating to the physical development of preschoolers might help parents and caregivers in their care of children?

- *From a health-care worker's perspective:* How might biology and environment combine to affect the physical growth of a child adopted as an infant from a developing country and reared in a more industrialized one?

Intellectual Development

Three-year-old Sam was talking to himself. As his parents listened with amusement from another room, they could hear him using two very different voices. "Find your shoes," he said in a low voice. "Not today. I'm not going. I hate the shoes," he said in a higher-pitched voice. The lower voice answered, "You are a bad boy. Find the shoes, bad boy." The higher-voiced response was "No, no, no."

Sam's parents realized that he was playing a game with his imaginary friend, Gill. Gill was a bad boy who often disobeyed his mother, at least in Sam's imagination. In fact, according to Sam's musings, Gill often was guilty of the very same misdeeds for which his parents blamed Sam.

In some ways, the intellectual sophistication of 3-year-olds is astounding. Their creativity and imagination leap to new heights, their language is increasingly sophisticated, and they reason and think about the world in ways that would have been impossible even a few months earlier. But what underlies the dramatic advances in intellectual development that start in the preschool years and continue throughout that period? We have discussed the general outlines of the brain development that underlies cognitive development in preschoolers. Let's now consider several approaches to children's thinking, starting with a look at Piaget's findings on the cognitive changes that occur during the preschool years.

Piaget's Stage of Preoperational Thinking

Swiss psychologist Jean Piaget, whose stage approach to cognitive development we discussed in Chapter 5, saw the preschool years as a time of both stability and great change. He suggests that the preschool years fit entirely into a single stage of cognitive development—the preoperational stage—which lasts from the age of 2 years until around 7 years.

During the **preoperational stage,** children's use of symbolic thinking grows, mental reasoning emerges, and the use of concepts increases. Seeing Mom's car keys may prompt a question, "Go to store?" as the child comes to see the keys a symbol of a car ride. In this way, children become better at representing events internally, and they grow less dependent on the use of direct sensorimotor activity to understand the world around them. Yet they are still not capable of **operations:** organized, formal, logical mental processes that characterize school-age children. It is only at the end of the preoperational stage that the ability to carry out operations comes into play.

According to Piaget, a key aspect of preoperational thought is *symbolic function,* the ability to use a mental symbol, a word, or an object to stand for or represent something that is not physically present. For example, during this stage, preschoolers can use a mental symbol for a car (the word "car"), and they likewise understand that a small toy car is representative of the real thing. Because of their ability to use symbolic function, children have no need to get behind the wheel of an actual car to understand its basic purpose and use.

preoperational stage according to Piaget, the stage from approximately age 2 to age 7 in which children's use of symbolic thinking grows, mental reasoning emerges, and the use of concepts increases.

operations organized, formal, logical mental processes.

The Relation Between Language and Thought.   Symbolic function is at the heart of one of the major advances that occurs in the preoperational period: the increasingly sophisticated use of language. As we discuss later in this chapter, children make substantial progress in language skills during the preschool period.

Piaget suggests that language and thinking are tightly interconnected and that the advances in language that occur during the preschool years reflect several improvements over the type of thinking that is possible during the earlier sensorimotor period. For instance, thinking embedded in sensorimotor activities is relatively slow, since it depends on actual movements of the body that are bound by human physical limitations. In contrast, the use of symbolic thought, such as the development of an imaginary friend, allows preschoolers to represent actions symbolically, permitting much greater speed.

Even more important, the use of language allows children to think beyond the present to the future. Consequently, rather than being grounded in the immediate here-and-now, preschoolers can imagine future possibilities through language in the form of sometimes elaborate fantasies and daydreams.

Do the improved language abilities of preschoolers lead to improvements in thinking, or is it the other way around, with the improvements in thinking during the preoperational period leading to enhancements in language ability? This question—whether thought determines language or language determines thought—is one of the enduring and most controversial questions within the field of psychology. Piaget's answer is that language grows out of cognitive advances, rather than the other way around. He argues that improvements during the earlier sensorimotor period are necessary for language development and that continuing growth in cognitive ability during the preoperational period provides the foundation for language ability.

Centration: What You See Is What You Think.   Place a dog mask on a cat and what do you get? According to 3- and 4-year-old preschoolers, a dog. To them, a cat with a dog mask ought to bark like a dog, wag its tail like a dog, and eat dog food. In every respect, the cat has been transformed into a dog (deVries, 1969).

To Piaget, the root of this belief is centration, a key element, and limitation, of the thinking of children in the preoperational period. **Centration** is the process of concentrating on one limited aspect of a stimulus and ignoring other aspects.

Preschoolers are unable to consider all available information about a stimulus. Instead, they focus on superficial, obvious elements that are within their sight. These external elements come to dominate preschoolers' thinking, leading to inaccuracy in thought.

When preschoolers are shown two rows of buttons, one with 10 buttons that are spaced closely together and the other with 8 buttons spread out to form a longer row (see Figure 7-6), and asked which of the rows contains more buttons, children who are 4 or 5 usually choose the row that looks longer, rather than the one that actually contains more buttons. This occurs in spite of the fact that children this age know quite well that 10 is more than 8.

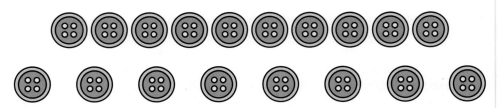

FIGURE 7-6   **WHICH ROW CONTAINS MORE BUTTONS?**

When preschoolers are shown these two rows and asked which row has more buttons, they usually respond that the lower row of buttons contains more, because it looks longer. They answer in this way even though they know quite well that 10 is greater than 8. Do you think preschoolers can be *taught* to answer correctly?

centration   the process of concentrating on one limited aspect of a stimulus and ignoring other aspects.

The cause of the children's mistake is that the visual image of the longer row dominates their thinking. Rather than taking into account their understanding of quantity, they focus on appearance. To a preschooler, appearance is everything. Preschoolers' focus on appearances might be related to another aspect of preoperational thought, the lack of conservation.

Conservation: Learning That Appearances Are Deceiving.   Consider the following scenario:

Four-year-old Jaime is shown two drinking glasses of different shapes. One is short and broad; the other is tall and thin. A teacher half-fills the short, broad glass with apple juice. The teacher then pours the juice into the tall, thin glass. The juice fills the tall glass almost to the brim. The teacher asks Jaime a question: Is there more juice in the second glass than there was in the first?

If you view this as an easy task, so do children like Jaime. They have no trouble answering the question. However, they almost always get the answer wrong.

Most 4-year-olds respond that there is more apple juice in the tall, thin glass than there was in the short, broad one. In fact, if the juice is poured back into the shorter glass, they are quick to say that there is now less juice than there was in the taller glass (see Figure 7-7).

The reason for the error in judgment is that children of this age have not mastered conservation. **Conservation** is the knowledge that quantity is unrelated to the arrangement and physical appearance of objects. Because they are unable to conserve, preschoolers can't understand that changes in one dimension (such as a change in appearance) does not necessarily mean that other dimensions (such as quantity) change. For example, children who do not yet understand the principle of conservation feel quite comfortable in asserting that the amount of liquid changes as it is poured between glasses of different sizes. They simply are unable to realize that the transformation in appearance does not imply a transformation in quantity.

The lack of conservation also manifests itself in children's understanding of area, as illustrated by Piaget's cow-in-the-field problem (Piaget, Inhelder, & Szeminska, 1960). In the problem, two sheets of green paper, equal in size, are shown to a child, and a toy cow is placed in each field. Next, a toy barn is placed in each field, and children are asked which cow has more to eat. The typical—and, so far, correct—response is that the cows have the same amount.

In the next step, a second toy barn is placed in each field. But in one field, the barns are placed adjacent to one another, while in the second field, they are separated from one another. Children who have not mastered conservation usually say that the cow in the field with the adjacent barns has more grass to eat than the cow in the field with the separated barns. In contrast, children who can conserve answer, correctly, that the amount available is identical. (Some other conservation tasks are shown in Figure 7-8).

Why do children in the preoperational stage make errors on tasks that require conservation? Piaget suggests that the main reason is that their tendency toward centration prevents them from focusing on the relevant features of the situation. Furthermore, they cannot follow the sequence of transformations that accompanies changes in the appearance of a situation.

Incomplete Understanding of Transformation.   A preoperational, preschool child who sees several worms during a walk in the woods may believe that they are all the same worm. The reason: She views each sighting in isolation, and she is unable to understand that a transformation would be necessary for a worm to be able to move quickly from one location to the next.

As Piaget used the term, **transformation** is the process in which one state is changed into another. For instance, adults know that if a pencil that is held upright is allowed to fall down, it passes through a series of successive stages until it reaches its final, horizontal resting spot

FIGURE 7-7   WHICH GLASS CONTAINS MORE?

Most 4-year-old children believe that the amount of liquid in these two glasses differs because of the differences in the containers' shapes, even though they may have seen equal amounts of liquid being poured into each.

VIDEO CLIP

CONSERVATION

- - - - - - - - - - - - - - - -

conservation   the knowledge that quantity is unrelated to the arrangement and physical appearance of objects.

transformation   the process in which one state is changed into another.

Type of Conservation	Modality	Change in Physical Appearance	Average Age Invariance Is Grasped
Number	Number of elements in a collection	Rearranging or dislocating elements	6–7 years
Substance (mass)	Amount of a malleable substance (e.g., clay or liquid)	Altering shape	7–8 years
Length	Length of a line or object	Altering shape or configuration	7–8 years
Area	Amount of surface covered by a set of plane figures	Rearranging the figures	8–9 years
Weight	Weight of an object	Altering shape	9–10 years
Volume	Volume of an object (in terms of water displacement)	Altering shape	14–15 years

FIGURE 7-8   COMMON TESTS OF CHILDREN'S UNDERSTANDING OF THE PRINCIPLE OF CONSERVATION

Why is a sense of conservation important?

(see Figure 7-9). In contrast, children in the preoperational period are unable to envision or recall the successive transformations that the pencil followed in moving from the upright to the horizontal position. If asked to reproduce the sequence in a drawing, they draw the pencil upright and lying down, with nothing in between. Basically, they ignore the intermediate steps.

Egocentrism: The Inability to Take Others' Perspectives.   Another hallmark of the preoperational period is egocentric thinking. **Egocentric thought** is thinking that does not take into account the viewpoints of others. Preschoolers do not understand that others have different perspectives from their own. Egocentric thought takes two forms: the lack of awareness that others see things from a different physical perspective and the failure to realize that others may hold thoughts, feelings, and points of view that differ from theirs. (Note what egocentric thought does *not* imply: that preoperational children intentionally think in a selfish or inconsiderate manner.)

mydevelopmentlab

VIDEO CLIP

EGOCENTRISM

egocentric thought   thinking that does not take into account the viewpoints of others.

Egocentric thinking is what is behind children's lack of concern over their nonverbal behavior and the impact it has on others. For instance, a 4-year-old who is given an unwanted gift of socks when he was expecting something more desirable may frown and scowl as he opens the package, unaware that his face can be seen by others, and may reveal his true feelings about the gift (Feldman, 1992).

Egocentrism lies at the heart of several types of behavior during the preoperational period. For instance, preschoolers may talk to themselves, even in the presence of others, and at times they simply ignore what others are telling them. Rather than being a sign of eccentricity, such behavior illustrates the egocentric nature of preoperational children's thinking: the lack of awareness that their behavior acts as a trigger to others' reactions and responses. Consequently, a considerable amount of verbal behavior on the part of preschoolers has no social motivation behind it but is meant for the preschoolers' own consumption.

Similarly, egocentrism can be seen in hiding games with children during the preoperational stage. In a game of hide-and-seek, 3-year-olds may attempt to hide by covering their faces with a pillow—even though they remain in plain view. Their reasoning: If they cannot see others, others cannot see them. They assume that others share their view.

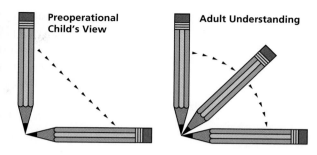

FIGURE 7-9   THE FALLING PENCIL

Children in Piaget's preoperational stage do not understand that as a pencil falls from the upright to the horizontal position it moves through a series of intermediary steps. Instead, they think that there are no intermediate steps in the change from the upright to horizontal position.

The Emergence of Intuitive Thought.

Because Piaget labeled the preschool years as the "*pre*operational period," it is easy to assume that this is a period of marking time, waiting for the more formal emergence of operations. As if to support this view, many of the characteristics of the preoperational period highlight deficiencies, cognitive skills that the preschooler has yet to master. However, the preoperational period is far from idle. Cognitive development proceeds steadily, and in fact several new types of ability emerge. A case in point: the development of intuitive thought.

Intuitive thought refers to preschoolers' use of primitive reasoning and their avid acquisition of knowledge about the world. From about age 4 through 7, children's curiosity blossoms. They constantly seek out the answers to a wide variety of questions, asking, "Why?" about nearly everything. At the same time, children may act as if they are authorities on particular topics, feeling certain that they have the correct—and final—word on an issue. If pressed, they are unable to explain how they know what they know. In other words, their intuitive thought leads them to believe that they know answers to all kinds of questions, but there is little or no logical basis for this confidence in their understanding of the way the world operates. This may lead a preschooler to state authoritatively that airplanes can fly because they move their wings up and down like a bird, even if they have never seen an airplane's wings moving in that way.

In the late stages of the preoperational period, children's intuitive thinking does have certain qualities that prepare them for more sophisticated forms of reasoning. For instance, preschoolers come to understand that pushing harder on the pedals makes a bicycle move faster, or that pressing a button on a remote control makes the television change channels. By the end of the preoperational stage, preschoolers begin to understand the notion of *functionality*, the idea that actions, events, and outcomes are related to one another in fixed patterns. Children also begin to show an awareness of the concept of identity in the later stages of the preoperational period. *Identity* is the understanding that certain things stay the same, regardless of changes in shape, size, and appearance. For instance, knowledge of identity allows one to understand that a lump of clay contains the same amount of clay regardless of whether it is clumped into a ball or stretched out like a snake. Comprehension of identity is necessary for children to develop an understanding of conservation, the ability to understand that quantity is not related to physical appearances, as we discussed earlier. Piaget regarded children's development of conservation as a skill that marks the transition from the preoperational period to the next stage, concrete operations, which we will discuss in Chapter 9.

intuitive thought thinking that reflects preschoolers' use of primitive reasoning and their avid acquisition of knowledge about the world.

Evaluating Piaget's Approach to Cognitive Development.   Piaget, a masterful observer of children's behavior, provided a detailed portrait of preschoolers' cognitive abilities. The broad outlines of his approach has given us a useful way of thinking about the progressive advances in cognitive ability that occur during the preschool years (Siegal, 1997).

However, it is important to consider Piaget's approach to cognitive development within the appropriate historical context and in light of more recent research findings. As we discussed in Chapter 5, his theory is based on extensive observations of relatively few children. Despite his insightful and groundbreaking observations, recent experimental investigations suggest that in certain regards, Piaget underestimated children's capabilities.

Take, for instance, Piaget's views of how children in the preoperational period understand numbers. He contended that preschoolers' thinking is seriously handicapped, as evidenced by their performance on tasks involving conservation and reversibility, the understanding that a transformation can be reversed to return something to its original state. Yet more recent experimental work suggests otherwise. For instance, developmental psychologist Rochel Gelman has found that children as young as 3 can easily tell the difference between rows of two and three toy animals, regardless of the animals' spacing. Older children are able to note differences in number, performing tasks such as identifying which of two numbers is larger and indicating that they understand some rudiments of addition and subtraction problems (Wynn, 1992; Sophian, Garyantes, & Chang, 1997; Vilette, 2002; Gelman, 2006).

Based on such evidence, Gelman concludes that children have an innate ability to count, one akin to the ability to use language that some theorists see as universal and genetically determined. Such a conclusion is clearly at odds with Piagetian notions, which suggest that children's numerical abilities do not blossom until after the preoperational period.

Some developmentalists (particularly those who favor the information processing approach, as we'll see later in the chapter) also believe that cognitive skills develop in a more continuous manner than Piaget's stage theory implies. They believe that rather than thought changing in quality, as Piaget argues, developmental changes are more quantitative in nature, improving gradually. The underlying processes that produce cognitive skill are regarded by such critics as undergoing only minor changes with age (Gelman & Baillargeon, 1983; Case, 1991).

There are further difficulties with Piaget's view of cognitive development. His contention that conservation does not emerge until the end of the preoperational period, and in some cases even later, has not stood up to careful experimental scrutiny. Children can be taught to answer correctly on conservation tasks following certain training and experiences. The fact that one can improve children's performance on these tasks argues against the Piagetian view that children in the preoperational period have not reached a level of cognitive maturity that would permit them to understand conservation (Siegler, 1995).

Clearly, children are more capable at an earlier age than Piaget's account would lead us to believe. Why did Piaget underestimate children's cognitive abilities? One answer is that his questioning of children used language that was too difficult to allow children to answer in a way that would provide a true picture of their skills. In addition, as we've seen, Piaget tended to concentrate on preschoolers' *deficiencies* in thinking, focusing his observations on children's lack of logical thought. By focusing more on children's competence, more recent theorists have found increasing evidence for a surprising degree of capability in preschoolers.

Information Processing Approaches to Cognitive Development

Even as an adult, Paco has clear recollections of his first trip to a farm, which he took when he was 3 years old. He was visiting his godfather, who lived in Puerto Rico, and the two of them went to a nearby farm. Paco recounts seeing what seemed like hundreds of chickens, and he clearly recalls his fear of the pigs, who seemed huge, smelly, and frightening. Most of all, he recalls the thrill of riding on a horse with his godfather.

The fact that Paco has a clear memory of his farm trip is not surprising: Most people have unambiguous, and seemingly accurate, memories dating as far back as the age of 3. But are the processes used to form memories during the preschool years similar to those that operate later in life? More broadly, what general changes in the processing of information occur during the preschool years?

Information processing approaches focus on changes in the kinds of "mental programs" that children use when approaching problems. They view the changes that occur in children's cognitive abilities during the preschool years as analogous to the way a computer program becomes more sophisticated as a programmer modifies it on the basis of experience. In fact, for many child developmentalists, information processing approaches represent the dominant, most comprehensive, and ultimately the most accurate explanation of how children develop cognitively (Siegler, 1994; Lacerda, von Hofsten, & Heimann, 2001).

We'll focus on two areas that highlight the approach taken by information processing theorists: understanding of numbers and memory development during the preschool years.

Preschoolers' Understanding of Numbers.   As we saw earlier, one of the flaws critics have noticed in Piaget's theory is that preschoolers have a greater understanding of numbers than Piaget thought. Researchers using information processing approaches to cognitive development have found increasing evidence for the sophistication of preschoolers' understanding of numbers. The average preschooler is able not only to count, but to do so in a fairly systematic, consistent manner (Siegler, 1998).

For instance, developmental psychologist Rochel Gelman suggests that preschoolers follow a number of principles in their counting. Shown a group of several items, they know they should assign just one number to each item and that each item should be counted only once. Moreover, even when they get the *names* of numbers wrong, they are consistent in their usage. For instance, a 4-year-old who counts three items as "1, 3, 7" will say "1, 3, 7" when counting another group of different items. And she will probably say that there are 7 items in the group, if asked how many there are (Gelman & Cordes, 2001; Gelman, 2006).

In short, preschoolers may demonstrate a surprisingly sophisticated understanding of numbers, although their understanding is not totally precise. Still, by the age of 4, most are able to carry out simple addition and subtraction problems by counting, and they are able to compare different quantities quite successfully (Donlan, 1998).

Memory: Recalling the Past.   Think back to your own earliest memory. If you are like Paco, described earlier, and most other people too, it probably is of an event that occurred after the age of 3. **Autobiographical memory,** memory of particular events from one's own life, achieves little accuracy until after 3 years of age. Accuracy then increases gradually and slowly throughout the preschool years (Sutton, 2002; Ross & Wilson, 2003; De Roten, Favez, & Drapeau, 2004; Nelson & Fivush, 2004).

Preschool children's recollections of events that happened to them are sometimes, but not always, accurate. For instance, 3-year-olds can remember central features of routine occurrences, such as the sequence of events involved in eating at a restaurant, fairly well. In addition, preschoolers are typically accurate in their responses to open-ended questions, such as "What rides did you like best at the amusement park?" (Price & Goodman, 1990; Wang, 2006).

The accuracy of preschoolers' memories is partly determined by how soon the memories are assessed. Unless an event is particularly vivid or meaningful, it is not likely to be remembered at all. Moreover, not all autobiographical memories last into later life. For instance, a child may remember the first day of kindergarten 6 months or a year later, but later in life might not remember that day at all.

Memories are also affected by cultural factors. For example, Chinese college students' memories of early childhood are more likely to be unemotional and reflect activities involving social roles, such as working in a family store, whereas U.S. college students' earliest memories are

autobiographical memory memory of particular events from one's own life.

This preschooler may recall this ride in six months, but by the time he is 12, it will probably be forgotten. Can you explain why?

more emotionally elaborate and focus on specific events such as the birth of a sibling (Wang, 2001, 2004, 2006).

Preschoolers' autobiographical memories not only fade, but what is remembered may not be wholly accurate. For example, if an event happens often, such as a trip to a grocery store, it may be hard to remember one specific time it happened. Preschoolers' memories of familiar events are often organized in terms of **scripts,** broad representations in memory of events and the order in which they occur. For example, a young preschooler might represent eating in a restaurant in terms of a few steps: talking to a waitress, getting the food, and eating. With age, the scripts become more elaborate: getting in the car, being seated at the restaurant, choosing food, ordering, waiting for the meal to come, eating, ordering dessert, and paying for the food. Because events that are frequently repeated tend to be melded into scripts, particular instances of a scripted event are recalled with less accuracy than those that are unscripted in memory (Fivush, Kuebli, & Clubb, 1992; Sutherland, Pipe, & Schick, 2003).

There are other reasons why preschoolers may not have entirely accurate autobiographical memories. Because they have difficulty describing certain kinds of information, such as complex causal relationships, they may oversimplify recollections. For example, a child who has witnessed an argument between his grandparents may only remember that grandma took the cake away from grandpa, not the discussion of his weight and cholesterol that led up to the action. And, as we consider next, preschoolers' memories are also susceptible to the suggestions of others. This is a special concern when children are called upon to testify in legal situations, such as when abuse is suspected, as we consider next.

Children's Eyewitness Testimony: Memory on Trial.

I was looking and then I didn't see what I was doing and it got in there somehow. . . . The mousetrap was in our house because there's a mouse in our house. . . . The mousetrap is down in the basement, next to the firewood. . . . I was playing a game called "Operation" and then I went downstairs and said to Dad, "I want to eat lunch," and then it got stuck in the mousetrap. . . . My daddy was down in the basement collecting firewood. . . . [My brother] pushed me [into the mousetrap]. . . . It happened yesterday. The mouse was in my house yesterday. I caught my finger in it yesterday. I went to the hospital yesterday. (Ceci & Bruck, 1993, p. A23)

Despite the detailed account by this 4-year-old boy of his encounter with a mousetrap and subsequent trip to the hospital, there's a problem: The incident never happened, and the memory is entirely false.

The 4-year-old's explicit recounting of a mousetrap incident that had not actually occurred was the product of a study on children's memory. Each week for 11 weeks, the 4-year-old boy was told, "You went to the hospital because your finger got caught in a mousetrap. Did this ever happen to you?"

The first week, the child quite accurately said, "No. I've never been to the hospital." But by the second week, the answer changed to, "Yes, I cried." In the third week, the boy said, "Yes. My mom went to the hospital with me." By the 11th week, the answer had expanded to the quote above (Ceci & Bruck, 1993; Bruck & Ceci, 2004).

The research study that elicited the child's false memories is part of a new and rapidly growing field: forensic developmental psychology. *Forensic developmental psychology* focuses on the reliability of children's autobiographical memories in the context of the legal system. It considers children's abilities to recall events in their lives and the reliability of children's courtroom accounts when they are witnesses or victims (Bruck & Ceci, 2004; Goodman, 2006).

The embellishment of a completely false incident is characteristic of the fragility, impressionability, and inaccuracy of memory in young children. Young children may recall things quite mistakenly, but with great conviction, contending that events occurred which never really happened, and forgetting events that did occur.

Children's memories are susceptible to the suggestions of adults asking them questions. This is particularly true of preschoolers, who are considerably more vulnerable to suggestion than

scripts broad representations in memory of events and the order in which they occur.

either adults or school-age children. Preschoolers are also more prone to make inaccurate inferences about the reasons behind others' behavior and are less able to draw appropriate conclusions based on their knowledge of a situation (e.g., "He was crying because he didn't like the sandwich.") (Principe & Ceci, 2002; Ceci, Fitneva, & Gilstrap, 2003; Loftus, 2004; Goodman & Melinder, 2007).

Of course, preschoolers recall many things accurately; as we discussed earlier; children as young as 3 recall some events in their lives without distortion. However, not all recollections are accurate, and certain events that are recalled with seeming accuracy never actually occurred.

The error rate for children is heightened when the same question is asked repeatedly. False memories—of the type reported by the 4-year-old who "remembered" going to the hospital after his finger was caught in a mousetrap—in fact may be more persistent than actual memories. In addition, when questions are highly suggestive (that is, when questioners attempt to lead a person to particular conclusions), children are more apt to make mistakes in recall (Powell, Thomson, & Ceci, 2003; Bruck & Ceci, 2004; Loftus & Bernstein, 2005; Krähenbühl & Blades, 2006).

Information Processing in Perspective. According to information processing approaches, cognitive development consists of gradual improvements in the ways people perceive, understand, and remember information. With age and practice, preschoolers process information more efficiently and with greater sophistication, and they are able to handle increasingly complex problems. In the eyes of proponents of information processing approaches, it is these quantitative advances in information processing—and not the qualitative changes suggested by Piaget—that constitute cognitive development (Case & Okamoto, 1996; Goswami, 1998; Zhe & Siegler, 2000).

For supporters of information processing approaches, the reliance on well-defined processes that can be tested, with relative precision, by research is one of the perspective's most important features. Rather than relying on concepts that are somewhat vague, such as Piaget's notions of assimilation and accommodation, information processing approaches provide a comprehensive, logical set of concepts.

For instance, as preschoolers grow older, they have longer attention spans, can monitor and plan what they are attending to more effectively, and become increasingly aware of their cognitive limitations. As discussed earlier in this chapter, these advances may be due to brain development. Such increasing attentional abilities place some of Piaget's findings in a different light. For instance, increased attention allows older children to attend to both the height *and* the width of tall and short glasses into which liquid is poured. This permits them to understand that the amount of liquid in the glasses stays the same when it is poured back and forth. Preschoolers, in contrast, are unable to attend to both dimensions simultaneously, and thus are less able to conserve (Miller & Seier, 1994; Hudson, Sosa, & Shapiro, 1997).

Proponents of information processing theory have also been successful in focusing on important cognitive processes to which alternative approaches traditionally have paid little attention, such as the contribution of mental skills like memory and attention to children's thinking. They suggest that information processing provides a clear, logical, and full account of cognitive development.

Yet information processing approaches have their detractors, who raise significant points. For one thing, the focus on a series of single, individual cognitive processes leaves out of consideration some important factors that appear to influence cognition. For instance, information processing theorists pay relatively little attention to social and cultural factors—a deficiency that the approach we'll consider next attempts to remedy.

An even more important criticism is that information processing approaches "lose the forest for the trees." In other words, information processing approaches pay so much attention to the detailed, individual sequence of processes that compose cognitive processing and development

Russian developmental psychologist Lev Vygotsky proposed that the focus of cognitive development should be on a child's social and cultural world, as opposed to the Piagetian approach concentrating on individual performance.

that they never adequately paint a whole, comprehensive picture of cognitive development—which Piaget clearly did quite well.

Developmentalists using information processing approaches respond to such criticisms by saying that their model of cognitive development has the advantage of being precisely stated and capable of leading to testable hypotheses. They also argue that there is far more research supporting their approach than there is for alternative theories of cognitive development. In short, they suggest that their approach provides a more accurate account than any other.

Information processing approaches have been highly influential over the past several decades. They have inspired a tremendous amount of research that has helped us gain some insights into how children develop cognitively.

Vygotsky's View of Cognitive Development: Taking Culture into Account

> *As her daughter watches, a member of the Chilcotin Indian tribe prepares a salmon for dinner. When the daughter asks a question about a small detail of the process, the mother takes out another salmon and repeats the entire process. According to the tribal view of learning, understanding and comprehension can come only from grasping the total procedure, and not from learning about the individual subcomponents of the task. (Tharp, 1989)*

The Chilcotin view of how children learn about the world contrasts with the prevalent view of Western society, which assumes that only by mastering the separate parts of a problem can one fully comprehend it. Do differences in the ways particular cultures and societies approach problems influence cognitive development? According to Russian developmental psychologist Lev Vygotsky, who lived from 1896 to 1934, the answer is a clear "yes."

Vygotsky viewed cognitive development as a result of social interactions in which children learn through guided participation, working with mentors to solve problems. Instead of concentrating on individual performance, as Piaget and many alternative approaches do, Vygotsky's increasingly influential view focuses on the social aspects of development and learning.

Vygotsky saw children as apprentices, learning cognitive strategies and other skills from adult and peer mentors who not only present new ways of doing things, but also provide assistance, instruction, and motivation. Consequently, he focused on the child's social and cultural world as the source of cognitive development. According to Vygotsky, children gradually grow intellectually and begin to function on their own because of the assistance that adult and peer partners provide (Vygotsky, 1979, 1926/1997; Tudge & Scrimsher, 2003).

Vygotsky contends that the nature of the partnership between developing children and adults and peers is determined largely by cultural and societal factors. For instance, culture and society establish the institutions, such as preschools and play groups, that promote development by providing opportunities for cognitive growth. Furthermore, by emphasizing particular tasks, culture and society shape the nature of specific cognitive advances. Unless we look at what is important and meaningful to members of a given society, we may seriously underestimate the nature and level of cognitive abilities that ultimately will be attained (Tappan, 1997; Schaller & Crandall, 2004).

For example, children's toys reflect what is important and meaningful in a particular society. In Western society, preschoolers commonly play with toy wagons, automobiles, and other vehicles, in part reflecting the mobile nature of the culture.

Societal expectations about gender also play a role in how children come to understand the world. For example, one study conducted at a science museum found that parents provided more detailed scientific explanations to boys than to girls at museum displays. Such differences in level of explanation may lead to more sophisticated understanding of science in boys and ultimately may produce later gender differences in science learning (Crowley et al., 2001).

Vygotsky's approach is therefore quite different from that of Piaget. Where Piaget looked at developing children and saw junior scientists, working by themselves to develop an independent understanding of the world, Vygotsky saw cognitive apprentices, learning from master teachers the skills that are important in the child's culture. In Vygotsky's view, then, children's cognitive development is dependent on interaction with others (Kitchener, 1996; Fernyhough, 1997).

The Zone of Proximal Development and Scaffolding: Foundations of Cognitive Development.
Vygotsky proposed that children's cognitive abilities increase through exposure to information that is new enough to be intriguing, but not too difficult for the child to contend with. He called this the **zone of proximal development,** or **ZPD,** the level at which a child can *almost,* but not fully, perform a task independently, but can do so with the assistance of someone more competent. When appropriate instruction is offered within the zone of proximal development, children are able to increase their understanding and master new tasks. In order for cognitive development to occur, then, new information must be presented—by parents, teachers, or more skilled peers—within the zone of proximal development. For example, a preschooler might not be able to figure out by herself how to get a handle to stick on the clay pot she's building, but she could do it with some advice from her childcare teacher (Blank & White, 1999; Chaiklin, 2003; Kozulin, 2004).

The concept of the zone of proximal development suggests that even though two children might be able to achieve the same amount without help, if one child receives aid, he or she may improve substantially more than the other. The greater the improvement that comes with help, the larger is the zone of proximal development (see Figure 7-10).

The assistance or structuring provided by others has been termed *scaffolding*. **Scaffolding** is the support for learning and problem solving that encourages independence and growth (Puntambekar & Hübscher, 2005).

To Vygotsky, the process of scaffolding not only helps children solve specific problems, but also aids in the development of their overall cognitive abilities. Scaffolding takes its name from the scaffolds that are put up to aid in the construction of a building and are removed once the building is complete. In education, scaffolding involves, first of all, helping children think about and frame a task in an appropriate manner. In addition, a parent or teacher is likely to provide clues to task completion that are appropriate to the child's level of development and to model behavior that can lead to completion of the task. As in construction, the scaffolding that more competent people provide, which facilitates the completion of identified tasks, is removed once children are able to solve a problem on their own (Rogoff, 1995; Warwick & Maloch, 2003).

zone of proximal development (ZPD) according to Vygotsky, the level at which a child can *almost,* but not fully, perform a task independently, but can do so with the assistance of someone more competent.

scaffolding the support for learning and problem solving that encourages independence and growth.

VIDEO CLIP
ZONE OF PROXIMAL DEVELOPMENT

VIDEO CLIP
SCAFFOLDING

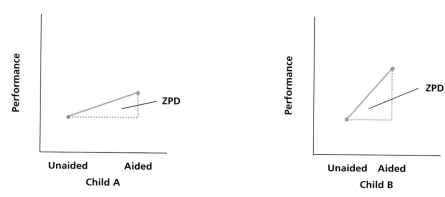

FIGURE 7-10 SAMPLE ZONES OF PROXIMAL DEVELOPMENT (ZPD) FOR TWO CHILDREN

Although the two children's performance is similar when working at a task without aid, Child B benefits more from aid and therefore has a larger ZPD. Is there any way to measure a child's ZPD? Can it be enlarged?

To illustrate how scaffolding operates, consider the following conversation between mother and son:

Mother: Do you remember how you helped me make the cookies before?
Child: No.
Mother: We made the dough and put it in the oven. Do you remember that?
Child: When Grandma came?
Mother: Yes, that's right. Would you help me shape the dough into cookies?
Child: OK.
Mother: Can you remember how big we made the cookies when Grandma was here?
Child: Big.
Mother: Right. Can you show me how big?
Child: We used the big wooden spoon.
Mother: Good boy, that's right. We used the wooden spoon, and we made big cookies. But let's try something different today by using the ice cream scoop to form the cookies.

Although this conversation isn't particularly sophisticated, it illustrates the practice of scaffolding. The mother is supporting her son's efforts, and she gets him to respond conversationally. In the process, she not only expands her son's abilities by using a different tool (the scoop instead of the spoon), she models how conversations proceed.

In some societies parental support for learning differs by gender. In one study, Mexican mothers were found to provide more scaffolding than fathers. A possible explanation is that mothers may be more aware of their children's cognitive abilities than are fathers (Tenenbaum & Leaper, 1998; Tamis-LeMonda & Cabrera, 2002).

One key aspect of the aid that more accomplished individuals provide to learners comes in the form of cultural tools. *Cultural tools* are actual, physical items (e.g., pencils, paper, calculators, computers, and so forth) as well as an intellectual and conceptual framework for solving problems. The intellectual and conceptual framework available to learners includes the language that is used within a culture, its alphabetical and numbering schemes, its mathematical and scientific systems, and even its religious systems. These cultural tools provide a structure that can be used to help children define and solve specific problems, as well as an intellectual point of view that encourages cognitive development.

For example, consider the cultural differences in how people talk about distance. In cities, distance is usually measured in blocks ("the store is about 15 blocks away"). To a child from a rural background, such a unit of measurement is meaningless, and more meaningful distance-related terms may be used, such as yards, miles, such practical rules of thumb as "a stone's throw," or references to known distances and landmarks ("about half the distance to town"). To make matters more complicated, "how far" questions are sometimes answered in terms not of distance, but of time ("it's about 15 minutes to the store"), which will be understood variously to refer to walking or riding time, depending on context—and, if riding time, to different forms of riding. For some children the ride to the store will be conceived of as being by ox cart, for others, by bicycle, bus, canoe, or automobile, again depending on cultural context. The nature of the tools available to children to solve problems and perform tasks is highly dependent on the culture in which they live.

Evaluating Vygotsky's Contributions. Vygotsky's view—that the specific nature of cognitive development can be understood only by taking into account cultural and social context—has become increasingly influential in the last decade. In some ways, this is surprising, in light of the fact that Vygotsky died over seven decades ago at the young age of 37 (Winsler, 2003; Vanderburg, 2006).

Several factors explain Vygotsky's growing influence. One is that until recently he was largely unknown to developmentalists. His writings are only now becoming widely disseminated in the United States due to the growing availability of good English translations. In fact, for most of the 20th century Vygotsky was not widely known even within his native land. His work was banned for some time, and it was not until the breakup of the Soviet Union that it became freely available in the formerly Soviet countries. Thus, Vygotsky, long hidden from his fellow developmentalists, didn't emerge onto the scene until long after his death.

Even more important, though, is the quality of Vygotsky's ideas. They represent a consistent theoretical system and help explain a growing body of research attesting to the importance of social interaction in promoting cognitive development. The idea that children's comprehension of the world is an outcome of their interactions with their parents, peers, and other members of society is both appealing and well supported by research findings. It is also consistent with a growing body of multicultural and cross-cultural research, which finds evidence that cognitive development is shaped, in part, by cultural factors (Daniels, 1996; Scrimsher & Tudge, 2003).

Of course, not every aspect of Vygotsky's theorizing has been supported, and he can be criticized for a lack of precision in his conceptualization of cognitive growth. For instance, such broad concepts as the zone of proximal development are not terribly precise, and they do not always lend themselves to experimental tests (Wertsch, 1999; Daniels, 2006).

Furthermore, Vygotsky was largely silent on how basic cognitive processes such as attention and memory develop and how children's natural cognitive capabilities unfold. Because of his emphasis on broad cultural influences, he did not focus on how individual bits of information are processed and synthesized. These processes, which must be taken into account if we are to have a complete understanding of cognitive development, are more directly addressed by information processing theories.

Still, Vygotsky's melding of the cognitive and social worlds of children has been an important advance in our understanding of cognitive development. We can only imagine what his impact would have been if he had lived a longer life.

Review and Apply

Review

- According to Piaget, children in the preoperational stage develop symbolic function, a qualitative change in their thinking that is the foundation of further cognitive advances.

- Preoperational children use intuitive thought to explore and draw conclusions about the world, and their thinking begins to encompass the important notions of functionality and identity.

- Recent developmentalists, while acknowledging Piaget's gifts and contributions, take issue with his emphasis on children's limitations and his underestimation of their capabilities.

- Proponents of information processing approaches argue that quantitative changes in children's processing skills largely account for their cognitive development.

- Vygotsky believed that children develop cognitively within a context of culture and society. His theory includes the concepts of the zone of proximal development and scaffolding.

Applying Lifespan Development

- In your view, how do thought and language interact in preschoolers' development? Is it possible to think without language? How do children who have been deaf from birth think?

- *From an educator's perspective:* If children's cognitive development is dependent on interactions with others, what obligations does society have regarding such social settings as preschools and neighborhoods?

syntax   the way in which an individual combines words and phrases to form sentences.

fast mapping   instances in which new words are associated with their meaning after only a brief encounter.

The Growth of Language and Learning

I tried it out and it was very great!

This is a picture of when I was running through the water with Mommy.

Where are you going when I go to the fireworks with Mommy and Daddy?

I didn't know creatures went on floats in pools.

We can always pretend we have another one.

And the teacher put it up on the counter so no one could reach it.

I really want to keep it while we're at the park.

You need to get your own ball if you want to play "hit the tree."

When I grow up and I'm a baseball player, I'll have my baseball hat, and I'll put it on, and I'll play baseball. (Schatz, 1994, p. 179)

Listen to Ricky, at the age of 3. In addition to recognizing most letters of the alphabet, printing the first letter of his name, and writing the word "HI," he is readily capable of producing the complex sentences quoted above.

During the preschool years, children's language skills reach new heights of sophistication. They begin the period with reasonable linguistic capabilities, although with significant gaps in both comprehension and production. In fact, no one would mistake the language used by a 3-year-old for that of an adult. However, by the end of the preschool years, they can hold their own with adults, both comprehending and producing language that has many of the qualities of adults' language. How does this transformation occur?

Language Development

Language blooms so rapidly between the later months of age 2 and the mid-3s that researchers have yet to understand the exact pattern. What is clear is that sentence length increases at a steady pace, and the ways in which children at this age combine words and phrases to form sentences—known as **syntax**—doubles each month. By the time a preschooler is 3, the various combinations reach into the thousands (see Table 7-3 for an example of one child's growth in the use of language; Wheeldon, 1999, Pinker, 2005).

In addition to the increasing complexity of sentences, there are enormous leaps in the number of words children use. By age 6, the average child has a vocabulary of around 14,000 words. To reach this number, preschoolers acquire vocabulary at a rate of nearly one new word every 2 hours, 24 hours a day. They manage this feat through a process known as **fast mapping,** in which new words are associated with their meaning after only a brief encounter (Clark, 1983; Fenson et al., 1994; Ganger & Brent, 2004).

By the age of 3, preschoolers routinely use plurals and possessive forms of nouns (such as "boys" and "boy's"), employ the past tense (adding "-ed" at the end of words), and use articles ("the" and "a"). They can ask, and answer, complex questions ("Where did you say my book is?" and "Those are trucks, aren't they?").

Preschoolers' skills extend to the appropriate formation of words that they have never before encountered. For example, in one classic experiment, preschool children were shown cards with drawings of a cartoon-like bird, such as those shown in Figure 7-11 (Berko, 1958). The experimenter told the children that the figure was a "wug," and then showed them a card with two of the cartoon figures. "Now there are two of them," the children were told, and they were then asked to supply the missing word in the sentence, "There are two_____" (the answer to which, of course, is "wugs").

Not only did children show that they knew rules about the plural forms of nouns, but they understood possessive forms of nouns and the third-person singular and past-tense forms of

This is a wug.

**Now there is another one.
There are two of them.
There are two _____ .**

FIGURE 7-11   APPROPRIATE FORMATION OF WORDS

Even though no preschooler—like the rest of us—is likely to have ever before encountered a wug, preschoolers are able to produce the appropriate word to fill in the blank (which, for the record, is *wugs*).

(*Source:* Adapted from Berko, 1958.)

Table 7-3 Growing Speech Capabilities

Over the course of just a year, the sophistication of the language of a boy named Adam increases amazingly, as these speech samples show:

2 years, 3 months:	Play checkers. Big drum I got horn. A bunny-rabbit walk.
2 years, 4 months:	See marching bear go? Screw part machine. That busy bulldozer truck.
2 years, 5 months:	Now put boots on. Where wrench go? Mommy talking bout lady. What that paper clip doing?
2 years, 6 months:	Write a piece of paper. What that egg doing? I lost a shoe. No, I don't want to sit seat.
2 years, 7 months:	Where piece a paper go? Ursula has a boot on. Going to see kitten. Put the cigarette down. Dropped a rubber band. Shadow has hat just like that. Rintintin don't fly, Mommy.
2 years, 8 months:	Let me get down with the boots on. Don't be afraid a horses. How tiger be so healthy and fly like kite? Joshua throw like a penguin.
2 years, 9 months:	Where Mommy keep her pocket book? Show you something funny. Just like turtle make mud pie.
2 years, 10 months:	Look at that train Ursula brought. I simply don't want put in chair. You don't have paper. Do you want little bit, Cromer? I can't wear it tomorrow.
2 years, 11 months:	That birdie hopping by Missouri in bag. Do want some pie on your face? Why you mixing baby chocolate? I finish drinking all up down my throat. I said why not you coming in? Look at that piece of paper and tell it. Do you want me tie that round? We going turn light on so you can't see.
3 years, 0 months:	I going come in fourteen minutes. I going wear that to wedding. I see what happens. I have to save them now. Those are not strong mens. They are going sleep in wintertime. You dress me up like a baby elephant.
3 years, 1 month:	I like to play with something else. You know how to put it back together. I gon' make it like a rocket to blast off with. I put another one on the floor. You went to Boston University? You want to give me some carrots and some beans? Press the button and catch it, sir. I want some other peanuts. Why you put the pacifier in his mouth? Doggies like to climb up.
3 years, 2 months:	So it can't be cleaned? I broke my racing car. Do you know the light wents off? What happened to the bridge? When it's got a flat tire it's need a go to the station. I dream sometimes. I'm going to mail this so the letter can't come off. I want to have some espresso. The sun is not too bright. Can I have some sugar? Can I put my head in the mailbox so the mailman can know where I are and put me in the mailbox? Can I keep the screwdriver just like a carpenter keep the screwdriver?

(*Source:* Pinker, 1994.)

verbs—all for words that they never had previously encountered, since they were nonsense words with no real meaning (O'Grady & Aitchison, 2005).

Preschoolers also learn what *cannot* be said as they acquire the principles of grammar. **Grammar** is the system of rules that determine how our thoughts can be expressed. For instance, preschoolers come to learn that "I am sitting" is correct, while the similarly structured "I am knowing [that]" is incorrect. Although they still make frequent mistakes of one sort or another, 3-year-olds follow the principles of grammar most of the time. Some errors are very noticeable—such as the use of "mens" and "catched"—but these errors are actually quite rare. In fact, young preschoolers are correct in their grammatical constructions more than 90% of the time (deVilliers & deVilliers, 1992; Pinker, 1994; Guasti, 2002).

Private Speech and Social Speech.   In even a short visit to a preschool, you're likely to notice some children talking to themselves during play periods. A child might be reminding a doll that the two of them are going to the grocery store later, or another child, while playing with a toy racing car, might speak of an upcoming race. In some cases, the talk is sustained, as when a child working on a puzzle says things like, "This piece goes here. . . . Uh-oh, this one doesn't fit. . . . Where can I put this piece? . . . This can't be right."

Some developmentalists suggest that **private speech,** speech by children that is spoken and directed to themselves, performs an important function. For instance, Vygotsky suggested that

grammar the system of rules that determines how our thoughts can be expressed.

private speech speech by children that is spoken and directed to themselves.

pragmatics   the aspect of language that relates to communicating effectively and appropriately with others.

social speech   speech directed toward another person and meant to be understood by that person.

private speech is used as a guide to behavior and thought. By communicating with themselves through private speech, children are able to try out ideas, acting as their own sounding boards. In this way, private speech facilitates children's thinking and helps them control their behavior. (Have you ever said to yourself, "Take it easy" or "Calm down" when trying to control your anger over some situation?) In Vygotsky's view, then, private speech ultimately serves an important social function, allowing children to solve problems and reflect upon difficulties they encounter. He also suggested that private speech is a forerunner to the internal dialogues that we use when we reason with ourselves during thinking (Winsler, De Leon, & Wallace, 2003; Winsler et al., 2006).

In addition, private speech may be a way for children to practice the practical skills required in conversation, known as *pragmatics*. **Pragmatics** is the aspect of language relating to communicating effectively and appropriately with others. The development of pragmatic abilities permits children to understand the basics of conversations—turn-taking, sticking to a topic, and what should and should not be said, according to the conventions of society. When children are taught that the appropriate response to receiving a gift is "thank you," or that they should use different language in various settings (on the playground with their friends versus in the classroom with their teacher), they are learning the pragmatics of language.

The preschool years also mark the growth of social speech. **Social speech** is speech directed toward another person and meant to be understood by that person. Before the age of 3, children may seem to be speaking only for their own entertainment, apparently uncaring as to whether anyone else can understand. However, during the preschool years, children begin to direct their speech to others, wanting others to listen and becoming frustrated when they cannot make themselves understood. As a result, they begin to adapt their speech to others through pragmatics, as just discussed. Recall that Piaget contended that most speech during the preoperational period was egocentric: Preschoolers were seen as taking little account of the effect their speech was having on others. However, more recent experimental evidence suggests that children are somewhat more adept in taking others into account than Piaget initially suggested.

Poverty and Language Development.   The language that preschoolers hear at home has profound implications for future cognitive success, according to results of a landmark series of studies by psychologists Betty Hart and Todd Risley (Hart & Risley, 1995; Hart, 2000, 2004). The researchers studied the language used over a 2-year period by a group of parents of varying levels of affluence as they interacted with their children. Their examination of some 1,300 hours of everyday interactions between parents and children produced several major findings:

- The greater the affluence of the parents, the more they spoke to their children. As shown in Figure 7-12, the rate at which language was addressed to children varied significantly according to the economic level of the family. The greater the affluence of the parents, the more they spoke to their children.

- In a typical hour, parents classified as professionals spent almost twice as much time interacting with their children as parents who received welfare assistance.

- By the age of 4, children in families that received welfare assistance were likely to have been exposed to some 13 million fewer words than those in families classified as professionals.

- The kind of language used in the home differed among the various types of families. Children in families that received welfare assistance were apt to hear prohibitions ("no" or "stop," for example) twice as frequently as those in families classified as professionals.

Ultimately, the study found that the type of language to which children were exposed was associated with their performance on tests of intelligence. The greater the number and variety of words children heard, for instance, the better their performance at age 3 on a variety of measures of intellectual achievement.

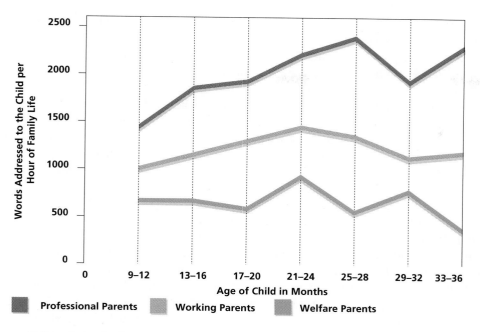

FIGURE 7-12   DIFFERENT LANGUAGE EXPOSURE

Parents at differing levels of economic affluence provide different language experiences. Professional parents and working parents address more words to their children, on average, than parents on welfare. Why do you think this is so?

(*Source:* Hart & Risley, 1995.)

Although the findings are correlational, and thus cannot be interpreted in terms of cause and effect, they clearly suggest the importance of early exposure to language, in terms of both quantity and variety. They also suggest that intervention programs that teach parents to speak to their children more often and use more varied language may be useful in alleviating some of the potentially damaging consequences of poverty.

The research is also consistent with an increasing body of evidence that family income and poverty have powerful consequences for children's general cognitive development and behavior. By the age of 5, children raised in poverty tend to have lower IQ scores and do not perform as well on other measures of cognitive development as children raised in affluence. Furthermore, the longer children live in poverty, the more severe the consequences. Poverty not only reduces the educational resources available to children, it also has such negative effects on parents that it limits the psychological support they can provide their families. In short, the consequences of poverty are severe, and they linger (Ramey & Ramey, 1998; Whitehurst & Fischel, 2000; Bornstein & Bradley, 2003; Farah et al., 2006).

Learning from the Media: Television and the Internet

It's a Thursday afternoon at Unitel Studio on Ninth Avenue, where Sesame Street *is taping its nineteenth season. Hanging back in the wings is a newcomer on the set, a compact young woman with short blonde hair named Judy Sladky. Today is her screen test. Other performers come to New York aspiring to be actresses, dancers, singers, comedians. But Sladky's burning ambition is to be Alice, a shaggy mini-mastodon who will make her debut later this season as the devoted baby sister of Aloysius Snuffle-upagus, the biggest creature on the show.* (Hellman, 1987, p. 50)

Ask almost any preschooler, and she or he will be able to identify Snuffle-upagus, as well as Big Bird, Bert, Ernie, and a host of other characters: the members of the cast of *Sesame Street*. *Sesame Street* is the most successful television show in history targeted at preschoolers; its audience is in the millions.

But *Sesame Street* is not all that preschoolers are watching or doing, for—as we first noted in Chapter 5—television, and more recently the Internet and computers, play a central role in many U.S. households. Television, in particular, is one of the most potent and widespread stimuli to which children are exposed, with the average preschooler watching more than 21 hours of TV a week. More than a third of households with children 2 to 7 years of age say that the television is on "most of the time" in their homes. In comparison, preschoolers spend three-quarters of an hour reading on the average day (see Figure 7-13; Robinson & Bianchi, 1997; Roberts et al., 1999; Bryant & Bryant, 2001, 2003).

Computers are also becoming influential in the lives of preschoolers. Seventy percent of preschoolers between the ages of 4 and 6 have used a computer, and a quarter of them use one every day. Those who use a computer spend an average of an hour a day in computer activities, and the majority use it by themselves. With help from their parents, almost one-fifth have sent an e-mail (Rideout, Vandewater, & Wartella, 2003).

It's too early to know the effects of computer usage—and other new media such as video games—on preschoolers. However, there is a wealth of research on the consequences of viewing television, as we begin to consider next.

Television: Controlling Exposure.   Despite the introduction of a number of high-quality educational programs over the past decade, many children's programs are not of high quality or are not appropriate for a preschool audience. Accordingly, the American Academy of Pediatrics recommends that exposure to television should be limited. They suggest that until the age of 2, children watch *no* television, and after that age, no more than 1 to 2 hours of quality programming each day (American Academy of Pediatrics, 1999).

What are the limits of preschoolers' "television literacy"? When they do watch television, preschool children often do not fully understand the plots of the stories they are viewing, particularly in longer programs. They are unable to recall significant story details after viewing a program, and the inferences they make about the motivations of characters are limited and often erroneous. Moreover, preschool children may have difficulty separating fantasy from reality in television programming, with some believing, for example, that there is a real Big Bird living on *Sesame Street* (Rule & Ferguson, 1986; Wright et al., 1994).

Preschool-age children exposed to advertising on television are not able to critically understand and evaluate the messages to which they are exposed. Consequently, they are likely to fully accept advertisers' claims about their product. The likelihood of children believing advertising messages is so high that the American Psychological Association has recommended that advertising targeting children under the age of 8 be restricted (Kunkel et al., 2004).

In short, the world to which preschoolers are exposed on TV is imperfectly understood and unrealistic. On the other hand, as they get older and their information processing capabilities improve, preschoolers' understanding of the material they see on television improves. They remember things more accurately, and they become better able to focus on the central message of a show. This improvement suggests that the powers of the medium of television may be harnessed to bring about cognitive gains—exactly what the producers of *Sesame Street* set

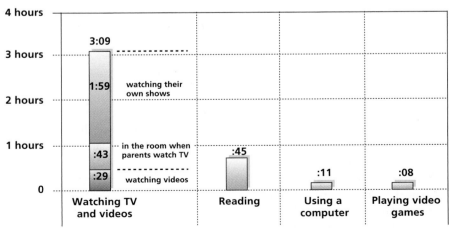

FIGURE 7-13   TELEVISION TIME

Though 2- to 7-year-olds spend more time reading than playing video games or using a computer, they spend considerably more time watching television.

(*Source:* Roberts et al., 1999.)

Times are presented in hours: minutes. Numbers cannot be summed to calculate children's total media use time because they may have used more than one medium at a time. Reading includes amount of time children are read to.

out to do (Singer & Singer, 2000; Crawley, Anderson, & Santomero, 2002; Berry, 2003; Uchikoshi, 2006).

Sesame Street: A Teacher in Every Home? *Sesame Street* is, without a doubt, the most popular educational program for children in the United States. Almost half of all preschoolers in the United States watch the show, and it is broadcast in almost 100 different countries and in 13 foreign languages. Characters like Big Bird and Elmo have become familiar throughout the world to both adults and preschoolers (Bickham, Wright, & Huston, 2000; Cole, Arafat, & Tidhar, 2003).

Sesame Street was devised with the express purpose of providing an educational experience for preschoolers. Its specific goals include teaching letters and numbers, increasing vocabulary, and teaching preliteracy skills. Has *Sesame Street* achieved its goals? Most evidence suggests that it has.

For example, a 2-year longitudinal study compared three groups of 3- and 5-year-olds: those who watched cartoons or other programs, those who watched the same amount of *Sesame Street,* and those who watched little or no TV. Children who watched *Sesame Street* had significantly larger vocabularies than those who watched other programs or those who watched little television. These findings held regardless of the children's gender, family size, and parent education and attitudes. Such findings are consistent with earlier evaluations of the program, which concluded that viewers showed dramatic improvements in skills that were directly taught, such as alphabet recitation, and improvements in other areas that were not directly taught, such as reading words (Bogatz & Ball, 1972; Rice et al., 1990).

Formal evaluations of the show find that preschoolers living in lower-income households who watch the show are better prepared for school, and they perform significantly higher on several measures of verbal and mathematics ability at ages 6 and 7 than those who do not watch it. Furthermore, viewers of *Sesame Street* spend more time reading than nonviewers. And by the time they are 6 and 7, viewers of *Sesame Street* and other educational programs tend to be better readers and are judged more positively by their teachers (Wright et al., 1995; Augustyn, 2003).

On the other hand, *Sesame Street* has not been without its critics. For instance, some educators claim the frenzied pace at which different scenes are shown makes viewers less receptive to the traditional forms of teaching that they will experience when they begin school. However, careful evaluations of the program find no evidence that viewing *Sesame Street* leads to declines in enjoyment of traditional schooling. Indeed, the most recent findings regarding *Sesame Street* and other informative programs like it show quite positive outcomes for viewers (Wright et al., 2001).

Early Childhood Education: Taking the "Pre" Out of the Preschool Period

The term "preschool period" is something of a misnomer: Almost three-quarters of children in the United States are enrolled in some form of care outside the home, much of which is designed either explicitly or implicitly to teach skills that will enhance intellectual as well as social abilities (see Figure 7-14). There are several reasons for this increase, but one major factor—as we considered in Chapter 6 when we discussed infant care centers—is the rise in the number of families in which both parents work outside the home. For instance, a high proportion of fathers work outside the home, and close to 60% of women with children under 6 are employed, most of them full-time (Gilbert, 1994; Borden, 1998; Tamis-LeMonda & Cabrera, 2002).

However, there is another reason, one less tied to the practical considerations of child care: Developmental psychologists have found increasing evidence that children can benefit substantially from involvement in some form of educational activity before they enroll in formal schooling, which typically takes place at age 5 or 6 in the United States. When compared to children who stay at home and have no formal educational involvement, those children enrolled in good preschools experience clear cognitive and social benefits (NICHO, 1999, 2000; Campbell, Ramey, & Pungello, 2002).

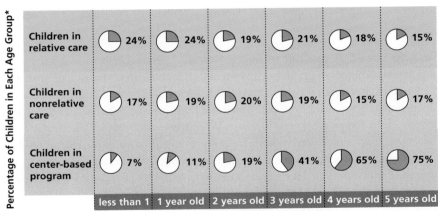

FIGURE 7-14   CARE OUTSIDE THE HOME

Approximately 75% of children in the United States are enrolled in some form of care outside the home—a trend that is the result of more parents employed full time. Evidence suggests that children can benefit from early childhood education.

(*Source:* U.S. Department of Education, National Center for Child Health, 2003)

The Varieties of Early Education.

The variety of early education alternatives is vast. Some outside-the-home care for children is little more than babysitting, while other options are designed to promote intellectual and social advances. Among the major choices of the latter type are the following:

- *Childcare centers* typically provide care for children outside the home, while their parents are at work. (Childcare centers were previously referred to as daycare centers. However, because a significant number of parents work nonstandard schedules and therefore require care for their children at times other than the day, the preferred label has changed to childcare centers.)

  Although many childcare centers were first established as safe, warm environments where children could be cared for and could interact with other children, today their purpose tends to be broader, aimed at providing some form of intellectual stimulation. Still, their primary purpose tends to be more social and emotional than cognitive.

- Some child care is provided in *family childcare centers*, small operations run in private homes. Because centers in some areas are unlicensed, the quality of care can be uneven, and parents should consider whether a family childcare center is licensed before enrolling their children. In contrast, providers of center-based care, which is offered in institutions such as school classrooms, community centers, and churches and synagogues, are typically licensed and regulated by governmental authorities. Because teachers in such programs are more often trained professionals than those who provide family child care, the quality of care is often higher.

- *Preschools* are explicitly designed to provide intellectual and social experiences for children. They tend to be more limited in their schedules than family care centers, typically providing care for only 3 to 5 hours per day. Because of this limitation, preschools mainly serve children from middle and higher socioeconomic levels, in cases where parents don't need to work full time.

  Like childcare centers, preschools vary enormously in the activities they provide. Some emphasize social skills, while others focus on intellectual development. Some do both. For instance, Montessori preschools, which use a method developed by Italian educator Maria Montessori, employ a carefully designed set of materials to create an environment that fosters sensory, motor, and language development. Children are provided with a variety of activities to choose from, with the option of moving from one to another (Gutek, 2003).

  Similarly, in the Reggio Emilia preschool approach—another Italian import—children participate in what is called a "negotiated curriculum" that emphasizes the joint participation of children and teachers. The curriculum builds on the interests of children, promoting their cognitive development through the integration of the arts and participation in week-long projects (Hong & Trepanier-Street, 2004; Rankin, 2004).

- *School child care* is provided by some local school systems in the United States. Almost half the states in the United States fund prekindergarten programs for 4-year-olds, often aimed at disadvantaged children. Because they typically are staffed by better-trained teachers than less-regulated childcare centers, school childcare programs are often of higher quality than other early education alternatives.

The Effectiveness of Child Care.   How effective are such programs? Most research suggests that preschoolers enrolled in childcare centers show intellectual development that at least matches that of children at home, and often is better. For instance, some studies find that preschoolers in child care are more verbally fluent, show memory and comprehension advantages, and even achieve higher IQ scores than at-home children. Other studies find that early and long-term participation in child care is particularly helpful for children from impoverished home environments or who are otherwise at risk (Campbell et al., 2002; Clarke-Stewart & Allhusen, 2002; Vandell, 2004).

Similar advantages are found for social development. Children in high-quality programs tend to be more self-confident, independent, and knowledgeable about the social world in which they live than those who do not participate. On the other hand, not all the outcomes of outside-the-home care are positive: Children in child care have been found to be less polite, less compliant, less respectful of adults, and sometimes more competitive and aggressive than their peers. Furthermore, as we discussed in Chapter 6, children who spend more than 10 hours a week in preschools have a slightly higher likelihood of being disruptive in class extending through the sixth grade (Clarke-Stewart & Allhusen, 2002; NICHD Early Child Care Research Network, 2003; Belsky et al., 2007).

It is important to keep in mind that not all early childhood care programs are equally effective. As we observed of infant child care in Chapter 6, one key factor is program *quality:* High-quality care provides intellectual and social benefits, while low-quality care not only is unlikely to furnish benefits, but actually may harm children (Maccoby & Lewis, 2003; Votruba-Drzal, Coley, & Chase-Lansdale, 2004; NICHD Early Child Care Research Network, 2006).

The Quality of Child Care.   How can we define "high quality"? Several characteristics are important; they are analogous to those that pertain to infant child care (see Chapter 6). The major characteristics of high-quality care include the following (Love et al., 2003; Vandell, Shumow, & Posner, 2005; Lavzer & Goodson, 2006; Maxwell, 2007):

- The care providers are well trained.

- The childcare center has an appropriate overall size and ratio of care providers to children. Single groups should not have many more than 14 to 20 children, and there should be no more than 5 to 10 3-year-olds per caregiver, or 7 to 10 4- or 5-year-olds per caregiver.

- The curriculum of a childcare facility is not left to chance, but is carefully planned out and coordinated among the teachers.

- The language environment is rich, with a great deal of conversation.

- The caregivers are sensitive to children's emotional and social needs, and they know when and when not to intervene.

- Materials and activities are age appropriate.

- Basic health and safety standards are followed.

No one knows how many programs in the United States can be considered "high quality," but there are many fewer than desirable. In fact, the United States lags behind almost every other industrialized country in the quality of its child care as well as in its quantity and affordability (Zigler & Finn-Stevenson, 1995; Scarr, 1998).

Developmental Diversity

Preschools Around the World: Why Does the United States Lag Behind?

In France and Belgium, access to preschool is a legal right. Sweden and Finland provide child care for preschoolers whose parents want it. Russia has an extensive system of state-run *yasli-sads*, nursery schools and kindergartens, attended by 75% of children age 3 to 7 in urban areas.

In contrast, the United States has no coordinated national policy on preschool education—or on the care of children in general. There are several reasons for this. For one, decisions about education have traditionally been left to the states and local school districts. For another, the United States has no tradition of teaching preschoolers, unlike other countries in which preschool-age children have been enrolled in formal programs for decades. Finally, the status of preschools in the United States has been traditionally low. Consider, for instance, that preschool and nursery school teachers are the lowest paid of all teachers. (Teacher salaries increase as the age of students rises. Thus, college and high school teachers are paid the highest salaries, while preschool and elementary school teachers are paid the lowest salaries.)

Preschools also differ significantly from one country to another according to differing societal views of the purpose of early childhood education (Lamb et al., 1992). For instance, in a cross-country comparison of preschools in China, Japan, and the United States, researchers found that parents in the three countries view the purpose of preschools very differently. Whereas parents in China tend to see preschools primarily as a way of giving children a good start academically, Japanese parents view them primarily as a way of giving children the opportunity to be members of a group. In the United States, in comparison, parents regard the primary purpose of preschools as making children more independent and self-reliant, although obtaining a good academic start and having group experience are also important (see Figure 7-15; Tobin, Wu, & Davidson, 1989; Huntsinger et al., 1997; Johnson et al., 2003).

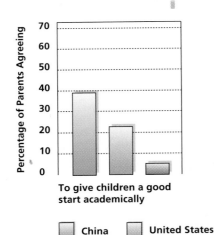
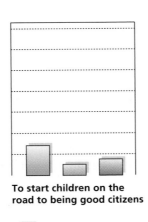
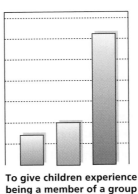
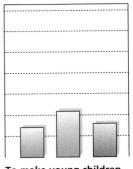

Percentage of Parents Agreeing

To give children a good start academically

To start children on the road to being good citizens

To give children experience being a member of a group

To make young children more independent and self-reliant

☐ China   ☐ United States   ☐ Japan

FIGURE 7-15   THE PURPOSE OF PRESCHOOL

To parents in China, Japan, and the United States, the main purpose of preschools is very different. Whereas parents in China see preschools mainly as a way of giving children a good start academically, parents in Japan see them primarily as a means of giving children the experience of being a member of a group. In contrast, parents in the United States view preschools as a way of making children more independent, although obtaining a good academic start and group experience are also important. How do you interpret these findings?

(*Source:* Based on Tobin, Wu, & Davidson, 1989.)

Preparing Preschoolers for Academic Pursuits: Does Head Start Truly Provide a Head Start? Although many programs designed for preschoolers focus primarily on social and emotional factors, some are geared primarily toward promoting cognitive gains and preparing preschoolers for the more formal instruction they will experience when they start kindergarten. In the United States, the best-known program designed to promote future academic success is Head Start. Born in the 1960s when the United States declared a War on Poverty, the program has served over 13 million children and their families. The program, which stresses parental involvement, was designed to serve the "whole child," including children's physical health, self-confidence, social responsibility, and social and emotional development (Ripple et al., 1999; Zigler & Styfco, 2004; Vinovakis, 2005).

Whether Head Start is seen as successful or not depends on the lens through which one is looking. If, for instance, the program is expected to provide long-term increases in IQ scores, it is a disappointment. Although graduates of Head Start programs tend to show immediate IQ gains, these increases do not last. On the other hand, it is clear that Head Start is meeting its goal of getting preschoolers ready for school. Preschoolers who participate in Head Start are better prepared for future schooling than those who do not. Furthermore, graduates of Head Start programs have better future school adjustment than their peers, and they are less likely to be in special education classes or to be retained in their grade. Finally, some research suggests that Head Start graduates even show higher academic performance at the end of high school, although the gains are modest (Schnur & Belanger, 2000; Brooks-Gunn, 2003; Kronholz, 2003).

In addition to Head Start programs, other types of preschool readiness programs also provide advantages throughout the school years. Studies show that those who participate and graduate from such preschool programs are less likely to repeat grades, and they complete school more frequently than those who are not in the programs. Preschool readiness programs also appear to be cost-effective. According to a cost-benefit analysis of one readiness program, for every dollar spent on the program, taxpayers saved seven dollars by the time the graduates reached the age of 27 (Schweinhart, Barnes, & Weikart, 1993; Friedman, 2004; Gormley et al., 2005).

The most recent comprehensive evaluation of early intervention programs, suggests that, taken as a group, they can provide significant benefits, and that government funds invested early in life may ultimately lead to a reduction in future costs. For instance, compared with children who did not participate in early intervention programs, participants in various programs showed gains in emotional or cognitive development, better educational outcomes, increased economic self-sufficiency, reduced levels of criminal activity, and improved health-related behaviors. Although not every program produced all these benefits, and not every child benefited to the same extent, the results of the evaluation suggested that the potential benefits of early intervention can be substantial (Wigfield, & Galper, 1999; Schnur & Belanger, 2000; Campbell et al., 2001; NICHD Early Child Care Research Network & Duncan, 2003).

Of course, traditional programs such as Head Start, which emphasize academic success brought about by traditional instruction, are not the only approach to early intervention that has proven effective. As we consider in the *From Research to Practice* box, Montessori schools, which have their own unique philosophy and approach, have also proven valuable.

Are We Pushing Children Too Hard and Too Fast? Not everyone agrees that programs that seek to enhance academic skills during the preschool years are a good thing. In fact, according to developmental psychologist David Elkind, U.S. society tends to push children so rapidly that they begin to feel stress and pressure at a young age (Elkind, 1994).

Elkind argues that academic success is largely dependent upon factors out of parents' control, such as inherited abilities and a child's rate of maturation. Consequently, children of a particular age cannot be expected to master educational material without taking into account their current level of cognitive development. In short, children require **developmentally appropriate educational practice,** which is education that is based on both typical development and the unique characteristics of a given child (Copple & Bredekamp, 1997; Robinson & Stark, 2005).

developmentally appropriate educational practice education that is based on both typical development and the unique characteristics of a given child.

From Research to Practice

The Montessori Approach: Is It Effective?

In immaculately ordered and naturally lit classrooms, materials play a prominent role. Children ages 3 to 6 pick their tools—a wet sponge, a textured globe, a model dinosaur skeleton—and work quietly, either alone or in groups of two or three. Down the hall, their peers do yoga on 10 mats in the library. (MacDonald, 2007, p. 9D)

In the early 1900s, Dr. Maria Montessori developed an alternative to the traditional approach to educating young children in an effort to improve educational access for the poor. Montessori rejected traditional methods such as tests and grades because she felt they fostered competition and discouraged collaborative learning. Instead, she embraced self-directed exploration and discovery through hands-on, active learning. Montessori education emphasizes children's active participation in their own learning. In Montessori classrooms, teachers act more as facilitators within multiage classrooms where pupils engage in individual and small-group activities that help them learn social skills as well as academic lessons (Montessori, 1964).

Montessori argued that the traditional educational approach treated children as adults and that her method was better tailored to the distinctive ways in which children think and learn. Thousands of private schools in the United States employ the Montessori method, and Montessori programs are available at several hundred public schools.

While Montessori education is clearly a different experience from the traditional classroom, does it in fact produce better educational outcomes for children? Recent research provides compelling evidence that it does.

Researchers Angeline Lillard and Nicole Else-Quest compared two groups of 3-to-6-year-old children: one group was completing the primary level of education at a Montessori school while the other group was completing the equivalent level at various non-Montessori schools (mainly urban public schools). These two groups were known to be equivalent before they entered their respective schools, as they had all originally applied for admission to the Montessori school, with admission being determined by a random lottery. Consequently, any differences between the groups on outcome measures could be attributed to the different educational programs (Lillard & Else-Quest, 2006).

The researchers examined a variety of cognitive/academic and social/behavioral skills that are generally important to life success. To examine differences in cognitive/academic skills, the researchers used a test that measures school readiness. The Montessori students performed significantly better that the non-Montessori group on standardized measures of reading and math skills. Moreover, the Montessori students performed better on a test of executive function that involved applying different decision rules in a card-sorting task.

The benefits weren't just academic, either. The children were asked their solutions to several social problems (such as a child not sharing a playground swing). The children from the Montessori school were significantly more likely than those from the comparison school group to make appeals to justice or fairness in trying to persuade the problem child to do the right thing. On the playground, Montessori children were more likely to engage in positive shared play and less likely to engage in ambiguous rough play, such as wrestling. Finally, Montessori children were more likely to show an understanding of false beliefs, a milestone in development that we will discuss in Chapter 8.

Further research is needed to determine what specific components of a Montessori education are responsible for producing these beneficial outcomes. Still, taking the Montessori approach as a whole, the advantages it produces over traditional educational programs are compelling evidence of its effectiveness.

- *Can you think of any potential drawbacks to Montessori education? Would it be appropriate for every pupil? Keep in mind that in this comparison, all of the parents originally wanted their children to attend a Montessori school. What about children whose parents aren't as supportive of the Montessori method?*

- *In what ways does the Montessori method relate to Vygotsky's view of cognitive development?*

Rather than arbitrarily expecting children to master material at a particular age, Elkind suggests that a better strategy is to provide an environment in which learning is encouraged, but not pushed. By creating an atmosphere in which learning is facilitated—for instance, by reading to preschoolers—parents will allow children to proceed at their own pace rather than at one that pushes them beyond their limits (Reese & Cox, 1999; van Kleeck & Stahl, 2003).

Although Elkind's suggestions are appealing—it is certainly hard to disagree that increases in children's anxiety levels and stress should be avoided—they are not without their detractors. For instance, some educators have argued that pushing children is largely a phenomenon of the middle and higher socioeconomic levels, possible only if parents are relatively affluent. For poorer children, whose parents may not have substantial resources available to push their children nor the easy ability to create an environment that promotes learning, the benefits of formal programs that promote learning are likely to outweigh their drawbacks.

Review and Apply

Review

- In the preschool years, children rapidly increase in linguistic ability, developing an improved sense of grammar and shifting gradually from private to social speech.

- Poverty can affect children's language development by limiting the opportunities for parents and other caregivers to interact linguistically with children.

- Preschoolers watch television at high levels. The effects of television on preschoolers are mixed, with benefits from some programs and clear disadvantages due to other aspects of viewing.

- Preschool educational programs are beneficial if they are of high quality, with trained staff, good curriculum, proper group sizes, and small staff-to-student ratios.

- Preschool children are likely to benefit from a developmentally appropriate, individualized, and supportive environment for learning.

Applying Lifespan Development

- Is private speech egocentric or useful? Do adults ever use private speech? What functions does it serve?

- *From an educator's perspective:* Do you accept the view that children in U.S. society are "pushed" academically to the extent that they feel too much stress and pressure at a young age? Why?

Epilogue

In this chapter, we looked at children in the preschool years, focusing on their physical development, growth, nutritional needs, overall health, brain growth, and advances in gross and fine motor skills. We discussed cognitive development from the Piagetian perspective, with its description of the characteristics of thought in the preoperational stage, and from the perspective of information processing theorists and Lev Vygotsky, who emphasized the social and cultural influences on cognitive development. We then discussed the burst in linguistic ability that occurs during the preschool years and the influence of television on preschoolers' development. We concluded with a discussion of preschool education and its effects.

Before moving on to a discussion of children's social and personality development in the next chapter, turn back for a moment to this chapter's prologue, which describes Aaron's excursion across the kitchen counter and into the sink (with a stop along the way at the cookie jar). Consider these questions:

1. Why, specifically, do you think Aaron climbed up on the counter? Was it merely to get a cookie?

2. What gross and fine motor skills were involved in Aaron's journey across the counter and into the sink?

3. What dangers did Aaron face in this incident?

4. What could Aaron's father, who had left the room for only a moment, have done to prevent Aaron from climbing into the sink?

Looking
Back

- **What is the state of children's bodies and overall health during the preschool years?**

  - In addition to gaining height and weight, the bodies of preschool children undergo changes in shape and structure. Children grow more slender, and their bones and muscles strengthen.

  - Children in the preschool years are generally quite healthy. Obesity in these years is caused by genetic and environmental factors. The greatest health threats are accidents and environmental factors.

- **How do preschool children's brains and physical skills develop?**

  - Brain growth is particularly rapid during the preschool years, with the number of interconnections among cells and the amount of myelin around neurons increasing greatly. The halves of the brain begin to specialize in somewhat different tasks—a process called lateralization.

  - Both gross and fine motor skills advance rapidly during the preschool years. Gender differences begin to emerge, fine motor skills are honed, and handedness begins to assert itself.

- **How does Piaget interpret cognitive development during the preschool years?**

  - During the stage that Piaget has described as *preoperational,* children are not yet able to engage in organized, formal, logical thinking. However, their development of symbolic function permits quicker and more effective thinking as they are freed from the limitations of sensorimotor learning.

  - According to Piaget, children in the preoperational stage engage in intuitive thought for the first time, actively applying rudimentary reasoning skills to the acquisition of world knowledge.

- **How do other views of cognitive development differ from Piaget's?**

  - A different approach to cognitive development is taken by proponents of information processing theories, who focus on preschoolers' storage and recall of information and on quantitative changes in information processing abilities (such as attention).

  - Lev Vygotsky proposed that the nature and progress of children's cognitive development are dependent on the children's social and cultural context.

■ **How does children's language develop in the preschool years?**

- Children rapidly progress from two-word utterances to longer, more sophisticated expressions that reflect their growing vocabularies and emerging grasp of grammar.

- The development of linguistic abilities is affected by socioeconomic status. The result can be lowered linguistic—and, ultimately, academic—performance by poorer children.

■ **What effects does television have on preschoolers?**

- The effects of television are mixed. Preschoolers' sustained exposure to emotions and situations that are not representative of the real world have raised concerns. On the other hand, preschoolers can derive meaning from such targeted programs as *Sesame Street,* which are designed to bring about cognitive gains.

■ **What kinds of preschool educational programs are available?**

- Early childhood educational programs, offered as center-based or school-based child care or as preschool, can lead to cognitive and social advances.

- The United States lacks a coordinated national policy on preschool education. The major federal initiative in U.S. preschool education has been the Head Start program, which has yielded mixed results.

Key Terms and Concepts

obesity (p. 214)
lateralization (p. 216)
myelin (p. 218)
handedness (p. 221)
preoperational stage
  (p. 223)
operations (p. 223)
centration (p. 224)
conservation (p. 225)

transformation (p. 225)
egocentric thought (p. 226)
intuitive thought (p. 227)
autobiographical memory
  (p. 229)
scripts (p. 230)
zone of proximal
  development (ZPD)
  (p. 233)

scaffolding (p. 233)
syntax (p. 236)
fast mapping (p. 236)
grammar (p. 237)
private speech (p. 237)
pragmatics (p. 238)
social speech (p. 238)
developmentally appropriate
  educational practice (p. 245)

8 Social and Personality Development in the Preschool Years

Chapter Overview

FORMING A SENSE OF SELF

Psychosocial Development: Resolving the Conflicts

Self-Concept in the Preschool Years: Thinking About the Self

Gender Identity: Developing Femaleness and Maleness

FRIENDS AND FAMILY: PRESCHOOLERS' SOCIAL LIVES

The Development of Friendships

Playing by the Rules: The Work of Play

Preschoolers' Theory of Mind: Understanding What Others Are Thinking

Preschoolers' Family Lives

Effective Parenting: Teaching Desired Behavior

Child Abuse and Psychological Maltreatment: The Grim Side of Family Life

Resilience: Overcoming the Odds

MORAL DEVELOPMENT AND AGGRESSION

Developing Morality: Following Society's Rights and Wrongs

Aggression and Violence in Preschoolers: Sources and Consequences

Prologue: Feeling His Mother's Pain

When Alison Gopnik got home from the lab one day, she was overcome with the feeling that she was a lousy teacher, an incompetent scientist and a bad mother. A student had argued with a grade, a grant proposal had been rejected and the chicken legs she'd planned for dinner were still in the freezer. So the University of California, Berkeley, developmental psychologist collapsed on the couch and started to cry. Her son, almost 2, sized up the situation like a little pro. He dashed to the bathroom, fumbled around for what he needed and returned with Band-Aids—which he proceeded to stick all over his sobbing (and now startled) mother, figuring that eventually he would find the place that needed patching. (Begley, 2000, p. 25)

During the preschool years, a child's ability to understand others' emotions begins to grow.

Like most 2-year-olds, Gopnik's son could not only share his mother's pain but was able to find a way to try to soothe it. During the preschool years, children's ability to understand others' emotions begins to grow, and it colors their relationships with others.

In this chapter, we address social and personality development during the preschool period, a time of enormous growth and change. We begin by examining how preschool-age children continue to form a sense of self, focusing on how they develop their self-concepts. We especially examine issues of self relating to gender, a central aspect of children's views of themselves and others.

Preschoolers' social lives are the focus of the next part of the chapter. We look at how children play with one another, examining the various types of play. We consider how parents and other authority figures use discipline to shape children's behavior.

Finally, we examine two key aspects of preschool-age children's social behavior: moral development and aggression. We consider how children develop a notion of right and wrong and how that development can lead them to be helpful to others. We also look at the other side of the coin—aggression—and examine the factors that lead preschool-age children to behave in a way that hurts others. We end on an optimistic note: considering how we may help preschool-age children to be more moral and less aggressive individuals.

After reading this chapter, you will be able to answer these questions:

■ **How do preschool-age children develop a concept of themselves?**

■ **How do children develop their sense of racial identity and gender?**

■ **In what sorts of social relationships and play do preschool-age children engage?**

■ **What sorts of disciplinary styles do parents employ, and what effects do they have?**

■ **What factors contribute to child abuse and neglect?**

■ **How do children develop a moral sense?**

■ **How does aggression develop in preschool-age children?**

Forming a Sense of Self

Although the question "Who am I?" is not explicitly posed by most preschool-age children, it underlies a considerable amount of development during the preschool years. During this period, children wonder about the nature of the self, and the way they answer the "Who am I?" question may affect them for the rest of their lives.

Psychosocial Development: Resolving the Conflicts

The view of the self that preschoolers develop depends in part on the culture in which they grow up.

Mary-Alice's preschool teacher raised her eyebrows slightly when the 4-year-old took off her coat. Mary-Alice, usually dressed in well-matched play suits, was a medley of prints. She had on a pair of flowered pants, along with a completely clashing plaid top. The outfit was accessorized with a striped headband, socks in an animal print, and Mary-Alice's polka-dotted rain boots. Mary-Alice's mom gave a slightly embarrassed shrug. "Mary-Alice got dressed all by herself this morning," she explained as she handed over a bag containing spare shoes, just in case the rain boots became uncomfortable during the day.

Psychoanalyst Erik Erikson may well have praised Mary-Alice's mother for helping Mary-Alice develop a sense of initiative (if not of fashion). The reason: Erikson (1963) suggested that, during the preschool years, children face a key conflict relating to psychosocial development that involves the development of initiative.

As we discussed in Chapter 6, **psychosocial development** encompasses changes both in individuals' understanding of themselves and their understanding of others' behavior. According to Erikson, society and culture present the developing person with particular challenges, which shift as people age. Erikson believed that people pass through eight distinct stages, each characterized by a crisis or conflict that the person must resolve. Our experiences as we try to resolve these conflicts lead us to develop ideas about ourselves that can last for the rest of our lives.

In the early part of the preschool period, children are ending the autonomy-versus-shame-and-doubt stage, which lasts from around 18 months to 3 years. In this period, children either become more independent and autonomous if their parents encourage exploration and freedom or they experience shame and self-doubt if they are restricted and overprotected.

The preschool years largely encompass what Erikson called the **initiative-versus-guilt stage,** which lasts from around age 3 to age 6. During this period, children's views of themselves change as preschool-age children face conflicts between, on the one hand, the desire to act independently of their parents and do things on their own, and, on the other hand, the guilt that comes from failure when they don't succeed. They are eager to do things on their own ("Let *me* do it" is a popular refrain among preschoolers), but they feel guilt if their efforts fail. They come to see themselves as persons in their own right, and they begin to make decisions on their own.

Parents, such as Mary-Alice's mother, who react positively to this transformation toward independence can help their children resolve the opposing feelings that are characteristic of this period. By providing their children with opportunities to act self-reliantly, while still giving them direction and guidance, parents can support and encourage their children's initiative. On the other hand, parents who discourage their children's efforts to seek independence may contribute to a sense of guilt that persists throughout their lives as well as affects their self-concept, which begins to develop during this period.

Self-Concept in the Preschool Years: Thinking About the Self

If you ask preschool-age children to specify what makes them different from other kids, they readily respond with answers like, "I'm a good runner" or "I like to color" or "I'm a big girl." Such answers relate to **self-concept**—their identity, or their set of beliefs about what they are like as individuals (Brown, 1998; Tessor, Felson, & Suls, 2000; Marsh, Ellis, & Craven, 2002).

The statements that describe children's self-concepts are not necessarily accurate. In fact, preschool children typically overestimate their skills and knowledge across all domains of expertise. Consequently, their view of the future is quite rosy: They expect to win the next game they play, to beat all opponents in an upcoming race, to write great stories when they grow up. Even when they have just experienced failure at a task, they are likely to expect to do well in the future. This optimistic view is held, in part, because they have not yet started to compare themselves and their performance against others. Their inaccuracy is also helpful, freeing them to take chances and try new activities (Dweck, 2002; Wang, 2004).

Preschool-age children's view of themselves also reflects the way their particular culture considers the self. For example, many Asian societies tend to have a **collectivistic orientation,** promoting the notion of interdependence. People in such cultures tend to regard themselves as parts of a larger social network in which they are interconnected with and responsible to others. In contrast, children in Western cultures are more likely to develop a view of the self reflecting an **individualistic orientation** that emphasizes personal identity and the uniqueness of the individual. They are more apt to see themselves as self-contained and autonomous, in competition with others for scarce resources. Consequently, children in Western cultures are more likely to focus on what sets them apart from others—what makes them special.

Such views pervade a culture, sometimes in subtle ways. For instance, one well-known saying in Western cultures states that "the squeaky wheel gets the grease." Preschoolers who are

psychosocial development according to Erikson, development that encompasses changes both in the understandings individuals have of themselves as members of society and in their comprehension of the meaning of others' behavior.

initiative-versus-guilt stage according to Erikson, the period during which children aged 3 to 6 years experience conflict between independence of action and the sometimes negative results of that action.

self-concept a person's identity, or set of beliefs about what one is like as an individual.

collectivistic orientation a philosophy that promotes the notion of interdependence.

individualistic orientation a philosophy that emphasizes personal identity and the uniqueness of the individual.

race dissonance   the phenomenon in which minority children indicate preferences for majority values or people.

exposed to this perspective are encouraged to gain the attention of others by standing out and making their needs known. On the other hand, children in Asian cultures are exposed to a different perspective; they are told that "the nail that stands out gets pounded down." This perspective suggests to preschoolers that they should attempt to blend in and refrain from making themselves distinctive (Markus & Kitayama, 1991; Dennis et al., 2002; Lehman, Chiu, & Schaller, 2004; Wang, 2004, 2006).

Preschoolers' developing self-concepts can also be affected by their culture's attitudes toward various racial and ethnic groups. As we'll see in the *Developmental Diversity* feature, preschoolers' awareness of their ethnic or racial identity develops slowly, and is subtly influenced by the attitudes of the people, schools, and other cultural institutions with which they come into contact in their community.

Developmental Diversity

Developing Racial and Ethnic Awareness

The preschool years mark an important turning point for children. Their answer to the question of who they are begins to take into account their racial and ethnic identity.

For most preschool-age children, racial awareness comes relatively early. Certainly, even infants are able to distinguish different skin colors; their perceptual abilities allow for such color distinctions quite early in life. However, it is only later that children begin to attribute meaning to different racial characteristics.

By the time they are 3 or 4 years of age, preschool-age children notice differences among people based on skin color, and they begin to identify themselves as a member of a particular group such as "Hispanic" or "black." Although early in the preschool years they do not realize that ethnicity and race are enduring features of who they are, later they begin to develop an understanding of the significance that society places on ethnic and racial membership (Bernal & Knight, 1993; Sheets & Hollins, 1999; Hall & Rowan, 2003).

Some preschoolers have mixed feelings about their racial and ethnic identity. Some experience **race dissonance,** the phenomenon in which minority children indicate preferences for majority values or people. For instance, some studies find that as many as 90% of African American children, when asked about their reactions to drawings of black and white children, react more negatively to the drawings of black children than to those of white children. However, these negative reactions did not translate into lower self-esteem for the African American subjects. Instead, their preferences appear to be a result of the powerful influence of the dominant white culture, rather than a disparagement of their own racial characteristics (Holland, 1994).

Ethnic identity emerges somewhat later than racial identity, because it is usually less conspicuous than race. For instance, in one study of Mexican American ethnic awareness, preschoolers displayed only a limited knowledge of their ethnic identity. However, as they became older, they grew more aware of the significance of their ethnicity. Preschoolers who were bilingual, speaking both Spanish and English, were most apt to be aware of their ethnic identity (Bernal, 1994).

Gender Identity: Developing Femaleness and Maleness

Boys' awards: Very Best Thinker, Most Eager Learner, Most Imaginative, Most Enthusiastic, Most Scientific, Best Friend, Mr. Personality, Hardest Worker, Best Sense of Humor.

Girls' awards: All-Around Sweetheart, Sweetest Personality, Cutest Personality, Best Sharer, Best Artist, Biggest Heart, Best Manners, Best Helper, Most Creative.

What's wrong with this picture? To one parent, whose daughter received one of the girls' awards during a kindergarten graduation ceremony, quite a bit. While the girls were getting pats on the back for their pleasing personalities, the boys were receiving awards for their intellectual and analytic skills (Deveny, 1994).

Such a situation is not rare: Girls and boys often live in very different worlds. Differences in the ways males and females are treated begin at birth, continue during the preschool years, and—as we'll see later—extend into adolescence and beyond (Coltrane & Adams, 1997; Maccoby, 1999; Martin & Ruble, 2004).

Gender, the sense of being male or female, is well established by the time children reach the preschool years. (As we first noted in Chapter 6, "gender" and "sex" do not mean the same thing. *Sex* typically refers to sexual anatomy and sexual behavior, while *gender* refers to the perception of maleness or femaleness related to membership in a given society). By the age of 2, children consistently label themselves and those around them as male or female (Poulin-Dubois et al., 1994; Raag, 2003; Campbell, Shirley, & Candy, 2004).

One way gender shows up is in play. Preschool boys spend more time than girls in rough-and-tumble play, while preschool girls spend more time than boys in organized games and role-playing. During this time boys begin to play more with boys, and girls play more with girls, a trend that increases during middle childhood. Girls begin to prefer same-sex play-mates a little earlier than boys. They first have a clear preference for interacting with other girls at age 2, while boys don't show much preference for same-sex playmates until age 3 (Boyatzis, Mallis, & Leon, 1999; Martin & Fabes, 2001; Raag, 2003).

During the preschool period, differences in play according to gender become more pronounced. In addition, boys tend to play with boys, and girls with girls.

Such same-sex preferences appear in many cultures. For instance, studies of kindergartners in mainland China show no examples of mixed-gender play. Similarly, gender "outweighs" ethnic variables when it comes to play: A Hispanic boy would rather play with a white boy than with a Hispanic girl (Whiting & Edwards, 1988; Martin, 1993; Aydt & Corsaro, 2003).

Preschool-age children often have very strict ideas about how boys and girls are supposed to act. In fact, their expectations about gender-appropriate behavior are even more gender-stereotyped than those of adults and may be less flexible during the preschool years than at any other point in the life span. Beliefs in gender stereotypes become increasingly pronounced up to age 5, and although they become somewhat less rigid by age 7, they do not disappear. In fact, the gender stereotypes held by preschoolers resemble those held by traditional adults in society (Eichstedt, Serbin, & Poulin-Dubois, 2002; Serbin, Poulin-Dubois, & Eichstedt, 2002; Lam & Leman, 2003).

And what is the nature of preschoolers' gender expectations? Like adults, preschoolers expect that males are more apt to have traits involving competence, independence, forceful-ness, and competitiveness. In contrast, females are viewed as more likely to have traits such as warmth, expressiveness, nurturance, and submissiveness. Although these are *expectations*, and say nothing about the way that men and women actually behave, such expectations provide the lens through which preschool-age children view the world and thus affect their behavior as well as the way they interact with peers and adults (Durkin & Nugent, 1998; Blakemore, 2003; Gelman, Taylor, & Nguyen, 2004).

The prevalence and strength of preschoolers' gender expectations, and differences in behavior between boys and girls, have proven puzzling. Why should gender play such a powerful role during the preschool years (as well as during the rest of the life span)? Developmentalists have proposed several explanations.

Biological Perspectives on Gender. Since gender relates to the sense of being male or female, and sex refers to the physical characteristics that differentiate males and females, it would hardly be surprising to find that the biological characteristics associated with sex might them-selves lead to gender differences. This has been shown to be true.

According to social learning approaches, children learn gender-related behavior and expectations from their observations of others.

Hormones are one sex-related biological characteristic that have been found to affect gender-based behaviors. Girls exposed to unusually high levels of *androgens* (male hormones) prenatally are more likely to display behaviors associated with male stereotypes than are their sisters who were not exposed to androgens (Money & Ehrhardt, 1972; Hines, Golombok, & Rust, 2002; Servin, Nordenstroem, & Larsson, 2003).

Androgen-exposed girls preferred boys as playmates and spent more time than other girls playing with toys associated with the male role, such as cars and trucks. Similarly, boys exposed prenatally to atypically high levels of female hormones are apt to display more behaviors that are stereotypically female than is usual (Berenbaum & Hines, 1992; Hines & Kaufman, 1994; Servin et al., 2003; Knickmeyer & Baron-Cohen, 2006).

Moreover, as we first noted in Chapter 7, some research suggests that biological differences exist in the structure of female and male brains. For instance, part of the *corpus callosum*, the bundle of nerves that connects the hemispheres of the brain, is proportionally larger in women than in men. To some theoreticians, evidence such as this suggests that gender differences may be produced by biological factors like hormones (Benbow, Lubinski, & Hyde, 1997; Westerhausen et al., 2004).

Before accepting such contentions, however, it is important to note that alternative explanations abound. For example, it may be that the corpus callosum is proportionally larger in women as a result of certain kinds of experiences that influence brain growth in particular ways. We know, as discussed in Chapter 6, that girls are spoken to more than boys as infants, which might produce certain kinds of brain development. If this is true, environmental experience produces biological change—and not the other way around.

Other developmentalists see gender differences as serving the biological goal of survival of the species through reproduction. Basing their work on an evolutionary approach, these theorists suggest that our male ancestors who showed more stereotypically masculine qualities, such as forcefulness and competitiveness, may have been able to attract females who were able to provide them with hardy offspring. Females who excelled at stereotypically feminine tasks, such as nurturing, may have been valuable partners because they could increase the likelihood that children would survive the dangers of childhood (Geary, 1998; Browne, 2006; Ellis, 2006).

As in other domains that involve the interaction of inherited biological characteristics and environmental influences, it is difficult to attribute behavioral characteristics unambiguously to biological factors. Because of this problem, we must consider other explanations for gender differences.

Psychoanalytic Perspectives.   You may recall from Chapter 1 that Freud's psychoanalytic theory suggests that we move through a series of stages related to biological urges. To Freud, the preschool years encompass the *phallic stage*, in which the focus of a child's pleasure relates to genital sexuality.

Freud argued that the end of the phallic stage is marked by an important turning point in development: the Oedipal conflict. According to Freud, the *Oedipal conflict* occurs at around the age of 5, when the anatomical differences between males and females become particularly evident. Boys begin to develop sexual interests in their mothers, viewing their fathers as rivals. As a consequence, boys conceive a desire to kill their fathers—just as Oedipus did in the ancient Greek tragedy. However, because they view their fathers as all-powerful, boys develop a fear of retaliation, which takes the form of *castration anxiety*. In order to overcome this fear, boys repress their desires for their mothers and instead begin to identify with their fathers, attempting to be as similar to them as possible. **Identification** is the process in which children attempt to be similar to their same-sex parent, incorporating the parent's attitudes and values.

Girls, according to Freud, go through a different process. They begin to feel sexual attraction toward their fathers and experience *penis envy*—a view that not unexpectedly has led to

identification   the process in which children attempt to be similar to their same-sex parent, incorporating the parent's attitudes and values.

accusations that Freud viewed women as inferior to men. In order to resolve their penis envy, girls ultimately identify with their mothers, attempting to be as similar to them as possible.

In the cases of both boys and girls, the ultimate result of identifying with the same-sex parent is that the children adopt their parents' gender attitudes and values. In this way, says Freud, society's expectations about the ways females and males "ought" to behave are perpetuated into new generations.

You may find it difficult to accept Freud's elaborate explanation of gender differences. So do most developmentalists, who believe that gender development is best explained by other mechanisms. In part, they base their criticisms of Freud on the lack of scientific support for his theories. For example, children learn gender stereotypes much earlier than the age of 5. Furthermore, this learning occurs even in single-parent households. However, some aspects of psychoanalytic theory have been supported, such as findings indicating that preschool-age children whose same-sex parents support sex-stereotyped behavior tend to demonstrate that behavior also. Still, far simpler processes can account for this phenomenon, and many developmentalists have searched for explanations of gender differences other than Freud's (Martin & Ruble, 2004).

Social Learning Approaches.   As their name implies, social learning approaches see children as learning gender-related behavior and expectations by observing others. Children watch the behavior of their parents, teachers, siblings, and even peers. A little boy sees the glory of a major league baseball player and becomes interested in sports. A little girl watches her high-school neighbor practicing cheerleading moves and begins to try them herself. The observation of the rewards that these others attain for acting in a gender-appropriate manner leads the children to conform to such behavior themselves (Rust et al., 2000).

Books and the media, and in particular television and video games, also play a role in perpetuating traditional views of gender-related behavior from which preschoolers may learn. Analyses of the most popular television shows, for example, find that male characters outnumber female characters by two to one. Furthermore, females are more apt to appear with males, whereas female–female relationships are relatively uncommon (Calvert et al., 2003).

Television also presents men and women in traditional gender roles. Television shows typically define female characters in terms of their relationships with males. Females are more likely to appear as victims than males (Wright et al., 1995; Turner-Bowker, 1996). They are less likely to be presented as productive or as decision-makers, and more likely to be portrayed as characters interested in romance, their homes, and their families. Such models, according to social learning theory, are apt to have a powerful influence on preschoolers' definitions of appropriate behavior (Browne, 1998; Nathanson, Wilson, & McGee, 2002; Scharrer et al., 2006).

In some cases, learning of social roles does not involve models, but occurs more directly. For example, most of us have heard preschool-age children being told by their parents to act like a "little girl" or "little man." What this generally means is that girls should behave politely and courteously, or that boys should be tough and stoic—traits associated with society's traditional stereotypes of men and women. Such direct training sends a clear message about the behavior expected of a preschool-age child (Witt, 1997; Leaper, 2002).

Cognitive Approaches.   In the view of some theorists, one aspect of the desire to form a clear sense of identity is the desire to establish a **gender identity,** a perception of themselves as male or female. To do this, they develop a **gender schema,** a cognitive framework that organizes information relevant to gender (Martin, 2000; Barberá, 2003; Martin & Ruble, 2004).

Gender schemas are developed early in life and serve as a lens through which preschoolers view the world. For instance, preschoolers use their increasing cognitive abilities to develop "rules" about what is right and what is inappropriate for males and females. Thus, some girls decide that wearing pants is inappropriate for a female and apply the rule so rigidly that they refuse to wear anything but dresses. Or a preschool boy may reason that since makeup is

gender identity   the perception of oneself as male or female.

gender schema   a cognitive framework that organizes information relevant to gender.

gender constancy   the belief that people are permanently males or females, depending on fixed, unchangeable biological factors.

androgynous   a state in which gender roles encompass characteristics thought typical of both sexes.

mydevelopmentlab

VIDEO CLIP

GENDER CONSISTENCY

typically worn by females, it is inappropriate for him to wear makeup even when he is in a preschool play and all the other boys and girls are wearing it.

According to *cognitive-developmental theory*, proposed by Lawrence Kohlberg, this rigidity is in part a reflection of preschoolers' understanding of gender (Kohlberg, 1966). Rigid gender schemas are influenced by the preschooler's erroneous beliefs about sex differences. Specifically, young preschoolers believe that sex differences are based not on biological factors but on differences in appearance or behavior. Employing this view of the world, a girl may reason that she can be a father when she grows up, or a boy may think he could turn into a girl if he put on a dress and tied his hair in a ponytail. However, by the time they reach the age of 4 or 5, children develop an understanding of **gender constancy,** the awareness that people are permanently males or females, depending on fixed, unchangeable biological factors.

Interestingly, research on children's growing understanding of gender constancy during the preschool period indicates that it has no particular effect on gender-related behavior. In fact, the appearance of gender schemas occurs well before children understand gender constancy. Even young preschool-age children assume that certain behaviors are appropriate—and others are not—on the basis of stereotypic views of gender (Warin, 2000; Martin, Ruble, & Szkrybalo, 2002; Martin & Ruble, 2004).

Is it possible to avoid viewing the world in terms of gender schemas? According to Sandra Bem (1987), one way is to encourage children to be **androgynous,** a state in which gender roles encompass characteristics thought typical of both sexes. For instance, parents and caregivers can encourage preschool children to see males as assertive (typically viewed as a male-appropriate trait) but at the same time warm and tender (usually viewed as female-appropriate traits). Similarly, girls might be encouraged to see the female role as both empathetic and tender (typically seen as female-appropriate traits) and competitive, assertive, and independent (typical male-appropriate traits).

Like the other approaches to gender development (summarized in Table 8-1), the cognitive perspective does not imply that differences between the two sexes are in any way improper or inappropriate. Instead, it suggests that preschoolers should be taught to treat others as individuals. Furthermore, preschoolers need to learn the importance of fulfilling their own talents, acting as individuals and not as representatives of a particular gender.

Table 8-1	Four Approaches to Gender Development	
Perspective	**Key Concepts**	**Applying the Concepts to Preschool Children**
Biological	Our ancestors who behaved in ways that are now stereotypically feminine or masculine may have been more successful in reproducing. Brain differences may lead to gender differences.	Girls may be genetically "programmed" by evolution to be more expressive and nurturing, while boys are "programmed" to be more competitive and forceful. Abnormal hormone exposure before birth has been linked to both boys and girls behaving in ways typically expected of the other gender.
Psychoanalytic	Gender development is the result of identification with the same-sex parent, achieved by moving through a series of stages related to biological urges.	Girls and boys whose parents of the same sex behave in stereotypically masculine or feminine ways are likely to do so, too, perhaps because they identify with those parents.
Social Learning	Children learn gender-related behavior and expectations from their observation of others' behavior.	Children notice that other children and adults are rewarded for behaving in ways that conform to standard gender stereotypes— and sometimes punished for violating those stereotypes.
Cognitive	Through the use of gender schemas, developed early in life, preschoolers form a lens through which they view the world. They use their increasing cognitive abilities to develop "rules" about what is appropriate for males and females.	Preschoolers are more rigid in their rules about proper gender behavior than people at other ages, perhaps because they have just developed gender schemas that don't yet permit much variation from stereotypical expectations.

Review and Apply

Review

- According to Erikson's psychosocial development theory, preschool-age children move from the autonomy-versus-shame-and-doubt stage to the initiative-versus-guilt stage.

- During the preschool years, children develop their self-concepts, beliefs about themselves that they derive from their own perceptions, their parents' behaviors, and society.

- Racial and ethnic awareness begins to form in the preschool years.

- Gender awareness also develops in the preschool years. Explanations of this phenomenon include biological, psychoanalytical, learning, and cognitive approaches.

Applying Lifespan Development

- What sorts of activities might you encourage a preschool boy to undertake to encourage him to adopt a less stereotypical gender schema?

- *From a child-care provider's perspective:* How would you relate Erikson's stages of trust versus mistrust, autonomy versus shame and doubt, and initiative versus guilt to the issue of secure attachment discussed in an earlier chapter?

Friends and Family: Preschooler's Social Lives

When Juan was 3, he had his first best friend, Emilio. Juan and Emilio, who lived in the same apartment building in San Jose, were inseparable. They played incessantly with toy cars, racing them up and down the apartment hallways until some of the neighbors began to complain about the noise. They pretended to read to one another, and sometimes they slept over at each other's home—a big step for a 3-year-old. Neither boy seemed more joyful than when he was with his "best friend"—the term each used of the other.

An infant's family can provide nearly all the social contact he or she needs. As preschoolers, however, many children, like Juan and Emilio, begin to discover the joys of friendship with their peers. Although they may expand their social circles considerably, parents and family nevertheless remain very influential in the lives of preschoolers. Let's take a look at both of these sides of preschoolers' social development, friends and family.

The Development of Friendships

Before the age of 3, most social activity involves simply being in the same place at the same time, without real social interaction. However, at around the age of 3, children begin to develop real friendships like Juan and Emilio's as peers come to be seen as individuals who hold some special qualities and rewards. While preschoolers' relations with adults reflect children's needs for care, protection, and direction, their relations with peers are based more on the desire for companionship, play, and fun.

As preschoolers age, their ideas about friendship gradually evolve. They come to view friendship as a continuing state, a stable relationship that takes place not just in the immediate moment, but also offers the promise of future activity (Harris, 1998, 2000; Hay, Payne, & Chadwick, 2004).

As preschoolers get older, their conception of friendship evolves and the quality of their interactions changes.

In parallel play, children play with similar toys, in a similar manner, but don't necessarily interact with one another.

The quality and kinds of interactions children have with friends change during the preschool period. For 3-year-olds, the focus of friendship is the enjoyment of carrying out shared activities—doing things together and playing jointly, as when Juan and Emilio played with their toy cars in the hallway. Older preschoolers, however, pay more attention to abstract concepts such as trust, support, and shared interests (Park, Lay, & Ramsay, 1993). Throughout the preschool years, playing together remains an important part of all friendships. Like friendships, these play patterns change during the preschool years.

Playing by the Rules: The Work of Play

In Rosie Graiff's class of 3-year-olds, Minnie bounces her doll's feet on the table as she sings softly to herself. Ben pushes his toy car across the floor, making motor noises. Sarah chases Abdul around and around the perimeter of the room.

Play is more than what children of preschool age do to pass the time. Instead, play helps preschoolers develop socially, cognitively, and physically (Roopnarine, 2002; Lindsey & Colwell, 2003; Blundon & Schaefer, 2006; Samuelsson & Johansson, 2006).

VIDEO CLIP

PARTEN'S PLAY CATEGORIES

Categorizing Play.   At the beginning of the preschool years, children engage in **functional play**—simple, repetitive activities typical of 3-year-olds. Functional play may involve objects, such as dolls or cars, or repetitive muscular movements such as skipping, jumping, or rolling and unrolling a piece of clay. Functional play, then, involves doing something for the sake of being active rather than with the aim of creating some end product (Rubin, Fein, & Vandenberg, 1983; Bober, Humphry, & Carswell, 2001; Kantrowitz & Evans, 2004).

As children get older, functional play declines. By the time they are 4, children become involved in a more sophisticated form of play. In **constructive play** children manipulate objects to produce or build something. A child who builds a house out of Legos or puts a puzzle together is involved in constructive play: He or she has an ultimate goal—to produce something. Such play is not necessarily aimed at creating something novel, since children may repeatedly build a house of blocks, let it fall into disarray, and then rebuild it.

Constructive play gives children a chance to test their developing physical and cognitive skills and to practice their fine muscle movements. They gain experience in solving problems about the ways and the sequences in which things fit together. They also learn to cooperate with others—a development we observe as the social nature of play shifts during the preschool period. Consequently, it's important for adults who care for preschoolers to provide a variety of toys that allow for both functional and constructive play (Power, 1999; Edwards, 2000; Shi, 2003).

The Social Aspects of Play.   If two preschoolers are sitting at a table side by side, each putting a different puzzle together, are they engaged jointly in play?

According to pioneering work done by Mildred Parten (1932), the answer is "yes." She suggests that these preschoolers are engaged in **parallel play,** in which children play with similar toys, in a similar manner, but do not interact with each other. Parallel play is typical for children during the early preschool years. Preschoolers also engage in another form of play, a highly passive one: onlooker play. In **onlooker play,** children simply watch others at play, but do not actually participate themselves. They may look on silently, or they may make comments of encouragement or advice.

As they get older, however, preschool-age children engage in more sophisticated forms of social play that involve a greater degree of interaction. In **associative play** two or more children actually interact with one another by sharing or borrowing toys or materials, although they do not do the same thing. In **cooperative play,** children genuinely play with one another, taking turns, playing games, or devising contests. (The various types of play are summarized in Table 8-2.)

---

functional play   play that involves simple, repetitive activities typical of 3-year-olds.

constructive play   play in which children manipulate objects to produce or build something.

parallel play   action in which children play with similar toys, in a similar manner, but do not interact with each other.

onlooker play   action in which children simply watch others at play, but do not actually participate themselves.

associative play   play in which two or more children actually interact with one another by sharing or borrowing toys or materials, although they do not do the same thing.

cooperative play   play in which children genuinely interact with one another, taking turns, playing games, or devising contests.

Table 8-2	Preschoolers' Play	
Type of Play	**Description**	**Examples**
General Categories		
Functional play	Simple, repetitive activities typical of 3-year-olds. May involve objects or repetitive muscular movements.	Moving dolls or cars repetitively. Skipping, jumping, rolling or unrolling a piece of clay.
Constructive play	More sophisticated play in which children manipulate objects to produce or build something. Developed by age 4, constructive play lets children test physical and cognitive skills and practice fine muscle movements.	Building a dollhouse or car garage out of Legos, putting together a puzzle, making an animal out of clay.
Social Aspects of Play (Parten's Categories)		
Parallel play	Children use similar toys in a similar manner at the same time, but do not interact with each other. Typical of children during the early preschool years.	Children sitting side by side, each playing with his or her own toy car, putting together his or her own puzzle, or making an individual clay animal.
Onlooker play	Children simply watch others at play, but do not actually participate. They may look on silently or they may make comments of encouragement or advice. Common among preschoolers and can be helpful when a child wishes to join a group already at play.	One child watches as a group of others plays with dolls, cars, or clay; builds with Legos, or works on a puzzle together.
Associative play	Two or more children interact, sharing or borrowing toys or materials, although they do not do the same thing.	Two children, each building his or her own Lego garage, may trade bricks back and forth.
Cooperative play	Children genuinely play with one another, taking turns, playing games, or devising contests.	A group of children working on a puzzle may take turns fitting in the pieces. Children playing with dolls or cars may take turns making the dolls talk or may agree on rules to race the cars.

Usually associative and cooperative play do not typically become common until children reach the end of the preschool years. But children who have had substantial preschool experience are more apt to engage in more social forms of behavior, such as associative and cooperative play, fairly early in the preschool years than those with less experience (Roopnarine, Johnson, & Hooper, 1994; Brownell, Ramani, & Zerwas, 2006; Dyer & Moneta, 2006).

Solitary and onlooker play continue in the later stages of the preschool period. There are simply times when children prefer to play by themselves. And when newcomers join a group, one strategy for becoming part of the group—often successful—is to engage in onlooker play, waiting for an opportunity to join the play more actively (Howes, Unger, & Seidner, 1989; Hughes, 1995; Lindsey & Colwell, 2003).

The nature of pretend, or make-believe, play also changes during the preschool period. In some ways, pretend play becomes increasingly *un*realistic—and even more imaginative—as preschoolers change from using only realistic objects to using less concrete ones. Thus, at the start of the preschool period, children may pretend to listen to a radio only if they actually have a plastic radio that looks realistic. Later, however, they are more likely to use an entirely different object, such as a large cardboard box, as a pretend radio (Bornstein et al., 1996).

Russian developmentalist Lev Vygotsky, who we discussed in Chapter 7, argued that pretend play, particularly if it involves social play, is an important means for expanding preschool-age children's cognitive skills. Through make-believe play, children are able to "practice" activities (such as pretending to use a computer or read a book) that are a part of their particular culture and broaden their understanding of the way the world functions.

According to developmentalist Lev Vygotsky, children are able, through make-believe play, to practice activities that are part of their particular culture and broaden their understanding of the way the world functions.

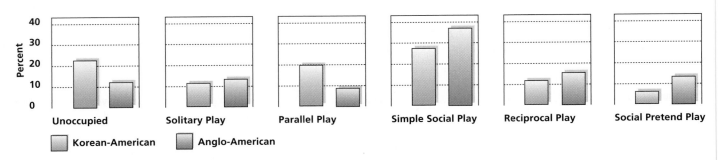

FIGURE 8-1 COMPARING PLAY COMPLEXITY

An examination of Korean American and Anglo-American preschoolers' play complexity finds clear differences in patterns of play. Can you think of any explanation for this finding?

(*Source:* Adapted from Farver, Kim, & Lee-Shin, 1995.)

VIDEO CLIP

SOCIODRAMATIC PLAY

Culture also affects children's styles of play. For example, Korean American children engage in a higher proportion of parallel play than their Anglo-American counterparts, while Anglo-American preschoolers are involved in more pretend play (see Figure 8-1; Farver, Kim, & Lee-Shin, 1995; Farver & Lee-Shin, 2000; Bai, 2005).

Preschoolers' Theory of Mind: Understanding What Others Are Thinking

One reason behind the changes in children's play is the continuing development of preschoolers' theory of mind. As we first discussed in Chapter 6, *theory of mind* refers to knowledge and beliefs about how the mind operates. Using their theory of mind, preschool children are able to come up with explanations for how *others* think and reasons for why they behave the way they do.

One of the main reasons for children's emerging play and social skills is that during the preschool years, children increasingly can see the world from others' perspectives. Even children as young as 2 are able to understand that others have emotions. By the age of 3 or 4, preschoolers can distinguish between something in their minds and physical actuality. For instance, 3-year-olds know that they can imagine something that is not physically present, such as a zebra, and that others can do the same. They can also pretend that something has happened and react as if it really had occurred, a skill that becomes part of their imaginative play. And they know that others have the same capability (Cadinu & Kiesner, 2000; Mauritzson & Saeljoe, 2001; Andrews, Halford, & Bunch, 2003).

Preschool-age children also become more insightful regarding the motives and reasons behind people's behavior. They begin to understand that their mother is angry because she was late for an appointment, even if they themselves haven't seen her be late. Furthermore, by the age of 4, preschool-age children's understanding that people can be fooled and mistaken by physical reality (such as magic tricks

"We've done a lot of important playing here today."

involving sleight-of-hand) becomes surprisingly sophisticated. This increase in understanding helps children become more socially skilled as they gain insight into what others are thinking (Nguyen & Frye, 1999; Fitzgerald & White, 2002; Eisbach, 2004).

There are limits, however, to 3-year-olds' theory of mind. Although they understand the concept of "pretend" by the age of 3, their understanding of "belief" is still not complete. The difficulty experienced by 3-year-olds in comprehending "belief" is illustrated by their performance on the *false belief* task. In the false belief task, preschoolers are shown a doll named Maxi who places chocolate in a cabinet and then leaves. After Maxi is gone, though, his mother moves the chocolate somewhere else.

After viewing these events, a preschooler is asked where Maxi will look for the chocolate when he returns. Three-year-olds answer (erroneously) that Maxi will look for it in the new location. In contrast, 4-year-olds correctly realize that Maxi has the erroneous false belief that the chocolate is still in the cabinet, and that's where he will look for it (Wimmer & Gschaider, 2000; Ziv & Frye, 2003; Flynn, O'Malley, & Wood, 2004; Amsterlaw & Wellman, 2006).

By the end of the preschool years, most children easily solve false belief problems. Certain children have considerable difficulties with false belief problems throughout their lifetimes: children with autism. *Autism* is a psychological disorder that produces significant language and emotional difficulties. Children with autism find it particularly difficult to relate to others, in part because they find it difficult to understand what others are thinking. Occurring in about 4 in 10,000 people, particularly males, autism is characterized by a lack of connection to other people, even parents, and an avoidance of interpersonal situations. Individuals with autism are bewildered by false belief problems no matter how old they are (Begeer, Rieffe, & Terwogt, 2003; Heerey, Keltner, & Capps, 2003; Ropar, Mitchell, & Ackroyd, 2003).

The Emergence of Theory of Mind.   What factors are involved in the emergence of theory of mind? Certainly, brain maturation is an important factor. As myelination within the frontal lobes becomes more pronounced, preschoolers develop more emotional capacity involving self-awareness. In addition, hormonal changes seem to be related to emotions that are more evaluative in nature (Sroufe, 1996; Davidson, 2003; Schore, 2003).

Developing language skills are also related to the increasing sophistication of children's theory of mind. In particular, the ability to understand the meaning of words such as "think" and "know" is important in helping preschool-age children understand the mental lives of others (Astington & Baird, 2005; Farrant, Fletcher, & Maybery, 2006).

As much as the child's developing theory of mind promotes more engaged social interactions and play, the process is reciprocal: Opportunities for social interaction and make-believe play are also critical in promoting the development of theory of mind. For example, preschool-age children with older siblings (who provide high levels of social interaction) have more sophisticated theories of mind than those without older siblings. In addition, abused children show delays in delays in their ability to correctly answer the false belief task, in part due to reduced experience with normal social interaction (Watson, 2000; Cicchetti et al., 2003; Cicchetti, 2004, 2004; McAlister & Peterson, 2006).

Cultural factors also play an important role in the development of theory of mind and the interpretations that children bring to bear on others' actions. For example, children in more industrialized Western cultures may be more likely to see others' behavior as due to the kind of people they are, a function of the people's personal traits and characteristics ("She won the race because she is really fast"). In contrast, children in non-Western cultures may see others' behavior as produced by forces that are less under their personal control ("She won the race because she was lucky") (Lillard, 1998; Tardif, Wellman, & Cheung, 2004; Wellman et al., 2006).

Preschoolers' Family Lives

Four-year-old Benjamin was watching TV while his mom cleaned up after dinner. After a while, he wandered in and grabbed a towel, saying, "Mommy, let me help you do the dishes." Surprised by this unprecedented behavior, she asked him, "Where did you learn to do dishes?"

"I saw it on Leave It to Beaver," *he replied, "Only it was the dad helping. Since we don't have a dad, I figured I'd do it."*

For an increasing number of preschool-age children, life does not mirror what we see in reruns of old sitcoms. Many face the realities of an increasingly complicated world. For instance, as we noted in Chapter 6, and will discuss in greater detail in Chapter 10, children are increasingly likely to live with only one parent. In 1960, less than 10% of all children under the age of 18 lived with one parent. In 2000, a single parent headed 21% of white families, 35% of Hispanic families, and 55% of African American families.

Still, for most children the preschool years are not a time of upheaval and turmoil. Instead, the period encompasses a growing interaction with the world at large. As we've seen, for instance, preschoolers begin to develop genuine friendships with other children, in which close ties emerge. One central factor leading preschoolers to develop friendships comes when parents provide a warm, supportive home environment. A good deal of research finds that strong, positive relationships between parents and children encourage children's relationships with others (Sroufe, 1994; Howes, Galinsky, & Kontos, 1998). How do parents nurture that relationship?

Effective Parenting: Teaching Desired Behavior

While she thinks no one is looking, Maria goes into her brother Alejandro's bedroom, where he has been saving the last of his Halloween candy. Just as she takes his last Reese's Peanut Butter Cup, the children's mother walks into the room and immediately takes in the situation.

If you were Maria's mother, which of the following reactions seems most reasonable?

1. Tell Maria that she must go to her room and stay there for the rest of the day, and that she is going to lose access to her favorite blanket, the one she sleeps with every night and during naps.

2. Mildly tell Maria that what she did was not such a good idea, and she shouldn't do it in the future.

3. Explain why her brother Alejandro would be upset by her actions, and tell her that she must go to her room for an hour as punishment.

4. Forget about it, and let the children sort it out themselves.

Each of these four alternative responses represents one of the major parenting styles identified by Diana Baumrind (1971, 1980) and updated by Eleanor Maccoby and colleagues (Baumrind, 1971, 1980; Maccoby & Martin, 1983).

Authoritarian parents respond as in the first alternative. They are controlling, punitive, rigid, cold. Their word is law, and they value strict, unquestioning obedience from their children. They also do not tolerate expressions of disagreement.

Permissive parents, in contrast, provide lax and inconsistent feedback, as in the second alternative. They require little of their children, and they don't see themselves as holding much responsibility for how their children turn out. They place little or no limits or control on their children's behavior.

Authoritative parents are firm, setting clear and consistent limits. Although they tend to be relatively strict, like authoritarian parents, they are loving and emotionally supportive. They also try to reason with their children, giving explanations for why they should behave in a particular way ("Alejandro is going to be upset"), and communicating the rationale for any punishment they may impose. Authoritative parents encourage their children to be independent.

authoritarian parents parents who are controlling, punitive, rigid, and cold, and whose word is law.

permissive parents parents who provide lax and inconsistent feedback and require little of their children.

authoritative parents parents who are firm, setting clear and consistent limits, but who try to reason with their children, giving explanations for why they should behave in a particular way.

Finally, **uninvolved parents** show virtually no interest in their children, displaying indifferent, rejecting behavior. They are detached emotionally and see their role as no more than feeding, clothing, and providing shelter for their child. In its most extreme form, uninvolved parenting results in *neglect*, a form of child abuse. (The four patterns are summarized in Table 8-3.)

Does the particular style of discipline that parents use result in differences in children's behavior? The answer is very much yes—although, as you might expect, there are many exceptions (Collett et al., 2001; Snyder, Cramer, & Afrank, 2005; Arredondo et al., 2006; Simons & Conger, 2007):

- Children of authoritarian parents tend to be withdrawn, showing relatively little sociability. They are not very friendly, often behaving uneasily around their peers. Girls who are raised by authoritarian parents are especially dependent on their parents, whereas boys are unusually hostile.

- Permissive parents have children who, in many ways, share the undesirable characteristics of children of authoritarian parents. Children with permissive parents tend to be dependent and moody, and they are low in social skills and self-control.

- Children of authoritative parents fare best. They generally are independent, friendly with their peers, self-assertive, and cooperative. They have strong motivation to achieve, and they are typically successful and likable. They regulate their own behavior effectively, both in terms of their relationships with others and emotional self-regulation.

uninvolved parents parents who show almost no interest in their children and indifferent, rejecting behavior.

Table 8-3 Parenting Styles

How Demanding Parents Are of Children ▶ How Responsive Parents Are to a Child ▼	Demanding Authoritative	Undemanding Permissive
Highly Responsive	**Characteristics:** firm, setting clear and consistent limits **Relationship with Children:** Although they tend to be relatively strict, like authoritarian parents, they are loving and emotionally supportive and encourage their children to be independent. They also try to reason with their children, giving explanations for why they should behave in a particular way, and communicate the rationale for any punishment they may impose.	**Characteristics:** lax and inconsistent feedback **Relationship with Children:** They require little of their children, and they don't see themselves as holding much responsibility for how their children turn out. They place little or no limits or control on their children's behavior.
	Authoritarian	**Uninvolved**
Low Responsive	**Characteristics:** controlling, punitive, rigid, cold **Relationship with Children:** Their word is law, and they value strict, unquestioning obedience from their children. They also do not tolerate expressions of disagreement.	**Characteristics:** displaying indifferent, rejecting behavior **Relationship with Children:** They are detached emotionally and see their role as only providing food, clothing, and shelter. In its extreme form, this parenting style results in neglect, a form of child abuse.

Children with authoritative parents tend to be well adjusted, in part because the parents are supportive and take the time to explain things. What are the consequences of parents who are too permissive? Too authoritarian? Too uninvolved?

- Some authoritative parents also display several characteristics that have come to be called *supportive parenting*, including parental warmth, proactive teaching, calm discussion during disciplinary episodes, and interest and involvement in children's peer activities. Children whose parents engage in such supportive parenting show better adjustment and are better protected from the consequences of later adversity they may encounter (Pettit, Bates, & Dodge, 1997; Belluck, 2000; Kaufmann et al., 2000).

- Children whose parents show uninvolved parenting styles are the worst off. Their parents' lack of involvement disrupts their emotional development considerably, leading them to feel unloved and emotionally detached, and impedes their physical and cognitive development as well.

Though such classification systems are useful ways of categorizing and describing parents' behavior, they are not a recipe for success. Parenting and growing up are more complicated than that! For instance, in a significant number of cases the children of authoritarian and permissive parents develop quite successfully.

Furthermore, most parents are not entirely consistent: Although the authoritarian, permissive, authoritative, and uninvolved patterns describe general styles, sometimes parents switch from their dominant mode to one of the others. For instance, when a child darts into the street, even the most laid-back and permissive parent is likely to react in a harsh, authoritarian manner, laying down strict demands about safety. In such cases, authoritarian styles may be most effective (Janssens & Dekovic, 1997; Holden & Miller, 1999; Eisenberg & Valiente, 2002; Gershoff, 2002).

Cultural Differences in Child-Rearing Practices.   It's important to keep in mind that the findings regarding child-rearing styles we have been discussing are chiefly applicable to Western societies. The style of parenting that is most successful may depend quite heavily on the norms of a particular culture—and what parents in a particular culture are taught regarding appropriate child-rearing practices (Claes, Lacourse, & Bouchard, 2003; Giles-Sims & Lockhart, 2005; Dwairy et al., 2006; Hulei, Zevenbergen, & Jacobs, 2006).

The style of parenting that is most effective depends on what parents in a particular culture are taught regarding appropriate childbearing practices.

For example, the Chinese concept of *chiao shun* suggests that parents should be strict, firm, and in tight control of their children's behavior. Parents are seen to have a duty to train their children to adhere to socially and culturally desirable standards of behavior, particularly those manifested in good school performance. Children's acceptance of such an approach to discipline is seen as a sign of parental respect (Chao, 1994; Wu, Robinson, & Yang, 2002).

Parents in China are typically highly directive with their children, pushing them to excel and controlling their behavior to a considerably higher degree than parents typically do in Western countries. And it works: Children of Asian parents tend to be quite successful, particularly academically (Steinberg, Dornbusch, & Brown, 1992; Nelson et al., 2006).

In contrast, U.S. parents are generally advised to use authoritative methods and explicitly to avoid authoritarian measures. It is interesting to note that it wasn't always this way. Until World War II, the point of view that dominated the advice literature was authoritarian, apparently founded on Puritan religious influences that suggested that children had "original sin" or that they needed to have their wills broken (Smuts & Hagen, 1985).

In short, the child-rearing practices that parents are urged to follow reflect cultural perspectives about the nature of children as well as about the appropriate role of parents and their support system (see the *From Research to Practice* box). No single parenting pattern or style, then, is likely to be universally appropriate or likely invariably to produce successful children (Harwood et al., 1996; Hart et al., 1998; Wang & Tamis-LeMonda, 2003.)

Similarly, it is important to keep in mind that child-rearing practices are not the sole influence on children's development. For example, sibling and peer influences play a significant

From Research to Practice

Parenting Coaches: Teaching Parents to Teach Their Children

What tripped Lisa D'Annolfo Levey's maternal tolerance meter on a recent Tuesday afternoon was not just the toy football her 7-year-old son, Skylar, zinged across the living room, nearly toppling her teacup. Or the karate kick sprung by her 4-year-old, Forrest, which Ms. Levey ducked, barely.

The clincher was the full-throttle duel with foam swords, her boys whooping and squealing, flailing their weapons at the blue leather couch, the yellow kidney-shaped rug, and, ultimately, their mother.

"Forrest, how about you come up and hug Skylar instead of whacking him in the head?" Ms. Levey implored. "This is stressing me out, guys." (Belluck, 2005, p. A1)

And then she called her personal parent coach to find out how to deal with the situation.

Personal parent coach? In a new and growing phenomenon, parents are turning to members of a profession that didn't exist only few years ago called *parent coaching* to help them navigate the trials of parenthood.

Less expensive than formal therapy, but more systematic than the advice one might receive from one's next-door neighbor, parent coaching provides a combination of advice and support. Some parent coaches offer specific child-rearing strategies, while others teach parents the basics of child development so that they

put their child's behavior in perspective (Marchant, Young, & West, 2004).

For some parents, parent coaching is a lifeline. It provides a way for parents who might not have access to the advice of other, more experienced parents to learn how to deal with the challenges of children. It also provides a relationship with another adult who can offer social support (Smith, 2005).

Although many parents swear by the value of parent coaches, the effectiveness of parent coaching has not been established by much scientific research. In part, the lack of data is a reflection of the newness of the field. In addition, there is great heterogenity in the qualificaitons of parent coaches. While some have had formal training in child development, the only qualifications of other coaches is having raised a child themselves (Leonard, 2005).

Because there is no licensing of parent coaches, parents should adopt a buyer-beware attitude. Anyone can call themselves a parent coach, and parents should examine the credentials of prospective coaches carefully. Until the field becomes more regulated—and the value of parent coaches has been formally established—parents should be cautious.

- *If you were conducting an interview with a potential parent coach, what kind of questions would you ask?*

- *Do you think parent coaches should be licensed by the government? Why or why not? What kind of qualifications do you think should be required to get a license?*

---

role in children's development. Furthermore, children's behavior is in part produced by their unique genetic endowments, and their behavior can in turn shape parental behavior. In sum, parents' child-rearing practices are just one of a rich array of environmental and genetic influences that influence children (Boivin et al., 2005; Loehlin, Neiderhiser, & Reiss, 2005).

Child Abuse and Psychological Maltreatment: The Grim Side of Family Life

The figures are gloomy and disheartening: At least five children are killed by their parents or caretakers every day, and 140,000 others are physically injured every year. Around 3 million children are abused or neglected in the United States each year. The abuse takes several forms, ranging from actual physical abuse to psychological mistreatment (see Figure 8-2; Briere et al., 1996; Parnell & Day, 1998; National Clearinghouse on Child Abuse and Neglect Information, 2004; U.S. Department of Health and Human Services, 2007).

Physical Abuse.　Child abuse can occur in any household, regardless of economic well-being or the social status

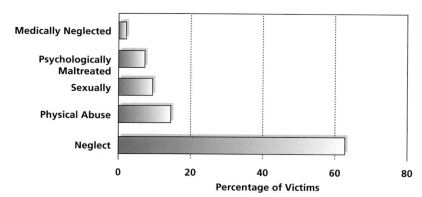

The percentages add up to numbers higher than 100 percent because some victims were exposed to multiple types of maltreatment. 62.8 percent of victims experienced neglect.

FIGURE 8-2　TYPES OF CHILD ABUSE

Neglect is the most frequent form of abuse. How can educators and healthcare providers help identify cases of child abuse?

(*Source:* U.S. Department of Health and Human Services, Administration on Children, Youth and Families, 2007).

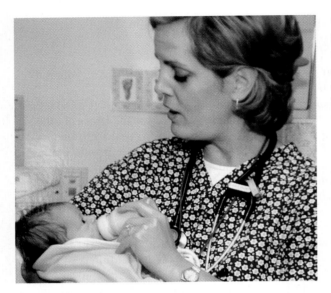

This nine-day-old infant, named Baby Vinnie, was found after being abandoned on the steps behind a church. He later was adopted by a foster family.

of the parents. It is most frequent in families living in stressful environments. Poverty, single parenthood, and higher-than-average levels of marital conflict help create such environments. Stepfathers are more likely to commit abuse against stepchildren than genetic fathers are against their own offspring. Child abuse is also more likely when there is a history of violence between spouses (Kitzmann, Gaylord, & Holt, 2003; Litrownik, Newton, & Hunter, 2003; Osofsky, 2003; Evans, 2004). Table 8-4 lists some of the warning signs of abuse.

Abused children are more likely to be fussy, resistant to control, and not readily adaptable to new situations. They have more headaches and stomachaches, experience more bedwetting, are generally more anxious, and may show developmental delays. Children in certain age groups are also more likely to be the targets of abuse: Three- and 4-year-olds and 15- to 17-year-olds are somewhat more likely to be abused by their parents than children of other ages (Straus & Gelles, 1990; Ammerman & Patz, 1996; Haugaard, 2000).

As you consider this information about the characteristics of abused children, keep in mind that labeling children as being at higher risk for receiving abuse does not make them responsible for their abuse; the family members who carry out the abuse are at fault. Statistical findings simply suggest that children with such characteristics are more at risk of being the recipients of family violence.

Reasons for Physical Abuse. Why does physical abuse occur? Most parents certainly do not intend to hurt their children. In fact, most parents who abuse their children later express bewilderment and regret about their own behavior.

One reason for child abuse is the vague demarcation between permissible and impermissible forms of physical violence. Societal folklore in the United States says that spanking is not

---

Table 8-4 What Are the Warning Sings of Child Abuse?

Because child abuse is typically a secret crime, identifying the victims of abuse is particularly difficult. Still, there are several signs in a child that indicate that he or she is the victim of violence (Robbins, 1990):

- visible, serious injuries that have no reasonable explanation
- bite or choke marks
- burns from cigarettes or immersion in hot water
- feelings of pain for no apparent reason
- fear of adults or care providers
- inappropriate attire in warm weather (long sleeves, long pants, high-necked garments)—possibly to conceal injuries to the neck, arms, and legs
- extreme behavior—highly aggressive, extremely passive, extremely withdrawn
- fear of physical contact

If you suspect a child is a victim of aggression, it is your responsibility to act. Call your local police or the department of social services in your city or state, or call Childhelp U.S.A. at 1-800-422-4453. Talk to a teacher or a member of the clergy. Remember, by acting decisively you can literally save someone's life.

merely acceptable, but often necessary and desirable. Almost half of mothers with children less than 4 years of age have spanked their child in the previous week, and close to 20% of mothers believe it is appropriate to spank a child less than 1 year of age. In some other cultures, physical discipline is even more common (Straus, Gelles, & Steinmetz, 2003; Lansford et al., 2005; Deb & Adak, 2006; Shor, 2006).

Unfortunately, the line between "spanking" and "beating" is not clear, and spankings begun in anger can escalate into abuse. In fact, increasing scientific evidence suggests that spanking should be avoided entirely. Although physical punishment may produce immediate compliance— children typically stop the behavior spanking is meant to end—there are a number of serious long-term side effects. For example, spanking is associated with lower quality of parent–child relationships, poorer mental health for both child and parent, higher levels of delinquency, and more antisocial behavior. Spanking also teaches children that violence is an acceptable solution to problems by serving as a model of violent, aggressive behavior. Consequently, according to the American Academy of Pediatrics, the use of physical punishment of any sort is *not* recommended (American Academy of Pediatrics, 1998; Gershoff, 2002; Kazdin & Benjet, 2003; Afifi et al., 2006).

Two of the children in this large family allegedly were singled out for abuse by their parents and were severely malnourished, while the other children were seemingly well-cared for. What might account for this unusual situation?

Another factor that leads to high rates of abuse is the privacy in which child care is conducted in Western societies. In many other cultures child rearing is seen as the joint responsibility of several people and even society as a whole. In most Western cultures— and particularly the United States—children are raised in private, isolated households. Because child care is seen as the sole responsibility of the parent, other people are typically not available to help out when a parent's patience is tested (Chaffin, 2006; Elliott & Urquiza, 2006).

Sometimes abuse is the result of an adult's unrealistically high expectations regarding children's abilities to be quiet and compliant at a particular age. Children's failure to meet these unrealistic expectations may provoke abuse (Peterson, 1994).

The Cycle of Violence Hypothesis.   Many times, those who abuse children were themselves abused as children. According to the **cycle of violence hypothesis,** the abuse and neglect that children suffer predispose them as adults to abuse and neglect their own children (Miller-Perrin & Perrin, 1999; Widom, 2000; Heyman & Slep, 2002).

According to this hypothesis, victims of abuse have learned from their childhood experiences that violence is an appropriate and acceptable form of discipline. Violence may be perpetuated from one generation to another, as each generation learns to behave abusively (and fails to learn the skills needed to solve problems and instill discipline without resorting to physical violence) through its participation in an abusive, violent family (Straus, Sugarman, & Giles-Sims, 1997; Blumenthal, 2000; Ethier, Couture, & Lacharite, 2004).

Being abused as a child does not inevitably lead to abuse of one's own children. In fact, statistics show that only about one-third of people who were abused or neglected as children abuse their own children; the remaining two-thirds of people abused as children do not turn out to be child abusers. Clearly, suffering abuse as a child is not the full explanation for child abuse in adults (Cicchetti, 1996; Straus & McCord, 1998).

Psychological Maltreatment.   Children may also be the victims of more subtle forms of mistreatment. **Psychological maltreatment** occurs when parents or other caregivers harm children's behavioral, cognitive, emotional, or physical functioning. It may be the result of either overt behavior or neglect (Hart, Brassard, & Karlson, 1996; Higgins & McCabe, 2003).

For example, abusive parents may frighten, belittle, or humiliate their children, thereby intimidating and harassing them. Children may be made to feel like disappointments or failures, or they may be constantly reminded that they are a burden to their parents. Parents may tell

cycle of violence hypothesis   the theory that the abuse and neglect that children suffer predispose them as adults to abuse and neglect their own children.

psychological maltreatment   abuse that occurs when parents or other caregivers harm children's behavioral, cognitive, emotional, or physical functioning.

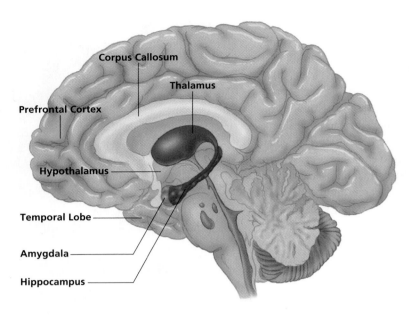

FIGURE 8-3   ABUSE ALTERS THE BRAIN

The limbic system, comprised of the hippocampus and amygdala, can be permanently altered as a result of childhood abuse.

(*Source: Scientific American*, 2002.)

their children that they wish they had never had children and specifically that they wish that their children had never been born. Children may be threatened with abandonment or even death. In other instances, older children may be exploited. They may be forced to seek employment and then to give their earnings to their parents.

In other cases of psychological maltreatment, the abuse takes the form of neglect. Parents may ignore their children or act emotionally unresponsive to them. In such cases, children may be given unrealistic responsibilities or may be left to fend for themselves. No one is certain how much psychological maltreatment occurs each year, because figures separating psychological maltreatment from other types of abuse are not routinely gathered. Most maltreatment occurs in the privacy of people's homes.

Furthermore, psychological maltreatment typically causes no physical damage, such as bruises or broken bones, to alert physicians, teachers, and other authorities. Consequently, many cases of psychological maltreatment probably are not identified. However, it is clear that profound neglect that involves children who are unsupervised or uncared for is the most frequent form of psychological maltreatment (Hewitt, 1997).

What are the consequences of psychological maltreatment? Some children are sufficiently resilient to survive the abuse and grow into psychologically healthy adults. In many cases, however, lasting damage results. For example, psychological maltreatment has been associated with low self-esteem, lying, misbehavior, and underachievement in school. In extreme cases, it can produce criminal behavior, aggression, and murder. In other instances, children who have been psychologically maltreated become depressed and even commit suicide (Shonk & Cicchetti, 2001; Eigsti & Cicchetti, 2004; Koenig, Cicchetti, & Rogosch, 2004).

One reason that psychological maltreatment—as well as physical abuse—produces so many negative consequences is that the brains of victims undergo permanent changes due to the abuse (see Figure 8-3). For example, childhood maltreatment can lead to reductions in the size of the amygdala and hippocampus in adulthood. The stress, fear, and terror produced by abuse may also produce permanent changes in the brain due to overstimulation of the limbic system. Because the limbic system is involved in the regulation of memory and emotion, the result can be antisocial behavior during adulthood (Teicher et al., 2002; Bremner, 2003; Teicher et al., 2003; Watts-English et al., 2006).

Resilience: Overcoming the Odds

Given the seriousness of child abuse in all its forms, and the physical, psychological, and neurological damage it can cause, it's remarkable that not all children who have been abused are permanently scarred by it. In fact, some do surprisingly well, considering the type of problems they have encountered. What enables some children to overcome the stress and trauma that in most cases haunts others for life?

The answer appears to be a quality that psychologists have termed resilience. **Resilience** is the ability to overcome circumstances that place a child at high risk for psychological or physical damage, such as extremes of poverty, prenatal stress, or homes that are racked with violence or other forms of social disorder. Several factors seem to reduce and, in certain cases, eliminate some children's reactions to difficult circumstances that produce profoundly

resilience the ability to overcome circumstances that place a child at high risk for psychological or physical damage.

negative consequences in others (Luthar, Cicchetti, & Becker, 2000; Trickett, Kurtz, & Pizzigati, 2004).

According to developmental psychologist Emmy Werner, resilient children tend to have temperaments that evoke positive responses from a wide variety of caregivers. They tend to be affectionate, easygoing, and good natured. They are easily soothed as infants, and they are able to elicit care from the most nurturant people in any environment in which they find themselves. In a sense, then, resilient children are successful in making their own environments by drawing out behavior in others that is necessary for their own development (Werner, 1995; Werner & Smith, 2002).

Similar traits are associated with resilience in older children. The most resilient school-age children are those who are socially pleasant, outgoing, and have good communication skills. They tend to be relatively intelligent, and they are independent, feeling that they can shape their own fate and are not dependent on others or luck (Curtis & Cicchetti, 2003; Kim & Cicchetti, 2003; Haskett et al., 2006).

The characteristics of resilient children suggest ways to improve the prospects of children who are at risk from a variety of developmental threats. For instance, in addition to decreasing their exposure to factors that put them at risk in the first place, we need to increase their competence by teaching them ways to deal with their situation. In fact, programs that have been successful in helping especially vulnerable children have a common thread: They provide competent and caring adult models who can teach the children problem-solving skills and help them to communicate their needs to those who are in a position to help them (Davey et al., 2003; Maton, Schellenbach, & Leadbeater, 2004; Condly, 2006). (Also see the *Careers in Lifespan Development* box.)

mydevelopmentlab

VIDEO CLIP

TEMPERAMENT

Careers in Lifespan Development

Debra A. Littler

Education: BA Psychology, Arizona State University; Master of Counseling, Arizona State University

Position: Clinical Director, Child Crisis Center, Mesa, Arizona

More than 3 million children a year are victims of child abuse. To deal with this epidemic, many organizations across the country are dedicated to both prevention of child abuse and providing a safe haven for children who have been abused. Among them is the nonprofit Child Crisis Center in Mesa, Arizona.

The Center has served more than 10,000 children, from birth through 12 years of age, over the past 25 years. The goal of the Center is to prevent child abuse by supporting and strengthening families and providing a safe environment for children to heal and grow. With 40 beds, it provides emergency shelter for children who have experienced child abuse.

According to the Center's clinical director, Debra Littler, "Children come to the Center through two pathways. One is through the state Child Protection Services, where children have been removed from their caretakers because of substantiated or alleged abuse.

"The other way is where the child is taken for a minimum 24-hour stay, an early prevention and intervention so the child is not at further risk," she added. "This is usually the result of a family crisis such as homelessness or incarceration."

Littler's counseling responsibilities range from when a child enters the clinic to when he or she leaves.

"I see newly admitted children who have behavioral and/or emotional distress of some type," Littler said, "and they need to be told information which may be traumatic, difficult, or significant in some way. For example, I might have to tell a child they are leaving for a foster home without their sibling, or talk to a child about a parent's incarceration.

"We provide 24/7 care-giving in a homelike environment," Littler noted, "and we have counselors provide one-to-one counseling. We use a child-directed play therapy in fully equipped playrooms where children see a counselor at least once a week and often more frequently.

"Many children come in with serious behavioral problems and we work from a cognitive behavioral model, depending on age, to have the child learn more appropriate ways of expressing feelings," she said.

Becoming an Informed Consumer of Development

Disciplining Children

The question of how best to discipline children has been raised for generations. Answers from developmentalists today include the following advice (O'Leary, 1995; Brazelton & Sparrow, 2003; Flouri, 2005):

- **For most children in Western cultures, authoritative parenting works best.** Parents should be firm and consistent, providing clear direction for desirable behavior. Authoritative disciplinarians provide rules, but they explain why those rules make sense, using language that children can understand.

- **Spanking is *never* an appropriate discipline technique,** according to the American Academy of Pediatrics. Not only is spanking less effective than other techniques in curbing undesirable behavior, but it leads to additional, unwanted outcomes, such as the potential for more aggressive behavior (American Academy of Pediatrics, 1998).

- **Use *time-out* for punishment,** in which children are removed from a situation where they have misbehaved and are not permitted to engage in enjoyable activities for a set period of time.

- **Tailor parental discipline to the characteristics of the child and the situation.** Try to keep the child's particular personality in mind, and adapt discipline to it.

- **Use routines (such as a bath routine or a bedtime routine) to avoid conflict.** For instance, bedtime can be the source of a nightly struggle between a resistant child and an insistent parent. Parental strategies for gaining compliance that involve making the situation predictably enjoyable—such as routinely reading a bedtime story or engaging in a nightly "wrestling" match with the child—can defuse potential battles.

Review and Apply

Review

- In the preschool years, children develop their first true friendships on the basis of personal characteristics, trust, and shared interests.

- The character of preschoolers' play changes over time, growing more sophisticated, interactive, and cooperative, and relying increasingly on social skills.

- There are several distinct child-rearing styles, including authoritarian, permissive, authoritative, and uninvolved.

- Child-rearing styles show strong cultural influences.

- Some children suffer abuse from their own family members.

Applying Lifespan Development

- What cultural and environmental factors in the United States may have contributed to the shift from an authoritarian parenting style to an authoritative one since World War II? Is another shift under way?

- *From an educator's perspective:* How might a nursery school teacher encourage a shy child to join a group of preschoolers who are playing?

Moral Development and Aggression

moral development the changes in people's sense of justice and of what is right and wrong, and in their behavior related to moral issues.

During snack time at preschool, playmates Jan and Meg inspected the goodies in their lunch boxes. Jan found two appetizing cream-filled cookies. Meg's snack offered less tempting carrot and celery sticks. As Jan began to munch on one of her cookies, Meg looked at the cut-up vegetables and burst into tears. Jan responded to Meg's distress by offering her companion one of her cookies, which Meg gladly accepted. Jan was able to put herself in Meg's place, understand Meg's thoughts and feelings, and act compassionately. (Katz, 1989, p. 213)

In this short scenario we see many of the key elements of morality, as it is played out among preschool-age children. Changes in children's views of what is ethically right and what is the right way to behave are an important element of growth during the preschool years.

At the same time, the kind of aggression displayed by preschoolers is also changing. We can consider the development of morality and aggression as two sides of the coin of human conduct, and both involve a growing awareness of others.

Developing Morality: Following Society's Rights and Wrongs

Moral development refers to changes in people's sense of justice and of what is right and wrong, and in their behavior related to moral issues. Developmentalists have considered moral development in terms of children's reasoning about morality, their attitudes toward moral lapses, and their behavior when faced with moral issues. In the process of studying moral development, several approaches have evolved (Langford, 1995; Grusec & Kuczynski, 1997).

Piaget's View of Moral Development. Child psychologist Jean Piaget was one of the first to study questions of moral development. He suggested that moral development, like cognitive development, proceeds in stages (Piaget, 1932). The earliest stage is a broad form of moral thinking he called *heteronomous morality*, in which rules are seen as invariant and unchangeable. During this stage, which lasts from about age 4 through age 7, children play games rigidly, assuming that there is one, and only one, way to play and that every other way is wrong. At the same time, though, preschool-age children may not even fully grasp game rules. Consequently, a group of children may be playing together, with each child playing according to a slightly different set of rules. Nevertheless, they enjoy playing with others. Piaget suggests that every child may "win" such a game, because winning is equated with having a good time, as opposed to truly competing with others.

This rigid heteronomous morality is ultimately replaced by two later stages of morality: incipient cooperation and autonomous cooperation. As its name implies, in the *incipient cooperation stage*, which lasts from around age 7 to age 10, children's games become more clearly social. Children learn the actual formal rules of games, and they play according to this shared knowledge. Consequently, rules are still seen as largely unchangeable. There is a "right" way to play the game, and children in the incipient cooperation stage play according to these formal rules.

It is not until the *autonomous cooperation stage*, which begins at about age 10, that children become fully aware that formal game rules can be modified if the people who play them agree. The later transition into more sophisticated forms of moral development—which we will consider in Chapter 12—also is reflected in school-age children's understanding that rules of law are created by people and are subject to change according to the will of people.

Until these later stages are reached, however, children's reasoning about rules and issues of justice is bounded in the concrete. For instance, consider the following two stories:

A little boy who is called John is in his room. He is called to dinner. He goes into the dining room. But behind the door there was a chair, and on the chair there was a tray with fifteen cups on it. John couldn't have known there was all this behind the door. He goes in, the door knocks against the tray, bang go the fifteen cups, and they all get broken!

Once there was a little boy whose name was Marcello. One day when his mother was out he tried to get some jam out of the cupboard. He climbed up on to a chair and stretched out

Preschoolers believe in immanent justice. This child may worry that he/she will be punished even if no one sees him/her carrying out the misdeed.

his arm. But the jam was too high up and he couldn't reach it and have any. But while he was trying to get it he knocked over a cup. The cup fell down and broke. (Piaget, 1932, p. 122)

Piaget found that a preschool child in the heteronomous morality stage judges the child who broke the 15 cups as being worse than the one who broke just 1 cup. In contrast, children who have moved beyond the heteronomous morality stage consider the child who broke the one cup as being naughtier. The reason: Children in the heteronomous morality stage do not take *intention* into account.

Children in the heteronomous stage of moral development also believe in immanent justice. *Immanent justice* is the notion that rules that are broken earn immediate punishment. Preschool children believe that if they do something wrong, they will be punished instantly—even if no one sees them carrying out their misdeeds. In contrast, older children understand that punishments for misdeeds are determined and meted out by people. Children who have moved beyond the heteronomous morality stage have come to understand that one must make judgments about the severity of a transgression based on whether the person intended to do something wrong.

Evaluating Piaget's Approach to Moral Development.   Recent research suggests that although Piaget was on the right track in his description of how moral development proceeds, his approach suffers from the same problem we encountered in his theory of cognitive development. Specifically, Piaget underestimated the age at which children's moral skills are honed.

It is now clear that preschool-age children understand the notion of intentionality by about age 3, and this allows them to make judgments based on intent at an earlier age than Piaget supposed. Specifically, when provided with moral questions that emphasize intent, preschool children judge someone who is intentionally bad as more "naughty" than someone who is unintentionally bad, but who creates more objective damage. Moreover, by the age of 4, they judge intentional lying as being wrong (Yuill & Perner, 1988; Bussey, 1992).

Social Learning Approaches to Morality.   Social learning approaches to moral development stand in stark contrast to Piaget's approach. While Piaget emphasizes how limitations in preschoolers' cognitive development lead to particular forms of moral *reasoning*, social learning approaches focus more on how the environment in which preschoolers operate produces **prosocial behavior,** helping behavior that benefits others (Eisenberg et al., 1999; Eisenberg, 2004).

Social learning approaches build upon the behavioral approaches that we first discussed in Chapter 1. They acknowledge that some instances of children's prosocial behavior stem from situations in which they have received positive reinforcement for acting in a morally appropriate way. For instance, when Claire's mother tells her she has been a "good girl" for sharing a box of candy with her brother Dan, Claire's behavior has been reinforced. As a consequence, she is more likely to engage in sharing behavior in the future.

However, social learning approaches go a step further, arguing that not all prosocial behavior has to be directly performed and subsequently reinforced for learning to occur. According to social learning approaches, children also learn moral behavior more indirectly by observing the behavior of others, called *models* (Bandura, 1977). Children imitate models who receive reinforcement for their behavior, and ultimately they learn to perform the behavior themselves. For example, when Claire's friend Jake watches Claire share her candy with her brother, and Claire is praised for her behavior, Jake is more likely to engage in sharing behavior himself at some later point.

Quite a few studies illustrate the power of models and of social learning more generally in producing prosocial behavior in preschool-age children. For example, experiments have shown that children who view someone behaving generously or unselfishly are apt to follow the model's example, subsequently behaving in a generous or unselfish manner themselves when put in a similar situation (Midlarsky & Bryan, 1972; Kim & Stevens, 1987). The opposite also holds true: If a model behaves selfishly, children who observe such behavior tend to behave more selfishly themselves (Staub, 1971; Grusec, 1982, 1991).

Not all models are equally effective in producing prosocial responses. For instance, preschoolers are more apt to model the behavior of warm, responsive adults than of adults who

prosocial behavior   helping behavior that benefits others.

appear colder. Furthermore, models viewed as highly competent or high in prestige are more effective than others (Yarrow, Scott, & Waxler, 1973; Bandura, 1977).

Children do more than simply mimic unthinkingly behavior that they see rewarded in others. By observing moral conduct, they are reminded of society's norms about the importance of moral behavior as conveyed by parents, teachers, and other powerful authority figures. They notice the connections between particular situations and certain kinds of behavior. This increases the likelihood that similar situations will elicit similar behavior in the observer.

Consequently, modeling paves the way for the development of more general rules and principles in a process called **abstract modeling.** Rather than always modeling the particular behavior of others, older preschoolers begin to develop generalized principles that underlie the behavior they observe. After observing repeated instances in which a model is rewarded for acting in a morally desirable way, children begin the process of inferring and learning the general principles of moral conduct (Bandura, 1991).

Empathy and Moral Behavior.   According to some developmentalists, **empathy**—the understanding of what another individual feels—lies at the heart of some kinds of moral behavior. Think back to the example in this chapter's prologue, of Alison Gropnik's son who used Band-Aids to try to heal whatever was making his mother cry. For her son to understand that Alison needed comforting, it was necessary for him to feel empathy with her unhappiness. Although he may have been confused about the source of her pain, Alison's son realized that she seemed hurt and warranted sympathy.

The roots of empathy grow early. One-year-old infants cry when they hear other infants crying. By ages 2 and 3, toddlers will offer gifts and spontaneously share toys with other children and adults, even if they are strangers (Stanjek, 1978; Radke-Yarrow, Zahn-Wexler, & Chapman, 1983; Zahn-Wexler & Radke-Yarrow, 1990).

During the preschool years, empathy continues to grow as children's ability to monitor and regulate their emotional and cognitive responses increases. Some theorists believe that increasing empathy—as well as other positive emotions, such as sympathy and admiration—leads children to behave in a more moral fashion. In addition, some negative emotions—such as anger at an unfair situation or shame over previous transgressions—also may promote moral behavior (Miller & Jansen op de Haar, 1997; Valiente, Eisenberg, & Fabes, 2004; Decety & Jackson, 2006).

The notion that negative emotions may promote moral development is one that Freud first suggested in his theory of psychoanalytic personality development. Recall from Chapter 1 that Freud argued that a child's *superego,* the part of the personality that represents societal do's and don'ts, is developed through resolution of the *Oedipal conflict.* Children come to identify with their same-sex parent, incorporating that parent's standards of morality in order to avoid unconscious guilt raised by the Oedipal conflict.

Whether or not we accept Freud's account of the Oedipal conflict and the guilt it produces, his theory is consistent with more recent findings. These suggest that preschoolers' attempts to avoid experiencing negative emotions sometimes lead them to act in more moral, helpful ways. For instance, one reason children help others is to avoid the feelings of personal distress that they experience when they are confronted with another person's unhappiness or misfortune (Eisenberg & Fabes, 1991; Valiente et al., 2004; Eisenberg, Valiente, & Champion, 2004).

abstract modeling   the process in which modeling paves the way for the development of more general rules and principles.

empathy   the understanding of what another individual feels.

The roots of empathy grow early, and by the time children reach the age of 2 or 3 are able to offer gifts and spontaneously share toys with other children and adults.

Aggression and Violence in Preschoolers: Sources and Consequences

Four-year-old Duane could not contain his anger and frustration anymore. Although he usually was mild mannered, when Eshu began to tease him about the split in his pants and kept it up for several minutes, Duane finally snapped. Rushing over to Eshu, Duane pushed

aggression intentional injury or harm to another person.

emotional self-regulation the capability to adjust emotions to a desired state and level of intensity.

instrumental aggression aggression motivated by the desire to obtain a concrete goal.

relational aggression nonphysical aggression that is intended to hurt another person's psychological well-being.

mydevelopmentlab

VIDEO CLIP

RELATIONAL AGGRESSION
REACTIVE AGGRESSION

him to the ground and began to hit him with his small, closed fists. Because he was so distraught, Duane's punches were not terribly effective, but they were severe enough to hurt Eshu and bring him to tears before the preschool teachers could intervene.

Aggression among preschoolers is quite common, though attacks such as this are not. The potential for verbal hostility, shoving matches, kicking, and other forms of aggression is present throughout the preschool period, although the degree to which aggression is acted out changes as children become older.

Eshu's taunting was also a form of aggression. **Aggression** is intentional injury or harm to another person. Infants don't act aggressively; it is hard to contend that their behavior is *intended* to hurt others, even if they inadvertently manage to do so. In contrast, by the time they reach preschool age, children demonstrate true aggression.

During the early preschool years, some of the aggression is addressed at attaining a desired goal, such as getting a toy away from another person or using a particular space occupied by another person. Consequently, in some ways the aggression is inadvertent, and minor scuffles may in fact be a typical part of early preschool life. It is the rare child who does not demonstrate at least an occasional act of aggression.

On the other hand, extreme and sustained aggression is a cause of concern. In most children, the amount of aggression declines as they move through the preschool years, as does the frequency and average length of episodes of aggressive behavior (Cummings, Iannotti, & Zahn-Waxler, 1989; Persson, 2005).

The child's personality and social development contribute to this decline in aggression. Throughout the preschool years, children become better at controlling the emotions that they are experiencing. **Emotional self-regulation** is the capability to adjust emotions to a desired state and level of intensity. Starting at age 2, children are able to talk about their feelings, and they engage in strategies to regulate them. As they get older, they develop more effective strategies, learning to better cope with negative emotions. In addition to their increasing self-control, children are also, as we've seen, developing sophisticated social skills. Most learn to use language to express their wishes, and they become increasingly able to negotiate with others (Eisenberg & Zhou, 2000; Philippot & Feldman, 2005; Zeman et al., 2006).

Despite these typical declines in aggression, some children remain aggressive throughout the preschool period. Furthermore, aggression is a relatively stable characteristic: The most aggressive preschoolers tend to be the most aggressive children during the school-age years, and the least aggressive preschoolers tend to be the least aggressive school-age children (Rosen, 1998; Tremblay, 2001; Schaeffer, Petras, & Ialongo, 2003).

Boys typically show higher levels of physical, instrumental aggression than girls. **Instrumental aggression** is aggression motivated by the desire to obtain a concrete goal, such as playing with a desirable toy that another child is playing with.

On the other hand, although girls show lower levels of instrumental aggression, they may be just as aggressive, but in different ways from boys. Girls are more likely to practice **relational aggression,** which is nonphysical aggression that is intended to hurt another person's feelings. Such aggression may be demonstrated through name-calling, withholding friendship, or simply saying mean, hurtful things that make the recipient feel bad (Underwood, 2003; Werner & Crick, 2004; Murray-Close, Ostrov, & Crick, 2007).

The Roots of Aggression. How can we explain the aggression of preschoolers? Some theoreticians suggest that to behave aggressively is an instinct, part and parcel of the human condition. For instance, Freud's psychoanalytic theory suggests that we all are motivated by sexual and aggressive instincts (Freud, 1920). According to ethologist Konrad Lorenz, an expert in animal behavior, animals—including humans—share a fighting instinct that stems

Aggression, both physical and verbal, is present throughout the preschool period.

from primitive urges to preserve territory, maintain a steady supply of food, and weed out weaker animals (Lorenz, 1966, 1974).

Similar arguments are made by evolutionary theorists and *sociobiologists,* scientists who consider the biological roots of social behavior. They argue that aggression leads to increased opportunities to mate, improving the likelihood that one's genes will be passed on to future generations. In addition, aggression may help to strengthen the species and its gene pool as a whole, because the strongest survive. Ultimately, then, aggressive instincts promote the survival of one's genes to pass on to future generations (McKenna, 1983; Reiss, 1984).

Although instinctual explanations of aggression are logical, most developmentalists believe they are not the whole story. Not only do instinctual explanations fail to take into account the increasingly sophisticated cognitive abilities that humans develop as they get older, but they also have relatively little experimental support. Moreover, they provide little guidance in determining when and how children, as well as adults, will behave aggressively, other than noting that aggression is an inevitable part of the human condition. Consequently, developmentalists have turned to other approaches to explain aggression and violence.

Social Learning Approaches to Aggression.   The day after Duane lashed out at Eshu, Lynn, who had watched the entire scene, got into an argument with Ilya. They verbally bickered for a while, and suddenly Lynn balled her hand into a fist and tried to punch Ilya. The preschool teachers were stunned: It was rare for Lynn to get upset, and she had never displayed aggression before.

Is there a connection between the two events? Most of us would answer yes, particularly if we subscribed to the view, suggested by social learning approaches, that aggression is largely a learned behavior. Social learning approaches to aggression contend that aggression is based on observation and prior learning. To understand the causes of aggressive behavior, then, we should look at the system of rewards and punishments that exists in a child's environment.

Social learning approaches to aggression emphasize how social and environmental conditions teach individuals to be aggressive. These ideas grow out of behavioral perspectives, which suggest that aggressive behavior is learned through direct reinforcement. For instance, preschool-age children may learn that they can continue to play with the most desirable toys by aggressively refusing their classmates' requests for sharing. In the parlance of traditional learning theory, they have been reinforced for acting aggressively (by continued use of the toy), and they are more likely to behave aggressively in the future.

But social learning approaches suggest that reinforcement also comes in less direct ways. A good deal of research suggests that exposure to aggressive models leads to increased aggression, particularly if the observers are themselves angered, insulted, or frustrated. For example, Albert Bandura and his colleagues illustrated the power of models in a classic study of preschool-age children (Bandura, Ross, & Ross, 1963). One group of children watched a film of an adult playing aggressively and violently with a Bobo doll (a large, inflated plastic clown designed as a punching bag for children that always returns to an upright position after being pushed down). In comparison, children in another condition watched a film of an adult playing sedately with a set of Tinkertoys (see Figure 8-4). Later, the preschool-age children were allowed to play with a number of toys, which included both the Bobo doll and the Tinkertoys. But first, the children were led to feel frustration by being refused the opportunity to play with a favorite toy.

As predicted by social learning approaches, the preschool-age children modeled the behavior of the adult. Those who had seen the aggressive model playing with the Bobo doll were considerably more aggressive than those who had watched the calm, unaggressive model playing with the Tinkertoys.

Later research has supported this early study, and it is clear that exposure to aggressive models increases the likelihood that aggression on the part of observers will follow. These findings have profound consequences, particularly for children who live in communities in which violence is prevalent. For instance, one survey conducted in a city public hospital found that 1 in 10 children under the age of 6 said they had witnessed a shooting or stabbing. Other research

FIGURE 8-4   MODELING AGGRESSION

This series of photos is from Albert Bandura's classic Bobo doll experiment, designed to illustrate social learning of aggression. The photos clearly show how the adult model's aggressive behavior (in the first row) is imitated by children who had viewed the aggressive behavior (second and third rows).

Social learning explanations of aggression suggest that children's observation of aggression on television can result in actual aggression.

indicates that one-third of the children in some urban neighborhoods have seen a homicide and that two-thirds have seen a serious assault. Such frequent exposure to violence certainly increases the probability that observers will behave aggressively themselves (Osofsky, 1995b; Farver & Frosch, 1996; Farver et al., 1997; Evans, 2004).

Viewing Violence on TV: Does It Matter? Even the majority of preschool-age children who are not witnesses to real-life violence are typically exposed to aggression via the medium of television. Children's television programs actually contain higher levels of violence (69%) than other types of programs (57%). In an average hour, children's programs contain more than twice as many violent incidents than other types of programs (see Figure 8-5; Wilson, 2002).

This high level of televised violence coupled with Bandura and others' research findings on modeling violence raise a significant question: Does viewing aggression increase the likelihood that children (and later adults) will enact actual—and ultimately deadly—aggression? It is hard to answer the question definitively. Although it is clear that laboratory observation of aggression on television leads to higher levels of aggression, evidence showing that real-world viewing of aggression is associated with subsequent aggressive behavior is correlational. (Think, for a moment, of what would be required to conduct a true experiment involving children's viewing habits. It would require that we control children's viewing of television in their homes for extended periods, exposing some to a steady diet of violent shows and others to nonviolent ones—something that most parents would not agree to.)

Despite the fact, then, that the results are primarily correlational, the overwhelming weight of research evidence is clear in suggesting that observation of televised aggression does lead to subsequent aggression. Longitudinal studies have found that children's preferences for violent television shows at age 8 are related to the seriousness of criminal convictions by age 30. Other evidence supports the notion that observation of media violence can lead to a greater readiness

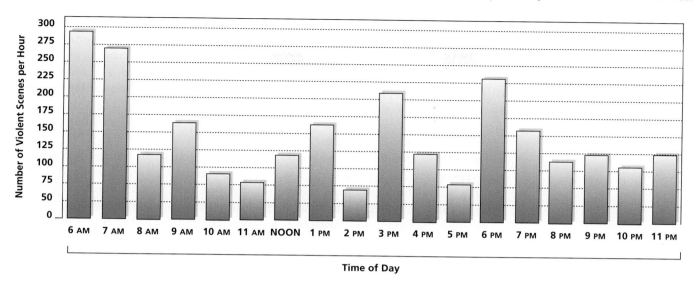

FIGURE 8-5 ACTS OF VIOLENCE

A survey of the violence shown on the major TV networks and several cable channels on one particular weekday found acts of violence during every time period. Do you think depictions of violence on TV should be regulated?

(*Source:* Center for Media and Public Affairs, 1995.)

to act aggressively, bullying, and to an insensitivity to the suffering of victims of violence (Huesmann, Moise-Titus, & Podolski, 2003; Anderson et al., 2003; Slater, Henry, & Swaim, 2003; Ostrov, Gentile, & Crick, 2006).

Television is not the only source of media violence. Many video games contain a significant amount of aggressive behavior, and children are playing such games at high rates. For example, 14% of children age 3 and younger and around 50% of those age 4 to 6 play video games. Because research conducted with adults shows that playing violent video games is associated with behaving aggressively, children who play video games containing violence may be at higher risk for behaving aggressively (Bushman & Anderson, 2001, 2002; Funk, Buchman, & Jenks, 2003; Rideout, Vandewater, & Wartella, 2003; Anderson et al., 2004).

Fortunately, social learning principles that lead preschoolers to learn aggression from television and video games suggest ways to reduce the negative influence of the medium. For instance, children can be explicitly taught to view violence with a more skeptical, critical eye. Being taught that violence is not representative of the real world, that the viewing of violence can affect them negatively, and that they should refrain from imitating the behavior they have seen on television can help children interpret the violent programs differently and be less influenced by them (Farhi, 1995; Persson & Musher-Eizenman, 2003; Donnerstein, 2005).

Furthermore, just as exposure to aggressive models leads to aggression, observation of *non*aggressive models can *reduce* aggression. Preschoolers don't just learn from others how to be aggressive; they can also learn how to avoid confrontation and to control their aggression, as we'll discuss later.

Cognitive Approaches to Aggression: The Thoughts Behind Violence.   Two children, waiting for their turn in a game of kickball, inadvertently knock into one another. One child's reaction is to apologize; the other's is to shove, saying angrily, "Cut it out."

Despite the fact that each child bears the same responsibility for the minor event, very different reactions result. The first child interprets the event as an accident, while the second sees it as a provocation and reacts with aggression.

The cognitive approach to aggression suggests that the key to understanding moral development is to examine preschoolers' interpretations of others' behavior and of the environmental context in which a behavior occurs. According to developmental psychologist Kenneth Dodge and his colleagues, some children are more prone than others to assume that actions are aggressively motivated. They are unable to pay attention to the appropriate cues in a situation and are unable to interpret the behaviors in a given situation accurately. Instead, they assume—often erroneously—that what is happening is related to others' hostility. Subsequently, in deciding how to respond, they base their behavior on their inaccurate interpretation of behavior. In sum, they may behave aggressively in response to a situation that never, in fact, existed (Dodge & Coie, 1987; Dodge & Crick, 1990; Petit & Dodge, 2003).

For example, consider Jake, who is drawing at a table with Gary. Jake reaches over and takes a red crayon that Gary had just decided he was going to use next. Gary is instantly certain that the Jake "knew" that he was going to use the red crayon, and that Jake is taking it just to be mean. With this interpretation in mind, Gary hits Jake for "stealing" his crayon.

Although the cognitive approach to aggression provides a description of the process that leads some children to behave aggressively, it is less successful in explaining how certain children come to be inaccurate perceivers of situations in the first place. Furthermore, it fails to explain why such inaccurate perceivers so readily respond with aggression, and why they assume that aggression is an appropriate and even desirable response.

On the other hand, cognitive approaches to aggression are useful in pointing out a means to reduce aggression: By teaching preschool-age children to be more accurate interpreters of a situation, we can induce them to be less prone to view others' behavior as motivated by hostility, and consequently less likely to respond with aggression themselves. The guidelines in *Becoming an Informed Consumer of Development* are based on the various theoretical perspectives on aggression and morality that we've discussed in this chapter.

Becoming an Informed Consumer of Development

Increasing Moral Behavior and Reducing Aggression in Preschool-Age Children

The numerous points of view on the causes of aggression in preschool children are useful for the various methods for encouraging preschoolers' moral conduct and reducing the incidence of aggression they suggest. Here are some of the most practical and readily accomplished strategies (Goldstein, 1999; Bor & Bor, 2004):

- **Provide opportunities for preschool-age children to observe others acting in a cooperative, helpful, prosocial manner.** Encourage them to interact with peers in joint activities in which they share a common goal. Such cooperative activities can teach the importance and desirability of working with—and helping—others.

- **Do not ignore aggressive behavior.** Parents and teachers should intervene when they see aggression in preschoolers, and send a clear message that aggression is an unacceptable means to resolve conflicts.

- **Help preschoolers devise alternative explanations for others' behavior.** This is particularly important for children who are prone to aggression and who may be apt to view others' conduct as more hostile than it actually is. Parents and teachers should help such children see that the behavior of their peers has several possible interpretations.

- **Monitor preschoolers' television viewing, particularly the violence that they view.** There is good evidence that observation of televised aggression results in subsequent increases in children's levels of aggression. Encourage preschoolers to watch particular shows that are designed, in part, to increase the level of moral conduct, such as *Sesame Street, Dora the Explorer, Mr. Rogers' Neighborhood,* and *Barney.*

- **Help preschoolers understand their feelings.** When children become angry—and all children do—they need to learn how to deal with their feelings in a constructive manner. Tell them *specific* things they can do to improve the situation ("I see you're really angry with Jake for not giving you a turn. Don't hit him, but tell him you want a chance to play with the game.")

- **Explicitly teach reasoning and self-control.** Preschoolers can understand the rudiments of moral reasoning, and they should be reminded why certain behaviors are desirable. For instance, explicitly saying "If you take all the cookies, others will have no dessert" is preferable to saying, "Good children don't eat all the cookies."

Review and Apply

Review

- Piaget believed that preschoolers are in the heteronomous morality stage of moral development, in which rules are seen as invariant and unchangeable.

- Social learning approaches to moral development emphasize the importance of reinforcement for moral actions and the observation of models of moral conduct. Psychoanalytical and other theories focus on children's empathy with others and their wish to help others so they can avoid unpleasant feelings of guilt themselves.

- Aggression typically declines in frequency and duration as children become more able to regulate their emotions and to use language to negotiate disputes.

- Ethologists and sociobiologists regard aggression as an innate human characteristic, while proponents of social learning and cognitive approaches focus on learned aspects of aggression.

Applying Lifespan Development

- If high-prestige models of behavior are particularly effective in influencing moral attitudes and actions, are there implications for individuals in such industries as sports, advertising, and entertainment?

- *From an educator's perspective:* How might a preschool teacher or parent help children notice the violence in the programs they watch and protect them from its effects?

Epilogue

This chapter examined the social and personality development of preschool-age children, including their development of self-concept. The changing social relationships of preschool-age children can be seen in the changing nature of play. We considered typical styles of parental discipline and their effects later in life, and we examined the factors that lead to child abuse. We discussed the development of a moral sense from several developmental perspectives, and we concluded with a discussion of aggression.

Before moving on to the next chapter, take a moment to reread the prologue to this chapter, about Alison Gopnik's 2-year-old son, and answer the following questions:

1. In what ways do the actions of Alison Gopnik's son indicate that he is developing a theory of mind?

2. Is Erikson's framework of moral development helpful in interpreting the boy's actions in this instance? Why or why not?

3. Do you think the boy's reaction would have been different if his father had collapsed on the couch after a bad day instead of his mother? Why or why not? Can you think of a hypothesis to test based on this question? Could an experiment be devised to examine the hypothesis?

4. How might social learning approaches to morality and the concept of empathy explain the son's actions in helping his mother?

5. Can you discuss the boy's actions in terms of emotional self-regulation?

Looking Back

■ **How do preschool-age children develop a concept of themselves?**

- According to Erik Erikson, preschool-age children initially are in the autonomy-versus-shame-and-doubt stage (18 months to 3 years) in which they develop independence and mastery over their physical and social worlds or feel shame, self-doubt, and unhappiness. Later, in the initiative-versus-guilt stage (ages 3 to 6), preschool-age children face conflicts between the desire to act independently and the guilt that comes from the unintended consequences of their actions.

- Preschoolers' self-concepts are formed partly from their own perceptions and estimations of their characteristics, partly from their parents' behavior toward them, and partly from cultural influences.

■ **How do children develop a sense of racial identity and gender?**

- Preschool-age children form racial attitudes largely in response to their environment, including parents and other influences. Gender differences emerge early and conform to social stereotypes about what is appropriate and inappropriate for each sex.

- The strong gender expectations held by preschoolers are explained in different ways by different theorists. Some point to genetic factors as evidence for a biological explanation of gender expectations. Freud's psychoanalytic theories use a framework based on the subconscious. Social learning theorists focus on environmental influences, including parents, teachers, peers, and the media, while cognitive theorists propose that children form gender schemas, cognitive frameworks that organize information that the children gather about gender.

■ **In what sorts of social relationships and play do preschoolers engage?**

- Preschool social relationships begin to encompass genuine friendships, which involve trust and endure over time.

- Older preschoolers engage in more constructive play than functional play. They also engage in more associative and cooperative play than younger preschoolers, who do more parallel and onlooker playing.

■ **What kinds of disciplinary styles do parents employ, and what effects do they have?**

- Disciplinary styles differ both individually and culturally. In the United States and other Western societies, parents' styles tend to be mostly authoritarian, permissive, uninvolved, and authoritative. The authoritative style is regarded as the most effective.

- Children of authoritarian and permissive parents may develop dependency, hostility, and low self-control, while children of uninvolved parents may feel unloved and emotionally detached. Children of authoritative parents tend to be more independent, friendly, self-assertive, and cooperative.

- **What factors contribute to child abuse and neglect?**

  - Child abuse, which may be either physical or psychological, occurs especially in stressful home environments. Firmly held notions regarding family privacy and the use of physical punishment in child rearing contribute to the high rate of abuse in the United States. Moreover, the cycle of violence hypothesis points to the likelihood that persons who were abused as children may turn into abusers as adults.

- **How do children develop a moral sense?**

  - Piaget believed that preschool-age children are in the heteronomous morality stage of moral development, characterized by a belief in external, unchangeable rules of conduct and sure, immediate punishment for all misdeeds.

  - In contrast, social learning approaches to morality emphasize interactions between environment and behavior in moral development, in which models of behavior play an important role.

- Some developmentalists believe that moral behavior is rooted in a child's development of empathy. Other emotions, including the negative emotions of anger and shame, may also promote moral behavior.

- **How does aggression develop in preschool-age children?**

  - Aggression, which involves intentional harm to another person, begins to emerge in the preschool years. As children age and improve their language skills, acts of aggression typically decline in frequency and duration.

  - Some ethologists, such as Konrad Lorenz, believe that aggression is simply a biological fact of human life, a belief held also by many sociobiologists, who focus on competition within species to pass genes on to the next generation.

  - Social learning theorists focus on the role of the environment, including the influence of models and social reinforcement as factors influencing aggressive behavior.

  - The cognitive approach to aggression emphasizes the role of interpretations of the behaviors of others in determining aggressive or nonaggressive responses.

Key Terms and Concepts

psychosocial development (p. 253)
initiative-versus-guilt stage (p. 253)
self-concept (p. 253)
collectivistic orientation (p. 253)
individualistic orientation (p. 253)
race dissonance (p. 254)
identification (p. 256)
gender identity (p. 257)
gender schema (p. 257)
gender constancy (p. 258)

androgynous (p. 258)
functional play (p. 260)
constructive play (p. 260)
parallel play (p. 260)
onlooker play (p. 260)
associative play (p. 260)
cooperative play (p. 260)
authoritarian parents (p. 264)
permissive parents (p. 264)
authoritative parents (p. 264)
uninvolved parents (p. 265)
cycle of violence hypothesis (p. 269)

psychological maltreatment (p. 267)
resilience (p. 270)
moral development (p. 273)
prosocial behavior (p. 274)
abstract modeling (p. 275)
empathy (p. 275)
aggression (p. 276)
emotional self-regulation (p. 276)
instrumental aggression (p. 276)
relational aggression (p. 276)

9 Physical and Cognitive Development in Middle Childhood

Chapter Overview

PHYSICAL DEVELOPMENT

The Growing Body

Motor Development

Health During Middle Childhood

Psychological Disorders

Children with Special Needs

Attention Deficit Hyperactivity Disorder

INTELLECTUAL DEVELOPMENT

Piagetian Approaches to Cognitive Development

Information Processing in Middle Childhood

Vygotsky's Approach to Cognitive Development and Classroom Instruction

Language Development: What Words Mean

Bilingualism: Speaking in Many Tongues

SCHOOLING: THE THREE Rs (AND MORE) OF MIDDLE CHILDHOOD

Schooling Around the World and Across Genders: Who Gets Educated?

Reading: Learning to Decode the Meaning Behind Words

Educational Trends: Beyond the Three Rs

Intelligence: Determining Individual Strengths

Intelligence Benchmarks: Differentiating the Intelligent from the Unintelligent

Below and Above Intelligence Norms: Mental Retardation and the Intellectually Gifted

Prologue: La-Toya Pankey and The Witches

There are few books in La-Toya Pankey's apartment on 102nd Street near Amsterdam Avenue in Manhattan, and even fewer places for an 8-year-old girl to steal away to read them.

There is no desk, no bookshelf, no reading lamp or even a bureau in La-Toya's small room, one of only two bedrooms in the apartment she shares with seven other people: her mother, her five sisters, and her infant brother.

At night, there is little light, save a couple of bare bulbs mounted on the peeling, beige walls. And there are few places to sit, except a lone, wooden chair at a battered kitchen table, which La-Toya must wait her turn to occupy.

Yet there was La-Toya, on a rainy evening earlier this month, leaning against that table and reading aloud, flawlessly, to her mother from the Roald Dahl classic *The Witches*, which she had borrowed from the makeshift library in her third-grade classroom. (Steinberg, 1997, p. B1)

During middle childhood, children's physical, cognitive, and social skills increase to new heights.

It was a significant moment for La-Toya. It marked a shift from the first-grade-level books that she had previously chosen to read to a far more challenging one, written at a grade level 2 years higher than her own.

Middle childhood is characterized by moments such as these, as children's physical, cognitive, and social skills ascend to new heights. Beginning at age 6 and continuing to the start of adolescence at around age 12, the period of middle childhood is often referred to as the "school years" because it marks the beginning of formal education for most children. Sometimes the physical and cognitive growth that occurs during middle childhood is gradual; other times it is sudden; but always it is remarkable.

We begin our consideration of middle childhood by examining physical and motor development. We discuss how children's bodies change and the twin problems of malnutrition and—the other side of the coin—childhood obesity. We also consider the development of children with special needs.

Next, we turn to the development of children's cognitive abilities in middle childhood. We examine several approaches put forward to describe and explain cognitive development, including Piagetian and information processing theories and the important ideas of Vygotsky. We look at language development and the questions surrounding bilingualism—an increasingly pressing social policy issue in the United States.

Finally, we consider several issues involving schooling. After discussing the scope of education throughout the world, we examine the critical skill of reading and the nature of multicultural education. The chapter ends with a discussion of intelligence, a characteristic closely tied to school success. We look at the nature of IQ tests and at the education of children who are either significantly below or above the intellectual norm.

After reading this chapter, you will be able to answer these questions:

- In what ways do children grow during the school years, and what factors influence their growth?

- What are the main health concerns of school-age children?

- What sorts of special needs may become apparent in children at this age, and how can they be met?

- In what ways do children develop cognitively during these years, according to major theoretical approaches?

- How does language develop during the middle childhood period?

- What are some trends in schooling today?

- How can intelligence be measured, and how are exceptional children educated?

Physical Development

Cinderella, dressed in yella, went upstairs to kiss her fellah. But she made a mistake and she kissed a snake. How many doctors did it take? One, two, . . .

While the other girls chanted the classic jump-rope rhyme, Kat proudly displayed her newly developed ability to jump backwards. In second grade, Kat was starting to get quite good at jumping rope. In first grade, she simply had not been able to master it. But over the summer, she had spent many hours practicing, and now that practice seemed to be paying off.

As Kat is gleefully experiencing, middle childhood is a time when children make great physical strides, mastering all kinds of new skills as they grow bigger and stronger. How does this progress occur? We'll first consider typical physical growth during middle childhood and then turn our attention to a look at exceptional children.

The Growing Body

Slow but steady. If three words could characterize the nature of growth during middle childhood, it would be these. Especially when compared to the swift growth during the first 5 years of life and the remarkable growth spurt characteristic of adolescence, middle childhood is relatively tranquil. On the other hand, the body has not shifted into neutral. Physical growth continues, although at a more stately pace than it did during the preschool years.

Variations of six inches in height between children of the same age are not unusual and well within normal ranges.

Height and Weight Changes.   While they are in elementary school, children in the United States grow, on average, 2 to 3 inches a year. By the age of 11, the average height for girls is 4 feet, 10 inches and the average height for boys is slightly shorter at 4 feet, 9 1/2 inches. This is the only time during the life span when girls are, on average, taller than boys. This height difference reflects the slightly more rapid physical development of girls, who start their adolescent growth spurt around the age of 10.

Weight gain follows a similar pattern. During middle childhood, both boys and girls gain around 5 to 7 pounds a year. Weight is also redistributed. As the rounded look of "baby fat" disappears, children's bodies become more muscular and their strength increases.

These average height and weight increases disguise significant individual differences, as anyone who has seen a line of fourth graders walking down a school corridor has doubtless noticed. It is not unusual to see children of the same age who are 6 or 7 inches apart in height.

Cultural Patterns of Growth.   Most children in North America receive sufficient nutrients to grow to their full potential. In other parts of the world, however, inadequate nutrition and disease take their toll, producing children who are shorter and who weigh less than they would if they had sufficient nutrients. The discrepancies can be dramatic: Children in poorer areas of cities such as Calcutta, Hong Kong, and Rio de Janeiro are smaller than their counterparts in affluent areas of the same cities.

In the United States, most variations in height and weight are the result of different people's unique genetic inheritance, including genetic factors relating to racial and ethnic background. For instance, children from Asian and Oceanic Pacific backgrounds tend to be shorter, on average, than those with northern and central European heritages. In addition, the rate of growth during childhood is generally more rapid for blacks than for whites (Meredith, 1971; Deurenberg, Deurenberg-Yap, Guricci, 2002; Deurenberg et al., 2003).

Of course, even within particular racial and ethnic groups, there is significant variation between individuals. Moreover, we cannot attribute racial and ethnic differences solely to genetic factors, because dietary customs as well as possible variations in levels of affluence also may contribute to the differences. In addition, severe stress—brought on by factors such as parental conflict or alcoholism—can affect the functioning of the pituitary gland, thereby affecting growth (Powell, Brasel, & Blizzard, 1967; Koska et al., 2002).

Promoting Growth with Hormones: Should Short Children Be Made to Grow?
Being tall is considered an advantage in most of U.S. society. Because of this cultural preference, parents sometimes worry about their children's growth if their children are short. To the manufacturers of Protropin, an artificial human growth hormone that can make short children taller, there's a simple solution: Administer the drug to make the children grow taller than they naturally would (Kolata, 1994; Sandberg & Voss, 2002; Hall, 2005).

Is being short so much of a social disadvantage that children should receive artificial growth hormones to make them taller?

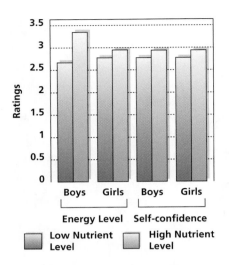

FIGURE 9-1   NUTRITIONAL BENEFITS

Children who received higher levels of nutrients had more energy and felt more self-confident than those whose nutritional intake was lower. What policy implications does this finding suggest?

(*Source:* Adapted from Barrett & Radke-Yarrow, 1985.)

Should children be given such drugs? The question is a relatively new one: Artificial hormones to promote growth have become available only in the last two decades. Although tens of thousands of children who have insufficient natural growth hormone are taking such drugs, some observers question whether shortness is a serious enough problem to warrant the use of the drug. Certainly, one can function well in society without being tall. Furthermore, the drug is costly and has potentially dangerous side effects. In some cases, the drug may lead to the premature onset of puberty, which may—ironically—restrict later growth.

On the other hand, there is no denying that artificial growth hormones are effective in increasing children's height, in some cases adding well over a foot in height to extremely short children, placing them within normal height ranges. Ultimately, until long-term studies of the safety of such treatments are completed, parents and medical personnel must carefully weigh the pros and cons before administering the drug to their children (Gohlke & Stanhope, 2002; Heyman et al., 2003; Ogilvy-Stuart & Gleeson, 2004).

Nutrition.   As we discussed earlier, there is a rather obvious relationship between size and nutrition. But size isn't the only area affected by children's levels of nutrition. For instance, longitudinal studies over many years in Guatemalan villages show that children's nutritional backgrounds are related to several dimensions of social and emotional functioning at school age. Children who had received more nutrients were more involved with their peers, showed more positive emotion, and had less anxiety than their peers who had received less adequate nutrition. Better nutrition also made children more eager to explore new environments, more persistent in frustrating situations, and more alert at some types of activities, and these children displayed generally higher energy levels and more self-confidence (Barrett & Frank, 1987; see Figure 9-1).

Nutrition is also linked to cognitive performance. For instance, in one study, children in Kenya who were well nourished performed better on a test of verbal abilities and on other cognitive measures than those who had mild to moderate undernutrition. Other research suggests that malnutrition may influence cognitive development by dampening children's curiosity, responsiveness, and motivation to learn (McDonald et al., 1994; Brown & Pollitt, 1996; Wachs, 2002; Grigorenko, 2003).

Although undernutrition and malnutrition clearly lead to physical, social, and cognitive difficulties, in some cases *over*nutrition—the intake by a child of too many calories—presents problems of its own, particularly when it leads to childhood obesity.

Inadequate nutrition and disease affect growth significantly. Children in poorer areas of cities such as Calcutta, Hong Kong, and Rio de Janeiro are smaller than their counterparts in affluent areas of the same cities.

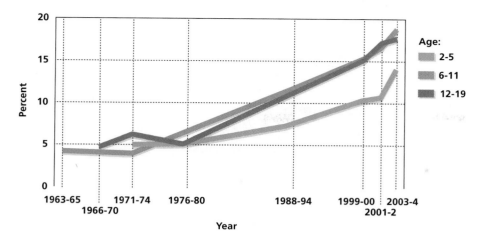

Note: Overweight is defined as BMI > = gender-and weight-specific 95th percentile from the 2000CDC Growth Charts.

FIGURE 9-2 OBESITY IN CHILDREN

Obesity in children ages 6 to 12 has risen dramatically over the past four decades by more than three-fold.

(*Source:* National Center for Health Statistics, 2001.)

Childhood Obesity. When Ruthellen's mother asks if she would like a piece of bread with her meal, Ruthellen replies that she better not—she thinks that she may be getting fat. Ruthellen, who is of normal weight and height, is 6 years old.

Although height can be of concern to both children and parents during middle childhood, maintaining the appropriate weight is an even greater worry for some. In fact, concern about weight can border on an obsession, particularly among girls. For instance, many 6-year-old girls worry about becoming "fat," and some 40% of 9- and 10-year-olds are trying to lose weight. Why? Their concern is most often the result of the U.S. preoccupation with being slim, which permeates every sector of society (Schreiber et al., 1996; Greenwood & Pietromonaco, 2004).

In spite of this widely held view that thinness is a virtue, increasing numbers of children are becoming obese. *Obesity* is defined as body weight that is more than 20% above the average for a person of a given age and height. By this definition, 15% of U.S. children are obese—a proportion that has tripled since the 1960s (see Figure 9-2; Brownlee, 2002; Dietz, 2004; Mann, 2005).

The costs of childhood obesity last a lifetime. Children who are obese are more likely to be overweight as adults, and have a greater risk of heart disease, diabetes, and other diseases. In fact, some scientists believe that an epidemic of obesity may be leading to a decline in life span in the United States (Freedman et al., 2004; Olshansky et al, 2005; Krishnamoorthy, Hart, & Jelalian, 2006).

Obesity is caused by a combination of genetic and social characteristics as well as diet. Particular inherited genes are related to obesity and predispose certain children to be overweight. For example, adopted children tend to have weights that are more similar to those of their birth parents than to those of their adoptive parents (Zhang et al., 1994; Whitaker et al., 1997).

Social factors also enter into children's weight problems. Children need to learn to control their eating themselves. Parents who are particularly controlling and directive regarding their children's eating may produce children who lack internal controls to regulate their own food intake (Johnson & Birch, 1994; Faith, Johnson, & Allison, 1997; Wardle, Guthrie, & Sanderson, 2001).

Of course, poor diets also contribute to obesity. Despite their knowledge that certain foods are necessary for a balanced, nutritious diet, many parents provide their children with too few fruits and vegetables and

"Remember when we used to have to fatten the kids up first?"

MyPyramid for Kids reminds you to be physically active every day, or most days, and to make healthy food choices. Every part of the new symbol has a message for you. Can you figure it out?

Be Physically Active Every Day
The person climbing the stairs reminds you to do something active every day, like running, walking the dog, playing, swimming, biking, or climbing lots of stairs.

Eat More From Some Food Groups Than Others
Did you notice that some of the color stripes are wider than others? The different sizes remind you to choose more foods from the food groups with the widest stripes.

Choose Healthier Foods From Each Group
Why are the colored stripes wider at the bottom of the pyramid? Every food group has foods that you should eat more often than others; these foods are at the bottom of the pyramid.

Every Color Every Day
The colors orange, green, red, yellow, blue, and purple represent the five different food groups plus oils. Remember to eat foods from all food groups every day.

Grains Vegetables Fruits Oils Milk Meat & Beans

Make Choices That Are Right for You
MyPyramid.gov is a Web site that will give everyone in the family personal ideas on how to eat better and exercise more.

Take One Step at a Time
You do not need to change overnight what you eat and how you exercise. Just start with one new, good thing, and add a new one every day.

MyPyramid.gov
STEPS TO A HEALTHIER YOU

U.S. Department of Agriculture Food and Nutrition Service September 2005 FNS-388
USDA is an equal opportunity provider and employer.

FIGURE 9-3   BALANCED DIET?

Recent studies have found that the diet of children is almost the opposite of that recommended by the U.S. Department of Agriculture, a situation which can lead to an increase in obesity. The typical 10-year-old is 10 pounds heavier than a decade ago.
(*Source:* USDA, 1999; NPD Group, 2004.)

more fats and sweets than recommended (see Figure 9-3). School lunch programs have sometimes contributed to the problem by failing to provide nutritious options.

Given how energetic children in middle childhood can be, it is surprising that a major factor in childhood obesity is a lack of exercise. School-age children, by and large, tend to engage in relatively little exercise and are not particularly fit. For instance, around 40% of boys age 6 to 12 are unable to do more than one pull-up, and a quarter can't do any. Furthermore, children have shown little or no improvement in the amount of exercise they get, despite national efforts to increase the level of fitness of school-age children, in part because many schools have reduced the time available for recess and gym classes. From the ages of 6 to 18, boys decrease their physical activity by 24% and girls by 36% (Moore, Gao, & Bradlee, 2003; Sallis & Glanz, 2006; Weiss & Raz, 2006).

Why, when our visions of childhood include children running happily on school playgrounds, playing sports, and chasing one another in games of tag, is the actual level of exercise relatively low? One answer is that many kids are inside their homes, watching television and computer screens. Such sedentary activities not only keep children from exercising, but they often snack while viewing TV or surfing the Web (Gable & Lutz, 2000; Giammattei et al., 2003; Rideout, Vandewater, & Wartella, 2003; Tartamella, Herscher, & Woolston, 2005; Anderson & Butcher, 2006; Taveras et al., 2006).

Motor Development

Diet, genetics, and a lack of exercise all contribute to the rapidly growing rate of obesity in the United States.

The fact that the fitness level of school-age children is not as high as we would desire does not mean that such children are physically incapable. In fact, even without regular exercise, children's gross and fine motor skills develop substantially over the course of the school years.

Gross Motor Skills. One important improvement in gross motor skills is in the realm of muscle coordination. When watching a softball player pitch a ball past a batter to her catcher, a runner reach the finish line in a race, or Kat, the jump-roper described earlier in the chapter, we are struck by the huge strides that these children have made since the more awkward days of preschool.

During middle childhood, children master many types of skills that earlier they could not perform well. For instance, most school-age children can readily learn to ride a bike, ice skate, swim, and skip rope (Cratty, 1986; see Figure 9-4).

Do boys and girls differ in their motor skills? Years ago developmentalists concluded that gender differences in gross motor skills became increasingly pronounced during these years, with boys outperforming girls (Espenschade, 1960). However, when comparisons are made between boys and girls who regularly take part in similar activities—such as softball—gender variations in gross motor skills are minimal (Hall & Lee, 1984; Jurimae & Saar, 2003).

Why the change? Expectations probably played a role. Society did not expect girls to be highly physically active and told girls that they would do worse than boys in sports, and the girls' performance reflected that message.

Today, however, society's message has changed, at least officially. For instance, the American Academy of Pediatrics suggests that boys and girls should engage in the same sports and games, and that they can do so together in mixed-gender groups. There is no reason to separate the sexes in physical exercise and sports until puberty, when the smaller size of females begins to make them more susceptible to injury in contact sports (Raudsepp & Liblik, 2002; Vilhjalmsson & Kristjansdottir, 2003; American Academy of Pediatrics, 1989, 2004).

During middle childhood, children master many types of skills that earlier they could not perform well, such as riding a bike, ice skating, swimming, and skipping rope. Is this the same for children of other cultures?

6 Years	7 Years	8 Years	9 Years	10 Years	11 Years	12 Years
Girls superior in accuracy of movement; boys superior in more forceful, less complex acts.	Can balance on one foot with eyes closed.	Can grip objects with 12 pounds of pressure.	Girls can jump vertically 8.5 inches over their standing height plus reach; boys can jump vertically 10 inches.	Can judge and intercept directions of small balls thrown from a distance.	Boys can achieve standing broad jump of 5 feet; girls can achieve standing broad jump of 4.5 feet.	Can achieve high jump of 3 feet.
Can throw with the proper weight shift and step.	Can walk on a 2-inch-wide balance beam without falling off.	Can engage in alternate rhythmical hopping in a 2-2, 2-3, or 3-3 pattern.	Boys can run 16.6 feet per second and throw a small ball 41 feet; girls can run 16 feet per second and throw a small ball 41 feet.	Both girls and boys can run 17 feet per second.		
Acquire the ability to skip.	Can hop and jump accurately into small squares (hopscotch).	Girls can throw a small ball 33 feet; boys can throw a small ball 59 feet.				
	Can correctly execute a jumping-jack exercise.	The number of games participated in by both sexes is the greatest at this age.				

FIGURE 9-4 **GROSS MOTOR SKILLS**

Gross motor skills developed by children between the ages of 6 and 12 years.
(*Source:* Adapted from Cratty, 1979, p. 222.)

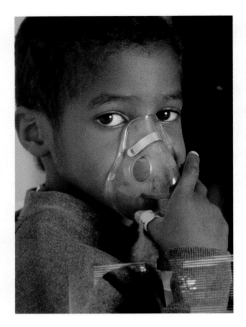

The incidence of asthma, a chronic respiratory condition, has increased dramatically over the last several decades.

Fine Motor Skills.   Typing at a computer keyboard. Writing in cursive with pen and pencil. Drawing detailed pictures. These are just some of the accomplishments that depend on improvements in fine motor coordination that occur during early and middle childhood. Six- and 7-year-olds are able to tie their shoes and fasten buttons; by age 8, they can use each hand independently; and by 11 and 12, they can manipulate objects with almost as much capability as they will show in adulthood.

One of the reasons for advances in fine motor skills is that the amount of myelin in the brain increases significantly between the ages of 6 and 8 (Lecours, 1982). *Myelin* provides protective insulation that surrounds parts of nerve cells. Because increased levels of myelin raise the speed at which electrical impulses travel between neurons, messages can reach muscles more rapidly and control them better.

Health During Middle Childhood

Imani was miserable. Her nose was running, her lips were chapped, and her throat was sore. Although she had been able to stay home from school and spend the day watching old reruns on TV, she still felt that she was suffering mightily.

Despite her misery, Imani's situation is not so bad. She'll get over the cold in a few days and be no worse for having experienced it. In fact, she may be a little *better* off, for she is now immune to the specific cold germs that made her ill in the first place.

Imani's cold may end up being the most serious illness that she gets during middle childhood. For most children, this is a period of robust health, and most of the ailments they do contract tend to be mild and brief. Routine immunizations during childhood have produced a considerably lower incidence of the life-threatening illnesses that 50 years ago claimed the lives of a significant number of children.

However, illness is not uncommon. For instance, more than 90% of children are likely to have at least one serious medical condition over the 6-year period of middle childhood, according to the results of one large survey. And although most children have short-term illnesses, about one in nine has a chronic, persistent condition, such as repeated migraine headaches. And some illnesses are actually becoming more prevalent (Dey & Bloom, 2005).

asthma   a chronic condition characterized by periodic attacks of wheezing, coughing, and shortness of breath.

Asthma.   Asthma is among the diseases that have shown a significant increase in prevalence over the last several decades. **Asthma** is a chronic condition characterized by periodic attacks of wheezing, coughing, and shortness of breath. More than 15 million U.S. children suffer from the disorder, and worldwide the number is more than 150 million (see Figure 9-5; Doyle, 2000; Johnson, 2003; Dey & Bloom, 2005).

Asthma occurs when the airways leading to the lungs constrict, partially blocking the passage of oxygen. Because the airways are obstructed, more effort is needed to push air through them, making breathing more difficult. As air is forced through the obstructed airways, it makes the whistling sound called wheezing.

Asthma attacks can be frightening, both for children and their parents. The anxiety and agitation produced by their breathing difficulties may actually make the attack worse. In some cases, breathing becomes so difficult that further physical symptoms develop, including sweating, an increased heart rate, and—in the most severe cases—a blueness in the face and lips due to a lack of oxygen (Israel, 2005).

One of the most puzzling questions about asthma is why more and more children have been suffering from it over the last two decades. Some researchers suggest that increasing air

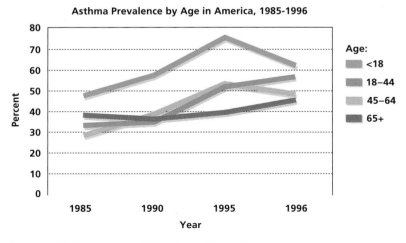

Asthma Prevalence by Age in America, 1985-1996

Age:
- ■ <18
- ■ 18–44
- ■ 45–64
- ■ 65+

FIGURE 9-5   RISING RATES OF ASTHMA

Since the early 1980s, the rate of asthma among children has almost doubled. A number of factors explain the rise, including increased air pollution and better means of detecting the disease.

(*Source:* Centers for Disease Control, 1999.)

pollution has led to the rise; others believe that cases of asthma that might have been missed in the past are simply being identified more accurately. Still others have suggested that exposure to "asthma triggers," such as dust, may be increasing, because new buildings are more weather-proof—and therefore less drafty—than old ones, and consequently the flow of air within them is more restricted (Poulain et al., 2006).

Finally, poverty may play an indirect role. Children living in poverty have a higher incidence of asthma than other children, probably due to poorer medical care and less sanitary living conditions. For instance, poor youngsters are more likely than more affluent ones to be exposed to triggering factors that are associated with asthma, such as dust mites, cockroach feces and body parts, and rodent feces and urine (Nossiter, 1995; Johnson, 2003; Pearlman et al., 2006).

Although asthma and other illnesses are threats to children's well-being during middle childhood, the greater potential risk comes from the possibility of injury. During this period, children are more likely to suffer a life-threatening injury from an accident than a severe illness, as we discuss next (Woolf & Lesperance, 2003).

Accidents.   The increasing independence and mobility of school-age children lead to new safety issues. Between the ages of 5 and 14, the rate of injury for children increases. Boys are more apt to be injured than girls, probably because their overall level of physical activity is greater (Noonan, 2003a).

The increased mobility of school-age children is a source of several kinds of accidents. For instance, children who regularly walk to school on their own, many traveling such a distance alone for the first time in their lives, face the risk of being hit by cars and trucks. Because of their lack of experience, they may misjudge distances when calculating just how far they are from an oncoming vehicle. Furthermore, bicycle accidents pose an increasing risk, particularly as children more frequently venture out onto busy roads (Thomson et al., 1998).

The most frequent source of injury to children is automobile accidents. Auto crashes annually kill 5 out of every 100,000 children between the ages 5 and 9. Fires and burns, drowning, and gun-related deaths follow in frequency (Field & Behrman, 2002; Schiller & Bernadel, 2004).

Two ways to reduce auto and bicycle injuries are to use seat belts consistently inside the car and to wear appropriate protective gear outside. Bicycle helmets have significantly reduced head injuries, and in many localities their use is mandatory. Similar protection is available for other activities; for example, knee and elbow pads have proven to be important sources of injury reduction for roller-blading and skateboarding (American Academy of Pediatrics Committee on Accident and Poison Prevention, 1990; Lee, Schofer, & Koppelman, 2005).

Safety in Cyberspace.   The newest threat to the safety of school-age children comes from a source that just a decade ago was unheard of: the Internet and the World Wide Web. Although claims that cyberspace is overrun with pornography and child molesters are exaggerated—and the benefits of going online are many—it is true that cyberspace makes available material that many parents find objectionable (Brant, 2003).

Although computer software developers have devised programs that will block particular computer sites, most experts feel that the most reliable safeguard is close supervision by parents. According to the National Center for Missing and Exploited Children (2002), a nonprofit organization that works with the U.S. Department of Justice, parents should warn their children never to provide personal information, such as home addresses or telephone numbers, to people on public computer "bulletin boards" or in chat rooms. In addition, children should not be allowed to hold face-to-face meetings with people they meet via computer, at least not without a parent present.

We do not yet have statistics that provide a true sense of the risk presented by exposure to cyberspace. But certainly a potential hazard exists, and parents must offer their children guidance in the use of this computer resource. It would be erroneous to think that just because children are in the supposed safety of their own rooms, logged on to home computers, they are truly safe.

Psychological Disorders

Tyler Whitley, 7, is 4 feet 4 inches and weighs 74 pounds. He has blond hair, blue eyes, a generous spirit—and bipolar disorder, a serious mental illness. Highly irritable and angry one minute, he'll be laughing hysterically the next. Grand illusions kick in: he can leap to the ground from the top of a tall tree or jump from a grocery cart and fly. And then there are the heart-wrenching bouts of depression when Tyler tells his parents, "I should never have been born. I need to go to heaven so people can be happy." (Kalb, 2003, p. 68)

Bipolar disorder such as Tyler's is diagnosed when a person cycles back and forth between two emotional states: unrealistically high spirits and energy at one extreme, and depression on the other. For years most people neglected the symptoms of such psychological disorders in children, and even today parents and teachers may overlook their presence. Yet it is a common problem: one in five children and adolescents has a psychological disorder that produces at least some impairment. For example, about 5% of preteens suffer from childhood depression, and 13% of children between 9 and 17 experience an anxiety disorder (Kalb, 2003; Beardslee & Goldman, 2003; Tolan & Dodge, 2005; Cicchetti & Cohen, 2006).

In part, the neglect of children's psychological disorders occurs because children's symptoms are not entirely consistent with the ways adults express similar disorders. Even when childhood psychological disorders are diagnosed, the correct treatment is not always apparent. For example, the use of antidepressant drugs has become a popular treatment for a variety of childhood psychological disorders, including depression and anxiety. In 2002, more than 10 million prescriptions were written for children under the age of 18. Surprisingly, though, antidepressant drugs have never been approved by governmental regulators for use with children. Still, because the drugs have received approval for adult use, it is perfectly legal for physicians to write prescriptions for children (Goode, 2004).

Advocates for the increased use of antidepressants such as Prozac, Zoloft, Paxil, and Wellbutrin for children suggest that depression and other psychological disorders can be treated quite successfully using drug therapies. In many cases, more traditional nondrug therapies that largely employ verbal methods simply are ineffective. In such cases, drugs can provide the only form of relief. Furthermore, at least one clinical test has shown that the drugs are effective with children (Emslie et al., 1997; Garland, 2004).

Critics, however, contend that there is little evidence for the long-term effectiveness of antidepressants with children. Even worse, no one knows the consequences of the use of antidepressants on the developing brains of children, nor the long-term consequences more generally. Little is known about the correct dosages for children of given ages or sizes. Furthermore, some observers suggest that the use of special children's versions of the drugs, in orange- or mint-flavored syrups, might lead to overdoses or perhaps eventually encourage the use of illegal drugs (Strauch, 1997; Goode, 2004).

Finally, there is some evidence linking the use of antidepressant medication with an increased risk of suicide. Although the link has not been firmly established, the U.S. Federal Drug Administration issued a warning about the use of a class of antidepressants known as SSRIs in 2004. Some experts have urged that the use of these antidepressants in children and adolescents be banned completely (Satel, 2004; Vedantam, 2004).

Although the use of antidepressant drugs to treat children is controversial, what is clear is that childhood depression and other psychological disorders remain a significant problem for many children. Childhood psychological disorders must not be ignored. Not only are the disorders disruptive during childhood, but those who suffer from psychological problems as children are at risk for future disorders during adulthood (Marmer, Neylan, & Schoenfeld, 2002; Marx & Pennington, 2003; Wals & Verhulst, 2005).

As we'll see next, adults also need to pay attention to other, ongoing special needs that affect many school-age children.

Children with Special Needs

visual impairment a difficulty in seeing that may include blindness or partial sightedness.

auditory impairment a special need that involves the loss of hearing or some aspect of hearing.

Andrew Mertz was a very unhappy little boy. . . . Third grade was a disaster, the culmi-nation of a crisis that had been building since he entered kindergarten in suburban Maryland. He couldn't learn to read, and he hated school. "He would throw temper tantrums in the morning because he didn't want to go," recalls his mother, Suzanne. The year before, with much prodding from Suzanne, the school had authorized diagnostic tests for Andrew. The results revealed a host of brain processing problems that explained why he kept mixing up letters and sounds. Andrew's problem now had a label—he was officially classified as learning disabled—and he was legally entitled to help. (Wingert & Kantrowitz, 1997)

Andrew joined millions of other children who are classified as learning disabled, one of several types of special needs that children can have. Although every child has different specific capa-bilities, children with *special needs* differ significantly from typical children in terms of physi-cal attributes or learning abilities. Furthermore, their needs present major challenges for both care providers and teachers.

We turn now to the most prevalent exceptionalities that affect children of normal intelli-gence: sensory difficulties, learning disabilities, and attention deficit disorders. (We will con-sider the special needs of children who are significantly below and above average in intelligence later in the chapter.)

Sensory Difficulties: Visual, Auditory, and Speech Problems.   Anyone who has tem-porarily lost his or her eyeglasses or a contact lens has had a glimpse of how difficult even rudi-mentary, everyday tasks must be for those with sensory impairments. To function with less than typical vision, hearing, or speech can be a tremendous challenge.

Visual impairment can be considered in both a legal and an educational sense. The defini-tion of legal impairment is quite straightforward: *Blindness* is visual acuity of less than 20/200 after correction (meaning the inability to see even at 20 feet what a typical person can see at 200 feet), while *partial sightedness* is visual acuity of less than 20/70 after correction.

Even if a person is not so impaired as to be legally blind, his or her visual problems may still seriously affect schoolwork. For one thing, the legal criterion pertains solely to distance vision, while most educational tasks require close-up vision. In addition, the legal definition does not consider abilities in the perception of color, depth, and light—all of which might influence a student's educational success. About one student in a thousand requires special education ser-vices relating to a visual impairment.

Most severe visual problems are identified fairly early, but it sometimes happens that an impairment goes undetected. Visual problems can also emerge gradually as children develop physiologically and changes occur in the visual apparatus of the eye. Parents and teachers need to be aware of the signals of visual problems in children. Frequent eye irritation (redness, sties, or infection), continual blinking and facial contortions when reading, holding reading material unusually close to the face, difficulty in writing, and frequent headaches, dizziness, or burning eyes are some of the signs of visual problems.

Auditory impairments can also cause academic problems, and they can produce social difficulties as well, since considerable peer interaction takes place through informal conversation. Hearing loss, which affects some 1% to 2% of the school-age population, is not simply a matter of not hearing enough. Rather, auditory problems can vary along a number of dimensions (Yoshinaga-Itano, 2003; Smith, Bale, & White, 2005).

In some cases of hearing loss, the child's hearing is impaired at only a lim-ited range of frequencies, or pitches. For example, the loss may be great at pitches in the nor-mal speech range yet quite minor in other frequencies, such as those of very high or low

Auditory impairments can produce both academic and social difficulties, and they may lead to speech difficulties.

speech impairment   speech that deviates so much from the speech of others that it calls attention to itself, interferes with communication, or produces maladjustment in the speaker.

stuttering   substantial disruption in the rhythm and fluency of speech; the most common speech impairment.

learning disabilities   difficulties in the acquisition and use of listening, speaking, reading, writing, reasoning, or mathematical abilities.

sounds. A child with this kind of loss may require different levels of amplification at different frequencies; a hearing aid that indiscriminately amplifies all frequencies equally may be ineffective because it will amplify the sounds the person can hear to an uncomfortable degree.

How a child adapts to this impairment depends on the age at which the hearing loss begins. If the loss of hearing occurs in infancy, the effects will probably be much more severe than if it occurs after the age of 3. Children who have had little or no exposure to the sound of language are unable to understand or produce oral language themselves. On the other hand, loss of hearing after a child has learned language will not have serious consequences on subsequent linguistic development.

Severe and early loss of hearing is also associated with difficulties in abstract thinking. Because children with hearing impairment may have limited exposure to language, they may have more trouble mastering abstract concepts that can be understood fully only through the use of language than concrete concepts that can be illustrated visually. For example, it is difficult to explain the concept of "freedom" or "soul" without use of language (Butler & Silliman, 2002; Marschark, Spencer, & Newsom, 2003).

Auditory difficulties are sometimes accompanied by speech impairments, one of the most public types of exceptionality: Every time the child speaks aloud, the impairment is obvious to listeners. In fact, the definition of **speech impairment** suggests that speech is impaired when it deviates so much from the speech of others that it calls attention to itself, interferes with communication, or produces maladjustment in the speaker. In other words, if a child's speech sounds impaired, it probably is. Speech impairments are present in around 3% to 5% of the school-age population (Bishop & Leonard, 2001).

Stuttering, which involves a substantial disruption in the rhythm and fluency of speech, is the most common speech impairment. Despite a great deal of research, no specific cause has been identified. Occasional stuttering is not unusual in young children—and occasionally occurs in normal adults—but chronic stuttering can be a severe problem. Not only does stuttering hinder communication, but it can produce embarrassment and stress in children, who may become inhibited from conversing with others and speaking aloud in class (Whaley & Parker, 2000; Altholz & Golensky, 2004).

Parents and teachers can adopt several strategies for dealing with stuttering. For starters, attention should not be drawn to the stuttering, and children should be given sufficient time to finish what they begin to say, no matter how protracted the statement becomes. It does not help stutterers to finish their sentences for them or otherwise correct their speech (Ryan, 2001).

Learning Disabilities: Discrepancies Between Achievement and Capacity to Learn.   Like Andrew Mertz, who was described at the beginning of this section, some 1 in 10 school-age children are labeled as having learning disabilities. **Learning disabilities** are characterized by difficulties in the acquisition and use of listening, speaking, reading, writing, reasoning, or mathematical abilities. A somewhat ill-defined, grab-bag category, learning disabilities are diagnosed when there is a discrepancy between children's actual academic performance and their apparent potential to learn (Lerner, 2002; Bos & Vaughn, 2005).

Such a broad definition encompasses a wide and extremely varied range of difficulties. For instance, some children suffer from *dyslexia*, a reading disability that can result in the misperception of letters during reading and writing, unusual difficulty in sounding out letters, confusion between left and right, and difficulties in spelling. Although dyslexia is not fully understood, one likely explanation for the disorder is a problem in the part of the brain responsible for breaking words into the sound elements that make up language (Paulesu et al., 2001; McGough, 2003; Lachmann et al., 2005).

The causes of learning disabilities in general are not well understood. Although they are generally attributed to some form of brain dysfunction, probably due to genetic factors, some experts suggest that they are produced by such environmental causes as poor early nutrition or allergies (Shaywitz, 2004).

Attention Deficit Hyperactivity Disorder

Dusty Nash, an angelic-looking blond child of 7, awoke at five one recent morning in his Chicago home and proceeded to throw a fit. He wailed. He kicked. Every muscle in his 50-pound body flew in furious motion. Finally, after about 30 minutes, Dusty pulled himself together sufficiently to head downstairs for breakfast. While his mother bustled about the kitchen, the hyperkinetic child pulled a box of Kix cereal from the cupboard and sat on a chair.

But sitting still was not in the cards this morning. After grabbing some cereal with his hands, he began kicking the box, scattering little round corn puffs across the room. Next he turned his attention to the TV set, or rather, the table supporting it. The table was covered with checkerboard Con-Tact paper, and Dusty began peeling it off. Then he became intrigued with the spilled cereal and started stomping it to bits. At this point his mother interceded. In a firm but calm voice she told her son to get the stand-up dust pan and broom and clean up the mess. Dusty got out the dust pan but forgot the rest of the order. Within seconds he was dismantling the plastic dust pan, piece by piece. His next project: grabbing three rolls of toilet paper from the bathroom and unraveling them around the house.

It was only 7:30 A.M. (Wallis, 1994, p. 43)

Seven-year-old Dusty Nash's high energy and low attention span is due to attention deficit hyperactivity disorder, which occurs in 3 to 5 % of the school-age population.

Dusty suffers from a disorder that no one had heard of just a few decades ago—attention deficit hyperactivity disorder. **Attention deficit hyperactivity disorder,** or **ADHD,** is marked by inattention, impulsiveness, a low tolerance for frustration, and generally a great deal of inappropriate activity. All children show such traits some of the time, but for those diagnosed with ADHD, such behavior is common and interferes with their home and school functioning (American Academy of Pediatrics, 2000b; Nigg, 2001; Whalen et al., 2002).

What are the most common signs of ADHD? It is often difficult to distinguish between children who simply have a high level of activity and those with ADHD. Some of the most common symptoms include:

attention deficit hyperactivity disorder (ADHD) a learning disability marked by inattention, impulsiveness, a low tolerance for frustration, and generally a great deal of inappropriate activity.

- persistent difficulty in finishing tasks, following instructions, and organizing work
- inability to watch an entire television program
- frequent interruption of others or excessive talking
- a tendency to jump into a task before hearing all the instructions
- difficulty in waiting or remaining seated
- fidgeting, squirming

Because there is no simple test to identify whether a child has ADHD, it is hard to know for sure how many children have the disorder. Most estimates put the number between 3% to 7% of those under the age of 18. Only a trained clinician can make an accurate diagnosis following an extensive evaluation of the child and interviews with parents and teachers (Sax & Kautz, 2003).

The treatment of children with ADHD has been a source of considerable controversy. Because it has been found that doses of Ritalin or Dexadrine (which, paradoxically, are stimulants) reduce activity levels in hyperactive children, many physicians routinely prescribe drug treatment (Volkow et al., 2001; Kaplan et al., 2004; HMHL, 2005).

Although in many cases such drugs are effective in increasing attention span and compliance, in some cases the side effects (such as irritability, reduced appetite, and depression) are considerable, and the long-term health consequences of this treatment are unclear. It is also true that though the drugs often help scholastic performance in the short run, the long-term evidence for continuing improvement is mixed. In fact, some studies suggest that after a few years, children treated with drugs do not perform academically any better than untreated children with ADHD. Nonetheless the drugs are being prescribed with increasing frequency (see Figure 9-6; Hallahn, Kauffman, & Lloyd, 2000; Marshall, 2000; Zernike & Petersen, 2001).

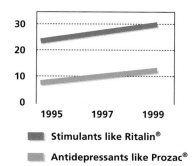

30		
20		
10		
0		
1995	**1997**	**1999**

■ **Stimulants like Ritalin®**

■ **Antidepressants like Prozac®**

FIGURE 9-6 OVERPRESCRIBING RITALIN?

The number of children being given drugs for psychological disorders has increased significantly over the last decade.

(*Source:* U.S. Surgeon General, 2000.)

In addition to the use of drugs for treating ADHD, behavior therapy is often employed. With behavior therapy, parents and teachers are trained in techniques for improving behavior, primarily involving the use of rewards (such as verbal praise) for desired behavior. In addition, teachers can increase the structure of classroom activities and use other class management techniques to help children with ADHD, who have great difficulty with unstructured tasks (Chronis, Jones, & Raggi, 2006; DuPaul & Weyandt, 2006).

Finally, because some research has shown links between ADHD and children's diet, particularly in terms of fatty acids or food additives, dietary treatments have sometimes been prescribed. However, dietary treatments are usually insufficient by themselves (Cruz & Bahna, 2006; Stevenson, 2006). (Parents and teachers can receive support from the Children and Adults with Attention-Deficit/Hyperactivity Disorder organization at www.chadd.org.)

Becoming an Informed Consumer of Development

Keeping Children Fit

Here is a brief portrait of a contemporary American: Sam works all week at a desk and gets no regular physical exercise. On weekends he spends many hours sitting in front of the TV, often snacking on sodas and sweets. Both at home and at restaurants, his meals feature high-calorie, fat-saturated foods. (Segal & Segal, 1992, p. 235)

Although this sketch could apply to many adult men and women, Sam is actually a 6-year-old. He is one of many school-age children in the United States who get little or no regular exercise and who consequently are physically unfit and at risk for obesity and other health problems.

Several things can be done to encourage children to become more physically active (Tyre & Scelfo, 2003; Okie, 2005):

- *Make exercise fun.* In order for children to build the habit of exercising, they need to find it enjoyable. Activities that keep children on the sidelines or that are overly competitive may give children with inferior skills a lifelong distaste for exercise.

- *Be an exercise role model.* Children who see that exercise is a regular part of the lives of their parents, teachers, or adult friends may come to think of fitness as a regular part of their lives, too.

- *Gear activities to the child's physical level and motor skills.* For instance, use child-size equipment that can make participants feel successful.

- *Encourage the child to find a partner.* It could be a friend, a sibling, or a parent. Exercising can involve a variety of activities, such as snowboarding or hiking, but almost all activities are carried out more readily if someone else is doing them too.

- *Start slowly.* Sedentary children—those who aren't used to regular physical activity—should start off gradually. For instance, they could start with 5 minutes of exercise a day, 7 days a week. Over 10 weeks, they could move toward a goal of 30 minutes of exercise 3 to 5 days a week.

- *Urge participation in organized sports activities, but do not push too hard.* Not every child is athletically inclined, and pushing too hard for involvement in organized sports may backfire. Make participation and enjoyment the goals of such activities, not winning.

- *Don't make physical activity, such as jumping jacks or push-ups, a punishment for unwanted behavior.* Instead, schools and parents should encourage children to participate in organized programs that seek to involve children in ways that are enjoyable.
- *Provide a healthy diet.* Children who eat a healthy diet will have more energy to engage in physical activitiy than those who have a diet heavy in soda and snack foods.

Review and Apply

Review

- During the middle childhood years, the body grows at a slow but steady pace that is influenced by both genetic and social factors.
- Adequate nutrition is important for physical, social, and cognitive development, but overnutrition may lead to obesity.
- Children substantially improve their gross and fine motor skills during the school years, with muscular coordination and manipulative skills advancing to near-adult levels.
- The incidence of asthma and childhood depression has increased significantly over the last several decades.
- Many school-age children have special needs, particularly in the areas of vision, hearing, and speech. Some also have learning disabilities.
- Attention deficit hyperactivity disorder, marked by attention, organization, and activity problems, affects between 3% and 5% of the school-age population. Treatment through the use of drugs is highly controversial.

Applying Lifespan Development

- What are some aspects of U.S. culture that may contribute to obesity among school-age children?
- *From a healthcare provider's perspective:* Under what circumstances would you recommend the use of a growth hormone such as Protropin? Is shortness primarily a physical or a cultural problem?

Intellectual Development

Jared's parents were delighted when he came home from kindergarten one day and explained that he had learned why the sky was blue. He talked about the earth's atmosphere—although he didn't pronounce the word correctly—and how tiny bits of moisture in the air reflected the sunlight. Although his explanation had rough edges (he couldn't quite grasp what the "atmosphere" was), he still had the general idea, and that, his parents felt, was quite an achievement for their 5-year-old.

***

Fast-forward six years. Jared, now 11, had already spent an hour laboring over his evening's homework. After completing a two-page worksheet on multiplying and dividing fractions, he had begun work on his U.S. Constitution project. He was taking notes for his report, which would explain what political factions had been involved in the writing of the document and how the Constitution had been amended since its creation.

concrete operational stage the period of cognitive development between 7 and 12 years of age, which is characterized by the active, and appropriate, use of logic.

decentering the ability to take multiple aspects of a situation into account.

VIDEO CLIP

CONSERVATION

Research conducted in such places as more remote areas of Australia show that, contrary to Piaget's assertion, not everyone reaches the concrete operational stage.

Jared is not alone in having made vast intellectual advances during middle childhood. During this period, children's cognitive abilities broaden, and they become increasingly able to understand and master complex skills. At the same time, though, their thinking is still not fully adultlike.

What are the advances, and the limitations, in thinking during childhood? Several perspectives explain what goes on cognitively during middle childhood.

Piagetian Approaches to Cognitive Development

Let's return for a moment to Jean Piaget's view of the preschooler, which we considered in Chapter 7. From Piaget's perspective, the preschooler thinks *preoperationally*. This type of thinking is largely egocentric, and preoperational children lack the ability to use *operations*—organized, formal, logical mental processes.

The Rise of Concrete Operational Thought. All this changes, according to Piaget, during the concrete operational period, which coincides with the school years. The **concrete operational stage,** which occurs between 7 and 12 years of age, is characterized by the active, and appropriate, use of logic. Concrete operational thought involves applying *logical operations* to concrete problems. For instance, when children in the concrete operational stage are confronted with a conservation problem (such as determining whether the amount of liquid poured from one container to another container of a different shape stays the same), they use cognitive and logical processes to answer, no longer being influenced solely by appearance. They are able to reason correctly that since none of the liquid has been lost, the amount stays the same. Because they are less egocentric, they can take multiple aspects of a situation into account, an ability known as **decentering.** Jared, the sixth grader described at the beginning of this section, was using his decentering skills to consider the views of the different factions involved in creating the U.S. Constitution.

The shift from preoperational thought to concrete operational thought does not happen overnight, of course. During the 2 years before children move firmly into the concrete operational period, they shift back and forth between preoperational and concrete operational thinking. For instance, they typically pass through a period when they can answer conservation problems correctly but can't articulate why they did so. When asked to explain the reasoning behind their answers, they may respond with an unenlightening, "Because."

However, once concrete operational thinking is fully engaged, children show several cognitive advances. For instance, they attain the concept of *reversibility*, which is the notion that processes transforming a stimulus can be reversed, returning it to its original form. Grasping reversibility permits children to understand that a ball of clay that has been squeezed into a long, snake-like rope can be returned to its original state. More abstractly, it allows school-age children to understand that if 3 + 5 equals 8, then 5 + 3 also equals 8—and, later during the period, that 8 − 3 equals 5.

Concrete operational thinking also permits children to understand such concepts as the relationship between time and speed. For instance, consider the problem shown in Figure 9-7, in which two cars start and finish at the same points in the same amount of time, but travel different routes. Children who are just entering the concrete operational period reason that the cars are traveling at the same speed. However, between the ages of 8 and 10, children begin to draw the right conclusion: that the car traveling the longer route must be moving faster if it arrives at the finish point at the same time as the car traveling the shorter route.

Despite the advances that occur during the concrete operational stage, children still experience one critical limitation in their thinking. They remain tied to concrete, physical reality. Furthermore, they are unable to understand truly abstract or hypothetical questions, or ones that involve formal logic, such as concepts like free will or determinism.

Piaget in Perspective: Piaget Was Right, Piaget Was Wrong. As we learned in our prior consideration of Piaget's views in Chapters 5 and 7, researchers following in Piaget's footsteps have found much to cheer about—as well as much to criticize.

Piaget was a virtuoso observer of children, and his many books contain pages of brilliant, careful observations of children at work and play. Furthermore, his theories have powerful educational

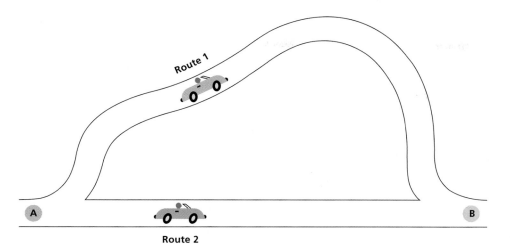

FIGURE 9-7 ROUTES TO CONSERVATION

After being told that the two cars traveling the Routes 1 and 2 start and end their journeys in the same amount of time, children who are just entering the concrete operational period still reason that the cars are traveling at the same speed. Later, however, they reach the correct conclusion: that the car traveling the longer route must be moving at a higher speed if it starts and ends its journey at the same time as the car traveling the shorter route.

implications, and many schools employ principles derived from his views to guide the nature and presentation of instructional materials (Flavell, 1996; Siegler & Ellis, 1996; Brainerd, 2003).

In some ways, then, Piaget's approach was quite successful in describing cognitive development (Lourenco & Machado, 1996). At the same time, though, critics have raised compelling and seemingly legitimate grievances about his approach. As we have noted before, many researchers argue that Piaget underestimated children's capabilities, in part because of the limited nature of the mini-experiments he conducted. When a broader array of experimental tasks is used, children show less consistency within stages than Piaget would predict (Siegler, 1994; Bjorklund, 1997b).

Furthermore, Piaget seems to have misjudged the age at which children's cognitive abilities emerge. As might be expected from our earlier discussions of Piaget's stages, increasing evidence suggests that children's capabilities emerge earlier than Piaget envisioned. Some children show evidence of a form of concrete operational thinking before the age of 7, the time at which Piaget suggested these abilities first appear.

Still, we cannot dismiss the Piagetian approach. Although some early cross-cultural research seemed to imply that children in certain cultures never left the preoperational stage, failing to master conservation and to develop concrete operations, more recent research suggests otherwise. For instance, with proper training in conservation, children in non-Western cultures who do not conserve can readily learn to do so. For instance, in one study, urban Australian children—who develop concrete operations on the same timetable as Piaget suggested—were compared to rural Aborigine children, who typically do not demonstrate an understanding of conservation at the age of 14 (Dasen, Ngini, & Lavallee, 1979). When the rural Aborigine children were given training, they showed conservation skills similar to their urban counterparts, although with a time lag of around 3 years (see Figure 9-8).

Furthermore, when children are interviewed by researchers from their own culture, who know the language and customs of the culture well and who use reasoning tasks that are related to domains important to the culture, the children are considerably more likely to display concrete operational thinking (Nyiti, 1982; Jahoda, 1983). Ultimately, such research suggests that Piaget was right when he argued that concrete operations were universally achieved during middle childhood. Although school-age children in some cultures may differ from Westerners in the demonstration of certain cognitive skills, the most probable explanation of the difference is that the non-Western children have had different sorts of experiences from those that permit children in Western societies to perform well on Piagetian measures of conservation and concrete operations. The progress of cognitive development, then, cannot be understood without looking at the nature of a child's culture (Beilin & Pufall, 1992; Berry et al., 1992; Mishra, 1997; Lau, Lee, & Chiu, 2004).

Cognitive development makes substantial advances in middle childhood.

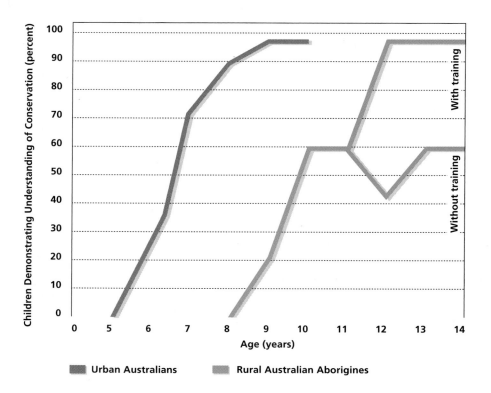

FIGURE 9-8   CONSERVATION TRAINING

Rural Australian Aborigine children trail their urban counterparts in the development of their understanding of conservation; with training, they later catch up. Without training, around half of 14-year-old Aborigines do not have an understanding of conservation. What can be concluded from the fact that training influences the understanding of conservation?

(*Source:* Adapted from Dasen, Ngini, & Lavallee, 1979.)

Information Processing in Middle Childhood

It is a significant achievement for first graders to learn basic math tasks, such as addition and subtraction of single-digit numbers, as well as the spelling of simple words such as "dog" and "run." But by the time they reach the sixth grade, children are able to work with fractions and decimals, like the fractions worksheet that Jared, the boy in the example at the start of this section, completed for his sixth-grade homework. They can also spell such words as "exhibit" and "residence."

According to *information processing approaches*, children become increasingly sophisticated in their handling of information. Like computers, they can process more data as the size of their memories increases and the "programs" they use to process information become increasingly sophisticated (Kuhn et al., 1995; Kail, 2003; Zelazo et al., 2003).

Memory.   As we saw in Chapter 5, **memory** in the information processing model is the ability to encode, store, and retrieve information. For a child to remember a piece of information, the three processes must all function properly. Through *encoding*, the child initially records the information in a form usable to memory. Children who were never taught that 5 + 6 = 11, or who didn't pay attention when they were exposed to this fact, will never be able to recall it. They never encoded the information in the first place.

But mere exposure to a fact is not enough; the information also has to be *stored*. In our example, the information that 5 + 6 = 11 must be placed and maintained in the memory system. Finally, proper functioning of memory requires that material that is stored in memory must be *retrieved*. Through retrieval, material in memory storage is located, brought into awareness, and used.

During middle childhood, short-term memory (also referred to as *working memory*) capacity improves significantly. For instance, children are increasingly able to hear a string of digits ("1-5-6-3-4") and then repeat the string in reverse order ("4-3-6-5-1"). At the start of the preschool period, they can remember and reverse only about two digits; by the beginning of adolescence, they can perform the task with as many as six digits. In addition, they use more sophisticated strategies for recalling information, which can be improved with training (Bjorklund et al., 1994; Halford et al., 1994; Cowan, Saults, & Elliot, 2002).

memory   the process by which information is initially recorded, stored, and retrieved.

Memory capacity may shed light on another issue in cognitive development. Some developmental psychologists suggest that the difficulty children experience in solving conservation problems during the preschool period may stem from memory limitations (Siegler & Richards, 1982). They argue that young children simply may not be able to recall all the necessary pieces of information that enter into the correct solution of conservation problems.

Metamemory, an understanding about the processes that underlie memory, also emerges and improves during middle childhood. By the time they enter first grade and their theory of mind becomes more sophisticated, children have a general notion of what memory is, and they are able to understand that some people have better memories than others (Schneider & Pressley, 1989; Lewis & Mitchell, 1994; Cherney, 2003).

School-age children's understanding of memory becomes more sophisticated as they grow older and increasingly engage in *control strategies*—conscious, intentionally used tactics to improve cognitive processing. For instance, school-age children are aware that rehearsal, the repetition of information, is a useful strategy for improving memory, and they increasingly employ it over the course of middle childhood. Similarly, they progressively make more effort to organize material into coherent patterns, a strategy that permits them to recall it better. For instance, when faced with remembering a list including cups, knives, forks, and plates, older school-age children are more likely to group the items into coherent patterns—cups and plates, forks and knives—than children just entering the school-age years (Weed, Ryan, & Day, 1990; Pressley & Van Meter, 1993; Sang, Miao, & Deng, 2002).

Improving Memory. Can children be trained to be more effective in the use of control strategies? Definitely. School-age children can be taught to use particular strategies, although such teaching is not a simple matter. For instance, children need to know not only how to use a memory strategy, but also when and where to use it most effectively.

Take, for example, an innovative technique called the keyword strategy, which can help students learn the vocabulary of a foreign language, the capitals of the states, or other information in which two sets of words or labels are paired. In the *keyword strategy,* one word is paired with another that sounds like it (Pressley & Levin, 1983; Pressley, 1987). For instance, in learning foreign language vocabulary, a foreign word is paired with a common English word that has a similar sound. The English word is the keyword. Thus, to learn the Spanish word for duck (*pato,* pronounced *pot-o*), the keyword might be "pot"; for the Spanish word for horse (*caballo,* pronounced *cob-eye-yo*), the keyword might be "eye." Once the keyword is chosen, children then form a mental image of the two words interacting with one another. For instance, a student might use an image of a duck taking a bath in a pot to remember the word *pato,* or a horse with bulging eyes to remember the word *caballo.*

Vygotsky's Approach to Cognitive Development and Classroom Instruction

Learning environments can encourage children to learn these strategies as well. Recall from Chapter 7 that Russian developmentalist Lev Vygotsky proposed that cognitive advances occur through exposure to information within a child's *zone of proximal development,* or ZPD. The ZPD is the level at which a child can almost, but not quite, understand or perform a task.

Vygotsky's approach has been particularly influential in the development of several classroom practices based on the proposition that children should actively participate in their educational experiences (e.g., Holzman, 1997). Consequently, classrooms are seen as places where children should have the opportunity to experiment and try out new activities (Vygotsky, 1926/1997).

According to Vygotsky, education should focus on activities that involve interaction with others. Both child–adult and child–child interactions can provide the potential for cognitive growth. The nature of the interactions must be carefully structured to fall within each individual child's zone of proximal development.

metamemory an understanding about the processes that underlie memory, which emerges and improves during middle childhood.

mydevelopmentlab

VIDEO CLIP

THEORY OF MIND

Students working in cooperative groups benefit from the insights of others.

Several current and noteworthy educational innovations have borrowed heavily from Vygotsky's work. For example, *cooperative learning*, in which children work together in groups to achieve a common goal, incorporates several aspects of Vygotsky's theory. Students working in cooperative groups benefit from the insights of others, and if they get off onto the wrong track, they may be brought back to the correct course by others in their group. On the other hand, not every peer is equally helpful to members of a cooperative learning group: As Vygotsky's approach would imply, individual children benefit most when at least some of the other members of the group are more competent at the task and can act as experts (Slavin, 1995; Karpov & Haywood, 1998; Gillies & Boyle, 2006).

Reciprocal teaching is another educational practice that reflects Vygotsky's approach to cognitive development. *Reciprocal teaching* is a technique to teach reading comprehension strategies. Students are taught to skim the content of a passage, raise questions about its central point, summarize the passage, and finally predict what will happen next. A key to this technique is its reciprocal nature, its emphasis on giving students a chance to take on the role of teacher. In the beginning, teachers lead students through the comprehension strategies. Gradually, students progress through their zones of proximal development, taking more and more control over use of the strategies, until the students are able to take on a teaching role. The method has shown impressive success in raising reading comprehension levels, particularly for students experiencing reading difficulties (Palincsar, Brown, & Campione, 1993; Greenway, 2002; Takala, 2006).

Language Development: What Words Mean

If you listen to what school-age children say to one another, their speech, at least at first hearing, sounds not too different from that of adults. However, the apparent similarity is deceiving. The linguistic sophistication of children—particularly at the start of the school-age period—still requires refinement to reach adult levels of expertise.

Mastering the Mechanics of Language.   Vocabulary continues to increase during the school years at a fairly rapid clip. For instance, the average 6-year-old has a vocabulary of from 8,000 to 14,000 words, whereas the vocabulary grows by another 5,000 words between the ages of 9 and 11.

School-age children's mastery of grammar also improves. For instance, the use of the passive voice is rare during the early school-age years (as in "The dog was walked by Jon," compared with the active-voice "Jon walked the dog"). Six- and 7-year-olds only infrequently use conditional sentences, such as "If Sarah will set the table, I will wash the dishes." However, over the course of middle childhood, the use of both passive voice and conditional sentences increases. In addition, children's understanding of *syntax*, the rules that indicate how words and phrases can be combined to form sentences, grows during middle childhood.

By the time they reach first grade, most children pronounce words quite accurately. However, certain *phonemes*, units of sound, remain troublesome. For instance, the ability to pronounce *j, v, th,* and *zh* sounds develops later than the ability to pronounce other phonemes.

School-age children also may have difficulty decoding sentences when the meaning depends on *intonation*, or tone of voice. For example, consider the sentence, "George gave a book to David and he gave one to Bill." If the word "he" is emphasized, the meaning is "George gave a book to David and David gave a different book to Bill." But if the intonation emphasizes the word "and," then the meaning changes to "George gave a book to David and George also gave a book to Bill." School-age children cannot easily sort out subtleties such as these (Moshman, Glover, & Bruning, 1987; Woolfolk, 1993).

In addition to language skills, conversational skills also develop during middle childhood. Children become more competent in their use of *pragmatics*, the rules governing the use of language to communicate in a given social setting.

For example, although children are aware of the rules of conversational turn-taking at the start of the early childhood period, their use of these rules is sometimes primitive. Consider the following conversation between 6-year-olds Yonnie and Max:

Yonnie: My dad drives a FedEx truck.
Max: My sister's name is Molly.
Yonnie: He gets up really early in the morning.
Max: She wet her bed last night.

Later, however, conversations show more give-and-take, with the second child actually responding to the comments of the first. For instance, this conversation between 11-year-olds Mia and Josh reflects a more sophisticated mastery of pragmatics:

Mia: I don't know what to get Claire for her birthday.
Josh: I'm getting her earrings.
Mia: She already has a lot of jewelry.
Josh: I don't think she has that much.

Metalinguistic Awareness.   One of the most significant developments in middle childhood is children's increasing understanding of their own use of language, or **metalinguistic awareness.** By the time children are 5 or 6, they understand that language is governed by a set of rules. Whereas in the early years they learn and comprehend these rules implicitly, during middle childhood children come to understand them more explicitly (Kemper & Vernooy, 1994; Benelli et al., 2006).

Metalinguistic awareness helps children achieve comprehension when information is fuzzy or incomplete. For instance, when preschoolers are given ambiguous or unclear information, such as directions for how to play a complicated game, they rarely ask for clarification, and they tend to blame themselves if they do not understand. By the time they reach the age of 7 or 8, children realize that miscommunication may be due to factors attributable not only to themselves, but to the person communicating with them as well. Consequently, school-age children are more likely to ask for clarifications of information that is unclear to them (Beal & Belgrad, 1990; Kemper & Vernooy, 1994; Apperly & Robinson, 2002).

metalinguistic awareness   an understanding of one's own use of language.

bilingualism the use of more than one language.

How Language Promotes Self-Control.   The growing sophistication of their language helps school-age children control and regulate their behavior. For instance, in one experiment, children were told that they could have one marshmallow treat if they chose to eat one immediately, but two treats if they waited. Most of the children, who ranged in age from 4 to 8, chose to wait, but the strategies they used while waiting differed significantly.

The 4-year-olds often chose to look at the marshmallows while waiting, a strategy that was not terribly effective. In contrast, 6- and 8-year-olds used language to help them overcome temptation, although in different ways. The 6-year-olds spoke and sang to themselves, reminding themselves that if they waited they would get more treats in the end. The 8-year-olds focused on aspects of the marshmallows that were not related to taste, such as their appearance, which helped them to wait.

In short, children used "self-talk" to help regulate their own behavior. Furthermore, the effectivness of their self-control grew as their linguistic capabilities increased.

Bilingualism: Speaking in Many Tongues

For picture day at New York's P.S. 217, a neighborhood elementary school in Brooklyn, the notice to parents was translated into five languages. That was a nice gesture, but insufficient: More than 40% of the children are immigrants whose families speak any one of twenty-six languages, ranging from Armenian to Urdu. (Leslie, 1991, p. 56)

From the smallest towns to the biggest cities, the voices with which children speak are changing. Nearly one in five people in the United States speaks a language other than English at home, and that percentage is growing. **Bilingualism**—the use of more than one language—is growing increasingly common (Shin & Bruno, 2003; Graddol, 2004; see Figure 9-9).

Children who enter school with little or no English proficiency must learn both the standard curriculum and the language in which that curriculum is taught. One approach to educating non-English speakers is *bilingual education*, in which children are initially taught in their native language, while at the same time learning English. With bilingual instruction, students are able to develop a strong foundation in basic subject areas using their native language. The ultimate goal of most bilingual education programs is to gradually shift instruction into English.

In contrast to immersion programs, in which students receive instruction only in English, in bilingual education, children are initially taught in their own language, while also learning English.

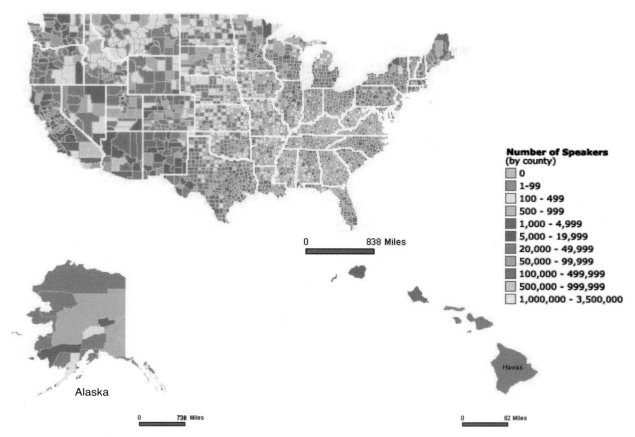

Number of Speakers
(by county)
- 0
- 1-99
- 100 - 499
- 500 - 999
- 1,000 - 4,999
- 5,000 - 19,999
- 20,000 - 49,999
- 50,000 - 99,999
- 100,000 - 499,999
- 500,000 - 999,999
- 1,000,000 - 3,500,000

0   838 Miles

Hawaii

Alaska

0   738 Miles   0   82 Miles

FIGURE 9-9   THE TOP 10 LANGUAGES OTHER THAN ENGLISH SPOKEN IN THE UNITED STATES

These figures show the number of U.S. residents over the age of 5 who speak a language other than English at home. With increases in the number and variety of languages spoken in the United States, what types of approaches might an educator use to meet the needs of bilingual students?

(*Source:* Modern Language Association, www.mla.org/census_ map, 2005; U.S. Census Bureau, 2000.)

An alternative approach is to immerse students in English, teaching solely in that language. To proponents of this approach, initially teaching students in a language other than English hinders students' efforts to learn English and slows their integration into society.

The two quite different approaches have been highly politicized, with some politicians arguing in favor of "English-only" laws, while others urge school systems to respect the challenges faced by nonnative speakers by offering some instruction in their native language. Still, the psychological research is clear in suggesting that knowing more than one language offers several cognitive advantages. Because they have a wider range of linguistic possibilities to choose from as they assess a situation, speakers of two languages show greater cognitive flexibility. They can solve problems with greater creativity and versatility. Furthermore, learning in one's native tongue is associated with higher self-esteem in minority students (Romaine, 1994; Wright & Taylor, 1995; Barker, Giles, & Noels, 2001).

Bilingual students often have greater metalinguistic awareness, understanding the rules of language more explicitly. They even may score higher on tests of intelligence, according to some research. For example, one survey of French- and English-speaking schoolchildren in Canada found that bilingual students scored significantly higher on both verbal and nonverbal tests of intelligence than those who spoke only one language (Lambert & Peal, 1972; Bochner, 1996; Crutchley, 2003; Swanson, Saez, & Gerber, 2004).

Finally, because many linguists contend that universal processes underlie language acquisition, as we noted in Chapter 5, instruction in a native language may enhance instruction in a second language. In fact, as we discuss next, many educators believe that second-language learning should be a regular part of elementary schooling for *all* children (Perozzi & Sanchez, 1992; Yelland, Pollard, & Mercuri, 1993; Kecskes & Papp, 2000).

Review and Apply

Review

- According to Piaget, school-age children are in the concrete operational stage, characterized by the application of logical processes to concrete problems.
- Information processing approaches focus on quantitative improvements in memory and in the sophistication of the mental programs that school-age children use.
- According to Vygotsky's approach, children in the school years should have the opportunity to experiment and participate actively with their colleagues in their educational experiences.
- The memory processes—encoding, storage, and retrieval—come under increasing control during the school years, and the development of metamemory improves cognitive processing and memorization.
- Language development is characterized by improvements in vocabulary, syntax, and pragmatics; by the growth of metalinguistic awareness; and by the use of language as a self-control device.
- Bilingualism can produce improvements in cognitive flexibility, and metalinguistic awareness.

Applying Lifespan Development

- Do adults use language (and talking to themselves) as a self-control device? How?
- *From an educator's perspective:* Suggest how a teacher might use Vygotsky's approach to teach 10-year-olds about colonial America.

Schooling: The Three Rs (and More) of Middle Childhood

As the eyes of the six other children in his reading group turned to him, Glenn shifted uneasily in his chair. Reading had never come easily to him, and he always felt anxious when it was his turn to read aloud. But as his teacher nodded in encouragement, he plunged in, hesitantly at first, then gaining momentum as he read the story about a mother's first day on a new job. He found that he could read the passage quite nicely, and he felt a surge of happiness and pride at his accomplishment. When he was done, he broke into a broad smile as his teacher said simply, "Well done, Glenn."

Small moments such as these, repeated over and over, make—or break—a child's educational experience. Schooling marks a time when society formally attempts to transfer to new generations its accumulated body of knowledge, beliefs, values, and wisdom. The success with which this transfer is managed determines, in a very real sense, the future fortunes of the world, as well as the individual success of each student.

In almost all developing countries, more males than females receive formal education.

Schooling Around the World and Across Genders: Who Gets Educated?

In the United States, as in most developed countries, a primary school education is both a universal right and a legal requirement. Virtually all children are provided with a free education through the 12th grade.

Children in other parts of the world are not so fortunate. More than 160 million of the world's children do not have access to even a primary school education. An additional 100 million children do not progress beyond a level comparable to our elementary school education, and overall close to a billion individuals (two-thirds of them women) are illiterate throughout their lives (see Figure 9-10; World Conference on Education for All, 1990; International Literacy Institute, 2001).

In almost all developing countries, fewer females than males receive formal education, a discrepancy found at every level of schooling. Even in developed countries, women lag behind men in their exposure to science and technological topics. These differences reflect widespread and deeply held cultural and parental biases that favor males over females. Educational levels in the United States are more nearly equal between men and women. Especially in the early years of school, boys and girls share equal access to educational opportunities.

Reading: Learning to Decode the Meaning Behind Words

The efforts of La-Toya Pankey (described in the chapter prologue) to improve her reading are no small matter, for there is no other task that is more fundamental to schooling than learning to read. Reading involves a significant number of skills, from low-level cognitive skills (the identification of single letters and associating letters with sounds) to higher-level skills (matching written words with meanings located in long-term memory and using context and background knowledge to determine the meaning of a sentence).

Beginning around the fourth grade, children begin to use reading as a primary source of learning.

Reading Stages.   Development of reading skill generally occurs in several broad and frequently overlapping stages (Chall, 1979, 1992; see Table 9-1). In *Stage 0*, which lasts from birth to the start of first grade, children learn the essential prerequisites for reading, including

FIGURE 9-10   THE PLAGUE OF ILLITERACY

Illiteracy remains a significant worldwide problem, particularly for women. Across the world, close to a billion people are illiterate throughout their lives.

(*Source:* UNESCO, 2006.)

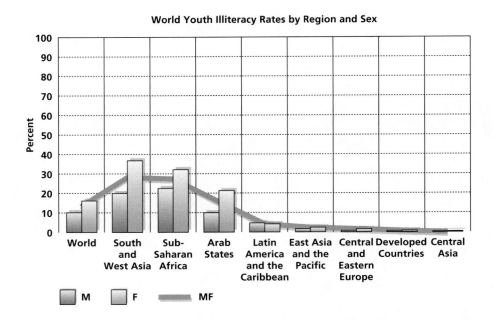

World Youth Illiteracy Rates by Region and Sex

Table 9-1	Development of Reading Skills

Stage	Age	Key Characteristics
Stage 0	Birth to start of first grade	Learns prerequisites for reading, such as identification of the letters
Stage 1	First and second grades	Learns phonological recoding skills, starts reading
Stage 2	Second and third grades	Reads aloud fluently, but without much meaning
Stage 3	Fourth to eighth grades	Uses reading as a means for learning
Stage 4	Eighth grade and beyond	Understands reading in terms of reflecting multiple points of view

(*Source:* Based on Challe, 1979.)

identification of the letters in the alphabet, sometimes writing their names, and reading a few very familiar words (such as their own names or *stop* on a stop sign).

Stage 1 brings the first real type of reading, but it largely involves *phonological recoding* skill. At this stage, which usually encompasses the first and second grade, children can sound out words by blending the letters together. Children also complete the job of learning the names of letters and the sounds that go with them.

In *Stage 2*, typically around second and third grades, children learn to read aloud with fluency. However, they do not attach much meaning to the words, because the effort involved in simply sounding out words is usually so great that relatively few cognitive resources are left over to process the meaning of the words. La-Toya's flawless reading of *The Witches* shows that she has reached at least this stage of reading development.

The next period, *Stage 3*, extends from fourth to eighth grade. Reading becomes a means to an end—in particular, a way to learn. Whereas earlier reading was an accomplishment in and of itself, by this point children use reading to learn about the world. However, even at this age, understanding gained from reading is not complete. For instance, one limitation children have at this stage is that they are able to comprehend information only when it is presented from a single perspective.

In the final period, *Stage 4,* children are able to read and process information that reflects multiple points of view. This ability, which begins during the transition into high school,

From Research to Practice

Making the Grade: Are We Pushing Too Hard?

Brian and Tiffany Aske of Oakland, Calif., desperately want their daughter, Ashlyn, to succeed in first grade. . . . When they started Ashlyn in kindergarten last year, they had no reason to worry. A bright child with twinkling eyes, Ashlyn was eager to learn, and the neighborhood school had a great reputation. But by November, Ashlyn, then 5, wasn't measuring up. No matter how many times she was tested, she couldn't read the 130-word list her teacher gave her: words like "our," "house" and "there." She became so exhausted and distraught over homework—including a weekly essay on "my favorite animal" or "my family vacation"—that she would put her head down on the dining-room table and sob. "She would tell me, 'I can't write a story, Mama. I just can't do it,'" said Tiffany. (Tyre 2006, p. 34)

The No Child Left Behind Act of 2002 aimed to ensure that all children would be able to read by the time they reached the third grade. The law requires school principals to meet this goal or risk losing their jobs and their school funding. While the intentions of this law may have been good, an unforeseen outcome in some cases has been so much focus on reading that other important topics such as social studies and music and activities such as recess are excluded from the school day. Worse, some schools' reading programs have become so intense that some children are simply burning out (Abril & Gault, 2006; Paige, 2006).

When once kindergarten was a time for finger painting, story time, and free play, children are increasingly beginning reading lessons at that level. Frequent testing to ensure that children are meeting short-term and long-term literacy goals has become more commonplace. The experience of failure—and of competitive pressure to be at the top of the class—is hitting children at younger ages than before.

One trend that has many parents and educators concerned is an increase in the amount of homework assigned. A study conducted by the Institute for Social Research at the University of Michigan determined that children are spending a lot more time on academics today than they did 20 years ago. The time spent in school for children ages 6 to 8 has increased from about 5 hours to about 7 hours per weekday. Time spent studying and reading has increased over that time period, while play time, sports, and other outdoor activities have decreased (Juster, Ono, & Stafford, 2004).

But is the extra homework worth the cost? While time spent on homework is associated with greater academic achievement in secondary school, the relationship gets less strong for the lower grades; below grade 5, the relationship disappears. Experts explain this finding in terms of younger children's inability to tune out distractions as well as their yet undeveloped study skills. Moreover, research with older children shows that more homework is not necessarily better. In fact, some research indicates that the benefits of homework may reach a plateau beyond which additional time spent on homework produces no further benefits (Cooper & Valentine, 2001; Trautwein et al., 2006).

Some educational experts fear that the social and emotional development of children are taking a back seat to literacy education, and that the pressure, the testing, the accelerated programs, and the time spent in school—as well as in after-school programs and on homework—is robbing kids of opportunities to just be kids. Some parents, such as the Askes, are worried that their children are just becoming frustrated and discouraged with learning (Kohn, 2006).

Ultimately, the Askes found their own solution to the pressure that Ashylyn was facing: they moved to a different state where Ashlyn could attend a less-intense public school that offered more more flexibility and less pressure.

- *Why might it be the case that students who spend a lot of time doing homework tend not to have better academic success than students who spend a moderate amount of time?*

- *Do you agree with the Askes that the challenges Ashlyn was facing were just excessive? Why do you think more parents aren't expressing the same concerns?*

---

permits children to develop a far more sophisticated understanding of material. This explains why great works of literature are not read at an earlier stage of education. It is not so much that younger children do not have the vocabulary to understand such works (although this is partially true); it is that they lack the ability to understand the multiple points of view that sophisticated literature invariably presents.

How Should We Teach Reading?   Educators have long been engaged in an ongoing debate regarding the most effective means of teaching reading. At the heart of this debate is a disagreement about the nature of the mechanisms by which information is processed during reading. According to proponents of *code-based approaches to reading*, reading should be taught by presenting the basic skills that underlie reading. Code-based approaches emphasize the components of reading, such as the sounds of letters and their combinations—phonics—and how letters and sounds are combined to make words. They suggest that reading consists of processing the individual components of words, combining them into words, and then using the words to derive the meaning of written sentences and passages (Vellutino, 1991; Jimenez & Guzman, 2003; Gray et al., 2007).

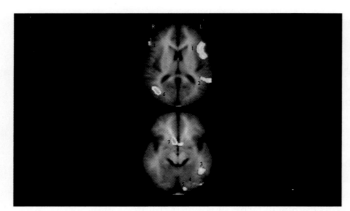

FIGURE 9-11

Students with reading difficulties who were tutored in phonics showed improved reading proficiency and increased activity in brain areas related to skilled reading.

(*Source:* Shaywitz et al., 2004.)

In contrast, some educators argue that reading is taught most successfully by using a whole-language approach. In *whole-language approaches to reading*, reading is viewed as a natural process, similar to the acquisition of oral language. According to this view, children should learn to read through exposure to complete writing—sentences, stories, poems, lists, charts, and other examples of actual uses of writing. Instead of being taught to sound out words, children are encouraged to make guesses about the meaning of words based on the context in which they appear. Through such a trial-and-error approach, children come to learn whole words and phrases at a time, gradually becoming proficient readers (Shaw, 2003; Sousa, 2005; Donat, 2006).

A growing body of research suggests that the code-based approach to reading instruction is superior to whole-language approaches. For example, one study found that a group of children tutored in phonics for a year not only improved substantially in their reading, compared to a group of good readers, but that the neural pathways involved in reading became closer to that of good readers (see Figure 9-11; Shaywitz et al., 2004).

Based on research such as this, the National Reading Panel and National Research Council now support reading instruction using code-based approaches. Their position signals that an end may be near to the debate over which approach to teaching reading is most effective (Rayner et al., 2002).

Educational Trends: Beyond the Three Rs

Schooling in the 21st century is very different from what it was as recently as a decade ago. In fact, U.S. schools are experiencing a return to the educational fundamentals embodied in the traditional three Rs (reading, writing, and arithmetic). The focus on the fundamentals marks a departure from educational trends of prior decades when the emphasis was on their social well-being and on allowing students to choose study topics on the basis of their interests instead of following a set curriculum (Schemo, 2003; Yinger, 2004).

Elementary school classrooms today also stress individual accountability, both for teachers and students. Teachers are more likely to be held responsible for their students' learning, and both students and teachers are more likely to be required to take tests, developed at the state or national level, to assess their competence. As we discuss in the *From Research to Practice* box on page 311, pressures on students to succeed have grown (McDonnell, 2004).

As the U. S. population has become more diverse, elementary schools have also paid increased attention to issues involving student diversity and multiculturalism. And with good reason: Cultural, as well as language, differences affect students socially and educationally. The demographic makeup of students in the United States is undergoing an extraordinary shift. For instance, the proportion of Hispanics will in all likelihood more than double in the next 50 years. Moreover, by the year 2050, non-Hispanic Caucasians will likely become a minority of the total population of the United States (U.S. Bureau of Census, 2001, see Figure 9-12). Consequently, educators have been increasingly serious about multicultural concerns. The following *Developmental Diversity* feature, on multicultural education, discusses how the goals for educating students from different cultures have changed significantly over the years and are still being debated today.

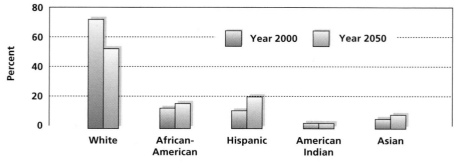

FIGURE 9-12   THE CHANGING FACE OF AMERICA

Current projections of the population makeup of the United States show that by the year 2050, the proportion of non-Hispanic whites will decline as the proportion of minority group members increases. What will be some of the impacts on social workers as the result of changing demographics?

(*Source:* U.S. Census Bureau, 2000.)

Developmental Diversity

Multicultural Education

It has always been the case that classrooms in the United States have been populated by individuals from a broad range of backgrounds and experiences. Yet it is only recently that variations in student backgrounds have been viewed as one of the major challenges—and opportunities—that educators face.

In fact, the diversity of background and experience in the classroom relates to a fundamental objective of education, which is to provide a formal mechanism to transmit the information a society deems important. As the famous anthropologist Margaret Mead (1942) once said, "In its broadest sense, education is the cultural process, the way in which each newborn human infant, born with a potentiality for learning greater than that of any other mammal, is transformed into a full member of a specific human society, sharing with the other members of a specific human culture" (p. 633).

Pupils and teachers exposed to a diverse group could better understand the world and gain a greater sensitivity to the values and needs of others. What are some ways of developing greater sensitivity in the classroom?

multicultural education a form of education in which the goal is to help minority students develop competence in the culture of the majority group while maintaining positive group identities that build on their original cultures.

cultural assimilation model the model that fostered the view of American society as the proverbial melting pot.

Culture, then, can be thought of as a set of behaviors, beliefs, values, and expectations shared by members of a particular society. But culture is not just a relatively broad context, as in "Western culture" or "Asian culture," it is also made up of particular *subcultural* groups. Membership in a cultural or subcultural group might be of only passing interest to educators were it not for the fact that students' cultural backgrounds have a substantial impact on the way that they—and their peers—experience school. In recent years a considerable amount of thought has gone into establishing **multicultural education,** a form of education in which the goal is to help minority students develop competence in the culture of the majority group while maintaining positive group identities that build on their original cultures (Nieto, 2005).

Cultural Assimilation or Pluralistic Society? Multicultural education developed in part as a reaction to a **cultural assimilation model** in which the goal of education was to assimilate individual cultural identities into a unique, unified American culture. In practical terms this meant, for example, that non-English-speaking students were discouraged from speaking their native tongues and were totally immersed in English.

pluralistic society model the concept that American society is made up of diverse, coequal cultural groups that should preserve their individual cultural features.

bicultural identity Maintaining one's original cultural identity while integrating oneself into the dominant culture.

In the early 1970s, however, educators and members of minority groups began to suggest that the cultural assimilation model ought to be replaced by a **pluralistic society model.** According to this conception, American society is made up of diverse, coequal cultural groups that should preserve their individual cultural features.

The pluralistic society model grew in part from the belief that teachers, by emphasizing the dominant culture and discouraging students who were nonnative speakers from using their native tongues, had the effect of devaluing minority subcultural heritages and lowering those students' self-esteem. Instructional materials, such as readers and history lessons, inevitably feature culture-specific events and understandings; children who never saw examples representing their own cultural heritage might never be exposed to important aspects of their backgrounds. For example, English-language texts rarely present some of the great themes that appear throughout Spanish literature and history (such as the search for the Fountain of Youth and the Don Juan legend). Hispanic students immersed in such texts might never come to understand important components of their own heritage.

Over the past decade or so, educators began to argue that the presence of students from diverse cultures enriched and broadened the educational experience of all students. Pupils and teachers exposed to people from different backgrounds could better understand the world and gain greater sensitivity to the values and practices of others.

Fostering a Bicultural Identity. Today, most educators agree that minority children should be encouraged to develop a **bicultural identity.** They recommend that school systems encourage children to maintain their original cultural identities while they integrate themselves into the dominant culture. This view suggests that an individual can live as a member of two cultures, with two cultural identities, without having to choose one over the other (Lu, 2001; Oyserman et al., 2003; Vyas, 2004).

The best way to achieve this goal of biculturalism is not clear. Consider, for example, children who enter a school speaking only Spanish. The traditional "melting-pot" technique would be to immerse the children in classes taught in English while providing a crash course in English language instruction (and little else) until the children demonstrate a suitable level of proficiency. Unfortunately, the traditional approach has a considerable drawback: Until the children master English, they fall further and further behind their peers who entered school already knowing English (First & Cardenas, 1986).

More contemporary approaches emphasize a bicultural strategy in which children are encouraged to maintain simultaneous membership in more than one culture. In the case of Spanish-speaking children, for example, instruction begins in the child's native language and shifts as rapidly as possible to include English. At the same time, the school conducts a program of multicultural education for all students, in which teachers present material on the cultural backgrounds and traditions of all the students in the school. Such instruction is designed to enhance the self-image of speakers from both majority and minority cultures (Wright & Taylor, 1995; Bracey, Bamaca, & Umana-Taylor, 2004; Fowers & Davidov, 2006).

Although most educational experts favor bicultural approaches, the general public does not always agree. For instance, the national "English-only" movement mentioned earlier has as one of its goals the prohibition of school instruction in any language other than English. Whether such a perspective will prevail remains to be seen.

Intelligence: Determining Individual Strengths

"Why should you tell the truth?" "How far is Los Angeles from New York?" "A table is made of wood; a window of _____."

As 10-year-old Hyacinth sat hunched over her desk, trying to answer a long series of questions like these, she tried to guess the point of the test she was taking in her fifth-grade classroom. Clearly, the test didn't cover material that her teacher, Ms. White-Johnston, had talked about in class.

"What number comes next in this series: 1, 3, 7, 15, 31, _____?"

As she continued to work her way through the questions, she gave up trying to guess the rationale for the test. She'd leave that to her teacher, she sighed to herself. Rather than attempting to figure out what it all meant, she simply tried to do her best on the individual test items.

Hyacinth was taking an intelligence test. She might be surprised to learn that she was not alone in questioning the meaning and import of the items on the test. Intelligence test items are painstakingly prepared, and intelligence tests show a strong relationship to success in school (for reasons we'll soon discuss). Many developmentalists, however, would admit to harboring their own doubts as to whether questions such as those on Hyacinth's test are entirely appropriate to the task of assessing intelligence.

Understanding just what is meant by the concept of intelligence has proven to be a major challenge for researchers interested in delineating what separates intelligent from unintelligent behavior. Although nonexperts have their own conceptions of intelligence (one survey found, for instance, that laypersons believe that intelligence consists of three components: problem-solving ability, verbal ability, and social competence), it has been more difficult for experts to concur (Sternberg et al., 1981; Howe, 1997). Still, a general definition of intelligence is possible: **Intelligence** is the capacity to understand the world, think with rationality, and use resources effectively when faced with challenges (Wechsler, 1975).

Part of the difficulty in defining intelligence stems from the many—and sometimes unsatisfactory—paths that have been followed over the years in the quest to distinguish more intelligent people from less intelligent ones. To understand how researchers have approached the task of assessing intelligence by devising *intelligence tests*, we need to consider some of the historical milestones in the area of intelligence.

> **intelligence** the capacity to understand the world, think with rationality, and use resources effectively when faced with challenges.

Intelligence Benchmarks: Differentiating the Intelligent from the Unintelligent

The Paris school system was faced with a problem at the turn of the 20th century: A significant number of children were not benefiting from regular instruction. Unfortunately, these children—many of whom we would now call mentally retarded—were generally not identified early enough to shift them to special classes. The French minister of instruction approached psychologist Alfred Binet with this problem and asked him to devise a technique for the early identification of students who might benefit from instruction outside the regular classroom.

Binet's Test. Binet tackled his task in a thoroughly practical manner. His years of observing school-age children suggested to him that previous efforts to distinguish intelligent from unintelligent students—some of which were based on reaction time or keenness of sight—were off the mark. Instead, he launched a trial-and-error process in which items and tasks were administered to students who had been previously identified by teachers as being either "bright" or "dull." Tasks that the bright students completed correctly and the dull students failed to complete correctly were retained for the test. Tasks that did not discriminate between the two groups were discarded. The end result of this process was a test that reliably distinguished students who had previously been identified as fast or slow learners.

Binet's pioneering efforts in intelligence testing left three important legacies. The first was his pragmatic approach to the construction of intelligence tests. Binet did not have theoretical preconceptions about what intelligence was. Instead, he used a trial-and-error approach to psychological measurement that continues to serve as the predominant approach to test construction today. His definition of intelligence as *that which his test measured* has been adopted by many modern researchers, and it is particularly popular among test developers who respect the widespread utility of intelligence tests but wish to avoid arguments about the underlying nature of intelligence.

mental age the typical intelligence level found for people at a given chronological age.

chronological (or physical) age the actual age of the child taking the intelligence test.

intelligence quotient (or IQ score) a measure of intelligence that takes into account a student's mental *and* chronological age.

Binet's legacy extends to his linking of intelligence and school success. Binet's procedure for constructing an intelligence test ensured that intelligence—defined as performance on the test—and school success would be virtually one and the same. Thus, Binet's intelligence test, and today's tests that follow in Binet's footsteps, have become reasonable indicators of the degree to which students possess attributes that contribute to successful school performance. On the other hand, they do not provide useful information regarding a vast number of other attributes that are largely unrelated to academic proficiency, such as social skills or personality characteristics.

Finally, Binet developed a procedure of linking each intelligence test score with a **mental age,** the age of the children taking the test who, on average, achieved that score. For example, if a 6-year-old girl received a score of 30 on the test, and this was the average score received by 10-year-olds, her mental age would be considered 10 years. Similarly, a 15-year-old boy who scored a 90 on the test—thereby matching the mean score for 15-year-olds—would be assigned a mental age of 15 years.

Although assigning a mental age to students provides an indication of whether or not they are performing at the same level as their peers, it does not permit adequate comparisons between students of different **chronological (or physical) ages.** By using mental age alone, for instance, it would be assumed that a 15-year-old responding with a mental age of 17 years would be as bright as a 6-year-old responding with a mental age of 8 years, when actually the 6-year-old would be showing a much greater *relative* degree of brightness.

A solution to this problem comes in the form of the **intelligence quotient,** or **IQ,** a score that takes into account a student's mental *and* chronological age. The traditional method of calculating an IQ score uses the following formula, in which MA stands for mental age and CA for chronological age:

$$\text{IQ score} = \frac{\text{MA}}{\text{CA}} \times 100$$

As a bit of trial-and-error with this formula demonstrates, people whose mental age (MA) is equal to their chronological age (CA) will always have an IQ of 100. Furthermore, if the

The Wechsler Intelligence Scale for Children-Fourth Edition (WISC-IV) is widely used as an intelligence test that measures verbal and performance (nonverbal) skills.

chronological age exceeds the mental age—implying below-average intelligence—the score will be below 100; and if the chronological age is lower than the mental age—suggesting above-average intelligence—the score will be above 100.

Using this formula, we can return to our earlier example of a 15-year-old who scores at a 17-year-old mental age. This student's IQ is $\frac{17}{15} \times 100$, or 113. In comparison, the IQ of a 6-year-old scoring at a mental age of 8 is $\frac{8}{6} \times 100$, or 133—a higher IQ score than the 15-year-old's.

IQ scores today are calculated in a more mathematically sophisticated manner and are known as *deviation IQ scores*. The average deviation IQ score remains set at 100, but tests are now devised so that the degree of deviation from this score permits the calculation of the proportion of people who have similar scores. For instance, approximately two-thirds of all people fall within 15 points of the average score of 100, achieving scores between 85 and 115. As scores rise or fall beyond this range, the percentage of people in the same score category drops significantly.

Measuring IQ: Present-Day Approaches to Intelligence.

Since the time of Binet, tests of intelligence have become increasingly accurate measures of IQ. Most of them can still trace their roots to his original work in one way or another. For example, one of the most widely used tests—the **Stanford-Binet Intelligence Scales, Fifth Edition (SB5)**—began as an American revision of Binet's original test. The test consists of a series of items that vary according to the age of the person being tested. For instance, young children are asked to answer questions about everyday activities or to copy complex figures. Older people are asked to explain proverbs, solve analogies, and describe similarities between groups of words. The test is administered orally and test-takers are given progressively more difficult problems until they are unable to proceed.

The **Wechsler Intelligence Scale for Children—Fourth Edition (WISC-IV)** is another widely used intelligence test. The test (which stems from its adult counterpart, the *Wechsler Adult Intelligence Scale*) provides separate measures of verbal and performance (or nonverbal) skills, as well as a total score. As you can see from the sample items in Figure 9-13, the verbal tasks are traditional word problems testing skills such as understanding a passage, while typical nonverbal tasks are copying a complex design, arranging pictures in a logical order, and assembling objects. The separate portions of the test allow for easier identification of any specific problems a test-taker may have. For example, significantly higher scores on the performance part of the test than on the verbal part may indicate difficulties in linguistic development (Zhu & Weiss, 2005).

The **Kaufman Assessment Battery for Children, Second Edition (KABC-II)** takes a different approach than the Stanford-Binet and WISC-IV. In the KABC-II, children are tested on their ability to integrate different kinds of stimuli simultaneously and to use step-by-step thinking. A special virtue of the KABC-II is its flexibility. It allows the person giving the test to use alternative wording or gestures, or even to pose questions in a different language, in order to maximize a test-taker's performance. This capability of the KABC-II makes testing more valid and equitable for children to whom English is a second language (Kaufman et al., 2005).

What do the IQ scores derived from IQ tests mean? For most children, IQ scores are reasonably good predictors of their school performance. That's not surprising, given that the initial impetus for the development of intelligence tests was to identify children who were having difficulties in school (Sternberg & Grigorenko, 2002).

But when it comes to performance outside of academic spheres, the story is different. For instance, although people with higher IQ scores are apt to finish more years of schooling, once this is statistically controlled for, IQ scores are not closely related to income and later success in life. Furthermore, IQ scores are frequently inaccurate when it comes to predicting a particular individual's future success. For example, two people with different IQ scores may both finish their bachelor's degrees at the same college, and the person with a lower IQ might end up with a higher income and a more successful career. Because of these difficulties with traditional IQ scores, researchers have turned to alternative approaches to intelligence (McClelland, 1993).

Stanford-Binet Intelligence Scales, Fifth Edition (SB5) a test that consists of a series of items that vary according to the age of the person being tested.

Wechsler Intelligence Scale for Children—Fourth Edition (WISC-IV) a test for children that provides separate measures of verbal and performance (or nonverbal) skills, as well as a total score.

Kaufman Assessment Battery for Children, Second Edition (KABC-II) an intelligence test that measures children's ability to integrate different stimuli simultaneously and step-by-step thinking.

Name	Goal of Item	Example
Verbal Scale		
Information	Assess general information	How many nickels make a dime?
Comprehension	Assess understanding and evaluation of social norms and past experience	What is the advantage of keeping money in the bank?
Arithmetic	Assess math reasoning through verbal problems	If two buttons cost 15 cents, what will be the cost of a dozen buttons?
Similarities	Test understanding of how objects or concepts are alike, tapping abstract reasoning	In what way are an hour and a week alike?
Performance Scale		
Digit symbol	Assess speed of learning	Match symbols to numbers using key. 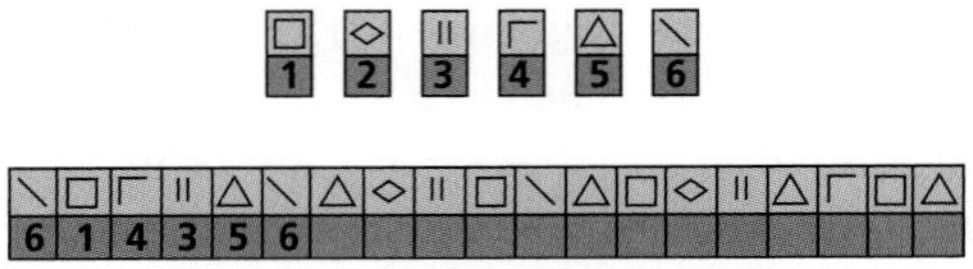
Picture completion	Visual memory and attention	Identify what is missing. 
Object assembly	Test understanding of relationship of parts to wholes	Put pieces together to form a whole. 

FIGURE 9-13   MEASURING INTELLIGENCE

The Wechsler Intelligence Scales for Children (WISC-IV) includes items such as these. What do such items cover? What do they miss?

What IQ Tests Don't Tell: Alternative Conceptions of Intelligence.   The intelligence tests used most frequently in school settings today are based on the idea that intelligence is a single factor, a unitary mental ability. This one main attribute has commonly been called *g* (Spearman, 1927; Lubinski, 2004). The *g* factor is assumed to underlie performance on every aspect of intelligence, and it is the *g* factor that intelligence tests presumably measure.

However, many theorists dispute the notion that intelligence is unidimensional. Some developmentalists suggest that in fact two kinds of intelligence exist: fluid intelligence and crystallized intelligence (Catell, 1967, 1987). **Fluid intelligence** reflects information processing capabilities, reasoning, and memory. For example, a student asked to group a series of letters according to some criterion or to remember a set of numbers would be using fluid intelligence. In contrast, **crystallized intelligence** is the accumulation of information, skills, and strategies that people have learned through experience and that they can apply in problem-solving situations. A student would likely be relying on crystallized intelligence to solve a puzzle or deduce the solution to a mystery, in which it was necessary to draw on past experience (McGrew, 2005; Alfonso, Flanagan, & Radwan, 2005).

Other theorists divide intelligence into an even greater number of parts. For example, psychologist Howard Gardner suggests that we have at least eight distinct intelligences, each relatively independent (see Figure 9-14). Gardner suggests that these separate intelligences operate not in isolation, but together, depending on the type of activity in which we are engaged (Gardner, 2000, 2003; Chen & Gardner, 2005; Gardner & Moran, 2006).

Russian psychologist Lev Vygotsky, whose approach to cognitive development we first discussed in Chapter 1, took a very different approach to intelligence. He suggested that to assess intelligence, we should look not only at those cognitive processes that are fully developed, but at those that are currently being developed as well. To do this, Vygotsky contended that assessment tasks should involve cooperative interaction between the individual who is being assessed and the person who is doing the assessment—a process called *dynamic assessment*. In short, intelligence is seen as being reflected not only in how children can perform on their own, but in terms of how well they perform when helped by adults (Vygotsky, 1927/1976; Daniels, 1996; Brown & Ferrara, 1999).

Taking yet another approach, psychologist Robert Sternberg (1987, 1990, 2003a) suggests that intelligence is best thought of in terms of information processing. In this view, the way in which people store material in memory and later use it to solve intellectual tasks provides the most precise conception of intelligence. Rather than focusing on the various subcomponents that make up the *structure* of intelligence, then, information processing approaches examine the *processes* that underlie intelligent behavior.

Studies of the nature and speed of problem-solving processes show that people with higher intelligence levels differ from others not only in the number of problems they ultimately are able to solve, but in their method of solving the problems as well. People with high IQ scores spend more time on the initial stages of problem solving, retrieving relevant information from memory. In contrast, those who score lower on traditional IQ tests tend to spend less time on the initial stages, instead skipping ahead and making less informed guesses. The processes used in solving problems, then, may reflect important differences in intelligence (Sternberg, 1982, 1990).

Sternberg's work on information processing approaches to intelligence led him to develop the **triarchic theory of intelligence.** According to this model, intelligence consists of three aspects of information processing: the componential element, the experiential element, and the contextual element. The componential aspect of intelligence reflects how efficiently people can process and analyze information. Efficiency in these areas allows people to infer relationships among different parts of a problem, solve the problem, and then evaluate their solution. People who are strong on the componential element score highest on traditional tests of intelligence (Sternberg, 2005).

The *experiential* element is the insightful component of intelligence. People who have a strong experiential element can easily compare new material with what they already know and can combine and relate facts that they already know in novel and creative ways. Finally, the *contextual* element of intelligence concerns practical intelligence, or ways of dealing with the demands of the everyday environment.

Bodily kinesthetic intelligence, as displayed by dancers, ballplayers, and gymnasts is one of Gardner's eight intelligences. What are some examples of other Gardner intelligences?

fluid intelligence   intelligence that reflects information processing capabilities, reasoning, and memory.

crystallized intelligence   the accumulation of information, skills, and strategies that people have learned through experience and that they can apply in problem-solving situations.

triarchic theory of intelligence   a model that states that intelligence consists of three aspects of information processing: the componential element, the experiential element, and the contextual element.

1. *Musical intelligence* (skills in tasks involving music). Case example:
When he was 3, Yehudi Menuhin was smuggled into the San Francisco Orchestra concerts by his parents. The sound of Louis Persinger's violin so entranced the youngster that he insisted on a violin for his birthday and Louis Persinger as his teacher. He got both. By the time he was 10 years old, Menuhin was an international performer.

2. *Bodily kinesthetic intelligence* (skills in using the whole body or various portions of it in the solution of problems or in the construction of products or displays, exemplified by dancers, athletes, actors, and surgeons). Case example:
Fifteen-year-old Babe Ruth played third base. During one game, his team's pitcher was doing poorly and Babe loudly criticized him from third base. Brother Mathias, the coach, called out, "Ruth, if you know so much about it, *you* pitch!" Babe was surprised and embarrassed because he had never pitched before, but Brother Mathias insisted. Ruth said later that at the very moment he took the pitcher's mound, he *knew* he was supposed to be a pitcher.

3. *Logical mathematical intelligence* (skills in problem solving and scientific thinking). Case example:
Barbara McClintock won the Nobel Prize in medicine for her work in microbiology. She describes one of her breakthroughs, which came after thinking about a problem for half an hour...: "Suddenly I jumped and ran back to the [corn] field. At the top of the field [the others were still at the bottom] I shouted, 'Eureka, I have it!'"

4. *Linguistic intelligence* (skills involved in the production and use of language). Case example:
At the age of 10, T.S. Elliot created a magazine called *Fireside*, to which he was the sole contributor. In a 3-day period during his winter vacation, he created eight complete issues.

5. *Spatial intelligence* (skills involving spatial configurations, such as those used by artists and architects). Case example:
Navigation around the Caroline Islands...is accomplished without instruments....During the actual trip, the navigator must envision mentally a reference island as it passes under a particular star and from that he computes the number of segments completed, the proportion of the trip remaining, and any corrections in heading.

6. *Interpersonal intelligence* (skills in interacting with others, such as sensitivity to the moods, temperaments, motivations, and intentions of others). Case example:
When Anne Sullivan began instructing the deaf and blind Helen Keller, her task was one that had eluded others for years. Yet, just 2 weeks after beginning her work with Keller, Sullivan achieved a great success. In her words, "My heart is singing with joy this morning. A miracle has happened! The wild little creature of 2 weeks ago has been transformed into a gentle child."

7. *Intrapersonal intelligence* (knowledge of the internal aspects of oneself; access to one's own feelings and emotions). Case example:
In her essay "A Sketch of the Past," Virginia Woolf displays deep insight into her own inner life through these lines, describing her reaction to several specific memories from her childhood that still, in adulthood, shock her: "Though I still have the peculiarity that I receive these sudden shocks, they are now always welcome; after the first surprise, I always feel instantly that they are particularly valuable. And so I go on to suppose that the shock-receiving capacity is what makes me a writer."

8. *Naturalist intelligence* (ability to identify and classify patterns in nature). Case example:
In prehistoric periods, hunter-gatherers required naturalist intelligence in order to identify what types of plants were edible.

FIGURE 9-14 GARDNER'S EIGHT INTELLIGENCES

Howard Gardner has theorized that there are eight distinct intelligences, each relatively independent.

(*Source:* Adapted from Walters & Gardner, 1986.)

In Sternberg's view, people vary in the degree to which each of these three elements is present. Our level of success at any given task reflects the match between the task and our own specific pattern of strength on the three components of intelligence (Sternberg, 1991, 2003b, 2007).

Group Differences in IQ.

A "jontry" is an example of a

(a)   rulpow

(b)   flink

(c)   spudge

(d)   bakwoe

If you were to find an item composed of nonsense words such as this on an intelligence test, your immediate—and quite legitimate—reaction would likely be to complain. How could a test that purports to measure intelligence include test items that incorporate meaningless terminology?

Yet for some people, the items actually used on traditional intelligence tests might appear equally nonsensical. To take a hypothetical example, suppose children living in rural areas were asked details about subways, while those living in urban areas were asked about the mating practices of sheep. In both cases, we would expect that the previous experiences of test-takers would have a substantial effect on their ability to answer the questions. And if questions about such matters were included on an IQ test, the test could rightly be viewed as a measure of prior experience rather than of intelligence.

Although the questions on traditional IQ tests are not so obviously dependent upon test-takers' prior experiences as our examples, cultural background and experience do have the potential to affect intelligence test scores. In fact, many educators suggest that traditional measures of intelligence are subtly biased in favor of white, upper- and middle-class students and against groups with different cultural experiences (Ortiz & Dynda, 2005).

Explaining Racial Differences in IQ.

The issue of how cultural background and experience influence IQ test performance has led to considerable debate among researchers. The debate has been fueled by the finding that IQ scores of certain racial groups are consistently lower, on average, than the IQ scores of other groups. For example, the mean score of African Americans tends to be about 15 IQ points lower than the mean score of whites—although the measured difference varies a great deal depending on the particular IQ test employed (Fish, 2001; Maller, 2003).

The question that emerges from such differences, of course, is whether they reflect actual differences in intelligence or, instead, are caused by bias in the intelligence tests themselves in favor of majority groups and against minorities. For example, if whites perform better on an IQ test than African Americans because of their greater familiarity with the language used in the test items, the test hardly can be said to provide a fair measure of the intelligence of African Americans. Similarly, an intelligence test that solely used African American Vernacular English could not be considered an impartial measure of intelligence for whites.

The question of how to interpret differences between intelligence scores of different cultural groups lies at the heart of one of the major controversies in child development: To what degree is an individual's intelligence determined by heredity, and to what degree by environment? The issue is important because of its social implications. For instance, if intelligence is primarily determined by heredity and is therefore largely fixed at birth, attempts to alter cognitive abilities later in life, such as schooling, will meet with limited success. On the other hand, if intelligence is largely environmentally determined, modifying social and educational conditions is a more promising strategy for bringing about increases in cognitive functioning (Weiss, 2003).

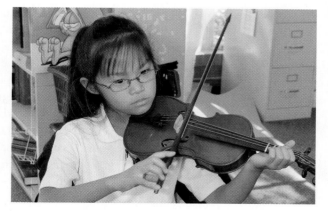

The issue of whether racial differences in IQ exist is highly controversial and ultimately relates to questions of the genetic and environmental determinants of intelligence.

Performance on traditional IQ tests is dependent in part on test-takers' prior experiences and cultural background.

***The Bell Curve* Controversy.** Although investigations into the relative contributions of heredity and environment to intelligence have been conducted for decades, the smoldering debate became a raging fire with the publication of a book by Richard J. Herrnstein and Charles Murray (1994), titled *The Bell Curve.* In the book, Herrnstein and Murray argue that the average 15-point IQ difference between whites and African Americans is due primarily to heredity rather than environment. Furthermore, they argue that this IQ difference accounts for the higher rates of poverty, lower employment, and higher use of welfare among minority groups as compared with majority groups.

The conclusions reached by Herrnstein and Murray raised a storm of protest, and many researchers who examined the data reported in the book came to conclusions that were quite different. Most developmentalists and psychologists responded by arguing that the racial differences in measured IQ can be explained by environmental differences between the races. In fact, when a variety of indicators of economic and social factors are statistically taken into account simultaneously, mean IQ scores of black and white children turn out to be actually quite similar. For instance, children from similar middle-class backgrounds, whether African American or white, tend to have similar IQ scores (Brooks-Gunn, Klebanov, & Duncan, 1996; Alderfer, 2003).

Furthermore, critics maintained that there is little evidence to suggest that IQ is a cause of poverty and other social ills. In fact, some critics suggested, as mentioned earlier in this discussion, that IQ scores were unrelated in meaningful ways to later success in life (e.g., McClelland, 1993; Nisbett, 1994; Sternberg, 1985, 1997; Reifman, 2000).

Finally, members of cultural and social minority groups may score lower than members of the majority group due to the nature of the intelligence tests themselves. It is clear that traditional intelligence tests may discriminate against minority groups who have not had exposure to the same environment as majority group members have experienced.

Most traditional intelligence tests are constructed using white, English-speaking, middle-class populations as their test subjects. As a result, children from different cultural backgrounds may perform poorly on the tests—not because they are less intelligent, but because the tests use questions that are culturally biased in favor of majority group members. In fact, a classic study found that in one California school district, Mexican American students were 10 times more likely than whites to be placed in special education classes (Mercer, 1973). More recent findings show that nationally, twice as many African American students as white students are classified as mildly retarded, a difference that experts attribute primarily to cultural bias and poverty (Reschly, 1996; Terman et al., 1996). Although certain IQ tests (such as the *System of Multicultural Pluralistic Assessment,* or *SOMPA*) have been designed to be equally valid regardless of the cultural background of test-takers, no test can be completely without bias (Sandoval et al., 1998).

In short, most experts in the area of IQ were not convinced by *The Bell Curve* contention that differences in group IQ scores are largely determined by genetic factors. Still, we cannot put the issue to rest, largely because it is impossible to design a definitive experiment that can determine the cause of differences in IQ scores between members of different groups. (Thinking about how such an experiment might be designed shows the futility of the enterprise: One cannot ethically assign children to different living conditions to find the effects of environment, nor would one wish to genetically control or alter intelligence levels in unborn children.)

Today, IQ is seen as the product of *both* nature and nurture interacting with one another in a complex manner. Rather than seeing intelligence as produced by either genes or experience, genes are seen to affect experiences, and experiences are viewed as influencing the expression of genes. For instance, psychologist Eric Turkheimer has found evidence that while environmental factors play a larger role in influencing the IQ of poor children, genes are more influential in the IQ of affluent children (Turkheimer et al., 2003).

Ultimately, it may be less important to know the absolute degree to which intelligence is determined by genetic and environmental factors than it is to learn how to improve children's living conditions and educational experiences. By enriching the quality of children's environments, we will be in a better position to permit all children to reach their full potential and to maximize their contributions to society, whatever their individual levels of intelligence (Wachs, 1996; Wickelgren, 1999; Posthuma & de Geus, 2006).

least restrictive environment the setting that is most similar to that of children without special needs.

Below and Above Intelligence Norms: Mental Retardation and the Intellectually Gifted

Although Connie kept pace with her classmates in kindergarten, by the time she reached first grade, she was academically the slowest in almost every subject. It was not that she didn't try, but rather that it took her longer than other students to catch on to new material, and she regularly required special attention to keep up with the rest of the class.

On the other hand, in some areas she excelled: When asked to draw or produce something with her hands, she not only matched her classmates' performance but exceeded it, producing beautiful work that was much admired by her classmates. Although the other students in the class felt that there was something different about Connie, they were hard-pressed to identify the source of the difference, and in fact they didn't spend much time pondering the issue.

Connie's parents and teacher, though, knew what made her special. Extensive testing in kindergarten had shown that Connie's intelligence was well below normal, and she was officially classified as a special needs student.

If Connie had been attending school before 1975, she would most likely have been removed from her regular class as soon as her low IQ was identified, and placed in a class taught by a special needs teacher. Such classes, often consisted of students with a hodgepodge of afflictions, including emotional difficulties, severe reading problems, and physical disabilities such as multiple sclerosis, as well those with lower IQs, were traditionally kept separate and apart from the regular educational process.

All that changed in 1975 when Congress passed Public Law 94–142, the Education for All Handicapped Children Act. The intent of the law—an intent that has been largely realized—was to ensure that children with special needs received a full education in the **least restrictive environment,** the setting most similar to that of children without special needs (Yell, 1995).

This boy with mental retardation is mainstreamed into this fifth-grade class.

mainstreaming an educational approach in which exceptional children are integrated to the extent possible into the traditional educational system and are provided with a broad range of educational alternatives.

mental retardation a significantly subaverage level of intellectual functioning that occurs with related limitations in two or more skill areas.

In practice, the law has meant that children with special needs must be integrated into regular classrooms and regular activities to the greatest extent possible, as long as doing so is educationally beneficial. Children are to be isolated from the regular classroom only for those subjects that are specifically affected by their exceptionality; for all other subjects, they are to be taught with nonexceptional children in regular classrooms. Of course, some children with severe handicaps still need a mostly or entirely separate education, depending on the extent of their condition. But the goal of the law is to integrate exceptional children and typical children to the fullest extent possible (Yell, 1995).

This educational approach to special education, designed to end the segregation of exceptional students as much as possible, has come to be called mainstreaming. In **mainstreaming,** exceptional children are integrated as much as possible into the traditional educational system and are provided with a broad range of educational alternatives (Hocutt, 1996; Belkin, 2004).

Ending Segregation by Intelligence Levels: The Benefits of Mainstreaming. In many respects, the introduction of mainstreaming—while clearly increasing the complexity of classroom teaching—was a reaction to failures of traditional special education. For one thing, there was little research support for the advisability of special education for exceptional students. Research that examined such factors as academic achievement, self-concept, social adjustment, and personality development generally failed to discern any advantages for special needs children placed in special, as opposed to regular, education classes. Furthermore, systems that compel minorities to be educated separately from majorities historically tend to be less effective—as an examination of schools that were once segregated on the basis of race clearly demonstrates (Wang, Peverly, & Catalano, 1987; Wang, Reynolds, & Walberg, 1996).

Ultimately, though, the most compelling argument in favor of mainstreaming is philosophical: Because special needs students must ultimately function in a normal environment, greater experience with their peers ought to enhance their integration into society, as well as positively affect their learning. Mainstreaming, then, provides a mechanism to equalize the opportunities available to all children. The ultimate objective of mainstreaming is to ensure that all persons, regardless of ability or disability, have access to a full range of educational opportunities and, ultimately, a fair share of life's rewards (Fuchs & Fuchs, 1994; Scherer, 2004).

Does the reality of mainstreaming live up to its promise? To some extent, the benefits extolled by proponents have been realized. However, classroom teachers must receive substantial support in order for mainstreaming to be effective. It is not easy to teach a class in which students' abilities are significantly different from one another (Kauffman, 1993; Daly & Feldman, 1994; Scruggs & Mastropieri, 1994).

The benefits of mainstreaming have led some professionals to promote an alternative educational model known as full inclusion. *Full inclusion* is the integration of all students, even those with the most severe disabilities, into regular classes. In such a system, separate special education programs would cease to operate. Full inclusion is controversial, and it remains to be seen how widespread such a practice will become (Kavale & Forness, 2000; Kavale, 2002; Brehm, 2003; Gersten & Dimino, 2006).

Below the Norm: Mental Retardation. Approximately 1% to 3% of the school-age population is considered to be mentally retarded. Estimates vary so widely because the most commonly accepted definition of mental retardation is one that leaves a great deal of room for interpretation. According to the American Association on Mental Retardation (AAMR), **mental retardation** is a disability characterized by significant limitations both in intellectual functioning and in adaptive behavior involving conceptual, social, and practical adaptive skills (AAMR, 2002).

Most cases of mental retardation are classified as *familial retardation,* in which no cause is apparent, but there is a history of retardation in the family. In other cases, there is a clear biological cause. The most common biological causes are *fetal alcohol syndrome,* which is produced by a mother's use of alcohol while pregnant, and *Down syndrome,* which results from the presence of an extra chromosome. Birth complications, such as a temporary lack of oxygen, may also produce retardation (Burd et al., 2003; Plomin, 2005; West & Blake, 2005; Manning & Hoyme, 2007).

Although limitations in intellectual functioning can be measured in a relatively straightforward manner—using standard IQ tests—it is more difficult to determine how to gauge limitations in other areas. Ultimately, this imprecision leads to a lack of uniformity in the ways experts apply the label of "mental retardation." Furthermore, it has resulted in significant variation in the abilities of people who are categorized as mentally retarded. Accordingly, mentally retarded people range from those who can be taught to work and function with little special attention to those who are virtually untrainable and who never develop speech or such basic motor skills as crawling or walking.

The vast majority of the mentally retarded—some 90%—have relatively low levels of deficits. Classified with **mild retardation,** they score in the range of 50 or 55 to 70 on IQ tests. Typically, their retardation is not even identified before they reach school, although their early development often is slower than average. Once they enter elementary school, their retardation and their need for special attention usually become apparent, as it did with Connie, the first grader profiled at the beginning of this discussion. With appropriate training, these students can reach a third- to sixth-grade educational level, and although they cannot carry out complex intellectual tasks, they are able to hold jobs and function quite independently and successfully.

Intellectual and adaptive limitations become more apparent, however, at higher levels of mental retardation. People whose IQ scores range from around 35 or 40 to 50 or 55 are classified with **moderate retardation.** Composing between 5% and 10% of those classified as mentally retarded, the moderately retarded display distinctive behavior early in their lives. They are slow to develop language skills, and their motor development is also affected. Regular schooling is usually not effective in training people with moderate retardation to acquire academic skills, because generally they are unable to progress beyond the second-grade level. Still, they are capable of learning occupational and social skills, and they can learn to travel independently to familiar places. Typically, they require moderate levels of supervision.

At the most significant levels of retardation—those who are classified with **severe retardation** (IQs ranging from around 20 or 25 to 35 or 40) and **profound retardation** (IQs below 20 or 25)—the ability to function is severely limited. Usually, such people have little or no speech, have poor motor control, and may need 24-hour nursing care. At the same time, though, some people with severe retardation are capable of learning basic self-care skills, such as dressing and eating, and they may even develop the potential to become partially independent as adults. Still, the need for relatively high levels of care continues throughout the life span, and most severely and profoundly retarded people are institutionalized for the majority of their lives. (Also see the *Careers in Lifespan Development* feature.)

Above the Norm: The Gifted and Talented.

Before her second birthday, Audrey Walker recognized sequences of five colors. When she was 6, her father, Michael, overheard her telling a little boy: "No, no, no, Hunter, you don't understand. What you were seeing was a flashback."

At school, Audrey quickly grew bored as the teacher drilled letters and syllables until her classmates caught on. She flourished, instead, in a once-a-week class for gifted and talented children where she could learn as fast as her nimble brain could take her. (Schemo, 2004, p. A18)

It sometimes strikes people as curious that the gifted and talented are considered to have a form of exceptionality. Yet the 3% to 5% of school-age children who are gifted and talented present special challenges of their own.

Which students are considered to be **gifted and talented**? Little agreement exists among researchers on a single definition of this rather broad category of students. However, the federal government considers the term *gifted* to include "children who give evidence of high performance capability in areas such as intellectual, creative, artistic, leadership capacity, or specific

---

mild retardation retardation in which IQ scores fall in the range of 50 or 55 to 70.

moderate retardation retardation in which IQ scores range from around 35 or 40 to 50 or 55.

severe retardation retardation in which IQ scores range from around 20 or 25 to 35 or 40.

profound retardation retardation in which IQ scores fall below 20 or 25.

gifted and talented children who show evidence of high performance capability in areas such as intellectual, creative, artistic, leadership capacity, or specific academic fields.

academic fields, and who require services or activities not ordinarily provided by the school in order to fully develop such capabilities" (Sec 582, P.L. 97–35). Intellectual capabilities, then, represent only one type of exceptionality; unusual potential in areas outside the academic realm are also included in the concept. Gifted and talented children have so much potential that they, no less than students with low IQs, warrant special concern—although special school programs for them are often the first to be dropped when school systems face budgetary problems (Robinson, Zigler, & Gallagher, 2000; Schemo, 2004; Mendoza, 2006).

Despite the stereotypic description of the gifted—particularly those with exceptionally high intelligence—as "unsociable," "poorly adjusted," and "neurotic," most research suggests that highly intelligent people tend to be outgoing, well adjusted, and popular (Howe, 2004; Bracken & Brown, 2006; Shaunessy et al., 2006).

For instance, one landmark, long-term study of 1,500 gifted students, which began in the 1920s, found that not only were the gifted smarter than average, but they were healthier, better coordinated, and psychologically better adjusted than their less intelligent classmates. Furthermore, their lives played out in ways that most people would envy. The subjects received more awards and distinctions, earned more money, and made many more contributions in art and literature than the average person. For instance, by the time they had reached the age of 40, they had collectively produced more than 90 books, 375 plays and short stories, and 2,000 articles, and they had registered more than 200 patents. Perhaps not surprisingly, they reported greater satisfaction with their lives than the nongifted (Terman & Oden, 1959; Sears, 1977; Shurkin, 1992; Reis & Renzulli, 2004).

Yet being gifted and talented is no guarantee of success in school, as we can see if we consider the particular components of the category. For example, the verbal abilities that allow the eloquent expression of ideas and feelings can equally permit the expression of glib and persuasive statements that happen to be inaccurate. Furthermore, teachers may sometimes misinterpret the

Careers in Lifespan Development

Vikas M. Darji

Position: Math/Science Teacher, Gables Academy, Stone Mountain, Georgia

Education: BS Degree, Applied Mathematics, Georgia Tech University

Home: Snellville, Georgia

School provides an abundance of challenges for any child, but it can be especially demanding for students with special needs. It is in this case where special education teachers become a critical asset to the development of children with learning disabilities.

Vikas Darji, a math and science teacher at Gables Academy, a small private school that works exclusively with students with learning disabilities, notes that patience and a specialized approach to teaching are important.

"I have to provide a lot of experimental and hands-on activities," Darji said. "If we're doing math I have to show real money, measure real things, and figure out real angles in geometry. I also use number games as well as flash cards and dice."

"You also have to do a lot of one-on-one work. Even though I only have four or five students in one class, I have to circle around and work with everyone. Each student is on a different level," he added.

Working in a class with fewer students is a plus, according to Darji, who was recognized as an outstanding teacher by the National Association of Special Education Teachers.

"When you have a class of 30 or 35 students, you just can't give individual attention," he said. "In this situation I can set my own pace. I also know a child's strengths and weaknesses in advance from psycho-educational testing. Even though I may teach them all the same thing, they will be tested individually and taught differently," he explained.

Working with students who have a variety of learning disabilities that include dyslexia and attention deficit hyperactivity disorder, Darji stresses patience as a key approach used by special education teachers.

"You have to give students with special needs a break and try to understand them and their difficulties," he noted. "You should try to encourage them and look for positive things and progress. Talk to them outside of class and ask them about their home lives, letting them know you are interested in them."

"There is always a lack of self-confidence or lack of knowledge, and sometimes both. You have to learn where the student's ability lies and go from there," Darji said.

humor, novelty, and creativity of unusually gifted children, and see their intellectual fervor as disruptive or inappropriate. And peers are not always sympathetic: Some very bright children try to hide their intelligence in an effort to fit in better with other students (Swiatek, 2002).

Educating the Gifted and Talented. Educators have devised two approaches to teaching the gifted and talented: acceleration and enrichment. **Acceleration** allows gifted students to move ahead at their own pace, even if this means skipping to higher grade levels. The materials that students receive under acceleration programs are not necessarily different from what other students receive; they simply are provided at a faster pace than for the average student.

An alternative approach is **enrichment,** through which students are kept at grade level but are enrolled in special programs and given individual activities to allow greater depth of study on a given topic. In enrichment, the material provided to gifted students differs not only in the timing of its presentation, but in its sophistication as well. Thus, enrichment materials are designed to provide an intellectual challenge to the gifted student, encouraging higher-order thinking (Worrell, Szarko, & Gabelko, 2001).

Acceleration programs can be remarkably effective. Most studies have shown that gifted students who begin school even considerably earlier than their age-mates do as well as or better than those who begin at the traditional age. One of the best illustrations of the benefits of acceleration is the "Study of Mathematically Precocious Youth," an ongoing program at Vanderbilt University. In this program, seventh and eighth graders who have unusual abilities in mathematics participate in a variety of special classes and workshops. The results have been nothing short of sensational, with students successfully completing college courses and sometimes even enrolling in college early. Some students have even graduated from college before the age of 18 (Achter et al., 1999; Lubinski & Benbow, 2001; Webb, Lubinski, & Benbow, 2001).

acceleration special programs that allow gifted students to move ahead at their own pace, even if this means skipping to higher grade levels.

enrichment an approach through which students are kept at grade level but are enrolled in special programs and given individual activities to allow greater depth of study on a given topic.

Review and Apply

Review

- The development of reading skill generally occurs in several stages. A combination of elements from code-based (i.e., phonics) approaches and whole-language approaches appears to offer the most promise.

- Multicultural education is in transition from a melting-pot model of cultural assimilation to a pluralistic society model.

- The measurement of intelligence has traditionally been a matter of testing skills that promote academic success.

- Recent theories of intelligence suggest that there may be several distinct intelligences or several components of intelligence that reflect different ways of processing information.

- U.S. educators are attempting to deal with substantial numbers of exceptional persons whose intellectual and other skills are significantly lower or higher than normal.

Applying Lifespan Development

- Should one goal of society be to foster cultural assimilation of children from other cultures? Why or why not?

- *From an educator's perspective:* Does Howard Gardner's theory of multiple intelligences suggest that classroom instruction should be modified from an emphasis on the traditional 3Rs of reading, writing, and arithmetic?

Epilogue

In this chapter, we discussed children's physical and cognitive development during the middle childhood years. We considered physical growth and its related nutrition, and health concerns. We also looked at the intellectual growth that occurs at this time as interpreted by Piaget, information processing approaches, and Lev Vygotsky. Children at this age show increased capabilities in memory and language, which facilitate and support gains in many other areas. We looked at some aspects of schooling worldwide and, especially, in the United States, concluding with an examination of intelligence: how it is defined, how it is tested, and how children who fall significantly below or above the intellectual norm are educated and treated.

Look back to the prologue, about La-Toya Pankey's development of reading skills, and answer the following questions:

1. Judging from the cues provided in the prologue, how would you have estimated La-Toya's chances for academic success before you learned about her ability to read? Why?

2. If you wished to isolate the factors in La-Toya's genetic or environmental background that contributed to her interest and ability in reading, how would you proceed? Which factors would you examine? What questions would you ask?

3. Given her circumstances, what threats to academic accomplishment does La-Toya still face? What advantages does she seem to have?

4. Discuss La-Toya's situation in light of the premises of the authors of *The Bell Curve*. If La-Toya succeeds academically, outperforming students of higher socioeconomic status, how would the authors explain this phenomenon? How do you explain it?

Looking Back

■ In what ways do children grow during the school years, and what factors influence their growth?

- The middle childhood years are characterized by slow and steady growth. Weight is redistributed as baby fat disappears. In part, growth is genetically determined, but societal factors such as affluence, dietary habits, nutrition, and disease also contribute significantly.

- During the middle childhood years, great improvements occur in gross motor skills. Cultural expectations appear to underlie most gross motor skill differences between boys and girls. Fine motor skills also develop rapidly.

■ What are the main health concerns of school-age children?

- Adequate nutrition is important because of its contributions to growth, health, social and emotional functioning, and cognitive performance.

- Obesity is partially influenced by genetic factors, but is also associated with children's failure to develop internal controls, overeating, overindulgence in sedentary activities such as television viewing, and lack of physical exercise.

- Asthma and childhood depression are fairly prevalent among children of school age.

■ What sorts of special needs may become apparent in children of this age, and how can they be met?

- Visual, auditory, and speech impairments, as well as other learning disabilities, can lead to academic and social problems and must be handled with sensitivity and appropriate assistance.

- Children with attention deficit hyperactivity disorder exhibit another form of special need. ADHD is characterized by inattention, impulsiveness, failure to complete tasks, lack of organization, and excessive amounts of uncontrollable activity. Treatment of ADHD by drugs is highly controversial because of unwanted side effects and doubts about long-term consequences.

■ In what ways do children develop cognitively during these years, according to major theoretical approaches?

- According to Piaget, school-age children enter the concrete operational period and for the first time become capable of applying logical thought processes to concrete problems.

- According to information processing approaches, children's intellectual development in the school years can be attributed to substantial increases in memory capacity and the sophistication of the "programs" children can handle.

- Vygotsky recommends that students focus on active learning through child–adult and child–child interactions that fall within each child's zone of proximal development.

■ **How does language develop during the middle childhood period?**

- The language development of children in the school years is substantial, with improvements in vocabulary, syntax, and pragmatics. Children learn to control their behavior through linguistic strategies, and they learn more effectively by seeking clarification when they need it.

- Bilingualism can be beneficial in the school years. Children who are taught all subjects in the first language, with simultaneous instruction in English, appear to experience few deficits and attain several linguistic and cognitive advantages.

■ **What are some trends in schooling today?**

- Schooling, which is available to nearly all children in most developed countries, is not as accessible to children, especially girls, in many less developed countries.

- The development of reading skill, which is fundamental to schooling, generally occurs in several stages: identifying letters, reading highly familiar words, sounding out letters and blending sounds into words, reading words with fluency but with little comprehension, reading with comprehension and for practical purposes, and reading material that reflects multiple points of view.

- Multiculturalism and diversity are significant issues in U.S. schools, where the melting-pot society, in which minority cultures are assimilated to the majority culture, is being replaced by the pluralistic society, in which individual cultures maintain their own identities while participating in the definition of a larger culture.

■ **How can intelligence be measured, and how are exceptional children educated?**

- Intelligence testing has traditionally focused on factors that differentiate successful academic performers from unsuccessful ones. The intelligence quotient, or IQ, reflects the ratio of a person's mental age to his or her chronological age. Other conceptualizations of intelligence focus on different types of intelligence or on different aspects of the information processing task.

- In today's schools, exceptional children—including children with intellectual deficits—are to be educated in the least restrictive environment, typically the regular classroom. If done properly, this strategy can benefit all students and permit the exceptional student to focus on strengths rather than weaknesses.

- Gifted and talented children can benefit from special educational programs, including acceleration programs and enrichment programs.

Key Terms and Concepts

asthma (p. 292)
visual impairment (p. 295)
auditory impairment (p. 295)
speech impairment (p. 296)
stuttering (p. 296)
learning disabilities (p. 296)
attention deficit hyperactivity disorder (ADHD) (p. 297)
concrete operational stage (p. 300)
decentering (p. 300)
memory (p. 302)
metamemory (p. 303)
metalinguistic awareness (p. 305)
bilingualism (p. 306)
multicultural education (p. 313)
cultural assimilation model (p. 313)

pluralistic society model (p. 314)
bicultural identity (p. 314)
intelligence (p. 315)
mental age (p. 316)
chronological (or physical) age (p. 316)
intelligence quotient (or IQ score) (p. 316)
Stanford-Binet Intelligence Scales, Fifth Edition (SB5) (p. 317)
Wechsler Intelligence Scale for Children—Fourth Edition (WISC-IV) (p. 317)
Kaufman Assessment Battery for Children, Second edition (KABC—II) (p. 317)
fluid intelligence (p. 319)
crystallized intelligence (p. 319)

triarchic theory of intelligence (p. 319)
least restrictive environment (p. 323)
mainstreaming (p. 324)
mental retardation (p. 324)
mild retardation (p. 325)
moderate retardation (p. 325)
severe retardation (p. 325)
profound retardation (p. 325)
gifted and talented (p. 325)
acceleration (p. 327)
enrichment (p. 327)

10 Social and Personality Development in Middle Childhood

Chapter Overview

THE DEVELOPING SELF

Psychosocial Development in Middle Childhood: Industry Versus Inferiority

Understanding One's Self: A New Response to "Who Am I?"

Self-Esteem: Developing a Positive—or Negative—View of the Self

Moral Development

RELATIONSHIPS: BUILDING FRIENDSHIP IN MIDDLE CHILDHOOD

Stages of Friendship: Changing Views of Friends

Individual Differences in Friendship: What Makes a Child Popular?

Bullying: Schoolyard and Online Victimization

Gender and Friendships: The Sex Segregation of Middle Childhood

Cross-Race Friendships: Integration in and out of the Classroom

FAMILY AND SCHOOL: SHAPING CHILDREN'S BEHAVIOR IN MIDDLE CHILDHOOD

Family: The Changing Home Environment

School: The Academic Environment

Prologue: Play Time

On a bright weekday afternoon, six boys are playing under the endless Nevada sky. Bryan and Christopher Hendrickson are third graders, 9-year-old twins, and as on so many afternoons, their garage is headquarters.

The twins, their younger brother, Andrew, and three friends pull two enormous boxes from the garage—one each from a recently purchased washer and dryer—and set to work transforming them.

"We're making our spaceship," says Bryan. "With guns included."

Why does the spaceship need guns?

"For evil, don't you know?" says Bryan. He sprays machine gun sounds.

As the sun sets, an ever-larger clan of kids, now including the twins' older sister, Lindsay, invades the backyard. The boxes become forts, the group divides in two, and a furious round of capture-the-stuffed-tiger ensues. . .

Around 6 o'clock, mom Judy summons all the kids—now nearly a dozen—inside for dinner of pizza and juice. Later, the game resumes for another hour or so by moonlight before exhausting itself. Some children wander home. Others are picked up by their parents. (Fishman, 1999, p. 56)

During middle childhood, play involves the development of friendships and social relationships.

For Bryan and Christopher, afternoons like these represent more than just a way of passing time. They also pave the way for the formation of friendships and social relationships, a key developmental task during middle childhood.

In this chapter, we focus on social and personality development during middle childhood. It is a time when children's views of themselves undergo significant changes, they form new bonds with friends and family, and they become increasingly attached to social institutions outside the home.

We start our consideration of personality and social development during middle childhood by examining the changes that occur in the ways children see themselves. We discuss how they view their personal characteristics, and we examine the complex issue of self-esteem.

Next, the chapter turns to relationships during middle childhood. We discuss the stages of friendship and the ways gender and ethnicity affect how and with whom children interact. We also examine how to improve children's social competence.

The last part of the chapter explores the central societal institution in children's lives: the family. We consider the consequences of divorce, self-care children, and the phenomenon of group care.

After reading this chapter, you will be able to answer these questions:

■ **In what ways do children's views of themselves change during middle childhood?**

■ **Why is self-esteem important during these years?**

■ **How does children's sense of right and wrong change as children age?**

■ **What sorts of relationships and friendships are typical of middle childhood?**

■ **How do gender and ethnicity affect friendships?**

■ **How do today's diverse family and care arrangements affect children?**

■ **How do children's social and emotional lives affect their school performance?**

Looking Ahead

The Developing Self

Nine-year-old Karl Haglund is perched in his eagle's nest, a treehouse built high in the willow that grows in his backyard. Sometimes he sits there alone among the tree's spreading branches, his face turned toward the sky, a boy clearly enjoying his solitude. . . .

This morning Karl is busy sawing and hammering. "It's fun to build," he says. "I started the house when I was 4 years old. Then when I was about 7, my dad built me this platform. 'Cause all my places were falling apart and they were crawling with carpenter ants. So we destroyed them and then built me a deck. And I built on top of it. It's stronger now. You can have privacy here, but it's a bad place to go when it's windy 'cause you almost get blown off." (Kotre & Hall, 1990, p. 116)

Karl's growing sense of competence is reflected in this passage, as he describes how he and his father built his treehouse. Conveying what psychologist Erik Erikson calls "industriousness," Karl's quiet pride in his accomplishment illustrates one of the ways in which children's views of themselves evolve.

Psychosocial Development in Middle Childhood: Industry Versus Inferiority

According to Erik Erikson, whose approach to psychosocial development we last discussed in Chapter 8, middle childhood is very much about competence. Lasting from roughly age 6 to age 12, the **industry-versus-inferiority stage** is characterized by a focus on efforts to meet the challenges presented by parents, peers, school, and the other complexities of the modern world.

As they move through middle childhood, children direct their energies not only to mastering what they are presented in school—an enormous body of information—but to making a place for themselves in their social worlds. Success in this stage brings with it feelings of mastery and proficiency and a growing sense of competence, like those expressed by Karl when he talks

industry-versus-inferiority stage the period from age 6 to 12 characterized by a focus on efforts to attain competence in meeting the challenges presented by parents, peers, school, and the other complexities of the modern world.

about his building experience. On the other hand, difficulties in this stage lead to feelings of failure and inadequacy. As a result, children may withdraw both from academic pursuits, showing less interest and motivation to excel, and from interactions with peers.

Children such as Karl may find that attaining a sense of industry during the middle childhood years has lasting consequences. For example, one study examined how childhood industriousness and hard work were related to adult behavior by following a group of 450 men over a 35-year period, starting in early childhood (Vaillant & Vaillant, 1981). The men who were most industrious and hard-working during childhood were most successful as adults, both in occupational attainment and in their personal lives. In fact, childhood industriousness was more closely associated with adult success than was intelligence or family background.

Understanding One's Self: A New Response to "Who Am I?"

During middle childhood, children continue their efforts to answer the question "Who am I?" as they seek to understand the nature of the self. Although the question does not yet have the urgency it will assume in adolescence, elementary-school-age children still seek to pin down their place in the world.

The Shift in Self-Understanding from the Physical to the Psychological. Children are on a quest for self-understanding during middle childhood. Helped by the cognitive advances that we discussed in the previous chapter, they begin to view themselves less in terms of external, physical attributes and more in terms of psychological traits (Marsh & Ayotte, 2003; Sotiriou & Zafiropoulou, 2003; Lerner, Theokas, & Jelicic, 2005).

For instance, 6-year-old Carey describes herself as "a fast runner and good at drawing"—both characteristics dependent on skill in external activities relying on motor skills. In contrast, 11-year-old Meiping characterizes herself as "pretty smart, friendly, and helpful to my friends." Meiping's view of herself is based on psychological characteristics, inner traits that are more abstract than the younger child's descriptions. The use of inner traits to determine self-concept results from the child's increasing cognitive skills, a development that we discussed in Chapter 9.

In addition to shifting focus from external characteristics to internal, psychological traits, children's views of who they are became less simplistic and have greater complexity. In Erikson's view, children are seeking endeavors where they can be successfully industrious. As they get older, children discover that they may be good at some things and not so good at others. Ten-year-old Ginny, for instance, comes to understand that she is good at arithmetic but not very good at spelling; 11-year-old Alberto determines that he is good at softball but doesn't have the stamina to play soccer very well.

Children's self-concepts become divided into personal and academic spheres. In fact, as can be seen in Figure 10-1, children evaluate themselves in four major areas, and each of these areas can be broken down even further. For instance, the nonacademic self-concept includes the components of physical appearance, peer relations, and physical ability. Academic self-concept is similarly divided. Research on students' self-concepts in English, mathematics, and nonacademic realms has found that the separate self-concepts are not always correlated, although there is overlap among them. For example, a child who sees herself as a star math student is not necessarily going to feel she is great at English (Burnett & Proctor, 2002; Marsh & Ayotte, 2003; Marsh & Hau, 2004).

Social Comparison. If someone asks you how good you are at math, how would you respond? Most of us would compare our performance to others who are roughly of the same age and educational level. It is unlikely that we'd answer the question by comparing ourselves either to Albert Einstein or to a kindergartner just learning about numbers.

Elementary-school-age children begin to follow the same sort of reasoning when they seek to understand how able they are. When they were younger, they tended to consider their abilities in terms of some hypothetical standard, making a judgment that they are good or bad in an absolute sense. Now they begin to use social comparison processes, comparing themselves to others, to determine their levels of accomplishment during middle childhood (Weiss, Ebbeck, & Horn, 1997).

As children become older, they begin to characterize themselves in terms of their psychological attributes as well as their physical achievements.

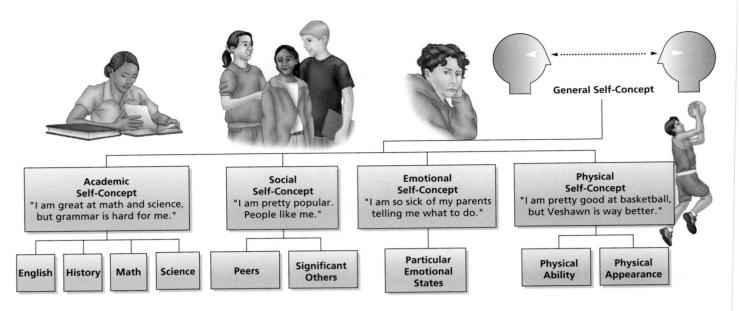

FIGURE 10-1 **LOOKING INWARD: THE DEVELOPMENT OF SELF**

As children get older, their views of self become more differentiated, comprising several personal and academic spheres. What cognitive changes make this possible?

(*Source:* Adapted from Shavelson, Hubner, & Stanton, 1976.)

Social comparison is the desire to evaluate one's own behavior, abilities, expertise, and opinions by comparing them to those of others. According to a theory first suggested by psychologist Leon Festinger (1954), when concrete, objective measures of ability are lacking, people turn to *social reality* to evaluate themselves. Social reality refers to understanding that is derived from how others act, think, feel, and view the world.

But who provides the most adequate comparison? When they cannot objectively evaluate their ability, children during middle childhood increasingly look to others who are similar to themselves (Suls & Wills, 1991; Summers, Schallert, & Ritter, 2003).

Downward Social Comparison. Although children typically compare themselves to similar others, in some cases—particularly when their self-esteem is at stake—they choose to make *downward social comparisons* with others who are obviously less competent or successful (Aspinwall & Taylor, 1993; Vohs & Heatherton, 2004).

Downward social comparison protects children's self-esteem. By comparing themselves to those who are less able, children ensure that they will come out on top and thereby preserve an image of themselves as successful.

Downward social comparison helps explain why some students in elementary schools with generally low achievement levels are found to have stronger academic self-esteem than very capable students in schools with high achievement levels. The reason seems to be that students in the low-achievement schools observe others who are not doing terribly well academically, and they feel relatively good by comparison. In contrast, students in the high-achievement schools may find themselves competing with a more academically proficient group of students, and their perception of their performance may suffer in comparison. At least in terms of self-esteem, then, it is better to be a big fish in a small pond than a small fish in a big one (Marsh & Hau, 2003; Borland & Howsen, 2003).

Self-Esteem: Developing a Positive— or Negative—View of the Self

Children don't dispassionately view themselves just in terms of an itemization of physical and psychological characteristics. Instead, they make judgments about themselves as being good or

social comparison the desire to evaluate one's own behavior, abilities, expertise, and opinions by comparing them to those of others.

According to Erik Erikson, middle childhood encompasses the industry-versus-inferiority stage, characterized by a focus on meeting the challenges presented by the world.

bad in particular ways. **Self-esteem** is an individual's overall and specific positive and negative self-evaluation. Whereas self-concept reflects beliefs and cognitions about the self (*I am good at trumpet; I am not so good at social studies*), self-esteem is more emotionally oriented (*Everybody thinks I'm a nerd.*) (Baumeister, 1993; Davis-Kean & Sandler, 2001; Bracken & Lamprecht, 2003).

Self-esteem develops in important ways during middle childhood. As we've noted, children increasingly compare themselves to others, and as they do, they assess how well they measure up to society's standards. In addition, they increasingly develop their own internal standards of success, and they can see how well they compare to those. One of the advances that occurs during middle childhood is that, like self-concept, self-esteem becomes increasingly differentiated. At the age of 7, most children have self-esteem that reflects a global, fairly simple view of themselves. If their overall self-esteem is positive, they believe that they are relatively good at all things. Conversely, if their overall self-esteem is negative, they feel that they are inadequate at most things (Harter, 1990b; Lerner et al., 2005).

As children progress into the middle childhood years, however, their self-esteem is higher for some areas and lower in others. For example, a boy's overall self-esteem may be composed of positive self-esteem in some areas (such as the positive feelings he gets from his artistic ability) and more negative self-esteem in others (such as the unhappiness he feels over his athletic skills).

Change and Stability in Self-Esteem.

Generally, overall self-esteem is high during middle childhood, but it begins to decline around the age of 12. Although there are probably several reasons for the decline, the main one appears to be the school transition that typically occurs around this age: Students leaving elementary school and entering either middle school or junior high school show a decline in self-esteem, which then gradually rises again (Twenge & Campbell, 2001; Robins & Trzesniewski, 2005).

On the other hand, some children have chronically low self-esteem. Children with low self-esteem face a tough road, in part because their self-esteem becomes enmeshed in a cycle of failure that grows increasingly difficult to break. Assume, for instance, that Harry, a student with chronically low self-esteem, is facing an important test. Because of his low self-esteem, he expects to do poorly. As a consequence, he is quite anxious—so anxious that he is unable to concentrate well and study effectively. Furthermore, he may decide not to study much, because he figures that if he's going to do badly anyway, why bother studying?

self-esteem an individual's overall and specific positive and negative self-evaluation.

**FIGURE 10-2   A CYCLE OF LOW
SELF-ESTEEM**

Because children with low self-esteem may
expect to do poorly on a test, they may
experience high anxiety and not work as
hard as those with higher self-esteem. As a
result, they actually do perform badly on the
test, which in turn confirms their negative
view of themselves. In contrast, those with
high self-esteem have more positive expectations, which leads to lower anxiety and
higher motivation. As a consequence, they
perform better, reinforcing their positive
self-image. How would a teacher help
students with low self-esteem break out of
their negative cycle?

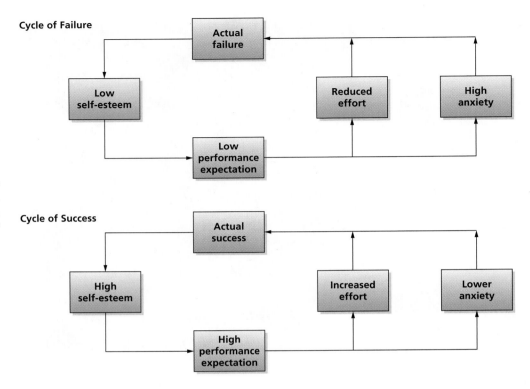

Ultimately, of course, Harry's high anxiety and lack of effort bring about the result he
expected: He does poorly on the test. This failure, which confirms Harry's expectation, reinforces his low self-esteem, and the cycle of failure continues (see Figure 10-2).

On the other hand, students with high self-esteem travel a more positive path, falling into a
cycle of success. Having higher expectations leads to increased effort and lower anxiety, increasing
the probability of success. In turn, this helps affirm their higher self-esteem that began the cycle.

Parents can help break the cycle of failure by promoting their children's self-esteem. The best
way to do this is through the use of the *authoritative* child-rearing style that we discussed in
Chapter 8. Authoritative parents are warm and emotionally supportive, while still setting clear
limits for their children's behavior. In contrast, other parenting styles have less positive effects
on self-esteem. Parents who are highly punitive and controlling send a message to their
children that they are untrustworthy and unable to make good decisions—a message that can
undermine children's sense of adequacy. Highly indulgent parents, who indiscriminately praise
and reinforce their children regardless of their actual performance, can create a false sense of
self-esteem in their children, which ultimately may be just as damaging to children (DeHart,
Pelham, & Tennen, 2006; Rudy & Grusec, 2006; Bender et al., 2007).

Race and Self-Esteem.   If you were a member of a racial group whose members routinely
experienced prejudice and discrimination, it seems reasonable to predict that your self-esteem
would be affected. Early research confirmed that hypothesis and found that African Americans
had lower self-esteem than whites. For example, a set of pioneering studies a generation ago
found that African American children shown black and white dolls preferred the white dolls
over the black ones (Clark & Clark, 1947). The interpretation that was drawn from the study:
The self-esteem of the African American children was low.

However, more recent research has shown these early assumptions to be overstated. The
picture is more complex regarding relative levels of self-esteem between members of different
racial and ethnic groups. For example, although white children initially show higher
self-esteem than black children, black children begin to show slightly higher self-esteem than
white children around the age of 11. This shift occurs as African American children become

In pioneering research conducted several
decades ago, African American girls' preference for white dolls was viewed as an indication of low self-esteem. More recent evidence, however, suggests that whites and
African American children show little difference in self-esteem.

more identified with their racial group, develop more complex views of racial identity, and increasingly view the positive aspects of their group membership (Gray-Little & Hafdahl, 2000; Oyserman et al., 2003; Tatum, 2007).

Hispanic children also show an increase in self-esteem toward the end of middle childhood, although even in adolescence their self-esteem still trails that of whites. In contrast, Asian American children show the opposite pattern: their self-esteem in elementary school is higher than that of whites and blacks, but by the end of childhood, their self-esteem is lower than that of whites (Twenge & Crocker, 2002; Umana-Taylor, Diveri, & Fine, 2002; Tropp & Wright, 2003).

One explanation for the complex relationship between self-esteem and minority group status comes from *social identity theory*. According to the theory, members of a minority group are likely to accept the negative views held by a majority group only if they perceive that there is little realistic possibility of changing the power and status differences between the groups. If minority group members feel that prejudice and discrimination can be reduced, and they blame society for the prejudice and not themselves, self-esteem should not differ between majority and minority groups (Tajfel, 1982; Turner & Onorato, 1999).

In fact, as group pride and ethnic awareness on the part of minority group members has grown, differences in self-esteem between members of different ethnic groups have narrowed. This trend has further been supported by an increased sensitivity to the importance of multiculturalism (Goodstein & Ponterotto, 1997; Negy, Shreve, & Jensen, 2003; Lee, 2005; Tatum, 2007).

Developmental Diversity

Are Children of Immigrant Families Well Adjusted?

Immigration to the United States has risen significantly in the last 30 years. More than 13 million children in the United States are either foreign born or the children of immigrants—some one-fifth of the total population of children.

How well are these children of immigrants faring? Quite well. In fact, in some ways they are better off than their nonimmigrant peers. For example, they tend to have equal or better grades in school than children whose parents were born in the United States. Psychologically, they also do quite well, showing similar levels of self-esteem as nonimmigrant children, although they do report feeling less popular and less in control of their lives (Kao & Tienda, 1995; Kao, 2000; Harris, 2000).

Why is the adjustment of immigrant children to U.S. culture so generally positive? One answer is that often their socioeconomic status is relatively higher. In spite of stereotypes that immigrant families come from lower social classes, many in fact are well educated and come to the United States seeking greater opportunities.

But socioeconomic status is only part of the story. Even the immigrant children who are not financially well off are often more highly motivated to succeed and place greater value on education than do children in nonimmigrant families. In addition, many immigrant children come from societies that emphasize collectivism, and consequently they may feel more obligation and duty toward their family to succeed. Finally, their country of origin may give some immigrant children a strong enough cultural identity to prevent them from adopting undesirable "American" behaviors—such as materialism or selfishness (Fuligini, Tseng, & Lam, 1999; Fuligni & Yoshikawa, 2003).

During the middle childhood years, it thus appears that children in immigrant families typically do quite well in the United States. The story is less clear, however, when immigrant children reach adolescence and adulthood. Research is just beginning to clarify how effectively immigrants cope over the course of the life span (Fuligini, 1998; Portes & Rumbaut, 2001).

Immigrant children tend to fare quite well in the United States, partly because many come from societies that emphasize collectivism, and consequently may feel more obligation and duty to their family to succeed. What are some other cultural differences that can lead to the success of immigrant children?

VIDEO CLIP
MORAL DEVELOPMENT

Moral Development

Your wife is near death from an unusual kind of cancer. One drug exists that the physicians think might save her—a form of radium that a scientist in a nearby city has recently developed. The drug, though, is expensive to manufacture, and the scientist is charging ten times what the drug costs him to make. He pays $1,000 for the radium and charges $10,000 for a small dose. You have gone to everyone you know to borrow money, but you can get together only $2,500—one-quarter of what you need. You've told the scientist that your wife is dying and asked him to sell it more cheaply or let you pay later. But the scientist has said, "No, I discovered the drug and I'm going to make money from it." In desperation, you consider breaking into the scientist's laboratory to steal the drug for your wife. Should you do it?

According to developmental psychologist Lawrence Kohlberg and his colleagues, the answer that children give to this question reveals central aspects of their sense of morality and justice. He suggests that people's responses to moral dilemmas such as this one reveal the stage of moral development they have attained—as well as yield information about their general level of cognitive development (Kohlberg, 1984; Colby & Kohlberg, 1987).

Kohlberg contends that people pass through a series of stages as their sense of justice evolves and in the kind of reasoning they use to make moral judgments. Primarily due to cognitive characteristics that we discussed earlier, younger school-age children tend to think either in terms of concrete, unvarying rules ("It is always wrong to steal" or "I'll be punished if I steal") or in terms of the rules of society ("Good people don't steal" or "What if everyone stole?").

By the time they reach adolescence, however, individuals are able to reason on a higher plane, typically having reached Piaget's stage of formal operations. They are capable of comprehending abstract, formal principles of morality, and they consider cases such as the one just presented in terms of broader issues of morality and of right and wrong ("Stealing may be acceptable if you are following your own conscience and doing the right thing").

Kohlberg suggests that moral development emerges in a three-level sequence, which is further subdivided into six stages (see Table 10-1). At the lowest level, *preconventional morality* (Stages 1 and 2), people follow rigid rules based on punishments or rewards. For example, a student at the preconventional level might evaluate the moral dilemma posed in the story by saying that it was not worth stealing the drug because if you were caught, you would go to jail.

Table 10-1   Kohlberg's Sequence of Moral Reasoning

Level	Stage	SAMPLE MORAL REASONING	
		In Favor of Stealing	Against Stealing
LEVEL 1 **Preconventional morality:** At this level, the concrete interests of the individual are considered in terms of rewards and punishments.	**STAGE 1** Obedience and punishment orientation: At this stage, people stick to rules in order to avoid punishment, and obedience occurs for its own sake.	"If you let your wife die, you will get in trouble. You'll be blamed for not spending the money to save her, and there'll be an investigation of you and the druggist for your wife's death."	"You shouldn't steal the drug because you'll get caught and sent to jail if you do. If you do get away, your conscience will bother you thinking how the police will catch up with you at any minute."
	STAGE 2 Reward orientation: At this stage, rules are followed only for a person's own benefit. Obedience occurs because of rewards that are received.	"If you do happen to get caught, you could give the drug back and you wouldn't get much of a sentence. It wouldn't bother you much to serve a little jail term, if you have your wife when you get out."	"You may not get much of a jail term if you steal the drug, but your wife will probably die before you get out, so it won't do much good. If your wife dies, you shouldn't blame yourself; it isn't your fault she has cancer."
LEVEL 2 **Conventional morality:** At this level, people approach moral problems as members of society. They are interested in pleasing others by acting as good members of society.	**STAGE 3** "Good boy" morality: Individuals at this stage show an interest in maintaining the respect of others and doing what is expected of them.	"No one will think you're bad if you steal the drug, but your family will think you're an inhuman husband if you don't. If you let your wife die, you'll never be able to look anybody in the face again."	"It isn't just the druggist who will think you're a criminal; everyone else will, too. After you steal the drug, you'll feel bad thinking how you've brought dishonor on your family and yourself; you won't be able to face anyone again."
	STAGE 4 Authority and social-order-maintaining morality: People at this stage conform to society's rules and consider that "right" is what society defines as right.	"If you have any sense of honor, you won't let your wife die just because you're afraid to do the only thing that will save her. You'll always feel guilty that you caused her death if you don't do your duty to her."	"You're desperate and you may not know you're doing wrong when you steal the drug. But you'll know you did wrong after you're sent to jail. You'll always feel guilty for your dishonesty and law-breaking."
LEVEL 3 **Postconventional morality:** At this level, people use moral principles, which are seen as broader than those of any particular society.	**STAGE 5** Morality of contract, individual rights, and democratically accepted law: People at this stage do what is right because of a sense of obligation to laws which are agreed upon within society. They perceive that laws can be modified as part of changes in an implicit social contract.	"You'll lose other people's respect, not gain it, if you don't steal. If you let your wife die, it will be out of fear, not out of reasoning. So you'll just lose self-respect and probably the respect of others, too."	"You'll lose your standing and respect in the community and violate the law. You'll lose respect for yourself if you're carried away by emotion and forget the long-range point of view."
	STAGE 6 Morality of individual principles and conscience: At this final stage, a person follows laws because they are based on universal ethical principles. Laws that violate the principles are disobeyed.	"If you don't steal the drug, and if you let your wife die, you'll always condemn yourself for it afterward. You won't be blamed and you'll have lived up to the outside rule of the law, but you won't have lived up to your own standards of conscience."	"If you steal the drug, you won't be blamed by other people, but you'll condemn yourself because you won't have lived up to your own conscience and standards of honesty."

(*Source*: Adapted from Kohlberg, 1969.)

In the next level, that of *conventional morality* (Stages 3 and 4), people approach moral problems in terms of their own position as good, responsible members of society. Some at this level would decide *against* stealing the drug because they think they would feel guilty or dishonest for violating social norms. Others would decide *in favor* of stealing the drug because if they did nothing in this situation, they would be unable to face others. All of these people would be reasoning at the conventional level of morality.

Finally, individuals using *postconventional morality* (Level 3; Stages 5 and 6) invoke universal moral principles that are considered broader than the rules of the particular society in which they live. People who feel that they would condemn themselves if they did not steal the drug because they would not be living up to their own moral principles would be reasoning at the postconventional level.

Kohlberg's theory proposes that people move through the periods of moral development in a fixed order and that they are unable to reach the highest stage until adolescence, due to deficits in cognitive development that are not overcome until then (Kurtines & Gewirtz, 1987). However, not everyone is presumed to reach the highest stages: Kohlberg found that postconventional reasoning is relatively rare.

Although Kohlberg's theory provides a good account of the development of moral *judgments,* the links with moral *behavior* are less strong. Still, students at higher levels of moral reasoning are less likely to engage in antisocial behavior at school (such as breaking school rules) and in the community (engaging in juvenile delinquency; Richards et al., 1992; Langford, 1995; Carpendale, 2000).

Furthermore, one experiment found that 15% of students who reasoned at the postconventional level of morality—the highest category—cheated when given the opportunity, although they were not as likely to cheat as those at lower levels, where more than half of the students cheated. Clearly, though, knowing what is morally right does not always mean acting that way (Snarey, 1995; Killen & Hart, 1995; Hart, Burock, & London, 2003; Semerci, 2006).

Kohlberg's theory has also been criticized because it is based solely on observations of members of Western cultures. In fact, cross-cultural research finds that members of more industrialized, technologically advanced cultures move through the stages more rapidly than members of nonindustrialized countries. Why? One explanation is that Kohlberg's higher stages are based on moral reasoning involving governmental and societal institutions such as the police and the court system. In less industrialized areas, morality may be based more on relationships between people in a particular village. In short, the nature of morality may differ in diverse cultures, and Kohlberg's theory is more suited for Western cultures (Fu et al., 2007).

An aspect of Kohlberg's theory that has proved even more problematic is the difficulty it has explaining *girls'* moral judgments. Because the theory initially was based largely on data from males, some researchers have argued that it does a better job describing boys' moral development than girls' moral development. This would explain the surprising finding that women typically score at a lower level than men on tests of moral judgments using Kohlberg's stage sequence. This result has led to an alternative account of moral development for girls.

Moral Development in Girls.   Psychologist Carol Gilligan (1982, 1987) has suggested that differences in the ways boys and girls are raised in our society lead to basic distinctions in how men and women view moral behavior. According to Gilligan, boys view morality primarily in terms of broad principles such as justice or fairness, while girls see it in terms of responsibility toward individuals and willingness to sacrifice themselves to help specific individuals within the context of particular relationships. Compassion for individuals, then, is a more prominent factor in moral behavior for women than it is for men (Gilligan, Ward, & Taylor, 1988; Gilligan, Lyons, & Hammer, 1990; Gump, Baker, & Roll, 2000).

Gilligan views morality as developing among females in a three-stage process (summarized in Table 10-2). In the first stage, called "orientation toward individual survival," females

Table 10-2	Gilligan's Three Stages of Moral Development for Women	
Stage	**Characteristics**	**Example**
Stage 1 Orientation toward individual survival	Initial concentration is on what is practical and best for self. Gradual transition from selfishness to responsibility, which includes thinking about what would be best for others.	A first grader may insist on playing only games of her own choosing when playing with a friend.
Stage 2 Goodness as self-sacrifice	Initial view is that a woman must sacrifice her own wishes to what other people want. Gradual transition from "goodness" to "truth," which takes into account needs of both self and others.	Now older, the same girl may believe that to be a good friend, she must play the games her friend chooses, even if she herself doesn't like them.
Stage 3 Morality of nonviolence	A moral equivalence is established between self and others. Hurting anyone—including one's self—is seen as immoral. Most sophisticated form of reasoning, according to Gilligan.	The same girl may realize that both friends must enjoy their time together and look for activities that both she and her friend can enjoy.

first concentrate on what is practical and best for them, gradually making a transition from selfishness to responsibility, in which they think about what would be best for others. In the second stage, termed "goodness as self-sacrifice," females begin to think that they must sacrifice their own wishes to what other people want. Ideally, women make a transition from "goodness" to "truth," in which they take into account their own needs plus those of others. This transition leads to the third stage, "morality of nonviolence," in which women come to see that hurting anyone is immoral—including hurting themselves. This realization establishes a moral equivalence between themselves and others and represents, according to Gilligan, the most sophisticated level of moral reasoning.

It is obvious that Gilligan's sequence of stages is quite different from Kohlberg's, and some developmentalists have suggested that her rejection of Kohlberg's work is too sweeping and that gender differences are not as pronounced as first thought (Colby & Damon, 1987). For instance, some researchers argue that both males and females use similar

Lawrence Kohlberg and Carol Gilligan present contrasting explanations for children's moral development, with Gilligan focusing on gender differences in how males and females view morality.

"justice" and "care" orientations in making moral judgments. Clearly, the question of how boys and girls differ in their moral orientations, as well as the nature of moral development in general, is far from settled (Tangney & Dearing, 2002; Weisz & Black, 2002; Jorgensen, 2006; Tappan, 2006).

Review and Apply

Review

- According to Erikson, children at this time are in the industry-versus-inferiority stage.
- In the middle childhood years, children begin to use social comparison and self-concepts based on psychological rather than physical characteristics.
- During the middle childhood years, self-esteem is based on comparisons with others and internal standards of success; if self-esteem is low, the result can be a cycle of failure.
- According to Kohlberg, moral development proceeds from a concern with rewards and punishments, through a focus on social conventions and rules, toward a sense of universal moral principles. Gilligan has suggested, however, that girls may follow a somewhat different progression of moral development.

Applying Lifespan Development

- Kohlberg and Gilligan each suggest there are three major levels of moral development. Are any of their levels comparable? In which level of either theory do you think that the largest discrepancy between males and females would be observed?
- *From an educator's perspective:* What can teachers do to help children whose low self-esteem is causing them to fail? How can this cycle of failure be broken?

Relationships: Building Friendship in Middle Childhood

In Lunch Room Number Two, Jamillah and her new classmates chew slowly on sandwiches and sip quietly on straws from cartons of milk. . . . Boys and girls look timidly at the strange faces across the table from them, looking for someone who might play with them in the schoolyard, someone who might become a friend.

For these children, what happens in the schoolyard will be just as important as what happens in the school. And when they're out on the playground, there will be no one to protect them. No child will hold back to keep from beating them at a game, humiliating them in a test of skill, or harming them in a fight. No one will run interference or guarantee membership in a group. Out on the playground, it's sink or swim. No one automatically becomes your friend. (Kotre & Hall, 1990, pp. 112–113)

As Jamillah and her classmates demonstrate, friendship comes to play an increasingly important role during middle childhood. Children grow progressively more sensitive to the importance of friends, and building and maintaining friendships becomes a large part of children's social lives.

Mutual trust is considered to be the centerpiece of friendship during middle childhood.

Friends influence children's development in several ways. For instance, friendships provide children with information about the world and other people as well as about themselves. Friends provide emotional support that allows children to respond more effectively to stress. Having friends makes a child less likely to be the target of aggression, and it can teach children how to manage and control their emotions and help them interpret their own emotional experiences (Berndt, 2002).

Friendships in middle childhood also provide a training ground for communicating and interacting with others. They also can foster intellectual growth by increasing children's range of experiences (Harris, 1998; Nangle & Erdley, 2001; Gifford-Smith & Brownell, 2003).

Although friends and other peers become increasingly influential throughout middle childhood, they are not more important than parents and other family members. Most developmentalists believe that children's psychological functioning and their development in general is the product of a combination of factors, including peers and parents (Harris, 2000; Vandell, 2000; Parke, Simpkins, & McDowell, 2002). For that reason, we'll talk more about the influence of family later in this chapter.

Stages of Friendship: Changing Views of Friends

During middle childhood, a child's conception of the nature of friendship undergoes some profound changes. According to developmental psychologist William Damon, a child's view of friendship passes through three distinct stages (Damon & Hart, 1988).

Stage 1: Basing Friendship on Others' Behavior.   In the first stage, which ranges from around 4 to 7 years of age, children see friends as others who like them and with whom they share toys and other activities. They view the children with whom they spend the most time as their friends. For instance, a kindergartner who was asked, "How do you know that someone is your best friend?" responded in this way:

> I sleep over at his house sometimes. When he's playing ball with his friends he'll let me play. When I slept over, he let me get in front of him in 4-squares. He likes me. (Damon, 1983, p. 140)

What children in this first stage don't do much of, however, is to take others' personal qualities into consideration. For instance, they don't see their friendships as being based upon their peers' unique positive personal traits. Instead, they use a very concrete approach to deciding who is a friend, primarily dependent upon others' behavior. They like those who share and with whom they can share, while they don't like those who don't share, who hit, or who don't play with them. In sum, in the first stage, friends are viewed largely in terms of presenting opportunities for pleasant interactions.

Stage 2: Basing Friendship on Trust.   In the next stage, however, children's view of friendship becomes more complicated. Lasting from around age 8 to age 10, this stage covers a period in which children take others' personal qualities and traits as well as the rewards they provide into consideration. But the centerpiece of friendship in this second stage is mutual trust. Friends are seen as those who can be counted on to help out when they are needed. This means that violations of trust are taken very seriously, and friends cannot make amends for such violations just by engaging in positive play, as they might at earlier ages. Instead, the expectation is that formal explanations and formal apologies must be provided before a friendship can be reestablished.

Stage 3: Basing Friendship on Psychological Closeness.   The third stage of friendship begins toward the end of middle childhood, from 11 to 15 years of age. During this period, children begin to develop the view of friendship that they hold during adolescence. Although we'll discuss this perspective in detail in Chapter 12, the main criteria for friendship shift toward intimacy and loyalty. Friendship at this stage is characterized by feelings of closeness, usually brought on by sharing personal thoughts and feelings through mutual disclosure. They are also somewhat exclusive. By the time they reach the end of middle childhood, children seek out friends who will be loyal, and they come to view friendship not so much in terms of shared activities as in terms of the psychological benefits that friendship brings (Newcomb & Bagwell, 1995).

Children also develop clear ideas about which behaviors they seek in their friends—and which they dislike. As can be seen in Table 10-3, fifth and sixth graders most enjoy others who invite them to participate in activities and who are helpful, both physically and psychologically. In contrast, displays of physical or verbal aggression, among other behaviors, are disliked.

Individual Differences in Friendship: What Makes a Child Popular?

Why is it that some children are the schoolyard equivalent of the life of the party, while others are social isolates whose overtures toward their peers are dismissed or disdained?

Developmentalists have attempted to answer this question by examining individual differences in popularity, seeking to identify the reasons why some children climb the ladder of popularity while others remain firmly on the ground.

Status Among School-Age Children: Establishing One's Position.   Who's on top? Although school-age children are not likely to articulate such a question, the reality of children's friendships is that they exhibit clear hierarchies in terms of status. **Status** is the evaluation of a role or person by other relevant members of a group. Children who have higher status have greater access to available resources, such as games, toys, books, and information. In contrast, lower-status children are more likely to follow the lead of children of higher status.

Status can be measured in several ways. Most frequently, children are asked directly how much they like or dislike particular classmates. They also may be asked whom they would most (and least) like to play with or to carry out some task with.

status   the evaluation of a role or person by other relevant members of a group.

Table 10-3	The Most-Liked and Least-Liked Behaviors That Children Note in their Friends, in Order of Importance	

Most-Liked Behaviors	Least-Liked Behaviors
Having a sense of humor	Verbal aggression
Being nice or friendly	Expressions of anger
Being helpful	Dishonesty
Being complimentary	Being critical or criticizing
Inviting one to participate in games, etc.	Being greedy or bossy
Sharing	Physical aggression
Avoiding unpleasant behavior	Being annoying or bothersome
Giving one permission or control	Teasing
Providing instructions	Interfering with achievements
Loyalty	Unfaithfulness
Performing admirably	Violating of rules
Facilitating achievements	Ignoring others

(*Source:* Adapted from Zarbatany Hartmann, & Rankin, 1990.)

Status is an important determinant of children's friendships. High-status children tend to form friendships with higher-status individuals, while lower-status children are more likely to have friends of lower status. Status is also related to the number of friends a child has: Higher-status children are more apt to have a greater number of friends than those of lower status.

But it is not only the quantity of social interactions that separates high-status children from lower-status children; the nature of their interactions is also different. Higher-status children are more likely to be viewed as friends by other children. They are more likely to form cliques, groups that are viewed as exclusive and desirable, and they tend to interact with a greater number of other children. In contrast, children of lower status are more likely to play with younger or less popular children (Ladd, 1983).

In short, popularity is a reflection of children's status. School-age children who are mid to high in status are more likely to initiate and coordinate joint social behavior, making their general level of social activity higher than that of children low in social status (Erwin, 1993).

What Personal Characteristics Lead to Popularity?   Popular children share several personality characteristics. They are usually helpful, cooperating with others on joint projects. Popular children are also funny, tending to have good senses of humor and to appreciate others' attempts at humor. Compared with children who are less popular, they are better able to read others' nonverbal behavior and understand others' emotional experiences. They also can control their nonverbal behavior more effectively, thereby presenting themselves well. In short, popular children are high in **social competence**, the collection of individual social skills that permits individuals to perform successfully in social settings (Feldman, Philippot, & Custrini, 1991; Feldman, Tomasian, & Coats, 1999).

social competence   the collection of social skills that permits individuals to perform successfully in social settings.

A variety of factors lead some children to be unpopular and socially isolated from their peers.

Although generally popular children are friendly, open, and cooperative, one subset of popular boys displays an array of negative behaviors, including being aggressive, disruptive, and causing trouble. Despite these behaviors, they may be viewed as cool and tough by their peers, and they are often remarkably popular. This popularity may occur in part because they are seen as boldly breaking rules that others feel constrained to follow (Farmer, Estell, & Bishop, 2003; de Bruyn & Cillessen, 2006; Vaillancourt & Hymel, 2006).

Social Problem-Solving Abilities.   Another factor that relates to children's popularity is their skill at social problem-solving. **Social problem-solving** refers to the use of strategies for solving social conflicts in ways that are satisfactory both to oneself and to others. Because social conflicts among school-age children are a frequent occurrence—even among the best of friends—successful strategies for dealing with them are an important element of social success (Laursen, Hartup, & Koplas, 1996; Rose & Asher, 1999; Murphy & Eisenberg, 2002).

According to developmental psychologist Kenneth Dodge, successful social problem-solving proceeds through a series of steps that correspond to children's information processing strategies (see Figure 10-3). Dodge argues that the manner in which children solve social problems is a consequence of the decisions that they make at each point in the sequence (Dodge, & Crick, 1990; Dodge & Price, 1994; Dodge, Lansford, & Burks, 2003).

By carefully delineating each of the stages, Dodge provides a means by which interventions can be targeted toward a specific child's deficits. For instance, some children routinely misinterpret the meaning of other children's behavior (Step 2), and then respond according to their misinterpretation.

Suppose Max, a fourth grader, is playing a game with Will. While playing the game, Will begins to get angry because he is losing and complains about the rules. If Max is not able to understand that much of Will's anger is frustration at not winning, he is likely to react in an angry way himself, defending the rules, criticizing Will, and making the situation worse. If

social problem-solving   the use of strategies for solving social conflicts in ways that are satisfactory both to oneself and to others.

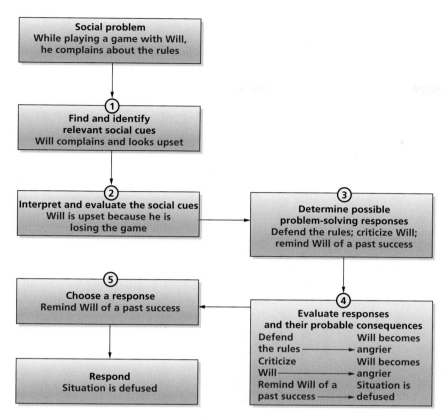

FIGURE 10-3 **PROBLEM-SOLVING STEPS**

Children's problem solving proceeds through several steps involving different information processing strategies.

(*Source:* Based on Dodge, 1985.)

Max interprets the source of Will's anger more accurately, Max may be able to behave in a more effective manner, perhaps by reminding Will, "Hey, you beat me at Connect Four," thereby defusing the situation.

Generally, children who are popular are better at interpreting the meaning of others' behavior accurately. Furthermore, they possess a wider inventory of techniques for dealing with social problems. In contrast, less popular children tend to be less effective at understanding the causes of others' behavior, and because of this their reactions to others may be inappropriate. In addition, their strategies for dealing with social problems are more limited; they sometimes simply don't know how to apologize or help someone who is unhappy feel better (Vitaro & Pelletier, 1991; Rose & Asher, 1999; Rinaldi, 2002).

Teaching Social Competence. Can anything be done to help unpopular children learn social competence? Happily, the answer appears to be yes. Several programs have been developed to teach children a set of social skills that seem to underlie general social competence. For example, in one experimental program, a group of unpopular fifth and sixth graders was taught how to hold a conversation with friends. They were taught ways to disclose material about themselves, to learn about others by asking questions, and to offer help and suggestions to others in a nonthreatening way.

Compared with a group of children who did not receive such training, the children who were in the experiment interacted more with their peers, held more conversations, developed higher self-esteem, and—most critically—were more accepted by their peers than before training (Bierman & Furman, 1984; Asher & Rose, 1997).

mydevelopmentlab

VIDEO CLIP

BULLYING

Bullying: Schoolyard and Online Victimization

For some children, school represents a virtual battleground in which they live in constant fear of being the victim of a bully. In fact, according to the National Association of School Psychologists, 160,000 U.S. schoolchildren stay home from school each day because they are afraid of being bullied. Furthermore, bullying is a worldwide problem: cross-cultural studies find significant bullying problems in Asian and European countries (Eslea et al., 2004; Espelage & Swearer, 2004; Kanetsuna, Smith, & Morita, 2006).

The newest form of bullying takes place virtually on the Web. Cyberbullies may use the Web to make fun of others, start rumors, or post doctored photos. It often takes place anonymously, and victims may not be able to identify the bully—making them feel particularly vulnerable and helpless. The public nature of cyberbullying makes victims experience humiliation that may be deeply damaging (Ybarra & Mitchell, 2004; Patchin & Hinduja, 2006; Thomas, 2006; Raskauskas & Stoltz, 2007).

About 10% to 15% of students bully others at one time or another. About half of all bullies come from abusive homes. They watch more television containing violence, and they misbehave more at home and at school than nonbullies. When their bullying gets them into trouble, they may try to lie their way out of the situation, and they show little remorse for their victimization of others. Compared with their peers, bullies are more likely to break the law as adults (Kaltiala-Heino et al., 2000; Haynie et al., 2001; Ireland & Archer, 2004).

The victims of bullies typically share several characteristics. Most often they are loners who are fairly passive. They often cry easily, and they tend to lack the social skills that might otherwise defuse a bullying situation. For example, they tend not to think of humorous comebacks to bullies' taunts. But though children such as these are more likely to be bullied, even children without these characteristics occasionally are bullied during their school careers: Some 90% of middle school students report being bullied at some point in their time at school, beginning as early as the preschool years (Schwartz et al., 1997; Egan & Perry, 1998; Crick, Casas, & Ku, 1999; Ahmed & Braithwaite, 2004).

mydevelopmentlab

VIDEO CLIP

GENDER CONSTANCY

Gender and Friendships: The Sex Segregation of Middle Childhood

Girls rule; boys drool.

Boys are idiots. Girls have cooties.

Boys go to college to get more knowledge; girls go to Jupiter to get more stupider.

At least, those are some of the views of boys and girls regarding members of the other sex during the elementary school years. Avoidance of the other sex becomes quite pronounced during those years, to the degree that the social networks of most boys and girls consist almost entirely of same-sex groupings (Adler, Kless, & Adler, 1992; Lewis & Phillipsen, 1998; McHale, Dariotis, & Kauh, 2003).

Interestingly, the segregation of friendships according to gender occurs in almost all societies. In nonindustrialized societies, same-gender segregation may be the result of the types of activities that children engage in. For instance, in many cultures, boys are assigned one type of chore and girls another (Whiting & Edwards, 1988). Participation in different activities may not provide the whole explanation for sex segregation, however: Even children in more developed countries, who attend the same schools and participate in many of the same activities, still tend to avoid members of the other gender.

When boys and girls make occasional forays into the other gender's territory, the action often has romantic overtones. For instance, girls may threaten to kiss a boy, or boys might

Though same-sex groupings dominate in middle childhood, when boys and girls do make occasional forays into each others' territory, there are often romantic overtones. Such behavior has been termed "border work."

try to lure girls into chasing them. Such behavior, termed "border work," helps to emphasize the clear boundaries that exist between the two sexes. In addition, it may pave the way for future interactions that do involve romantic or sexual interests, when school-age children reach adolescence and cross-sex interactions become more socially endorsed (Thorne, 1986; Beal, 1994).

The lack of cross-gender interaction in the middle childhood years means that boys' and girls' friendships are restricted to members of their own sex. Furthermore, the nature of friendships within these two groups is quite different (Lansford & Parker, 1999; Rose, 2002).

Boys typically have larger networks of friends than girls, and they tend to play in groups, rather than pairing off. Differences in status within the group are usually quite pronounced, with an acknowledged leader and members falling into particular levels of status. Because of the fairly rigid rankings that represent the relative social power of those in the group, known as the **dominance hierarchy**, members of higher status can safely question and oppose children lower in the hierarchy (Beal, 1994).

Boys tend to be concerned with their place in the dominance hierarchy, and they attempt to maintain their status and improve upon it. This makes for a style of play known as *restrictive*. In restrictive play, interactions are interrupted when a child feels that his status is challenged. Thus, a boy who feels that he is unjustly challenged by a peer of lower status may attempt to end the interaction by scuffling over a toy or otherwise behaving assertively. Consequently, boys' play tends to come in bursts, rather than in more extended, tranquil episodes (Boulton & Smith, 1990; Benenson & Apostoleris, 1993).

The language of friendship used among boys reflects their concern over status and challenge. For instance, consider this conversation between two boys who were good friends:

Child 1: Why don't you get out of my yard?
Child 2: Why don't you *make* me get out of the yard?
Child 1: I *know* you don't want that.
Child 2: You're not gonna make me get out the yard cuz you can't.
Child 1: Don't force me.
Child 2: You can't. Don't force me to hurt you (*snickers*). (Goodwin, 1990, p. 37)

Friendship patterns among girls are quite different. Rather than having a wide network of friends, school-age girls focus on one or two "best friends" who are of relatively equal status. In contrast to boys, who seek out status differences, girls profess to avoid differences in status, preferring to maintain friendships at equal-status levels.

Conflicts among school-age girls are usually solved through compromise, by ignoring the situation, or by giving in, rather than by seeking to make one's own point of view prevail. In sum, the goal is to smooth over disagreements, making social interaction easy and nonconfrontational (Goodwin, 1990).

According to developmental psychologist Carole Beal, the motivation of girls to solve social conflict indirectly does not stem from a lack of self-confidence or from apprehension over the use of more direct approaches. In fact, when school-age girls interact with other girls who are not considered friends or with boys, they can be quite confrontational. However, among friends their goal is to maintain equal-status relationships—ones lacking a dominance hierarchy (Beal, 1994).

The language used by girls tends to reflect their view of relationships. Rather than blatant demands ("Give me the pencil"), girls are more apt to use language that is less confrontational and directive. Girls tend to use indirect forms of verbs, such as "Let's go to the movies" or "Would you want to trade books with me?" rather than "I want to go to the movies" or "Let me have these books" (Goodwin, 1980, 1990).

dominance hierarchy rankings that represent the relative social power of those in a group.

As children age, there is a decline in the number of and depth of friendships outside their own racial group. What are some ways in which schools can foster mutual acceptance?

Cross-Race Friendships: Integration in and out of the Classroom

Are friendships color-blind? For the most part, the answer is no. Children's closest friendships tend largely to be with others of the same race. In fact, as children age there is a decline in the number and depth of friendships outside their own racial group. By the time they are 11 or 12, it appears that African American children become particularly aware of and sensitive to the prejudice and discrimination directed toward members of their race. At that point, they are more like to make distinctions between members of ingroups (groups to which people feel they belong) and members of outgroups (groups to which people do not perceive membership) (Bigler, Jones, & Lobliner, 1997; Aboud, Mendelson, & Purdy, 2003; Kao & Vaquera, 2006).

For instance, when third graders from one long-integrated school were asked to name a best friend, around one-quarter of white children and two-thirds of African American children chose a child of the other race. In contrast, by the time they reached 10th grade, less than 10% of whites and 5% of African Americans named a different-race best friend (Singleton & Asher, 1979; Asher, Singleton, & Taylor, 1982).

On the other hand, although they may not choose each other as best friends, whites and African Americans—as well as members of other minority groups—can show a high degree of mutual acceptance. This pattern is particularly true in schools with ongoing integration efforts. This makes sense: A good deal of research supports the notion that contact between majority and minority group members can reduce prejudice and discrimination (Kerner & Aboud, 1998; Hewstone, 2003).

Becoming an Informed Consumer of Development

Increasing Children's Social Competence

It is clear that building and maintaining friendships is critical in children's lives. Is there anything that parents and teachers can do to increase children's social competence?

The answer is a clear yes. Among the strategies that can work are the following:

- *Encourage social interaction.* Teachers can devise ways in which children are led to take part in group activities, and parents can encourage membership in such groups as Brownies and Cub Scouts or participation in team sports.
- *Teach listening skills to children.* Show them how to listen carefully and respond to the underlying meaning of a communication as well as its overt content.
- *Make children aware that people display emotions and moods nonverbally* and that consequently they should pay attention to others' nonverbal behavior, not just to what they are saying on a verbal level.
- *Teach conversational skills, including the importance of asking questions and self-disclosure.* Encourage students to use "I" statements in which they clarify their own feelings or opinions, and avoid making generalizations about others.
- *Don't ask children to choose teams or groups publicly.* Instead, assign children randomly: It works just as well in ensuring a distribution of abilities across groups and avoids the public embarrassment of a situation in which some children are chosen last.

Review and Apply

Review

- Children's understanding of friendship changes from the sharing of enjoyable activities, through the consideration of personal traits that can meet their needs, to a focus on intimacy and loyalty.

- Friendships in childhood display status hierarchies. Improvements in social problem-solving and social information processing can lead to better interpersonal skills and greater popularity.

- Boys and girls engage increasingly in same-sex friendships, with boys' friendships involving group relationships and girls' friendships characterized by pairings of girls with equal status.

- Interracial friendships decrease in frequency as children age, but contact as peers among members of different races can promote mutual acceptance and appreciation.

- Many children are the victims of bullies during their school years, but both victims and bullies can be taught ways to reduce bullying.

Applying Lifespan Development

- Do you think the stages of friendship are a childhood phenomenon, or do adults' friendships display similar stages?

- *From a social worker's perspective:* How might it be possible to decrease the segregation of friendships along racial lines? What factors would have to change in individuals or in society?

Family and School: Shaping Children's Behavior in Middle Childhood

Tamara's mother, Brenda, waited outside the door of her second-grade classroom for the end of the school day. Tamara came over to greet her mother as soon as she spotted her. "Mom, can Anna come over to play today?" Tamara demanded. Brenda had been looking forward to spending some time alone with Tamara, who had spent the last three days at her dad's house. But, Brenda reflected, Tamara hardly ever got to ask kids over after school, so she agreed to the request. Unfortunately, it turned out today wouldn't work for Anna's family, so they tried to find an alternate date. "How about Thursday?" Anna's mother suggested. Before Tamara could reply, her mother reminded her, "You'll have to ask your dad. You're at his house that night." Tamara's expectant face fell. "OK," she mumbled.

How will Tamara's adjustment be affected from dividing her time between the two homes where she lives with her divorced parents? What about the adjustment of her friend, Anna, who lives with both her parents, both of whom work outside the home? These are just a few of the

coregulation a period in which parents and children jointly control children's behavior.

questions we need to consider as we look at the ways that children's schooling and home life affect their lives during middle childhood.

Family: The Changing Home Environment

The original plot goes like this: First comes love. Then comes marriage. Then comes Mary with a baby carriage. But now there's a sequel: John and Mary break up. John moves in with Sally and her two boys. Mary takes the baby Paul. A year later Mary meets Jack, who is divorced with three children. They get married. Paul, barely 2 years old, now has a mother, a father, a stepmother, a stepfather, and five stepbrothers and stepsisters—as well as four sets of grandparents (biological and step) and countless aunts and uncles. And guess what? Mary's pregnant again. (Katrowitz & Wingert, 1990, p. 24)

We've already noted in earlier chapters the changes that have occurred in the structure of the family over the last few decades. With an increase in the number of parents who both work outside of the home, a soaring divorce rate, and a rise in single-parent families, the environment faced by children passing through middle childhood in the 21st century is very different than that faced by prior generations.

One of the biggest challenges facing children and their parents is the increasing independence that characterizes children's behavior during middle childhood. During the period, children move from being almost completely controlled by their parents to increasingly controlling their own destinies—or at least their everyday conduct. Middle childhood, then, is a period of **coregulation** in which children and parents jointly control behavior. Increasingly, parents provide broad, general guidelines for conduct, while children have control over their everyday behavior. For instance, parents may urge their daughter to buy a balanced, nutritious school lunch each day, but their daughter's decision to regularly buy pizza and two desserts is very much her own.

Family Life. During the middle years of childhood, children spend significantly less time with their parents. Still, parents remain the major influence in their children's lives, and they are seen as providing essential assistance, advice, and direction (Furman & Buhrmester, 1992; Parke, 2004).

Siblings also have an important influence on children during middle childhood, for good and for bad. Although brothers and sisters can provide support, companionship, and a sense of security, they can also be a source of strife.

Sibling rivalry can occur, with siblings competing or quarreling with one another. Such rivalry can be most intense when siblings are similar in age and of the same sex. Parents may intensify sibling rivalry by being perceived as favoring one child over another. Such perceptions may or may not be accurate. For example, older siblings may be permitted more freedom, which the younger sibling may interpret as favoritism. In some cases, perceived favoritism not only leads to sibling rivalry, but may damage the self-esteem of the younger sibling. On the other hand, sibling rivalry is not inevitable, as we discuss in the accompanying *From Research to Practice* box (Howe & Ross, 1990; Ciricelli, 1995; Branje et al., 2004; McHale, Kim & Whiteman, 2006).

What about children who have no siblings? As an only child, there is no opportunity to develop sibling rivalry; they also miss out on the benefits that siblings can bring. Generally, despite the stereotype that only children are spoiled and self-centered, the reality is that they are as well-adjusted as children with brothers and sisters. In fact, in some ways, only children are better adjusted, often having higher self-esteem and stronger motivation to achieve. This is particularly good news for parents in the People's Republic of China, where a strict one-child policy is in effect. Studies there show that Chinese only-children often academically outperform children with siblings (Jiao, Ji, & Jing, 1996; Miao & Wang, 2003).

From Research to Practice

Learning to Get Along: How Children Are Influenced by Their Siblings

Alejandra and Sofia Romero, 5-year-old fraternal twins growing up in New York City, entered the world at almost the same instant but have gone their own ways ever since—at least in terms of temperament. Alejandra has more of a tolerance—even a taste—for rules and regimens. Sofia. . . distinguished herself as the looser, less disciplined of the two. Sofia is also the more garrulous, and Alejandra eventually became the more taciturn. "Sofie served as their mouthpiece," says Lisa Dreyer, 39, the girls' mother, "and Alejandra was perfectly happy to let her do it." (Kluger, 2006, p. 52)

Siblings Alejandra and Sofia Romero couldn't be more different. But like other siblings, they share a special relationship with one another—one that will likely last a lifetime. Unlike our relationships with peers and parents, sibling relationships are likely to endure across the life span. Developmental scientists are uncovering the ways in which early relationships between siblings shape the ways in which we relate to others as well as the choices we make later in life (McHale et al., 2006).

What are relationships with siblings like? Romanticized notions of brotherly love aside, siblings in middle childhood bicker and fight a lot—as often as one conflict every 20 minutes or so (Kramer, Perozynski, & Chung 1999). But beyond the fighting, the jealousy, and the jostling for attention, sibling relationships have a special quality that sets them apart: unlike friends or spouses, people don't choose their siblings. The influence of siblings is unsurprising when you consider just how much time they spend together in childhood and even into adolescence—more time, in fact, than they spend with friends, teachers, and other family members. Strategies learned for getting along with one's siblings, especially in terms of resolving conflicts, seem to carry over into later social settings. For example, children who negotiate well with their siblings in early childhood enjoy better relations with their teachers and classmates in middle childhood, whereas destructive conflict solving between siblings is associated with continued aggressiveness in boys (McGuire, McHale, & Updegrff, 1996; Vondra et al., 1999; Garcia et al., 2000; Criss & Shaw, 2005).

Older children also can function as role models for their younger siblings, but not always in a positive way. For example, younger sisters of teenage mothers are more than four times as likely to become teenage mothers themselves. But younger children can also learn what *not* to do from an older sibling—and it may not simply be because they learned from the older child's mistakes. In some cases, they seem to be more motivated by the idea of distinguishing themselves from their big brother or sister.

For example, one study of childhood smoking found that while children take after their older siblings in picking up the habit, their tendency to do so is weaker the closer they are in age (and presumably, the more motivated they therefore are to distinguish themselves). Consequently, big brothers and big sisters seem to inspire behavior in their younger siblings in two ways: often by emulation, but sometimes in the opposite direction to set themselves apart (Bard & Rodgers, 2003; East & Khoo, 2005).

The desire to be different from an older sibling—a phenomenon called *de-identification*—also influences gender-role behavior. In one study, children with opposite-sex siblings tended not only to adhere more closely to gender-linked traits themselves, but also to have friends who did as well. Specifically, boys with sisters tended to choose friends who were more masculine and more focused on shared activities, while girls with brothers tended to choose friends who were more feminine in terms of preferring emotional closeness and intimacy (Updegraff, McHale, & Crouter, 2000; McHale et al., 2004).

But while having an opposite-sex sibling may exaggerate same-gender identification in childhood, it also seems to improve cross-gender relations later in life. In one study, college students were put together in opposite-sex pairs and given a chance to casually interact. When they later rated the quality of these interactions, the students who had older, opposite sex siblings were rated as more interactive and more likable by their opposite-sex conversation partners (Ickes & Turner, 1983; Updegraff et al., 2000).

- *What might determine whether a child chooses to model an older sibling's behavior or to de-identify with him or her?*

- *Why might sibling relationships have a more pronounced effect than peer relationships on how children learn to get along with others?*

When Both Parents Work Outside the Home: How Do Children Fare? In most cases, children whose parents both work full time outside of the home fare quite well. Children whose parents are loving, are sensitive to their children's needs, and provide appropriate substitute care typically develop no differently from children in families in which one of the parents does not work (Harvey, 1999).

The good adjustment of children whose mothers and fathers both work relates to the psychological adjustment of the parents, especially mothers. In general, women who are satisfied

FIGURE 10-4   HOW KIDS SPEND THEIR TIME

While the amount of time spent on some activities of children has remained constant over the years, the amount of time spent on others, such as playing and eating, has shown significant changes. What might account for these changes?

(*Source:* Hofferth & Sandberg, 1998.)

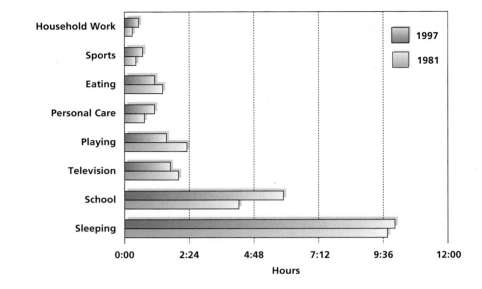

VIDEO CLIP

NEGLECTED CHILDREN

self-care children   children who let themselves into their homes after school and wait alone until their caretakers return from work; previously known as *latchkey children.*

The consequences of being a self-care child are not necessarily harmful, and they may even lead to a greater sense of independence and competence.

with their lives tend to be more nurturing with their children. When work provides a high level of satisfaction, then, mothers who work outside of the home may be more psychologically supportive of their children. Thus, it is not so much a question of whether a mother chooses to work full time, to stay at home, or to arrange some combination of the two. What matters is how satisfied she is with the choices she has made (Barnett & Rivers, 1992; Gilbert, 1994; Haddock & Rattenborg, 2003).

Although we might expect that children whose parents both work would spend comparatively less time with their parents than children with one parent at home full time, research suggests otherwise. Children with mothers and fathers who work full time spend essentially the same amount of time with family, in class, with friends, and alone as children in families where one parent stays at home (Richards & Duckett, 1994; Gottfried, Gottfried, & Bathurst, 2002).

What are children doing during the day? The activities that take the most time are sleeping and school. The next most frequent activities are watching television and playing, followed closely by personal care and eating. This has changed little over the past 20 years (see Figure 10-4). What has changed is the amount of time spent in supervised, structured settings. In 1981, 40% of a child's day was free time; by the late 1990s, only 25% of a child's day was unscheduled (Hofferth & Sandberg, 1998).

Home and Alone: What Do Children Do?

When 10-year-old Johnetta Colvin comes home after finishing a day at Martin Luther King Elementary School, the first thing she does is grab a few cookies and turn on the computer. She takes a quick look at her email, and then goes over to the television and typically spends the next hour watching. During commercials, she takes a look at her homework.

What she doesn't do is chat with her parents, neither of whom are there. She's home alone.

Johnetta is a **self-care child,** the term for children who let themselves into their homes after school and wait alone until their parents return from work. She is far from unique. Some 12% to 14% of children in the United States between the ages of 5 and 12 spend some time alone after school, without adult supervision (Lamorey et al., 1998; Berger, 2000).

In the past, concern about self-care children centered on their lack of supervision and the emotional costs of being alone. In fact, such children were previously called *latchkey children,* raising connotations of sad, pathetic, and neglected children. However, a new view of self-care children is emerging. According to sociologist Sandra Hofferth, given the hectic schedule of many children's lives, a few hours alone may provide a helpful period of decompression. Furthermore, it may provide the opportunity for children to develop a greater sense of autonomy (Hofferth & Sandberg, 2001).

Research has identified few differences between self-care children and children who return to homes with parents. Although some children report negative experiences while at home by themselves (such as loneliness), they do not seem emotionally damaged by the experience. In addition, if they stay at home by themselves rather than "hanging out" unsupervised with friends, they may avoid involvement in activities that can lead to difficulties (Long & Long, 1983; Belle, 1999; Goyette-Ewing, 2000).

In sum, the consequences of being a self-care child are not necessarily harmful. In fact, children may develop an enhanced sense of independence and competence. Furthermore, the time spent alone provides an opportunity to work uninterrupted on homework and school or personal projects. In fact, children with employed parents may have higher self-esteem because they feel they are contributing to the household in significant ways (Goyette-Ewing, 2000).

Divorce.   Having divorced parents, like Tamara, the second-grader who was described earlier, is no longer very distinctive. Only around half the children in the United States spend their entire childhoods living in the same household with both their parents. The rest will live in single-parent homes or with stepparents, grandparents, or other nonparental relatives; and some will end up in foster care (Harvey & Fine, 2004).

How do children react to divorce? The answer depends on how soon you ask the question following a divorce as well as how old the children are at the time of the divorce. Immediately after a divorce, both children and parents may show several types of psychological maladjustment for a period that may last from 6 months to 2 years. For instance, children may be anxious, experience depression, or show sleep disturbances and phobias. Even though children most often live with their mothers following a divorce, the quality of the mother–child relationship declines in the majority of cases, often because children see themselves as caught in

Based on current trends almost three-quarters of American children will spend some portion of their lives in a single-parent family. What are some possible consequences for a child in a single-parent family?

the middle between their mothers and fathers (Holyrod & Sheppard, 1997; Wallerstein, Lewis, & Blakeslee, 2000; Amato & Afifi, 2006).

During the early stage of middle childhood, children whose parents are divorcing often blame themselves for the breakup. By the age of 10, children feel pressure to choose sides, taking the position of either the mother or the father. Because of this, they experience some degree of divided loyalty (Shaw, Winslow, & Flanagan, 1999).

Although researchers agree that the short-term consequences of divorce can be quite difficult, the longer-term consequences are less clear. Some studies have found that 18 months to 2 years later, most children begin to return to their predivorce state of psychological adjustment. For many children, there are minimal long-term consequences (Hetherington & Kelly, 2002; Guttmann & Rosenberg, 2003; Harvey & Fine, 2004).

On the other hand, other evidence suggests that the fallout from divorce lingers. For example, twice as many children of divorced parents enter psychological counseling as children from intact families (although sometimes counseling is mandated by a judge as part of the divorce). In addition, people who have experienced parental divorce are more at risk for experiencing divorce themselves later in life (Wallerstein et al., 2000; Amato & Booth, 2001; Wallerstein & Resnikoff, 2005; Huurre, Junkkari, & Aro, 2006).

How children react to divorce depends on several factors. One is the economic standing of the family the child is living with. In many cases, divorce brings a decline in both parents' standards of living. When this occurs, children may be thrown into poverty (Ozawa & Yoon, 2003).

In other cases, the negative consequences of divorce are less severe because the divorce reduces the hostility and anger in the home. If the household before the divorce was overwhelmed by parental strife—as is the case in around 30% of divorces—the greater calm of a postdivorce household may be beneficial to children. This is particularly true for children who maintain a close, positive relationship with the parent with whom they do not live (Davies et al., 2002).

For some children, then, divorce is an improvement over living with parents who have an intact but unhappy marriage, high in conflict. But in about 70% of divorces, the predivorce level of conflict is not high, and children in these households may have a more difficult time adjusting to divorce (Amato & Booth, 1997).

Single-Parent Families.   Almost one-quarter of all children under the age of 18 in the United States live with only one parent. If present trends continue, almost three-quarters of American children will spend some portion of their lives in a single-parent family before they are 18 years old. For minority children, the numbers are even higher: Almost 60% of African American children and 35% of Hispanic children under the age of 18 live in single-parent homes (U.S. Bureau of the Census, 2000; see Figure 10-5).

In rare cases, death is the reason for single parenthood. More frequently, either no spouse was ever present (that is, the mother never married), the spouses have divorced, or the spouse is absent. In the vast majority of cases, the single parent who is present is the mother.

What consequences are there for children living in homes with just one parent? This is a difficult question to answer. Much depends on whether a second parent was present earlier and the nature of the parents' relationship at that time. Furthermore, the economic status of the single-parent family plays a role in determining the consequences for children. Single-parent families are often less well-off financially than two-parent families, and living in relative poverty has a negative impact on children (Davis, 2003; Harvey & Fine, 2004).

In sum, the impact of living in a single-parent family is not, by itself, invariably negative or positive. Given the large number of single-parent households, the stigma that once existed toward such families has largely declined. The ultimate consequences for children depend on a

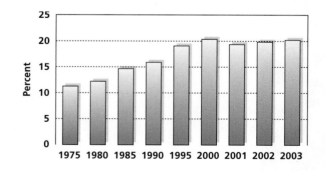

FIGURE 10-5   INCREASE OF SINGLE MOTHERS, 1975–2003

The number of mothers without spouses has increased significantly over the last two decades.

(*Source:* U. S. Bureau of the Census, 2004.)

variety of factors that accompany single parenthood, such as the economic status of the family, the amount of time that the parent is able to spend with the child, and the degree of stress in the household.

Multigenerational Families.   Some households consist of several generations, in which children, parents, and grandparents live together. The presence of multiple generations in the same house can make for a rich living experience for children, who experience the influence both of their parents and grandparents. On the other hand, multigenerational families also have the potential for conflict, with several adults acting as disciplinarians without coordinating what they do.

The prevalence of three-generation families who live together is greater among African Americans than among Caucasians. In addition, African American families, which are more likely than white families to be headed by single parents, often rely substantially on the help of grandparents in everyday child care, and cultural norms tend to be highly supportive of grandparents taking an active role (Budris, 1998; Baydar & Brooks-Gunn, 1998; Baird, John, & Hayslip, 2000; Crowther & Rodriguez, 2003).

Living in Blended Families.   For many children, the aftermath of divorce includes the subsequent remarriage of one or both parents. In fact, more than 10 million households in the United States contain at least one spouse who has remarried. More than 5 million remarried couples have at least one stepchild living with them in what have come to be called **blended families**. Overall, 17% of all children in the United States live in blended families (U.S. Bureau of the Census, 2001; Bengtson et al., 2004).

Living in a blended family is challenging for the children involved. There often is a fair amount of *role ambiguity*, in which roles and expectations are unclear. Children may be uncertain about their responsibilities, how to behave toward stepparents and stepsiblings, and how to make a host of decisions that have wide-ranging implications for their role in the family. For instance, a child in a blended family may have to choose which parent to spend each vacation and holiday with, or to decide between the conflicting advice coming from biological parent and stepparent (Dainton, 1993; Cath & Shopper, 2001; Belcher, 2003).

blended families   a remarried couple that has at least one stepchild living with them.

Blended families occur when previously married husbands and wives with children remarry.

In many cases, however, school-age children in blended families often do surprisingly well. In comparison to adolescents, who have more difficulties, school-age children often adjust relatively smoothly to blended arrangements, for several reasons. For one thing, the family's financial situation is often improved after a parent remarries. In addition, in a blended family there are more people to share the burden of household chores. Finally, the simple fact that the family contains more individuals increases the opportunities for social interaction (Hetherington & Clingempeel, 1992; Greene, Anderson, & Hetherington, 2003; Hetherington & Elmore, 2003).

On the other hand, not all children adjust well to life in a blended family. Some find the disruption of routine and of established networks of family relationships difficult. For instance, a child who is used to having her mother's complete attention may find it difficult to observe her mother showing interest and affection to a stepchild. The most successful blending of families occurs when the parents create an environment that supports children's self-esteem and create a climate in which all family members feel a sense of togetherness. Generally, the younger the children, the easier the transition is within a blended family (Sage, 2003; Jeynes, 2007; Kirby, 2006).

Families with Gay and Lesbian Parents. An increasing number of children have two mothers or two fathers. Estimates suggest there are between 1 and 5 million families headed by two lesbians or two gay parents in the United States, and some 6 million children have lesbian or gay parents (Patterson & Friel, 2000).

Relatively little research has been done on the effects of same-sex parenting on children. However, most studies find that the children in lesbian and gay households develop similarly to the children of heterosexual families. Their sexual orientation is unrelated to that of their parents; their behavior is no more or less gender-typed; and they seem equally well adjusted (Patterson, 2002, 2003, 2006; Parke, 2004).

Furthermore, children of lesbian and gay parents have similar relationships with their peers as children of heterosexual parents. They also relate to adults—both those who are gay and those who are straight—no differently from children whose parents are heterosexual. And when they reach adolescence, their romantic relationships and sexual behavior are no different from those of adolescents living with opposite-sex parents (Patterson, 1995; Golombok et al., 2003; Wainright, Russell, & Patterson, 2004).

In short, a growing body of research suggests that there is little developmental difference between children whose parents are gay and lesbian and those who have heterosexual parents. What is clearly different for children with same-sex parents is the possibility of discrimination and prejudice due to their parents' homosexuality. As U.S. citizens engage in an ongoing and highly politicized debate regarding the legality of gay and lesbian marriage, children of such unions may feel singled out and victimized because of societal stereotypes and discrimination. (We'll consider more about gay and lesbian relationships in Chapter 14.)

Race and Family Life. Although there are as many types of families as there are individuals, research does find some consistencies related to race (Parke, 2004). For example, African American families often have a particularly strong sense of family. Members of African American families are frequently willing to offer welcome and support to extended family members in their homes. Because there is a relatively high level of female-headed households among African Americans, the social and economic support of extended family often is critical. In addition, there is a relatively high proportion of families headed by older adults, such as grandparents, and some studies find that children in grandmother-headed households are particularly well adjusted (McLoyd et al., 2000; Smith & Drew, 2002; Taylor, 2002).

Hispanic families also often stress the importance of family life, as well as community and religious organizations. Children are taught to value their ties to their families, and they come to see themselves as a central part of an extended family. Ultimately, their sense of who they are becomes tied to the family. Hispanic families also tend to be relatively larger, with an average size of 3.71, compared to 2.97 for Caucasian families and 3.31 for African American families (Cauce & Domenech-Rodriguez, 2002; U.S. Census Bureau, 2003; Halgunseth, Ispa, & Rudy, 2006).

Although relatively little research has been conducted on Asian American families, emerging findings suggest that fathers are more apt to be powerful figures, maintaining discipline. In keeping with the more collectivist orientation of Asian cultures, children tend to believe that family needs have a higher priority than personal needs, and males, in particular, are expected to care for their parents throughout their lifetimes (Ishi-Kuntz, 2000).

Poverty and Family Life.   Regardless of race, children living in families who are economically disadvantaged face significant hardships. Poor families have fewer basic everyday resources, and there are more disruptions in children's lives. For example, parents may be forced to look for less expensive housing or may move the entire household in order to find work. The result frequently is family environments in which parents are less responsive to their children's needs and provide less social support (Evans, 2004).

The stress of difficult family environments, along with other stress in the lives of poor children—such as living in unsafe neighborhoods with high rates of violence and attending inferior schools—ultimately takes its toll. Economically disadvantaged children are at risk for poorer academic performance, higher rates of aggression, and conduct problems. In addition, declines in economic well-being have been linked to mental health problems (Solantaus, Leinonen, & Punamaki, 2004; Sapolsky, 2005; Morales & Guerra, 2006).

Group Care: Orphanages in the 21st Century.   The term "orphanage" evokes images of pitiful youngsters clothed in rags, eating porridge out of tin cups, and housed in huge, prison-like institutions. The reality today is different. Even the word "orphanage" is rarely used, having been replaced by *group home* or *residential treatment center*. Typically housing a relatively small number of children, group homes are used for children whose parents are no longer able to care for them adequately. They are typically funded by a combination of federal, state, and local aid.

Group care has grown significantly in the last decade. In fact, in the 5-year period from 1995 to 2000, the number of children in foster care increased by more than 50%. Today, more than one-half million children in the United States live in foster care (Berrick, 1998; Roche, 2000; Jones-Harden, 2004).

Although the orphanages of the early 1900s were crowded and institutional (left), today the equivalent, called group homes or residential treatment centers (right), are much more pleasant.

About three-quarters of children in group care are victims of neglect and abuse. Each year, 300,000 children are removed from their homes. Most of them can be returned to their homes following intervention with their families by social service agencies. But the remaining one-quarter are so psychologically damaged due to abuse or other causes that once they are placed in group care, they are likely to remain there throughout childhood. Children who have developed severe problems, such as high levels of aggression or anger, have difficulty finding adoptive families, and in fact it is often difficult to find even temporary foster families who are able to cope with their emotional and behavior problems (Bass, Shields, & Behrman, 2004; Chamberlain et al., 2006).

Although some politicians have suggested that an increase in group care is a solution to complex social problems associated with unwed mothers who become dependent on welfare, experts in providing social services and psychological treatment are not so sure. For one thing, group homes cannot always consistently provide the support and love potentially available in a family setting. Moreover, group care is hardly cheap: It can cost some $40,000 per year to support a child in group care—about 10 times the cost of maintaining a child in foster care or on welfare (Roche, 2000; Allen & Bissell, 2004).

Other experts argue that group care is neither inherently good nor bad. Instead, the consequences of living away from one's family may be quite positive, depending on the particular

Table 10-4	Personal Characteristics of the Best and Worst Child and Youth Care Workers	
The Best Workers:	**The Worst Workers:**
Flexible	Exhibit pathology
Mature	Selfish
Integrity	Defensive
Good judgment	Dishonest
Common sense	Abusive
Appropriate values	Abuse drugs/alcohol
Responsible	Uncooperative
Good self-image	Poor self-esteem
Self-control	Rigid
Responsive to authority	Irresponsible
Interpersonally adept	Critical
Stable	Passive-aggressive
Unpretentious	Inappropriate boundaries
Predictable/consistent	Unethical
Nondefensive	Authoritarian/coercive
Nurturant/firm	Inconsistent/unpredictable
Self-aware	Avoidant
Empowering	Don't learn from experience
Cooperative	Poor role model
Good role model	Angry/explosive

(*Source:* Adapted from Shealy, 1995.)

characteristics of the staff of the group home and whether child and youth care workers are able to develop an effective, stable, and strong emotional bond with a specific child. On the other hand, if a child is unable to form a meaningful relationship with a worker in a group home, the results may well be harmful (Shealy, 1995; McKenzie, 1997; Reddy & Pfeiffer, 1997). (Table 10-4 shows the personal characteristics of the best—and worst—child and youth care workers.)

School: The Academic Environment

Children spend more of their day in the classroom than anywhere else. It is not surprising, then, that schools have a profound impact on children's lives, shaping and molding not only their ways of thinking but the ways they view the world. We turn now to a number of aspects of schooling in middle childhood that can have a profound effect on children.

attributions people's explanations for the reasons behind their behavior.

How Children Explain Academic Success and Failure. Most of us, at one time or another, have done poorly on a test. Think back to how you felt when you received a bad grade. Did you feel shame? Anger at the teacher? Fear of the consequences? According to psychologist Bernard Weiner (1985, 1994), your response in such situations is determined largely by how you explained the failure to yourself. The explanation you come up with may ultimately determine how hard you strive to do well on future tests.

Weiner has proposed a theory of motivation based on people's **attributions**, their explanations for the reasons behind their behavior. He suggests that people react to failure (as well as success) by considering whether the cause is due to *dispositional factors* ("I'm not such a smart person") or due to *situational* factors ("I didn't get enough sleep last night"). In addition, they consider if the cause is stable ("I usually do poorly") or unstable ("I didn't try very hard this time"). Finally, they consider whether the cause is controllable ("If I study harder, I might do better") or uncontrollable ("I can't control the instructor's behavior").

How people feel about their performance in a situation is a factor of the attributions they make for that performance. For example, when a success is attributed to internal factors ("I'm smart"), students tend to feel pride; but failure attributed to internal factors ("I'm so stupid") causes shame. The stability dimension determines future expectations about success and failure. Specifically, when students attribute success or failure to factors that are relatively stable and invariant, they are apt to expect similar performance in the future. In contrast, when they attribute performance to unstable factors such as effort or luck, their expectations about future performance are relatively unaffected.

Finally, the controllability dimension affects emotions that are directed toward others. If children feel that failure was due to factors within their control—for example, lack of effort—they are apt to experience anger at themselves and others; but if the failure was uncontrollable, they are likely to feel sadness.

Cultural Comparisons: Individual Differences in Attribution. Not everyone comes to the same conclusions about the sources of success and failure. In addition to individual differences, among the strongest influences on people's attributions are their race, ethnicity, and socioeconomic status. Attribution is a two-way street. While our attributions can affect our future performance, it is also true that different experiences give us different perceptions about the ways things in the world fit together. For this reason, it is not surprising that there are subcultural differences in how achievement-related behaviors are understood and explained.

One important difference is related to racial factors: African Americans are less likely than whites to attribute success to internal rather than external causes. African American children tend to feel that aspects such as how difficult a task is and luck (external causes) are the major determinants of their performance outcomes. They are likely to believe that even if they put in maximum effort, prejudice and discrimination (external causes) will prevent them from succeeding (Friend & Neale, 1972; Ogbu, 1988; Graham, 1990, 1994).

Such an attributional pattern, one that overemphasizes the importance of external causes, reduces a student's sense of personal responsibility for success or failure. When attributions are based on internal factors, they suggest that a change in behavior—such as increased effort—can bring about a change in success (Graham, 1986, 1990; Glasgow et al., 1997).

African Americans are not the only group susceptible to maladaptive attributional patterns. Women, for example, often attribute their unsuccessful performance to low ability, an uncontrollable factor. Ironically, though, they do not attribute successful performance to high ability, but to factors outside their control. A belief in this pattern suggests the conclusion that even with future effort, success will be unattainable. Females who hold these views may be less inclined to expend the effort necessary to improve their rate of success (Dweck, 1991; Nelson & Cooper, 1997; Dweck, 2002). By contrast, the success rate of Asian students in school, as described in the following *Developmental Diversity* section, illustrates the power of internal attributions.

Developmental Diversity

Explaining Asian Academic Success

Consider two students, Ben and Hannah, each performing poorly in school. Suppose you thought that Ben's poor performance was due to unalterable, stable causes, such as a lack of intelligence, while Hannah's was produced by temporary causes, such as a lack of hard work. Who would you think would ultimately do better in school?

If you are like most people, you'd probably predict that the outlook was better for Hannah. After all, Hannah could always work harder, but it is hard for someone like Ben to develop higher intelligence.

According to psychologist Harold Stevenson, this reasoning lies at the heart of the superior school performance of Asian students compared with students in the United States. Stevenson's research suggests that teachers, parents, and students in the United States are likely to attribute school performance to stable, internal causes, while people in Japan, China, and other East Asian countries are more likely to see temporary, situational factors as the cause of their performance. The Asian view, which stems in part from ancient Confucian writings, tends to accentuate the necessity of hard work and perseverance (Stevenson & Lee, 1996; Stevenson, Lee, & Mu, 2000; Yang & Rettig, 2004; Phillipson, 2006).

This cultural difference in attributional styles is displayed in several ways. For instance, surveys show that mothers, teachers, and students in Japan and Taiwan all believe strongly that students in a typical class tend to have the same amount of ability. In contrast, mothers, teachers, and students in the United States are apt to disagree, arguing that there are significant differences in ability among the various students (see Figure 10-6).

It is easy to imagine how such different attributional styles can influence teaching approaches. If, as in the United States, students and teachers seem to believe that ability is fixed and locked in, poor academic performance will be greeted with a sense of failure and reduced motivation to work harder to overcome it. In contrast, Japanese teachers and students are apt to see failure as a temporary setback due to their lack of hard work. After making such an attribution, they are more apt to expend increased effort on future academic activities.

These different attributional orientations may explain the fact that Asian students frequently outperform American students in international comparisons of student achievement, according to some developmentalists (Linn, 1997; Wheeler, 1998). Because Asian

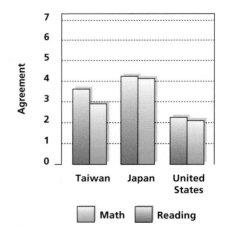

FIGURE 10-6 MOTHERS' BELIEFS IN CHILDREN'S ABILITY

Compared to mothers in Taiwan and Japan, U.S. mothers were less apt to believe that all children have the same degree of underlying, innate ability. Subjects responded using a 7-point scale, where 1 = strongly disagree and 7 = strongly agree. What are the implications of this finding for schooling in the United States?

(*Source:* Stevenson & Lee, 1990.)

students tend to assume that academic success results from hard work, they may put greater effort into their schoolwork than American students, who believe that their inherent ability determines their performance. These arguments suggest that the attributional style of students and teachers in the United States might well be maladaptive. They also argue that the attributional styles taught to children by their parents may have a significant effect on their future success (Eaton & Dembo, 1997; Little & Lopez, 1997; Little, Miyashita, & Karasawa, 2003).

Expectation Effects: How Others' Expectancies Influence Children's Behavior.
Imagine yourself as an elementary school teacher. Suppose you were told at the beginning of a new school year that the children in your class had taken a test described in this way:

> All children show hills, plateaus, and valleys in their scholastic progress. A study being conducted at Harvard with the support of the National Science Foundation is interested in those children who show an unusual forward spurt of academic progress. These spurts can and do occur at any level of academic and intellectual functioning. When these spurts occur in children who have not been functioning too well academically, the result is familiarly referred to as "late blooming."
>
> As part of our study we are further validating a test which predicts the likelihood that a child will show an inflection point or "spurt" within the near future. This test which will be administered in your school will allow us to predict which youngsters are most likely to show an academic spurt. . . . The development of the test for predicting inflections or "spurts" is not yet such that *every* one of the top 20 percent will show the spurt or "blooming" effect. But the top 20 percent of the children *will* show a more significant inflection or spurt within the next year or less than will the remaining 80 percent of the children. (Rosenthal & Jacobson, 1968, p. 66)

Consider your reaction to the children on the list of "bloomers" identified by the test. Would you treat them differently from the children who were not so designated?

If the results of a classic but controversial study are any guide, your answer should be affirmative: Teachers do in fact seem to treat children for whom they have expectations of improvement differently from those for whom they have no such expectations (Rosenthal & Jacobson, 1968). In the experiment, elementary school teachers were told at the beginning of a new school year that five children in their classes would be likely to "bloom" in the upcoming year, based on the test just described. In reality, however, the information was bogus: The names of the children had simply been picked at random, although the teachers didn't know that. The teachers received no further details from the experimenters for the rest of the year.

Research shows that teachers' expectations regarding student performance can create a self-fulfilling prophecy. In what ways is the child affected by the self-fulfilling prophecy? The teacher?

At the end of the year, the children completed an intelligence test that was identical to one taken a year earlier. According to the experimenters, the results showed that clear differences existed in the intellectual growth of the so-called "bloomers" compared with that of the other members of their classes. Those randomly designated as likely to make significant gains did in fact improve more than the other children. However, the results were not uniform: The greatest differences were found for children in first and second grades, with smaller differences for children in grades 3 through 6.

When the findings of the experiment, reported in a book dubbed *Pygmalion in the Classroom,* were published, they caused an immediate stir among educators—and among the public at large. The reason for this furor was the implication of the results: If merely holding high expectations is sufficient to bring about gains in achievement, wouldn't holding low expectations lead to slowed achievement? And since teachers sometimes may hold low expectations about children from lower socioeconomic and minority backgrounds, did this mean that children from such backgrounds were destined to show low achievement throughout their educational careers?

Despite some criticism of the original experiment on methodological and statistical grounds (Snow, 1969; Wineburg, 1987), there has been enough new evidence supporting the study's findings to make it clear that the expectations of teachers *are* communicated to their students and can bring about the expected performance. The phenomenon has come to be called the **teacher expectancy effect**—the cycle of behavior in which a teacher transmits an expectation about a child and actually brings about the expected behavior (Babad, 1992).

The teacher expectancy effect can be viewed as a special case of a broader concept known as the *self-fulfilling prophecy,* in which a person's expectation is capable of bringing about an outcome (Snyder, 1974). For instance, physicians have long known that providing patients with placebos (fake, inactive drugs) can sometimes "cure" them, simply because the patients expect the medicine to work.

In the case of teacher expectancy effects, the basic explanation seems to be that teachers, after forming an initial expectation about a child's ability, transmit it to the child through a complex

teacher expectancy effect   the cycle of behavior in which a teacher transmits an expectation about a child and thereby actually brings about the expected behavior.

series of verbal and nonverbal cues. These communicated expectations in turn indicate to the child what behavior is appropriate, and the child behaves accordingly (Rosenthal, 2002).

Once teachers have developed expectations about a child, how are those expectations communicated to the student? Teachers transmit their expectations through four channels (Rosenthal, 1994, 2002):

- *Classroom social-emotional climate.* Teachers are warm and more accepting of children for whom they hold high expectations than those they expect less from. They convey more positive attitudes by smiling and nodding more often, and they look at high-expectation children more frequently.

- *Input to children.* Children who are expected to do well are given more materials—books, worksheets, articles—from their teachers, and they are asked to complete more difficult material. Consequently, they are given more opportunities to perform well.

- *Output from teachers.* The overall number of contacts between teachers and high-expectation children is higher than with low-expectation children. As a result, high-expectation children have more opportunities to respond in class.

- *Feedback.* When teachers hold high expectations for a child, they provide more positive evaluations of the child's work and they are more accepting of the child's ideas. In contrast, low-expectation children receive more criticism and little or no feedback in some situations. Even when low-expectation children do well, the kind of feedback teachers offer is less positive than when a high-expectation child does well.

The child is the final link in the chain of events that encompasses the teacher expectation effect. Given the way expectations can color teacher behaviors, it is hardly surprising that a child's performance would be significantly affected. Clearly, children who encounter a warm social-emotional climate, who are given more material to complete, who have more contact with teachers, and who are the recipients of more feedback from their teachers are going to develop more positive self-concepts, be more motivated, and work harder than those who receive negative treatment or neglect. Ultimately, the high-expectation children are likely to perform better in class.

The cycle, then, is complete: A teacher who expects a child to do better treats that child more positively. The child responds to such treatment and eventually performs in accord with the teacher's expectations. But note that the cycle does not stop there: Once children behave congruently with the teacher's expectations, the expectations are reinforced. As a consequence, a child's behavior ultimately may cement the expectation initially held by the teacher (see Figure 10-7).

Expectations operate in every classroom and are not the province of teachers alone. For instance, children develop their own expectations about their teacher's competence, based on rumors and other bits of information, and they communicate their expectations to those teachers through the things they say and their nonverbal behavior. In the end, a teacher's behavior may be brought about in significant measure by children's expectations (Feldman & Prohaska, 1979; Feldman & Theiss, 1982; Jamieson et al., 1987).

Finally, remember that the classroom is not the only place in which expectations operate. *Any* setting in which one person holds an expectation about a child, and vice versa, may produce analogous expectancy effects. Clearly, children's views of themselves and of their behavior are in part a consequence of what others expect of them (Eden, 1990; Harris et al., 1992).

Beyond the 3Rs: Should Schools Teach Emotional Intelligence?

In many elementary schools, the hottest topic in the curriculum has little to do with the traditional 3Rs. Instead, a significant educational trend for educators in many elementary schools throughout the United States is the use of techniques to increase students' **emotional intelligence**, the skills

emotional intelligence the set of skills that underlies the accurate assessment, evaluation, expression, and regulation of emotions.

FIGURE 10-7 **TEACHER EXPECTATIONS AND STUDENT PERFORMANCE**

Teachers' expectations about their students— positive or negative—can actually bring about positive or negative performance from their students. How does this relate to what we know about self-esteem?

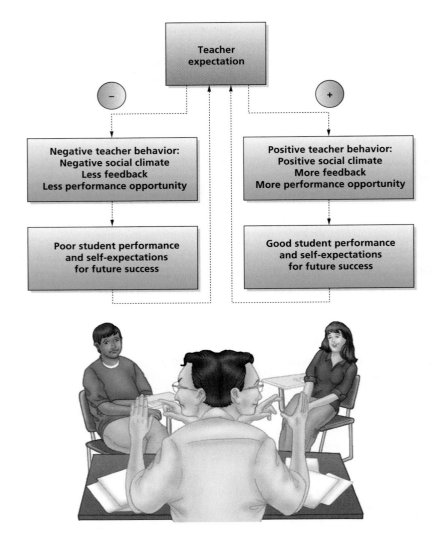

that underlie the accurate assessment, evaluation, expression, and regulation of emotions (Mayer, Salovey, & Caruso, 2000; Mayer, 2001; Pfeiffer, 2001; Salovey & Pizarro, 2003).

Psychologist Daniel Goleman (1995), who wrote a best-seller entitled *Emotional Intelligence*, argues that emotional literacy should be a standard part of the school curriculum. He points to several programs that are effective in teaching students to manage their emotions more effectively. For instance, in one program, children are provided with lessons in empathy, self-awareness, and social skills. In another, children are taught about caring and friendship as early as first grade through exposure to stories in which characters exhibit these positive qualities.

Programs meant to increase emotional intelligence have not been met with universal acceptance. Critics suggest that the nurturance of emotional intelligence is best left to students' families and that schools ought to concentrate on more traditional curriculum matters. Others suggest that adding emotional intelligence to an already crowded curriculum may reduce time spent on academics. Finally, some critics argue that there is no well-specified set of criteria for what constitutes emotional intelligence, and consequently it is difficult to develop appropriate, effective curriculum materials (Humphrey et al., 2007).

Still, most people consider emotional intelligence to be something that is worthy of nurturance. Certainly, it is clear that emotional intelligence is quite different from traditional conceptions of intelligence. For example, most of us can think of individuals who, while quite intelligent in a traditional sense, are also insensitive and socially unskilled. The goal of emotional intelligence training is to produce people who are not only cognitively sophisticated but able to manage their emotions effectively (Schulman & Mekler, 1994; Sleek, 1997).

Review and Apply

Review

- Self-care children may develop independence and enhanced self-esteem from their experience.
- How divorce affects children depends on such factors as financial circumstances and the comparative levels of tension in the family before and after the divorce.
- The effects of being raised in a single-parent household depend on financial circumstances, the amount of parent–child interaction, and the level of tension in the family.
- Attributional patterns differ along individual, cultural, and gender dimensions.
- Expectancies, particularly those of parents and teachers, can affect behavior and produce outcomes that reflect and confirm the expectancies.
- Emotional intelligence—the skills that underlie the accurate assessment, evaluation, expression, and regulation of emotions—is becoming accepted as an important aspect of social intelligence.

Applying Lifespan Development

- Politicians often speak of "family values." How does this term relate to the diverse family situations covered in this chapter, including divorced parents, single parents, blended families, working parents, self-care children, abusive families, and group care?
- *From a health-care worker's perspective:* How might the development of self-esteem in middle childhood be affected by a divorce? Can constant hostility and tension between parents lead to a child's health problems?

Epilogue

Self-esteem and moral development are two key areas in social and personality development in the middle childhood years. Children at this age tend to develop and rely on deeper relationships and friendships, and we looked at the ways gender and race can affect friendships. The changing nature of family arrangements can also affect social and personality development. So can the ways children and teachers explain school successes and failures. Finally, we concluded with a discussion of emotional intelligence, a set of qualities that enhances children's ability to feel empathy for others and to control and express their emotions.

Return to the prologue—about Bryan and Christopher Hendrickson—and answer the following questions.

1. In what ways do the Hendrickson twins' activities exemplify Erikson's industry-versus-inferiority stage of development?

2. How does the children's play with the boxes differ from the way they would have played during the preschool years?

3. What would you expect is the basis of the friendship between the twins and the other kids in the prologue?

4. What educated guesses can you make about the popularity, status, and social competence of the twins based on the information in the prologue?

Looking Back

■ **In what ways do children's views of themselves change during middle childhood?**

- According to Erikson, children in the middle childhood years are in the industry-versus-inferiority stage, focusing on achieving competence and responding to a wide range of personal challenges.

- Children in the middle childhood years begin to view themselves in terms of psychological characteristics and to differentiate their self-concepts into separate areas. They use social comparison to evaluate their behavior, abilities, expertise, and opinions.

■ **Why is self-esteem important during these years?**

- Children in these years are developing self-esteem; those with chronically low self-esteem can become trapped in a cycle of failure in which low self-esteem feeds on itself by producing low expectations and poor performance.

■ **How does children's sense of right and wrong change as children age?**

- According to Kohlberg, people pass from preconventional morality (motivated by rewards and punishments), through conventional morality (motivated by social reference), to postconventional morality (motivated by a sense of universal moral principles). Gilligan has sketched out an alternative progression for girls, from an orientation toward individual survival, through goodness as self-sacrifice, to the morality of nonviolence.

■ **What sorts of relationships and friendships are typical of middle childhood?**

- Children's friendships display status hierarchies, and their understanding of friendship passes through stages, from a focus on mutual liking and time spent together, through the consideration of personal traits and the rewards that friendship provides, to an appreciation of intimacy and loyalty.

- Popularity in children is related to traits that underlie social competence. Because of the importance of social interactions and friendships, developmental researchers have engaged in efforts to improve social problem-solving skills and the processing of social information.

■ **How do gender and ethnicity affect friendships?**

- Boys and girls in middle childhood increasingly prefer same-gender friendships. Male friendships are characterized by groups, status hierarchies, and restrictive play. Female friendships tend to involve one or two close relationships, equal status, and a reliance on cooperation.

- Cross-race friendships diminish in frequency as children age. Equal-status interactions among members of different racial groups can lead to improved understanding, mutual respect and acceptance, and a decreased tendency to stereotype.

How do today's diverse family and care arrangements affect children?

- Children in families in which both parents work outside the home generally fare well. Self-care children who fend for themselves after school may develop independence and a sense of competence and contribution.

- Immediately after a divorce, the effects on children in the middle childhood years can be serious, depending on the financial condition of the family and the hostility level between spouses before the divorce.

- The consequences of living in a single-parent family depend on the financial condition of the family and, if there had been two parents, the level of hostility that existed between them. Blended families present challenges to the child but can also offer opportunities for increased social interaction.

- Children in group care tend to have been victims of neglect and abuse. Many can be helped and placed with their own or other families, but about 25% of them will spend their childhood years in group care.

How do children's social and emotional lives affect their school performance?

- People attach attributions to their academic successes and failures. Differences in attributional patterns are not only individual, but appear to be influenced by culture and gender as well.

- The expectancies of others, particularly teachers, can produce outcomes that conform to those expectancies by leading students to modify their behavior.

- Emotional intelligence is the set of skills that permits people to manage their emotions effectively.

Key Terms and Concepts

industry-versus-inferiority stage (p. 332)
social comparison (p. 334)
self-esteem (p. 335)
status (p. 344)
social competence (p. 345)

social problem-solving (p. 346)
dominance hierarchy (p. 349)
coregulation (p. 352)
self-care children (p. 354)

blended families (p. 357)
attributions (p. 361)
teacher expectancy effect (p. 364)
emotional intelligence (p. 365)

11 Physical and Cognitive Development in Adolescence

Chapter Overview

PHYSICAL MATURATION

Growth During Adolescence: The Rapid Pace of Physical and Sexual Maturation

Puberty: The Start of Sexual Maturation

Nutrition, Food, and Eating Disorders: Fueling the Growth of Adolescence

Brain Development and Thought: Paving the Way for Cognitive Growth

COGNITIVE DEVELOPMENT AND SCHOOLING

Piagetian Approaches to Cognitive Development: Using Formal Operations

Information Processing Perspectives: Gradual Transformations in Abilities

Egocentrism in Thinking: Adolescents' Self-Absorption

School Performance

Cyberspace: Adolescents Online

THREATS TO ADOLESCENTS' WELL-BEING

Illegal Drugs

Alcohol: Use and Abuse

Tobacco: The Dangers of Smoking

Sexually Transmitted Infections

Prologue: A Teenager's Day

5:45 AM. The alarm goes off in Wendy Vacarro's bedroom.

5:55 AM. The alarm goes off for the second time; this time Wendy gets up.

6:10 AM. After washing and dressing, Wendy grabs a bagel and heads out the door to wait for the school bus.

7:05 AM. The school bus deposits Wendy at Glenwood High School, where Wendy spends most of the day in her classes. Today, they consist of English, algebra, advanced biology, criminal justice, German, and phys ed, with lunch and orchestra practice sandwiched in.

3:00 PM. Field hockey practice begins. For 2 hours, Wendy runs laps and participates in two scrimmages.

5:30 PM. Sue catches a bus for a 1½ hour ride home.

7:15 PM. She eats dinner by herself; the rest of her family already ate earlier.

7:30 PM. Wendy watches a rerun of *Friends*, while looking over her homework for the evening.

8:00 PM. She spends an hour working on a criminal justice paper, doing research on the Web while text messaging with her friends. Then she does an algebra assignment and finishes a bio lab. Her major task is to study for the next day's German test. She's up until 11:30 going over vocabulary and grammar, interrupted by a few phone calls.

During adolescence, teenagers' lives become increasingly complex.

adolescence the developmental stage that lies between childhood and adulthood.

11:30 PM.   Trying to unwind a bit, she watches the *Daily Show*.

12:00 midnight.   Goes to bed. Sets her alarm for 5:15 AM to be able to get in some extra study time for her German test.

This was a usual day for Wendy Vacarro, whose life is a pressure-cooker of academic and social demands that fill virtually every waking moment. It's also typical of the lives of many adolescents, who struggle to meet society's—and their own—demands as they traverse the challenges of the teenage years. With bodies that are conspicuously changing, temptations of sex, alcohol, and other drugs, cognitive advances that make the world seem increasingly complex, social networks that are in constant flux, and careening emotions, adolescents find themselves in a period of life that evokes excitement, anxiety, glee, and despair, sometimes in equal measure.

In this chapter and the next, we consider the basic issues and questions that underlie adolescence. **Adolescence** is the developmental stage that lies between childhood and adulthood. It is generally viewed as starting just before the teenage years and ending just after them. It is a transitional stage. Adolescents are considered no longer children, but not yet adults. It is a time of considerable physical and psychological growth and change.

This chapter focuses on physical and cognitive growth during adolescence. It is a time of extraordinary physical maturation, triggered by the onset of puberty. We discuss the consequences of early and late maturation, as well as nutrition and eating disorders.

Next, we turn to a consideration of cognitive development during adolescence. After reviewing several approaches to understanding changes in cognitive capabilities, we examine school performance, focusing on the ways that socioeconomic status, ethnicity, and race affect scholastic achievement.

The chapter concludes with a discussion of several of the major threats to adolescents' well-being. We will focus on drug, alcohol, and tobacco use as well as sexually transmitted infections.

After reading this chapter, you will be able to answer these questions:

- **What physical changes do adolescents experience?**

- **What are the consequences of early and late maturation?**

- **What nutritional needs and concerns do adolescents have?**

- **In what ways does cognitive development proceed during adolescence?**

- **What factors affect adolescent school performance?**

- **What dangerous substances do adolescents use and why?**

- **What dangers do adolescent sexual practices present, and how can these dangers be avoided?**

Physical Maturation

For the male members of the Awa tribe, the beginning of adolescence is signaled by an elaborate and—to Western eyes—gruesome ceremony marking the transition from childhood to adulthood. The boys are whipped for 2 or 3 days with sticks and prickly branches. Through the whipping, the boys atone for their previous infractions and honor tribesmen who were killed in warfare. But that's just for starters; the ritual continues for days more.

Most of us probably feel gratitude that we did not have to endure such physical trials when we entered adolescence. But members of Western cultures do have their own rites of passage into adolescence, admittedly less fearsome, such as bar mitzvahs and bat mitzvahs at age 13 for Jewish boys and girls, and confirmation ceremonies in many Christian denominations (Dunham, Kidwell, & Wilson, 1986; Delaney, 1995; Herdt, 1998; Eccles, Templeton, & Barber, 2003; Hoffman, 2003).

Regardless of the nature of the ceremonies celebrated by various cultures, their underlying purpose tends to be similar from one culture to the next: symbolically celebrating the onset of the physical changes that turn a child's body into an adult body capable of reproduction. With these changes the child exits childhood and arrives at the doorstep of adulthood.

Growth During Adolescence: The Rapid Pace of Physical and Sexual Maturation

In only a few months, adolescents can grow several inches and require a virtually new wardrobe as they are transformed, at least in physical appearance, from children to young adults. One aspect of this transformation is the adolescent growth spurt, a period of very rapid growth in height and weight. On average, boys grow 4.1 inches a year and girls 3.5 inches a year. Some adolescents grow as much as 5 inches in a single year (Tanner, 1972; Caino et al., 2004).

Boys' and girls' adolescent growth spurts begin at different times. As you can see in Figure 11-1, girls begin their spurts around age 10, while boys start at about age 12. During the 2-year period starting at age 11, girls tend to be taller than boys. But by the age of 13, boys, on average, are taller than girls—a state of affairs that persists for the remainder of the life span.

Puberty: The Start of Sexual Maturation

Puberty, the period during which the sexual organs mature, begins when the pituitary gland in the brain signals other glands in children's bodies to begin producing the sex hormones,

puberty the period during which the sexual organs mature.

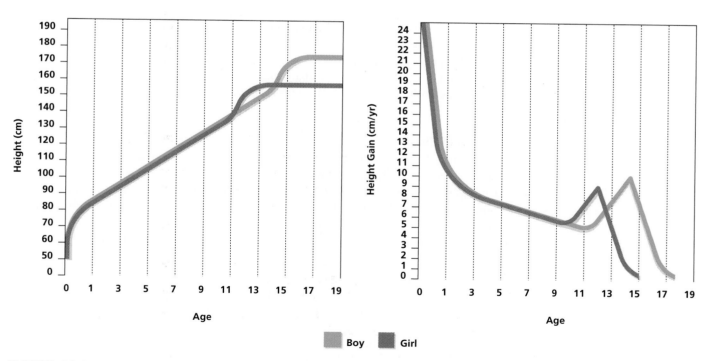

Boy **Girl**

FIGURE 11-1 GROWTH PATTERNS

Patterns of growth are depicted in two ways. The first figure shows height at a given age, while the second shows the height *increase* that occurs from birth through the end of adolescence. Notice that girls begin their growth spurt around age 10, while boys begin the growth spurt at about age 12. However, by the age of 13, boys tend to be taller than girls. What are the social consequences of being taller or shorter than average for boys and girls?

(*Source:* Adapted from Cratty, 1986.)

Note the changes that have occurred in just a few years in these pre- and post-puberty photos of the same boy.

androgens (male hormones) or *estrogens* (female hormones), at adult levels. (Males and females produce both types of sex hormones, but males have a higher concentration of androgens and females a higher concentration of estrogens.) The pituitary gland also signals the body to increase production of growth hormones that interact with the sex hormones to cause the growth spurt and puberty. In addition, the hormone *leptin* appears to play a role in the start of puberty.

Like the growth spurt, puberty begins earlier for girls than for boys. Girls start puberty at around age 11 or 12, and boys begin at around age 13 or 14. However, there are wide variations among individuals. For example, some girls begin puberty as early as 7 or 8 or as late as 16 years of age.

Puberty in Girls.   It is not clear why puberty begins at a particular time. What is clear is that environmental and cultural factors play a role. For example, **menarche,** the onset of menstruation and probably the most obvious signal of puberty in girls, varies greatly in different parts of the world. In poorer, developing countries, menstruation begins later than in more economically advantaged countries. Even within wealthier countries, girls in more affluent groups begin to menstruate earlier than less affluent girls (see Figure 11-2).

Consequently, it appears that girls who are better nourished and healthier are more apt to start menstruation at an earlier age than those who suffer from malnutrition or chronic disease. In fact, some studies have suggested that weight or the proportion of fat to muscle in the body might play a critical role in the timing of menarche. For example, in the United States, athletes with a low percentage of body fat may start menstruating later than less active girls. Conversely, obesity—which results in an increase in the secretion of leptin, a hormone associated with the onset of menstruation—leads to earlier puberty (Richards, 1996; Vizmanos & Marti-Henneberg, 2000; Woelfle, Harz, & Roth, 2007).

Other factors can affect the timing of menarche. For instance, environmental stress due to such factors as parental divorce or high levels of family conflict can bring about an early onset (Hulanicka, 1999; Kim & Smith, 1999; Kaltiala-Heino, Kosunen, & Rimpela, 2003; Ellis, 2004).

Over the past 100 years or so, girls in the United States and other cultures have been experiencing puberty at earlier ages. Near the end of the 19th century, menstruation began, on average,

menarche   the onset of menstruation.

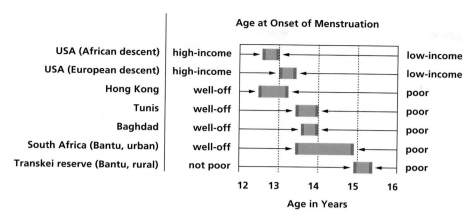

Age at Onset of Menstruation

USA (African descent)	high-income		low-income
USA (European descent)	high-income		low-income
Hong Kong	well-off		poor
Tunis	well-off		poor
Baghdad	well-off		poor
South Africa (Bantu, urban)	well-off		poor
Transkei reserve (Bantu, rural)	not poor		poor

Age in Years

FIGURE 11-2 ONSET OF MENSTRUATION

The onset of menstruation occurs earlier in more economically advantaged countries than in those that are poorer. But even in wealthier countries, girls living in more affluent circumstances begin to menstruate earlier than those living in less affluent situations. Why is this the case?

(*Source:* Adapted from Eveleth & Tanner, 1976.)

around age 14 or 15, compared with today's 11 or 12. Other indicators of puberty, such as the age at which adult height and sexual maturity are reached, have also appeared at earlier ages, probably due to reduced disease and improved nutrition.

The earlier start of puberty is an example of a significant **secular trend,** a pattern of change occurring over several generations. Secular trends occur when a physical characteristic changes over the course of several generations, such as earlier onset of menstruation or increased height that has occurred as a result of better nutrition over the centuries.

Menstruation is just one of several changes in puberty that are related to the development of primary and secondary sex characteristics. **Primary sex characteristics** are associated with the development of the organs and structures of the body that directly relate to reproduction. In contrast, **secondary sex characteristics** are the visible signs of sexual maturity that do not involve the sex organs directly.

In girls, the development of primary sex characteristics involves changes in the vagina and uterus. Secondary sex characteristics include the development of breasts and pubic hair. Breasts begin to grow at around the age of 10, and pubic hair beings to appear at about age 11. Underarm hair appears about 2 years later.

For some girls, indications of puberty start unusually early. One out of 7 Caucasian girls develops breasts or pubic hair by age 8. Even more surprisingly, the figure is 1 out of 2 for African American girls. The reasons for this earlier onset of puberty are unclear, and the demarcation between normal and abnormal onset of puberty is a point of controversy among specialists (Lemonick, 2000; The Endocrine Society, 2001; Ritzen, 2003).

Puberty in Boys.   Boys' sexual maturation follows a somewhat different course. The penis and scrotum begin to grow at an accelerated rate around the age of 12, and they reach adult size about 3 or 4 years later. As boys' penises enlarge, other primary sex characteristics are developing with enlargement of the prostate gland and seminal vesicles, which produce semen (the fluid that carries sperm). A boy's first ejaculation, known as *spermarche,* usually occurs around the age of 13, more than a year after the body has begun producing sperm. At first, the semen contains relatively few sperm, but the amount of sperm increases significantly with age. Secondary sex characteristics are also developing. Pubic hair begins to grow around the age of 12, followed by the growth of underarm and facial hair. Finally, boys' voices deepen as the vocal cords become longer and the larynx larger. (Figure 11-3 summarizes the changes that occur in sexual maturation during early adolescence.)

The surge in production of hormones that triggers the start of adolescence also may lead to rapid swings in mood. For example, boys may have feelings of anger and annoyance that are associated with higher hormone levels. In girls, the emotions produced by hormone production are somewhat different: Higher levels of hormones are associated with anger and depression (Buchanan, Eccles, & Becker, 1992).

secular trend   a pattern of change occurring over several generations.

primary sex characteristics   characteristics associated with the development of the organs and structures of the body that directly relate to reproduction.

secondary sex characteristics   the visible signs of sexual maturity that do not directly involve the sex organs.

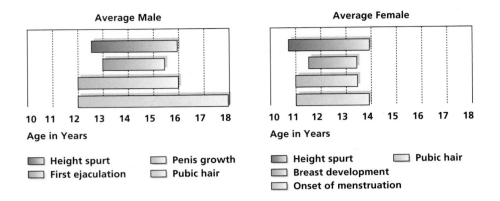

FIGURE 11-3   SEXUAL MATURATION

The changes in sexual maturation that occur for males and females during early adolescence.

(*Source:* Adapted from Tanner, 1978.)

Body Image: Reactions to Physical Changes in Adolescence.   Unlike infants, who also undergo extraordinarily rapid growth, adolescents are well aware of what is happening to their bodies, and they may react with horror or joy, spending long periods in front of mirrors. Few, though, are neutral about the changes they are witnessing (Mehran, 1997).

Some of the changes of adolescence do not show up in physical changes, but carry psychological weight. In the past, girls tended to react to menarche with anxiety because Western society tended to emphasize the more negative aspects of menstruation, such as the potential of cramps and messiness. Today, however, society's view of menstruation tends to be more positive, in part because menstruation has been demystified and discussed more openly. (For instance, television commercials for tampons are commonplace.) As a consequence, menarche is typically accompanied by an increase in self-esteem, a rise in status, and greater self-awareness, as adolescent girls see themselves as becoming adults (Brooks-Gunn & Reiter, 1990; Johnson, Roberts, & Worell, 1999; Matlin, 2003).

A boy's first ejaculation is roughly equivalent to menarche in a girl. However, while girls generally tell their mothers about the onset of menstruation, boys rarely mention their first ejaculation to their parents or even their friends (Stein & Reiser, 1994). Why? One reason is that girls require tampons or sanitary napkins, and mothers provide them. It also may be that boys see the first ejaculation as an indication of their budding sexuality, an area about which they are quite uncertain and therefore reluctant to discuss with others.

Menstruation and ejaculations occur privately, but changes in body shape and size are quite public. Consequently, teenagers entering puberty frequently are embarrassed by the changes that are occurring. Girls, in particular, are often unhappy with their new bodies. Ideals of beauty in many Western countries call for an unrealistic thinness that is quite different from the actual shape of most women. Puberty brings a considerable increase in the amount of fatty tissue, as well as enlargement of the hips and buttocks—a far cry from the slenderness that society seems to demand (Attie & Brooks-Gunn, 1989; Crawford & Unger, 2004). How children react to the onset of puberty depends in part on when it happens. Girls and boys who mature either much earlier or later than most of their peers are especially affected by the timing of puberty.

The Timing of Puberty: The Consequences of Early and Late Maturation.   Why does it matter when a boy or girl reaches puberty? There are social consequences of early or late maturation. And as we shall see, social consequences are very important to adolescents.

Early Maturation. For boys, early maturation is largely a plus. Early-maturing boys tend to be more successful at athletics, presumably because of their larger size. They also tend to be more popular and to have a more positive self-concept.

On the other hand, early maturation in boys does have a downside. Boys who mature early are more apt to have difficulties in school, and they are more likely to become involved in delinquency and substance abuse. The reason: Their larger size makes it more likely that they will seek out the company of older boys who may involve them in activities that are inappropriate for their age. Furthermore, although early-maturers are more responsible and cooperative in later life, they are also more conforming and lacking in humor. Overall, though, the pluses seem to outweigh the minuses for early-maturing boys (Weichold, Silbereisen, & Schmitt-Rodermund, 2003; Taga, Markey, & Friedman, 2006; Costello et al., 2007; Lynne et al., 2007).

The story is a bit different for early-maturing girls. For them, the obvious changes in their bodies—such as the development of breasts—may lead them to feel uncomfortable and different from their peers. Moreover, because girls, in general, mature earlier than boys, early maturation tends to come at a very young age in the girl's life. Early-maturing girls may have to endure ridicule from their less mature classmates (Williams & Currie, 2000; Franko & Striegel-Moore, 2002; Olivardia & Pope, 2002).

On the other hand, early maturation is not a completely negative experience for girls. Girls who mature earlier tend to be sought after more as potential dates, and their popularity may enhance their self-concepts. This attention has a price, however. They may not be socially ready to participate in the kind of one-on-one dating situations that most girls deal with at a later age, and such situations may be psychologically challenging for early-maturing girls. Moreover, the conspicuousness of their deviance from their later-maturing classmates may have a negative effect, producing anxiety, unhappiness, and depression (Kaltiala-Heino et al., 2003).

Cultural norms and standards regarding how women should look play a big role in how girls experience early maturation. For instance, in the United States, the notion of female sexuality is looked upon with a degree of ambivalence, being promoted in the media yet frowned upon socially. Girls who appear "sexy" attract both positive and negative attention. Consequently, unless a young girl who has developed secondary sex characteristics early can handle the disapproval she may encounter when she conspicuously displays her growing sexuality, the outcome of early maturation may be negative. In countries in which attitudes about sexuality are more liberal, the results of early maturation may be more positive. For example, in Germany, which has a more open view of sex, early-maturing girls have higher self-esteem than such girls in the United States. Furthermore, the consequences of early maturation vary even within the United States, depending on the views of girls' peer groups and on prevailing community standards regarding sex (Silbereisen et al., 1989; Richards et al., 1990; Petersen, 2000).

Late Maturation. As with early maturation, the situation with late maturation is mixed, although in this case boys fare worse than girls. For instance, boys who are smaller and lighter than their more physically mature peers tend to be viewed as less attractive. Because of their smaller size, they are at a disadvantage when it comes to sports activities. Furthermore, boys are expected to be bigger than their dates, so the social lives of late-maturing boys may suffer. Ultimately, if these difficulties lead to a decline in self-concept, the disadvantages of late maturation for boys could extend well into adulthood. More positively, coping with the challenges of late maturation may actually help males in some ways. Late-maturing boys grow up to have several positive qualities such as assertiveness and insightfulness, and they are more creatively playful than early-maturers (Livson & Peskin, 1980; Kaltiala-Heino et al., 2003).

The picture for late-maturing girls is actually quite positive. In the short-term, girls who mature later may be overlooked in dating and other mixed-sex activities during junior high school and middle school, and they may have relatively low social status (Apter et al., 1981; Clarke-Stewart & Friedman, 1987). However, by the time they are in the 10th grade and have begun to mature visibly, late-maturing-girls' satisfaction with themselves and their bodies may be greater than that of early-maturers. In fact, late-maturing girls may end up with fewer

Boys who mature early tend to be more successful in athletics and have a more positive self-concept. But what might be the downside to early maturation?

emotional problems. The reason? Late-maturing girls are more apt to fit the societal ideal of a slender, "leggy" body type than early-maturers, who tend to look heavier in comparison (Simmons & Blythe, 1987; Peterson, 1988).

In sum, the reactions to early and late maturation present a complex picture. As we have seen repeatedly, we need to take into consideration the complete constellation of factors affecting individuals in order to understand their development. Some developmentalists suggest that other factors, such as changes in peer groups, family dynamics, and particularly schools and other societal institutions, may be more pertinent in determining an adolescent's behavior than early and later maturation, and the effects of puberty in general (Paikoff & Brooks-Gunn, 1990; Dorn, Susman, & Ponirakis, 2003; Stice, 2003).

Nutrition, Food, and Eating Disorders: Fueling the Growth of Adolescence

A rice cake in the afternoon, an apple for dinner. That was Heather Rhodes's typical diet her freshman year at St. Joseph's College in Rensselaer, Indiana, when she began to nurture a fear (exacerbated, she says, by the sudden death of a friend) that she was gaining weight. But when Rhodes, now 20, returned home to Joliet, Illinois, for summer vacation a year and a half ago, her family thought she was melting away. "I could see the outline of her pelvis in her clothes . . ." says Heather's mother . . . , so she and the rest of the family confronted Heather one evening, placing a bathroom scale in the middle of the family room. "I told them they were attacking me and to go to hell," recalls Heather, who nevertheless reluctantly weighed herself. Her 5'7" frame held a mere 85 pounds—down 22 pounds from her senior year in high school. "I told them they rigged the scale," she says. It simply didn't compute with her self-image. "When I looked in the mirror," she says, "I thought my stomach was still huge and my face was fat." (Sandler, 1994, p. 56)

Heather's problem: a severe eating disorder, anorexia nervosa. As we have seen, the cultural ideal of slim and fit favors late-developing girls. But when those developments do occur, how do girls and, increasingly, boys cope when the image in the mirror deviates from the ideal presented in the popular media?

The rapid physical growth of adolescence is fueled by an increase in food consumption. Particularly during the growth spurt, adolescents eat substantial quantities of food, increasing their intake of calories rather dramatically. During the teenage years, the average girl requires some 2,200 calories a day, and the average boy requires 2,800.

Of course, not just any calories help nourish adolescents' growth. Several key nutrients are essential, including, in particular, calcium and iron. The calcium provided by milk helps bone growth, which may prevent the later development of osteoporosis—the thinning of bones— that affects 25% of women later in their lives. Similarly, iron is necessary to prevent iron-deficiency anemia, an ailment that is not uncommon among teenagers.

For most adolescents, the major nutritional issue is ensuring the consumption of a sufficient balance of appropriate foods. Two extremes of nutrition can be a major concern for a substantial minority and can create a real threat to health. Among the most prevalent problems: obesity and eating disorders like the one afflicting Heather Rhodes.

Obesity.   The most common nutritional concern during adolescence is obesity. One in 5 adolescents is overweight, and 1 in 20 can be formally classified as obese (body weight that is more than 20% above average). Moreover, the proportion of female adolescents who are classified as obese increases over the course of adolescence (Brook & Tepper, 1997; Critser, 2003; Kimm et al., 2003).

Although adolescents are obese for the same reasons as younger children, the psychological consequences may be particularly severe during a time of life when body image is of special concern. Furthermore, the potential health consequences of obesity during adolescence are

Obesity has become the most common nutritional concern during adolescence. In addition to issues of health, what are some psychological concerns about obesity in adolescence?

also problematic. For instance, obesity taxes the circulatory system, increasing the likelihood of high blood pressure and diabetes. Finally, obese adolescents stand an 80% chance of becoming obese adults (Blaine, Rodman, & Newman, 2007).

Lack of exercise is one of the main culprits. One survey found that by the end of the teenage years, most females get virtually no exercise outside of physical education classes in school. In fact, the older they are, the less exercise female adolescents engage in. The problem is particularly pronounced for older black female adolescents, more than half of whom report *no* physical exercise outside of school, compared with about a third of white adolescents who report no exercise (see Figure 11-4; Kimm et al., 2002; Burke et al., 2006; Deforche, De Bourdeaudhuij, & Tanghe, 2006; Delva, O'Malley, & Johnston, 2006).

Why do adolescent women get so little exercise? It may reflect a lack of organized sports or good athletic facilities for women. It may even be the result of lingering cultural norms suggesting that athletic participation is more the realm of boys than girls. Whatever the reason, it is clear that this lack of exercise feeds into the growing problem of obesity.

Anorexia Nervosa and Bulimia.

The fear of fat and desire to avoid obesity sometimes become so strong that they turn into a problem. For instance, Heather Rhodes suffered from **anorexia nervosa,** a severe eating disorder in which individuals refuse to eat. Their troubled body image leads them to deny that their behavior and appearance, which may become skeletal, are out of the ordinary.

Anorexia is a dangerous psychological disorder; some 15% to 20% of its victims literally starve themselves to death. It primarily afflicts women between the ages of 12 and 40; those most susceptible are intelligent, successful, and attractive white adolescent girls from affluent homes. Anorexia is also becoming a problem for more boys. About 10% of victims are male, a percentage that is increasing and is associated with the use of steroids (Robb & Dadson, 2002; Jacobi et al., 2004; Ricciardelli & McCabe, 2004; Crisp et al., 2006).

Even though they eat little, anorexics are often focused on food. They may go shopping often, collect cookbooks, talk about food, or cook huge meals for others. Although they may be incredibly thin, their body images are so distorted that they see their reflections in mirrors as disgustingly fat and try to lose more and more weight. Even when they look like skeletons, they are unable to see what they have become.

Bulimia, another eating disorder, is characterized by *bingeing,* eating large quantities of food, followed by *purging* of the food through vomiting or the use of laxatives. Bulimics may eat an entire gallon of ice cream or a whole package of tortilla chips. But after such a binge, sufferers experience powerful feelings of guilt and depression, and they intentionally rid themselves of the food.

Although the weight of a person with bulimia remains fairly normal, the disorder is quite hazardous. The constant vomiting and diarrhea of the binge-and-purge cycles may produce a chemical imbalance that can lead to heart failure.

The exact reasons for the occurrence of eating disorders are not clear, although several factors appear to be implicated. Dieting often precedes the development of eating disorders, as even normal-weight individuals are spurred on by societal standards of slenderness to seek to lower their weight. The feelings of control and success may encourage them to lose more and more weight. Furthermore, girls who mature earlier than their peers and who have a higher level of body fat are more susceptible to eating disorders during later adolescence as they try to bring their maturing bodies back into line with the cultural standard of a thin, boyish physique. Adolescents who are clinically depressed are also more likely to develop eating disorders later, perhaps seeking to withhold from themselves (Pratt, Phillips, & Greydanus, 2003; Walcott, Pratt, & Patel, 2003; Giordana, 2005).

Some experts suggest that a biological cause lies at the root of both anorexia nervosa and bulimia. In fact, twin studies suggest there are genetic components to the disorders. In addition, hormonal imbalances sometimes occur in sufferers (Condit, 1990; Irwin, 1993; Treasure & Tiller, 1993; Kaye et al., 2004).

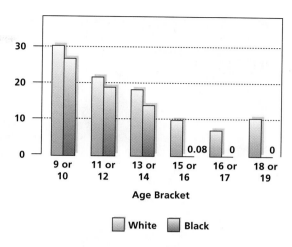

FIGURE 11-4   NO SWEAT

Physical activity among both white and black adolescent females declines substantially over the course of adolescence. What might be the reasons for this decline?

(*Source:* Kimm et al., 2002.)

- -

anorexia nervosa   a severe eating disorder in which individuals refuse to eat, while denying that their behavior and appearance, which may become skeletal, are out of the ordinary.

bulimia   an eating disorder characterized by binges on large quantities of food, followed by purges of the food through vomiting or the use of laxatives.

This young woman suffers from anorexia nervosa, a severe eating disorder in which people refuse to eat, while denying that their behavior and appearance are out of the ordinary.

Other attempts to explain the eating disorders emphasize psychological and social factors. For instance, some experts suggest that the disorders are a result of perfectionistic, overdemanding parents or by-products of other family difficulties. Culture also plays a role. Anorexia nervosa, for instance, is found only in cultures that idealize slender female bodies. Because in most places such a standard does not hold, anorexia is not prevalent outside the United States (Haines & Neumark-Sztainer, 2006; Harrison & Hefner, 2006).

For example, anorexia is nonexistent in all of Asia, with two interesting exceptions: the upper classes of Japan and of Hong Kong, where Western influence is greatest. Furthermore, anorexia nervosa is a fairly recent disorder. It was not seen in the 17th and 18th centuries, when the ideal of the female body was a plump corpulence. The increasing number of boys with anorexia in the United States may be related to a growing emphasis on a muscular male physique that features little body fat (Keel, Leon, & Fulkerson, 2001; Mangweth, Hausmann, & Walch, 2004; Makino et al., 2006; Greenberg, Cwikel, & Mirsky, 2007).

Because anorexia nervosa and bulimia are products of both biological and environmental causes, treatment typically involves a mix of approaches. For instance, both psychological therapy and dietary modifications are likely to be needed for successful treatment. In more extreme cases, hospitalization may be necessary (Porzelius, Dinsmore, & Staffelbach, 2001; Stice & Shaw, 2004; Robergeau, Joseph, & Silber, 2006).

Brain Development and Thought: Paving the Way for Cognitive Growth

Adolescence brings greater independence. Teenagers tend to assert themselves more and more. This independence is, in part, the result of changes in the brain that pave the way for the significant advances that occur in cognitive abilities during adolescence, as we'll consider in the next part of the chapter. As the number of neurons (the cells of the nervous system) continue to grow, and their interconnections become richer and more complex, adolescent thinking also becomes more sophisticated (Thompson & Nelson, 2001; Toga & Thompson, 2003).

The prefrontal cortex, the area of the brain responsible for impulse control, is biologically immature during adolescence, leading to some of the risk and impulsive behavior associated with the age group.

The brain produces an oversupply of gray matter during adolescence, which is later pruned back at the rate of 1% to 2% per year (see Figure 11-5). Myelination—the process in which nerve cells are insulated by a covering of fat cells—increases and continues to make the transmission of neural messages more efficient. Both the pruning process and increased myelination contribute to the growing cognitive abilities of adolescents (Sowell et al., 2001; Sowell et al., 2003).

One specific area of the brain that undergoes considerable development throughout adolescence is the prefrontal cortex, which is not fully developed until around the early 20s. The *prefrontal cortex* is the part of the brain that allows people to think, evaluate, and make complex judgments in a uniquely human way. It underlies the increasingly complex intellectual achievements that are possible during adolescence.

During adolescence, the prefrontal cortex becomes increasingly efficient in communicating with other parts of the brain. This helps build a communication system within the brain that is more distributed and sophisticated, permitting the different areas of the brain to process information more effectively (Scherf, Sweeney, & Luna, 2006).

The prefrontal cortex also provides for impulse control. Rather than simply reacting to emotions such as anger or rage, an individual with a fully developed prefrontal cortex is able to inhibit the desire for action that stems from such emotions.

Because during adolescence the prefrontal cortex is biologically immature, the ability to inhibit impulses is not fully developed (see Figure 11-6). As we discuss in the *From Research to Practice* box, this brain immaturity may lead to some of the risky and impulsive behaviors that are characteristic of adolescence—and some behaviors that are even more extreme (Weinberger, 2001; Steinberg & Scott, 2003).

Adolescent brain development also produces changes in regions involving dopamine sensitivity and production. As a result of these alterations, adolescents may become less susceptible to the effects of alcohol, and it requires more drinks for adolescents to experience its reinforcing qualities—leading to higher alcohol intake. In addition, alterations in dopamine sensitivity may make adolescents more sensitive to stress, leading to further alcohol use (Spear, 2002).

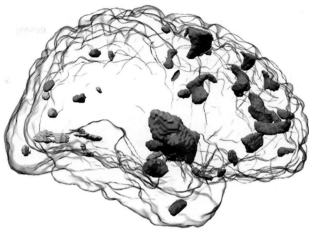

FIGURE 11-5   PRUNING GRAY MATTER

This three-dimensional view of the brain shows areas of gray matter that are pruned from the brain between adolescence and adulthood.

(*Source:* Sowell et al., 1999.)

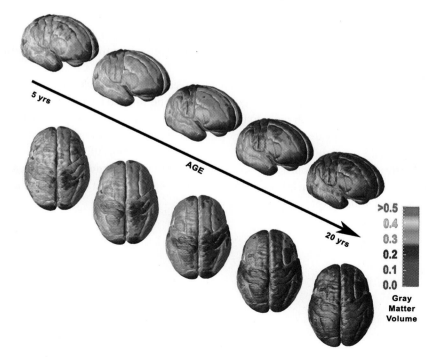

FIGURE 11-6   CONTINUING BRAIN MATURATION

Even in the late teenage years, gray matter is replaced throughout the cortex.

(*Source:* Beckman, 2004.)

From Research to Practice

The Immature Brain Argument: Too Young for the Death Penalty?

Just after 2 AM on September 9, 1993, Christopher Simmons, 17, and Charles Benjamin, 15, broke into a trailer south of Fenton, Misouri, just outside of St. Louis. They woke Shirley Ann Crook, a 46-year-old truck driver who was inside, and proceeded to tie her up and cover her eyes and mouth with silver duct tape. They then put her in the back of her minivan, drove her to a railroad bridge and pushed her into the river below, where her body was found the next day. Simmons and Benjamin later confessed to the abduction and murder, which had netted them $6. (Raeburn, 2004, p. 26)

This horrific case sent Benjamin to life in prison, and Simmons was given the death penalty. But Simmons's lawyers appealed, and ultimately the U.S. Supreme Court ruled that he—and anyone else under the age of 18—could not be executed because of their youth.

Among the evidence that the Supreme Court weighed in its decision was evidence from neuroscientists and child developmentalists that the brains of adolescents are still developing in important ways and that therefore they lack judgment because of this brain immaturity. According to this reasoning, adolescents are not fully capable of making reasonable decisions because their brains are not yet wired like those of adults.

The argument that adolescents may not be as responsible for their crimes stems from research showing that the brain continues to grow and mature during the teenage years, and sometimes beyond. For example, neurons that make up unnecessary gray matter of the brain begin to disappear during adolescence. In their place, the volume of white matter of the brain begins to increase. The decline in gray matter and increase in white matter permits more sophisticated, thoughtful cognitive processing (Beckman, 2004).

For instance, when the frontal lobes of the brain contain more white matter, they are better at restraining impulsivity. As neuroscientist Ruben Gur puts it, "If you've been insulted, your emotional brain says, 'Kill,' but your frontal lobe says you're in the middle of a cocktail party, 'so let's respond with a cutting remark'"(Beckman, 2004, p. 597).

In adolescents, that censoring process may not occur as efficiently. As a result, teenagers may act impulsively, responding with emotion rather than reason. Furthermore, adolescents' ability to foresee the consequences of their actions may also be hindered as a result of their less mature brains.

Are the brains of adolescents so immature that teenage offenders should receive less harsh punishment for their crimes than those with older, and therefore more mature, brains? It is not a simple question, and the answer probably will come more from those studying morality than from scientists.

- *Do you think that the penalty for criminal behavior should be tied to the maturity of a criminal's brain? Why or why not?*

- *Are there other aspects of physical development that should be taken into consideration in determining a person's responsibility for criminal activity?*

Sleep Deprivation. With increasing academic and social demands placed upon them, adolescents go to bed later and get up earlier. As a result, they often lead their lives in something of a sleep-deprived daze.

The sleep deprivation comes at a time when adolescents' internal clocks shift. Older adolescents in particular experience the need to go to bed later and to sleep later in the morning, and they require 9 hours of sleep each night to feel rested. Because they typically have early morning classes but don't feel sleepy until late at night, they end up getting far less sleep than their bodies crave (National Sleep Foundation, 2002; Dorofaeff & Denny, 2006; Fuligni & Hardway, 2006).

Sleep deprivation takes its toll. Sleepy teens have lower grades, are more depressed, and have greater difficulty controlling their moods. In addition, they are at great risk for auto accidents (Fredriksen et al., 2004).

Review and Apply

Review

- Adolescence is a period of rapid physical growth, including the changes associated with puberty.
- Puberty can cause reactions in adolescents ranging from confusion to increased self-esteem.
- Early or late maturation can bring advantages and disadvantages, depending on gender as well as emotional and psychological maturity.
- Adequate nutrition is essential in adolescence because of the need to fuel physical growth. Changing physical needs and environmental pressures can induce obesity or eating disorders.
- The two most common eating disorders are anorexia nervosa and bulimia. Both must be treated with a combination of physical and psychological therapies.
- Brain development paves the way for significant cognitive growth, although the brain is not fully developed until the early 20s.

Applying Lifespan Development

- How can societal and environmental influences contribute to the emergence of an eating disorder?
- *From an educator's perspective:* Why do you think the passage to adolescence is regarded in many cultures as such a significant transition that it calls for unique ceremonies?

Cognitive Development and Schooling

Mrs. Kirby smiled as she read a particularly creative paper. As part of her eighth-grade American Government class every year, she asked students to write about what their lives would be like if America had not won its war for independence from Britain. She had tried something similar with her sixth graders, but many of them seemed unable to imagine anything different from what they already knew. By eighth grade, however, they were able to come up with some very interesting scenarios. One boy imagined that he would be known as Lord Lucas; a girl imagined that she would be a servant to a rich landowner; another that she would be helping to plot an overthrow of the government.

What is it that sets adolescents' thinking apart from that of younger children? One of the major changes is the ability to think beyond the concrete, current situation to what *might* or *could* be. Adolescents are able to keep in their heads a variety of abstract possibilities, and they can see issues in relative, as opposed to absolute, terms. Instead of viewing problems as having black-and-white solutions, they are capable of perceiving shades of gray (Keating, 1980, 1990).

Once again we can use several approaches to explain adolescents' cognitive development. We'll begin by returning to Piaget's theory, which has had a significant influence on how developmentalists think about thinking during adolescence.

Piagetian Approaches to Cognitive Development: Using Formal Operations

Fourteen-year-old Leigh is asked to solve a problem that anyone who has seen a grandfather's clock may have pondered: What determines the speed at which a pendulum moves back and

formal operational stage   the stage at which people develop the ability to think abstractly.

forth? In the version of the problem that she is asked to solve, Leigh is given a weight hanging from a string. She is told that she can vary several things: the length of the string, the weight of the object at the end of the string, the amount of force used to push the string, and the height to which the weight is raised in an arc before it is released.

Leigh doesn't remember, but she was asked to solve the same problem when she was 8 years old, as part of a longitudinal research study. At that time, she was in the concrete operational period, and her efforts to solve the problem were not very successful. She approached the problem haphazardly, with no systematic plan of action. For instance, she simultaneously tried to push the pendulum harder *and* shorten the length of the string *and* increase the weight on the string. Because she was varying so many factors at once, when the speed of the pendulum changed she had no way of knowing which factor or factors made a difference.

Now, however, Leigh is much more systematic. Rather than immediately beginning to push and pull at the pendulum, she stops a moment and thinks about what factors to take into account. She considers how she might test which of those factors is important, forming a hypothesis about which is most important. Then, just like a scientist conducting an experiment, she varies only one factor at a time. By examining each variable separately and systematically, she is able to come to the correct solution: The length of the string determines the speed of the pendulum.

Using Formal Operations to Solve Problems.   Leigh's approach to the pendulum question, a problem devised by Piaget, illustrates that she has moved into the formal operational period of cognitive development (Piaget & Inhelder, 1958). The **formal operational stage** is the stage at which people develop the ability to think abstractly. Piaget suggested that people reach it at the start of adolescence, around the age of 12. Leigh was able to think about the various aspects of the pendulum problem in an abstract manner, and to understand how to test out the hypotheses that she had formed.

By bringing formal principles of logic to bear on problems they encounter, adolescents are able to consider problems in the abstract rather than only in concrete terms. They are able to test their understanding by systematically carrying out rudimentary experiments on problems and situations, and observing what their experimental "interventions" bring about.

Like scientists who form hypotheses, adolescents in the formal operational stage use systematic reasoning. They start with a general theory about what produces a particular outcome and then deduce explanations for specific situations in which they see that particular outcome.

Adolescents are able to use formal reasoning, in which they start with a general theory about what produces a particular outcome, and then deduce explanations for specific situations in which they see that particular outcome. Like the scientists who form hypotheses that we discussed in Chapter 1, they can then test their theories. What distinguishes this kind of thinking from earlier cognitive stages is the ability to start with abstract possibilities and move to the concrete; in previous stages, children are tied to the concrete here-and-now. For example, at age 8, Leigh just started moving things around to see what would happen in the pendulum problem, a concrete approach. At age 12, however, she started with the abstract idea that each variable—the string, the size of the weight, and so forth—should be tested separately.

Adolescents also are able to employ propositional thought during the formal operational stage. *Propositional thought* is reasoning that uses abstract logic in the absences of concrete examples. For example, propositional thinking allows adolescents to understand that if certain premises are true, then a conclusion must also be true. For example, consider the following:

All men are mortal.	*[premise]*
Socrates is a man.	*[premise]*
Therefore, Socrates is mortal.	*[conclusion]*

Not only can adolescents understand that if both premises are true, then so is the conclusion, but they are also capable of using similar reasoning when premises and conclusions are stated more abstractly, as follows:

All As are B.	*[premise]*
C is an A.	*[premise]*
Therefore, C is a B.	*[conclusion]*

Although Piaget proposed that children enter the formal operational stage at the beginning of adolescence, you may recall that he also hypothesized that—as with all the stages of cognitive development—full capabilities do not emerge suddenly, at one stroke. Instead, they gradually unfold through a combination of physical maturation and environmental experiences. According to Piaget, it is not until adolescents are around 15 years old that they are fully settled in the formal operational stage.

mydevelopmentlab

VIDEO CLIP

DEDUCTIVE REASONING

In fact, some evidence suggests that a sizable proportion of people hone their formal operational skills at a later age, and in some cases, never fully employ formal operational thinking at all. For instance, most studies show that only 40% to 60% of college students and adults achieve formal operational thinking completely, and some estimates run as low as 25%. But many of those adults who do not show formal operational thought in every domain are fully competent in *some* aspects of formal operations (Keating & Clark, 1980; Sugarman, 1988).

One of the reasons adolescents differ in their use of formal operations relates to the culture in which they were raised. For instance, people who live in isolated, scientifically unsophisticated societies and who have little formal education are less likely to perform at the formal operational level than formally educated persons living in more technologically sophisticated societies (Jahoda, 1980; Segall et al., 1990).

Does this mean that adolescents (and adults) from cultures in which formal operations tend not to emerge are incapable of attaining them? Not at all. A more probable conclusion is that the scientific reasoning that characterizes formal operations is not equally valued in all societies. If everyday life does not require or promote a certain type of reasoning, it is unreasonable to expect people to employ that type of reasoning when confronted with a problem (Greenfield, 1976; Shea, 1985; Gauvain, 1998).

The Consequences of Adolescents' Use of Formal Operations.   Adolescents' ability to reason abstractly, embodied in their use of formal operations, leads to a change in their everyday behavior. Whereas earlier they may have unquestioningly accepted rules and explanations set out for them, their increased abstract reasoning abilities may lead them to question their parents and other authority figures far more strenuously.

In general, adolescents become more argumentative. They enjoy using abstract reasoning to poke holes in others' explanations, and their increased abilities to think critically make them acutely sensitive to parents' and teachers' perceived shortcomings. For instance, they may note the inconsistency in their parents' arguments against using drugs, such as when they know that their parents used drugs when they were adolescents and nothing much came of it. At the same time, adolescents can be indecisive, as they are able to see the merits of multiple sides to issues (Elkind, 1996).

Coping with the increased critical abilities of adolescents can be challenging for parents, teachers, and other adults who deal with adolescents. But it also makes adolescents more interesting, as they actively seek to understand the values and justifications that they encounter in their lives.

Evaluating Piaget's Approach.   Each time we've considered Piaget's theory in previous chapters, several concerns have cropped up. Let's summarize some of the issues here:

- Piaget suggests that cognitive development proceeds in universal, step-like advances that occur at particular stages. Yet we find significant differences in cognitive abilities from one person to the next, especially when we compare individuals from different cultures. Furthermore, we find inconsistencies even within the same individual. People may be able to accomplish some tasks that indicate they have reached a certain level of thinking, but not others. If Piaget were correct, a person ought to perform uniformly well once she or he reaches a given stage (Siegler, 1994).

- The notion of stages proposed by Piaget suggests that cognitive abilities do not grow gradually or smoothly. Instead, the stage point of view implies that cognitive growth is typified by relatively rapid shifts from one stage to the next. In contrast, many developmentalists argue that cognitive development proceeds in a more continuous fashion, increasing not so much in qualitative leaps forward as in quantitative accumulations. They also contend that Piaget's theory is better at *describing* behavior at a given stage than *explaining* why the shift from one stage to the next occurs (Gelman & Baillargeon, 1983; Case, 1991).

- Because of the nature of the tasks Piaget employed to measure cognitive abilities, critics suggest that he underestimated the age at which certain capabilities emerge. It is now widely accepted that infants and children are more sophisticated at an earlier age than Piaget asserted (Bornstein & Sigman, 1986).

- Piaget had a relatively narrow view of what is meant by *thinking* and *knowing*. To Piaget knowledge consists primarily of the kind of understanding displayed in the pendulum problem. However, as we discussed in Chapter 9, developmentalists such as Howard Gardner suggest that we have many kinds of intelligence, separate from and independent of one another (Gardner, 2000).

Adolescents' ability to reason abstractly leads them to question accepted rules and explanations.

- Finally, some developmentalists argue that formal operations do not represent the epitome of thinking and that more sophisticated forms of thinking do not actually emerge until early adulthood. For instance, developmental psychologist Giesela Labouvie-Vief (1980, 1986) argues that the complexity of society requires thought that is not necessarily based on pure logic. Instead, a kind of thinking is required that is flexible, allows for interpretive processes, and reflects the fact that reasons behind events in the real world are subtle—something that Labouvie-Vief calls *postformal thinking*. (We'll examine Labouvie-Vief's ideas on postformal thinking in more detail in Chapter 13.)

These criticisms and concerns regarding Piaget's approach to cognitive development have considerable merit. On the other hand, Piaget's theory has been the impetus for an enormous number of studies on the development of thinking capacities and processes, and it also spurred a good deal of classroom reform. Finally, his bold statements about the nature of cognitive development provided a fertile soil from which many opposing positions on cognitive development bloomed, such as the information processing perspective, to which we turn next (Zigler & Gilman, 1998; Taylor, 2005).

Information Processing Perspectives: Gradual Transformations in Abilities

From the perspective of proponents of information processing approaches to cognitive development, adolescents' mental abilities grow gradually and continuously. Unlike Piaget's view that the increasing cognitive sophistication of the adolescent is a reflection of stage-like spurts, the **information processing perspective** sees changes in adolescents' cognitive abilities as evidence of gradual transformations in the capacity to take in, use, and store information. A number of progressive changes occur in the ways people organize their thinking about the world, develop strategies for dealing with new situations, sort facts, and achieve advances in memory capacity and perceptual abilities (Wellman & Gelman, 1992; Pressley & Schneider, 1997; Wyer, 2004).

Adolescents' general intelligence—as measured by traditional IQ tests—remains stable, but there are dramatic improvements in the specific mental abilities that underlie intelligence. Verbal, mathematical, and spatial abilities increase, making many adolescents quicker with a comeback, impressive sources of information, and accomplished athletes. Memory capacity grows, and adolescents become more adept at effectively dividing their attention across more than one stimulus at a time—such as simultaneously studying for a biology test and listening to a Ludactis CD.

Furthermore, as Piaget noted, adolescents grow increasingly sophisticated in their understanding of problems, their ability to grasp abstract concepts and to think hypothetically, and their comprehension of the possibilities inherent in situations. This permits them, for instance, to endlessly dissect the course that their relationships might hypothetically take.

Adolescents know more about the world, too. Their store of knowledge increases as the amount of material to which they are exposed grows and their memory capacity enlarges. Taken as a whole, the mental abilities that underlie intelligence show a marked improvement during adolescence (Kail, 2003, 2004).

According to information processing explanations of cognitive development during adolescence, one of the most important reasons for advances in mental abilities is the growth of metacognition. **Metacognition** is the knowledge that people have about their own thinking processes, and their ability to monitor their cognition. Although school-age children can use some metacognitive strategies, adolescents are much more adept at understanding their own mental processes.

For example, as adolescents improve their understanding of their memory capacity, they get better at gauging how long they need to study a particular kind of material to memorize it for a test. Furthermore, they can judge when they have fully memorized the material considerably more accurately than when they were younger. These improvements in metacognitive abilities

information processing perspective the model that seeks to identify the way that individuals take in, use, and store information.

metacognition the knowledge that people have about their own thinking processes, and their ability to monitor their cognition.

adolescent egocentrism a state of self-absorption in which the world is viewed from one's own point of view.

imaginary audience an adolescent's belief that his or her own behavior is a primary focus of others' attentions and concerns.

permit adolescents to comprehend and master school material more effectively (Nelson, 1994; Kuhn, 2000; Desoete, Roeyers, & De Clercq, 2003).

These new abilities also can make adolescents particularly introspective and self-conscious—two hallmarks of the period which, as we see next, may produce a high degree of egocentrism.

Egocentrism in Thinking: Adolescents' Self-Absorption

Carlos thinks of his parents as "control freaks"; he cannot not figure why his parents insist that when he borrows their car, he call home and let them know where he is. Jeri is thrilled that Molly bought earrings just like hers, thinking it is the ultimate compliment, even though it's not clear that Molly even knew that Jeri had a similar pair when she bought them. Lu is upset with his biology teacher, Ms. Sebastian, for giving a long, difficult midterm exam on which he didn't do well.

Adolescents' newly sophisticated metacognitive abilities enable them to readily imagine that others are thinking about them, and they may construct elaborate scenarios about others' thoughts. It is also the source of the egocentrism that sometimes dominates adolescents' thinking. **Adolescent egocentrism** is a state of self-absorption in which the world is viewed as focused on oneself. This egocentrism makes adolescents highly critical of authority figures such as parents and teachers, unwilling to accept criticism, and quick to find fault with others' behavior (Elkind, 1985; Rycek et al., 1998; Greene, Krcmar, & Rubin, 2002).

The kind of egocentrism we see in adolescence helps explain why adolescents sometimes perceive that they are the focus of everyone else's attention. In fact, adolescents may develop what has been called an **imaginary audience,** fictitious observers who pay as much attention to the adolescents' behavior as adolescents do themselves.

Because of adolescents' newly sophisticated metacognitive abilities, they readily imagine that others are thinking about them, and they may construct elaborate scenarios about others' thoughts. The imaginary audience is usually perceived as focusing on the one thing that adolescents think most about: themselves. Unfortunately, these scenarios may suffer from the same kind of egocentrism as the rest of their thinking. For instance, a student sitting in a class may be

Adolescents' personal fables may lead them to feel invulnerable and to engage in risky behavior, like these Brazilian boys (known as "surfistas") riding on the roof of a high-speed train.

sure a teacher is focusing on her, and a teenager at a basketball game is likely to be convinced that everyone around is focusing on the pimple on his chin.

Egocentrism leads to a second distortion in thinking: the notion that one's experiences are unique. Adolescents develop **personal fables,** the view that what happens to them is unique, exceptional, and shared by no one else. For instance, teenagers whose romantic relationships have ended may feel that no one has ever experienced the hurt they feel, that no one has ever been treated so badly, that no one can understand what they are going through.

Personal fables also may make adolescents feel invulnerable to the risks that threaten others. Much of adolescents' risk taking may well be traced to the personal fables they construct for themselves. They may think that there is no need to use condoms during sex because, in the personal fables they construct, pregnancy and sexually transmitted infections such as AIDS only happen to other kinds of people, not to them. They may drive after drinking because their personal fables paint them as careful drivers, always in control (Greene et al., 2000; Vartanian, 2000; Reyna & Farley, 2006).

personal fables the view held by some adolescents that what happens to them is unique, exceptional, and shared by no one else.

School Performance

Do the advances that occur in metacognition, reasoning, and other cognitive abilities during adolescence translate into improvements in school performance? If grades are used as the

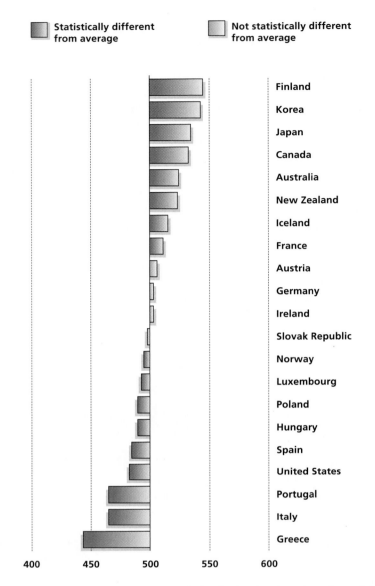

Statistically different from average

Not statistically different from average

Finland
Korea
Japan
Canada
Australia
New Zealand
Iceland
France
Austria
Germany
Ireland
Slovak Republic
Norway
Luxembourg
Poland
Hungary
Spain
United States
Portugal
Italy
Greece

400   450   500   550   600

FIGURE 11-7   NOT AT THE TOP OF THE CLASS: U.S. MATH PERFORMANCE LAGS

When compared to the math performance of students across the world, U.S. students perform at below-average levels.

(*Source:* Adapted from OECD, 2005.)

measure, the clear answer is "yes." Grades awarded to high school students have shifted upward in the last decade. The mean grade point average for college-bound seniors was 3.3 (out of a scale of 4), compared with 3.1 a decade ago. More than 40% of seniors reported average grades of A+, A, or A– (College Board, 2005).

At the same time, though, independent measures of achievement, such as SAT scores, have not risen. Consequently, a more likely explanation for the higher grades is the phenomenon of grade inflation. According to this view, it is not that students have changed. Instead, instructors have become more lenient, awarding higher grades for the same performance (Cardman, 2004).

Further evidence for grade inflation comes from the relatively poor achievement of students in the United States when compared to students in other countries. For instance, students in the United States score lower on standardized math and science tests when compared to students in other industrialized countries (see Figure 11-7; OECD, 2005).

There is no single reason for this gap in the educational achievement of U.S. students, but a combination of factors, such as less time spent in classes and less intensive instruction, are at work. Furthermore, the broad diversity of the U.S. school population may affect performance relative to other countries, in which the population attending school is more homogeneous and affluent (Stedman, 1997; Schemo, 2001).

The poorer accomplishments of U.S. students is also reflected in high school graduation rates. Although it once stood first in the percentage of the population who graduates from high school, the United States has dropped to 24th among industrialized countries. Only 78% of U.S. high school students graduate—a rate considerably lower than other developed countries (OECD, 1998, 2001).

In addition, the performance of students in the United States on math and science is poor when compared to that of students in other industrialized countries, and performance in geography is only average. There is no single reason for this gap in the educational achievement of U.S. students, but a combination of factors, such as less time spent in classes and less intensive instruction, is at work. Furthermore, the broad diversity of the U.S. school population may affect performance relative to other countries, in which the population attending school is more homogeneous and affluent. Certainly, as we discuss next, differences in socioeconomic status are reflected in school performance within the United States (Stedman, 1997; Schemo, 2001).

Socioeconomic Status and School Performance: Individual Differences in Achievement.   All students are entitled to the same opportunity in the classroom, but it is very clear that certain groups have more educational advantages than others. One of the most telling indicators of this reality is the relationship between educational achievement and socioeconomic status (SES).

Middle- and high-SES students, on average, earn higher grades, score higher on standardized tests of achievement, and complete more years of schooling than students from lower-SES homes. Of course, this disparity does not start in adolescence; the same findings hold for children in lower grades. However, by the time students are in high school, the effects of socioeconomic status become even more pronounced.

Why do students from middle- and high-SES homes show greater academic success? There are several reasons. For one thing, children living in poverty lack many of the advantages enjoyed by other children. Their nutrition and health may be less adequate. Often living in crowded conditions and attending inadequate schools, they may have few places to do homework. Their homes may lack the books and computers commonplace in more economically advantaged households (Adams & Singh, 1998; Bowen & Bowen, 1999; Prater, 2002).

For these reasons, students from impoverished backgrounds may be at a disadvantage from the day they begin their schooling. As they grow older, their school performance may continue to lag, and in fact their disadvantage may snowball. Because later school success builds heavily on basic skills presumably learned early in school, children who experience early problems may find themselves falling increasingly behind the academic eight ball as adolescents (Huston, 1991; Phillips et al., 1994).

Ethnic and Racial Differences in School Achievement.   Achievement differences between ethnic and racial groups are significant, and they paint a troubling picture of American education. For instance, data on school achievement indicate that, on average, African American and Hispanic students tend to perform at lower levels, receive lower grades, and score lower on standardized tests of achievement than Caucasian students. In contrast, Asian American students tend to receive higher grades than Caucasian students (National Center for Educational Statistics, 2003).

What is the source of such ethnic and racial differences in academic achievement? Clearly, much of the difference is due to socioeconomic factors: Because more African American and Hispanic families live in poverty, their economic disadvantage may be reflected in their school performance. In fact, when we take socioeconomic levels into account by comparing different ethnic and racial groups at the same socioeconomic level, achievement differences diminish, but they do not vanish (Meece & Kurtz-Costes, 2001; Cokley, 2003; Guerrero et al., 2006).

John Ogbu notes that Korean children whose parents emigrated voluntarily to the United States do better in school than their counterparts in Japan whose parents were forced to emigrate from Korea during WWII.

Anthropologist John Ogbu (1988, 1992) argues that members of certain minority groups may perceive school success as relatively unimportant. They may believe that societal prejudice in the workplace will dictate that they will not succeed, no matter how much effort they expend. The conclusion is that hard work in school will have no eventual payoff.

Ogbu suggests that members of minority groups who enter a new culture voluntarily are more likely to be successful in school than those who are brought into a new culture against their will. For instance, he notes that Korean children who are the sons and daughters of voluntary immigrants to the United States tend to be, on average, quite successful in school. On the other hand, Korean children in Japan, whose parents were forced to immigrate during World War II and work as forced laborers, tend to do relatively poorly in school. The reason for the disparity? The process of involuntary immigration apparently leaves lasting scars, reducing the motivation to succeed in subsequent generations. Ogbu suggests that in the United States, the involuntary immigration, as slaves, of the ancestors of many African American students might be related to their motivation to succeed (Ogbu, 1992; Gallagher, 1994).

Another factor in the differential success of various ethnic and racial group members has to do with attributions for academic success. As we discussed in Chapter 10, students from many Asian cultures tend to view achievement as the consequence of temporary situational factors, such as how hard they work. In contrast, African American students are more apt to view success as the result of external causes over which they have no control, such as luck or societal biases. Students who subscribe to the belief that effort will lead to success, and then expend that effort, are more likely to do better in school than students who believe that effort makes less of a difference (Stevenson, Chen, & Lee, 1992; Fuligni, 1997; Saunders, Davis, & Williams, 2004).

Adolescents' beliefs about the consequences of not doing well in school may also contribute to the racial and ethnic differences in school performance. Specifically, it may be that African American and Hispanic students tend to believe that they can succeed *despite* poor school performance. This belief may cause them to put less effort into their studies. In contrast, Asian American students tend to believe that if they do not do well in school, they are unlikely to get good jobs and be successful. Asian Americans, then, are motivated to work hard in school by a fear of the consequences of poor academic performance (Steinberg, Dornbusch, & Brown, 1992).

Cyberspace: Adolescents Online

Students at McClymonds High School in Oakland, California, have a mission: In conjunction with local entomologists, they are creating an online collection of insects in the neighborhood. By placing their "collection" on the World Wide Web, they expect to provide a long-term resource for local residents. (Harmon, 1997)

The widespread availability of the Internet and the Web is producing significant changes in the lives of adolescents. Easy access to far-reaching information and contacts is bringing benefits and, at the same time, dangers that are both real and virtual.

The educational promise of the Internet is significant. Through the Web, students can tap into a vast array of information, ranging from library catalogs to government statistics to views of the landscape of Mars transmitted by cameras actually sitting on that planet. And adolescents are quite adept with computers, using them in a variety of ways (see Figure 11-8).

Although it is clear that the Internet is having an impact on education, it is not yet obvious how it will change education or whether the impact will be uniformly positive. For instance, schools must change their curricula to include specific instruction in a key skill for deriving value from the Internet: learning to sort through huge bodies of information to identify what is most useful and discard what is not. To obtain the full benefits of the Web, then, students

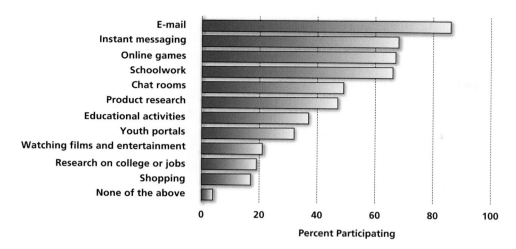

FIGURE 11-8 **TEENAGE ONLINE ACTIVITY**

Today, a large majority of teenagers use the Internet to communicate via email and instant messaging, and many also use the new technology for education-related material and research. How will this trend affect the way educators will teach in the future?

(*Source:* Yankee Group Interactive Consumer Survey, 2001.)

must obtain the ability to search, choose, and integrate information in order to create new knowledge (Oblinger & Rush, 1997; Trotter, 2004).

Despite the substantial benefits of the Web, its use also has a downside. Claims that cyberspace is overrun with child molesters may be exaggerated, but it is true that cyberspace makes available material that many parents and other adults find highly objectionable. In addition, there is a growing problem of Internet gambling. High school and college students can easily bet on sports events and participate in games such as poker on the Web using credit cards (Dowling, Smith, & Thomas, 2005; Winters, Stinchfield, & Botzet, 2005; Fleming et al., 2006; Mitchell, Wolak, & Finkelhor, 2007).

The growing use of computers also presents a challenge involving socioeconomic status, race, and ethnicity. Poorer adolescents and members of minority groups have less access to computers than more affluent adolescents and members of socially advantaged groups—a phenomenon known as the *digital divide.* For example, 77% of black students reported using a personal computer frequently, compared with 87% of white students and 81% of Hispanic/Latino students. Asian American students had the highest rate of use of computers, at 91.2%. How society reduces these discrepancies is a matter of considerable importance (Sax et al., 2004; Fetterman, 2005).

Dropping Out of School. Most students complete high school, but as we have said, some half million students each year drop out prior to graduating. The consequences of dropping out are severe. High school dropouts earn 42% less than high school graduates, and the unemployment rate for dropouts is 50%.

Adolescents who leave school do so for a variety of reasons. Some leave because of pregnancy or problems with the English language. Some must leave for economic reasons, needing to support themselves or their families.

Dropout rates differ according to gender and ethnicity. Males are more likely to drop out of school than females. In addition, although the dropout rate for all ethnicities has been declining somewhat over the last two decades, Hispanics and African American students still are more likely to leave high school before graduating than non-Hispanic white students. On the other hand, not all minority groups show higher dropout rates: Asians, for instance, drop out at a lower rate than Caucasians (National Center for Educational Statistics, 2003; Stearns & Glennie, 2006).

Poverty plays a large role in determining whether a student completes high school. Students from lower-income households are three times more likely to drop out than those from middle- and upper-income households. Because economic success is so dependent on education, dropping out often perpetuates a cycle of poverty (National Center for Educational Statistics, 2002).

Review and Apply

Review

- Adolescence corresponds to Piaget's formal operations period, a stage characterized by abstract reasoning and an experimental approach to problems.

- According to the information processing perspective, the cognitive advances of adolescence are quantitative and gradual, involving improvements in many aspects of thinking and memory. Improved metacognition enables the monitoring of thought processes and of mental capacities.

- Adolescents are susceptible to adolescent egocentrism and the perception that an imaginary audience is constantly observing their behavior. They also construct personal fables that stress their uniqueness and immunity to harm.

- Academic performance is linked in complex ways to socioeconomic status and to race and ethnicity.

Applying Lifespan Development

- When faced with complex problems, such as what kind of computer or car to buy, do you think most adults spontaneously apply formal operations like those used to solve the pendulum problem? Why or why not?

- *From a social worker's perspective:* In what ways does adolescent egocentrism complicate adolescents' social and family relationships? Do adults entirely outgrow egocentrism and personal fables?

Threats to Adolescents' Well-Being

Like most parents, I had thought of drug use as something you worried about when your kids got to high school. Now I know that, on the average, kids begin using drugs at 11 or 12, but at the time that never crossed our minds. Ryan had just begun attending mixed parties. He was playing Little League. In the eighth grade, Ryan started getting into a little trouble—one time he and another fellow stole a fire extinguisher, but we thought it was just a prank. Then his grades began to deteriorate. He began sneaking out at night. He would become belligerent at the drop of a hat, then sunny and nice again. . . .

It wasn't until Ryan fell apart at 14 that we started thinking about drugs. He had just begun McLean High School, and to him, it was like going to drug camp every day. Back then, everything was so available. He began cutting classes, a common tip-off, but we didn't hear from the school until he was flunking everything. It turned out that he was going to school for the first period, getting checked in, then leaving and smoking marijuana all day. (Shafer, 1990, p. 82)

Ryan's parents learned that marijuana was not the only drug Ryan was using. As his friends later admitted, Ryan was what they called a "garbage head." He would try anything. Despite efforts to curb his use of drugs, he never succeeded in stopping. He died at the age of 16, hit by a passing car after wandering into the street during an episode of drug use.

Few cases of adolescent drug use produce such extreme results, but the use of drugs, as well as other kinds of substance use and abuse, is one of several kinds of threats to health during adolescence, usually one of the healthiest periods of life. While the extent of risky behavior is difficult to gauge, preventable problems such as drug, alcohol, and tobacco use, as well as sexually transmitted infections, represent serious threats to adolescents' health and well-being.

Illegal Drugs

How common is illegal drug use during adolescence? Very. For instance, the most recent annual survey of nearly 50,000 U.S. students shows that almost 50% of high school seniors and almost 20% of eighth graders report having used marijuana within the past year. Although marijuana usage (as well as use of other drugs) has declined over the last few years, the data on drug use still represents substantial adolescent involvement (Johnston, Bachman, & O'Malley, 2003; Nanda & Konnur, 2006; see Figure 11-9).

Adolescents have a variety of reasons for using drugs. Some use them for the pleasurable experience drugs supposedly provide. Others use them to try to escape from the pressures of everyday life, however temporarily. Some adolescents try drugs simply for the thrill of doing something illegal. The alleged drug use of well-known role models, such as singer Britney Spears, may also contribute. Finally, peer pressure plays a role: Adolescents, as we'll discuss in greater detail in Chapter 12, are particularly susceptible to the perceived standards of their peer groups (Urberg, Luo, & Pilgrim, 2003; Nation & Heflinger, 2006; Young et al., 2006).

The use of illegal drugs is dangerous in several respects. For instance, some drugs are addictive. **Addictive drugs** are drugs that produce a biological or psychological dependence in users, leading to increasingly powerful cravings for them.

addictive drugs drugs that produce a biological or psychological dependence in users, leading to increasingly powerful cravings for them.

The use of marijuana among high school students has decreased since the late 1990s.

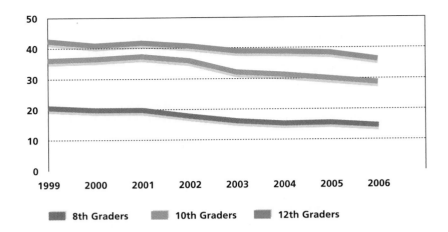

FIGURE 11-9 DOWNWARD TREND

According to an annual survey, the proportion of students reporting marijuana use over the past 12 months has decreased since 1999. What might account for the decline in drug use?

(*Source:* Johnston et al., 2006.)

8th Graders   10th Graders   12th Graders

Careers in Lifespan Development

Daniel W. Prior

Education: BS, Psychology and Sociology, Evangel College, Springfield, Missouri; MS, Psychology, Pittsburg State University, Pittsburg, Kansas; PhD, Counseling Psychology, Kansas State University, Manhattan, Kansas

Position: Program Manager/Counselor, The Pathway Home

Home: Anchorage, Alaska

While substance abuse cuts across all age groups, adolescents are particularly vulnerable to the threats posed by drugs, alcohol, and tobacco. As a result, treatment centers such as The Pathway Home in Anchorage, Alaska, have been established to deal with the problems and help youth get back on track with their lives.

According to program manager Daniel Prior, The Pathway Home serves a maximum of 30 Alaskan Native youth in an environment that offers nurturance and personal growth.

"Most of the youth that come here have a co-occurring disorder, meaning they have a substance abuse issue and some mental health issues as well," Prior noted. "As a result, we believe in creating an environment that offers a lot of nurturance and personal growth.

"For example the building was designed as an open structure, since many of the kids are used to being outdoors a lot," he said.

"We found that environmental factors are critical since adolescents like a lot of freedom."

The approach taken to helping adolescents at The Pathway Home is based on psychologist Abraham Maslow's hierarchy of motivational needs. Maslow suggested that certain basic needs must be satisfied before more sophisticated, higher-order needs can be fulfilled. In his view, the most basic needs are physiological needs, safety and security needs, and needs for love and a sense of belongingness.

"Based on Maslow's theory, the first needs we address are physiological needs," said Prior. "Because kids come in influenced by various unhealthy substances, we strive to get them on a balanced diet and physically fit. This usually takes two to three months.

"The second of Maslow's needs are safety and security needs. Here we work hard to help them set boundaries, teaching them how to stay safe and how not to engage in risky behaviors," Prior added. "Finally, to address love and belongingness needs, we teach them how to have a meaningful relationship since many, because of trauma, are suspicious and skeptical of authority and others."

In addition to counseling services, The Pathway Home provides an in-house school that includes shops to teach the residents how to work with their hands. In addition, courses are offered on the Alaskan Native culture.

"Many youth come in with mixed identity issues," Prior explained. "We offer a significant cultural program that teaches young people the good aspects of their culture with emphasis on native drumming, dancing and singing."

When drugs produce a biological addiction, their presence in the body becomes so common that the body is unable to function in their absence. Furthermore, addiction causes actual physical—and potentially lingering—changes in the nervous system. In such cases, drug intake no longer may provide a "high," but may be necessary simply to maintain the perception of everyday normalcy (Cami & Farré, 2003; Munzar, Cami, & Farré, 2003).

In addition to physical addiction, drugs also can produce psychological addiction. In such cases, people grow to depend on drugs to cope with the everyday stress of life. If drugs are used as an escape, they may prevent adolescents from confronting—and potentially solving—the problems that led them to drug use in the first place. Finally, drugs may be dangerous because even casual users of less hazardous drugs can escalate to more danger-ous forms of substance abuse (Toch, 1995; Segal & Stewart, 1996). (Also see the *Careers in Lifespan Development* interview.)

Alcohol: Use and Abuse

More than 75% of college students have something in common: They've consumed at least one alcoholic drink during the last 30 days. More than 40% say they've had 5 or more drinks within the past 2 weeks, and some 16% drink 16 or more drinks per week. High school students, too, are drinkers: Some 76% of high school seniors report having had an alcoholic drink in the last year, and in some subgroups—such as male athletes—the proportion of drinkers is even higher (NIAAA, 1990; Carmody, 1990; Center on Addiction and Substance Abuse, 1994; Carr, Kennedy, & Dimick, 1996).

Binge drinking is a particular problem on college campuses. Binge drinking is defined for men as drinking five or more drinks in one sitting; for women, who tend to weigh less and whose bodies absorb alcohol less efficiently, binge drinking is defined as four drinks in one sitting. Surveys find that almost half of male college students and over 40% of female college students say they participated in binge drinking during the previous 2 weeks (see Figure 11-10).

Binge drinking affects even those who don't drink or drink very little. Two-thirds of lighter drinkers reported that they had been disturbed by drunken students while sleep-ing or studying. Around a third had been insulted or humiliated by a drunken student, and 25% of women said they had been the target of an unwanted sexual advance by a drunk classmate (Wechsler et al., 2000, 2002, 2003).

Why do adolescents start to drink? There are many reasons. For some—especially male athletes, whose rate of drinking tends to be higher than that of the general adolescent population—drinking is seen as a way of proving they can drink as much as anybody. Others drink for the same reason that some use drugs: It releases inhibitions and tension and reduces stress. Many begin because the conspicuous examples of drunkeness strewn around campus cause them to assume that everyone is drinking heavily, something known as the *false consensus effect* (Pavis, Cunningham-Burley, & Amos, 1997; Nelson & Wechsler, 2003; Weitzman, Nelson, & Wechsler, 2003).

For some adolescents, alcohol use becomes a habit that cannot be controlled. **Alcoholics,** those with alcohol problems, learn to depend on alcohol and are unable to control their drinking. They also become increasingly able to tolerate alcohol, and therefore need to drink ever-larger amounts of liquor in order to bring about the positive effects they crave. Some drink throughout the day, while others go on binges in which they consume huge quantities of alcohol (NIAAA, 1990; Morse & Flavin, 1992).

The reasons that some adolescents–or anyone—become alcoholics are not fully under-stood. Genetics plays a role: Alcoholism runs in families. For those adolescents with a family history of alcohol use, alcoholism may be triggered by efforts to deal with the stress that

Alcoholism is a serious problem for some adolescents.

alcoholics persons with alcohol problems who have learned to depend on alcohol and are unable to control their drinking.

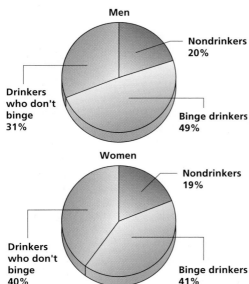

FIGURE 11-10 **BINGE DRINKING AMONG COLLEGE STUDENTS**

For men, binge drinking was defined as con-suming five or more drinks in one sitting; for women, the total was four or more. Why is binge drinking popular?

(*Source:* Wechsler et al., 2003.)

having an alcoholic parent or family member can cause. On the other hand, not all alcoholics have family members with alcohol problems (Bushman, 1993; Boyd, Howard, & Zucker, 1995; Berenson, 2005).

Of course, the origins of an adolescent's problems with alcohol or drugs are less important than getting help. Parents, teachers, and friends can provide the help a teen needs to address the problem—if they realize there is a problem. How can concerned friends and family members tell if an adolescent they know is having difficulties with alcohol or drugs? Some of the telltale signs are described next.

Becoming an Informed Consumer of Development

Hooked on Drugs or Alcohol?

Although it is not always easy to determine if an adolescent has a drug or alcohol abuse problem, there are some signals. Among them:

Identification with the drug culture
- Drug-related magazines or slogans on clothing
- Conversation and jokes that are preoccupied with drugs
- Hostility discussing drugs
- Collection of beer cans

Signs of physical deterioration
- Memory lapses, short attention span, difficulty concentrating
- Poor physical coordination; slurred or incoherent speech
- Unhealthy appearance; indifference to hygiene and grooming
- Bloodshot eyes, dilated pupils

Dramatic changes in school performance
- Marked downturn in grades—not just from C's to F's, but from A's to B's and C's; assignments not completed
- Increased absenteeism or tardiness

Changes in behavior
- Chronic dishonesty (lying, stealing, cheating); trouble with the police
- Changes in friends; evasiveness in talking about new ones
- Possession of large amounts of money
- Increasing and inappropriate anger, hostility, irritability, secretiveness
- Reduced motivation, energy, self-discipline, self-esteem
- Diminished interest in extracurricular activities and hobbies (adapted from Franck & Brownstone, 1991, pp. 593–594)

If an adolescent—or anyone else, for that matter—fits any of these descriptors, help is probably needed. A good place to start is a national hotline run by the National Institute on Drug Abuse at (800) 662-4357 or its website at www.nida.nih.gov. In addition, those who need advice can find a local listing for Alcoholics Anonymous in the telephone book.

Tobacco: The Dangers of Smoking

Most adolescents are well aware of the dangers of smoking, but many still indulge in it. Recent figures show that, overall, a smaller proportion of adolescents smoke than in prior decades, but the numbers remain substantial; and within certain groups the numbers are increasing. Smoking is on the rise among girls, and in several countries, including Austria, Norway, and Sweden, the proportion of girls who smoke is higher than the proportion of boys. There are racial differences, as well: White children and children in lower-socioeconomic-status households are more likely to experiment with cigarettes and to start smoking earlier than African American children and children living in higher-socioeconomic-status households. Also, significantly more white males of high school age smoke than do African American males in high school, although the differences have narrowed in recent years (Harrell et al., 1998; Stolberg, 1998; Baker, Brandon, & Chassin, 2004; Fergusson et al., 2007).

Smoking is becoming a habit that is harder and harder to maintain. There are growing social sanctions against it. It's becoming more difficult to find a comfortable place to smoke: More places, including schools and places of business, have become "smoke-free." Even so, a good number of adolescents still smoke, despite knowing the dangers of smoking and of secondhand smoke.

Developmental Diversity

Selling Death: Pushing Smoking to the Less Advantaged

In Dresden, Germany, three women in miniskirts offer passers-by a pack of Lucky Strikes and a leaflet that reads "You just got hold of a nice piece of America." Says a local doctor, "Adolescents time and again receive cigarettes at such promotions."

A Jeep decorated with the Camel logo pulls up to a high school in Buenos Aires. A woman begins handing out free cigarettes to 15- and 16-year-olds during their lunch recess.

At a video arcade in Taipei, free American cigarettes are strewn atop each game. At a disco filled with high school students, free packs of Salems are on each table. (Ecenbarger, 1993, p. 50)

If you are a cigarette manufacturer and you find that the number of people using your product is declining, what do you do? U.S. companies have sought to carve out new markets by turning to the least advantaged groups of people, both at home and abroad. For instance, in the early 1990s the R.J. Reynolds tobacco company designed a new brand of cigarettes it named "Uptown." The advertising used to herald its arrival made clear who the target was: African Americans living in urban areas (Quinn, 1990). Because of subsequent protests, the tobacco company withdrew "Uptown" from the market.

In addition to seeking new converts in the United States, tobacco companies aggressively recruit adolescent smokers abroad. In many developing countries the number of smokers is still low. Tobacco companies are seeking to increase this number through marketing strategies designed to hook adolescents on the habit by means of free samples. In addition, in countries where American culture and products are held in high esteem, advertising suggests that the use of cigarettes is an American—and consequently prestigious—habit (Sesser, 1993).

The strategy is effective. For instance, in some Latin American cities as many as 50% of teenagers smoke. According to the World Health Organization, smoking will prematurely kill some 200 million of the world's children and adolescents, and overall, 10% of the world's population will die because of smoking (Ecenbarger, 1993).

Krista Blake contracted AIDS at the age of 16. She later died from the disease.

Why do adolescents begin to smoke and maintain the habit? For one thing, adolescents are influenced by advertisements for cigarettes in the media, even if the ads aren't targeting their age group. In addition, the number of images of attractive, popular actors smoking in films viewed by adolescents is increasing. As a result, among at least some adolescents, smoking is viewed as a "cool" activity (Aloise-Young, Slater, & Cruickshank, 2006; Weiss et al., 2006; Golmier, Chebat, & Gelinas-Chebat, 2007; Sargent, Tanski, & Gibson, 2007).

Cigarettes are also very addicting. Nicotine, the active chemical ingredient of cigarettes, can produce biological and psychological dependency very quickly. Although one or two cigarettes generally do not usually produce a lifetime smoker, it takes only a little more to start the habit. In fact, people who smoke as few as 10 cigarettes early in their lives stand an 80% chance of becoming habitual smokers (Bowen et al., 1991; Stacy et al., 1992; Haberstick et al., 2007).

Smoking produces a pleasant emotional state that smokers seek to maintain. Seeing parents and peers smoking increases the chances that an adolescent will take up the habit. Finally, smoking is sometimes seen as an adolescent rite of passage, a sign of growing up (Botvin, et al., 1994; Webster, Hunter, & Keats, 1994; Kodl & Mermelstein, 2004).

Sexually Transmitted Infections

Krista Blake was 18 and looking forward to her first year at Youngstown State University in Ohio. She and her boyfriend were talking about getting married. Her life was, she says, "basic, white-bread America." Then she went to the doctor, complaining about a backache, and found out she had the AIDS virus.

Blake had been infected with HIV, the virus that causes AIDS, two years earlier by an older boy, a hemophiliac. "He knew that he was infected, and he didn't tell me," she says. "And he didn't do anything to keep me from getting infected, either." (Becahy, 1992, p. 49)

AIDS.   Krista Blake, who later died from the disorder, was not alone: *Acquired immunodeficiency syndrome*, or *AIDS*, is one of the leading causes of death among young people. AIDS has no cure and ultimately brings death to those who are infected with the HIV virus that produces the disease.

Because AIDS is spread primarily through sexual contact, it is classified as a **sexually transmitted infection (STI)**. Although it began as a problem that primarily affected homosexuals, it has spread to other populations, including heterosexuals and intravenous drug users. Minorities have been particularly hard hit. For example, African Americans account for 49% of new diagnoses of the AIDS virus, and 19% of those with the disease are Hispanic American.

sexually transmitted infection (STI) an infection that is spread through sexual contact.

FIGURE 11-11 AIDS AROUND THE WORLD

The number of people carrying the AIDS virus varies substantially by geographic region. By far the most cases are found in Africa and the Middle East, although the disease is a growing problem in Asia.

(*Source:* UNAIDS & World Health Organization, 2006.)

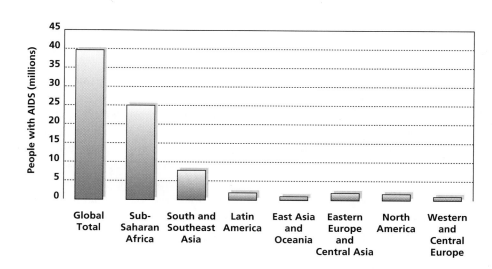

Already, 20 million people have died due to AIDS, and the number of people living with the disease numbers almost 40 million worldwide (see Figure 11-11; Centers for Disease Control, 2006; UNAIDS & World Health Organization, 2006).

Other Sexually Transmitted Infections. Although AIDS is the deadliest of sexually transmitted infections, there are a number of other STIs that are far more common (see Figure 11-12). In fact, one out of four adolescents contracts an STI before graduating from high school. Overall, around 2.5 million teenagers contract an STI, such as the ones listed here, each year (Leary, 1996; Weinstock, Berman, & Cates, 2004):

The most common STI is *human papilloma virus (HPV)*. HPV can be transmitted through genital contact without intercourse. Most infections do not have symptoms, but HPV can produce genital warts and in some cases lead to cervical cancer. A vaccine that protects against some kinds of HPV is now available. The U.S. Centers for Disease Control and Prevention recommends it be routinely administered to girls 11 to 12 years of age—a recommendation that has provoked considerable political reaction (Friedman et al., 2006; Kahn, 2007).

Another common STI is *trichomoniasis*, an infection in the vagina or penis that is caused by a parasite. Initially without symptoms, it can eventually cause a painful discharge. *Chlamydia*, a bacterial infection, initially has few symptoms, but later it causes burning urination and a discharge from the penis or vagina. It can lead to pelvic inflammation and even to sterility. Chlamydial infections can be treated successfully with antibiotics (Nockels & Oakshott, 1999; Fayers et al., 2003).

Genital herpes is a virus not unlike the cold sores that sometimes appear around the mouth. The first symptoms of herpes are often small blisters or sores around the genitals, which may break open and become quite painful. Although the sores may heal after a few weeks, the infection often recurs after an interval, and the cycle repeats itself. When the sores reappear, the infection, for which there is no cure, is contagious.

Gonorrhea and *syphilis* are the STIs that have been recognized for the longest time; cases were recorded by ancient historians. Until the advent of antibiotics, both infections were deadly. However, today both can be treated quite effectively.

Contracting an STI is not only an immediate problem during adolescence, but could become a problem later in life, too. Some infections increase the chances of future infertility and cancer.

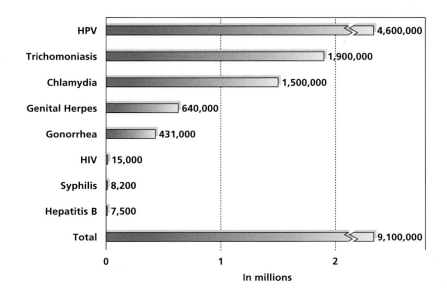

FIGURE 11-12 SEXUALLY TRANSMITTED INFECTIONS (STIs) AMONG ADOLESCENTS

Why are adolescents in particular in danger of contracting an STI?

(*Sources:* Alan Guttmacher Institute, 1993a; Weinstock, Berman & Cates, 2004.)

Table 11-1	Safer Sex Practices

The only foolproof method of avoiding a sexually transmitted infection (STI) is abstinence. However, by following the "safer sex" practices listed here, one can significantly reduce the risk of contracting an STI:

- *Know your sexual partner—well.* Before having sex with someone, learn about his or her sexual history.

- *Use condoms.* For those in sexual relationships, condoms are the most reliable means of preventing transmission of STIs.

- *Avoid the exchange of bodily fluids, particularly semen.* In particular, avoid anal intercourse. The AIDS virus in particular can spread through small tears in the rectum, making anal intercourse without condoms particularly dangerous. Oral sex, once thought relatively safe, is now viewed as potentially dangerous for contracting the AIDS virus.

- *Stay sober.* Using alcohol and drugs impairs judgment and can lead to poor decisions—and it makes using a condom correctly more difficult.

- *Consider the benefits of monogamy.* People in long-term, monogamous relationships with partners who have been faithful are at a lower risk of contracting STIs.

Avoiding STIs.   Short of abstinence, there is no certain way to avoid STIs. However, there are things that can be done to make sex safer; these are listed in Table 11-1.

Still, even when adolescents have been exposed to substantial sex education, the use of safer sex practices is far from universal. As we discussed earlier the chapter, teens are prone to feel invulnerable and are therefore more likely to engage in risky behavior, believing their chances of contracting STIs are minimal. This is particularly true when adolescents perceive that their partner is "safe"—someone they know well and with whom they are involved in a relatively long-term relationship (Freiberg, 1998; Lefkowitz, Sigman, & Kit-fong Au, 2000; Tinsley, Lees, & Sumartojo, 2004).

Unfortunately, unless an individual knows the complete sexual history and STI status of a partner, unprotected sex remains a risky business. And learning a partner's complete sexual history is difficult. Not only is it embarrassing to ask, partners may not be accurate reporters, whether from ignorance of their own exposure, embarrassment, a sense of privacy, or simply forgetfulness. As a result, STIs remain a significant problem among adolescents.

Review and Apply

Review

- Illegal drug use is prevalent among adolescents as a way to find pleasure, avoid pressure, or gain the approval of peers.

- The use of alcohol is also popular among adolescents, often to appear adult or to lessen inhibitions.

- Despite the well-known dangers of smoking, adolescents often smoke to enhance their images or emulate adults.

- AIDS is the most serious of the sexually transmitted infections, ultimately causing death. Safe-sex practices or sexual abstinence can prevent AIDS, although adolescents often ignore these strategies.

- Other sexually transmitted infections affect adolescents, such as chlamydia, genital herpes, trichomoniasis, gonorrhea, and syphilis.

Applying Lifespan Development

- How do adolescents' concerns about self-image and their perception that they are the center of attention contribute to smoking and alcohol use?

- *From a healthcare provider's perspective:* Why do adolescents' increased cognitive abilities, including the ability to reason and to think experimentally, fail to deter them from irrational behavior such as drug and alcohol abuse, tobacco use, and unsafe sex practices? How might you use these abilities to design a program to help prevent these problems?

Epilogue

To call adolescence a period of great change in people's lives is an understatement. This chapter looked at the significant physical, psychological, and cognitive changes that adolescents undergo and at some of the consequences of entering and living through adolescence.

Before turning to the next chapter, return for the moment to the opening prologue of this one, about Wendy Vacarro. In light of what you now know about adolescence, consider the following questions about Wendy:

1. Wendy's days are filled with activities of one sort or another, and that probably leads to a high level of stress. What might be the short- and long-term consequences of such stress?

2. How might Wendy reduce the stress in her life?

3. Do you believe that Wendy's participation in field hockey makes her more or less susceptible to the health-related risks that characterize adolescence? Why or why not?

4. What arguments would you use that could convince Wendy to avoid the typical health-related risks of adolescence?

Looking Back

■ **What physical changes do adolescents experience?**

- The adolescent years are marked by a physical growth spurt, which for girls begins around age 10, and for boys, around age 12.

- Puberty begins in girls at around age 11 and in boys at around age 13. The physical changes of puberty often have psychological effects, such as an increase in self-esteem and self-awareness, as well as confusion and uncertainty about sexuality.

■ **What are the consequences of early and late maturation?**

- Early maturation has different effects on boys and girls. For boys, being bigger and more developed can lead to increased athleticism, greater popularity, and a more positive self-concept. For girls, early maturation can lead to increased popularity with older boys and an enhanced social life, but also embarrassment over their bodies, which suddenly look quite different from everyone else's.

- For the short-term, late maturation can be a physical and social disadvantage that affects boys' self-concept. Girls who mature late may suffer neglect by their peers, but ultimately they appear to suffer no lasting ill effects and may even benefit.

■ **What nutritional needs and concerns do adolescents have?**

- While most adolescents have no greater nutritional worries other than fueling their growth with appropriate foods, some are obese or overweight. Excessive concern about obesity can cause some adolescents, especially girls, to develop an eating disorder such as anorexia nervosa or bulimia.

■ **In what ways does cognitive development proceed during adolescence?**

- Cognitive growth during adolescence is rapid, with gains in abstract thinking, reasoning, and the ability to view possibilities in relative rather than absolute terms.

- Adolescence coincides with Piaget's formal operations period of development, when people begin to engage in abstract thought and scientific reasoning.

- According to information processing approaches, cognitive growth during adolescence is gradual and quantitative, involving improvements in memory capacity, mental strategies, metacognition, and other aspects of cognitive functioning.

- Adolescents also grow in the area of metacognition, which permits them to monitor their thought processes and accurately assess their cognitive capabilities.

- Adolescents' developing cognitive abilities may also promote a form of adolescent egocentrism, a self-absorption related to their developing sense of themselves as independent identities. This can make it hard for adolescents to accept criticism and tolerate authority figures. Adolescents may play to an imaginary audience of critical observers, and they may develop personal fables.

■ **What factors affect adolescent school performance?**

- School performance tends to decline during the adolescent years. School achievement is linked with socioeconomic status, race, and ethnicity. While many academic achievement differences are due to socioeconomic factors, attributional patterns regarding success factors and belief systems regarding the link between school success and success in life also play a part.

■ **What dangerous substances do adolescents use, and why?**

● The use of illicit drugs, alcohol, and tobacco is very prevalent among adolescents, who are motivated by pleasure seeking, pressure avoidance, the desire to flout authority, or the imitation of role models.

■ **What dangers do adolescent sexual practices present, and how can these dangers be avoided?**

● AIDS is one of the leading causes of death among young people, affecting minority populations with particular severity. Adolescent behavior patterns and attitudes, such as shyness, self-absorption, and a belief in personal invulnerability, work against the use of safe-sex practices that can prevent the disease.

● Other sexually transmitted infections, including chlamydia, genital herpes, trichomoniasis, gonorrhea, and syphilis, occur frequently among the adolescent population and can also be prevented by safe-sex practices or abstinence.

Key Terms and Concepts

adolescence (p. 372)
puberty (p. 373)
menarche (p. 374)
secular trend (p. 375)
primary sex characteristics (p. 375)
secondary sex characteristics (p. 375)

anorexia nervosa (p. 379)
bulimia (p. 379)
formal operational stage (p. 384)
information processing perspective (p. 387)
metacognition (p. 387)

adolescent egocentrism (p. 388)
imaginary audience (p. 388)
personal fables (p. 389)
addictive drugs (p. 395)
alcoholics (p. 397)
sexually transmitted infection (STI) (p. 400)

12 Social and Personality Development in Adolescence

Chapter Overview

IDENTITY: ASKING "WHO AM I?"

Self-Concept: What Am I Like?

Self-Esteem: How Do I Like Myself?

Identity Formation: Change or Crisis?

Marcia's Approach to Identity Development: Updating Erikson

Identity, Race, and Ethnicity

Depression and Suicide: Psychological Difficulties in Adolescence

RELATIONSHIPS: FAMILY AND FRIENDS

Family Ties: Changing Relations with Relations

Relationships with Peers: The Importance of Belonging

Popularity and Rejection

Conformity: Peer Pressure in Adolescence

Juvenile Delinquency: The Crimes of Adolescence

DATING, SEXUAL BEHAVIOR, AND TEENAGE PREGNANCY

Dating: Close Relationships in the 21st Century

Sexual Relationships

Sexual Orientation: Heterosexuality, Homosexuality, and Bisexuality

Teenage Pregnancies

Prologue: Adolescent Trio

Carly, a freshman at Benjamin Franklin High School, a school for gifted kids, says she has no interest in politics or social issues. "It's probably because of my mom—she's racked my brain with statistics and feminism and the environment," she says. "I'm like, 'Well, what do you want me to do?' . . . So what *is* she passionate about? "My friends."

***

Trevor is the third of four sons of Richard Kelson, 56, a retired truck driver, and his wife, JoAnn, 46, a medical tape transcriber. The family lives in a four-bedroom home across from Hunter Junior High School, where Trevor is in ninth grade. He spent the summer volunteering in a leadership-training program at the Sugar House Boys & Girls Club in Salt Lake City. "I guess it gives you a good feeling to help somebody else," he says.

***

At 16, Purva Chawla holds good rankings in school and loves competing in drama and elocution contests. The New Delhi student is "head girl" of her school and plays for a table-tennis team. Recently, she won a public-speaking contest. . . . Even with all her extracurricular activities, she still makes it home for dinner with her parents and goes out to the movies with them twice a week. "I talk with them very freely about what's happening with my friends, boyfriends,

Although the social lives of adolescents take varied forms, certain rituals are common.

whatever," she says. (Fields-Meyer, 1995, pp. 52, 53; Kantrowitz & Springen, 2005, p. 50)

Although Carly, Trevor, and Purva lead very different lives, they are remarkably similar in their focus on friends, family, and school. And they also are far more typical of adolescent life than the stereotype of wild and confused teenagers might have one believe.

Despite the reputation of adolescence as a time of confusion and rebellion, most teenagers pass through the period without much turmoil. Although they may "try on" different roles and flirt with activities that their parents find objectionable, the majority of adolescents find adolescence an exciting time during which friendships grow, intimate relationships develop, and their sense of themselves deepens.

This is not to say that the transitions adolescents pass through are unchallenging. As we shall see in this chapter, where we discuss personality and social development, adolescence brings about major changes in the ways in which individuals must deal with the world.

We begin by considering how adolescents form their views of themselves. We look at self-concept, self-esteem, and identity development. We also examine two major psychological difficulties: depression and suicide.

Next, we discuss relationships during adolescence. We consider how adolescents reposition themselves within the family and how the influence of family members declines in some spheres as peers take on new importance. We also examine the ways in which adolescents interact with their friends, and the ways in which popularity is determined.

Finally, the chapter considers dating and sexual behavior. We look at the role of dating and close relationships in adolescents' lives, and we consider sexual behavior and the standards that govern adolescents' sex lives. We conclude by looking at teenage pregnancy and at programs that seek to prevent unwanted pregnancy.

After reading this chapter, you will be able to answer these questions:

■ **How does the development of self-concept, self-esteem, and identity proceed during adolescence?**

■ **What dangers do adolescents face as they deal with the stresses of adolescence?**

■ **How does the quality of relationships with family and peers change during adolescence?**

■ **What are gender, race, and ethnic relations like in adolescence?**

■ **What does it mean to be popular and unpopular in adolescence, and how do adolescents respond to peer pressure?**

■ **What are the functions and characteristics of dating during adolescence?**

■ **How does sexuality develop in the adolescent years?**

Looking Ahead

Identity: Asking "Who Am I?"

"Thirteen is a hard age, very hard. A lot of people say you have it easy, you're a kid, but there's a lot of pressure being 13—to be respected by people in your school, to be liked, always feeling like you have to be good. There's pressure to do drugs, too, so you try not to succumb to that. But you don't want to be made fun of, so you have to look cool. You gotta wear the right shoes, the right clothes."—Carlos Quintana (1998, p. 66)

The thoughts of 13-year-old Carlos Quintana demonstrate a clear awareness—and self-consciousness—regarding his newly forming place in society and life. During adolescence, questions like "Who am I?" and "Where do I belong in the world?" begin to take a front seat.

Why should issues of identity become so important during adolescence? One reason is that adolescents' intellectual capacities become more adultlike. They are able to see how they stack up to others and become aware that they are individuals, apart not just from their parents, but from all others. The dramatic physical changes during puberty make adolescents acutely aware of their own bodies and aware that others are reacting to them in ways to which they are unaccustomed. Whatever the cause, adolescence often brings substantial changes in teenagers' self-concepts and self-esteem—in sum, their notions of their own identity.

Self-Concept: What Am I Like?

Ask Valerie to describe herself, and she says, "Others look at me as laid-back, relaxed, and not worrying too much. But really, I'm often nervous and emotional."

The fact that Valerie distinguishes others' views of her from her own perceptions represents a developmental advance of adolescence. In childhood, Valerie would have characterized herself according to a list of traits that would not differentiate her view of herself and others' perspectives. However, adolescents are able to make the distinction, and when they try to describe who they are, they take both their own and others' views into account (Harter, 1990a; Cole et al., 2001; Updegraff et al., 2004).

Adolescents' sense of who they are takes their own and others' views into account.

This broader view of themselves is one aspect of adolescents' increasing understanding of who they are. They can see various aspects of the self simultaneously, and this view of the self becomes more organized and coherent. They look at the self from a psychological perspective, viewing traits not as concrete entities but as abstractions (Adams, Montemayor, & Gullotta, 1996). For example, teenagers are more likely than younger children to describe themselves in terms of their ideology (saying something like "I'm an environmentalist") than in terms of physical characteristics (such as "I'm the fastest runner in my class").

In some ways, however, this broader, more multifaceted self-concept is a mixed blessing, especially during the earlier years of adolescence. At that time, adolescents may be troubled by the multiple aspects of their personalities. During the beginning of adolescence, for instance, teenagers may want to view themselves in a certain way ("I'm a sociable person and love to be with people"), and they may become concerned when their behavior is inconsistent with that view ("Even though I want to be sociable, sometimes I can't stand being around my friends and just want to be alone"). By the end of adolescence, however, teenagers find it easier to accept that different situations elicit different behaviors and feelings (Harter, 1990b; Pyryt & Mendaglio, 1994; Trzesniewski, Donnellan, & Robins, 2003; Hitlin, Brown, & Elder, 2006).

Self-Esteem: How Do I Like Myself?

Knowing who you are and *liking* who you are are two different things. Although adolescents become increasingly accurate in understanding who they are (their self-concept), this knowledge does not guarantee that they like themselves (their self-esteem) any better. In fact, their increasing accuracy in understanding themselves permits them to see themselves fully—warts and all. It's what they do with these perceptions that leads them to develop a sense of their self-esteem.

The same cognitive sophistication that allows adolescents to differentiate various aspects of the self also leads them to evaluate those aspects in different ways (Chan, 1997; J. Cohen, 1999). For instance, an adolescent may have high self-esteem in terms of academic performance, but lower self-esteem in terms of relationships with others. Or it may be just the opposite, as articulated by this adolescent:

> How much do I *like* the kind of person I am? Well, I like some things about me, but I don't like others. I'm glad that I'm popular since it's really important to me to have friends. But in school I don't do as well as the really smart kids. That's OK, because if you're too smart you'll lose your friends. So being smart is just not that important. Except to my parents. I feel like I'm letting them down when I don't do as well as they want. (Harter, 1990b, p. 364)

Gender Differences in Self-Esteem.   What determines an adolescent's self-esteem? Several factors make a difference. One is gender: Particularly during early adolescence, girls' self-esteem tends to be lower and more vulnerable than boys' (Watkins, Dong, & Xia, 1997; Byrne, 2000b; Miyamoto et al., 2000; Ah-Kion, 2006).

One reason is that, compared to boys, girls tend to be more concerned about physical appearance and social success—in addition to academic achievement. Although boys are also concerned about these things, their attitudes are often more casual. In addition, societal messages suggesting that female academic achievement is a roadblock to social success can put girls in a difficult bind: If they do well academically, they jeopardize their social success. No wonder that the self-esteem of adolescent girls is more fragile than that of boys (Unger, 2001; Ricciardelli & McCabe, 2003).

Although generally self-esteem is higher in adolescent boys than girls, boys do have vulnerabilities of their own. For example, society's stereotypical gender expectations may lead boys to feel that they should be confident, tough, and fearless all the time. Boys facing difficulties, such as not making a sports team or rejection from a girl they wanted to date, are likely to feel not only miserable about the defeat they face, but also incompetent, since they don't measure up to the stereotype (Pollack, 1999; Pollack, Shuster, & Trelease, 2001).

Socioeconomic Status and Race Differences in Self-Esteem.   Socioeconomic status (SES) and race also influence self-esteem. Adolescents of higher SES generally have higher self-esteem than those of lower SES, particularly during middle and later adolescence. It may be that the social status factors that especially enhance one's standing and self-esteem—such as having

more expensive clothes or a car—become more conspicuous in the later periods of adolescence (Savin-Williams & Demo, 1983; Van Tassel-Baska, Olszewski, Kubilius, & Kulieke, 1994).

Race and ethnicity also play a role in self-esteem, but their impact has lessened as prejudicial treatment of minorities has eased. Early studies argued that minority status would lead to lower self-esteem, and this was initially supported by research. African Americans and Hispanics, researchers explained, had lower self-esteem than Caucasians because prejudicial attitudes in society made them feel disliked and rejected, and this feeling was incorporated into their self-concepts. More recent research paints a different picture. Most findings suggest that African American adolescents differ little from whites in their levels of self-esteem (Harter, 1990b). Why should this be? One explanation is that social movements within the African American community that bolster racial pride help support African American adolescents. In fact, research finds that a stronger sense of racial identity is related to a higher level of self-esteem in African Americans and Hispanics (Phinney, Lochner, & Murphy, 1990; Gray-Little & Hafdahl, 2000; Verkuyten, 2003).

Another reason for overall similarity in self-esteem levels between adolescents of different racial groups is that teenagers in general focus their preferences and priorities on those aspects of their lives at which they excel. Consequently, African American youths may concentrate on the things that they find most satisfying and gain self-esteem from being successful at them (Gray-Little & Hafdahl, 2000; Yang & Blodgett, 2000; Phinney, 2005).

Finally, self-esteem may be influenced not by race alone, but by a complex combination of factors. For instance, some developmentalists have considered race and gender simultaneously, coining the term *ethgender* to refer to the joint influence of race and gender. One study that simultaneously took both race and gender into account found that African American and Hispanic males had the highest levels of self-esteem, while Asian and Native American females had the lowest levels (Dukes & Martinez, 1994; King, 2003; Romero & Roberts, 2003; Saunders, Davis, & Williams, 2004; Biro et al., 2006).

A strong sense of racial identity during adolescence is tied to higher levels of self-esteem.

Identity Formation: Change or Crisis?

According to Erik Erikson, whose theory we last discussed in Chapter 10, the search for identity inevitably leads some adolescents into substantial psychological turmoil as they encounter the adolescent identity crisis (Erikson, 1963). Erikson's theory regarding this stage, which is summarized with his other stages in Table 12-1, suggests that teenagers try to figure out what is unique and distinctive about themselves—something they are able to do with increasing sophistication because of the cognitive gains that occur during adolescence.

Erikson argues that adolescents strive to discover their particular strengths and weaknesses and the roles they can best play in their future lives. This discovery process often involves "trying on" different roles or choices to see if they fit an adolescent's capabilities and views about himself or herself. Through this process, adolescents seek to understand who they are by narrowing and making choices about their personal, occupational, sexual, and political commitments. Erikson call this the **identity-versus-identity-confusion stage.**

In Erikson's view, adolescents who stumble in their efforts to find a suitable identity may go off course in several ways. They may adopt socially unacceptable roles as a way of expressing what they do *not* want to be, or they may have difficulty forming and maintaining long-lasting close personal relationships. In general, their sense of self becomes "diffuse," failing to organize around a central, unified core identity.

On the other hand, those who are successful in forging an appropriate identity set a course that provides a foundation for future psychosocial development. They learn their unique capabilities and believe in them, and they develop an accurate sense of who they are. They are prepared to set out on a path that takes full advantage of what their unique strengths permit them to do (Blustein, & Palladino, 1991; Archer & Waterman, 1994; Allison & Schultz, 2001).

During the identity-versus-identity-confusion stage, teenagers seek to understand who they are by narrowing and making choices about their personal, occupational, sexual, and political commitments. Can this stage be applied to teenagers in other cultures? Why or why not?

identity-versus-identity-confusion stage the period during which teenagers seek to determine what is unique and distinctive about themselves.

Table 12-1	A Summary of Erikson's Stages		
Stage	**Approximate Age**	**Positive Outcomes**	**Negative Outcomes**
1. Trust-versus-mistrust	Birth–1.5 years	Feelings of trust from others' support	Fear and concern regarding others
2. Autonomy versus shame and doubt	1.5–3 years	Self-sufficiency if exploration is encouraged	Doubts about self; lack of independence
3. Initiative versus guilt	3–6 years	Discovery of ways to initiate actions	Guilt from actions and thoughts
4. Industry versus inferiority	6–12 years	Development of sense of competence	Feelings of inferiority; little sense of mastery
5. Identity versus identity confusion	Adolescence	Awareness of uniqueness of self; knowledge of roles	Inability to identify appropriate roles in life
6. Intimacy versus isolation	Early adulthood	Development of loving, sexual relationships and close friendships	Fear of relationships with others
7. Generativity versus stagnation	Middle adulthood	Sense of contribution to continuity of life	Trivialization of one's activities
8. Ego-integrity versus despair	Late adulthood	Sense of unity in life's accomplishments	Regret over lost opportunities of life

(*Source:* Erikson, 1963.)

Societal Pressures and Reliance on Friends and Peers.   As if teenagers' self-generated identity issues were not difficult enough, societal pressures are also high during the identity-versus-identity-confusion stage, as any student knows who has been repeatedly asked by parents and friends "What's your major?" and "What are you going to do when you graduate?" Adolescents feel pressure to decide whether their post-high-school plans include work or college and, if they choose work, which occupational track to follow. Up to this point in their development, their educational lives have been pretty much programmed by U.S. society, which lays out a universal educational track. However, the track ends at high school, and consequently, adolescents face difficult choices about which of several possible future paths they will follow (Kidwell et al., 1995).

During this period, adolescents increasingly rely on their friends and peers as sources of information. At the same time, their dependence on adults declines. As we discuss later in the chapter, this increasing dependence on the peer group enables adolescents to forge close relationships. Comparing themselves to others helps them clarify their own identities.

This reliance on peers to help adolescents define their identities and learn to form relationships is the link between this stage of psychosocial development and the next stage Erikson proposed, known as intimacy versus isolation. It also relates to the subject of gender differences in identity formation. When Erikson developed his theory, he suggested that males and females move through the identity-versus-identity-confusion period differently. He argued that males are more likely to proceed through the social development stages in the order they are shown in Table 12-1, developing a stable identity before committing to an intimate relationship with another person. In contrast, he suggested that females reverse the order, seeking intimate relationships and then defining their identities through these relationships. These ideas largely reflect the social conditions at the time he was writing, when women were less likely to go to college or establish their own careers and instead often married early. Today, however, the experiences of boys and girls seem relatively similar during the identity-versus-confusion period.

Psychological Moratorium.   Because of the pressures of the identity-versus-identity-confusion period, Erikson suggested that many adolescents pursue a "psychological moratorium."

The *psychological moratorium* is a period during which adolescents take time off from the upcoming responsibilities of adulthood and explore various roles and possibilities. For example, many college students take a semester or year off to travel, work, or find some other way to examine their priorities.

On the other hand, many adolescents cannot, for practical reasons, pursue a psychological moratorium involving a relatively leisurely exploration of various identities. Some adolescents, for economic reasons, must work part time after school and then take jobs immediately after graduation from high school. As a result, they have little time to experiment with identities and engage in a psychological moratorium. Does this mean such adolescents will be psychologically damaged in some way? Probably not. In fact, the satisfaction that can come from successfully holding a part-time job while attending school may be a sufficient psychological reward to outweigh the inability to try out various roles.

mydevelopmentlab

VIDEO CLIP

IDENTITY DEVELOPMENT

Limitations of Erikson's Theory. One criticism that has been raised regarding Erikson's theory is that he uses male identity development as the standard against which to compare female identity. In particular, he saw males as developing intimacy only after they have achieved a stable identity, which is viewed as the normative pattern. To critics, Erikson's view is based on male-oriented concepts of individuality and competitiveness. In an alternative conception, psychologist Carol Gilligan has suggested that women develop identity through the establishment of relationships. In this view, a key component of a woman's identity is the building of caring networks between herself and others (Gilligan, Brown, & Rogers, 1990; Gilligan, 2004; Kroger, 2006).

Marcia's Approach to Identity Development: Updating Erikson

Using Erikson's theory as a springboard, psychologist James Marcia suggests that identity can be seen in terms of which of two characteristics—crisis or commitment—is present or absent. *Crisis* is a period of identity development in which an adolescent consciously chooses between various alternatives and makes decisions. *Commitment* is psychological investment in a course of action or an ideology. We can see the difference between an adolescent who careens from one activity to another, with nothing lasting more than a few weeks, compared with one who becomes totally absorbed in volunteer work at a homeless shelter, for example (Marcia, 1980; Peterson, Marcia, & Carpendale, 2004).

After conducting lengthy interviews with adolescents, Marcia proposed four categories of adolescent identity (see Table 12-2).

Table 12-2 **Marcia's Four Categories of Adolescent Development**

		COMMITMENT	
		Present	Absent
CRISIS/EXPLORATION	PRESENT	**Identity achievement** "I love animals; I'm going to become a vet."	**Moratorium** "I'm going to work at the mall while I figure out what to do next."
	ABSENT	**Identity foreclosure** "I am going into law, just like Mom."	**Identity diffusion** "I don't have a clue."

(*Source:* Marcia, 1980.)

According to Marcia's approach, psychologically-healthy identity development can be seen in adolescents who choose to commit to a course of action or ideology.

1. **Identity achievement.** Teenagers within this identity status have successfully explored and thought through who they are and what they want to do. Following a period of crisis during which they considered various alternatives, these adolescents have committed to a particular identity. Teens who have reached this identity status tend to be the most psychologically healthy, higher in achievement motivation and moral reasoning than adolescents of any other status.

2. **Identity foreclosure.** These are adolescents who have committed to an identity, but who did not do it by passing through a period of crisis in which they explored alternatives. Instead, they accepted others' decisions about what was best for them. Typical adolescents in this category are a son who enters the family business because it is expected of him, and a daughter who decides to become a physician simply because her mother is one. Although foreclosers are not necessarily unhappy, they tend to have what can be called "rigid strength": Happy and self-satisfied, they also have a high need for social approval and tend to be authoritarian.

3. **Moratorium.** Although adolescents in the moratorium category have explored various alternatives to some degree, they have not yet committed themselves. As a consequence, Marcia suggests, they show relatively high anxiety and experience psychological conflict. On the other hand, they are often lively and appealing, seeking intimacy with others. Adolescents of this status typically settle on an identity, but only after something of a struggle.

4. **Identity diffusion.** Adolescents in this category neither explore nor commit to considering various alternatives. They tend to be flighty, shifting from one thing to the next. While they may seem carefree, according to Marcia, their lack of commitment impairs their ability to form close relationships. In fact, they are often socially withdrawn.

It is important to note that adolescents are not necessarily stuck in one of the four categories. In fact, some move back and forth between moratorium and identity achievement in what has been called a "MAMA" cycle (**m**oratorium—identity **a**chievement—**m**oratorium—identity **a**chievement). For instance, even though a forecloser may have settled upon a career path during early adolescence with little active decision making, he or she may reassess the choice later and move into another category. For some individuals, then, identity formation may take place beyond the period of adolescence. However, identity gels in the late teens and early 20s for most people (Kroger, 2000; Meeus, 1996, 2003).

identity achievement the status of adolescents who commit to a particular identity following a period of crisis during which they consider various alternatives.

identity foreclosure the status of adolescents who prematurely commit to an identity without adequately exploring alternatives.

moratorium the status of adolescents who may have explored various identity alternatives to some degree, but have not yet committed themselves.

identity diffusion the status of adolescents in this category neither explore nor commit to consider various alternatives.

Identity, Race, and Ethnicity

Although the path to forming an identity is often difficult for adolescents, it presents a particular challenge for members of racial and ethnic groups that have traditionally been discriminated against. Society's contradictory values are one part of the problem. On the one hand, adolescents are told that society should be color blind, that race and ethnic background should not matter in terms of opportunities and achievement, and that if they do achieve, society will accept them. Based on a traditional *cultural assimilation model,* this view holds that individual cultural identities should be assimilated into a unified culture in the United States—the proverbial melting-pot model.

On the other hand, the *pluralistic society model* suggests that U.S. society is made up of diverse, coequal cultural groups that should preserve their individual cultural features. The pluralistic society model grew in part from the belief that the cultural assimilation model denigrates the cultural heritage of minorities and lowers their self-esteem. According to this view, then, racial and ethnic factors become a central part of adolescents' identity and are not submerged in an attempt to assimilate into the majority culture.

There is a middle ground. Minority group members can form a *bicultural identity* in which they draw from their own cultural identity while integrating themselves into the dominant culture. This view suggests that an individual can live as a member of two cultures, with two cultural identities, without having to choose one over the other (LaFromboise, Coleman, & Gerton, 1993). The choice of a bicultural identity is increasingly common. In fact, the number of individuals who think of themselves as belonging to more than one race is considerable, according to data from the 2000 U.S. Census (see Figure 12-1; Schmitt, 2001).

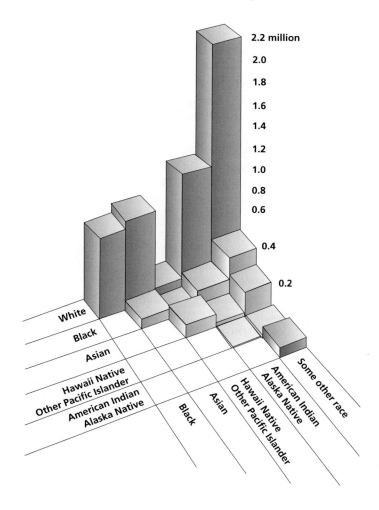

FIGURE 12-1   INCREASE IN BICULTURAL IDENTITY

On the 2000 U.S. Census, almost 7 million people indicated they were multiracial. Bars represent the number of people who chose various combinations of races.

(*Source:* U.S. Census Bureau, 2000.)

The process of identity formation is not simple for anyone and may be doubly difficult for minority group members. Racial and ethnic identity takes time to form, and for some individuals it may occur over a prolonged period. Still, the ultimate result can be the formation of a rich, multifaceted identity (Roberts et al., 1999; Grantham & Ford, 2003; Nadal, 2004; Umana-Taylor & Fine, 2004).

Depression and Suicide: Psychological Difficulties in Adolescence

Brianne Camilleri had it all: Two involved parents, a caring older brother and a comfortable home near Boston. But that didn't stop the overwhelming sense of hopelessness that enveloped her in ninth grade. "It was like a cloud that followed me everywhere," she says. "I couldn't get away from it."

Brianne started drinking and experimenting with drugs. One Sunday she was caught shoplifting at a local store and her mother, Linda, drove her home in what Brianne describes as a "piercing silence." With the clouds in her head so dark she believed she would never see light again, Brianne went straight for the bathroom and swallowed every Tylenol and Advil she cound—a total of 74 pills. She was only 14, and she wanted to die. (Wingert & Kantrowitz, 2002, p. 54)

Although by far the majority of teenagers weather the search for identity—as well as the other challenges presented by the period—without major psychological difficulties, some find adolescence particularly stressful. Some, in fact, develop severe psychological problems. Two of the most serious are adolescent depression and suicide.

Adolescent Depression.   No one is immune to periods of sadness and bad moods, and adolescents are no exception. The end of a relationship, failure at an important task, the death of a loved one—all may produce profound feelings of sadness, loss, and grief. In situations such as these, depression is a fairly typical reaction.

How common are feelings of depression in adolescence? More than a quarter of adolescents report feeling so sad or hopeless for two or more weeks in a row that they stop doing their normal activities. Almost two-thirds of teenagers say they have experienced such feelings at one time or another. On the other hand, only a small minority of adolescents—some 3%—experience *major depression,* a full-blown psychological disorder in which depression is severe and lingers for long periods (Cicchetti & Toth, 1998; Grunbaum et al., 2001; Galambos, Leadbeater, & Barker, 2004).

Gender, ethnic, and racial differences also are found in depression rates. As is the case among adults, adolescent girls, on average, experience depression more often than boys. Some studies have found that African American adolescents have higher rates of depression than white adolescents, although not all research supports this conclusion. Native Americans, too, have higher rates of depression (Stice, Presnell, & Bearman, 2001; Jacques & Mash, 2004; Hightower, 2005; Li, DiGiuseppe, & Froh, 2006).

In cases of severe, long-term depression, biological factors are often involved. Although some adolescents seem to be genetically predisposed to experience depression, environmental and social factors relating to the extraordinary changes in the social lives of adolescents are also important influences. An adolescent who experiences the death of a loved one, for example, or one who grows up with an alcoholic or depressed parent, is at a higher risk of depression. In addition, being unpopular, having few close friends, and experiencing rejection are associated with adolescent depression (Lau & Kwok, 2000; Goldsmith et al., 2002; Eley, Liang, & Plomin, 2004; Zalsman et al., 2006).

Between 25 and 40 percent of girls, and 20 to 35 percent of boys, experience occasional episodes of depression during adolescence, although the incidence of major depression is far lower.

One of the most puzzling questions about depression is why its incidence is higher among girls than boys. There is little evidence it is linked to hormone differences or a particular gene. Instead, some psychologists speculate that stress is more pronounced for girls than for boys in adolescence due to the many, sometimes conflicting demands of the traditional female gender role. Recall, for instance, the situation of the adolescent girl who was quoted in our discussion of self-esteem. She is worried both about doing well in school and about being popular. If she feels that academic success undermines her popularity, she is placed in a difficult bind that can leave her feeling helpless. Added to this is the fact that traditional gender roles still give higher status to men than women (Nolen-Hoeksema, 2003; Gilbert, 2004).

Girls' generally higher levels of depression during adolescence may reflect gender differences in ways of coping with stress, rather than gender differences in mood. Girls may be more apt than boys to react to stress by turning inward, thereby experiencing a sense of helplessness and hopelessness. In contrast, boys more often react by externalizing the stress and acting more impulsively or aggressively, or by turning to drugs and alcohol (Hankin & Abramson, 2001; Winstead & Sanchez, 2005).

Adolescent Suicide.   The rate of adolescent suicide in the United States has tripled in the last 30 years. In fact, one teenage suicide occurs every 90 minutes, for an annual rate of 12.2 suicides per 100,000 adolescents. Moreover, the reported rate may actually understate the true number of suicides; parents and medical personnel are often reluctant to report a death as suicide, preferring to label it an accident. Even with underreporting, suicide is the third most common cause of death in the 15-to-24-year-old age group, after accidents and homicide. It is important to keep in mind, however, that although the rate of suicide for adolescents has risen more than for other age groups, the highest rate of suicide is found in the period of late adulthood (Healy, 2001; Grunbaum et al., 2002; Joe & Marcus, 2003; Conner & Goldston, 2007).

In adolescence, the rate of suicide is higher for boys than girls, although girls *attempt* suicide more frequently. Suicide attempts among males are more likely to result in death because of the methods they use: Boys tend to use more violent means, such as guns, while girls are more apt to choose the more peaceful strategy of drug overdose. Some estimates suggest that there are as many as 200 attempted suicides by both sexes for every successful one (Gelman, 1994; Joseph, Reznik, & Mester, 2003; Dervic et al., 2006).

The reasons behind the increase in adolescent suicide over past decades are unclear. The most obvious explanation is that the stress experienced by teenagers has increased, leading those who are most vulnerable to be more likely to commit suicide (Elkind, 1984). But why should stress have increased only for adolescents? The suicide rate for other segments of the population has remained fairly stable over the same time period. Although we are not yet sure why adolescent suicide has increased, it is clear that certain factors heighten the risk of suicide. One factor is depression. Depressed teenagers who are experiencing a profound sense of hopelessness are at greater risk of committing suicide (although most depressed individuals do not commit suicide). In addition, social inhibition, perfectionism, and a high level of stress and anxiety are related to a greater risk of suicide. The easy availability of guns—which are more prevalent in the United States than in other industrialized nations—also contributes to the suicide rate (Huff, 1999; Goldston, 2003).

In addition to depression, some cases of suicide are associated with family conflicts and relationship or school difficulties. Some stem from a history of abuse and neglect. The rate of suicide among drug and alcohol abusers is also relatively high. As can be seen in Figure 12-2, teens who called in to a hotline because they were thinking of killing themselves mentioned several other factors as well (Lyon et al., 2000; Bergen, Martin, & Richardson, 2003; Wilcox, Conner, & Caine, 2004).

Some suicides appear to be caused by exposure to the suicide of others. In *cluster suicide,* one suicide leads to attempts by others to kill themselves. For instance, some high schools have

The rate of adolescent suicide has tripled in the last 30 years. These girls console one another following the suicide of a classmate.

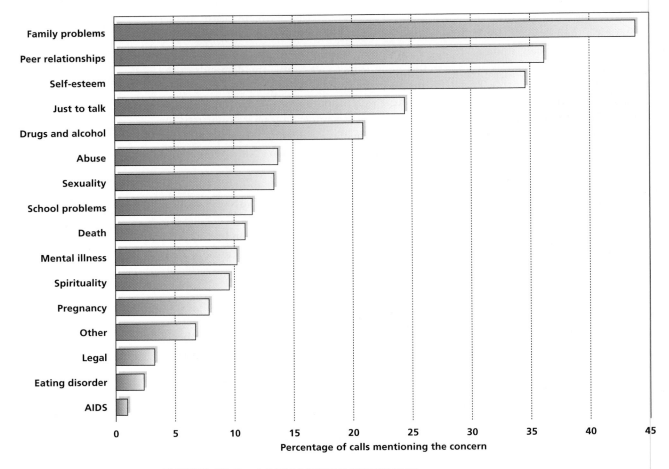

FIGURE 12-2 ADOLESCENT DIFFICULTIES

Family, peer relationships, and self-esteem problems were most often mentioned by adolescents contemplating suicide, according to a review of phone calls to a telephone help line.
(*Source:* Boehm & Campbell, 1995.)

experienced a series of suicides following a well-publicized case. As a result, many schools have established crisis intervention teams to counsel students when one student commits suicide (Haas, Hendin, & Mann, 2003; Arenson, 2004).

There are several warning signs that should sound an alarm regarding the possibility of suicide. Among them:

- Direct or indirect talk about suicide, such as "I wish I were dead" or "You won't have me to worry about any longer"

- School difficulties, such as missed classes or a decline in grades

- Making arrangements as if preparing for a long trip, such as giving away prized possessions or arranging for the care of a pet

- Writing a will

- Loss of appetite or excessive eating

- General depression, including a change in sleeping patterns, slowness and lethargy, and uncommunicativeness

- Dramatic changes in behavior, such as a shy person suddenly acting outgoing

- Preoccupation with death in music, art, or literature.

Talking about suicide, contrary to popular opinion, does not encourage it. In fact, it actually helps to provide support and breaks down the sense of isolation many suicidal people experience.

Becoming an Informed Consumer of Development

Preventing Adolescent Suicide

If you suspect that an adolescent, or anyone else for that matter, is contemplating suicide, don't stand idly by. Act! Here are several suggestions:

- Talk to the person, listen without judging, and give the person an understanding forum in which to try to talk things through.

- Talk specifically about suicidal thoughts, asking such questions as: Does the person have a plan? Has he or she bought a gun? Where is it? Has he or she stockpiled pills? Where are they? The Public Health Service notes that, "contrary to popular belief, such candor will not give a person dangerous ideas or encourage a suicidal act."

- Evaluate the situation, trying to distinguish between general upset and more serious danger, as when suicide plans *have* been made. If the crisis is acute, *do not leave the person alone.*

- Be supportive, let the person know you care, and try to break down his or her feelings of isolation.

- Take charge of finding help, without concern about invading the person's privacy. Do not try to handle the problem alone; get professional help immediately.

- Make the environment safe, removing from the premises (not just hiding) weapons such as guns, razors, scissors, medication, and other potentially dangerous household items.

- Do not keep suicide talk or threats secret; these are calls for help and call for immediate action.

- Do not challenge, dare, or use verbal shock treatment on suicidal persons in an effort to make them realize the errors in their thinking. These can have tragic effects.

- Make a contract with the person, getting a promise or commitment, preferably in writing, not to make any suicidal attempt until you have talked further.

- Don't be overly reassured by a sudden improvement of mood. Such seemingly quick recoveries sometimes reflect the relief of finally deciding to commit suicide or the temporary release of talking to someone, but most likely the underlying problems have not been resolved.

For immediate help with a suicide-related problem, call (800) 784-2433 or (800) 621-4000, national hotlines staffed with trained counselors.

Review and Apply

Review

- Self-concept during adolescence grows more differentiated as the view of the self becomes more organized, broader, and more abstract, and takes account of the views of others.

- Self-esteem, too, grows increasingly differentiated as the adolescent develops the ability to place different values on different aspects of the self.

- Both Erikson's identity-versus-identity-confusion stage and Marcia's four identity statuses focus on the adolescent's struggle to determine an identity and a role in society.

- One of the dangers that adolescents face is depression, which affects girls more than boys.

- Suicide is the third most common cause of death among 15- to 24-year-olds.

Applying Lifespan Development

- What are some consequences of the shift from reliance on adults to reliance on peers? Are there advantages? Dangers?

- *From a social worker's perspective:* Do you believe that all four of Marcia's identity statuses can lead to reassessment and different choices later in life? Are there stages in Marcia's theory of development that may be more difficult to achieve for adolescents who live in poverty? Why?

Relationships: Family and Friends

Leah is dressed up and ready to go to the first real formal dance of her life. True, the smashing effect of her short beaded black dress is marred slightly by the man's shirt she insists on wearing to cover her bare shoulders. And she is in a sulk. Her boyfriend, Sean Moffitt, is four minutes late, and her mother, Linda, refuses to let her stay out all night at a coed sleepover party after the dance. . . . Leah's father, George, suggests a 2 a.m. curfew: Leah hoots incredulously. Sean pitches the all-nighter, stressing that the party will be chaperoned. Leah's mother has already talked to the host's mother, mortifying Leah with her off-hand comment that a coed sleepover seemed "weird." Rolling her eyes, Leah persists: "It's not like anybody's really going to sleep!" (E. Graham, 1995, p. B1)

The social world of adolescents is considerably wider than that of younger children. As adolescents' relationships with people outside the home grow increasingly important, their interactions with their families evolve and take on a new, and sometimes difficult, character (Collins, Gleason, & Sesma, 1997; Collins & Andrew, 2004).

Family Ties: Changing Relations with Relations

When Paco Lizzagara entered junior high school, his relationship with his parents changed drastically. What had been a good relationship had become tense by the middle of seventh grade. Paco felt his parents always seemed to be "on his case." Instead of giving him more freedom, which he felt he deserved at age 13, they actually seemed to be becoming more restrictive.

Paco's parents would probably see things differently. They would likely suggest that they were not the source of the tension in the household—Paco was. From their point of view, Paco, with whom they'd established what seemed to be a close, stable, loving relationship throughout much of his childhood, suddenly seemed transformed. They felt he was shutting them out of his life, and when he did speak with them, it was merely to criticize their politics, their dress, their preferences in TV shows. To his parents, Paco's behavior was upsetting and bewildering.

The Quest for Autonomy. Parents are sometimes angered, and even more frequently puzzled, by adolescents' conduct. Children who have previously accepted their parents' judgments, declarations, and guidelines begin to question—and sometimes rebel against—their parents' views of the world.

One reason for these clashes are the shifting roles both children and parents must deal with during adolescence. Adolescents increasingly seek **autonomy**, independence and a

Adolescents seek increasing autonomy, independence, and a sense of control over their lives.

autonomy having independence and a sense of control over one's life.

sense of control over their lives. Most parents intellectually realize that this shift is a normal part of adolescence, representing one of the primary developmental tasks of the period, and in many ways they welcome it as a sign of their children's growth. However, in many cases the day-to-day realities of adolescents' increasing autonomy may prove difficult for them to deal with (Smetana, 1995). But understanding this growing independence intellectually and agreeing to allow a teen to attend a party when no parents will be present are two different things. To the adolescent, her parents' refusal indicates a lack of trust or confidence. To the parent, it's simple good sense: "I trust you," they may say. "It's everyone else who will be there that I worry about."

In most families, teenagers' autonomy grows gradually over the course of adolescence. For instance, one study of changes in adolescents' views of their parents found that increasing autonomy led them to perceive parents less in idealized terms and more as persons in their own right. For example, rather than seeing their parents as authoritarian disciplinarians mindlessly reminding them to do their homework, they may come to see their parents' emphasis on excelling in school as evidence of parental regrets about their own lack of education and a wish to see their children have more options in life. At the same time, adolescents come to depend more on themselves and to feel more like separate individuals (see Figure 12-3).

The increase in adolescent autonomy changes the relationship between parents and teenagers. At the start of adolescence, the relationship tends to be asymmetrical: Parents hold most of the power and influence over the relationship. By the end of adolescence, however, power and influence have become more balanced, and parents and children end up in a more symmetrical, or egalitarian, relationship. Power and influence are shared, although parents typically retain the upper hand.

Culture and Autonomy. The degree of autonomy that is eventually achieved varies from one family and one child to the next. Cultural factors play an important role. In Western societies, which tend to value individualism, adolescents seek autonomy at a relatively early stage of adolescence. In contrast, Asian societies are collectivistic; they promote the idea that the well-being of the group is more important than that of the individual. In such societies, adolescents' aspirations to achieve autonomy are less pronounced (Kim et al., 1994; Raeff, 2004).

Adolescents from different cultural backgrounds also vary in the degree of obligation to their family that they feel. Those in more collectivistic cultures tend to feel greater obligation to their families, in terms of fulfilling their expectations about their duty to provide assistance, show respect, and support their families in the future, than those from more individualistic societies. In such societies, the push for autonomy is less strong, and the timetable during which autonomy is expected to develop is slower (see Figure 12-4; Fuligni, Tseng, & Lam, 1999; Chao, 2001; Fuligni & Zhang, 2004; Leung, Pe-Pua, & Karnilowicz, 2006).

For example, when asked at what age an adolescent would be expected to carry out certain behaviors (such as going to a concert with friends), adolescents and parents provide different answers depending on their cultural background. In comparison to Asian adolescents and parents, Caucasian adolescents and parents indicate an earlier timetable, anticipating greater autonomy at an earlier age (Feldman & Rosenthal, 1991; Feldman & Wood, 1994).

Does the more extended timetable for the development of autonomy in more collectivistic cultures have negative consequences for adolescents in those cultures? Apparently not.

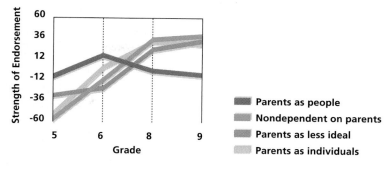

FIGURE 12-3   CHANGING VIEWS OF PARENTS

As adolescents become older, they come to perceive their parents in less idealized terms and more as individuals. What effect is this likely to have on family relations?

(*Source:* Adapted from Steinberg & Silverberg, 1986.)

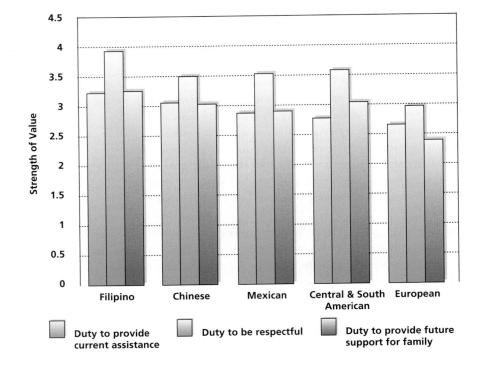

FIGURE 12-4 FAMILY OBLIGATIONS

Adolescents from Asian and Latin American groups felt a greater sense of respect and obligation toward their families than those adolescents with European backgrounds.

(*Source:* Fulgini, Tseng, & Lam, 1999.)

Compared with adolescents from more individualistic societies, adolescents from more collectivistic cultures tend to feel greater obligation to their families.

● ● ● ● ● ● ● ● ● ● ● ● ● ● ● ● ● ● ●

generation gap a divide between parents and adolescents in attitudes, values, aspirations, and world views.

The more important factor is the degree of match between cultural expectations and developmental patterns. What probably matters most is how well the development of autonomy matches societal expectations, not the specific timetable of autonomy (Rothbaum et al., 2000; Zimmer-Gembeck & Collins, 2003; Updegraff et al., 2006).

In addition to cultural factors affecting autonomy, gender also plays a role. In general, male adolescents are permitted more autonomy at an earlier age than female adolescents. The encouragement of male autonomy is consistent with more general traditional male stereotypes, in which males are perceived as more independent and females, conversely, more dependent on others. In fact, the more parents hold traditional stereotypical views of gender, the less likely they are to encourage their daughters' autonomy (Bumpus, Crouter, & McHale, 2001).

The Myth of the Generation Gap. Teen movies often depict adolescents and their parents with totally opposing points of view about the world. For example, the parent of an environmentalist teen might turn out to own a polluting factory. These exaggerations are often funny because we assume there is a kernel of truth in them, in that parents and teenagers often don't see things the same way. According to this argument, there is a **generation gap,** a deep divide between parents and children in attitudes, values, aspirations, and world views.

The reality, however, is quite different. The generation gap, when it exists, is really quite narrow. Adolescents and their parents tend to see eye-to-eye in a variety of domains. Republican parents generally have Republican children; members of the Christian right have children who espouse similar views; parents who advocate for abortion rights have children who are pro-abortion. On social, political, and religious issues, parents and adolescents tend to be in synch, and children's worries mirror those of their parents. Adolescents' concerns about society's problems (see Figure 12-5) are ones with which most adults would probably agree (Flor & Knap, 2001; Knafo & Schwartz, 2003; Smetana, 2005).

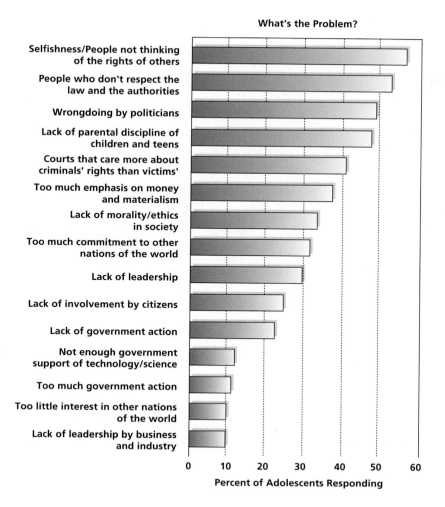

What's the Problem?

Selfishness/People not thinking of the rights of others

People who don't respect the law and the authorities

Wrongdoing by politicians

Lack of parental discipline of children and teens

Courts that care more about criminals' rights than victims'

Too much emphasis on money and materialism

Lack of morality/ethics in society

Too much commitment to other nations of the world

Lack of leadership

Lack of involvement by citizens

Lack of government action

Not enough government support of technology/science

Too much government action

Too little interest in other nations of the world

Lack of leadership by business and industry

Percent of Adolescents Responding

FIGURE 12-5   WHAT'S THE PROBLEM?

Adolescents' views of society's ills are ones with which their parents would be likely to agree.

(*Source:* PRIMEDIA/Roper National Youth Survey, 1999.)

As we've said, most adolescents and their parents get along quite well. Despite their quest for autonomy and independence, most adolescents have deep love, affection, and respect for their parents—and parents feel the same way about their children. Although some parent–adolescent relationships are seriously troubled, the majority of relationships are more positive than negative and help adolescents avoid the kind of peer pressure we'll discuss later in the chapter (Gavin & Furman, 1996; Resnick et al., 1997; Black, 2002).

Even though adolescents spend decreasing amounts of time with their families in general, the amount of time they spend alone with each parent remains remarkably stable across adolescence (see Figure 12-6). In short, there is no evidence suggesting that family problems are worse during adolescence than at any other stage of development (Steinberg, 1993; Larson et al., 1996; Granic, Hollenstein, & Dishion, 2003).

Conflicts with Parents.   Of course, if most adolescents get along with their parents most of the time, that means some of the time they don't. No relationships are always sweetness and light. Parents and teens may hold similar attitudes about social and political issues, but they often hold different views on matters of personal taste, such as music preferences and styles of dress. Also, as we've seen, parents and children may run into disagreements when children seek to achieve autonomy and independence sooner than parents feel is right. Consequently, parent–child conflicts are more likely to occur during adolescence, particularly during the early stages, although it's important to remember that not every family is affected to the same degree (Sagrestano et al., 1999; Arnett, 2000; Smetana, Daddis, & Chuang, 2003).

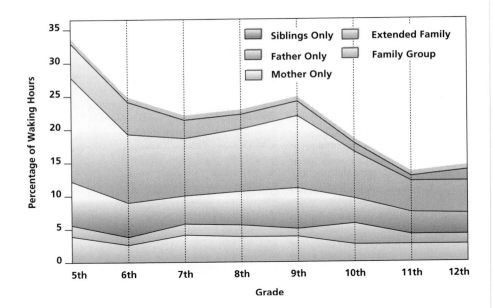

FIGURE 12-6   TIME SPENT BY ADOLESCENTS WITH PARENTS

Despite their quest for autonomy and independence, most adolescents have deep love, affection, and respect for their parents, and the amount of time they spend alone with each parent (the lower two segments) remains remarkably stable across adolescence.

(*Source:* Larson et al., 1996.)

Why should conflict be greater during early adolescence than at later stages of the period? According to developmental psychologist Judith Smetana, the reason involves differing definitions of, and rationales for, appropriate and inappropriate conduct. Parents may feel, for instance, that getting one's ear pierced in three places is inappropriate because society traditionally deems it inappropriate. On the other hand, adolescents may view the issue in terms of personal choice (Smetana, Yau, & Hanson, 1991; Smetana, 2005).

Furthermore, the newly sophisticated reasoning of adolescents (discussed in the previous chapter) leads teenagers to think about parental rules in more complex ways. Arguments that might be convincing to a school-age child ("Do it because I tell you to do it") are less compelling to an adolescent.

The argumentativeness and assertiveness of early adolescence at first may lead to an increase in conflict, but in many ways these qualities play an important role in the evolution of parent–child relationships. While parents may initially react defensively to the challenges that their children present, and may grow inflexible and rigid, in most cases they eventually come to realize that their children *are* growing up and that they want to support them in that process.

As parents come to see that their adolescent children's arguments are often compelling and not so unreasonable, and that their daughters and sons can in fact be trusted with more freedom, they become more yielding, allowing and eventually perhaps even encouraging independence. As this process occurs during the middle stages of adolescence, the combativeness of early adolescence declines.

Of course, this pattern does not apply for all adolescents. Although the majority of teenagers maintain stable relations with their parents throughout adolescence, as many as 20% pass through a fairly rough time (Dryfoos, 1990; Dmitrieva, Chen, & Greenberger, 2004).

Cultural Differences in Parent–Child Conflicts During Adolescence.   Although parent–child conflicts are found in every culture, there does seem to be less conflict between parents and their teenage children in "traditional," preindustrial cultures. Teens in such traditional cultures also experience fewer mood swings and instances of risky behavior than do teens in industrialized countries (Schlegel & Barry, 1991; Arnett, 2000; Nelson, Badger, & Wu, 2004).

Why? The answer may relate to the degree of independence that adolescents expect and adults permit. In more industrialized societies, in which the value of individualism is typically high, independence is an expected component of adolescence. Consequently, adolescents and their parents must negotiate the amount and timing of the adolescent's increasing independence—a process that often leads to strife.

The argumentativeness of adolescents can bring about an evolution in parent–child relationships, as parents can at times see that some of their child's arguments are not unreasonable.

In contrast, in more traditional societies, individualism is not valued as highly, and therefore adolescents are less inclined to seek out independence. With diminished independence-seeking on the part of adolescents, the result is less parent–child conflict (Dasen & Mishra, 2000, 2002).

Relationships with Peers: The Importance of Belonging

In the eyes of many parents, the most fitting symbols of adolescence are the cell phone or perhaps the computer, on which incessant instant messaging occurs. For many of their sons and daughters, communicating with friends is experienced as an indispensable lifeline, sustaining ties to individuals with whom they may have already spent many hours earlier in the day.

The seemingly compulsive need to communicate with friends demonstrates the role that peers play in adolescence. Continuing the trend that began in middle childhood, adolescents spend increasing amounts of time with their peers, and the importance of peer relationships grows as well. In fact, there is probably no period of life in which peer relationships are as important as they are in adolescence (Youniss & Haynie, 1992).

Social Comparison.   Peers become more important for a number of reasons in adolescence. For one thing, they provide each other with the opportunity to compare and evaluate opinions, abilities, and even physical changes—a process called *social comparison*. Because physical and cognitive changes of adolescence are so unique to this age group and so pronounced, especially during the early stages of puberty, adolescents turn increasingly to others who share, and consequently can shed light on, their own experiences (Paxton et al., 1999; Schutz, Paxton, & Wertheim, 2002; Rankin, Lane, & Gibbons, 2004).

Parents are unable to provide social comparison. Not only are they well beyond the changes that adolescents undergo, but adolescents' questioning of adult authority and their motivation to become more autonomous make parents, other family members, and adults in general inadequate and invalid sources of knowledge. Who is left to provide such information? Peers.

Reference Groups.   As we have said, adolescence is a time of experimentation, of trying out new identities, roles, and conduct. Peers provide information about what roles and behavior are most acceptable by serving as a reference group. **Reference groups** are groups of people with whom one compares oneself. Just as a professional ballplayer is likely to compare his performance against that of other professional players, so do teenagers compare themselves to those who are similar to them.

Reference groups present a set of *norms*, or standards, against which adolescents can judge their abilities and social success. An adolescent need not even belong to a group for it to serve as a reference group. For instance, unpopular adolescents may find themselves belittled and rejected by members of a popular group, yet use that more popular group as a reference group (Berndt, 1999).

Cliques and Crowds: Belonging to a Group.   One of the consequences of the increasing cognitive sophistication of adolescents is the ability to group others in more discriminating ways. Consequently, even if they do not belong to the group they use for reference purposes, adolescents typically are part of some identifiable group. Rather than defining people in concrete terms relating to what they do ("football players" or "musicians") as a younger school-age child might, adolescents use more abstract terms packed with greater subtleties ("jocks" or "skaters" or "stoners") (Brown, 1990; Montemayor, Adams, & Gulotta, 1994).

There are actually two types of groups to which adolescents tend to belong: cliques and crowds. **Cliques** are groups of 2 to 12 people whose members have frequent social interactions with one another. In contrast, **crowds** are larger, comprising individuals who share particular characteristics but who may not interact with one another. For instance, "jocks" and "nerds" are representative of crowds found in many high schools.

reference groups groups of people with whom one compares oneself.

cliques groups of 2 to 12 people whose members have frequent social interactions with one another.

crowds larger groups than cliques, composed of individuals who share particular characteristics but who may not interact with one another.

sex cleavage sex segregation in which boys interact primarily with boys and girls primarily with girls.

Membership in particular cliques and crowds is often determined by the degree of similarity with members of the group. One of the most important dimensions of similarity relates to substance use; adolescents tend to choose friends who use alcohol and other drugs to the same extent that they do. Their friends are also often similar in terms of their academic success, although this is not always true. For instance, during early adolescence, attraction to peers who are particularly well behaved seems to decrease while, at the same time, those who behave more aggressively become more attractive (Bukowski, Sippola, & Newcomb, 2000; Farmer, Estell, & Bishop, 2003; Kupersmidt & Dodge, 2004).

The emergence of distinct cliques and crowds during adolescence reflects in part the increased cognitive capabilities of adolescents. Group labels are abstractions, requiring teens to make judgments of people with whom they may interact only rarely and of whom they have little direct knowledge. It is not until mid-adolescence that teenagers are sufficiently sophisticated cognitively to make the subtle judgments that underlie distinctions between different cliques and crowds (Burgess & Rubin, 2000; Brown & Klute, 2003).

Gender Relations.   As children enter adolescence from middle childhood, their groups of friends are composed almost universally of same-sex individuals. Boys hang out with boys; girls hang out with girls. Technically, this sex segregation is called the **sex cleavage.**

However, the situation changes as members of both sexes enter puberty. Boys and girls experience the hormonal surge that marks puberty and causes the maturation of the sex organs (see Chapter 11). At the same time, societal pressures suggest that the time is appropriate for romantic involvement. These developments lead to a change in the ways adolescents view the opposite sex. Where a 10-year-old is likely to see every member of the other sex as "annoying" and "a pain," heterosexual teenage boys and girls begin to regard each other with greater interest in terms of both personality and sexuality. (For gays and lesbians, pairing off holds other complexities, as we will discuss later when we consider adolescent dating.)

As they move into puberty, boys' and girls' cliques, which previously had moved along parallel but separate tracks, begin to converge. Adolescents begin to attend boy–girl dances or parties, although mostly the boys still spend their time with boys, and the girls with girls (Richards et al., 1998).

A little later, however, adolescents increasingly spend time with members of the other sex. New cliques emerge, composed of both males and females. Not everyone participates

The sex segregation of childhood continues during the early stages of adolescence. However, by the time of middle adolescence, this segregation decreases, and boys' and girls' cliques begin to converge.

initially: Early on, the teenagers who are leaders of the same-sex cliques and who have the highest status lead the way. Eventually, however, most adolescents find themselves in cliques that include boys and girls.

Cliques and crowds undergo yet another transformation at the end of adolescence: They become less influential and may dissolve as a result of the increased pairing off that occurs.

Developmental Diversity

Race Segregation: The Great Divide of Adolescence

When Philip McAdoo, a [student] at the University of North Carolina, stopped one day to see a friend who worked on his college campus, a receptionist asked if he would autograph a basketball for her son. Because he was African American and tall, "she just assumed that I was on the basketball team," recounted McAdoo.

Jasme Kelly, an African American sophomore at the same college, had a similar story to tell. When she went to see a friend at a fraternity house, the student who answered the door asked if she was there to apply for the job of cook.

White students, too, find racial relations difficult and in some ways forbidding. For instance, Jenny Johnson, a white 20-year-old junior, finds even the most basic conversation with African American classmates difficult. She describes a conversation in which African American friends "jump at my throat because I used the word 'black' instead of African American. There is just such a huge barrier that it's really hard . . . to have a normal discussion." (Sanoff & Minerbrook, 1993, p. 58)

The pattern of race segregation found at the University of North Carolina is repeated over and over in schools and colleges throughout the United States: Even when they attend desegregated schools with significant ethnic and racial diversity, people of different ethnicities and races interact very little. Moreover, even if they have a friend of a different ethnicity within the confines of a school, most adolescents don't interact with that friend outside of school (DuBois & Hirsch, 1990).

It doesn't start out this way. During elementary school and even during early adolescence, there is a fair amount of integration among students of differing ethnicities. However, by middle and late adolescence, the amount of segregation is striking (Shrum, Cheek, & Hunter, 1988; Spencer & Dornbusch, 1990; Spencer, 1991; Ennett & Bauman, 1996).

Why should racial and ethnic segregation be the rule, even in schools that have been desegregated for some time? One reason is that minority students may actively seek support from others who share their minority status (where "minority" is used in its sociological sense to indicate a subordinate group whose members lack power, compared to members of a dominant group). By associating primarily with other members of their own group, members of minority groups are able to affirm their own identity.

Members of different racial and ethnic groups may be segregated in the classroom as well. As we discussed in Chapter 10, because certain groups have been historically discriminated against, members of these minority groups tend to experience less school success than members of the majority group. It may be that ethnic and racial segregation in high school is based not on ethnicity itself, but on academic achievement.

If minority group members experience less academic success, they may find themselves in classes with proportionally fewer majority group members. Similarly, majority students may be in classes with few minority students. Such class assignment practices, then, may inadvertently maintain and promote racial and ethnic segregation. This pattern would be particularly prevalent in schools where rigid academic tracking is practiced, with students assigned to "low," "medium," and "high" tracks depending on their prior achievement (Lucas & Behrends, 2002).

The lack of contact among students of different racial and ethnic backgrounds in school may also reflect prejudice, both perceived and real, toward members of other groups. Students of color may feel that the white majority is prejudiced, discriminatory, and hostile, and they may prefer to stick to same-race groups. Conversely, white students may assume that minority group members are antagonistic and unfriendly. Such mutually destructive attitudes reduce the likelihood that meaningful interaction can take place (Phinney, Ferguson, & Tate, 1997; Tropp, 2003).

Is this sort of voluntary segregation along racial and ethnic lines found during adolescence inevitable? No. Adolescents who have interacted regularly and extensively with those of different races earlier in their lives are more likely to have friends of different races. Schools that actively promote contact among members of different ethnicities in classes help create an environment in which cross-race friendships can flourish (Hewstone, 2003).

Still, the task is daunting. Many societal pressures act to keep members of different races from interacting with one another. Peer pressure, too, may encourage this as some cliques may actively promote norms that discourage group members from crossing racial and ethnic lines to form new friendships.

Popularity and Rejection

Most adolescents have well-tuned antennae when it comes to determining who is popular and who is not. In fact, for some teenagers, concerns over popularity—or lack of it—may be a central focus of their lives.

Actually, the social world of adolescents is divided not only into popular and unpopular individuals; the differentiations are more complex (see Figure 12-7). For instance, some adolescents are controversial; in contrast to *popular* adolescents, who are mostly liked, **controversial adolescents** are liked by some and disliked by others. For example, a controversial adolescent may be highly popular within a particular group such as the string orchestra, but not popular among other classmates. Furthermore, there are **rejected adolescents**, who are uniformly disliked, and **neglected adolescents**, who are neither liked nor disliked. Neglected adolescents are the forgotten students—the ones whose status is so low that they are overlooked by almost everyone.

In most cases, popular and controversial adolescents tend to be similar in that their overall status is higher, while rejected and neglected adolescents share a generally lower status.

controversial adolescents   children who are liked by some peers and disliked by others.

rejected adolescents   children who are actively disliked, and whose peers may react to them in an obviously negative manner.

neglected adolescents   children who receive relatively little attention from their peers in the form of either positive or negative interactions.

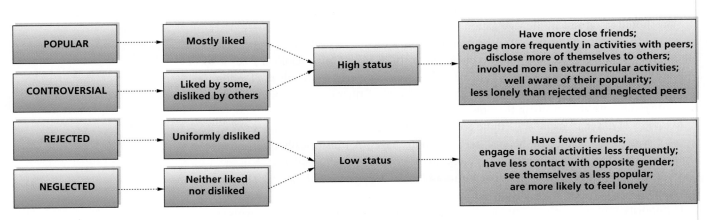

FIGURE 12-7   **THE SOCIAL WORLD OF ADOLESCENCE**

An adolescent's popularity can fall into one of four categories, depending on the opinions of his or her peers. Popularity is related to differences in status, behavior, and adjustment.

Unpopular adolescents fall into several categories. Controversial adolescents are liked by some and disliked by others; rejected adolescents are uniformly disliked; and neglected adolescents are neither liked nor disliked.

Popular and controversial adolescents have more close friends, engage more frequently in activities with their peers, and disclose more about themselves to others than less popular students. They are also more involved in extracurricular school activities. In addition, they are well aware of their popularity, and they are less lonely than their less popular classmates (Englund et al., 2000; Farmer et al., 2003; Zettergren, 2003; Becker & Luthar, 2007).

In contrast, the social world of rejected and neglected adolescents is considerably less pleasant. They have fewer friends, engage in social activities less frequently, and have less contact with the opposite sex. They see themselves—accurately, it turns out—as less popular, and they are more likely to feel lonely.

What is it that determines status in high school? As illustrated in Table 12-3, men and women have different perceptions. For example, college men suggest that physical attractiveness is the most important factor in determining high school girls' status, while college women believe it is a high school girl's grades and intelligence (Suitor et al., 2001).

Conformity: Peer Pressure in Adolescence

Whenever Aldos Henry said he wanted to buy a particular brand of sneakers or a certain style of shirt, his parents complained that he was just giving in to peer pressure and told him to make up his own mind about things.

Table 12-3	High School Status		
WHAT MAKES HIGH SCHOOL GIRLS HIGH IN STATUS:		**WHAT MAKES HIGH SCHOOL BOYS HIGH IN STATUS:**	
According to college men:	**According to college women:**	**According to college men:**	**According to college women:**
1. Physical attractiveness	1. Grades/intelligence	1. Participation in sports	1. Participation in sports
2. Grades/intelligence	2. Participation in sports	2. Grades/intelligence	2. Grades/intelligence
3. Participation in sports	3. General sociability	3. Popularity, with girls	3. General sociability
4. General sociability	4. Physical attractiveness	4. General sociability	4. Physical attractiveness
5. Popularity with boys	5. Clothes	5. Car	5. School clubs/government

Note: Students at the following universities were asked in which ways adolescents in their high schools had gained prestige with their peers: Louisiana State University, Southeastern Louisiana University, State University of New York at Albany, State University of New York at Stony Brook, University of Georgia, and the University of New Hampshire.

(*Source:* Suitor et al., 2001.)

peer pressure the influence of one's peers to conform to their behavior and attitudes.

undersocialized delinquents adolescent delinquents who are raised with little discipline or with harsh, uncaring parental supervision.

As they grow more confident of their own decisions, adolescents become less likely to conform to peers and parents.

Undersocialized delinquents are raised with little discipline or by harsh, uncaring parents, and they begin anti-social activities at a relatively early age. In contrast, socialized delinquents know and usually follow the norms of society, and they are highly influenced by their peers.

In arguing with Aldos, his parents were subscribing to a view of adolescence that is quite prevalent in U.S. society: that teenagers are highly susceptible to **peer pressure,** the influence of one's peers to conform to their behavior and attitudes. Were his parents correct?

The research suggests that it all depends. In some cases, adolescents *are* highly susceptible to the influence of their peers. For instance, when considering what to wear, whom to date, and what movies to see, adolescents are apt to follow the lead of their peers. Wearing the right clothes, down to a particular brand, sometimes can be a ticket to membership in a popular group. It shows you know what's what. On the other hand, when it comes to many nonsocial matters, such as choosing a career path or trying to solve a problem, they are more likely to turn to an experienced adult (Phelan, Yu, & Davidson, 1994).

In short, particularly in middle and late adolescence, teenagers turn to those they see as experts on a given dimension. If they have social concerns, they turn to the people most likely to be experts—their peers. If the problem is one about which parents or other adults are most likely to have expertise, teenagers tend to turn to them for advice and are most susceptible to their opinions (Young & Ferguson, 1979; Perrine & Aloise-Young, 2004).

Overall, then, it does not appear that susceptibility to peer pressure suddenly soars during adolescence. Instead, adolescence brings about a change in the people to whom an individual conforms. Whereas children conform fairly consistently to their parents during childhood, in adolescence conformity shifts to the peer group, in part because pressures to conform to peers increase as adolescents seek to establish their identity apart from their parents.

Ultimately, however, adolescents conform less to both peers *and* adults as they develop increasing autonomy over their lives. As they grow in confidence and in the ability to make their own decisions, adolescents are more apt to remain independent and to reject pressures from others, no matter who those others are. Before they learn to resist the urge to conform to their peers, however, teenagers may get into trouble, often along with their friends (Steinberg, 1993; Crockett & Crouter, 1995). (For a look at a growing problem among adolescents, see the *From Research to Practice* box.)

Juvenile Delinquency: The Crimes of Adolescence

Adolescents, along with young adults, are more likely to commit crimes than any other age group. This is a misleading statistic in some respects: Because certain behaviors (such as drinking) are illegal for adolescents but not for older individuals, it is rather easy for adolescents to break the law by doing something that, were they a few years older, would be legal. But even when such crimes are disregarded, adolescents are disproportionately involved in violent crimes, such as murder, assaults, and rape, and in property crimes involving theft, robbery, and arson.

Although the number of violent crimes committed by U.S. adolescents over the past decade has shown a decline of 40%, probably due to the strength of the economy, delinquency among some teenagers remains a significant problem. Overall, 16% of all arrests for serious crimes involved a person under the age of 18.

Why do adolescents become involved in criminal activity? Some offenders, known as **undersocialized delinquents,** are adolescents who are raised with little discipline or with harsh, uncaring parental supervision. Although they are influenced by their peers, these children have not been socialized appropriately by their parents and were not taught standards of conduct to regulate their own behavior. Undersocialized delinquents typically begin criminal activities at an early age, well before the onset of adolescence.

Undersocialized delinquents share several characteristics. They tend to be relatively aggressive and violent fairly early in life, characteristics that lead to rejection by peers and academic failure. They also are more likely to have been diagnosed with attention deficit disorder as children, and they tend to be less intelligent than average (Henry et al., 1996; Silverthorn & Frick, 1999; Rutter, 2003).

From Research to Practice

Know When to Fold 'Em: The Growing Problem of Online Gambling

Greg Hogan Jr., a 19-year-old Lehigh University sophomore, was on tilt—the poker term for a spell of insanity that often follows a run of bad luck—for months now. Alone at the computer, usually near the end of one of his long online gambling sessions, the thought "I'm on tilt" would occur to him. Dude, he'd tell himself, you gotta stop. These thoughts sounded the way a distant fire alarm sounds in the middle of a warm bath. He would ignore them and go back to playing poker. "The side of me that said, 'Just one more hand,' was the side that always won," he reported months later. "I couldn't get away from it, not until all my money was gone." In a little more than a year, he had lost $7,500 playing poker online. (Schwartz, 2006, p. 52)

Greg Hogan's addiction to Internet gambling shortly came to an end when, in desperation, he held up a local bank and was quickly caught and arrested. While the ending of Hogan's story may be extreme, the events that sent him down the path of self-destruction are becoming alarmingly common among adolescent males.

A survey conducted by the Annenberg Public Policy Center found that adolescent gambling—especially on card games—is on the rise. The rate of monthly card playing among 14- to 22-year-old males rose from 35% to 42% between 2004 and 2005—an increase of 20% in just one year. The rate was even higher among men in college: some 50%. Over 1 million young people—mostly males—currently use online gambling sites at least once a month (Annenberg Public Policy Center, 2005, 2006).

Adolescent card players were particularly likely to report gambling on the Internet—a phenomenon that more than doubled in the same 1-year period. This trend is troubling, in part because gamblers who use the Internet for gaming are more than three times as likely as gamblers using non-Internet gaming venues to exhibit serious levels of problematic or pathological gambling. In addition, the Annenberg Center study showed that over half of young people who gambled at least once a week reported at least one symptom of problem gambling, with card players reporting more symptoms than other kinds of gamblers (Ladd & Petry, 2002).

Whether Internet venues foster more serious gambling problems or merely tend to attract people who already have such problems remains unclear. For example, one study of female gamblers found that gambling was associated with higher levels of hyperactivity at age 6 and higher levels of drug use within the prior year. Other research finds that problem gambling is associated with greater drug and alcohol problems, as well as engaging in unprotected sex (Huang et al., 2007; Martins et al, 2007).

Easy access to the Internet as well its anonymity make online gambling a behavior in which it is easy to become involved, as well as to keep secret from others. It's simply much easier for adolescents to hide a gambling problem from friends and family when they never have to leave their dorm room.

- *Why might gambling be particularly problematic among adolescents in college?*

- *Why do you think male adolescents are more attracted to gambling than are female adolescents?*

Undersocialized delinquents often suffer from psychological difficulties, and as adults fit a psychological pattern called antisocial personality disorder. They are relatively unlikely to be successfully rehabilitated, and many undersocialized delinquents live on the margins of society throughout their lives (Rönkä & Pulkkinen, 1995; Lynam, 1996; Frick et al., 2003).

A larger group of adolescent offenders are socialized delinquents. **Socialized delinquents** know and subscribe to the norms of society; they are fairly normal psychologically. For them, transgressions committed during adolescence do not lead to a life of crime. Instead, most socialized delinquents pass through a period during adolescence when they engage in some petty crimes (such as shoplifting), but they do not continue lawbreaking into adulthood.

Socialized delinquents are typically highly influenced by their peers, and their delinquency often occurs in groups. In addition, some research suggests that parents of socialized delinquents supervise their children's behavior less closely than other parents. But like other aspects of adolescent behavior, these minor delinquencies are often a result of giving in to group pressure or seeking to establish one's identity as an adult (Dornbusch et al., 1985; Windle, 1994; Fletcher et al., 1995; Thornberry & Krohn, 1997).

socialized delinquents adolescent delinquents who know and subscribe to the norms of society and who are fairly normal psychologically.

Review and Apply

Review

- The search for autonomy may cause a readjustment in relations between teenagers and their parents, but the generation gap is less wide than is generally thought.

- Cliques and crowds serve as reference groups in adolescence and offer a ready means of social comparison. Sex cleavage gradually diminishes, until boys and girls begin to pair off.

- Racial separation increases during adolescence, bolstered by socioeconomic status differences, different academic experiences, and mutually distrustful attitudes.

- Degrees of popularity in adolescence include popular, controversial, neglected, and rejected adolescents.

- Adolescents tend to conform to their peers in areas in which they regard their peers as experts, and to adults in areas of perceived adult expertise.

- Adolescents are disproportionately involved in criminal activities, although most do not commit crimes. Juvenile delinquents can be categorized as undersocialized or socialized delinquents.

Applying Lifespan Development

- Thinking back to your own high school days, what was the dominant clique in your school, and what factors were related to group membership?

- *From a social worker's perspective:* In what ways do you think parents with different styles—authoritarian, authoritative, permissive, and uninvolved—react to attempts to establish autonomy during adolescence? Are the styles of parenting different for a single parent? Are there cultural differences?

Dating, Sexual Behavior, and Teenage Pregnancy

It took him almost a month, but Sylvester Chiu finally got up the courage to ask Jackie Durbin to go to the movies. It was hardly a surprise to Jackie, though. Sylvester had first told his friend Erik about his resolve to ask Jackie out, and Erik had told Jackie's friend Cynthia about Sylvester's plans. Cynthia, in turn, had told Jackie, who was primed to say "yes" when Sylvester finally did call.

Welcome to the complex world of dating, an important and changing ritual of adolescence. We'll consider dating, as well as several other aspects of adolescents' relationships with one another, in the remainder of the chapter.

Dating: Close Relationships in the 21st Century

When and how adolescents begin to date is determined by cultural factors that change from one generation to another. Until fairly recently, exclusively dating a single individual was seen as something of a cultural ideal, viewed in the context of romance. In fact, society often encouraged dating in adolescence, in part as a way for adolescents to explore relationships that might eventually lead to marriage. Today, some adolescents believe that the concept of dating is outmoded and limiting, and in some places the practice of "hooking up"—a vague term that covers everything from kissing to sexual intercourse—is viewed as more appropriate. Despite changing cultural norms, dating remains the dominant form of social interaction that leads to intimacy among adolescents (Larson, Clore, & Wood, 1999; Denizet-Lewis, 2004; Manning, Giordano, & Longmore, 2006).

The Functions of Dating.   Although on the surface dating is part of a pattern of courtship that can potentially lead to marriage, it actually serves other functions as well, especially early on. Dating is a way to learn how to establish intimacy with another individual. It can provide entertainment and, depending on the status of the person one is dating, prestige. It even can be used to develop a sense of one's own identity (Skipper & Nass, 1966; Savin-Williams & Berndt, 1990; Sanderson & Cantor, 1995).

Just how well dating serves such functions, particularly the development of psychological intimacy, is an open question. What specialists in adolescence do know, however, is surprising: Dating in early and middle adolescence is not terribly successful at facilitating intimacy. On the contrary, dating is often a superficial activity in which the participants so rarely let down their guards that they never become truly close and never expose themselves emotionally to each other. Psychological intimacy may be lacking even when sexual activity is part of the relationship (Savin-Williams & Berndt, 1990; Collins, 2003; Furman & Shaffer, 2003).

True intimacy becomes more common during later adolescence. At that point, the dating relationship may be taken more seriously by both participants, and it may be seen as a way to select a mate and as a potential prelude to marriage (an institution we consider in Chapter 14).

For homosexual adolescents, dating presents special challenges. In some cases, blatant homophobic prejudice expressed by classmates may lead gays and lesbians to date members of the other sex in efforts to fit in. If they do seek relationships with other gays and lesbians, they may find it difficult to find partners, who may not openly express their sexual orientation. Homosexual couples who do openly date face possible harassment, making the development of a relationship all the more difficult (Savin-Williams, 2003a).

Dating, Race, and Ethnicity.   Culture influences dating patterns among adolescents of different racial and ethnic groups, particularly those whose parents have immigrated to the United States from other countries. Parents may try to control their children's dating behavior in an effort to preserve their culture's traditional values or ensure that their child dates within his or her racial or ethnic group.

For example, Asian parents may be especially conservative in their attitudes and values, in part because they themselves may have had no experience of dating. (In many cases, the parents' marriage was arranged by others, and the entire concept of dating is unfamiliar.) They may insist that dating be conducted with chaperones, or not at all. As a consequence, they may find themselves involved in substantial conflict with their children (Kibria, 2003; Hamon & Ingoldsby, 2003; Hoelterk, Axinn, & Ghimire, 2004).

Sexual Relationships

The hormonal changes of puberty not only trigger the maturation of the sexual organs, but also produce a new range of feelings in the form of sexuality. Sexual behavior and thoughts are among the central concerns of adolescents. Almost all adolescents think about sex, and many think about it a good deal of the time (Kelly, 2001; Ponton, 2001).

Masturbation.   The first type of sex in which adolescents engage is often solitary sexual self-stimulation or **masturbation.** By the age of 15, some 80% of teenage boys and 20% of teenage girls report that they have masturbated. The frequency of masturbation in males occurs more in the early teens and then begins to decline, while in females, the frequency is lower initially and increases throughout adolescence. In addition, patterns of masturbation frequency show differences according to race. For example, African American men and women masturbate less than whites (Oliver & Hyde, 1993; Schwartz, 1999; Hyde & DeLamater, 2004).

masturbation   sexual self-stimulation.

Although masturbation is widespread, it still may produce feelings of shame and guilt. There are several reasons for this. One is that adolescents may believe that masturbation signifies the inability to find a sexual partner—an erroneous assumption, since statistics show that three-quarters of married men and 68% of married women report masturbating between 10 and 24 times a year (Hunt, 1974; Davidson, Darling, & Norton, 1995).

For some there is also a sense of shame about masturbation, the result of a lingering legacy of misguided views of masturbation. For instance, 19th-century physicians and laypersons warned of horrible effects of masturbation, including "dyspepsia, spinal disease, headache, epilepsy, various kinds of fits . . . impaired eyesight, palpitation of the heart, pain in the side and bleeding at the lungs, spasm of the heart, and sometimes sudden death" (Gregory, 1856). Suggested remedies included bandaging the genitals, covering them with a cage, tying the hands, male circumcision without anesthesia (so that it might better be remembered), and for girls, the administration of carbolic acid to the clitoris. One physician, J. W. Kellogg, believed that certain grains would be less likely to provoke sexual excitation—leading to his invention of corn flakes (Hunt, 1974; Michael et al., 1994).

The reality of masturbation is different. Today, experts on sexual behavior view it as a normal, healthy, and harmless activity. In fact, some suggest that it provides a useful way to learn about one's own sexuality (Hyde & DeLamater, 2004).

Sexual Intercourse.   Although it may be preceded by many different types of sexual intimacy, including deep kissing, massaging, petting, and oral sex, sexual intercourse remains a major milestone in the perceptions of most adolescents. Consequently, the main focus of researchers investigating sexual behavior has been on the act of heterosexual intercourse.

The average age at which adolescents first have sexual intercourse has been steadily declining over the last 50 years, and about one in five adolescents have had sex before the age of 15. Overall, around half of adolescents begin having intercourse between the ages of 15 and 18, and at least 80% have had sex before the age of 20 (see Figure 12-8). At the same time, though, many teenagers are postponing sex, and the number of adolescents who say they have never had sexual intercourse increased by nearly 10% from 1991 to 2001, largely as a response to the threat of infection by the virus that causes AIDS (Seidman & Reider, 1994; Centers for Disease Control and Prevention, 1998; NCPYP, 2003).

FIGURE 12-8 ADOLESCENTS AND SEXUAL ACTIVITY

The age at which adolescents have sexual intercourse for the first time is declining, and 80% have had sex before the age of 20.

(*Source:* Kantrowitz & Wingert, 1999.)

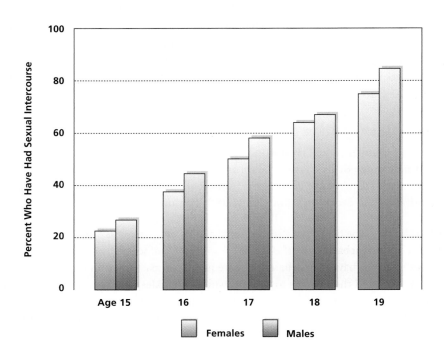

It is impossible to consider sexual activities without also looking at the societal norms governing sexual conduct. The prevailing norm several decades ago was the *double standard* in which premarital sex was considered permissible for males but not for females. Women were told by society that "nice girls don't," while men heard that premarital sex was permissible—although they should be sure to marry virgins.

Today, however, the double standard has begun to give way to a new norm, called *permissiveness with affection.* According to this standard, premarital intercourse is viewed as permissible for both men and women if it occurs in the context of a long-term, committed, or loving relationship (Hyde & DeLamater, 2004).

The demise of the double standard is far from complete, however. Attitudes toward sexual conduct are still typically more lenient for males than for females, even in relatively socially liberal cultures. And in some cultures, the standards for men and women are quite distinct. For example, in North Africa, the Middle East, and the majority of Asian countries, most women conform to societal norms suggesting that they abstain from sexual intercourse until they are married. In Mexico, where there are strict standards against premarital sex, males are also considerably more likely than females to have premarital sex. In contrast, in Sub-Saharan Africa, women are more likely to have sexual intercourse prior to marriage, and intercourse is common among unmarried teenage women (Liskin, 1985; Spira et al., 1992; Johnson et al., 1992; Peltzer & Pengpid, 2006).

Sexual Orientation: Heterosexuality, Homosexuality, and Bisexuality

When we consider adolescents' sexual development, the most frequent pattern is *heterosexuality*, sexual attraction and behavior directed to the other sex. Yet some teenagers are *homosexual*, in which their sexual attraction and behavior is oriented to members of their own sex. (Many male homosexuals prefer the term *gay* and female homosexuals the label *lesbian*, because they refer to a broader array of attitudes and lifestyle than the term *homosexual*, which focuses on the sexual act.) Other people find they are *bisexual*, sexually attracted to people of both sexes.

Many teens experiment with homosexuality. At one time or another, around 20% to 25% of adolescent boys and 10% of adolescent girls have at least one same-sex sexual encounter. In fact, homosexuality and heterosexuality are not completely distinct sexual orientations. Alfred Kinsey, a pioneer sex researcher, argued that sexual orientation should be viewed as a continuum in which "exclusively homosexual" is at one end and "exclusively heterosexual" at the other (Kinsey, Pomeroy, & Martin, 1948). In between are people who show both homosexual and heterosexual behavior. Although accurate figures are difficult to obtain, most experts believe that between 4% and 10% of both men and women are exclusively homosexual during extended periods of their lives (Kinsey, Pomeroy, & Martin, 1948; McWhirter, Sanders, & Reinisch, 1990; Michael et al., 1994; Diamond, 2003a, 2003b; Russell & Consolacion, 2003).

The determination of sexual orientation is further complicated by distinctions between sexual orientation and gender identity. While sexual orientation relates to the object of one's sexual interests, *gender identity* is the gender a person believes he or she is psychologically. Sexual orientation and gender identity are not necessarily related to one another: A man who has a strong masculine gender identity may be attracted to other men. Consequently, the extent to which men and women enact traditional "masculine" or "feminine" behavior is not necessarily related to their sexual orientation or gender identity (Hunter & Mallon, 2000).

Some people feel they have been born the wrong physical sex, believing, for example, that they are women trapped in men's bodies. These *transgendered* individuals may pursue sexual reassignment surgery, a prolonged course of treatment in which they receive hormones and reconstructive surgery so they are able to take on the physical characteristics of the other sex.

The stresses of adolescence are magnified for homosexuals, who often face societal prejudice. Eventually, however, most adolescents come to grips and embrace their sexual orientation.

What Determines Sexual Orientation?   The factors that induce people to develop as heterosexual, homosexual, or bisexual are not well understood. Evidence suggests that genetic and biological factors may play an important role. Studies of twins show that identical twins are more likely to both be homosexual than pairs of siblings who don't share their genetic makeup. Other research finds that various structures of the brain are different in homosexuals and heterosexuals, and hormone production also seems to be linked to sexual orientation (Meyer-Bahlburg et al., 1995; Lippa, 2003; Rahman & Wilson, 2003; Kraemer et al., 2006).

Other researchers have suggested that family or peer environmental factors play a role. For example, Freud argued that homosexuality was the result of inappropriate identification with the opposite-sex parent (Freud, 1922/1959). The difficulty with Freud's theoretical perspective and other, similar perspectives that followed is that there simply is no evidence to suggest that any particular family dynamic or child-rearing practice is consistently related to sexual orientation. Similarly, explanations based on learning theory, which suggest that homosexuality arises because of rewarding, pleasant homosexual experiences and unsatisfying heterosexual ones, do not appear to be the complete answer (Bell & Weinberg, 1978; Isay, 1990; Golombok & Tasker, 1996).

In short, there is no accepted explanation of why some adolescents develop a heterosexual orientation and others a homosexual orientation. Most experts believe that sexual orientation develops out of a complex interplay of genetic, physiological, and environmental factors (LeVay & Valente, 2003).

What is clear is that adolescents who find themselves attracted to members of the same sex may face a more difficult time than other teens. U.S. society still harbors great ignorance and prejudice regarding homosexuality, persisting in the belief that people have a choice in the matter—which they do not. Gay and lesbian teens may be rejected by their family or peers, or even harassed and assaulted if they are open about their orientation. The result is that adolescents who find themselves to be homosexual are at greater risk for depression, and suicide rates are significantly higher for homosexual adolescents than heterosexual adolescents (Ryan & Rivers, 2003; C. M. Harris, 2004; Murdock & Bolch, 2005; Koh & Ross, 2006; Lester, 2006).

Ultimately, though, most people are able to come to grips with their sexual orientation and become comfortable with it. Although lesbian, gay, and bisexuals may experience mental health difficulties as a result of the stress, prejudice, and discrimination they face, homosexuality is not considered a psychological disorder by any of the major psychological or medical associations. All of them endorse efforts to reduce discrimination against homosexuals (Stone, 2003; van Wormer & McKinney, 2003; Davison, 2005).

Teenage Pregnancies

Feedings at 3:00 AM, diaper changes, and visits to the pediatrician are not part of most people's vision of adolescence. Yet, every year, tens of thousands of adolescents in the United States give birth.

The good news, though, is that the number of teenage pregnancies is declining. In the last 10 years, the teenage birthrate has dropped 30%. Births to African American teenagers have shown the steepest decline, with births down by more than 40% in a decade. Overall the pregnancy rate of teenagers is 43 births per 1,000, a historic low (see Figure 12-9; Centers for Disease Control and Prevention, 2003; Colen, Geronimus, & Phipps, 2006).

Several factors explain the drop in teenage pregnancies:

- New initiatives have raised awareness among teenagers of the risks of unprotected sex. For example, about two-thirds of high schools in the United States have established comprehensive sex education programs (Villarosa, 2003; Corcoran & Pillai, 2007).

- The rates of sexual intercourse among teenagers have declined. The percent of teenage girls who have ever had sexual intercourse dropped from 51% to 43% from 1991 to 2001.

- The use of condoms and other forms of contraception has increased. For example, 57% of sexually active high school students reported using condoms.

This 16-year-old mother and her child are representative of a major social problem: teenage pregnancy. Why is teenage pregnancy a greater problem in the United States than in other countries?

- Substitutes for sexual intercourse may be more prevalent. For example, data from the 1995 National Survey of Adolescent Males found that about half of 15- to 19-year-old boys reported having received oral sex, an increase of 44% since the late 1980s. It is possible that oral sex, which many teenagers do not even consider "sex," may increasingly be viewed as an alternative to sexual intercourse (Bernstein, 2004).

One thing that apparently hasn't led to a reduction in teenage pregnancies is asking adolescents to take a virginity pledge. Public pledges to refrain from premarital sex—a centerpiece of some forms of sex education—apparently are ineffective. For example, in one study of 12,000 teenagers, 88% reported eventually having sexual intercourse. However, pledges did delay the start of sex an average of 18 months (Bearman & Bruckner, 2004).

Even with the decline in the birth rate for U.S. teenagers, the rate of teenage pregnancy in the United States is 2 to 10 times higher compared to that of other industrialized countries. The results of an unintended pregnancy can be devastating to both mother and child. In comparison to earlier times, teenage mothers today are much less likely to be married. In a high percentage of cases, mothers care for their children without the help of the father. Without financial or emotional support, a mother may have to abandon her own education, and consequently she may be relegated to unskilled, poorly paying jobs for the rest of her life. In other cases, she may develop long-term dependency on welfare. An adolescent mother's physical and mental health may suffer as she faces unrelenting stress due to continual demands on her time (Manlove et al., 2004; Gillmore et al., 2006; Oxford et al., 2006).

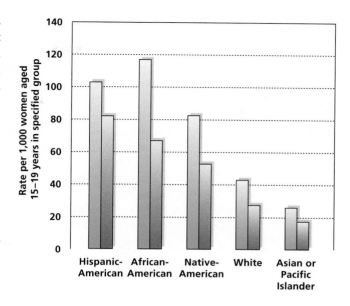

FIGURE 12-9 **TEENAGE PREGNANCY RATES**

The rate of teenage pregnancy in the United States has declined significantly among all ethnic groups.

(*Source:* Centers for Disease Control, 2003.)

Review and Apply

Review

- Dating in adolescence serves a number of functions including intimacy, entertainment, and prestige.

- Masturbation, once viewed very negatively, is now generally regarded as a normal and harmless practice that continues into adulthood.

- Sexual intercourse is a major milestone that most people reach during adolescence. The age of first intercourse reflects cultural differences and has been declining over the last 50 years.

- Sexual orientation, which is most accurately viewed as a continuum rather than categorically, develops as the result of a complex combination of factors.

- Teenage pregnancy is a problem in the United States, with negative consequences for adolescent mothers and their children.

Applying Lifespan Development

- What aspects of the social world of adolescents work against the achievement of true intimacy in dating?

- *From the viewpoint of a medical care provider:* A parent asks you how to prevent her 14-year-old son from engaging in sexual activity until he is older. What would you tell her?

Epilogue

We continued our consideration of adolescence in this chapter, looking at social and personality issues. Self-concept, self-esteem, and identity develop during adolescence, and it can be a period of self-discovery. We looked at adolescents' relationships with family and peers, and at gender, race, and ethnic relations during adolescence. Our discussion concluded with a look at dating, sexuality, and sexual orientation.

Return for a moment to the opening prologue, in which we looked at three adolescents, Carly, Trevor, and Purva. In light of what you now know about adolescent social and personality development, consider the following questions:

1. In what ways does each of these three adolescents appear to be dealing with the issues of self-concept, self-esteem, and identity?

2. How is each one dealing with the issues of belonging and relationships with peers?

3. In what ways is Carly's avoidance of politics an example of the quest for autonomy? Is this evidence of a deep generation gap in Carly's family?

4. Does Trevor show any signs of entering or being in any of Marcia's identity statuses: identity achievement, identity foreclosure, identity diffusion, or moratorium? What evidence is there that he may be exploring his identity?

Looking Back

■ **How does the development of self-concept, self-esteem, and identity proceed during adolescence?**

- During adolescence, self-concept differentiates to encompass others' views as well as one's own and to include multiple aspects simultaneously. Differentiation of self-concept can cause confusion as behaviors reflect a complex definition of the self.

- Adolescents also differentiate their self-esteem, evaluating particular aspects of themselves differently.

- According to Erik Erikson, adolescents are in the identity-versus-identity-confusion stage, seeking to discover their individuality and identity. They may become confused and exhibit dysfunctional reactions, and they may rely for help and information more on friends and peers than on adults.

- James Marcia identifies four identity statuses that individuals may experience in adolescence and in later life: identity achievement, identity foreclosure, identity diffusion, and moratorium.

- The formation of an identity is challenging for members of racial and ethnic minority groups, many of whom appear to be embracing a bicultural identity approach.

■ **What dangers do adolescents face as they deal with the stresses of adolescence?**

- Many adolescents have feelings of sadness and hopelessness, and some experience major depression. Biological, environmental, and social factors contribute to depression, and there are gender, ethnic, and racial differences in its occurrence.

- The rate of adolescent suicide is rising, with suicide now the third most common cause of death in the 15- to 24-year-old bracket.

■ **How does the quality of relationships with family and peers change during adolescence?**

- Adolescents' quest for autonomy often brings confusion and tension to their relationships with their parents, but the actual "generation gap" between parents' and teenagers' attitudes is usually small.

- Peers are important during adolescence because they provide social comparison and reference groups against which to judge social success. Relationships among adolescents are characterized by the need to belong.

- **What are gender, race, and ethnic relations like in adolescence?**

  - During adolescence, boys and girls begin to spend time together in groups and, toward the end of adolescence, to pair off.

  - In general, segregation between people of different races and ethnicities increases in middle and late adolescence, even in schools with a diverse student body.

- **What does it mean to be popular and unpopular in adolescence, and how do adolescents respond to peer pressure?**

  - Degrees of popularity during adolescence include popular and controversial adolescents (on the high end of popularity) and neglected and rejected adolescents (on the low end).

  - Peer pressure is not a simple phenomenon. Adolescents conform to their peers in areas in which they feel their peers are expert, and to adults in areas of adult expertise. As adolescents grow in confidence, their conformity to both peers and adults declines.

- Although most adolescents do not commit crimes, adolescents are disproportionately involved in criminal activities. Juvenile delinquents can be categorized as undersocialized or socialized delinquents.

- **What are the functions and characteristics of dating during adolescence?**

  - During adolescence, dating provides intimacy, entertainment, and prestige. Achieving psychological intimacy, which is difficult at first, becomes easier as adolescents mature, gain confidence, and take relationships more seriously.

- **How does sexuality develop in the adolescent years?**

  - For most adolescents, masturbation is often the first step into sexuality. The age of first intercourse, which is now in the teens, has declined as the double standard has faded and the norm of permissiveness with affection has gained ground. However, as more and more adolescents have become aware of the threat of STDs and AIDS, the rate of sexual intercourse has declined.

  - Sexual orientation develops out of a complex interplay of genetic, physiological, and environmental factors.

Key Terms and Concepts

identity-versus-identity-confusion stage (p. 411)
identity achievement (p. 414)
identity foreclosure (p. 414)
moratorium (p. 414)
identity diffusion (p. 414)
autonomy (p. 420)
generation gap (p. 422)

reference groups (p. 425)
cliques (p. 425)
crowds (p. 425)
sex cleavage (p. 426)
controversial adolescents (p. 428)
rejected adolescents (p. 428)

neglected adolescents (p. 428)
peer pressure (p. 430)
undersocialized delinquents (p. 430)
socialized delinquents (p. 431)
masturbation (p. 433)

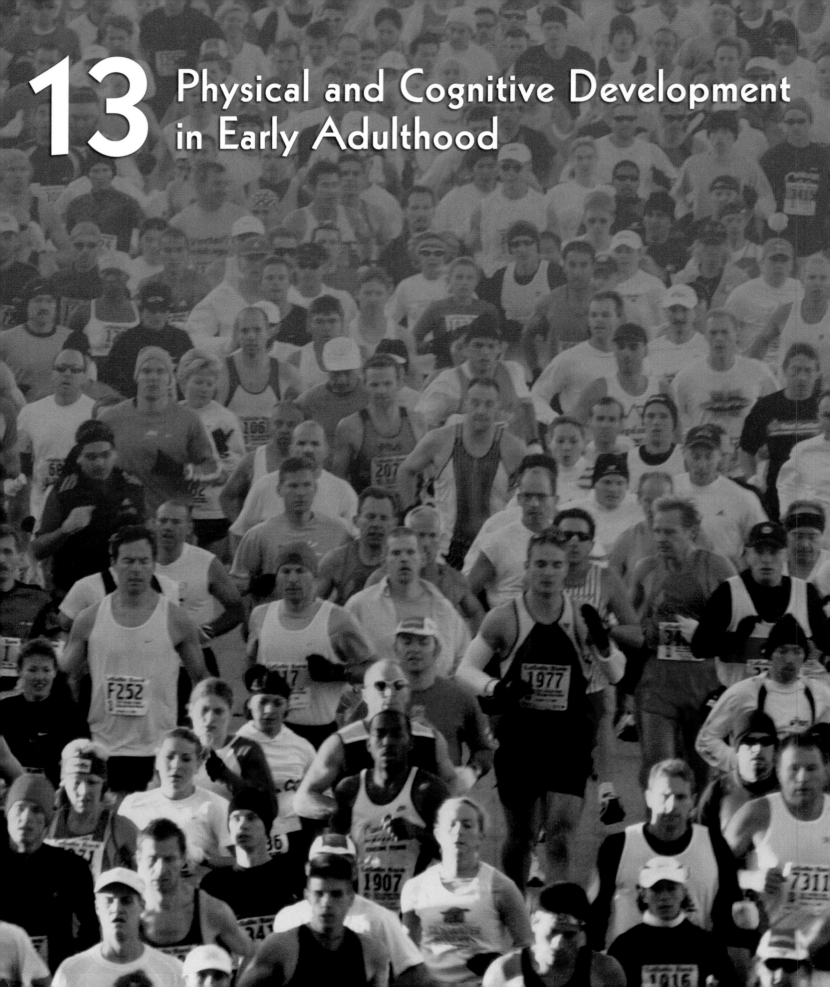

13 Physical and Cognitive Development in Early Adulthood

Chapter Overview

PHYSICAL DEVELOPMENT

Physical Development and the Senses

Motor Functioning, Fitness, and Health: Staying Well

Eating, Nutrition, and Obesity: A Weighty Concern

Physical Disabilities: Coping with Physical Challenge

Stress and Coping: Dealing with Life's Challenges

COGNITIVE DEVELOPMENT

Intellectual Growth in Early Adulthood

Postformal Thought

Perry's Approach to Postformal Thinking

Schaie's Stages of Development

Intelligence: What Matters in Early Adulthood?

Life Events and Cognitive Development

COLLEGE: PURSUING HIGHER EDUCATION

The Demographics of Higher Education

College Adjustment: Reacting to the Demands of College Life

Gender and College Performance

Stereotype Threat and Disidentification with School

Dropping Out of College

Prologue: A Tale of Two Students

For Enrico Vasquez, there was never any doubt: He was headed for college. Enrico, the son of a wealthy Cuban immigrant who had made a fortune in the medical supply business after fleeing Cuba 5 years before Enrico's birth, had always had the importance of education drummed into him by his family. In fact, the question was never *whether* he would go to college, but what college he would be able to get into. As a consequence, Enrico found high school to be a pressure cooker: Every grade and extracurricular activity was seen as helping—or hindering—his chances of admission to a "good" college.

***

Armando Williams's letter of acceptance to Dallas County Community College is framed on the wall of his mother's apartment. To her, the letter represents nothing short of a miracle, an answer to her prayers. Growing up in a neighborhood saturated with drugs and drive-by shootings, Armando had always been a hard worker and a "good boy," in his mother's view. But when he was growing up, she never even entertained the possibility of his making it to college. To see him reach this stage in his education fills her with joy.

College campuses, like the rest of society, reflect increasing diversity.

Although Enrico Vasquez's and Armando Williams's lives have followed two very different paths, they share the single goal of obtaining a college education. They represent the increasing diversity in family background, socioeconomic status, race, and ethnicity that is coming to characterize college populations today.

Whether they attend college or not, people in early adulthood are at the height of their cognitive abilities. Physically, too, they are at their peak. The body acts as if it's on automatic pilot: Physical health and fitness are never better.

At the same time, though, considerable development goes on during early adulthood, which starts at the end of adolescence (around age 20) and continues until roughly the start of middle age (around age 40). As we see throughout this and the following chapter, significant changes occur as new opportunities arise and people choose to take on (or to forgo) a new set of roles as spouse, parent, and worker.

This chapter focuses on physical and cognitive development during this period. It begins with a look at the physical changes that extend into early adulthood. Though more subtle than the physical changes of adolescence, growth continues and various motor skills change as well. We look at diet and weight, examining the prevalence of obesity in this age group. We also consider stress and coping during the early years of adulthood.

The chapter then turns to cognitive development. Although traditional approaches to cognitive development regarded adulthood as an inconsequential plateau, we will examine some new theories that suggest that significant cognitive growth occurs during adulthood. We also consider the nature of adult intelligence and the impact of life events on cognitive development.

The last part of the chapter considers college, the institution that shapes intellectual growth for those who attend. We examine who goes to college, and how gender and race can influence achievement. We end by looking at some reasons why students drop out of college and examining some of the adjustment problems that college students face.

After reading this chapter, you will be able to answer these questions:

- How does the body develop during early adulthood, and to what risks are young adults exposed?

- What are the effects of stress, and what can be done about it?

- Does cognitive development continue in young adulthood?

- How is intelligence defined today, and what causes cognitive growth in young adults?

- Who attends college today, and how is the college population changing?

- What do students learn in college, and what difficulties do they face?

Looking Ahead

Physical Development

Grady McKinnon grinned as his mountain bike left the ground briefly. The 27-year-old financial auditor was delighted to be out for a camping and biking weekend with four of his college buddies. Grady had been worried that an upcoming deadline at work would make him miss this trip. When they were still in school, Grady and his friends used to go biking nearly every weekend. But jobs, marriage—and even a child for one of the guys—started taking up a lot of their attention. This was their only trip this summer. He was sure glad he hadn't missed it.

Grady and his friends were probably in the best physical condition of their lives when they first started to go mountain biking regularly in college. Even now, as Grady's life becomes more complicated and sports starts to take a backseat to work and other personal demands, he is still enjoying one of the healthiest periods of his life. As we will see, although most people, like

Grady, reach the height of their physical capacities in young adulthood, at the same time, they must try to cope with the stress produced by the challenges of their adult lives.

senescence   the natural physical decline brought about by aging.

Physical Development and the Senses

In most respects, physical development and maturation are complete at early adulthood. Most people are at the peak of their physical capabilities. They have attained their full height, and their limbs are proportional to their size, rendering the gangliness of adolescence a memory. People in their early 20s tend to be healthy, vigorous, and energetic. Although **senescence,** the natural physical decline brought about by increasing age, has begun, age-related changes are not usually very obvious to people until later in their lives.

At the same time, some growth still is going on during early adulthood. For example, some people, particularly late maturers, continue to gain height in their early 20s.

Certain parts of the body also come to reach full maturity. For example, the brain grows in both size and weight, reaching its maximum during early adulthood (and then subsequently contracting in size later in life). The gray matter of the brain continues to be pruned back, and myelination (the process in which nerve cells are insulated by a covering of fat cells) continues to increase. These changes in the brain help support the cognitive advances that occur during early adulthood (Sowell et al., 2001; Toga, Thompson, & Sowell, 2006).

The senses are as sharp as they will ever be. Although there are changes in the elasticity of the eye—a continuation of an aging process that may begin as early as age 10—they are so minor that they produce no deterioration in vision. It is not until the 40s that eyesight changes sufficiently to be noticeable—as we will see in Chapter 15.

Hearing, too, is at its peak. However, a gender difference emerges: Women can detect higher tones more readily than men (McGuinness, 1972). In general, though, the hearing of both men and women is quite good. Under quiet conditions, the average young adult can hear the ticking of a watch 20 feet away.

The other senses, including taste, smell, and sensitivity to touch and pain, are quite good, and they remain that way throughout early adulthood. These senses do not begin to deteriorate until the 40s or 50s.

Motor Functioning, Fitness, and Health: Staying Well

If you are a professional athlete, most people probably consider you to be over the hill by the time you leave your 20s. Although there are notable exceptions (think of baseball star Roger Clemens, who continued pitching into his 40s), even athletes who train constantly tend to lose their physical edge once they reach their 30s. In some sports, the peak passes even sooner. Swimmers are at their best in their late teens, and gymnasts peak even earlier (Schultz & Curnow, 1988).

The rest of us are also at the peak of our psychomotor abilities during early adulthood. Reaction time is quicker, muscle strength is greater, and eye–hand coordination is better than at any other period (Salthouse, 1993; Sliwinski et al., 1994).

Physical Fitness.   The physical prowess that typically characterizes early adulthood doesn't come naturally, however; nor does it come to everyone. In order to reach their physical potential, people must exercise and maintain a proper diet.

The benefits of exercise are hardly secret: In the United States, yoga and aerobics classes, Nautilus workouts, and jogging and swimming are seemingly common activities. Yet, the conspicuousness of exercise activities is misleading. Less than 10% of Americans are

People in their early twenties tend to be healthy, vigorous, and energetic, but they often experience quite a lot of stress.

It's not just professional athletes such as tennis star Serena Williams and Yankee baseball great Derek Jeter who are at the height of athleticism in early adulthood. Most everyone reaches their peak of physical fitness during this period.

FIGURE 13-1 THE RESULT OF FITNESS: LONGEVITY

The greater the fitness level, the lower the death rate tends to be for both men and women.

(*Source:* Blair et al., 1989.)

involved in sufficient regular exercise to keep them in good physical shape, and less than a quarter engage in even moderate regular exercise. Furthermore, the opportunity to exercise is largely an upper- and middle-class phenomenon; people of lower socioeconomic status (SES) often have neither the time nor the money to engage in regular exercise (Estabrook, Lee, & Gyurcsik, 2003; Bove & Olson, 2006; Delva, O'Malley, & Johnston, 2006; Proper, Cerin, & Owen, 2006).

The amount of exercise required to yield significant health benefits is not enormous. According to recommendations from the American College of Sports Medicine and the Centers for Disease Control and Prevention, people should accumulate at least 30 minutes of moderate physical activity at least 5 days a week. The time spent exercising can be continuous or occur in bouts of at least 10 minutes, as long as it totals 30 minutes each day. Moderate activity includes walking briskly at 3 to 4 mph, biking at speeds up to 10 mph, golfing while carrying or pulling clubs, fishing by casting from shore, playing ping pong, or canoeing at 2 to 4 mph. Even common household chores, such as weeding, vacuuming, and mowing with a power mower, provide moderate exercise (American College of Sports Medicine, 1997).

The advantages to those who do become involved in regular exercise programs are many. Exercise increases cardiovascular fitness, meaning that the heart and circulatory system operate more efficiently. Furthermore, lung capacity increases, raising endurance. Muscles become stronger, and the body is more flexible and maneuverable. The range of movement is greater, and the muscles, tendons, and ligaments are more elastic. Moreover, exercise during this period helps reduce *osteoporosis*, the thinning of the bones, in later life.

Exercise also may optimize the immune response of the body, helping it fight off disease. Exercise may even decrease stress and anxiety and reduce depression. It can provide people with a sense of control over their bodies, as well as impart a feeling of accomplishment (Mutrie, 1997; Faulkner & Biddle, 2004; Harris, Cronkite, & Moos, 2006; Wise et al., 2006).

Regular exercise offers the possibility of another, ultimately more important, reward: It is associated with increased longevity (see Figure 13-1; Stevens et al., 2002).

Health.   Although a lack of exercise may produce poor health (and worse), health risks in general are relatively slight during early adulthood. During this period, people are less susceptible to colds and other minor illnesses than they were as children, and when they do come down with illnesses, they usually get over them quickly.

Adults in their 20s and 30s stand a higher risk of dying from accidents, primarily those involving automobiles, than from most other causes. But there are other killers: Among the leading sources of death for people age 25 to 34 are AIDS, cancer, heart disease, and suicide. Amid the grim statistics of mortality, the age 35 represents a significant milestone. It is at that point that illness and disease overtake accidents as the leading cause of death—the first time this is true since infancy.

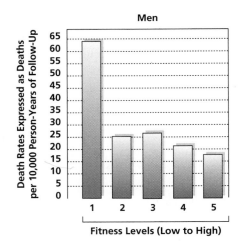

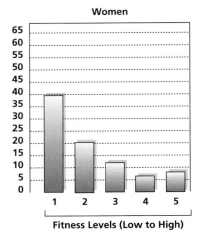

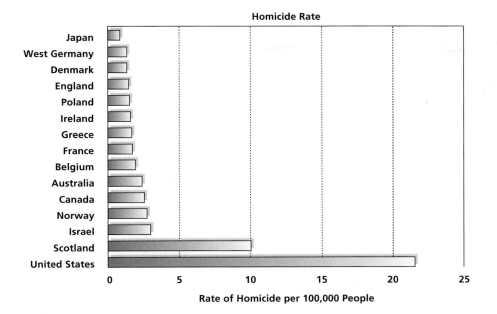

Homicide Rate

Rate of Homicide per 100,000 People

FIGURE 13-2 TRACKING MURDER

The murder rate (per 100,000 men) is far higher in the United States than in any other developed country. What features of U.S. society contribute to this state of affairs?

(*Source:* Fingerhut & Kleinman, 1990.)

Not all people fare equally well during early adulthood. Lifestyle decisions, including the use—or abuse—of alcohol, tobacco, or drugs or engaging in unprotected sex, can hasten *secondary aging*, physical declines brought about by environmental factors or an individual's behavioral choices. These substances can also increase a young adult's risk of dying from illness and disease.

As the definition of secondary aging implies, cultural factors, including gender and race, are also related to the risk of dying in young adulthood. For instance, men are more apt to die than women, primarily due to their higher involvement in automobile accidents. Furthermore, African Americans have twice the death rate of Caucasians, and minorities in general have a higher likelihood of dying than the Caucasian majority.

Another major cause of death for men in this age group is violence, particularly in the United States. The murder rate is significantly higher in the United States than in any other developed country (see Figure 13-2). Compare, for instance, the U.S. murder rate of 21.9 per 100,000 men to Japan's 0.5 murders per 100,000 men—a difference in magnitude of more than

The murder rate in the United States is significantly higher than in any other developed country.

4,000%. Statistics like this one have led some observers to conclude that violence is "as American as apple pie" (Fingerhut & Kleinman, 1990; Berkowitz, 1993).

Murder rates also depend significantly on racial factors. Although murder is the fifth most frequent cause of death for young adult white Americans, it is *the* most likely cause of death for African Americans, and it is a significant factor for Hispanic Americans. In some areas of the country, a young black male has a higher probability of being murdered than a soldier in the Vietnam War had of being killed. Overall, an African American male has a 1 in 21 chance of being murdered during his lifetime. In contrast, a white male has a 1 in 131 chance of being murdered (Centers for Disease Control, 1991; Berkowitz, 1993; Triandis, 1994).

Cultural factors influence not only causes of death, but, as examined in the *Developmental Diversity* feature, also young adults' lifestyles and health-related behavior.

Developmental Diversity

How Cultural Beliefs Influence Health and Health Care

Manolita recently suffered a heart attack. She was advised by her doctor to change her eating and activity habits or face the risk of another life-threatening heart attack. During the period that followed, Manolita dramatically changed her eating and activity habits. She also began going to church and praying extensively. After a recent check-up, Manolita is in the best shape of her life. What are some of the reasons for Manolita's amazing recovery? (Murguia, Peterson, & Zea, 1997, p. 16)

After reading this passage, would you conclude that Manolita recovered her health because (a) she changed her eating and activity habits; (b) she became a better person; (c) God was testing her faith; or (d) her doctor prescribed the correct changes?

In response to a survey asking this question, more than two-thirds of Latino immigrants from Central America, South America, or the Caribbean believed that "God was testing her faith" had a moderate or great effect on her recovery, although most also agreed that a change in eating and activity habits was important (Murguia et al., 1997).

The findings help explain why Latinos are the least likely of any Western ethnic group to seek the help of a physician when they are ill. According to psychologists Alejandro Murguia, Rolf Peterson, and Maria Zea (1997), cultural health beliefs, along with demographic and psychological barriers, reduce people's use of physicians and medical care.

Specifically, they suggest that Latinos, as well as members of some other non-Western groups, are more likely than non-Hispanic whites to believe in supernatural causes of illness. For instance, members of these groups may attribute illness to a punishment from God, a lack of faith, or a hex. Such beliefs may reduce the motivation to seek medical care from a physician (Landrine & Klonoff, 1994). Money also plays a role. Lower socioeconomic status reduces the ability to pay for traditional medical care, which is expensive and may indirectly encourage the continued reliance on less-traditional and less-expensive methods. In addition, the lower level of involvement in the mainstream culture that is characteristic of recent immigrants to the United States is associated with a lower likelihood of visiting a physician and obtaining mainstream medical care (Pachter & Weller, 1993; Landrine & Klonoff, 1994; Antshel & Antshel, 2002).

Health-care providers need to take cultural beliefs into account when treating members of different cultural groups. For example, if a patient believes that the source of his or her illness is a spell cast by a jealous romantic rival, the patient may not comply with medical regimens that ignore that perceived source. To provide effective health care, then, health care providers must be sensitive to such cultural health beliefs.

Eating, Nutrition, and Obesity: A Weighty Concern

Most young adults know which foods are nutritionally sound and how to maintain a balanced diet; they just don't bother to follow the rules—even though the rules are not all that difficult to follow.

Good Nutrition.   According to guidelines provided by the U.S. Department of Agriculture, people can achieve good nutrition by eating foods that are low in fat, including vegetables, fruits, whole-grain foods, fish, poultry, lean meats, and low-fat dairy products. In addition, whole-grain foods and cereal products, vegetables (including dried beans and peas), and fruit are beneficial in another way: They help people raise the amount of complex carbohydrates and fiber they ingest. Milk and other sources of calcium are also needed to prevent osteoporosis. Finally, people should reduce salt intake (USDA, 2006).

During adolescence, a poor diet does not always present a significant problem. For instance, teenagers don't suffer too much from a diet high in junk foods and fat, because they are undergoing such tremendous growth. The story changes when they reach young adulthood, however. With growth tapering off, young adults must reduce the caloric intake they were used to during adolescence.

Many do not. Although most people enter young adulthood with bodies of average height and weight, they gradually put on weight if their poor dietary habits remain unchanged (Insel & Roth, 1991).

Obesity.   The adult population of the United States is growing—in more ways than one. Obesity, defined as body weight that is 20% or more above the average weight for a person of a given height, is on the rise in the United States. In just the 1-year period from 1998 to 1999, obesity increased 6%. Some 12% of those age 18 to 29 are obese, and the numbers edge up throughout adulthood: As age increases, more and more people are classified as obese (see Figure 13-3; Centers for Disease Control and Prevention, 2000).

Weight control is a difficult, and often losing, battle for many young adults. Most people who diet ultimately regain the weight they have lost, and they become involved in a see-saw cycle of weight gain and loss. In fact, some obesity experts now argue that the rate of dieting failure is so great that people may want to avoid dieting altogether. Instead, if people eat the foods they really want in moderation, they may be able to avoid the binge eating that often occurs when diets fail. Even though obese people may never reach their desired weight, they may, according to this reasoning, ultimately control their weight more effectively (Polivy & Herman, 2002; Lowe, 2004; Putterman & Linden, 2004; Quatromoni et al., 2006; Annunziato & Lowe, 2007; see also the *Careers in Lifespan Development* box).

Some 12% of those age 18 to 29 are obese, and the proportion of those obese increases throughout adulthood.

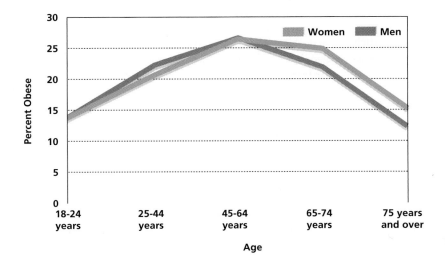

FIGURE 13-3   OBESITY ON THE RISE

In spite of greater awareness of the importance of good nutrition, obesity among American adults has risen dramatically over the past decade. Why do you think this rise has occurred?

(*Source:* Centers for Disease Control and Prevention, 2001.)

Careers in Lifespan Development

Martin Binks, Behavioral Health Clinician

Education: BA, Psychology, Concordia University, Montreal, Quebec; MA and PhD, Clinical Psychology, Farleigh Dickinson University, Teaneck, New Jersey

Position: Director of Behavioral Health, Duke Diet and Fitness Center

Home: Durham, North Carolina

Despite the popularity of the weight control programs such as the Atkins and South Beach diets, few people are able to lose weight on their own. In fact, the incidence of obesity has doubled in the last 20 years.

As a result, more effective interventions in treating obesity are required to not only deal with gains in weight, but also to treat a variety of other medical problems associated with obesity. The rise in obesity has led to the establishment of a number of organizations, such as the Duke Diet and Fitness Center, to treat people with weight problems.

"The client populations that we serve face severe obesity and have a body mass index (BMI) of 40 or greater," said behavioral health director Martin Binks, adding that the average BMI is about 25.

"We offer various types of interventions, and we make sure the individual's needs are met," Binks said. "Some who come have fairly active lifestyles in terms of fitness, while others have had their weight render them inactive with significant joint pain or arthritis."

The Duke Center is an entirely residential facility, and each person attends a 5-day intensive evaluation, after which a plan of treatment is recommended.

"In most cases, the primary intervention is with lifestyle," he said. "We use a cognitive behavioral approach that includes mind/body strategies, meditation, and stress management. We try to find a balance between avoiding stress and dealing with it.

"Very often people use food as a coping mechanism and this makes eating an emotional issue," Binks noted. "We try to help people identify their barriers and make some changes in the structure of their lives."

The Duke Diet and Fitness Center, affiliated with Duke University, currently serves between 60 and 80 patients at a time. Binks noted that the approach to treating obesity has dramatically changed over the years.

"There have been major evolutions in obesity treatment," he said. "In the 1970s the original approach focused on drastically reducing calories, and less on lifestyle changes. Contemporary innovations involve an increase in the health psychology and behavioral medicine components, and utilizing mind/body approaches. These have been important improvements."

Physical Disabilities: Coping with Physical Challenge

Over 50 million people in the United States are physically or mentally challenged, according to the official definition of *disability*—a condition that substantially limits a major life activity such as walking or vision. People with disabilities face a difficult, challenging path.

Statistics paint a picture of a minority group that is undereducated and underemployed. Fewer than 10% of people with major handicaps have finished high school, fewer than 25% of disabled men and 15% of disabled women work full time, and unemployment rates are high. Furthermore, even if people with disabilities do find work, the positions they find are often routine and low-paying jobs (Schaefer & Lamm, 1992; Albrecht, 2005).

Individuals with disabilities face several kinds of barriers to leading full lives that are completely integrated into the broader society. Some barriers are physical. Despite passage in 1990 of the landmark Americans with Disabilities Act (ADA), which mandates full access to public establishments such as stores, office buildings, hotels, and theaters, people in wheelchairs still cannot gain access to many older buildings.

Another barrier—sometimes harder to overcome than a physical one—is prejudice and discrimination. People with disabilities sometimes face pity or avoidance from nondisabled people. Some nondisabled people focus so much on the disability that they overlook other characteristics, reacting to a person with a disability only as a problem category and not as an individual. Others treat people with disabilities as if they were children. Ultimately, such treatment can take its toll on the way people with disabilities think about themselves (French & Swain, 1997).

Despite the passage of the Americans with Disabilities Act (ADA), people with physical disabilities still cannot gain access to many older buildings.

Stress and Coping: Dealing with Life's Challenges

It's 5:00 PM. Rosa Convoy, a 25-year-old single mother, has just finished her work as a receptionist at a dentist's office and is on her way home. She has exactly 2 hours to pick up her daughter Zoe from child care, get home, make and eat dinner, pick up and return with a babysitter from down the street, say goodbye to Zoe, and get to her 7 o'clock programming class at a local community college. It's a marathon she runs every Tuesday and Thursday night, and she knows she doesn't have a second to spare if she wants to reach the class on time.

It doesn't take an expert to know what Rosa Convoy is experiencing: **stress,** the physical and emotional response to events that threaten or challenge us. How well Rosa, and everyone, can cope with stress depends on a complex interplay between physical and psychological factors (Hetherington & Blechman, 1996).

Stress is a part of nearly everyone's existence, and our lives are crowded with events and circumstances, known as stressors, that produce threats to our well-being. Stressors need not be unpleasant events: Even the happiest events, such as starting a long-sought job or planning a wedding, can produce stress (Crowley, Hayslip, & Hobdy, 2003; Shimizu & Pelham, 2004).

Researchers in the new field of **psychoneuroimmunology** (**PNI**)—the study of the relationship among the brain, the immune system, and psychological factors—have found that stress produces several outcomes. The most immediate is typically a biological reaction, as certain hormones, secreted by the adrenal glands, cause a rise in heart rate, blood pressure, respiration rate, and sweating. In some situations, these immediate effects may be beneficial because they produce an "emergency reaction" in the sympathetic nervous system by which people are better able to defend themselves from a sudden, threatening situation (Parkes, 1997; Ray, 2004).

On the other hand, long-term, continuous exposure to stressors may result in a reduction of the body's ability to deal with stress. As stress-related hormones are constantly secreted, the heart, blood vessels, and other body tissues may deteriorate. As a consequence, people become more susceptible to diseases as their ability to fight off germs declines (Cohen, Tyrrell, & Smith, 1997; Lundberg, 2006).

stress   the physical and emotional response to events that threaten or challenge us.

psychoneuroimmunology (PNI)   the study of the relationship among the brain, the immune system, and psychological factors.

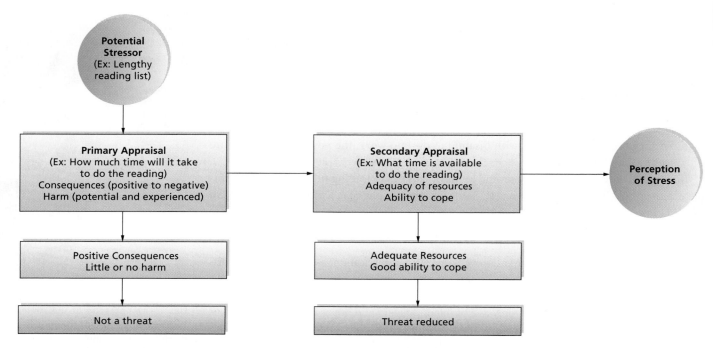

FIGURE 13-4   STEPS IN THE PERCEPTION OF STRESS

The way an individual appraises a potential stressor determines whether the individual will experience stress.

(*Source:* Adapted from Kaplan, Sallis, & Patterson, 1993.)

The effects of major stress stemming from situations like that facing this woman, whose home was destroyed by fire, can be long-lasting.

primary appraisal   the assessment of an event to determine whether its implications are positive, negative, or neutral.

secondary appraisal   the assessment of whether one's coping abilities and resources are adequate to overcome the harm, threat, or challenge posed by the potential stressor.

The Origins of Stress.   Experienced job interviewers, college counselors, and owners of bridal shops all know that not everyone reacts the same way to a potentially stressful event. What makes the difference in people's reactions? According to psychologists Arnold Lazarus and Susan Folkman, people move through a series of stages, depicted in Figure 13-4, that determine whether they will experience stress (Lazarus & Folkman, 1984; Lazarus, 1968, 1991).

Primary appraisal is the first step—the individual's assessment of an event to determine whether its implications are positive, negative, or neutral. If a person sees the event as primarily negative, he or she appraises it in terms of the harm that it has caused in the past, how threatening it is likely to be, and how likely it is that the challenge can be resisted successfully. For example, you are likely to feel differently about an upcoming French test if you passed the last one with flying colors than you would if you did poorly.

Secondary appraisal follows. **Secondary appraisal** is the person's answer to the question, "Can I handle it?," an assessment of whether his or her coping abilities and resources are adequate to overcome the challenge posed by the potential stressor. At this point in the process, people try to determine if they will be able to meet the dangers in the situation. If resources are lacking, and the potential threat is great, they will experience stress. A traffic ticket is upsetting to anyone, but to those for whom the fine is an economic hardship, the stress is considerably greater.

Stress varies with the person's appraisal, and that appraisal varies with the person's temperament and circumstances. There are some general principles that help predict when an event will be appraised as stressful. Psychologist Shelley Taylor (1991) suggests the following:

- Events and circumstances that produce negative emotions are more likely to lead to stress than events that are positive. For example, planning for the adoption of a new baby produces less stress than dealing with the illness of a loved one.

- Situations that are uncontrollable or unpredictable are more likely to produce stress than those that can be controlled and predicted. Professors who give surprise quizzes in their classes, then, produce more stress than those whose quizzes are scheduled in advance.

- Events and circumstances that are ambiguous and confusing produce more stress than those that are unambiguous and clear. If people cannot easily understand a situation, they must struggle simply to comprehend it, rather than dealing with it directly. Taking a new job that does not have a clear job description is likely to produce more stress than starting in a well-defined position.

- People who must accomplish simultaneously many tasks that strain their capabilities are more likely to experience stress than those who have fewer things to do. A graduate student who is expecting her first child during the same month she is scheduled to take her dissertation oral exam is likely to be feeling quite a bit of stress, for example.

The Consequences of Stress. Over the long run, the constant wear and tear caused by the physiological arousal that occurs as the body tries to fight off stress produces negative effects. If enough stress is experienced, it can have formidable costs. For instance, headaches, backaches, skin rashes, indigestion, chronic fatigue, and even the common cold are stress-related illnesses (Cohen, Tyrrell, & Smith, 1993, 1997; Suinn, 2001).

In addition, the immune system—the complex of organs, glands, and cells that constitutes our bodies' natural line of defense in fighting disease—may be damaged by stress. Because stress overstimulates the immune system, it may begin to attack the body itself, damaging healthy tissue, rather than fighting invading bacteria and viruses. In addition, stress can prevent the immune system from reacting effectively, which can permit germs to reproduce more easily or allow cancer cells to spread more rapidly (Ader, Felten, & Cohen, 2001; Miller & Cohen, 2001; Cohen et al., 2002).

Consequently, stress may lead to **psychosomatic disorders,** medical problems caused by the interaction of psychological, emotional, and physical difficulties. For instance, ulcers, asthma, arthritis, and high blood pressure may—although not invariably—be produced by stress (Lepore, Palsane, & Evans, 1991).

In sum, stress affects people in a number of ways. It can increase the risk of becoming ill, it may actually produce illness, it makes it more difficult to recover from illness, and it may reduce one's ability to cope with future stress. (To get a sense of how much stress you have in your own life, complete the questionnaire in Table 13-1.) Keep in mind that although stress occurs at all stages of life, as we age, we may learn to cope with stress better. As we see next, coping takes a variety of forms.

psychosomatic disorders medical problems caused by the interaction of psychological, emotional, and physical difficulties.

Although we commonly think of negative events, such as auto mishaps, as leading to stress, even welcome events, like getting married, can be stressful.

Table 13-1 How Stressed Are You?

Test your level of stress by answering these questions, and adding the score from each box. Questions apply to the last month only. A key below will help you determine the extent of your stress.

1. How often have you been upset because of something that happened unexpectedly?
   □ 0 = never, 1 = almost never, 2 = sometimes, 3 = fairly often, 4 = very often

2. How often have you felt that you were unable to control the important things in your life?
   □ 0 = never, 1 = almost never, 2 = sometimes, 3 = fairly often, 4 = very often

3. How often have you felt nervous and "stressed"?
   □ 0 = never, 1 = almost never, 2 = sometimes, 3 = fairly often, 4 = very often

4. How often have you felt confident about your ability to handle your personal problems?
   □ 4 = never, 3 = almost never, 2 = sometimes, 1 = fairly often, 0 = very often

5. How often have you felt that things were going your way?
   □ 4 = never, 3 = almost never, 2 = sometimes, 1 = fairly often, 0 = very often

6. How often have you been able to control irritations in your life?
   □ 4 = never, 3 = almost never, 2 = sometimes, 1 = fairly often, 0 = very often

7. How often have you found that you could not cope with all the things that you had to do?
   □ 0 = never, 1 = almost never, 2 = sometimes, 3 = fairly often, 4 = very often

8. How often have you felt that you were on top of things?
   □ 4 = never, 3 = almost never, 2 = sometimes, 1 = fairly often, 0 = very often

9. How often have you been angered because of things that were outside your control?
   □ 0 = never, 1 = almost never, 2 = sometimes, 3 = fairly often, 4 = very often

10. How often have you felt difficulties were piling up so high that you could not overcome them?
    □ 0 = never, 1 = almost never, 2 = sometimes, 3 = fairly often, 4 = very often

How You Measure Up

Stress levels vary among individuals—compare your total score to the averages below:

Age		Gender	
18–29	14.2	Men	12.1
30–44	13.0	Women	13.7
45–54	12.6		
55–64	11.9		
65 & over	12.0		

Marital Status

Widowed	12.6
Married or living with	12.4
Single or never wed	14.1
Divorced	14.7
Separated	16.6

(*Source:* Sheldon Cohen, Dept. of Psychology, Carnegie Mellon University.)

Coping with Stress.   Stress is a normal part of life, something that everyone encounters. Yet, some young adults are better than others at **coping,** the effort to control, reduce, or learn to tolerate the threats that lead to stress. What is the key to successful coping?

Some people use problem-focused coping, by which they attempt to manage a stressful problem or situation by directly changing the situation to make it less stressful. For example, a man who is having on-the-job difficulties may speak to his boss and ask that his responsibilities be modified, or he may look for another job.

Other people employ *emotion-focused coping*, which involves the conscious regulation of emotion. For instance, a mother who is having trouble finding appropriate care for her child while she is at work may tell herself that she should look at the bright side: At least she has a job in a difficult economy (Folkman & Lazarus, 1980, 1988).

Sometimes people acknowledge that they are in a stressful situation that cannot be changed, but they cope by managing their reactions. For example, they may take up meditation or exercise to reduce their physical reactions.

Coping is also aided by the presence of *social support*, assistance and comfort supplied by others. Turning to others in the face of stress can provide both emotional support (in the form

coping the effort to control, reduce, or learn to tolerate the threats that lead to stress.

of a shoulder to cry on) and practical, tangible support (such as a temporary financial loan) (Spiegel, 1993; Giacobbi, Lynn, & Wetherington, 2004; Jackson, 2006).

Finally, even if people do not consciously cope with stress, some psychologists suggest that they may use unconscious defensive coping mechanisms of which they are unaware and that aid in stress reduction. **Defensive coping** involves unconscious strategies that distort or deny the true nature of a situation. For instance, people may deny the seriousness of a threat, trivializing a life-threatening illness, or they may say to themselves that academic failure on a series of tests is unimportant.

Another type of defensive coping is emotional insulation. In *emotional insulation*, people unconsciously try to prevent themselves from experiencing emotions. By attempting to remain unaffected by negative (or positive) experiences, they try to avoid the pain brought about by the experience. If defensive coping becomes a habitual response to stress, it can prevent the person from dealing with the reality of the situation by offering a way to avoid or ignore the problem (Ormont, 2001).

In some cases, people use drugs or alcohol to escape from stressful situations. Like defensive coping, drinking and drug use do not help address the situation causing the stress, and they can increase a person's difficulties. For example, people may become addicted to the substances that initially provided them with a pleasurable sense of escape.

Hardiness, Resilience, and Coping.   The success with which young adults deal with stress depends in part on their *coping style*, their general tendency to deal with stress in a particular way. For example, people with a "hardy" coping style are especially successful in dealing with stress. **Hardiness** is a personality characteristic associated with a lower rate of stress-related illness.

Hardy individuals are take-charge people who revel in life's challenges. It is not surprising, then, that people who are high in hardiness are more resistant to stress-related illness than those who show less hardiness. Hardy people react to potentially threatening stressors with optimism, feeling that they can respond effectively. By turning threatening situations into

defensive coping   coping that involves unconscious strategies that distort or deny the true nature of a situation.

hardiness   a personality characteristic associated with a lower rate of stress-related illness.

Assistance and comfort by others in times of stress can provide both emotional and practical support.

challenging ones, they are less apt to experience high levels of stress (Horner, 1998; Maddi, 2006; Maddi et al., 2006).

For people who face the most profound of life's difficulties—such as the unexpected death of a loved one or a permanent injury such as spinal cord damage—a key factor in their reactions is their level of resilience. As we first discussed in Chapter 8, *resilience* is the ability to withstand, overcome, and actually thrive following profound adversity (Bonanno, 2004; Werner, 2005; Norlander et al., 2005; Kim-Cohen, 2007).

Resilient young adults tend to be easy-going, good-natured, and have good social and communication skills. They are independent, feeling that they can shape their own fate and are not dependent on others or luck. In short, they work with what they have and make the best of whatever situation in which they find themselves (Humphreys, 2003; Spencer et al., 2003; Deshields et al., 2005; Friborg et al., 2005).

Becoming an Informed Consumer of Development

Coping with Stress

Although no single formula can cover all cases of stress, some general guidelines can help all of us cope with the stress that is part of our lives. Among them are the following (Sacks, 1993; Kaplan, Sallis, & Patterson, 1993; Bionna, 2006).

- Seek control over the situation producing the stress. Putting yourself in charge of a situation that is producing stress can take you a long way toward coping with it. For example, if you are feeling stress about an upcoming test, do something about it—such as starting to study.
- Redefine "threat" as "challenge." Changing the definition of a situation can make it seem less threatening. "Look for the silver lining" is not bad advice. For example, if you're fired, look at it as an opportunity to get a new, and potentially better, job.
- Find social support. Almost any difficulty can be faced more easily with the help of others. Friends, family members, and even telephone hotlines staffed by trained counselors can provide significant support. (For help in identifying appropriate hotlines, the U.S. Public Health Service maintains a "master" toll-free number that can provide phone numbers and addresses of many national groups. Call 800-336-4794.)
- Use relaxation techniques. Reducing the physiological arousal brought about by stress can be a particularly effective way of coping with stress. A variety of techniques that produce relaxation, such as transcendental meditation, Zen and yoga, progressive muscle relaxation, and even hypnosis, have been shown to be effective in reducing stress. One that works particularly well was devised by physician Herbert Benson and is illustrated in Table 13-2 (Benson, 1993).
- Try to maintain a healthy lifestyle that will reinforce your body's natural coping mechanisms. Exercise, eat nutritiously, get enough sleep, and avoid or moderate use of alcohol, tobacco, or other drugs.
- If all else fails, keep in mind that a life without any stress at all would be a dull one. Stress is a natural part of life, and successfully coping with it can be a gratifying experience.

Table 13-2	How to Elicit the Relaxation Response

Some general advice on regular practice of the relaxation response:

- Try to find 10 to 20 minutes in your daily routine; before breakfast is a good time.
- Sit comfortably.
- For the period you will practice, try to arrange your life so you won't have distractions. Put on the answering machine, and ask someone else to watch the kids.
- Time yourself by glancing periodically at a clock or watch (but don't set an alarm). Commit yourself to a specific length of practice, and try to stick to it.

There are several approaches to eliciting the relaxation response. Here is one standard set of instructions:

Step 1. Pick a focus word or short phrase that's firmly rooted in your personal belief system. For example, a nonreligious individual might choose a neutral word like *one* or *peace* or *love*. A Christian person desiring to use a prayer could pick the opening words of Psalm 23, *The Lord is my shepherd*; a Jewish person could choose *Shalom*.

Step 2. Sit quietly in a comfortable position.

Step 3. Close your eyes.

Step 4. Relax your muscles.

Step 5. Breathe slowly and naturally, repeating your focus word or phrase silently as you exhale.

Step 6. Throughout, assume a passive attitude. Don't worry about how well you're doing. When other thoughts come to mind, simply say to yourself, "Oh, well," and gently return to the repetition.

Step 7. Continue for 10 to 20 minutes. You may open your eyes to check the time, but do not use an alarm. When you finish, sit quietly for a minute or so, at first with your eyes closed and later with your eyes open. Then do not stand for one or two minutes.

Step 8. Practice the technique once or twice a day.

(*Source:* Benson, 1993.)

Review and Apply

Review

- By young adulthood, the body and the senses are at their peak, but growth is proceeding, particularly in the brain.
- Young adults are generally as fit and healthy as they will ever be, and accidents present the greatest risk of death. In the United States, violence is also a significant risk, particularly for nonwhite males.
- Even in young adulthood, health must be maintained by proper diet and exercise. Obesity is increasingly a problem for young adults.
- People with physical disabilities face not only physical barriers but also psychological barriers caused by prejudice and stereotyping.
- Stress, which is a healthy reaction in small doses, can be harmful to body and mind if it is frequent or of long duration.

Applying Lifespan Development

- Describe and discuss your own coping style(s). What do you do when faced with stress? What works and what doesn't?
- *From a social worker's perspective:* What sorts of interpersonal barriers do people with disabilities face? How can those barriers be removed?

The nature of thought changes qualitatively during early adulthood.

Cognitive Development

Ben is known to be a heavy drinker, especially when he goes to parties. Tyra, Ben's wife, warns him that if he comes home drunk one more time, she will leave him and take the children. Tonight Ben is out late at an office party. He comes home drunk. Does Tyra leave Ben?

An adolescent who hears this situation (drawn from research by Adams and Labouvie-Vief, 1986) may find the case to be open-and-shut: Tyra leaves Ben. But in early adulthood, the answer becomes a bit less clear. As people enter adulthood, they become less concerned with the sheer logic of situations and instead take into account real-life concerns that may influence and temper behavior in particular instances.

Intellectual Growth in Early Adulthood

If cognitive development were to follow the same pattern as physical development, we would expect to find little new intellectual growth in early adulthood. In fact, Piaget, whose theory of cognitive development played such a prominent role in our earlier discussions of intellectual change, argued that by the time people left adolescence, their thinking, at least qualitatively, had largely become what it would be for the rest of their lives. People might gather more information, but the ways in which they think about it would not change.

Was Piaget's view correct? Increasing evidence suggests that he was mistaken.

Postformal Thought

Developmental psychologist Giesela Labouvie-Vief suggests that the nature of thinking changes qualitatively during early adulthood. She asserts that thinking based solely on formal operations (Piaget's final stage, reached during adolescence) is insufficient to meet the demands placed on young adults. The complexity of society, which requires specialization, and the increasing challenge of finding one's way through all that complexity require thought that is not necessarily based on logic alone, but on practical experience, moral judgments, and values (Labouvie-Vief, 1990, 2006).

For example, imagine a young, single woman in her first job. Her boss, a married man she respects greatly and who is in a position to help her career, invites her to go with him to make an important presentation to a client. When the presentation, which has gone very well, is over, he suggests they go out to dinner and celebrate. Later that evening, after sharing a bottle of wine, he attempts to accompany her to her hotel room. What should she do?

Logic alone doesn't answer such questions. Labouvie-Vief suggests that as young adults are increasingly exposed to ambiguous situations like these, their thinking must develop to handle them. She suggests that young adults learn to use analogies and metaphors to make comparisons, confront society's paradoxes, and become comfortable with a more subjective understanding. Such thinking requires weighing all the aspects of a situation according to one's values and beliefs. It allows for interpretive processes and reflects the fact that reasons behind events in the real world are subtle, painted in shades of gray rather than in black and white (Labouvie-Vief, 1990; Sinnott, 1998b; Thornton, 2004).

To demonstrate how this sort of thinking develops, Labouvie-Vief presented experimental subjects, ranging in age from 10 to 40, with scenarios similar to the Ben and Tyra scenario at the beginning of this section. Each story had a clear, logical conclusion. However, the story could be interpreted differently if real-world demands and pressures were taken into account.

In responding to the scenarios, adolescents relied heavily on the logic inherent in formal operations. For instance, they would predict that Tyra would immediately pack up her bags and leave with the children when Ben came home drunk. After all, that's what she said she would do.

In contrast, young adults were less prone to use strict logic in determining a character's likely course of action. Instead, they would consider various possibilities that might come into the picture in a real-life situation: Would Ben be apologetic and beg Tyra not to leave? Did Tyra really mean it when she said she would leave? Does Tyra have some alternative place to go?

Young adults exhibited what Labouvie-Vief calls postformal thinking. **Postformal thought** is thinking that goes beyond Piaget's formal operations. Rather than being based on purely logical processes, with absolutely right and wrong answers to problems, postformal thought acknowledges that adult predicaments must sometimes be solved in relativistic terms.

Postformal thought also encompasses *dialectical thinking*, an interest in and appreciation for argument, counterargument, and debate (Basseches, 1984). Dialectical thinking accepts that issues are not always clear-cut, and that answers to questions are not always absolutely right or wrong but must sometimes be negotiated.

According to psychologist Jan Sinnott (1998a), postformal thought also takes into account real-world considerations when solving problems. Postformal thinkers can shift back and forth between an abstract, ideal solution and real-world constraints that might prevent the solution from being successfully implemented. In addition, postformal thinkers understand that just as there can be multiple causes of a situation, there can be multiple solutions.

In short, postformal thought and dialectical thinking acknowledge a world that sometimes lacks clearly right and wrong solutions to problems, a world in which logic may fail to resolve complex human questions. Instead, finding the best resolution to difficulties may involve drawing upon and integrating prior experiences.

> **postformal thought** thinking that acknowledges that adult predicaments must sometimes be solved in relativistic terms.

Perry's Approach to Postformal Thinking

To psychologist William Perry (1970, 1981), early adulthood represents a period of developmental growth that encompasses mastery not just of particular bodies of knowledge, but of ways of understanding the world. Perry examined the ways in which students grew intellectually and morally during college. In comprehensive interviews with a group of students at Harvard University, he found that students entering college tended to use *dualistic thinking* in their views of the world. For instance, they reasoned that something was right, or it was wrong; people were good, or they were bad; and others were either for them, or against them.

However, as these students encountered new ideas and points of view from other students and their professors, their dualistic thinking declined. Consistent with the notion of changes in postformal thinking, students increasingly realized that issues can have more than one plausible side. Furthermore, they understood more clearly that it is possible to hold multiple perspectives on an issue. This multiple thinking was characterized by a shift in the way the students viewed authorities: Instead of presupposing that experts had all the answers, they began to assume that their own thinking on an issue had validity if their position was well thought out and rational.

In fact, according to Perry, they had entered a stage in which knowledge and values were regarded as relativistic. Rather than seeing the world as having absolute standards and values, they argued that different societies, cultures, and individuals could have different standards and values, and all of them could be equally valid.

It's important to keep in mind that Perry's theory is based on a sample of interviews conducted with well-educated students attending an elite college. His findings may not apply as well to people who are not taught to examine multiple points of view as is common in a college education. Still, his notion that thinking continues to develop during early adulthood is widely accepted. In fact, as we consider next, other theories suggest that thinking changes in significant ways throughout adulthood.

Schaie's Stages of Development

Developmental psychologist K. Warner Schaie offers another perspective on postformal thought. Taking up where Piaget left off, Schaie suggests that adults' thinking follows a set pattern of stages (illustrated in Figure 13-5). But Schaie focuses on the ways in which information

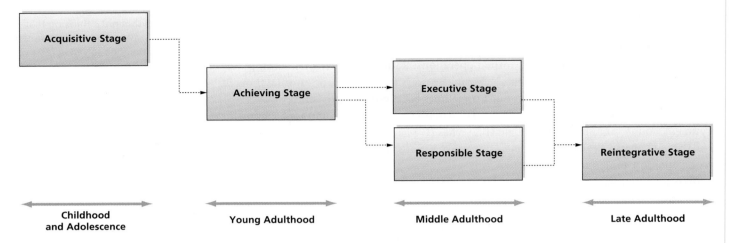

FIGURE 13-5 SCHAIE'S STAGES OF ADULT DEVELOPMENT
(*Source:* Schaie, 1977–1978.)

is *used* during adulthood, rather than on changes in the acquisition and understanding of new information, as in Piaget's approach (Schaie & Willis, 1993; Schaie & Zanjani, 2006).

Schaie suggests that before adulthood, the main cognitive developmental task is acquisition of information. Consequently, he labels the first stage of cognitive development, which encompasses all of childhood and adolescence, the **acquisitive stage.** Information gathered before we grow up is largely squirreled away for future use. In fact, much of the rationale for education during childhood and adolescence is to prepare people for future activities.

The situation changes considerably in early adulthood, however. Instead of targeting the future use of knowledge, the focus shifts to the "here and now." According to Schaie, young adults are in the achieving stage, applying their intelligence to attaining long-term goals regarding their careers, family, and contributions to society. During the **achieving stage,** young adults must confront and resolve several major issues, and the decisions they make—such as what job to take and whom to marry—have implications for the rest of their lives.

During the late stages of early adulthood and in middle adulthood, people move into what Schaie calls the responsible and executive stages. In the **responsible stage,** middle-aged adults are mainly concerned with protecting and nourishing their spouses, families, and careers.

Sometime later, further into middle adulthood, many people (but not all) enter the **executive stage** in which they take a broader perspective, becoming more concerned about the larger world (Sinnott, 1997). Rather than focusing only on their own lives, people in the executive stage also put energy into nourishing and sustaining societal institutions. They may become involved in town government, religious congregations, service clubs, charitable groups, factory unions—organizations that have a larger purpose in society. People in the executive stage, then, look beyond their individual situations.

Old age, according to Schaie's model, marks entry into the final period, the **reintegrative stage,** the period of late adulthood during which they focus on tasks that have personal meaning. In this stage, people no longer focus on acquiring knowledge as a means of solving potential problems that they may encounter. Instead, their information acquisition is directed toward particular issues that specifically interest them.

Furthermore, they have less interest in—and patience for—things that they do not see as having some immediate application to their lives. Thus, the abstract issue of whether the federal budget should be balanced may be of less concern to an elderly individual than whether the government should provide universal health care.

acquisitive stage according to Schaie, the first stage of cognitive development, encompassing all of childhood and adolescence, in which the main developmental task is to acquire information.

achieving stage the point reached by young adults in which intelligence is applied to specific situations involving the attainment of long-term goals regarding careers, family, and societal contributions.

responsible stage the stage where the major concerns of middle-aged adults relate to their personal situations, including protecting and nourishing their spouses, families, and careers.

executive stage the period in middle adulthood when people take a broader perspective than earlier, including concerns about the world.

reintegrative stage the period of late adulthood during which the focus is on tasks that have personal meaning.

Schaie's perspective on cognitive development reminds us that cognitive change doesn't stop at adolescence, as Piaget would contend. Instead, there are significant changes that continue throughout early adulthood and onward.

Intelligence: What Matters in Early Adulthood?

Your year on the job has been generally favorable. Performance ratings for your department are at least as good as they were before you took over, and perhaps even a little better. You have two assistants. One is quite capable. The other just seems to go through the motions and is of little real help. Even though you are well liked, you believe that there is little that would distinguish you in the eyes of your superiors from the nine other managers at a comparable level in the company. Your goal is rapid promotion to an executive position. (Based on Wagner & Sternberg, 1985, p. 447)

How do you meet your goal?

The way adults answer this question has a great deal to do with their future success, according to psychologist Robert Sternberg. The question is one of a series designed to assess a particular type of intelligence that may have more of an impact on future success than the type of intelligence measured by traditional IQ tests (of the sort we discussed in Chapter 9).

In his **triarchic theory of intelligence,** Sternberg suggests that intelligence is made up of three major components: componential, experiential, and contextual (see Figure 13-6). The *componential* aspect includes the mental components involved in analyzing data used in solving problems, especially problems involving rational behavior. It relates to people's ability to select and use formulas, to choose appropriate problem-solving strategies, and in general to make use of what they have been taught. The *experiential* component refers to the relationship between intelligence, people's prior experience, and their ability to cope with new situations. This is the insightful aspect of intelligence, which allows people to relate

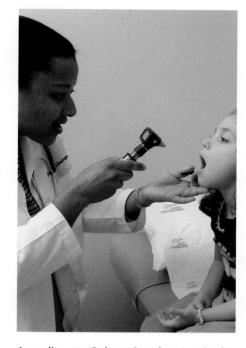

According to Robert Sternberg's triarchic theory of intelligence, practical intelligence is as important as traditional academic intelligence in determining success.

Componential Aspect of Intelligence
(Analysis of data to solve problems, using previously-learned information)

Contextual Aspect of Intelligence
(How intelligence is used to face real-world demands; practical intelligence)

Experiential Aspect of Intelligence
(How prior experiences are used in problem solving; abililty to cope with new situations)

FIGURE 13-6   STERNBERG'S TRIARCHIC THEORY OF INTELLIGENCE
(*Source:* Based on Sternberg, 1985, 1991.)

practical intelligence   according to Sternberg, intelligence that is learned primarily by observing others and modeling their behavior.

emotional intelligence   the set of skills that underlie the accurate assessment, evaluation, expression, and regulation of emotions.

what they already know to a new situation and an array of facts never before encountered. Finally, the *contextual* component of intelligence involves the degree of success people demonstrate in facing the demands of their everyday, real-world environments. For instance, the contextual component is involved in adapting to on-the-job professional demands (Sternberg, 2005).

Traditional intelligence tests, which yield an IQ score, tend to focus on the componential aspect of intelligence. Yet increasing evidence suggests that a more useful measure, particularly when one is looking for ways to compare and predict adult success, is the contextual component—the aspect of intelligence that has come to be called practical intelligence.

Practical and Emotional Intelligence.   According to Robert Sternberg, the IQ score that most traditional tests produce relates quite well to academic success. However, IQ seems to be unrelated to other types of achievement, such as career success. For example, although it is clear that success in business settings requires some minimal level of the sort of intelligence measured by IQ tests, the rate of career advancement and the ultimate success of business executives is only marginally related to IQ scores (Ree & Carretta, 2002; Cianciolo et al., 2006; Sternberg, 2006).

Sternberg contends that success in a career necessitates a type of intelligence—called practical intelligence—that is substantially different from that involved in traditional academic pursuits (Sternberg et al., 1997). While academic success is based on knowledge of particular types of information, obtained largely from reading and listening, **practical intelligence** is learned primarily by observing others and modeling their behavior. People who are high in practical intelligence have a good "social radar." They are able to understand and handle even new situations effectively, reading people and circumstances insightfully, based on their previous experiences. (See Figure 13-7 for sample items from a test of practical intelligence).

Related to this sort of mental ability is another type of intelligence involving emotional domains. **Emotional intelligence** is the set of skills that underlies the accurate assessment, evaluation, expression, and regulation of emotions. Emotional intelligence is what gives some people the ability to get along well with others, to understand what others are feeling and experiencing, and to respond appropriately to the needs of others. It permits a person to tune into others' feelings, allowing an individual to respond appropriately. Emotional intelligence is also of obvious value to career and personal success as a young adult (Zeidner, Matthews, & Roberts, 2004; Mayer, Salovey, Caruso, 2004; Carmeli & Josman, 2006; Sy, Tram, & O'Hara, 2006).

Creativity: Novel Thought.   The hundreds of musical compositions of Wolfgang Amadeus Mozart, who died at the age of 35, were largely written during early adulthood. The same is true of many other creative individuals: Their major works were produced during early adulthood (Dennis, 1966a; see Figure 13-8 on page 462).

One reason for the higher productivity of early adulthood may be that after early adulthood, creativity can be stifled by a situation that psychologist Sarnoff Mednick (1963) described as "familiarity breeds rigidity." By this he meant that the more people know about a subject, the less likely they are to be creative in that area. According to such reasoning, people in early adulthood may be at the peak of their creativity because many of the problems they encounter on a professional level are novel—or at least new to them. As they get older, however, and become more familiar with the problems, their creativity may be stymied.

On the other hand, not everybody seems to have this problem. Many people do not reach their pinnacle of creativity until much later in life. For instance, Buckminster Fuller did not devise his major contribution, the geodesic dome, until he was in his 50s. Frank Lloyd Wright designed the Guggenheim Museum in New York at age 70. Charles Darwin and Jean Piaget were still writing influential works well into their 70s, and Picasso was painting in his 90s. Furthermore, when we look at overall productivity, as opposed to the period of a person's most important output, we

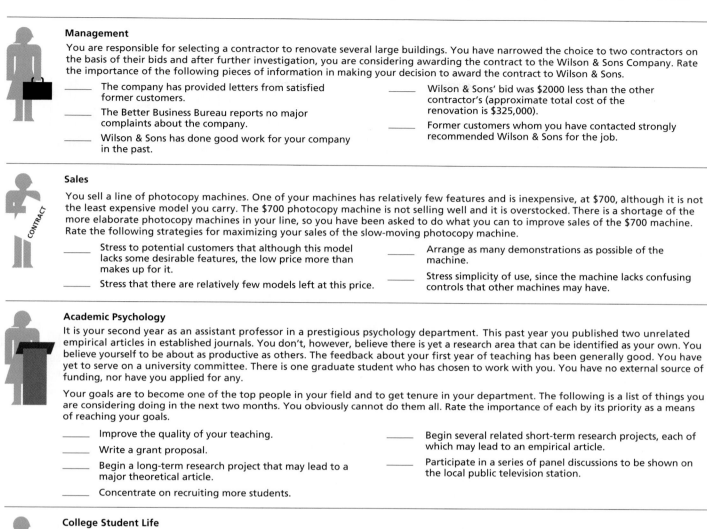

Management

You are responsible for selecting a contractor to renovate several large buildings. You have narrowed the choice to two contractors on the basis of their bids and after further investigation, you are considering awarding the contract to the Wilson & Sons Company. Rate the importance of the following pieces of information in making your decision to award the contract to Wilson & Sons.

_____ The company has provided letters from satisfied former customers.

_____ The Better Business Bureau reports no major complaints about the company.

_____ Wilson & Sons has done good work for your company in the past.

_____ Wilson & Sons' bid was $2000 less than the other contractor's (approximate total cost of the renovation is $325,000).

_____ Former customers whom you have contacted strongly recommended Wilson & Sons for the job.

Sales

You sell a line of photocopy machines. One of your machines has relatively few features and is inexpensive, at $700, although it is not the least expensive model you carry. The $700 photocopy machine is not selling well and it is overstocked. There is a shortage of the more elaborate photocopy machines in your line, so you have been asked to do what you can to improve sales of the $700 machine. Rate the following strategies for maximizing your sales of the slow-moving photocopy machine.

_____ Stress to potential customers that although this model lacks some desirable features, the low price more than makes up for it.

_____ Stress that there are relatively few models left at this price.

_____ Arrange as many demonstrations as possible of the machine.

_____ Stress simplicity of use, since the machine lacks confusing controls that other machines may have.

Academic Psychology

It is your second year as an assistant professor in a prestigious psychology department. This past year you published two unrelated empirical articles in established journals. You don't, however, believe there is yet a research area that can be identified as your own. You believe yourself to be about as productive as others. The feedback about your first year of teaching has been generally good. You have yet to serve on a university committee. There is one graduate student who has chosen to work with you. You have no external source of funding, nor have you applied for any.

Your goals are to become one of the top people in your field and to get tenure in your department. The following is a list of things you are considering doing in the next two months. You obviously cannot do them all. Rate the importance of each by its priority as a means of reaching your goals.

_____ Improve the quality of your teaching.

_____ Write a grant proposal.

_____ Begin a long-term research project that may lead to a major theoretical article.

_____ Concentrate on recruiting more students.

_____ Begin several related short-term research projects, each of which may lead to an empirical article.

_____ Participate in a series of panel discussions to be shown on the local public television station.

College Student Life

You are enrolled in a large introductory lecture course. Requirements consist of three exams and a final. Please indicate how characteristic it would be of your behavior to spend time doing each of the following if your goal were to receive an A in the course.

_____ Attend class regularly.

_____ Attend optional weekly review sections with the teaching fellow.

_____ Read assigned text chapters thoroughly.

_____ Take comprehensive class notes.

_____ Speak with the professor after class and during office hours.

FIGURE 13-7 SAMPLE ITEMS FROM A TEST THAT TAPS FOUR DOMAINS OF PRACTICAL INTELLIGENCE

(_Source:_ Sternberg, 1993.)

find that productivity remains fairly steady throughout adulthood, particularly in the humanities (Dennis, 1966b; Simonton, 1989).

Overall, the study of creativity reveals few consistent developmental patterns. One reason for this is the difficulty of determining just what constitutes an instance of **creativity,** which is defined as combining responses or ideas in novel ways. Because definitions of what is "novel" may vary from one person to the next, it is hard to identify a particular behavior unambiguously as creative (Isaksen & Murdock, 1993; Sasser-Coen, 1993).

That ambiguity hasn't stopped psychologists from trying. For instance, one important component of creativity is a person's willingness to take risks that may result in potentially high payoffs. Creative people are analogous to successful stock market investors, who try to follow

creativity the combination of responses or ideas in novel ways.

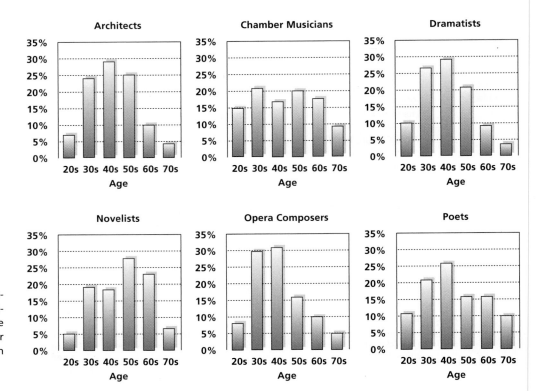

FIGURE 13-8 CREATIVITY AND AGE

The period of maximum creativity differs depending on the particular field. The percentages refer to the percent of total lifetime major works produced during the particular age period. Why do poets peak earlier than novelists?

(*Source:* Based on Dennis, 1966.)

the "buy low, sell high" rule. Creative people develop and endorse ideas that are unfashionable or regarded as wrong ("buying low"). They assume that eventually others will see the value of the ideas and embrace them ("selling high"). According to this theory, creative adults take a fresh look at ideas or problem solutions that might initially be discarded, particularly if the problem is a familiar one. They are flexible enough to move away from the way they have typically had done things and to consider new approaches and opportunities (Sternberg & Lubart, 1992; Sternberg, Kaufman, & Peretz, 2002).

Life Events and Cognitive Development

Marriage. The death of a parent. Starting a first job. The birth of a child. Buying a house. The course of life comprises many events such as these—important milestones on the path through the life span. Such occurrences, whether they are welcome or unwanted, clearly may bring about stress, as we saw earlier in this chapter. But do they also cause cognitive growth?

Although the research is still spotty and largely based on case studies, some evidence suggests that major life events may lead to cognitive growth. For instance, the birth of a child—a profound event—may trigger fresh insights into the nature of one's relationships with relatives and ancestors, one's broader place in the world, and the role one has in perpetuating humanity. Similarly, the death of a loved one may cause people to reevaluate what is important to them and to look anew at the manner in which they lead their lives (Haan, 1985; Aldwin, 1994; Woike & Matic, 2004).

Experiencing the ups and downs of life events may lead young adults to think about the world in novel, more complex and sophisticated, and often less rigid ways. Rather than applying formal logic to situations—a strategy of which they are fully capable—they instead apply the broader perspective of postformal thought that we described earlier in this chapter, seeing trends and patterns, personalities and choices. Such thinking allows them to deal more effectively with the complex social worlds (discussed in Chapter 14) of which they are a part.

Profound events such as the birth of a child or the death of a loved one can stimulate cognitive development by offering an opportunity to reevaluate our place in the world. What are some other profound events that might stimulate cognitive development?

Review and Apply

Review

- Cognitive development continues into young adulthood with the emergence of postformal thought, which goes beyond logic to encompass interpretive and subjective thinking.

- Perry suggests that people move from dualistic thinking to relativistic thought during early adulthood.

- According to Schaie, people pass through five stages in the way they use information: acquisitive, achieving, responsible, executive, and reintegrative.

- New views of intelligence encompass the triarchic theory, practical intelligence, and emotional intelligence.

- Creativity seems to peak during early adulthood, with young adults viewing even long-standing problems as novel situations.

- Major life events contribute to cognitive growth by providing opportunities and incentives to rethink one's self and one's world.

Applying Lifespan Development

- What does "familiarity breeds rigidity" mean? Can you think of examples of this phenomenon from your own experience?

- *From an educator's perspective:* Can you think of situations that you would deal with differently as an adult than as an adolescent? Do the differences reflect postformal thinking?

College: Pursuing Higher Education

It's 4:30 in the morning. Marion Mealey, a college student who has returned to school at the age of 27, looks in on her son, walks her dogs, and begins to study for a biology exam.

By 6:00 AM, she leaves the house, taking her breakfast and lunch that she had readied the night before. Her son and her mother are still asleep. Her mother, who helps care for Mealey's son, will soon wake up herself, and get her grandson off to school.

Before she returns home at the end of the day, Mealey will have spent four hours in transit, fitting in some additional study time along the way, four hours in class, and three hours at a job that pays her family's living expenses. After spending a few hours with her family, she still has to read for classes tomorrow. (Adapted from Dembner, 1995)

Marion Mealey, one of the one-third of college students who are above the age of 24, faces unusual challenges as she pursues the goal of a college degree. Older students like her are just one aspect of the increasing diversity—in family background, socioeconomic status, race, and ethnicity—that characterizes college campuses today. We noted this phenomenon in the chapter prologue, in which we met Armando Williams, a student who might never have been able to attend college just a few years ago.

For any student, though, attending college is a significant accomplishment. Although you may believe that college attendance is commonplace, this is not the case at all: Nationwide, high school graduates who enter college are actually in the minority.

The number of older students, starting or returning to college, continues to grow. More than a third of college students are 25 years old or older. Why are so many older, nontraditional students taking college courses?

The Demographics of Higher Education

What types of students enter college? As in the U.S. population as a whole, U.S. college students are primarily white and middle class. Although nearly 69% of white high school graduates enter college, only 61% of African American and 47% of Hispanic graduates do so. Even more striking, although the absolute number of minority students enrolled in college has increased, the overall *proportion* of the minority population that does enter college has *decreased* over the past decade—a decline that most education experts attribute to changes in the availability of financial aid (U.S. Bureau of the Census, 1998, 2000; see Figure 13-9).

Furthermore, the proportion of students who enter college but ultimately never graduate is substantial. Only around 40% of those who start college finish 4 years later with a degree. Although about half of those who don't receive a degree in 4 years eventually do finish, the other half never obtain a college degree. For minorities, the picture is even worse: The national

FIGURE 13-9 COLLEGE ENROLLMENT BY RACIAL GROUP

The proportion of nonwhites who attend college has increased in the last few decades.

(*Source:* National Center for Education Statistics, 2004.)

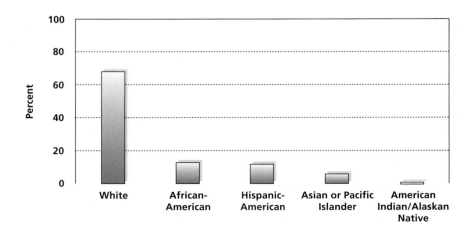

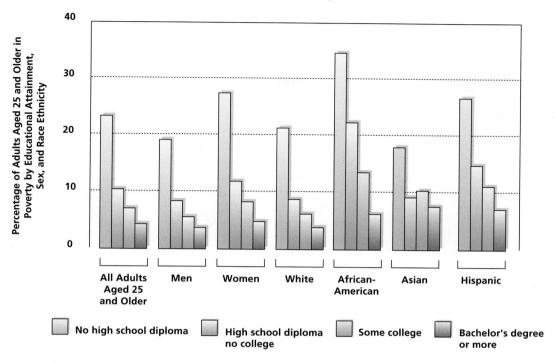

FIGURE 13-10 **EDUCATION AND ECONOMIC SECURITY**

Education provides more than knowledge; it is also an important means to attain economic security for both men and women.

(*Source:* U.S. Census Bureau, 1996.)

dropout rate for African American college students stands at 70% (American Council on Education, 1995; American College Testing Program, 2001).

For students who do not attend or complete college, the consequences can be significant. Higher education is an important way for people to improve their economic well-being. Just 3% of adults who have a college education live below the poverty line. Compare that with high school dropouts: They are 10 times more likely to be living in poverty (see Figure 13-10; O'Hare, 1997; U.S. Census Bureau, 2003).

The decline in the proportion of minority students attending college has implications for the kind of educational experience a college can offer *all* its students. As we consider in the *From Research to Practice* box, a diverse student body can actually enhance cognitive development.

The Gender Gap in College Attendance. More women than men attend college, and the proportion of women, relative to men, is increasing. There already are more women than men enrolled in college, with women receiving 133 bachelor's degrees for every 100 men receive. The gender gap is even more evident for minority students, with 166 African American women attending college for every 100 African American men (Sum, Fogg, & Harrington, 2003).

Why is there a gender gap in college attendance? It may be that men have more opportunities to earn money when they graduate from high school, and they find these immediate opportunities more seductive than college. For instance, the military, trade unions, and jobs that require physical strength may be more attractive to men, and consequently more men than women may perceive that good options other than college are available. Furthermore, as affirmative action has become less of a factor in admissions, women often have better high school academic records than men, and they may be admitted to college at greater rates (Dortch, 1997; Buchmann & DiPrete, 2006; England & Li, 2006).

The availability of higher paying jobs that do not require a college education is one reason why enrollment of men in college is increasing more slowly than women.

From Research to Practice

Does a Racially Diverse College Campus Make for a Richer Learning Environment?

Sitting in a bustling basement coffee shop at the University of Chicago, 21-year-old Anthonia Akitunde said the new faces in many of her classes this semester are "definitely noticeable."

"I'm used to being one of the only black people in classes," she said, as indie rock plays in the background. "Now I'm one of three."

The freshman class at University of Chicago is the most diverse group of students to enroll at the Hyde Park campus, school officials say. One of four new students is either black, Hispanic or from a foreign country. (Newbart, 2006, p. A09)

One factor students sometimes consider in choosing a college to attend is the diversity of the student body. Some applicants—perhaps those seeking to learn about people from different backgrounds—are attracted to campuses with a diverse ethnic mixture. But the benefits of studying in a racially diverse environment may actually extend beyond learning about others, to learning how to think more effectively and critically.

It seems reasonable that diversity should stimulate critical thinking. For example, members of homogenous groups, who have similar backgrounds and perspectives, bring similarities in thinking to situations in which they engage in problem solving. On the other hand, diverse groups, representing a variety of backgrounds and perspectives, bring greater variety in ideas and perspectives that the group must integrate in their discussions. This engagement with different outlooks on a problem tends to increase the complexity of the group members' thinking (Nemeth, 1992).

To test this hypothesis in racially diverse groups, one recent study assigned white college students to small discussion groups in which they discussed a problematic social issue. The students' responses to a previous survey were used to ensure that all members of each discussion group shared the same opinion on the social issue they would discuss.

Each discussion group included a research confederate who posed as a discussant. These confederates were sometimes black (creating racial diversity) and sometimes white (leaving the group homogenous). Additionally, the black and the white confederates would agree with the majority opinion in some groups and disagree with it in others. After discussing the issue, group members then wrote essays on their positions on the issue that was discussed (Antonio et al., 2006).

When a black confederate was added to an otherwise white discussion group, the white members indicated that he or she made them think more about the issue in different ways, introduced a more novel perspective, and influenced the group more compared to a white confederate. This was the case even when the black confederate agreed with the group opinion. What makes this finding particularly surprising is that the black and white confederates followed scripts; that is, their contributions were actually equal. The difference was in how they were perceived by the group.

Moreover, exposing white discussants to a confederate who espoused a contrary viewpoint (regardless of the confederate's race) led to more complex thinking, as did the presence of a black confederate. These findings suggest that racial diversity—and the associated diversity of opinions and perspectives—leads college students to engage in more complex critical thinking, even within the limited context of a brief encounter.

Perhaps most tellingly, the white discussants who had a history of higher levels of diverse racial contact also tended to show more complex thinking in their essays, suggesting that prolonged interracial contact is associated with more complex cognition. Taken together, these findings lend support to the position that a diverse student body produces a richer educational environment for young adults.

These findings are congruent with a growing body of research that finds that exposure to other students who represent the range of cultures, ethnicities, and races has important consequences. Not only do students benefit socially in terms of increased multicultural understanding, but their cognitive development is also enhanced. In short, diversity has significant cogntive benefits, leading to more critical thinking and other sorts of cognitive advances (Gurin, Nagda, & Lopez, 2004; Nagda, Gurin, & Johnson, 2005).

■ *Why might students perceive the contributions of a black discussant to be more novel and influential than the contributions of a white discussant, even when they say the same things?*

■ *Why might the race of the confederates alone (and not their contributions to the discussion, which were the same) have made a difference in how the white discussants thought about the topic?*

The Changing College Student: Never Too Late to Go to College?   If the phrase "average college student" brings to mind an image of an 18- or 19-year-old, you should begin to rethink your view. Increasingly, students are older. In fact 26% of students taking college courses for credit in the United States are between the ages of 25 and 35, like Marion Mealey, the 27-year-old student profiled earlier. Thirty six percent of community college students are over 30 years old (Dortch, 1997; U.S. Department of Education, 2005).

Why are so many older, nontraditional students taking college courses? One reason is economic. As a college degree becomes increasingly important in obtaining a job, some workers feel compelled to get the credential. Many employers encourage or require workers to undergo training to learn new skills or update their old ones.

In addition, as people age, they may begin to feel the need to settle down with a family. This change in attitude can reduce their risk-taking behavior and make them focus more on acquiring the ability to support their family—a phenomenon that has been labeled *maturation reform.*

According to developmental psychologist Sherry Willis (1985), several broad goals underlie adults' participation in learning experiences. First, adults may be seeking to understand their own aging. As they get older, they try to figure out what is happening to them and what to expect in the future. Second, adults seek education in order to understand more fully the rapid technological and cultural changes that characterize modern life.

Furthermore, adult learners may be seeking a practical edge in combating obsolescence on the job. Some individuals also may be attempting to acquire new vocational skills. Finally, adult educational experiences may be seen as helpful in preparing for future retirement. As adults get older, they become increasingly concerned with shifting from a work orientation to a leisure orientation, and they may see education as a means of broadening their possibilities.

College Adjustment: Reacting to the Demands of College Life

When you began college, did you feel depressed, lonely, anxious, and withdrawn from others? If you did, you weren't alone. Many students, particularly those who are recent high school graduates and who are living away from home for the first time, experience difficulties in adjustment during their first year in college. The **first-year adjustment reaction** is a cluster of psychological symptoms, including loneliness, anxiety, and depression, relating to the college experience. Although any first-year student may suffer from one or more of the symptoms of first-year adjustment reaction, it is particularly likely to occur among students who have been unusually successful, either academically or socially, in high school. When they begin college, their sudden change in status may cause them distress.

Students who have been successful and popular in high school are particularly vulnerable to first-year adjustment reaction in college. Counseling, as well as increasing familiarity with campus life, can help a student adjust.

first-year adjustment reaction a cluster of psychological symptoms, including loneliness, anxiety, withdrawal, and depression, relating to the college experience suffered by first-year college students.

Most often, first-year adjustment reaction passes as students make friends, experience academic success, and integrate themselves into campus life. In other cases, though, the problems remain and may fester, leading to more serious psychological difficulties.

Becoming an Informed Consumer of Development

When Do College Students Need Professional Help with Their Problems?

A college friend comes to you and says that she has been feeling depressed and unhappy and can't seem to shake the feeling. She doesn't know what to do and thinks that she may need professional help. How do you answer her?

Although there are no hard-and-fast rules, several signals can be interpreted to determine if professional help is warranted (Engler & Goleman, 1992). Among them are the following:

- psychological distress that lingers and interferes with a person's sense of well-being and ability to function (such as depression so great that someone has trouble completing his or her work)
- feelings that one is unable to cope effectively with the stress
- hopeless or depressed feelings, with no apparent reason
- the inability to build close relationships with others
- physical symptoms such as headaches, stomach cramps, and skin rashes that have no apparent underlying cause

If some of these signals are present, it would be helpful to discuss them with some kind of help-provider—such as a counseling psychologist, clinical psychologist, or other mental health worker. The best place to start is the campus medical center. A personal physician, neighborhood clinic, or local board of health can also provide a referral.

How prevalent are concerns about psychological problems? Surveys find that almost half of college students report having at least one significant psychological issue. Other research found that more than 40% of students who visited a college counseling center reported being depressed (see Figure 13-11). Remember, though, that these figures include only those students who sought help from the counseling center and not those who did not seek treatment. Consequently, the figures are not representative of the entire college population (Benton et al., 2003).

Gender and College Performance

I registered for a calculus course my first year at DePauw. Even twenty years ago I was not timid, so on the very first day I raised my hand and asked a question. I still have a vivid memory of the professor rolling his eyes, hitting his head with his hand in frustration, and announcing to everyone, "Why do they expect me to teach calculus to girls?" I never asked another question. Several weeks later I went to a football game, but I had forgotten to bring my ID. My calculus professor was at the gate checking IDs, so I went up to him and said, "I forgot my ID but you know me, I'm in your class." He looked right at me and said, "I don't remember you in my class." I couldn't believe that someone who changed my life and whom I remember to this day didn't even recognize me. (Sadker & Sadker, 1994, p. 162)

Although such incidents of blatant sexism are less likely to occur today, prejudice and discrimination directed at women are still a fact of college life. For instance, the next time you are in class, consider the gender of your classmates—and the subject matter of the class. Although men and women attend college in roughly equal proportions, there is significant variation in

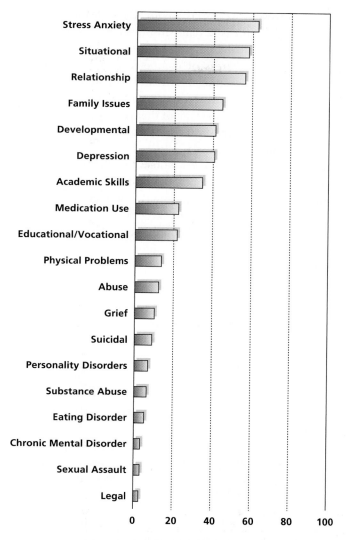

FIGURE 13-11 **COLLEGE PROBLEMS**

The difficulties most frequently reported by college students visiting a campus counseling center.

(*Source:* Benton et al., 2003.)

the classes they take. Classes in education and the social sciences, for instance, typically have a larger proportion of women than men; and classes in engineering, the physical sciences, and mathematics tend to have more men than women.

Even women who start out in mathematics, engineering, and the physical sciences are more likely than men to drop out. For instance, the attrition rate for women in such fields during the college years is two-and-one-half times greater than the rate for men. And although the number of women seeking graduate degrees in science and engineering has been increasing, women still lag behind men in the numbers seeking to enter those fields (National Science Foundation, 2002).

The differences in gender distribution and attrition rates across subject areas are no accident. They reflect the powerful influence of gender stereotypes that operate throughout the world of education—and beyond. For instance, when women in their first year of college are asked to name a likely career choice, they are much less apt to choose careers that have traditionally been dominated by men, such as engineering or computer programming, and more likely to choose professions that have traditionally been populated by women, such as nursing and social work (Glick, Zion, & Nelson, 1988; CIRE, 1990).

Women also expect to earn less than men, both when they start their careers and when they are at their peaks (Jackson, Gardner, & Sullivan, 1992; Desmarais & Curtis, 1997; Pelham & Hetts, 2001). These expectations jibe with reality: On average, women earn 77 cents for every dollar that men earn. Moreover, women who are members of minority groups do even worse: African

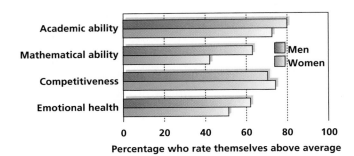

FIGURE 13-12 THE GREAT GENDER DIVIDE

During their first year of college, men, compared to women, are more apt to view themselves as above average on several spheres relevant to academic success. What is the root of this difference?

(*Source:* The American Freshman: National Norms for Fall, 1990; Astin, Korn, & Berz. Higher Education Research Institute, UCLA.)

American women earn 63 cents for every dollar men make, while for Hispanic women the figure is 52 cents (Institute for Women's Policy Research, 2006).

Male and female college students also have different expectations regarding their areas of competence. For instance, one survey asked first-year college students whether they were above or below average on a variety of traits and abilities. As shown in Figure 13-12, men were more likely than women to think of themselves as above average in overall academic and mathematical ability, competitiveness, and emotional health.

Both male and female college professors treat men and women differently in their classes, even though the different treatment is largely unintentional and the professors are unaware of their actions. For instance, professors call on men in class more frequently than women, and they make more eye contact with men than with women. Furthermore, male students are more likely than women to receive extra help from their professors. Finally, the quality of the responses received by male and female students differs, with male students receiving more positive reinforcement for their comments than female students—exemplified by the startling illustration in Table 13-3 (Epperson, 1988; AAUW, 1992; Sadker & Sadker, 1994).

Benevolent Sexism: When Being Nice Is Not So Nice. Although some cases of unequal treatment of women represent *hostile sexism*, in which people treat women in a way that is overtly harmful, in other cases women are the victims of benevolent sexism. *Benevolent*

Table 13-3 Gender Bias in the Classroom

The course on the U.S. Constitution is required for graduation, and more than 50 students, approximately half male and half female, file in. The professor begins by asking if there are questions on next week's midterm. Several hands go up.

BERNIE: Do you have to memorize names and dates in the book? Or will the test be more general?

PROFESSOR: You do have to know those critical dates and people. Not every one but the important ones. If I were you, Bernie, I would spend time learning them. Ellen

ELLEN: What kind of short-answer questions will there be?

PROFESSOR: All multiple choice.

ELLEN: Will we have the whole class time?

PROFESSOR: Yes, we'll have the whole class time. Anyone else?

BEN (calling out): Will there be an extra-credit question?

PROFESSOR: I hadn't planned on it. What do you think?

BEN: I really like them. They take some of the pressure off. You can also see who is doing extra work.

PROFESSOR: I'll take it under advisement. Charles?

CHARLES: How much of our final grade is this?

PROFESSOR: The midterm is 25 percent. But remember, class participation counts as well. Why don't we begin?

The professor lectures on the Constitution for 20 minutes before he asks a question about the electoral college. The electoral college is not as hot a topic as the midterm, so only four hands are raised. The professor calls on Ben.

BEN: The electoral college was created because there was a lack of faith in the people. Rather than have them vote for the president, they voted for the electors.

PROFESSOR: I like the way you think. (He smiles at Ben, and Ben smiles back.) Who could vote? (Five hands go up, five out of fifty.) Angie?

ANGIE: I don't know if this is right, but I thought only men could vote.

BEN (calling out): That was a great idea. We began going downhill when we let women vote. (Angie looks surprised but says nothing. Some of the students laugh, and so does the professor. He calls on Barbara.)

BARBARA: I think you had to be pretty wealthy, own property—JOSH *(not waiting for Barbara to finish, calls out):* That's right. There was a distrust of the poor, who could upset the democracy. But if you had property, if you had something at stake, you could be trusted not to do something wild. Only property owners could be trusted.

PROFESSOR: Nice job, Josh. But why do we still have electors today? Mike?

MIKE: Tradition, I guess.

PROFESSOR: Do you think it's tradition? If you walked down the street and asked people their views of the electoral college, what would they say?

MIKE: Probably they'd be clueless. Maybe they would think that it elects the Pope. People don't know how it works.

PROFESSOR: Good, Mike. Judy, do you want to say something? (Judy's hand is at "half-mast," raised but just barely. When the professor calls her name, she looks a bit startled.)

JUDY (speaking very softly): Maybe we would need a whole new constitutional convention to change it. And once they get together to change that, they could change anything. That frightens people, doesn't it? (As Judy speaks, a number of students fidget, pass notes, and leaf through their books; a few even begin to whisper.)

(*Source:* Sadker & Sadker, 1994.)

As a result of the powerful influence of gender stereotypes in the world of education, women are underrepresented in the areas of physical science, math, and engineering. What can be done to reverse this trend?

sexism is a form of sexism in which women are placed in stereotyped and restrictive roles that appear, on the surface, to be positive.

Benevolent sexism even seems, at first, to be beneficial to women. For instance, a male college professor may compliment a female student on her good looks or offer to give her an easier research project so she won't have to work so hard. While the professor may feel that he is merely being thoughtful, in fact he may be making the woman feel that she is not taken seriously and undermining her view of her competence. In short, benevolent sexism can be just as harmful as hostile sexism (Glick et al., 2000; Greenwood & Isbell, 2002).

Stereotype Threat and Disidentification with School

African Americans don't do well in academic pursuits. Women lack ability in math and science. So say erroneous, damaging, and yet persistent stereotypes about African Americans and women. And in the real world these stereotypes play out in vicious ways. For instance, when

Both male and female college professors may unintentionally favor their male students over their female students, calling on their male students more and making more eye contact with them than with their female students. Why do you think unconscious sexism like this persists?

African Americans start elementary school, their standardized test scores are only slightly lower than those of Caucasian students, and yet a 2-year gap emerges by the sixth grade. And even though more African American high school graduates are enrolling in college, the increase has not been as large as for other groups (American Council on Education, 1995–1996).

Analagously, even though boys and girls perform virtually identically on standardized math tests in elementary school and middle school, this changes when they reach high school. At that level, and even more so in college, men tend to do better in math than women. In fact, when women take college math, science, and engineering courses, they are more likely to do poorly than men who enter college with the same level of preparation and identical SAT scores. Strangely, though, this phenomenon does not hold true for other areas of the curriculum, where men and women perform at similar levels (Hyde, Fennema, & Lamon, 1990).

According to psychologist Claude Steele, the reason behind the declining levels of performance for both women and African Americans is the same: *academic disidentification*, a lack of personal identification with an academic domain. For women, disidentification is specific to math and science; for African Americans, it is more generalized across academic domains. In both cases, negative societal stereotypes produce a state of **stereotype threat** in which members of the group fear that their behavior will indeed confirm the stereotype (Steele, 1997).

For instance, women seeking to achieve in nontraditional fields that rely on math and science may be hindered as they become distracted by worries about the failure that society predicts for them. In some cases, a woman may decide that failure in a male-dominated field, because it would confirm societal stereotypes, presents such great risks that, paradoxically, the struggle to succeed is not worth the effort. In that instance, the woman may not even try very hard (Inzlicht & Ben-Zeev, 2000).

Similarly, African Americans may work under the pressure of feeling that they must disconfirm the negative stereotype regarding their academic performance. The pressure can be anxiety-provoking and threatening, and can reduce their performance below their true ability level. Ironically, stereotype threat may be most severe for better, more confident students, who have not internalized the negative stereotype to the extent of questioning their own abilities (Steele, 1997).

Rather than ignoring negative stereotypes, women and African Americans may perform less well and, ultimately, disidentify with schooling and academic pursuits relevant to the stereotype. In support of such reasoning, Steele and colleagues conducted an experiment in which two groups of African American and white students were given identical tests composed of difficult verbal-skills items from the Graduate Record Exam. However, the stated purpose of the test was varied across participant groups. Some participants were told that the test measured "psychological factors involved in solving verbal problems"—information that presumably had little to do with underlying ability. It was stressed that the test would not evaluate their ability. In contrast, other participants were told that the test was concerned with various "personal factors involved in performance on problems requiring reading and verbal reasoning abilities," and that the test would be helpful in identifying their personal strengths and weaknesses.

The results provided clear evidence for the stereotype vulnerability hypothesis. African American participants who thought the test measured psychological factors performed as well as white participants. But African American participants who thought the test measured core abilities and limitations scored significantly lower than the white participants. In contrast, white participants scored equally well, regardless of the test description. Clearly, having to contend with the stereotype resulted in poorer performance (Steele & Aronson, 1995).

In short, members of groups that are traditionally discriminated against are vulnerable to expectations regarding their future success. Happily, though, there is room for optimism. Even relatively subtle changes in a situation—such as the way an assessment is described—can reduce vulnerability to stereotyping. Intervention programs designed to inform members of minority groups about the consequences of society's negative stereotypes may offer a means of reducing the impact of the stereotypes (Lesko & Corpus, 2006; McGlone & Aronson, 2006; McGlone, Aronson, & Kobrynowicz, 2006; Rosenthal & Crisp, 2006).

Dropping Out of College

Not everyone who enters college completes it. Six years after starting college, only 63% have graduated. The picture is even worse for some demographic groups. Less than half of African American students and less than half of Hispanic students graduate in 6 years (NAACP Education Department, 2003; Carey, 2004).

Why is the college dropout rate so high? There are several reasons. One has to do with finances: Given the high cost of college, many students are unable to afford the continued expense or the strain of juggling the demands of a job and the demands of college. Other people leave college because of changes in their life situations, such as marriage, the birth of a child, or the death of a parent.

Academic difficulties also may play a role. Some students simply find that they are not successful in their studies, and they are either forced by academic authorities to drop out or they leave on their own. However, in most cases students who drop out are not in academic jeopardy (Rotenberg & Morrison, 1993).

College students who drop out in early adulthood—intending to return one day, but never making it back because they become enmeshed in the nitty-gritty of everyday life—can experience real difficulties. They may become stuck as young adults in undesirable, low-paying jobs for which they are intellectually overqualified. A college education becomes a lost opportunity.

On the other hand, dropping out is not always a step backward in a young adult's life path. In some cases, it gives people breathing room to reassess their goals. For instance, students who view the college experience as simply marking time until they can get on with their "real" lives by earning a living can sometimes benefit from a period of full-time work. During the hiatus from college, they often get a different perspective on the realities of both work and school. Other individuals simply benefit by having some time off from school in which to mature socially or psychologically, as we'll discuss further in the next chapter.

Review and Apply

Review

- Rates of college enrollment differ across racial and ethnic lines.
- The average age of college students is steadily increasing as more adults return to college.
- New students often find the transition to college difficult and experience first-year adjustment reaction.
- In college, students learn not only a body of knowledge, but also a way of understanding the world that generally accepts more viewpoints and sees values in relativistic terms.
- Gender differences in treatment and expectations cause men and women to make different choices and engage in different behaviors in college.
- The phenomena of academic disidentification and stereotype threat help explain the lower performance of women and African Americans in certain academic domains.

Applying Lifespan Development

- How would you educate college professors who behave differently toward male and female students? What factors contribute to this phenomenon? Can this situation be changed?
- *From an educator's perspective:* How is the presence of older students likely to affect the college classroom, given what you know about human development? Why?

Epilogue

In this chapter we discussed physical and cognitive development in early adulthood. We looked at overall health and fitness and at intellectual growth, which proceeds through stages that profit from young adults' increasing experience and subtlety. We also looked at college, noting demographic trends and differences in treatment and academic performance that affect some groups of college students. We discussed the advantages of college and the adjustment reaction that some first-year college students experience as they encounter the new realities of college life.

Return to the prologue of this chapter, in which we met college students Enrico Vasquez and Armando Williams. In light of what you now know about physical and cognitive development in early adulthood, answer the following questions:

1. How do you think family expectations about education affected the two students' decisions to enroll in college?

2. As a Cuban American student from a wealthy background, what challenges is Enrico likely to encounter if he enters a college in which Hispanic students are a small minority?

3. Is academic disidentification likely to be a problem for Armando, with his "mean streets" background? Why or why not?

4. How might the phenomenon of stereotype threat affect both Enrico and Armando?

5. Which student do you think may have the more difficult adjustment to college? Which is more likely to drop out of college? Why?

Looking
Back

How does the body develop during early adulthood, and to what risks are young adults exposed?

- The body and the senses generally reach their peak in early adulthood. Health risks are minimal, with accidents presenting the greatest risk of death, followed by AIDS. In the United States, violence is a significant cause of death, particularly among nonwhite segments of the population.

- Many young adults begin to put on weight because they fail to change poor eating habits developed earlier, and the percentage of obese adults increases with every year of aging.

- People with physical disabilities face physical and material difficulties as well as psychological difficulties, including prejudice and stereotyping.

What are the effects of stress, and what can be done about it?

- Moderate, occasional stress is biologically healthy, but long exposure to stressors produces damaging physical and psychosomatic effects. In reacting to potentially stressful situations, people pass through primary appraisal of the situation itself and secondary appraisal of their own coping abilities.

- People cope with stress in a number of healthy and unhealthy ways, including problem-focused coping, emotion-focused coping, social support, and defensive coping.

Does cognitive development continue in young adulthood?

- Some theorists find increasing evidence of postformal thought, which goes beyond formal logic to produce more flexible and subjective thinking that takes account of real-world complexity and yields subtler answers than those found during adolescence.

- According to Schaie, the development of thinking follows a set pattern of stages: the acquisitive stage, the achieving stage, the responsible stage, the executive stage, and the reintegrative stage.

How is intelligence defined today, and what causes cognitive growth in young adults?

- Traditional views that equated IQ with intelligence are being questioned. According to Sternberg's triarchic theory, intelligence is made up of componential, experiential, and contextual components. Practical intelligence seems to be related most closely with career success, and emotional intelligence underlies social interactions and responsiveness to others' needs.

- Creativity often peaks in young adulthood, possibly because young people view problems in novel ways rather than in the familiar ways of their older peers.

- Important life events, such as births and deaths, seem to contribute to cognitive growth by generating new insights into the self and revised views of the world.

■ **Who attends college today, and how is the college population changing?**

- The profile of the U.S. college student has been changing, with many students beyond the traditional 19- to 22-year-old age range. Compared to white high school graduates, a smaller percent of African American and Hispanic American high school graduates enter college.

■ **What do students learn in college, and what difficulties do they face?**

- Many college students, particularly those who experience a decline in status from their high school days, fall victim to the first-year adjustment reaction—feelings of depression, anxiety, and withdrawal that typically pass quickly as the students integrate themselves into their new surroundings.

- In college, students learn different ways of understanding the world, shifting from dualistic thinking to multiple thinking and to a more relativistic view of values.

- Gender differences exist in the fields of study chosen by students, students' expectations regarding their future careers and earnings, and professors' treatment of students.

- Academic disidentification is the tendency of some students (especially females and African Americans) to abandon personal identification with an academic domain because of negative stereotypes that predict their failure in that domain. The concept of stereotype threat, the fear of confirming the negative stereotypes, may explain this phenomenon.

Key Terms and Concepts

senescence (p. 443)

stress (p. 449)

psychoneuroimmunology (PNI) (p. 449)

primary appraisal (p. 450)

secondary appraisal (p. 450)

psychosomatic disorders (p. 451)

coping (p. 452)

defensive coping (p. 453)

hardiness (p. 453)

postformal thought (p. 457)

acquisitive stage (p. 458)

achieving stage (p. 458)

responsible stage (p. 458)

executive stage (p. 458)

reintegrative stage (p. 458)

triarchic theory of intelligence (p. 459)

practical intelligence (p. 460)

emotional intelligence (p. 460)

creativity (p. 461)

first-year adjustment reaction (p. 467)

stereotype threat (p. 472)

14 Social and Personality Development in Early Adulthood

Chapter Overview

FORGING RELATIONSHIPS: INTIMACY, LIKING, AND LOVING DURING EARLY ADULTHOOD

The Components of Happiness: Fulfilling Psychological Needs

The Social Clocks of Adulthood

Seeking Intimacy: Erikson's View of Young Adulthood

Friendship

Falling in Love: When Liking Turns to Loving

Passionate and Companionate Love: The Two Faces of Love

Sternberg's Triangular Theory: The Three Faces of Love

Choosing a Partner: Recognizing Mr. or Ms. Right

Attachment Styles and Romantic Relationships: Do Adult Loving Styles Reflect Attachment in Infancy?

THE COURSE OF RELATIONSHIPS

Marriage, POSSLQ, and Other Relationship Choices: Sorting Out the Options of Early Adulthood

What Makes Marriage Work?

Parenthood: Choosing to Have Children

Gay and Lesbian Parents

Staying Single: I Want to Be Alone

WORK: CHOOSING AND EMBARKING ON A CAREER

Identity During Young Adulthood: The Role of Work

Picking an Occupation: Choosing Life's Work

Gender and Career Choices: Women's Work

Why Do People Work? More Than Earning a Living

Prologue: Love Without Borders

Ah, the weddings. The hair, the makeup, the layers of fabric. They're enough to frazzle the calmest of brides. But when Taiwanese-American Grace Tsai married Japanese-Canadian Richard Tsuyuki, she took wedding-day stress to a whole new level. After a Roman Catholic ceremony in a New Jersey church, the wedding party dashed to a banquet hall in Philadelphia's Chinatown. There was the waltz, the cake and the bouquet toss. Then the new Mrs. Tsuyuki rushed to a back room, took off her white gown and returned in a slim-fitting, high-necked Chinese *chipao* dress for a customary tea ceremony. As guests dug into a 13-course Chinese meal, she dashed out, changed into an elaborate Japanese kimono and reappeared for a sake-drinking ritual. By the time the bride raised her tiny cup of Japanese wine, she was ready for a drink. "It was totally crazy and exhausting," she says. "But it was important for us to melt together our different cultures." (Clemetson, 2000, p. 62)

Weddings of brides and grooms of different ethnicities, races, and religions produce a melding of cultural customs.

Life hasn't gotten any less complicated for Grace and Richard. Expecting their first child, they are outfitting the baby's room with the ABCs on one wall, Chinese characters on another, and Japanese characters on a third.

Early adulthood, as Grace and Richard are discovering, is a period during which we face a variety of developmental tasks (see Table 14-1). During this period, we come to grips with the notion that we are no longer other people's children. We begin to perceive ourselves as adults, full members of society with significant responsibilities (Arnett, 2000).

This chapter examines those challenges, concentrating on the development and course of relationships with others. We will consider first how we establish and maintain love for others, looking at the differences between liking and loving, and the different types of love. The chapter will examine how people choose partners and how their choices are influenced by societal and cultural factors.

Close relationships are a major preoccupation for most young adults. We will examine the choice of whether to marry and the factors that influence the course and success of marriage. We also consider how having a child influences a couple's happiness and the kinds of roles children play within a marriage. Families today come in all shapes and sizes, representing the complexity of relationships that are the stuff of life for most people during early adulthood.

Table 14-1   The Developmental Tasks of Adulthood

Adulthood (Ages 20–40)	Middle Adulthood (Ages 40–60)	Late Adulthood (Ages 60+)
1. Psychological separation from parents.	1. Dealing with body changes or illness and altered body image.	1. Maintaining physical health.
2. Accepting responsibility for one's own body.	2. Adjusting to middle-life changes in sexuality.	2. Adapting to physical infirmities or permanent impairment.
3. Becoming aware of one's personal history and time limitation.	3. Accepting the passage of time.	3. Using time in gratifying ways.
4. Integrating sexual experience (homosexual or heterosexual).	4. Adjusting to aging.	4. Adapting to losses of partner and friends.
5. Developing a capacity for intimacy with a partner.	5. Living through illness and death of parents and contemporaries.	5. Remaining oriented to present and future, not preoccupied with the past.
6. Deciding whether to have children.	6. Dealing with realities of death.	6. Forming new emotional ties.
7. Having and relating to children.	7. Redefining relationship to spouse or partner.	7. Reversing roles of children and grandchildren (as caretakers).
8. Establishing adult relationships with parents.	8. Deepening relations with grown children or grandchildren.	8. Seeking and maintaining social contacts: companionship vs. isolation and loneliness.
9. Acquiring marketable skills.	9. Maintaining longstanding friendships and creating new ones.	9. Attending to sexual needs and (changing) expressions.
10. Choosing a career.	10. Consolidating work identity.	10. Continuing meaningful work and play (satisfying use of time).
11. Using money to further development.	11. Transmitting skills and values to the young.	11. Using financial resources wisely, for self and others.
12. Assuming a social role.	12. Allocating financial resources effectively.	12. Integrating retirement into new lifestyle.
13. Adapting ethical and spiritual values.	13. Accepting social responsibility.	
	14. Accepting social change.	

(*Source:* Colarusso & Nemiroff, 1981.)

Careers are another preoccupation of young adulthood. We see how identity during early adulthood is often tied to one's job and how people decide on the kind of work they wish to do. The chapter ends with a discussion of the reasons people work—not only to earn money—and techniques for choosing a career.

After reading this chapter, you will be able to answer these questions:

■ **How do young adults form loving relationships, and how does love change over time?**

■ **How do people choose spouses, and what makes relationships work and cease working?**

■ **How does the arrival of children affect a relationship?**

■ **Why is choosing a career such an important issue for young adults, and what factors influence the choice of a career?**

■ **Why do people work, and what elements of a job bring satisfaction?**

Looking Ahead

Forging Relationships: Intimacy, Liking, and Loving During Early Adulthood

Asia Kaia Linn, whose parents chose her name while looking through a world atlas, met Chris Applebaum about six years ago at Hampshire College in Massachusetts and fell in love with him one Saturday night while they were dancing.

Although many women might swoon over a guy with perfect hair and fluid dance steps, it was his silly haircut and overall lack of coordination that delighted her. "He's definitely a funny dancer, and he spun me around and we were just being goofy," Ms. Linn recalled. "I realized how much fun we were having, and I thought this is ridiculous and fabulous and I love him." (Brady, 1995, p. 47)

Asia followed her first instincts: Ultimately, she and Chris were married in an unconventional wedding ceremony at an art gallery. Guests were dressed in a psychedelic mix of fashion, and the ring-bearer delivered the wedding ring by steering a remote-control truck down the aisle of the gallery.

Not everyone falls in love quite as easily as Asia. For some, the road to love is tortuous, meandering through soured relationships and fallen dreams; for others, it is a road never taken. For some, love leads to marriage and a life befitting society's storybook view of home, children, and long years together as a couple. For many, it leads to a less happy ending, prematurely concluding in divorce and custody battles.

Intimacy and forming relationships are major considerations during early adulthood. Young adults' happiness stems, in part, from their relationships, and many worry about whether or not they are developing serious relationships "on time." Even those who are not interested in forming a long-term relationship typically are focused, to some extent, on connecting with others.

The Components of Happiness: Fulfilling Psychological Needs

Think back over the last 7 days of your life. What made you happiest? According to research on young adults, it probably wasn't money or material objects that brought you happiness. Instead, happiness usually is derived from feelings of independence, competence, self-esteem, or relating well to other people (Sheldon et al., 2001).

If you ask young adults to recall a time when they were happy, they are most likely to mention an experience or moment when they felt their psychological needs rather than material needs had been satisfied. Being chosen for a new job, developing a deep relationship, or

social clock the culturally determined psychological timepiece providing a sense of whether we have reached the major benchmarks of life at the appropriate time in comparison to our peers.

moving into their own apartment or home are examples of the kinds of experiences that might be recalled. Conversely, when they remember times when they were least satisfied, they mention incidents in which basic psychological needs were left unfulfilled.

It's interesting to compare these findings, based on research in the United States, with studies conducted in Asian countries. For example, young adults in Korea more often associate satisfaction with experiences involving other people, whereas young adults in the United States experienced satisfaction from experiences relating to the self and self-esteem. Apparently, culture influences which psychological needs are most important in determining happiness (Sheldon et al., 2001; Diener, Oishi, & Lucas, 2003; Sedikides, Gaertner, & Toguchi, 2003; Jongudomkarn & Camfield, 2006).

The Social Clocks of Adulthood

Having children. Receiving a promotion. Getting divorced. Changing jobs. Becoming a grandparent. Each of these events marks a moment on what has been called the social clock of life.

The **social clock** is a term used to describe the psychological timepiece that records the major milestones in people's lives. Each of us has such a social clock that provides us with a sense of whether we have reached the major benchmarks of life early, late, or right on time in comparison to our peers. Our social clocks are culturally determined: They reflect the expectations of the society in which we live.

Until the middle of the 20th century, the social clocks of adulthood were fairly uniform—at least for upper-class and middle-class people in Western society. Most people moved through a series of developmental stages closely aligned with particular ages. For example, the typical man completed his education by his early 20s, started a career, married in his mid-20s, and was working to provide for a growing family by the time he was in his 30s. Women also followed a set pattern, which focused on getting married and raising children—but not, in most cases, entering a profession and developing a career.

Today, there is considerably more heterogeneity in the social clocks of both men and women. The timing at which major life events occur has changed considerably. Furthermore, as we consider next, women's social clocks have changed dramatically as a result of social and cultural changes.

Women's Social Clocks. Developmental psychologist Ravenna Helson and colleagues suggest that people have several social clocks from which to choose, and the selection they make has substantial implications for personality development during middle adulthood. Focusing on a sample of women who graduated from college during the early 1960s, Helson's longitudinal research has examined women whose social clocks were focused either on their families, on careers, or on a more individualistic target (Helson & Moane, 1987).

Helson found several broad patterns. Over the course of the study, which assessed participants at the ages of 21, 27, and 43, the women generally became more self-disciplined and committed to their duties. They also felt greater independence and confidence, and they were able to cope with stress and adversity more effectively. Finding a spouse and embarking on a journey toward motherhood meant that many women exhibited what Helson called traditional feminine behavior from about age 21 to 27. But as children grew up and maternal duties diminished, women took on less traditional roles. The study also found some intriguing similarities in personality development in women who chose to focus on family compared with those who focused on career. Both groups tended to show generally positive changes. In contrast, women who had no strong focus on either family or career tended to show either little change or more negative shifts in personality development, such as becoming less satisfied over time.

Helson's conclusion is that the particular social clock that a woman chooses may not be the critical factor in determining the course of personality development. Instead, the process of

Always culturally determined, women's social clocks have changed over the years.

choosing a particular social clock may be important in producing growth, whether that social clock involves motherhood or a career path. It is less important whether a woman chooses to first develop a career and then embark toward motherhood, or chooses the opposite pattern, or follows some other path entirely. What is more critical is investing in and focusing on a particular trajectory.

It is important to keep in mind that social clocks are culturally determined. The timing of motherhood and the type and course of a woman's career are both influenced by the social, economic, and cultural worlds in which the woman lives (Helson, Stewart, & Ostrove, 1995; Stewart & Ostrove, 1998).

Despite changes in the nature of women's (and men's) social clocks, one aspect of adulthood still remains a central feature: the development and maintenance of relationships with others. As we consider next, those relationships are a key part of development during early adulthood.

intimacy-versus-isolation stage according to Erikson, the period of postadolescence into the early 30s that focuses on developing close relationships with others.

Seeking Intimacy: Erikson's View of Young Adulthood

Erik Erikson regarded young adulthood as the time of the **intimacy-versus-isolation stage.** As we first noted in Chapter 12 (see Table 12-1), the intimacy-versus-isolation stage spans the period of postadolescence into the early 30s. During this period, the focus is on developing close, intimate relationships with others.

Erikson's idea of intimacy comprises several aspects. One is a degree of selflessness, involving the sacrifice of one's own needs to those of another. A further component involves sexuality, the experience of joint pleasure from focusing not just on one's own gratification but also on that of one's partner. Finally, there is deep devotion, marked by efforts to fuse one's identity with the identity of a partner.

According to Erikson, those who experience difficulties during this stage are often lonely, isolated, and fearful of relationships with others. Their difficulties may stem from an earlier failure to develop a strong identity. In contrast, young adults who are able to form intimate relationships with others on a physical, intellectual, and emotional level successfully resolve the crisis posed by this stage of development.

Although Erikson's approach has been influential, some aspects of his theory trouble today's developmentalists. For instance, Erikson's view of healthy intimacy was limited to adult heterosexuality, the goal of which was to produce children. Consequently, homosexual partnerships, couples who were childless by choice, and other relationships that deviated from what Erikson saw as the ideal were thought of as less than satisfactory. Furthermore, Erikson focused more on men's development than on women's, and did not consider racial and ethnic identity, greatly limiting the applicability of his theory (Yip, Sellers, & Seaton, 2006).

Still, Erikson's work has been influential historically because of its emphasis on examining the continued growth and development of personality throughout the life span. Furthermore, it inspired other developmentalists to consider psychosocial growth during young adulthood and the range of intimate relationships we develop, from friendship to mates for life.

Friendship

Most of our relationships with others involve friends, and for most people maintaining such relationships is an important part of adult life. Why? One reason is that there is a basic *need for belongingness* that leads people in early adulthood to establish and maintain at least a minimum number of relationships with others. Most people are driven toward forming and preserving relationships that allow them to experience a sense of belonging with others (Manstead, 1997; Rice, 1999).

But how do particular people end up becoming our friends? One of the most important reasons is simple proximity—people form friendships with others who live nearby and with

People are most attracted to those who can keep confidences, and are loyal, warm, and affectionate.

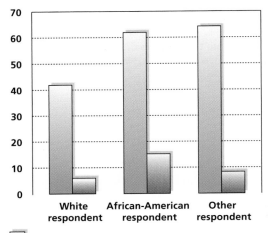

FIGURE 14-1   REPHRASING THE QUESTION

Although a relatively high percentage of whites and blacks claim to have a close friend who is a member of a different race, only a small majority actually name a person of another race or ethnicity when asked to list the names of their close friends.

(*Source:* General Social Survey, 1998.)

Legend:
- Percent who say they have a close friend who is black or white
- Percent who name a close friend who is of a different race

whom they come in contact most frequently. Because of their accessibility, people who are in close proximity can obtain rewards of friendship, such as companionship, social approval, and the occasional helping hand, at relatively little cost.

Similarity also plays an important role in friendship formation. Birds of a feather *do* flock together: People are more attracted to others who hold attitudes and values similar to their own (McCaul et al., 1995; Simpkins et al., 2006; Morry, 2007).

The importance of similarity becomes particularly evident when we consider cross-race friendships. As we noted in Chapter 12, by the time of adolescence, the number of cross-race close friendships dwindles, a pattern that continues throughout the remainder of the life span. In fact, although most adults claim on surveys to have a close friend of a different race, when they are queried regarding the names of close friends, few include a person of a different race (see Figure 14-1).

We also choose friends on the basis of their personal qualities. What's most important? According to results of surveys, people are most attracted to others who keep confidences and are loyal, warm, and affectionate. In addition, people tend to like those who are supportive, frank, and have a good sense of humor (Parlee, 1979; Hartup & Stevens, 1999).

Falling in Love: When Liking Turns to Loving

After a few chance encounters at the laundromat where they wash their clothes each week, Rebecca and Jerry begin to talk with one another. They find they have a lot in common, and they begin to look forward to what are now semi-planned meetings. After several weeks, they go out on their first official date and discover that they are well suited to each other.

If such a pattern seems predictable, it is: Most relationships develop in a fairly similar way, following a surprisingly regular progression (Burgess & Huston, 1979; Berscheid, 1985):

- Two people interact with each other more often and for longer periods of time. Furthermore, the range of settings increases.
- The two people increasingly seek out each other's company.
- They open up to each other more and more, disclosing more intimate information about themselves. They begin to share physical intimacies.
- The couple is more willing to share both positive and negative feelings, and they may offer criticism in addition to praise.
- They begin to agree on the goals they hold for the relationship.
- Their reactions to situations become more similar.
- They begin to feel that their own psychological well-being is tied to the success of the relationship, viewing it as unique, irreplaceable, and cherished.
- Finally, their definition of themselves and their behavior changes: They begin to see themselves and act as a couple, rather than as two separate individuals.

Another view of the way in which a relationship evolves was put forward by psychologist Bernard Murstein (Murstein, 1976, 1986, 1987). According to **stimulus-value-role (SVR) theory,** relationships proceed in a fixed order of three stages.

In the first stage, the *stimulus stage*, relationships are built on surface, physical characteristics such as the way a person looks. Usually, this represents just the initial encounter. The second stage, the *value stage*, usually occurs between the second and the seventh encounter. In the value stage, the relationship is characterized by increasing similarity of values and beliefs. Finally, in the third stage, the *role stage*, the relationship is built on specific roles played by the participants. For instance, the couple may define themselves as boyfriend–girlfriend or husband–wife.

stimulus-value-role (SVR) theory   the theory that relationships proceed in a fixed order of three stages: stimulus, value, and role.

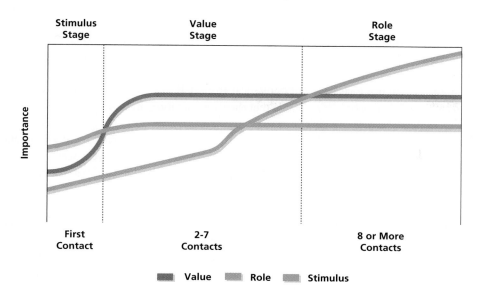

FIGURE 14-2 **THE PATH OF RELATIONSHIPS**

According to stimulus-value-role (SVR) theory, relationships proceed through a fixed series of stages.

(*Source:* Murstein, 1987.)

Although stimulus, value, and role factors each dominate at a particular stage, they also contribute at other junctures in the developing relationship. For instance, consider Figure 14-2, which illustrates the course of a typical relationship.

Of course, not every relationship follows a similar pattern, and this has led to criticism of SVR theory (Gupta & Singh, 1982; Sternberg, 1986). For instance, there seems to be no logical reason why value factors, rather than stimulus factors, could not predominate early in a relationship. Two people who first encounter each other at a political meeting, for example, could be attracted to each other's views of current issues. Consequently, additional approaches have been devised to explain the course of relationship development.

Passionate and Companionate Love: The Two Faces of Love

Is "love" just a lot of "liking"? Most developmental psychologists would answer negatively; love not only differs quantitatively from liking, it represents a qualitatively different state. For example, love, at least in its early stages, involves relatively intense physiological arousal, an all-encompassing interest in another individual, recurrent fantasies about the other individual, and rapid swings of emotion (Lamm & Wiesman, 1997). As distinct from liking, love includes elements of closeness, passion, and exclusivity (Walster & Walster, 1978; Hendrick & Hendrick, 2003).

Not all love is the same. We don't love our mothers the same way we love girlfriends or boyfriends, brothers or sisters, or lifelong friends. What distinguishes these different types of love? Some psychologists suggest that our love relationships can fall into two different categories: passionate or companionate.

Passionate (or romantic) love is a state of powerful absorption in someone. It includes intense physiological interest and arousal, and caring for another's needs. In comparison, **companionate love** is the strong affection that we have for those with whom our lives are deeply involved (Hecht, Marston, & Larkey, 1994; Lamm & Wiesman, 1997; Hendrick & Hendrick, 2003).

What is it that fuels the fires of passionate love? According to one theory, anything that produces strong emotions—even negative ones such as jealousy, anger, or fear of rejection—may be the source of deepening passionate love.

In psychologists Elaine Hatfield and Ellen Berscheid's **labeling theory of passionate love,** individuals experience romantic love when two events occur together: intense physiological arousal and situational cues that indicated that "love" is the appropriate label for the feelings they are experiencing (Berscheid & Walster, 1974a). The physiological arousal can be produced by sexual arousal, excitement, or even negative emotions such as jealousy. Whatever the cause,

passionate (or romantic) love   a state of powerful absorption in someone.

companionate love   the strong affection for those with whom our lives are deeply involved.

labeling theory of passionate love   the theory that individuals experience romantic love when two events occur together: intense physiological arousal and situational cues suggesting that the arousal is due to love.

The idea of romantic love is predominately a western concept. How do you think members of other cultures view romantic or passionate love?

intimacy component the component of love that encompasses feelings of closeness, affection, and connectedness.

passion component the component of love that comprises the motivational drives relating to sex, physical closeness, and romance.

decision/commitment component the third aspect of love that embodies both the initial cognition that one loves another person and the longer-term determination to maintain that love.

if that arousal is subsequently labeled as "I must be falling in love" or "she makes my heart flutter" or "he really turns me on," then the experience is attributed to passionate love.

The theory is particularly useful in explaining why people may feel deepened love even when they experience continual rejection or hurt from their assumed lover. It suggests that such negative emotions can produce strong physiological arousal. If this arousal is interpreted as being caused by "love," then people may decide that they are even more in love than they were before they experienced the negative emotions.

But why should people label an emotional experience as "love" when there are so many possible alternatives? One answer is that in Western cultures, romantic love is seen as possible, acceptable, desirable—an experience to be sought. The virtues of passion are extolled in love ballads, commercials, television shows, and films. Consequently, young adults are primed and ready to experience love in their lives (Dion & Dion, 1988; Hatfield & Rapson, 1993; Florsheim, 2003).

It is interesting to note that this is not the way it is in every culture. For instance, in many cultures, passionate, romantic love is a foreign concept. Marriages may be arranged on the basis of economic and status considerations. Even in Western cultures, the concept of love is of relatively recent origin. For instance, the notion that couples need to be in love was not "invented" until the Middle Ages, when social philosophers first suggested that love ought to be a requirement for marriage. Their goal in making such a proposal: to provide an alternative to the raw sexual desire that had served as the primary basis for marriage before (Lewis, 1958; Xiaohe & Whyte, 1990; Haslett, 2004).

Sternberg's Triangular Theory: The Three Faces of Love

To psychologist Robert Sternberg, love is more complex than a simple division into passionate and companionate types. He suggests instead that love is made up of three components: intimacy, passion, and decision/commitment. The **intimacy component** encompasses feelings of closeness, affection, and connectedness. The **passion component** comprises the motivational drives relating to sex, physical closeness, and romance. This component is exemplified by intense, physiologically arousing feelings of attraction. Finally, the third aspect of love, the **decision/commitment component,** embodies both the initial cognition that one loves another person and the longer-term determination to maintain that love (Sternberg, 1986, 1988, 1997b).

These components can be combined to form eight different types of love depending on which of the three components is either present or missing from a relationship (see Table 14-2).

Table 14-2	The Combinations of Love			
	Component			
Type of Love	Intimacy	Passion	Decision/Commitment	Example
Nonlove	Absent	Absent	Absent	The way you might feel about the person who takes your ticket at the movies.
Liking	Present	Absent	Absent	Good friends who have lunch together at least once or twice a week.
Infatuated love	Absent	Present	Absent	A "fling" or short-term relationship based only on sexual attraction.
Empty love	Absent	Absent	Present	An arranged marriage or a couple who have decided to stay married "for the sake of the children."
Romantic love	Present	Present	Absent	A couple who have been happily dating a few months, but have not made any plans for a future together.
Companionate love	Present	Absent	Present	A couple who enjoy each other's company and their relationship, although they no longer feel much sexual interest in each other.
Fatuous love	Absent	Present	Present	A couple who decides to move in together after knowing each other for only two weeks.
Consummate love	Present	Present	Present	A loving, sexually vibrant, long-term relationship.

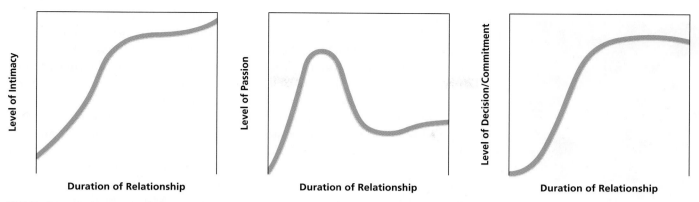

FIGURE 14-3 THE SHAPE OF LOVE

Over the course of a relationship, the three aspects of love—intimacy, passion, and decision/commitment—vary in strength. How do these change as a relationship develops?
(*Source:* Sternberg, 1986.)

For instance, nonlove refers to people who have only the most casual of relationships; it consists of the absence of the three components of intimacy, passion, and decision/commitment. *Liking* develops when only intimacy is present; *infatuated love* exists when only passion is felt; and *empty love* exists when only decision/commitment is present.

Other types of love involve a mix of two or more components. For instance, romantic love occurs when intimacy and passion are present, and *companionate love* when intimacy and decision/commitment occur jointly. When two people experience romantic love, they are drawn together physically and emotionally, but they do not necessarily view the relationship as lasting. Companionate love, on the other hand, may occur in long-lasting relationships in which physical passion has taken a back seat.

Fatuous love exists when passion and decision/commitment, without intimacy, are present. Fatuous love is a kind of mindless loving in which there is no emotional bond between the partners.

Finally, the eighth kind of love is *consummate love*. In consummate love, all three components of love are present. Although we might assume that consummate love represents the "ideal" love, such a view may well be mistaken. Many long-lasting and entirely satisfactory relationships are based on types of love other than consummate love. Furthermore, the type of love that predominates in a relationship varies over time. As shown Figure 14-3, in strong, loving relationships the level of decision/commitment peaks and remains fairly stable. By contrast, passion tends to peak early in a relationship, but then declines and levels off. Intimacy also increases fairly rapidly, but can continue to grow over time.

Sternberg's triangular theory of love emphasizes both the complexity of love and its dynamic, evolving quality. As people and relationships develop and change over time, so does their love.

Choosing a Partner: Recognizing Mr. or Ms. Right

For many young adults, the search for a partner is a major pursuit during early adulthood. Certainly society offers a great deal of advice on how to succeed in this endeavor, as a glance at the array of magazines at any supermarket check-out counter confirms. Despite all the counsel, however, the road to identifying an individual to share one's life is not always easy.

Seeking a Spouse: Is Love the Only Thing That Matters? Most people have no hesitation in articulating that the major factor in choosing a husband or wife is love. Most people in the United States, that is: If we ask people in other societies, love becomes a secondary consideration. For instance, consider the results of a survey in which college students were

What traits are valued in matters of the heart? There are both commonalities and differences across cultures in what are seen as important traits. In China, men see good health as an important consideration; Chinese women value emotional stability and maturity.

asked if they would marry someone they did not love. Hardly anyone in the United States, Japan, or Brazil would consider it. On the other hand, a goodly proportion of college students in Pakistan and India would find it acceptable to marry without love (Levine, 1993).

If love is not the only important factor, what else matters? The characteristics differ considerably from one culture to another (see Table 14-3). For instance, a survey of nearly 10,000 people from around the world found that although people in the United States believed that love and mutual attraction were the primary characteristics, in China men ranked good health most important and women rated emotional stability and maturity most critical. In contrast, in South Africa men from a Zulu background rated emotional stability first, and Zulu women rated dependable character as being of greatest concern (Buss et al., 1990; Buss, 2003).

On the other hand, there are commonalities across cultures. For instance, love and mutual attraction, even if not at the top of a specific culture's list, were relatively highly desired across all cultures. Furthermore, traits such as dependability, emotional stability, pleasing disposition, and intelligence were highly valued almost universally.

Certain gender differences in the preferred characteristics of a mate were similar across cultures—findings that have been confirmed by other surveys (e.g., Sprecher, Sullivan, & Hatfield, 1994). Men, more than women, prefer a potential marriage partner who is physically attractive. In contrast, women, more than men, prefer a potential spouse who is ambitious and industrious.

One explanation for cross-cultural similarities in gender differences rests on evolutionary factors. According to psychologist David Buss and colleagues (Buss, 2004), human beings, as a

Table 14-3 Most Desired Characteristics in a Marriage Partner

	China		South African (Zulu)		United States	
	Males	**Females**	**Males**	**Females**	**Males**	**Females**
Mutual Attraction—Love	4	8	10	5	1	1
Emotional Stability and Maturity	5	1	1	2	2	2
Dependable Character	6	7	3	1	3	3
Pleasing Disposition	13	16	4	3	4	4
Education and Intelligence	8	4	6	6	5	5
Good Health	1	3	5	4	6	9
Sociability	12	9	11	8	8	8
Desire for Home and Children	2	2	9	9	9	7
Refinement, Neatness	7	10	7	10	10	12
Ambition and Industriousness	10	5	8	7	11	6
Good Looks	11	15	14	16	7	13
Similar Education	15	12	12	12	12	10
Good Financial Prospects	16	14	18	13	16	11
Good Cook and Housekeeper	9	11	2	15	13	16
Favorable Social Status or Rating	14	13	17	14	14	14
Similar Religious Background	18	18	16	11	15	15
Chastity (no prior sexual intercourse)	3	6	13	18	17	18
Similar Political Background	17	17	15	17	18	17

Note: numbers indicate rank ordering of characteristics.
(*Source:* Buss et al., 1990.)

species, seek out certain characteristics in their mates that are likely to maximize the availability of beneficial genes. He argues that males in particular are genetically programmed to seek out mates with traits that indicate they have high reproductive capacity. Consequently, physically attractive, younger women might be more desirable since they are more capable of having children over a longer time period.

In contrast, women are genetically programmed to seek out men who have the potential to provide scarce resources in order to increase the likelihood that their offspring will survive. Consequently, they are attracted to mates who offer the highest potential of providing economic well-being (Walter, 1997; Kasser & Sharma, 1999; Li et al., 2002).

The evolutionary explanation for gender differences has come under heavy fire from critics. First, there is the problem that the explanation is untestable. Furthermore, the similarities across cultures relating to different gender preferences may simply reflect similar patterns of gender stereotyping that have nothing to do with evolution. In addition, although some of the gender differences in what men and women prefer are consistent across cultures, there are numerous inconsistencies as well.

Finally, some critics of the evolutionary approach suggest that finding that women prefer a partner who has good earning potential may have nothing to do with evolution and everything to do with the fact that men generally hold more power, status, and other resources fairly consistently across different cultures. Consequently, it is a rational choice for women to prefer a high-earning-potential spouse. On the other hand, because men don't need to take economic considerations into account, they can use more inconsequential criteria—like physical attractiveness—in choosing a spouse. In short, the consistencies that are found across cultures may be due to the realities of economic life that are similar throughout different cultures (Eagly & Wood, 2003).

Filtering Models: Sifting Out a Spouse.　While surveys assist in identifying the characteristics that are highly valued in a potential spouse, they are less helpful in determining how a specific individual is chosen as a partner. One approach that helps explain this is the filtering model developed by psychologists Louis Janda and Karen Klenke-Hamel (1980). They suggest that people seeking a mate screen potential candidates through successively finer-grained filters, just as we sift flour in order to remove undesirable material (see Figure 14-4).

The model assumes that people first filter for factors relating to broad determinants of attractiveness. Once these early screens have done their work, more sophisticated types of screening are used. The end result is a choice based on compatibility between the two individuals.

What determines compatibility? It is not only a matter of pleasing personality characteristics; several cultural factors also play an important role. For instance, people often marry according to the principle of homogamy. **Homogamy** is the tendency to marry someone who is similar in age, race, education, religion, and other basic demographic characteristics. Homogamy has traditionally been the dominant standard for most marriages in the United States.

On the other hand, the importance of homogamy is declining, particularly among certain ethnic groups. For example, the rate of intermarriage among African American men increased by three-quarters in the 1990s. Still, for other groups—such as Hispanic and Asian immigrants—the principle of homogamy still has considerable influence (also see Figure 14-5 on page 489; Suro, 1999; Qian & Lichter, 2007).

The marriage gradient represents another societal standard that determines who marries whom. The **marriage gradient** is the tendency for men to marry women who are slightly younger, smaller, and lower in status, and women to marry men who are slightly older, larger, and higher in status (Bernard, 1982).

The marriage gradient, which has a powerful influence on marriage in the United States, has important, and unfortunate, effects on partner choice. For one thing, it limits the number of potential mates for women, especially as they age, while allowing men a wider choice of partners as their age increases. Furthermore, some men do not marry because they cannot find

homogamy　the tendency to marry someone who is similar in age, race, education, religion, and other basic demographic characteristics.

marriage gradient　the tendency for men to marry women who are slightly younger, smaller, and lower in status, and women to marry men who are slightly older, larger, and higher in status.

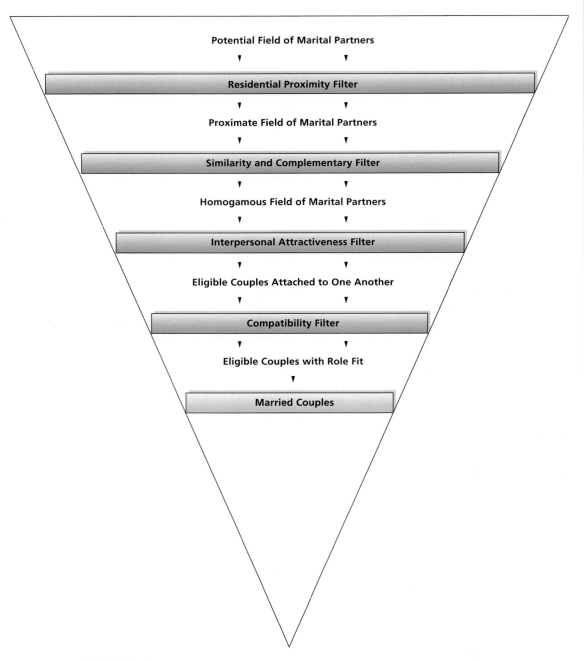

FIGURE 14-4   FILTERING POTENTIAL MARRIAGE PARTNERS

According to one approach, we screen potential mates through successively finer-grained filters in order to settle on an appropriate spouse.

(*Source:* Adapted from Janda & Klenke-Hamel, 1980.)

women of low enough status to meet the demands of the gradient, or cannot find women of the same or higher status who are willing to accept them as mates. Consequently, they are, in the words of sociologist Jessie Bernard (1982), "bottom of the barrel" men. On the other hand, some women will be unable to marry because they are higher in status or seek someone of higher status than anyone in the available pool of men—"cream of the crop" women, in Bernard's words.

The marriage gradient makes finding a spouse particularly difficult for well-educated African American women. Fewer African American men attend college than African American women,

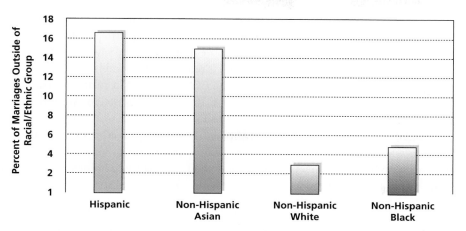

FIGURE 14-5 MARRIAGE OUTSIDE OF RACIAL/ETHNIC GROUP

Although homogamy has been the standard for most marriages in the United States, the rate of marriages crossing ethnic and racial lines is substantial.

(*Source:* Based on data from William H. Grey, Milken Institute, reported in *American Demographics,* Nov. 1999.)

making the potential pool of men who are suitable—as defined by society and the marriage gradient—relatively small. Consequently, relative to women of other races, African American women are more apt to marry men who are less educated than they are—or not marry at all (Tucker & Mitchell-Kernan, 1995; Kiecolt & Fossett, 1997; Willie & Reddick, 2003).

Attachment Styles and Romantic Relationships: Do Adult Loving Styles Reflect Attachment in Infancy?

"I want a girl just like the girl that married dear old Dad." So go the lyrics of an old song, suggesting that the songwriter would like to find someone who loves him as much as his mother did. Is this just a corny tune, or is there a kernel of truth in this sentiment? Put more broadly, is the kind of attachment that people experience during infancy reflected in their adult romantic relationships?

Increasing evidence suggests that it very well may be. As you may recall, attachment refers to the positive emotional bond that develops between a child and a particular individual (see Chapter 6). Most infants fall into one of three attachment categories: securely attached children, who have healthy, positive, trusting relationships with their caregivers; avoidant infants, who are relatively indifferent to caregivers and who avoid interactions with them; and ambivalent infants, who show great distress when separated from a caregiver, but who appear angry upon the caregiver's return.

According to psychologist Phillip Shaver and his colleagues, attachment styles continue into adulthood and affect the nature of romantic relationships (Tracy, Shaver, & Albino, 2003; Davis et al., 2006; Mikulincer & Shaver, 2007). For instance, consider the following statements:

(1) I find it relatively easy to get close to others and am comfortable depending on them and having them depend on me. I don't often worry about being abandoned or about someone getting too close to me.

(2) I am somewhat uncomfortable being close to others; I find it difficult to trust them completely, difficult to allow myself to depend on them. I am nervous when anyone gets too close, and often love partners want me to be more intimate than I feel comfortable being.

(3) I find that others are reluctant to get as close as I would like. I often worry that my partner doesn't really love me or won't want to stay with me. I want to merge completely with another person, and this desire sometimes scares people away. (Shaver, Hazan, & Bradshaw, 1988)

According to Shaver's research, agreement with the first statement reflects a secure attachment style. Adults who agree with this statement readily enter into relationships and feel happy and confident about the future success of their relationships. Most young adults—just over half—display the secure style of attachment (Hazan & Shaver, 1987).

Some psychologists believe that our attachment style as infants is repeated in the quality of our intimate relationships as adults.

Research finds that the quality of lesbian and gay relationships differs little from that of heterosexual relationships.

In contrast, adults who agree with the second statement typically display the avoidant attachment style. These individuals, who make up about a quarter of the population, tend to be less invested in relationships, have higher break-up rates, and often feel lonely.

Finally, agreement with the third category is reflective of an ambivalent style. Adults with an ambivalent style have a tendency to become overly invested in relationships, have repeated break-ups with the same partner, and have relatively low self-esteem. Around 20% of adults, gay and straight, fall into this category (Simpson, 1990).

Attachment style is also related to the nature of care that adults give to their romantic partners when they need assistance. For instance, secure adults tend to provide more sensitive and supportive care, being responsive to their partner's psychological needs. In comparison, anxious adults are more likely to provide compulsive, intrusive (and ultimately less helpful) aid to partners (Shaver, 1994; Feeney & Collins, 2001, 2003; Gleason, Iida, & Bolger, 2003).

It seems clear that there are continuities between infants' attachment styles and their behavior as adults. People who are having difficulty in relationships might well look back to their infancy to identify the root of their problem (Brennan & Shaver, 1995; Rholes et al., 2007). Insight into the roots of our current behavior can sometimes help us learn more adaptive skills as adults.

Developmental Diversity

Gay and Lesbian Relationships: Men with Men and Women with Women

Most research conducted by developmental psychologists has examined heterosexual relationships, but an increasing number of studies have looked at relationships involving gay men and those involving lesbian women. The findings suggest that gay relationships are quite similar to relationships between heterosexuals.

For example, gay men describe successful relationships in ways that are similar to heterosexual couples' descriptions. They believe that successful relationships involve greater appreciation for the partner and the couple as a whole, less conflict, and more positive feelings toward the partner. Similarly, lesbian women in a relationship show high levels of attachment, caring, intimacy, affection, and respect (Brehm, 1992; Beals, Impett, & Peplau, 2002; Kurdek, 2006).

Furthermore, the age preferences expressed in the marriage gradient for heterosexuals also extend to partner preferences for homosexual men. Like heterosexual men, homosexual men prefer partners who are the same age or younger. On the other hand, lesbians' age preferences fall somewhere between those of heterosexual women and heterosexual men (Kenrick et al., 1995).

Finally, despite the stereotype that gay males, in particular, find it difficult to form relationships and are interested in only sexual alliances, the reality is different. Most gays and lesbians seek loving, long-term, and meaningful relationships that differ little qualitatively from those desired by heterosexuals (Division 44, 2000; Diamond, 2003; Diamond & Savin-Williams, 2003).

There are virtually no scientific data regarding gay and lesbian marriage, which became a major social issue when the first legal homosexual marriages were conducted in the United States in 2004. It is clear that the question produces strong reactions, but more, it turns out, among older adults than younger ones. Although only 18% of those older than 65 support the legalization of gay marriage, a clear majority—61%—of people younger than 30 support the practice (Deakin, 2004).

Review and Apply

Review

- According to Erikson, young adults are in the intimacy-versus-isolation stage.
- The course of relationships typically follows a pattern of increasing interaction, intimacy, and redefinition. SVR theory regards relationships as passing successively through stimulus, value, and role stages.
- According to the labeling theory of passionate love, people experience love when intense physiological arousal is accompanied by situational cues that the experience should be labeled "love."
- Types of love include passionate and companionate love. Sternberg's triangular theory identifies three basic components (intimacy, passion, and decision/commitment).
- In many Western cultures, love is the most important factor in selecting a partner.
- According to filtering models, people apply increasingly fine filters to potential partners, eventually choosing a mate according to the principles of homogamy and the marriage gradient.
- Attachment styles in infants appear to be linked to the ability to form romantic relationships in adulthood.
- In general, the values applied to relationships by heterosexual, gay, and lesbian couples are more similar than different.

Applying Lifespan Development

- Consider a long-term marriage with which you are familiar. Do you think the relationship involves passionate love or companionate love (or both)? What changes when a relationship moves from passionate to companionate love? From companionate to passionate love? In which direction is it more difficult for a relationship to move? Why?

- *From a social worker's perspective:* How do the principles of homogamy and the marriage gradient work to limit options for high-status women? How do they affect men's options?

The Course of Relationships

He wasn't being a chauvinist or anything, expecting me to do everything and him nothing. He just didn't volunteer to do things that obviously needed doing, so I had to put down some ground rules. Like if I'm in a bad mood, I may just yell: "I work eight hours just like you. This is half your house and half your child, too. You've got to do your share!" Jackson never changed the kitty litter box once in four years, but he changes it now, so we've made great progress. I just didn't expect it to take so much work. We planned this child together and we went through Lamaze together, and Jackson stayed home for the first two weeks. But then—wham—the partnership was over. (Cowan & Cowan, 1992, p. 63)

Relationships, like the individuals who make them up, face a variety of challenges. As men and women move through early adulthood, they encounter significant changes in their lives as they work at starting and building their careers, having children, and establishing, maintaining, and sometimes ending relationships with others. One of the primary questions young adults face is whether and when to marry.

FIGURE 14-6 **POSSLQs**

The number of POSSLQs, or persons of the opposite sex sharing living quarters, has risen considerably in the last three decades. Why do you think this is the case?

(*Source:* U.S. Bureau of the Census, 2001.)

cohabitation couples living together without being married.

POSSLQs, or Persons of the Opposite Sex Sharing Living Quarters, now make up about 10 percent of all couples in the United States—almost 7.5 million people.

Marriage, POSSLQ, and Other Relationship Choices: Sorting Out the Options of Early Adulthood

For some people, the primary issue is not identifying a potential spouse, but whether to marry at all. Although surveys show that most heterosexuals (and a growing number of homosexuals) say they want to get married, a significant number choose some other route. For instance, the past three decades have seen both a decline in the number of married couples and a significant rise in couples living together without being married, a status known as **cohabitation** (see Figure 14-6). These people, whom the U.S. Census Bureau calls *POSSLQs,* or *persons of the opposite sex sharing living quarters,* now make up around 10% of all couples in the United States. In fact, married couples now make up a minority of households: as of 2005, 49.7% of all U.S. households contained a married couple (Fields & Casper, 2001; Doyle, 2004b; Roberts, 2006).

POSSLQs tend to be young: Almost a quarter of cohabiting women and over 15% of cohabiting men are under 25. African Americans are more likely to cohabit than whites. Countries other than the U.S. have even higher cohabitation rates, such as Sweden, where cohabitation is the norm. In Latin America, cohabitation has a long history and is widespread (Tucker & Mitchell-Kernan, 1995).

Why do some couples choose to cohabit rather than to marry? Some feel they are not ready to make a lifelong commitment. Others feel that cohabitation provides "practice" for marriage. Some reject the institution of marriage altogether, maintaining that marriage is outmoded and that it is unrealistic to expect a couple to spend a lifetime together (Hobart & Grigel, 1992; Cunningham & Antill, 1994; Martin, Martin, & Martin, 2001).

Those who feel that cohabiting increases their subsequent chances of a happy marriage are incorrect. On the contrary, the chances of divorce are somewhat higher for those who have previously cohabited, according to data collected in both the United States and Western Europe (Brown, 2003; Doyle, 2004; Hohmann-Marriott, 2006; Rhoades, Stanley, & Markman, 2006).

Despite the prevalence of cohabitation, marriage remains the preferred alternative for most people during early adulthood. Many see marriage as the appropriate culmination of a loving relationship, while others feel it is the "right" thing to do after reaching a particular age in early adulthood. Others seek marriage because of the various roles that a spouse can fill. For instance, a spouse can play an economic role, providing security and financial well-being. Spouses also fill a sexual role, offering a means of sexual gratification and fulfillment that is fully accepted by society. Another role is therapeutic and recreational: Spouses provide a sounding board to discuss one another's problems and act as partners for activities. Marriage also offers the only means of having children that is fully accepted by all segments of society. Finally, marriage offers legal benefits and protections, such as being eligible for medical insurance under a spouse's policy and eligibility for survivor benefits such as Social Security benefits (Lillard & Waite, 1995; Furstenberg, 1996; DeVita, 1996).

Although marriage remains important, it is not a static institution. For example, fewer U.S. citizens are now married than at any time since the late 1890s. Part of this decline in marriage is attributable to higher divorce rates (which we discuss in Chapter 16), but the decision of people to marry later in life is also a contributing factor. The median age of first marriage in the United States is now 27 for men and 25 for women—the oldest age for women since national statistics were first collected in the 1880s (see Figure 14-7; Furstenberg, 1996; U.S. Bureau of the Census, 2001).

In many European countries, legal alternatives to marriage are growing. For instance, France offers "Civil Solidarity Pacts," in which couples receive many of the same legal rights as married couples. What differs is that there is no legal lifetime commitment that they would be asked to make if they married; Civil Solidarity Pacts can be dissolved more easily than marriages (Lyall, 2004).

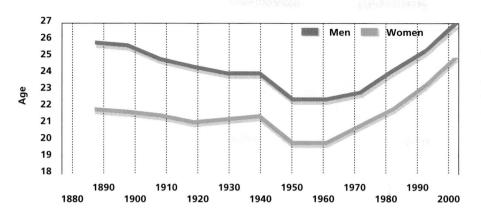

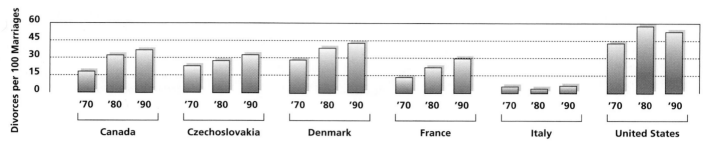

FIGURE 14-8   DIVORCE AROUND THE WORLD

Increases in divorce rates are not just a U.S. phenomenon: Data from other countries also show significant increases.

(*Source:* Population Council Report, 1995.)

Early Marital Conflict.   Conflict in marriage is not unusual. According to some statistics, nearly half of newly married couples experience a significant degree of conflict. One of the major reasons is that partners may initially idealize one another, perceiving each other through the proverbial "starry eyes." However, as the realities of day-to-day living together and interacting begin to sink in, they become more aware of flaws, like the wife whose quotation began this section of the chapter. In fact, perceptions of marital quality over the first 10 years of marriage on the part of both wives and husbands show a decline in the early years, followed by a period of stabilization, and then additional decline (see Figure 14-9; Kurdek, 1999, 2002, 2003a; Huston et al., 2001; Karney & Bradbury, 2005).

There are many sources of marital conflict. Husbands and wives may have difficulty making the transition from being children of their parents to being autonomous adults. Others have difficulty developing an identity apart from their spouses, while some struggle to find a satisfactory allocation of time to share with the spouse, compared with time spent with friends and other family members (Fincham, 1998; Caughlin, 2002; Crawford, Houts, & Huston, 2002; Murray, Bellavia, & Rose, 2003).

On the other hand, most married couples view the early years of marriage as deeply satisfying. For them, marriage can be a kind of extension of courtship. As they negotiate changes in

Successful marriage involves companionship and mutual enjoyment of various activities.

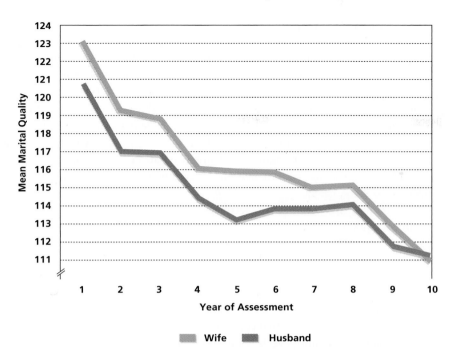

FIGURE 14-9 PERCEPTIONS OF MARITAL QUALITY

At the beginning of marriage, partners see each other in a more idealized manner. But as time passes, the perception of the quality of the marriage declines.

(*Source:* Kurdek, 1999.)

their relationship and learn more about each other, many couples find themselves more deeply in love than before marriage. In fact, the newlywed period is for many couples one of the happiest of their entire married lives (Bird & Melville, 1994; Orbuch et al., 1996; McNulty & Karney, 2004).

Parenthood: Choosing to Have Children

Deciding whether to have children is one of the most important decisions couples make. What makes a couple decide to have children? Child rearing certainly isn't economically advantageous: According to one estimate, a middle-class family with two children spends around $233,000 for each child by the time the child reaches the age of 18. Add in the costs of college and the figure comes to over $300,000 per child (Lino, 2001).

Instead, young adults typically cite psychological reasons for having children. They expect to derive pleasure from watching their children grow, fulfillment from their children's accomplishments, satisfaction from seeing them become successful, and enjoyment from forging a close bond with their children. But there also may be a self-serving element in the decision to have children. For example, parents-to-be may hope that their children will provide for them in their old age, maintain a family business or farm, or simply offer companionship. Others have children because to do so is such a strong societal norm: More than 90% of all married couples have at least one child (Mackey, White, & Day, 1992).

For some couples, there is no decision to have children. Some children are unplanned, the result of the failure or absence of birth control methods. In some cases, the couple may have planned to have children at some point in the future, and so the pregnancy is not regarded as particularly undesirable and may even be welcomed. But in families that had actively not wanted to have children, or already had what they considered "enough" children, the pregnancy can be viewed as problematic (Clinton & Kelber, 1993; Leathers & Kelley, 2000; Pajulo, Helenius, & MaYes, 2006).

The couples who are most likely to have unwanted pregnancies are often the most vulnerable in society. Unplanned pregnancies occur most frequently in younger, poorer, and less educated couples. Happily, there has been a dramatic rise in the use and effectiveness of contraceptives, and the incidence of undesired pregnancies has declined in the last several decades (Centers for Disease Control, 2003; Villarosa, 2003).

Family Size.   The availability and use of effective contraceptives has also dramatically decreased the number of children in the average American family. Almost 70% of Americans polled in the 1930s agreed that the ideal number of children was three or more, but by the 1990s the percentage had shrunk to less than 40%. Today, most families seek to have no more than two children—although most say that three or more is ideal if money is no object (Kate, 1998; Gallup Poll, 2004).

These preferences have been translated into changes in the actual birth rate. In 1957, the *fertility rate* reached a post–World War II peak in the United States of 3.7 children per woman and then began to decline. Today, the rate is at 2.1 children per woman, which is less than the *replacement level*, the number of children that one generation must produce to be able to replenish its numbers. In contrast, in some underdeveloped countries, the fertility rate is as high as 6.9 (World Bank, 2004).

What has produced this decline in the fertility rate? In addition to the availability of more reliable birth control methods, one reason is that increasing numbers of women have joined the workforce. The pressures of simultaneously holding a job and raising a child have convinced many women to have fewer children.

Furthermore, many women who work outside the home are choosing to have children later in their childbearing years in order to develop their careers. In fact, women between the ages of 30 and 34 are the only ones whose rate of births has actually increased over earlier decades. Still, because women who have their first children in their 30s have fewer years in which to have children, they ultimately cannot have as many children as women who begin childbearing in their 20s. Research suggesting that there are health benefits for mothers in terms of spacing children further apart may lead families to ultimately have fewer children (Marcus, 2004).

Some of the traditional incentives for having children—such as their potential for providing economic support in old age—may also no longer be as attractive. Potential parents may view Social Security and other pensions as a more predictable means of support when they are elderly than relying on their children. There is also, as mentioned earlier, the sheer cost of raising a child, particularly the well-publicized increase in the cost of college. This, too, may act as a disincentive for bearing larger numbers of children.

Finally, some couples avoid having children because they fear they will not be good parents or simply don't want the work and responsibility involved in child rearing. Women may also fear that they will share a disproportionate amount of the effort involved in child rearing—a perception that may be an accurate reading of reality, as we consider next.

Dual-Earner Couples.   One of the major historical shifts affecting young adults that began in the last half of the 20th century is the increase in families in which both parents work. Close to three-quarters of married women with school-aged children are employed outside the home, and more than half of mothers with children under the age of 6 are working. In the mid-1960s, only 17% of mothers of 1-year-olds worked full time; now, more than 50% do. In the majority of families, both husband and wife work (Darnton, 1990; Carnegie Task Force, 1994; Barnett & Hyde, 2001).

The income that is generated when both partners work provides economic benefits, but it also takes a toll, particularly on women. Even when both spouses work similar hours, the wife generally spends more time taking care of the children than the husband does (Huppe & Cyr, 1997; Kitterod & Pettersen, 2006). And even though men are spending more time with their children than in the past (the amount of time has increased by one-quarter in the last 20 years), wives still spend more time with their children than husbands do (Families and Work Institute, 1998).

Furthermore, the nature of husbands' contributions to the household often differs from wives'. For instance, husbands tend to carry out chores such as mowing the lawn or house repairs that are more easily scheduled in advance (or sometimes postponed), while women's household chores tend to be devoted to things that need immediate attention, such as child care and meal preparation. As a result, wives experience greater levels of anxiety and stress (Barnett & Shen, 1997; Juster, Ono, & Stafford, 2000; Haddock & Rattenborg, 2003; Lee, Vernon-Feagans, & Vazquez, 2003; see Figure 14-10).

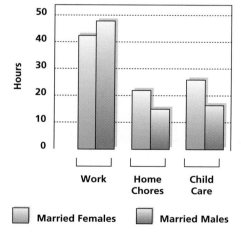

FIGURE 14-10   DIVISION OF LABOR

Although husbands and wives generally work at their paying jobs a similar number of hours each week, wives are apt to spend more time than their husbands doing home chores and in child-care activities. Why do you think this pattern exists?

(*Source:* Googans & Burden, 1987.)

As increasing numbers of women have joined the workforce, more are choosing to have fewer children and have them later.

The Transition to Parenthood: Two's a Couple, Three's a Crowd?   Consider this quote from a spouse who just became a parent:

We had no idea what we were getting into when our first child was born. We certainly prepared for the event, reading magazine articles and books and even attending a class on child care. But when Sheanna was actually born, the sheer enormity of the task of taking care of her, her presence at every moment of the day, and the awesome responsibility of raising another human being weighed on us like nothing else we'd ever faced. Not that it was a burden. But it did make us look at the world with an entirely different perspective.

The arrival of a child alters virtually every aspect of family life, in positive and, sometimes, negative ways. The addition of a child to a household brings about a dramatic shift in the roles spouses must play. They are suddenly placed in new roles—"mother" and "father"—and these new positions may overwhelm their ability to respond in their older, although continuing, roles of "wife" and "husband." In addition, the birth of a child produces significant physical and psychological demands, including near-constant fatigue, new financial responsibilities, and an increase in household chores (Meijer & van den Wittenboer, 2007).

Furthermore, in contrast to many non-Western cultures, in which child rearing is seen as a task that involves the entire community, Western culture's emphasis on individualism views child rearing as a primarily private enterprise. Thus, mothers and fathers in Western society are largely left to forge their own paths after the birth of a child, often without significant community support (Rubin & Chung, 2006; Lamm & Keller, 2007).

Consequently, for many couples, the strains accompanying the birth of a child produce the lowest level of marital satisfaction of any point in their marriage. This is particularly true for

Parenthood expands the roles of both husbands and wives into that of fathers and mothers, a process that can have profound effects on couples' relationships.

women, who tend to be more dissatisfied than men with their marriages after the arrival of children. The most likely reason for this gender difference is that wives often experience a greater increase in their responsibilities than husbands do, even in families in which parents seek to share child-rearing chores (Levy-Shiff, 1994; Laflamme, Pomerleau, & Malcuit, 2002; Lu, 2006).

On the other hand, not all couples experience a decrease in marital satisfaction upon the birth of a child. According to work by John Gottman and colleagues (Shapiro, Gottman, & Carrère, 2000), marital satisfaction can stay steady, and actually rise, with the birth of a child. They identified three factors that permitted couples to successfully weather the increased stress that follows the birth of a child:

- Working to build fondness and affection toward one's partner
- Remaining aware of events in one's spouse's life, and responding to those events
- Considering problems as controllable and solvable

In particular, those couples who were well satisfied with their marriages as newlyweds were more likely to continue to be satisfied as they raised their children. Couples who harbor realistic expectations regarding the extent of child-rearing effort and other household responsibilities they face when children are born also tend to be more satisfied after they become parents. Furthermore, parents who work together as a *coparenting team*, in which they thoughtfully adopt common child-rearing goals and strategies, are more apt to be satisfied with their parenting roles (Schoppe-Sullivan et al., 2006; McHale & Rotman, 2007).

In short, having children can well lead to greater marital satisfaction—at least for couples who are already satisfied with their marriage. For marriages in which satisfaction is low, having children may make a bad situation worse (Shapiro et al., 2000; Driver, Tabares, & Shapiro, 2003).

Gay and Lesbian Parents

In increasing numbers, children are being raised in families in which there are two moms or two dads. Rough estimates suggest that some 20% of gay men and lesbian women are parents (Falk, 1989; Turner, Scadden, & Harris, 1990).

How do lesbian and gay households compare to heterosexual households? To answer the question, we first need to consider some characteristics of gay and lesbian couples without children. According to studies comparing gay, lesbian, and heterosexual couples, labor tends to be divided more evenly in homosexual households than in heterosexual households. Each partner in a homosexual relationship is more likely to carry out approximately the same number of different chores, compared with heterosexual partners. Furthermore, gay and lesbian couples cling more strongly to the ideal of an egalitarian allocation of household work than heterosexual couples do (Patterson, 1992, 1994; Parks, 1998; Kurdek, 1993, 2003b).

However, as with heterosexual couples, the arrival of a child (usually through adoption or artificial insemination) changes the dynamics of household life considerably in homosexual couples. As in heterosexual unions, a specialization of roles develops. According to recent research on lesbian mothers, for instance, child rearing tends to fall more to one member of the couple, while the other spends more time in paid employment. Although both partners usually say they share household tasks and decision making equally, biological mothers are more involved in child care. Conversely, the nonbiological mother in the couple is more likely to report spending greater time in paid employment (Patterson, 1995).

The evolution of homosexual couples when children arrive appears to be more similar to that of heterosexual couples than dissimilar, particularly in the increased role specialization occasioned by the requirements of child care. The experience for children of being in a household with two parents of the same sex is also similar. Most research suggests that children raised in households in which the parents are homosexual show no differences in terms of eventual

"If Heather has two mommies, and each of them has two brothers, and one of those brothers has another man for a 'roommate,' how many uncles does Heather have?"

longitudinal study of a large group of male graduates of Harvard, begun when they were freshmen in the 1930s, Vaillant found a general pattern of psychological development (Vaillant, 1977; Vaillant & Vaillant, 1990).

In their early 20s, the men tended to be influenced by their parents' authority. But in their late 20s and early 30s, they started to act with greater autonomy. They married and began to have and raise children. At the same time, they started and began to focus on their careers—the period of career consolidation.

Based on his data, Vaillant drew a relatively uninspiring portrait of people in the career consolidation stage. The participants in his study worked very hard because they were working their way up the corporate ladder. They tended to be rule-followers who sought to conform to the norms of their professions. Rather than showing the independence and questioning that they had displayed earlier, while still in college, they threw themselves unquestioningly into their work.

Vaillant argues that work played such an important role in the lives of the men he studied that the career consolidation stage should be seen as an addition to Erikson's intimacy-versus-isolation stage of psychosocial identity. In Vaillant's view, career concerns come to supplant the focus on intimacy, and the career consolidation stage marks a bridge between Erikson's intimacy-versus-isolation stage and Erikson's next period, that of generativity-versus-stagnation. (Generativity refers to an individual's contribution to society, as we discuss in Chapter 16.)

However, the reaction to Vaillant's viewpoint has been mixed. Critics point out, for instance, that Vaillant's sample, although relatively large, comprised a highly restricted, unusually bright group of people, all of them men. It is hard to know how generalizable the results are. Furthermore, societal norms have changed considerably since the time the study was begun in the late 1930s, and people's views of the importance of work may have shifted. Finally, the lack of women in the sample and the fact that there have been major changes in the role of work in *women's* lives make Vaillant's conclusions even less generalizable.

Still, it is hard to argue about the importance of work in most people's lives, and current research suggests that it makes up a significant part of both men's and women's identity—if for no other reason than that many people spend more time working than they do on any other activity (Deaux et al., 1995). We turn now to how people decide what careers to follow—and the implications of that decision.

Picking an Occupation: Choosing Life's Work

Some people know from childhood that they want to be physicians or firefighters or to go into business, and they follow invariant paths toward their goals. For others, the choice of a career is very much a matter of chance, of turning to the want ads and seeing what's available. Many of us fall somewhere between these two extremes.

Ginzberg's Career Choice Theory.   According to Eli Ginzberg (1972), people typically move through a series of stages in choosing a career. The first stage is the **fantasy period,** which lasts until a person is around 11. During the fantasy period, career choices are made, and discarded, without regard to skills, abilities, or available job opportunities. Instead, choices are made solely on the basis of what sounds appealing. Thus, a child may decide he wants to be a rock star —despite the fact that he cannot carry a tune.

People begin to take practical considerations into account during the **tentative period,** which spans adolescence. They begin to think more practically about the requirements of various jobs and how their own abilities and interests might fit with them. They also consider their personal values and goals, exploring how well a particular occupation might satisfy them.

Finally, in early adulthood, people enter the realistic period. In the **realistic period,** young adults explore specific career options either through actual experience on the job or through training for a profession. After initially exploring what they might do, people begin to narrow their choices to a few alternative careers and eventually make a commitment to a particular one.

fantasy period   according to Ginzberg, the period, lasting until about age 11, when career choices are made, and discarded, without regard to skills, abilities, or available job opportunities.

tentative period   the second stage of Ginzberg's theory, which spans adolescence, when people begin to think in pragmatic terms about the requirements of various jobs and how their own abilities might fit with them.

realistic period   the third stage of Ginzberg's theory, which occurs in early adulthood, when people begin to explore specific career options, either through actual experience on the job or through training for a profession, and then narrow their choices and make a commitment.

According to one theory, people move through a series of life stages in choosing a career. The first stage is the fantasy period, which lasts until a person is around 11 years old.

According to John Holland's personality type theory, the greater the correspondence between career choices and personality traits, the happier people will be in their career choice.

Although Ginzberg's theory makes sense, critics have charged that it oversimplifies the process of choosing a career. Because Ginzberg's research was based on subjects from middle socioeconomic levels, it may overstate the choices and options available to people in lower socioeconomic levels. Furthermore, the ages associated with the various stages may be too rigid. For instance, a person who does not attend college but begins to work immediately after high school graduation is likely to be making serious career decisions at a much earlier point than a person who attends college. In addition, economic shifts have caused many people to change careers at different points in their adult lives.

Holland's Personality Type Theory.   Other theories of career choice emphasize how an individual's personality affects decisions about a career. According to John Holland, for instance, certain personality types match particularly well with certain careers. If the correspondence between personality and career is good, people will enjoy their careers more and be more likely to stay in them; but if the match is poor, they will be unhappy and more likely to shift into other careers (Holland, 1973, 1987; Gottfredson & Holland, 1990).

According to Holland, six personality types are important in career choice:

- *Realistic.* These people are down-to-earth, practical problem-solvers, and physically strong, but their social skills are mediocre. They make good farmers, laborers, and truck drivers.

- *Intellectual.* Intellectual types are oriented toward the theoretical and abstract. Although not particularly good with people, they are well suited to careers in math and science.

- *Social.* The traits associated with the social personality type are related to verbal skills and interpersonal relations. Social types are good at working with people, and consequently make good salespersons, teachers, and counselors.

- *Conventional.* Conventional individuals prefer highly structured tasks. They make good clerks, secretaries, and bank tellers.

- *Enterprising.* These individuals are risk-takers and take-charge types. They are good leaders and may be particularly effective as managers or politicians.

- *Artistic.* Artistic types use art to express themselves, and they often prefer the world of art to interactions with people. They are best suited to occupations involving art.

Although Holland's enumeration of personality types is sensible, it suffers from a central flaw: Not everyone fits neatly into particular personality types. Furthermore, there are certainly exceptions to the typology, with jobs being held by people who don't have the particular personality that Holland would predict. Still, the basic notions of the theory have been validated, and they form the foundation of several of the "job quizzes" that people can take to see what occupations they might especially enjoy (Randahl, 1991).

Gender and Career Choices: Women's Work

WANTED: Full-time employee for small family firm. DUTIES: Including but not limited to general cleaning, cooking, gardening, laundry, ironing and mending, purchasing, bookkeeping and money management. Child care may also be required. HOURS: Avg. 55/wk but standby duty required 24 hours/day, 7 days/wk. Extra workload on holidays. SALARY AND BENEFITS: No salary, but food, clothing, and shelter provided at employer's discretion; job security and benefits depend on continued goodwill of employer. No vacation. No retirement plan. No opportunities for advancement. REQUIREMENTS: No previous experience necessary, can learn on the job. Only women need apply. (Unger & Crawford, 1992, p. 446)

A generation ago, many women entering early adulthood assumed that this admittedly exaggerated job description matched the work for which they were best suited and to which they aspired: housewife. Even those women who sought work outside the home were relegated to certain professions. For instance, until the 1960s, employment ads in newspapers throughout the United States were almost always divided into two sections: "Help Wanted: Male" and "Help Wanted: Female." The men's job listings encompassed such professions as police officer, construction worker, and legal counsel; the women's listings were for secretaries, teachers, cashiers, and librarians.

The breakdown of jobs deemed appropriate for men and women reflected society's traditional view of what the two genders were best suited for. Traditionally, women were considered most appropriate for **communal professions,** occupations associated with relationships, such as nursing. In contrast, men were perceived as best suited for agentic professions. **Agentic professions** are associated with getting things accomplished, such as carpentry. It is probably no coincidence that communal professions typically have lower status and pay than agentic professions (Eagly & Steffen, 1984, 1986; Hattery, 2000).

Although discrimination based on gender is far less blatant today than it was several decades ago—it is now illegal, for instance, to advertise a position specifically for a man or a woman— remnants of traditional gender role prejudice persist. As we discussed in Chapter 13, women are less likely to be found in traditionally male-dominated professions such as engineering and computer programming. As shown in Figure 14-11, although significant progress in closing the gender wage gap was made in the last 40 years, women's weekly earnings still lag behind those of men. In fact, women in many professions earn significantly less than men in identical jobs (Frome et al., 2006; U.S. Bureau of the Census, 2006).

More women are working outside the home than ever before, despite status and pay that are often lower than men's. Between 1950 and 2003, the percent of the female population (aged 16 and over) in the U.S. labor force increased from around 35% to over 60%, and women today make up around 55% of the labor force, a figure comparable to their presence in the general population. Almost all women expect to earn a living, and almost all do at some point in their lives. Furthermore, in about one-half of U.S. households, women earn about as much as their husbands (Lewin, 1995; U.S. Bureau of Labor Statistics, 2003).

Opportunities for women are considerably greater than they were in earlier years. Women are more likely to be physicians, lawyers, insurance agents, and bus drivers than they were in the past. However, as noted earlier, within specific job categories, there are still notable gender differences. For example, female bus drivers are more apt to have part-time school bus routes, while men hold better-paying full-time routes in cities. Similarly, female pharmacists are more likely to work in hospitals, while men work in higher-paying jobs in retail stores (Unger & Crawford, 2003).

In the same way, women (and minorities, too) in high-status, visible professional roles may hit what has come to be called the glass ceiling. The glass ceiling is an invisible barrier within

communal professions occupations that are associated with relationships.

agentic professions occupations that are associated with getting things accomplished.

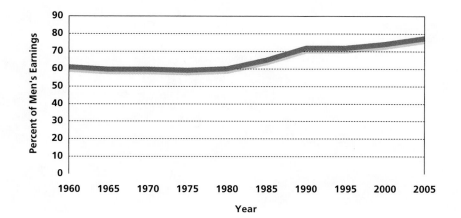

FIGURE 14-11 THE GENDER WAGE GAP

Women's weekly earnings as a percent of men's has increased since 1979, but still is only a bit more than 75% and has remained steady over the past 3 years.

(*Source:* U.S. Bureau of the Census, 2006.)

extrinsic motivation motivation that drives people to obtain tangible rewards, such as money and prestige.

intrinsic motivation motivation that causes people to work for their own enjoyment, not for the rewards work may bring.

status the evaluation of a role or person by other relevant members of a group or society.

an organization that, because of discrimination, prevents individuals from being promoted beyond a certain level. It operates subtly, and often the people responsible for keeping the glass ceiling in place are unaware of how their actions perpetuate discrimination against women and minorities (Goodman, Fields, & Blum, 2003; Stockdale & Crosby, 2004).

Why Do People Work? More Than Earning a Living

This may seem an easy question to answer: People work to earn a living. Yet the reality is different, for young adults express many reasons for seeking a job.

Intrinsic and Extrinsic Motivation. Certainly, people work in order to obtain various concrete rewards, or out of extrinsic motivation. **Extrinsic motivation** drives people to obtain tangible rewards, such as money and prestige (Singer, Stacey, & Lange, 1993).

People also work for their own enjoyment, for personal rewards, not just for the financial rewards a job may bring. This is known as **intrinsic motivation.** People in many Western societies tend to subscribe to the Puritan work ethic, the notion that work is important in and of itself. According to this view, working is a meaningful act that brings psychological and (at least in the traditional view) even spiritual well-being and satisfaction.

Work also brings a sense of personal identity. Consider, for instance, what people say about themselves when they first meet someone. After mentioning their names and where they live, they very typically tell what they do for a living. What people do is a large part of who they are.

Work also may be a central element in people's social lives. Because so much time is spent in work settings, work can be a source of young adults' friends and social activities. Social relationships forged at work may spill over into other parts of people's lives. In addition, there are often social obligations—dinner with the boss, or the annual seasonal party in December—that are related to work.

Finally, the kind of work that people do is a factor in determining status. **Status** is the evaluation by society of the role a person plays. Various jobs are associated with a certain status, as

Extrinsic motivation drives people as a way of obtaining tangible rewards, such as money, prestige, or an expensive automobile. How might extrinsic motivation be illustrated in a less developed, nonwestern culture?

Table 14-4 Status Hierarchy of Various Professions			
Occupation	**Score**	**Occupation**	**Score**
Physicians and surgeons	100	Court/municipal clerks	53
Lawyers	99	Heavy vehicle mechanics	52
Computer software engineers	94	Sheet metal workers	50
Psychologists	93	Massage therapists	48
Architects	92	Utility meter readers	46
College professors	86	Home appliance repairers	45
High school teachers	86	Animal control workers	44
Health services managers	85	Tax preparers	44
Human resources managers	82	Medical assistants	42
Special education teachers	80	Paper hangers	41
Editors	79	Telephone operators	39
Social workers	77	Chefs	39
Firefighters	77	Tellers	36
Writers/authors	76	Carpenters	35
Funeral directors	75	Dancers/choreographers	32
Clergy	75	Barbers	31
Dental hygienists	74	Motion picture projectionists	27
Private detectives	72	Nonfarm animal caretakers	25
Aircraft mechanics	72	Child care workers	21
Real estate brokers	70	Telemarketers	20
Postal service clerks	69	Personal/home care aides	19
EMTs and paramedics	65	Crossing guards	11
Correctional officers	60	Maids and housekeeping personnel	7
Electricians	58	Food prep workers	3
Physical therapists	56	Counter attendants	1
Actors	55	Dishwashers	1

(*Source:* Nam & Boyd, 2004.)

indicated in Table 14-4. For instance, physicians and lawyers are near the top of the status hierarchy, while counter attendants and dishwashers fall to the bottom.

Satisfaction on the Job. The status associated with particular jobs affects people's satisfaction with their work. As might be expected, the higher the status of the job, the more satisfied people tend to be. Furthermore, the status of the job of the major wage-earner can affect the status of the other members of the family (Green, 1995; Schieman, McBrier, & van Gundy, 2003).

Of course, status isn't everything: Worker satisfaction depends on a number of factors, not the least of which is the nature of the job itself. For example, consider the plight of Patricia

Alford, who worked at the Equitable Life Assurance Company. Her job consisted of entering data into a computer 9 hours each day except for two 15-minute breaks and an hour off for lunch. She never knew how much she was earning, because her salary depended on how many insurance claims she entered into the computer each day. The pay standards were so complicated that her pay varied from $217 to $400 a week, providing her with a weekly surprise at paycheck time (Booth, 1987; Ting, 1997).

Other people who work at computers are monitored on a minute-by-minute basis; supervisors can consistently see how many keystrokes they are entering. In some firms in which workers use the telephone for sales or to take customer orders, their conversations are monitored by supervisors. Workers' Internet use and email are also monitored or restricted by a large number of employers. Not surprisingly, such forms of job stress produce worker dissatisfaction (MacDonald, 2003).

Job satisfaction is higher when workers have input into the nature of their jobs and feel their ideas and opinions are valued. They also prefer jobs that offer variety, requiring many different types of skills, over those that require only a few. Finally, the more influence employees have over others, either directly as supervisors or more informally, the greater their job satisfaction (Steers & Porter, 1991; Peterson & Wilson, 2004; Thompson & Prottas, 2006).

Becoming an Informed Consumer of Development

Choosing a Career

One of the greatest challenges people face in early adulthood is making a decision that will have lifelong implications: the choice of a career. Although there is no single correct choice—most people can be happy in any of several different jobs—the options can be daunting. Following are some guidelines for at least starting to come to grips with the question of what occupational path to follow:

- Systematically evaluate a variety of choices. Libraries contain a wealth of information about potential career paths, and most colleges and universities have career centers that can provide occupational data and guidance.

- Know yourself. Evaluate your strengths and weaknesses, perhaps by completing a questionnaire at a college career center that can provide insight into your interests, skills, and values.

- Create a "balance sheet" listing the potential gains and losses that you will incur from a particular profession. First list the gains and losses that you will experience directly, and then list gains and losses for others, such as family members. Next, write down your projected self-approval or self-disapproval from the potential career. Finally, write down the projected social approval or disapproval you are likely to receive from others. By systematically evaluating a set of potential careers according to each of these criteria, you will be in a better position to compare different possibilities.

- "Try out" different careers through paid or unpaid internships. By seeing a job first-hand, interns are able to get a better sense of what an occupation is truly like.

- Remember that if you make a mistake, you can change careers. In fact, people today increasingly change careers in early adulthood and even beyond. No one should feel locked into a decision made earlier in life. As we have seen throughout this book, people develop substantially over the course of their lives.

- It is reasonable to expect that shifting values, interests, abilities, and life circumstances might make a different career more appropriate later in life than the one chosen during early adulthood.

Review and Apply

Review

- Choosing a career is an important step in early adulthood, so important that George Vaillant considers career consolidation a developmental stage on a par with Erikson's intimacy-versus-isolation stage.

- According to Eli Ginzberg, people pass through three stages in considering careers: the fantasy period, the tentative period, and the realistic period.

- Other theories of career choice, such as John Holland's, attempt to match personality types to suitable careers.

- Gender stereotypes are changing, but women still experience subtle prejudice in career choices, roles, and wages.

- People work because of both extrinsic and intrinsic motivation factors.

Applying Lifespan Development

- If Vaillant's study were performed today on women, in what ways do you think the results would be similar to or different from those of the original study?

- *From a social worker's perspective:* How does the division of jobs into communal and agentic relate to traditional views of male–female differences?

Epilogue

Our examination of early adulthood revealed a period less dramatic than others in terms of evident growth, but no less important or less characterized by change and development. We witnessed individuals at the peak of health and the height of their intellectual powers entering a period of their lives in which true independence is the challenge and the goal.

In this chapter we looked at some of the most significant issues of early adulthood: forming relationships, falling in love and potentially getting married, and finding a career. We explored the factors that lead to loving relationships, the considerations that affect the choice of whether and whom to marry, and the characteristics of good—and not so good—marriages. We also discussed factors that people consider in choosing careers and the features of careers that make them satisfying.

Before we move on to middle adulthood in the next chapter, recall the prologue that began this chapter, about the marriage of Grace Tsai and Richard Tsuyuki. In light of your knowledge of relationships and careers in early adulthood, answer the following questions:

1. How does this couple's insistence on performing three ceremonies underline the cultural importance of marriage?

2. How does the concept of homogamy relate to Grace and Richard's marriage? In what ways are the two individuals similar, and in what ways are they different?

3. Assuming that Grace and Richard are typical, what steps did their courtship probably follow?

4. What advice would you give Grace and Richard about keeping their marriage happy once their baby arrives?

Looking Back

■ **How do young adults form loving relationships, and how does love change over time?**

- Young adults face Erikson's intimacy-versus-isolation stage, with those who resolve this conflict being able to develop intimate relationships with others.

- According to stimulus-value-role theory, relationships pass through the consideration of surface characteristics, values, and finally the roles played by the participants.

- Passionate love is characterized by intense physiological arousal, intimacy, and caring, while companionate love is characterized by respect, admiration, and affection.

- Psychologist Robert Sternberg suggests that three components of love (intimacy, passion, and decision/commitment) combine to form eight types of love, through which a relationship can dynamically evolve.

■ **How do people choose spouses, and what makes relationships work and cease working?**

- Although in Western cultures love tends to be the most important factor in selecting a partner, other cultures emphasize other factors.

- According to filtering models, people filter potential partners initially for attractiveness and then for compatibility, generally conforming to the principle of homogamy and the marriage gradient.

- Gays and lesbians generally seek the same qualities in relationships as heterosexual men and women: attachment, caring, intimacy, affection, and respect.

- In young adulthood, while cohabitation is popular, marriage remains the most attractive option. The median age of first marriage is rising for both men and women.

- Divorce is prevalent in the United States, affecting nearly half of all marriages.

■ **How does the arrival of children affect a relationship?**

- More than 90% of married couples have at least one child, but the size of the average family has decreased, due partly to birth control and partly to the changing roles of women in the workforce.

- Children bring pressures to any marriage, shifting the focus of the marriage partners, changing their roles, and increasing their responsibilities. Gay and lesbian couples with children experience similar changes in their relationships.

■ **Why is choosing a career such an important issue for young adults, and what factors influence the choice of a career?**

- According to Vaillant, career consolidation is a developmental stage in which young adults are involved in defining their careers and themselves.

- A model developed by Ginzberg suggests that people typically move through three stages in choosing a career: the fantasy period of youth, the tentative period of adolescence, and the realistic period of young adulthood.

- Other approaches, such as that of Holland, attempt to match people's personality types with suitable careers. This sort of research underlies most career-related inventories and measures used in career counseling.

- Gender role prejudice and stereotyping remain a problem in the workplace and in preparing for and selecting careers. Women tend to be pressured into certain occupations and out of others, and they earn less money for the same work.

■ **Why do people work, and what elements of a job bring satisfaction?**

- People are motivated to work by both extrinsic factors, such as the need for money and prestige, and intrinsic factors, such as the enjoyment of work and its personal importance. Work helps determine a person's identity, social life, and status.

- Job satisfaction is the result of many factors, including the nature and status of one's job, the amount of input one has into its nature, the variety of one's responsibilities, and the influence one has over others.

Key Terms and Concepts

social clock (p. 480)
intimacy-versus-isolation
   stage (p. 481)
stimulus-value-role (SVR)
   theory (p. 482)
passionate (or romantic)
   love (p. 483)
companionate love (p. 483)
labeling theory of
   passionate love (p. 483)

intimacy component (p. 484)
passion component (p. 484)
decision/commitment
   component (p. 484)
homogamy (p. 487)
marriage gradient (p. 487)
cohabitation (p. 492)
career consolidation (p. 500)
fantasy period (p. 501)

tentative period (p. 501)
realistic period (p. 501)
communal professions
   (p. 503)
agentic professions (p. 503)
extrinsic motivation (p. 504)
intrinsic motivation (p. 504)
status (p. 504)

15 Physical and Cognitive Development in Middle Adulthood

Chapter Overview

PHYSICAL DEVELOPMENT

Physical Transitions: The Gradual Change in the Body's Capabilities

Height, Weight, and Strength: The Benchmarks of Change

The Senses: The Sights and Sounds of Middle Age

Reaction Time: Not-so-Slowing Down

Sex in Middle Adulthood: The Ongoing Sexuality of Middle Age

HEALTH

Wellness and Illness: The Ups and Downs of Middle Adulthood

Stress in Middle Adulthood

The A's and B's of Coronary Heart Disease: Linking Health and Personality

The Threat of Cancer

COGNITIVE DEVELOPMENT

Does Intelligence Decline in Adulthood?

The Development of Expertise: Separating Experts from Novices

Memory: You Must Remember This

Prologue: Fit for Life

Twenty-eight days, 222 hours of riding time and 1,939 miles on a solo bicycle trip into the Yukon . . . will cause you to lose weight, which Pat Rodden, a 46-year-old Whidbey Island man, needed. But whizzing through desolation and past grizzlies, sharing in the kindness of strangers, and depending on yourself, not convenience, will provide a far more lasting gift. . .

The last 460 miles, all mud and gravel, were the hardest physically, but the first 500 miles were the hardest because quitting was an easier option then. Through the month-long ride, his only injury was a sore upper back from miles of traversing bumpy ground. . . .

About halfway through, Rodden crossed a mental barrier: from hoping he could do it to knowing he could. He needed the confidence and resolve as the road to Inuvik in the Arctic Mackenzie Delta got tougher.

"I regained what I thought I had lost forever as a middle-aged person," Rodden says. "But I found people doing all kinds of things that would amaze you." (Seven, 2006, p. 6)

For many people, middle adulthood is a period in which physical activity remains at high levels.

Pat Rodden's enthusiastic rediscovery of cross-country bicycling is indicative of a revolution that is occurring in terms of the physical activity of people in middle adulthood. People reaching the midcentury mark are joining health clubs in record numbers, seeking to maintain their health and agility as they age.

They are doing this because it is during middle adulthood, roughly defined as the period from 40 to 65 years of age, that many people first face visible reminders that time is passing. Their bodies and, to some extent, their cognitive abilities begin to change in unwelcome ways. As we look at the physical, cognitive, and social changes of middle adulthood in this chapter and the next, we see that the news isn't all bad. This is also a period when many individuals are at the height of their capabilities, when they are engaged in the process of shaping their lives as never before.

We begin the chapter by considering physical development. We consider changes in height, weight, and strength, and discuss the subtle declines in various senses. We also look at the role of sexuality in middle adulthood.

We examine both health and illness during middle age, and pay particular attention to two of the major health problems of the period, heart disease and cancer.

The second part of the chapter focuses on cognitive development in middle age. We look at the tricky question of whether or what kind of intelligence declines during the period, and we consider the difficulty of answering the question fully. We also look at memory, examining the ways in which memory capabilities change during middle adulthood.

After reading this chapter, you will be able to answer these questions:

■ **What sorts of physical changes affect people in middle adulthood?**

■ **What changes in sexuality do middle-aged men and women experience?**

■ **Is middle adulthood a time of health or disease for men and women?**

■ **What sorts of people are likely to get coronary heart disease?**

■ **What causes cancer, and what tools are available to diagnose and treat it?**

■ **What happens to a person's intelligence in middle adulthood?**

■ **How does aging affect memory, and how can memory be improved?**

Looking Ahead

Physical Development

It crept up gradually on Sharon Boker-Tov. Soon after reaching the age of 40, she noticed that it took her a bit longer to bounce back from minor illnesses such as colds and the flu. Then she became conscious of changes in her eyesight: She needed more light to read fine print, and she had to adjust how far she held newspapers from her face in order to read them easily. Finally, she couldn't help but notice that the strands of gray hair on her head, which had begun to appear gradually in her late 20s, were becoming a virtual forest.

Physical Transitions: The Gradual Change in the Body's Capabilities

Middle adulthood is the time when most people become increasingly aware of the gradual changes in their bodies that mark the aging process. As we saw in Chapter 13, some of the aging that people experience is the result of senescence, or naturally occurring declines related to age. Other changes, however, are the result of lifestyle choices, such as diet, exercise, smoking, and alcohol or drug use. As we'll see throughout this chapter, people's lifestyle choices can have a major impact on their physical, and even cognitive, fitness during middle age.

Of course, physical changes occur throughout the entire life span. Yet these changes take on new significance during middle adulthood, particularly in Western cultures that place a high value on youthful appearance. For many people, the psychological significance of such changes far exceeds the relatively minor and gradual changes that they are experiencing. Sharon Boker-Tov had found gray hairs even in her 20s, but in her 40s they multiplied in a way that she could not ignore. She was no longer young.

People's emotional reactions to the physical changes of middle adulthood depend in part on their self-concepts. For those whose self-image is tied closely to their physical attributes—such as highly athletic men and women or those who are physically quite attractive—middle adulthood can be particularly difficult. The signs of aging they see in the mirror signal not just a reduction in their physical attractiveness, but also aging and mortality. On the other hand, because most people's views of themselves are not so closely tied to physical attributes, middle-aged adults generally report no less satisfaction with their body images than younger adults (Berscheid, Walster, & Bohrnstedt, 1973; Eitel, 2003).

Physical appearance often plays an especially important role in determining how women see themselves. This is particularly true in Western cultures, where women face strong societal pressures to retain a youthful appearance. In fact, society applies a double standard to men and women in terms of appearance: Whereas older women tend to be viewed in unflattering terms, aging men are more frequently perceived as displaying a maturity that enhances their stature (Katchadourian, 1987; Harris, 1994).

Height, Weight, and Strength: The Benchmarks of Change

Most people reach their maximum height during their 20s and remain relatively close to that height until around age 55. At that point, people begin a "settling" process in which the bones attached to the spinal column become less dense. Although the loss of height is very slow, ultimately women average a 2-inch decline and men a 1-inch decline over the rest of the life span (Rossman, 1977).

Women are more prone to a decline in height because they are at greater risk of osteoporosis. **Osteoporosis,** a condition in which the bones become brittle, fragile, and thin, is often brought about by a lack of calcium in the diet. As we discuss further in Chapter 17, osteoporosis, although it has a genetic component, is one of the aspects of aging that can be affected by a person's lifestyle choices. Women—and men, for that matter—can reduce the risk of osteoporosis by maintaining a diet high in calcium (which is found in milk, yogurt, cheese, and other dairy products) and by exercising regularly (Prince et al., 1991; Alvarez-Leon, Roman-Vinas, & Serra-Majem, 2006; Prentice et al., 2006).

During middle adulthood the amount of body fat also tends to grow in the average person. "Middle-age spread" is a visible symptom of this problem. Even those who have been relatively slim all their lives may begin to put on weight. Because height is not increasing, and actually may be declining, these weight and body fat gains lead to an increase in the numbers of people who become obese.

This weight gain usually doesn't have to happen. Lifestyle choices play a major role. In fact, people who maintain an exercise program during middle age tend to avoid obesity, as do individuals living in cultures where the typical life is more active and less sedentary than that of many Western cultures.

Changes in height and weight are also accompanied by declines in strength. Throughout middle adulthood, strength gradually decreases, particularly in the back and leg muscles. By the time they are 60, people have lost, on average, about 10% of their maximum strength. Still, such a loss in strength is relatively minor, and most people are easily able to compensate for it (Troll, 1985; Spence, 1989). Again, lifestyle choices can make a difference. People who exercise regularly are likely to feel stronger and to have an easier time compensating for any losses than those who are sedentary.

osteoporosis a condition in which the bones become brittle, fragile, and thin, often brought about by a lack of calcium in the diet.

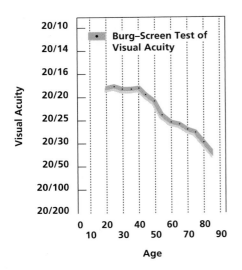

FIGURE 15-1   THE DECLINE OF VISUAL ACUITY

Beginning around the age of 40, the ability to discern fine detail begins to drop.

(*Source:* Adapted from Pitts, 1982.)

presbyopia   a nearly universal change in eyesight during middle adulthood that results in some loss of near vision.

glaucoma   a condition in which pressure in the fluid of the eye increases, either because the fluid cannot drain properly or because too much fluid is produced.

presbycusis   loss of the ability to hear sounds of high frequency.

Beginning at or around the age of 40, visual acuity, the ability to discern fine spatial detail, begins to drop. Most people begin to suffer from presbyopia, a decline in near vision.

The Senses: The Sights and Sounds of Middle Age

Sharon Boker-Tov's experiences with needing extra light to read and holding the newspaper a little farther away are so common that reading glasses and bifocals have become almost a stereotypical emblem of middle age. Like Sharon, most people notice unmistakable changes in the sensitivity not only of their eyes, but also of other sense organs. Although all the organs seem to shift at roughly the same rate, the changes are particularly noticeable in vision and hearing.

Vision.   Starting at around age 40, *visual acuity*—the ability to discern fine spatial detail in both close and distant objects—begins to decline (see Figure 15-1). The shape of the eye's lens changes, and its elasticity deteriorates, which makes it harder to focus images sharply onto the retina. The lens becomes less transparent, so less light passes through the eye (Pitts, 1982; DiGiovanna, 1994).

A nearly universal change in eyesight during middle adulthood is the loss of near vision, called **presbyopia**. Even people who have never needed glasses or contact lenses find themselves holding reading matter at an increasing distance from their eyes in order to bring it into focus. Eventually, they need reading glasses. For those who were previously near-sighted, presbyopia may require bifocals or two sets of glasses (Kalsi, Heron, & Charman, 2001; Koopmans & Kooijman, 2006).

Other changes in vision also begin in middle adulthood. There are declines in depth perception, distance perception, and the ability to view the world in three dimensions. The loss of elasticity in the lens also means that people's ability to adapt to darkness is impaired, and they are less able to see in dimly lit environments. Such visual reductions may make it more difficult to climb stairs or to navigate around a dark room (Artal et al., 1993; Spear, 1993).

Although changes in vision are most often brought about by the gradual processes of normal aging, in some cases disease is involved. One of the most frequent causes of eye problems is glaucoma, which may, if left untreated, ultimately produce blindness. **Glaucoma** occurs when pressure in the fluid of the eye increases, either because the fluid cannot drain properly or because too much is produced. Around 1% to 2% of people over the age of 40 are afflicted by the disorder, and African Americans are particularly susceptible (Wilson, 1989).

Initially, the increased pressure in the eye may constrict the neurons involved in peripheral vision and lead to tunnel vision. Ultimately, the pressure can become so high that all nerve cells are constricted, which causes complete blindness. Fortunately, glaucoma can be treated if it is detected early enough. Medication can reduce the pressure in the eye, as can surgery to restore normal drainage of eye fluid (Plosker & Keam, 2006).

Hearing.   Like vision, hearing undergoes a gradual decline in acuity starting in middle adulthood. For the most part, however, the changes are less evident than those involving eyesight.

Some of the hearing losses of middle adulthood result from environmental factors. For instance, people whose professions keep them near loud noises—such as airplane mechanics and construction workers—are more apt to suffer debilitating and permanent hearing loss.

However, many changes are simply related to aging. For instance, age brings a loss of *cilia* or *hair cells* in the inner ear, which transmit neural messages to the brain when vibrations bend them. Like the lens of the eye, the eardrum also becomes less elastic with age, reducing sensitivity to sound (Wiley et al., 2005).

The ability to hear high-pitched, high-frequency sounds usually degrades first, a problem called **presbycusis**. About 12% of people between ages 45 and 65 suffer from presbycusis. There is also a gender difference: Men are more prone to hearing loss than women, starting at around age 55. People who have hearing difficulties may also have problems identifying the direction and origin of a sound, a process called *sound localization*. Sound localization can deteriorate because it depends on comparing the discrepancy in sound perceived by the two ears. For example, a sound on the right will stimulate the right ear first and then, a tiny time later, register in the left ear. Because hearing loss may not affect both ears equally, sound localization can suffer (Schneider, 1997; Willott, Chisolm, & Lister, 2001; Veras & Mattos, 2007).

Declines in sensitivity to sounds do not markedly affect most people in middle adulthood. Most people are able to compensate for the losses that do occur relatively easily—by asking people to speak up, turning up the volume of a television set, or paying greater attention to what others are saying.

Reaction Time: Not-So-Slowing Down

One common concern about aging is the notion that people begin to slow down once they reach middle adulthood. How valid is such a worry?

In most cases, not very. There is an increase in reaction time (meaning that it takes longer to react to a stimulus), but usually the increase is fairly mild and hardly noticeable. For instance, reaction time on simple tasks such as reacting to a loud noise increases by around 20% from age 20 to 60. More complex tasks, which require the coordination of various skills—such as driving a car—show less of an increase. Still, it takes a bit more time for drivers to move the foot from the gas pedal to the brake when they are faced with an emergency situation. Increases in reaction time are largely produced by changes in the speed with which the nervous system processes nerve impulses (Nobuyuki, 1997; Roggeveen, Prime, & Ward, 2007).

Despite the increase in reaction time, middle-aged drivers have fewer accidents than younger ones. Why would this be? Part of the reason is that older drivers tend to be more careful and to take fewer risks than younger ones. Much of the cause for their better performance, however, is older drivers' greater amount of practice in the skill. The minor slowing of reaction time is made up for by their expertise. In the case of reaction time, then, practice may indeed make perfect (MacDonald, Hultsch, & Dixon, 2003; Marczinski, Milliken, & Nelson, 2003).

Can slowing down be slowed down? In many cases, the answer is yes. Lifestyle choices once more come into play. Specifically, involvement in an active exercise program retards the effects of aging, producing several important outcomes, such as better health and improved muscle strength and endurance (see Figure 15-2). "Use it or lose it" is an aphorism with which developmentalists would agree (Conn, 2003).

Slowing down can be slowed down. In many cases, it's "use it or lose it."

FIGURE 15-2   THE BENEFITS OF EXERCISE

Many benefits accrue from maintaining a high level of physical activity throughout life. (*Source:* DiGiovanna, 1994.)

The advantages of exercise include

Muscle System

Slower decline in energy molecules, muscle cell thickness, number of muscle cells, muscle thickness, muscle mass, muscle strength, blood supply, speed of movement, stamina

Slower increase in fat and fibers, reaction time, recovery time, development of muscle soreness

Nervous System

Slower decline in processing impulses by the central nervous system

Slower increase in variations in speed of motor neuron impulses

Circulatory System

Maintenance of lower levels of LDLs and higher HDL/cholesterol and HDL/LDL ratios

Decreased risk of high blood pressure, atherosclerosis, heart attack, stroke

Skeletal System

Slower decline in bone minerals

Decreased risk of fractures and osteoporosis

Ψ

Psychological Benefits

Enhanced mood

Feelings of well-being

Reduces stress

Sexuality continues to be a vital part of most couples' lives in middle adulthood.

Sex in Middle Adulthood: The Ongoing Sexuality of Middle Age

Sexuality remains an important part of life for many, if not most, middle-aged people. The frequency of sexual intercourse declines with age (see Figure 15-3), but sexual pleasure remains a vital part of most middle-aged adults' lives. About half of men and women age 45 to 59 report having sexual intercourse about once a week or more. Similarly, sex remains an important activity for gay and lesbian couples during middle adulthood (Michael et al., 1994; Gabbay & Wahler, 2002; Cain, Johannes, & Avis, 2003; Kimmel & Sang, 2003; Duplassie & Daniluk, 2007).

For many, middle adulthood brings a kind of sexual enjoyment and freedom that was missing during their earlier lives. With their children grown and away from home, middle-aged married couples have more time to engage in uninterrupted sexual activities. Women who have passed through menopause are liberated from the fear of pregnancy and no longer need to employ birth control techniques (Sherwin, 1991; Lamont, 1997).

Both men and women can face some challenges to their sexuality during middle adulthood. For instance, a man typically needs more time to achieve an erection, and it takes longer after an orgasm to have another. The volume of fluid that is ejaculated declines. Finally, the production of *testosterone*, the male sex hormone, declines with age (Hyde & DeLamater, 2003).

For women, the walls of the vagina become thinner and less elastic. The vagina begins to shrink and its entrance becomes compressed, which can make intercourse painful. For most women, though, the changes are not so great as to reduce sexual pleasure. Those women who do experience declines in enjoyment from sexual intercourse can find help from an increasing array of drugs, such as topical creams and testosterone patches, being developed to increase sexual pleasure (Laumann, Paik, & Rosen, 1999; Freedman & Ellison, 2004).

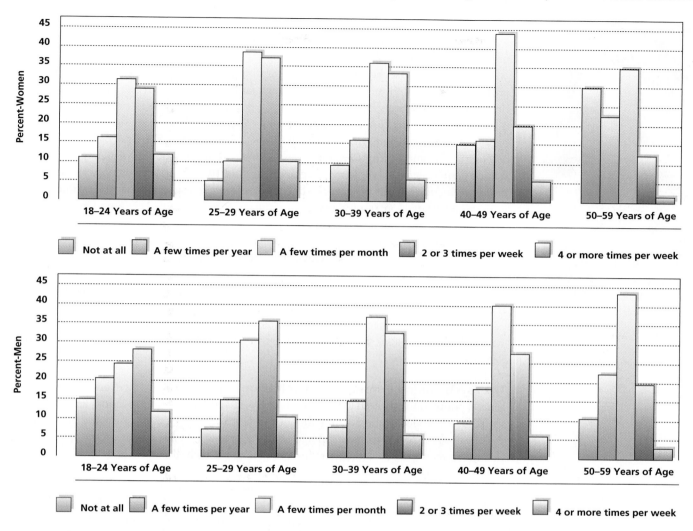

FIGURE 15-3   **FREQUENCY OF SEXUAL INTERCOURSE**

As people age, the frequency of sexual intercourse declines.

(*Source:* Adapted from Michael et al., 1994.)

The Female Climacteric and Menopause.   Starting at around age 45, women enter a period known as the climacteric that lasts for some 15 to 20 years. The **female climacteric** marks the transition from being able to bear children to being unable to do so.

The most notable sign of the female climacteric is menopause. **Menopause** is the cessation of menstruation. For most women, menstrual periods begin to occur irregularly and less frequently during a 2-year period starting at around age 47 or 48, although this process may begin as early as age 40 or as late as age 60. After a year goes by without a menstrual period, menopause is said to have occurred.

Menopause is important for several reasons. For one thing, it marks the point at which a traditional pregnancy is no longer possible (although eggs implanted in a postmenopausal woman can produce a pregnancy). In addition, the production of estrogen and progesterone, the female sex hormones, begins to drop, producing a variety of hormone-related age changes (Schwenkhagen, 2007).

The changes in hormone production may produce a variety of symptoms, although the degree to which a woman experiences them varies significantly. One of the best-known and most prevalent symptoms is "hot flashes," in which a woman senses an unexpected feeling of heat

female climacteric   the period that marks the transition from being able to bear children to being unable to do so.

menopause   the cessation of menstruation.

While women in some cultures anticipate menopause with dread, Mayan women have no notion of hot flashes, and they generally look forward to the end of their childbearing years.

from the waist up. A woman may get red and begin to sweat when a hot flash occurs. Afterwards, she may feel chilled. Some women experience hot flashes several times a day; others never experience hot flashes.

During menopause, headaches, feelings of dizziness, heart palpitations, and aching joints are other relatively common symptoms, though far from universal. In one survey, for instance, only half of the women reported experiencing hot flashes. In general, only about one-tenth of all women experience severe distress during menopause. And many—perhaps as many as half—have no significant symptoms at all (Hyde & DeLamater, 2003; Grady, 2006).

For many women, symptoms of menopause may begin a decade before menopause actually occurs. *Perimenopause* is the period beginning around 10 years prior to menopause when hormone production begins to change. Perimenopause is marked by sometimes radical fluctuations in hormone production, resulting in some of the same symptoms that are found in menopause.

Symptoms of menopause also differ by race. Compared with Caucasians, Japanese and Chinese women generally report fewer overall symptoms. African American women experience more hot flashes and night sweats, and Hispanic women report a higher level of several other symptoms, including heart pounding and vaginal dryness. Although the reason for these differences is unclear, it may be related to systematic racial differences in hormonal levels (Avis et al., 2001; Cain, Johannes, & Avis, 2003; Winterich, 2003; Shea, 2006).

For some women, the symptoms of perimenopause and menopause can be considerable. Treating those problems, though, has proven to be no easy task, as we consider in the *From Research to Practice* box.

The Psychological Consequences of Menopause. Traditionally, experts, as well as the general population, believed that menopause was linked directly to depression, anxiety, crying spells, lack of concentration, and irritability. In fact, some researchers estimated that as many as 10% of menopausal women suffered severe depression. It was assumed that physiological changes in menopausal women's bodies brought about such disagreeable outcomes (Schmidt & Rubinow, 1991).

Today, however, most researchers view menopause from a different perspective. It now seems more reasonable to regard menopause as a normal part of aging that does not, by itself, produce psychological symptoms. Certainly, some women experience psychological difficulties, but they do at other points in life as well (Dell & Stewart, 2000; Matthews et al., 2000; Freeman, Sammel, & Liu, 2004; Somerset et al., 2006).

A woman's expectations about menopause can make a significant difference in her experience of it, according to research. Women who expect to have difficulties during menopause are more likely to attribute every physical symptom and emotional swing to it. On the other hand, those with more positive attitudes toward menopause may be less apt to attribute physical sensations to menopausal physiological changes. A woman's attribution of physical symptoms, then, may affect her perception of the rigors of menopause—and ultimately her actual experience of the period (Dell & Stewart, 2000; Breheny & Stephens, 2003).

The nature and extent of menopausal symptoms also differ according to a woman's ethnic and cultural background. Women in non-Western cultures often have vastly different menopausal experiences from those in Western cultures. For instance, women of high castes in India report few symptoms of menopause. In fact, they look forward to menopause because being postmenopausal produces several social advantages, such as an end to taboos associated with menstruation and a perception of increased wisdom due to age. Similarly, Mayan women have no notion of hot flashes, and they generally look forward to the end of their childbearing years (Beck, 1992; Avis et al., 2001; Avis, Crawford, & Johannes, 2002; Robinson, 2002).

The Male Climacteric. Do men experience the equivalent of menopause? Not really. Because they have never weathered anything akin to menstruation, they would have difficulty experiencing its discontinuation. On the other hand, men experience some changes during

From Research to Practice

The Dilemma of Hormone Therapy: No Easy Answer

Not long ago, a forty-something friend of ours stopped at a convenience store to pick up a sports drink for her 13-year-old son. As she was about to pay, she felt a sensation of intense heat throughout her body and became nauseated and dizzy. The alarmed cashier asked if she needed help. Our friend shook her head and quickly made her way outside. But when she and her son got back in the car, she panicked and told him to call 911 on her cell phone because she was sure she was having a heart attack. Within minutes, she heard sirens coming closer. It was only then, as the heat dissipated and she began to sweat, that our friend realized what all these symptoms meant. She'd had her first hot flash! (Wingert & Kantrowitz, 2007, p. 38)

A few years ago, physicians would have had a straightforward remedy for hot flashes and other uncomfortable symptoms caused by the onset of menopause: They would have prescribed regular doses of a hormone replacement drug.

For millions of women who experienced similar difficulties, it was a solution that worked. In *hormone therapy* (HT), estrogen and progesterone are administered to alleviate the worst of the symptoms experienced by menopausal women. HT clearly reduces a variety of problems, such as hot flashes and loss of skin elasticity. In addition, HT may reduce coronary heart disease by changing the ratio of "good" cholesterol to "bad" cholesterol. HT also decreases the thinning of the bones related to osteoporosis, which, as we discussed, becomes a problem for many people in late adulthood (Palan et al., 2005; McCauley, 2007).

Furthermore, some studies show that HT is associated with reduced risks of stroke and colon cancer. Estrogen may even slow the mental deterioration found in people suffering from Alzheimer's disease, and some research shows that it improves memory and cognitive performance in healthy women. Finally, increased estrogen may lead to a greater sex drive (Sarrel, 2000; O'Hara et al., 2005; Stephens, Pachana, & Bristow, 2006; Schwenkhagen, 2007).

Although hormone therapy may sound like a cure-all, in fact since it became popular in the early 1990s, it has been well understood that there were risks involved. For instance, it seemed to increase the risk of breast cancer and blood clots. The thinking was, though, that the benefits of HT outweighed the risks.

All that changed after 2002, when a large study conducted by the Women's Health Initiative determined that the long-term risks of HT outweighed the benefits. Women taking a combination of estrogen and progestin were found to be at higher risk for breast cancer, stroke, pulmonary embolism, and heart disease. Increased risk of stroke and pulmonary embolism were later found to be associated with estrogen-alone therapy (Parker-Pope, 2003 October).

The results of the Women's Health Initiative study led to a profound rethinking of the benefits of HT, calling into question the wisdom that HT could protect postmenopausal women against chronic disease. Many women stopped taking hormone replacement drugs, choosing instead to use alternative herbal and dietary therapies for menopausal symptoms; unfortunately, the most popular of such remedies have proven to be no more effective than a placebo (Ness, Aronow, & Beck, 2006; Newton et al., 2006).

The sharp decline among menopausal women using HT is probably an overreaction, however. The most recent thinking among medical experts is that it's not a simple all-or-nothing proposition; some women are simply better candidates for HT than others. While HT seems to be less appropriate for older, postmenopausal women (such as those who participated in the Women's Health Initiative study) because of the increased risk of coronary heart disease and other health complications, younger women at the onset of menopause and who are experiencing severe symptoms might still benefit from the therapy, at least on a short-term basis (Lobo et al., 2006; Rossouw, 2006; Plonczynski & Plonczynski, 2007; Rossouw et al., 2007).

Ultimately, HT remains something of a gamble. Women nearing menopause need to read literature on the topic, consult their physicians, and ultimately come to an informed decision about how to proceed.

- *How might the fact that the medical advice of experts on hormone therapy has changed frequently over the last decade affect women's decisions about what course of action to follow?*

- *What are the most important factors a woman should take into account in deciding whether or not to embark on a course of hormone therapy?*

---

middle age that are collectively referred to as the male climacteric. The **male climacteric** is the period of physical and psychological change in the reproductive system that occurs during late middle age, typically in a man's 50s.

Because the changes happen gradually, it is hard to pinpoint the exact period of the male climacteric. For instance, despite progressive declines in the production of testosterone and sperm, men continue to be able to father children throughout middle age. Furthermore, it is no easier in men than in women to attribute psychological symptoms to subtle physiological changes.

One physical change that does occur quite frequently is enlargement of the *prostate gland*. By the age of 40, around 10% of men have enlarged prostates, and the percentage increases to

male climacteric the period of physical and psychological change relating to the male reproductive system that occurs during late middle age.

half of all men by the age of 80. Enlargement of the prostate produces problems with urination, including difficulty starting urination or a need to urinate frequently at night.

Furthermore, sexual problems increase as men age. In particular, *erectile dysfunction*, in which men are unable to achieve or maintain an erection, becomes more common. Drugs such as Viagra, Levitra, and Cialis, as well as patches that deliver doses of the hormone testosterone, often are effective in treating the problem (Hitt, 2000; Noonan, September 29, 2003; Kim & Park, 2006).

Although the physical changes associated with middle age are unequivocal, it's not clear whether they are the direct cause of any particular psychological symptoms or changes. Men, like women, clearly undergo psychological development during middle adulthood, but the extent to which psychological changes—which we discuss more in the next chapter—are associated with changes in reproductive or other physical capabilities remains an open question.

Review and Apply

Review

- People in middle adulthood experience gradual changes in physical characteristics and appearance.
- The acuity of the senses, particularly vision and hearing, and speed of reaction declines slightly during middle age.
- Sexuality in middle adulthood changes slightly, but middle-aged couples, freed from concerns about children, can often progress to a new level of intimacy and enjoyment.
- Physiological changes relating to sexuality occur in both men and women. Both the female climacteric, which includes menopause, and the male climacteric seem to have physical and perhaps psychological symptoms.

Applying Lifespan Development

- Would you rather fly on an airplane with a middle-aged pilot or a young one? Why?
- *From the perspective of a healthcare professional:* What cultural factors in the United States might contribute to a woman's negative experience of menopause? How?

Health

It was an average exercise session for Jerome Yanger. After the alarm went off at 5:30 AM, he climbed onto his exercise bike and began vigorously peddling, trying to maintain, and exceed, his average speed of 14 miles per hour. Stationed in front of the television set, he used the remote control to tune to the morning business news. Occasionally glancing up at the television, he began reading a report he had not finished the night before, swearing under his breath at some of the poor sales figures he was seeing. By the time he had completed exercising a half-hour later, he had gotten through the report, had managed to sign a few letters his administrative assistant had typed for him, and had even left two voice-mail messages for some colleagues.

Most of us would be ready to head back to bed after such a packed half-hour. For Jerome Yanger, however, it was routine: He consistently tried to accomplish several activities at the same time. Jerome thought of such behavior as efficient. Developmentalists might view it in another light, however: as symptomatic of a style of behavior that makes Jerome a likely candidate for coronary heart disease.

Although most people are relatively healthy in middle adulthood, they also become increasingly susceptible to a variety of health-related concerns. We will consider some of the typical health problems of middle age, focusing in particular on coronary heart disease and cancer.

Wellness and Illness: The Ups and Downs of Middle Adulthood

Health concerns become increasingly important to people during middle adulthood. In fact, surveys asking adults what they worry about show health—as well as safety and money—to be an issue of concern. For instance, more than half of adults surveyed say they are either "afraid" or "very afraid" of having cancer (see Figure 15-4).

Health becomes increasingly of concern during middle adulthood.

For most people, however, middle age is a period of health. According to census figures, the vast majority of middle-aged adults report no chronic health difficulties and face no limitations on their activities.

In fact, in some ways people are better off, healthwise, in middle adulthood than in earlier periods of life. People between the ages of 45 and 65 are less likely than younger adults to experience infections, allergies, respiratory diseases, and digestive problems. They may contract fewer of these diseases now because they may have already experienced them and built up immunities during younger adulthood (Sterns, Barrett, & Alexander, 1985).

Certain chronic diseases do begin to appear during middle adulthood. Arthritis typically begins after the age of 40, and diabetes is most likely to occur in people between the ages of 50 and 60, particularly if they are overweight. Hypertension (high blood pressure) is one of the most frequent chronic disorders found in middle age. Sometimes called the "silent killer" because it is symptomless, hypertension, if left untreated, greatly increases the risk of strokes and heart disease. For such reasons, a variety of preventive and diagnostic medical tests are routinely recommended for adults during middle adulthood (see Table 15-1).

As a result of the onset of chronic diseases, the death rate among middle-aged individuals is higher than it is in earlier periods of life. Still, death remains a rare occurrence: Statistically, only three out of every hundred 40-year-olds would be expected to die before the age of 50, and eight out of every hundred 50-year-olds would be expected to die before the age of 60.

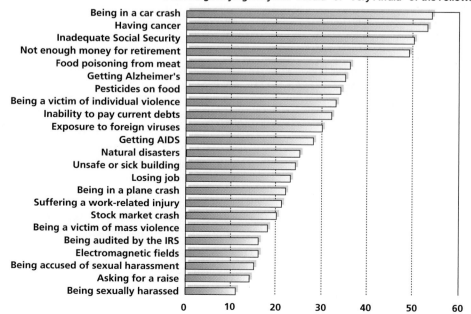

Percentage Saying They Are "Afraid" or "Very Afraid" of the Following:

- Being in a car crash
- Having cancer
- Inadequate Social Security
- Not enough money for retirement
- Food poisoning from meat
- Getting Alzheimer's
- Pesticides on food
- Being a victim of individual violence
- Inability to pay current debts
- Exposure to foreign viruses
- Getting AIDS
- Natural disasters
- Unsafe or sick building
- Losing job
- Being in a plane crash
- Suffering a work-related injury
- Stock market crash
- Being a victim of mass violence
- Being audited by the IRS
- Electromagnetic fields
- Being accused of sexual harassment
- Asking for a raise
- Being sexually harassed

0 10 20 30 40 50 60

FIGURE 15-4 WORRIES OF ADULTHOOD

As people enter middle adulthood, health and safety concerns become increasingly important, followed by financial worries.

(*Source: USA Weekend,* 1997.)

Table 15-1 Adult Preventive Health-Care Screening Recommendations

These are general guidelines for healthy adults who have no symptoms of disease

Screening	Description	Ages 40–49	Ages 50–59	Age 60+
ALL ADULTS				
BLOOD PRESSURE	Used to detect hypertension, which can lead to heart attack, stroke, or kidney disease	Every 2 years	Every 2 years	Every 2 years, Every year If family history of hypertension.
CHOLESTEROL—TOTAL/HDL	Used to detect high cholesterol levels, which increase risk of heart disease	All adults should receive total cholesterol screening, HDL cholesterol, LDL cholesterol, and triglycerides AT LEAST ONCE. Cardiac risk factors and lipoprotein results will determine frequency of follow-up by your health care provider.		
EYE EXAMINATION	Used to determine if glasses required and check for eye disease	Every 2–4 years Diabetics—Every year	Every 2–4 years Diabetics—Every year	Every 2–4 years. At age 65 and over, every 1–2 years. Diabetics—Every year
FLEXIBLE SIGMOIDOSCOPY OR DOUBLE CONTRAST BARIUM ENEMA OR COLONOSCOPY	A procedure using a scope or x-ray to detect cancer of the colon and rectum		Baseline at age 50. Every 3–5 years after initial test	Every 3–5 years. Age to stop depends on health. Follow up normal colonoscopy in 8–10 yrs
FECAL OCCULT BLOOD SCREENING	Detects unseen blood in stool, which is early warning sign for colon cancer		Every year	Every year
RECTAL EXAM (DIGITAL)	Examination of prostate or ovaries to detect cancer		Every year	Every year
URINALYSIS SCREENING	Examination to detect presence of excess of protein in urine	Every 5 years	Every 5 years	Every 3–5 years
IMMUNIZATIONS (SHOTS): Tetanus	Protection against infection after injury	Every 10 years	Every 10 years	Every 10 years
Influenza (Flu)	Protection against the influenza virus	Any person with chronic medical conditions such as heart, lung, kidney disease, diabetes	Annually, age 50 and over	Annually, age 65 and over
Pneumococcal	Protection against pneumonia			At age 65, then every 6 years
ADDITIONAL GUIDELINES FOR WOMEN				
BREAST SELF-EXAM/ BREAST EXAM BY PROVIDER	Examination to detect changes in breast that may indicate cancer	Every month/ Every year	Every month/ Every year	Every month/ Every year
MAMMOGRAM	Low-dose x-ray used to locate tumors for early detection of breast cancer	Every year	Every year	Every year
PAP SMEAR	Test that takes small sample of cells to detect cervical cancer or precancer cells	After 3 normal tests in a row, screen every 2–3 years unless at special risk.	After 3 normal tests in a row, screen every 2–3 years unless at special risk	Women 70 and older with 3 normal tests in a row and no abnormal tests in the 10 years prior to age 70 may cease having Pap test
PELVIC EXAM	Examination to detect pelvic abnormality	Every year (if ovaries remain after hysterectomy)	Every year (if ovaries remain after hysterectomy)	Every year (if ovaries remain after hysterectomy)
ADDITIONAL GUIDELINES FOR MEN				
PROSTATE SPECIFIC ANTIGEN	Blood test used to detect cancer of the prostate gland	Positive family history cancer— Every year (African Americans: Every year)	Every year upon doctor's advice	Until age 75, every year upon doctor's advice
TESTICULAR SELF-EXAM	Examination to detect changes in testicles that may indicate cancer	Every month	Every month	Every month

(*Source:* Adapted from Ochsner Clinic Foundation, 2003.)

Furthermore, the death rate for people between 40 and 60 has declined dramatically over the past 50 years. For instance, the death rate now stands at just half of what it was in the 1940s. There also are cultural variations in health, as we consider next (Smedley & Syme, 2000).

Developmental Diversity

Individual Variation in Health: Ethnic and Gender Differences

Masked by the overall figures describing the health of middle-aged adults are vast individual differences. While most people are relatively healthy, some are beset by a variety of ailments. Part of the cause is genetic. For instance, hypertension often runs in families.

Some of the causes of poor health are related to social and environmental factors. For instance, the death rate for middle-aged African Americans in the United States is twice the rate for Caucasians. Why should this be true?

Socioeconomic status (SES) seems to play a large role. For instance, when whites and African Americans of the same SES level are compared, the death rate for African Americans actually falls below that of whites. The lower a family's income, the more likely it is that a member will experience a disabling illness. There are a number of reasons for this. People living in lower SES households are more apt to work in occupations that are dangerous, such as mining or construction work. Lower income also often translates into inferior health-care coverage. In addition, the crime rates and environmental pollutants are generally higher in lower-income neighborhoods. Ultimately, then, a higher incidence of accidents and health hazards, and thus a higher death rate, are linked to lower levels of income (U.S. Bureau of the Census, 1990b; Fingerhut & MaKuc, 1992; Dahl & Birkelund, 1997; see Figure 15-5).

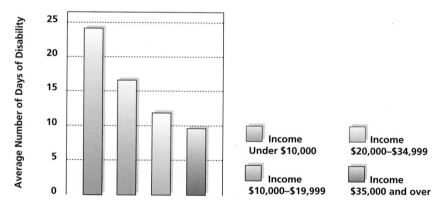

FIGURE 15-5   DISABILITY AND INCOME LEVEL

Workers living in poverty are more likely to become disabled than those with higher income levels. Why?

(*Source:* U.S. Bureau of the Census, 1990b.)

Gender, like SES, also makes a difference in health. Even though women's overall mortality rate is lower than men's—a trend that holds true from the time of infancy—the incidence of illness among middle-aged women is higher than it is among men.

Women are more likely to experience minor, short-term illness and chronic, but non-life-threatening diseases such as migraine headaches, and men are more apt to experience more serious illnesses such as heart disease. Furthermore, the rate of cigarette smoking is lower among women than men, which reduces their susceptibility to cancer and heart disease; women drink less alcohol than men, which reduces the risk of cirrhosis of the liver and auto accidents; and they work at less dangerous jobs (McDonald, 1999).

The discrepancies in the lives of people of higher and lower socioeconomic status are associated with differences in death rates between the two groups.

Another possible reason for the higher incidence of illness in women may be the greater medical research targeted toward men and the types of disorders from which they suffer. The vast majority of medical research money is aimed at preventing life-threatening diseases faced mostly by men rather than at chronic conditions such as heart disease that may cause disability and suffering, but not necessarily death. Typically, when research is carried out on diseases that strike both men and women, much of it has focused on men as subjects rather than on women. Although this bias is now being addressed in initiatives announced by the U.S. National Institutes of Health, the historical pattern has been one of gender discrimination by the traditionally male-dominated research community (Vidaver, 2000).

Stress in Middle Adulthood

Stress continues to have a significant impact on health during middle adulthood, as it did in young adulthood, although the nature of what is stressful may have changed. For example, parents may experience stress over their adolescent children's potential drug use rather than worry about whether their toddler is ready to give up his pacifier.

No matter what events trigger stress, the results are similar. As we first discussed in Chapter 13, *psychoneuroimmunologists,* who study the relationship between the brain, the immune system, and psychological factors, note that stress produces three main consequences, summarized in Figure 15-6. First, stress has direct physiological outcomes, ranging from increased

FIGURE 15-6   THE CONSEQUENCES OF STRESS

Stress produces three major consequences: direct physiological effects, harmful behaviors, and indirect health-related behaviors.

(*Source:* Adapted from Baum, 1994.)

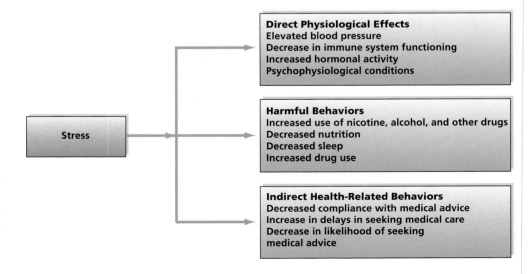

Direct Physiological Effects
Elevated blood pressure
Decrease in immune system functioning
Increased hormonal activity
Psychophysiological conditions

Harmful Behaviors
Increased use of nicotine, alcohol, and other drugs
Decreased nutrition
Decreased sleep
Increased drug use

Indirect Health-Related Behaviors
Decreased compliance with medical advice
Increase in delays in seeking medical care
Decrease in likelihood of seeking medical advice

Stress

blood pressure and hormonal activity to decreased immune system response. Second, stress also leads people to engage in unhealthy behaviors, such as cutting back on sleep, smoking, drinking, or taking other drugs. Finally, stress has indirect effects on health-related behavior. People under a lot of stress may be less likely to seek out good medical care, exercise, or to comply with medical advice (Suinn, 2001; Suls & Wallston, 2003; Zellner et al., 2006). All of these can lead to or affect serious health conditions, including such major problems as heart disease.

The A's and B's of Coronary Heart Disease: Linking Health and Personality

More men die in middle age from diseases relating to the heart and circulatory system than from any other cause. Women are less vulnerable, as we'll see, but they are not immune. Each year such diseases kill around 200,000 people under the age of 65, and they are responsible for more loss of work and disability days due to hospitalization than any other cause (American Heart Association, 1988).

Risk Factors for Heart Disease. Although heart and circulatory diseases are a major problem, they are not an equal threat for all people—some people have a much lower risk than others. For instance, the death rate in some countries, such as Japan, is only a quarter of the rate in the United States. A few other countries have a considerably higher death rate (see Figure 15-7). Why should this be true?

The answer is that both genetic and experiential characteristics are involved. Some people seem genetically predisposed to develop heart disease. If a person's parents suffered from it, the likelihood is greater that she or he will too. Similarly, sex and age are risk factors: Men are more likely to suffer from heart disease than women, and the risk rises as people age.

However, environment and lifestyle choices are also important. Cigarette smoking, a diet high in fats and cholesterol, and a relative lack of physical exercise all increase the likelihood of heart disease. Such factors may explain country-to-country variations in the incidence of heart disease. For example, the death rate attributable to heart disease in Japan is relatively low and may be due to differences in diet: The typical diet in Japan is much lower in fat than the typical diet in the United States (Zhou et al., 2003; Wilcox et al., 2006; De Meersman & Stein, 2007).

But diet is not the only factor. Psychological factors, particularly those related to the perception and experience of stress, appear to be associated with heart disease. In particular, a set of

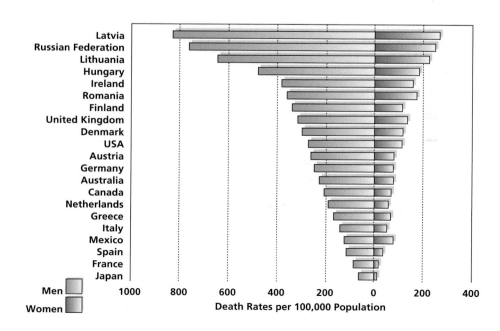

FIGURE 15-7   DEATH FROM HEART DISEASE WORLDWIDE

The risk of dying from cardiovascular disease differs significantly depending on the country in which one lives. What cultural or environmental factors might help to explain this fact?

(*Source:* World Health Organization, 1999.)

Type A behavior pattern behavior characterized by competitiveness, impatience, and a tendency toward frustration and hostility.

Type B behavior pattern behavior characterized by noncompetitiveness, patience, and a lack of aggression.

personality characteristics appears to be related to the development of middle-aged adults' coronary heart disease—the Type A behavior pattern.

Type A's and Type B's. For a certain proportion of adults, waiting patiently in a long line at the grocery store is a near impossibility. Sitting in their cars at a long red light makes them seethe. And an encounter with a slow, inept clerk at a retail store turns them furious.

People like this—and those similar to Jerome Yanger, who uses his exercise program as an opportunity to accomplish more work—have a set of characteristics known as the Type A behavior pattern. The **Type A behavior pattern** is characterized by competitiveness, impatience, and a tendency toward frustration and hostility. Type A people are driven to accomplish more than others, and they engage in *polyphasic activities*—multiple activities carried out simultaneously. They are the true multitaskers whom you might see talking on their phones while working on their laptop computers while riding the commuter train—and eating breakfast. They are easily angered and become both verbally and nonverbally hostile if they are prevented from reaching a goal they seek to accomplish.

In contrast to the Type A behavior pattern, many people have virtually the opposite characteristics in a pattern known as the Type B behavior pattern. The **Type B behavior pattern** is characterized by noncompetitiveness, patience, and a lack of aggression. In contrast to Type A's, Type B's experience little sense of time urgency, and they are rarely hostile.

Most people are not purely Type A's or Type B's. In fact, Type A and Type B represent the ends of a continuum, with most people falling somewhere in between the two endpoints. Still, most people come closer to one or the other of the two categories. Which category a person falls into is of some importance, particularly by middle adulthood, because a great deal of research suggests that the distinction is related to the incidence of coronary heart disease. For example, Type A men have twice the rate of coronary heart disease, a greater number of fatal heart attacks, and five times as many heart problems overall as Type B men (Rosenman, 1990; Strube, 1990; Wielgosz & Nolan, 2000).

Although it is not certain why Type A behavior increases the risk of heart problems, the most likely explanation is that when Type A's are in stressful situations, they become excessively aroused physiologically. Heart rate and blood pressure rise, and production of the hormones epinephrine and norepinephrine increases. The wear and tear on the body's circulatory system is what seems to ultimately produce coronary heart disease (Raikkonen et al., 1995; Sundin et al., 1995; Williams, Barefoot, & Schneiderman, 2003).

It's important to note that not every component of the Type A behavior pattern is harmful. The key component that links Type A behavior and heart disease is *hostility*. Furthermore, the links between Type A behavior and coronary heart disease are correlational. No definitive evidence has been found that Type A behavior *causes* coronary heart disease. In fact, some evidence suggests that only certain components of Type A behavior are most involved in producing disease, and not the entire constellation of behaviors associated with the pattern. For instance, there is a growing consensus that the hostility and anger related to the Type A behavior pattern may be the central link to coronary heart disease (Kahn, 2004; Eaker et al., 2004; Demaree & Everhart, 2004; Myrtek, 2007).

In addition to being characterized as competitive, people with Type A personalities also tend to engage in polyphasic activities, or doing a number of things at once. Does a Type A personality deal with stress differently than a Type B personality?

Although the relationship between at least some Type A behaviors and heart disease is clear, this does not mean that all middle-aged adults who can be characterized as Type A's are destined to suffer from coronary heart disease. For one thing, almost all the research conducted to date has focused on men, primarily because the incidence of coronary heart disease is much higher for males than for females. In addition, other types of negative emotions besides the hostility found in Type A behavior have been linked to heart disease. For example, psychologist Johan Denollet has identified behavior he calls *Type D*—for "distressed"—that is linked to coronary heart disease. He believes that insecurity, anxiety, and having a negative outlook put people at risk for heart attacks (Denollet & Brutsaert, 1998; Denollet, 2005; Schiffer et al., 2005; Schiffer et al., 2006).

The Threat of Cancer

Brenda surveyed the crowd as she stood in line to start the annual "Race for the Cure," a running and walking event that raised funds to fight breast cancer. It was a sobering sight. She spotted a group of five women, all wearing the bright pink shirts that marked them as cancer survivors. Several other racers had photos of loved ones who had lost their battles with the disease pinned to their jerseys.

Few diseases are as frightening as cancer, and many middle-aged individuals view a cancer diagnosis as a death sentence. Although the reality is different—many forms of cancer respond quite well to medical treatment, and 40% of people diagnosed with the disease are still alive 5 years later—the disease raises many fears. And there is no denying that cancer is the second-leading cause of death in the United States (Smedley & Syme, 2000).

The precise trigger for cancer is still not known, but the process by which cancer spreads is straightforward. For some reason, particular cells in the body begin to multiply uncontrollably and rapidly. As they increase in number, these cells form tumors. If left unimpeded, they draw nutrients from healthy cells and body tissue. Eventually, they destroy the body's ability to function properly.

Like heart disease, cancer is associated with a variety of risk factors, some genetic and others environmental. Some kinds of cancer have clear genetic components. For example, a family history of breast cancer—which is the most common cause of cancer death among women—raises the risk for a woman.

However, several environmental and behavioral factors are also related to the risk of cancer. For instance, poor nutrition, smoking, alcohol use, exposure to sunlight, exposure to radiation, and particular occupational hazards (such as exposure to certain chemicals or asbestos) are all known to increase the chances of developing cancer.

After a diagnosis of cancer, several forms of treatment are possible, depending on the type of cancer. One treatment is *radiation therapy,* in which the tumor is the target of radiation designed to destroy it. Patients undergoing *chemotherapy* ingest controlled doses of toxic substances meant, in essence, to poison the tumor. Finally, surgery may be used to remove the tumor (and often the surrounding tissue). The exact form of treatment is a result of how far the cancer has spread throughout a patient's body when it is first identified.

Because early cancer detection improves a patient's chances, diagnostic techniques that help identify the first signs of cancer are of great importance. This is particularly true during middle adulthood, when the risk of contracting certain kinds of cancer increases.

Consequently, physicians urge that women routinely examine their breasts and men regularly check their testicles for signs of cancer. In addition, cancer of the prostate gland, which is the most frequent type of cancer in men, can be detected by routine rectal exams and by a blood test to identify the presence of prostate-specific antigen (PSA).

Mammograms, which provide internal scans of women's breasts, also help identify early-stage cancer. However, the question of when women should begin to routinely have the procedure has been controversial.

Routine Mammograms: At What Age Should Women Start?

I found the lump in February . . . . Buried deep in my left breast, it was rock-hard, the size of a BB, and it hurt. I wondered if it might be cancer. Like blue eyes and a sense of humor, the disease runs in my family. But not breast cancer. And not me. I was too young. OK. I had recently turned 40, but I was healthy. I worked out three times a week and I was almost a vegetarian. My next physical was only a month away. I'd have it checked then. (Driedger, 1994, p. 46)

For Sharon Driedger, feeling healthy, exercising, and eating a good diet was not enough: She did have cancer. But she was also lucky. After aggressive treatment with radiation therapy, she stands a good chance of a full recovery.

Women should routinely examine their breasts for signs of breast cancer.

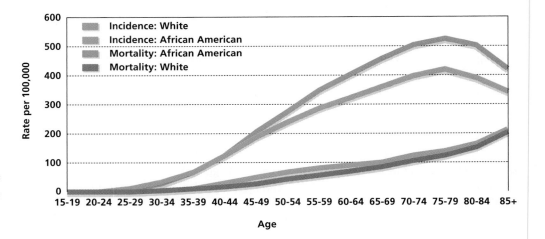

FIGURE 15-8   AGE AND THE RISK OF BREAST CANCER

Starting around the age of 30, the risk of breast cancer becomes increasingly likely, as these annual incidence figures show.

(*Source:* Adapted from American Cancer Society, 2003.)

In part, her good luck is a result of the early identification of her cancer. Statistically, the earlier breast cancer is diagnosed, the better a woman's chances of survival. But just how to accomplish early identification has produced some degree of contention in the medical field. Specifically, the controversy surrounds the age at which *mammograms,* a kind of weak x-ray used to examine breast tissue, should be routinely administered to women.

Mammograms are among the best means of detecting breast cancer in its earliest stages. The technique allows physicians to identify tumors while they are still very small. Patients have time for treatment before the tumor grows and spreads to other parts of the body. Mammograms have the potential for saving many lives, and nearly all medical professionals suggest that at some point during middle adulthood women should routinely obtain them.

But at what age should women start having annual mammograms? As shown in Figure 15-8, the risk of breast cancer begins to grow at around the age of 30 and then becomes increasingly more likely. Ninety-five percent of new cases occur in women aged 40 and above (SEER, 2005).

Determining the age to begin routine screening mammograms is complicated by two considerations. First, there is the problem of *false positives,* instances in which the test suggests something is wrong when in fact there is no problem. Because the breast tissue of younger women is denser than that of older women, younger women are more likely to have false positives. In fact, some estimates suggest that as many as a third of all younger women who have repeated mammograms are likely to have a false positive that necessitates further testing or a biopsy. Furthermore, the opposite problem also may occur: *false negatives,* in which a mammogram does not detect indications of cancer (Miller, 1991; Baines et al., 1997; Wei et al., 2007).

A second problem with routine mammograms is their expense, which runs around $125 on average. If the incidence of breast cancer at age 40 is 112 cases out of 100,000, this means that it will cost $12.5 million to detect just 112 cases. Medical costs being high already, coverage of routine mammograms has not been eagerly embraced by insurers.

The current consensus, at least among medical care providers, is that age 40 is the most reasonable age to begin routine annual screenings using mammograms. Although the debate is not over, the American Cancer Society, American Medical Association, and the National Cancer Institute now recommend annual screening mammograms for women aged 40 and above (Rimer et al., 2001).

Psychological Factors Relating to Cancer: Mind over Tumor?   Increasing evidence suggests that cancer is related not only to physiological causes, but to psychological factors as well (Edelman & Kidman, 1997). In particular, some research indicates that the emotional responses of people with cancer can influence their recovery. In one study, for instance, a group

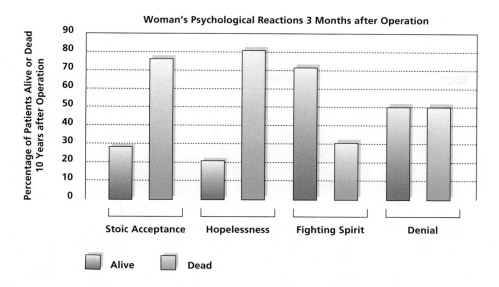

Woman's Psychological Reactions 3 Months after Operation

FIGURE 15-9 ATTITUDE AND SURVIVING CANCER

A fighting spirit pays off. A woman's psychological reaction 3 months after her cancer operation was clearly associated with whether she was alive 10 years later. What does this suggest about potential treatment approaches?

(*Source:* Pettingale et al., 1985.)

of women who recently had had a breast removed as part of their treatment for breast cancer were categorized according to their attitudes. Some felt their situation was hopeless, while others stoically accepted their cancer, voicing no complaints. Other women expressed a "fighting spirit," contending that they would lick the disease. Finally, some simply denied that they had cancer, refusing to accept the diagnosis.

Ten years later, the researchers looked again at the group of women. They found clear-cut evidence that initial attitude was related to survival. A larger percentage of the women who had stoically accepted their cancer or had felt hopeless had died. The death rate was much lower for those who had a "fighting spirit" or who had denied that they had the disease (Pettingale et al., 1985; see Figure 15-9).

Personality factors may also play a role in cancer. For example, cancer patients who are habitually optimistic report less physical and psychological distress than those who are less optimistic (Carver & Scheier, 1993; Bolger et al., 1996; Gerend, Aiken, & West, 2004).

Related to the idea that psychological factors can help prevent or improve cancer treatment success is evidence that participation in psychological therapy may give cancer patients an edge in treatment. For example, one study found that women in the advanced stages of breast cancer who participated in group therapy lived at least 18 months longer than those who did not participate in therapy. Furthermore, the women who participated also experienced less anxiety and pain (Spiegel et al., 1989; Spiegel, 1993, 1996; Spiegel & Giese-Davis, 2003).

How, exactly, might a person's psychological state be linked to his or her prognosis with cancer? Cancer treatment is intricate, complex, and often unpleasant. It may be that patients who have the most positive attitudes and are involved in therapy might be more likely to adhere to medical treatments. Consequently, such patients are more likely to experience treatment success (Holland & Lewis, 1993; Sheridan & Radmacher, 2003).

There's another possibility: It may be that a positive psychological outlook bolsters the body's immune system, the natural line of defense against disease. A positive outlook may energize the immune system to produce "killer" cells that fight the cancerous cells. In contrast, negative emotions and attitudes may impair the ability of the body's natural killer cells to fight off the cancer (Seligman, 1995; Ironson & Schneiderman, 2002; Gidron et al., 2006).

It is important to keep in mind that the link between attitudes, emotions, and cancer is far from proven. Furthermore, it is unjustified and unfair to assume that a cancer patient would be doing better if only he or she had a more positive attitude. What the data do suggest is that psychological therapy might be warranted as a routine component of cancer treatment, even if it does nothing more than improve the patient's psychological state and raise his or her morale (Holland & Lewis, 1993; Owen et al., 2004; Weber et al., 2004).

Although some studies suggest that the degree of social support in a person's life may be related to a decreased risk of cancer, the link between attitudes, emotions, and cancer is far from proven.

Review and Apply

Review

- In general, middle adulthood is a period of good health, although susceptibility to chronic diseases, such as arthritis, diabetes, and hypertension, increases.
- Heart disease is a risk for middle-aged adults. Both genetic and environmental factors contribute to heart disease, including the Type A behavior pattern.
- The incidence of cancer begins to be significant in middle adulthood.
- Therapies such as radiation therapy, chemotherapy, and surgery can successfully treat cancer, and psychological factors, such as a fighting attitude and a refusal to accept the finality of cancer, can influence survival rates.

Applying Lifespan Development

- What social policies might be developed to lower the incidence of disabling illness among members of lower-socioeconomic groups?

- *From the perspective of a healthcare professional:* Does the effect of psychological attitude on cancer survival suggest that nontraditional healing techniques—such as the use of meditation—might have a place in cancer treatment? Why or why not?

Cognitive Development

It began innocently enough. Forty-five-year-old Bina Clingman couldn't remember whether she had mailed the letter that her husband had given her, and she wondered, in passing, whether this was a sign of aging. The very next day, her feelings were reinforced when she had to spend 20 minutes looking for a phone number that she knew she had written down on a piece of paper—somewhere. By the time she had found it, she was surprised and even a little anxious. "Am I losing my memory?" she asked herself, with both annoyance and some degree of concern.

Many people in their 40s will tell you that they feel more absentminded than they did 20 years earlier and that they harbor at least some concern about becoming less mentally able than when they were younger. Common wisdom suggests that people lose some mental sharpness as they age. But how accurate is this notion?

Does Intelligence Decline in Adulthood?

For years, experts provided a clear, unwavering response when asked whether intelligence declined during adulthood. It was a response that most adults were not happy to hear: Intelligence peaks at age 18, stays fairly steady until the mid-20s, and then begins a gradual decline that continues until the end of life.

Today, however, developmentalists have come to see that the answers to questions about changes in intelligence across the life span are more complicated—and they have come to different, and more complex, conclusions.

The Difficulties in Answering the Question. The conclusion that intelligence starts to diminish in the mid-20s was based on extensive research. In particular, *cross-sectional studies*—which test people of different ages at the same point in time—clearly showed that older subjects were more likely to score less well than younger subjects on traditional intelligence tests, of the sort we first discussed in Chapter 9.

But consider the drawbacks of cross-sectional research—in particular the possibility that it may suffer from *cohort effects*. Recall from Chapter 1 that cohort effects are influences associated with growing up at a particular historical time that affect persons of a particular age. For instance, suppose that compared to the younger people, the older people in a cross-sectional study had had less adequate educations, were exposed to less stimulation in their jobs, or were relatively less healthy. In that case, the lower IQ scores of the older group could hardly be attributed solely, or perhaps even partially, to differences in intelligence between younger and older individuals. In sum, because they do not control for cohort effects, cross-sectional studies may well *underestimate* intelligence in older subjects.

In an effort to overcome the cohort problems of cross-sectional studies, developmentalists began to turn to *longitudinal studies,* in which the same people are studied periodically over a span of time. These studies began to reveal a different developmental pattern for intelligence: Adults tended to show fairly stable and even increasing intelligence test scores until they reached their mid-30s, and in some cases up to their 50s. At that point, though, scores began to decline (Bayley & Oden, 1955).

But let's step back a moment and consider the drawbacks of longitudinal studies. For instance, people who take the same intelligence test repeatedly may perform better simply because they become more familiar—and comfortable—with the testing situation. Similarly, because they have been exposed to the same test regularly over the years, they may even begin to remember some of the test items. Consequently, practice effects may account for the relatively superior performance of people on longitudinal measures of intelligence as opposed to cross-sectional measures.

Furthermore, it is difficult for researchers using longitudinal studies to keep their samples intact. Participants in a study may move away, decide they no longer want to participate, or become ill and die. In fact, as time goes on, the participants who remain in the study may represent a healthier, more stable, and more psychologically positive group of people than those who are no longer part of the sample. If this is the case, then longitudinal studies may mistakenly *overestimate* intelligence in older subjects.

fluid intelligence   reflects information processing capabilities, reasoning, and memory.

crystallized intelligence   the accumulation of information, skills, and strategies that people have learned through experience and that they can apply in problem-solving situations.

Crystallized and Fluid Intelligence. The ability of developmentalists to draw conclusions about age-related changes in intelligence faces still more hurdles. For instance, many IQ tests include sections based on physical performance, such as arranging a group of blocks. These sections are timed and scored on the basis of how quickly a question is completed. If older people take longer on physical tasks—and remember that reaction time slows with age, as we discussed earlier in the chapter—then their poorer performance on IQ tests may be a result of physical rather than cognitive changes (Schaie, 1991; Nettelbeck & Rabbit, 1992).

To complicate the picture even further, many researchers believe that there are two kinds of intelligence: fluid intelligence and crystallized intelligence. As we first noted in Chapter 9, **fluid intelligence** reflects information processing capabilities, reasoning, and memory. For instance, a person who is asked to arrange a series of letters according to some rule or to memorize a set of numbers uses fluid intelligence. In contrast, **crystallized intelligence** is the accumulation of information, skills, and strategies that people have learned through experience and that they can apply in problem-solving situations. Someone who is solving a crossword puzzle or attempting to identify the murderer in a mystery story is using crystallized intelligence, relying on his or her past experience as a resource.

Initially, researchers believed that fluid intelligence was largely determined by genetic factors, and crystallized intelligence primarily by experiential, environmental factors. However, they later abandoned this distinction, largely because they found that crystallized intelligence is determined in part by fluid intelligence. For instance, a person's ability to solve a crossword puzzle (which involves crystallized intelligence) is a result of that person's proficiency with letters and patterns (a manifestation of fluid intelligence).

When developmentalists looked at the two kinds of intelligence separately, they arrived at a new answer to the question of whether intelligence declines with age. Actually, they arrived at two answers: yes and no. Yes, because in general, fluid intelligence does decline with age; no, because crystallized intelligence holds steady and in some cases actually improves (Ryan, Sattler, & Lopez, 2000; Salthouse, Atkinson, & Berish, 2003; Bugg et al., 2006; see Figure 15-10).

If we look at more specific types of intelligence, true age-related differences and developments in intelligence begin to show up. According to developmental psychologist K. Warner Schaie (1994), who has conducted extensive longitudinal research on the course of adult

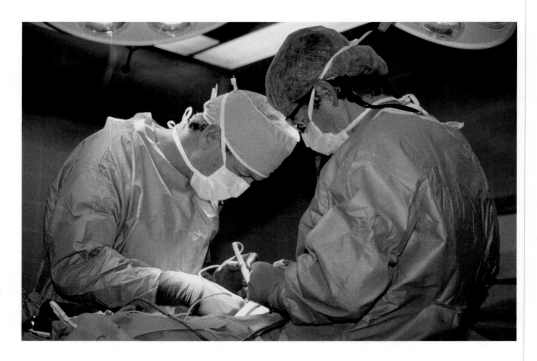

It is difficult to evaluate cognitive abilities in middle adulthood. While some types of mental abilities may begin to decline, crystallized intelligence holds steady and actually may increase.

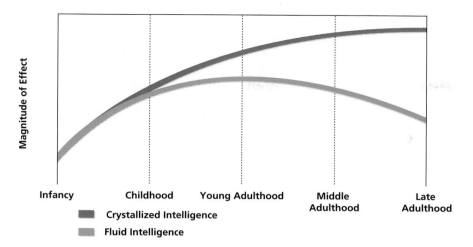

FIGURE 15-10 **CHANGES IN CRYSTALLIZED AND FLUID INTELLIGENCE**

Although crystallized intelligence increases with age, fluid intelligence begins to decline in middle age. What are the implications for general competence in middle adulthood? (*Source:* Schaie, 1985.)

intellectual development, we should consider many particular types of ability, such as spatial orientation, numeric ability, verbal ability, and so on rather than the broad divisions of crystallized and fluid intelligence.

When looked at in this way, the question of how intelligence changes in adulthood yields yet another answer, a more specific one. Schaie has found that certain abilities, such as inductive reasoning, spatial orientation, perceptual speed, and verbal memory, begin to decline very gradually at around age 25 and continue to decline through old age. Numeric and verbal abilities show a quite different pattern. Numeric ability tends to increase until the mid-40s, is lower at age 60, and then stays steady throughout the rest of life. Verbal ability rises until about the start of middle adulthood, around age 40, and stays fairly steady throughout the rest of the life span (Schaie, 1994).

Why do these changes occur? One reason is that brain functioning begins to change in middle adulthood. For example, researchers have found that 20 genes that are vital to learning, memory, and mental flexibility begin to function less efficiently as early as age 40 (Lu et al., 2004).

Reframing the Issue: What Is the Source of Competence During Middle Adulthood? Despite the gradual declines in particular cognitive abilities during middle adulthood, it is during this part of the life span that people come to hold some of the most important and powerful positions in society. How can we explain such continuing, and even growing, competence in the face of apparently ongoing declines in certain cognitive skills?

One answer comes from psychologist Timothy Salthouse (1989, 1990, 1994a), who suggests that there are four reasons why this discrepancy exists. For one thing, it is possible that typical measures of cognitive skills tap a different type of cognition than what is required to be successful in particular occupations. Recall the discussion of practical intelligence in Chapter 13, in which we found that traditional IQ tests fail to measure cognitive abilities that are related to occupational success. Perhaps we would find no discrepancy between intelligence and cognitive abilities in middle adulthood if we used measures of practical intelligence rather than traditional IQ tests to assess intelligence.

A second factor also relates to the measurement of IQ and occupational success. It is possible that the most successful middle-aged adults are not representative of middle-aged adults in general. It may be that only a small proportion of people are highly successful, and the rest, who experience only moderate or little success, may have changed occupations, retired, or become sick and died. If we look at highly successful people, then, we are examining an unrepresentative sample of individuals.

It is also conceivable that the degree of cognitive ability required for professional success is simply not that high. According to this argument, people can be quite successful professionally

Cognitive development during middle and later adulthood is a mixture of growth and decline. As people begin to lose certain abilities due to biological deterioration, they also advance in other areas by strengthening their skills.

and still be on the decline in certain kinds of cognitive abilities. In other words, their cognitive declines are not all that important; they have brains to spare.

Finally, it may be that older people are successful because they have developed specific kinds of expertise and particular competencies. Whereas IQ tests measure reactions to novel situations, occupational success may be influenced by very specific sorts of well-practiced abilities. Consequently, although their overall intellectual skills may show a decline, middle-aged individuals may maintain and even expand the distinctive talents they need for professional accomplishment. This explanation has generated a whole area of research on expertise, as we'll see later in the chapter.

For example, developmental psychologists Paul Baltes and Margaret Baltes have studied a strategy called selective optimization. **Selective optimization** is the process by which people concentrate on particular skill areas to compensate for losses in other areas. Baltes suggests that cognitive development during middle and later adulthood is a mixture of growth and decline. As people begin to lose certain abilities due to biological deterioration, they advance in other areas by strengthening their skills. Because they are able to compensate for their losses, they avoid showing any practical deterioration. Overall cognitive competence, then, ultimately remains stable and may even improve (Bajor & Baltes, 2003; Baltes & Carstensen, 2003; Baltes & Freund, 2003; Ebner, Freund, & Baltes, 2006).

For instance, recall that reaction time lengthens as people get older. Because reaction time is a component of typing skill, we would expect that older typists would be slower than younger ones. However, this is not the case. Why? The answer is that while their reaction time is increasing, older typists look further ahead in the material they are to type. This allows them to compensate for their lengthier reaction time. Similarly, although a business executive may be less quick in recalling names, he may have a mental file of deals he has completed in the past and be able to forge new agreements easily because of it.

Selective optimization is only one of the strategies adults with expertise in various fields use to maintain high performance. What are some other characteristics of experts?

The Development of Expertise: Separating Experts from Novices

If you were ill and needed a diagnosis, would you rather visit a newly minted young physician who had just graduated from medical school, or a more experienced, middle-aged physician?

If you chose the older physician, it's probably because you assumed that he or she would have a higher level of expertise. **Expertise** is the acquisition of skill or knowledge in a particular area. More focused than broader intelligence, expertise develops as people devote attention and practice to particular domains and, in so doing, gain experience, either because of their profession or because they simply enjoy a given area. For example, physicians become better at diagnosing the symptoms of a medical problem in their patients as they gain experience. Similarly, a person who enjoys cooking and does a lot of it begins to know beforehand how a recipe will taste if certain modifications are made.

What separates experts from those who are less skilled in a given area? While beginners use formal procedures and rules, often following them very strictly, experts rely on experience and intuition, and they often bend the rules. Because experts have so much experience, their processing of information is often automatic, performed without the need for much thought. Experts often are not very articulate at explaining how they draw conclusions; their solutions often just seem right to them—and *are* more likely to be right. Brain imaging studies show that experts, compared to novices, use different neural pathways to solve problems (Grabner, Neubauer, & Stern, 2006).

Finally, when difficulties arise, experts develop better strategies for solving them than non-experts, and they're more flexible in approaching problems. Their experience has provided

selective optimization the process by which people concentrate on particular skill areas to compensate for losses in other areas.

expertise the acquisition of skill or knowledge in a particular area.

Expertise develops as people become more experienced in a particular domain and are able to be flexible with procedures and rules.

them with alternative routes to the same problem, and this increases the probability of success (Willis, 1996; Clark, 1998; Arts, Gijselaers, & Boshuizen, 2006).

Of course, not everyone develops expertise in some particular area during middle adulthood. Professional responsibilities, amount of leisure time, educational level, income, and marital status all affect the development of expertise.

Memory: You Must Remember This

Whenever Mary Donovan can't find her car keys, she mutters to herself that she is "losing her memory." Like Bina Clingman, who was worried about forgetting things like letters and phone numbers, Mary probably believes that memory loss is pretty common in middle age.

However, if she fits the pattern of most people in middle adulthood, her assessment is not necessarily accurate. According to research on memory changes in adulthood, most people show only minimal memory losses, and many exhibit none at all, during middle adulthood. Furthermore, because of societal stereotypes about aging, people in middle adulthood may be prone to attribute their absentmindedness to aging, even though they have been absentminded throughout their lives. Consequently, it is the *meaning* they give to their forgetfulness that changes, rather than their actual ability to remember (Erber, Rothberg, & Szuchman, 1991).

Types of Memory. To understand the nature of memory changes, it is necessary to consider the different types of memory. Memory is traditionally viewed in terms of three sequential components: sensory memory, short-term memory (also called working memory), and long-term memory. *Sensory memory* is an initial, momentary storage of information that lasts only an instant. Information is recorded by an individual's sensory system as a raw, meaningless stimulus. Next, information moves into *short-term memory*, which holds it for 15 to 25 seconds. Finally, if the information is rehearsed, it is moved into *long-term memory*, where it is stored on a relatively permanent basis.

Both sensory memory and short-term memory show virtually no weakening during middle adulthood. The story is a bit different for long-term memory, which declines with age for some people. It appears, however, that the reason for the decline is not a fading or a complete loss of memory, but rather that with age, people register and store information less efficiently.

Understanding a tale told by Native-American storytellers may require familiarity with the culture, due to the existence of particular schemas.

. . . .

schemas organized bodies of information stored in memory.

mnemonics formal strategies for organizing material in ways that make it more likely to be remembered.

In addition, age makes people less efficient in retrieving information that is stored in memory. In other words, even if the information was adequately stored in long-term memory, it may become more difficult to locate or isolate it (Schieber et al., 1992; Salthouse, 1994b).

It is important to keep in mind that memory declines in middle age are relatively minor, and most can be compensated for by various cognitive strategies. As mentioned earlier, paying greater attention to material when it is first encountered can aid in its later recall. Your lost car keys may have relatively little to do with memory declines, instead reflecting your inattentiveness when you put them down.

Many middle adults find it hard to pay attention to particular things for some of the same reasons expertise develops. They are used to using memory shortcuts, *schemas*, to ease the burden of remembering all the many things that each of us experiences every day.

Memory Schemas. One of the ways that people recall information is through the use of **schemas,** organized bodies of information stored in memory. Schemas help people represent the way the world is organized, and allow them to categorize and interpret new information (Fiske & Taylor, 1991). For example, we may have a schema for eating out in a restaurant. We don't need to treat a meal in a new restaurant as a completely new experience. We know that when we go there, we will be seated at a table or counter and offered a menu from which to select food. Our schema for eating out tells us how to relate to the server, what sorts of food to eat first, and that we should leave a tip at the end of the meal.

People hold schemas for particular individuals (such as the particular behavior patterns of one's mother, wife, or child) as well as for categories of people (mail carriers, lawyers, or professors) and behaviors or events (dining in a restaurant or visiting the dentist). People's schemas serve to organize their behavior into coherent wholes and help them to interpret social events. For example, a person who knows the schema for a visit to the doctor is not likely to be surprised when he is asked to remove his clothes.

Schemas also convey cultural information. Psychologists Susan Fiske and Shelley Taylor (1991) give an example of an old Native American folktale in which the hero participates with several companions in a battle and is shot by an arrow. However, he feels no pain from the arrow. When he returns to his home and tells the story, something black emerges from his mouth, and he dies the next morning.

This tale is puzzling to most Westerners because they are unschooled in the particular Native American culture to which the story belongs. However, to someone familiar with the Native American culture, the story makes perfect sense: The hero feels no pain because his companions are ghosts, and the "black thing" coming from his mouth is his departing soul.

For a Native American, it may be relatively easy to later recall the story, because it makes sense in a way that it doesn't to members of other cultures. Furthermore, material that is consistent with existing schemas is more likely to be recalled than material that is inconsistent (Van Manen & Pietromonaco, 1993). For example, a person who usually puts her keys in a certain spot may lose them because she doesn't recall putting them down somewhere other than in the usual place.

Becoming an Informed Consumer of Development

Effective Strategies for Remembering

All of us are forgetful at one time or another. However, there are techniques that can help us remember more effectively and make it less likely that we will forget things that we wish to remember. **Mnemonics** (pronounced "nee-MON-iks") are formal strategies for organizing material in ways that make it more likely to be remembered. Among the mnemonics that work not only in middle adulthood, but at other points of the life span, are the following (Bellezza, Six, & Phillips, 1992; Guttman, 1997; Bloom & Lamkin, 2006; Morris & Fritz, 2006):

- *Get organized.* For people who have trouble keeping track of where they left their keys or remembering appointments, the simplest approach is for them to become more organized. Using an appointment book, hanging one's keys on a hook, or using Post-It notes can help jog one's memory.

- *Pay attention.* You can improve your recall by initially paying attention when you are exposed to new information, and by purposefully thinking that you wish to recall it in the future. If you are particularly concerned about remembering something, such as where you parked your car, pay particular attention at the moment you park the car, and remind yourself that you really want to remember.

- *Use the encoding specificity phenomenon.* According to the encoding specificity phenomenon, people are most likely to recall information in environments that are similar to those in which they initially learned ("encoded") it (Tulving & Thompson, 1973). For instance, people are best able to recall information on a test if the test is held in the room in which they studied.

- *Visualize.* Making mental images of ideas can help you recall them later. For example, if you want to remember that global warming may lead to rising oceans, think of yourself on a beach on a hot day, with the waves coming closer and closer to where you've set out your beach blanket.

- *Rehearse.* In the realm of memory, practice makes perfect, or if not perfect, at least better. Adults of all ages can improve their memories if they expend more effort in rehearsing what they want to remember. By practicing what they wish to recall, people can substantially improve their recall of the material.

Review and Apply

Review

- The question of whether intelligence declines in middle adulthood is complicated by limitations in cross-sectional studies and longitudinal studies.

- Intelligence appears to be divided into components, some of which decline while others hold steady or even improve.

- In general, cognitive competence in middle adulthood holds fairly steady despite declines in some areas of intellectual functioning.

- Memory may appear to decline in middle age, but in fact long-term memory deficits are probably due to ineffective strategies of storage and retrieval.

Applying Lifespan Development

- How might crystallized and fluid intelligence work together to help middle-aged people deal with novel situations and problems?

- *From the perspective of an educator:* How do you think the apparent discrepancy between declining IQ scores and continuing cognitive competence in middle adulthood would affect the learning ability of middle adults who return to school?

Epilogue

People's physical abilities and health in middle adulthood are generally still good. Subtle changes are occurring, but individuals often find it easy to compensate for them because of the strengths of other cognitive skills. The incidence of chronic and life-threatening diseases increases, especially heart disease and cancer. In the cognitive realm intelligence and memory decline very gradually in some areas, but this decline is hidden by compensatory strategies and gains in other areas.

Return to the prologue of this chapter, about Pat Rodden's bicycle trek, and answer these questions:

1. What changes in physical functions during middle adulthood are likely to affect Rodden's performance?

2. What adjustments could Rodden make to compensate for his changes in ability?

3. Does Rodden seem to have more of a Type A or a Type B personality? Why do you think so?

4. Do you think that Rodden's ability to pick up a long-neglected activity is typical or atypical of people in middle adulthood?

5. If Rodden continues with his rediscovered enthusiasm for bike riding, what physical and psychological benefits can he expect to result?

6. If Rodden were to return to school in middle adulthood, what cognitive challenges would he face compared with his younger classmates?

Looking
Back

■ **What sorts of physical changes affect people in middle adulthood?**

- During middle adulthood, roughly the period from 40 to 65, people typically decline slowly in height and strength, and gain in weight. Height loss, especially in women, may be associated with osteoporosis, a thinning of the bones brought about by a lack of calcium in the diet. The best antidote for physical and psychological deterioration appears to be a healthful lifestyle, including regular exercise.

- Visual acuity declines during this period as the eyes' lens changes. People in middle adulthood tend to experience declines in near vision, depth and distance perception, adaptation to darkness, and the ability to perceive in three dimensions. In addition, the incidence of glaucoma, a disease that can cause blindness, increases in middle adulthood.

- Hearing acuity also declines slightly in this period, typically involving some loss of the ability to hear high-frequency sounds and a deterioration of sound localization.

- Reaction time of middle-aged people begins to increase gradually, but slower reactions are largely offset in complex tasks by increased skill due to years of task rehearsal.

■ **What changes in sexuality do middle-aged men and women experience?**

- Adults in middle age experience changes in sexuality, but these are less dramatic than commonly supposed, and many middle-aged couples experience new sexual freedom and enjoyment.

- Women in middle age experience the female climacteric, the change from being able to bear children to no longer being able to do so. The most notable sign is menopause, which is often accompanied by physical and emotional discomfort. Therapies and changing attitudes toward menopause appear to be lessening women's fears and experience of difficulty regarding menopause.

- Hormone therapy (HT) is a therapy that aims to decrease symptoms related to menopause and slow the deterioration associated with aging by replacing the female body's estrogen. Despite evidence of positive effects, some studies have suggested that the risks of HT can outweigh the benefits.

- Men also undergo changes in their reproductive systems, sometimes referred to as the male climacteric. Generally, the production of sperm and testosterone declines and the prostate gland enlarges, causing difficulties with urination.

■ **Is middle adulthood a time of health or disease for men and women?**

- Middle adulthood is generally a healthy period, but people become more susceptible to chronic diseases, including arthritis, diabetes, and hypertension, and they have a higher death rate than before. However, the death rate among people in middle adulthood in the United States has been steadily declining.

- Overall health in middle adulthood varies according to socioeconomic status and gender. People of higher SES are healthier and have lower death rates than people of lower SES. Women have a lower mortality rate than men, but a higher incidence of illness. Researchers have generally paid more attention to the life-threatening diseases experienced by men than to the less fatal but chronic diseases typical of women.

■ **What sorts of people are likely to get coronary heart disease?**

• Heart disease begins to be a significant factor in middle adulthood. Genetic characteristics, such as age, gender, and a family history of heart disease, are associated with the risk of heart disease, as are environmental and behavioral factors, including smoking, a diet high in fats and cholesterol, and a lack of exercise.

• Psychological factors also play a role in heart disease. A pattern of behaviors associated with competitiveness, impatience, frustration, and particularly hostility—called the Type A behavior pattern—is associated with a high risk of heart problems.

■ **What causes cancer, and what tools are available to diagnose and treat it?**

• Like heart disease, cancer becomes a threat in middle adulthood and is related to genetic and environmental factors. Treatments include radiation therapy, chemotherapy, and surgery.

• Psychological factors appear to play a role in cancer. Cancer patients who refuse to accept that they have the disease or who fight back against it seem to have a higher survival rate than patients who stoically accept their diagnosis or fall into hopelessness. Furthermore, persons with strong family and social ties appear to be less likely to develop cancer than persons who lack such ties.

• Breast cancer is a significant risk for women in middle adulthood. Mammography can help identify cancerous tumors early enough for successful treatment, but the age at which women should begin to have routine mammograms—40 or 50—is a matter of controversy.

■ **What happens to a person's intelligence in middle adulthood?**

• The question of whether intelligence declines in middle adulthood is challenging to answer because the two basic methods of addressing it have significant limitations.

Cross-sectional methods, which study many subjects of different ages at one point in time, suffer from cohort effects. Longitudinal studies, which focus on the same subjects at several different points in time, are plagued by the difficulty of keeping a sample of subjects intact over many years.

• Because intelligence appears to have several components, the question of intellectual declines is complex. Those who divide intelligence into two main types—fluid and crystallized—generally find that fluid intelligence slowly declines through middle adulthood while crystallized intelligence holds steady or even improves. Those who divide intelligence into greater numbers of components find an even more complicated pattern.

• People in middle adulthood generally display a high degree of overall cognitive competence despite demonstrated declines in particular areas of intellectual functioning. People tend to focus on and exercise specific areas of competence that generally compensate for areas of loss, a strategy known as selective optimization.

• Experts maintain, and even increase, cognitive competence in a particular subject through attention and practice. Experts process information about their field significantly differently from novices.

■ **How does aging affect memory, and how can memory be improved?**

• Memory in middle adulthood may seem to be on the decline, but the problem is not with either sensory memory or short-term memory. Even apparent problems with long-term memory may have more to do with people's storage and retrieval strategies rather than with overall memory deterioration, and the problems are minor and relatively easy to overcome.

• People interpret, store, and recall information in the form of memory schemas, which organize related bits of information, set up expectations, and add meaning to phenomena. Schemas are based on prior experiences and facilitate interpretation of new situations and recall of information that fits the schema.

• Mnemonic devices can help people improve their ability to recall information by forcing them to pay attention to information as they store it (the keyword technique), to use cues to enable retrieval (the encoding specificity phenomenon), or to practice information retrieval (rehearsal).

Key Terms and Concepts

osteoporosis (p. 513)
presbyopia (p. 514)
glaucoma (p. 514)
presbycusis (p. 514)
female climacteric (p. 514)
menopause (p. 514)

male climacteric (p. 519)
Type A behavior pattern (p. 526)
Type B behavior pattern (p. 526)
fluid intelligence (p. 532)

crystallized intelligence (p. 532)
selective optimization (p. 534)
expertise (p.534)
schemas (p. 536)
mnemonics (p. 536)

16 Social and Personality Development in Middle Adulthood

Chapter Overview

PERSONALITY DEVELOPMENT

Two Perspectives on Adult Personality Development: Normative-Crisis Versus Life Events

Erikson's Stage of Generativity Versus Stagnation

Stability Versus Change in Personality

RELATIONSHIPS: FAMILY IN MIDDLE AGE

Marriage

Divorce

Family Evolutions: From Full House to Empty Nest

Becoming a Grandparent: Who, Me?

Family Violence: The Hidden Epidemic

WORK AND LEISURE

Work and Careers: Jobs at Midlife

Challenges of Work: On-the-Job Dissatisfaction

Unemployment: The Dashing of the Dream

Switching—and Starting—Careers at Midlife

Leisure Time: Life Beyond Work

Prologue: From Boxer to Poetry Professor

When Perry Nicholas—a former boxer who also worked in construction—hit 50, he decided to go for a lifelong goal of becoming a full-time teacher.

The once-amateur middleweight contender knocks 'em out with his poetry, having been nominated for a 2007 Pushcart [Poetry] Prize.

"I've taken a somewhat strange route," concedes the Erie Community College professor. . . . For me, life's been a combination of my Buffalo West Side childhood, Greek-American upbringing, various passions such as amateur boxing, literature, and the circuitous route of working in the construction world."

From age 20 to 30, Nicholas boxed, and today he testifies in his lyrics to "slicing the air with straight rights, the crack of a perfect crisp jab."

Nicholas studied at the University at Buffalo, when poets like Robert Creeley and John Logan taught there. He received a master's degree in English.

"At that time, due to the shortage of teaching jobs, I became involved in the painting and contracting business. For the next 25 years, I worked on numerous commercial and industrial projects," including supervision of rigging, sandblasting, and painting sections of the Peace Bridge.

However, it's never too late to pursue a dream. He taught part time at Erie Community College and Niagara County Community College. But it fueled a growing commitment to language and literature, helping him to land in 2004 a full-time teaching job. (Continelli, 2006, p. B3)

During middle age, adults often seek out new challenges.

The twists and turns in Perry Nicholas's life path are not unusual: Few lives follow a set, predictable pattern through middle adulthood. In fact, one of the remarkable characteristics of middle age is its variety, as the paths that different people travel continue to diverge.

In this chapter we focus on the personality and social development that occurs in midlife. We begin by examining the personality changes that typify this period. We also explore some of the controversies that underlie developmental psychologists' understandings of midlife, including whether the midlife crisis, a phenomenon popularized in modern media, is fact or fiction.

Next we consider the relationships that evolve during middle adulthood, the various familial ties that bind people together (or come unglued) during this period, including marriage, divorce, the empty nest, and grandparenting. We also look at a bleaker side of family relations: family violence, which is surprisingly prevalent.

Finally, the chapter examines the role of work and leisure during middle adulthood. We will examine the changing role of work in people's lives and some of the difficulties associated with work, such as burnout and unemployment. The chapter concludes with a discussion of leisure time, which becomes more important during middle age.

After reading this chapter, you will be able to answer these questions:

- **In what ways does personality develop during middle adulthood?**

- **Is there continuity in personality development during middle adulthood?**

- **What are typical patterns of marriage and divorce in middle adulthood?**

- **What changing family situations do middle-aged adults face?**

- **What are the causes and characteristics of family violence in the United States?**

- **What are the characteristics of work and career in middle adulthood?**

Looking Ahead

Personality Development

My 40th birthday was not an easy one. It's not that I woke up one morning and felt different—that's never been the case. But what did happen during my 40th year was that I came to the realization of the finiteness of life, and that the die was cast. I began to understand that I probably wasn't going to be president of the United States—a secret ambition—or a CEO of a major corporation. Time was no longer on my side, but something of an adversary. But it was curious: Rather than following my traditional pattern of focusing on the future, planning to do this or do that, I began to appreciate what I had. I looked around at my life, was pretty well satisfied with some of my accomplishments, and began to focus on the things that were going right, not the things that I was lacking. But this state of mind didn't happen in a day; it took several years after turning 40 before I felt this way. Even now, it is hard to fully accept that I am middle-aged.

In Western Society, turning 40 represents an important milestone.

As this 47-year-old man suggests, the realization that one has entered middle adulthood does not always come easily, nor is it generally welcome. In many Western societies, the age of 40 has special meaning, bringing with it the inescapable fact that one is now middle-aged—at least in the view of others—and the suggestion, embodied in everyday common wisdom, that one is about to experience the throes of a "midlife crisis." Is this view correct? As we'll see, it depends on your perspective.

Two Perspectives on Adult Personality Development: Normative-Crisis Versus Life Events

Traditional views of personality development during adulthood have suggested that people move through a fixed series of stages, each tied fairly closely to age. These stages are related to specific crises in which an individual goes through an intense period of questioning and even psychological turmoil. This traditional perspective is a feature of what are called normative-crisis models of personality development. **Normative-crisis models** see personality development in terms of fairly universal stages, tied to a sequence of age-related crises. For example, Erik Erikson's psychosocial theory predicts that people move through a series of stages and crises throughout the life span.

In contrast, some critics suggest that normative-crisis approaches may be outmoded. They arose at a time when society had fairly rigid and uniform roles for people. Traditionally, men were expected to work and support a family; women were expected to stay at home, be housewives, and take care of the children. And the roles of men and women played out at relatively uniform ages.

Today, however, there is considerable variety in both the roles and the timing. Some people marry and have children at 40. Others have children and marry later. Others never marry, and live with a partner of the same or opposite sex and perhaps adopt a child or forego children altogether. In sum, changes in society have called into question normative-crisis models that are tied closely to age (Fugate & Mitchell, 1997; Barnett & Hyde, 2001; Fraenkel, 2003).

Because of all this variation, some theorists, such as Ravenna Helson, focus on what may be called **life events models,** which suggest that it is the particular events in an adult's life, rather than age per se, that determines the course of personality development. For instance, a woman who has her first child at age 21 may experience psychological forces similar to those experienced by a woman who has her first child at age 39. The result is that the two women, despite their very different ages, share certain commonalities of personality development (Helson & Wink, 1992; Helson & Srivastava, 2001; Roberts, Helson, & Klohnen, 2002).

It is not clear whether the normative-crisis view or the life events perspective will ultimately paint the more accurate picture of personality development and change during the course of adulthood. What is clear is that developmental theorists from a range of perspectives all agree that middle adulthood is a time of continuing—and significant—psychological growth.

Erikson's Stage of Generativity Versus Stagnation

As we first discussed in Chapter 12, psychoanalyst Erik Erikson suggested that middle adulthood encompasses a period he characterized as one of **generativity versus stagnation.** One's middle adulthood, according to Erikson, is either spent in what he called generativity, making a personal contribution to family, community, work, and society as a whole, or in stagnation. Generative people strive to play a role in guiding and encouraging future generations. Often, people find generativity through parenting, but other roles can fill this need too. People may work directly with younger individuals, acting as mentors, or they may satisfy their need for generativity through creative and artistic output, seeking to leave a lasting contribution. The focus of those who experience generativity, then, is beyond themselves, as they look toward the continuation of their own lives through others (Pratt et al., 2001; McAdams & Logan, 2004; An & Cooney, 2006; Peterson, 2006).

On the other hand, a lack of psychological growth in this period means that people become stagnant. Focusing on the triviality of their own activity, people may come to feel that they have made only limited contributions to the world, that their presence has counted for little. In fact, some individuals find themselves floundering, still seeking new and potentially more fulfilling careers. Others become frustrated and bored.

Although Erikson provides a broad overview of personality development, some psychologists have suggested that we need a more precise look at changes in personality during middle adulthood. We'll consider three alternative approaches.

Building on Erikson's Views: Vaillant, Gould, and Levinson. Developmentalist George Vaillant (1977) argues that an important period between about ages 45 and 55 is "keeping the meaning" versus rigidity. During that period, adults seek to extract the meaning from their lives, and they seek to "keep the meaning" by developing an acceptance of the strengths and weaknesses of others. Although they recognize that the world is not perfect and has many

normative-crisis models the approach to personality development that is based on fairly universal stages tied to a sequence of age-related crises.

life events models the approach to personality development that is based on the timing of particular events in an adult's life rather than on age per se.

generativity-versus-stagnation stage according to Erikson, the stage during middle adulthood in which people consider their contributions to family and society.

Table 16-1	Gould's Transformations in Adult Development	
Stage	**Approximate Age**	**Development(s)**
1	16 to 18	Desire to escape parental control
2	18 to 22	Leaving the family; peer group orientation
3	22 to 28	Developing independence; commitment to a career and to children
4	29 to 34	Questioning self; role confusion; marriage and career vulnerable to dissatisfaction
5	35 to 43	Period of urgency to attain life's goals; awareness of time limitation; realignment of life's goals
6	43 to 53	Settling down; acceptance of one's life
7	53 to 60	More tolerance; acceptance of past; less negativism; general mellowing

(*Source:* From *Transformations*, by R. L. Gould & M. D. Gould, 1978, New York: Simon & Schuster.)

shortcomings, they strive to safeguard their world, and they are relatively content. The man quoted at the beginning of this section, for example, seems to be content with the meaning he has found in his life. People who are not able to keep the meaning in their lives risk becoming rigid and increasingly isolated from others.

Psychiatrist Roger Gould (1978, 1980) offered an alternative to both Erikson's and Vaillant's views. While he agrees that people move through a series of stages and potential crises, he suggests that adults pass through a series of seven stages associated with specific age periods (see Table 16-1). According to Gould, people in their late 30s and early 40s begin to feel a sense of urgency in terms of attaining life's goals as they realize that their time is limited. Coming to grips with the reality that life is finite can propel people toward adult maturity.

Gould based his model of adult development on a relatively small sample and relied heavily on his own clinical judgments. In fact, little research has supported his description of the various stages, which was heavily influenced by the psychoanalytic perspective.

Another alternative to Erikson's work is psychologist Daniel Levinson's *seasons of life* theory. According to Levinson (1986, 1992), who intensively interviewed a group of men, the early 40s are a period of transition and crisis. Levinson suggests that adult men pass through a series of stages beginning with their entry into early adulthood at around age 20 and continuing into middle adulthood. The beginning stages have to do with leaving one's family and entering the adult world.

However, at around age 40 or 45, people move into a period that Levinson calls the midlife transition. The *midlife transition* is a time of questioning. People begin to focus on the finite nature of life, and they begin to question some of their everyday, fundamental assumptions. They experience the first signs of aging, and they confront the knowledge that they will be unable to accomplish all their aims before they die.

In Levinson's view, this period of assessment may lead to a **midlife crisis,** a stage of uncertainty and indecision brought about by the realization that life is finite. Facing signs of physical aging, men may also discover that even the accomplishments of which they are proudest have brought them less satisfaction than they expected. Looking toward the past, they may seek to define what went wrong and look for ways to correct their past mistakes. The midlife crisis, then, is a painful and tumultuous period of questioning.

Levinson's view is that most people are susceptible to a fairly profound midlife crisis. But before accepting his perspective, we need to consider some critical drawbacks in his research. First, his initial theorizing was based on a group of only 40 men, and his work with women was carried out years later and once again on only a small sample. Furthermore, Levinson overstated the consistency and generality of the patterns he found in the samples he used to derive his theory. In fact, as we consider next, the notion of a universal midlife crisis has come under considerable criticism (McCrae & Costa, 1990; Stewart & Ostrove, 1998).

midlife crisis   a stage of uncertainty and indecision brought about by the realization that life is finite.

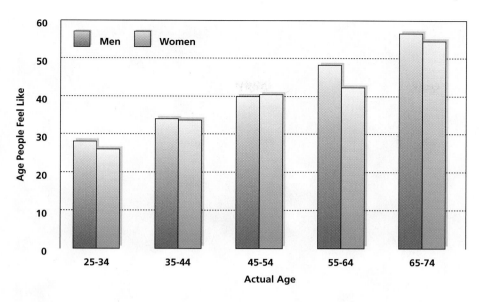

FIGURE 16-1   WHAT AGE DO YOU FEEL MOST OF THE TIME?

Throughout adulthood, most people say they feel younger than they actually are.

(*Source:* The John D. and Catherine T. MacArthur Foundation Research Network on Successful Midlife Development, 1999.)

The Midlife Crisis: Reality or Myth?   Central to Levinson's model of the seasons of life is the concept of midlife crisis, a period in the early 40s presumed to be marked by intense psychological turmoil. The notion has taken on a life of its own: There is a general expectation in U.S. society that the age of 40 represents an important psychological juncture.

There's a problem, though, with such a view: The evidence for a widespread midlife crisis is simply lacking. In fact, most research suggests that for most people, the passage into middle age is relatively tranquil. The majority of people regard midlife as a particularly rewarding time. If they are parents, for example, their children often have passed the period when child rearing is physically demanding, and in some cases children have left the home altogether, allowing parents the opportunity to rekindle an intimacy that they may have lost. Many middle-aged people find that their careers have blossomed—as we discuss later in this chapter—and far from being in crisis, they may feel quite content with their lot in life. Rather than looking toward the future, they focus on the present, seeking to maximize their ongoing involvement with family, friends, and other social groups. Those who feel regret over the course of their lives may be motivated to change the direction of their lives, and those who do change their lives end up better off psychologically (Stewart & Vandewater, 1999).

Furthermore, by the time they approach and enter middle adulthood, most people feel younger than they actually are, as can be seen in Figure 16-1 (Miller, Hemesath, & Nelson, 1997; Wethington, Cooper, & Holmes, 1997).

In short, the evidence for a midlife crisis experienced by most people is no more compelling than the evidence for a stormy adolescence that we discussed in Chapter 12. Yet, like that notion, the idea that the midlife crisis is nearly universal seems unusually well entrenched in "common wisdom." Why is this the case?

One reason may be that people who do experience turmoil during middle age tend to be relatively obvious and easily remembered by observers. For instance, a 40-year-old man who divorces his wife, replaces his sedate Ford Taurus station wagon with a red Saab convertible, and marries a much younger woman is likely to be more conspicuous than a happily married man who remains with his spouse (and Taurus) throughout middle adulthood. As a consequence, we are more likely to notice and recall marital difficulties more readily than the lack of them. In this way the myth of a blustery and universal midlife crisis is perpetuated. The reality, though, is quite different: For most people, a midlife crisis is more the stuff of fiction than of reality. In fact, for some people midlife may not bring many changes at all. And as we consider in the Developmental Diversity segment, in some cultures, middle age is not even considered a separate period of life.

In spite of there being no strong evidence that people universally experience "midlife crisis," the belief that it is commonplace remains. Why is this belief so prevalent?

Developmental Diversity

Middle Age: In Some Cultures It Doesn't Exist

There's no such thing as middle age.

At least one can draw that conclusion by looking at the lives of women living in the Oriya culture in Orissa, India. According to research carried out by developmental anthropologist Richard Shweder, who studied how high-caste Hindu women viewed the process of aging, a distinct period of middle age does not exist. These women view their life course not on the basis of chronological age, but on the nature of one's social responsibility, family management issues, and moral sense at a given time (Shweder, 1998, 2003).

The model of aging of the Oriyan women is based on two phases of life: life in her father's house (*bapa gharo*), followed by life in her husband's mother's house (*sasu gharo*). These two segments make sense in the context of Oriyan family life, which consists of multigenerational households in which marriages are arranged. After they are married, husbands remain with their parents and wives are expected to move into the husband's parents' household. At the time of marriage, a wife is seen as having changed social status from a child (someone's daughter) to a sexually active female (a daughter-in-law).

The shift from child to daughter-in-law typically occurs around the age of 18 to 20. However, chronological age, per se, does not mark significant boundaries in life for Oriyan women, nor do physical changes, such as the onset of menstruation and its cessation at menopause. Instead, it is the change from daughter to daughter-in-law that brings about a significant alteration in social responsibility. For instance, women must shift their focus from their own parents to the parents of their husband, and they must become sexually active in order to reproduce the husband's family line.

To a Western eye, the description of the life course of these Indian women suggests that they might perceive their lives as restricted, because in most cases they have no careers outside the home, but they do not see themselves in this light. In fact, in the Oriya culture, domestic work is highly respected and valued. Furthermore, Oriyan women perceive themselves as more cultured and civilized than men, who must work outside the home.

In short, the notion of a separate middle age is clearly a cultural construction. The significance of a particular age range differs significantly depending on the culture in which one lives.

Stability Versus Change in Personality

Harry Hennesey, age 53 and a vice president of an investment banking firm, says that inside, he still feels like a kid.

VIDEO CLIP

ADULTHOOD

Many middle-aged adults would agree with such a sentiment. Although most people tend to say that they have changed a good deal since they reached adolescence—and mostly for the better—many also contend that in terms of basic personality traits, they perceive important similarities between their present selves and their younger selves.

The degree to which personality is stable across the life span or changes as we age is one of the major issues of personality development during middle adulthood. Theorists such as Erikson and Levinson clearly suggest that there is substantial change over time. Erikson's stages and Levinson's seasons describe set patterns of change. The change may be predictable and related to age, but it is substantial.

On the other hand, an impressive body of research suggests that at least in terms of individual traits, personality is quite stable and continuous over the life span. Developmental psychologists Paul Costa and Robert McCrae find remarkable stability in particular traits. Even-tempered 20-year-olds are even-tempered at age 75; affectionate 25-year-olds become affectionate 50-year-olds; and disorganized 26-year-olds are still disorganized at age 60. Similarly, self-concept at age 30 is a good indication of self-concept at age 80 (Costa & McCrae, 2002; McCrae & Costa, 2003; Srivastava, John, & Gosling, 2003; Terracciano, Costa, & McCrae, 2006; also see Figure 16-2).

There is also evidence that people's traits actually become more ingrained as they age. For instance, some research suggests that confident adolescents become more confident in their mid-50s, while shy people become more diffident over the same time frame.

Stability and Change in the "Big Five" Personality Traits.   Quite a bit of research has centered on the personality traits that have come to be known as the "Big Five"—because they represent the five major clusters of personality characteristics. These include:

- neuroticism, the degree to which a person is moody, anxious, and self-critical

- extroversion, how outgoing or shy a person is

- openness, a person's level of curiosity and interest in new experiences

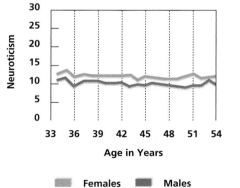
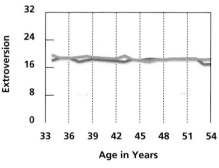
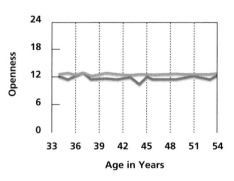

Females   Males

FIGURE 16-2   THE STABILITY OF PERSONALITY

According to Paul Costa and Robert McCrae, basic personality traits such as neuroticism, extroversion, and openness are stable and consistent throughout adulthood.

(*Source:* Adapted from Costa et al., 1986, p. 148.)

While Erikson and Levinson suggest there is substantial personality change over time, other research has shown that personality in terms of individual traits remains stable over the life span. How many of these high school swimmers do you think are still physically active after 40 years? Why?

- agreeableness, how easygoing and helpful a person tends to be
- conscientiousness, a person's tendencies to be organized and responsible

The majority of studies find that the Big Five traits are relatively stable past the age of 30, although there are some variations in specific traits. In particular, neuroticism, extraversion, and openness to experience decline somewhat from early adulthood through middle adulthood, while agreeableness and conscientiousness increase to a degree—findings that are consistent across cultures. The basic pattern, however, is one of stability through adulthood (McCrae & Costa, 2003; Srivastava et al., 2003).

Does evidence for the stability of personality traits contradict the perspective of personality change championed by theorists such as Erikson, Gould, and Levinson? Not necessarily, for on closer inspection the contradictions of the two approaches may be more apparent than real.

People's basic traits do appear to show continuity, particularly over the course of their adult lives. On the other hand, people are also susceptible to changes in their lives, and adulthood is jam-packed with major events, such as changes in family status, career, and even the economy. Furthermore, physical changes due to aging, illness, the death of a loved one, and an increased understanding of a finite life span can provide the impetus for changes in the ways people view themselves and the world at large (Krueger & Heckhausen, 1993; Roberts, Walton, & Viechtbauer, 2006).

Happiness Across the Life Span.   Suppose you hit it big on *Jeopardy*. Would you be a happier person?

For most people, the answer would be no. According to a growing body of research, adults' sense of *subjective well-being* or general happiness remains stable over their lives. Even winning the lottery doesn't do much to change happiness; despite an initial surge of subjective well-being, one year later people's happiness tends to return to pre-lottery levels (Diener, 2000).

The steadiness of subjective well-being suggests that most people have a general "set point" for happiness, a level of happiness that is consistent despite the day-to-day ups and downs of life. Although specific events may temporarily elevate or depress a person's mood (for example, a surprisingly high job evaluation or being laid off from work), people eventually return to their general level of happiness.

Most people's happiness set points seem to be fairly high. For example, some 30% of people in the United States rate themselves as "very happy," while only 10% rate themselves as "not too happy." Most people say they are "pretty happy." These findings are similar across different social groups. Men and women rate themselves as equally happy, and African Americans rate themselves as "very happy" at only slightly lower rates than whites. Regardless of where they stand economically, residents of countries across the world have similar levels of happiness (Schkade & Kahneman, 1998; Diener, 2000; Diener, Oishi, & Lucas, 2003; Kahneman et al., 2006).

Ultimately, it seems clear that people generally feel they are happy, regardless of their economic situation. The conclusion: Money doesn't buy happiness.

Review and Apply

Review

- Normative-crisis models portray people as passing through age-related stages of development; life events models focus on specific changes in response to varying life events.
- According to Erikson, middle adulthood encompasses the "generativity-versus-stagnation" stage, while Vaillant sees it as the "keeping the meaning versus rigidity" period.
- Gould suggests that people move through seven stages during adulthood.
- Levinson argues that the midlife transition can lead to a midlife crisis, but there is little evidence for this in the majority of middle-aged people.
- Broad, basic personality characteristics are relatively stable. Specific aspects of personality do seem to change in response to life events.

Applying Lifespan Development

- How do you think the midlife transition is different for a middle-aged person whose child has just entered adolescence versus a middle-aged person who has just become a parent for the first time?
- *From a social worker's perspective:* In what ways might normative-crisis models of personality development be specific to Western culture?

Relationships: Family in Middle Age

For Kathy and Bob, accompanying their son Jon to his college orientation was like nothing they had ever experienced in the life of their family. When Jon had been accepted at a college on the other side of the country, the reality that he would be leaving home didn't really register. It wasn't until the time came to leave him on his new campus, that the sense that their family would be changing in ways they could barely fathom hit them. It was a wrenching experience. Not only did Kathy and Bob worry about their son in the ways that parents always

Indian women view their life course not on the basis of chronological age, but on the nature of one's social responsibility, family management issues, and moral sense at a given period.

worry about their children, but they felt a sense of profound loss—that, to a large extent, their job of raising their son was over. Now he was largely on his own. It was a thought that filled them with pride and anticipation for his future, but with great sadness as well. They would miss him.

For members of many non-Western cultures who live in traditional extended families in which multiple generations spend their lives in the same household or village, middle adulthood is not particularly special. But in Western cultures, family dynamics undergo significant change during middle adulthood. It is in middle age that most parents experience major changes in their relationships not only with their children, but with other family members as well. It is a period of shifting role relationships that, in 21st-century Western cultures, encompasses an increasing number of combinations and permutations. We'll start by looking at the ways in which marriage develops and changes over this period and then consider some of the many alternative forms that family life takes today (Kaslow, 2001).

Marriage

Fifty years ago, midlife was similar for most people. Men and women who had married during early adulthood were still married to one another. One hundred years ago, when life expectancy was much shorter than it is today, people in their 40s were most likely married—but necessarily not to the same persons they had first married. Spouses often died; people might be well into their second marriage by the time of middle age.

Today, however, the story is different and, as we said earlier, more varied. More people are single during middle adulthood, having never married. Single people may live alone or with a partner. Gay and lesbian adults, for example, may have committed relationships even though marriage is typically not an option for them. Among heterosexuals, some have divorced, lived alone, and then remarried. During middle adulthood, many people's marriages end in divorce, and many families "blend" together into new households, containing children and stepchildren from previous marriages. Other couples still spend between 40 and 50 years together, the bulk of those years during middle adulthood. Many people experience the peak of marital satisfaction during middle age.

The Ups and Downs of Marriage. Even for happily married couples, marriage has its ups and downs, with satisfaction rising and falling over the course of the marriage. In the past, most research has suggested that marital satisfaction follows the U-shaped configuration shown in Figure 16-3 (Figley, 1973). Specifically, marital satisfaction begins to decline just after the marriage, and it continues to fall until it reaches its lowest point following the births of the couple's children. However, at that point, satisfaction begins to grow, eventually returning to the same level that it held before the marriage (Karney & Bradbury, 1995; Noller, Feeney, & Ward, 1997; Harvey & Weber, 2002).

On the other hand, newer research is calling the U-shaped pattern into question. As we discuss in the *From Research to Practice* box on the next page, several recent studies, using more sophisticated research designs, suggest that the upturn in satisfaction that occurs later in life may be illusory and that marital satisfaction continues to decline across the life span.

It is too early to reject the U-shaped view of marital satisfaction, and it may be that individual differences in marriages account for the discrepancy in findings. What is clear is that middle-aged couples cite several sources of marital satisfaction. For instance, both men and women typically state that their spouse is "their best friend" and that they like their spouses as people. They also view marriage as a long-term commitment and agree on their aims and goals. Finally, most also feel that their spouses have grown more interesting over the course of the marriage (Levenson, Carstensen, & Gottman, 1993).

Sexual satisfaction is related to general marital satisfaction. What matters is not how often married people have sex. Instead, satisfaction is related to *agreeing* about their sex lives (Goleman, 1985; Spence 1997; Litzinger & Gordon, 2005).

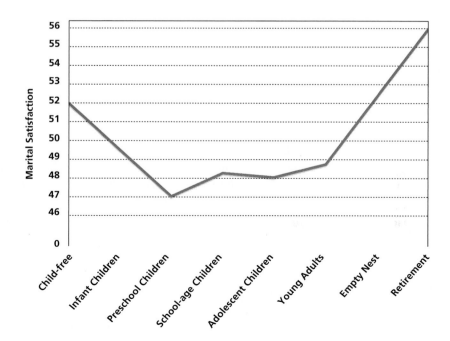

FIGURE 16-3   THE PHASES OF MARITAL SATISFACTION

For many couples, marital satisfaction falls and rises in a U-shaped configuration. It begins to decline after the birth of children but increases when the youngest child leaves home and eventually returns to a level of satisfaction similar to that at the start of marriage. Why do you think this pattern of satisfaction occurs?

(*Source:* Adapted from Rollins & Cannon, 1974.)

From Research to Practice

After the Vows: Changes in Marital Satisfaction over Time

"I can't believe you're watching this," said my downer of a husband. I ignored him. In fact, I turned the volume up on the TV.

"I'm going downstairs to check on the sump pumps," he said. Fine, I thought. Be that way. Run to your sump pumps instead of supporting me in my hour of need. I wasn't angry, exactly. Just . . . alone. (Laskas, 2006, p. W35)

The vast majority of Americans are married at least once in their lives, and with good reason. Marriage confers a number of benefits, including economic and sexual ones as well as health advantages and social support, to name a few. Whereas marriage is traditionally considered a lifelong commitment, social scientists have long been interested in the trajectory of marital satisfaction over the course of a typical marriage relationship. Much of their research shows that marital satisfaction follows a U-shaped curve, declining over time from the start of the marriage until the arrival of children, when it bottoms out, and then steadily growing during subsequent years until it reaches its original level.

Much of the research establishing this U-shaped pattern has used cross-sectional research, surveying different people who are at different points in their marriages. However, more recent research has employed longitudinal research, in which the marital satisfaction of the same couples is tracked over substantial time periods, and the results of these studies are painting a somewhat different picture (VanLaningham, Johnson, & Amato, 2001; Umberson et al., 2005).

One longitudinal study assessed changes in marriage quality over a period of 8 years and another did the same over 17 years. Both studies confirmed earlier findings that marital satisfaction declines in the years just after marriage, but both also failed to find evidence of a subsequent upswing after the childbearing years. Rather, when assessed over time, marriage quality seems to continue to decline over the course of a marriage (or at best to reach a low point and level out) (Umberson et al., 2005).

Two explanations help to shed light on these inconsistent findings. One is that unhappy marriages tend to terminate. Consequently, cross-sectional research on couples who have been married for a long time captures only the more happily married couples whose marriages tend to last that long. Another explanation is that couples who have long been married tend to be older, and they were married during a time when marriage was more highly valued and more in line with the social climate.

Age itself may play an important role in marital satisfaction. One study examined the contribution of age separately from marital duration and found that older couples tend to have happier marriages both at the outset and in the later years. It may be the case that people tend to become less emotionally reactive to marital discord as they age, or that their standards for evaluating their partners become more mellow. Furthermore, parenting plays a role in the developmental path of marriage quality—but not a straightforward one. While parenting puts extra strain on a marriage in the early years, it also seems to enhance marital satisfaction in the later years. Finally, different couples have different levels of marital satisfaction even at the outset; those who are happiest with their marriage in the earliest years may be less affected by the decline that follows (Umberson et al., 2005).

- *Why might couples who have children tend to experience better marital satisfaction later in life than do childless couples?*

- *Given these findings, how might you advise a newlywed couple on what to expect as their years of marriage progress?*

Divorce

Jane Burroughs knew 10 years into her marriage that it wasn't working. She and her husband argued constantly. He made all the decisions; she felt she had no say. But instead of divorcing, she stayed for 21 more years. It wasn't until she was 50, when her children were grown with kids of their own, that she finally got up the nerve to leave. Although she had wanted the divorce for years—and her husband eventually did, too—Burroughs, now 58, concedes it was the most difficult experience of her life and one that triggered conflicting emotions. "The hardest part was learning how to be alone," she says. "But I liked being independent." (Enright, 2004, p. 54)

Although the overall divorce rate has declined in the last two decades, divorce among couples during midlife is actually rising. One woman in eight who is in her first marriage will get divorced after the age of 40 (Uhlenberg, Cooney, & Boyd, 1990; Stewart et al., 1997; Enright, 2004).

Why do marriages unravel? There are many causes. One is that people in middle adulthood spend less time together than in earlier years. In individualistic Western cultures, people feel concerned with their own personal happiness. If their marriage is not satisfying, they feel that divorce may be the answer to increasing their happiness. Divorce is also more socially acceptable than in the past, and there are fewer legal impediments to divorces. In some cases—but certainly not all—the financial costs are not high. Furthermore, as the opportunities for women grow, wives may feel less dependent on their husbands, both from an emotional and an economic standpoint (Wallerstein, Lewis, & Blakeslee, 2000; Amato & Previti, 2003; Fincham, 2003).

Another reason for divorce is that, as we discussed in Chapter 14, feelings of romantic, passionate love may subside over time. Because Western culture emphasizes the importance of romance and passion, members of marriages in which passion has declined may feel that that is a sufficient reason to divorce. Finally, there is a great deal of stress in households in which both parents work, and this stress puts a strain on marriages. Much of the energy directed toward families and maintaining relationships in the past is now directed toward work and other institutions outside the home (Macionis, 2001).

Whatever the causes, divorce can be especially difficult for men and women in midlife. It can be particularly hard for women who have followed the traditional female role of staying with their children and never performing substantial work outside the home. They may face prejudice against older workers, finding that they are less likely to be hired than younger people, even in jobs with minimal requirements. Without a good deal of training and support, these divorced women, lacking recognized job skills, may remain virtually unemployable (Stewart et al., 1997; McDaniel & Coleman, 2003; Williams & Dunne-Bryant, 2006).

On the other hand, many people who divorce in midlife end up happy with the decision. Women, in particular, are apt to find that developing a new, independent self-identity is a positive outcome. Furthermore, both men and women who divorce during midlife are likely to enter new relationships, and—as we will see—they typically remarry (Enright, 2004).

Remarriage.   Many of the people who divorce—some 75 to 80%—end up marrying again, usually within 2 to 5 years. They are most likely to marry people who have also been divorced, partly because divorced people tend to be the ones in the available pool, but also because those who have gone through divorce share similar experiences (DeWitt, 1992).

Although the overall rate of remarriage is high, it is far higher in some groups than in others. For instance, it is harder for women to remarry than men, particularly older women. Whereas 90% of women under the age of 25 remarry after divorce, less than one-third of women over the age of 40 remarry (Bumpass, Sweet, & Martin, 1990; Besharov & West, 2002).

The reason for this age difference stems from the *marriage gradient* that we first discussed in Chapter 14: Societal norms push men to marry women who are younger, smaller, and lower in status than themselves. As a consequence, the older a woman is, the fewer the socially acceptable men she has available to her since those men her age are likely to be looking for younger women. In addition, women have the disadvantage of societal double standards regarding physical attractiveness. Older women tend to be perceived as unattractive, while older men tend to be seen as "distinguished" and "mature" (Bernard, 1982; Buss, 2003; Doyle, 2004a).

There are several reasons divorced people may find getting married again more appealing than remaining single. One motivation to remarry is to avoid the social consequences of divorce. Even in the 21st century, when the breakup of marriages is common, divorce carries with it a certain stigma that people may attempt to overcome by remarrying. In addition, divorced people overall report lower levels of satisfaction with life than married people (Lucas, 2005).

Divorced people miss the companionship that marriage provides. Divorced men in particular report feeling lonely and experience an increase in physical and mental health problems following divorce. Finally, marriage provides clear economic benefits, such as sharing the cost of a house and medical benefits reserved for spouses (Ross, Microwsky, & Goldsteen, 1991; Stewart et al., 1997).

Second marriages are not the same as first marriages. Older couples tend to be more mature and realistic in their expectations of a partner and a marriage. They tend to look at marriage

Around three-quarters of people who divorce remarry again, usually within 2 to 5 years.

empty nest syndrome the experience that relates to parents' feelings of unhappiness, worry, loneliness, and depression resulting from their children's departure from home.

in less romantic terms than younger couples, and they are more cautious. They are also likely to show greater flexibility in terms of roles and duties; they share household chores more equitably and make decisions in a more participatory manner (Hetherington, 1999).

Unfortunately, though, this doesn't make second marriages more durable than first ones. In fact, the divorce rate for second marriages is slightly higher than for first marriages. Several factors explain this phenomenon. One is that second marriages may be subject to stresses that are not present in first marriages, such as the strain of blending different families. For another, having experienced and survived divorce before, partners in second marriages may be less committed to relationships and more ready to walk away from unsatisfactory ones. Finally, they may have personality and emotional characteristics that don't make them easy to live with (Cherlin, 1993; Warshak, 2000; Coleman, Ganong, & Weaver, 2001).

Despite the high divorce rate for second marriages, many people settle into remarriage quite successfully. In such cases, remarried couples report as great a degree of satisfaction as couples in successful first marriages (Bird & Melville, 1994; Michaels, 2006).

Family Evolutions: From Full House to Empty Nest

For many parents, a major transition that typically occurs during middle adulthood is the departure of children, who may be either going to college, getting married, joining the military, or taking a job far from home. Even people who become parents at relatively late ages are likely to experience this transition at some point during middle adulthood, since the period spans nearly a quarter century. As we saw in the description of Kathy and Bob, a child's departure can be a wrenching experience—so wrenching, in fact, that it has been labeled the "empty nest syndrome." The **empty nest syndrome** refers to instances in which parents experience unhappiness, worry, loneliness, and depression from their children's departure from home (Lauer & Lauer, 1999).

Many parents report that major adjustments are required. Particularly for women who have stayed home to rear their children, the loss can be difficult. Certainly, if traditional homemakers have little or nothing else in their lives except their children, they do face a challenging period.

While coping with the feelings of loss can be difficult, parents can also find that some aspects of this era of middle adulthood are quite positive. Even mothers who have not worked outside the home find they have time for other outlets for their physical and psychological energies, such as community or recreational activities, when the children leave. Moreover, they may feel that they now have the opportunity to get a job or to go back to school. Finally, many mothers find that the period of motherhood is not easy; surveys show that most people feel that being a mother is harder than it used to be. Such mothers may now feel liberated from a comparatively difficult set of responsibilities (Heubusch, 1997; Morfei et al., 2004).

Leaving their youngest child at college marks the start of a significant transition for parents, who face an "empty nest."

Consequently, though some feelings of loss over the departure of children are common for most people, there is little, if any, evidence to suggest that the departure of children produces anything more than temporary feelings of sadness and distress. This is especially true for women who have been working outside the home (Antonucci, 2001; Crowley, Hayslip, & Hobdy, 2003).

In fact, there are some discernible benefits when children leave home. Married spouses have more time for one another. Married or unmarried people can throw themselves into their own work without having to worry about helping the kids with homework, carpools, and the like. The house stays neater, and the telephone rings less often.

Keep in mind that most research examining the so-called empty nest syndrome has focused on women. Because men traditionally are not as involved as women in child rearing, it was assumed that the transition when children left home would be relatively smooth for men. However, at least some research suggests that men also experience feelings of loss when their children depart, although the nature of that loss may be different from that experienced by women.

One survey of fathers whose children had left home found that although most fathers expressed either happy or neutral feelings about the departure of their children, almost a quarter felt unhappy (Lewis, Freneau, & Roberts, 1979). Those fathers tended to mention lost opportunities, regretting things that they had not done with their children. For instance, some felt that they had been too busy for their children or hadn't been sufficiently nurturing or caring.

The concept of the empty nest syndrome first arose at a time when children, after growing up, tended to leave home for good. However, times change, and the empty nest frequently becomes replenished with what have been called "boomerang children," as we discuss next.

Boomerang Children: Refilling the Empty Nest.

Carole Olis doesn't know what to make of her 23-year-old son, Rob. He has been living at home since his graduation from college more than 2 years ago. Her six older children returned to the nest for just a few months and then bolted.

"I ask him, 'Why don't you move out with your friends?'" says Mrs. Olis, shaking her head. Rob has a ready answer: "They all live at home, too."

Carole Olis is not alone in being surprised and somewhat perplexed by the return of her son. There has been a significant increase in the United States in the number of young adults who come back to live in the homes of their middle-aged parents.

Known as **boomerang children,** these returning offspring typically cite economic issues as the main reason for returning. Because of a difficult economy, many young adults cannot find jobs after college, or the positions they do find pay so little that they have difficulty making ends meet. Others return home after the breakup of a marriage. Around half of all 18- to 24 year-olds live with their parents, and overall, about 14% of young adults live with their parents in the United States. In some European countries, the proportion is even higher (Bianchi & Casper, 2000; Lewin, December 2003; Buss, 2005).

Parents' reactions to the return of their children vary, largely according to the reasons for it. If their children are unemployed, their return to the previously empty nest may be a major irritant. Fathers in particular may not grasp the realities of a difficult job market that college graduates may encounter, and may be decidedly unsympathetic to their children's return. Moreover, there may be some subtle parent–child rivalry for the attention of the spouse (Gross, J., 1991; Wilcox, 1992; Mitchell, 2006).

In contrast, mothers tend to be more sympathetic to children who are unemployed. Single mothers in particular may welcome the help and security provided by returning children. Both mothers and fathers feel fairly positive about returning sons and daughters who work and contribute to the functioning of the household (Quinn, 1993; Veevers & Mitchell, 1998).

The Sandwich Generation: Between Children and Parents.

At the same time children are leaving the nest, or perhaps even returning as boomerang children, many middle-aged adults face another challenge: growing responsibility for the care of their own aging parents. The term **sandwich generation** has come to be applied to these middle adults who feel squeezed between the needs of both their children and their aging parents (Riley & Bowen, 2005; Grundy & Henretta, 2006).

Being part of the sandwich generation is a relatively new phenomenon, produced by several converging trends. First, both men and women are marrying later and having children at an older age. At the same time, people are living longer. Consequently, the likelihood is growing that those in middle adulthood will simultaneously have children who still require a significant amount of nurturing and parents who are still alive and in need of care.

boomerang children   young adults who return, after leaving home for some period, to live in the homes of their middle-aged parents.

sandwich generation   couples who in middle adulthood must fulfill the needs of both their children and their aging parents.

"I'm in the sandwich generation—my parents don't approve of me and my kids hate me."

The care of aging parents can be psychologically tricky. For one thing, there is a significant degree of role reversal, with children taking on the parental role and parents in a more dependent position. As we'll discuss further in Chapter 18, elderly people, who were previously independent, may resent and resist their children's efforts to help. They certainly do not want to be burdens on their children. For instance, almost all elderly people who live alone report that they do not wish to live with their children (CFCEPLA, 1986; Merrill, 1997).

People in middle adulthood provide a range of care for their parents. In some cases, the care is merely financial, such as helping them make ends meet on meager pensions. In other situations, it takes the form of help in managing a household, such as taking down storm windows in the spring or shoveling snow in the winter.

In more extreme cases, elderly parents may be invited to live in the home of a son or daughter. Census data reveal that the multigenerational household, which includes three or more generations, is the fastest-growing household arrangement of any sort. Multigenerational households increased by more than a third between 1990 and 2000, and they represent 4% of all households (Navarro, 2006).

Multigenerational families present a tricky situation, as parental and children's roles are renegotiated. Typically, the adult children in the middle generation—who, after all, are no longer children—are in charge of the household. Both they and their parents must adjust to the changing relationships and find some common ground in making decisions. Elderly parents may find the loss of independence particularly difficult, and this can be wrenching for their adult child as well. The youngest generation may resist the inclusion of the oldest generation.

In many cases, the burden of caring for aging parents is not shared equally, with the larger share most often taken on by women. Even in married couples where both husband and wife are in the labor force, middle-aged women tend to be more involved in the day-to-day care of aging parents, even when the parent or parents are their in-laws (Soldo, 1996; Putney & Bengtson, 2001).

Culture also influences how caregivers view their roles. For example, members of Asian cultures, which are more collectivistic, are more likely to view caregiving as a traditional and not-out-of-the-ordinary duty. In contrast, members of more individualistic cultures may perceive familial ties as less central, and caring for a member of an older generation may be experienced as more burdensome (Ho et al., 2003; Kim & Lee, 2003).

Despite the burden of being sandwiched in the middle of two generations, which can stretch the caregiving child's resources, there are also significant rewards. The psychological attachment between middle-aged children and their elderly parents can continue to grow. Both partners in the relationship can see each other more realistically. They can become closer, more accepting of each other's weaknesses and more appreciative of each other's strengths (Mancini & Blieszner, 1991; Vincent, Phillipson, & Downs, 2006).

Becoming a Grandparent: Who, Me?

When her eldest son and daughter-in-law had their first child, Leah couldn't believe it. At age 54, she had become a grandmother! She kept telling herself that she felt far too young to be considered anybody's grandparent.

Middle adulthood often brings one of the unmistakable symbols of aging: becoming a grandparent. For some people, becoming a grandparent has been eagerly awaited. They may miss the energy and excitement and even demands of young children, and they may see grandparenthood as the next stage in the natural progression of life. Others are less pleased with the prospect of grandparenthood, seeing it as a clear signpost of aging.

Grandparenting tends to fall into different styles. *Involved* grandparents are actively engaged in grandparenting and have influence over their grandchildren's lives. They hold clear expectations about the ways their grandchildren should behave. A retired grandmother or grandfather who takes care of a grandchild several days a week while her parents are at work is an example of an involved grandparent (Cherlin & Furstenberg, 1986; Mueller, Wilhelm, & Elder, 2002).

One reason that African American grandparents are more involved with their grandchildren than white grandparents is the greater prevalence of three-generation families living together in African American households.

In contrast, *companionate* grandparents are more relaxed. Rather than taking responsibility for their grandchildren, companionate grandparents act as supporters and buddies to them. Grandparents who visit and call frequently, and perhaps occasionally take their grandchildren on vacations or invite them to visit without their parents, are practicing the companionate style of grandparenting.

Finally, the most aloof type of grandparents are *remote*. Remote grandparents are detached and distant, and they show little interest in their grandchildren. Remote grandparents, for example, would rarely make visits to see their grandchildren and might complain about their childish behavior when they did see them.

There are marked gender differences in the extent to which people enjoy grandparenthood. Generally, grandmothers are more interested and experience greater satisfaction than grandfathers, particularly when they have a high level of interaction with younger grandchildren (Smith, 1995; Smith & Drew, 2002).

Furthermore, African American grandparents are more apt to be involved with their grandchildren than white grandparents. The most reasonable explanation for this phenomenon is that the prevalence of three-generation families who live together is greater among African Americans than among Caucasians. In addition, African American families, which are more likely than white families to be headed by single parents, often rely substantially on the help of grandparents in everyday child care, and cultural norms tend to be highly supportive of grandparents taking an active role (Baydar & Brooks-Gunn, 1998; Baird, John, & Hayslip, 2000; Crowther & Rodriguez, 2003; Stevenson, Henderson, & Baugh, 2007).

Family Violence: The Hidden Epidemic

After finding an unidentified earring, the wife accused her husband of being unfaithful. His reaction was to throw her against the wall of their apartment, and then to toss her clothes out the window. In another incident, the husband became angry. Screaming at his wife, he threw her against a wall, and then picked her up and literally threw her out of the house. Another time, the wife called 911, begging for the police to protect her. When the police came, the woman, with a black eye, a cut lip, and swollen cheeks, hysterically screamed, "He's going to kill me."

If nothing else was clear about what was called the murder trial of the century, there is ample evidence that the spousal abuse just described was an ingredient in the lives of O. J. Simpson and Nicole Brown Simpson. The allegations of abuse that came out during the trial were both chilling and yet all too familiar.

The Prevalence of Spousal Abuse.   Domestic violence is one of the ugly truths about marriage in the United States, occurring at epidemic levels. Some form of violence happens in one-fourth of all marriages, and more than half the women who were murdered in one recent 10-year period were murdered by a partner. Between 21% and 34% of women will be slapped, kicked, beaten, choked, or threatened or attacked with a weapon at least once by an intimate partner. In fact, close to 15% of all marriages in the United States are characterized by continuing, severe violence. Furthermore, domestic violence is a worldwide problem. Estimates suggest that one in three women throughout the globe experience some form of violent victimization during their lives (Browne, 1993; Walker, 1999; Garcia-Moreno et al., 2005).

In the United States, no segment of society is immune from spousal abuse. Violence occurs across social strata, races, ethnic groups, and religions. Both gay and straight partnerships can be abusive. It also occurs across genders: Although in the vast majority of cases of abuse a husband batters a wife, in about 8% of the cases wives physically abuse their husbands (Emery & Laumann-Billings, 1998; de Anda & Becerra, 2000; Harway, 2000; Cameron, 2003; Dixon & Browne, 2003).

Certain factors increase the likelihood of abuse. For instance, spousal abuse is more likely to occur in large families in which there is continuing economic concern and a high level of verbal aggression than families in which such factors are not present. Those husbands and wives

Parents who abuse their own spouses and children were often victims of abuse themselves as children, reflecting a cycle of violence.

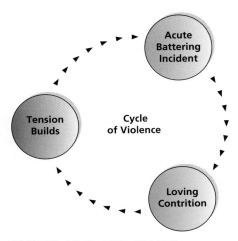

FIGURE 16-4   THE STAGES OF VIOLENCE
(*Source:* Adapted from Walker, 1979, 1984; Gondolf, 1985.)

who grew up in families where violence was present are more likely to be violent themselves (Straus & Yodanis, 1996; Ehrensaft, Cohen, & Brown, 2003; Lackey, 2003).

The factors that put a family at risk are similar to those associated with child abuse, another form of family violence. Child abuse occurs most frequently in stressful environments, in lower socioeconomic levels, in single-parent families, and in situations with high levels of marital conflict. Families with four or more children have higher rates of abuse, and those with incomes lower than $15,000 a year have abuse rates that are seven times higher than families with higher incomes. But not all types of abuse are higher in poorer families: Incest is more likely to occur in affluent families (Dodge, Bates, & Pettit, 1990; APA, 1996; Cox, Kotch, & Everson, 2003).

Marital aggression by a husband typically occurs in three stages (Walker, 1989; see Figure 16-4). The first is the *tension building* stage in which a batterer becomes upset and shows dissatisfaction initially through verbal abuse. He may also show some preliminary physical aggression in the form of shoving or grabbing. The wife may desperately try to avoid the impending violence, attempting to calm her spouse or withdraw from the situation. Such behavior may serve only to enrage the husband, who senses his wife's vulnerability, and her efforts to escape may lead to an escalation of his anger.

The next stage consists of an *acute battering incident*, when the physical abuse actually occurs. It may last from several minutes to hours. Wives may be shoved against walls, choked, slapped, punched, kicked, and stepped on. Their arms may be twisted or broken, they may be shaken severely, thrown down a flight of stairs, or burned with cigarettes or scalding liquids. About a quarter of wives are forced to engage in sexual activities during this period, which takes the form of aggressive sexual acts and rape.

Finally, in some—but not all—cases, the episode moves into the *loving contrition* stage. At this point, the husband feels remorse and apologizes for his actions. He may minister to his wife, providing first aid and sympathy, and assuring her that he will never act violently again. Because wives may feel that in some way they were partly at fault in triggering the aggression, they may be motivated to accept the apology and forgive their husbands. They want to believe that the aggression will never occur again.

The loving contrition stage helps explain why many wives remain with abusive husbands and are the continuing victims of abuse. Wishing desperately to keep their marriages intact, and believing that they have no good alternatives, some wives remain out of a vague sense that they are responsible for the abuse. Others remain out of fear: They are afraid their husbands may come after them if they leave.

The Cycle of Violence.   Still other wives stay with batterers because they, like their husbands, have learned a seemingly unforgettable lesson from childhood: that violence is an acceptable means of settling disputes.

Individuals who abuse their spouses and children were often as children the victims of abuse themselves. According to the **cycle of violence hypothesis,** abuse and neglect of children leads them to be predisposed to abusiveness as adults. In line with social learning theory, the cycle of violence hypothesis suggests that family aggression is perpetuated from one generation to another as family members follow the lead of the previous generation. It is a fact that individuals who abuse their wives often have been raised in households in which they have witnessed spousal abuse, just as parents who abuse their children frequently have been the victims of abuse themselves as children (McCloskey & Bailey, 2000; Serbin & Karp, 2004; Renner & Slack, 2006).

Growing up in a home where abuse occurs does not invariably lead to abusiveness as an adult. Only about one-third of people who were abused or neglected as children abuse their own children as adults, and two-thirds of abusers were not themselves abused as children. The cycle of violence, then, does not tell the full story of abuse (Jacobson & Gottman, 1998).

Whatever the causes of abuse, there are ways to deal with it, as we consider next.

cycle of violence hypothesis   the theory that abuse and neglect of children leads them to be predisposed to abusiveness as adults.

Becoming an Informed Consumer of Development

Dealing with Spousal Abuse

Despite the fact that spousal abuse occurs in some 25% of all marriages, efforts to deal with victims of abuse are underfunded and inadequate to meet current needs. In fact, some psychologists argue that the same factors that led society to underestimate the magnitude of the problem for many years now hinder the development of effective interventions. Still, there are several measures to help the victims of spousal abuse (Dutton, 1992; Browne, 1993; Koss et al., 1993):

- **Teach both wives and husbands a basic premise.** Physical violence is *never*, under *any* circumstances, an acceptable means of resolving disagreements.

- **Call the police.** It is against the law to assault another person, including a spouse. Although it may be difficult to involve law enforcement officers, this is a realistic way of dealing with domestic abuse. Judges can also issue restraining orders requiring abusive husbands to stay away from their wives.

- **Understand that the remorse shown by a spouse, no matter how heartfelt, may have no bearing on the possibility of future violence.** Even if a husband shows loving regret after a battering session and vows that he will never be violent again, such a promise is no guarantee against future abuse.

- **If you are the victim of abuse, seek a safe haven.** Many communities have shelters for the victims of domestic violence that can house women and their children. Because addresses of shelters are kept confidential, an abusive spouse will not be able to find you. Telephone numbers are listed in the yellow or blue pages of phone books, and local police should also have the numbers.

- **If you feel in danger from an abusive partner, seek a restraining order** from a judge in court. Under a restraining order a spouse is forbidden to come near you, under penalty of law.

- **Call the National Domestic Violence Hotline at 1-800-799-7233** for immediate advice.

Spousal Abuse and Society: The Cultural Roots of Violence.

After Dong Lu Chen beat his wife to death, he was sentenced to five years' probation. He had confessed to the act but claimed that his wife had been unfaithful to him. His lawyer (and an anthropologist) had argued in court that traditional Chinese values might have led to his violent reaction to his wife's purported infidelity.

After Lee Fong, a Laotian immigrant, had abducted a 16-year-old girl, he was acquitted of kidnapping, sexual assault, and menacing. During his trial, his lawyer argued that "bride stealing" is a traditional custom among the Hmong people of Laos.

Both cases were decided in courts in the United States. In both cases, lawyers based their arguments on the claim that in the Asian countries from which the defendants had emigrated, the use of violence against women was common and may even have received social approval. The juries obviously agreed with this "cultural defense" justification. (Findlen, 1990)

Although the tendency often is to see marital violence and aggression as a particularly North American phenomenon, in fact other cultures have traditions in which violence is regarded as acceptable (Rao, 1997). For instance, wife battering is particularly prevalent in cultures in which women are viewed as inferior to men and are treated as property.

In Western societies too, wife beating was acceptable at one time. According to English common law, which formed the foundation of the legal system in the United States, husbands were allowed to beat their wives. In the 1800s this law was modified to permit only certain kinds of beating. Specifically, a husband could not beat his wife with a stick or rod that was thicker than his thumb—the origin of the phrase "rule of thumb." It was not until the late 19th century that this law was removed from the books in the United States (Davidson, 1977).

Some experts on abuse suggest that the traditional power structure under which women and men function is a root cause of abuse. They argue that the more a society differentiates between men and women in terms of status, the more likely it is that abuse will occur.

As evidence, they point to research examining the legal, political, educational, and economic roles of women and men. For example, some research has compared battering statistics across the various states in the United States. Abuse is more likely to occur in states where women are of particularly low or high status compared with women's status in other states. Apparently, relatively low status makes women easy targets of violence. Conversely, unusually high status may make husbands feel threatened and consequently more likely to behave abusively (Dutton, 1994; Vandello & Cohen, 2003).

Review and Apply

Review

- For most couples, marital satisfaction rises during middle adulthood.
- Family changes in middle adulthood include the departure of children. In recent years, the phenomenon of "boomerang children" has emerged.
- Middle-aged adults often have increasing responsibilities for their aging parents.
- A further change is grandparenthood. Typically, grandparents may be involved, companionate, or remote.
- Marital violence tends to pass through three stages: tension building, an acute battering incident, and loving contrition.
- The incidence of family violence is highest in families of lower socioeconomic status. A "cycle of violence" affords a partial explanation. Cultural norms may also play a role.

Applying Lifespan Development

- Are the phenomena of the empty nest, boomerang children, the sandwich generation, and grandparenting culturally dependent? Why might such phenomena be different in societies where multigenerational families are the norm?

- *From the perspective of a healthcare provider:* What can be done to end the cycle of violence, in which people who were abused as children grow up to be abusers of others?

Work and Leisure

Enjoying a weekly game of golf . . . starting a neighborhood watch program . . . coaching a Little League baseball team . . . joining an investment club . . . traveling . . . taking a cooking class . . . attending a theater series . . . running for the local town council . . . going to the movies with friends . . . hearing lectures on Buddhism . . . fixing up a porch in the back of the house . . . chaperoning a high school class on an out-of-state trip . . . lying on a beach in Duck, North Carolina, reading a book during an annual vacation . . .

When we look at what people in the middle years of adulthood actually do, we find activities as varied as the individuals themselves. Although for most people middle adulthood represents the peak of on-the-job success and earning power, it is also a time when people throw themselves into leisure and recreational activities. In fact, middle age may be the period when work and leisure activities are balanced most easily. No longer feeling that they must prove themselves on the job, and increasingly valuing the contributions they are able to make to family, community, and—more broadly—society, middle-aged adults may find that work and leisure complement one another in ways that enhance overall happiness.

burnout a situation that occurs when highly trained professionals experience dissatisfaction, disillusionment, frustration, and weariness from their jobs.

Work and Careers: Jobs at Midlife

For many, middle age is the time of greatest productivity, success, and earning power. It is also a time when occupational success may become considerably less alluring than it once was. This is particularly the case for those who may not have achieved the occupational success they had hoped for when they began their careers. In such cases, work becomes less valued, while family and other off-the-job interests become more important (Howard, 1992; Simonton, 1997).

The factors that make a job satisfying change during middle age. Younger adults are interested in abstract and future-oriented concerns, such as the opportunity for advancement or the possibility of recognition and approval. Middle-aged employees care more about the here-and-now qualities of work. For instance, they are more concerned with pay, working conditions, and specific policies, such as the way vacation time is calculated. Furthermore, as at earlier stages of life, changes in overall job quality are associated with changes in stress levels for both men and women (Hattery, 2000; Peterson & Wilson, 2004; Cohrs, Abele, & Dette, 2006).

In general, though, the relationship between age and work seems to be positive: The older workers are, the more overall job satisfaction they experience. This pattern is not altogether surprising, since younger adults who are dissatisfied with their positions will quit them and find new positions that they like better. Furthermore, older workers have fewer opportunities to change positions. Consequently, they may learn to live with what they have, and accept that the position they have is the best they are likely to get. Such acceptance may ultimately be translated into satisfaction (Tangri, Thomas, & Mednick, 2003).

Challenges of Work: On-the-Job Dissatisfaction

Job satisfaction is not universal in middle adulthood. For some people, in fact, work becomes increasingly stressful as dissatisfaction with working conditions or with the nature of the job mounts. In some cases, conditions become so bad that the result is burnout or a decision to change jobs.

Burnout. For 44-year-old Peggy Augarten, early-morning shifts in the intensive care unit of the suburban hospital where she worked were becoming increasingly difficult. Although it had always been hard to lose a patient, recently she found herself breaking into tears over her patients at the strangest moments: while she was doing the laundry, washing the dishes, or watching TV. When she began to dread going to work in the morning, she knew that her feelings about her job were undergoing a fundamental change.

Augarten's response can probably be traced to the phenomenon of burnout. **Burnout** occurs when workers experience dissatisfaction, disillusionment, frustration, and weariness from their jobs. It occurs most often in jobs that involve helping others, and it often strikes those who initially were the most idealistic and driven. In some ways, in fact, such workers may be over-committed to their jobs, and the realization that they can make only minor dents in huge societal problems such as poverty and medical care can be disappointing and demoralizing (Demir, Ulusoy, & Ulusoy, 2003; Taris, van Horn, & Schaufeli, 2004; Bakker & Heuven, 2006).

Burnout occurs when a worker experiences dissatisfaction, disillusionment, frustration, or weariness from his or her job. Those who experience it grow increasingly cynical or indifferent toward their work.

One of the consequences of burnout is a growing cynicism about one's work. For instance, an employee might say to himself, "What am I working so hard on this for? No one is even going to notice that I've come in on budget for the last two years." In addition, workers may feel indifference and lack of concern about how well they do their job. The idealism with which a worker may have entered a profession is replaced by pessimism and the attitude that it is impossible to provide any kind of meaningful solution to a problem (Lock, 1992).

People can combat burnout, even those in professions with high demands and seemingly insurmountable burdens. For example, the nurse who despairs of not having enough time for every patient can be helped to realize that a more feasible goal—such as giving patients a quick backrub—can be equally important. Jobs can also be structured so that workers (and their supervisors) pay attention to small victories in their daily work, such as the pleasure of a client's gratitude, even though the "big picture" of disease, poverty, racism, and an inadequate educational system may look gloomy.

Unemployment: The Dashing of the Dream

The dream is gone—probably forever. And it seems like it tears you apart. It's just disintegrating away. You look alongside the river banks . . . there's all flat ground. There used to be a big scrap pile there where steel and iron used to be melted and used over again, processed. That's all leveled off. Many a time I pass through and just happen to see it. It's hard to visualize it's not there anymore. (Kotre & Hall, 1990, p. 290)

It is hard not to view 52-year-old Matt Nort's description of an obsolete Pittsburgh steel mill as symbolic of his own life. Because he has been unemployed for several years, Matt's dreams for occupational success in his own life have died along with the mill in which he once worked.

For many workers, unemployment is a hard reality of life, and the implications of not being able to find work are as much psychological as they are economic. For those who have been fired, laid-off by corporate downsizing, or forced out of jobs by technological advances, being out of work can be psychologically and even physically devastating (Sharf, 1992).

Unemployment can leave people feeling anxious, depressed, and irritable. Their self-confidence may plummet, and they may be unable to concentrate. In fact, according to one analysis, every time the unemployment rate goes up 1%, there is a 4% rise in suicide, and admissions to psychiatric facilities go up by some 4% for men and 2% for women (Kates, Grieff, & Hagen, 1990; Connor, 1992; Inoue et al., 2006).

Even aspects of unemployment that might at first seem positive, such as having more time, can produce disagreeable consequences. Perhaps because of feelings of depression and having too much time on one's hands, unemployed people are less apt to participate in community activities, use libraries, and read than employed people. They are more likely to be late for appointments and even for meals (Ball & Orford, 2002; Tyre & McGinn, 2003).

And these problems may linger. Middle-aged adults who lose their jobs tend to stay unemployed longer than younger workers, and have fewer opportunities for gratifying work as they age. Furthermore, employers may discriminate against older job applicants and make it more difficult to obtain new employment. Ironically, such discrimination is not only illegal, but is based on misguided assumptions: Research finds that older workers show less absenteeism than younger ones, hold their jobs longer, are more reliable, and are more willing to learn new skills (Allan, 1990; Birsner, 1991; Connor, 1992).

In sum, midlife unemployment is a shattering experience. And for some people, especially those who never find meaningful work again, it taints their entire view of the world. For people forced into such involuntary—and premature—retirement, the loss of a job can lead to pessimism, cynicism, and despondency. Overcoming such feelings often takes time and a good deal of psychological adjustment to come to terms with the situation. There are challenges for those who *do* find a new career, too (Trippet, 1991; Waters & Moore, 2002).

Becoming unemployed in midlife can be a shattering experience. It can taint your view of the world.

Switching—and Starting—Careers at Midlife

For some people, middle adulthood brings with it a hunger for change. For such individuals, who may be experiencing dissatisfaction with their jobs, switching careers after a period of unemployment, or simply returning to a job market they left years before, their developmental paths lead to new careers.

People who change careers in middle adulthood do so for several reasons. It may be that their jobs offer little challenge; they have achieved mastery, and what was once difficult is now routine. Other people change because their jobs have changed in ways they do not like, or they may have lost their job. They may be asked to accomplish more with fewer resources, or technological advances may have made such drastic changes in their day-to-day activities that they no longer enjoy what they do.

Still others are unhappy with the status they have achieved and wish to make a fresh start. Some are burned out or feel that they are on a treadmill. In addition, some people simply do not like to think of themselves doing the same thing for the rest of their lives. For them, middle age is seen as the last point at which they can make a meaningful occupational change (Steers & Porter, 1991).

Finally, a significant number of people, almost all of them women, return to the job market after having taken time off to raise children. Some may need to find paying work after a divorce. Since the mid-1980s, the number of women in the workforce who are in their 50s has grown significantly. Around half of women between the ages of 55 and 64—and an even larger percentage of those who graduated from college—are now in the workforce (see Figure 16-5). (For more on the challenges of finding a new career in midlife, see the *Careers in Lifespan Development* box on page 565.)

People may enter new professions with unrealistically high expectations and be disappointed by the realities of the situation. Furthermore, middle-aged people who start new careers may find themselves in entry-level positions. As a consequence, their peers on the job may be considerably younger than they are (Sharf, 1992; Barnett & Hyde, 2001). But in the long run, taking on a new career in middle adulthood can be invigorating. Those who switch or start new careers may be especially valued employees (Adelmann, Antonucci, & Crohan, 1990; Connor, 1992; Bromberger & Matthews, 1994).

Some forecasters suggest that career changes may become the rule rather than the exception. According to this point of view, technological advances will occur so rapidly that people will be forced periodically to change what they do to earn a living, often dramatically. In such a scenario, people will have not one, but several, careers during their lifetimes. As the Developmental Diversity segment makes clear, this is especially true for those who make the major life and career change: immigrating to another country as adults.

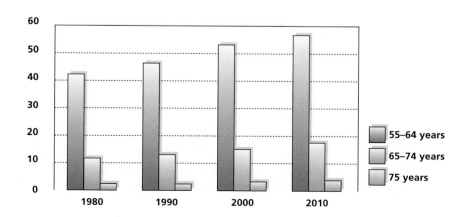

FIGURE 16-5 **WOMEN AT WORK**

The percentage of women aged 55 to 64 who are in the labor force has steadily increased since 1980, and is slated to continue to grow over the current decade.

(*Source:* Monthly Labor Review, 2001.)

Developmental Diversity

Immigrants on the Job: Making It in America

Seventeen years ago, Mankekolo Mahlangu-Ngcobo was placed in solitary confinement for 21 days in South Africa's Moletsane police station, falsely accused of terrorism. In 1980, once again in danger of imprisonment for her anti-apartheid protests, she fled to Botswana, leaving her 12-year-old son Ratijawe with her mother. She came to the U.S. in 1981, won political asylum in 1984 and now lives with her 13-year-old daughter Ntokozo in a $60,000 Baltimore row house. Her experiences left her with a deep appreciation of her adopted land. "If you have never lived somewhere else," she says, "you cannot know how much freedom you have here."

Ngcobo also found prosperity here. As with many of her fellow immigrants, the key was education. Since her arrival, she has earned a bachelor's degree, two master's and a doctorate in theology—which she paid for largely with scholarships or with her own money. Her academic credentials and dedication to helping others have won her two soul-satisfying careers, as a lecturer in public health at Baltimore's Morgan State University and as assistant minister at the Metropolitan African Methodist Episcopal Church in Washington, D.C. (Kim, 1995, p. 133)

Mankekolo Mahlangu-Ngcobo, who fled Botswana, is now a lecturer and minister in the United States.

If we rely solely on public opinion, we would probably view immigrants to the United States as straining the educational, prison, welfare, and health-care systems while contributing little to U.S. society. But—as the story of Mankekolo Mahlangu-Ngcobo exemplifies—the assumptions that underlie anti-immigrant sentiment are in fact quite wrong.

With the number of immigrants entering the United States hovering around 1.2 million each year, residents born outside the country now represent 10% of the population, more than twice the percentage in 1970. First- and second-generation immigrants comprise almost a quarter of the population of the United States (see Figure 16-6; Deaux, 2006).

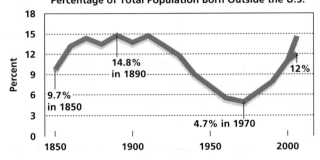

Percentage of Total Population Born Outside the U.S.

- 14.8% in 1890
- 9.7% in 1850
- 4.7% in 1970
- 12%

FIGURE 16-6   IMMIGRANTS IN THE UNITED STATES

Since 1970 the number of immigrants in the United States has steadily climbed and is approaching a historic high, especially if the estimated 9 million undocumented immigrants are included.

Today's immigrants are somewhat different from those of the earlier waves at the beginning of the 20th century. Only a third are white, compared with almost 90% of immigrants who arrived before 1960. Critics argue that many new immigrants lack the skills that will allow them to make a contribution to the high-tech economy of the 21st century.

However, the critics are wrong in many fundamental respects. For instance, consider the following data (Topolnicki, 1995; Camarota, 2001):

- **Most legal *and* illegal immigrants ultimately succeed financially.** For example, although they initially experience higher rates of poverty than native-born Americans, immigrants who arrived in the United States prior to 1980 and have had a chance to establish themselves actually have a higher family income than native-born Americans. Immigrants have the same rate of entrepreneurship as non-immigrants, with one in nine owning their own business.

- **Only a few immigrants come to the United States to get on welfare.** Instead, most say they come because of opportunities to work and prosper in the United States. Non-refugee immigrants who are old enough to work are less likely to be on welfare than native-born U.S. citizens.

- **Given time, immigrants contribute more to the economy than they take away.** Although initially costly to the government, often because they hold low-paying jobs and therefore pay no income taxes, immigrants become more productive as they get older. Ultimately, immigrants pay $25 billion to $30 billion a year more in taxes than they use in government services.

Why are immigrants often ultimately financially successful? One explanation is that immigrants who voluntarily choose to leave their native countries are particularly motivated and driven to be successful, whereas those who choose *not* to immigrate may be relatively less motivated.

In short, the reality is that the majority of immigrants ultimately become contributing members of U.S. society. For instance, they may alleviate labor shortages, and the money they send to relatives who remain at home may invigorate the world economy (World Bank, 2003).

Careers in Lifespan Development

Cathy Goodwin, Career Counselor

Education: BA, Political Science, Barnard College; MBA, Wharton School of Business; PhD, Marketing and Consumer Behavior, University of California at Berkeley

Home: Silver City, New Mexico

For many people, midlife is a time when they feel most content, concentrating on maintaining their careers and their family and friends. For some, though, it is a time to move in different directions, such as the pursuit of a new career.

While such a move can prove beneficial psychologically, several things should be considered before making a major career change, according to career counselor Cathy Goodwin.

"Once someone voluntarily decides they want to leave their profession, the biggest challenge they will face is an identity challenge. At this point in your life you are going to have built an identity involving your career, your family, and where you live," Goodwin explained. "When you make the decision to change careers, you have to ask yourself how your identity will change."

Goodwin suggests that people thinking about a career change should first test the waters. "Tell a few friends what your plans are, and think about how you feel introducing yourself in your new profession," she added.

From her experience counseling people making midlife career changes, Goodwin has identified two categories of people: jumpers and clingers.

"Jumpers thrive on energy, enthusiasm, and luck, while clingers thrive on careers that offer security, money, and identity," she noted. "If you ask most people, they would know right off whether they are a jumper or a clinger. You can be a jumper in one area, such as buying a house, but a clinger when it comes to your career.

"It is a truism that in midlife some things that worked in the past are not going to work now. What made you a success in your career is not necessarily going to work for you in a new career," Goodwin noted.

Leisure Time: Life Beyond Work

With the typical work week hovering between 35 and 40 hours—and becoming shorter for most people—most middle-aged adults have some 70 waking hours per week at their disposal (Kacapyr, 1997). What do they do with their leisure time?

For one thing, they watch television. On average, middle-aged people watch around 15 hours of television each week. But middle-aged adults do much more with their leisure time than watch television. In fact, for many people, middle adulthood represents a renewed opportunity to become involved in activities outside the home. As children leave home, parents have substantial time freed up to participate more extensively in leisure activities, such as taking

Table 16-2	Pace of Life Worldwide			
	Overall Pace	**Walking 60 Feet**	**Postal Service**	**Public Clock**
Switzerland	1	3	2	1
Ireland	2	1	3	11
Germany	3	5	1	8
Japan	4	7	4	6
Italy	5	10	12	2
England	6	4	9	13
Sweden	7	13	5	7
Austria	8	23	8	3
Netherlands	9	2	14	25
Hong Kong	10	14	6	14
France	11	8	18	10
Poland	12	12	15	8
Costa Rica	13	16	10	15
Taiwan	14	18	7	21
Singapore	15	25	11	4
United States	16	6	23	20
Canada	17	11	21	22

up sports, or civic participation, such as joining town committees. Middle-aged adults in the United States spend about 6 hours each week socializing (Robinson & Godbey, 1997; Lindstrom et al., 2005).

A significant number of people find the allure of leisure so great that they take early retirement. For those who make such a choice, and who have adequate financial resources to last the dozens of years that likely remain to them, life can be quite gratifying. Early retirees tend to be in good health, and they may take up a variety of new activities (Cliff, 1991; Ransom, Sutch, & Williamson, 1991).

Although middle adulthood presents the opportunity for more leisure activities, most people report that the pace of their lives does not seem slower. Because they are involved in a variety of activities, much of their free time is scattered throughout the week in 15- and 30-minute chunks. Consequently, despite a documented increase of 5 hours of weekly leisure time since 1965, many people feel they have no more free time than they did earlier (Robinson & Godbey, 1997).

One reason why extra leisure time may not be noticeable is that the pace of life in the United States is still considerably faster than in many countries. By measuring the length of time average pedestrians cover 60 feet, the time it takes for a customer to purchase a stamp, and the accuracy of public clocks, research has compared the tempo of living in a variety of countries. According to a composite of these measures, the United States has a quicker tempo than many other countries, particularly Latin American, Asian, Middle Eastern, and African countries. On the other hand, many countries outpace the United States. For example, Western European countries and Japan operate more quickly than the United States, with Switzerland ranking first (see Table 16-2; Levine, 1997a, 1997b).

	Overall Pace	Walking 60 Feet	Postal Service	Public Clock
South Korea	18	20	20	16
Hungary	19	19	19	18
Czech Republic	20	21	17	23
Greece	21	14	13	29
Kenya	22	9	30	24
China	23	24	25	12
Bulgaria	24	27	22	17
Romania	25	30	29	5
Jordan	26	28	27	19
Syria	27	29	28	27
El Salvador	28	22	16	31
Brazil	29	31	24	28
Indonesia	30	26	26	30
Mexico	31	17	31	26

Rank of 31 countries for overall pace of life and for three measures: minutes downtown pedestrians take to walk 60 feet; minutes it takes a postal clerk to complete a stamp purchase transaction; and accuracy in minutes of public clocks.

(*Source:* Adapted from Levine, 1997a.)

Review and Apply

Review

- People in middle age look at their jobs differently than before, placing more emphasis on short-term factors and less on career striving and ambition.

- Job satisfaction tends to be high for most middle-aged people, but some are dissatisfied because of disappointment with their accomplishments and for other reasons. Burnout is a factor, especially for people in the helping professions.

- Unemployment in midlife can have negative economic, psychological, and physical effects.

- Midlife career changes are becoming more prevalent, motivated usually by dissatisfaction, the need for more challenge or status, or the desire to return to the workforce after child rearing.

- People in middle adulthood usually have more leisure time than previously. Often they use it to become more involved outside the home in recreational and community activities.

Applying Lifespan Development

- Why might striving for occupational success be less appealing in middle age than before? What cognitive and personality changes might contribute to this phenomenon?

- *From the perspective of a social worker:* Why do you think immigrants' ambition and achievements are widely underestimated? Does the occurrence of conspicuous negative examples play a role (as it does in perceptions of the midlife crisis and stormy adolescence)?

Epilogue

Despite the lingering beliefs that middle adulthood is a time of stagnation, crisis, and dissatisfaction, we have seen that people continue to grow and change during this period. Physically, they experience gradual declines and become more susceptible to some diseases. Cognitively, middle-aged adults experience both gains in some areas and losses in others, and generally they learn to compensate rather well for any declining capacities.

As for the realm of social and personality development, we witnessed people facing and dealing successfully with a large number of changes in family relationships and work life. We also saw that to characterize this as a time of crisis is to overstate the negative and to ignore the positive aspects of the period, which is usually characterized by satisfaction and successful adjustment. Most typically, people in middle age successfully fill many roles, engaging with others from many periods of the life span, including their children, parents, spouses, friends, and coworkers.

In this chapter, we examined theories of the stages of midlife development and viewed some of the major controversies that emerge from this period of life. We have also considered the status of relationships during middle adulthood, particularly relationships with children, parents, and spouses. We have seen that changes in these areas are especially likely to affect adults at this time of their lives. Finally, we discussed work and leisure time during midlife—a time when career and retirement issues are likely to be uniquely salient.

Before turning to the next chapter, recall the prologue to this one, about Perry Nicholas's midlife journey. Using your knowledge of the midlife period, consider these questions:

1. Do Perry Nicolas's reasons for changing careers in midlife seem typical or unusual? Does it seem that dissatisfaction played an important role in his particular career trajectory?

2. In what ways does Nicholas's career progression seem to be the reverse of the typical pattern?

3. How might Nicholas benefit from having found a career that also incorporates his leisure-time passions?

4. Does Nicholas's experience seem to fit best with Erikson's, Vaillant's, or Levinson's view on midlife? Why do you think so?

5. Does Nicholas display any of the signs of a midlife crisis? Why or why not?

6. How do you think Nicholas might appraise his life in terms of a dial clock?

7. Can you interpret Nicholas's life more accurately in terms of a normative-crisis model of personality development or a life events model? Why?

Looking
Back

■ **In what ways does personality change during middle adulthood?**

- There are differing opinions as to whether people pass through age-related developmental stages in a more or less uniform progression, as normative-crisis models indicate, or respond to a varying series of major life events at different times and in different orders, as life events models suggest.

- Erik Erikson suggests that the developmental conflict of the age is generativity-versus-stagnation, involving a shift in focus from oneself to the world beyond. George Vaillant views the main developmental issue as keeping the meaning versus rigidity, in which people seek to extract meaning from their lives and accept the strengths and weaknesses of others.

- According to Roger Gould, people move through seven stages during adulthood. Daniel Levinson's theory of the seasons of life focuses on the creation of "The Dream"—a global vision of one's future—in early adulthood, followed by the midlife transition of the early 40s, during which people confront their mortality and question their accomplishments, often inducing a midlife crisis. Levinson has been criticized for the methodological limitations of his study, which focused on a small sample of men.

- The notion of the midlife crisis has been discredited for lack of evidence. Even the concept of a distinct "middle age" appears to be cultural in nature, achieving significance in some cultures and not in others.

Is there continuity in personality development during middle adulthood?

- It appears that, in general, the broad personality may be relatively stable over time, with particular aspects changing in response to life changes.

What are typical patterns of marriage and divorce in middle adulthood?

- Middle adulthood is, for most married couples, a time of satisfaction, but for many couples marital satisfaction declines steadily and divorce results.

- Most people who divorce remarry, usually to another divorced person. Because of the marriage gradient, women over 40 find it harder to remarry than men.

- People who marry for a second time tend to be more realistic and mature than people in first marriages, and to share roles and responsibilities more equitably. However, second marriages end in divorce even more often than first marriages.

What changing family situations do middle-aged adults face?

- The empty nest syndrome, a supposed psychological upheaval following the departure of children, is probably exaggerated. The permanent departure of children is often delayed as "boomerang" children return home for a number of years after having faced the harsh realities of economic life.

- Adults in the middle years often face responsibilities for their children and for their aging parents. Such adults, who have been called the sandwich generation, face significant challenges.

- Many middle-aged adults become grandparents for the first time. Researchers have identified three grandparenting styles: involved, companionate, and remote. Styles tend to differ by gender and race.

What are the causes and characteristics of family violence in the United States?

- Family violence in the United States has reached epidemic proportions, with some form of violence occurring in a quarter of all marriages. The likelihood of violence is highest in families that are subject to economic or emotional stresses. In addition, people who were abused as children have a higher likelihood of becoming abusers as adults—a phenomenon termed the "cycle of violence."

- Marital aggression typically proceeds through three stages: a tension building stage, an acute battering incident, and a loving contrition stage. Despite contrition, abusers tend to remain abusers unless they get effective help.

What are the characteristics of work and career in middle adulthood?

- For most persons, midlife is a time of job satisfaction. Career ambition becomes less of a force in the lives of middle-aged workers and outside interests begin to be more valued.

- Job dissatisfaction can result from disappointment with one's achievements and position in life or from the feeling that one has failed to make a difference in the insurmountable problems of the job. This latter phenomenon, termed "burnout," often affects those in the helping professions.

- Some people in middle adulthood must face unexpected unemployment, which brings economic, psychological, and physical consequences.

- A growing number of people voluntarily change careers in midlife, some to increase job challenge, satisfaction, and status, and others to return to a workforce they left years earlier to rear children.

- Middle-aged people have substantial leisure time at their disposal, which many spend in social, recreational, and community activities. Leisure activities in midlife serve as a good preparation for retirement.

Key Terms and Concepts

normative-crisis models (p. 543)
life events models (p. 543)
generativity-versus-stagnation stage (p. 543)
midlife crisis (p. 544)

empty nest syndrome (p. 554)
boomerang children (p. 555)
sandwich generation (p. 555)

cycle of violence hypothesis (p. 558)
burnout (p. 561)

17 Physical and Cognitive Development in Late Adulthood

Chapter Overview

PHYSICAL DEVELOPMENT IN LATE ADULTHOOD

Aging: Myth and Reality

Physical Transitions in Older People

Slowing Reaction Time

The Senses: Sight, Sound, Taste, and Smell

HEALTH AND WELLNESS IN LATE ADULTHOOD

Health Problems in Older People: Physical and Psychological Disorders

Wellness in Late Adulthood: The Relationship Between Aging and Illness

Sexuality in Old Age: Use It or Lose It

Approaches to Aging: Why Is Death Inevitable?

Postponing Aging: Can Scientists Find the Fountain of Youth?

COGNITIVE DEVELOPMENT IN LATE ADULTHOOD

Intelligence in Older People

Recent Conclusions About the Nature of Intelligence in Older People

Memory: Remembrance of Things Past—and Present

Learning in Later Life: Never Too Late to Learn

Prologue: Cycling Through Late Adulthood

Remarkable. Unbelievable. Inspirational.

Pick your adjective. They all apply to Carol Deland, [who] recently accomplished a feat that would intimidate a buff 20-year-old with bulging muscles, a strong heart and unlimited lung capacity.

But Deland isn't 20. Far from it. She's a divorced 66-year-old retired physical education teacher. . . .

"I go by a wonderful expression," she said. "'If you rest, you rust.'"

Rust won't form on Deland anytime soon. . . . [She] proved that recently when she biked across the country—starting March 8 in San Diego, Calif., and finishing May 4 in St. Augustine, Fla. That's a total of 3,115 miles in just 58 days—an average of more than 50 miles per day. . . .

When it was over, she was greeted at the beach in Florida by her three children and her sister.

"The last day, we had a 47-mile ride going into the ocean. It was a real feeling of accomplishment," Deland said. "My children are all real active, so I really had their support. They thought Mom was pretty cool. And so did Mom." (Heiser, 2007, p. 1)

Gerontologists have found that people in late adulthood can be as vigorous and active as those many years younger.

gerontologists specialists who study aging.

Carol Deland is not alone when it comes to showing extraordinary vitality in late adulthood, nor is she by any means the oldest. For instance, consider runner Philip Rabinowitz, who, at the age of 100, broke the centenarian 100-meter world record with a time of 30.86 seconds. For an increasing number of people in late adulthood, vigorous physical activity remains an important part of their everyday life.

Old age used to be equated with loss: loss of brain cells, loss of intellectual capabilities, loss of energy, loss of sex drive. Increasingly, however, that view is being displaced as **gerontologists**, specialists who study aging, paint a very different picture of late adulthood. Rather than being viewed as a period of decline, late adulthood is now seen as a stage in which people continue to change—to grow in some areas and, yes, to decline in others.

Even the definition of "old" is changing, for many of those in the period of late adulthood, which begins at around age 65 and continues to death, are as vigorous and involved with life as people several decades younger. The reality, then, is that we cannot define old age by chronological years alone; we also must take into account people's physical and psychological well-being, their *functional ages*. Some researchers of aging divide people into three groups according to their functional ages: the *young old* are healthy and active; the *old old* have some health problems and difficulties with daily activities; and the *oldest old* are frail and in need of care.

Although a person's chronological age can predict which group they are most likely to fall into, it is not a sure thing. An active, healthy 100-year-old would be considered young old. In comparison, a 65-year-old in the late stages of emphysema would be considered among the oldest old, according to functional age.

In this chapter, we will consider both physical and cognitive development during late adulthood. We begin with a discussion of the myths and realities of aging, examining some of the stereotypes that color our understanding of late adulthood. We look at the outward and inward signs of aging and the ways the nervous system and senses change with age.

Next, we consider health and well-being in late adulthood. After examining some of the major disorders that affect older people, we look at what determines wellness and what it is about aging that makes old people susceptible to disease. We also focus on various theories that seek to explain the aging process, as well as on gender, race, and ethnic differences in life expectancy.

Finally, the chapter discusses intellectual development during late adulthood. We look at the nature of intelligence in older people and the various ways cognitive abilities change. We also assess how different types of memory fare during late adulthood, and we consider ways to reverse intellectual declines in older people.

After reading this chapter, you will be able to answer these following questions:

■ **What is it like to grow old in the United States today?**

■ **What sorts of physical changes occur in old age?**

■ **How are the senses affected by aging?**

■ **What is the general state of health of older people, and to what disorders are they susceptible?**

■ **Can wellness and sexuality be maintained in old age?**

■ **How long can people expect to live, and why do they die?**

■ **How well do older people function intellectually?**

■ **Do people lose their memories in old age?**

Physical Development in Late Adulthood

Astronaut-turned-senator John Glenn was 77 years old when he returned to outer space as part of a 10-day space mission to help NASA study how the elderly adjust to space travel. Although the magnitude of Glenn's accomplishment sets him apart from most others, many people lead active, vigorous lives during late adulthood, and they are fully engaged with life.

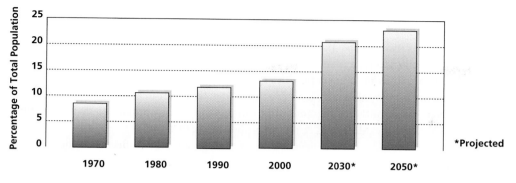

FIGURE 17-1 **THE FLOURISHING ELDERLY**

The percentage of people over the age of 65 is projected to rise to almost 25% of the population by the year 2050. Can you name two factors that contribute to this?

(*Source:* Adapted from U.S. Bureau of the Census, 2000.)

ageism prejudice and discrimination directed at older people.

Aging: Myth and Reality

Late adulthood holds a unique distinction among the periods of human life: Because people are living longer, late adulthood is actually increasing in length. Whether we peg the start of the period at age 65 or 70, there is today a greater proportion of people alive in late adulthood than at any time in world history. In fact, because the period has begun to last so long for so many people, demographers have taken to dividing their measurements of the elderly population by age. They use the same terms as researchers who refer to functional aging, but with different meanings (so be sure to clarify if someone is using one of these terms). For demographers, the *young old* are those 65 to 74 years old. The *old old* are between 75 and 84, and the *oldest old* are people 85 and older.

The Demographics of Late Adulthood.

One out of every eight people in the United States is 65 years of age or older. And projections suggest that by the year 2050, nearly one-quarter of the population will be age 65 and above. The number of people over the age of 85 is projected to increase from the current 4 million to 18 million by 2050 (see Figure 17-1; Schneider, 1999; Administration on Aging, 2003).

The fastest growing segment of the population is the oldest old—people who are 85 or older. In the last two decades, the size of this group has nearly doubled. The population explosion among older people is not limited to the United States. In fact, the rate of increase is much higher in developing countries. As can be seen in Figure 17-2, the sheer numbers of elderly are increasing substantially in countries around the globe. By 2050, the number of adults worldwide over the age 60 will exceed the number of people under the age of 15 for the first time in history (Sandis, 2000; United Nations Population Division, 2002).

Ageism: Confronting the Stereotypes of Late Adulthood.

Crotchety. Old codger. Old coot. Senile. Geezer. Old hag. Such are the labels of late adulthood. If you find that they don't draw a pretty picture, you're right: Such words are demeaning and biased, representing both overt and subtle ageism. **Ageism** is prejudice and discrimination directed at older people.

Ageism is manifested in several ways. It is found in widespread negative attitudes toward older people, suggesting that they are in less than full command of their mental faculties. For example, the results of many attitude studies have found that older adults are viewed more negatively than younger ones on a variety of traits, particularly those having to do with general competence and attractiveness (Thornton, 2002; Cuddy & Fiske, 2004; Angus & Reeve, 2006).

Furthermore, identical behavior carried out by an older and a younger person often is interpreted quite differently. Imagine you hear someone describing his search for his house keys. How would your perception of the person change if you knew he was 20 or 80? Older adults who show memory lapses are viewed as chronically forgetful and likely to be suffering from some mental disorder. Similar behavior on the part of young adults is judged more charitably,

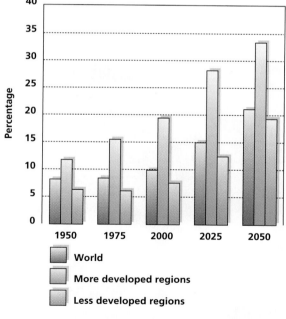

FIGURE 17-2 **THE ELDERLY POPULATION WORLDWIDE**

Longer life is transforming population profiles worldwide, with the proportion of those over the age of 60 predicted to increase substantially by the year 2050.

(*Source:* United Nations Population Division, 2002.)

merely as evidence of temporary forgetfulness produced by having too much on their minds (Erber, Szuchman, & Rothberg, 1990; Nelson, 2004).

This negative view of older people is connected to the reverence of youth and youthful appearance that characterizes many Western societies. It is the rare advertisement that includes an elderly person, unless it is for a product specifically designed for older adults. And when older persons are portrayed in television programming, they are often presented as someone's mother, father, grandmother, or grandfather rather than as individuals in their own right (Vernon, 1990; McVittie, McKinlay, & Widdicombe, 2003).

The ageism that produces such negative views of older people is reflected in the way they are treated. For instance, elderly individuals seeking jobs may face open prejudice, being told in job interviews that they lack the stamina for particular jobs. Or they sometimes are relegated to jobs for which they are overqualified. Such job discrimination persists even though it is illegal (Hays-Thomas, 2004; Hedge, Borman, & Lammlein, 2006; Rupp, Vodanovich, & Credé, 2006).

An older person doesn't need to be employed to experience ageist treatment. Older adults in nursing homes, for example, are often addressed in "baby talk," the language and tone of voice that adults use to speak to infants (the type we discussed in Chapter 5). An 84-year-old woman might be addressed as "honey" or "baby," for example, and told that she has to go "night-night" (Whitbourne & Wills, 1993; Whitbourne & Sneed, 2004).

The ageism directed toward people in late adulthood is, in some ways, a peculiarly modern and Western cultural phenomenon. In the colonial period of U.S. history, a long life was an indication that a person had been particularly virtuous, and older people were held in high esteem. Similarly, people in most Asian societies venerate those who have reached old age because elders have attained special wisdom as a consequence of living so long. Likewise, many Native American societies traditionally have viewed older people as storehouses of information about the past (Cowgill & Holmes, 1972; Palmore, 1999; Ng, 2002).

Today, however, negative views of older people prevail in U.S. society, and they are based on widespread misinformation. For instance, to test your knowledge about aging, try answering the questions posed in Table 17-1. Most people score no higher than chance on the items, averaging about 50% correct (Palmore, 1988, 1992). Given the prevalence of ageist stereotypes in Western societies today, it is reasonable to ask how accurate these views are. Is there a kernel of truth in them?

The answer is largely no. Aging produces consequences that vary greatly from one person to the next. Although some elderly people are in fact physically frail, have cognitive difficulties, and require constant care, others, like Carol Deland, are vigorous and independent—and sharp, brilliant, and shrewd thinkers. Furthermore, some problems that at first glance seem attributable to old age are actually a result of illness, improper diet, or insufficient nutrition. As we will see, the autumn and winter of life can bring change and growth on a par with—and sometimes even greater than—earlier periods of the life span (Whitbourne, 1996).

Physical Transitions in Older People

"Feel the burn." That's what the exercise tape says, and many of the 14 women in the group are doing just that. As the exercise tape continues through a variety of drills, the women participate to varying degrees. Some stretch and reach vigorously, while others mostly appear to be just swaying in time to the pounding beat of the music. It's not much different from thousands of exercise classes all over the United States. Yet to a youthful observer, there is one surprise: The youngest woman in this exercise group is 66 years old, and the oldest, dressed in sleek Spandex leotards, is 81.

The surprise registered by this observer reflects a popular stereotype of elderly persons. Many people view those over 65 as sedentary and sedate, an image that certainly does not incorporate involvement in vigorous exercise.

What do you see when you look at this woman? Ageism is found in widespread negative attitudes toward older people, suggesting that they are in less than full command of their faculties.

Table 17-1	The Myths of Aging

1. The majority of old people (age 65 and older) have defective memory, are disoriented, or demented. T or F?
2. The five senses (sight, hearing, taste, touch, and smell) all tend to weaken in old age. T or F?
3. The majority of old people have no interest in, nor capacity for, sexual relations. T or F?
4. Lung capacity tends to decline in old age. T or F?
5. The majority of old people are sick most of the time. T or F?
6. Physical strength tends to decline in old age. T or F?
7. At least one-tenth of the aged are living in long-stay institutions (such as nursing homes, mental hospitals, and homes for the aged). T or F?
8. Aged drivers have fewer accidents per driver than those under age 65. T or F?
9. Older workers usually cannot work as effectively as younger workers. T or F?
10. Over three-fourths of the aged are healthy enough to carry out their normal activities. T or F?
11. The majority of old people are unable to adapt to change. T or F?
12. Old people usually take longer to learn something new. T or F?
13. It is almost impossible for the average old person to learn something new. T or F?
14. Older people tend to react slower than do younger people. T or F?
15. In general, old people tend to be pretty much alike. T or F?
16. The majority of old people say they are seldom bored. T or F?
17. The majority of old people are socially isolated. T or F?
18. Older workers have fewer accidents than do younger workers. T or F?

Scoring

All odd-numbered statements are false; all even-numbered statements are true. Most college students miss about six, and high school students miss about nine. Even college instructors miss an average of about three.

(*Source:* Adapted from Palmore, 1988; Rowe & Kahn, 1999.)

primary aging aging that involves universal and irreversible changes that, due to genetic programming, occur as people get older.

secondary aging changes in physical and cognitive functioning that are due to illness, health habits, and other individual differences, but which are not due to increased age itself and are not inevitable.

The reality, however, is different. Although the physical capabilities of elderly people are not the same as they were in earlier stages of life, many older persons remain remarkably agile and physically fit in later life (Fiatarone & Garnett, 1997; Riebe, Burbank, & Garber, 2002).

Still, the changes in the body that began subtly during middle adulthood become unmistakable during old age. Both the outward indications of aging and those related to internal functioning become incontestable.

As we discuss aging, it is important to remember the distinction, introduced in Chapters 13 and 15, between primary and secondary aging. **Primary aging,** or *senescence,* involves the universal and irreversible changes that occur as people get older due to genetic programming. It reflects the inevitable changes that all of us experience from the time we are born. In contrast, **secondary aging** encompasses changes that are due to illness, health habits, and other individual differences, but which are not due to increased age itself and are not inevitable. Although the physical and cognitive changes that involve secondary aging are more common as people become older, they are potentially avoidable and can sometimes be reversed.

Even in late adulthood, exercise is possible—and beneficial.

Outward Signs of Aging.   One of the most obvious signs of aging is the changes in a person's hair. Most people's hair becomes distinctly gray and eventually white, and it may thin out. The face and other parts of the body become wrinkled as the skin loses elasticity and *collagen,* the protein that forms the basic fibers of body tissue (Bowers & Thomas, 1995; Medina, 1996).

People may become noticeably shorter, with some shrinking as much as 4 inches. Although this shortening is partially due to changes in posture, the primary cause is that the cartilage in the discs of the backbone has become thinner. This is particularly true for women, who are more susceptible than men to **osteoporosis,** or thinning of the bones, largely because of a reduction in production of estrogen.

Osteoporosis affects 25% of women over the age of 60 and is a primary cause of broken bones among elderly women and men. It is largely preventable if people's calcium and protein intake are sufficient in earlier parts of life and if they have engaged in adequate exercise. In addition, osteoporosis can be treated and even prevented through use of drugs such as Fosamax (alendronate) (Moyad, 2004; Picavet & Hoeymans, 2004).

Although negative stereotypes against appearing old operate for both men and women, they are particularly potent for women. In fact, in Western cultures there is a *double standard* for appearance, by which women who show signs of aging are judged more harshly than men. For instance, gray hair in men is often viewed as "distinguished," a sign of character; the same characteristic in women is a signal that they are "over the hill" (Sontag, 1979; Bell, 1989).

As a consequence of the double standard, women are considerably more likely than men to feel compelled to hide the signs of aging. For instance, older women are much more likely than men to dye their hair and to have cosmetic surgery, and women's use of cosmetics is designed to make them look younger than their years (Unger & Crawford, 1992). This is changing, however. Men are also becoming more interested in maintaining a youthful appearance, another sign of the dominance of a youth orientation in Western culture. For example, more cosmetic products, such as wrinkle creams, are available for men. This may be interpreted as a sign that the double standard is easing as well as a sign that ageism is becoming more of a concern for both sexes.

Internal Aging.   As the outward physical signs of aging become increasingly apparent, significant changes occur in the internal functioning of the organ systems. The capacities of many functions decline with age (see Figure 17-3; Whitbourne, 2001; Aldwin & Gilmer, 2004).

The brain becomes smaller and lighter with age, although, in the absence of disease, it retains its structure and function. As the brain shrinks, it pulls away from the skull, and the amount of space between brain and skull doubles from age 20 to age 70. Blood flow is reduced within the brain, which also uses less oxygen and glucose. The number of neurons, or brain

Although gray hair is often characterized as "distinguished" in men, the same trait in women is viewed more often as a sign of being "over the hill"—a clear double standard.

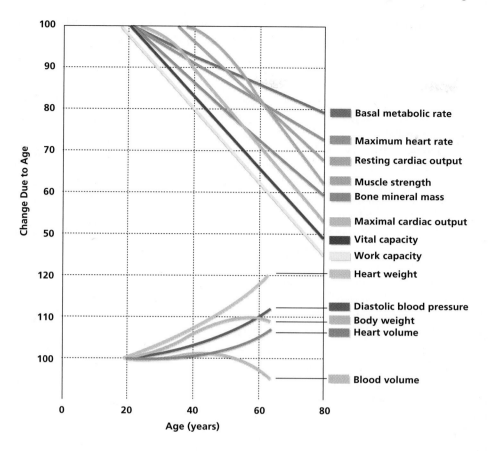

FIGURE 17-3 CHANGING PHYSICAL CAPACITIES

As people age, significant changes occur in the functioning of various systems of the body.

(*Source:* Whitbourne, 2001.)

cells, declines in some parts of the brain, although not as much as was once thought. For instance, recent research suggests that the number of cells in the brain's cortex may drop only minimally or not at all. In fact, some evidence suggests that certain types of neuronal growth may continue throughout the life span (Tisserand & Jolles, 2003; Lindsey & Tropepe, 2006; Raz et al., 2007; see Figure 17-4).

The reduced flow of blood in the brain is due in part to the heart's reduced capacity to pump blood throughout the circulatory system. Because of hardening and shrinking of blood vessels throughout the body, the heart is forced to work harder, and it is typically unable to compensate fully. A 75-year-old man pumps less than three-quarters of the blood that he was able to pump during early adulthood (Kart, 1990; Yildiz, 2007).

Other bodily systems work at lower capacity than they did earlier in life. For instance, the respiratory system is less efficient with age. The digestive system produces less digestive juice and is less efficient in pushing food through the system—which produces a higher incidence of constipation. Some hormones are produced at lower levels with increasing age. Furthermore, muscle fibers decrease both in size and in amount, and they become less efficient at using oxygen from the bloodstream and storing nutrients (Fiatarone & Garnett, 1997; Lamberts, van den Beld, & van der Lely, 1997).

Although all of these changes are part of the normal process of aging, they often occur earlier in people who have less healthy lifestyles. For example, smoking accelerates declines in cardiovascular capacity at any age.

Lifestyle factors can also slow the changes associated with aging. For instance, people whose exercise program includes weightlifting may lose muscle fiber at a slower rate than those who are sedentary. Similarly, physical fitness is related to better performance on mental tests, may prevent a loss of brain tissue, and may even aid in the development of new neurons. In fact, an increasing number of studies suggest that sedentary older adults who begin aerobic fitness

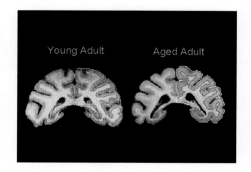

FIGURE 17-4 BRAIN CELL DECLINE

These MRI images show loss of white, but not gray, matter in the brain of a 32-year-old rhesus monkey (right). The young adult is 5 years old.

(*Source:* Rosene et al., 1996.)

peripheral slowing hypothesis the theory suggesting that overall processing speed declines in the peripheral nervous system with increasing age.

generalized slowing hypothesis the theory that processing in all parts of the nervous system, including the brain, is less efficient.

training ultimately show cognitive benefits (Elder, DeGasperi, & GamaSosa, 2006; Colcombe et al., 2006; Kramer, Erickson, & Colcombe, 2006; Pereira et al., 2007).

Slowing Reaction Time

Karl winced as the "game over" message came up on his grandson's video game system. He enjoyed trying out their games, but he just couldn't shoot down those bad guys as quickly as his grandkids could.

As people get older, they take longer: longer to put on a tie, longer to reach a ringing phone, longer to press the buttons in a video game. One reason for this slowness is a lengthening of reaction time. As we discussed first in Chapter 15, reaction time begins to increase in middle age, and by late adulthood the rise can be significant (Fozard et al., 1994; Benjuya, Melzer, & Kaplanski, 2004; Der & Deary, 2006).

It is not clear why people slow down. One explanation, known as the **peripheral slowing hypothesis**, suggests that overall processing speed declines in the peripheral nervous system. According to this notion, the peripheral nervous system, which encompasses the nerves that branch out from the spinal cord and brain and reach the extremities of the body, becomes less efficient with age. Because of this decrease in efficiency, it takes longer for information from the environment to reach the brain and longer for commands from the brain to be transmitted to the body's muscles (Salthouse, 1989, 2006).

Other researchers have proposed an alternative explanation. According to the **generalized slowing hypothesis,** processing in all parts of the nervous system, including the brain, is less efficient. As a consequence, slowing occurs throughout the body, including the processing of both simple and complex stimuli and the transmission of commands to the muscles of the body (Cerella, 1990).

Although we don't know which explanation provides the more accurate account, it is clear that the slowing of reaction time and general processing results in a higher incidence of accidents for elderly persons. Because their reaction and processing time is slowed, they are unable to efficiently receive information from the environment that may indicate a dangerous situation, their decision-making processes may be slower, and ultimately their ability to remove themselves from harm's way is impaired. Drivers over the age of 70 have as many fatal accidents as teenagers when accidents are figured in terms of miles of driving (Whitbourne, Jacobo, & Munoz-Ruiz, 1996; see Figure 17-5).

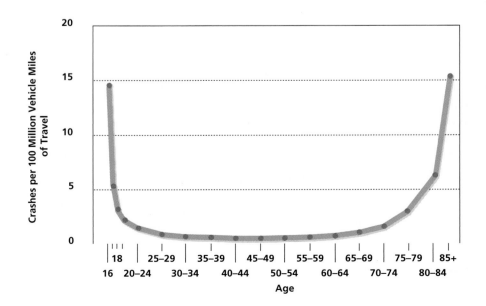

FIGURE 17-5 VEHICLE FATALITIES ACROSS THE LIFE SPAN

Drivers over age 70 have a fatal accident record comparable to that of teenagers when crashes are calculated per mile of driving. Why is this the case?

(*Source:* National Highway Traffic Safety Administration, 1994.)

Although it takes older individuals longer to respond, the *perception* of time seems to increase with age. The days and weeks seem to go by more quickly; generally time seems to rush by faster for older adults than younger ones. The reason may be due to changes in the way the brain coordinates its internal time clock (Mangan, 1997).

The Senses: Sight, Sound, Taste, and Smell

Old age brings with it distinct declines in the sense organs of the body, although in this area there is a great deal of variation. Sensory declines are of major psychological consequence because the senses serve as people's link with the world outside the mind.

Vision.   Age-related changes in the physical apparatus of the eye—the cornea, lens, retina, and optic nerve—lead to a decrease in visual abilities. For instance, the lens becomes considerably less transparent: The amount of light arriving at the retina of a healthy 60-year-old is only a third as much as that of a 20-year-old. The optic nerve becomes less efficient in transmitting nerve impulses (Scheiber et al., 1992; Gawande, 2007).

As a result, vision declines along several dimensions. We see distant objects less clearly, need more light to see clearly, and it takes longer to adjust from dark to light places and vice versa.

These changes in vision produce everyday difficulties. Driving, particularly at night, becomes more challenging. Similarly, reading requires more lighting, and eye strain occurs more easily. On the other hand, eyeglasses and contact lenses can correct many of these problems, and the majority of older people can see reasonably well (Horowitz, 1994; Ball & Rebok, 1994; Owsley, Stalvey, & Phillips, 2003).

Several eye diseases become more common during late adulthood. For instance, *cataracts* —cloudy or opaque areas on the lens of the eye that interfere with passing light—frequently develop. People with cataracts have blurred vision and tend to experience glare in bright light. If cataracts are left untreated, the lens becomes milky white and blindness is the eventual result. However, cataracts can be surgically removed, and eyesight can be restored through the use of eyeglasses, contact lenses, or *intraocular lens implants,* in which a plastic lens is permanently placed in the eye (Walker, Anstey, & Lord, 2006).

Another serious problem that afflicts many elderly individuals is glaucoma. As we noted first in Chapter 15, *glaucoma* occurs when pressure in the fluid of the eye increases, either because the fluid cannot drain properly or because too much fluid is produced. Glaucoma, too, can be treated by drugs or surgery if it is detected early enough.

The most common cause of blindness in people over the age of 60 is *age-related macular degeneration (AMD).* This disorder affects the *macula,* a yellowish area of the eye located near the retina at which visual perception is most acute. When a portion of the macula thins and degenerates, eyesight gradually deteriorates (see Figure 17-6). If diagnosed early, macular degeneration can sometimes be treated with medication or lasers. In addition, there is some evidence that a diet rich in antioxidant vitamins (C, E, and A) can reduce the risk of the disease (Mayo Clinic, 2000; Sun & Nathans, 2001; Rattner & Nathans, 2006; Wiggins & Uwaydat, 2006).

Hearing.   Around 30% of adults between the ages of 65 and 74 have some degree of hearing loss, and the figure rises to 50% among people over the age of 75. Overall, more than 10 million elderly people in the United States have hearing impairments of one kind or another (*HHL,* 1997; Chisolm, Willott, & Lister, 2003).

FIGURE 17-6   THE WORLD THROUGH MACULAR DEGENERATION

Macular degeneration leads to a gradual deterioration of the center of the retina, leaving only peripheral vision. This is an example of what a person with macular degeneration might see.

(*Source:* AARP, 2005, p. 34.)

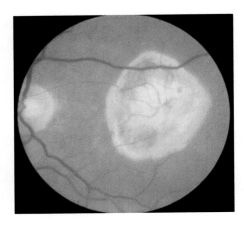

Age-related macular degeneration affects the macula, a yellowish area of the eye located near the retina. Eyesight gradually deteriorates once the portion of the macula thins and degenerates.

Aging particularly affects a person's ability to hear higher frequencies. Loss of these frequencies makes it hard to hear conversations when there is considerable background noise or when several people are speaking simultaneously. Furthermore, some elderly persons actually find loud noises painful.

Although hearing aids can help compensate for these losses and would probably be helpful in around 75% of the cases of permanent hearing loss, only 20% of elderly people wear them. One reason is that hearing aids are far from perfect. They amplify background noises as much as they amplify conversations, making it difficult for wearers to separate what they want to hear from other sounds. An elderly person trying to follow a conversation in a restaurant may be jolted by the sound of a fork clattering onto a plate. Many elderly people feel that the use of hearing aids makes them appear even older than they really are and encourages others to treat them as if their minds were disabled (Lesner, 2003; Meister & von Wedel, 2003).

Hearing loss can be especially damaging to the social lives of older people. Unable to hear conversations fully, some elderly people with hearing problems withdraw from others, avoiding situations in which many people are present. They may also be unwilling to respond to others, since they are unsure of what was said to them. Hearing loss can lead to feelings of paranoia as the person fills in the blanks according to his or her mental fears rather than reality. For example, someone may say "I *hate* going to the mall," and the impaired listener may decide that they have said, "I hate going to Maude's." Because they are able to catch only fragments of conversations, a hearing-impaired older adult can easily feel left out and lonely (Knutson & Lansing, 1990; Myers, 2000).

Furthermore, hearing loss may hasten cognitive declines in the elderly. As they struggle to understand what is being said, older people who have hearing problems may use considerable mental resources simply to try to perceive what is being said—mental resources that might otherwise be processing the information being conveyed. The result can be difficulties in remembering and understanding information (Wingfield, Tun, & McCoy, 2005).

Taste and Smell.   Elderly people who have enjoyed eating throughout their lives may experience a real decline in the quality of life because of changes in sensitivity to taste and smell. Both senses become less discriminating in old age, causing food to taste and smell less appetizing than it did earlier (Kaneda et al., 2000; Nordin, Razani, & Markison, 2003).

The reason for the decrease in taste and smell sensitivity can be traced to physical changes. Most older people have fewer taste buds in the tongue than they did when they were younger. Furthermore, the olfactory bulbs in the brain begin to shrivel, which reduces the ability to smell. Because smell is responsible in part for taste, the shrinkage of the olfactory bulbs makes food taste even blander.

The loss of taste and smell sensitivity has an unfortunate side effect: Because food does not taste as good, people eat less and open the door to malnutrition. They may also over-salt their food to compensate for the loss of taste buds, thereby increasing their chances of developing *hypertension,* or high blood pressure, one of the most common health problems of old age (Smith et al., 2006).

Review and Apply

Review

- Older people are often the victims of ageism—prejudice and discrimination against old people.
- Old age brings both external changes (thinning and graying hair, wrinkles, and shorter stature) and internal changes (decreased brain size, reduced blood flow within the brain, and diminished efficiency in circulation, respiration, and digestion).

- The two main hypotheses to explain the increase in reaction time in old age are the peripheral slowing hypothesis and the generalized slowing hypothesis.

- Vision may become more difficult at distances, in dim light, and when moving from darkness to light and vice versa.

- Hearing, especially of high frequencies, may diminish, causing social and psychological difficulties, and taste and smell may become less discriminating, leading to nutritional problems.

Applying Lifespan Development

- *From the perspective of a social worker:* When older people win praise and attention for being "vigorous," "active," and "youthful," is this a message that combats or supports ageism?

- Should strict examinations for renewal of driver's licenses be imposed on older people? What issues should be taken into consideration?

Health and Wellness in Late Adulthood

For an actor, there is no greater loss than the loss of his audience. I can part the Red Sea, but I can't part with you, which is why I won't exclude you from this stage in my life.

For now, I'm not changing anything. I'll insist on work when I can; the doctors will insist on rest when I must.

If you see a little less spring to my step, if your name fails to leap to my lips, you'll know why. And if I tell you a funny story for the second time, please laugh anyway. (Heston, 2002)

With these words, actor Charlton Heston announced that he had joined the 4.5 million Americans who suffer from Alzheimer's disease, a debilitating condition that saps both the physical and mental powers of its victims. In some ways, Alzheimer's disease—which led to the death of former president Ronald Reagan in 2004—symbolizes our view of elderly people, who, according to popular stereotypes, are more apt to be ill than healthy.

However, the reality is different: Most elderly people are in relatively good health for most of old age. According to surveys conducted in the United States, almost three-quarters of people 65 years old and above rate their health as good, very good, or excellent (USDHHS, 1990; Kahn & Rowe, 1999).

On the other hand, to be old is to be susceptible to a host of diseases. We now consider some of the major physical and psychological problems that beset older people.

Before his death at the age of 93, former President Ronald Reagan suffered from Alzheimer's disease for a decade.

Health Problems in Older People: Physical and Psychological Disorders

Most of the illnesses and diseases found in late adulthood are not peculiar to old age; people of all ages suffer from cancer and heart disease, for instance. However, the incidence of these and many other diseases rises with age, raising the odds that an elderly person will be ill during the period. Moreover, while younger people can readily rebound from a variety of health problems, older persons bounce back more slowly from illnesses. And ultimately, the illness may get the best of an older person, preventing a full recovery.

Common Physical Disorders.　The leading causes of death in elderly people are heart disease, cancer, and stroke. Close to three-quarters of people in late adulthood die from these problems. Because aging is associated with a weakening of the body's immune system, older adults are also more susceptible to infectious diseases (Feinberg, 2000). In addition to their risk of fatal diseases and conditions, most older people have at least one chronic, long-term condition (AARP, 1990). For instance, *arthritis,* an inflammation of one or more joints, afflicts roughly half of older people. Arthritis can cause painful swelling in various parts of the body, and it can be disabling. Sufferers can find themselves unable to carry out the simplest of everyday activities, such as unscrewing the cap of a jar of food or turning a key in a lock. Although aspirin and other drugs can relieve some of the swelling and reduce the pain, the condition cannot be cured (Burt & Harris, 1994).

Around one-third of older people have *hypertension,* or high blood pressure. Many people who have high blood pressure are unaware of their condition because it does not have any symptoms, which makes it more dangerous. Over time, higher tension within the circulatory system can result in deterioration of the blood vessels and heart, and can raise the risk of cerebrovascular disease, or stroke, if it is not treated (Wiggins & Uwaydat, 2006).

Psychological and Mental Disorders.　Some 15% to 25% of those over age 65 are thought to show some symptoms of psychological disorder, although this represents a lower prevalence rate than in younger adults. The behavioral symptoms related to these disorders are sometimes different in those over 65 than those displayed by younger adults (Haight, 1991; Whitbourne, 2001).

One of the more prevalent problems is major depression, which is characterized by feelings of intense sadness, pessimism, and hopelessness. One obvious reason older people may become depressed is because they suffer cumulative losses with the death of spouses and friends. Their own declining health and physical capabilities, which may make them feel less independent and in control, may contribute to the prevalence of depression (Penninx et al., 1998; Kahn, Hessling, & Russell, 2003).

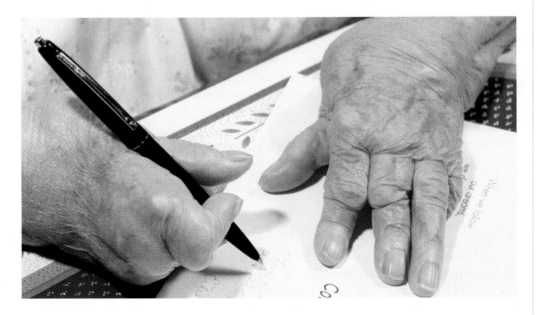

Arthritis can produce swelling and inflammation in the joints of the hands.

These explanations make sense, but it is not yet entirely clear that depression is a significantly worse problem in late adulthood than it is earlier in life. Some studies suggest that the rate of depression actually may be lower during late adulthood. One reason for this contradictory finding is that there may be two kinds of depression in older adulthood: depression that continues from earlier stages of life and depression that occurs as a result of aging (Gatz, 1997).

It is not unusual for some elderly people to suffer from drug-induced psychological disorders brought about by combinations of drugs they may be taking for various medical conditions. Because of changes in metabolism, a dose of a particular drug that would be appropriate for a 25-year-old might be much too large for a person of 75. The effects of drug interactions can be subtle, and they can manifest themselves in a variety of psychological symptoms, such as drug intoxication or anxiety. Because of these possibilities, older people who take medications must be careful to inform their physicians and pharmacists of every drug they take. They should also avoid medicating themselves with over-the-counter drugs, because a combination of nonprescription and prescription drugs may be dangerous, or even deadly.

The most common mental disorder of elderly people is **dementia,** a broad category of serious memory loss accompanied by declines in other mental functioning, which encompasses a number of diseases. Although dementia has many causes, the symptoms are similar: declining memory, lessened intellectual abilities, and impaired judgment. The chances of experiencing dementia increase with age. Less than 2% of people between 60 and 65 years are diagnosed with dementia, but the percentages double for every 5-year period past 65. Consequently, almost one-third of people over the age of 85 suffer from some sort of dementia. There are some ethnic differences, too, with African Americans and Hispanics showing higher levels of dementia than Caucasians (National Research Council, 1997).

The most common form of dementia is Alzheimer's disease. Alzheimer's represents one of the most serious mental health problems faced by the aging population.

Alzheimer's Disease.   **Alzheimer's disease,** a progressive brain disorder that produces loss of memory and confusion, leads to the deaths of 100,000 people in the United States each year. Nineteen percent of people age 75 to 84 have Alzheimer's, and nearly half of people over the age of 85 are affected by the disease. In fact, unless a cure is found, some 14 million people will be victims of Alzheimer's by 2050—more than three times more than the current number (Cowley, January 2000).

The symptoms of Alzheimer's disease develop gradually. Generally, the first sign is unusual forgetfulness. A person may stop at a grocery store several times during the week, forgetting that he or she has already done the shopping. People may also have trouble recalling particular words during conversations. At first, recent memories are affected, and then older memories fade. Eventually, people with the disease are totally confused, unable to speak intelligibly or to recognize even their closest family and friends. In the final stages of the disease, they lose voluntary control of their muscles and are bedridden. Because victims of the disorder are initially aware that their memories are failing and often understand quite well the future course of the disease, they may suffer from anxiety, fear, and depression—emotions not difficult to understand, given the grim prognosis.

Biologically, Alzheimer's occurs when production of the protein *beta amyloid precursor protein*—a protein that normally helps the production and growth of neurons—goes awry, producing large clumps of cells that trigger inflammation and deterioration of nerve cells. The brain shrinks, and several areas of the hippocampus and frontal and temporal lobes show deterioration. Furthermore, certain neurons die, which leads to a shortage of various neurotransmitters, such as acetylcholine

dementia the most common mental disorder of the elderly, it covers several diseases, each of which includes serious memory loss accompanied by declines in other mental functioning.

Alzheimer's disease a progressive brain disorder that produces loss of memory and confusion.

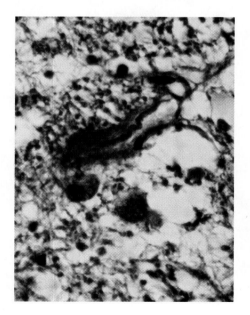

Brain scans of a patient with Alzheimer's disease show twisted clumps of nerve cells that are characteristic of the disease.

The enormous physical and emotional demands of caring for an Alzheimer's patient lead many caregivers to frustration, anger and exhaustion. What can ease the stress of the caregiver?

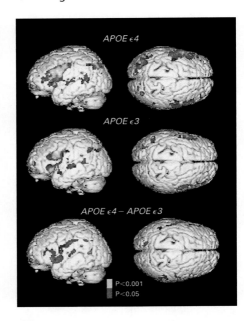

FIGURE 17-7 A DIFFERENT BRAIN?

Brain scans during memory recall tasks show differences between the brains of people who have an inherited tendency toward Alzheimer's disease and those who do not. The brains at the top are a composite of those at risk; the brains in the middle are a composite of normal brains. The bottom row indicates areas of difference between the first two rows.

(*Source:* Bookheimer et al., 2000.)

(Lanctot, Herrmann, & Mazzotta, 2001; Blennow & Vanmechelen, 2003; Wolfe, 2006; Medeiros et al., 2007).

Although the physical changes in the brain that produce the symptoms of Alzheimer's are clear, what is not known is what triggers the problem in the first place. Several explanations have been advanced. For instance, as we saw in Chapter 2, genetics clearly plays a role, with some families showing a much higher incidence of Alzheimer's than others. In fact, in certain families half the children appear to inherit the disease from their parents. Furthermore, years before the actual symptoms of Alzheimer's emerge, people who are genetically at high risk for the disease show differences in brain functioning when they are trying to recall information, as illustrated in the brain scans in Figure 17-7 (Bookheimer et al., 2000; Nelson et al., 2007; Coon et al., 2007; Thomas & Fenech, 2007).

Most evidence suggests that Alzheimer's is an inherited disorder, but nongenetic factors such as high blood pressure or diet may increase susceptibility to the disease. In one cross-cultural study, poor black residents in a Nigerian town were less likely to develop Alzheimer's than a comparable sample of African Americans living in the United States. The researchers speculate that variations in diet between the two groups—the residents of Nigeria ate mainly vegetables—might account for the differences in the Alzheimer's rates (Hendrie et al., 2001; Friedland, 2003; Wu, Zhou, & Chen, 2003; Lahiri et al., 2007).

Other explanations for the disease have also been investigated. For example, scientists are studying certain kinds of viruses, dysfunctions of the immune system, and hormone imbalances that may produce the disease. Other studies have found that lower levels of linguistic ability in the early 20s are associated with declines in cognitive capabilities due to Alzheimer's much later in life (Small et al., 1995; Snowdon et al., 1996; Alisky, 2007).

At the present time, there is no cure for Alzheimer's disease; treatment deals only with the symptoms. While understanding of the causes of Alzheimer's is incomplete, several drug treatments for Alzheimer's appear promising, although none is effective in the long term. The most promising drugs are related to the loss of the neurotransmitter acetylcholine (Ach) that occurs in some forms of Alzheimer's disease. Donepezil (Aricept), galantamine (Razadyne), rivastigmine (Exelon), and tacrine (Cognex) are among the most common drugs prescribed, and they alleviate some of the symptoms of the disease. Still, they are effective in only half of Alzheimer's patients, and only temporarily (Corliss, 1996; de Jesus Moreno Moreno, 2003).

Other drugs being studied include anti-inflammatory drugs, which may reduce the brain inflammation that occurs in Alzheimer's. In addition, the chemicals in vitamins C and E are being tested, since some evidence suggests that people who take such vitamins are at lower risk for developing the disorder. Still, at this point, it is clear that no drug treatment is truly effective (Alzheimer's Association, 2004).

As victims lose the ability to feed and clothe themselves, or even to control bladder and bowel functions, they must be cared for 24 hours a day. Because such care is typically impossible for even the most dedicated families, most Alzheimer's victims end their lives in nursing homes. Patients with Alzheimer's make up some two-thirds of those in nursing homes (Prigerson, 2003).

People who care for the victims of Alzheimer's often become secondary victims of the disease. It is easy to become frustrated, angry, and exhausted by the demands of Alzheimer's patients, whose needs may be overpowering. In addition to the physical chore of providing total care, caregivers face the loss of a loved one, who not only is visibly deteriorating but can act emotionally unstable and even fly into rages. The burdens of caring for a person with Alzheimer's can be overwhelming (Schulz, 2000; Ferrario, Vitaliano, & Zotti, 2003; Danhauer, McCann, & Gilley, 2004; Kosmala & Kloszewska, 2004; Thomas et al., 2006).

Becoming an Informed Consumer of Development

Caring for People with Alzheimer's Disease

Alzheimer's disease is one of the most difficult illnesses to deal with, as a friend or loved one progressively deteriorates both mentally and physically. However, several steps can be taken to help both patient and caregiver deal with Alzheimer's:

- Make patients feel secure in their home environments by keeping them occupied in everyday tasks of living as long as possible.

- Provide labels for everyday objects, furnish calendars and detailed but simple lists, and give oral reminders of time and place.

- Keep clothing simple: Provide clothes with few zippers and buttons, and lay them out in the order in which they should be put on.

- Put bathing on a schedule. People with Alzheimer's may be afraid of falling and of hot water, and may therefore avoid needed bathing.

- Prevent people with the disease from driving. Although patients often want to continue driving, their accident rate is high—some 20 times higher than average.

- Monitor the use of the telephone. Alzheimer patients who answer the phone have been victimized by agreeing to requests of telephone salespeople and investment counselors.

- Provide opportunities for exercise, such as a daily walk. This prevents muscle deterioration and stiffness.

- Caregivers should remember to take time off. Although caring for an Alzheimer's patient can be a full-time chore, caregivers need to lead their own lives. Seek out support from community service organizations.

- Call or write the Alzheimer's Association, which can provide support and information. The Association can be reached at 225 N. Michigan Ave. Fl. 17, Chicago, IL 60601-7633; Tel. 1-800-272-3900; *http://www.alz.org*.

Wellness in Late Adulthood: The Relationship Between Aging and Illness

Is getting sick an inevitable part of old age? Not necessarily. Whether an older person is ill or well depends less on age than on a variety of factors, including genetic predisposition, past and present environmental factors, and psychological factors.

Certain diseases, such as cancer and heart disease, have a clear genetic component. Some families have a higher incidence of breast cancer, for instance, than others. At the same time, though, a genetic predisposition does not automatically mean that a person will get a particular illness. People's lifestyles—whether or not they smoke, the nature of their diets, their exposure to cancer-causing agents such as sunlight or asbestos—may raise or lower their chances of coming down with such a disease.

Furthermore, economic well-being also plays a role. For instance, as at all stages of life, living in poverty restricts access to medical care. Even relatively well-off people may have difficulties finding affordable health care. In 2002, for example, older individuals averaged $3,600 in out-of-pocket health-care expenditures, an increase of 45% in 10 years. Furthermore, older people spend almost 13% of their total expenditures on healthcare, more than two times more than younger individuals. Because the United States lacks a healthcare insurance system that provides for universal medical coverage, many elderly individuals face grave financial burdens in obtaining affordable health care. As a result, many receive inadequate care. They are less likely to have regular checkups, and when they finally go for treatment, their illnesses may be more advanced (Administration on Aging, 2003).

Finally, psychological factors play an important role in determining people's susceptibility to illness—and ultimately the likelihood of death. For example, having a sense of control over one's environment, even in terms of making choices involving everyday matters, leads to a better psychological state and superior health outcomes (Taylor, 1991; Levy et al., 2002).

Promoting Good Health.   People can do specific things to enhance their physical well-being—as well as their longevity—during old age. It is probably no surprise that the right things to do are no different from what people should do during the rest of the life span: Eat a proper diet, exercise, and avoid obvious threats to health, such as smoking (see Figure 17-8). Medical and social services providers who work with elderly people have begun to emphasize the importance of these lifestyle choices for older adults. The goal of many such professionals has become not just to keep older adults from illness and death, but to extend people's *active life spans,* the amount of time they remain healthy and able to enjoy their lives (Burns, 2000; Resnick, 2000; Sawatzky & Naimark, 2002; Gavin & Myers, 2003; Katz & Marshall, 2003).

Sometimes, however, older people experience difficulties that prevent them from following even these simple guidelines. For instance, varying estimates suggest that between 15% and 50% of elderly people do not have adequate nutrition, and several million experience hunger every day (McCarthy, 1994; Burt & Harris, 1994; deCastro, 2002; Donini, Savina, & Cannella, 2003).

The reasons for such malnutrition and hunger are varied. Some elderly people are too poor to purchase adequate food, and some are too frail to shop or cook for themselves. Others feel little motivation to prepare and eat proper meals, particularly if they live alone or are depressed. For those who have experienced significant declines in taste and smell sensitivity, eating well-prepared food may no longer be enjoyable. And some older people may never have eaten well-balanced meals in earlier periods of their lives (Horwath, 1991; Wolfe, Olson, & Kendall, 1998).

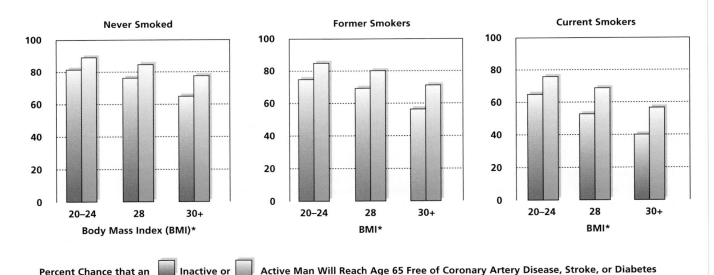

Percent Chance that an ▮ Inactive or ▯ Active Man Will Reach Age 65 Free of Coronary Artery Disease, Stroke, or Diabetes

FIGURE 17-8   BENEFITS OF EXERCISE AND A HEALTHY DIET

A recent study of more than 7,000 men, aged 40 to 59, found that not smoking, keeping weight down, and exercising regularly can greatly reduce the risk of coronary heart disease, stroke, and diabetes. Although the study included only men, a healthy lifestyle can benefit women too. *To find your body mass index (BMI) multiply your weight in pounds by 705. Divide the result by your height in inches, then divide by your height again.

(*Source:* Adapted from Wannamethee et al., 1998.)

Obtaining sufficient exercise may also prove problematic for older persons. Physical activity increases muscle strength and flexibility, reduces blood pressure and the risk of heart attack, and produces several other benefits, but many older people do not get sufficient exercise to experience any of these benefits.

For instance, illness may prevent older adults from exercising, and even inclement weather during the winter may restrict a person's ability to get out of the house. Furthermore, problems can combine: A poor person with insufficient money to eat properly may as a consequence have little energy to put into physical activity.

Sexuality in Old Age: Use It or Lose It

Do your grandparents have sex? Quite possibly, yes. Although the answer may surprise you, increasing evidence suggests that people are sexually active well into their 80s and 90s. This happens in spite of societal stereotypes suggesting that it is somehow improper for two 75-year-olds to have sexual intercourse, and even worse for a 75-year-old to masturbate. Such negative attitudes are a function of societal expectations in the United States. In many other cultures, elderly people are expected to remain sexually active, and in some societies, people are expected to become less inhibited as they age (Winn & Newton, 1982; Hyde, 1994; Hillman, 2000).

Two major factors determine whether an elderly person will engage in sexual activity (Masters, Johnson, & Kolodny, 1982). One is good physical and mental health. People need to be physically healthy and to hold generally positive attitudes about sexual activity in order for sex to take place. The other determinant of sexual activity during old age is previous regular sexual activity. The longer elderly men and women have gone without sexual activity, the less likely is future sexual activity. "Use it or lose it" seems an accurate description of sexual functioning in older people. Sexual activity can and often does continue throughout the life span. Furthermore, there's some intriguing evidence that having sex may have some unexpected side benefits: One study found that having sex regularly is associated with a lower risk of death (Purdy, 1995; Davey, Frankel, & Yarnell, 1997; Gelfand, 2000; Kellett, 2000; Henry & McNab, 2003)!

One survey found that 43% of men and 33% of women over the age of 70 masturbated. The average frequency for those who masturbated was once per week. Around two-thirds of married men and women had sex with their spouses, again averaging around once per week. In addition, the percentage of people who view their sexual partners as physically attractive actually increases with age (see Figure 17-9; Brecher et al., 1984; Budd, 1999).

Of course, there are some changes in sexual functioning related to age. Testosterone, the male hormone, declines during adulthood, with some research finding a decrease of approximately 30% to 40% from the late 40s to the early 70s. It takes a longer time, and more stimulation, for

Economic well-being is an important factor in the relationship between aging and illness, in part because poverty restricts access to medical care.

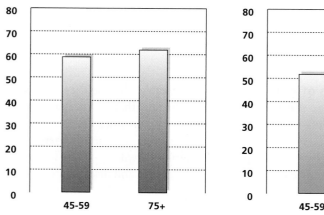

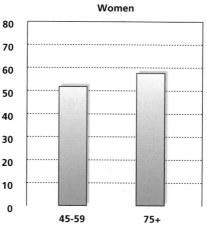

FIGURE 17-9 ATTRACTIVENESS OVER TIME

More than 50% of Americans over age 45 find their partners attractive, and as time goes on, more attractive.

(*Source:* AARP/Modern Maturity Sexuality Study, 1999.)

genetic programming theories of aging theories that suggest that our body's DNA genetic code contains a built-in time limit for the reproduction of human cells.

wear-and-tear theories the theory that the mechanical functions of the body simply wear out with age.

mydevelopmentlab

VIDEO CLIP

ADULTHOOD

men to get a full erection. The refractory period—the time following an orgasm during which men are unable to become aroused again—may last as long as a day or even several days. Women's vaginas become thin and inelastic, and they produce less natural lubrication, making intercourse more difficult (Frishman, 1996; Seidman, 2003). Even in the elderly, sex must be approached responsibly. Older adults—like younger ones—are susceptible to sexually trans-mitted diseases. In fact, 10% of people diagnosed with AIDS are over the age of 50 (National Institute of Aging, 2004).

Approaches to Aging: Why Is Death Inevitable?

Hovering over our discussion of health in late adulthood is the specter of death. At some point, no matter how healthy we have been throughout life, we know that we will experience physical declines and that life will end. But why?

There are two major approaches to explaining why we undergo physical deterioration and death: genetic programming theories and wear-and-tear theories.

Genetic Programming Theories of Aging.
Genetic programming theories of aging suggest that our body's DNA genetic code contains a built-in time limit for the reproduction of human cells. After a certain amount of time has gone by—determined genetically—the cells are no longer able to divide, and the individual begins to deteriorate (Jazwinski, 1996; Finch & Tanzi, 1997; Rattan, Kristensen, & Clark, 2006).

There are actually several variations of the genetic programming approach. One is that the genetic material contains a "death gene" that is programmed to direct the body to deteriorate and die. Researchers who take an evolutionary viewpoint, described first in Chapter 1, suggest that survival of the species would require that people live long enough to reproduce. A long life span after the reproductive years, however, would be unnecessary. According to this view, genetically related diseases that tend to strike later in life would continue to exist, because they allow people time to have children, thus passing along genes that are "programmed" to cause diseases and death.

A variation of the genetic programming view is that the cells of the body can only duplicate a certain number of times. Throughout our lives, new cells are being made, through cell duplication, to repair and replenish all of our various tissues and organs. According to this view, however, the genetic instructions for running the body can be read only a certain number of times before they become illegible. (Think of a computer disk containing a program that is used over and over and eventually just gives out.) As these instructions become incomprehensible, cells stop reproducing. Because the body is not being renewed at the same rate, people begin to experience bodily deterioration and ultimately death (Hayflick, 1974; Thoms, Kuschal, & Emmert, 2007).

Evidence for the genetic programming theory comes from research showing that when human cells are permitted to divide in the laboratory, they can do so successfully only around 50 times. Each time they divide, *telomeres,* which are tiny, protective areas of DNA at the tip of chromosomes, grow shorter. When a cell's telomere has just about disappeared, the cell stops replicating, making it susceptible to damage and producing signs of aging (Chung et al., 2007).

Wear-and-Tear Theories of Aging.
The other general set of theories to explain aging and physical decline are **wear-and-tear theories,** which argue that the mechanical functions of the body simply wear out—the way cars and washing machines do. In addition, some wear-and-tear theorists suggest that the body's constant manufacture of energy to fuel its activities creates by-products. These by-products, combined with the toxins and threats of everyday life (such as radiation, chemical exposure, accidents, and disease), eventually reach such high levels that they impair the body's normal functioning. The ultimate result is dete-rioration and death.

One specific category of by-products that has been related to aging includes free radicals, electrically charged molecules or atoms that are produced by the cells of the body. Because of their electrical charge, free radicals may cause negative effects on other cells of the body. A great deal of research suggests that oxygen free radicals may be implicated in a number of age-related problems, including cancer, heart disease, and diabetes (Vajragupta et al., 2000; Birlouez-Aragon & Tessier, 2003; Poon et al., 2004; Sierra, 2006).

Reconciling the Theories of Aging.   Genetic programming theories and wear-and-tear theories make different suggestions about the inevitability of death. Genetic programming theories suggest that there is a built-in time limit to life—it's programmed in the genes, after all. On the other hand, wear-and-tear theories, particularly those that focus on the toxins that are built up during the course of life, paint a somewhat more optimistic view. They suggest that if a means can be found to eliminate the toxins produced by the body and by exposure to the environment, aging might well be slowed.

We don't know which class of theories provides the more accurate account of the reasons for aging. Each is supported by some research, and each seems to explain certain aspects of aging. Ultimately, then, just why the body begins to deteriorate and die remains something of a mystery (Horiuchi, Finch, & Mesle, 2003).

Life Expectancy: How Long Have I Got?   Although the reasons for deterioration and death are not fully apparent, conclusions about average life expectancy can be stated quite clearly: Most of us can expect to live into old age. The **life expectancy**—the average age of death for members of a population—of a person born in 2007, for instance, is 78 years of age. This is of course a far cry from the 100 years achieved by the individual we met in the chapter prologue, but even that life span is not as uncommon as it once was.

Average life expectancy has been steadily increasing. In 1776, average life expectancy in the United States was just 35. By the early 1900s, it had risen to 47. And in only four decades, from 1950 to 1990, it increased from 68 to over 75 years. Predictions are that it will continue to rise steadily, possibly reaching age 80 by the year 2050 (see Figure 17-10).

There are several reasons for the steady increase in life expectancy over the past 200 years. Health and sanitation conditions are generally better, with many diseases, such as smallpox, wiped out entirely. Other diseases that used to kill people at early ages, such as measles and mumps, are now better controlled through vaccines and preventive measures. People's working conditions are generally better, and many products are safer than they once were. As we've seen, many people are becoming aware of lifestyle choices such as keeping their weight down, eating lots of fresh fruit and vegetables, and exercising, which can extend their lives. As environmental factors continue to improve, we can predict that life expectancy will continue to

life expectancy   the average age of death for members of a population.

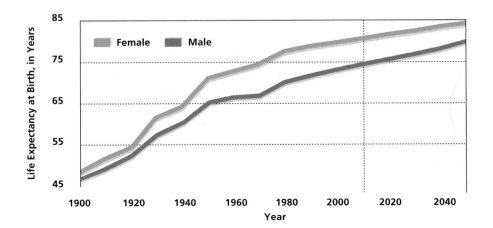

FIGURE 17-10   LIVING TO AGE 100

If increases in life expectancy continue, it may be a common occurrence for people to live to be 100 by the end of this century. What implications does this have for society? (*Source:* U.S. Bureau of the Census, 1997.)

According to genetic preprogramming theories of aging, our DNA genetic code contains a built-in limit on the length of life.

increase. Also, as we've seen, many people are becoming aware of the importance of lifestyle choices for extending not just the length of their lives, but their active life spans, the years they spend in health and enjoyment of life.

One major question for gerontologists is just how far the lifespan can be increased. The most common answer is that the upper limit of life hovers around 120 years, the age reached by Jeanne Calment, who was the oldest person in the world until she died in 1997 at the age of 122. Living beyond this age would probably require some major genetic alterations in humans, and that seems both technically and ethically improbable. Still, as we consider next, several scientific and technological advances that have occurred in the last decade suggest that significantly extending the life span is not an impossibility.

Postponing Aging: Can Scientists Find the Fountain of Youth?

Are researchers close to finding the scientific equivalent of the mythical fountain of youth that can postpone aging?

They haven't found it yet, but they're getting closer, at least in nonhuman species. Researchers have made significant strides in the last decade in identifying potential ways that aging may be held off. For instance, studies involving nematodes, microscopic, transparent worms that typically live for just 9 days, have found that it is possible to extend their lives to 50 days, which is the equivalent of having a human live to the age of 420 years. Fruit flies' lives have also been extended, doubling their life expectancy (Whitbourne, 2001; Libert et al., 2007; Ocorr et al., 2007).

According to new findings in several areas, there is no single mechanism that is likely to postpone aging. Instead, it is probable that a combination of some of the following most promising avenues for increasing the length of life will prove effective:

- *Telomere therapy.* As noted earlier, telomeres are the tiny areas at the tip of chromosomes that grow shorter each time a cell divides and eventually disappear, ending cell replication. Some scientists believe that if telomeres could be lengthened, age-related problems could be slowed. Researchers are now attempting to find genes that control the natural production of telomerase, an enzyme that seems to regulate the length of telomeres (Steinert, Shay, & Wright, 2000; Urquidi, Tarin, & Goodison, 2000; Chung et al., 2007).

- *Unlocking longevity genes.* Certain genes control the body's ability to overcome environmental challenges, making it better able to overcome physical adversity. If those genes can be harnessed, they may provide a way of increasing the life span. One particularly promising family of genes is *sirtuins,* which may regulate and promote longer life (Guarente, 2006; Sinclair & Guarente, 2006).

- *Reducing free radicals through antioxidant drugs.* As mentioned earlier, free radicals are unstable molecules that are a by-product of normal cell functioning that may drift through the body, damaging other cells and leading to aging. Although antioxidant drugs designed to reduce the number of free radicals have not yet been proven effective, some scientists think that they may eventually be perfected. Furthermore, some speculate it may be possible to insert in human cells genes that produce enzymes that act as antioxidants. In the meantime, nutritionists urge a diet rich in antioxidant vitamins, which are found in fruits and vegetables (Vajragupta et al., 2000; Birlouez-Aragon & Tessier, 2003; Kedziora-Kornatowska et al., 2007).

- *Restricting calories.* For at least the last decade, researchers have known that laboratory rats who are fed an extremely low-calorie diet, one that provides 30% to 50% of their normal intake, often live 30% longer than better-fed rats, provided that they obtain all the vitamins and minerals that they require. The reason appears to be that fewer free radicals are produced in the hungry rats. Researchers hope to develop drugs that mimic the effects of calorie restriction without forcing people to feel hungry all the time (Lee et al., 1999; Mattson, 2003; Ingram, Young, & Mattison, 2007).

- *The bionic solution: replacing worn-out organs.* Heart transplants . . . liver transplants . . . lung transplants. We live in an age where the removal of damaged or diseased organs and their replacement with better-functioning ones seems nearly routine.

However, despite significant advances in organ transplantation, transplants frequently fail because the body rejects the foreign tissue. To overcome this problem, some researchers suggest that replacement organs can be grown from a recipient's cloned cells, thereby solving the rejection problem. In an even more radical advance, genetically engineered cells from nonhumans that do not evoke rejection could be cloned, harvested, and transplanted into people who require transplants. Finally, it is possible that technical advances permitting the development of artificial organs that can completely replace diseased or damaged ones will become common (Cascalho, Ogle, & Platt, 2006; Kwant et al., 2007; Li & Zhu, 2007).

Ultimately, all these possibilities for the extension of the human life span remain unproven. Furthermore, a more immediate problem to solve is the reduction in the significant disparities in life expectancies between members of different racial and ethnic groups, as discussed in the following *Developmental Diversity* segment. These differences have important implications for society at large.

Developmental Diversity

Gender, Race, and Ethnic Differences in Average Life Expectancy: Separate Lives, Separate Deaths

- The average white child born in the United States is likely to live 78 years. The average African American child is likely to live 5 years less.
- A child born in Japan has a life expectancy of 79 years; for a child born in Gambia, life expectancy is less than 45 years.
- A male born in the United States today is most likely to live to the age of 73; a female will probably live some 7 years longer.

A child born in Japan has a life expectancy of 79 years. In countries like Gambia, people have an average life expectancy of 45.

T here are several reasons for these discrepancies. Consider, for example, the gender gap in life expectancy, which is particularly pronounced. Across the industrialized world, women live longer than men by some 4 to 10 years (Holden, 1987). This female advantage begins just after conception: Although slightly more males are conceived, males are more likely to die during the prenatal period, infancy, and childhood. Consequently, by the age of 30 there are roughly equal numbers of men and women. But by the age of 65, 84% of females and only 70% of males are still alive. For those over 85, the gender gap gapes wider: For every male, 2.57 women are still alive (AARP, 1990).

There are several explanations for the gender gap. One is that the naturally higher levels of hormones such as estrogen and progesterone in women provide some protection from diseases such as heart attacks. It is also possible that women engage in healthier behavior during their lives, such as eating well. However, no conclusive evidence supports any of these explanations fully (DiGiovanna, 1994).

Whatever its cause, the gender gap has continued to increase. During the early part of the 20th century, there was only a 2-year difference in favor of women, but in the 1980s this gap grew to 7 years. The size of the gap now seems to have leveled off, largely due to the fact that men are more likely than previously to engage in positive health behaviors (such as smoking less, eating better, and exercising more).

The racial and ethnic differences are troubling. They point out the disparities in socioeconomic well-being of various groups in the United States. For example, life expectancy is almost 10% greater for Caucasians than for African Americans (see Figure 17-11). Furthermore, in contrast to Caucasians, whose life expectancy keeps edging up, African Americans have actually experienced slight declines in life expectancy in recent years.

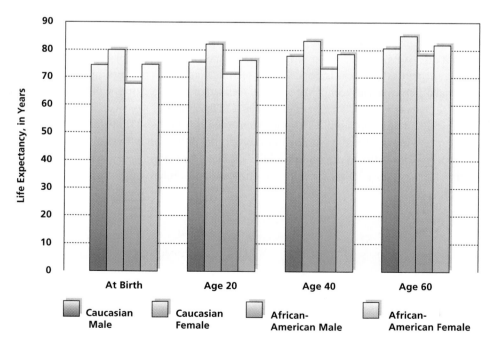

FIGURE 17-11 **LIFE EXPECTANCY OF AFRICAN AMERICANS AND WHITES**

Both male and female African Americans have a shorter life expectancy than male and female Caucasians. Are the reasons for this genetic, cultural, or both?

(*Source:* Anderson, 2001.)

Review and Apply

Review

- Although most older people are healthy, the incidence of some serious diseases rises in old age, and most people have at least one chronic ailment before they die.

- Older people are susceptible to psychological disorders such as depression.

- The most prevalent and damaging brain disorder among older people is Alzheimer's disease.

- Proper diet, exercise, and avoidance of health risks can lead to prolonged wellness during old age, and sexuality can continue throughout the life span in healthy adults.

- Whether death is caused by genetic programming or by general physical wear and tear is an unresolved question. Life expectancy, which has risen for centuries, varies with gender, race, and ethnicity.

- New approaches to increasing life expectancy include telomere therapy, reducing free radicals through antioxidant drugs, restricting caloric intake, and replacing worn-out organs.

Applying Lifespan Development

- In what ways is socioeconomic status related to wellness in old age and to life expectancy?

- *From the perspective of a healthcare professional:* Given what you've learned about explanations of life expectancy, what might you do to try to extend your own life?

Cognitive Development in Late Adulthood

Three women were talking about the inconveniences of growing old.

"Sometimes," one of them confessed, "when I go to my refrigerator, I can't remember if I'm putting something in or taking something out."

"Oh, that's nothing," said the second woman. "There are times when I find myself at the foot of the stairs wondering if I'm going up or if I've just come down."

"Well, my goodness!" exclaimed the third woman. "I'm certainly glad I don't have any problems like that"—and she knocked on wood. "Oh," she said, starting up out of her chair, "there's someone at the door." (Dent, 1984, p. 38)

This old joke summons up the stereotypic view of aging. In fact, not too long ago many gerontologists would have subscribed to the view that older people are befuddled and forgetful.

Today, however, the view has changed dramatically. Researchers no longer see the cognitive abilities of older people as inevitably declining. Overall intellectual ability and specific cognitive skills, such as memory and problem solving, are more likely to remain strong. In fact, with the appropriate practice and exposure to certain kinds of environmental stimuli, cognitive skills can actually improve.

Intelligence in Older People

The notion that older people become less cognitively adept initially arose from misinterpretations of research evidence. As we first noted in Chapter 15, early research on how intelligence changed as a result of aging typically drew a simple comparison between younger and older people's performance on the same IQ test, using traditional cross-sectional experimental methods. For example, a group of 30-year-olds and a group of 70-year-olds might have been given the same test and had their performance compared.

However, there are several drawbacks to such a procedure, as we noted in Chapter 1. One is that cross-sectional methods do not take into account *cohort effects*—influences attributable to growing up in a particular era. For example, if the younger group—because of when they grew up—has more education, on average, than the older group, we might expect the younger group to do better on the test for that reason alone. Furthermore, because some traditional intelligence tests include timed portions or reaction-time components, the slower reaction time of older people might account for their inferior performance.

To try to overcome such problems, developmental psychologists turned to longitudinal studies, which followed the same individuals for many years. However, because of repeated exposure to the same test, subjects may, over time, become familiar with the test items. Furthermore, participants in longitudinal studies may move away, quit participating, become ill, or die, leaving a smaller and possibly more cognitively skilled group of people. In short, longitudinal studies have their drawbacks, and their use initially led to some erroneous conclusions about older people.

Recent Conclusions About the Nature of Intelligence in Older People

More recent research has attempted to overcome the drawbacks of both cross-sectional and longitudinal methods. In what is probably the most ambitious—and still ongoing—study of intelligence in older people, developmental psychologist K. Warner Schaie has employed sequential methods. As we discussed in Chapter 1, *sequential studies* combine cross-sectional and longitudinal methods by examining several different age groups at a number of points in time.

In Schaie's massive study, carried out in Seattle, Washington, a battery of tests of cognitive ability was given to a group of 500 randomly chosen individuals. The people belonged to different age groups, starting at age 20 and extending at 5-year intervals to age 70. The participants were tested, and continue to be tested, every 7 years, and more people are recruited to participate every year. At this point, more than 5,000 participants have been tested (Schaie, 1994).

The study, along with other research, supports several generalizations about the nature of intellectual change during old age. Among the major ones are the following (Schaie, 1994; Craik & Salthouse, 1999; Salthouse, 2006):

- Some abilities gradually decline throughout adulthood, starting at around age 25, while others stay relatively steady (see Figure 17-12). There is no uniform pattern in adulthood of age-related changes across all intellectual abilities. In addition, as we discussed in Chapter 15, fluid intelligence (the ability to deal with new problems and situations) declines with age, while crystallized

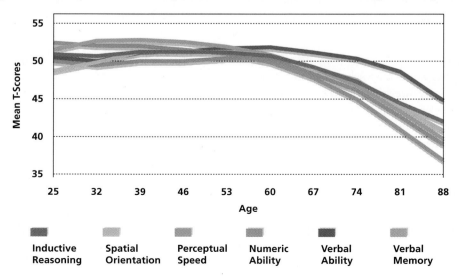

FIGURE 17-12   CHANGES IN INTELLECTUAL FUNCTIONING

Although some intellectual abilities decline across adulthood, others stay relatively steady.

(*Source:* Schaie, 1994, p. 307.)

intelligence (the store of information, skills, and strategies that people have acquired) remains steady and in some cases actually improves (Baltes & Schaie, 1974; Schaie, 1993).

- For the average person, some cognitive declines are found in all abilities by age 67. However, these declines are minimal until the 80s. Even at age 81, less than half of the people tested showed consistent declines over the previous 7 years.

- Significant individual differences are found in the patterns of change in intelligence. Some people begin to show intellectual declines in their 30s, while others do not experience any decreases until they are in their 70s. In fact, around a third of those in their 70s score higher than the average young adult.

- Environmental and cultural factors play a role in intellectual decline. People with an absence of chronic disease, higher socioeconomic status (SES), involvement in an intellectually stimulating environment, a flexible personality style, being married to a bright spouse, maintenance of good perceptual processing speed, and feelings of self-satisfaction with one's accomplishments in midlife or early old age showed less decline.

> **plasticity**   the degree to which a developing structure or behavior is susceptible to experience.

The relationship between environmental factors and intellectual skills suggests that with the proper stimulation, practice, and motivation, older people can maintain their mental abilities. Such **plasticity** in cognitive skills illustrates that there is nothing fixed about the changes that occur in intellectual abilities during late adulthood. In mental life, as in so many other areas of human development, the motto "use it or lose it" is quite fitting. Based on this principle, some developmentalists have sought to develop interventions to help older adults maintain their information processing skills, as we discuss in the *From Research to Practice* box on the next page.

It is important to note that not all developmentalists believe the "use it or lose it" hypothesis. For example, developmental psychologist Timothy Salthouse suggests that the rate of true, underlying cognitive decline in late adulthood is unaffected by mental exercise. Instead, he argues that some people—the kind who have consistently engaged throughout their lives in high levels of mental activity such as completing crossword puzzles—enter late adulthood with a "cognitive reserve." This cognitive reserve allows them to continue to perform at relatively high mental levels, even though underlying declines are actually happening. His hypothesis is controversial, though, and most developmentalists accept the hypothesis that mental exercise is beneficial (Salthouse, 2006).

Memory: Remembrance of Things Past—and Present

Composer Aaron Copland summed up what had happened to his memory in old age by remarking, "I have no trouble remembering everything that had happened 40 or 50 years ago—dates, places, faces, music. But I'm going to be 90 my next birthday, November 14th, and I find I can't remember what happened yesterday" (*Time*, 1980, p. 57). Our confidence in the accuracy of Copland's analysis is strengthened by an error in his statement: On his next birthday, he would be only 80 years old!

Is memory loss an inevitable part of aging? Not necessarily. For instance, cross-cultural research reveals that in societies where older people are held in relatively high esteem, such as in China, people are less likely to show memory losses than in societies where they are held in less regard. In such cultures, the more positive expectations regarding aging may lead people to think more positively about their own capabilities (Levy & Langer, 1994; Hess, Auman, & Colcombe, 2003).

Even when memory declines that can be directly traced to aging do occur, they are limited primarily to *episodic memories*, which relate to specific life experiences such as recalling the year you first visited New York City. In contrast, other types of memory, such as *semantic memories* (general knowledge and facts, such as the fact that 2 + 2 = 4 or the name of the capital of North Dakota) and *implicit memories* (memories about which people are not consciously aware, such as how to ride a bike), are largely unaffected by age (Nilsson et al., 1997; Dixon, 2003; Nilsson, 2003).

Memory loss is not as common among Chinese elderly as it is in the West. What are some factors that contribute to cultural differences in memory loss of the elderly?

From Research to Practice

Exercising the Aging Brain

My friend Joyce walks six miles a day, unless the weather is rotten: then she does just three or four. She's a voracious reader and contributes to various philosophical e-discussion groups. Joyce is in her 70s and is one of those people whose life, far from becoming empty in retirement, has filled almost to overflowing. Keen to speak to her, I found I had to leave several phone messages and send a number of e-mails: she is always busy. (McCartney, 2006, p. 1)

Cognitive decline in old age is far from inevitable. Research shows that continued intellectual stimulation keeps cognitive abilities sharp, although as people pass retirement age, their opportunities and motivation for cognitive challenges may decline. Recent studies on the effectiveness of mental workouts suggest that a relatively small investment of time and effort can pay big dividends in intellectual functioning among older adults.

Researcher Sherry L. Willis and her colleagues examined the long term, real-world benefits of cognitive training in older adults. Participants in Willis's study were healthy adults over age 65 with good cognitive and functional abilities. Participants received 10 cognitive training sessions lasting about an hour each, with each successive session becoming increasingly challenging. Three groups of participants received memory training (such as mnemonic strategies for memorizing word lists), reasoning training (such as finding the pattern in a series of numbers), or processing speed training (such as identifying objects that flashed briefly on a computer screen). Some participants also received "booster" training 1 year later and again 3 years later, each time consisting of four more sessions (Willis et al., 2006).

Remarkably, cognitive benefits were evident five years after the original training sessions. Compared to a control group that received no training, participants who received reasoning training performed 40% better on reasoning tasks at the 5-year mark, those who received memory training performed 75% better on memory tasks, and those who received speed training performed a staggering 300% better on speed tasks. To put these results in perspective, imagine spending just 2 weeks working out at the gym for an hour a day and then giving up entirely—but still seeing noticeable improvement 5 years later (Vedantam, 2006; Willis et al., 2006)!

In terms of benefits to real-world functioning (such as interpreting labels on medicine bottles or looking up a telephone number), only the participants who received the processing speed training followed by booster sessions showed improvement at the 5-year mark. However, participants in all three cognitive training groups did report having more confidence in their ability to complete cognitively complex daily tasks such as housework, meal preparation, finances, and shopping. Such confidence is

important by itself, because it is associated with greater independence, less reliance on health services, and better longevity (Willis et al., 2006).

Willis interprets these findings as evidence that mental exercise works much the same as physical exercise for older adults. While it doesn't stop decline entirely, it does seem to slow it down—and the specific activity that you choose to do isn't as important as doing it regularly. Games and puzzles such as chess or crosswords can be both stimulating and fun. Engaging in some form of mental workout consistently—and continually increasing the level of difficulty to keep yourself challenged—is the key to success (Vedantam, 2006; Willis et al., 2006).

Although some aspects of intelligence decline during late adulthood—as well as throughout earlier adulthood—crystallized intelligence (the store of information, skills, and strategies that people have acquired) remains steady and actually may improve.

■ *Why might the benefits of cognitive training in healthy, well-functioning older adults become evident 5 years afterward?*

■ *If you were the director of a community center for older adults, how might you apply this research in creating new programs to improve cognitive functioning in the center's patrons?*

Memory capacities do change during old age. For instance, *short-term memory* slips gradually during adulthood until age 70, when the decline becomes more pronounced. The largest drop is for information that is presented quickly and verbally, such as when someone staffing a computer helpline rattles off a series of complicated steps for fixing a problem with a computer. In addition, information about things that are completely unfamiliar is more difficult to recall. For example, declines occur in memory for prose passages, names and faces of people, and even such critical information as the directions on a medicine label, possibly because new information is not registered and processed as effectively when it is initially encountered. Although these age-related changes are generally minor, and their impact on everyday life negligible (because most elderly people automatically learn to compensate for them), memory losses are real (Cherry & Park, 1993; Carroll, 2000; Light, 2000).

Autobiographical Memory: Recalling the Days of Our Lives.

When it comes to **autobiographical memory,** memories of information about one's own life, older people are subject to some of the same principles of recall as younger individuals. For instance, memory recall frequently follows the *Pollyanna principle,* in which pleasant memories are more likely to be recalled than unpleasant memories. Similarly, people tend to forget information about their past that is not congruent with the way they currently see themselves. They are more likely to make the material that they do recall "fit" their current conception of themselves, like a strict parent who forgets that she got drunk at her high school prom (Rubin, 1996; Eacott, 1999; Rubin & Greenberg, 2003; Skowronski, Walker, & Betz, 2003; Loftus, 2003).

Everyone tends to recall particular periods of life better than others. As can be seen in Figure 17-13, 70-year-olds tend to recall autobiographical details from their 20s and 30s best. In contrast, 50-year-olds are likely to have more memories of their teenage years and their 20s. In both cases, recall of earlier years is better than recall of somewhat more recent decades, but not as complete as recall of very recent events (Fromholt & Larsen, 1991; Rubin, 2000).

Explaining Memory Changes in Old Age.

Explanations for apparent changes in memory among older people tend to focus on three main categories: environmental factors, information processing deficits, and biological factors.

- *Environmental factors.* Certain short-term factors that cause declines in memory may be found more frequently in older people. For example, older people are more apt than younger ones to take the kinds of prescription drugs that hinder memory. The lower performance of older people on memory tasks may be related to drug taking and not to age per se.

   Similarly, declines in memory can sometimes be traced to life changes in late adulthood. For instance, retirees, no longer facing intellectual challenges from their jobs, may become less practiced in using memory. Also, their motivation to recall information may be lower than previously, accounting for lower performance on tasks involving memory. They also may be less motivated than younger people to do their best in testing situations in experiments.

- *Information processing deficits.* Memory declines may also be linked to changes in information processing capabilities. For example, as we reach later adulthood, our ability to inhibit irrelevant information and thoughts may decrease, and these irrelevant thoughts interfere with successful problem solving. Similarly, the speed of information processing may decline, perhaps in a similar way to the slowing of reaction times that we discussed earlier, leading to the memory impairments observed in old age (Bashore, Ridderinkhof, & van der Molen, 1998; Palfai, Halperin, & Hoyer, 2003; Salthouse, Atkinson, & Berish, 2003).

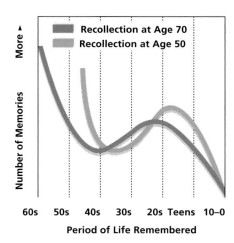

FIGURE 17-13   REMEMBRANCES OF THINGS PAST

Recall of autobiographical memories varies with age, with 70-year-olds recalling details from their 20s and 30s best, and 50-year-olds recalling memories from their teenage years and 20s. People of both ages also recall more recent memories best of all.

(*Source:* Rubin, 1986.)

autobiographical memory   memories of information about one's own life.

Another information processing view suggests that older adults concentrate on new material less effectively than younger individuals and have greater difficulty paying attention to appropriate stimuli and organizing material in memory. This information-processing-deficit approach, which has received the most research support, suggests that memory declines are due to changes in the ability to pay attention to and organize tasks involving memory skills. According to this view, older people also use less efficient processes to retrieve information from memory. These information processing deficits subsequently lead to declines in recall abilities (Craik, 1994; Castel & Craik, 2003).

- *Biological factors.* The last of the major approaches to explaining changes in memory during late adulthood concentrates on biological factors. According to this view, memory changes are a result of brain and body deterioration.

  For instance, declines in episodic memory may be related to the deterioration of the frontal lobes of the brain or a reduction in estrogen. Some studies also show a loss of cells in the hippocampus, which is critical to memory. However, specific sorts of memory deficits occur in many older people without any evidence of underlying biological deterioration (Shaywitz et al., 1999; Eberling et al., 2004; Lye et al., 2004).

Learning in Later Life: Never Too Late to Learn

The University of Arkansas campus is buzzing with talk of midterms and football. In a cafeteria, students are grousing about the food.

"Where are the dinner rolls?" says one. "I'm a vegetarian, and all they have is meat," complains another. Soon, though, everyone has moved on to complaining about classes.

A typical college scene—except for all the canes, hearing aids and white hair in evidence. This is Elderhostel, a program for people 60 and older run by a Boston nonprofit organization, formed in 1975, that recruits colleges to conduct weeklong educational sessions in everything from genealogy to the archaeology of ancient Egypt. (Stern, 1994, p. A1)

Dorothy McAlpin is one of the more than 250,000 people who enroll annually in thousands of classes organized by the Elderhostel program, the largest educational program for people in late adulthood. Represented on college campuses across the world, the Elderhostel movement is among the increasing evidence that intellectual growth and change continue to be important throughout people's lives, including late adulthood. In fact, as we saw in our examination of research on cognitive training, exercising specific cognitive skills may be especially important to older adults who want to maintain their intellectual functioning (Sack, 1999; Simson, Wilson, & Harlow-Rosentraub, 2006).

The popularity of programs such as Elderhostel is part of a growing trend among older people. Because the majority of older people have retired, they have time to pursue further education and delve into subjects in which they have always been interested.

Although not everyone is able to afford tuitions charged by Elderhostels, many public colleges encourage senior citizens to enroll in classes by providing them with free tuition. In addition, some retirement communities are located at or near college campuses, such as those constructed by the University of Michigan and Penn State University (Beck, 1991; Masunaga, 1998; Powell, 2004).

Although some elderly people are doubtful about their intellectual capabilities and consequently avoid regular college classes in which they compete with younger students, their concern is largely misplaced. Older adults often have no trouble maintaining their standing in rigorous college classes. Furthermore, professors and other students generally find the presence of older people, with their varied and substantial life experiences, a real educational benefit (Simpson, Simon, & Wilson, 2001; Simson, Wilson, & Harlow-Rosentaub, 2006).

Review and Apply

Review

● Although some intellectual abilities gradually decline throughout adulthood, starting at around age 25, others stay relatively steady.

● The intellect retains considerable plasticity and can be maintained with stimulation, practice, and motivation.

● Declines in memory affect mainly episodic memories and short-term memory.

● Explanations of memory changes in old age have focused on environmental factors, information processing declines, and biological factors.

Applying Lifespan Development

● Do you think steady or increasing crystallized intelligence can partially or fully compensate for declines in fluid intelligence? Why or why not?

● *From the perspective of a healthcare professional:* How might cultural factors, such as the esteem in which a society holds its older members, work to affect an older person's memory performance?

Epilogue

Who are the old and how old are they? In this chapter we began by reviewing the demographics of old age and looking at the phenomenon of ageism. We discussed health and wellness during late adulthood and found that older people can extend their well-being through good diet, good habits, and good exercise. We also discussed the length of the life span and explored some of the reasons why life expectancy has been increasing. We ended with an examination of cognitive abilities among the elderly, and evidence showing that there are considerable discrepancies between stereotypical views of older people's intellectual abilities and memory and reality.

Return to the prologue of this chapter, about Carol Deland's bike trip across the country, and answer the following questions:

1. In what ways does Deland contradict the stereotypes of older people and life in late adulthood?

2. In what ways does she confirm these stereotypes?

3. What elements of Deland's life may have contributed to her high level of activity? What do you think she was like as a younger person?

4. What are the likely cognitive results of Deland's vigorous exercise?

Looking Back

■ **What is it like to grow old in the United States today?**

- The number and proportion of older people in the United States and many other countries are larger than ever, and elderly people are the fastest growing segment of the U.S. population. Older people as a group are subjected to stereotyping and discrimination, a phenomenon referred to as *ageism*.

■ **What sorts of physical changes occur in old age?**

- Old age is a period in which outward physical changes unmistakably indicate aging, but many older people remain fit, active, and agile well into the period.

- Older people experience a decrease in brain size and a reduction of blood flow (and oxygen) to all parts of the body, including the brain. The circulatory, respiratory, and digestive systems all work with less efficiency.

- Reaction time among the elderly is slower, a fact that is explained by the peripheral slowing hypothesis (processing speed in the peripheral nervous system slows down) and the generalized slowing hypothesis (processing in all parts of the nervous system slows down).

■ **How are the senses affected by aging?**

- Physical changes in the eye bring declines in vision, and several eye diseases become more prevalent in old age, including cataracts, glaucoma, and age-related macular degeneration (AMD).

- Hearing also declines, particularly the ability to hear higher frequencies. Hearing loss has psychological and social consequences, since it discourages older people from engaging in social interactions. Declines in the senses of taste and smell can have health consequences.

■ **What is the general state of health of older people, and to what disorders are they susceptible?**

- Although some people are healthy, the incidence of certain serious diseases rises in old age and the ability to recuperate declines. Most older people suffer from at least one long-term ailment. The leading causes of death in old age are heart disease, cancer, and stroke.

- Older people are also susceptible to psychological disorders, such as depression and brain disorders, especially Alzheimer's disease.

Can wellness and sexuality be maintained in old age?

- Psychological and lifestyle factors can influence wellness in old age. A sense of control over one's life and environment can have positive effects, as can a proper diet, exercise, and the avoidance of risk factors, such as smoking.

- Despite some changes in sexual functioning, sexuality continues throughout old age, provided both physical and mental health are good.

How long can people expect to live, and why do they die?

- The inevitability of death is unquestioned but unexplained. Genetic programming theories claim that the body has a built-in time limit on life, while wear-and-tear theories maintain that the body simply wears out.

- Life expectancy has been rising steadily for centuries and continues to do so, with differences according to gender, race, and ethnicity. The life span may be further increased by technological advances such as telomere therapy, the use of antioxidant drugs to reduce free radicals, development of low-calorie diets, and organ replacement.

How well do older people function intellectually?

- According to sequential studies, such as those conducted by K. Warner Schaie, intellectual abilities tend to decline slowly throughout old age, but different abilities change in different ways. Training, stimulation, practice, and motivation can help older people maintain their mental abilities.

Do people lose their memories in old age?

- Loss of memory in old age is not general, but specific to certain kinds of memory. Episodic memories are most affected, while semantic and implicit memories are largely unaffected. Short-term memory declines gradually until age 70, then deteriorates quickly.

- Explanations of memory changes may focus on environmental factors, information processing declines, and biological factors. Which approach is most accurate is not entirely settled.

Key Terms and Concepts

gerontologists (p. 572)

ageism (p. 573)

primary aging (p. 575)

secondary aging (p. 575)

osteoporosis (p. 576)

peripheral slowing
   hypothesis (p. 578)

generalized slowing
   hypothesis (p. 578)

dementia (p. 583)

Alzheimer's disease (p. 583)

genetic programming
   theories of aging (p. 588)

wear-and-tear theories
   (p. 588)

life expectancy (p. 589)

plasticity (p. 595)

autobiographical memory
   (p. 597)

18 Social and Personality Development in Late Adulthood

Chapter Overview

PERSONALITY DEVELOPMENT AND SUCCESSFUL AGING

Continuity and Change in Personality During Late Adulthood

Age Stratification Approaches to Late Adulthood

Does Age Bring Wisdom?

Successful Aging: What Is the Secret?

THE DAILY LIFE OF LATE ADULTHOOD

Living Arrangements: The Places and Spaces of Their Lives

Financial Issues: The Economics of Late Adulthood

Work and Retirement in Late Adulthood

RELATIONSHIPS: OLD AND NEW

Marriage in the Later Years: Together, Then Alone

The Social Networks of Late Adulthood

Family Relationships: The Ties That Bind

Elder Abuse: Relationships Gone Wrong

Prologue: Late Love

Photos of their late spouses gaze over the bed of Geraldine Mooers, 76, and Dick Thomas, 73. "They helped us become who we are. We're honoring them, just as we honor each other," Mooers said . . . .

They met at a singles picnic five years ago. He was a staunch Republican and she a liberal Democrat. He was an overweight retired cook, she a retired dietitian who loved to exercise. They belonged to different churches. Both were widowed and had children and grandchildren.

"What an unlikely pair," Thomas said. "But I'll tell you, I love this woman. We can talk, we can disagree and we don't go to bed mad, ever."

Gradually, he moved into her condo but kept his, now rented out as an investment. They were married in church, but not with a wedding license. "Her accountant and my lawyer advised us not to complicate the inheritance issues, and we agreed," Thomas said. "In our eyes, we're married. . . ."

In recent years Thomas has had a pacemaker for his heart, stomach-stapling surgery to lose weight and last year a penile implant "because I wanted to have intercourse with Gerry. It was worth it."

As they age, "with any luck, we'll have a lot of good years to travel, do stuff with others, take classes and just be together," Mooers said. "We've each lost a spouse, and we know one of us will go through that again. All we have is now. And for now we're the best of friends and the best of lovers."
(Wolfe, 2007, p. 1E)

Romance can bloom during late adulthood, and it can be as intense and fulfilling as in earlier stages of life.

The warmth and affection between Geraldine and Dick are unmistakable. Their relationship is central to their lives, and their mutual love and admiration reach the heights of human interconnectedness.

We turn in this chapter to the social and emotional aspects of late adulthood, which remain as central an aspect of life as in earlier stages of the life span. We begin by considering how personality continues to develop in elderly individuals, and then turn to an examination of various ways people can age successfully.

Next, we consider how various societal factors affect the day-to-day living conditions of older adults. We discuss options in living arrangements, as well as ways economic and financial issues influence people's lives. We also look at how culture governs the way we treat older people, and we examine the influence of work and retirement on elderly individuals, considering the ways retirement can be optimized.

Finally, we consider relationships in late adulthood, not only among married couples, but also among other relatives and friends. We will see how the social networks of late adulthood continue to play an important—and sustaining—role in people's lives. We examine how events such as the divorce of a parent, decades earlier, can still have a critical impact on the course of people's lives. We end with a discussion of the growing phenomenon of elder abuse.

Looking Ahead

After reading this chapter, you will be able to answer these questions:

■ **In what ways does personality develop during late adulthood?**

■ **How do people deal with aging?**

■ **In what circumstances do older people live, and what difficulties do they face?**

■ **What is it like to retire?**

■ **How do marriages in late adulthood fare?**

■ **What happens when an elderly spouse dies?**

■ **What sorts of relationships are important in late adulthood?**

Personality Development and Successful Aging

Greta Roach has a puckish manner, a habit of nudging you when she is about to say something funny. This happens often, because that is how she views the world. Even last year's knee injury, which forced her to drop out of her bowling league and halted the march of blue-and-chrome trophies across her living-room table, is not—in her mind—a frailty of age.

Roach, 93, takes the same spirited approach to life in her 90s as she did in her 20s, something not all elders can do. . . . "I enjoy life. I belong to all the clubs. I love to talk on the telephone. I write to my old friends." She pauses. "Those that are still alive." (Pappano, 1994, pp. 19, 30)

In many ways, Roach, with her wit, high spirits, and enormous activity level, is much the same person she was in earlier years. Yet for other older adults, time and circumstances seem to bring changes in their outlook on life, in their views of themselves, and perhaps even in their basic personalities. In fact, one of the fundamental questions asked by lifespan developmentalists concerns the degree to which personality either remains stable or changes in later adulthood.

Continuity and Change in Personality During Late Adulthood

Is personality relatively stable throughout adulthood, or does it vary in significant ways? The answer, it turns out, depends on which facets of personality we wish to consider. According to developmental psychologists Paul Costa and Robert McCrae, whose work we first discussed in Chapter 16, the "Big Five" basic personality traits (neuroticism, extroversion, openness, agreeableness, and conscientiousness) are remarkably stable across adulthood. For instance, even-tempered people at age 20 are still even-tempered at age 75, and people who hold positive self-concepts early in adulthood still view themselves positively in late adulthood (Costa & McCrae, 1988, 1989, 1997; McCrae & Costa, 1990, 2003).

For example, at age 93, Greta Roach is still active and humorous, as she was in her 20s. Similarly, other longitudinal investigations have found that personality traits remain quite stable. Consequently, there seems to be a fundamental continuity to personality (Field & Millsap, 1991).

Despite this general stability of basic personality traits, there is still the possibility of change over time. As we noted in Chapter 16, the profound changes that occur throughout adulthood in people's social environments may produce fluctuations and changes in personality. What is important to a person at age 80 is not necessarily the same as what was important at age 40.

In order to account for these sorts of changes, some theorists have focused their attention on the discontinuities of development. As we'll see next, the work of Erik Erikson, Robert Peck, Daniel Levinson, and Bernice Neugarten has examined the changes in personality that occur as a result of new challenges that appear in later adulthood.

Ego Integrity Versus Despair: Erikson's Final Stage.

Psychoanalyst Erik Erikson's final word on personality concerns late adulthood, the time, he suggested, when elderly people move into the last of life's eight stages of psychosocial development. Labeled the **ego-integrity-versus-despair stage,** this last period is characterized by a process of looking back over one's life, evaluating it, and coming to terms with it.

People who are successful in this stage of development experience a sense of satisfaction and accomplishment, which Erikson terms "integrity." When people achieve integrity, they feel that they have realized and fulfilled the possibilities that have come their way in life, and they have few regrets. On the other hand, some people look back on their lives with dissatisfaction. They may feel that they have missed important opportunities and have not accomplished what they wished. Such individuals may be unhappy, depressed, angry, or despondent over what they have done, or failed to do, with their lives—in short, they despair.

Peck's Developmental Tasks.

Although Erikson's approach provides a picture of the broad possibilities of later adulthood, other theorists offer a more differentiated view of what occurs in the final stage of life. For instance, psychologist Robert Peck (1968) suggests that personality development in elderly people is occupied by three major developmental tasks or challenges.

In Peck's view—which is part of a comprehensive description of change across adulthood—the first task in old age is that people must redefine themselves in ways that do not relate to their work roles or occupations. He labels this stage **redefinition of self versus preoccupation with work role.** As we will see when we discuss retirement, the changes that occur when people stop working can trigger a difficult adjustment that has a major impact on the way people view themselves. Peck suggests that people must adjust their values to place less emphasis on themselves as workers or professionals and more on attributes that don't involve work, such as being a grandparent or a gardener.

The second major developmental task in late adulthood, according to Peck, is **body transcendence versus body preoccupation.** As we saw in Chapter 17, elderly individuals can undergo significant changes in their physical capabilities as a result of aging. In the body-transcendence-versus-body-preoccupation stage, people must learn to cope with and move beyond those physical changes (transcendence). If they don't, they become preoccupied with their physical deterioration, to the detriment of their personality development. Greta Roach, who just gave up bowling in her 90s, is an example of someone who is coping well with the physical changes of aging.

ego-integrity-versus-despair stage
Erikson's final stage of life, characterized by a process of looking back over one's life, evaluating it, and coming to terms with it.

redefinition of self versus preoccupation with work role   the theory that those in old age must redefine themselves in ways that do not relate to their work roles or occupations.

body transcendence versus body preoccupation   a period in which people must learn to cope with and move beyond changes in physical capabilities as a result of aging.

Finally, the third developmental task faced by those in old age is **ego transcendence versus ego preoccupation,** in which elderly people must come to grips with their coming death. They need to understand that although death is inevitable, and probably not too far off, they have made contributions to society. If people in late adulthood see these contributions, which can take the form of children or work- and civic-related activities, as lasting beyond their own lives, they will experience ego transcendence. If not, they may become preoccupied with the question of whether their lives had value and worth to society.

Levinson's Final Season: The Winter of Life. Daniel Levinson's theory of adult development does not focus as much as Erikson's and Peck's theories on the challenges that aging adults must overcome. Instead, he looks at the processes that can lead to personality change as we grow old. According to Daniel Levinson, people enter late adulthood by passing through a transition stage that typically occurs around age 60 to 65 (Levinson, 1986, 1992). During this transition period, people come to view themselves as entering late adulthood—or, ultimately, as being "old." Knowing full well what society's stereotypes about elderly individuals are, and how negative they can be, people struggle with the notion that they are now in this category.

ego transcendence versus ego preoccupation the period in which elderly people must come to grips with their coming death.

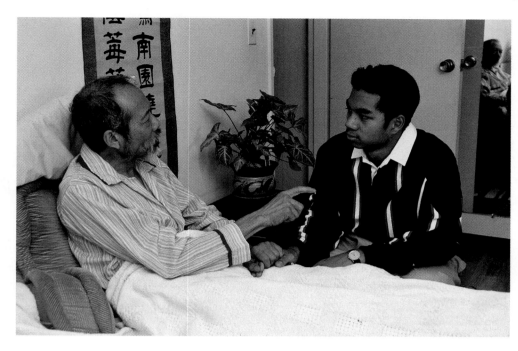

Older adults may become "venerated elders," whose advice is sought and relied upon.

According to Levinson, with age people come to realize that they are no longer on the center stage of life, but are increasingly playing bit parts. This loss of power, respect, and authority may be difficult for individuals accustomed to having control in their lives.

On the other hand, people in late adulthood can serve as resources to younger individuals, and they may find themselves regarded as "venerated elders" whose advice is sought and relied upon. Furthermore, old age can bring with it a new freedom to do things for the simple sake of the enjoyment and pleasure they bring, rather than because they are obligations.

Coping with Aging: Neugarten's Study.   Rather than focusing on the commonalities of aging, or the processes and tasks involved in aging, Bernice Neugarten (1972, 1977)—in what became a classic study—examined the different ways that people cope with aging. Neugarten found four different personality types in her research on people in their 70s:

- *Disintegrated and disorganized personalities.* Some people are unable to accept aging, and they experience despair as they get older. They are often found in nursing homes or are hospitalized.

- *Passive-dependent personalities.* Others become fearful with age—fear of falling ill, fear of the future, fear of their own inability to cope. They are so fearful that they may seek out help from family and care providers, even when they don't need it.

- *Defended personalities.* Others respond to the fear of aging in a quite different manner. They try to stop it in its tracks. They may attempt to act young, exercising vigorously and engaging in youthful activities. Unfortunately, they may set up unrealistic expectations for themselves and run the risk of feeling disappointed as a result.

- *Integrated personalities.* The most successful individuals cope comfortably with aging. They accept becoming older and maintain a sense of self-dignity.

Neugarten found that the majority of the people she studied fell into the final category. They acknowledged aging and were able to look back at their lives and gaze into the future with acceptance.

Life Review and Reminiscence: The Common Theme of Personality Development.   Looking back over one's life is a major thread running through the work of Erikson, Peck, Neugarten, and Levinson's views of personality development in old age. In

The process of life review can improve memory and foster feelings of interconnectedness.

fact, **life review,** in which people examine and evaluate their lives, is a common theme for most personality theorists who focus on late adulthood.

According to gerontologist Robert Butler (2002), life review is triggered by the increasingly obvious prospect of one's death. As people age, they look back on their lives, remembering and reconsidering what has happened to them. We might at first suspect that such reminiscence may be harmful, as people relive the past, wallow in past problems, and revive old wounds, but this is not the case at all. By reviewing the events of their lives, elderly people often come to a better understanding of their past. They may be able to resolve lingering problems and conflicts that they had with particular people, such as an estrangement from a child, and they may feel they can face their current lives with greater serenity (Bohlmeijer, Smit, & Cuijpers, 2003; Arkoff, Meredith, & Dubanoski, 2004; McKee et al., 2005).

Life review offers other benefits. For example, reminiscence may lead to a sense of sharing and mutuality, a feeling of interconnectedness with others. Moreover, it can be a source of social interaction, as older adults seek to share their prior experiences with others (Sherman, 1991; Parks, Sanna, & Posey, 2003).

Reminiscence may even have cognitive benefits, improving memory in older people. By reflecting on the past, people activate a variety of memories about people and events in their lives. In turn, these memories may trigger other, related memories, and may bring back sights, sounds, and even smells of the past (Thorsheim & Roberts, 1990; Kartman, 1991).

On the other hand, the outcomes of life review and reminiscence are not always positive. People who become obsessive about the past, reliving old insults and mistakes that cannot be rectified, may end up feeling guilt, depression, and anger against people from the past who may not even still be alive. In such cases, reminiscence produces declines in psychological functioning (DeGenova, 1993).

Overall, though, the process of life review and reminiscence can play an important role in the ongoing lives of elderly individuals. It provides continuity between past and present, and may increase awareness of the contemporary world. It also can provide new insights into the past and into others, allowing people to continue personality growth and to function more effectively in the present (Stevens-Ratchford, 1993; Turner & Helms, 1994; Webster & Haight, 2002; Coleman, 2005; Haber, 2006).

life review   the point in life in which people examine and evaluate their lives.

Age Stratification Approaches to Late Adulthood

Age, like race and gender, provides a way of ranking people within a given society. **Age stratification theories** suggest that economic resources, power, and privilege are distributed unequally among people at different stages of the life course. Such inequality is particularly pronounced during late adulthood.

Even as advances in medical technologies have led to a longer life span, power and prestige for the elderly have eroded, at least in industrialized societies. For example, the peak earning years are the 50s; later, earnings tend to decline. Further, younger people have more independence and are often physically removed from their elders, making them less dependent on older adults. In addition, rapidly changing technology causes older adults to be seen as lacking important skills. Ultimately, older adults are seen as not particularly productive members of society and in some cases simply irrelevant (Cohn, 1982; Macionis, 2001). As Levinson's theory emphasizes, people are certainly aware of the declines in status that accompany growing old in Western societies. Levinson considers adjusting to them to be the major transition of late adulthood.

Age stratification theories help explain why aging is viewed more positively in less industrialized societies. For example, in cultures in which agricultural activities predominate, older people can accumulate control over important resources such as animals and land. In such societies, in which the concept of retirement is unknown, older individuals (especially older males) are exceptionally respected, in part because they continue to be involved in daily activities central to the society. Furthermore, because agricultural practices change at a less rapid pace than the technological advances that characterize more industrialized societies, people in late adulthood are seen as possessing considerable wisdom. Cultural values that stress respect for elders are not limited to less industrialized countries. They shape how elderly adults are treated in a variety of societies, as discussed in the *Developmental Diversity* feature.

age stratification theories the view that an unequal distribution of economic resources, power, and privilege exists among people at different stages of the life course.

Developmental Diversity

How Culture Shapes the Way We Treat People in Late Adulthood

The view we hold of late adulthood is colored by the culture in which we live. For example, Asian societies, in general, hold elderly people, particularly members of their own families, in higher esteem than Western cultures tend to. Although the strength of this standard has been declining in areas of Asia in which industrialization has been increasing rapidly, such as Japan, the view of aging and the treatment of people in late adulthood still tend to be more positive than in Western cultures. Indeed, incidents such as the deaths of nearly 15,000 French elderly (who had been left uncared for by their vacationing children during a blazing heat wave in 2003) fuel the view that members of Western cultures hold those in late adulthood in little esteem (Fry, 1985; Ikels, 1989; Cobbe, 2003; Degnen, 2007).

What is it about Asian cultures that leads to higher levels of esteem for old age? In general, cultures that hold the elderly in high regard are relatively homogeneous in socioeconomic terms. In addition, the roles that people play in those societies entail greater responsibility with increasing age, and elderly people control resources to a relatively large extent.

Moreover, the roles played by people in Asian society display more continuity throughout the life span than in Western cultures, and older adults continue to engage in activities that are valued by society. Finally, Asian cultures are more organized around extended families in which the older generations are well integrated into the family structure (Fry, 1985; Sangree, 1989). In such an arrangement, younger family members may come to see older members as having accumulated a great deal of wisdom, which they can share.

What aspects of Asian cultures lead them to hold higher levels of esteem for old age?

On the other hand, even those societies that articulate strong ideals regarding the treatment of older adults do not always live up to those standards. For instance, the Chinese people, whose admiration, respect, and even worship for individuals in late adulthood are strong, show that people's actual behavior, in almost every segment of the society except for the most elite, fails to be as positive as their attitudes are. Furthermore, it is typically sons and their wives who are expected to care for elderly parents; parents with just daughters may find themselves with no one to care for them in late adulthood. In short, conduct toward elderly people in particular cultures is not uniform, and it is important not to make broad, global statements about how older adults are treated in a given society (Harrell, 1981; Comunian & Gielen, 2000).

It is not just Asian cultures that hold the elderly in particular esteem. For example, in Latino cultures, the elderly are thought to have a special inner strength, and they are assumed to be a valuable resource for younger individuals in a family. In many African cultures, reaching an old age is seen as a sign of divine intervention, and the elderly are called "big person" in a number of African languages (Diop, 1989; Holmes & Holmes, 1995; Lehr, Seiler, & Thomae, 2000).

Does Age Bring Wisdom?

One of the benefits of age is supposed to be wisdom. But does the average elderly person have wisdom, and do people gain wisdom as they become older?

Although it seems reasonable to believe that we get wiser as we get older, we don't know for sure, because the concept of **wisdom**—expert knowledge in the practical aspects of life—has, until recent years, received little attention from gerontologists and other researchers. In part, this lack of attention stems from the difficulty in defining and measuring the concept, which is unusually vague (Helmuth, 2003; Brugman, 2006).

Wisdom can be seen as reflecting an accumulation of knowledge, experience, and contemplation, and by this definition, older age may be necessary, or at least helpful, to acquiring true

wisdom   expert knowledge in the practical aspects of life.

wisdom (Baltes & Staudinger, 2000; Dixon & Cohen, 2003; Wink & Dillon, 2003; Kunzmann & Baltes, 2005).

Wisdom is not the same as intelligence, but distinguishing these two qualities can be tricky. Some researchers suggest that a primary distinction is related to timing: While knowledge that is derived from intelligence is related to the here-and-now, wisdom is a more timeless quality. While intelligence may permit a person to think logically and systematically, wisdom provides an understanding of human behavior. According to psychologist Robert Sternberg, who has conducted research related to practical intelligence, as we discussed in Chapter 13, intelligence permits humans to invent the atom bomb, while wisdom prevents them from using it (Seppa, 1997). Measuring wisdom is difficult. Ursula Staudinger and Paul Baltes (2000) designed a study that has shown that it is possible to assess people reliably on the concept. Pairs of people ranging in age from 20 to 70 years discussed difficulties relating to life events. One problem involved someone who gets a phone call from a good friend who says that he or she is planning to commit suicide. Another involved a 14-year-old girl who wanted to move out of her family home immediately. Participants were asked what they should do and consider.

Although there were no absolute right or wrong answers to these problems, the responses were evaluated against several criteria, including the amount of factual knowledge the participants brought to bear on the problem; their knowledge about decision-making strategies such as considering the consequences of a decision; how well the participants considered the problem within the context of the central character's life span and the values that the central character may hold; and whether the participants recognized that there may not be a single, absolute solution.

Using these criteria, participants' responses were rated as relatively wise or unwise. For instance, an example of a response to the suicide problem rated as particularly wise is the following:

On the one hand this problem has a pragmatic side, one has to react one way or another. On the other hand, it also has a philosophical side whether human beings are allowed to kill themselves etc. . . . First one would need to find out whether this decision is the result of a longer process or whether it is a reaction to a momentary life situation. In the latter case, it is uncertain how long this condition will last. There can be conditions that make suicide conceivable. But I think no one should be easily released from life. They should be forced to "fight" for their death if they really want it. . . . It seems that one has a responsibility to try to show the person alternative pathways. Currently, for example, there seems to be a trend in our society that it becomes more and more accepted that old people commit suicide. This can also be viewed as dangerous. Not because of the suicide itself but because of its functionality for society. (Staudinger & Baltes, 1996, p. 762)

The Staudinger and Baltes study also found that the older participants benefited more from an experimental condition designed to promote wise thinking, and other research suggests that the very wisest individuals may be older adults.

Other research has looked at wisdom in terms of the development of theory of mind—the ability to make inferences about others' thoughts, feelings, and intentions, their mental states. Older adults, with their added years of experience to draw upon, appear to be able to utilize a more sophisticated theory of mind (Happe, Winner, & Brownell, 1998).

Successful Aging: What Is the Secret?

At age 77, Elinor Reynolds spends most of her time at home, leading a quiet, routine existence. Never married, Elinor receives visits from her two sisters every few weeks, and some of her nieces and nephews stop by on occasion. But for the most part, she keeps to herself. When asked, she says she is quite happy.

disengagement theory the period in late adulthood that marks a gradual withdrawal from the world on physical, psychological, and social levels.

In contrast, Carrie Masterson, also 77, is involved in something different almost every day. If she is not visiting the senior center, participating in some kind of activity, she is out shopping. Her daughter complains that Carrie is "never home" when she tries to reach her by phone, and Carrie replies that she has never been busier—or happier.

Clearly, there is no single way to age successfully. How people age depends on personality factors and the circumstances in which people find themselves. Some people become progressively less involved with day-to-day events, while others maintain active ties to people and their areas of personal interest. Three major approaches provide explanations: disengagement theory, activity theory, and continuity theory. While disengagement theory suggests that successful aging is characterized by gradual withdrawal, activity theory argues that successful aging occurs when people maintain their engagement with the world. Continuity theory takes a compromise position, suggesting that what is important is maintaining a desired level of involvement. We'll consider each approach in turn.

Disengagement Theory: Gradual Retreat.   According to **disengagement theory,** late adulthood often involves a gradual withdrawal from the world on physical, psychological, and social levels (Cummings & Henry, 1961). On a physical level, elderly people have lower energy levels and tend to slow down progressively. Psychologically, they begin to withdraw from others, showing less interest in the world around them and spending more time looking inward. Finally, on a social level, they engage in less interaction with others, in terms of both day-to-day, face-to-face encounters and participation in society as a whole. Older adults also become less involved and invested in the lives of others (Quinnan, 1997).

Disengagement theory suggests that withdrawal is a mutual process. Because of norms and expectations about aging, society in general begins to disengage from those in late adulthood. For example, mandatory retirement ages compel elderly people to withdraw from work-related roles, thereby accelerating the process of disengagement.

Contrary to what we might expect, such withdrawal is not necessarily a negative experience for those in old age. In fact, most theorists who subscribe to disengagement theory argue that the outcomes of disengagement are largely positive. According to this view, the gradual withdrawal

While disengagement theory suggests that people in late adulthood begin to gradually withdraw from the world, activity theory argues that successful aging occurs when people maintain their involvement with others.

of people in late adulthood permits them to become more reflective about their own lives and less constrained by social roles. Furthermore, people can become more discerning in their social relationships, focusing on those who best meet their needs. In a sense, then, disengagement can be liberating (Carstensen, 1995; Settersten, 2002; Wrosch, Bauer, & Scheier, 2005).

Similarly, decreased emotional investment in others can be viewed as beneficial. By investing less emotional energy in their social relationships with others, people in late adulthood are better able to adjust to the increasing frequency of serious illness and death among their peers.

Evidence for disengagement comes from a study examining close to 300 people aged 50 to 90 which found that specific events, such as retirement or the death of a spouse, were accompanied by a gradual disengagement in which the level of social interaction with others plummeted (Cummings & Henry, 1961). According to these results, disengagement was related to successful aging.

Activity Theory: Continued Involvement.

Although early findings were consistent with disengagement theory, later research was not so supportive. For example, a follow-up study found that although some of the subjects were happily disengaged, others, who had remained quite involved and active, were as happy—and sometimes happier—than those who showed signs of disengagement. Furthermore, in many non-Western cultures, people remain engaged, active, and busy throughout old age, and the expectation is that people will remain actively involved in everyday life. Clearly, disengagement is not an automatic, universal process (Havighurst, 1973; Palmore, 1975; Bergstrom & Holmes, 2000; Crosnoe & Elder, 2002).

The lack of support for disengagement theory led to an alternative, known as activity theory. **Activity theory** suggests that successful aging occurs when people maintain the interests and activities they pursued during middle age and resist any decrease in the amount and type of social interaction they have with others. According to this perspective, happiness and satisfaction with life are assumed to spring from a high level of involvement with the world. Moreover, successful aging occurs when older adults adapt to inevitable changes in their environments not by withdrawing, but by resisting reductions in their social involvement (Bell, 1978; Charles, Reynolds, & Gatz, 2001; Consedine, Magai, & King, 2004; Hutchinson & Wexler, 2007).

Activity theory suggests that successful aging in late adulthood reflects a continuation of activities in which elderly people participated earlier. Even in cases in which it is no longer possible to participate in certain activities—such as work, following retirement—activity theory argues that successful aging occurs when replacement activities are found.

But activity theory, like disengagement theory, is not the full story. For one thing, activity theory makes little distinction between various types of activities. Surely not every activity will have an equal impact on a person's happiness and satisfaction with life, and being involved in various activities just for the sake of remaining engaged is unlikely to be satisfying. In sum, the specific nature and quality of the activities in which people engage are likely to be more critical than the mere quantity or frequency of their activities (Burrus-Bammel & Bammel, 1985; Adams, 2004).

A more significant concern is that for some people in late adulthood, the principle of "less is more" clearly holds. For such individuals, less activity brings greater enjoyment of life. They are able to slow down and do only the things that bring them the greatest satisfaction (Ward, 1984). In fact, some people view the ability to moderate their pace as one of the bounties of late adulthood. For them, a relatively inactive, and perhaps even solitary, existence is welcomed (Hansson & Carpenter, 1994).

In short, neither disengagement theory nor activity theory provides a complete picture of successful aging. For some people, a gradual disengagement occurs, and this leads to relatively high levels of happiness and satisfaction. For others, preserving a significant level of activity and involvement leads to greater satisfaction (Johnson & Barer, 1992; Rapkin & Fischer, 1992; Ouwehand, de Ridder, & Bensing, 2007).

activity theory the theory suggesting that successful aging occurs when people maintain the interests, activities, and social interactions with which they were involved during middle age.

Continuity Theory: A Compromise Position.   The current view of successful aging is a compromise between disengagement theory and activity theory. **Continuity theory** suggests that people simply need to maintain their desired level of involvement in society in order to maximize their sense of well-being and self-esteem (Whitbourne, 2001; Atchley, 2003).

According to continuity theory, those who were highly active and social will be happiest if they largely remain so. Those more retiring individuals, who enjoy solitude and solitary interests, such as reading or walks in the woods, will be happiest if they are free to pursue that level of sociability (Maddox & Campbell, 1985; Holahan & Chapman, 2002).

It is also clear that, regardless of the level of activity in which older adults engage, most experience positive emotions as frequently as younger individuals. Furthermore, they become more skilled in regulating their emotions.

Other factors enhance feelings of happiness during late adulthood. For instance, good physical and mental health is clearly important in determining an elderly person's overall sense of well-being. Similarly, having enough financial security to provide for basic needs, including food, shelter, and medical care, is critical. In addition, a sense of autonomy, independence, and personal control over one's life is a significant advantage (Carstensen et al., 2000; Lawton, 2001; Morris, 2001; Charles, Mather, & Carstensen, 2003).

Finally, as we first discussed in Chapter 17, the way elderly people perceive old age can influence their happiness and satisfaction. Those who view late adulthood in terms of positive attributes—such as the possibility of gaining knowledge and wisdom—are apt to perceive themselves in a more positive light than those who view old age in a more pessimistic and unfavorable way (Thompson, 1993; Levy, Slade, & Kasl, 2002; Levy, 2003).

Selective Optimization with Compensation: A General Model of Successful Aging.   In considering the factors that lead to successful aging, developmental psychologists Paul Baltes and Margret Baltes focus on the "selective optimization with compensation" model. As we first noted in Chapter 15, the assumption underlying the model is that late adulthood brings with it changes and losses in underlying capabilities, which vary from one person to another. However, it is possible to overcome such shifts in capabilities through selective optimization.

Selective optimization is the process by which people concentrate on particular skill areas to compensate for losses in other areas. They do this by seeking to fortify their general motivational, cognitive, and physical resources, while also, through a process of selection, focusing on particular areas of special interest. A person who has run marathons all her life may have to cut back or give up entirely other activities in order to increase her training. By giving up other activities, she may be able to maintain her running skills through concentration on them (Bajor & Baltes, 2003; Baltes & Carstensen, 2003; Baltes & Freund, 2003a, 2003b; Rapp, Krampe, & Baltes, 2006).

At the same time, the model suggests that elderly individuals engage in compensation for the losses that they have sustained due to aging. Compensation may take the form, for instance, of employing a hearing aid to offset losses in hearing. Piano virtuoso Arthur Rubinstein provides another example of selective optimization with compensation. In his later years, he maintained his concert career and was acclaimed for his playing. To manage this, he used several strategies that illustrate the model of selective optimization with compensation.

First, Rubinstein reduced the number of pieces he played at concerts—an example of being selective in what he sought to accomplish. Second, he practiced those pieces more often, thus using optimization. Finally, in an example of compensation, he slowed down the tempo of musical passages immediately preceding faster passages, thereby fostering the illusion that he was playing just as fast as he had ever played (Baltes & Baltes, 1990).

In short, the model of selective optimization with compensation (summarized in Figure 18-1) illustrates the fundamentals of successful aging. Although late adulthood may bring about

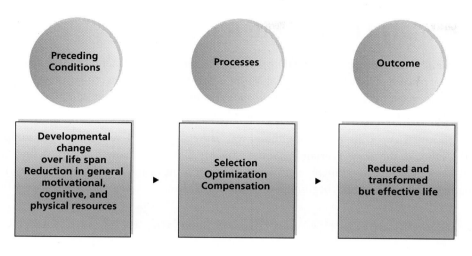

FIGURE 18-1 SELECTIVE OPTIMIZATION WITH COMPENSATION

According to the model proposed by Paul Baltes and Margret Baltes, successful aging occurs when an older adult focuses on his or her most important areas of functioning and compensates for losses in other areas. Is this unique to old age?

(*Source:* Adapted from Baltes & Baltes, 1990.)

various changes in underlying capabilities, people who focus on making the most of their achievements in particular areas may well be able to compensate for any limitations and losses that do occur. The outcome is a life that is reduced in some areas, but is also transformed and modified and, ultimately, is effective and successful.

Review and Apply

Review

- While some aspects of personality remain stable, others change to reflect the social environments through which people pass as they age.

- Erikson calls older adulthood the ego-integrity-versus-despair stage, focusing on individuals' feelings about their lives, while Peck focuses on three tasks that define the period.

- According to Levinson, after struggling with the notion of being old, people can experience liberation and self-regard. Neugarten focuses on the ways people cope with aging.

- Age stratification theories suggest that the unequal distribution of economic resources, power, and privilege becomes particularly pronounced during late adulthood.

- Societies in which elderly people are respected are generally characterized by social homogeneity, extended families, responsible roles for older people, and control of significant resources by older people.

- Disengagement theory suggests that older people gradually withdraw from the world, which can lead to reflection and satisfaction. In contrast, activity theory suggests that the happiest people continue to be engaged with the world. A compromise position—that of continuity theory—may be the most useful approach.

- The most successful model for aging may be selective optimization with compensation.

Applying Lifespan Development

- How might personality traits account for success or failure in achieving satisfaction through the life review process?

- *From the perspective of a social worker:* How might cultural factors affect an older person's likelihood of pursuing either the disengagement strategy or the activity strategy?

continuing-care community a community that offers an environment in which all the residents are of retirement age or older and need various levels of care.

The Daily Life of Late Adulthood

I hear all these retired folks complaining that they don't have this and they don't have that. . . . I'm not pinched. . . . My house is paid for. My car is paid for. Both my sons are grown up. I don't need many new clothes. Every time I go out and eat somewhere, I get a senior citizen's discount. This is the happiest period of my life. These are my golden years. (Gottschalk, 1983, p. 1)

This positive view of life in late adulthood was expressed by a 74-year-old retired shipping clerk. Although the story is certainly not the same for all retirees, many, if not most, find their post-work lives happy and involving. We will consider some of the ways in which people lead their lives in late adulthood, beginning with where they live.

Living Arrangements: The Places and Spaces of Their Lives

Think "old age," and if you are like most people, your thoughts soon turn to nursing homes. Popular stereotypes place most elderly people in lonely, unpleasant, institutional surroundings, under the care of strangers.

The reality, however, is quite different. Although it is true that some people finish their lives in nursing homes, they are a tiny minority—only 5%. Most people live out their entire lives in home environments, typically in the company of at least one other family member.

Living at Home. A large number of older adults live alone. People over 65 represent a quarter of America's 9.6 million single-person households. Roughly two-thirds of people over the age of 65 live with other members of the family. In most cases they live with spouses. Some older adults live with their siblings, and others live in multigenerational settings with their children, grandchildren, and even occasionally great-grandchildren.

The consequences of living with a family member are quite varied, depending on the nature of the setting. For married couples, living with a spouse represents continuity with earlier life. On the other hand, for people who move in with their children, the adjustment to life in a multigenerational setting can be jarring. Not only is there a potential loss of independence and privacy, but older adults may feel uncomfortable with the way their children are raising their grandchildren. Unless there are some ground rules about the specific roles that people are to play in the household, conflicts can arise (Sussman & Sussman, 1991; Navarro, 2006).

For some groups, living in extended families is more typical than for other groups. For instance, as mentioned in Chapter 15, African Americans are more likely than whites to live in multigenerational families. Furthermore, the amount of influence that family members have over one another and the interdependence of extended families are generally greater in African American, Asian American, and Hispanic families than in Caucasian families (Becker, Beyene, & Newsom, 2003).

Specialized Living Environments. For some 10% of those in late adulthood, home is an institution. As we'll see, there is a broad range of different types of specialized environments in which elderly people live.

One of the more recent innovations in living arrangements is the **continuing-care community.** Such communities typically offer an environment in which all the residents are of retirement age or older. Residents may need various levels of care, which is provided by the community. Residents sign contracts under which the community makes a commitment to provide care at whatever level is needed. In many such communities, people start out living in separate houses or apartments, either independently or with occasional home care. As they age and their needs increase, residents may eventually move into *assisted living*, in which people live in independent housing but are supported by medical providers to the extent required. Continuing care ultimately extends all the way to full-time nursing care, which is often provided at an on-site nursing home.

Living in a multigenerational setting with children and their families can be rewarding and helpful for those in late adulthood. Are there any disadvantages to this type of situation? What are some solutions?

Continuing-care communities tend to be fairly homogeneous in terms of religious, racial, and ethnic backgrounds, and they are often organized by private or religious organizations. Because joining may involve a substantial initial payment, members of such communities tend to be relatively well-off financially. Increasingly, though, continuing-care communities are making efforts to raise the level of diversity. Furthermore, they are attempting to increase opportunities for intergenerational interaction by establishing day-care centers on the premises and developing programs that involve younger populations (Barton, 1997; Chaker, 2003; Berkman, 2006).

Several types of nursing institutions exist, ranging from those that provide part-time day care to homes that offer 24-hour-a-day, live-in care. In **adult day-care facilities,** elderly individuals receive care only during the day, but spend nights and weekends in their own homes. During the time that they are at the facility, people receive nursing care, take their meals, and participate in scheduled activities. Sometimes adult facilities are combined with infant and child day-care programs, an arrangement that allows for interaction between the old and the young (Quade, 1994; Ritchie, 2003; Tse & Howie, 2005; Gitlin et al., 2006).

Other institutional settings offer more extensive care. The most intensive institutions are **skilled-nursing facilities,** which provide full-time nursing care for people who have chronic illnesses or are recovering from a temporary medical condition. While only 4.5% of those age 65 and older live in nursing homes, the number increases dramatically with age. The percentages are 1.1 for persons 65 to 74 years old, 4.7 for those 75 to 84, and 18.2 for persons 85 and older. Approximately 5% of the elderly live in a variety of self-described senior housing environments that offer a number of supportive services (Administration on Aging, 2006).

The greater the extent of nursing home care, the greater the adjustment required of residents. Although some newcomers adjust relatively rapidly, the loss of independence brought about by institutional life may lead to difficulties. In addition, elderly people are as susceptible as other members of society to society's stereotypes about nursing homes, and their expectations may be particularly negative. They may see themselves as just marking time until they eventually die, forgotten and discarded by a society that venerates youth (Biedenharn & Normoyle, 1991; Baltes, 1996).

Institutionalism and Learned Helplessness.

Although the fears of those in nursing homes may be exaggerated, they can lead to **institutionalism,** a psychological state in which people develop apathy, indifference, and a lack of caring about themselves. Institutionalism is brought about, in part, by a sense of *learned helplessness,* a belief that one has no control over one's environment (Butler & Lewis, 1981; Peterson & Park, 2007).

The sense of helplessness brought about by institutionalism can literally have deadly consequences. Consider, for instance, what happens when people enter nursing homes in late adulthood. One of the most conspicuous changes from their independent past is that they no longer have control over their most basic activities. They may be told when and what to eat, their sleeping schedules may be arranged by others, and even their visits to the bathroom may be regulated (Kane et al., 1997; Wolinsky, Wyrwich, & Babu, 2003).

A classic experiment showed the consequences of such a loss of control. Psychologists Ellen Langer and Irving Janis (1979) divided elderly residents of a nursing home into two groups. One group of residents was encouraged to make a variety of choices about their day-to-day activities. The other group was given no choices and was encouraged to let the nursing home staff care for them. The results were clear. The participants who had choices were not only happier, they were also healthier. In fact, 18 months after the experiment began, only 15% of the choice group had died—compared to 30 percent of the comparison group.

In short, the loss of control over certain aspects of their daily life experienced by residents of nursing homes and other institutions can have a profound effect on their well-being. Keep in mind that not all nursing homes are the same, however. The best go out of their way to permit residents to make basic life decisions, and they attempt to give people in late adulthood a sense of control over their lives.

adult day-care facilities settings in which elderly individuals receive care only during the day, but spend nights and weekends in their own homes.

skilled-nursing facilities settings that provide full-time nursing care for people who have chronic illnesses or are recovering from a temporary medical condition.

institutionalism a psychological state in which people in nursing homes develop apathy, indifference, and a lack of caring about themselves.

Financial Issues: The Economics of Late Adulthood

People in late adulthood, like people in all other stages of life, range from one end of the socioeconomic spectrum to the other. Like the man quoted earlier in this section of the chapter, those who were relatively affluent during their working years tend to remain relatively affluent, while those who were poor at earlier stages of life tend to remain poor when they reach late adulthood.

However, the social inequities that various groups experience during their earlier lives become magnified with increasing age. At the same time, people who reach late adulthood today may experience growing economic pressure as a result of the ever-increasing human life span that means it is more likely they will run through their savings.

Overall, 10% of people age 65 and older live in poverty, a proportion that is quite close to that for people less than age 65. However, there are significant differences in gender and racial groups. For instance, women are almost twice as likely as men to be living in poverty. Of those elderly women living alone, around one-fourth live on incomes below the poverty line. A married woman may also slip into poverty if she becomes widowed, for she may have used up savings to pay for her husband's final illness, and the husband's pension may cease with his death (Spraggins, 2003; see Figure 18-2).

Furthermore, 8% of whites in late adulthood live below the poverty level, 19% of Hispanics, and 24% of African Americans. Minority women fare the worst of any category. For example, divorced black women aged 65 to 74 had a poverty rate of 47% (Rank & Hirschl, 1999; Federal Interagency Forum on Age-Related Statistics, 2000; U.S. Bureau of the Census, 2005).

One source of financial vulnerability for people in late adulthood is the reliance on a fixed income for support. Unlike that of a younger person, the income of an elderly person, which typically comes from a combination of Social Security benefits, pensions, and savings, rarely keeps up with inflation. Consequently, as inflation drives up the price of goods such as food and clothing, income does not rise as quickly. What may have been a reasonable income at age 65 is worth much less 20 years later, as the elderly person gradually slips into poverty.

The rising cost of health care is another source of financial vulnerability in older adults. The average older person spends close to 20% of his or her income for health-care costs. For those who require care in nursing home facilities, the financial costs can be staggering, running an average of more than $75,190 a year (MetLife Mature Market Institute, 2007).

FIGURE 18-2 **POVERTY AND THE ELDERLY**

While 10% of those 65 years of age and older live in poverty, women are almost twice as likely as men to be living in poverty.

(*Source:* U.S. Bureau of the Census, 2005.)

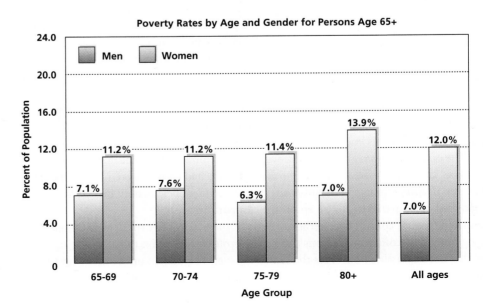

During late adulthood, the range of socioeconomic well-being mirrors that of earlier years.

Unless major changes are made in the way that Social Security and Medicare are financed, the costs borne by younger U.S. citizens in the workforce must rise significantly. Increasing expenditures mean that a larger proportion of younger people's pay must be taxed to fund benefits for the elderly. Such a situation is apt to lead to increasing friction and segregation between younger and older generations. Indeed, as we'll see, Social Security payments are one key factor in many people's decisions about how long to work.

Work and Retirement in Late Adulthood

It's 5 a.m., and Arthur Winston pulls into his parking space and clocks in, just as he has every workday for 70 years.

"They tell me I'm a workaholic," says Winston.

Winston, a cleaning supervisor at a Los Angeles bus yard, turned 98 this month. He's never been late, never called in sick and never punched out early.

"I just love to come to work here," he says . . .

So what's his secret?

"I don't smoke, and I don't drink and I don't fool with these credit cards," he says . . .

Asked if he has any desire to retire, Winston says, "No, no, no, no."

Maybe when he's 100. Until then, he'll take it one day at a time.

"It's nice to walk out in the morning and say, 'Thank God. Let me see another day that I've never seen before. Just one,'" says Winston. (Whitaker, 2004)

Deciding when to retire is a major decision faced by the majority of individuals in late adulthood. Some, like Arthur Winston, wish to work as long as they can. Others retire the moment their financial circumstances permit it.

When they do retire, many people experience a fair amount of difficulty in making the identity shift from "worker" to "retiree." They lack a professional title, they may no longer have people asking them for advice, and they can't say "I work for the Diamond Company."

For others, though, retirement represents a major opportunity, offering the chance to lead, perhaps for the first time in adulthood, a life of leisure. Because a significant number of people retire as early as age 55 or 60, and because people's life spans are expanding, many people spend far more time in retirement than in previous generations. Moreover, because the number of people in late adulthood continues to increase, retirees are an increasingly significant and influential segment of the U.S. population. (For more on retirement, see the *From Research to Practice* box.)

Older Workers: Combating Age Discrimination. Many other people continue to work, either full or part time, for some part of late adulthood. That they can do so is largely because of legislation that was passed in the late 1970s, in which mandatory retirement ages were made illegal in almost every profession. Part of broader legislation that makes age discrimination illegal, these laws gave most workers the opportunity either to remain in jobs they held previously or to begin working in entirely different fields (Lindemann & Kadue, 2003).

Whether older adults continue to work because they enjoy the intellectual and social rewards that work provides or because they need to work for financial reasons, many encounter age discrimination. Age discrimination remains a reality despite laws making it illegal. Some

From Research to Practice

Retirement: Looking Back and Looking Forward

> *Darlyn and Chuck Davenport could easily be idling away their retirement in the south of France or some other far-flung resort destination.*
>
> *But most days, you can find the couple reporting for duty gratis at an unlikely storefront.*
>
> *The Windmill Thrift Shop has become something of a second home to the Davenports, who have turned the once-lagging store into a font of revenue for two local nonprofits.*
>
> *"Been there, done that," exclaimed Darlyn Davenport the other day in explaining why she would rather be raising money for charity than be on permanent vacation in a posh overseas villa. (Green, 2005, p. C1)*

Many people think of retirement as a time of slowing down, perhaps withdrawing from an active lifestyle to sit out the rest of one's days in a rocking chair. But the reality is that there are many different possible approaches to retirement, including options for staying just as active while retired as in the preretirement years. Rather than the closing of a book, retirement represents the turning of a new chapter—and the story that unfolds in that new chapter has a lot to do with the retiree's expectations, goals, and preretirement plans (Dittmann, 2004; Goodman, Schlossberg, & Anderson, 2006; Nuttman-Shwartz, 2007).

Based on an extensive series of interviews, psychologist Nancy Schlossberg (2004) has identified six basic paths of retirement:

- *Continuers* use part-time or volunteer work to remain at least partially active in their preretirement work.

- *Involved spectators* take more of a back-seat role in staying connected with their previous fields.

- *Adventurers*, on the other hand, use retirement as a time to explore entirely new pursuits, perhaps including a new field of work.

- *Searchers* try different activities in search of a suitable way to spend their retirement.

- *Easy gliders* don't fret about retirement much and take each day as it comes.

- *Retreaters* become depressed and withdrawn and stop searching for a meaningful pathway through retirement.

The path that a person takes can change over the course of retirement, too, underscoring another fundamental point: Retirement is less of a destination than it is a journey. People who negotiate retirement most successfully are those who see it not as a time of withdrawal and stagnation but as an opportunity for development and exploration (Greer, 2004; Wang, 2007).

For many people, retirement occurs in stages as they withdraw slowly from work—perhaps by dropping to part-time work for a period before retiring altogether. Others put off retirement as long as they can; some simply enjoy their work, while others are increasingly finding that they simply do not have the financial means to retire as employers scale back pension plans and health benefits for retirees (Porter & Walsh, 2005).

Research suggests that it's just as important to prepare psychologically for retirement as it is to prepare financially. Some important considerations include the climate at work and the opportunities for future growth in one's career, relationships with family members, and community ties and activities. It's important for older adults to keep in mind that they don't just retire from work, but they also retire to a new lifestyle. Planning for what that lifestyle will be like—whether it will include part-time work, volunteer work, travel, or other activities, for example—can make a difference in adjustment to retirement (Dittmann, 2004).

- *Besides finances, what do you think are some important factors in deciding on the right time to retire?*

- *What factors might contribute to the specific retirement path a given person takes?*

employers encourage older workers to leave their jobs in order to replace them with younger employees whose salaries will be considerably lower. Furthermore, some employers believe that older workers are not up to the demands of the job or are less willing to adapt to a changing workplace—stereotypes about the elderly that are enduring, despite legislative changes (Moss, 1997).

There is little evidence to support the idea that older workers' ability to perform their jobs declines. In many fields, such as art, literature, science, politics, and even entertainment, it is easy to find examples of people who have made some of their greatest contributions during late adulthood. Even in those few professions that were specifically exempted from laws prohibiting mandatory retirement ages—those involving public safety—the evidence does not support the notion that workers should be retired at an arbitrary age.

For instance, one large-scale, careful study of older police officers, firefighters, and prison guards came to the conclusion that age was not a good predictor of whether a worker was likely to be incapacitated on the job, or the level of his or her general work performance. Instead, a case-by-case analysis of individual workers' performance was a more accurate predictor (Landy & Conte, 2004).

Although age discrimination remains a problem, market forces may help reduce its severity. As baby boomers retire and the workforce drastically shrinks, companies may begin to offer incentives to older adults to either remain in the workforce or to return to it after they have retired. Still, for most older adults, retirement is the norm.

Retirement: Filling a Life of Leisure.   Why do people decide to retire? Although the basic reason seems apparent—to stop working—the retirement decision is actually based on a variety of factors. For instance, sometimes workers are burned out after a lifetime of work; they seek a respite from the tension and frustration of their jobs and from the sense that they are not accomplishing as much as they once wished they could. Others retire because their health has declined, and still others because they are offered incentives by their employers in the form of bonuses or increased pensions if they retire by a certain age. Finally, some people have planned for years to retire and intend to use their increased leisure to travel, study, or spend more time with their children and grandchildren (Beehr et al., 2000; Nimrod & Adoni, 2006; Sener, Terzioglu, & Karabulut, 2007).

Whatever the reason they retire, people often pass through a series of retirement stages, summarized in Table 18-1. Retirement may begin with a *honeymoon* period, in which former workers engage in a variety of activities, such as travel, that were previously hindered by full-time work. The next phase may be *disenchantment*, in which retirees conclude that retirement

Table 18-1	Stages of Retirement
Stage	**Characteristic**
Honeymoon	In this period, former workers engage in a variety of activities, such as travel, that were previously hindered by working full time.
Disenchantment	In this stage, retirees feel that retirement is not all that they thought it would be. They may miss the stimulation of a job or may find it difficult to keep busy.
Reorientation	At this point, retirees reconsider their options and become engaged in new, more fulfilling activities. If successful, it leads them to the next stage.
Retirement Routine	Here the retiree comes to grips with the realities of retirement and feels fulfilled with this new phase of life. Not all reach this stage; some may feel disenchanted with retirement for years.
Termination	Although some people terminate retirement by going back to work, termination occurs for most people because of major physical deterioration where their health becomes so bad they can no longer function independently.

(*Source:* Atchley, 1982.)

Retirement is a different journey for each individual. Some are content with a more sedate lifestyle, while others continue to remain active and in some cases pursue new activities. Can you explain why many non-Western cultures do not follow the disengagement theory of retirement?

is not all they thought it would be. They may miss the stimulation and companionship of their previous jobs, or they may find it hard to keep busy (Atchley, 1985; Atchley & Barusch, 2005).

The next phase is *reorientation*, in which retirees reconsider their options and become engaged in new, more fulfilling activities. If successful, this leads to the *retirement routine* stage, in which they come to grips with the realities of retirement and feel fulfilled in this new phase of life. Not all people reach this stage; some may feel disenchanted with retirement for years.

Finally, the last phase of the retirement process is *termination*. Although some people terminate retirement by going back to work, termination for most people results from major physical deterioration. In this case, health becomes so bad that the person can no longer function independently. Obviously, not everyone passes through all these stages, and the sequence is not universal. In large measure, a person's reactions to retirement stem from the reasons he or she retired in the first place. For example, a person forced into retirement for health reasons will have a very different experience from a person who eagerly chose to retire at a particular age. Similarly, the retirement of people who loved their jobs may be a quite different experience from that of people who despised their work.

In short, the psychological consequences of retirement vary a great deal from one individual to the next. For many people, though, retirement is a continuation of a life well lived, and they use it to the fullest. Moreover, as we see in the *Becoming an Informed Consumer of Development* feature, there are several things one can do to plan a good retirement.

Becoming an Informed Consumer of Development

Planning for—and Living—a Good Retirement

What makes for a good retirement? Gerontologists suggest that several factors are related to success (Kreitlow & Kreitlow, 1997; Rowe & Kahn, 1998):

- **Plan ahead financially.** Because most financial experts suggest that Social Security pensions will be inadequate in the future, personal savings are critical. Similarly, having adequate healthcare insurance is essential.

- **Consider tapering off from work gradually.** Sometimes it is possible to enter into retirement by shifting from full-time to part-time work. Such a transition may be helpful in preparing for eventual full-time retirement.
- **Explore your interests before you retire.** Assess what you like about your current job and think how that might be translated into leisure activities.
- **If you are married or in a long-term partnership, spend some time discussing your views of the ideal retirement with your partner.** You may find that you need to negotiate a vision that will suit you both.
- **Consider where you want to live.** Try out, temporarily, a community to which you are thinking of moving.
- **Determine the advantages and disadvantages of downsizing your current home.**
- **Plan to volunteer your time.** People who retire have an enormous wealth of skills, and these are often needed by nonprofit organizations and small businesses. Organizations such as the Retired Senior Volunteer Program and the Foster Grandparent Program can help match your skills with people who need them.

Review and Apply

Review

- Elderly people live in a variety of settings, although most live at home with a family member.
- Financial issues can trouble older people, largely because their incomes are fixed, healthcare costs are increasing, and the life span is lengthening.
- People may pass through stages, including a honeymoon period, disenchantment, reorientation, retirement routine, and termination, as they adjust to retirement.

Applying Lifespan Development

- Based on the research on successful aging, what advice would you give someone who is nearing retirement?
- *From the perspective of a healthcare professional:* What policies might a nursing home institute to minimize the chances that its residents will develop "institutionalism"? Why are such policies relatively uncommon?

Relationships: Old and New

"Well, I tell you," says Eva Solymosi, and so she does, starting at the beginning when she first met Joseph. The youngest of 13, she was a poor cook in Hungary, befriended by an old woman who shared this advice: "When a kind face comes by, keep him."

Eva saw Joseph, an 18-year-old chimney sweep, getting a drink of cold water by the public well. "He had a kind face. So that's it," she says and shrugs. They married the next year, moved to the U.S., and have been together since. She is 97 and he is 93....

They are partners. When one is telling a story, the other quietly gets up and fetches a pertinent picture or letter. They share the chores and praise the other's efforts....

When Joseph is shopping or watching the news, Eva will spend hours going through her dozen photo albums. There is Joseph as a young man reading the newspaper, Eva eating an ear of corn in the 1920s, their first Christmas tree . . . She comes across a picture of him when he was 18. "Ah ha, that is the kind face I fell in love with. In my eyes he is still as handsome." He says nothing, but gently taps her cane with his. (Ansberry, 1995, pp. A1, A17)

The warmth and affection between Joseph and Eva are unmistakable. Their relationship, spanning eight decades, continues to bring them quiet joy, and their life is the sort to which many couples aspire. Yet it is also something of a rarity for those in the last stage of life. For every older person who is part of a couple, many more are alone.

What is the nature of the social world of people in late adulthood? To answer the question, we will first consider the nature of marriage in that period.

Marriage in the Later Years: Together, Then Alone

It's a man's world—at least when it comes to marriage after the age of 65. The proportion of men who are married at this age is far greater than that of women (see Figure 18-3). One reason for this disparity is that 70% of women outlive their husbands by at least a few years. Because there are fewer men available (many have died), these women are unlikely to remarry (Barer, 1994).

Furthermore, the marriage gradient that we first discussed in Chapter 14 is still a powerful influence. Reflecting societal norms that suggest that women should marry men older than themselves, the marriage gradient works to keep women single even in the later years of life. At the same time, it makes remarriage for men much easier, since the available pool of eligible partners is much larger (Treas & Bengtson, 1987; AARP, 1990).

The vast majority of people who are still married in later life report that they are satisfied with their marriages. Their partners provide substantial companionship and emotional support. Because at this period in life they have typically been together for a long time, they have great insight into their partners (Brubaker, 1991; Levenson, Carstensen, & Gottman, 1993; Jose & Alfons, 2007).

At the same time, not every aspect of marriage is equally satisfying, and marriages may undergo severe stress as spouses experience changes in their lives. For instance, the retirement of one or both spouses can bring about a shift in the nature of a couple's relationship (Askham, 1994; Henry, Miller, & Giarrusso, 2005).

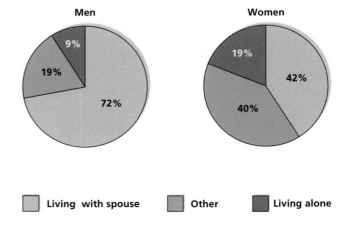

FIGURE 18-3 LIVING PATTERNS OF OLDER AMERICANS

What, if anything, do these patterns suggest about the relative health and adjustment of older men and women?

(*Source:* Administration on Aging, 2006.)

 Living with spouse ▪ Other ▪ Living alone

For some couples, the stress is so great that one spouse or the other seeks a divorce. Although the exact numbers are hard to come by, at least 2% of divorces in the United States involve women over the age of 60 (Uhlenberg, Cooney, & Boyd, 1990).

The reasons for divorce at such a late stage of life are varied. Often, women who divorce do so because their husbands are abusive or alcoholic. But in the more frequent case of a husband seeking a divorce from his wife, the reason is often that he has found a younger woman. Often the divorce occurs soon after retirement, when men who have been highly involved in their careers are in psychological turmoil (Cain, 1982; Solomon et al., 1998).

Divorce so late in life is particularly difficult for women. Between the marriage gradient and the limited size of the potential pool of eligible men, it is unlikely that an older divorced woman will remarry. Divorce in late adulthood can be devastating. For many women, marriage has been their primary role and the center of their identities, and they may view divorce as a major failure. As a consequence, happiness and the quality of life for divorced women often plummet (Goldscheider, 1994; Davies & Denton, 2002).

Seeking a new relationship becomes a priority for many men and women who are divorced or whose spouses have died. As in earlier stages of life, people seeking to develop relationships use a variety of strategies to meet potential partners, such as joining singles organizations or even using the Internet to seek out companionship (Durbin, 2003).

It is important to keep in mind that some people enter late adulthood having never married. For those who have remained single throughout their lives—about 5% of the population—late adulthood may bring fewer transitions, since the status of living alone does not change. In fact, never-married individuals report feeling less lonely than do most people their age, and they have a greater sense of independence (Essex & Nam, 1987; Newston & Keith, 1997).

Dealing with Retirement: Too Much Togetherness?   When Morris Abercrombie finally stopped working full time, his wife, Roxanne, found some aspects of his increased presence at home troubling. Although their marriage was strong, his intrusion into her daily routine and his constant questioning about whom she was on the phone with and where she was going when she went out were irksome. Finally, she began to wish he would spend less time around the house. It was an ironic thought: She had passed much of Morris's preretirement years wishing that he would spend more time at home.

The situation in which Morris and Roxanne found themselves is not unique. For many couples, retirement means that relationships need to be renegotiated. In some cases, retirement results in a couple's spending more time together than at any other point in their marriage. In others, retirement alters the longstanding distribution of household chores, with men taking on more responsibility than before for the everyday functioning of the household.

In fact, research suggests that an interesting role reversal often takes place. In contrast to the early years of marriage, when wives, more than husbands, typically desire greater companionship with their spouses, in late adulthood husbands' companionship needs tend to be greater than their wives'. The power structure of marriage also changes: Men become more affiliative and less competitive following retirement. At the same time, women become more assertive and autonomous (Blumstein & Schwartz, 1989; Bird & Melville, 1994).

Caring for an Aging Spouse.   The shifts in health that accompany late adulthood sometimes require women and men to care for their spouses in ways that they never envisioned. Consider, for example, one woman's comments of frustration:

> I cry a lot because I never thought it would be this way. I didn't expect to be mopping up the bathroom, changing him, doing laundry all the time. I was taking care of babies at twenty; now I'm taking care of my husband. (Doress et al., 1987, pp. 199–200)

At the same time, some people view caring for an ailing and dying spouse in a more positive light, regarding it in part as a final opportunity to demonstrate love and devotion. In fact,

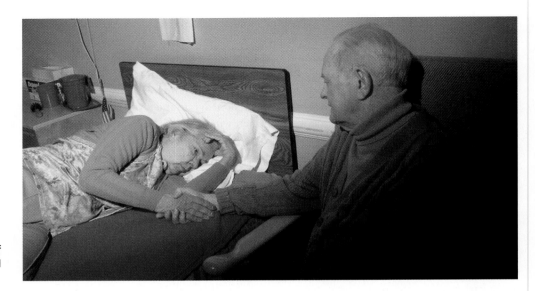

One of the most difficult responsibilities of later adulthood can be caring for one's ill spouse.

some caregivers report feeling quite satisfied as a result of fulfilling what they see as their responsibility to their spouse. And some of those who experience emotional distress initially find that the distress declines as they successfully adapt to the stress of caregiving (Lawton et al., 1989; Townsend et al., 1989; Zarit & Reid, 1994).

Yet even if giving care is viewed in such a light, there is no getting around the fact that it is an arduous chore, made more difficult by the fact that the spouses providing the care are probably not in the peak of physical health themselves. In fact, caregiving may be detrimental to the provider's own physical and psychological health. For instance, caregivers report lower levels of satisfaction with life than do noncaregivers (Vitaliano, Dougherty, & Siegler, 1994; Grant, Weaver, & Elliott, 2004; Choi & Marks, 2006).

In most cases, it should be noted, the spouse who provides the care is the wife. Just under three-quarters of people who provide care to a spouse are women. Part of the reason is demographic: Men tend to die earlier than women, and consequently they contract the diseases leading to death earlier than women. A second reason, though, relates to society's traditional gender roles, which view women as "natural" caregivers. As a consequence, health-care providers may be more likely to suggest that a wife care for her husband than that a husband care for his wife (Polansky, 1976; Unger & Crawford, 1992).

The Death of a Spouse: Becoming Widowed. Hardly any event is more painful and stressful than the death of one's spouse. Especially for those who married young, the death of a spouse leads to profound feelings of loss and often brings about drastic changes in economic and social circumstances. If the marriage has been a good one, the death of the partner means the loss of a companion, a lover, a confidante, a helper.

Upon a partner's death, spouses suddenly assume a new and unfamiliar societal role: widowhood. At the same time, they lose the role with which they were most familiar: spouse. Abruptly, widowed people are no longer part of a couple; instead they are viewed by society, and themselves, solely as individuals. All this occurs as they are dealing with profound and sometimes overwhelming grief (which we discuss more in Chapter 19).

Widowhood brings a variety of new demands and concerns. There is no longer a companion with whom to share the day's events. If the deceased spouse primarily carried out household chores, the surviving spouse must learn how to do these tasks and must perform them every day. Although initially family and friends provide a great deal of support, this assistance quickly fades into the background, and newly widowed people are left to make the adjustment to being single on their own (Wortman & Silver, 1990; Hanson & Hayslip, 2000).

People's social lives often change drastically following the death of a spouse. Married couples tend to socialize with other married couples; widowed individuals may feel like "fifth wheels" as they seek to maintain the friendships they enjoyed as a member of a couple. Eventually, such friendships may cease, although they may be replaced by friendships with other single people (van den Hoonaard, 1994).

Economic issues are of major concern to many widowed people. Although many have insurance, savings, and pensions to provide economic security, some individuals, most often women, experience a decline in their economic well-being as the result of a spouse's death, as noted earlier in this chapter. In such cases, the change in financial status can force wrenching decisions, such as selling the house in which the couple spent their entire married lives (Meyer, Wolf, & Himes, 2006).

The process of adjusting to widowhood encompasses three stages (see Figure 18-4). In the first stage, *preparation*, spouses prepare, in some cases years and even decades ahead of time, for the eventual death of the partner. Consider, for instance, the purchase of life insurance, the preparation of a will, and the decision to have children who may eventually provide care in one's old age. Each of these actions helps prepare for the eventuality that one will be widowed and will require some degree of assistance (Heinemann & Evans, 1990; Roecke & Cherry, 2002).

The second stage of adjustment to widowhood, *grief and mourning*, is an immediate reaction to the death of a spouse. It starts with the shock and pain of loss and continues as

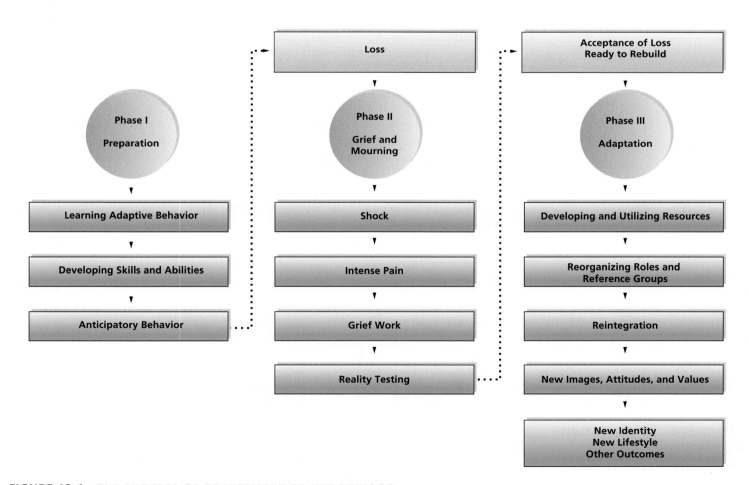

FIGURE 18-4   THE PROCESS OF ADJUSTMENT TO WIDOWHOOD

Do you think the process of adjustment is identical for men and women?

(*Source:* Based on Heinemann & Evans, 1990.)

the survivor works through the period of emotions the loss brings up. The length of time a person spends in this period depends on the degree of support received from others, as well as on personality factors. In some cases, the grief and mourning period may last for years, while in others it lasts a few months.

The last stage of adjustment to the death of a spouse is *adaptation*. In adaptation, the widowed individual starts a new life. The period begins with the acceptance of one's loss and continues with the reorganization of roles and the formation of new friendships. The adaptation stage also encompasses a period of reintegration in which a new identity—as an unmarried person—is developed.

It is important to keep in mind that this three-stage model of loss and change does not apply to everyone. Furthermore, the timing of the various stages in the model differs substantially from one person to the next. Still, for most people, life returns to normal and becomes enjoyable once again.

Without exception, the death of a spouse is a profound event in any period of life. During late adulthood, its implications are particularly powerful, since it can be seen as a forewarning of one's own mortality. Friends can help the surviving spouse move forward.

The Social Networks of Late Adulthood

Elderly people enjoy friends as much as younger people do, and friendships play an important role in the lives of those in late adulthood. In fact, time spent with friends is often valued more highly during late adulthood than time spent with family, and friends are often seen as more important providers of support than family members. Furthermore, around a third of older persons report that they made a new friend within the past year, and many older adults engage in significant interaction (see Figure 18-5; Hartshorne, 1994; Hansson & Carpenter, 1994; Ansberry, 1997).

Friendship: Why Friends Matter in Late Adulthood.   One reason for the importance of friendship relates to the element of control. In friendship relationships, unlike family relationships, we choose whom we like and whom we dislike, meaning that we have considerable control. Because late adulthood may bring with it a gradual loss of control in other areas, such as in one's health, the ability to maintain friendships may take on more importance than in other stages of life (Krause & Borawski-Clark, 1994; Pruchno & Rosenbaum, 2003; Stevens, Martina, & Westerhof, 2006).

FIGURE 18-5   SOCIAL ACTIVITY IN LATE ADULTHOOD

Friends and family play an important role in the social activities of the elderly.

(*Source:* Federal Interagency Forum on Age Related Statistics, 2000.)

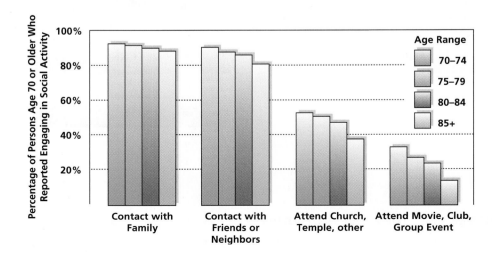

In addition, friendships—especially ones that have developed recently—may be more flexible than family ties, given that recent friendships are not likely to have a history of obligations and past conflicts. In contrast, family ties may have a long and sometimes stormy record that can reduce the emotional sustenance they provide (Hartshorne, 1994; Magai & McFadden, 1996).

Another reason for the importance of friendships in late adulthood relates to the increasing likelihood, over time, that one will be without a marital partner. When a spouse dies, people typically seek out the companionship of friends to help deal with their loss and also for some of the companionship that was provided by the deceased spouse.

Of course, it isn't only spouses who die during old age; friends die too. The way adults view friendship in late adulthood determines how vulnerable they are to the death of a friend. If the friendship has been defined as irreplaceable, then the loss of the friend may be quite difficult. On the other hand, if the friendship is defined as one of many friendships, then the death of a friend may be less traumatic. In such cases, older adults are more likely to become involved subsequently with new friends (Hartshorne, 1994).

It has been found that the benefits of social support are considerable, benefiting both the provider and receiver. What is the importance of reciprocity as a factor of social support?

Social Support: The Significance of Others.   Friendships also provide one of the basic social needs: social support. **Social support** is assistance and comfort supplied by a network of caring, interested people. Such support plays a critical role in successful aging (Antonucci, 1990; Antonucci & Akiyama, 1991; Avlund, Lund, & Holstein, 2004).

The benefits of social support are considerable. For instance, people can provide emotional support by lending a sympathetic ear and providing a sounding board for one's concerns. Furthermore, social support from people who are experiencing similar problems—such as the loss of a spouse—can provide an unmatched degree of understanding and a pool of helpful suggestions for coping strategies that would be less credible coming from others.

Finally, people can furnish material support, such as helping with rides or picking up groceries. They can provide help in solving problems, such as dealing with a difficult landlord or fixing a broken appliance.

The benefits of social support extend not only to the recipient of the support, but to the provider. People who offer support experience feelings of usefulness and heightened self-esteem, knowing that they are making a contribution to others' welfare.

What kinds of social support are most effective and appropriate? It can vary from preparing food, accompanying someone to a movie, or inviting someone to dinner. But the opportunity for reciprocity is important, too. Reciprocity is the expectation that if someone provides something positive to another person, eventually, the favor will be returned. In Western societies, older adults—like younger people—value relationships in which reciprocity is possible (Clark & Mills, 1993; Becker, Beyene, & Newsom, 2003).

With increasing age, it may be progressively more difficult to reciprocate the social support that one receives. As a consequence, relationships may become more asymmetrical, placing the recipient in a difficult psychological position (Roberto, 1987; Selig, Tomlinson, & Hickey, 1991).

Family Relationships: The Ties That Bind

Even after the death of a spouse, most older adults are part of a larger family unit. Connections with siblings, children, grandchildren, and even great-grandchildren continue, and they may provide an important source of comfort to adults in the last years of their lives.

social support   assistance and comfort supplied by another person or a network of caring, interested people.

Siblings may provide unusually strong emotional support during late adulthood. Because they often share old, pleasant memories of childhood, and because they usually represent the oldest existing relationships a person has, siblings can provide important support. While not every memory of childhood may be pleasant, continuing interaction with brothers and sisters still provides substantial emotional support during late adulthood (Bengston, Rosenthal, & Burton, 1990; Moyer 1992).

Children.   Even more important than siblings, however, are children and grandchildren. Even in an age in which geographic mobility is high, most parents and children remain fairly close, both geographically and psychologically. Some 75% of children live within a 30-minute drive of their parents, and parents and children visit and talk with one another frequently. Daughters tend to be in more frequent contact with their parents than sons, and mothers tend to receive more communication more frequently than fathers (Field & Minkler, 1988; Krout, 1988; Ji-liang, Li-qing, & Yan, 2003).

Because the great majority of older adults have at least one child who lives fairly close, family members still provide significant aid to one another. Moreover, parents and children tend to share similar views of how adult children should behave toward their parents (see Table 18-2). In particular, they expect that children should help their parents understand their resources, provide emotional support, and talk over matters of importance such as

Table 18-2	Parents and Children Share Similar Views of How Adult Children Should Behave Toward Their Parents	
Item	**Children's Rank**	**Parent's Rank**
Help understand resources	1	2
Give emotional support	2	3
Discuss matters of importance	3	1
Make room in home in emergency	4	7
Sacrifice personal freedom	5	6
Care when sick	6	9
Be together on special occasions	7	5
Provide financial help	8	13
Give parents advice	9	4
Adjust family schedule to help	10	10
Feel responsible for parent	11	8
Adjust work schedule to help	12	12
Believe that parent should live with child	13	15
Visit once a week	14	11
Live close to parent	15	16
Write once a week	16	14

(*Source:* Adapted from Hamon & Blieszner, 1990.)

medical issues. Furthermore, it is most often children who end up caring for their aging parents when they require assistance (Wolfson et al., 1993; Dellmann-Jenkins & Brittain, 2003; Ron, 2006).

The bonds between parents and children are sometimes asymmetrical, with parents seeking a closer relationship and children a more distant one. Parents have a greater *developmental stake* in close ties, since they see their children as perpetuating their beliefs, values, and standards. On the other hand, children are motivated to maintain their autonomy and live independently from their parents. These divergent perspectives make parents more likely to minimize conflicts they experience with their children, and children more likely to maximize them (Bengston et al., 1985; O'Connor, 1994).

For parents, their children remain a source of great interest and concern. Some surveys show, for instance, that even in late adulthood parents talk about their children nearly every day, particularly if the children are having some sort of problem. At the same time, children may turn to their elderly parents for advice, information, and sometimes tangible help, such as money (Greenberg & Becker, 1988).

Grandchildren and Great-Grandchildren.   As we discussed first in Chapter 16, not all grandparents are equally involved with their grandchildren. Even those grandparents who take great pride in their grandchildren may be relatively detached from them, avoiding any direct care role (Cherlin & Furstenberg, 1986).

As we saw, grandmothers tend to be more involved with their grandchildren than grandfathers; similarly, there are gender differences in the feelings grandchildren have toward their grandparents. Specifically, most young adult grandchildren feel closer to their grandmothers than to their grandfathers. In addition, most express a preference for their maternal grandmothers over their paternal grandmothers (Kalliopuska, 1994; Chan & Elder, 2000; Hayslip, Shore, & Henderson, 2000; Lavers-Preston & Sonuga-Barke, 2003).

African American grandparents tend to be more involved with their grandchildren than white grandparents, and African American grandchildren often feel closer to their grandparents. Moreover, grandfathers seem to play a more central role in the lives of African American children than in the lives of white children. The reason for these racial differences probably stems in large measure from the higher proportion of multigenerational families among African Americans than among whites. In such families, grandparents usually play a central role in child rearing (Taylor et al., 1991; Crowther & Rodriguez, 2003; Stevenson, Henderson, & Baugh, 2007).

Great-grandchildren play less of a role in the lives of both white and African American great-grandparents. Most great-grandparents do not have close relationships with their great-grandchildren. Close relationships tend to occur only when the great-grandparents and great-grandchildren live relatively near one another (Doka & Mertz, 1988).

There are several explanations for the relative lack of involvement of great-grandparents with great-grandchildren. One is that by the time they reach great-grandparenthood, elderly adults are so old that they do not have much physical or psychological energy to expend on forming relationships with their great-grandchildren. Another is that there may be so many great-grandchildren that great-grandparents do not feel strong emotional ties to them. In fact, it is not uncommon for a great-grandparent who has had a large number of children to have so many great-grandchildren that they are difficult to keep track of. For example, when President John Kennedy's mother, Rose Kennedy (who had given birth to a total of nine children), died at the age of 104, she had 30 grandchildren and 41 great-grandchildren!

Still, even though most great-grandparents may not have close relationships with their great-grandchildren, they still profit emotionally from the mere fact that they have great-grandchildren.

elder abuse   the physical or psychological mistreatment or neglect of elderly individuals.

For instance, great-grandparents may see their great-grandchildren as representing both their own and their family's continuation, as well as providing a concrete sign of their longevity (Doka & Mertz, 1988).

Elder Abuse: Relationships Gone Wrong

With good health and a sizable pension, 76-year-old Mary T. should have been enjoying a comfortable retirement. But in fact, her life was made miserable by a seemingly endless barrage of threats, insults, and indignities from her live-in adult son.

A habitual gambler and drug user, the son was merciless: he spat at Mary, brandished a knife in her face, stole her money, and sold her possessions. After several emergency room trips and two hospitalizations, social workers convinced Mary to move out and join a support group of other elderly people abused by their loved ones. With a new apartment and understanding friends, Mary finally had some peace. But her son found her, and feeling a mother's guilt and shame, Mary took him back—and opened another round of heartache. (Minaker & Frishman, 1995, p. 9)

It would be easy to assume that such cases are rare. The truth of the matter, however, is that they are considerably more common than we would like to believe. According to some estimates, **elder abuse**, the physical or psychological mistreatment or neglect of elderly individuals, may affect as many as 2 million people above the age of 60 each year. Even these estimates may be too low, since people who are abused are often too embarrassed or humiliated to report their plight. And as the number of elderly people increases, experts believe that the number of cases of elder abuse will also rise (Brubaker, 1991).

Elder abuse is most frequently directed at family members and particularly at elderly parents. Those most at risk are likely to be less healthy and more isolated than the average person in late adulthood, and they are more likely to be living in a caregiver's home. Although there is no single cause for elder abuse, it often is the result of a combination of economic, psychological, and social pressures on caregivers who must provide high levels of care 24 hours a day. Thus, people with Alzheimer's disease or other sorts of dementia are particularly likely to be targets of abuse (Dyer et al., 2000; Arai, 2006; Jayawardena & Liao, 2006; Nahmiash, 2006; Tauriac & Scruggs, 2006; Baker, 2007).

The best approach to dealing with elder abuse is to prevent it from occurring in the first place. Family members caring for an older adult should take occasional breaks. Social support agencies can be contacted; they can provide advice and concrete support. For instance, the National Family Caregivers Association (800-896-3650) maintains a caregivers' network and publishes a newsletter. Anyone suspecting that an elderly person is being abused should contact local authorities, such as their state's Adult Protective Services or Elder Protective Services.

Review and Apply

Review

- While marriages in older adulthood are generally happy, stresses due to aging can bring divorce.
- Retirement often requires a reworking of power relationships within the marriage.
- The death of a spouse brings highly significant psychological, social, and material changes to the survivor.
- Friendships are very important in later life, providing social support and companionship from peers who are likely to understand the older adult's feelings and problems.
- Family relationships are a continuing part of most older people's lives, especially relationships with siblings and children.
- Elder abuse typically involves a socially isolated elderly parent in poor health and a caregiver who feels burdened by the parent.

Applying Lifespan Development

- What are some ways the retirement of a spouse can bring stress to a marriage? Is retirement likely to be less stressful in households where both spouses work, or twice as stressful?
- *From the perspective of a social worker:* What are some factors that can combine to make older adulthood a more difficult time for women than for men?

Epilogue

Social and personality development continues in the last years of life. In this chapter, we focused on the question of change versus stability in personality and the sorts of life events that can affect personality development. We debunked a few stereotypes as we looked at the ways older people live and at the effects of retirement. Relationships, especially marital and family relationships but also friendships and social networks, are important to the well-being of older adults.

Turn back to the prologue of this chapter, about the late-in-life marriage of Geraldine Mooers and Dick Thomas, and answer the following questions:

1. What aspects of Geraldine's and Dick's personalities can be deduced from the prologue?

2. Based on evidence in the prologue, how do you think they are managing what Erikson calls the ego-integrity-versus-despair stage? How about Peck's developmental tasks?

3. In what ways are they accomplishing life review? Does this process appear to be harmful or helpful to them?

4. If Geraldine and Dick chose disengagement as a strategy in late adulthood, what would you expect their lives to be like? What if they chose the activity strategy? Is there evidence to suggest which approach they are taking?

5. Geraldine and Dick still live together in their own home. In what ways might their lives differ from those of other elderly individuals who have lost a spouse or live under different circumstances?

Looking Back

■ **In what ways does personality develop during late adulthood?**

• In Erikson's ego-integrity-versus-despair stage of psychosocial development, as people reflect on their lives, they may feel either satisfaction, which leads to integration, or dissatisfaction, which can lead to despair and a lack of integration.

• Robert Peck identifies the three main tasks of this period as redefinition of self versus preoccupation with work role, body transcendence versus body preoccupation, and ego transcendence versus ego preoccupation.

• Daniel Levinson identifies a transitional stage that people pass through on the way to late adulthood, during which they struggle with being "old" and with societal stereotypes. A successful transition can lead to liberation and self-respect.

• Bernice Neugarten identified four personality types according to the way they cope with aging: disintegrated and disorganized, passive-dependent, defended, and integrated.

• Life review, a common theme of developmental theories of late adulthood, can help people resolve past conflicts and achieve wisdom and serenity, but some people become obsessive about past errors and slights.

• Age stratification theories suggest that the unequal distribution of economic resources, power, and privilege is particularly pronounced during late adulthood. In general, Western societies do not hold elderly people in as high esteem as many Asian societies.

■ **How do people deal with aging?**

• Disengagement theory and activity theory present opposite views of ways to deal successfully with aging. People's choices depend partly on their prior habits and personalities.

• The model of selective optimization with compensation involves focusing on personally important areas of functioning and compensating for ability losses in those areas.

■ **In what circumstances do older people live, and what difficulties do they face?**

• Living arrangement options include staying at home, living with family members, participating in adult day care, residing in continuing-care communities, and living in skilled-nursing facilities.

• Elderly people may become financially vulnerable because they must cope with rising health-care expenses and other costs on a fixed income.

■ **What is it like to retire?**

• People who retire must fill an increasingly longer span of leisure time. Those who are most successful plan ahead and have varied interests.

• People who retire often pass through stages, including a honeymoon period, disenchantment, reorientation, a retirement routine stage, and termination.

■ **How do marriages in late adulthood fare?**

• Marriages in later life generally remain happy, although stresses brought about by major life changes that accompany aging can cause rifts. Divorce is usually harder on the woman than the man, partly because of the continuing influence of the marriage gradient.

• Deterioration in the health of a spouse can cause the other spouse—typically the wife—to become a caregiver, which can bring both challenges and rewards.

■ **What happens when an elderly spouse dies?**

• The death of a spouse forces the survivor to assume a new societal role, accommodate to the absence of a companion and chore-sharer, create a new social life, and resolve financial problems.

• Sociologists Gloria Heinemann and Patricia Evans have identified three stages in adjusting to widowhood: preparation, grief and mourning, and adaptation. Some people never reach the adaptation stage.

■ **What sorts of relationships are important in late adulthood?**

• Friendships are important in later life because they offer personal control, companionship, and social support.

• Family relationships, especially with siblings and children, provide a great deal of emotional support for people in later life.

• In the increasingly prevalent phenomenon of elder abuse, parents who are socially isolated and in poor health may be abused by children who are forced to act as caregivers.

Key Terms and Concepts

ego-integrity-versus-despair stage (p. 605)

redefinition of self versus preoccupation with work role (p. 605)

body transcendence versus body preoccupation (p. 605)

ego transcendence versus ego preoccupation (p. 606)

life review (p. 608)

age stratification theories (p. 609)

wisdom (p. 610)

disengagement theory (p. 612)

activity theory (p. 613)

continuity theory (p. 614)

selective optimization (p. 614)

continuing-care community (p. 616)

adult day-care facilities (p. 617)

skilled-nursing facilities (p. 617)

institutionalism (p. 617)

social support (p. 629)

elder abuse (p. 632)

19 Death and Dying

Chapter Overview

DYING AND DEATH ACROSS THE LIFE SPAN

Defining Death: Determining the Point at Which Life Ends

Death Across the Life Span: Causes and Reactions

Can Death Education Prepare Us for the Inevitable?

CONFRONTING DEATH

Understanding the Process of Dying: Are There Steps Toward Death?

Choosing the Nature of Death: Is DNR the Way to Go?

Caring for the Terminally Ill: The Place of Death

GRIEF AND BEREAVEMENT

Mourning and Funerals: Final Rites

Bereavement and Grief: Adjusting to the Death of a Loved One

Prologue: Choosing Death

Ted Soulis knew he was about to die. He'd made his peace and said his goodbyes. His family was gathered around him, and he was not afraid. He closed his eyes and slumped over in his chair. His wife let out a gasp.

A hush fell over the room.

And then Mr. Soulis lifted his head, grinned like the devil and said, "Just a little joke."

The room erupted in laughter. It was exactly what everyone would expect of Ted Soulis, a man of great joie de vivre who lived life on his terms.

Mr. Soulis, 69, died a few hours later, with his wife and daughter at his side.

Mr. Soulis was diagnosed last month with an especially aggressive form of brain cancer.

Rather than endure the agony of chemotherapy to eke out a few more months of life, he chose to return home, surround himself with loved ones, and let the cancer run its course. The doctors gave him two weeks to live, so he bought a lot of food and a lot of wine and threw a party that drew 300 people and went on for hours.

"He went out in style," said his daughter, Shana Soulis. "I can't imagine it any differently. It was peaceful, it was beautiful, and it was on his terms." (Squatriglia, 2007, p. B7)

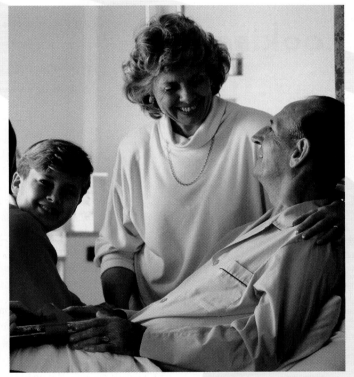

Many people choose a shorter, but higher quality-of-life when given the option.

If ever death can be said to be good, this was a good death. After 69 years, Ted Soulis slipped away in the company of those he loved.

Death is an experience that will happen to all of us at some time, as universal to the human condition as birth. As such, it is a milestone of life that is central to an understanding of the life span.

Only in the past several decades have lifespan developmentalists given serious study to the developmental implications of dying. In this chapter we will discuss death and dying from several perspectives. We begin by considering how we define death—a determination that is more complex than it seems. We then examine how people view and react to death at different points in the life span. And we consider the very different views of death held by various societies.

Next, we look at how people confront their own deaths. We discuss one theory that people move through several stages as they come to grips with their approaching death. We also look at how people use living wills and assisted suicide.

Finally, we consider bereavement and grief. We examine the difficulties in distinguishing normal from unhealthy grief, and we discuss the consequences of a loss. The chapter also looks at mourning and funerals, discussing how people can prepare themselves for the inevitability of death.

After reading this chapter, you will be able to answer these questions:

- **What is death, and what does it mean at different stages of the life span?**
- **In what ways do people face the prospect of their own death?**
- **How do survivors react to and cope with death?**

Looking Ahead

Dying and Death Across the Life Span

It took a major legal and political battle, but eventually Terri Schaivo's husband won the right to remove a feeding tube that had been keeping her alive for 15 years. Lying in a hospital bed all those years in what physicians called a "persistent vegetative state," Schaivo was never expected to regain consciousness after suffering brain damage due to respiratory and cardiac arrest. After a series of court battles, her husband—despite the wishes of her parents—was allowed to direct caretakers to remove the feeding tube; Schaivo died soon afterward.

Was Schaivo's husband right in seeking to remove her feeding tube? Was she already dead when it was removed? Were her constitutional rights unfairly ignored by her husband's action?

The difficulty of answering such questions illustrates the complexity of what are, literally, matters of life and death. Death is not only a biological event; it involves psychological aspects as well. We need to consider not only issues relating to the definition of death, but also the ways in which our conception of death changes across various points in the life span.

Defining Death: Determining the Point at Which Life Ends

What is death? Although the question seems straightforward, defining the point at which life ceases and death occurs is surprisingly complex. Over the last few decades, medicine has advanced to the point where some people who would have been considered dead a few years ago would now be considered alive.

Functional death is defined by an absence of heartbeat and breathing. Although this definition seems unambiguous, it is not completely straightforward. For example, a person whose heart has stopped beating and whose breathing has ceased for as long as 5 minutes may be resuscitated and suffer little damage as a consequence of the experience. Does this mean that the person who is now alive was dead, as the functional definition would have it?

functional death   the absence of a heartbeat and breathing.

Because of this imprecision, heartbeat and respiration are no longer used to determine the moment of death. Medical experts now measure brain functioning. In **brain death**, all signs of brain activity, as measured by electrical brain waves, have ceased. When brain death occurs, there is no possibility of restoring brain functioning.

Some medical experts suggest that a definition of death that relies only on a lack of brain waves is too restrictive. They argue that losing the ability to think, reason, feel, and experience the world may be sufficient to declare a person dead. In this view, which takes psychological considerations into account, a person who suffers irreversible brain damage, who is in a coma, and who will never experience anything approaching a human life can be considered dead. In such a case, the argument goes, death can be judged to have arrived, even if some sort of primitive brain activity is still occurring (Ressner, 2001).

Not surprisingly, such an argument, which moves us from strictly medical criteria to moral and philosophical considerations, is controversial. As a result, the legal definition of death in most localities in the United States relies on the absence of brain functioning, although some laws still include a definition relating to the absence of respiration and heartbeat. The reality is that no matter where a death occurs, in most cases people do not bother to measure brain waves. Usually, the brain waves are closely monitored only in certain circumstances—when the time of death is significant, when organs may potentially be transplanted, or when criminal or legal issues might be involved.

The difficulty in establishing legal and medical definitions of death may reflect some of the changes in understanding and attitudes about death that occur over the course of people's lives.

Death Across the Life Span: Causes and Reactions

Death is something we associate with old age. However, for many individuals, death comes earlier. In such cases, in part because it seems "unnatural" for a younger person to die, the reactions to death are particularly extreme. In the United States today, in fact, some people believe that children should be sheltered—that it is wrong for them to know much about death. Yet people of every age can experience the death of friends and family members, as well as their own death. How do our reactions to death evolve as we age? We will consider several age groups.

Death in Infancy and Childhood. Despite its economic wealth, the United States has a relatively high infant mortality rate, as we first discussed in Chapter 3. Although the rate has declined since the mid-1960s, the United States ranks behind 35 other countries in the proportion of infants who die during the first year of life (Centers for Disease Control, 2004).

As these statistics indicate, the number of parents who experience the death of an infant is substantial, and their reactions may be profound. The loss of a child typically brings up all the same reactions one would experience on the death of an older person, and sometimes even more severe effects as family members struggle to deal with a death at such an early age. One of the most common reactions is extreme depression (DeFrain et al., 1991; Brockington, 1992; Murphy, Johnson, & Wu, 2003).

One kind of death that is exceptionally difficult to deal with is prenatal death, or *miscarriage*, a topic touched on in Chapters 2 and 3. Parents typically form psychological bonds with their unborn child, and consequently they often feel profound grief if it dies before it is born. Moreover, friends and relatives often fail to understand the emotional impact of miscarriage on parents, making parents feel their loss all the more keenly (McGreal, Evans, & Burrows, 1997; Wheeler & Austin, 2001).

Another form of death that produces extreme stress, in part because it is so unanticipated, is sudden infant death syndrome. As we discussed in Chapter 3, in **sudden infant death syndrome**, or **SIDS**, a seemingly healthy baby stops breathing and dies of unexplained causes. Usually occurring between the ages of 2 and 4 months, SIDS strikes unexpectedly; a robust, hardy baby is placed into a crib at nap time or night time and never wakes up.

brain death a diagnosis of death based on the cessation of all signs of brain activity, as measured by electrical brain waves.

sudden infant death syndrome (SIDS) the unexplained death of a seemingly healthy baby.

The most frequent causes of death during childhood are due to motor vehicle crashes, fires, and drowning. However, a substantial number of children in the United States are victims of homicide.

In cases of SIDS, parents often feel intense guilt, and acquaintances may be suspicious of the "true" cause of death. As we discussed in Chapter 3, however, there is no known cause for SIDS, which seems to strike randomly, and parents' guilt is unwarranted (Dyregrov, Nordanger, & Dyregrov, 2003; Hunt & Hauck, 2006; Krueger, 2006; Paterson et al., 2006).

During childhood, the most frequent cause of death is accidents, most of them due to motor vehicle crashes, fires, and drowning. However, a substantial number of children in the United States are victims of homicides, which have nearly tripled in number since 1960. By the early 1990s, death by homicide had become the fourth leading cause of death for children between the ages of 1 and 9 (Finkelhor, 1997; Centers for Disease Control, 2004).

For parents, the death of a child produces the most profound sense of loss and grief. In fact, there is no worse death in the eyes of most parents, including the loss of a spouse or of one's own parents. Parents' extreme reaction is partly based on the sense that the natural order of the world, in which children "should" outlive their parents, has somehow collapsed. Their reaction is often coupled with the feeling that it is their primary responsibility to protect their children from any harm, and they may feel that they have failed in this task when a child dies (Gilbert, 1997; Strength, 1999).

Parents are almost never well equipped to deal with the death of a child, and they may obsessively ask themselves afterward, over and over, why the death occurred. Because the bond between children and parents is so strong, parents sometimes feel that a part of themselves has died as well. The stress is so profound that the loss of a child significantly increases the chances of admission to a hospital for a mental disorder (Stroebe, Stroebe, & Hansson, 1993; Wayment & Vierthaler, 2002; Li et al., 2005; Mahgoub & Lantz, 2006).

Childhood Conceptions of Death. Children themselves do not really begin to develop a concept of death until around the age of 5. Although they are well aware of death before that time, they are apt to think of it as a temporary state that involves a reduction in living, rather than a cessation. For instance, a preschool-age child might say, "dead people don't get hungry—well, maybe a little" (Kastenbaum, 1985, p. 629).

Some preschool-age children think of death in terms of sleep—with the consequent possibility of waking up, just as Sleeping Beauty was awakened in the fairy tale. For children who believe this, death is not particularly fearsome; rather, it is something of a curiosity. If people merely tried hard enough—by administering medicine, providing food, or using magic—dead people might "return" (Lonetto, 1980).

In some cases, children's misunderstanding of death can produce devastating emotional consequences. Children sometimes leap to the erroneous conclusion that they are somehow responsible for a person's death. For instance, they may assume they could have prevented the death by being better behaved. In the same way, they may think that if the person who died really wanted to, she or he could return.

Around the age of 5, children better understand the finality and irreversibility of death. In some cases, children personify death as some kind of ghostlike or devilish figure. At first, though, they do not think of death as universal, but rather as something that happens only to certain people. By about age 9, however, they come to accept the universality of death and its finality (Nagy, 1948). By middle childhood, children also learn about some of the customs involved with death, such as funerals, cremation, and cemeteries.

Death in Adolescence. We might expect the significant advances in cognitive development that occur during adolescence to bring about a sophisticated, thoughtful, and reasoned view of death. However, in many ways, adolescents' views of death are as unrealistic as those of younger children, although along different lines.

Adolescents' views of death may be highly romanticized and dramatic.

While adolescents clearly understand the finality and irreversibility of death, they tend not to think it can happen to them, a fact that can lead to risky behavior. As we discussed in Chapter 11, adolescents develop a *personal fable,* a set of beliefs that causes them to feel unique and special—so special, in fact, that they may believe they are invulnerable and that the bad things that happen to other people won't happen to them (Elkind, 1985).

Many times, this risky behavior causes death in adolescence. For instance, the most frequent cause of death among adolescents is accidents, most often involving motor vehicles. Other frequent causes include homicide, suicide, cancer, and AIDS (National Center for Health Statistics, 1994).

When adolescent feelings of invulnerability confront the likelihood of death due to an illness, the results can be shattering. Adolescents who learn that they have a terminal illness often feel angry and cheated—that life has been unjust to them. Because they feel—and act—so negatively, it may be difficult for medical personnel to treat them effectively.

In contrast, some adolescents diagnosed with a terminal illness react with total denial. Feeling indestructible, they may find it impossible to accept the seriousness of their illness. If it does not interfere with their acceptance of medical treatment, some degree of denial may actually be useful, as it allows an adolescent to continue with his or her normal life as long as possible (Blumberg, Lewis, & Susman, 1984).

Death in Young Adulthood. Young adulthood is the time when most people feel primed to begin their lives. Past the preparatory time of childhood and adolescence, they are on the threshold of making their mark on the world. Because death at such a point in life seems close to unthinkable, its occurrence is particularly difficult. Because they are actively pursuing their goals for life, they are angry and impatient with any illness that threatens their future.

In early adulthood, the leading cause of death continues to be accidents, followed by suicide, homicide, AIDS, and cancer. By the end of early adulthood, however, disease becomes a more prevalent cause of death.

For those people facing death in early adulthood, several concerns are of particular importance. One is the desire to develop intimate relationships and express sexuality, each of which are inhibited, if not completely prevented, by a terminal illness. For instance, people who test positive for the AIDS virus may find it quite difficult to start new relationships. The role of sexual activities within evolving relationships presents even more challenging issues (Rabkin, Remien, & Wilson, 1994).

Another particular concern during young adulthood involves future planning. At a time when most people are mapping out their careers and deciding at what point to start a family, young adults who have a terminal illness face additional burdens. Should they marry, even though it is likely that the partner will soon end up widowed? Should a couple seek to conceive a child if the child is likely to be raised by only one parent? How soon should one's employer be told about a terminal illness, when it is clear that employers sometimes discriminate against unhealthy workers? None of these questions is easily answered.

Like adolescents, young adults sometimes make poor patients. They are outraged at their plight and feel the world is unfair, and they may direct their anger at care providers and loved ones. In addition, they may make the medical staff who provide direct care—nurses and orderlies—feel particularly vulnerable, since the staff themselves are often young (Cook & Oltjenbruns, 1989).

Death in Middle Adulthood. For people in middle adulthood, the shock of a life-threatening disease—which is the most common cause of death in this period—is not so great. In fact, by this point, people are well aware that they are going to die sometime, and they may be able to consider the possibility of death in a fairly realistic manner.

On the other hand, their sense of realism doesn't make the possibility of dying any easier. In fact, fears about death are often greater in middle adulthood than at any time previously—or even in later life. These fears may lead people to look at life in terms of the number of years they have remaining as opposed to their earlier orientation toward the number of years they have already lived (Levinson, 1992).

The most frequent cause of death in middle adulthood is heart attack or stroke. Although the unexpectedness of such a death does not allow for preparation, in some ways it is easier than a slow and painful death from a disease such as cancer. It is certainly the kind of death that most people prefer: When asked, they say they would like an instant and painless death that does not involve loss of any body part (Taylor, 1991).

Death in Late Adulthood. By the time they reach late adulthood, people know with some certainty that their time is coming to an end. Furthermore, they face an increasing number of deaths in their environment. Spouses, siblings, and friends may have already died, a constant reminder of their own mortality.

The most likely causes of death are cancer, stroke, and heart disease during late adulthood. What would happen if these causes of death were eliminated? According to demographers' estimates, the average 70-year-old's life expectancy would increase around 7 years (see Figure 19-1; Hayward, Crimmins, & Saito, 1997).

The prevalence of death in the lives of elderly people makes them less anxious about dying than they were at earlier stages of life. This does not mean that people in late adulthood

FIGURE 19-1 ADDING YEARS

If the major causes of death were eliminated, the average 70-year-old person would live another 7 years.

(*Source:* Hayward, Crimmins, & Saito, 1997.)

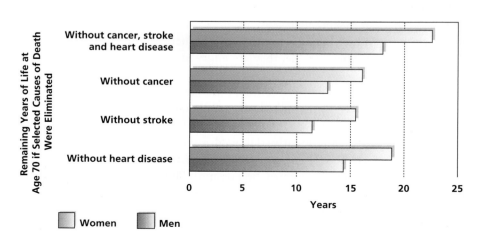

welcome death. Rather, it implies that they are more realistic and reflective about it. They think about death, and they may begin to make preparations for it. As discussed in Chapter 18, some begin to pull away from the world due to diminishing physical and psychological energy (Gesser, Wong, & Reker, 1988; Turner & Helms, 1994).

Impending death is sometimes accompanied by acceleration of declines in cognitive functioning. In what is known as the *terminal decline,* a significant drop in performance in cognitive areas such as memory and reading may foreshadow death within the next few years (Small & Bäckman, 1999; Wilson, Beckett, & Bienias, 2003; Sliwinski et al., 2006; Wilson et al., 2007).

Some elderly individuals actively seek out death, turning to suicide. In fact, the suicide rate for men climbs steadily during the course of late adulthood, and no age group has a higher rate of suicide than white men over the age of 85. (Adolescents and young adults commit suicide in greater numbers, but their *rate* of suicide—the number of suicides as a proportion of the general adolescent population—is actually lower.) Suicide is often a consequence of severe depression or some form of dementia, or it can be due to the loss of a spouse. And, as we will discuss later in the chapter, some individuals, struck down with a terminal illness, seek the assistance of others in committing suicide (Blazer, 1991; De Leo, Conforti, & Carollo, 1997; Chapple et al., 2006).

One particularly important issue for older adults suffering from a terminal illness is whether their lives still have value. More than younger individuals, elderly people who are dying harbor concerns that they are burdens to their family or to society. Furthermore, they may be given the message, sometimes inadvertently, that their value to society has ended and that they have attained the status of "dying" as opposed to being "very sick" (Kastenbaum, 2000).

Do older people wish to know if death is impending? The answer, in most cases, is yes. Like younger patients, who usually state that they wish to know the true nature of an ailment, older people want the details of their illnesses. Ironically, candor is not something caregivers wish to provide: Physicians usually prefer to avoid telling dying patients that their illnesses are terminal (Kaufman, 1992; Goold, Williams, & Arnold, 2000; Hagerty et al., 2004).

On the other hand, not all people wish to learn the truth about their condition or to know that they are dying. In fact, it is important to keep in mind that individuals react to death in substantially different ways. In part, their reaction is produced by personality factors. For example, people who are generally anxious are more concerned about death. In addition, there are significant cultural differences in how people view and react to death, as we consider in the *Developmental Diversity* feature.

Developmental Diversity

Differing Conceptions of Death

In the midst of a tribal celebration, an older man waits for his oldest son to place a cord around his neck. The older man has been sick, and he is ready to relinquish his ties to this earthly world. He asks that his son lift him to his death, and the son complies.

***

To Hindus in India, death is not an ending, but rather part of a continual cycle. Because they believe in reincarnation, death is thought to be followed by rebirth into a new life. Death, then, is seen as a companion to life.

People's responses to death take many forms, particularly in different cultures. But even within Western societies, reactions to death and dying are quite diverse. For instance, consider which is better: for a man to die after a full life in which he has raised a family and been successful in his job, or for a courageous and valiant young soldier to die defending his country in wartime. Has one person died a better death than the other?

Differing conceptions of death lead to different rituals, as this ceremony in India illustrates.

The answer depends on one's values, which are largely due to cultural and subcultural teachings, often shared through religious beliefs. For instance, some societies view death as a punishment or as a judgment about one's contributions to the world. Others see death as redemption from an earthly life of travail. Some view death as the start of an eternal life, while others believe that there is no heaven or hell and that an earthly life is all there is (Bryant, 2003).

Given that religious teachings regarding the meaning of life and death are quite diverse, it is not surprising that views of death and dying vary substantially. For instance, one study found that Christian and Jewish 10-year-olds tended to view death from a more "scientific" vantage point (in terms of the cessation of physical activity in the body) than Sunni Moslem and Druze children of the same age, who are more likely to see death in spiritual terms. We cannot be sure whether such differences are due to the different religious and cultural backgrounds of the children, or if differences in exposure to dying people influence the rate at which the understanding of death develops. However, it is clear that members of the various groups had very different conceptions of death (Florian & Kravetz, 1985; Thorson et al., 1997; Aiken, 2000).

For members of Native American tribes, death is seen as a continuation of life. For example, Lakota parents will tell their children, "Be kind to your brother, for someday he will die." When people die, they are assumed to move to a spirit land called "Wanagi Makoce," inhabited by all people and animals. Death, then, is not viewed with anger or seen as unfair (Huang, 2004).

Members of some cultures learn about death at an earlier age than others. For instance, exposure to high levels of violence and death may lead to an awareness of death earlier in some cultures than in cultures in which violence is less a part of everyday life. Research shows that children in Northern Ireland and Israel understood the finality, irreversibility, and inevitability of death at an earlier age than children in the United States and Britain (McWhirter, Young, & Majury, 1983; Atchley, 2000; Braun, Pietsch, & Blanchette, 2000).

Can Death Education Prepare Us for the Inevitable?

"When will Mom come back from being dead?"
"Why did Barry have to die?"
"Did Grandpa die because I was bad?"

Children's questions such as these illustrate why many developmentalists, as well as **thanatologists,** people who study death and dying, have suggested that death education should be an important component of everyone's schooling. Consequently, a relatively new area of instruction, termed death education, has emerged. *Death education* encompasses programs that teach about death, dying, and grief. Death education is designed to help people of all ages deal better with death and dying—both others' deaths and their own personal mortality.

Death education has evolved in part as a response to the way we hide death, at least in most Western societies. We typically give hospitals the task of dealing with dying people, and we do not talk to children about death or allow them to go to funerals for fear of disturbing them. Even those most familiar with death, such as emergency workers and medical specialists, are uncomfortable talking about the subject. Because it is discussed so little and is so removed from everyday life, people of all ages may have little opportunity to confront their feelings about death or to gain a more realistic sense of it (Kastenbaum, 1999; McGovern & Barry, 2000; Lowton & Higginson, 2003; Wass, 2004).

Several types of death education programs exist. Among them:

- *Crisis intervention education.* When the World Trade Center was attacked, children in the area were the subjects of several kinds of crisis intervention designed to deal with

thanatologists people who study death and dying.

their anxieties. Younger children, whose conceptions of death were shaky at best, needed explanations of the loss of life that day geared to their levels of cognitive development. Crisis intervention education is used in less extreme times as well. For example, it is common for schools to make emergency counseling available if a student is killed or commits suicide.

- *Routine death education.* Although there is relatively little curricular material on death available at the elementary school level, coursework in high schools is becoming increasingly common. For instance, some high schools have specific courses on death and dying. Furthermore, colleges and universities increasingly include courses relating to death in such departments as psychology, human development, sociology, and education.

- *Death education for members of the helping professions.* Professionals who will deal with death, dying, and grief as part of their careers have a special need for death education. Almost all medical and nursing schools now offer some form of death education to help their students. The most successful programs not only provide ways for providers to help patients deal with their own impending deaths and those of family members, but also allow students to explore their feelings about the topic (Downe-Wamboldt & Tamlyn, 1997; Kastenbaum, 1999).

Although no single form of death education will be sufficient to demystify death, the kinds of programs just described may help people come to grips more effectively with what is, along with birth, the most universal—and certain—of all human experiences.

Review and Apply

Review

- Death has been defined as the cessation of heartbeat and respiration (functional death), the absence of electrical brain waves (brain death), and the loss of human qualities.
- The death of an infant or young child can be particularly difficult for parents, and for an adolescent death appears to be unthinkable.
- Death in young adulthood can appear unfair, while people in middle adulthood have begun to understand the reality of death.
- By the time they reach late adulthood, people know they will die and begin to make preparations.
- Cultural differences in attitudes and beliefs about death strongly influence people's reactions to it.
- Thanatologists recommend that death education become a normal part of learning.

Applying Lifespan Development

- Do you think people who are going to die should be told? Does your response depend on the person's age?

- *From the perspective of an educator:* Given their developmental level and understanding of death, how do you think preschool children react to the death of a parent?

Confronting Death

Helen Reynolds, 63, had undergone operations in January and April to repair and then replace a heart valve that was not permitting a smooth flow of blood. But by May her feet had turned the color of overripe eggplants, their mottled purple black an unmistakable sign of gangrene. . . . In June she chose to have first her right leg, and then her left, amputated in hopes of stabilizing her condition. The doctors were skeptical about the surgery, but deferred to her wishes. . . .

But then Reynolds uncharacteristically began talking about her pain. On that Sunday afternoon in June, a nurse beckoned intern Dr. Randall Evans. Evans, a graduate of the University of New Mexico Medical School who planned a career in the critical-care field, was immensely popular with the nursing staff for his cordial and sympathetic manner. But, unlike the MICU nurses, he had difficulty reading Reynolds's lips (the ventilator made it impossible for her to speak aloud), and asked her to write down her request. Laboriously, she scrawled 16 words on the note pad: "I have decided to end my life as I do not want to live like this." (Begley, 1991, pp. 44–45)

Less than a week later, after the ventilator that helped her to breathe had been removed at her request, Helen Reynolds died.

Like other deaths, Reynolds's raises a myriad of difficult questions. Was her request to remove the respirator equivalent to suicide? Should the medical staff have complied with the request? Was she coping with her impending death effectively? How do people come to terms with death, and how do they react and adapt to it? Lifespan developmentalists and other specialists in death and dying have struggled to find answers to such questions.

Understanding the Process of Dying: Are There Steps Toward Death?

No individual has had a greater influence on our understanding of the way people confront death than Elisabeth Kübler-Ross. A psychiatrist, Kübler-Ross developed a theory of death and dying, built on extensive interviews with people who were dying and with those who cared for them (Kübler-Ross, 1969, 1982).

A hospice provides a warm and supportive environment for the dying. The emphasis is on making patients' lives as full as possible, not on squeezing out every additional moment of life at any cost. What are the advantages of hospice care to individuals and society?

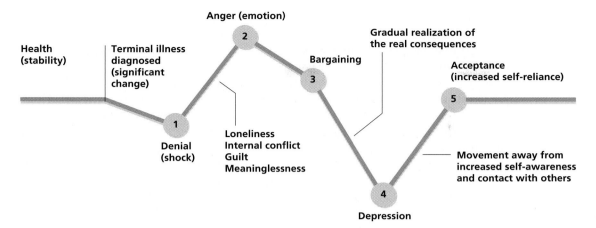

FIGURE 19-2   MOVING TOWARD THE END OF LIFE

The steps toward death, according to Kübler-Ross (1975). Do you think there are cultural differences in the steps?

Based on her observations, Kübler-Ross initially suggested that people pass through five basic steps as they move toward death (summarized in Figure 19-2).

Denial.   "No, I can't be dying. There must be some mistake." It is typical for people to protest in such a manner on learning that they have a terminal disease. Such objections represent the first stage of dying, *denial*. In denial, people resist the idea that they are going to die. They may argue that their test results have been mixed up, that an X-ray has been read incorrectly, or that their physician does not know what he or she is talking about.

Denial comes in several forms. A patient may flatly reject the diagnosis, simply refusing to believe the news. In extreme cases, memories of weeks in the hospital are forgotten. In other forms of denial, patients fluctuate between refusing to accept the news and at other times confiding that they know they are going to die (Teutsch, 2003).

Although we might view the loss of reality implied by denial as a sign of deteriorating mental health, in fact many experts view denial in positive terms. Denial is a defense mechanism that can permit people to absorb the unwelcome news on their own terms and at their own pace. Only when they are able to acknowledge the news can they move on and eventually come to grips with the reality that they are truly going to die.

Anger.   After they move beyond denial, people may be likely to express *anger*. A dying person may be angry at everyone: people who are in good health, their spouses and other family members, those who are caring for them, their children. They may lash out at others, and wonder—sometimes aloud—why *they* are dying and not someone else. They may be furious at God, reasoning that they have led good lives and that there are far worse people in the world who should be dying.

It may not be easy to be around people who are going through an anger stage. As they focus their anger on others, they may say and do things that are painful and sometimes unfathomable. Eventually, though, most patients move beyond the anger phase. This may lead to another development—bargaining.

Bargaining.   "If you're good, you'll be rewarded." Most people learn this equation in childhood, and many try to apply it to their impending death. In this case, "good" means promising to be a better person, and the "reward" is staying alive.

In *bargaining,* dying people try to negotiate their way out of death. They may declare that they will dedicate their lives to the poor if God saves them. They may promise that if they can just live long enough to see a son married, they will willingly accept death later.

However, the promises that are part of the bargaining process are rarely kept. If one request appears to be granted, people typically seek another, and yet another. Furthermore, they may be unable to fulfill their promises because their illnesses keep progressing and prevent them from achieving what they said they would do.

In some ways, bargaining seems to have positive consequences. Although death cannot be postponed indefinitely, having a goal of attending a particular event or living until a certain time may in fact delay death until then. For instance, death rates of Jewish people fall just before the holiday of Passover, and rise just after it. Similarly, the death rate among older Chinese women falls before and during important holidays, and rises after. It is as if the people involved have negotiated to stay alive until after the holidays have passed (Phillips & Smith, 1990; Philips, 1992).

In the end, of course, all the bargaining in the world is unable to overcome the inevitability of death. When people eventually realize that death is unavoidable, they often move into a stage of depression.

Depression.   Many dying people experience phases of *depression*. Realizing that the issue is settled and they cannot bargain their way out of death, people are overwhelmed with a deep sense of loss. They know that they are losing their loved ones and that their lives really are coming to an end.

The depression they experience may be of two types. In *reactive depression,* the feelings of sadness are based on events that have already occurred: the loss of dignity that may accompany medical procedures, the end of a job, or the knowledge that one will never return from the hospital to one's home.

Dying people also experience preparatory depression. In *preparatory depression,* people feel sadness over future losses. They know that death will bring an end to their relationships with others and that they will never see future generations. The reality of death is inescapable in this stage, and it brings about profound sadness over the unalterable conclusion of one's life.

Acceptance.   Kübler-Ross suggested that the final step of dying is *acceptance*. People who have developed a state of acceptance are fully aware that death is impending. Unemotional and uncommunicative, they have virtually no feelings—positive or negative—about the present or future. They have made peace with themselves, and they may wish to be left alone. For them, death holds no sting.

Evaluating Kübler-Ross's Theory.   Kübler-Ross has had an enormous impact on the way we look at death. As one of the first people to observe systematically how people approach their own deaths, she is recognized as a pioneer. Kübler-Ross was almost single-handedly responsible for bringing into public awareness the phenomenon of death, which previously had languished out of sight in Western societies. Her contributions have been particularly influential among those who provide direct care to the dying.

On the other hand, her work has drawn criticism. For one thing, there are some obvious limitations to her conception of dying. It is largely limited to those who are aware that they are dying and who die in a relatively leisurely fashion. To people who suffer from diseases in which the prognosis is uncertain as to when or even if they will die, her theory is not applicable.

The most important criticisms, however, concern the stage-like nature of Kübler-Ross's theory. Not every person passes through every step on the way to death, and some people move through the steps in a different sequence. Some people even go through the same steps several times. Depressed patients may show bursts of anger, and an angry patient may bargain for more time (Schulz & Aderman, 1976; Kastenbaum, 1992). This criticism of the theory has been especially important news for medical and other caregivers who work with dying people. Because Kübler-Ross's stages have become so well known, well-meaning caregivers have sometimes tried to encourage patients to work through the steps in a prescribed order, without enough consideration for their individual needs.

Furthermore, Kübler-Ross may have considered too limited a set of factors when she outlined her theory. For example, other researchers suggest that anxiety plays an important role throughout the process of dying. The anxiety may be about one's upcoming death, or it may relate to fear of the symptoms of the disease. A person with cancer, then, may fear death less than the uncontrollable pain that may be a future possibility (Taylor, 1991; Hayslip et al., 1997).

Finally, there are substantial differences in people's reactions to impending death. The specific cause of dying; how long the process of dying lasts; a person's age, sex, and personality; and the social support available from family and friends all influence the course of dying and people's responses to it (Stroebe, Stroebe, & Hansson, 1993; Carver & Scheier, 2002).

In short, there are significant concerns about the accuracy of Kübler-Ross's account of how people react to impending death. In response to some of these concerns, other theorists have developed some alternative ideas. Psychologist Edwin Shneidman, for example suggests that there are "themes" in people's reactions to dying that can occur—and recur—in any order throughout the dying process. These include such feelings and thoughts as incredulity, a sense of unfairness, fear of pain or even general terror, and fantasies of being rescued (Leenaars & Shneidman, 1999).

Another theorist, Charles Corr, suggests that, as in other periods of life, people who are dying face a set of psychological tasks. These include minimizing physical stress, maintaining the richness of life, continuing or deepening their relationships with other people, and fostering hope, often through spiritual searching (Corr & Doka, 2001; Corr, Nabe, & Corr, 2000, 2006).

Choosing the Nature of Death: Is DNR the Way to Go?

The letters "DNR" written on a patient's medical chart have a simple and clear meaning. Standing for "Do Not Resuscitate," DNR signifies that rather than administering any and every procedure that might possibly keep a patient alive, no extraordinary means are to be taken. For terminally ill patients, "DNR" may mean the difference between dying immediately or living additional days, months, or even years, kept alive only by the most extreme, invasive, and even painful medical procedures.

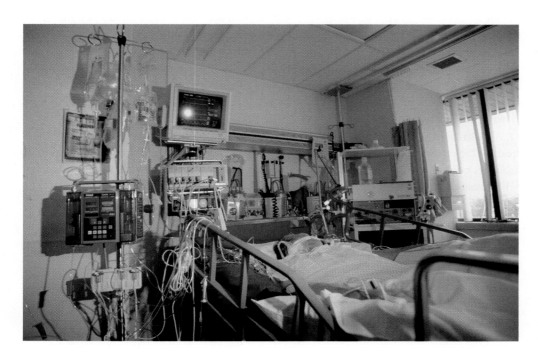

Many terminally ill patients choose "DNR," or "Do Not Resuscitate," as a way to avoid extraordinary medical interventions.

living wills   legal documents designating what medical treatments people want or do not want if they cannot express their wishes.

Table 19-1	Dying Hard: Experiences of 4,301 Patients with End-of-Life Care	
Terminal patients who did not want resuscitation		31%
Of those patients who did not want resuscitation, percentage whose physicians were aware of their preference		47%
Of those patients who did not want resuscitation, percentage whose preferences were entered on their charts		49%

(*Source:* Knaus et al., 1995.)

The decision to use or not to use extreme medical interventions entails several issues. One is the differentiation of "extreme" and "extraordinary" measures from those that are simply routine. There are no hard-and-fast rules; people making the decision must consider the needs of the specific patient, his or her prior medical history, and factors such as age and even religion. For instance, different standards might apply to a 12-year-old patient and an 85-year-old patient with the same medical condition.

Other questions concern quality of life. How can we determine an individual's current quality of life and whether it will be improved or diminished by a particular medical intervention? Who makes such decisions—the patient, a family member, or medical personnel?

One thing is clear: Medical personnel are reluctant to carry out the wishes of the terminally ill and their families to suspend aggressive treatment. Even when it is certain that a patient is going to die, and patients determine that they do not wish to receive further treatment, physicians often claim to be unaware of their patients' wishes. For instance, although one-third of the patients ask not to be resuscitated, less than half of these people's physicians state that they know of their patients' preference (see Table 19-1). In addition, only 49% of patients have their wishes entered on their medical charts. Physicians and other healthcare providers may be reluctant to act on DNR requests in part because they are trained to save patients, not permit them to die, and in part to avoid legal liability issues (Knaus et al., 1995; Goold, Williams, & Arnold, 2000; McArdle, 2002).

Living Wills.   In order to gain more control over decisions regarding the nature of their death, people are increasingly signing living wills. A **living will** is a legal document that designates the medical treatments a person does or does not want if the person cannot express his or her wishes (see Figure 19-3).

Some people designate a specific person, called a *healthcare proxy,* to act as their representative in making healthcare decisions. Health-care proxies are authorized either in living wills or in a legal document known as *durable power of attorney.* Healthcare proxies may be authorized to deal with all medical care problems (such as a coma) or only terminal illnesses.

As with DNR orders, living wills are ineffective unless people take steps to make sure their health-care proxies and doctors know their wishes. Although they may be reluctant to do so in advance, people should also have frank conversations clarifying their wishes with the representatives they choose as their healthcare proxies.

Euthanasia and Assisted Suicide.   Dr. Jack Kevorkian became well known in the 1990s for his invention and promotion of a "suicide machine," which allowed patients to push a button that releases anesthesia and a drug that stops the heart. By supplying the machine and the drugs, which patients administered themselves, Kevorkian was participating in a process known as *assisted suicide,* in which a person provides the means for a terminally ill individual to commit suicide. Kevorkian ended up spending 8 years in prison after being convicted of second-degree murder for his participation in an assisted suicide that was shown on the television show *60 Minutes.*

I,_____,
being of sound mind, make this statement as a directive to be followed if I become permanently unable to participate in decisions regarding my medical care. These instructions reflect my firm and settled commitment to decline medical treatment under the circumstances indicated below:

I direct my attending physician to withhold or withdraw treatment that merely prolongs my dying, if I should be in **an incurable or irreversible mental or physical condition** with no reasonable expectation of recovery, including but not limited to: (a) a **terminal condition**; (b) a **permanently unconscious condition**; or (c) a **minimally conscious condition in which I am permanently unable to make decisions or express my wishes**.

I direct that treatment be limited to measures to keep me comfortable and to relieve pain, including any pain that might occur by withholding or withdrawing treatment.
While I understand that I am not legally required to be specific about future treatments, **if I am in the condition(s) described above I feel especially strongly about the following treatments**:

I do not want cardiac resuscitation.
I do not want mechanical respiration.
I do not want tube feeding.
I do not want antibiotics.

However, I **do want** maximum pain relief, even if it may hasten my death.

Other directions (insert personal instructions):

These directions express my legal right to refuse treatment under federal and state law. I intend my instructions to be carried out, unless I have revoked them in a new writing or by clearly indicating that I have changed my mind.

Signed:_____ Date:_____

Address:_____

- -

Statement by Witnesses
I declare that the person who signed this document appears to be at least eighteen (18) years of age, of sound mind, and under no constraint or undue influence. The person who signed this document appeared to do so willingly and free from duress. He or she signed (or asked another to sign for him or her) this document in my presence.

Witness:_____

Address:_____

- -

Witness:_____

Address:_____

- -

FIGURE 19-3 A LIVING WILL

What steps can people take to make sure the wishes they write into their living wills are carried out?

euthanasia   the practice of assisting people who are terminally ill to die more quickly.

Assisted suicide continues to raise bitter conflict in the United States, and the practice is illegal in most states. The exception is the state of Oregon, which passed a "right to die law" in 1998. In the first decade that Oregon's law was in effect, less than 300 people took medication to end their own lives (Ganzini, Beer, & Brouns, 2006; Davey, 2007).

In many countries, assisted suicide is an accepted practice. For instance, in the Netherlands medical personnel may help end their patients' lives. However, several conditions must be met to make the practice permissible: At least two physicians must determine that the patient is terminally ill, there must be unbearable physical or mental suffering, the patient must give informed consent in writing, and relatives must be informed beforehand (Galbraith & Dobson, 2000; Rosenfeld et al., 2000; Naik, 2002; Kleespies, 2004).

Assisted suicide is one form of **euthanasia,** the practice of assisting terminally ill people to die more quickly. Popularly known as "mercy killing," euthanasia can take a range of forms. *Passive euthanasia* involves removing respirators or other medical equipment that may be sustaining a patient's life, to allow the individual to die naturally. This happens when medical staff follow a DNR order, for example. In *voluntary active euthanasia,* caregivers or medical staff act to end a person's life before death would normally occur, perhaps by administering a dose of pain medication that they know will be fatal. Assisted suicide, as we have seen, lies between passive and voluntary active euthanasia. Euthanasia is an emotional and controversial—although surprisingly widespread—practice.

No one knows how widespread euthanasia truly is. However, one survey of nurses in intensive care units found that 20% had deliberately hastened a patient's death at least once, and other experts assert that euthanasia is far from rare (Asch, 1996).

Euthanasia is highly controversial, in part because it centers on decisions about who should control life. Does the right belong solely to an individual, a person's physicians, his or her dependents, the government, or some deity? Because, at least in the United States, we assume that we all have the absolute right to create lives by bringing children into the world, some people argue that we should also have the absolute right to end our lives (Solomon, 1995; Lester, 1996; Allen et al., 2006).

On the other hand, many opponents of euthanasia argue that the practice is morally wrong. In their view, prematurely ending someone's life, no matter how willing that person may be, is the equivalent of murder. Others point out that physicians are often inaccurate in predicting how long a person's life will last. For example, a large-scale study known as SUPPORT—the Study to Understand Prognoses and Preferences for Outcomes and Risks of Treatment—found that patients often outlive physicians' predictions of when they will die. In fact, in some cases, patients have lived for years after being given no more than a 50% chance of living for 6 more months (Bishop, 2006; see Figure 19-4).

FIGURE 19-4   HOW LONG DO "TERMINAL" PATIENTS REALLY LIVE?

According to the large SUPPORT study, a significant percentage of a group of 3,693 patients given no more than a 50% chance of living for 6 months survived well beyond that period. Why do you think this happened?

(*Source:* Lynn et al., 1997.)

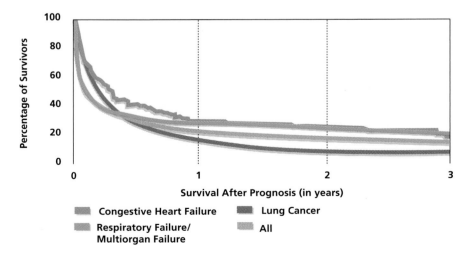

Another argument against euthanasia focuses on the emotional state of the patient. Even if patients ask or sometimes beg health-care providers to help them die, they may be suffering from a form of deep depression. In such cases, patients may be treated with antidepressant drugs that can alleviate the depression. Once the depression lifts, patients may change their minds about their earlier wish for death.

The debate over euthanasia is likely to continue. It is a highly personal issue, yet one that society increasingly must face as the world's elderly population increases (Becvar, 2000; Gostin, 2006).

home care   an alternative to hospitalization in which dying people stay in their homes and receive treatment from their families and visiting medical staff.

hospice care   care provided for the dying in institutions devoted to those who are terminally ill.

Caring for the Terminally Ill: The Place of Death

Recall the description of Helen Reynolds's last months of life, spent in the intensive care unit of a Boston hospital. Although family members visited her frequently, Helen also faced many lonely hours watching television as her condition deteriorated.

Like Reynolds, about half the people in the United States who die do so in hospitals. It need not be that way. In fact, there are several reasons why hospitals are among the least desirable locales in which to face death. Hospitals are typically impersonal, with staff rotating throughout the day. Because visiting hours are limited, people frequently die alone, without the comfort of loved ones at their bedside.

Furthermore, hospitals are designed to make people better, not to deal with the dying, and it is extraordinarily expensive to provide custodial care for dying people. Consequently, hospitals typically don't have the resources needed to deal adequately with the emotional requirements of terminally ill patients and their families.

Because of the limitations of traditional hospitals in dealing with the dying, there are now several alternatives to hospitalization. In **home care,** dying people stay in their homes and receive treatment from their families and visiting medical staff. Many dying patients prefer home care, because they can spend their final days in a familiar environment, with people they love and a lifetime accumulation of treasures around them.

Although the dying may prefer home care, it can be quite difficult for family members. Furnishing final care can offer family members a good deal of emotional solace because they are giving something precious to people they love. But, it is extraordinarily draining, both physically and emotionally, to be on call 24 hours a day. Furthermore, because most relatives are not trained in nursing, they may provide less than optimal medical care. Many people decide they just aren't equipped to care for a dying family member at home (Perreault, Fothergill-Bourbonnais, & Fiset, 2004).

For these families, another alternative to hospitalization that is becoming increasingly prevalent is hospice care. **Hospice care** is care for the dying provided in institutions devoted to those who are terminally ill. In the Middle Ages, hospices were facilities that provided comfort and hospitality to travelers. Drawing on that concept, today's hospices are designed to provide a warm, supportive environment for the dying. They do not focus on extending people's lives, but rather on making their final days pleasant and meaningful. Typically, people who go to hospices are removed from treatments that are painful, and no extraordinary or invasive means are employed to make their lives longer. The emphasis is on making patients' lives as full as possible, not on squeezing out every possible moment of life at any cost (Johnson, Kassner, & Kutner, 2004).

Although the research is far from conclusive, hospice patients appear to be more satisfied with the care they receive than those who receive treatment in more traditional settings (Tang, Aaronson, & Forbes, 2004). Hospice care, then, provides a clear alternative to traditional hospitalization for the terminally ill. (For more on hospice care, see the accompanying *Careers in Lifespan Development* box.)

Careers in Lifespan Development

Dina C. Bianga, Hospice Nurse

Education: Associates Degree, Nursing, LPN, RN, St. Clair County Community College, Port Huron, Michigan

Position: RN, Clinical Supervisor, Hospice of Michigan at Bloomfield Hills

Hometown: Harrison Township, Michigan

Although a relative newcomer to the health-care industry, hospice has greatly enhanced the quality of life of terminally ill patients and dramatically changed the way in which the medical field deals with death.

Dina Bianga, a registered nurse with the Hospice of Michigan, is one of many professionals who work to meet the physical and psychological needs of the terminally ill.

"As a nurse, you need to have compassion and a good clinical background," she noted. "You are also involved with so many different aspects of nursing. You go into the home, hospital, nursing home, adult foster care—wherever the patient is."

With a ratio of 1 nurse to approximately 10 to 12 patients, the process of care involves an interdisciplinary approach, according to Bianga.

"You have to work as a team with others who provide social work, spiritual care, home health aid, grief support, as well as people in the office who provide administrative support," she said.

One area that requires considerable care and sensitivity is dealing with families and friends of the patients.

"You have to teach them as much as you can about what is happening and also how to care for the patient," Bianga explained. "The more they are involved the better they often feel."

As part of the education process, Bianga discusses the symptoms that indicate that death is nearing.

"Families are frightened, and everything seems out of control to them," she said. "To help them deal with the situation, I go over the symptoms that revolve around this phase. Families are not always able to accept that death is coming soon, so you have to be careful and sensitive about how you word things. If they are well informed on what to expect, then the transition is smoother and a more comfortable atmosphere is created for the patient."

Review and Apply

Review

- Elisabeth Kübler-Ross has identified five steps toward dying: denial, anger, bargaining, depression, and acceptance. The stage nature of her theory has been criticized as too inflexible, and other theorists have suggested alternatives.

- Issues surrounding dying are highly controversial, including the degree of measures that physicians should apply to keep dying patients alive and who should make the decisions about those measures. Living wills are a way for people to take some control over the decision.

- Assisted suicide and, more generally, euthanasia are highly controversial and are illegal in most of the United States, although many people believe they should be legalized if they are regulated.

- Although most people in the United States die in hospitals, increasing numbers are choosing home care or hospice care for their final days.

Applying Lifespan Development

- Do you think assisted suicide should be permissible? What about other forms of euthanasia? Why or why not?

- *From the perspective of an educator:* Do you think Kübler-Ross's five steps of dying might be subject to cultural influences? Age differences? Why or why not?

Grief and Bereavement

No one ever told me that grief felt so like fear. I am not afraid, but the sensation is like being afraid. The same fluttering in the stomach, the same restlessness, the yawning. I keep on swallowing.

At other times it feels like being mildly drunk, or concussed. There is a sort of invisible blanket between the world and me. I find it hard to take in what anyone says. Or perhaps, hard to want to take it in. It is so uninteresting. (Lewis, 1985, p. 394)

For something that is a universal experience, most of us are surprisingly ill-prepared for the grief that follows the death of a loved one. Particularly in Western societies, where life expectancy is long and mortality rates are lower than at any time in history, people are apt to view death as an atypical event rather than an expected part of life. This attitude makes grief all the more difficult to bear, particularly when we compare the present day with historical eras in which people lived shorter lives and the death rate was considerably higher. The first step in grieving, for most survivors in Western countries, is some sort of funeral (Gluhoski, Leader, & Wortman, 1994; Nolen-Hoeksema & Larson, 1999; Bryant, 2003).

Mourning and Funerals: Final Rites

Death is a big business in the United States. The average funeral and burial costs $7,000. The purchase of an ornate, polished coffin, transportation to and from the cemetery in a limousine, and preparation of the body for preservation and viewing are among the services that people typically purchase in planning a funeral (AARP, 2004).

In part, the relatively grandiose nature of funerals is due to the vulnerability of those planning the funeral, who are typically close survivors of the deceased. Wishing to demonstrate love and affection, the survivors are susceptible to suggestions to "provide the best" for the deceased (Culver, 2003).

But it is not only the pressure of enterprising salespersons that leads many people to spend thousands of dollars on a funeral. In large measure, the nature of funerals, like that of weddings, is determined by social norms and customs. Because an individual's death represents an important transition, not only for loved ones but for an entire community, the rites associated

Because an individual's death represents an important transition, not only for loved ones but for an entire community, the rites associated with death take on an added importance. The emotional significance of death, combined with the pressure of enterprising salespersons, lead many to overspend on funerals.

with death take on an added importance. In a sense, then, a funeral is not only a public acknowledgment that an individual has died, but recognition of everyone's ultimate mortality and an acceptance of the cycle of life (DeSpelder & Strickland, 1992).

In Western societies, funeral rituals follow a typical pattern, despite some surface variations. Prior to the funeral, the body is prepared in some way and is dressed in special clothing. Funerals usually include the celebration of a religious rite, the delivery of a eulogy, a procession of some sort, and some formal period, such as the wake for Irish Catholics and shivah for Jews, in which relatives and friends visit the mourning family and pay their respects. Military funerals typically include the firing of weapons and a flag draped over the coffin.

Cultural Differences in Grieving.   Non-Western cultures include funeral rituals of quite different sorts. For instance, in some societies mourners shave their heads as a sign of grief, while in others they allow the hair to grow and men stop shaving for a period of time. In other cultures, mourners may be hired to wail and grieve. Sometimes noisy celebrations take place at funerals, while in other cultures silence is the norm. Even the nature of emotional displays, such as the amount and timing of crying, are determined culturally (Rosenblatt, 1988, 2001).

For example, mourners in Balinese funerals in Indonesia show little emotion, because they believe they must be calm in order for the gods to hear their prayers. In contrast, mourners at African American funerals are encouraged to show their grief, and the funeral rituals are meant to allow attendees to display their feelings (Rosenblatt, 1988; Rosenblatt & Wallace, 2005; Collins & Doolittle, 2006).

Historically, some cultures have developed funeral rites that strike us as extreme. For example, in *suttee,* a traditional Hindu practice in India that is now illegal, a widow was expected to throw herself into the fire that consumed her husband's body. In ancient China, servants were sometimes buried (alive) with their masters' bodies.

Ultimately, no matter what the particular ritual, all funerals basically serve the same underlying function: They serve as a way to mark the endpoint for the life of the person who has died—and provide a formal forum for the feelings of the survivors, a place where they can come together and share their grief and comfort one another.

Bereavement and Grief: Adjusting to the Death of a Loved One

After the death of a loved one, a painful period of adjustment follows, involving bereavement and grief. **Bereavement** is acknowledgment of the objective fact that one has experienced a death, while **grief** is the emotional response to one's loss. Everyone's grief is different, but there are certain similarities in the ways people in Western societies adjust to the loss.

Survivors' first stage of grief typically entails shock, numbness, disbelief, or outright denial. People may avoid the reality of the situation, trying to carry on with the usual routines of their lives, although the pain may break through, causing anguish, fear, and deep sorrow and distress. If the pain is too severe, however, the person may cycle back to numbness. In some ways, such a psychological state may be beneficial, since it permits the survivor to make funeral arrangements and carry out other psychologically difficult tasks. Typically, people pass through this stage in a few days or weeks, although in some cases it lasts longer.

In the next phase, people begin to confront the death and realize the extent of their loss. They fully experience their grief, and they begin to acknowledge the reality that the separation from the dead person will be permanent. In so doing, mourners may suffer deep unhappiness or even depression, a normal feeling in this situation and not one necessarily requiring treatment. They may yearn for the dead individual. Emotions can range from impatient to lethargic. However, they also begin to view their past relationship with the deceased realistically, good and bad. In so doing, they begin to free themselves from some of the bonds that tied them to their loved ones (de Vries et al., 1997).

After a death, people move through a painful period of bereavement and grief. These adolescents in Bosnia mourn the loss of a friend who was killed by enemy bombardment.

Finally, people who have lost a loved one reach the accommodation stage. They begin to pick up the pieces of their lives and to construct new identities. For instance, rather than seeing herself as someone's widowed spouse, a woman whose husband has died may come to regard herself as a single person. Still, there are moments when intense feelings of grief occur.

Ultimately, most people are able to emerge from the grieving process and live new lives, independent from the person who has died. They form new relationships, and some even find that coping with the death has helped them to grow as individuals. They become more self-reliant and more appreciative of life.

It is important to keep in mind that not everyone passes through the stages of grief in the same manner and in the same order. People display vast individual differences, partly due to their personalities, the nature of the relationship with the deceased, and the opportunities that are available to them for continuing their lives after the loss. As with Kübler-Ross's stages of dying, then, the stages of grieving do not unfold in the same way for all people.

As we consider in the *From Research to Practice* box, even the strength of one's relationship with the deceased—at least in the case of long-time spouses—can have an effect on the grieving process.

Differentiating Unhealthy Grief from Normal Grief. Although ideas abound about what separates normal grief from unhealthy grief, careful research has shown that many of the assumptions that both laypersons and clinicians hold are wrong. There is no particular timetable for grieving, particularly the common notion that grieving should be complete a year after a spouse has died. Increasing evidence suggests that for some people (but not all) grieving may take considerably longer than a year. Research also contradicts the common assumption that depression is widespread; only 15% to 30% of people show relatively deep depression following the loss of a loved one (Prigerson et al., 1995; Bonanno, Wortman, & Lehman, 2002; Hensley, 2006).

Similarly, it is often assumed that people who show little initial distress over a death are simply not facing up to reality, and that as a consequence they are likely to have problems later. This is not the case. In fact, those who show the most intense distress immediately after a death are

From Research to Practice

Moving on: Surviving the Loss of a Long-Time Spouse

Patty Limerick, 55, found solace in friends who surrounded her in the small hospital room the night her husband Jeff died suddenly of a stroke in 2005 and who stayed by her side in the weeks and months afterward. But she found she still needed time alone to grieve not only the death of her husband but also the end of their happy 26-year marriage. "For almost two months, I lay on the floor at night sobbing while listening to Marty Robbins sing 'At the End of a Long Lonely Day,'" she says, referring to the song played at Jeff's funeral. But as the weeks went by, the tears subsided. "It was gradual," she says, "but at some point, I realized I was listening to the song without crying." (Stitch, 2006, p. F3)

As you may well imagine, the death of a spouse is almost always a traumatic experience that is usually followed by intense grief and anguish. In the case of older couples who had been married for a very long time, losing a spouse can mean losing a lifelong companion and typically a partner's primary and sometimes sole source of emotional support. Intuition may therefore suggest that the period of grieving for such a loss would be particularly prolonged for a surviving spouse who had enjoyed a close and happy marriage.

But a growing body of research suggests otherwise: It seems, in fact, that people who had a successful marriage are better able to work through their mourning of a lost spouse and get on with the rest of their lives than those with less successful marriages. A recent longitudinal study of hundreds of married older adults revealed that almost half of those who reported having satisfying marriages were able to get past their grief within 6 months of the death of their spouses (Carr et al., 2000; Carr, Nesse, & Wortman, 2005; Carr & Ha, 2006).

One explanation for these findings is that people who enjoy close and happy marriages tend to have strong interpersonal skills on which to rely during their time of loss. They may be better equipped to call upon friends, family, and even a professional counselor if necessary to assist them through their grieving period. One way that others help the surviving spouse is by providing a diversion to keep him or her from dwelling on the loss and also by encouraging him or her to replace the void with new interests and activities. Strong interpersonal skills may also facilitate a positive approach to dating new people when the time is right (Carr et al., 2005; Stitch, 2006).

Another reason for the resiliency of surviving spouses of close marriages is the knowledge that they and their departed partner had culminated what they set out to achieve: a successful and satisfying relationship. Surviving partners of strained marriages might feel more sadness over never having achieved a desired level of closeness, or they might regret not having an opportunity to resolve lingering conflicts, or they might feel guilty about not working harder to make their marriage better when they had the chance.

On the other hand, surviving spouses who enjoyed a close marriage are more likely to have settled lingering issues and to have talked through what would happen after either of them died; they therefore are more likely to feel secure in knowing what their departed would have wanted for them in widowhood. Finally, spouses who have a close and secure relationship may simply have a better opportunity to say their final goodbyes as one of the partners' health fails (Bonanno et al., 2002).

Of course, having a secure marriage is no guarantee that life as a widow or widower will be lacking in pain. Even very resilient survivors grieve deeply in the immediate months following the death of their spouses. And indeed, it's possible to be too close to one's spouse, making the loss more difficult; men in particular may be hit hard by the loss of a wife who was their only emotional confidant. But in many cases, the final gift of a close and loving spouse is the security to move on with one's life within a reasonable time after his or her death (Boerner, Wortman, & Bonanno, 2005; Bonanno et al., 2005).

- *Do you think that these same findings would apply in the case of losing a spouse earlier in life? Why or why not?*

- *What other factors besides interpersonal closeness might affect the duration of grief after losing a long-time spouse?*

the most apt to have adjustment difficulties and health problems later on (Gluhoski, Leader, & Wortman, 1994; Boerner et al., 2005).

The Consequences of Grief and Bereavement. In a sense, death is catching, at least in terms of survivors' mortality. A good deal of evidence suggests that widowed people are particularly at risk of death. Some studies find that the risk of death is as much as seven times higher than normal in the first year after the death of a spouse. At particular risk are men and younger women who have been widowed. Remarriage seems to lower the risk of death for survivors. This is particularly true for men who have lost their wives, although the reasons are not clear (Gluhoski et al., 1994; Martikainen & Valkonen, 1996; Aiken, 2000).

Bereavement is more likely to produce depression or other negative consequences if the person who has lost a loved one is already insecure, anxious, or fearful and therefore less able to cope effectively. Furthermore, people whose relationships were marked by ambivalence before death are more apt to suffer poor post-death outcomes than those who were secure in their relationships. Those who were highly dependent on the person who died, and who therefore feel more vulnerable without them, are apt to suffer more after the death, as are those who spend a great deal of time reflecting on a loved one's death and their feelings of grief. Bereaved people who lack social support from family, friends, or a connection to some other group, religious or otherwise, are more likely to experience feelings of loneliness, and therefore are more at risk. Finally, people who are unable to make sense of the death or find meaning in it (such as a new appreciation of life) show less overall adjustment (Davis & Nolen-Hoeksema, 2001; Nolen-Hoeksema, 2001; Nolen-Hoeksema & Davis, 2002).

The suddenness of a loved one's death also appears to affect the course of grieving. People who unexpectedly lose their loved ones are less able to cope than those who were able to anticipate the death. For instance, in one study, people who experienced a sudden death still had not fully recovered 4 years later. In part, this may be because sudden, unanticipated deaths are often the result of violence, which occurs more frequently among younger individuals (Rando, 1993; Burton, Haley, & Small, 2006).

As we noted earlier in the chapter, and discussed further in the *Becoming an Informed Consumer of Development* feature, children may need special help understanding and mourning the death of someone they love.

Becoming an Informed Consumer of Development

Helping a Child Cope with Grief

Because of their limited understanding of death, younger children need special help in coping with grief. Among the strategies that can help are the following:

- **Be honest.** Don't say that a dead person is "sleeping" or "on a long trip." Use age-appropriate language to tell children the truth. Gently, but clearly, point out the irreversibility and the final and universal nature of death. For example, you might answer questions about whether grandma will be hungry by pointing out that, "No, after a person dies, their body doesn't work anymore, so it doesn't need food."

- **Encourage expressions of grief.** Don't tell children not to cry or show their feelings. Instead, tell them that it is understandable to feel terrible, and that they may always miss the deceased. Encourage them to draw a picture, write a letter, or express their feelings in some other way. At the same time, assure them that they will always have good memories of the person who has died.

- **Reassure children that they are not to blame for the death.** Children sometimes attribute a loved one's death to their own behavior—if they had not misbehaved, they mistakenly reason, the person would not have died.

- **Understand that children's grief may surface in unanticipated ways.** Children may show little or no grief at the time of the death, but later they may become upset for no apparent reason or revert to behaviors such as sucking their thumb or wanting to sleep with their parent or parents. Keep in mind that death can be overwhelming for a child, and try to be consistently loving and supportive.

- **Children may respond to books for young persons about death.** One especially effective book is *When Dinosaurs Die,* by Laurie Krasny Brown and Marc Brown.

Review and Apply

Review

- Bereavement refers to the loss of a loved one; grief refers to the emotional response to that loss.

- Funeral rites play a significant role in helping people acknowledge the death of a loved one, recognize their own mortality, and proceed with their lives.

- For many people, grief passes through denial, sorrow, and accommodation stages.

- Children need special help coping with grief.

Applying Lifespan Development

- Why do so many people in U.S. society feel reluctant to think and talk about death?

- *From the perspective of a social worker:* Why do you think the risk of death is so high for people who have recently lost a spouse? Why might remarriage lower the risk?

Epilogue

This chapter and the final part of the book focus on late adulthood and the end of life. Genuine physical and cognitive declines finally become the norm, but people can continue to lead healthy, engaged lives throughout most of the period—in defiance of stereotypes that characterize them as decrepit and doddering.

As in other periods of the life span, continuity and change are both evident in late adulthood. For example, we noticed that individual differences in cognitive performance, even as they show declines, reflect individual differences that were present in earlier years. We saw that lifestyle choices made earlier, such as exercise participation, contribute to health and longevity during this time.

Social and personality development can continue throughout late adulthood. We saw that although most people show similar personality traits to their earlier years, late adulthood also affords a unique perspective on the more turbulent years that have gone before. People defy stereotypes of late adulthood in the varied ways they live and the rich relationships they sustain in this period.

We ended the book with a consideration of the inevitable end of life. Even here, as we considered death and its meaning at various stages in the life span and across cultures, we saw that there are challenges to be faced and satisfaction to be drawn from a graceful departure from life whether in a hospital, hospice, or palliative or home care setting.

In sum, the story of the entire life span is one of fresh challenges and opportunities as we continuously undergo and adjust to physical and cognitive changes and learn to relate to new social situations. Development persists virtually to the point of death, and with preparation, we can appreciate and learn from all parts of the life span.

Before you close the book, return to the chapter prologue, about Ted Soulis's positive approach toward death. Based on your understanding of death and dying, answer the following questions:

1. To what extent do you think Soulis went through the stages described by Kübler-Ross?

2. How might Soulis have reacted differently to his impending death if he were a young man in his early 20s?

3. How might Soulis's celebratory and jocular attitude toward the ending of his life affected the bereavement process for his family?

4. How might Soulis's final days been different if he had elected to receive cancer treatment in the hospital? How might they have been different if he had required hospice care?

Looking Back

■ **What is death, and what does it mean at different stages of the life span?**

- The precise point of death is difficult to define. Functional death refers to the absence of heartbeat and respiration, from which people can be resuscitated, while brain death refers to the absence of electrical activity in the brain, which is irreversible.

- The death of an infant or a young child is among the most devastating experiences for parents, largely because it seems unnatural and entirely incomprehensible.

- Adolescents have an unrealistic sense of invulnerability that makes them susceptible to accidental death. Denial often makes it impossible for terminally ill adolescents to accept the seriousness of their condition.

- For young adults, death is virtually unthinkable. Young adults who are terminally ill can be difficult patients because of a strong sense of the injustice of their fate.

- In middle adulthood, disease becomes the leading cause of death, and awareness of the reality of death can lead to a substantial fear of death.

- People in late adulthood begin to prepare for death. Older people generally prefer to know if death is near, and the main issue they have to deal with is whether their lives continue to have value.

- Responses to death are in part determined by culture. Death may be regarded as a release from the pains of the world, the beginning of a pleasurable afterlife, a punishment or judgment, or simply the end to life.

- Death education can help people learn about death and consider their own mortality realistically.

■ **In what ways do people face the prospect of their own death?**

- Elisabeth Kübler-Ross suggests that people pass through five basic stages on their way to death: denial, anger, bargaining, depression, and acceptance. The stage nature of her theory has been criticized, and other theorists have suggested alternatives.

- A living will is a means of asserting control over decisions surrounding one's death through specification of desired medical treatments in life-threatening situations and designation of a health-care proxy to enforce one's wishes.

- Assisted suicide, a form of euthanasia, is illegal in most of the United States.

- Although most deaths in the United States occur in hospitals, an increasing number of terminal patients are opting for either home care or a hospice.

■ **How do survivors react to and cope with death?**

- Funeral rituals serve a dual function: acknowledging the death of a loved one and recognizing and anticipating the mortality of all who participate.

- The death of a loved one brings a period of adjustment involving bereavement and grief. Grief may proceed through stages of shock and denial, the beginning of acceptance, and accommodation. One consequence of bereavement is an increase in the risk of death for the survivor.

- Children need particular help in dealing with death, including honesty, encouragement of expressions of grief, reassurance that the death was not due to the child's behavior, and understanding that the child's grief may be delayed and indirect.

Key Terms and Concepts

functional death (p. 638)
brain death (p. 639)
sudden infant death
   syndrome (SIDS) (p. 639)

thanatologists (p. 644)
living wills (p. 650)
euthanasia (p. 652)
home care (p. 653)

hospice care (p. 653)
bereavement (p. 656)
grief (p. 656)

References

AAMR (American Association on Mental Retardation). (2002). *Mental retardation: Definition, classification, and systems of support.* Washington, DC: Author.

AARP (American Association of Retired Persons). (1990). *A profile of older Americans.* Washington, DC: Author.

AARP. (2004, May 25). Funeral arrangements and memorial service. Available online at http://www.aarp.org/griefandloss/articles/73_a.html.

AARP. (2005, October). I can see clearly now. *AARP Bulletin*, p. 34.

AAUW (American Association of University Women). (1992). *How schools shortchange women: The A.A.U.W. report.* Washington, DC: American Association of University Women Educational Foundation.

Aber, J. L., Bishop-Josef, S. J., Jones, S. M., McLearn, K. T., & Phillips, D. A. (Eds.). (2007). *Child development and social policy: Knowledge for action.* Washington, DC: American Psychological Association.

Aboud, F., Mendelson, M., and Purdy, K. (2003). Cross-race peer relations and friendship quality. *International Journal of Behavioral Development, 27,* 165–173.

Aboud, F. E., & Skerry, S. A. (1983). Self and ethnic concepts in relations to ethnic constancy. *Canadian Journal of Behavioral Science, 15,* 14–26.

Abril, C., & Gault, B. (2006, March). The state of music in the elementary school: The principal's perspective. *Journal of Research in Music Education, 54,* 6–20.

Abushaikha, L. (2007). Methods of coping with labor pain used by Jordanian women. *Journal of Transcultural Nursing, 18,* 35–40.

Achenbach, T. A. (1992). Developmental psychopathology. In M. H. Bornstein & M. E. Lamb (Eds.), *Developmental psychology: An advanced textbook.* Hillsdale, NJ: Erlbaum.

Achter, J. A., Lubinski, D., Benbow, C. P., & Eftekhari-Sanjani, H. (1999). Assessing vocational preferences among gifted adolescents adds incremental validity to abilities: A discriminant analysis of educational outcomes over a 10-year interval. *Journal of Educational Psychology, 91,* 777–786.

Ackerman, B. P., & Izard, C. E. (2004). Emotion cognition in children and adolescents: Introduction to the special issue. *Journal of Experimental Child Psychology, 89* [Special issue: Emotional cognition in children], 271–275.

Acocella, J. (August 18 & 25, 2003). Little people. *The New Yorker*, 138–143.

ACOG. (2002). *Guidelines for perinatal care.* Elk Grove, IN: Author.

Adams, C., & Labouvie-Vief, G. (1986, November 20). Modes of knowing and language processing. Symposium on developmental dimensions of adult adaptations. Perspectives in mind, self, and emotion. Paper presented at the meeting of the Gerontological Association of America, Chicago, IL.

Adams, C. R., & Singh, K. (1998). Direct and indirect effects of school learning variables on the academic achievement of African American 10th graders. *Journal of Negro Education, 67,* 48–66.

Adams, G. R., Montemayor, R., & Gullotta, T. P. (Eds.). (1996). *Psychosocial development during adolescence.* Thousand Oaks, CA: Sage Publications.

Adams, K. B. (2004). Changing investment in activities and interests in elders' lives: Theory and measurement. *International Journal of Aging and Human Development, 58,* 87–108.

Adams, R. J., Mauer, D., & Davis, M. (1986). Newborns' discrimination of chromatic from achromatic stimuli. *Journal of Experimental Child Psychology, 41,* 267–281.

Adams Hillard, P. J. (2001). Gynecologic disorders and surgery. In N. L. Stotland & D. E. Stewart. (Eds.), *Psychological aspects of women's health care: The interface between psychiatry and obstetrics and gynecology* (2nd ed.). Washington, DC: American Psychiatric Publishing.

Adamson, L., & Frick, J. (2003). The still face: A history of a shared experimental paradigm. *Infancy, 4,* 451–473.

Adelmann, P. K., Antonucci, T. C., & Crohan, S. E. (1990). A causal analysis of employment and health in midlife women. *Women and Health, 16,* 5–20.

Ader, R., Felten, D., & Cohen, N. (2001). *Psychoneuroimmunology* (3rd ed.) San Diego: Academic Press.

Adler, P. A., Kless, S. J., & Adler, P. (1992). Socialization to gender roles: Popularity among elementary school boys and girls. *Sociology of Education, 65,* 169–187.

Administration on Aging. (2003). *A profile of older Americans: 2003.* Washington, DC: U.S. Department of Health and Human Services.

Administration on Aging. (2006). *Profiles of older Americans 2005: Research report.* Washington, DC: U.S. Department of Health and Human Resources.

Adolph, K. E. (1997). Learning in the development of infant locomotion. With commentary by B. I. Bertenthal, S. M. Boker, E. C. Goldfield, & E. J. Gibson. *Monographs of the Society for Research in Child Development, 62,* 238–251.

Afifi, T., Brownridge, D., Cox, B., & Sareen, J. (2006, October). Physical punishment, childhood abuse and psychiatric disorders. *Child Abuse & Neglect, 30,* 1093–1103.

Aguiar, A., & Baillargeon, R. (2002). Developments in young infants' reasoning about occluded objects. *Cognitive Psychology, 45,* 267–336.

Ah-Kion, J. (2006, June). Body image and self-esteem: A study of gender differences among mid-adolescents. *Gender & Behaviour, 4,* 534–549.

Ahmed, E., & Braithwaite, V. (2004). Bullying and victimization: Cause for concern for both families and schools. *Social Psychology of Education, 7,* 35–54.

Ahn, W., Gelman, S., & Amsterlaw, J. (2000). Causal status effect in children's categorization. *Cognition, 76,* B35–B43.

Aiken, L. R. (2000). *Dying, death, and bereavement* (4th ed.). Mahwah, NJ: Erlbaum.

Ainsworth, M. D. S. (1973). The development of infant–mother attachment. In B. M. Caldwell & H. N. Ricciuti (Eds.), *Review of child development research* (Vol. 3). Chicago: University of Chicago Press.

Ainsworth, M. D. S. (1993). Attachment as related to mother–infant interaction. *Advances in Infancy Research, 8,* 1–50.

Ainsworth, M. D. S., Blehar, M. C., Waters, E., & Wall, S. (1978). *Patterns of attachment: A psychological study of the strange situation.* Hillsdale, NJ: Erlbaum.

Ainsworth, M. D. S., & Bowlby, J. (1991). An ethological approach to personality development. *American Psychologist, 46,* 333–341.

Aitken, R. J. (1995, July 7). The complexities of conception. *Science, 269,* 39–40.

Akmajian, A., Demers, R. A., & Harnish, R. M. (1984). *Linguistics.* Cambridge, MA: MIT Press.

Akshoomoff, N. (2006). Autism spectrum disorders: Introduction. *Child Neuropsychology, 12,* 245–246.

Alan Guttmacher Institute. (1993a). *Report on viral sexual diseases.* Chicago: Author.

Albers, L. L., & Krulewitch, C. J. (1993). Electronic fetal monitoring in the United States in the 1980s. *Obstetrics & Gynecology, 82,* 8–10.

Albers, L. L. Migliaccio, L., Bedrick, E. J., Teaf, D., & Peralta, P. (2007). Does epidural analgesia affect the rate of spontaneous obstetric lacerations in normal births? *Journal of Midwifery and Women's Health, 52,* 31–36.

Albrecht, G. L. (2005). *Encyclopedia of disability* (General ed.). Thousand Oaks, CA: Sage Publications.

Alderfer, C. (2003). The science and nonscience of psychologists' responses to *The Bell Curve. Professional Psychology: Research & Practice, 34,* 287–293.

Aldwin, C., & Gilmer, D. (2004). *Health, illness, and optimal aging: Biological and psychosocial perspectives.* Thousand Oaks, CA: Sage Publications, Inc.

Aldwin, C. M. (1994). *Stress, coping, and development: An integrative perspective.* New York: Guilford Press, 1994.

Ales, K. L., Druzin, M. L., & Santini, D. L. (1990). Impact of advanced maternal age on the outcome of pregnancy. *Surgery, Gynecology & Obstetrics, 171,* 209–216.

Alexander, G. M., & Hines, M. Sex differences in response to children's toys in nonhuman primates. (2002). *Evolution and Human Behavior, 23,* 467–479.

Alfonso, V. C., Flanagan, D. P., & Radwan, S. (2005). The impact of the Cattell-Horn-Carroll theory on test development and interpretation of cognitive and academic abilities. In D. P. Flanagan & P. L. Harrison (Eds.), *Contemporary intellectual assessment: Theories, tests, and issues.* New York, Guilford Press.

Alisky, J. M. (2007). The coming problem of HIV-associated Alzheimer's disease. *Medical Hypotheses, 12,* 47–55.

Allan, P. (1990). Looking for work after forty: Job search experiences of older unemployed managers and professionals. *Journal of Employment Counseling, 27,* 113–121.

Allen, J., Chavez, S., DeSimone, S., Howard, D., Johnson, K., LaPierre, L., et al. (2006, June). Americans' attitudes toward euthanasia and physician-assisted suicide, 1936–2002. *Journal of Sociology & Social Welfare, 33,* 5–23.

Allen, J. P., Philliber, S., Herrling, S., & Kuperminc, G. P. (1997). Preventing teen pregnancy and academic failure: Experimental evaluation of a developmentally based approach. *Child Development, 64,* 729–742.

Allen, M., & Bissell, M. (2004). Safety and stability for foster children: The policy context. *The Future of Children, 14,* 49–74.

Allison, A. C. (1954). Protection afforded by sickle cell trait against subtertian malarial infection. *British Medical Journal, 1,* 290–294.

Allison, B., & Schultz, J. (2001). Interpersonal identity formation during early adolescence. *Adolescence, 36*, 509–523.

Aloise-Young, P., Slater, M., & Cruickshank, C. (2006, April). Mediators and moderators of magazine advertisement effects on adolescent cigarette smoking. *Journal of Health Communication, 11*, 281–300.

Altemus, M., Deuster, P. A., Galliven, E., Carter, C. S., & Gold, P. W. (1995). Suppression of hypothalmic pituitary adrenal axis responses to stress in lactating women. *Journal of Clinical Endocrinology and Metabolism, 80*, 2954–2959.

Altholz, S., & Golensky, M. (2004). Counseling, support, and advocacy for clients who stutter. *Health & Social Work, 29*, 197–205.

Alvarez-Leon, E. E., Roman-Vinas, B., & Serra-Majem, L. (2006). Dairy products and health: A review of the epidemiological evidence. *British Journal of Nutrition, 96*, Supplement, S94–S99.

Alzheimer's Association. (2004, May 28). Standard prescriptions for Alzheimer's. Available online at http://www.alz.org/AboutAD/Treatment/Standard.asp.

Amato, P., & Afifi, T. (2006, February). Feeling caught between parents: Adult children's relations with parents and subjective well-being. *Journal of Marriage and Family, 68*, 222–235.

Amato, P., & Booth, A. (1997). *A generation at risk.* Cambridge, MA: Harvard University Press.

Amato, P., & Previti, D. (2003). People's reasons for divorcing: Gender, social class, the life course, and adjustment. *Journal of Family Issues, 24*, 602–626.

Amato, P. R., & Booth, A. (2001). The legacy of parents' marital discord: Consequences for children's marital quality. *Journal of Personality and Social Psychology, 81*, 627–638.

American Academy of Family Physicians. (2002). *Position paper on neonatal circumcision.* Leawood, KS: American Academy of Family Physicians.

American Academy of Pediatrics. (1995). *Policy statement on length of hospital stay following birth.* Washington, DC: Author.

American Academy of Pediatrics. (1997, April 16). Press release.

American Academy of Pediatrics. (1999, August). Media education. *Pediatrics, 104*, 341–343.

American Academy of Pediatrics. (2000). *Circumcision: Information for parents.* Washington, DC: American Academy of Pediatrics.

American Academy of Pediatrics (2000b). Clinical Practice Guideline: Diagnosis and evaluation of the child with attention-deficit/hyperactivity disorder. *Pediatrics,* http://www.pediatrics.org/cgi/content/full/105/5/1158.

American Academy of Pediatrics. (2004, June 3). *Sports programs.* Available online at http://www.medem.com/medlb/article_detaillb_for_printer.cfm?article_ID=ZZZD2QD5M7C&sub_cat=405.

American Academy of Pediatrics. (2005). Breastfeeding and the use of human milk: Policy Statement. *Pediatrics, 115*, 496–506.

American Academy of Pediatrics. (2005, May 12). *AAP endorses newborn screening report from the American College of Medical Genetics.* Press release.

American Academy of Pediatrics (Committee on Accident and Poison Prevention). (1990). Trampolines at home, school, and recreational centers. *Pediatrics, 103*, 1053–1056.

American Academy of Pediatrics (Committee on Psychosocial Aspects of Child and Family Health). (1998,

April). Guidance for effective discipline. *Pediatrics, 101*, 723–728.

American Academy of Pediatrics (Committee on Sports Medicine). (1988). Infant exercise programs. *Pediatrics, 82*, 800–825.

American Academy of Pediatrics (Committee on Sports Medicine and Committee on School Health). (1989). Organized athletics for preadolescent children. *Pediatrics, 84(3)*, 583–584.

American Academy of Pediatrics, Dietz, W. H., (Ed.), & Stern, L. (Ed.). (1999). *American Academy of Pediatrics guide to your child's nutrition: Making peace at the table and building healthy eating habits for life.* New York: Villard.

American College of Medical Genetics. (2006). *Genetics in Medicine, 8*, (5), Supplement.

American College of Sports Medicine. (1997, November 3). *Consensus development conference statement on physical activity and cardiovascular health.* Available online at: http://www.acsm.org/nhlbi.htm.

American College Testing Program. (2001). *National dropout rates.* Iowa City, IA: American College Testing Program.

American Council on Education. (1995–1996). *Minorities in higher education.* Washington, DC: Office of Minority Concerns.

American Heart Association. (1988). *Heart facts.* Dallas, TX: Author.

American Psychiatric Association. (1994). *Diagnostic and statistical manual of mental disorders* (4th ed.). Washington, DC: Author.

American Psychological Association. (1992). *Ethical principles of psychologists and code of conduct.* Washington, DC: Author.

American Psychological Association. (2002). *Ethical principles of psychologists and code of conduct. Updated.* Washington, DC: Author.

Amitai, Y., Haringman, M., Meiraz, H., Baram, N., & Leventhal, A. (2004). Increased awareness, knowledge and utilization of preconceptional folic acid in Israel following a national campaign. *Preventive Medicine: An International Journal Devoted to Practice and Theory, 39*, 731–737.

Ammerman, R. T., & Patz, R. J. (1996). Determinants of child abuse potential: Contribution of parent and child factors. *Journal of Clinical Child Psychology, 25*, 300–307.

Amsterlaw, J., & Wellman, H. (2006). Theories of mind in transition: A microgenetic study of the development of false belief understanding. *Journal of Cognition and Development, 7*, 139–172.

An, J., & Cooney, T. (2006, September). Psychological well-being in mid to late life: The role of generativity development and parent–child relationships across the lifespan. *International Journal of Behavioral Development, 30*, 410–421.

Anand, K. J. S., & Hickey, P. R. (1992). Halothane-morphine compared with high-dose sufentanil for anesthesia and post-operative analgesia in neonatal cardiac surgery. *New England Journal of Medicine, 326(1)*, 1–9.

Anders, T. F., & Taylor, T. (1994). Babies and their sleep environment. *Children's Environments, 11*, 123–134.

Anderson, C., Berkowitz, L., Donnerstein, E., Huesmann, L., Johnson, J., Linz, D., Malamuth, N., & Wartella, E. (2003). The influence of media violence on youth. *Psychological Science in the Public Interest, 4*, 81–110.

Anderson, C. A., Funk, J. B., & Griffiths, M. D. (2004). Contemporary issues in adolescent video game playing: Brief overview and introduction to the special issue. *Journal of Adolescence, 27*, 1–3.

Anderson, D., & Pempek, T. (2005). Television and very young children. *American Behavioral Scientist, 48*, 505–522.

Anderson, M. E., Johnson, D. C., & Batal, H. A. (2005). Sudden Infant Death Syndrome and prenatal maternal smoking: rising attributed risk in the Back to Sleep era. *BMC Medical Genetics, 11*, 4.

Anderson, P., & Butcher, K. (2006, March). Childhood obesity: Trends and potential causes. *The Future of Children, 16*, 19–45.

Anderson, R. N. (2001), *United States life tables, 1998. National vital statistics reports* (Vol. 48, No. 18). Hyattsville, MD: National Center for Health Statistics.

Andrews, G., Halford, G., & Bunch, K. (2003). Theory of mind and relational complexity. *Child Development, 74*, 1476–1499.

Angus, J., & Reeve, P. (2006, April). Ageism: A threat to "aging well" in the 21st century. *Journal of Applied Gerontology, 25*, 137–152.

Anisfeld, M. (1996). Only tongue protrusion modeling is matched by neonates. *Developmental Review, 16*, 149–161.

Annenberg Public Policy Center. (2005). *Card playing trend in young people continues.* Philadelphia, PA: Annenberg Public Policy Center.

Annenberg Public Policy Center. (2006). *More than 1 million young people use internet gambling sites each month.* Philadelphia, PA: Annenberg Public Policy Center.

Annunziato, R., & Lowe, M. (2007, April). Taking action to lose weight: Toward an understanding of individual differences. *Eating Behaviors, 8*, 185–194.

Ansberry, C. (1995, February 14). After seven decades, couple still finds romance in the 90s. *The Wall Street Journal*, pp. A1, A17.

Ansberry, C. (1997, November 14). Women of Troy: For ladies on a hill, friendships are a balm in the passages of life. *The Wall Street Journal*, pp. A1, A6.

Antonio, A., Chang, M., Hakuta, K., Kenny, D. Levin, S., & Milem, J. (2006). Effects of racial diversity on complex thinking in college students. *Psychological Science, 15*, 507–510.

Antonucci, T. C. (1990). Social supports and social relationships. In R. H. Binstock & L. K. George (Eds.), *Handbook of aging and the social sciences.* San Diego: Academic Press.

Antonucci, T. C. (2001). Social relations: An examination of social networks, social support, and sense of control. In J. E. Birren & K. W. Schaie (Eds.), *Handbook of the psychology of aging (5th ed.).* San Diego: Academic Press.

Antonucci, T. C., & Akiyama, H. (1991). Social relationships and aging well. *Generations, 15*, 39–44.

Antshel, K., & Antshel, K. (2002). Integrating culture as a means of improving treatment adherence in the Latino population. *Psychology, Health & Medicine, 7*, 435–449.

APA (American Psychological Association). (1996). *Violence and the family.* Washington, DC: Author.

APA Reproductive Choice Working Group. (2000). *Reproductive choice and abortion: A resource packet* Washington, DC: American Psychological Association.

Apperly, I., & Robinson, E. (2002). Five-year-olds' handling of reference and description in the domains of language and mental representation. *Journal of Experimental Child Psychology, 83*, 53–75.

Apter, A., Galatzer, A., Beth-Halachmi, N., & Laron, Z. (1981). Self-image in adolescents with delayed puberty and growth retardation. *Journal of Youth and Adolescence, 10,* 501–505.

Arai, M. (2006, January). Elder abuse in Japan. *Educational Gerontology, 32,* 13–23.

Archer, S. L., & Waterman, A. S. (1994). Adolescent identity development: Contextual perspectives. In C. B. Fisher & R. M. Lerner (Eds.), *Applied developmental psychology.* New York: McGraw-Hill.

Arcus, D. (2001). Inhibited and uninhibited children: Biology in the social context. In T. D. Wachs & G. A. Kohnstamm, (Eds.), *Temperament in context.* Mahwah, NJ: Lawrence Erlbaum Associates.

Arenson, K. W. (2004, December 3). Worried colleges step up efforts over suicide. *The New York Times,* p. A1.

Aries, P. (1962). *Centuries of childhood.* New York: Knopf.

Arkoff, A., Meredith, G., and Dubanoski, J. (2004). Gains in well-being achieved through retrospective proactive life review by independent older women. *Journal of Humanistic Psychology, 44,* 204–214.

Arlotti, J. B., Cottrell, B. H., Hughes, S. H. (1998). Breastfeeding among low-income women with and without peer support. *Journal of Community Health Nursing, 15,* 163–178.

Arnett, J. J. (2000). Emerging adulthood: A theory of development from the late teens through the twenties. *American Psychologist, 55,* 469–480. ·

Arnold, R., & Colburn, N. (2007). Brain food. *School Library Journal, 53,* 29.

Arredondo, E., Elder, J., Ayala, G., Campbell, N., Baquero, B., & Duerksen, S. (2006, December). Is parenting style related to children's healthy eating and physical activity in Latino families? *Health Education Research, 21,* 862–871.

Arseneault, L., Moffitt, T. E., & Caspi, A. (2003). Strong genetic effects on cross-situational antisocial behavior among 5-year-old children according to mothers, teachers, examiner-observers, and twins' self-reports. *Journal of Child Psychology and Psychiatry and Allied Disciplines, 44,* 832–848.

Artal, P., Ferro, M., Miranda, I., & Navarro, R. (1993). Effects of aging in retinal image quality. *Journal of the Optical Society of America, 10,* 1656–1662.

Arts, J. A. R., Gijselaers, W. H., & Boshuizen, H. P. A. (2006). Understanding managerial problem-solving, knowledge use and information processing: Investigating stages from school to the workplace. *Contemporary Educational Psychology, 31,* 387–410.

Asch, D. A. (1996, May 23). The role of critical care nurses in euthanasia and assisted suicide. *The New England Journal of Medicine, 334,* 1374–1379.

Asendorpf, J. (2002). Self-awareness, other-awareness, and secondary representation. In A. Meltzoffa & W. Prinz (Eds.), *The imitative mind: Development, evolution, and brain bases.* New York: Cambridge University Press.

Asendorpf, J. B., Warkentin, V., & Baudonniere, P. (1996). Self-awareness and other-awareness II: Mirror self-recognition, social contingency awareness, and synchronic imitation. *Developmental Psychology, 32,* 313–321.

Asher, S. R., Singleton, L. C., & Taylor, A. R. (1982). Acceptance vs. friendship. Paper presented at the meeting of the American Research Association, New York.

Ashwin, C., Baron-Cohen, S., Wheelwright, S., O'Riordan, M., & Bullmore, E. (2007). Differential activation of the amygdala and the "social brain" during fearful face-processing in Asperger syndrome. *Neuropsychologia, 45,* 2–14.

Askham, J. (1994). Marriage relationships of older people. *Reviews in Clinical Gerontology, 4,* 261–268.

Aslin, R. N. (1987). Visual and auditory development in infancy. In J. D. Osofsky (Ed.), *Handbook of infant development* (2nd ed.). New York: Wiley.

Aspinwall, O. G., & Taylor, S. E. (1993). Effects of social comparison direction, threat, and self-esteem on affect, evaluation, and expected success. *Journal of Personality and Social Psychology, 64,* 708–722.

Astington, J., & Baird, J. (2005). *Why language matters for theory of mind.* New York: Oxford University Press.

Atchley, R. C. (1982). Retirement: Leaving the world of work. *Annals of the American Academy of Political and Social Science, 464,* 120–131.

Atchley, R. C. (1985). *Social forces and aging: An introduction to social gerontology.* Belmont, CA: Wadsworth.

Atchley, R. C. (2000). *Social forces and aging* (9th ed.). Belmont, CA: Wadsworth Thomson Learning.

Atchley, R. (2003). Why most people cope well with retirement. In J. Ronch & J. Goldfield (Eds.), *Mental wellness in aging: Strengths-based approaches.* Baltimore, MD: Health Professions Press.

Atchley, R. C., & Barusch, A. (2005). *Social forces and aging (10th ed.).* Belmont, CA: Wadsworth.

Attie, I., & Brooks-Gunn, J. (1989). The development of eating problems in adolescent girls: A longitudinal study. *Developmental Psychology, 25,* 70–79.

Auestad, N., Scott, D. T., Janowsky, J. S., Jacobsen, C., Carroll, R. E., Montalto, M. B., Halter, R., Qiu, W., Jacobs, J. R., Connor, W. E., Connor, S. L., Taylor, J. A., Neuringer, M., Fitzgerald, K. M., & Hall, R. T. (2003). Visual cognitive and language assessments at 39 months: A follow-up study of children fed formulas containing long-chain polyunsaturated fatty acids to 1 year of age. *Pediatarics, 112,* e177–e183.

Augustyn, M. (2003). "G" is for growing. Thirty years of research on children and *Sesame Street. Journal of Developmental and Behavioral Pediatrics, 24,* 451.

Aviezer, O., Sagi, A., & Resnick, G. (2002). School competence in young adolescence: Links to early attachment relationships beyond concurrent self-perceived competence and representations of relationships. *International Journal of Behavioral Development, 26,* 397–409.

Avis, N. E., Stellato, R., Crawford, S., Bromberger, J., Ganz, P., Cain, V., & Kagawa-Singer, M. (2001). Is there a menopausal syndrome? Menopausal status and symptoms across racial/ethnic groups. *Social Science & Medicine, 52,* 345–356.

Avis, N., Crawford, S., & Johannes, C. (2002). Menopause. In G. Wingood & R. DiClemente (Eds.), *Handbook of women's sexual and reproductive health.* New York: Kluwer Academic/Plenum Publishers.

Avlund, K., Lund, R., & Holstein, B. (2004). Social relations as determinant of onset of disability in aging. *Archives of Gerontology & Geriatrics, 38,* 85–99.

Axia, G., Bonichini, S., & Benini, F. (1995). Pain in infancy: Individual differences. *Perceptual and Motor Skills, 81,* 142.

Aydt, H., & Corsaro, W. (2003). Differences in children's construction of gender across culture: An interpretive approach. *American Behavioral Scientist, 46,* 1306–1325.

Aylward, G. P., & Verhulst, S. J. (2000). Predictive utility of the Bayley Infant Neurodevelopmental Screener (BINS) risk status classifications: Clinical interpretation and application. *Developmental Medicine & Child Neurology, 42,* 25–31.

Ayoub, N. C. (2005, February 25). A pleasing birth: Midwives and maternity care in the Netherlands. *Chronicle of Higher Education,* p. 9.

Babad, E. (1992). Pygmalion—25 years after interpersonal expectations in the classroom. In P. D. Blanck (Ed.),

Interpersonal expectations: Theory, research and application. Cambridge, England: Cambridge University Press.

Bacchus, L., Mezey, G., & Bewley, S. (2006). A qualitative exploration of the nature of domestic violence in pregnancy. *Violence Against Women, 12,* 588–604.

Bader, A. P. (1995). Engrossment revisited: Fathers are still falling in love with their newborn babies. In J. L. Shapiro, M. J. Diamond, & M. Grenberg (Eds.), *Becoming a father.* New York: Springer.

Baer, J. S., Sampson, P. D., & Barr, H. M. (2003). A 21-year longitudinal analysis of the effects of prenatal alcohol exposure on young adult drinking. *Archives of General Psychiatry, 60,* 377–385.

Bai, L. (2005). Children at play: A childhood beyond the Confucian shadow. *Childhood: A Global Journal of Child Research, 12,* 9–32.

Bailey, J. M., Kirk, K. M., Zhu, G., Dunne, M. P., & Martin, N. G. (2000). Do individual differences in sociosexuality represent genetic or environmentally contingent strategies? Evidence from the Australian twin registry. *Journal of Personality and Social Psychology, 78,* 537–545.

Baillargeon, R. (2004). Infants' physical world. *Current Directions in Psychological Science, 13,* 89–94.

Baines, C. J., Vidmar, M., McKeown-Eyssen, G., & Tibshirani, R. (1997, August 15). Impact of menstrual phase on false-negative mammograms in the Canadian National Breast Screening Study. *Cancer, 80,* 720–724.

Baird, A., John, R., & Hayslip, Jr., B. (2000). Custodial grandparenting among African Americans: A focus group perspective. In B. Hayslip, Jr. & R. Goldberg-Glen (Eds.), *Grandparents raising grandchildren: Theoretical, empirical, and clinical perspectives.* New York: Springer.

Bajor, J., & Baltes, B. (2003). The relationship between selection optimization with compensation, conscientiousness, motivation, and performance. *Journal of Vocational Behavior, 63,* 347–367.

Baker, M. (2007, December). Elder mistreatment: Risk, vulnerability, and early mortality. *Journal of the American Psychiatric Nurses Association, 12,* 313–321.

Baker, T., Brandon, T., & Chassin, L. (2004). Motivational influences on cigarette smoking. *Annual Review of Psychology, 55,* 463–491.

Bakker, A., & Heuven, E. (2006, November). Emotional dissonance, burnout, and in-role performance among nurses and police officers. *International Journal of Stress Management, 13,* 423–440.

Balaban, M. T., Snidman, N., & Kagan, J. (1997). Attention, emotion, and reactivity in infancy and early childhood. In P. J. Lang, R. F. Simons, & M. T. Balaban (Eds.), *Attention and orienting: Sensory and motivational processes* (pp. 369–391). Mahwah, NJ: Erlbaum.

Ball, K., & Rebok, G. W. (1994). Evaluating the driving ability of older adults. [Special Issue: Research translation in gerontology: A behavioral and social perspective], *Journal of Applied Gerontology, 13,* 20–38.

Ball, M., & Orford, J. (2002). Meaningful patterns of activity amongst the long-term inner city unemployed: A qualitative study. *Journal of Community & Applied Social Psychology, 12,* 377–396.

Ballen, L., & Fulcher, A. (2006). Nurses and doulas: Complementary roles to provide optimal maternity care. *Journal of Obstetric, Gynecologic, & Neonatal Nursing: Clinical Scholarship for the Care of Women, Childbearing Families, & Newborns, 35,* 304–311.

Baltes, M., & Carstensen, L. (2003). The process of successful aging: Selection, optimization and compensation. In U. Staudinger & U. Lindenberger (Eds.),

Understanding human development: Dialogues with lifespan psychology. Netherlands: Kluwer Academic Publishers.

Baltes, M. M. (1995). Dependency in old age: Gains and losses. *Current Directions in Psychological Science, 4,* 14–19.

Baltes, M. M. (1996). *The many faces of dependency in old age.* New York: Cambridge University Press.

Baltes, P., & Freund, A. (2003a). Human strengths as the orchestration of wisdom and selective optimization with compensation. In L. Aspinwall & U. Staudinger (Eds.), *A psychology of human strengths: Fundamental questions and future directions for a positive psychology.* Washington, DC: American Psychological Association.

Baltes, P., & Freund, A. (2003b). The intermarriage of wisdom and selective optimization with compensation: Two meta-heuristics guiding the conduct of life. In C. Keyes & J. Haidt (Eds.), *Flourishing: Positive psychology and the life well-lived.* Washington, DC: American Psychological Association.

Baltes, P. B. (2003). On the incomplete architecture of human ontogeny: Selection, optimization and compensation as foundation of developmental theory. In U. M. Staudinger & U. Lindenberger (Eds.), *Understanding human development: Dialogues with lifespan psychology.* Dordrecht, Netherlands: Kluwer Academic Publishers.

Baltes, P. B., & Baltes, M. M. (1990). Psychological perspectives on successful aging: The model of selective optimization with compensation. In P. B. Baltes & M. M. Baltes (Eds.), *Successful aging: Perspectives from the behavioral sciences.* Cambridge, England: Cambridge University Press.

Baltes, P. B., & Schaie, K. W. (1974, March). The myth of the twilight years. *Psychology Today,* 35–38.

Baltes, P. B., & Staudinger, U. M. (2000). Wisdom: A metaheuristic (pragmatic) to orchestrate mind and virtue toward excellence. *American Psychologist, 55,* 122–136.

Baltes, P. B., Staudinger, U. M., & Lindenberger, U. (1999). Lifespan psychology: Theory and application to intellectual functioning. *Annual Review of Psychology, 50,* 471–507.

Baltes, P. B., Staudinger, U. M., Maercker, A., & Smith, J. (1995). People nominated as wise: A comparative study of wisdom-related knowledge. *Psychology and Aging, 10,* 155–166.

Bamshad, M. J., & Olson, S. E. (2003, December). Does race exist? *Scientific American,* 78–85.

Bamshad, M. J. et al. (2003). Human population genetic structure and inference of group membership. *American Journal of Human Genetics, 72,* 578–589.

Bandura, A. (1977). *Social learning theory.* Englewood Cliffs, NJ: Prentice-Hall.

Bandura, A. (1978). Social learning theory of aggression. *Journal of Communication, 28,* 12–29.

Bandura, A. (1986). *Social foundations of thought and action.* Englewood Cliffs, NJ: Prentice Hall.

Bandura, A. (1994). Social cognitive theory of mass communication. In J. Bryant & D. Zillmann (Eds.), *Media effects: Advances in theory and research. LEA's communication series.* Hillsdale, NJ: Erlbaum.

Bandura, A. (2002). Social cognitive theory in cultural context. *Applied Psychology: An International Review, 51* [*Special Issue*], 269–290.

Bandura, A., Grusec, J. E., & Menlove, F. L. (1967). Vicarious extinction of avoidance behavior. *Journal of Personality and Social Psychology, 5,* 16–23.

Bandura, A., Ross, D., & Ross, S. (1963). Vicarious extinction of avoidance behavior. *Journal of Personality and Social Psychology, 67,* 601–607.

Banich, M. T., & Nicholas, C. D. (1998). Integration of processing between the hemispheres in word recognition. In M. Beeman & C. Chiarello (Eds.), *Right hemisphere language comprehension: Perspectives from cognitive neuroscience* (pp. 349–371). Mahwah, NJ: Erlbaum.

Barberá, E. (2003). Gender schemas: Configuration and activation processes. *Canadian Journal of Behavioural Science, 35,* 176–180.

Bard, D., & Rodgers, J. (2003). Sibling influence on smoking behavior: A within-family look at explanations for a birth-order effect. *Journal of Applied Social Psychology, 33,* 1773–1795.

Barer, B. M. (1994). Men and women aging differently. *International Journal of Aging and Human Development, 38,* 29–40.

Barinaga, M. (2000, June 23). A critical issue for the brain. *Science, 288,* 2116–2119.

Barker, V., Giles, H., & Noels, K. (2001). The English-only movement: A communication analysis of changing perceptions of language vitality. *Journal of Communication, 51,* 3–37.

Barnett, R. C., & Hyde, J. S. (2001). Women, Men, Work, and Family. *American Psychologist, 56,* 781–796.

Barnett, R. C., & Rivers, C. (1992). The myth of the miserable working woman. *Working Woman, 2,* 62–65, 83–85.

Barnett, R. C., & Shen, Y-C. (1997). Gender, high- and low-schedule-control housework tasks, and psychological distress: A study of dual-earner couples. *Journal of Family Issues, 18,* 403–428.

Baron-Cohen, S. (2003). *The essential difference: Men, women and the extreme male brain.* London: Allen Lane/Penguin.

Baron-Cohen, S. (2005). Testing the extreme male brain (EMB) theory of autism: Let the data speak for themselves. *Cognitive Neuropsychiatry, 10,* 77–81.

Barr, R., & Hayne, H. (1999). Developmental changes in imitation from television during infancy. *Child Development, 70,* 1067–1081.

Barr, R., Marrott, H., & Rovee-Collier, C. (2003). The role of sensory preconditioning in memory retrieval by preverbal infants. *Learning & Behavior, 31,* 111–123.

Barr, R., Muentener, P., Garcia, A., Fujimoto, M., & Chávez, V. (2007). The effect of repetition on imitation from television during infancy. *Developmental Psychobiology, 49,* 196–207.

Barrett, D. E., & Frank, D. A. (1987). *The effects of undernutrition on children's behavior.* New York: Gordon & Breach.

Barrett, D. E., & Radke-Yarrow, M. R. (1985). Effects of nutritional supplementation on children's responses to novel, frustrating, and competitive situations. *American Journal of Clinical Nutrition, 42,* 102–120.

Barton, L. J. (1997, July). A shoulder to lean on: Assisted living in the U.S. *American Demographics,* 45–51.

Bashore, T. R., Ridderinkhof, K. R., & van der Molen, M. W. (1998). The decline of cognitive processing speed in old age. *Current Directions in Psychological Science, 6,* 163–169.

Bass, S., Shields, M. K., Behrman, R. E. (2004). Children, families, and foster care: Analysis and recommendations. *The Future of Children, 14,* 5–30.

Basseches, M. (1984). *Dialectical thinking and adult development.* Norwood, NJ: Ablex.

Bates, J. E., Marvinney, D., Kelly, T., Dodge, K. A., Bennett, D. S., & Pettit, G. S. (1994). Child-care history and kindergarten adjustment. *Developmental Psychology, 30,* 690–700.

Bauer, P. J. (1996). What do infants recall of their lives? Memory for specific events by 1- to 2-year-olds. *American Psychologist, 51,* 29–41.

Bauer, P. J. (2004). Getting explicit memory off the ground: Steps toward construction of a neuro-developmental account of changes in the first two years of life. *Developmental Review 24,* [Special Issue: Memory development in the new millennium], 347–373.

Bauer, P. J., Wenner, J. A., Dropik, P. L., & Wewerka, S. S. (2000). Parameters of remembering and forgetting in the transition from infancy to early childhood. With commentary by Mark L. Howe. *Monographs of the Society for Research in Child Development, 65,* 4.

Bauer, P. J., Wiebe, S. A., Carver, L. J., Waters, J. M., & Nelson, C. A. (2003). Developments in long-term explicit memory late in the first year of life: Behavioral and electrophysiological indices. *Psychological Science, 14,* 629–635.

Baum, A. (1994). Behavioral, biological, and environmental interactions in disease processes. In S. Blumenthal, K. Matthews, & S. Weiss (Eds.), *New research frontiers in behavioral medicine: Proceedings of the National Conference.* Washington, DC: NIH Publications.

Baumeister, R. F. (Ed.). (1993). *Self-esteem: The puzzle of low self-regard.* New York: Plenum.

Baumrind, D. (1971). Current patterns of parental authority. *Developmental Psychology Monographs, 4* (1, pt. 2).

Baumrind, D. (1980). New directions in socialization research. *Psychological Bulletin, 35,* 639–652.

Baydar, N., & Brooks-Gunn, J. (1998). Profiles of grandmothers who help care for their grandchildren in the United States. *Family Relations, 47,* 385–393.

Bayley, N. (1969). *Manual for the Bayley Scales of Infant Development.* New York: The Psychological Corporation.

Bayley, N., & Oden, M. (1955). The maintenance of intellectual ability in gifted adults. *Journal of Gerontology, 10,* 91–107.

Beach, B. A. (2003). Rural children's play in the natural environment. In D. E. Lytle (Ed.). *Play and educational theory and practice.* Westport, CT: Praeger Publishers/Greenwood Publishing Group.

Beal, C. R. (1994). *Boys and girls: The development of gender roles.* New York: McGraw-Hill.

Beal, C. R., & Belgrad, S. L. (1990). The development of message evaluation skills in young children. *Child Development, 61,* 705–712.

Beals, K., Impett, E., & Peplau, L. (2002). Lesbians in love: Why some relationships endure and others end. *Journal of Lesbian Studies, 6,* 53–63.

Bearce, K., & Rovee-Collier, C. (2006). Repeated priming increases memory accessibility in infants. *Journal of Experimental Child Psychology, 93,* 357–376.

Beardslee, W. R., & Goldman, S. (2003, September 22.) Living beyond sadness. *Newsweek,* p. 70.

Bearman, P., & Bruckner, H. (2004). Study on teenage virginity pledge. Paper presented at meeting of the National STD Prevention Conference, Phildadelphia, PA.

Beauchaine, T. P. (2003). Taxometrics and developmental psychopathology, *Development and Psychopathology: Special Issue, 15,* 501–527.

Becahy, R. (1992, August 3). AIDS epidemic. *Newsweek,* 49.

Beck, M. (1991, November 11). School days for seniors. *Newsweek,* 60–65.

Beck, M. (1992, May 25). Menopause. *Newsweek,* 71–79.

Becker, B., & Luthar, S. (2007, March). Peer-perceived admiration and social preference: Contextual correlates of positive peer regard among suburban and urban adolescents. *Journal of Research on Adolescence, 17,* 117–144.

Becker, G., Beyene, Y., & Newsom, E. (2003). Creating continuity through mutual assistance: Intergenerational reciprocity in four ethnic groups. *Journals of Gerontology: Series B: Psychological Sciences & Social Sciences, 58B,* S151–S159.

Beckman, M. (2004, July 30). Neuroscience: Crime, culpability, and the adolescent brain. *Science,* pp. 305, 596–599.

Becvar, D. S. (2000). Euthanasia decisions. In F. W. Kaslow et al. (Eds.), *Handbook of couple and family forensics: A sourcebook for mental health and legal professionals.* New York: Wiley.

Beeger, S., Rieffe, C., & Terwogt, M. M. (2003). Theory of mind-based action in children from the autism spectrum. *Journal of Autism and Developmental Disorders, 33,* 479–487.

Beehr, T. A., Glazer, S., Nielson, N. L., & Farmer, S. J. (2000). Work and nonwork predictors of employees' retirement ages. *Journal of Vocational Behavior, 57,* 206–225.

Begley, S. (1991, August 26). Choosing death. *Newsweek,* 43–46.

Begley, S. (1995, July 10). Deliver, then depart. *Newsweek,* 62.

Begley, S. (2000). Wired for thought. *Newsweek Special Issue: Your Child,* 25–30.

Beilin, H. (1996). Mind and meaning: Piaget and Vygotsky on causal explanation. *Human Development, 39,* 277–286.

Beilin, H., & Pufall, P. (Eds.). (1992). *Piaget's theory: Prospects and possibilities.* Hillsdale, NJ: Erlbaum.

Belcher, J. R. (2003). Stepparenting: Creating and recreating families in America today. *Journal of Nervous & Mental Disease, 191,* 837–838.

Belkin, L. (1999, July 25). Getting the girl. *The New York Times Magazine,* 26–35.

Belkin, L. (2004, September 12). The lessons of Classroom 506: What happens when a boy with cerebral palsy goes to kindergarten like all the other kids. *The New York Times Magazine,* 41–49.

Bell, A., & Weinberg, M. S. (1978). *Homosexuality: A study of diversities among men and women.* New York: Simon & Schuster.

Bell, I. P. (1989). The double standard: Age. In J. Freeman (Ed.), *Women: A feminist perspective* (4th ed.). Mountain View, CA: Mayfield.

Bell, J. Z. (1978). Disengagement versus engagement—A need for greater expectation. *Journal of American Geriatric Sociology, 26,* 89–95.

Bell, S. M., & Ainsworth, M. D. S. (1972). Infant crying and maternal responsiveness. *Child Development, 43,* 1171–1190.

Bella, D. (2006). *Singled out: How singles are stereotyped, stigmatized, and ignored, and still live happily every after.* New York: St. Martin's Press.

Belle, D. (1999). *The after-school lives of children: Alone and with others while parents work.* Mahwah, NJ: Erlbaum.

Bellezza, F. S., Six, L. S., & Phillips, D. S. (1992). A mnemonic for remembering long strings of digits. *Bulletin of the Psychonomic Society, 30,* 271–274.

Belluck, P. (2005, March 13). With mayhem at home, they call a parent coach. *New York Times,* pp. A1, A33.

Belluck, P. (2000, October 18). New advice for parents: Saying 'that's great!' may not be. *The New York Times,* A14.

Belsky, J. (2006). Early child care and early child development: Major findings from the NICHD Study of Early Child Care. *European Journal of Developmental Psychology, 3,* 95–110.

Belsky, J., Rovine, M., & Taylor, D. G. (1984). The Pennsylvania infant and family development project, III: The origins of individual differences in infant–mother attachment: Maternal and infant contributions. *Child Development, 55,* 718–728.

Belsky, J., Vandell, D. L., Burchinal, M., Clarke-Stewart, A. K., McCartney, K., & Owen, M. T. (2007). Are there long-term effects of early child care? *Child Development, 78,* 188–193.

Bem, S. (1987). Gender schema theory and its implications for child development: Raising gender-aschematic children in a gender-schematic society. In M. R. Walsh (Ed.), *The psychology of women: Ongoing debates.* New Haven, CT: Yale University Press.

Benbow, C. P., Lubinski, D., & Hyde, J. S. (1997). Mathematics: Is biology the cause of gender differences in performance? In M. R. Walsh (Ed.), *Women men & gender: Ongoing debates* (pp. 271–287). New Haven, CT: Yale University Press.

Bender, H., Allen, J., McElhaney, K., Antonishak, J., Moore, C., Kelly, H., et al. (2007, December). Use of harsh physical discipline and developmental outcomes in adolescence. *Development and Psychopathology, 19,* 227–242.

Benedict, H. (1979). Early lexical development: Comprehension and production. *Journal of Child Language, 6,* 183–200.

Benelli, B., Belacchi, C., Gini, G., & Lucangeli, D. (2006, February). "To define means to say what you know about things": The development of definitional skills as metalinguistic acquisition. *Journal of Child Language, 33,* 71–97.

Benenson, J. F., & Apostoleris, N. H. (1993, March). Gender differences in group interaction in early childhood. Paper presented at the biennial meeting of the Society for Research in Child Development, New Orleans, LA.

Bengtson, V. L., Acock, A. C., Allen, K. R., & Dilworth-Anderson, P. (Eds.). (2004). *Sourcebook of family theory and research.* Thousand Oaks, CA: Sage Publications.

Bengston, V. L., Cutler, N. E., Mangen, D. J., & Marshall, V. W. (1985). Generations, cohorts, and relations between age groups. In R. H. Binstock & E. Shanas (Eds.), *Handbook of aging and the social sciences* (2nd ed.). New York: Van Nostrand Reinhold.

Benjamin, J., Ebstein, R. P., & Belmaker, R. H. (2002). Personality genetics, 2002. *Israel Journal of Psychiatry and Related Sciences,* [Special Issue], 39, 271–279.

Benjuya, N., Melzer, I., & Kaplanski, J. (2004). Aging-induced shifts from a reliance on sensory input to muscle cocontraction during balanced standing. *Journal of Gerontology, Series A: Biological Sciences and Medical Sciences, 59,* 166–171.

Bennett, A. (1992, October 14). Lori Schiller emerges from the torments of schizophrenia. *The Wall Street Journal,* pp. A1, A10.

Benson, E. (2003, March). "Goo, gaa, grr?" *Monitor on Psychology,* 50–51.

Benson, H. (1993). The relaxation response. In D. Goleman & J. Guerin (Eds.), *Mind–body medicine: How to use your mind for better health.* Yonkers, NY: Consumer Reports Publications.

Benton, S.A., Robertson, J. M., Tseng, W-C., Newton, F. B., & Benton, S.L. (2003). Changes in counseling center client problems across 13 years. *Professional Psychology: Research and Practice, 34,* 66–72.

Berenbaum, S. A., & Bailey, J. M. (2003). Effects on gender identity of prenatal androgens and genital appearance: Evidence from girls with congenital adrenal hyperplasia. *Journal of Clinical Endocrinology and Metabolism, 88,* 1102–1106.

Berenbaum, S. A., & Hines, M. (1992). Early androgens are related to sex-typed toy preferences. *Psychological Science, 3,* 202–206.

Berenson, P. (2005). *Understand and treat alcoholism.* New York: Basic Books.

Bergen, H., Martin, G., & Richardson, A. (2003). Sexual abuse and suicidal behavior: A model constructed from a large community sample of adolescents. *Journal of the American Academy of Child & Adolescent Psychiatry, 42,* 1301–1309.

Berger, L. (2000, April 11). What children do when home and alone. *New York Times,* p. F8.

Bergeson, T. R., Pisoni, D. B., & Davis R. A. (2005). Development of audiovisual comprehension skills in prelingually deaf children with cochlear implants. *Ear and Hearing, 26,* 149–156.

Bergstrom, M. J., & Holmes, M. E. (2000). Lay theories of successful aging after the death of a spouse: A network text analysis of bereavement advice. *Health Communication, 12,* 377–406.

Berko, J. (1958). The child's learning of English morphology. *Word, 14,* 150–177.

Berkman, B. (2006). *Handbook of social work in health and aging.* New York: Oxford University Press.

Berkman, R. (Ed.), (2006). *Handbook of social work in health and aging.* New York: Oxford University Press.

Berkowitz, L. (1993). *Aggression: Its causes, consequences, and control.* New York: McGraw-Hill.

Berman, A. L., & Jobes, D. A. (1991). *Adolescent suicide: Assessment and intervention.* Washington, DC: American Psychological Association.

Bernal, M. E. (1994, August). *Ethnic identity of Mexican-American children.* Address at the annual meeting of the American Psychological Association, Los Angeles, CA.

Bernal, M. E., & Knight, G. P. (Eds.). (2003). *Ethnic identity: Formation and transmission among Hispanics and other minorities.* Albany: State University of New York Press.

Bernard, J. (1982). *The future of marriage.* New Haven, CT: Yale University Press.

Berndt, T. J. (1999). Friends' influence on students' adjustment to school. *Educational Psychologist, 34,* 15–28.

Berndt, T. J. (2002). Friendship quality and social development. *Current Directions in Psychological Science, 11,* 7–10.

Bernstein, N. (2004, March 7). Behind fall in pregnancy, a new teenage culture of restraint. *The New York Times,* pp. 1, 20.

Berrick, J. D. (1998). When children cannot remain home: Foster family care and kinship care. *Future of Children, 8,* 72–87.

Berry, G. L. (2003). Developing children and multicultural attitudes: The systemic psychosocial influences of television portrayals in a multimedia society. *Cultural Diversity and Ethnic Minority Psychology, 9,* 360–366.

Berry, J. W., Poortinga, Y. H., Segall, M. H., & Dasen, P. (1992). *Cross-cultural psychology: Research and application.* New York: Cambridge University Press.

Berscheid, E. (1985). Interpersonal attraction. In G. Lindzey & E. Aronson (Eds.), *Handbook of social psychology* (3rd ed.). New York: Random House.

Berscheid, E., & Walster, E. (1974a). Physical attractiveness. In G. Lindzey & E. Aronson (Eds.), *Handbook of social psychology* (3rd ed.). New York: Random House.

Berscheid, E., Walster, E., & Bohrnstedt, G. (1973). The happy American body: A survey report. *Psychology Today, 7*(6), 119–131.

Bertin, E., & Striano, T. (2006, April). The still-face response in newborn, 1.5-, and 3-month-old infants. *Infant Behavior & Development, 29,* 294–297.

Besharov, D. J., & West, A. (2002). African American marriage patterns. In A. Thernstrom & S. Thernstrom (Eds.), *Beyond the color line: New perspectives on race and ethnicity in America.* Stanford, CA: Hoover Institution Press.

Bianchi, S. M., & Casper, L. M. (2000). American Families. *Population Bulletin, 55*(4).

Bickham, D. S., Wright, J. C., & Huston, A. C. (2000). Attention, comprehension and the educational influences of television. In D. G. Singer & J. L. Singer (Eds.), *Handbook of children and the media.* Thousand Oaks, CA: Sage.

Biedenharn, B. J., & Normoyle, J. B. (1991). Elderly community residents' reactions to the nursing home: An analysis of nursing home-related beliefs. *Gerontologist, 31,* 107–115.

Bierman, K. L., & Furman, W. (1984). The effects of social skills training and peer involvement on the social adjustment of preadolescents. *Child Development, 55,* 151–162.

Bigelow, A., & Rochat, P. (2006). Two-month-old infants' sensitivity to social contingency in mother–infant and stranger–infant interaction. *Infancy, 9,* 313–325.

Bigler, R. S., Jones, L. C., & Lobliner, D. B. (1997). Social categorization and the formation of intergroup attitudes in children. *Child Development, 68,* 530–543.

Bijeljac-Babic, R., Bertoncini, J., & Mehler, J. (1993). How do 4-day-old infants categorize multisyllabic utterances? *Developmental Psychology, 29,* 711–721.

Bionna, R. (2006). *Coping with stress in a changing world.* New York: McGraw-Hill.

Birch, E. E., Garfield, S., Hoffman, D. R., Uauy, R., & Birch, D. G. (2000). A randomized controlled trail of early dietary supply of long-chain polyunsaturated fatty acids and mental development in term infants. *Developmental Medicine and Child Neurology, 42,* 174–181.

Bird, G., & Melville, K. (1994). *Families and intimate relationships.* New York: McGraw-Hill.

Birlouez-Aragon, I., & Tessier, F. (2003). Antioxidant vitamins and degenerative pathologies: A review of vitamin C. *Journal of Nutrition, Health & Aging, 7,* 103–109.

Biro, F., Striegel-Moore, R., Franko, D., Padgett, J., & Bean, J. (2006, October). Self-esteem in adolescent females. *Journal of Adolescent Health, 39,* 501–507.

Birsner, P. (1991). *Mid-career job hunting.* New York: Simon & Schuster.

Bishop, D. V. M., & Leonard, L. B. (Eds.). (2001). *Speech and language impairments in children: Causes, characteristics, intervention and outcome.* Philadelphia, PA: Psychology Press.

Bishop, J. (2006, April). Euthanasia, efficiency, and the historical distinction between killing a patient and allowing a patient to die. *Journal of Medical Ethics, 32,* 220–224.

Bjorklund, D. F. (1997a). In search of a metatheory of cognitive development (or Piaget is dead and I don't feel so good myself). *Child Development, 68,* 144–148.

Bjorklund, D. F., & Ellis, B. (2005). Evolutionary psychology and child development: An emerging synthesis.

In B. J. Ellis (Ed.), *Origins of the social mind: Evolutionary psychology and child development.* New York: Guilford Press.

Bjorklund, D. F., Schneider, W., Cassel, W. S., & Ashley, E. (1994). Training and extension of a memory strategy: Evidence of utilization deficiencies in the acquisition of an organizational strategy in high- and low-IQ children. *Child Development, 65,* 951–965.

Black, J. E., & Greenough, W. T. (1986). Induction of pattern in neural structure by experience: Implication for cognitive development. In M. E. Lamb, A. L. Brown, & B. Rogoff (Eds.), *Advances in developmental psychology* (Vol. 4). Hillsdale, NJ: Erlbaum.

Black, K. (2002). Associations between adolescent–mother and adolescent–best friend interactions. *Adolescence, 37,* 235–253.

Black, M. M., & Matula, K. (1999). *Essentials of Bayley Scales of Infant Development II assessment.* New York: Wiley.

Blaine, B. E., Rodman, J., & Newman, J. M. (2007). Weight loss treatment and psychological well-being: A review and meta-analysis. *Journal of Health Psychology, 12,* 66–82.

Blair, S. N., Kohl, H. W., Paffenberger, R. S., Clark, D. G., Cooper, K. H., & Gibbons, L. W. (1989). Physical fitness and all-cause mortality: A prospective study of healthy men and women. *Journal of the American Medical Association, 262,* 2395–2401.

Blake, J., & de Boysson-Bardies, B. (1992). Patterns in babbling: A cross-linguistic study. *Journal of Child Language, 19,* 51–74.

Blakemore, J. (2003). Children's beliefs about violating gender norms: Boys shouldn't look like girls, and girls shouldn't act like boys. *Sex Roles, 48,* 411–419.

Blakeslee, S. (1995, August 29). In brain's early growth, timetable may be crucial. *The New York Times,* pp. C1, C3.

Blank, M., & White, S. J. (1999). Activating the zone of proximal development in school: Obstacles and solutions. In P. Lloyd & C. Fernyhough (Eds.), *Lev Vygotsky: Critical assessments: The zone of proximal development, Vol. III.* New York: Routledge.

Blasi, H., & Bjorklund, D. F. (2003). Evolutionary developmental psychology: A new tool for better understanding human ontogeny. *Human Development, 46,* 259–281.

Blass, E. M., Ganchrow, J. R., & Steiner, J. E. (1984). Classical conditioning in newborn humans 2–48 hours of age. *Infant Behavior and Development, 7,* 223–235.

Blazer, D. (1991). Suicide risk factors in the elderly: An epidemiological study. *Journal of Geriatric Psychiatry, 24,* 175–190.

Blennow, K., & Vanmechelen, E. (2003). CSF markers for pathogenic processes in Alzheimer's disease: Diagnostic implications and use in clinical neurochemistry. *Brain Research Bulletin, 61,* 235–242.

Bloom, C., & Lamkin, D. (2006). The Olympian struggle to remember the cranial nerves: Mnemonics and student success. *Teaching of Psychology, 33,* 128–129.

Bloom, L. (1993). *The transition from infancy to language: Acquiring the power of expression.* New York: Cambridge University Press.

Blount, B. G. (1982). Culture and the language of socialization: Parental speech. In D. A. Wagner & H. W. Stevenson (Eds.), *Cultural perspectives on child development.* San Francisco: Freeman.

Blum, D. (2002). *Love at Goon Park: Harry Harlow and the science of affection.* New York: Perseus Publishing.

Blumberg, B. D., Lewis, M. J., & Susman, E. J. (1984). Adolescence: A time of transition. In M. G. Eisenberg,

L. C. Sutkin, & M. A. Jansen (Eds), *Chronic illness and disability through the life span: Effects on self and family.* New York: Springer.

Blumenthal, S. (2000). Developmental aspects of violence and the institutional response. *Criminal Behaviour & Mental Health, 10,* 185–198.

Blumstein, P., & Schwartz, P. (1989). *American couples: Money, work, sex.* New York: Morrow.

Blundon, J., & Schaefer, C. (2006). The role of parent–child play in children's development. *Psychology and Education: An Interdisciplinary Journal, 43,* 1–10.

Blustein, D. L., & Palladino, D. E. (1991). Self and identity in late adolescence: A theoretical and empirical integration. *Journal of Adolescent Research, 6,* 437–453.

Bober, S., Humphry, R., & Carswell, H. (2001). Toddlers' persistence in the emerging occupations of functional play and self-feeding. *American Journal of Occupational Therapy, 55,* 369–376.

Bochner, S. (1996). The learning strategies of bilingual versus monolingual students. *British Journal of Educational Psychology, 66,* 83–93.

Boehmer, U., Linde, R., & Freund, K. M. (2005). Sexual minority women's coping and psychological adjustment after a diagnosis of breast cancer. *Journal of Women's Health, 14,* 213–224.

Boerner, K., Wortman, C. B., Bonanno, G. A. (2005). Resilient or at risk? A 4-year study of older adults who initially showed high or low distress following conjugal loss. *Journal of Gerontology, B, Psychological Sciences and Social Sciences, 60,* P67–P73.

Bogatz, G. A., & Ball, S. (1972). *The second year of Sesame Street: A continuing evaluation.* Princeton, NJ: Educational Testing Service.

Bohlmeijer, E., Smit, F., & Cuijpers, P. (2003). Effects of reminiscence and life review on late-life depression: A meta-analysis. *International Journal of Geriatric Psychiatry, 18,* 1088–1094.

Bolger, N., Foster, M., Vinokur, A. D., & Ng, R. (1996). Close relationships and adjustments to a life crisis: The case of breast cancer. *Journal of Personality and Social Psychology, 70,* 283–294.

Bonanno, G., Galea, S., Bucciarelli, A., & Vlahov, D. (2006). Psychological resilience after disaster: New York City in the aftermath of the September 11th terrorist attack. *Psychological Science, 17,* 181–186.

Bonanno, G. A. (2004). Loss, trauma, and human resilience: Have we underestimated the human capacity to thrive after extremely aversive events? *American Psychologist, 59,* 20–28.

Bonanno, G. A., Moskowitz, J. T., Papa, A., & Folkman, S. (2005). Resilience to loss in bereaved spouses, bereaved parents, and bereaved gay men. *Journal of Personality and Social Psychology, 88,* 827–843.

Bonanno, G. A., Wortman, C. B., Lehman, D. R., Tweed, R. G., Haring, M., Sonnega, J., et al. (2002). Resilience to loss and chronic grief: A prospective study from preloss to 18-months postloss. *Journal of Personality and Social Psychology, 83,* 1150–1164.

Bonke, B., Tibben, A., Lindhout, D., Clarke, A. J., & Stijnen, T. (2005). Genetic risk estimation by healthcare professionals. *Medical Journal of Autism, 182,* 116–118.

Bookheimer, S. Y., Strojwas, M. H., Cophen, M. S., Saunders, A. M., Pericak-Vance, M. A., Mazziotta, J. C., & Small, G. W. (2000, August 17). Patterns of brain activation in people at risk for Alzheimer's disease. *New England Journal of Medicine, 343,* 450–456.

Bookstein, F. L., Sampson, P. D., Streissguth, A. P., & Barr, H. M. (1996). Exploiting redundant measurement of dose and developmental outcome: New methods from the behavioral teratology of alcohol. *Developmental Psychology, 32,* 404–415.

Booth, C., Kelly, J., & Spieker, S. (2003). Toddlers' attachment security to child-care providers: The Safe and Secure Scale. *Early Education & Development, 14,* 83–100.

Booth, W. (1987, October 2). Big Brother is counting your keystrokes. *Science, 238,* 17.

Bor, W., & Bor, W. (2004). Prevention and treatment of childhood and adolescent aggression and antisocial behaviour: A selective review. *Australian & New Zealand Journal of Psychiatry, 38,* 373–380.

Borden, M. E. (1998). *Smart start: The parents' complete guide to preschool education.* New York: Facts on File.

Boren, A. N., Moum, T., Bodtker, A. S., & Ekebert, O. (2005). Reasons for induced abortion and their relation to women's emotional distress: A prospective, two-year follow-up study. *General Hospital Psychiatry, 27,* 36–43.

Borland, M. V., & Howsen, M. (1998). Effect of student attendance on performance: Comment on Lamdin. *Journal of Educational Research, 91,* 195–197.

Borland, M. V., & Howsen, R. M. (2003). An examination of the effect of elementary school size on student academic achievement. *International Review of Education, 49,* 463–474.

Bornstein, M., & Arterberry, M. (2003). Recognition, discrimination and categorization of smiling by 5-month-old infants. *Developmental Science, 6,* 585–599.

Bornstein, M. H., & Bradley, R. H. (2003). *Socioeconomic status, parenting, and child development.* Mahwah, NJ: Lawrence Erlbaum.

Bornstein, M. H., Cote, L., & Maital, S. (2004). Cross-linguistic analysis of vocabulary in young children: Spanish, Dutch, French, Hebrew, Italian, Korean, and American English. *Child Development, 75,* 1115–1139.

Bornstein, M. H., & Lamb, M. E. (1992a). *Development in infancy: An introduction.* New York: McGraw-Hill.

Bornstein, M. H., & Lamb, M. E. (Eds.). (2005). *Developmental science.* Mahwah, NJ: Lawrence Erlbaum Associates.

Bornstein, M. H., Putnick, D. L., Suwalsky, T. D., & Gini, M. (2006). Maternal chronological age, prenatal and perinatal history, social support, and parenting of infants. *Child Development, 77,* 875–892.

Bornstein, M. H., & Sigman, M. D. (1986). Continuity in mental development from infancy. *Child Development, 57,* 251–274.

Boruch, R. F. (1998). Randomized controlled experiments for evaluation and planning. In L. Bickman & D. J. Rog (eds.), *Handbook of applied social research methods* (pp. 161–191). Thousand Oaks, CA: Sage.

Bos, C. S., & Vaughn, S. S. (2005). *Strategies for teaching students with learning and behavior problems,* (6th Ed.). Boston: Allyn & Bacon.

Bos, H., van Balen, F., & van den Boom, D. (2007, January). Child adjustment and parenting in planned lesbian-parent families. *American Journal of Orthopsychiatry, 77,* 38–48.

Botvin, G. J., Epstein, J. A., Schinke, S. P., & Diaz, T. (1994). Predictors of cigarette smoking among inner-city minority youth. *Journal of Developmental and Behavioral Pediatrics, 15,* 67–73.

Bouchard, T. J., Jr. (1997, September/October). Whenever the twain shall meet. *The Sciences,* 52–57.

Bouchard, T. J., Jr. (2004). Genetic influence on human psychological traits: A survey. *Current Directions in Psychological Science, 13,* 148–153.

Bouchard, T. J., Jr., Lykken, D. T., McGue, M., Segal, N. L., & Tellegen, A. (1990, October 12). Sources of human psychological differences: The Minnesota Study of twins reared apart. *Science, 250,* 223–228.

Bouchard, T. J., & McGue, M. (1981). Familial studies of intelligence: A review, *Science, 212,* 1055–1059.

Bouchard, T. J., Jr., & Pedersen, N. (1999). Twins reared apart: Nature's double experiment. In M. C. LaBuda, E. L. Grigorenko, et al. (Eds.), *On the way to individuality: Current methodological issues in behavioral genetics.* Commack, NY: Nova.

Boulton, M. J., & Smith, P. K. (1990). Affective bias in children's perceptions of dominance relationships. *Child Development, 61,* 221–229.

Bourne, V., & Todd, B. (2004). When left means right: An explanation of the left cradling bias in terms of right hemisphere specializations. *Developmental Science, 7,* 19–24.

Bove, C., & Olson, C. (2006). Obesity in low-income rural women: Qualitative insights about physical activity and eating patterns. *Women & Health, 44,* 57–78.

Bowen, D. J., Kahl, K., Mann, S. L., & Peterson, A. V. (1991). Descriptions of early triers. *Addictive Behaviors, 16,* 95–101.

Bowen, N. K., & Bowen, G. L. (1999). Effects of crime and violence in neighborhoods and schools on the school behavior and performance of adolescents. *Journal of Adolescent Research, 14,* 319–342.

Bower, B. (1985). The left hand of math and verbal talent. *Science News, 127,* 263.

Bower, T. G. R. (1977). *A primer of infant development.* San Francisco: Freeman.

Bowers, K. E., & Thomas, P. (1995, August). Handle with care. *Harvard Health Letter,* p. 6–7.

Bracey, J., Bamaca, M., & Umana-Taylor, A. (2004). Examining ethnic identity and self-esteem among biracial and monoracial adolescents. *Journal of Youth & Adolescence, 33,* 123–132.

Bracken, B., & Brown, E. (2006, June). Behavioral identification and assessment of gifted and talented students. *Journal of Psychoeducational Assessment, 24,* 112–122.

Bracken, B., & Lamprecht, M. (2003). Positive self-concept: An equal opportunity construct. *School Psychology Quarterly, 18,* 103–121.

Bradley, R. H., & Caldwell, B. M. (1995). Caregiving and the regulation of child growth and development: Describing proximal aspects of caregiving systems. *Developmental Review, 15,* 38–85.

Brady, L. S. (1995, January 29). Asia Linn and Chris Applebaum. *The New York Times,* p. 47.

Brainerd, C. (2003). Jean Piaget, learning research, and American education. In B. Zimmerman (Ed.), *Educational psychology: A century of contributions.* Mahwah, NJ: Lawrence Erlbaum Associates.

Branje, S. J. T., van Lieshout, C. F. M., van Aken, M. A. G., & Haselager, G. J. T. (2004). Perceived support in sibling relationships and adolescent adjustment. *Journal of Child Psychology and Psychiatry, 45,* 1385–1396.

Brant, M. (2003, September 8). Log on and learn. *Newsweek,* E14.

Branum, A. (2006). Teen maternal age and very preterm birth of twins. *Maternal & Child Health Journal, 10,* 229–233.

Braun, K. L., Pietsch, J. H., & Blanchette, P. L. (Eds.). (2000). *Cultural issues in end-of-life decision making.* Thousand Oaks, CA: Sage Publications.

Brazelton, T. B. (1969). *Infants and mothers: Differences in development.* (Rev. ed.) New York: Dell.

Brazelton, T. B. (1973). *The Neonatal Behavioral Assessment Scale.* Philadelphia: Lippincott.

Brazelton, T. B. (1983). *Infants and mothers: Differences in development* (Rev. ed.). New York: Dell.

Brazelton, T. B. (1990). Saving the bathwater. *Child Development, 61,* 1661–1671.

Brazelton, T. B. (1997). *Toilet training your child.* New York: Consumer Visions.

Brazelton, T. B., Christophersen, E. R., Frauman, A. C., Gorski, P. A., Poole, J. M., Stadtler, A. C. & Wright, C. L. (1999). Instruction, timeliness, and medical influences affecting toilet training. *Pediatrics, 103,* 1353–1358.

Brazelton, T. B., & Sparrow, J. D. (2003). *Discipline: The Brazelton way.* New York: Perseus.

Brazelton, T. B., & Sparrow, J. D. (2004). *Toilet training: The Brazelton way.* Cambridge, MA: DaCapo Press.

Brecher, E. M., & the Editors of Consumer Reports Books. (1984). *Love, sex, and aging.* Mount Vernon, New York: Consumers Union.

Breedlove, G. (2005). Perceptions of social support from pregnant and parenting teens using community-based doulas. *Journal of Perinatal Education, 14,* 15–22.

Breen, F., Plomin, R., & Wardle, J. (2006). Heritability of food preferences in young children. *Physiology & Behavior, 88,* 443–447.

Breheny, M., & Stephens, C. (2003). Healthy living and keeping busy: A discourse analysis of mid-aged women's attributions for menopausal experience. *Journal of Language & Social Psychology, 22,* 169–189.

Brehm, K. (2003). Lessons to be learned at the end of the day. *School Psychology Quarterly, 18,* 88–95.

Brehm, S. S. (1992). *Intimate relationships* (2nd ed.). New York: McGraw-Hill.

Bremmer, J. D. (2003). Long-term effects of childhood abuse on brain and neurobiology. *Child Adolescent Psychiatric Clinics of North America, 12,* 271–292.

Bremner, G., & Fogel, A. (Eds.), (2004). *Blackwell handbook of infant development.* Malden, MA: Blackwell Publishers.

Brennan, K. A., & Shaver, P. R. (1995). Dimensions of adult attachment, affect regulation, and romantic relationship functioning. *Personality and Social Psychology Bulletin, 21,* 267–283.

Bridges, J. S. (1993). Pink or blue: Gender-stereotypic perceptions of infants as conveyed by birth congratulations cards. *Psychology of Women Quarterly, 17,* 193–205.

Briere, J. N., Berliner, L., Bulkley, J., Jenny, C., & Reid, T. (Eds.). (1996). *The APSAC handbook on child maltreatment.* Thousand Oaks, CA: Sage.

Brockington, I. F. (1992). Disorders specific to the puerperium. *International Journal of Mental Health, 21,* 41–52.

Brody, N. (1993). Intelligence and the behavioral genetics of personality. In R. Plomin & G. E. McClearn (Eds.), *Nature, nurture, and psychology.* Washington, DC: American Psychological Association.

Bromberger, J. T., & Matthews, K. A. (1994). Employment status and depressive symptoms in middle-aged women: A longitudinal investigation. *American Journal of Public Health, 84,* 202–206.

Bronfenbrenner, U. (1989). Ecological systems theory. In R. Vasta (Ed.), *Six theories of child development.* Greenwich, CT: JAI Press.

Bronfenbrenner, U. (2000). Ecological theory. In A. Kazdin (Ed.), *Encyclopedia of psychology.* Washington, DC: American Psychological Association/Oxford University Press.

Bronstein, P. (1999). Differences in mothers' and fathers' behaviors toward children: A cross-cultural comparison. In L. A. Peplau, et al. (Eds). *Gender, culture, and ethnicity: Current research about women and men.* Mountain View, CA: Mayfield Publishing.

Brook, U., & Tepper, I. (1997). High school students' attitudes and knowledge of food consumption and body image: Implications for school-based education. *Patient Education & Counseling, 30,* 282–288.

Brooks, J., & Lewis, M. (1976). Infants' responses to strangers: Midget, adult, and child. *Child Development, 47,* 323–332.

Brooks-Gunn, J. (2003). Do you believe in magic?: What we can expect from early childhood intervention programs. *Social Policy Report, 17,* 1–16.

Brooks-Gunn, J., Klebanov, P. K., & Duncan, G. J. (1996). Ethnic differences in children's intelligence test scores: Role of economic deprivation, home environment, and maternal characteristics. *Child Development, 67,* 396–408.

Brown, A. L., & Ferrara, R. A. (1999). Diagnosing zones of proximal development. In P. Llyod & C. Fernyhough (Eds.), *Lev Vygotsky: Critical assessments: The zone of proximal development, Vol. III.* New York: Routledge.

Brown, B. (1990). Peer groups. In S. Feldman & G. Elliott (Eds.), *At the threshold: The developing adolescent.* Cambridge, MA: Harvard University Press.

Brown, J. D. (1998). *The self.* New York, McGraw-Hill.

Brown, J. L., & Pollitt, E. (1996, February). Malnutrition, poverty and intellectual development. *Scientific American,* 38–43.

Brown, J. V., Bakeman, R., Coles, C. D., Platzman, K. A., & Lynch, M. E. (2004). Prenatal cocaine exposure: A comparison of 2-year-old children in prenatal and non-parental care. *Child Development, 75,* 1282–1295.

Brown, R. (1973). *A first language.* Cambridge, MA: Harvard University Press.

Brown, S. (2003). Relationship quality dynamics of cohabitating unions. *Journal of Family Issues, 24,* 583–601.

Brown, S. (2006, March 3). A patient's story. *Australian Doctor.* Retrieved January 7, 2006 from LexisNexis Academic, http://www.australiandoctor.com.au/articles/93/0c03d093.asp?

Brown, W. M., Hines, M., & Fane, B. A. (2002). Masculinized finger length patterns in human males and females with congenital adrenal hyperplasia. *Hormones and Behavior, 42,* 380–386.

Browne, A. (1993). Violence against women by male partners: Prevalence, outcomes, and policy implications. *American Psychologist, 48,* 1077–1087.

Browne, B. A. (1998). Gender stereotypes in advertising on children's television in the 1990s: A cross-national analysis. *Journal of Advertising, 27,* 83–96.

Browne, K. (2006, March). Evolved sex differences and occupational segregation. *Journal of Organizational Behavior, 27,* 143–162.

Brownell, C. A., Ramani, G. B., & Zerwas, S. (2006). Becoming a social partner with peers: Cooperation and social understanding in one- and two-year-olds. *Child Development, 77,* 803–821.

Brownlee, S. (2002, January 21). Too heavy, too young. *Time,* 21–23.

Brubaker, T. (1991). Families in later life: A burgeoning research area. In A. Booth (Ed.), *Contemporary families.* Minneapolis, MN: National Council on Family Relations.

Bruck, M., & Ceci, S. (2004). Forensic developmental psychology: Unveiling four common misconceptions. *Current Directions in Psychological Science, 13,* 229–232.

Brueggeman, I. (1999). Failure to meet ICPD goals will affect global stability, health of environment, and well-being, rights and potential of people. *Asian Forum News,* 8.

Brugman, G. (2006). *Wisdom and aging.* Amsterdam, Netherlands: Elsevier.

Bryant, C. D. (Ed.). (2003). *Handbook of death and dying.* Thousand Oaks, CA: Sage Publications.

Bryant, J., & Bryant, J. (2003). Effects of entertainment televisual media on children. In E. Palmer & B.Young (Eds.), *The faces of televisual media: Teaching, violence, selling to children.* Mahwah, NJ: Lawrence Erlbaum Associates.

Bryant, J., & Bryant, J. A. (Eds.). (2001). *Television and the American family* (2nd ed.). Mahwah, NJ: Lawrence Erlbaum.

Buchanan, C. M., Eccles, J. S., & Becker, J. B. (1992). Are adolescents the victims of raging hormones? Evidence for activational effects of hormones on moods and behavior at adolescence. *Psychological Bulletin, 111,* 62–107.

Buchmann, C., & DiPrete, T. (2006, August). The growing female advantage in college completion: The role of family background and academic achievement. *American Sociological Review, 7,* 515–541.

Budd, K. (1999). The facts of life: Everything you wanted to know about sex (after 50). *Modern Maturity, 42,* 78.

Budris, J. (1998, April 26). Raising their children's children. *Boston Globe 55–Plus,* 8–9, 14–15.

Bugg, J., Zook, N., DeLosh, E., Davalos, D., & Davis, H. (2006, October). Age differences in fluid intelligence: Contributions of general slowing and frontal decline. *Brain and Cognition, 62,* 9–16.

Bukowski, W. M., Sippola, L. K., & Newcomb, A. F. (2000). Variations in patterns of attraction to same- and other-sex peers during early adolescence. *Developmental Psychology, 36,* 147–154.

Bullinger, A. (1997). Sensorimotor function and its evolution. In J. Guimon (Ed.), *The body in psychotherapy* (pp. 25–29). Basil, Switzerland: Karger.

Bumpass, L., Sweet, J., & Martin, T. (1990). Changing patterns of remarriage. *Journal of Marriage and the Family, 52,* 747–756.

Bumpus, M. F., Crouter, A. C., & McHale, S. M. (2001). Parental autonomy granting during adolescence: Exploring gender differences in context. *Developmental Psychology, 37,* 163–173.

Burd, L., Cotsonas-Hassler, T. M., Martsolf, J. T., & Kerbeshian, J. (2003). Recognition and management of fetal alcohol syndrome. *Neurotoxicological Teratology, 25,* 681–688.

Burdjalov, V. F., Baumgart, S., & Spitzer, A. R. (2003). Cerebral function monitoring: A new scoring system for the evaluation of brain maturation in neonates. *Pediatrics, 112,* 855–861.

Burgess, K. B., & Rubin, K. H. (2000). Middle childhood: Social and emotional development. In A. E. Kazdin (Ed.), *Encyclopedia of psychology, Vol. 5.* Washington, DC: American Psychological Association.

Burgess, R. L., & Huston, T. L. (Eds.). (1979). *Social exchanges in developing relationships.* New York: Academic Press.

Burke, V., Beilin, L., Durkin, K., Stritzke, W., Houghton, S., & Cameron, C. (2006, November). Television, computer use, physical activity, diet and fatness in Australian adolescents. *International Journal of Pediatric Obesity, 1,* 248–255.

Burkhammer, M. D., Anderson, G. C., & Chiu, S-H. (2004). Grief, anxiety, stillbirth, and perinatal problems: Healing with kangaroo care. *Journal of Obstetrics and Gynecological Neonatal Nursing, 33,* 774–782.

Burkhammer, M. D., Anderson, G. C., & Chiu, S. H. (2005). Theories of schizophrenia: A genetic-inflammatory-vascular synthesis. *BMC Medical Genetics, 11,* 7.

Burnett, P., & Proctor, R. (2002). Elementary school students' learner self-concept, academic self-concepts and approaches to learning. *Educational Psychology in Practice, 18,* 325–333.

Burnham, M., Goodlin-Jones, B., Gaylor, E. (2002). Nighttime sleep–wake patterns and self-soothing from birth to one year of age: A longitudinal intervention study. *Journal of Child Psychology & Psychiatry & Allied Disciplines, 43,* 713–725.

Burns, D. M. (2000). Cigarette smoking among the elderly: Disease consequences and the benefits of cessation. *American Journal of Health Promotion, 14,* 357–361.

Burrus-Bammel, L. L., & Bammel, G. (1985). Leisure and recreation. In J. E. Birren & K. W. Schaie (Eds.), *Handbook of the psychology of aging.* New York: Van Nostrand Reinhold.

Burt, V. L., & Harris, T. (1994). The third National Health and Nutrition Examination Survey: Contributing data on aging and health. *Gerontologist, 34,* 486–490.

Burton, A., Haley, W., & Small, B. (2006, May). Bereavement after caregiving or unexpected death: Effects on elderly spouses. *Aging & Mental Health, 10,* 319–326.

Bushman, B. J. (1993). Human aggression while under the influence of alcohol and other drugs: An integrative research review. *Current Directions in Psychological Science, 2,* 148–152.

Bushman, B. J., & Anderson, C. A. (2001). Media violence and the American public: Scientific facts versus media misinformation. *American Psychologist, 56,* 477–489.

Bushman, B. J., & Anderson, C. A. (2002). Violent video games and hostile expectations: A test of the general aggression model. *Personality and Social Psychology Bulletin, 28,* 1679–1689.

Buss, D. (2005, January 23). Sure, come back to the nest. Here are the rules. *The New York Times,* p. 8.

Buss, D. M. (2003a). The dangerous passion: Why jealousy is as necessary as love and sex: Book review. *Archives of Sexual Behavior, 32,* 79–80.

Buss, D. M. (2003b). *The evolution of desire: Strategies of human mating* (Revised ed.). New York: Basic Books.

Buss, D. M. (2004). *Evolutionary psychology: The new science of the mind [2nd Ed.].* Boston: Allyn & Bacon.

Buss, D. M., et al. (1990). International preferences in selecting mates: A study of 37 cultures. *Journal of Cross-Cultural Psychology, 21,* 5–47.

Buss, D. M., & Reeve, H. K. (2003). Evolutionary psychology and developmental dynamics: Comment on Lickliter and Honeycutt. *Psychological Bulletin, 129,* 848–853.

Buss, K. A., & Goldsmith, H. H. (1998). Feat and anger regulation in infancy: Effects on the temporal dynamics of affective expression. *Child Development, 69,* 359–374.

Buss, K. A., & Kiel, E. J. (2004). Comparison of sadness, anger, and fear facial expressions when toddlers look at their mothers. *Child Development, 75,* 1761–1773.

Bussey, K. (1992). Lying and truthfulness: Children's definition, standards, and evaluative reactions. *Child Development, 63,* 1236–1250.

Butler, D. (2004, May 18). Science of dieting: Slim pickings. *Nature*, 252–254.

Butler, K. G., & Silliman, E. R. (2002). *Speaking, reading, and writing in children with language learning disabilities: New paradigms in research and practice.* Mahwah, NJ: Lawrence Erlbaum Associates, Publishers, 2002.

Butler, R. N. (2002). The life review. *Journal of Geriatric Psychiatry, 35*, 7–10.

Butler, R. N., & Lewis, M. I. (1981). *Aging and mental health.* St. Louis: Mosby.

Butterworth, G. (1994). Infant intelligence. In J. Khalfa (Ed.), *What is intelligence? The Darwin College lecture series* (pp. 49–71). Cambridge, England: Cambridge University Press.

Buysse, D. J. (2005). Diagnosis and assessment of sleep and circadian rhythm disorders. *Journal of Psychiatric Practice, 11*, 102–115.

Byrne, A. (2000). Singular identities: Managing stigma, resisting voices. *Women's Studies Review, 7*, 13–24.

Byrne, B. (2000). Relationships between anxiety, fear, self-esteem, and coping strategies in adolescence. *Adolescence, 35*, 201–215.

Cadinu, M. R., & Kiesner, J. (2000). Children's development of a theory of mind. *European Journal of Psychology of Education, 15*, 93–111.

Cain, B. S. (1982, December 19). Plight of the gray divorcee. *The New York Times Magazine*, 89–93.

Cain, V., Johannes, C., & Avis, N. (2003). Sexual functioning and practices in a multi-ethnic study of midlife women: Baseline results from SWAN. *Journal of Sex Research, 40*, 266–276.

Caino, S., Kelmansky, D., Lejarraga, H., & Adamo, P. (2004). Short-term growth at adolescence in healthy girls. *Annals of Human Biology, 31*, 182–195.

Caldas, S. J., & Bankston, C. (1997). Effect of school population socioeconomic status on individual academic achievement. *Journal of Educational Research, 90*, 269–277.

Caldera, Y. M., & Sciaraffa, M. A. (1998). Parent–toddler play with feminine toys: Are all dolls the same? *Sex Roles, 39*, 657–668.

Calhoun, F., & Warren, K. (2007). Fetal alcohol syndrome: Historical perspectives. *Neuroscience & Biobehavioral Reviews, 31*, 168–171.

Callister, L. C., Khalaf, I., Semenic, S., Kartchner, R., Vehvilainen-Julkunen, K. (2003). The pain of childbirth: Perceptions of culturally diverse women. *Pain Management Nursing, 4*, 145–154.

Calvert, S. L., Kotler, J. A., Zehnder, S., & Shockey, E. (2003). Gender stereotyping in children's reports about educational and informational television programs. *Media Psychology, 5*, 139–162.

Camarota, S. A. (2001). *Immigrants in the United States — 2000: A snapshot of America's foreign-born population.* Washington, DC: Center for Immigration Studies.

Cameron, P. (2003). Domestic violence among homosexual partners. *Psychological Reports, 93*, 410–416.

Cami, J., & Farré, M., (2003). Drug addiction. *New England Journal of Medicine, 349*, 975–986.

Campbell, A., Shirley, L., & Candy, J. (2004). A longitudinal study of gender-related cognition and behaviour. *Developmental Science, 7*, 1–9.

Campbell, F., Ramey, C., & Pungello, E. (2002). Early childhood education: Young adult outcomes from the Abecedarian Project. *Applied Developmental Science, 6*, 42–57.

Campbell, F. A., Pungello, E. P., Miller-Johnson, S., Ramey, C. T., & Burchinal, M. (2001). The development of cognitive and academic abilities: Growth curves from an early childhood educational experiment. *Developmental Psychology, 37*, 231–242.

Campos, J. J., Langer, A., & Krowitz, A. (1970). Cardiac responses on the visual cliff in prelocomotor human infants. *Science, 170*, 196–197.

Camras, L. A., Malatesta, C., & Izard, C. E. (1991). The development of facial expressions in infancy. In R. S. Feldman & B. Rime (Eds.), *Fundamentals of nonverbal behavior.* Cambridge, England: Cambridge University Press.

Camras, L., Meng, Z., & Ujiie, T. (2002). Observing emotion in infants: Facial expression, body behavior, and rater judgments of responses to an expectancy-violating event. *Emotion, 2*, 179–193.

Camras, L. A., & Sachs, V. B. (1991). Social referencing and caretaker expressive behavior in a day care setting. *Infant Behavior and Development, 14*, 27–36.

Canals, J., Fernandez-Ballart, J., Esparo, G. (2003). Evolution of Neonatal Behavior Assessment Scale scores in the first month of life. *Infant Behavior & Development, 26*, 227–237.

Canfield, R. L., Smith, E. G., Breznyak, M. P., & Snow, K. L. (1997). Information processing through the first year of life: A longitudinal study using the visual expectation paradigm. With commentary by Richard N. Aslin, Marshall M. Hairth, Tara S. Wass, & Scott A. Adler. *Monographs of the Society for Research in Child Development, 62* (2, Serial No. 250).

Cano, A., Gillis, M., Heinz, W., Geisser, M., & Foran, H. (2004). Marital functioning, chronic pain, and psychological distress. *Pain, 107*, 99–106.

Cardalda, E. B., Miranda, S. E. Perez, M., & Sierra, E. M. (2003). Attitudes toward breastfeeding working mothers. *Puerto Rican Health Science Journal, 22*, 305–310.

Cardman, M. (2004). Rising GPAs, course loads a mystery to researchers. *Education Daily, 37*, 1–3.

Carey, K. (2004). A matter of degrees: *Improving graduation rates in four-year colleges and universities.* Washington, DC: Education Trust.

Carlson, E., & Hoem, J. M. (1999). Low-weight neonatal survival paradox in the Czech Republic: Original contributions. *American Journal of Epidemiology, 149*, 447–453.

Carmeli, A., & Josman, Z. (2006). The relationship among emotional intelligence, task performance, and organizational citizenship behaviors. *Human Performance, 19*, 403–419.

Carmichael, M. (2004, May 10). Have it your way: Redesigning birth. *Newsweek*, 70–72.

Carmody, D. (1990, March 7). College drinking: Changes in attitude and habit. *The New York Times.*

Carnegie Task Force on Meeting the Needs of Young Children. (1994). *Starting points: Meeting the needs of our youngest children.* New York: Carnegie Corporation.

Jones, C. (2004). *Supporting inclusion in the early years.* Maidenhead: England: Open University Press.

Caron, C., Gjelsvik, A., & Buechner, J. S. (2005). The impact of poverty on prevention practices and health status among persons with asthma. *Medicine Health Rhode Island, 88*, 60–62.

Carpendale, J. I. M. (2000). Kohlberg and Piaget on stages and moral reasoning. *Developmental Review, 20*, 181–205.

Carr, C. N., Kennedy, S. R., & Dimick, K. M. (1996). Alcohol use among high school athletes. *The Prevention Researcher, 3*, 1–3.

Carr, D. (2003). A "good death" for whom? Quality of spouse's death and psychological distress among older widowed persons. *Journal of Health and Social Behavior, 44*, 215–232.

Carr, D., & Ha, J. (2006). *Bereavement.* New York: Oxford University Press.

Carr, D., House, J. S., & Kessler, R. C. (2002). Marital quality and psychological adjustment to widowhood among older adults: A longitudinal analysis. *Journals of Gerontology: Series B: Psychological Sciences and Social Sciences, 55B*,(4), S197–S207.

Carr, D., Nesse, R., & Wortman, C. (2005). *Spousal bereavement in late life.* New York: Springer.

Carrere, S., Buehlman, K. T., Gottman, J. M., Coan, J. A., & Ruckstuhl, L. (2000). Predicting marital stability and divorce in newlywed couples. *Journal of Family Psychology, 14*, 42–58.

Carroll, L. (2000, February 1). Is memory loss inevitable? Maybe not. *The New York Times*, pp. D1, D7.

Carson, R. G. (2005). Neural pathways mediating bilateral interactions between the upper limbs. *Brain Research Review, 49*, 641–662.

Carstensen, L. L. (1995). Evidence for a life-span theory of socioemotional selectivity. *Current Directions in Psychological Science, 4*, 151–156.

Carstensen, L. L., Pasupathi, M., Mayr, U., Nesselroade, J. R. (2000). Emotional experience in everyday life across the adult life span. *Journal of Personality and Social Psychology, 79*, 644–655.

Carvajal, F., & Iglesias, J. (2000). Looking behavior and smiling in Down syndrome infants. *Journal of Nonverbal Behavior, 24*, 225–236.

Carver, C., & Scheier, M. (2002). Coping processes and adjustment to chronic illness. In A. Christensen & M. Antoni (Eds.), *Chronic physical disorders: Behavioral medicine's perspective* (pp. 47–68). Malden: Blackwell Publishers.

Carver, C. S., & Scheier, M. F. (1993). On the power of positive thinking: The benefits of being optimistic. *Current Directions in Psychological Science, 2*, 26–30.

Carver, L., Dawson, G., & Panagiotides, H. (2003). Age-related differences in neural correlates of face recognition during the toddler and preschool years. *Developmental Psychobiology, 42*, 148–159.

Carver, L., & Vaccaro, B. (2007, January). 12-month-old infants allocate increased neural resources to stimuli associated with negative adult emotion. *Developmental Psychology, 43*, 54–69.

Cascalho, M., Ogle, B. M., & Platt, J. L. (2006). The future of organ transplantation. *Annals of Transplantation, 11*, 44–47.

Case, R. (1991). Stages in the development of the young child's first sense of self. *Developmental Review, 11*, 210–230.

Case, R. (1999). Conceptual development. In M. Bennett, *Developmental psychology: Achievements and prospects.* Philadelphia, PA: Psychology Press.

Case, R., Demetriou, A., & Platsidou, M. (2001). Integrating concepts and tests of intelligence from the differential and developmental traditions. *Intelligence, 29*, 307–336.

Case, R., & Okamoto, Y. (1996). The role of central conceptual structures in the development of children's thought. *Monographs of the Society for Research in Child Development, 61*, v–265.

Caspi, A. (2000). The child is father of the man: Personality continuities from childhood to adulthood. *Journal of Personality and Social Psychology, 78*, 158–172.

Caspi, A., & Moffitt, T. E. (1991). Individual differences are accentuated during periods of social change: The sample case of girls at puberty. *Journal of Personality and Social Psychology, 61,* 157–168.

Caspi, A., & Moffitt, T. E. (1993). *Continuity amidst change: A paradoxical theory of personality coherence.* Manuscript submitted for publication.

Cassidy, J., & Berlin, L. J. (1994). The insecure/ambivalent pattern of attachment: Theory and research. *Child Development, 65,* 971–991.

Castel, A., & Craik, F. (2003). The effects of aging and divided attention on memory for item and associative information. *Psychology & Aging, 18,* 873–885.

Catell, R. B. (1967). *The scientific analysis of personality.* Chicago: Aldine.

Catell, R. B. (1987). *Intelligence: Its structure, growth, and action.* Amsterdam: North-Holland.

Cath, S., & Shopper, M. (2001). *Stepparenting: Creating and recreating families in America today.* Hillsdale, NJ: Analytic Press, Inc.

Cauce, A., & Domenech-Rodriguez, M. (2002). Latino families: myths and realities. In J.M. Contreras, J. K. A., Kerns, & A.M. Neal-Barnett (Eds.), *Latino children and families in the United States.* Westport, CT: Praeger.

Cauce, A. M., Steward, A., & Domenech-Rodriguez, M. (2003). Overcoming the odds? Adolescent development in the context of urban poverty. In S. S. Luthar (Ed.), *Resilience and vulnerability: Adaptation in the context of childhood adversities.*

Caughlin, J. (2002). The demand/withdraw pattern of communication as a predictor of marital satisfaction over time. *Human Communication Research, 28,* 49–85.

Cavallini, A., Fazzi, E., & Viviani, V. (2002).Visual acuity in the first two years of life in healthy term newborns: An experience with the Teller Acuity Cards.*Functional Neurology: New Trends in Adaptive & Behavioral Disorders, 17,* 87–92.

Cavallini, E., Pagnin, A., & Vecchi, T. (2003). Aging and everyday memory: The beneficial effect of memory training. *Archives of Gerontology & Geriatrics, 37,* 241–257.

Ceci, S. J., Fitneva, S. A., & Gilstrap, L. L. (2003). Memory development and eyewitness testimony. In A. Slater & G. Bremner, *An introduction to developmental psychology.* Malden, MA: Blackwell Publishers.

Center for Communication and Social Policy, University of California. (1998). *National television violence study, Vol. 2.* Thousand Oaks, CA: Sage.

Center on Addiction and Substance Abuse. (1994). *Report on college drinking.* New York: Columbia University.

Centers for Disease Control. (1991). *Preventing lead poisoning in young children: A statement by the Centers for Disease Control.* Atlanta, GA: U.S. Department of Health and Human Services.

Centers for Disease Control. (2003). Incidence-surveillance, epidemiology, and end results program, 1973–2000. Atlanta, GA: Author.

Centers for Disease Control. (2004). Health behaviors of adults: United States, 1999–2001. *Vital and Health Statistics, Series 10, no. 219.* Washington, DC: U.S. Department of Health and Human Services.

Centers for Disease Control and Prevention. (1998). *1997 youth risk behavior surveillance system.* Atlanta, GA: Author.

Centers for Disease Control and Prevention. (2000). *Obesity continues to climb in 1999 among American adults.* Division of Nutrition and Physical Activity, National Center for Chronic Disease Prevention and Health Promotions. Atlanta, GA: Author.

Centers for Disease Control and Prevention. (2006). *HIV/AIDS surveillance report.* Atlanta: Author.

Cerella, J. (1990). Aging and information-processing rate. In J. E. Birren & K. W. Schaie (Eds.), *Handbook of the psychology of aging* (3rd ed.). San Diego, CA: Academic Press.

CFCEPLA (Commonwealth Fund Commission on Elderly People Living Alone). (1986). *Problems facing elderly Americans living alone. New* York: Louis Harris & Associates.

Chaffin, M. (2006). The changing focus of child maltreatment research and practice within psychology. *Journal of Social Issues, 62,* 663–684.

Chaiklin, S. (2003). The zone of proximal development in Vygotsky's analysis of learning and instruction. In A. Kozulin & B. Gindis (Eds.), *Vygotsky's educational theory in cultural context.* New York: Cambridge University Press.

Chaker, A. M. (2003, September 23). Putting toddlers in a nursing home. *The Wall Street Journal,* D1.

Chall, J. (1992). The new reading debates: Evidence from science, art, and ideology. *Teachers College Record, 94,* 315–328.

Chall, J. S. (1979). The great debate: Ten years later, with a modest proposal for reading stages. In L. B. Resnick & P. A. Weaver (Eds.), *Theory and practice of early reading.* Hillsdale, NJ: Erlbaum.

Chamberlain, P., Price, J., Reid, J., Landsverk, J., Fisher, P., & Stoolmiller, M. (2006, April). Who disrupts from placement in foster and kinship care? *Child Abuse & Neglect, 30,* 409–424.

Chan, C. G., & Elder, G. H. Jr., (2000). Matrilineal advantage in grandchild-grandparent relations. *Gerontologist, 40,* 179–190.

Chan, D. W. (1997). Self-concept and global self-worth among Chinese adolescents in Hong Kong. *Personality & Individual Differences, 22,* 511–520.

Chao, R. K. (1994). Beyond parental control and authoritarian parenting style: Understanding Chinese parenting through the cultural notion of training. *Child Development, 65,* 1111–1119.

Chao, R. K. (2001). Extending research on the consequences of parenting style for Chinese Americans and European Americans. *Child Development, 72,* 1832–1843.

Chapple, A., Ziebland, S., McPherson, A., & Herxheimer, A. (2006, December). What people close to death say about euthanasia and assisted suicide: A qualitative study. *Journal of Medical Ethics, 32,* 706–710.

Charles, S. T., Mather, M., & Carstensen, L. L. (2003). Aging and emotional memory: The forgettable nature of negative images for older adults. *Journal of Experimental Psychology: General, 132,* 237–244.

Charles, S. T., Reynolds, C. A., & Gatz, M. (2001). Age-related differences and change in positive and negative affect over 23 years. *Journal of Personality and Social Psychology, 80,* 136–151.

Chatterji, M. (2004). Evidence on "What works": An argument for extended-term mixed-method (ETMM) evaluation designs. *Educational Researcher, 33,* 3–14.

Chen, C., Lee, S., & Stevenson, H. W. (1996). Long-term prediction of academic achievement of American, Chinese, and Japanese adolescents. *Journal of Educational Psychology, 88,* 750–759.

Chen, J., & Gardner, H. (2005). Assessment based on multiple-intelligences theory. In D. P. Flanagan & P. L. Harrison (Eds.), *Contemporary intellectual assessment: Theories, tests, and issues.* New York, Guilford Press.

Chen, X., Hastings, P. D., Rubin, K. H., Chen, H., Cen, G., & Stewart, S. L. (1998). Child-rearing attitudes and behavioral inhibition in Chinese and Canadian tod-

dlers: A cross-cultural study. *Developmental Psychology, 34,* 677–686.

Cherlin, A. (1993). *Marriage, divorce, remarriage.* Cambridge, MA: Harvard University Press.

Cherlin, A., & Furstenberg, F. (1986). *The new American grandparent.* New York: Basic Books.

Cherney, I. (2003). Young children's spontaneous utterances of mental terms and the accuracy of their memory behaviors: A different methodological approach. *Infant & Child Development, 12,* 89–105.

Cherney, I., Kelly-Vance, L., & Glover, K. (2003).The effects of stereotyped toys and gender on play assessment in children aged 18–47 months. *Educational Psychology, 23,* 95–105.

Cherry, K. E., & Park, D. C. (1993). Individual difference and contextual variables influence spatial memory in younger and older adults. *Psychology and Aging, 8,* 517–526.

Chicchetti, D., & Cohen, D. J. (Eds.). (2006). *Developmental psychopathology: Theory and Method, Vols 1–3.* New York: John Wiley & Sons.

Chien, S., Bronson-Castain, K., Palmer, J., & Teller, D. (2006). Lightness constancy in 4-month-old infants. *Vision Research, 46,* 2139–2148.

Child Health USA. (2002). *U.S. infant mortality rates by race of mother: 1980–2000.* Washington, DC: U.S. Dept of Health and Human Services.

Child Health USA. (2005). U.S. Department of Health and Human Services, Health Resources and Services Administration, Maternal and Child Health Bureau. *Child health USA 2005.* Rockville, MD: U.S. Department of Health and Human Services.

Child Health USA (2007). U.S. Department of Health and Human Services, Health Resources and Services Administration, Maternal and Child Health Bureau. *Child Health USA 2007.* Rockville, MD: U.S. Department of Health and Human Services.

Child Maltreatment. (2002). *Child maltreatment.* Washington, DC: U.S. Department of Health and Human Services.

Childs, B. (2003). *Genetic medicine: A logic of disease.* Baltimore: Johns Hopkins University Press.

ChildStats.gov. (2000). *America's children 2000.* Washington, DC: National Maternal and Child Health Clearinghouse.

ChildStats.gov. (2005). *America's children 2005.* Washington, DC: National Maternal and Child Health Clearinghouse.

Chisolm, T., Willott, J., & Lister, J. (2003). The aging auditory system: Anatomic and physiologic changes and implications for rehabilitation. *International Journal of Audiology, 42,* 2S3–2S10.

Choi, H. (2002). Understanding adolescent depression in ethnocultural context. *Advances in Nursing Science, 25,* 71–85.

Choi, H., & Marks, N. (2006, December). Transition to caregiving, marital disagreement, and psychological well-being: A prospective U.S. National Study. *Journal of Family Issues, 27,* 1701–1722.

Chomsky, N. (1968). *Language and mind.* New York: Harcourt Brace Jovanovich.

Chomsky, N. (1978). On the biological basis of language capacities. In G. A. Miller & E. Lennenberg (Eds.), *Psychology and biology of language and thought* (pp. 199–220). New York: Academic Press.

Chomsky, N. (1991). Linguistics and cognitive science: Problems and mysteries. In A. Kasher (Ed.), *The Chomskyan turn.* Cambridge, MA: Blackwell.

Chomsky, N. (1999). On the nature, use, and acquisition of language. In W. C. Ritchie & T. J. Bhatia (Eds.), *Handbook of child language acquisition.* San Diego: Academic Press.

Chomsky, N. (2005). Editorial: Universals of human nature. *Psychotherapy and Psychosomatics [serial online], 74,* 263–268.

Choy, C. M., Yeung, Q. S., Briton-Jones, C. M., Cheung, C. K., Lam, C. W., & Haines, C. J. (2002). Relationship between semen parameters and mercury concentrations in blood and in seminal fluid from subfertile males in Hong Kong. *Fertility and Sterility, 78,* 426–428.

Christophersen, E. R., Mortweet, S. L. (2003). Disciplining your child effectively. In E. R. Christophersen & S. L. Mortweet, *Parenting that works: Building skills that last a lifetime.* Washington, DC: American Psychological Association.

Chronis, A., Jones, H., & Raggi, V. (2006, June). Evidence-based psychosocial treatments for children and adolescents with attention-deficit/hyperactivity disorder. *Clinical Psychology Review, 26,* 486–502.

Chung, S. A., Wei, A. Q., Connor, D. E., Webb, G. C., Molloy, T., Pajic, M., & Diwan, A. D. (2007). Nucleus pulposus cellular longevity by telomerase gene therapy. *Spine, 15,* 1188–1196.

Cianciolo, A. T., Matthew, C., & Sternberg, R. J. (2006). Tacit knowledge, practical intelligence, and expertise. In K. A. Ericsson, N. Charness, P. J. Feltovich, & R. R. Hoffman, *The Cambridge handbook of expertise and expert performance.* New York: Cambridge University Press.

Cicchetti, D. (1996). Child maltreatment: Implications for developmental theory and research. *Human Development, 39,* 18–39.

Cicchetti, D. (2003). Neuroendocrine functioning in maltreated children. In D. Cicchetti and E. Walker (Eds.), *Neurodevelopmental mechanisms in psychopathology.* New York: Cambridge University Press.

Cicchetti, D. (2004). An odyssey of discovery: Lessons learned through three decades of research on child maltreatment. *American Psychologist, 59,* [Special issue: Awards Issue 2004], 731–741.

Cicchetti, D., & Cohen, D. J. (2006). *Developmental Psychopathology, Vol. 1: Theory and method, 2nd Edition.* Hoboken, NJ: John Wiley & Sons.

Cicchetti, D., Rogosch, F. A., Maughan, A., Toth, S., & Bruce, J. (2003). False belief understanding in maltreated children. *Journal of Development and Psychopathology, 15,* Special Issue, 1067–1091.

Cicchetti, D., & Toth, S. L. (1998). The development of depression in children and adolescents. *American Psychologist, 53,* 221–241.

Cillessen, A. H. N., & Mayeux, L. (2004). From censure to reinforcement: Developmental changes in the association between aggression and social status. *Child Development, 75,* 147–163.

CIRE (Cooperative Institutional Research Program of the American Council on Education). (1990). *The American freshman: National norms for fall 1990.* Los Angeles: American Council on Edcuation.

Ciricelli, V. G. (1995). *Sibling relationships across the life span.* New York: Plenum.

Cirulli, F., Berry, A., & Alleva, E. (2003). Early disruption of the mother–infant relationship: Effects on brain plasticity and implications for psychopathology. *Neuroscience & Biobehavioral Reviews, 27,* 73–82.

Claes, M., Lacourse, E., & Bouchard, C. (2003). Parental practices in late adolescence, a comparison of three countries: Canada, France and Italy. *Journal of Adolescence, 26,* 387–399.

Clark, E. (1983). Meanings and concepts. In J. Flavell & E. Markham (Eds.), *Handbook of child psychology: Cognitive development* (Vol. 3). New York: Wiley.

Clark, J. E., & Humphrey, J. H. (Eds.). (1985). *Motor development: Current selected research.* Princeton, NJ: Princeton Book Company.

Clark, K. B., & Clark, M. P. (1947). Racial identification and preference in Negro children. In T. M. Newcomb & E. L. Hartley (Eds.), *Readings in social psychology.* New York: Holt, Rinehart & Winston.

Clark, R. (1998). *Expertise.* Silver Spring, MD: International Society for Performance Improvement.

Clark, R., Hyde, J. S., Essex, M. J., & Klein, M. H. (1997). Length of maternity leave and quality of mother–infant interactions. *Child Development, 68,* 364–383.

Clarke-Stewart, A., & Friedman, S. (1987). *Child development: Infancy through adolescence.* New York: Wiley.

Clarke-Stewart, K., & Allhusen, V. (2002). Nonparental caregiving. (2002). In M. Bornstein (Ed.), *Handbook of parenting: Vol. 3: Being and becoming a parent* (2nd ed.). Mahwah, NJ: Lawrence Erlbaum Associates.

Claxton, L. J., Keen R., & McCarty, M. E. (2003). Evidence of motor planning in infant reaching behavior. *Psychological Science, 14,* 354–356.

Clearfield, M., & Nelson, N. (2006, January). Sex differences in mothers' speech and play behavior with 6-, 9-, and 14-month-old infants. *Sex Roles, 54,* 127–137.

Clemetson, L. (2000, September 18). Love without borders. *Newsweek,* 62.

Cliff, D. (1991). Negotiating a livable retirement: Further paid work and the quality of life in early retirement. *Aging and Society, 11,* 319–340.

Clifton, R. (1992). The development of spatial hearing in human infants. In L. A. Werner & E. W. Rubel (Eds.), *Developmental psychoacoustics* (pp. 135–157). Washington, DC: American Psychological Association.

Clinton, J. F., & Kelber, S. T. (1993). Stress and coping in fathers of newborns: Comparisons of planned versus unplanned pregnancy. *International Journal of Nursing Studies, 30,* 437–443.

Cnattingius, S., Berendes, H., & Forman, M. (1993). Do delayed childbearers face increased risks of adverse pregnancy outcomes after the first birth? *Obstetrics and Gynecology, 81,* 512–516.

CNN/USA Today/Gallup Poll. (1997, February). How many children? *The Gallup Poll Monthly.*

Cobbe, E. (2003, September 25). France ups heat toll. *CBS Evening News.*

Cohen, J. (1999, March 19). Nurture helps mold able minds. *Science, 283,* 1832–1833.

Cohen, L. B., & Cashon, C. H. (2003). Infant perception and cognition. In R. M. Lerner & M. A. Easterbrooks, (Eds.), *Handbook of psychology: Developmental psychology, (Vol. 6).* New York: John Wiley & Sons.

Cohen, S., Hamrick, N., Rodriguez, M. S., Feldman, P. J., Rabin B. S., & Manuck, S. B. (2002). Reactivity and vulnerability to stress-associated risk for upper respiratory illness. *Psychosomatic Medicine, 64,* 302–310.

Cohen, S., Tyrell, D. A., & Smith, A. P. (1993). Negative life events, perceived stress, negative affect, and susceptibility of the common cold. *Journal of Personality and Social Psychology, 64,* 131–140.

Cohen, S., Tyrell, D. A., & Smith, A. P. (1997). Psychological stress in humans and susceptibility to the common cold. In T. W. Miller (Ed.), *International Universities Press stress and health series, Monograph 7. Clinical disorders and stressful life events* (pp. 217–235). Madison, CT: International Universities Press.

Cohn, R. M. (1982). Economic development and status change of the aged. *American Journal of Sociology, 87,* 1150–1161.

Cohrs, J., Abele, A., & Dette, D. (2006, July). Integrating situational and dispositional determinants of job satisfaction: Findings from three samples of professionals. *Journal of Psychology: Interdisciplinary and Applied, 140,* 363–395.

Cokley, K. (2003). What do we know about the motivation of African American students? Challenging the "anti-intellectual" myth. *Harvard Educational Review, 73,* 524–558.

Colby, A., & Damon, W. (1987). Listening to a different voice: A review of Gilligan's in a different voice. In M. R. Walsh (Ed.), *The psychology of women.* New Haven, CT: Yale University Press.

Colby, A., & Kohlberg, L. (1987). *The measurement of moral adjudgment* (Vols. 1–2). New York: Cambridge University Press.

Colcombe, S. J., Erickson, K. I., Scalf, P. E., Kim, J. S., Prakash, R., McAuley, E., Elavsky, S., Marquez, D. X., Hu, L., & Kramer, A. F. (2006). Aerobic exercise training increases brain volume in aging humans. *Journal of Gerontology, A. Biological Sciences and Medical Sciences, 61,* 1166–1170.

Cole, C. F., Arafat, C., & Tidhar, C. (2003). The educational impact of Rechov Sumsum/Shara'a Simsim: A Sesame Street television series to promote respect and understanding among children living in Israel, the West Bank and Gaza. *International Journal of Behavioral Development, 27,* 409–422.

Cole, D. A., Maxwell, S. E., Martin, J. M., Peeke, L. G., Seroczynski, A. D., Tram, J. M., Joffman, K. B., Ruiz, M. D., Jacquez, F., & Maschman, T. (2001). The development of multiple domains of child and adolescent self-concept: A cohort sequential longitudinal design. *Child Development, 72,* 1723–1746.

Cole, M. (1992). Culture in development. In M. H. Bornstein & M. E. Lamb (Eds.), *Developmental psychology: An advanced textbook* (3rd ed.). Hillsdale, NJ: Erlbaum.

Cole, S. A. (2005). Infants in foster care: Relational and environmental factors affecting attachment. *Journal of Reproductive & Infant Psychology, 23,* 43–61.

Coleman, M., Ganong, L., & Weaver, S. (2001). Relationship maintenance and enhancement in remarried families. In J. Harvey & A. Wenzel (Eds.), *Close romantic relationships: Maintenance and enhancement.* Mahwah, NJ: Lawrence Erlbaum Associates.

Coleman, P. (2005, July). Editorial: Uses of reminiscence: Functions and benefits. *Aging & Mental Health, 9,* 291–294.

Colen, C., Geronimus, A., & Phipps, M. (2006, September). Getting a piece of the pie? The economic boom of the 1990s and declining teen birth rates in the United States. *Social Science & Medicine, 63,* 1531–1545.

Colino, S. (2002, February 26). Problem kid or label? *The Washington Post,* HE01.

College Board (2005). 2001 college bound seniors are the largest, most diverse group in history. New York: College Board.

Collett, B. R., Gimpel, G. A., Greenson, J. N., & Gunderson, T. L. (2001). Assessment of discipline styles among parents of preschool through school-age children. *Journal of Psychopathology and Behavioral Assessment, 23,* 163–170.

Collins, W. (2003). More than myth: The developmental significance of romantic relationships during adolescence. *Journal of Research on Adolescence, 13,* 1–24.

Collins, W., and Andrew, L. (2004). Changing relationships, changing youth: Interpersonal contexts of adolescent development. *Journal of Early Adolescence, 24,* 55–62.

Collins, W., & Doolittle, A. (2006, December). Personal reflections of funeral rituals and spirituality in a Kentucky African American family. *Death Studies, 30,* 957–969.

Collins, W. A., Gleason, T., & Sesma, A. (1997). Internalization, autonomy, and relationships: Development during adolescence. In J. E. Grusec & L. Kuczynski (Eds.), *Parenting and children's internalization of values: A handbook of contemporary theory* (pp. 78–99). New York: Wiley.

Colom, R., Lluis-Font, J. M., & Andrés-Pueyo, A. (2005). The generational intelligence gains are caused by decreasing variance in the lower half of the distribution: Supporting evidence for the nutrition hypothesis. *Intelligence, 33,* 83–91.

Colpin, H., & Soenen, S. (2004). Bonding. Through an adoptive mother's eyes. *Midwifery Today Int Midwife, 70,* 30–31.

Coltrane, S., & Adams, M. (1997). Children and gender. In T. Arendell (Ed.), *Contemporary parenting: Challenges and issues. Understanding Families* (Vol. 9, pp. 219–253). Thousand Oaks, CA: Sage.

Committee on Children, Youth and Families. (1994). *When you need child day care.* Washington, DC: American Psychological Association.

Compton, R., & Weissman, D. (2002). Hemispheric asymmetries in global-local perception: Effects of individual differences in neuroticism. *Laterality, 7,* 333–350.

Comunian, A. L., & Gielen, U. P. (2000). Sociomoral reflection and prosocial and antisocial behavior: Two Italian studies. *Psychological Reports, 87,* 161–175.

Condit, V. (1990). Anorexia nervosa: Levels of causation. *Human Nature, 1,* 391–413.

Condly, S. (2006, May). Resilience in children: A review of literature with implications for education. *Urban Education, 41,* 211–236.

Condry, J., & Condry, S. (1976). Sex differences: A study of the eye of the beholder. *Child Development, 47,* 812–819.

Conel, J. L. (1930/1963). *Postnatal development of the human cortex* (Vols. 1–6). Cambridge, MA: Harvard University Press.

Conklin, H. M., & Iacono, W. G. (2002). Schizophrenia: A neurodevelopmental perspective. *Current Directions in Psychological Science, 11,* 33–37.

Conn, V. S. (2003). Integrative review of physical activity intervention research with aging adults. *Journal of the American Geriatrics Society, 51,* 1159–1168.

Connell-Carrick, K. (2006). Early child care and early child development: Major findings of the NICHD Study of Early Child Care. *Child Welfare Journal, 85,* 819–836.

Conner, K., & Goldston, D. (2007, March). Rates of suicide among males increase steadily from age 11 to 21: Developmental framework and outline for prevention. *Aggression and Violent Behavior, 12(2),* 193–207.

Connor, R. (1992). *Cracking the over-50 job market.* New York: Penguin Books.

Consedine, N., Magai, C., & King, A. (2004). Deconstructing positive affect in later life: A differential functionalist analysis of joy and interest. *International Journal of Aging & Human Development, 58,* 49–68.

Continelli, L. (2006, December 24). From boxing to books. *Buffalo News,* p. B3.

Cook, A. S., & Oltjenbruns, K. A. (1989). *Dying and grieving: Lifespan and family perspectives.* New York: Holt, Rinehart & Winston.

Coon, K. D., Myers, A. J., Craig, D. W., Webster, J. A., Pearson, J. V., Lince, D. H., Zismann, V. L., Beach, T. G., Leung, D., Bryden, L., Halperin, R. F., Marlowe, L., Kaleem, M., Walker, D. G., Ravid, R., Heward, C. B., Rogers, J., Papassotiropoulos, A., Reiman, E. M., Hardy, J., & Stephan, D. A. (2007). A high-density whole-genome association study reveals that APOE is the major susceptibility gene for sporadic late-onset Alzheimer's disease. *Journal of Clinical Psychiatry, 68,* 613–618.

Coons, S., & Guilleminault, C. (1982). Developments of sleep-wake patterns and non-rapid-eye-movement sleep stages during the first six months of life in normal infants. *Pediatrics, 69(6),* 793–798.

Cooper, H., & Valentine, J. (2001). Using research to answer practical questions about homework. *Educational Psychologist, 36,* 143–153.

Cooperstock, M. S., Bakewell, J., Herman, A., & Schramm W. F. (1998). Effects of fetal sex and race on risk of very preterm birth in twins. *American Journal of Obstetrics & Gynecology, 179,* 762–765.

Copple, C., & Bredekamp, S. (1997). *Developmental appropriate practice in early childhood programs, (Revised ed.).* Washington, DC: National Association for the Education of Young Children.

Corballis, P. (2003). Visuospatial processing and the right-hemisphere interpreter. *Brain & Cognition, 53,* 171–176.

Corcoran, J., & Pillai, V. (2007, January). Effectiveness of secondary pregnancy prevention programs: A meta-analysis. *Research on Social Work Practice, 17,* 5–18.

Cordón, I. M., Pipe, M., Sayfan, L., Melinder, A., & Goodman, G. S. (2004). Memory for traumatic experiences in early childhood. *Developmental Review, 24,* 101–132.

Corliss, J. (1996, October 29). Alzheimer's in the news. *HealthNews,* 1–2.

Corr, C., & Doka, K. (2001). Master concepts in the field of death, dying, and bereavement: Coping versus adaptive strategies. *Omega: Journal of Death & Dying, 43,* 183–199.

Corr, C., Nabe, C., & Corr, D. (2006). *Death & dying, life & living.* Belmont, CA: Thomson Wadsworth.

Coscia, J., Ris, M., & Succop, P. (2003). Cognitive development of lead-exposed children from ages 6 to 15 years: An application of growth curve analysis. *Child Neuropsychology, 9,* 10–21.

Costa, P. T., & McCrae, R. R. (1997). Longitudinal stability of adult personality. In R. Hogan, J. A. Johnson, & S. R. Briggs (Eds.), *Handbook of personality psychology* (pp. 269–290). San Diego, CA: Academic Press.

Costa, P., & McCrae, R. (2002). Looking backward: Changes in the mean levels of personality traits from 80 to 12. In D. Cervone & W. Mischel (Eds.), *Advances in personality science.* New York: Guilford Press.

Costa, P. T., Jr., & McCrae, R. R. (1988). Personality in adulthood: A six-year longitudinal study of self-report and spouse ratings on the NEO Personality Inventory. *Journal of Personality and Social Psychology, 54,* 853–863.

Costa, P. T., Jr., & McCrae, R. R. (1989). Personality continuity and the changes of adult life. In M. Storandt & G. R. VandenBos (Eds.), *The adult years: Continuity and change.* Washington, DC: American Psychological Association.

Costello, E., Compton, S., & Keeler, G. (2003). Relationships between poverty and psychopathology: A natural experiment. *Journal of the American Medical Association, 290,* 2023–2029.

Costello, E., Sung, M., Worthman, C., & Angold, A. (2007, April). Pubertal maturation and the development of alcohol use and abuse. *Drug and Alcohol Dependence, 88,* S50–S59.

Côté, J. (2005). Editor's introduction. *Identity, 5,* 95–96.

Couperus, J., & Nelson, C. (2006). Early brain development and plasticity. *Blackwell handbook of early childhood development.* New York: Blackwell Publishing.

Courchesne, E., Carper, R., & Akshoomoff, N. (2003). Evidence of brain overgrowth in the first year of life in autism. *Journal of the American Medical Association, 290,* 337–344.

Couzin, J. (2002, June 21). Quirks of fetal environment felt decades later. *Science, 296,* 2167–2169.

Cowan, C. P., & Cowan, P. A. (1992). *When partners become parents.* New York: Wiley.

Cowan, N., Saults, J., & Elliot, E. (2002). The search for what is fundamental in the development of working memory. In R. Kail & H. Reese (Eds.), *Advances in child development and behavior* (Vol. 29). San Diego: Academic Press.

Cowgill, D. O., & Holmes, L. D. (1972). *Aging and modernization.* New York: Appleton-Century-Crofts.

Cowgill, D. O. (1968). The social life of the aging in Thailand. *Gerontologist, 8,* 159–163.

Cowley, G. (2000, January 31). Alzheimer's : Unlocking the mystery. *Newsweek,* 46–51.

Cox, C., Kotch, J., & Everson, M. (2003). A longitudinal study of modifying influences in the relationship between domestic violence and child maltreatment. *Journal of Family Violence, 18,* 5–17.

Craik, F., & Salthouse, T. A. (Eds.). (1999). *The handbook of aging and cognition* (2nd ed.). Mahwah, NJ: Erlbaum.

Craik, F. I. M. (1994). Memory changes in normal aging. *Current Directions in Psychological Science, 3,* 155–158.

Crane, E., & Morris, J. (2006). Changes in maternal age in England and Wales—Implications for Down syndrome. *Down Syndrome: Research & Practice, 10,* 41–43.

Cratty, B. (1979). *Perceptual and motor development in infants and children* (2nd ed.). Englewood Cliffs, NJ: Prentice-Hall.

Cratty, B. (1986). *Perceptual and motor development in infants and children* (3rd ed.). Englewood Cliffs, NJ: Prentice-Hall.

Crawford, D., Houts, R., & Huston, T. (2002). Compatiability, leisure, and satisfaction in marital relationships. *Journal of Marriage & Family, 64,* 433–449.

Crawford, M., & Unger, R. (2004). *Women and gender: A feminist psychology (4th ed).* New York: McGraw-Hill.

Crawley, A., Anderson, D., & Santomero, A. (2002). Do children learn how to watch television? The impact of extensive experience with *Blue's Clues* on preschool children's television viewing behavior. *Journal of Communication, 52,* 264–280.

Crews, D. (1993). The organizational concept and vertebrates without sex chromosomes. *Brain, Behavior, and Evolution, 42,* 202–214.

Crick, N. R., Casas, J. G., & Ku, H. (1999). Relational and physical forms of peer victimization in preschool. *Developmental Psychology, 35,* 376–385.

Crisp, A., Gowers, S., Joughin, N., McClelland, L., Rooney, B., Nielsen, S., et al. (2006, May). Anorexia nervosa in males: Similarities and differences to anorexia nervosa in females. *European Eating Disorders Review, 14,* 163–167.

Criss, M., & Shaw, D. (2005). Sibling relationships as contexts for delinquency training in low-income families. *Journal of Family Psychology, 19,* 592–600.

Critser, G. (2003). *Fat land: How Americans became the fattest people in the world.* Boston: Houghton Mifflin.

Crockenberg, S., & Leerkes, E. (2003). Infant negative emotionality, caregiving, and family relationships. In A. Crouter & A. Booth, (Eds.), *Children's influence on family dynamics: The neglected side of family relationships* (pp. 57–78). Mahwah, NJ: Lawrence Erlbaum Associates.

Crockett, L. J., & Crouter, A. C. (Eds.). (1995). *Pathways through adolescence: Individual development in relation to social contexts.* Hillsdale, NJ: Erlbaum.

Crosnoe, R., & Elder, G. H., Jr. (2002). Successful adaptation in the later years: A life course approach to aging. *Social Psychology Quarterly, 65,* 309–328.

Crowley, B., Hayslip, B., & Hobdy, J. (2003). Psychological hardiness and adjustment to life events in adulthood. *Journal of Adult Development, 10,* 237–248.

Crowley, K., Callaman, M. A., Tenenbaum, H. R., & Allen, E. (2001). Parents explain more often to boys than to girls during shared scientific thinking. *Psychological Science, 12,* 258–261.

Crowther, M., & Rodriguez, R. (2003). A stress and coping model of custodial grandparenting among African Americans. In B. Hayslip & J. Patrick (Eds.), *Working with custodial grandparents.* New York: Springer Publishing.

Crutchley, A. (2003). Bilingualism in development: Language, literacy and cognition. *Child Language Teaching & Therapy, 19,* 365–367.

Cruz, N., & Bahna, S. (2006, October). Do foods or additives cause behavior disorders? *Psychiatric Annals, 36,* 724–732.

Cuddy, A. J. C., & Fiske, S. T. (2004). Doddering but dear: Process, content, and function in stereotyping of older persons. In T. Nelson (Ed.), *Ageism: Stereotyping and prejudice against older persons.* Cambridge, MA: MIT Press.

Culbertson, J. L., & Gyurke, J. (1990). Assessment of cognitive and motor development in infancy and childhood. In J. H. Johnson & J. Goldman (Eds.), *Developmental assessment in clinical child psychology: A handbook* (pp. 100–131). New York: Pergamon Press.

Culver, V. (2003, August 26). Funeral expenses overwhelm survivors: $10,000-plus tab often requires aid. *The Denver Post,* p. B2.

Cummings, E., & Henry, W. E. (1961). *Growing old.* New York: Basic Books.

Cummings, E. M., Iannotti, R. J., & Zahn-Waxler, C. (1989). Aggression between peers in early childhood: Individual continuity and developmental change. *Child Development, 60,* 887–895.

Cunningham, J. D., & Antill, J. K. (1994). Cohabitation and marriage: Retrospective and predictive comparisons. *Journal of Social and Personal Relationships, 11,* 77–93.

Curtis, W. J., & Cicchetti, D. (2003). Moving research on resilience into the 21st century: Theoretical and methodological considerations in examining the biological contributors to resilience. *Development and Psychopathology, 15,* 126–131.

Cyna, A. M., Andrew, M. I., & McAuliffe, G. L. (2006). Antenatal self-hypnosis for labour and childbirth: A pilot study. *Anaestheology Intensive Care, 34,* 464–4699.

Cynader, M. (2000, March 17). Strengthening visual connections. *Science, 287,* 1943–1944.

Dahl, E., & Birkelund, E. (1997). Health inequalities in later life in a social democratic welfare state. *Social Science & Medicine, 44,* 871–881.

Dainton, M. (1993). The myths and misconceptions of the step-mother identity. *Family Relations, 42,* 93–98.

Daley, K. C. (2004). Update on sudden infant death syndrome. *Current Opinion in Pediatrics, 16,* 227–232.

Daly, T., & Feldman, R. S. (1994). Benefits of social integration for typical preschoolchildren. Unpublished manuscript.

Damon, W. (1983). *Social and personality development.* New York: Norton.

Damon, W., & Hart, D. (1988). *Self-understanding in childhood and adolescence.* New York: Cambridge University Press.

Danhauer, S., McCann, J., & Gilley, D. (2004). Do behavioral disturbances in persons with Alzheimer's disease predict caregiver depression over time? *Psychology & Aging, 19,* 198–202.

Daniels, H. (Ed.). (1996). *An introduction to Vygotsky.* New York: Routledge.

Daniels, H. (2006, February). The 'Social' in post-Vygotskian theory. *Theory & Psychology, 16,* 37–49.

Dapretto, M., Davies, M. S., Pfeifer, J. H., Scott, A. A., Sigman, M., Bookheimer, S. Y., & Iacoboni, M. (2006). Understanding emotions in others: Mirror neuron dysfunction in children with autism spectrum disorders. *Nature and Neuroscience, 9,* 28–30.

Dare, W. N., Noronha, C. C., Kusemiju, O. T., & Okanlawon, O. A. (2002). The effect of ethanol on spermatogenesis and fertility in male Sprague-Dawley rats pretreated with acetylsalicylic acid. *Nigeria Postgraduate Medical Journal, 9,* 194–198.

Darnton, N. (1990, June 4). Mommy vs. Mommy. *Newsweek,* 64–67.

Dasen, P., Inhelder, B., Lavallee, M., & Retschitzki, J. (1978). *Naissance de l'intelligence chez l'enfant Baoule de Cote d'Ivorie.* Berne: Hans Huber.

Dasen, P., Ngini, L., & Lavallee, M. (1979). Cross-cultural training studies of concrete operations. In L. H. Eckenberger, W. J. Lonner, & Y. H. Poortinga (Eds.), *Cross-cultural contributions to psychology.* Amsterdam: Swets & Zeilinger.

Dasen, P. R. (2000). Rapid social change and the turmoil of adolescence: A cross-cultural perspective. *International Journal of Group Tensions, 29,* 17–49.

Dasen, P. R., & Mishra, R. C. (2002). Cross-cultural views on human development in the third millennium. In W. W. Hartup & R. K. Silbereisen (Eds.), *Growing points in developmental science: An introduction.* Philadelphia, PA: Psychology Press.

Davey, M. (2007, June 2). Kevorkian freed after years in prison for aiding suicide. *The New York Times,* p. A1.

Davey, M., Eaker, D. G., & Walters, L. H. (2003). Resilience processes in adolescents: Personality profiles, self-worth, and coping. *Journal of Adolescent Research, 18,* 347–362.

Davey, S. G., Frankel S., & Yarnell, J. (1997). Sex and death: Are they related? Findings from the Caerphilly Cohort Study. *British Medical Journal, 315,* 1–4.

Davidson, J. K., Darling, C. A., & Norton, L. (1995). Religiosity and the sexuality of women: Sexual behavior and sexual satisfaction revisited. *Journal of Sex Research, 32,* 235–243.

Davidson, R. J. (2003). Affective neuroscience: A case for interdisciplinary research. In F. Kessel & P. L. Rosenfield (Eds.), *Expanding the boundaries of health and social science: Case studies in interdisciplinary innovation.* London: Oxford University Press.

Davidson, T. (1977). Wifebeating: A recurring phenomenon throughout history. In M. Roy (Ed.), *Battered women: A psychosociological study of domestic violence.* New York: Van Nostrand Reinhold.

Davies, P. G., Spencer, S. J., & Steele, C. M. (2005). Clearing the air: Identity safety moderates the effects of stereotype threat on women's leadership aspirations. *Journal of Personality & Social Psychology, 88,* 276–287.

Davies, P. T., Harold, G. T., Goeke-Morey, M. C., & Cummings, E. M. (2002). Child emotional security and interparental conflict. *Monographs of the Society for Research in Child Development, 67.*

Davies, S., & Denton, M. (2002). The economic well-being of older women who become divorced or separated in mid- or later life. *Canadian Journal on Aging, 21,* 477–493.

Davis, A. (2003). *Your divorce, your dollars: Financial planning before, during, and after divorce.* Bellingham, WA: Self-Counsel Press.

Davis, C., & Nolen-Hoeksema, S. (2001). Loss and meaning: How do people make sense of loss? *American Behavioral Scientist, 44,* 726–741.

Davis, D., Shaver, P., Widaman, K., Vernon, M., Follette, W., & Beitz, K. (2006, December). "I can't get no satisfaction": Insecure attachment, inhibited sexual communication, and sexual dissatisfaction. *Personal Relationships, 13,* 465–483.

Davis, M., & Emory, E. (1995). Sex differences in neonatal stress reactivity. *Child Development, 66,* 14–27.

Davis-Kean, P. E., & Sandler, H. M. (2001). A meta-analysis of measures of self-esteem for young children: A framework for future measures. *Child Development, 72,* 887–906.

Davison, G. C. (2005). Issues and nonissues in the gay-affirmative treatment of patients who are gay, lesbian, or bisexual. *Clinical Psychology: Science & Practice, 12,* 25–28.

de Anda, D., & Becerra, R. M. (2000). An overview of "Violence: Diverse populations and communities." *Journal of Multicultural Social Work, 8,* (1–2), 1–14.

de Bruyn, E., & Cillessen, A. (2006, November). Popularity in early adolescence: Prosocial and antisocial subtypes. *Journal of Adolescent Research, 21,* 607–627.

De Gelder, B. (2000). Recognizing emotions by ear and by eye. In R. D. Lane & L. Nadel et al. (Eds.), *Cognitive neuroscience of emotion. Series in affective science.* New York: Oxford University Press.

de Jesus Moreno Moreno, M. (2003). Cognitive improvement in mild to moderate Alzheimer's dementia after treatment with the acetylcholine precursor choline alfoscerate: A multicenter, double-blind, randomized, placebo-controlled trial. *Clinical Therapeutics: The International Peer-Reviewed Journal of Drug Therapy, 25,* 178–193.

De Leo, D., Conforti, D., & Carollo, G. (1997). A century of suicide in Italy: A comparison between the old and the young. *Suicide & Life-Threatening Behavior, 27,* 239–249.

De Meersman, R., & Stein, P. (2007, February). Vagal modulation and aging. *Biological Psychology, 74,* 165–173.

de Onis, M., Garza, C., Onyango, A. W., & Borghi, E. (2007). Comparison of the WHO child growth standards and the CDC 2000 growth charts. *Journal of Nutrition, 137,* 144–148.

de Rosnay, M., Cooper, P., Tsigaras, N., & Murray, L. (2006, August). Transmission of social anxiety from mother to infant: An experimental study using a social referencing paradigm. *Behaviour Research and Therapy, 44,* 1165–1175.

De Roten, Y., Favez, N., & Drapeau, M. (2003). Two studies on autobiographical narratives about an emotional event by preschoolers: Influence of the emotions experienced and the affective closeness with the interlocutor. *Early Child Development & Care, 173,* 237–248.

de Schipper, E. J., Riksen-Walraven, J. M., & Geurts, S. A. E. (2006). Effects of child–caregiver ratio on the interactions between caregivers and children in childcare centers: An experimental study. *Child Development, 77,* 861–874.

de St. Aubin, E., & McAdams, D. P. (Eds). (2004). *The generative society: Caring for future generations.* Washington, DC: American Psychological Association.

de St. Aubin, E., McAdams, D. P., & Kim, T. C. (Eds.), (2004). *The generative society: Caring for future generations.* Washington, DC: American Psychological Association.

de Vries, B., Davis, C. G., Wortman, C. B., & Lehman, D. R. (1997). Long-term psychological and somatic consequences of later life parental bereavement. *Omega—Journal of Death & Dying, 35,* 97–117.

Deakin, M. B. (2004, May 9). The (new) parent trap. *Boston Globe Magazine,* pp. 18–21, 28–33.

Deater-Deckard, K., & Cahill, K. (2006). Nature and nurture in early childhood. *Blackwell handbook of early childhood development* (pp. 3–21). New York: Blackwell Publishing.

Deaux, K. (2006). A nation of immigrants: Living our legacy. *Journal of Social Issues, 62,* 633–651.

Deaux, K., Reind, A., Mizrahi, K., & Ethier, K. A. (1995). Parameters of social identity. *Journal of Personality and Social Psychology, 68,* 280–291.

Deb, S., & Adak, M. (2006, July). Corporal punishment of children: Attitude, practice and perception of parents. *Social Science International, 22,* 3–13.

Decarrie, T. G. (1969). A study of the mental and emotional development of the thalidomide child. In B. M. Foss (Ed.), *Determinants of infant behavior* (Vol. 4). London: Methuen.

DeCasper, A. J., & Fifer, W. P. (1980). Of human bonding: Newborns prefer their mothers' voices. *Science, 208,* 1174–1176.

DeCasper, A. J., & Prescott, P. (1984). Human newborns' perception of male voices: Preference, discrimination, and reinforcing value. *Developmental Psychobiology, 17,* 481–491.

DeCasper, A. J., & Spence, M. J. (1986). Prenatal maternal speech influences newborns' perception of speech sounds. *Infant Behavior and Development, 9,* 133–150.

deCastro, J. (2002). Age-related changes in the social, psychological, and temporal influences on food intake in free-living, healthy, adult humans. *Journals of Gerontology: Series A: Biological Sciences & Medical Sciences, 57A,* M368–M377.

Decety, J., & Jackson, P. L. (2006). A social-neuroscience perspective on empathy. *Current Directions in Psychological Science, 15,* 54–61.

deChateau, P. (1980). Parent–neonate interaction and its long-term effects. In E. G. Simmel (Ed.), *Early experiences and early behavior.* New York: Academic Press.

Deforche, B., De Bourdeaudhuij, I., & Tanghe, A. (2006, May). Attitude toward physical activity in normal-weight, overweight and obese adolescents. *Journal of Adolescent Health, 38,* 560–568.

DeFrain, J., Martens, L., Stork, J., & Stork, W. (1991). The psychological effects of a stillbirth on surviving family members. *Omega—Journal of Death and Dying, 22,* 81–108.

DeGenova, M. K. (1993). Reflections of the past: New variables affecting life satisfaction in later life. *Educational Gerontology, 19,* 191–201.

Degnen, C. (2007). Minding the gap: The construction of old age and oldness amongst peers. *Journal of Aging Studies, 21,* 69–80.

Dehaene-Lambertz, G., Hertz-Pannier, L., & Dubois, J. (2006). Nature and nurture in language acquisition: Anatomical and functional brain-imaging studies in infants. *Neurosciences, 29, Special issue: Nature and nurture in brain development and neurological disorders,* 367–373.

DeHart, T., Pelham, B., & Tennen, H. (2006, January). What lies beneath: Parenting style and implicit self-esteem. *Journal of Experimental Social Psychology, 42,* 1–17.

Dejin-Karlsson, E., Hanson, B. S., Oestergren, P. O., Sjoeberg, N. O., & Marsal, K. (1998). Does passive smoking in early pregnancy increase the risk of small-for-gestational age infants? *American Journal of Public Health, 88,* 1523–1527.

Delaney, C. H. (1995). Rites of passage in adolescence. *Adolescence, 30,* 891–897.

DeLisi, L., & Fleischhaker, W. (2007). Schizophrenia research in the era of the genome, 2007. *Current Opinion in Psychiatry, 20,* 109–110.

Dell, D. L., & Stewart, D. E. (2000). Menopause and mood. Is depression linked with hormone changes?. *Postgraduate Medicine, 108,* 34–36, 39–43.

Dellmann-Jenkins, M., & Brittain, L. (2003). Young adults' attitudes toward filial responsibility and actual assistance to elderly family members. *Journal of Applied Gerontology, 22,* 214–229.

DeLoache, J. S., & Gottlieb, A. (2000). *A world of babies: Imagined childcare guides for seven societies.* New York: Cambridge University Press.

Delva, J., O'Malley, P., & Johnston, L. (2006, October). Racial/ethnic and socioeconomic status differences in overweight and health-related behaviors among American students: National trends 1986–2003. *Journal of Adolescent Health, 39,* 536–545.

Demaree, H. A., & Everhart, D. E. (2004). Healthy high-hostiles: Reduced parasympathetic activity and decreased sympathovagal flexibility during negative emotional processing. *Personality and Individual Differences, 36,* 457–469.

Dembner, A. (1995, October 15). Marion Mealey: A determination to make it. *Boston Globe,* p. 22.

Demir, A., Ulusoy, M., & Ulusoy, M. (2003). Investigation of factors influencing burnout levels in the professional and private lives of nurses. *International Journal of Nursing Studies, 40,* 807–827.

Denizet-Lewis, B. (2004, May 30). Friends, friends with benefits and the benefits of the local mall. *New York Times Magazine,* pp. 30–35, 54–58.

Dennis, T. A., Cole, P. M., Zahn-Wexler, C., & Mizuta, I. (2002). Self in context: Autonomy and relatedness in Japanese and U.S. mother–preschooler dyads. *Child Development, 73,* 1803–1817.

Dennis, W. (1966a). Age and creative productivity. *Journal of Gerontology, 21,* 1–8.

Dennis, W. (1966b). Creative productivity between the ages of 20 and 80 years. *Journal of Gerontology, 11,* 331–337.

Dennison, B., Edmunds, L., Stratton, H., & Pruzek, R. (2006). Rapid infant weight gain predicts childhood overweight. *Obesity, 14,* 491–499.

Denollet, J. (2005). DS14: Standard assessment of negative affectivity, social inhibition, and Type D personality. *Psychosomatic Medicine, 67,* 89–97.

DePaulo, B. (2004). *The scientific study of people who are single: An annotated bibliography.* Glendale, CA: Unmarried America.

DePaulo, B. M., & Morris W. L. (2006). The unrecognized stereotyping and discrimination against singles. *Current Directions in Psychological Science, 15,* 251–254.

Der, G., Batty, G., & Deary, I. (2006). Effect of breast feeding on intelligence in children: Prospective study, sibling pairs analysis, and meta-analysis. *BMJ: British Medical Journal, 333,* 723–732.

Der, G., & Deary, I. (2006, March). Age sex differences in reaction time in adulthood: Results from the United Kingdom health and lifestyle survey. *Psychology and Aging, 21*(1), 62–73.

Dervic, K., Friedrich, E., Oquendo, M., Voracek, M., Friedrich, M., & Sonneck, G. (2006, October). Suicide in Austrian children and young adolescents aged 14 and younger. *European Child & Adolescent Psychiatry, 15,* 427–434.

Deshields, T., Tibbs, T., Fan, M. Y., & Taylor, M. (2005, August 12). Differences in patterns of depression after treatment for breast cancer. *Psycho-Oncology,* published online, John Wiley & Sons.

Desmarias, S., & Curtis, J. (1997). Gender and perceived pay entitlement: Testing for effects of experience with income. *Journal of Personality and Social Psychology, 72,* 141–150.

Desoete, A., Roeyers, H., & De Clercq, A. (2003). Can offline metacognition enhance mathematical problem solving? *Journal of Educational Psychology, 95,* 188–200.

DeSpelder, L., & Strickland, A. L. (1992). *The last dance: Encountering death and dying* (3rd ed.). Palo Alto, CA: Mayfield.

Deurenberg, P., Deurenberg-Yap, M., & Guricci, S. (2002). Asians are different from Caucasians and from each other in their body mass index/body fat percent relationship. *Obesity Review, 3,* 141–146.

Deveny, K. (1994, December 5). Chart of kindergarten awards. *The Wall Street Journal,* p. B1.

deVilliers, P. A., & deVilliers, J. G. (1992). Language development. In M. H. Bornstein & M. E. Lamb (Eds.), *Developmental psychology: An advanced textbook.* Hillsdale, NJ: Erlbaum.

Devlin, B., Daniels, M., & Roeder, K. (1997). The heritability of IQ. *Nature, 388,* 468–471.

deVries, M. W. (1984). Temperament and infant mortality among the Masai of East Africa. American *Journal of Psychiatry, 141,* 1189–1194.

deVries, R. (1969). Constancy of generic identity in the years 3 to 6. *Monographs of the Society for Research in Child Development, 34* (3, Serial No. 127).

DeVries, R. (2005). *A pleasing birth.* Philadelphia, PA: Temple University Press.

DeWitt, P. M. (1992). The second time around. *American Demographics, 14,* 60–63.

Dey, A. N., & Bloom, B. (2005). Summary health statistics for U.S. children: National Health Interview Survey, 2003. *Vital Health Statistics 10, 223,* 1–78.

Diambra, L. & Menna-Barretio, L. (2004). Infradian rhythmicity in sleep/wake ratio in developing infants. *Chronobiology International, 21,* 217–227.

Diamond, L. (2003a). Love matters: Romantic relationships among sexual-minority adolescents. In P. Florsheim (Ed.), *Adolescent romantic relations and sexual behavior: Theory, research, and practical implications.* Mahwah, NJ: Lawrence Erlbaum Associates.

Diamond, L. (2003b). Was it a phase? Young women's relinquishment of lesbian/bisexual identities over a 5-year period. *Journal of Personality & Social Psychology, 84,* 352–364.

Diamond, L., & Savin-Williams, R. (2003). The intimate relationships of sexual-minority youths. In G.

Adams & M. Berzonsky (Eds.), *Blackwell handbook of adolescence.* Malden, MA: Blackwell Publishers.

Dick, D., Rose, R., & Kaprio, J. (2006). The next challenge for psychiatric genetics: Characterizing the risk associated with identified genes. *Annals of Clinical Psychiatry, 18,* 223–231.

Dick, D. M., & Rose, R. J. (2002). Behavior genetics: What's new? What's next? *Current Directions in Psychological Science, 11,* 70–74.

Diener, E. (2000). Subjective well-being: The science of happiness and a proposal for a national index. *American Psychologist, 55,* 34–43.

Diener, E., Oishi, S., & Lucas, R. (2003). Personality, culture, and subjective well-being: Emotional and cognitive evaluations of life. *Annual Review of Psychology, 54,* 403–425.

Dieter, J., Field, T., & Hernandez-Reif, M. (2003). Stable preterm infants gain more weight and sleep less after five days of massage therapy. *Journal of Pediatric Psychology, 28,* 403–411.

Dieter, J., Field, T., Hernandez-Reif, M., Emory, E. and Redzepi, M. (2003). Preterm infants gain more weight and sleep less following 5 days of massage therapy. *Journal of Pediatric Psychology, 28,* 403–411.

Dietz, W. (2004). Overweight in childhood and adolescence. *New England Journal of Medicine, 350,* 855–857.

Dietz, W. H., & Stern, L. (Eds.). (1999). *American Academy of Pediatrics guide to your child's nutrition: Making peace at the table and building healthy eating habits for life.* New York: Villard.

DiGiovanna, A. G. (1994). *Human aging: Biological perspectives.* New York: McGraw-Hill.

DiLalla, L. F., Thompson, L. A., Plomin, R., Phillips, K., Fagan, J. F., Haith, M. M., Cyphers, L. H., & Fulker, D. W. (1990). Infant predictors of preschool and adult IQ: A study of infant twins and their parents. *Developmental Psychology, 26,* 433–440.

Dildy, G. A. et al. (1996). Very advanced maternal age: Pregnancy after 45. *American Journal of Obstetrics and Gynecology, 175,* 668–674.

Dilworth-Bart, J., & Moore, C. (2006, March). Mercy mercy me: Social injustice and the prevention of environmental pollutant exposures among ethnic minority and poor children. *Child Development, 77,* 247–265.

DiMatteo, M. R., & Kahn, K. L. (1997). Psychosocial aspects of childbirth. In S. J. Gallant, G. P. Keita, & R. Royak-Schaler (Eds.), *Health care for women: Psychological, social, and behavioral influences.* Washington, DC: American Psychological Association.

Dion, K. L., & Dion, K. K. (1988). Romantic love: Individual and cultural perspectives. In R. J. Sternberg & M. L. Barnes (Eds.), *The psychology of love.* New Haven, CT: Yale University Press.

Diop, A. M. (1989). The place of the elderly in African society. *Impact of Science on Society, 153,* 93–98.

DiPietro, J. A., Bornstein, M. H., & Costigan, K. A. (2002). What does fetal movement predict about behavior during the first two years of life? *Developmental Psychobiology, 40,* 358–371.

DiPietro, J. A., Costigan, K. A., & Gurewitsch, E. D. (2005). Maternal psychophysiological change during the second half of gestation. *Biological Psychology, 69,* 23–39.

Dittman, M. (2005). Generational differences at work. *Monitor on Psychology, 36,* 54–55.

Dittmann, M. (2004, November). A new face to retirement. *Monitor on Psychology, 35,* 78.

Division 44/Committee on Lesbian, Gay, and Bisexual Concerns Joint Task Force on Guidelines for Psychotherapy with Lesbian, Gay, and Bisexual Clients. (2000). Guidelines for psychotherapy with lesbian, gay, and bisexual clients. *American Psychologist, 55,* 1440–1451.

Dixon, Jr., W. E. (2004). There's a long, long way to go. *PsycCRITIQUES.*

Dixon, L., & Browne, K. (2003). The heterogeneity of spouse abuse: A review. *Aggression & Violent Behavior, 8,* 107–130.

Dixon, R. (2003). Themes in the aging of intelligence: Robust decline with intriguing possibilities. In R. Sternberg &. Lautrey (Eds.), *Models of intelligence: International perspectives.* Washington, DC: American Psychological Association.

Dixon, R., & Cohen, A. (2003). Cognitive development in adulthood. In R. Lerner & M. Easterbrooks (Eds.), *Handbook of psychology: Developmental psychology, Vol. 6.* New York: John Wiley & Sons, Inc.

Dmitrieva, J., Chen, C., & Greenberg, E. (2004). Family relationships and adolescent psychosocial outcomes: Converging findings from Eastern and Western cultures. *Journal of Research on Adolescence, 14,* 425–447.

Dodge, K. A. (1985). A social information processing model of social competence in children. In M. Perlmutter (Ed.), *Minnesota Symposia on Child Psychology, 18,* 77–126.

Dodge, K. A., Bates, J. E., & Pettit, G. S. (1990, December 20). Mechanisms in the cycle of violence. *Science, 250,* 1678–1683.

Dodge, K. A., & Coie, J. D. (1987). Social information-processing factors in reactive and proactive aggression in children's peer groups. *Journal of Personality and Social Psychology, 53,* 1146–1158.

Dodge, K. A., & Crick, N. R. (1990). Social information-processing bases of aggressive behavior in children. *Personality and Social Psychology Bulletin, 16,* 8–22.

Dodge, K. A., & Price, J. M. (1994). On the relation between social information processing and socially competent behavior in early school-aged children. *Child Development, 65,* 1385–1397.

Dodge, K. A., Lansford, J. E., & Burks, V. S. (2003). Peer rejection and social information-processing factors in the development of aggressive behavior problems in children. *Child Development, 74,* 374–393.

Doka, K. J., & Mertz, M. E. (1988). The meaning and significance of great-grandparenthood. *Gerontologist, 28,* 192–197.

Doman, G., & Doman, J. (2002). *How to teach your baby to read.* Gentle Revolution Press.

Dombrowski, S., Noonan, K., & Martin, R. (2007). Low birth weight and cognitive outcomes: Evidence for a gradient relationship in an urban, poor, African American birth cohort. *School Psychology Quarterly, 22,* 26–43.

Dominguez, H. D., Lopez, M. F., & Molina, J. C. (1999). Interactions between perinatal and neonatal associative learning defined by contiguous olfactory and tactile stimulation. *Neurobiology of Learning and Memory, 71,* 272–288.

Donat, D. (2006, October). Reading their way: A balanced approach that increases achievement. *Reading & Writing Quarterly: Overcoming Learning Difficulties, 22,* 305–323.

Dondi, M., Simion, F., & Caltran, G. (1999). Can newborns discriminate between their own cry and the cry of another newborn infant? *Developmental Psychology, 35,* 418–426.

Donini, L., Savina, C., & Cannella, C. (2003). Eating habits and appetite control in the elderly: The anorexia of aging. *International Psychogeriatrics, 15,* 73–87.

Donlan, C. (1998). *The development of mathematical skills.* Philadelphia: Psychology Press.

Donnerstein, E. (2005, January). Media violence and children: What do we know, what do we do? Paper presented at the annual National Teaching of Psychology meeting, St. Petersburg Beach, FL.

Dorer, H., & Mahoney, J. (2006). Self-actualization in the corporate hierarchy. *North American Journal of Psychology, 8,* 397–410.

Doress, P. B., Siegal, D. L., & The Midlife and Old Women Book Project. (1987). *Ourselves, growing older.* New York: Simon & Schuster.

Dorn, L., Susman, E., & Ponirakis, A. (2003). Pubertal timing and adolescent adjustment and behavior: Conclusions vary by rater. *Journal of Youth & Adolescence, 32,* 157–167.

Dornbusch, S., Carlsmith, J., Bushwall, S., Ritter, P., Leiderman, P., Hastorf, A., & Gross, R. (1985). Single parents, extended households, and the control of adolescents. *Child Development, 56,* 326–341.

Dorofaeff, T., & Denny, S. (2006, September). Sleep and adolescence. Do New Zealand teenagers get enough? *Journal of Paediatrics and Child Health, 42,* 515–520.

Dortch, S. (1997, September). Hey guys: Hit the books. *American Demographics,* 4–12.

Doussard-Roosevelt, J. A., Porges, S. W., Scanlon, J. W., Alemi, B., & Scanlon, K. B. (1997). Vagal regulation of heart rate in the prediction of developmental outcome for very low birth weight preterm infants. *Child Development, 68,* 173–186.

Dowling, N., Smith, D., & Thomas, T. (2005). Electronic gaming machines: Are they the 'crack-cocaine' of gambling? *Addiction, 100,* 33–45.

Downe-Wamboldt, B., & Tamlyn, D. (1997). An international survey of death education trends in faculties of nursing and medicine. *Death Studies, 21,* 177–188.

Doyle, R. (2000, June). Asthma worldwide. *Scientific American, 28.*

Doyle, R. (2004a, January). Living together. *Scientific American,* p. 28.

Doyle, R. (2004b, April). By the numbers: A surplus of women. *Scientific American, 290,* 33.

Dreman, S. (Ed.). (1997). *The family on the threshold of the 21st century.* Mahwah, NJ: Erlbaum.

Drews, C. D., Murphy, C. C., Yeargin-Allsopp, M., & Decoufle, P. (1996). The relationship between idiopathic mental retardation and maternal smoking during pregnancy. *Pediatrics, 97,* 547–553.

Driver, J., Tabares, A., & Shapiro, A. (2003). Interactional patterns in marital success and failure: Gottman laboratory studies. In F. Walsh (Ed.), *Normal family processes: Growing diversity and complexity,* (3rd ed.). New York: Guilford Press.

Dromi, E. (1987). *Early lexical development.* Cambridge, England: Cambridge University Press.

Dryfoos, J. G. (1990). *Adolescents at risk: Prevalence and prevention.* New York: Oxford University Press.

DuBois, D. L., & Hirsch, B. J. (1990). School and neighborhood friendship patterns of blacks and whites in early adolescence. *Child Development, 61,* 524–536.

DuBreuil, S. C., Garry, M., & Loftus, E. F. (1998). Tales from the crib: Age regression and the creation of unlikely memories. In S. J. Lynn, & K. M. McConkey (Eds.), *Truth in memory.* New York: The Guilford Press.

Duenwald, M. (2003, July 15). After 25 years, new ideas in the prenatal test tube. *The New York Times*, p. D5.

Duenwald, M. (2004, May 11). For couples, stress without a promise of success. *The New York Times*, p. D3.

Dukes, R., & Martinez, R. (1994). The impact of gender on self-esteem among adolescents. *Adolescence, 29*, 105–115.

Dulitzki, M., Soriano, D., Schiff, E., Chetrit, A., Mashiach, S., & Seidman, D. S. (1998). Effect of very advanced maternal age on pregnancy outcome and rate of cesarean delivery. *Obstetrics and Gynecology, 92*, 935–939.

Duncan, G. J., & Brooks-Gunn, J. (2000). Family poverty, welfare reform, and child development. *Child Development, 71*, 188–196.

Dunham, R. M., Kidwell, J. S., & Wilson, S. M. (1986). Rites of passage at adolescence: A ritual process paradigm. *Journal of Adolescent Research, 1*, 139–153.

DuPaul, G., & Weyandt, L. (2006, June). School-based intervention for children with attention deficit hyperactivity disorder: Effects on academic, social, and behavioural functioning. *International Journal of Disability, Development and Education, 53*, 161–176.

Duplassie, D., & Daniluk, J. C. 2007). Sexuality: Young and middle adulthood. In A. Owens & M. Tupper (Eds.), *Sexual health: Volume 1, Psychological Foundations*. Westport, CT: Praeger.

Durbin, J. (2003, October 6). Internet sex unzipped. *McCleans*, p. 18.

Durik, A. M., Hyde, J. S., & Clark, R. (2000). Sequelae of cesarean and vaginal deliveries: Psychosocial outcomes for mothers and infants. *Developmental Psychology, 36*, 251–260.

Durkin, K., & Nugent, B. (1998). Kindergarten children's gender-role expectations for television actors. *Sex Roles, 38*, 387–402.

Dutton, D. G. (1994). *The domestic assault of women: Psychological and criminal justice perspectives* (2nd ed.). Vancouver, BC, Canada: University of British Columbia Press.

Dutton, M. A. (1992) *Empowering and healing the battered woman: A model of assessment and intervention*. New York: Springer.

Dwairy, M., Achoui, M., Abouserie, R., & Farah, A. (2006, May). Parenting styles, individuation, and mental health of Arab adolescents: A third cross-regional research study. *Journal of Cross-Cultural Psychology, 37*, 262–272.

Dweck, C. (2002). The development of ability conceptions. In A. Wigfield, Allan, & J. Eccles (Eds.), *Development of achievement motivation*. San Diego: Academic Press.

Dweck, C. S. (1991). Self-theories and goals: Their role in motivation, personality and development. In R. Dienstbier (Ed.), *Nebraska symposium on motivation* (Vol. 36). Lincoln: University of Nebraska Press.

Dyer, C. B., Pavlik, V. N., Murphy, K. P., & Hyman, D. J. (2000). The high prevalence of depression and dementia in elder abuse or neglect. *Journal of the American Geriatrics Society, 48*, 205–208.

Dyer, S., & Moneta, G. (2006). Frequency of parallel, associative, and co-operative play in British children of different socioeconomic status. *Social Behavior and Personality, 34*, 587–592.

Dyregrov, K., Nordanger, D., & Dyregrov, A. (2003). Predictors of psychosocial distress after suicide, SIDS and accidents. *Death Studies, 27*, 143–165.

Dyson, A. H. (2003). "Welcome to the jam": Popular culture, school literacy and making of childhoods. *Harvard Educational Review, 73*, 328–361.

Eacott, M. J. (1999). Memory of the events of early childhood. *Current Directions in Psychological Science, 8*, 46–49.

Eagly, A. H., & Steffen, V. J. (1984). Gender stereotypes stem from the distribution of women and men into social roles. *Journal of Personality and Social Psychology, 46*, 735–754.

Eagly, A. H., & Steffen, V. J. (1986). Gender and aggressive behavior: A meta-analytic review of the social psychological literature. *Psychological Bulletin, 100*, 309–330.

Eagly, A. H., & Wood, W. (2003). In C. B. Travis, *Evolution, gender, and rape*. Cambridge, MA: MIT Press.

Eaker, E. D., Sullivan, L. M., Kelly-Hayes, M., D'Agostino, R. B., Sr., & Benjamin, E. J. (2004). Anger and hostility predict the development of atrial fibrillation in men in the Framingham Offspring Study. *Circulation, 109*, 1267–1271.

East, P., & Khoo, S. (2005). Longitudinal pathways linking family factors and sibling relationship qualities to adolescent substance use and sexual risk behaviors. *Journal of Family Psychology, 19*, 571–580.

Eastman, Q. (2003, June 20). Crib death exoneration in new gene tests. *Science, 300*, 1858.

Eaton, M. J., & Dembo, M. H. (1997). Differences in the motivational beliefs of Asian American and non-Asian students. *Journal of Educational Psychology, 89*, 433–440.

Eaton, W. O., & Enns, L. R. (1986). Sex differences in human motor activity level. *Psychological Bulletin, 100*, 19–28.

Eaton, W. O., & Yu, A. P. (1989). Are sex differences in child motor activity level a function of sex differences in maturational status? *Child Development, 60*, 1005–1011.

Eberling, J. L., Wu, C., Tong-Turnbeaugh, R., & Jagust, W. J. (2004). Estrogen- and tamoxifen-associated effects on brain structure and function. *Neuroimage, 21*, 364–371.

Ebner, N., Freund, A., & Baltes, P. (2006, December). Developmental changes in personal goal orientation from young to late adulthood: From striving for gains to maintenance and prevention of losses. *Psychology and Aging, 21*, 664–678.

Ebstein, R. P., Novick, O., Umansky, R., Priel, B., Osher, Y., Blaine, D., Bennett, E. R., Nemanov, L., Katz, M., & Belmaker, R. H. (1996). Dopamine D4 receptor (1996) exon III polymorphism associated with the human personality trait of novelty seeking. *Nature and Genetics, 12*, 78–80.

Eccles, J., Templeton, J., & Barber, B. (2003). Adolescence and emerging adulthood: The critical passage ways to adulthood. In M. Bornstein & L. Davidson (Eds.), *Well-being: Positive development across the life course*. Mahwah, NJ: Lawrence Erlbaum Associates.

Ecenbarger, W. (1993, April 1). America's new merchants of death. *The Reader's Digest*, 50.

Eckerman, C., & Peterman, K. (2001). Peers and infant social/communicative development. In G. Bremner & A. Fogel (Eds.), *Blackwell handbook of infant development* (pp. 326–350). Malden, MA: Blackwell Publishers.

Eckerman, C. O., & Oehler, J. M. (1992). Very-low-birthweight newborns and parents as early social partners. In S. L. Friedman & M. D. Sigman (Eds.), *The psychological development of low-birthweight children*. Norwood, NJ: Ablex.

Edelman, S., & Kidman, A. D. (1997). Mind and cancer: Is there a relationship? A review of evidence. *Australian Psychologist, 32*, 79–85.

Eden, D. (1990). Pygmalion without interpersonal contrast effects: Whole groups gain from raising manager expectations. *Journal of Applied Psychology, 75*, 394–398.

Edwards, C. P. (2000). Children's play in cross-cultural perspective: A new look at the Six Cultures study. *Cross-Cultural Research: The Journal of Comparative Social Science, 34*, 318–338.

Edwards, S. (2005). Constructivism does not only happen in the individual: Sociocultural theory and early childhood education. *Early Child Development & Care, 175*, 37–47.

Egan, S. K., & Perry, D. G. (1998). Does low self-regard invite victimization? *Developmental Psychology, 34*, 299–309.

Ehrensaft, M., Cohen, P., & Brown, J. (2003). Intergenerational transmission of partner violence: A 20-year prospective study. *Journal of Consulting & Clinical Psychology, 71*, 741–753.

Eichstedt, J., Serbin, L., & Poulin-Dubois, D. (2002). Of bears and men: Infants' knowledge of conventional and metaphorical gender stereotypes. *Infant Behavior & Development, 25*, 296–310.

Eiden, R., Foote, A., & Schuetze, P. (2007). Maternal cocaine use and caregiving status: Group differences in caregiver and infant risk variables. *Addictive Behaviors, 32*, 465–476.

Eigsti, I., & Cicchetti, D. (2004). The impact of child maltreatment on expressive syntax at 60 months. *Developmental Science, 7*, 88–102.

Eimas, P. D., Siqueland, E. R., Jusczyk, P., & Vigorito, J. (1971). Speech perception in infants. *Science, 171*, 303–306.

Eisbach, A. O. (2004). Children's developing awareness of diversity in people's trains of thought. *Child Development, 75*, 1694–1707.

Eisenberg, N. (2004). Another slant on moral judgment. *psycCRITIQUES*, 12–15.

Eisenberg, N., & Fabes, R. (1991). Prosocial behavior and empathy: A multimethod, developmental perspective. In M. S. Clark (Ed.), *Review of personality and social psychology* (Vol. 12). Newbury Park, CA: Sage.

Eisenberg, N., Fabes, R. A., Guthrie, I. K., & Reiser, M. (2000). Dispositional emotionality and regulation: Their role in predicting quality of social functioning. *Journal of Personality and Social Psychology, 78*, 136–157.

Eisenberg, N., Guthrie, I. K., Murphy, B. C., Shepard, S. A., Cumberland, A., & Carlo, G. (1999). Consistency and development of prosocial dispositions: A longitudinal study. *Child Development, 70*, 1360–1372.

Eisenberg, N., & Valiente, C. (2002). Parenting and children's prosocial and moral development. In M. Bornstein (Ed.), *Handbook of parenting: Vol. 5: Practical issues in parenting*. Mahwah, NJ: Lawrence Erlbaum Associates.

Eisenberg, N., & Valiente, C. (2004). Empathy-related responding: Moral, social, and socialization correlates. In A. G. Miller (Ed.), *Social psychology of good and evil*. New York: Guilford Press.

Eisenberg, N., Valiente, C., & Champion, C. Empathy-related responding: Moral, social, and socialization correlates. In A. G. Miller (Ed.), *Social psychology of good and evil*. New York: Guilford Press.

Eisenberg, N., & Zhou, Q. (2000). Regulation from a developmental perspective. *Psychological Inquiry, 11*, 166–172.

Eitel, B. J. (2003). Body image satisfaction, appearance importance, and self-esteem: A comparison of Caucasian and African-American women across the adult lifespan. *Dissertation Abstracts International: Section B: The Sciences & Engineering, 63*, pp. 5511.

Ekman, P., & O'Sullivan, M. (1991). Facial expression: Methods, means, and moues. In R. S. Feldman &

B. Rime (Eds.), *Fundamentals of nonverbal behavior.* Cambridge, England: Cambridge University Press.

Elder, G. A., De Gasperi, R., & Gama Sosa, M. A. (2006). Research update: Neurogenesis in adult brain and neuropsychiatric disorders. *Mt. Sinai Journal of Medicine, 73,* 931–940.

Eley, T., Liang, H., & Plomin, R. (2004). Parental familial vulnerability, family environment, and their interactions as predictors of depressive symptoms in adolescents. *Child & Adolescent Social Work Journal, 21,* 298–306.

Eley, T. C., Bolton, D., & O'Connor, T. G. (2003). A twin study of anxiety-related behaviours in pre-school children. *Journal of Child Psychology and Psychiatry and Allied Disciplines, 44,* 103–121.

Eley, T. C., Lichtenstein, P., & Moffitt, T. E. (2003). A longitudinal behavioral genetic analysis of the etiology of aggressive and nonaggressive antisocial behavior. *Development and Psychopathology, 15,* 383–402.

Elkind, D. (1985). Egocentrism redux. *Developmental Review, 5,* 218–226.

Elkind, D. (1994). *Ties that stress: The new family imbalance.* Cambridge, MA: Harvard University Press.

Elkind, D. (1996). Inhelder and Piaget on adolescence and adulthood: A postmodern appraisal. *Psychological Science, 7,* 216–220.

Elliott, K., & Urquiza, A. (2006). Ethnicity, culture, and child maltreatment. *Journal of Social Issues, 62,* 787–809.

Ellis, B. J. (2004). Timing of pubertal maturation in girls: An integrated life history approach. *Psychological Bulletin, 130,* 920–958.

Ellis, L. (2006, July). Gender differences in smiling: An evolutionary neuroandrogenic theory. *Physiology & Behavior, 88,* 303–308.

Ellis, L., & Engh, T. (2000). Handedness and age of death: New evidence on a puzzling relationship. *Journal of Health Psychology, 5,* 561–565.

Elsayem, A., Swint, K., Fisch, M. J., Palmer, J. L., Reddy, S., Walker, P., Zhukovsky, D., Knight, P., & Bruera, E. (2004). Palliative care inpatient service in a comprehensive cancer center: Clinical and financial outcomes. *Journal of Clinical Oncology, 22,* 2008–2014.

Else-Quest, N. M., Hyde, J. S., & Clark, R. (2003). Breastfeeding, bonding, and the mother–infant relationship. *Merrill-Palmer Quarterly, 49,* 495–517.

Emery, R. E., & Laumann-Billings, L. (1998). An overview of the nature, causes, and consequences of abusive family relationships: Toward differentiating maltreatment and violence. *American Psychologist, 53,* 121–135.

Emslie, G. J., Rush, A. J., Weinberg, W. A., Kowatch, R. A., Hughes, C. W., Carmody, T., & Rintelmann, J. A. (1997). Double-blind, randomized, placebo-controlled trial of fluoxetine in children and adolescents with depression. *Archives of General Psychiatry, 54,* 1031–1037.

Endo, S. (1992). Infant–infant play from 7 to 12 months of age: An analysis of games in infant–peer triads. *Japanese Journal of Child and Adolescent Psychiatry, 33,* 145–162.

England, P., & Li, S. (2006, October). Desegregation stalled: The changing gender composition of college majors, 1971-2002. *Gender & Society, 20,* 657–677.

Engler, J., & Goleman, D. (1992). *The consumer's guide to psychotherapy.* New York: Simon & Schuster.

Englund, K., & Behne, D. (2006). Changes in infant directed speech in the first six months. *Infant and Child Development, 15*(2), 139–160.

Englund, M. M., Levy, A. K., Hyson, D. M., & Sroufe, L. A. (2000). Adolescent social competence: Effectiveness in a group setting. *Child Development, 71,* 1049–1060.

Ennett, S. T., & Bauman, K. E. (1996). Adolescent social networks: School, demographic, and longitudinal considerations. *Journal of Adolescent Research, 11,* 194–215.

Enright, E. (2004, July & August). A house divided. *AARP Magazine,* pp. 54, 57.

Ensenauer, R. E., Michels, V. V., & Reinke, S. S. (2005). Genetic testing: Practical, ethical, and counseling considerations. *Mayo Clinic Proceedings, 80,* 63–73.

Epperson, S. E. (1988, September 16). Studies link subtle sex bias in schools with women's behavior in the workplace. *The Wall Street Journal,* p. 19.

Erber, J. T., Rothberg, S. T., & Szuchman, L. T. (1991). Appraisal of everyday memory failures by middle-aged adults. *Educational Gerontology, 17,* 63–72.

Erber, J. T., Szuchman, L. T., & Rothberg, S. T. (1990). Everyday memory failure: Age differences in appraisal and attribution. *Psychology and Aging, 5,* 236–241.

Erikson, E. H. (1963). *Childhood and society.* New York: Norton.

Eron, L. D., & Huesmann, L. R. (1985). The control of aggressive behavior by changes in attitude, values, and the conditions of learning. In R. J. Blanchard & C. Blanchard (Eds.), *Advances in the study of aggression.* New York: Academic Press.

Erwin, P. (1993). *Friendship and peer relations in children.* Chichester, England: Wiley.

Eslea, M., Menesini, E., Morita, Y., O'Moore, M., Mora-Nerchan, J. A., Pereira, B., & Smith, P. K. (2004). Friendship and loneliness among bullies and victims: Data from seven countries. *Aggressive Behavior, 30,* 71–83.

Espelage, D. L., & Swearer, S. M. (2004). *Bullying in American schools.* Mahwah, NJ: Lawrence Erlbaum.

Espenschade, A. (1960). Motor development. In W. R. Johnson (Ed.), *Science and medicine of exercise and sports.* New York: Harper & Row.

Essex, M. J., & Nam, S. (1987). Marital status and loneliness among older women: The differential importance of close family and friends. *Journal of Marriage and the Family, 49,* 92–106.

Estabrook, P. A., Lee, R. E., & Gyurcsik, N. C. (2003). Resources for physical activity participation: Does availability and accessibility differ by neighborhood socioeconomic status? *Annals of Behavioral Medicine, 25,* 100–104.

Ethier, L., Couture, G., & Lacharite, C. (2004). Risk factors associated with the chronicity of high potential for child abuse and neglect. *Journal of Family Violence, 19,* 13–24.

Evans, G. W. (2004). The environment of childhood poverty. *American Psychologist, 59,* 77–92.

Eveleth, P., & Tanner, J. (1976). *Worldwide variation in human growth.* New York: Cambridge University Press.

Eyer, D. (1992). The bonding hype. In M. E. Lamb & J. B. Lancaster (Eds.), *Birth management: Biosocial perspectives.* Hawthorne, New York: Aldine de Gruyter.

Eyer, D. E. (1994). Mother–infant bonding: A scientific fiction. *Human Nature, 5,* 69–94.

Faith, M. S., Johnson, S. L., & Allison, D. B. (1997). Putting the behavior into the behavior genetics of obesity. *Behavior Genetics, 27,* 423–439.

Falck-Ytter, T., Gredeback, G., & von Hofsten, C. (2006). Infants predict other people's action goals. *Nature and Neuroscience, 9,* 878–879.

Falk, D. (2004). Prelinguistic evolution in early hominins: Whence motherese? *Behavioral and Brain Sciences, 27,* 491–503.

Falk, P. J. (1989). Lesbian mothers: Psychosocial assumptions in family law. *American Psychologist, 44,* 941–947.

Families and Work Institute. (1998). *Report on men spending more time with kids.* Washington, DC: Author.

Fangman, J. J., Mark, P. M., Pratt, L., Conway, K. K., Healey, M. L., Oswald, J. W., & Uden, D. L. (1994). Prematurity prevention programs. *American Journal of Obstetrical Gynecology, 170,* 744–750.

Fantz, R. (1963). Pattern vision in newborn infants. *Science, 140,* 296–297.

Fantz, R.L. (1961). The origin of form perception. *Scientific American, 72.*

Farah, M., Shera, D., Savage, J., Betancourt, L., Giannetta, J., Brodsky, N., et al. (2006, September). Childhood poverty: Specific associations with neurocognitive development. *Brain Research, 1110,* 166–174.

Farhi, P. (1995, June 21). Turning the tables on TV violence. *The Washington Post,* pp. F1, F2.

Farmer, T. W., Estell, D. B., Bishop, J. L., O'Neal, K. K., & Cairns, B. D. (2003). Rejected bullies or popular leaders? The social relations of aggressive subtypes of rural African American early adolescents. *Developmental Psychology, 39,* 992–1004.

Farrant, B., Fletcher, J., & Maybery, M. (2006, November). Specific language impairment, theory of mind, and visual perspective taking: Evidence for simulation theory and the developmental role of language. *Child Development, 77,* 1842–1853.

Farver, J. M., & Frosch, D. L. (1996). L.A. stories: Aggression in preschoolers' spontaneous narratives after the riots of 1992. *Child Development, 67,* 19–32.

Farver, J. M., & Lee-Shin, Y. (2000). Acculturation and Korean-American children's social and play behavior. *Social Development, 9,* 316–336.

Farver, J. M., Kim, Y. K., & Lee-Shin, Y. (1995). Cultural differences in Korean- and Anglo-American preschoolers' social interaction and play behaviors. *Child Development, 66,* 1088–1099.

Farver, J. M., Welles-Nystrom, B., Frosch, D. L., & Wimbarti, S. (1997). Toy stories: Aggression in children's narratives in the United States, Sweden, Germany, and Indonesia. *Journal of Cross-Cultural Psychology, 28,* 393–420.

Faulkner, G., & Biddle, S. (2004). Exercise and depression: Considering variability and contextuality. *Journal of Sport & Exercise Psychology, 26,* 3–18.

Federal Interagency Forum on Age-Related Statistics. (2000). *Older Americans 2000: Key indicators of well-being.* Hyattsville, MD: Federal Interagency Forum on Age-Related Statistics.

Federal Interagency Forum on Child and Family Statistics. (2003). *America's children: Key national indicators of well-Being, 2003.* Federal Interagency Forum on Child and Family Statistics. Washington, DC: U.S. Government Printing Office.

Feeney, B., & Collins, N. (2001). Predictors of caregiving in adult intimate relationships: An attachment theoretical perspective. *Journal of Personality & Social Psychology, 80,* 972–994.

Feldhusen, J. (2003). Precocity and acceleration. *Gifted Education International, 17,* 55–58.

Feldman, R., & Eidelman, A. (2003). Direct and indirect effects of breast milk on neurobehavioral and cognitive development of premature infants. *Developmental Psychobiology, 43,* 109–119.

Feldman, R., & Masalha, S. (2007). The role of culture in moderating the links between early ecological risk and young children's adaptation. *Development and Psychopathology, 19,* 1–21.

Feldman, R., Weller, A., Sirota, L., & Eidelman, A. I. (2003). Testing a family intervention hypothesis: The contribution of mother–infant skin-to-skin contact (Kangaroo Care) to family interaction, proximity, and touch. *Journal of Family Psychology, 17,* 94–107.

Feldman, R. S. (1982). *Development of nonverbal behavior in children.* New York: Springer-Verlag.

Feldman, R. S. (Ed.). (1992). *Applications of nonverbal behavioral theories and research.* Hillsdale, NJ: Erlbaum.

Feldman, R. S., Philippot, P., & Custrini, R. J. (1991). Social competence and nonverbal behavior. In R. S. Feldman & B. Rime (Eds.), *Fundamentals of nonverbal behavior.* Cambridge, England: Cambridge University Press.

Feldman, R. S., & Prohaska, T. (1979). The student as Pygmalion: Effect of student expectation on the teacher. *Journal of Educational Psychology, 4,* 485–493.

Feldman, R. S., & Rimé, B. (Eds.). (1991). *Fundamentals of nonverbal behavior.* Cambridge, England: Cambridge University Press.

Feldman, R. S., & Theiss, A. J. (1982). The teacher and student as Pygmalions: The joint effects of teacher and student expectation. *Journal of Educational Psychology, 74,* 217–223.

Feldman, R. S., Tomasian, J., & Coats, E. J. (1999). Adolescents' social competence and nonverbal deception abilities: Adolescents with higher social skills are better liars. *Journal of Nonverbal Behavior, 23,* 237–249.

Feldman, S. S., & Rosenthal, D. A. (1990). The acculturation of autonomy expectations in Chinese high schoolers residing in two Western nations. *International Journal of Psychology, 25,* 259–281.

Feldman, S. S., & Wood, D. N. (1994). Parents' expectations for preadolescent sons' behavioral autonomy: A longitudinal study of correlates and outcomes. *Journal of Research on Adolescence, 4,* 45–70.

Fenson, L., Dale, P. S., Reznick, J. S., Bates, E., Thal, D. J., & Pethick, S. J. (1994). Variability in early communicative development. *Monographs of the Society for Research in Child Development, 59*(5, Serial No. 242).

Fenwick, K., & Morrongiello, B. (1991). Development of frequency perception in infants and children. *Journal of Speech, Language Pathology, and Audiology, 15,* 7–22.

Fenwick, K. D., & Morrongiello, B. A. (1998). Spatial co-location and infants' learning of auditory-visual associations. *Behavior & Development, 21,* 745–759.

Fergusson, D., Horwood, L., Boden, J., & Jenkin, G. (2007, March). Childhood social disadvantage and smoking in adulthood: Results of a 25-year longitudinal study. *Addiction, 102,* 475–482.

Fergusson, D. M., Horwood, L. J., & Ridder, E. M. (2006). Abortion in young women and subsequent mental health. *Journal of Child Psychology and Psychiatry, 47,* 16–24.

Fernald, A. (2001). Hearing, listening, and understanding: Auditory development in infancy. In G. Bremner & A. Fogel (Eds.), *Blackwell handbook of infant development.* Malden, MA: Blackwell Publishers.

Fernald, A., & Morikawa, H. (1993). Common themes and cultural variations in Japanese and American mothers' speech to infants. *Child Development, 64,* 637–656.

Fernald, A., Taeschner, T., Dunn, J., Papousek, M., Boysson-Bardies, B., & Fukui, I. (1989). A cross-language study of prosodic modifications in mothers' and fathers' speech to preverbal infants. *Journal of Child Language, 16,* 477–501.

Fernyhough, C. (1997). Vygotsky's sociocultural approach: Theoretical issues and implications for current research. In S. Hala (Ed.), *The development of social cognition* (pp. 65–92). Hove, England: Psychology Press/Erlbaum, Taylor & Francis.

Ferrario, S., Vitaliano, P., & Zotti, A. (2003). Alzheimer's disease: Usefulness of the Family Strain Questionnaire and the Screen for Caregiver Burden in the study of caregiving-related problems. *International Journal of Geriatric Psychiatry, 18,* 1110–1114.

Festinger, L. (1954). A theory of social comparison processes. *Human Relations, 7,* 117–140.

Fetterman, D. M. (1998). Ethnography. In L. Bickman & D. J. Rog (Eds.), *Handbook of applied social research methods* (pp. 473–504). Thousand Oaks, CA: Sage.

Fetterman, D. M. (2005). Empowerment evaluation: From the digital divide to academic distsress. In D. Fetterman & A. Wandersman (Eds.), *Empowerment evaluation principles in practice.* New York: Guilford Press.

Fiatarone, M. S. A., & Garnett, L. R. (1997, March). Keep on keeping on. *Harvard Health Letter,* pp. 4–5.

Field, D., & Minkler, M. (1988). Continuity and change in social support between young-old and old-old or very-old age. *Journal of Gerontology, 43*(4), 100–106.

Field, M. J., & Behrman, R. E. (Eds.) (2002). *When children die.* Washington, DC: National Academies Press.

Field, T. (1990). *Infancy.* Cambridge, MA: Harvard University Press.

Field, T. (2001). Massage therapy facilitates weight gain in preterm infants. *Current Directions in Psychological Science, 10,* 51–54.

Field, T. (2003). *Touch.* Cambridge, MA: MIT Press.

Field, T., Diego, M., & Hernandez-Reif, M. (2006). Prenatal depression effects on the fetus and newborn: A review. *Infant Behavior & Development, 29,* 445–455.

Field, T., Greenberg, R., Woodson, R., Cohen, D., & Garcia, R. (1984). Facial expression during Brazelton neonatal assessments. *Infant Mental Health Journal, 5,* 61–71.

Field, T., Hernandez-Reif, M., & Diego, M. (2006). Newborns of depressed mothers who received moderate versus light pressure massage during pregnancy. *Infant Behavior & Development, 29*(1), 54–58.

Field, T., & Roopnarine, J. L. (1982). Infant–peer interactions. In T. Field, A. Huston, H. Quay, & G. Finley (Eds.), *Review of human development.* New York: Wiley.

Field, T., & Walden, T. (1982). Perception and production of facial expression in infancy and early childhood. In H. Reese & L. Lipsitt (Eds.), *Advances in child development and behavior* (Vol. 16). New York: Academic Press.

Field, T. M. (1982). Individual differences in the expressivity of neonates and young infants. In R. S. Feldman (Ed.), *Development of nonverbal behavior in children.* New York: Springer-Verlag.

Field, T. M. (Ed.). (1988). *Stress and coping across development.* Hillsdale, NJ: Erlbaum.

Field, T. M. (1990). Alleviating stress in newborn infants in the intensive care unit. In B. M. Lester & E. Z. Tronick (Eds.), *Stimulation and the preterm infant: The limits of plasticity.* Philadelphia: Saunders.

Field, T. M. (1995a). Infant massage therapy. In T. M. Field (Ed.), *Touch in early development.* Hillsdale, NJ: Erlbaum.

Field, T. M. (1995b). Massage therapy for infants and children. *Journal of Developmental & Behavioral Pediatrics, 16,* 105–111.

Field, T. M., & Millsap, R. E. (1991). Personality in advanced old age: Continuity or change? *Journal of Gerontology: Psychological Sciences, 46,* P299–P308.

Fields, J. & Casper, L. M. (2001). *America's families and living arrangements: March 2000.* Current Population Reports P20–537. U.S Census Bureau Washington DC.

Fields-Meyer, T. (1995, September 25). Having their say. *People,* 50–60.

Fifer, W. (1987). Neonatal preference for mother's voice. In N. A. Kasnegor, E. M. Blass, & M. A. Hofer (Eds.), *Perinatal development: A psychobiological perspective. Behavioral biology* (pp. 111–124). Orlando, FL: Academic Press.

Figley, C. R. (1973). Child density and the marital relationship. *Journal of Marriage and the Family, 35,* 272–282.

Finch, C. E., & Tanzi, R. E. (1997, October 17). Genetics of aging. *Science, 278,* 407–410.

Fincham, F. D. (1998). Child development and marital relations. *Child Development, 69,* 543–574.

Fincham, F. D. (2003). Marital conflict: Correlates, structure, and context. *Current Directions in Psychological Science, 12,* 23–27.

Fingerhut, L. A., & Kleinman, J. C. (1990). International and interstate comparisons of homicide among young males. *Journal of the American Medical Association, 263,* 3292–3295.

Fingerhut, L. A., & MaKuc, D. M. (1992). Mortality among minority populations in the United States. *American Journal of Public Health, 82,* 1168–1170.

Finkbeiner, A. K. (1996). *After the death of a child: Living with loss through the years.* New York: The Free Press.

Finkelhor, D. (1997). The homicides of children and youth: A developmental perspective. In G. K. Kantor & J. L. Janinski (Ed.), *Out of the darkness: Contemporary perspectives on family violence* (pp. 17–34). Thousand Oaks, CA: Sage.

Finkelstein, D. L., Harper, D. A., & Rosenthal, G. E. (1998). Does length of hospital stay during labor and delivery influence patient satisfaction? Results from a regional study. *American Journal of Managed Care, 4,* 1701–1708.

First, J. M., & Cardenas, J. (1986). A minority view on testing. *Educational Measurement Issues and Practice, 5,* 6–11.

Fischer, K. W., & Hencke, R. W. (1996). Infants' construction of actions in context: Piaget's contributions to research on early development. *Psychological Science, 7,* 204–210.

Fischer, K. W., & Rose, S. P. (1994). Dynamic development of coordination of components in brain and behavior: A framework for theory and research. In G. Dawson & K. W. Fischer (Eds.), *Human behavior and the developing brain.* New York: Guilfrod.

Fischer, K. W., & Rose, S. P. (1995). Concurrent cycles in the dynamic development of brain and behavior. *Newsletter of the Society for Research in Child Development,* p. 16.

Fish, J. M. (Ed.). (2001). *Race and intelligence: Separating science from myth.* Mahwah, NJ: Erlbaum.

Fisher, C. (2005). Deception research involving children: Ethical practices and paradoxes. *Ethics & Behavior, 15,* 271–287.

Fisher, C., & Tokura, H. (1996). Acoustic cues to grammatical structure in infant-directed speech: Cross-linguistic evidence. *Child Development, 67,* 3192–3218.

Fisher, C. B. (2003). *Decoding the ethics code: A practical guide for psychologists*. Thousand Oaks, CA: Sage Publications.

Fisher, C. B. (2004). Informed consent and clinical research involving children and adolescents: Implications of the revised APA Ethics Code and HIPAA. *Journal of Clinical Child & Adolescent Psychology, 33*, 832–839.

Fisher, J., Astbury, J., & Smith, A. (1997). Adverse psychological impact of obstetric interventions: A prospective longitudinal study. *Australian & New Zealand Journal of Psychiatry, 31*, 728–738.

Fishman, C. (1999, May). Watching the time go by. *American Demographics*, 56–57.

Fiske, S. T., & Taylor, S. E. (1991). *Social cognition* (2nd ed.). New York: McGraw-Hill.

Fitzgerald, D., & White, K. (2003). Linking children's social worlds: Perspective-taking in parent–child and peer contexts. *Social Behavior & Personality, 31*, 509–522.

Fivush, R., Kuebli, J., & Clubb, P.A. (1992). The structure of events and event representations: A developmental analysis. *Child Development, 63*, 188–201.

Flavell, J. H. (1994). Cognitive development: Past, present, and future. In R. D. Parke, P. A. Ornstein, J. J. Rieser, & C. Zahn-Waxler (Eds.), *A century of developmental psychology*. Washington, DC: American Psychological Association.

Flavell, J. H. (1996). Piaget's legacy. *Psychological Science, 7*, 200–203.

Flavell, J. H., Green, F. L., & Flavell, E. R. (1995). The development of children's knowledge about attentional focus. *Developmental Psychology, 31*, 706–712.

Flegal, K., Tabak, C., and Ogden, C. (2006). Overweight in children: Definitions and interpretation. *Health Education Research, 21*, 755–760.

Fleming, M., Greentree, S., Cocotti-Muller, D., Elias, K., & Morrison, S. (2006, December). Safety in cyberspace: Adolescents' safety and exposure online. *Youth & Society, 38*, 135–154.

Fleming, P., Tsogt, B., & Blair, P. (2006). Modifiable risk factors, sleep environment, developmental physiology and common polymorphisms: Understanding and preventing sudden infant deaths. *Early Human Development, 82*, 761–766.

Fletcher, A. C., Darling, N. E., Steinberg, L., & Dornbusch, S. M. (1995). The company they keep: Relation of adolescents' adjustment and behavior to their friends' perceptions of authoritative parenting in the social network. *Developmental Psychology, 31*, 300–310.

Flom, R., & Bahrick, L. (2007). The development of infant discrimination of affect in multimodal and unimodal stimulation: The role of intersensory redundancy. *Developmental Psychology, 43*, 238–252.

Flor, D. L., & Knap, N. F. (2001). Transmission and transaction: Predicting adolescents' internalization of parental religious values. *Journal of FamilyPsychology, 15*, 627–645.

Florian, V., & Kravetz, S. (1985). Children's concepts of death: A cross-cultural comparison among Muslims, Druze, Christians, and Jews in Israel. *Journal of Cross-Cultural Psychology, 16*, 174–189.

Florsheim, P. (2003). Adolescent romantic and sexual behavior: What we know and where we go from here. In P. Florsheim (Ed.), *Adolescent romantic relations and sexual behavior: Theory, research, and practical implications*. Mahwah, NJ: Lawrence Erlbaum Associates.

Flouri, E. (2005). *Fathering and child outcomes*. New York: Wiley & Sons.

Floyd, R. G. (2005). Information-processing approaches to interpretation of contemporary intellectual assessment instruments. In D. P. Flanagan, & P. L. Harrison, (Eds.), *Contemporary intellectual assessment: Theories, tests, and issues*. New York, Guilford Press.

Flynn, E., O'Malley, C., & Wood, D. (2004). A longitudinal, microgenetic study of the emergence of false belief understanding and inhibition skills. *Developmental Science, 7*, 103–115.

Fogel, A., de Koeyer, I., & Bellagamba, F. (2004). The dialogical self in the first two years of life: Embarking on a journey of discovery. *Theory & Psychology, 12* [Special issue: The dialogical self], 191–205.

Fogel, A., Hsu, H., Shapiro, A., Nelson-Goens, G., & Secrist, C. (2006, May). Effects of normal and perturbed social play on the duration and amplitude of different types of infant smiles. *Developmental Psychology, 42*, 459–473.

Fok, W. Y., Chan, L. Y., Tsui, M. H., Leung, T. N., Lau, T. K., & Chung, T. K. (2005). When to induce labor for post-term? A study of induction at 41 weeks versus 42 weeks. *European Journal of Obstetrics and Gynecological Reproductive Biology, 125*, 206–210.

Folkman, S., & Lazarus, R. S. (1980). An analysis of coping in a middle-aged community sample. *Journal of Health and Social Behavior, 21*, 219–239.

Folkman, S., & Lazarus, R. S. (1988). Coping as a mediator of emotion. *Journal of Personality and Social Psychology, 54*, 466–475.

Forrester, M. (2001). The embedding of the self in early interaction. *Infant & Child Development, 10*, 189–202.

Forste, R., Weiss, J., & Lippincott, E. (2001). The decision to breastfeed in the United States: Does race matter? *Pediatrics, 108*, 291–296.

Fowers, B. J., & Davidov, B. J. (2006). The virtue of multiculturalism: Personal transformation, character, and openness to the other. *American Psychologist, 61*, 581–594.

Fox, M., Pac, S., Devaney, B., & Jankowski L. (2004). Feeding infants and toddlers study: What foods are infants and toddlers eating? *Journal of the American Dietetic Association, 104*, 22–30.

Fozard, J. L., Vercruyssen, M., Reynolds, S. L., Hancock, P. A., et al. (1994). Age differences and changes in reaction time: The Baltimore Longitudinal Study of Aging. *Journal of Gerontology, 49*, 179–189.

Fraenkel, P. (2003). Contemporary two-parent families: Navigating work and family challenges. In F. Walsh (Ed.), *Normal family processes: Growing diversity and complexity* (3rd ed., pp. 61–95). New York: Guilford Press.

Fraley, R. C., & Spieker, S. J. (2003). Are infant attachment patterns continuously or categorically distributed? A taxometric analysis of Strange Situation behavior. *Developmental Psychology, 39*, 387–404.

Franck, I., & Brownstone, D. (1991). *The parent's desk reference*. New York: Prentice-Hall.

Frankel, M. and Chapman, A. (2000). *Human inheritable genetic modifications: Assessing scientific, ethical, religious, and policy issues*. Washington, DC: American Association for the Advancement of Science.

Frankenburg, W. K., Dodds, J., Archer, P., Shapiro, H., & Bresnick, B. (1992). The Denver II: A major revision and restandardization of the Denver Developmental Screening Test. *Pediatrics, 89*, 91–97.

Fransen, M., Meertens, R., & Schrander-Stumpel, C. (2006). Communication and risk presentation in genetic counseling: Development of a checklist. *Patient Education and Counseling, 61*, 126–133.

Fraser, S., Muckle, G., & Després, C. (2006, January). The relationship between lead exposure, motor function and behaviour in Inuit preschool children. *Neurotoxicology and Teratology, 28*, 18–27.

Frazier, L. M., Grainger, D. A., Schieve, L. A., & Toner, J. P. (2004). Follicle-stimulating hormone and estradiol levels independently predict the success of assisted reproductive technology treatment. *Fertility and Sterility, 82*, 834–840.

Fredriksen, K., Rhodes, J., Reddy, R., & Way, N. (2004). Sleepless in Chicago: Tracking the effects of adolescent sleep loss during the middle school years. *Child Development, 75*, 84–95.

Freedman, A. M., & Ellison, S. (2004, May 6). Testosterone patch for women shows promise. *The Wall Street Journal*, pp. A1, B2.

Freedman, D. G. (1979, January). Ethnic differences in babies. *Human Nature*, 15–20.

Freedman, D. S., Khan, L. K., Serdula, M. K., Dietz, W. H., Sriniasan, S. R., & Berenson, G. S. (2004). Interrelationships among childhood BMI, childhood height, and adult obesity: The Bogalusa Heart Study. *International Journal of Obesity and Related Metabolic Disorders, 28*, 10–16.

Freeman, E., Sammel, M., & Liu, L. (2004). Hormones and menopausal status as predictors of depression in women in transition to menopause. *Archives of General Psychiatry, 61*, 62–70.

Freiberg, P. (1998 February). We know how to stop the spread of AIDS: So why can't we? *APA Monitor, 32*.

French, S., & Swain, J. (1997). Young disabled people. In J. Roche & S. Tucker (Eds.), *Youth in society: Contemporary theory, policy and practice* (pp. 199–206). London, England: Sage.

Freud, S. (1920). *A general introduction to psychoanalysis*. New York: Boni & Liveright.

Freud, S. (1922/1959). *Group psychology and the analysis of the ego*. London: Hogarth.

Friborg, O., Barlaug, D., Martinussen, M., Rosenvinge, J. H., & Hjemdal, O. (2005). Resilience in relation to personality and intelligence. *International Journal of Methods in Psychiatric Research, 14*, 29–42.

Frick, P. J., Cornell, A. H., Bodin, S. D., Dane, H. A., Barry, C. T., & Loney, B. R. (2003). Callous-unemotional traits and developmental pathways to severe conduct problems. *Developmental Psychology, 39*, 246–260.

Fried, P. A., & Watkinson, B. (1990). 36- and 48-month neurobehavioral follow-up of children prenatally exposed to marijuana, cigarettes, and alcohol. *Developmental and Behavioral Pediatrics, 11*, 49–58.

Friedland, R. (2003). Fish consumption and the risk of Alzheimer disease: Is it time to make dietary recommendations? *Archives of Neurology, 60*, 923–924.

Friedman, D. E. (2004). *The new economics of preschool*. Washington, DC: Early Childhood Funders' Collaborative/NAEYC.

Friedman, L., Kahn, J., Middleman, A., Rosenthal, S., & Zimet, G. (2006, October). Human papillomavirus (HPV) vaccine: A position statement of the society for adolescent medicine. *Journal of Adolescent Health, 39*, 620–620.

Friend, R. M., & Neale, J. M. (1972). Children's perceptions of success and failure: An attributional analysis of the effects of race and social class. *Developmental Psychology, 7*, 124–128.

Frisch, M., Friis, S., Kjear, S. K., & Melbye, M. (1995). Falling incidence of penis cancer in an uncircumcised population (Denmark 1943–90). *British Medical Journal, 311*, 1471.

Frishman, R. (1996, October). Hormone replacement therapy for men. *Harvard Health Letter*, pp. 6–8.

Fritz, G., & Rockney, R. (2004). Summary of the practice parameter for the assessment and treatment of children and adolescents with enuresis. *Work Group on Quality Issues; Journal of the American Academy of Child & Adolescent Psychiatry, 43,* 123–125.

Frome, P., Alfeld, C., Eccles, J., & Barber, B. (2006, August). Why don't they want a male-dominated job? An investigation of young women who changed their occupational aspirations. *Educational Research and Evaluation, 12,* 359–372.

Fromholt, P., & Larsen, S. F. (1991). Autobiographical memory in normal, aging and primary degenerative dementia (dementia of the Alzheimer type). *Journal of Gerontology, 46,* 85–91.

Fry, C. L. (1985). Culture, behavior, and aging in the comparative perspective. In J. E. Birren & K. W. Schaie (Eds.), *Handbook of the psychology of aging.* New York: Van Nostrand Reinhold.

Fu, G., Xu, F., Cameron, C., Heyman, G., & Lee, K. (2007, March). Cross-cultural differences in children's choices, categorizations, and evaluations of truths and lies. *Developmental Psychology, 43*(2), 278–293.

Fuchs, D., & Fuchs, L. S. (1994). Inclusive schools movement and the radicalization of special education reform. *Exceptional Children, 60,* 294–309.

Fugate, W. N., & Mitchell, E. S. (1997). Women's images of midlife: Observations from the Seattle Midlife Women's Health Study. *Health Care for Women International, 18,* 439–453.

Fuligni, A., & Hardway, C. (2006, September). Daily variation in adolescents' sleep, activities, and psychological well-being. *Journal of Research on Adolescence, 16,* 353–378.

Fuligni, A., & Yoshikawa, H. (2003). Socioeconomic resources, parenting, and child development among immigrant families. In M. Bornstein & R. Bradley (Eds.), *Socioeconomic status, parenting, and child development.* Mahwah, NJ: Lawrence Erlbaum Associates.

Fuligni, A., & Zhang, W. (2004). Attitudes toward family obligation among adolescents in contemporary urban and rural China. *Child Development, 75,* 180–192.

Fuligini, A. J. (1997). The academic achievement of adolescents from immigrant families: The roles of family background, attitudes, and behavior. *Child Development, 68,* 351–368.

Fulgini, A. J. (1998). The adjustment of children from immigrant families. *Current Directions in Psychological Science, 7,* 99–103.

Fuligni, A. J., Tseng, V., & Lam, M. (1999). Attitudes toward family obligations among American adolescents with Asian, Latin American, and European backgrounds. *Child Development, 70,* 1030–1044.

Funk, J., Buchman, D., & Jenks, J. (2003). Playing violent video games, desensitization, and moral evaluation in children. *Journal of Applied Developmental Psychology, 24,* 413–436.

Furman, W., & Buhrmester, D. (1992). Age and sex differences in perceptions of networks of personal relationships. *Child Development, 63,* 103–115.

Furman, W., & Shaffer, L. (2003). The role of romantic relationships in adolescent development. In P. Florsheim (Ed.), *Adolescent romantic relations and sexual behavior: Theory, research, and practical implications.* Mahwah, NJ: Lawrence Erlbaum Associates.

Furnham, A., & Weir, C. (1996). Lay theories of child development. *Journal of Genetic Psychology, 157,* 211–226.

Furstenberg, Jr., F. F. (1996, June). The future of marriage. *American Demographics,* 34–40.

Gabbay, S., & Wahler, J. (2002). Lesbian aging: Review of a growing literature. *Journal of Gay & Lesbian Social Services: Issues in Practice, Policy & Research, 14,* 1–21.

Gable, S., & Lutz, S. (2000). Household, parent, and child contributions to childhood obesity. *Family Relations: Interdisciplinary Journal of Applied Family Studies, 49,* 293–300.

Gagnon, S. G., & Nagle, R. J. (2000). Comparison of the revised and original versions of the Bayley Scales of Infant Development. *School Psychology International, 21,* 293–305.

Galambos, N., Leadbeater, B., & Barker, E. (2004). Gender differences in and risk factors for depression in adolescence: A 4-year longitudinal study. *International Journal of Behavioral Development, 28,* 16–25.

Galbraith, K. M, & Dobson, K. S. (2000). The role of the psychologist in determining competence for assisted suicide/euthanasia in the terminally ill. *Canadian Psychology, 41,* 174–183.

Gallagher, J. J. (1994). Teaching and learning: New models. *Annual Review of Psychology, 45,* 171–195.

Gallagher, L., Becker, K., & Kearney, G. (2003). A case of autism associated with del(2)(q32.1q32.2) or (q32.2q32.3). *Journal of Autism and Developmental Disorders, 33,* 105–108.

Gallup Poll. (2004). How many children? *The Gallup Poll Monthly.*

Gallup, G. G., Jr. (1977). Self-recognition in primates: A comparative approach to the bidirectional properties of consciousness. *American Psychologist, 32,* 329–337.

Ganger, J., & Brent, M. R. (2004). Reexamining the vocabulary spurt. *Developmental Psychology, 40,* 621–632.

Ganzini, L., Beer, T., & Brouns, M. (2006, September). Views on physician-assisted suicide among family members of Oregon cancer patients. *Journal of Pain and Symptom Management, 32,* 230–236.

Garcia, C., Bearer, E. L., & Lerner, R. M. (Eds.). (2004). *Nature and nurture: The complex interplay of genetic and environmental influences on human behavior and development.* Mahwah: Lawrence Erlbaum Associates.

Garcia, M., Shaw, D., Winslow, E., & Yaggi, K. (2000). Destructive sibling conflict and the development of conduct problems in young boys. *Developmental Psychology, 36,* 44–53.

Garcia-Moreno, C., Heise, L., Jansen, H. A. F. M., Ellsberg, M., & Watts, C. (2005, November 25). Violence against women. *Science, 310,* 1282–1283.

Gardner, H. (2000). *Intelligence reframed: Multiple intelligences for the 21st century.* New York: Basic Books.

Gardner, H. (2003). Three distinct meanings of intelligence. In R. Sternberg & J. Lautrey (Eds.), *Models of intelligence: International perspectives.* Washington, DC: American Psychological Association.

Gardner, H., & Moran, S. (2006). The science of multiple intelligences theory: A response to Lynn Waterhouse. *Educational Psychologist, 41,* 227–232.

Garland, J. E. (2004). Facing the evidence: Antidepressant treatment in children and adolescents. *Canadian Medical Association Journal, 17,* 489–491.

Garlick, D. (2003). Integrating brain science research with intelligence research. *Current Directions in Psychological Science, 12,* 185–189.

Garrison, M., & Christakis, D. (2005). *A teacher in the living room? Educational media for babies, toddlers and preschoolers.* Menlo Park, CA: Kaiser Family Foundation.

Garrity, C., Jens, K., & Porter, W. W. (1996, August). Bully–victim problems in the school setting. Paper presented at the annual meeting of the American Psychological Association. Toronto, Canada.

Gartstein, M., Slobodskaya, H., & Kinsht, I. (2003). Cross-cultural differences in temperament in the first year of life: United States of America (US) and Russia. *International Journal of Behavioral Development, 27,* 316–328.

Gatz, M. (1997, August). Variations of depression in later life. Paper presented at the Annual Convention of the American Psychological Association, Chicago.

Gaulden, M. E. (1992). Maternal age effect: The enigma of Down syndrome and other trisomic conditions. *Mutation Research, 296,* 69–88.

Gauthier, Y. (2003). Infant mental health as we enter the third millennium: Can we prevent aggression? *Infant Mental Health Journal, 24,* 101–109.

Gauvain, M. (1998). Cognitive development in social and cultural context. *Current Directions in Psychological Science, 7,* 188–194.

Gavin, L. A., Furman, W. (1996). Adolescent girls' relationships with mothers and best friends. *Child Development, 67,* 375–386.

Gavin, T., & Myers, A. (2003). Characteristics, enrollment, attendance, and dropout patterns of older adults in beginner Tai-Chi and line-dancing programs. *Journal of Aging & Physical Activity, 11,* 123–141.

Gawande, A. (2007, April 30). The way we age now. *The New Yorker,* 49–59.

Gazmararian, J. A., Petersen, R., Spitz, A. M., Goodwin, M. M., Saltzman, L. E., & Marks, J. S. (2000). Violence and reproductive health: Current knowledge and future research directions. *Mat Child Health, 4,* 79–84.

Gazzaniga, M. S. (1983). Right-hemisphere language following brain bisection: A twenty-year perspective. *American Psychologist, 38,* 525–537.

Gee, H. (2004). *Jacob's ladder: The history of the human genome.* New York: Norton.

Gelfand, M. M. (2000). Sexuality among older women. *Journal of Womens Health & Gender-Based Medicine, 9*(Suppl 1), S-15–S-20.

Gelman, D. (1994, April 18). The mystery of suicide. *Newsweek,* 44–49.

Gelman, R. (2006, August). Young natural-number arithmeticians. *Current Directions in Psychological Science, 15,* 193–197.

Gelman, R., & Baillargeon, R. (1983). A review of some Piagetian concepts. In P. H. Mussen (Ed.), *Handbook of child psychology: Vol 3. Cognitive development* (4th ed., pp. 167–230). New York: Wiley.

Gelman, R., & Cordes, S. Counting in animals and humans. In E. Dupoux, *Language, brain, and cognitive development: Essays in honor of Jacques Mehler.* Cambridge, MA: The MIT Press.

Gelman, R., & Gallistel, C. R. (2004, October 15). Language and the origin of numerical concepts. *Science, 306,* 441–443.

Gelman, S. A., Taylor, M. G., & Nguyen, S. (2004). Mother–child conversations about gender. *Monographs of the Society for Research in Child Development, 69.*

General Social Survey. (1998). *National opinion research center.* Chicago: University of Chicago.

Genovese, J. (2006). Piaget, pedagogy, and evolutionary psychology. *Evolutionary Psychology, 4,* 127–137.

Gentilucci, M., & Corballis, M. (2006). From manual gesture to speech: A gradual transition. *Neuroscience & Biobehavioral Reviews, 30,* 949–960.

Gerard, C. M., Harris, K. A., & Thach, B. T. (2002). Spontaneous arousals in supine infants while swaddled and unswaddled during rapid eye movement and quiet sleep. *Pediatrics, 110,* 70.

Gerber, M. S. (October 9, 2002). Eighty million strong—the singles lobby. *The Hill,* p. 45.

Gerber, P., & Coffman, K. (2007). Nonaccidental head trauma in infants. *Child's Nervous System, 23,* 499–507.

Gerend, M., Aiken, L., & West, S. (2004). Personality factors in older women's perceived susceptibility to diseases of aging. *Journal of Personality, 72,* 243–270.

Gerhardt, P. (1999, August 10). Potty training: How did it get so complicated? *Daily Hampshire Gazette,* p. C1.

Gerrish, C. J., & Mennella, J. A. (2000). Short-term influence of breastfeeding on the infants' interaction with the environment. *Developmental Psychobiology, 36,* 40–48.

Gershkoff-Stowe, L., & Thelen, E. (2004). U-shaped changes in behavior: A dynamic systems perspective. *Journal of Cognition & Development, 5,* 88–97.

Gershoff, E. T. (2002). Parental corporal punishment and associated child behaviors and experiences: A meta-analytic and theoretical review. *Pychological Bulletin, 128,* 539–579.

Gersten, R., & Dimino, J. (2006, January). RTI (response to intervention): Rethinking special education for students with reading difficulties (yet again). *Reading Research Quarterly, 41,* 99–108.

Gesell, A. L. (1946). The ontogenesis of infant behavior. In L. Carmichael (Ed.), *Manual of child psychology.* New York: Harper.

Gesser, G., Wong, P. T., & Reker, G. T. (1988). Death attitudes across the life span: The development and validation of the Death Attitude Profile (DAP). *Omega: Journal of Death and Dying, 18,* 113–128.

Gewertz, C. (2005, April 6). Training focuses on teachers' expectations. *Education Week, 24,* 1–3.

Giacobbi, P., Lynn, T., & Wetherington, J. (2004). Stress and coping during the transition to university for first-year female athletes. *Sport Psychologist, 18,* 1–20.

Giammattei, J., Blix, G., Marshak, H. H., Wollitzer, A. O., & Petitt, D. J. (2003). Television watching and soft drink consumption: Associations with obesity in 11- to 13-year-old schoolchildren. *Archives of Pediatric Adolescence, 157,* 882–886.

Gibbs, N. (2002, April 15). Making time for a baby. *Time,* 48–54.

Gibson, E. J., & Walk, R. D. (1960). The "visual cliff." *Scientific American, 202,* 64–71.

Gibson, R. C. (1986). Older black Americans. *Generations, 10(4),* 35–39.

Gidron, Y., Russ, K., Tissarchondou, H., & Warner, J. (2006, July). The relation between psychological factors and DNA-damage: A critical review. *Biological Psychology, 72,* 291–304.

Gifford-Smith, M., & Brownell, C. (2003). Childhood peer relationships: Social acceptance, friendships, and peer networks. *Journal of School Psychology, 41,* 235–284.

Gilbert, K. R. (1997). Couple coping with the death of a child. In C. R. Figley, B. E. Bride, & N. Mazza (Eds.), *The series in trauma and loss. Death and trauma: The traumatology of grieving* (pp. 101–121). Washington, DC: Taylor & Francis.

Gilbert, L. A. (1994). Current perspectives on dual-career families. *Current Directions in Psychological Science, 3,* 101–105.

Gilbert, S. (2004, March 16). New clues to women veiled in black. *The New York Times,* pp. D1.

Gilbert, W. M., Nesbitt, T. S., & Danielsen, B. (1999). Childbearing beyond age 40: Pregnancy outcome in 24,032 cases. *Obstetrics and Gynecology, 93,* 9–14.

Giles-Sims, J., & Lockhart, C. (2005). Culturally shaped patterns of disciplining children. *Journal of Family Issues, 26,* 196–218.

Giligan, C. (2004). Recovering psyche: Reflections on life-history and history. *Annual of Psychoanalysis, 32,* 131–147.

Gillespie, N. A., Cloninger, C., R., & Heath, A. C. (2003). The genetic and environmental relationship between Cloninger's dimensions of temperament and character. *Personality and Individual Differences, 35,* 1931–1946.

Gillies, R., & Boyle, M. (2006, May). Ten Australian elementary teachers' discourse and reported pedagogical practices during cooperative learning. *The Elementary School Journal, 106,* 429–451.

Gilligan, C. (1982). *In a different voice: Psychological theory and women's development.* Cambridge, MA: Harvard University Press.

Gilligan, C., Lyons, N. P., & Hammer, T. J. (Eds.). (1990). *Making connections.* Cambridge, MA: Harvard University Press.

Gilligan, C., Ward, J. V., & Taylor, J. M. (Eds.). (1988). *Mapping the moral domain: A contribution of women's thinking to psychological theory and education.* Cambridge, MA: Harvard University Press.

Gilliland, A. L., & Verny, T. R. (1999). The effects of domestic abuse on the unborn child. *Journal of Prenatal and Perinatal Psychology and Health, 13* [Special Issue], 235–246.

Gillmore, M., Gilchrist, L., Lee, J., & Oxford, M. (2006, August). Women who gave birth as unmarried adolescents: Trends in substance use from adolescence to adulthood. *Journal of Adolescent Health, 39,* 237–243.

Ginzberg, E. (1972). Toward a theory of occupational choice: A restatement. *Vocational Guidance Quarterly, 12,* 10–14.

Giordana, S. (2005). *Understanding eating disorders: Conceptual and ethical issues in the treatment of anorexia (Issues in Biomedical Ethics).* New York: Oxford University Press.

Gitlin, L., Reever, K., Dennis, M., Mathieu, E., & Hauck, W. (2006, October). Enhancing quality of life of families who use adult day services: Short- and long-term effects of the Adult Day Services Plus Program. *The Gerontologist, 46,* 630–639.

Glasgow, K. L., Dornbusch, S. M., Troyer, L., Steinberg, L., & Ritter, P. L. (1997). Parenting styles, adolescents' attributions, and educational outcomes in nine heterogeneous high schools. *Child Development, 68,* 507–529.

Gleason, J., & Ely, R. (2002). Gender differences in language development. In A. McGillicuddy-De Lisi & R. De Lisi (Eds.), *Biology, society, and behavior: The development of sex differences in cognition* (pp. 127–154). Westport, CT: Ablex Publishing.

Gleason, J. B., Perlmann, R. U., Ely, R., & Evans, D. W. (1991). The babytalk register: Parents' use of diminutives. In J. L. Sokolov & C. E. Snow (Eds.), *Handbook of research in language development using CHILDES.* Hillsdale, NJ: Erlbaum.

Gleason, J. B., Perlmann, R. U., Ely, R., & Evans, D. W. (1994). The babytalk register: Parents' use of diminutives. In J. L. Sokolov & C. E. Snow (Eds.), *Handbook of research in language development using CHILDES.* Mahwah, NJ: Erlbaum.

Gleason, M., Iida, M., & Bolger, N. (2003). Daily supportive equity in close relationships. *Personality & Social Psychology Bulletin, 29,* 1036–1045.

Gleick, E., Reed, S., & Schindehette, S. (1994, October 24). The baby trap. *People Weekly,* 38–56.

Gleitman, L., & Landau, B. (1994). *The acquisition of the lexicon.* Cambridge, MA: Bradford.

Glick, P., Fiske, S. T., Mladinic, A., Saiz, J. L., et al. (2000). Beyond prejudice as simple antipathy: Hostile and benevolent sexism across cultures. *Journal of Personality and Social Psychology, 79,* 763–775.

Glick, P., Zion, C., & Nelson, C. (1988). What mediates sex discrimination in hiring decisions? *Journal of Personality and Social Psychology, 55,* 178–186.

Gluhoski, V., Leader, J., & Wortman, C. B. (1994). Grief and bereavement. In V. S. Ramachandran (Ed.), *Encyclopedia of human behavior.* San Diego: Academic Press.

Goetz, A., & Shackelford, T. (2006). Modern application of evolutionary theory to psychology: Key concepts and clarifications. *American Journal of Psychology, 119,* 567–584.

Gohlke, B. C., & Stanhope, R. (2002). Final height in psychosocial short stature: Is there complete catch-up? *Acta Paediatrica, 91,* 961–965.

Goldberg, A. E. (2004). But do we need universal grammar? Comment on Lidz et al. *Cognition, 94,* 77–84.

Goldberg, J., Pereira, L., & Berghella, V. (2002). Pregnancy after uterine artery emoblization. *Obstetrics and Gynecology, 100,* 869–872.

Goldfarb, Z. (2005, July 12). Newborn medical screening expands. *Wall Street Journal,* p. D6.

Goldman, R. (2004). Circumcision policy: A psychosocial perspective. *Pediatrics and Child Health, 9,* 630–633.

Goldscheider, F. K. (1994). Divorce and remarriage: Effects on the elderly population. *Reviews in Clinical Gerontology, 4,* 253–259.

Goldsmith, L. T. (2000). Tracking trajectories of talent: Child prodigies growing up. In R. C. Friedman & B. M. Shore et al. (Eds.), *Talents unfolding: Cognition and development.* Washington, DC: American Psychological Association.

Goldsmith, S. K., Pellmar, T. C., Kleinman, A. M., & Bunney, W. E. (2002). *Reducing suicide: A national imperative.* Washington, DC: The National Academies Press.

Goldstein, A. P. (1999). Aggression reduction strategies: Effective and ineffective. *Psychology Quarterly, 14,* 40–58.

Goldston, D. B. (2003). *Measuring suicidal behavior and risk in children and adolescents.* Washington, DC: American Psychological Association.

Goleman, D. (1985, February 5). Mourning: New studies affirm its benefits. *The New York Times,* pp. C1, C6.

Goleman, D. (1993, July 21). Baby sees, baby does, and classmates follow. *The New York Times,* p. C10.

Goleman, D. (1995). *Emotional intelligence.* New York: Bantam.

Goleman, D. (2005). What makes a leader? In R. L. Taylor & W. E. Rosenbach, *Military leadership: In pursuit of excellence* (5th ed.). Boulder, CO: Westview Press.

Golinkoff, R. M. (1993). When is communication a "meeting of minds"? *Journal of Child Language, 20,* 199–207.

Golmier, I., Cehbat, J. C., Gelinas-Chebat, C. (2007). Can cigarette warnings counterbalance effects of smoking scenes in movies? *Psychological Reports, 100,* 3–18.

Golombok, S., Golding, J., Perry, B., Burston, A., Murray, C., Mooney-Somers, J., & Stevens, M. (2003). Children with lesbian parents: A community study. *Developmental Psychology, 39,* 20–33.

Golombok, S., Murray, C., Vasanti, J., MacCallum, F., & Lycett, E. (2004). Families created through surrogacy arrangements: Parent–child relationships in the 1st year of life. *Developmental Psychology, 40*, 400–411.

Golombok, S., & Tasker, F. (1996). Do parents influence the sexual orientation of their children? Findings from a longitudinal study of lesbian families. *Developmental Psychology, 32*, 3–11.

Goode, E. (1999, January 12). Clash over when, and how, to toilet-train. *The New York Times*, pp. A1, A17.

Goode, E. (2004, February 3). Stronger warning is urged on antidepressants for teenagers. *The New York Times*, p. A12.

Goodlin-Jones, B. L., Burnham, M. M., & Anders, T. F. (2000). Sleep and sleep disturbances: Regulatory processes in infancy. In A. J. Sameroff & M. Lewis et al. (Eds.), *Handbook of developmental psychopathology* (2nd ed.). New York: Kluwer Academic/Plenum Publishers.

Goodman, G., & Melinder, A. (2007, February). Child witness research and forensic interviews of young children: A review. *Legal and Criminological Psychology, 12*, 1–19.

Goodman, G. S. (2006). Children's eyewitness memory: A modern history and contemporary commentary. *Journal of Social Issues, 62*, 811–832.

Goodman, J., Schlossberg, N. K., & Anderson, M. L. (2006). *Counseling adults in transition: Linking practice with theory*. New York: Springer.

Goodman, J. C., & Nusbaum, H. C. (Eds.). (1994). *The development of speech perception*. Cambridge, MA: Bradford.

Goodman, J. S., Fields, D. L., & Blum, T. C. (2003). Cracks in the glass ceiling: In what kinds of organizations do women make it to the top? *Group & Organization Management, 28*, 475–501.

Goodstein, R., & Ponterotto, J. G. (1997). Racial and ethnic identity: Their relationship and their contribution to self-esteem. *Journal of Black Psychology, 23*, 275–292.

Goodwin, M. H. (1980). Directive-response speech sequences in girls' and boys' task activities. In S. McConnell-Ginet, R. Borker, & N. Furman (Eds.), *Women and language in literature and society* (pp. 157–173). New York: Praeger.

Goodwin, M. H. (1990). Tactical uses of stories: Participation frameworks within girls' and boys' disputes. *Discourse Processes, 13*, 33–71.

Googans, B., & Burden, D. (1987). Vulnerability of working parents: Balancing work and home roles. *Social Work, 32*, 295–300.

Goold, S. D., Williams, B., & Arnold, R. M. (2000). Conflicts regarding decisions to limit treatment: A differential diagnosis. *Journal of the American Medical Association, 283*, 909–914.

Gopnik, A., Meltzoff, A. N., & Kuhl, P. K. (2002). *The scientist in the crib: What early learning tells us about the mind*. New York: HarperCollins.

Gordon, N. (2007). The cerebellum and cognition. *European Journal of Paediatric Neurology, 30*, 214–220.

Gormley, W. T., Jr., Gayer, T., Phillips, D., & Dawson, B. (2005). The effects of universal pre-K on cognitive development. *Developmental Psychology, 41*, 872–884.

Gostin, L. (2006, April). Physician-assisted suicide A legitimate medical practice? *JAMA: Journal of the American Medical Association, 295*, 1941–1943.

Gottesman, I. I. (1991). *Schizophrenia genesis: The origins of madness*. New York: Freeman.

Gottfredson, G. D., & Holland, J. L. (1990). A longitudinal test of the influence of congruence: Job satisfaction, competency utilization, and counterproductive behavior. *Journal of Counseling Psychology, 37*, 389–398.

Gottfried, A., Gottfried, A., & Bathurst, K. (2002). Maternal and dual-earner employment status and parenting. In M. Bornstein (Ed.), *Handbook of parenting: Vol. 2: Biology and ecology of parenting*. Mahwah, NJ: Lawrence Erlbaum Associates.

Gottlieb, G. (2003). On making behavioral genetics truly developmental. *Human Development, 46*, 337–355.

Gottlieb, G., & Blair, C. (2004). How early experience matters in intellectual development in the case of poverty. *Preventive Science, 5*, 245–52.

Gottman, J. M., Fainsilber-Katz, L., & Hooven, C. (1996). *Meta-emotion: How families communicate emotionally*. Mahwah, NJ: Erlbaum.

Gottschalk, E. C., Jr. (1983, February 21). Older Americans: The aging man gains in the 1970s, outpacing rest of the population. *The Wall Street Journal*, pp. 1, 20.

Gould, R. L. (1978). *Transformations: Growth and change in adult life*. New York: Simon Schuster.

Gould, S. J. (1977). *Ontogeny and phylogeny*. Cambridge, MA: Harvard University Press.

Goyette-Ewing, M. (2000). Children's after school arrangements: A study of self-care and developmental outcomes. *Journal of Prevention & Intervention in the Community, 20*, 55–67.

Grabner, R. H., Neubauer, A., C., & Stern, E. (2006). Superior performance and neural efficiency: The impact of intelligence and expertise. *Brain Research Bulletin, 69*, 422–439.

Graddol, D. (2004, February 27). The future of language. *Science, 303*, 1329–1331.

Grady, D. (2006, November). Management of menopausal symptoms. *New England Journal of Medicine, 355*, 2338–2347.

Graham, I., Carroli, G., Davies, C., & Medves, J. (2005). Episiotomy rates around the world: An update. *Birth: Issues in Perinatal Care, 32*, 219–223.

Graham, S. (1986). An attributional perspective on achievement motivation and black children. In R. S. Feldman (Ed.), *The social psychology of education: Current research and theory*. New York: Cambridge University Press.

Graham, S. (1990). Communicating low ability in the classroom: Bad things good teachers sometimes do. In S. Graham & V. S. Folkes (Eds.), *Attribution theory: Applications to achievement, mental health, and interpersonal conflict*. Hillsdale, NJ: Erlbaum.

Graham, S. (1992). "Most of the subjects were white and middle class": Trends in published research on African Americans in selected APA journals. *American Psychologist, 47*, 629–639.

Granic, I., Hollenstein, T., & Dishion, T. (2003). Longitudinal analysis of flexibility and reorganization in early adolescence: A dynamic systems study of family interactions. *Developmental Psychology, 39*, 606–617.

Grant, J., Weaver, M., & Elliott, T. (2004). Family caregivers of stroke survivors: Characteristics of caregivers at risk for depression. *Rehabilitation Psychology, 49*, 172–179.

Grantham, T., & Ford, D. (2003). Beyond self-concept and self-esteem: Racial identity and gifted African American students. *High School Journal, 87*, 18–29.

Grantham-McGregor, S., Ani, C., & Fernald, L. (2001). The role of nutrition in intellectual development. In R. J. Sternberg & E. L. Grigorenko (Eds.), *Environmental effects on cognitive abilities*. Mahwah, NJ: Erlbaum.

Grantham-McGregor, S., Powell, C., Walker, S., Chang, S., & Fletcher, P. (1994). The long-term follow-up of severely malnourished children who participated in an intervention program. *Child Development, 65*, 428–439.

Gratch, G., & Schatz, J. A. (1987). Cognitive development: The relevance of Piaget's infancy books. In J. D. Osofsky (Ed.), *Handbook of infant development* (2nd ed.). New York: Wiley.

Grattan, M. P., DeVos, E. S., Levy, J., & McClintock, M. K. (1992). Asymmetric action in the human newborn: Sex differences in patterns of organization. *Child Development, 63*, 273–289.

Gray, C., Ferguson, J., Behan, S., Dunbar, C., Dunn, J., & Mitchell, D. (2007, March). Developing young readers through the linguistic phonics approach. *International Journal of Early Years Education, 15*, 15–33.

Gray-Little, B., & Hafdahl, A. R. (2000). Factors influencing racial comparisons of self-esteem: A quantitative review. *Psychological Bulletin, 126*, 26–54.

Green, F. (2005, September 1). The golden-touch years. *San Diego Union-Tribune*, p. C1.

Green, M. H. (1995). Influences of job type, job status, and gender on achievement motivation. *Current Psychology: Developmental, Learning, Personality, Social, 14*, 159–165.

Greenberg, J., & Becker, M. (1988). Aging parents as family resources. *Gerontologist, 28*, 786–790.

Greenberg, L., Cwikel, J., & Mirsky, J. (2007, January). Cultural correlates of eating attitudes: A comparison between native-born and immigrant university students in Israel. *International Journal of Eating Disorders, 40*, 51–58.

Greene, K., Krcmar, M., & Rubin, D. (2002). Elaboration in processing adolescent health messages: The impact of egocentrism and sensation seeking on message processing. *Journal of Communication, 52*, 812–831.

Greene, K., Krcmar, M., Walters, L. H., Rubin, D L., & Hale, J. L. (2000). Targeting adolescent risk-taking behaviors: The contribution of egocentrism and sensation-seeking. *Journal of Adolescence, 23*, 439–461.

Greene, S., Anderson, E., & Hetherington, E. (2003). Risk and resilience after divorce. In F. Walsh (Ed.), *Normal family processes: Growing diversity and complexity*. New York: Guilford Press.

Greenfield, P. M. (1976). Cross-cultural research and Piagetian theory: Paradox and progress. In K. F. Riegel & J. A. Meacham (Eds.), *The developing individual in a changing world: Vol. 1*. The Hague, The Netherlands: Mouton.

Greenfield, P. M. (1997). You can't take it with you. Why ability assessments don't cross cultures. *American Psychologist, 52*, 1115–1124.

Greenway, C. (2002). The process, pitfalls and benefits of implementing a reciprocal teaching intervention to improve the reading comprehension of a group of year 6 pupils. *Educational Psychology in Practice, 18*, 113–137.

Greenwood, D., & Isbell, L. (2002). Ambivalent sexism and the dumb blonde: Men's and women's reactions to sexist jokes. *Psychology of Women Quarterly, 26*, 341–350.

Greenwood, D. N., & Piertomonaco, P. R. (2004). The interplay among attachment orientation, idealized media images of women, and body dissatisfaction: A social psychological analysis. In L. J. Shrum (Ed.), *Psychology of entertainment media: Blurring the lines between entertainment and persuasion*. Mahwah, NJ: Lawrence Erlbaum Associates.

Greer, M. (2004, November). Retirement's road map. *Monitor on Psychology, 35*, 80.

Gregory, K. (2005). Update on nutrition for preterm and full-term infants. *Journal of Obstetrics and Gynecological Neonatal Nursing, 34*, 98–108.

Gregory, S. (1856). *Facts for young women.* Boston.

Greve, T. (2003). Norway: The breastfeeding top of the world. *Midwifery Today International, 67,* 57–59.

Grey, W. H., (1999). Milken Institute, reported in Suro, R. (Nov. 1999). Mixed doubles. *American Demographics,* 57–62.

Griffith, D. R., Azuma, S. D., & Chasnoff, I. J. (1994). Three-year outcome of children exposed prenatally to drugs. *Journal of the American Academy of Child and Adolescent Psychiatry, 33,* 20–27.

Grigorenko, E. (2003). Intraindividual fluctuations in intellectual functioning: Selected links between nutrition and the mind. In R. Sternberg & J. Lautrey (Eds.), *Models of intelligence: International perspectives.* Washington, DC: American Psychological Association.

Groome, L. J., Swiber, M. J., Atterbury, J. L., Bentz, L. S., & Holland, S. B. (1997). Similarities and differences in behavioral state organization during sleep periods in the perinatal infant before and after birth. *Child Development, 68,* 1–11.

Groome, L. J., Swiber, M. J., Bentz, L. S., Holland, S. B., & Atterbury, J. L. (1995). Maternal anxiety during pregnancy: Effect on fetal behavior at 38 to 40 weeks of gestation. *Developmental and Behavioral Pediatrics, 16,* 391–396.

Groopman, J. (1998 February 8). Decoding destiny. *The New Yorker,* 42–47.

Gross, J. (1991, June 16). More young single men hang on to apron strings. *The New York Times,* pp. A1, A18.

Gross, P. A. (1991). *Managing your health: Strategies for lifelong good health.* Yonkers, NY: Consumer Reports Books.

Gross, R. T., Spiker, D., & Haynes, C. W. (Eds.). (1997). *Helping low-birthweight, premature babies: The Infant Health and Development Program.* Stanford, CA: Stanford University Press.

Grossmann, K. E., Grossman, K., Huber, F., & Wartner, U. (1982). German children's behavior towards their mothers at 12 months and their fathers at 18 months in Ainsworth's Strange Situation. *International Journal of Behavioral Development, 4,* 157–181

Grossman, K. E., Grossmann, K., & Waters, E. (Eds.). (2005). *Attachment from infancy to adulthood: The major longitudinal studies.* New York: Guilford Press.

Grossmann, T., Striano, T., & Friederici, A. (2006, May). Crossmodal integration of emotional information from face and voice in the infant brain. *Developmental Science, 9,* 309–315.

Grunbaum, J. A., Kann, L., Kinchen, S. A., Williams, B., Ross, J. G., Lowry, R., & Kolbe, S. (2002). *Youth risk behavior surveillance—United States, 2001.* Atlanta, GA: Centers for Disease Control.

Grunbaum, J. A., Lowry, R., & Kann, L. (2001). Prevalence of health-related behaviors among alternative high school students as compared with students attending regular high schools. *Journal of Adolescent Health, 29,* 337–343.

Grundy, E., & Henretta, J. (2006, September). Between elderly parents and adult children: A new look at the intergenerational care provided by the "sandwich generation." *Ageing & Society, 26,* 707–722.

Grusec, J. E. (1982). Socialization processes and the development of altruism. In J. P. Rushton & R. M. Sorrentino (Eds.), *Altruism and helping behavior.* Hillsdale, NJ: Erlbaum.

Grusec, J. E. (1991). The socialization of altruism. In M. S. Clark (Ed.), *Prosocial behavior.* Newbury Park, CA: Sage.

Grusec, J. E., & Kuczynski, L. E. (Eds.). (1997). *Parenting and children's internalization of values: A handbook of contemporary theory.* New York: Wiley.

Grych, J. H., & Clark, R. (1999). Maternal employment and development of the father–infant relationship in the first year. *Developmental Psychology, 35,* 893–903.

Guarente, L. (2006, December 14). Sirtuins as potential targets for metabolic syndrome. *Nature, 14,* 868–874.

Guasti, M. T. (2002). *Language acquisition: The growth of grammar.* Cambridge, MA: MIT Press.

Guerrero, A., Hishinuma, E., Andrade, N., Nishimura, S., & Cunanan, V. (2006, July). Correlations among socioeconomic and family factors and academic, behavioral, and emotional difficulties in Filipino adolescents in Hawaii. *International Journal of Social Psychiatry, 52,* 343–359.

Guerrini, I., Thomson, A., & Gurling, H. (2007). The importance of alcohol misuse, malnutrition and genetic susceptibility on brain growth and plasticity. *Neuroscience & Biobehavioral Reviews, 31,* 212–220.

Gump, L. S., Baker, R. C., & Roll, S. (2000). Cultural and gender differences in moral judgment: A study of Mexican Americans and Anglo-Americans. *Hispanic Journal of Behavioral Sciences, 22,* 78–93.

Gunnarsdottir, I., & Thorsdottir, I. (2003). Relationship between growth and feeding in infancy and body mass index at the age of 6 years. *International Journal of Obesity and Metabolic Disorders, 27,* 1523–1527.

Gupta, A., & State, M. (2007). Recent advances in the genetics of autism. *Biological Psychiatry, 61,* 429–437.

Gupta, U., & Singh, P. (1982). An exploratory study of love and liking and type of marriages. *Indian Journal of Applied Psychology, 19,* 92–97.

Gur, R. C., Gur, R. E., Obrist, W. D., Hungerbuhler, J. P., Younkin, D., Rosen, A. D., Skilnick, B. E., & Reivich, M. (1982). Sex and handedness differences in cerebral blood flow during rest and cognitive activity. *Science, 217,* 659–661.

Gurin, P., Nagda, B. R. A., & Lopez, G. E. (2004). The benefits of diversity in education for democratic citizenship. *Journal of Social Issues, 60,* 17–34.

Gutek, G. L. (2003). Maria Montessori: Contributions to educational psychology. In B. J. Zimmerman (Ed.), *Educational psychology: A century of contributions.* Mahwah, NJ: Lawrence Erlbaum Associates.

Guterl, F. (2002, November 11). What Freud got right. *Newsweek,* 50–51.

Guttman, M. (1997, May 16–18). Are you losing your mind? *USA Weekend,* pp. 4–5.

Guttmann, J., & Rosenberg, M. (2003). Emotional intimacy and children's adjustment: A comparison between single-parent divorced and intact families. *Educational Psychology, 23,* 457–472.

Haan, N., Millsap, R., & Hartka, E. (1986). As time goes by: Change and stability in personality over fifty years. *Psychology and Aging, 1,* 220–232.

Haas, A. P., Hendin, H., & Mann, J. J. (2003). Suicide in college students. *American Behavioral Scientist, 46,* [Special issue: Suicide in Youth], 1224–1240.

Haber, D. (2006). Life review: Implementation, theory, research, and therapy. *International Journal of Aging & Human Development, 63,* 153–171.

Haberstick, B. C., Timberlake, D., Ehringer, M. A., Lessem, J. M., Hopfer, C. J., Smolen, A., & Hewitt, J. K. (2007). Can cigarette warnings counterbalance effects of smoking scenes in movies? *Addiction, 102,* 655–665.

Haddock, S., & Rattenborg, K. (2003). Benefits and challenges of dual-earning: Perspectives of successful couples. *American Journal of Family Therapy, 31,* 325–344.

Hagerty, R. G., Butow, P. N., Ellis, P. A., Lobb, E. A., Pendlebury, S., Leighl, N., Goldstein, D., Lo, S. K., & Tattersall, M. H. (2004). Cancer patient preferences for communication of prognosis in the metastatic setting. *Journal of Clinical Oncology, 22,* 1721–1730.

Hahn, C-S., & DiPietro, J. A. (2001). In vitro fertilization and the family: Quality of parenting, family functioning, and child psychosocial adjustment. *Developmental Psychology, 37,* 37–48.

Haight, B. K. (1991). Psychological illness in aging. In E. M. Baines (Ed.), *Perspectives on gerontological nursing.* Newbury Park, CA: Sage.

Haight, W. L. (2002). *African-American children at church: A sociocultural perspective.* New York: Cambridge University Press.

Haines, J., & Neumark-Sztainer, D. (2006, December). Prevention of obesity and eating disorders: A consideration of shared risk factors. *Health Education Research, 21,* 770–782.

Haith, M. H. (1986). Sensory and perceptual processes in early infancy. *Journal of Pediatrics, 109(1),* 158–171.

Haith, M. H. (1991, April). Setting a path for the 90s: Some goals and challenges in infant sensory and perceptual development. Paper presented at the biennial meeting of the Society for Research in Child Development, Seattle, WA.

Hales, K. A., Morgan, M. A., & Thurnau, G. R. (1993). Influence of labor and route of delivery on the frequency of respiratory morbidity in term neonates. *International Journal of Gynecology & Obstetrics, 43,* 35–40.

Halford, G. S., Maybery, M. T., O'Hare, A. W., & Grant, P. (1994). The development of memory and processing capacity. *Child Development, 65,* 1338–1356.

Halgunseth, L. C., Ispa, J. M., & Rudy, D. (2006). Parental control in Latino families: An integrated review of the literature. *Child Development, 77,* 1282–1297.

Hall, E. G., & Lee, A. M. (1984). Sex differences in motor performance of young children: Fact or fiction? *Sex Roles, 10,* 217–230.

Hall, R. E., & Rowan, G. T. (2003). Identity development across the lifespan: Alternative model for biracial Americans. *Psychology and Education: An Interdisciplinary Journal, 40,* 3–12.

Hall, S. S. (2005, October 16). The short of it. *The New York Times Magazine,* 54–59.

Hallahan, D. P., Kauffman, J. M., & Lloyd, J. W. (2000). *Introduction to learning disabilities* (4th ed.). Boston: Allyn & Bacon.

Halliday, M. A. K. (1975). *Learning how to mean—Explorations in the development of language.* London: Edward Arnold.

Halpern, L. F., MacLean, W. E., & Baumeister, A. A. (1995). Infant sleep-wake characteristics: Relation to neurological status and the prediction of developmental outcome. *Developmental Review, 15,* 255–291.

Hamon, R. R., & Blieszner, R. (1990). Filial responsibility expectations among adult child–older parent pairs. *Journal of Gerontology, 45,* 110–112.

Hamon, R. R., & Ingoldsby, B. B. (Eds.) (2003). *Mate selection across cultures.* Thousand Oaks, CA: Sage Publications.

Hane, A., Feldstein, S., and Dernetz, V. (2003). The relation between coordinated interpersonal timing and maternal sensitivity in four-month-old infants. *Journal of Psycholinguistic Research, 32,* 525–539.

Hankin, B. L., & Abramson, L. Y. (2001). Development of gender differences in depression: An elaborated cognitive vulnerability-transactional stress theory. *Psychological Bulletin, 127,* 773–796.

Hanson, D. R., & Gottesman, I. I. (2005). Theories of schizophrenia: A genetic-inflammatory-vascular synthesis. *BMC Medical Genetics, 6*, 7.

Hanson, R., & Hayslip, B. (2000). Widowhood in later life. In J. Harvey & E. Miller (Eds.), *Loss and trauma: General and close relationship perspectives.* New York: Brunner-Routledge.

Hanson, R. F., & Spratt, E. G. (2000). Reactive attachment disorder: What we know about the disorder and implications for treatment. *Child Maltreatment, 5,* 137–145.

Hansson, R. O., & Carpenter, B. N. (1994). *Relationship in old age: Coping with the challenge of transition.* New York: Guilford Press.

Happe, F. G. E., Winner, E., & Brownell, H. (1998). The getting of wisdom: Theory of mind in old age. *Developmental Psychology, 34,* 358–362.

Hardy, L. T. (2007). Attachment theory and reactive attachment disorder: Theoretical perspectives and treatment implications. *Journal of Child and Adolescent Psychiatric Nursing, 20,* 27–39.

Harlow, H. F., & Zimmerman, R. R. (1959). Affectional responses in the infant monkey. *Science, 130,* 421–432.

Harman, S., Naftolin, F., Brinton, E., & Judelson, D. (2005). Is the estrogen controversy over? Deconstructing the Women's Health Initiative study: A critical evaluation of the evidence. In M. Singh & J. Simpkins (Eds.), *The future of hormone therapy: What basic science and clinical studies teach us.* New York: New York Academy of Sciences.

Harmon, A. (2004, August 26). Internet gives teenage bullies weapons to wound from afar. *The New York Times,* A1, A21.

Harrell, J. S., Bangdiwala, S. I., Deng, S., Webb, J. P., & Bradley, C. (1998). Smoking initiation in youth: The roles of gender, race, socioeconomics, and developmental status. *Journal of Adolescent Health, 23,* 271–279.

Harrell, S. (1981). Growing old in rural Taiwan. In P. T. Amoss & S. Harrell (Eds.), *Other ways of growing old.* Stanford, CA: Stanford University Press.

Harris, A., Cronkite, R., & Moos, R. (2006, July). Physical activity, exercise coping, and depression in a 10-year cohort study of depressed patients. *Journal of Affective Disorders, 93,* 79–85.

Harris, C. M. (2004). Personality and sexual orientation. *College Student Journal, 38,* 207–211.

Harris, G. (2005, March 3). Gene therapy is facing a crucial hearing. *The New York Times,* p. A16.

Harris, J., Vernon, P., & Jang, K. (2007). Rated personality and measured intelligence in young twin children. *Personality and Individual Differences, 42,* 75–86.

Harris, J. R. (1998). *The nurture assumption: Why children turn out the way they do.* New York: Free Press.

Harris, M. B. (1994). Growing old gracefully: Age concealment and gender. *Journals of Gerontology, 49,* 149–158.

Harris, M. J., Milich, R., Corbitt, E. M., Hoover, D. W., et al. (1992). Self-fulfilling effects of stigmatizing information on children's social interactions. *Journal of Personality and Social Psychology, 63,* 41–50.

Harris, P. L. (1983). Infant cognition. In M. Haith & J. J. Campos (Eds.) & P. H. Mussen (Gen. Ed.), *Handbook of child psychology: Vol 2. Infancy and developmental psychobiology.* New York: Wiley.

Harris, P. L. (1987). The development of search. In P. Sallapatek & L. Cohen (Eds.), *Handbook of infant perception: From perception to cognition* (Vol. 2, pp. 155–207). Orlando, FL: Academic Press.

Harrison, K., & Hefner, V. (2006, April). Media exposure, current and future body ideals, and disordered eating among preadolescent girls: A longitudinal panel study. *Journal of Youth and Adolescence, 35,* 153–163.

Harrison, R. V., Gordon, K. A., & Mount, R. J. (2005). Is there a critical period for cochlear implantation in congenitally deaf children? Analyses of hearing and speech perception performance after implantation. *Developmental Psychobiology, 46,* 252–261.

Harrist, A., & Waugh, R. (2002). Dyadic synchrony: Its structure and function in children's development. *Developmental Review, 22,* 555–592.

Hart, B. (2000). A natural history of early language experience. *Topics in Early Childhood Special Education, 20,* 28–32.

Hart, B. (2004). What toddlers talk about. *First Language, 24,* 91–106.

Hart, B., & Risley, T. R. (1995). *Meaningful differences in the everyday experience of young American children.* Baltimore, MD: Paul Brookes.

Hart, C. H., Yang, C., Nelson, D. A., Jin, S., Bazarskaya, N., & Nelson, L. (1998). Peer contact patterns, parenting practices, and preschoolers' social competence in China, Russia, and the United States. In P. Slee & K. Rigby (Eds.), *Peer relations amongst children: Current issues and future directions.* London: Routledge.

Hart, D., Burock, D., & London, B. (2003). Prosocial tendencies, antisocial behavior, and moral development. In A. Slater & G. Bremner (Eds.), *An introduction to developmental psychology.* Malden, MA: Blackwell Publishers.

Hart, S. N., Brassard, M. R., & Karlson, H. (1996). Psychological maltreatment. In J. N. Briere, L. Berliner, J. Bulkley, C. Jenny, & T. Reid (Eds.), *The APSAC handbook on child maltreatment.* Thousand Oaks, CA: Sage.

Harter, S. (1990a). Identity and self-development. In S. Feldman & G. Elliott (Eds.), *At the threshold: The developing adolescent.* Cambridge, MA: Harvard University Press.

Harter, S. (1990b). Issues in the assessment of self-concept of children and adolescents. In A. LaGreca (Ed.), *Through the eyes of a child.* Boston: Allyn & Bacon.

Hartshorne, T. S. (1994). Friendship. In V. S. Ramachandran (Ed.), *Encyclopedia of human behavior.* San Diego: Academic Press.

Hartup, W. W. (1983). Peer relations. In P. H. Mussen (Ed.), *Handbook of child psychology* (Vol. 4, 4th ed.). New York: Wiley.

Hartup, W. W., & Stevens, N. (1999). Friendships and adaptation across the life span. *Current Directions in Psychological Science, 8,* 76–79.

Harvey, E. (1999). Short-term and long-term effects of early parental employment on children of the National Longitudinal Survey of Youth. *Developmental Psychology, 35,* 445–459.

Harvey, J., & Weber, A. (2002). *Odyssey of the heart: Close relationships in the 21st century* (2nd ed.). Mahwah, NJ: Lawrence Erlbaum Associates.

Harvey, J. H., & Fine, M. A. (2004). *Children of divorce: Stories of loss and growth.* Mahwah, NJ: Lawrence Erlbaum Associates.

Harway, M. (2000). Families experiencing violence. In W. C. Nichols & M. A. Pace-Nichols et al. (Eds.), *Handbook of family development and intervention. Wiley series in couples and family dynamics and treatment.* New York: Wiley.

Harwood, R. L., Miller, J. G., & Irizarry, N. L. (1995). *Culture and attachment: Perceptions of the child in context.* New York: Guilford Press.

Harwood, R. L., Schoelmerich, A., Ventura-Cook, E., Schulze, P. A., & Wilson, S. P. (1996). Culture and class influences on Anglo and Puerto Rican mothers' beliefs regarding long-term socialization goals and child behavior. *Child Development, 67,* 2446–2461.

Hasher, L., & Zacks, R. T. (1984). Automatic processing of fundamental information: The case of frequency of occurrence. *American Psychologist, 39,* 1372–1388.

Haskett, M., Nears, K., Ward, C., & McPherson, A. (2006, October). Diversity in adjustment of maltreated children: Factors associated with resilient functioning. *Clinical Psychology Review, 26,* 796–812.

Haslam, C., & Lawrence, W. (2004). Health-related behavior and beliefs of pregnant smokers. *Health Psychology, 23,* 486–491.

Haslett, A. (2004, May 31). Love supreme. *The New Yorker,* 76–80.

Hastings, S. (2004, October 15). Emotional intelligence. *The Times Educational Supplement, London,* F1.

Hatfield, E., & Rapson, R. L. (1993). Historical and cross-cultural perspectives on passionate love and sexual desire. *Annual Review of Sex Research, 4,* 67–97.

Hattery, A. (2000). *Women, work, and family: Balancing and weaving.* Thousand Oaks, CA: Sage.

Haugaard, J. J. (2000). The challenge of defining child sexual abuse. *American Psychologist, 55,* 1036–1039.

Hauser, M., Chomsky, N., & Fitch, W. (2002). The faculty of language: What is it, who has it, and how did it evolve? *Science, 298,* 1569–1579.

Havighurst, R. J. (1973). Social roles, work, leisure, and education. In C. Eisdorfer & M. P. Lawton (Eds.), *The psychology of adult development and aging.* Washington, DC: American Psychological Association.

Hay, D., Payne, A., & Chadwick, A. (2004). Peer relations in childhood. *Journal of Child Psychology & Psychiatry & Allied Disciplines, 45,* 84–108.

Hay, D. F., Pawlby, S., & Angold, A. (2003). Pathways to violence in the children of mothers who were depressed postpartum. *Developmental Psychology, 39,* 1083–1094.

Hayflick, L. (1974). The strategy of senescence. *The Journal of Gerontology, 14,* 37–45.

Haynie, D. L., Nansel, T., Eitel, P., Crump, A. D., Saylor, K., Yu, K., & Simons-Morton, B. (2001). Bullies, victims, and bully/victims: Distinct groups of at-risk youth. *Journal of Early Adolescence, 21,* 29–49.

Hays-Thomas, R. (2004). Why now? The contemporary focus on managing diversity. In M. S. Stockdale & F. J. Crosby (Eds.), *Psychology and management of workplace diversity.* Malden, MA: Blackwell Publishers.

Hayslip, B., Servaty, H. L., Christman, T., & Mumy, E. (1997). Levels of death anxiety in terminally ill persons: A cross validation and extension. *Omega—Journal of Death & Dying, 34,* 203–217.

Hayslip, B., Jr., Shore, R. J., & Henderson, C. E. (2000). Perceptions of grandparents' influence in the lives of their grandchildren. In B. Hayslip, Jr., Goldberg, & G. Robin (Eds). *Grandparents raising grandchildren: Theoretical, empirical, and clinical perspectives.* New York: Springer.

Hayward, M., Crimmins, E., & Saito, Y. (1997). Cause of death and active life expectancy in the older population of the United States. *Journal of Aging and Health,* 122–131.

Hazan, C., & Shaver, P. (1987). Romantic love conceptualized as an attachment process. *Journal of Personality and Social Psychology, 52,* 511–524.

Health eLine. (2003, June 26). Baby's injury points to danger of kids imitating TV. *Health eLine*. www.reutershealth.com

Health News. (2004). Moderate exercise, without dieting, can prevent further weight gain. *Health News, 10*, 4.

Healy, P. (2001, March 3). Data on suicides set off alarm. *Boston Globe*, p. B1.

Hecht, M. L., Marston, P. J., & Larkey, L. K. (1994). Love ways and relationship quality in heterosexual relationships. *Journal of Social and Personal Relationships, 11*, 25–43.

Hedge, J., Borman, W., & Lammlein, S. (2006). *Age stereotyping and age discrimination*. Washington, DC: American Psychological Association.

Hedgepeth, E. (2005). Different lenses, different vision. *School Administrator, 62*, 36–39.

Heerey, E. A., Keltner, D., & Capps, L. M. (2003). Making sense of self-conscious emotion: Linking theory of mind and emotion in children with autism. *Emotion, 3*, 394–400.

Heimann, M. (2001). Neonatal imitation—a "fuzzy" phenomenon? In F. Lacerda & C. von Hofsten (Eds.), *Emerging cognitive abilities in early infancy*. Mahwah, NJ: Lawrence Erlbaum Associates.

Heimann, M. (Ed.). (2003). *Regression periods in human infancy*. Mahwah, NJ: Lawrence Erlbaum Associates.

Heimann, M., Strid, K., Smith, L., Tjus, T., Ulvund, S., & Meltzoff, A. (2006). Exploring the relation between memory, gestural communication, and the emergence of language in infancy: A longitudinal study. *Infant and Child Development, 15*, 233–249.

Heinemann, G. D., & Evans, P. L. (1990). Widowhood: Loss, change, and adaptation. In T. H. Brubaker (Ed.), *Family relationships in later life*. Newbury Park, CA: Sage.

Heiser, S. (2007, May 23). 66-year-old woman's cross-country cycling feat tough to beat. *York Dispatch*, p. 1.

Hellman, P. (1987, November 23). *Sesame Street* smart. *New York*, pp. 49–53.

Helms, J. E., Jernigan, M., & Mascher, J. (2005). The meaning of race in psychology and how to change it: A methodological perspective. *American Psychologist, 60*, 27–36.

Helmuth, L. (2003, February 28). The wisdom of the wizened. *Science, 299*, 1300–1302.

Helson R., & Moane, G. (1987). Personality change in women from college to midlife. *Journal of Personality and Social Psychology, 53*, 176–186.

Helson, R. & Srivastava, S. (2001). Three paths of adult development: Conservers, seekers, and achievers. *Journal of Personality and Social Psychology, 80*, 995–1010.

Helson, R., Stewart, A. J., & Ostrove, J. (1995). Identity in three cohorts of midlife women. *Journal of Personality and Social Psychology, 69*, 544–557.

Helson, R., & Wink, P. (1992). Personality change in women from the early 40s to the early 50s. *Psychology and Aging, 7*, 46–55.

Hendrick, C., & Hendrick, S. (2003). Romantic love: Measuring cupid's arrow. In S. Lopez & C. Snyder (Eds.), *Positive psychological assessment: A handbook of models and measures*. Washington, DC: American Psychological Association.

Hendrie, H. C., Ogunniyi, A., Hall, K. S., Baiyewu, O., Unverzagt, F. W., Gureje, O., Gao, S., Evans, R. M., Ogunseyinde, A. O., Adeyinka, A. O., Musick, B., & Hui, S. L. (2001). Incidence of dementia and Alzheimer disease in 2 communities: Yoruba residing in Ibadan, Nigeria, and African Americans residing in Indianapolis, Indiana. *Journal of the American Medical Association, 285*, 739–747.

Henig, R. M. (2003, June). Pandora's baby. *Scientific American*, 63–67.

Henry, J., & McNab, W. (2003). Forever young: A health promotion focus on sexuality and aging. *Gerontology & Geriatrics Education, 23*, 57–74.

Henry, R., Miller, R., & Giarrusso, R. (2005). Difficulties, disagreements, and disappointments in late-life marriages. *International Journal of Aging & Human Development, 61*, 243–264.

Hensley, P. (2006, July). Treatment of bereavement-related depression and traumatic grief. *Journal of Affective Disorders, 92*, 117–124.

Herbert, M. R., Ziegler, D. A., Deutsch, C. K., O'Brien, L. M., Kennedy, D. N., Filipek, P. A., Bakardjiev, A. I., Hodgson, J., Takeoka, M., Makris, N., & Caviness, Jr., V. S. (2005). Brain asymmetries in autism and developmental language disorder: A nested whole-brain analysis. *Brain, 128*, 213–226.

Herdt, G. H. (Ed.). (1998). *Rituals of manhood: Male initiation in Papua New Guinea*. Somerset, NJ: Transaction Books.

Hernandez-Reif, M., Field, T., Diego, M., Vera, Y., & Pickens, J. (2006, January). Brief report: Happy faces are habituated more slowly by infants of depressed mothers. *Infant Behavior & Development, 29*, 131–135.

Hernandez-Reif, M., Field, T., Krasnegor, J., Martinez, E., Schwartzmann, M., & Mavunda, K. (1999). Children with cystic fibrosis benefit from massage therapy. *Journal of Pediatric Psychology, 24*, 175–181.

Herrnstein, R. J., & Murray, C. (1994). *The bell curve: Intelligence and class structure in American life*. New York: Free Press.

Hertelendy, F., & Zakar, T. (2004). Prostaglandins and the mymetrium and cervix. *Prostaglandins, Leukotrienes and Essential Fatty Acids, 70*, 207–222.

Hertenstein, M. J. (2002). Touch: Its communicative functions in infancy. *Human Development, 45*, 70–94.

Hertenstein, M. J., & Campos, J. J. (2001). Emotion regulation via maternal touch. *Infancy, 2*, 549–566.

Hertenstein, M. J., & Campos, J. J. (2004). The retention effects of an adult's emotional displays on infant behavior. *Child Development, 75*, 595–613.

Heston, C. (2002, August 9). Quoted in Charlton Heston has Alzheimer's symptoms. Retrieved May 13, 2004 from http://www.cnn.com/2002/US/08/09/heston.illness/.

Hetherington, E., & Elmore, A. (2003). Risk and resilience in children coping with their parents' divorce and remarriage. In S. Luthar (Ed.), *Resilience and vulnerability: Adaptation in the context of childhood adversities*. New York: Cambridge University Press.

Hetherington, E. M. (Ed.) (1999). *Coping with divorce, single parenting, and remarriage: A risk and resiliency perspective*. Mahwah, NJ: Erlbaum.

Hetherington, E. M., & Blechman, E. A. (Eds.). (1996). *Stress, coping, and resiliency in children and families*. Hillsdale, NJ: Erlbaum.

Hetherington, E. M., & Clingempeel, W. (1992). Coping with marital transitions: A family systems perspective. *Monographs of the Society for Research in Child Development, 57*(2–3, Serial No. 227).

Hetherington, E. M., & Kelly, J. (2002). For better or worse: Divorce reconsidered. New York: Norton.

Hetheringon, E. M., Stanley-Hagan, M., & Anderson, E. (1989). Marital transitions: A child's perspective. *American Psychologist, 44*, 303–312.

Heubusch, K. (1997, September). A tough job gets tougher. *American Demographics*, p. 39.

Hewlett, B., & Lamb, M. (2002). Integrating evolution, culture and developmental psychology: Explaining caregiver-infant proximity and responsiveness in central Africa and the USA. In H. Keller & Y. Poortinga (Eds.), *Between culture and biology: Perspectives on ontogenetic development* (pp. 241–269). New York: Cambridge University Press.

Hewstone, M. (2003). Intergroup contact: Panacea for prejudice? *Psychologist, 16*, 352–355.

Heyman, J. D., Breu, G., Simmons, M., & Howard, C. (2003, September 15). Drugs can make short kids grow but is it right to prescribe them? *People Magazine*, 103–104.

Heyman, R., & Slep, A. M. (2002). Do child abuse and interparental violence lead to adulthood family violence? *Journal of Marriage & Family, 64*, 864–870.

HHL (Harvard Health Letter). (1997, May). *Turning up the volume*, p. 4.

HHS News. (2001, January 12). *Early Head Start shows significant results for low income children and parents*. Washington, DC: Health and Human Services.

Hietala, J., Cannon, T. D., & van Erp, T. G. M. (2003). Regional brain morphology and duration of illness in never-medicated first-episode patients with schizophrenia. *Schizophrenia, 64*, 79–81.

Higgins, D., & McCabe, M. (2003). Maltreatment and family dysfunction in childhood and the subsequent adjustment of children and adults. *Journal of Family Violence, 18*, 107–120.

Highley, J. R., Esiri, M. M., McDonald, B., Cortina-Borja, M., Herron, B. M., & Crow, T. J. (1999). The size and fibre composition of the corpus callosum with respect to gender and schizophrenia: A post-mortem study. *Brian, 122*, 99–110.

Hightower, J. R. R. (2004). Women and depression. In A. Barnes, *Handbook of women, psychology, and the law*. New York: John Wiley & Sons.

Hildreth, K., Sweeney, B., & Rovee-Collier, C. (2003). Differential memory-preserving effects of reminders at 6 months. *Journal of Experimental Child Psychology, 84*, 41–62.

Hill, S., & Flom, R. (2007, February). 18- and 24-month-olds' discrimination of gender-consistent and inconsistent activities. *Infant Behavior & Development, 30*, 168–173.

Hillman, J. (2000). *Clinical perspectives on elderly sexuality*. Dordrecht, Netherlands: Kluwer Academic Publishers.

Hines, M., & Kaufman, F. R. (1994). Androgen and the development of human sex-typical behavior: Rough-and-tumble play and sex of preferred playmates in children with congenital adrenal hyperplasi (CAH). *Child Development, 65*, 1042–1053.

Hinojosa, T., Sheu, C., & Michel, G. (2003). Infant hand-use preferences for grasping objects contributes to the development of a hand-use preference for manipulating objects. *Developmental Psychobiology, 43*, 328–334.

Hintermair, M., & Albertini, J. A. (2005). Ethics, deafness, and new medical technologies. *Journal of Deaf Studies & Deaf Education, 10*, 184–192.

Hirsch, H. V., & Spinelli, D. N. (1970). Visual experience modifies distribution of horizontally and vertically oriented receptive fields in cats. *Science, 168*, 869–871.

Hirshberg, L., & Svejda, M. (1990). When infants look to their parents: I. Infants' social referencing of mothers compared to fathers. *Child Development, 61*, 1175–1186.

Hirsh-Pasek, K., & Michnick-Golinkoff, R. (1995). *The origins of grammar: Evidence from early language comprehension*. Cambridge, MA: MIT Press.

Hitlin, S., Brown, J. S., & Elder, G. H., Jr. (2006). Racial self-categorization in adolescence: Multiracial development and social pathways. *Child Development, 77*, 1298–1308.

Hitt, J. (2000, February 20). The second sexual revolution. *The New York Times Magazine*, 34–62.

Hjelmstedt, A., Widström, A., & Collins, A. (2006). Psychological correlates of prenatal attachment in women who conceived after in vitro fertilization and women who conceived naturally. *Birth: Issues in Perinatal Care, 33*, 303–310.

HMHL (Harvard Mental Health Letter). (2005). The treatment of attention deficit disorder: New evidence. *Harvard Mental Health Letter, 21*, 6.

Ho, B., Friedland, J., Rappolt, S., Noh, S. (2003). Caregiving for relatives with Alzheimer's disease: Feelings of Chinese-Canadian women. *Journal of Aging Studies, 17*, 301–321.

Hoagland, J., & Enstin-Franklin, T. (1999, May 1). Life.

Hobart, C., & Grigel, F. (1992). Cohabitation among Canadian students at the end of the eighties. *Journal of Comparative Family Studies, 23*, 311–337.

Hocutt, A. M. (1996). Effectiveness of special education: Is placement the critical factor? *The Future of Children, 6*, 77–102.

Hoek, J., & Gendall, P. (2006). Advertising and obesity: A behavioral perspective. *Journal of Health Communication, 11*, 409–423.

Hoelterk L. F., Axinn, W. G., & Ghimire, D. J. (2004). Social change, premarital nonfamily experiences, and marital dynamics. *Journal of Marriage & Family, 66*, 1131–1151.

Hofer, M. A. (2006). Psychobiological roots of early attachment. *Current Directions in Psychological Science, 15*, 84–88.

Hofferth, S., & Sandberg, J. F. (2001). How American children spend their time. *Journal of Marriage and the Family, 63*, 295–308.

Hofferth, S. L., & Sandberg, J. (1998*). Changes in American children's time, 1981–1997*. Ann Arbor, MI: University of Michigan Institute for Social Research.

Hoffman, L. (2003). Why high schools don't change: What students and their yearbooks tell us. *High School Journal, 86*, 22–37.

Hohmann-Marriott, B. (2006, November). Shared beliefs and the union stability of married and cohabiting couples. *Journal of Marriage and Family, 68*, 1015–1028.

Holahan, C., & Chapman, J. (2002). Longitudinal predictors of proactive goals and activity participation at age 80. *Journals of Gerontology: Series B: Psychological Sciences & Social Sciences, 57B*, P418–P425.

Holden, C. (1987, October 9). Why do women live longer than men? *Science, 233*, 158–160.

Holden, G. W., & Miller, P. C. (1999). Enduring and different: A meta-analysis of the similarity in parents' child rearing. *Psychological Bulletin, 125*, 223–254.

Holland, J. C., & Lewis, S. (1993). Emotions and cancer: What do we really know? In D. Goleman & J. Gurin (Eds.), *Mind–body medicine*. Yonkers, NY: Consumer Reports Books.

Holland, J. L. (1973). *Making vocational choices: A theory of careers*. Englewood Cliffs, NJ: Prentice-Hall.

Holland, J. L. (1987). Current status of Holland's theory of careers: Another perspective. *Career Development Quarterly, 36*, 24–30.

Holland, N. (1994, August). Race dissonance—Implications for African American children. Paper presented at the annual meeting of the American Psychological Association, Los Angeles, CA.

Hollich, G. J., Hirsh-Pasek, K., Golinkoff, R. M., Brand, R. J., Brown, E. C., He, L., Hennon, E., & Rocrot, C. (2000). Breaking the language barrier: An emergentist coalition model of the origins of word learning. *Monographs of the Society for Research in Child Development, 65*(3, Serial No. 262).

Hollingworth, H. L. (1943/1990). *Letta Stetter Hollingworth: A biography*. Boston: Anker.

Holmes, E. R., & Holmes, L.D. (1995). *Other cultures, elder years*. Thousand Oaks, CA: Sage Publications.

Holowaka, S., & Petitto, L. A. (2002). Left hemisphere cerebral specialization for babies while babbling. *Science, 287*, 1515.

Holyrod, R., & Sheppard, A. (1997). Parental separation: Effects on children; implications for services. *Child: Care, Health & Development, 23*, 369–378.

Holzman, L. (1997). *Schools for growth: Radical alternatives to current educational models*. Mahwah, NJ: Erlbaum.

Honey, J. L., Bennett, P., & Morgan, M. (2003). Predicting postnatal depression. *Journal of Affective Disorders, 76*, 201–210.

Hong, S. B., & Trepanier-Street, M. (2004). Technology: A tool for knowledge construction in a Reggio Emilia inspired teacher education program. *Early Childhood Education Journal, 32*, 87–94.

Hopkins, B., & Westra, T. (1989). Maternal expectations of their infants' development: Some cultural differences. *Developmental Medicine and Child Neurology, 31*, 384–390.

Hopkins-Golightly, T., Raz, S., & Sander, C. (2003). Influence of slight to moderate risk for birth hypoxia on acquisition of cognitive and language function in the preterm infant: A cross-sectional comparison with preterm-birth controls. *Neuropsychology, 17*, 3–13.

Hoppe, M. J., Graham, L., Wilsdon, A., Wells, E. A., Nahom, D., & Morrison, D. M. (2004). Teens speak out about HIV/AIDS: Focus group discussions about risk and decision-making. *Journal of Adolescent Health, 35*, 27–35.

Horiuchi, S., Finch, C., & Mesle, F. (2003). Differential patterns of age-related mortality increase in middle age and old age. *Journals of Gerontology: Series A: Biological Sciences & Medical Sciences, 58A*, 495–507.

Horner, K. L. (1998). Individuality in vulnerability: Influences on physical health. *Journal of Health Psychology, 3*, 71–85.

Hornik, R., & Gunnar, M. R. (1988). A descriptive analysis of infant social referencing. *Child Development, 59*, 626–634.

Horowitz, A. (1994). Vision impairment and functional disability among nursing home residents. *Gerontologist, 34*, 316–323.

Horwath, C. C. (1991). Nutrition goals for older adults: A review. *Gerontologist, 31*, 811–821.

Houts, A. (2003). Behavioral treatment for enuresis. In A. Kazdin (Ed.), *Evidence-based psychotherapies for children and adolescents* (pp. 389–406). New York: Guilford Press.

Howard, A. (1992). Work and family crossroads spanning the career. In S. Zedeck (Ed.), *Work, families and organizations*. San Francisco: Jossey-Bass.

Howe, M. J. (1997). *IQ in question: The truth about intelligence*. London, England: Sage.

Howe, M. J. (2004). Some insights of geniuses into the causes of exceptional achievement. In L. V. Shavinina & M. Ferrari (Eds.), *Beyond knowledge: Extracognitive aspects of developing high ability*. Mahwah, NJ: Lawrence Erlbaum Associates.

Howe, M. L. (2003). Memories from the cradle. *Current Directions in Psychological Science, 12*, 62–65.

Howe, M. L., Courage, M. L., & Edison, S. C. (2004). When autobiographical memory begins. In S. Algarabel, A. Pitarque, T. Bajo, S. E. Gathercole, & M. A. Conway (Eds.), *Theories of memory: Vol. 3*. New York: Psychology Press.

Howe, N., & Ross, H. S. (1990). Socialization, perspective-taking, and the sibling relationship. *Developmental Psychology, 26*, 160–165.

Howes, C., Galinsky, E., & Kontos, S. (1998). Child care caregiver sensitivity and attachment. *Social Development, 7*, 25–36.

Howes, C., Unger, O., & Seidner, L. B. (1989). Social pretend play in toddlers: Parallels with social play and with solitary pretend. *Child Development, 60*, 77–84.

Huang, J. (2004). Death: Cultural traditions. From *On Our Own Terms: Moyers on Dying*. Retrieved May 24, 2004 from www.pbs.org.

Huang, J. H., Jacobs, D. F., Derevensky, J. L., Gupta, R. & Paskus, T. S. (2007). Gambling and health risk behaviors among U.S. college student-athletes: Findings from a national study. *Journal of Adolescent Health, 40*, 390–397.

Hubbs-Tait, L., Nation, J. R., Krebs, N. F., & Bellinger, D. C. (2005). Neurotoxicants, micronutrients, and social environments: Individual and combined effects on children's development. *Journal of the American Psychological Society, 6*, 57–101.

Hubel, D. H., & Wiesel, T. N. (1979). Brain mechanisms of vision. *Scientific American, 241*, 150–162.

Hubel, D. H., & Wiesel, T. N. (2004). *Brain and visual perception: The story of a 25-year collaboration*. New York: Oxford University Press.

Huddleston, J., & Ge, X. (2003). Boys at puberty: Psychosocial implications. In C. Hayward (Ed.), *Gender differences at puberty*. New York: Cambridge University Press.

Hudson, J. A., Sosa, B. B., & Shapiro, L. R. (1997). Scripts and plans: The development of preschool children's event knowledge and event planning. In S. L. Friedman & E. K. Scholnick (Eds.), *The developmental psychology of planning: Why, how and when do we plan* (pp. 77–102). Mahwah, NJ: Erlbaum.

Huesmann, L. R., Moise-Titus, J., & Podolski, C. L. (2003). Longitudinal relations between children's exposure to TV violence and their aggressive and violent behavior in young adulthood: 1977–1992. *Developmental Psychology, 39*, 201–221.

Huff, C. O. (1999). Source, recency, and degree of stress in adolescence and suicide ideation. *Adolescence, 34*, 81–89.

Hughes, F. P. (1995). *Children, play, and development* (2nd ed.). Boston: Allyn & Bacon.

Huizink, A., & Mulder, E. (2006). Maternal smoking, drinking or cannabis use during pregnancy and neurobehavioral and cognitive functioning in human offspring. *Neuroscience & Biobehavioral Reviews, 30*, 24–41.

Huizink, A., Mulder, E., & Buitelaar, J. (2004). Prenatal stress and risk for psychopathology: Specific effects or induction of general susceptibility? *Psychological Bulletin, 130*, 115–142.

Hulanicka, B. (1999). Acceleration of menarcheal age of girls from dysfunctional families. *Journal of Reproductive & Infant Psychology, 17*, 119–132.

Hulei, E., Zevenbergen, A., & Jacobs, S. (2006, September). Discipline behaviors of Chinese American and European American mothers. *Journal of Psychology: Interdisciplinary and Applied, 140*, 459–475.

Human Genome Program. (2003). *Genomics and its impact on science and society: A 2003 primer.* Washington, DC: U.S. Department of Energy.

Human Genome Project. (2006). Available online at http://www.ornl.gov/sci/techresources/Human_Genome/medicine/genetest.shtml

Humphrey, N., Curran, A., Morris, E., Farrell, P., & Woods, K. (2007, April). Emotional intelligence and education: A critical review. *Educational Psychology, 27,* 235–254.

Humphreys, J. (2003). Resilience in sheltered battered women. *Issues in Mental Health Nursing, 24,* 137–152.

Hunt, C., & Hauck, F. (2006). Sudden infant death syndrome. *Canadian Medical Association Journal, 174,* 1861–1869.

Hunt, M. (1974). *Sexual behaviors in the 1970s.* New York: Dell.

Hunt, M. (1993). *The story of psychology.* New York: Doubleday.

Hunter, J., & Mallon, G. P. (2000). Lesbian, gay, and bisexual adolescent development: Dancing with your feet tied together. In B. Greene & G. L. Croom (Eds.), *Education, research, and practice in lesbian, gay, bisexual, and transgendered psychology: A resource manual, Vol. 5.* Thousand Oaks, CA: Sage.

Huntsinger, C. S., Jose, P. E., Liaw, F., & Ching, W-D. (1997). Cultural differences in early mathematics learning: A comparison of Euro-American, Chinese-American, and Taiwan-Chinese families. *International Journal of Behavioral Development, 21,* 371–388.

Huppe, M., & Cyr, M. (1997). Division of household labor and marital satisfaction of dual income couples according to family life cycle. *Canadian Journal of Counseling, 31,* 145–162.

Huston, A. (Ed.). (1991). *Children in poverty: Child development and public policy.* Cambridge, England: Cambridge University Press.

Huston, T. L., Caughlin, J. P., Houts, R. M., & Smith, S. E. (2001). The connubial crucible: Newlywed years as predictors of marital delight, distress, and divorce. *Journal of Personality and Social Psychology, 80,* 237–252.

Hutchinson, A., Whitman, R., & Abeare, C. (2003). The unification of mind: Integration of hemispheric semantic processing. *Brain & Language, 87,* 361–368.

Hutchinson, S., & Wexler, B. (2007, January). Is "raging" good for health?: Older women's participation in the Raging Grannies. *Health Care for Women International, 28,* 88–118.

Hutton, P. H. (2004). *Phillippe Aries and the politics of French cultural history.* Amherst: University of Massachusetts Press.

Huurre, T., Junkkari, H., & Aro, H. (2006, June). Long-term psychosocial effects of parental divorce: A follow-up study from adolescence to adulthood. *European Archives of Psychiatry and Clinical Neuroscience, 256,* 256–263.

Hwang, S. (2004, January 19). As "doulas" enter delivery rooms, conflicts arise. *Wall Street Journal* pp. A1, A10.

Hyde, J. S. (1994). *Understanding human sexuality* (5th ed.). New York: McGraw-Hill.

Hyde, J. S., & DeLamater, J. D. (2003). *Understanding human sexuality* (8th ed.). New York: McGraw-Hill.

Hyde, J. S. & DeLamater, J. D. (2004). *Understanding human sexuality,* (9th ed.). Boston: McGraw Hill.

Hyde, J. S., Fennema, E., & Lamon, S. J. (1990). Gender differences in mathematics performance: A meta-analysis. *Psychological Bulletin, 107,* 139–155.

Hyde, J. S., Klein, M. H., Essex, M. J., & Clark, R. (1995). Maternity leave and women's mental health. *Psychology of Women Quarterly, 19,* 257–285.

Hyssaelae L., Rautava, P., & Helenius, H. (1995). Fathers' smoking and use of alcohol: The viewpoint of maternity health care clinics and well-baby clinics. *Family Practice, 12,* 22–27.

Ickes, W., & Turner, M. (1983). On the social advantages of having an older, opposite-sex sibling: Birth order influences in mixed-sex dyads. *Journal of Personality and Social Psychology, 45,* 210–222.

Iglesias, J., Eriksson, J., Grize, F., Tomassini, M., & Villa, A. E. (2005). Dynamics of pruning in simulated large-scale spiking neural networks. *Biosystems, 79,* 11–20.

Ikels, C. (1989). Becoming a human being in theory and practice: Chinese views of human development. In D. I. Kertzer & K. W. Schaie (Eds.), *Age structuring in comparative perspective.* Hillsdale, NJ: Erlbaum.

Ingersoll, E. W., & Thoman, E. B. (1999). Sleep/wake states of preterm infants: Stability, developmental change, diurnal variation, and relation with caregiving activity. *Child Development, 70,* 1–10.

Ingram, D. K., Young, J., & Mattison, J. A. (2007). Calorie restriction in nonhuman primates: Assessing effects on brain and behavioral aging. *Neuroscience, 14,* 1359–1364.

Inoue, K., Tanii, H., Abe, S., Kaiya, H., Nata, M., & Fukunaga, T. (2006, December). The correlation between rates of unemployment and suicide rates in Japan between 1985 and 2002. *International Medical Journal, 13,* 261–263.

Insel, P. M., & Roth, W. T. (1991). *Core concepts in health* (6th ed.). Mountain View, CA: Mayfield.

Institute for Women's Policy Research (2006). The best and worst state economies for women. *Briefing Paper, No. R334.* Washington, DC: Institute for Women's Policy Research.

International Cesarean Awareness Network. (2004). Available online at http://www.ican-online.org/ International Cesarean Awareness Network. (2007, April 10). Available online at http://www.birthchoiceuk.com.

International Human Genome Sequencing Consortium. (2001). Initial sequencing and analysis of the human genome. *Nature, 409,* 860–921.

International Literacy Institute. (2001). Literacy overview. Available online at http://www.literacyonline.org/explorer/.

Inzlicht, M., & Ben-Zeev, T. (2000). A threatening intellectual environment: Why females are susceptible to experiencing problem-solving deficits in the presence of males. *Psychological Science, 11,* 365–371.

Ireland, J. L., & Archer, J. (2004). Association between measures of aggression and bullying among juvenile young offenders. *Aggressive Behavior, 30,* 29–42.

Ironson, G., & Schneiderman, N. (2002). Psycholosical factors, spirituality/religiousness, and immune function in HIV/AIDS patients. In H. G. Koenig & H. J. Cohen (Eds.), *Link between religion and health: Psychoneuroimmunology and the faith factor.* London: Oxford University Press.

Irwin, E. G. (1993). A focused overview of anorexia nervosa and bulimia: I. Etiological issues. *Archives of Psychiatric Nursing, 7,* 342–346.

Isaksen, S. G., & Murdock, M. C. (1993). The emergence of a discipline: Issues and approaches to the study of creativity. In S. G. Isaksen, M. C. Murdock, R. L. Firestein, & D. J. Treffinger (Eds.), *The emergence of a discipline* (Vol. 1). Norwood, NJ: Ablex.

Isay, R. A. (1990). *Being homosexual: Gay men and their development.* New York: Avon.

Ishi-Kuntz, M. (2000). Diversity within Asian-American families. In D.H. Demo, K. R. Allen, & M.A. Fine (Eds.), *Handbook of family diversity.* New York: Oxford.

Israel, E. (2005). Introduction: The rise of the age of individualism—variability in the pathobiology, response to treatment, and treatment outcomes in asthma. *Journal of Allergy and Clinical Immunology, 115,* S525.

Izard, J., Haines, C., Crouch, R., Houston, S., & Neill, N. (2003). Assessing the impact of the teaching of modelling: Some implications. In S. Lamon, W. Parker, & K. Houston (Eds.), *Mathematical Modelling: A Way of Life: ICTMA 11.* Chichester, England: Horwood Publishing.

Jackson, H. (2006, November 27). Boosting brain power: Computer program gives retirees a workout to keep memory sharp, thinking clear. *St. Louis Post-Dispatch,* p. H4.

Jackson, L. A., Gardner, P. D., & Sullivan, L. A. (1992). Explaining gender differences in self-pay expectations: Social comparison standards and perceptions of fair pay. *Journal of Applied Psychology, 77,* 651–663.

Jackson, T. (2006, May). Relationships between perceived close social support and health practices within community samples of American women and men. *Journal of Psychology: Interdisciplinary and Applied, 140,* 229–246.

Jacobi, C., Hayward, C., de Zwaan, M., Kraemer, H. C., & Agras, W. S. (2004). Coming to terms with risk factors for eating disorders: Application of risk terminology and suggestions for a general taxonomy. *Psychological Bulletin, 130,* 19–65.

Jacobson, N., & Gottman, J. (1998). *When men batter women.* New York: Simon & Schuster.

Jacques, H., & Mash, E. (2004). A test of the tripartite model of anxiety and depression in elementary and high school boys and girls. *Journal of Abnormal Child Psychology, 32,* 13–25.

Jahoda, G. (1980). Theoretical and systematic approaches in mass-cultural psychology. In H. C. Triandis & W. W. Lambert (Eds.), *Handbook of cross-cultural psychology* (Vol. 1). Boston: Allyn & Bacon.

Jahoda, G. (1983). European "lag" in the development of an economic concept: A study in Zimbabwe. *British Journal of Developmental Psychology, 1,* 113–120.

James, W. (1890/1950). *The principles of psychology.* New York: Holt.

Jamieson, D. W., Lydon, J. E., Stewart, G., & Zanna, M. P. (1987). Pygmalion revisited: New evidence for student expectancy effects in the classroom. *Journal of Educational Psychology, 79,* 461–466.

Janda, L. H., & Klenke-Hamel, K. E. (1980). *Human sexuality.* New York: Van Nostrand.

Jansen, B. R. J., Van der Maas, W. L., & Black J. E. (2001). Evidence for the phase transition from rule I to rule II on the balance scale task. *Developmental Review, 21,* 450–494.

Janssens, J. M. A. M., & Dekovic, M. (1997). Child rearing, prosocial moral reasoning, and prosocial behaviour. *International Journal of Behavioral Development, 20,* 509–527.

Javawant, S., & Parr, J. (2007). Outcome following subdural hemorrhages in infancy. *Archives of the Disabled Child, 92,* 343–347.

Jayawardena, K., & Liao, S. (2006, January). Elder abuse at end of life. *Journal of Palliative Medicine, 9,* 127–136.

Jazwinski, S. M. (1996, July 5). Longevity, genes, and aging. *Science, 273,* 54–59.

Jehlen, A., & Winans, D. (2005). No child left behind—myth or truth? *NEA Today, 23,* 32–34.

Jeng, S., Yau, K. T., & Teng, R. (1998). Neurobehavioral development at term in very low-birthweight infants and normal term infants in Taiwan. *Early Human Development, 51,* 235–245.

Jensen, A. (2003). Do age-group differences on mental tests imitate racial differences? *Intelligence, 31,* 107–21.

Jeynes, W. (2007). The impact of parental remarriage on children: A meta-analysis. *Marriage & Family Review, 40,* 75–102.

Ji-liang, S., Li-qing, Z., & Yan, T. (2003). The impact of intergenerational social support and filial expectation on the loneliness of elder parents. *Chinese Journal of Clinical Psychology, 11,* 167–169.

Jiao, S., Ji, G., & Jing, Q. (1996). Cognitive development of Chinese urban only children and children with siblings. *Child Development, 67,* 387–395.

Jimenez, J., & Guzman, R. (2003). The influence of code-oriented versus meaning-oriented approaches to reading instruction on word recognition in the Spanish language. *International Journal of Psychology, 38,* 65–78.

Joe, S., & Marcus, S. (2003). Datapoints: Trends by race and gender in suicide attempts among U.S. adolescents, 1991–2001. *Psychiatric Services, 54,* 454.

Johannes, L. (2003, October 9). A better test for Down syndrome. *The Wall Street Journal,* pp. D1, D3.

Johnson, A. M., Wadsworth, J., Wellings, K., & Bradshaw, S. (1992). Sexual lifestyles and HIV risk. *Nature, 360,* 410–412.

Johnson, C. H., Vicary, J. R., Heist, C. L., & Corneal, D. A. (2001). Moderate alcohol and tobacco use during pregnancy and child behavior outcomes. *Journal of Primary Prevention, 21,* 367–379.

Johnson, C. L., & Barer, B. M. (1992). Patterns of engagement and disengagement among the oldest old. *Journal of Aging Studies, 6,* 351–364.

Johnson, D. C., Kassner, C. T., & Kutner, J. S. (2004). Current use of guidelines, protocols, and care pathways for symptom management in hospice. *American Journal of Hospital Palliative Care, 21,* 51–57.

Johnson, D. J., Jaeger, E., Randolph, S. M., Cauce, A. M., Ward, J., & National Institute of Child Health and Human Development: Early Child Care Research Network. (2003). Studying the effects of early child care experiences on the development of children of color in the United States: Toward a more inclusive research agenda. *Child Development, 74,* 1227–1244.

Johnson, J., Cohen, P., Smailes, E. M., Kasen, S., Brook, J. S. (2002, March 29). Television viewing and aggressive behavior during adolescence and adulthood. *Science, 295,* 2468–2471.

Johnson, J. L., Primas, P. J., & Coe, M. K. (1994). Factors that prevent women of low socioeconomic status from seeking prenatal care. *Journal of the American Academy of Nurse Practitioners, 6,* 105–111.

Johnson, K., & Eilers, A. (1998). Effects of knowledge and development on subordinate level categorization. *Cognitive Development, 13,* 515–545.

Johnson, M. H. (1998). The neural basis of cognitive development. In D. Kuhn & R. S. Siegler (Eds.), *Handbook of child psychology: Vol. 2: Cognition, perception, and language* (5th ed., pp. 1–49). New York: Wiley.

Johnson, M. J. (2003). Development of human brain functions. *Biological Psychiatry, 54,* 1312–1316.

Johnson, N. (2003). Psychology and health: Research, practice, and policy. *American Psychologist, 58,* 670–677.

Johnson, N. G., Roberts, M. C., & Worell, J. (Eds.). (1999). *Beyond appearance: A new look at adolescent girls.* Washington, DC: American Psychological Association.

Johnson, S. L., & Birch, L. L. (1994). Parents' and children's adiposity and eating style. *Pediatrics, 94,* 653–661.

Johnston, L. D., Bachman, J. G., & O'Malley, P. M. (2000). *Monitoring the future study.* Lansing, MI: University of Michigan.

Johnston, L. D., O'Malley, P. M., Bachman, J. G. & Schulenberg, J. E. (December 21, 2006). *Teen drug use continues down in 2006, particularly among older teens; but use of prescription-type drugs remains high.* University of Michigan News and Information Services: Ann Arbor, MI. [On-line]. Available: www.monitoringthefuture.org;accessed04/12/07.

Jones, A., & Crandall, R. (Eds.). (1991). Handbook of self-actualization. *Journal of Social Behavior and Personality, 6,* 1–362.

Jones, H. (2006). Drug addiction during pregnancy: Advances in maternal treatment and understanding child outcomes. *Current Directions in Psychological Science, 15,* 126–130.

Jones, H. E. (2006). Drug addiction during pregnancy: Advances in maternal treatment and understanding child outcomes. *Current Directions in Psychological Science, 15,* 126–132.

Jones, S. (2006). Exploration or imitation? The effect of music on 4-week-old infants' tongue protrusions. *Infant Behavior & Development, 29,* 126–130.

Jones-Harden, B. (2004). Safety and stability for foster children: A developmental perspective. *The Future of Children, 14,* 31–48.

Jongudomkarn, D., & Camfield, L. (2006, September). Exploring the quality of life of people in northeastern and southern Thailand. *Social Indicators Research, 78,* 489–529.

Jorgensen, G. (2006, June). Kohlberg and Gilligan: Duet or duel? *Journal of Moral Education, 35,* 179–196.

Jose, O., & Alfons, V. (2007). Do demographics affect marital satisfaction? *Journal of Sex and Marital Therapy, 33,* 73–85.

Joseph, H., Reznik, I., & Mester, R. (2003). Suicidal behavior of adolescent girls: Profile and meaning. *Israel Journal of Psychiatry & Related Sciences, 40,* 209–219.

Joseph, R. (1999). Environmental influences on neural plasticity, the limbic system, emotional development and attachment: A review. *Child Psychiatry & Human Development, 29,* 189–208.

Jost, H., & Songtag, L. (1944). The genetic factor in autonomic nervous system function. *Psychosomatic Medicine, 6,* 308–310.

Juhn, Y. J., Sauver, J. S., Katusic, S., Vargas, D., Weaver, A., & Yunginger, J. (2005). The influence of neighborhood environment on the incidence of childhood asthma: A multilevel approach. *Social Science Medicine, 60,* 2453–2464.

Jurimae, T., & Saar, M. (2003). Self-perceived and actual indicators of motor abilities in children and adolescents. *Perception and Motor Skills, 97,* 862–866.

Juster, F., Ono, H., & Stafford F. (2004). *Changing times of American youth: 1981–2003.* Ann Arbor, MI: Institute for Social Research.

Juster, T., Ono, H., & Stafford, F. (2000) *Time use.* Presented at the Sloan Centers on Work and Family Conference, San Francisco.

Kacapyr, E. (1997, October). Are we having fun yet? *American Demographics,* 28–30.

Kagan, J. (1981). Universals in human development. In R. H. Munroe, R. L. Munroe, & B. B. Whiting (Eds.), *Handbook of crosscultural human development* (pp. 53–62). New York: Garland.

Kagan, J. (2003a). An unwilling rebel. In R. J. Sternberg (Ed.), *Psychologists defying the crowd: Stories of those who battled the establishment and won.* Washington, DC: American Psychological Association.

Kagan, J., Arcus, D., & Snidman, N. (1993). The idea of temperament: Where do we go from here? In R. Plomin & G. E. McClearn (Eds.), *Nature, nurture, and psychology.* Washington, DC: American Psychological Association.

Kagan, J., Arcus, D., Snidman, N., Feng, W. Y., Hendler, J., & Greene, S. (1994). Reactivity in infants: A cross-national comparison. *Developmental Psychology, 30,* 342–345.

Kagan, J., Kearsley, R., & Zelazo, P. R. (1978). *Infancy: Its place in human development.* Cambridge, MA: Harvard University Press.

Kagan, J., & Snidman, N. (1991). Infant predictors of inhibited and uninhibited profiles. *Psychological Science, 2,* 40–44.

Kahn, A., Groswasser, J., Franco, P., Scaillet, S., Sawaguchi, T., Kelmanson, I., & Dan, B. (2003). Sudden infant deaths: Stress, arousal and SIDS. *Early Human Development, 75, Supplement,* 147–166.

Kahn, J. (2007, February). Maximizing the potential public health impact of HPV vaccines: A focus on parents. *Journal of Adolescent Health, 40,* 101–103.

Kahn, J., Hessling, R., & Russell, D. (2003). Social support, health, and well-being among the elderly: What is the role of negative affectivity? *Personality & Individual Differences, 35,* 5–17.

Kahn, J. P. (2004). Hostility, coronary risk, and alpha-adrenergic to beta-adrenergic receptor density ratio. *Psychosomatic Medicine, 66,* 289–297.

Kahn, R. L., & Rowe, J. W. (1999). *Successful aging.* New York: Dell.

Kahneman, D., Krueger, A., Schkade, D., Schwarz, N., & Stone, A. (2006, June). Would you be happier if you were richer? A focusing illusion. *Science, 312,* 1908–1910.

Kail, R. (2003). Information processing and memory. In M. Bornstein & L. Davidson (Eds.), *Well-being: Positive development across the life course.* Mahwah, NJ: Lawrence Erlbaum Associates.

Kail, R. V. (2004). Cognitive development includes global and domain-specific processes. *Merrill-Palmer Quarterly, 50.* [Special issue: 50th anniversary issue: Part II, the maturing of the human development sciences: Appraising past, present, and prospective agendas], 445–455.

Kaiser, L. L., Allen, L., & American Dietetic Association. (2002). Position of the American Dietetic Association: Nutrition and lifestyle for a healthy pregnancy outcome. *Journal of the American Dietetic Association, 102,* 1479–1490.

Kalb, C. (1997, Spring/Summer). The top 10 health worries. *Newsweek Special Issue,* 42–43.

Kalb, C. (2003, March 10). Preemies grow up. *Newsweek,* 50–51.

Kalb, C. (2004, January 26). Brave new babies. *Newsweek,* 45–53.

Kalb, C. (2006, December 11). Peering into the future. *Newsweek,* 52.

Kalichman, S. C. (1998). *Understanding AIDS, second edition: Advances in research and treatment.* Washington, DC: APA Books.

Kalliopuska, M. (1994). Relations of retired people and their grandchildren. *Psychological Reports, 75,* 1083–1088.

Kalsi, M., Heron, G., & Charman, W. (2001). Changes in the static accommodation response with age. *Ophthalmic & Physiological Optics, 21,* 77–84.

Kaltiala-Heino, R., Kosunen, E., & Rimpela, M. (2003). Pubertal timing, sexual behaviour and self-reported depression in middle adolescence. *Journal of Adolescence, 26,* 531–545.

Kaltiala-Heino, R., Rimpelae, M., Rantanen, P., & Rimpelae, A. (2000). Bullying at school—an indicator of adolescents at risk for mental disorders. *Journal of Adolescence, 23,* 661–674.

Kane, R. A., Caplan, A. L., Urv-Wong, E. K., & Freeman, I. C. (1997). Everyday matters in the lives of nursing home residents: Wish for and perception of choice and control. *Journal of the American Geriatrics Society, 45,* 1086–1093.

Kaneda, H., Maeshima, K., Goto, N., Kobayakawa, T., Ayabe-Kanamura, S., & Saito, S. (2000). Decline in taste and odor discrimination abilities with age, and relationship between gustation and olfaction. *Chemical Senses, 25,* 331–337.

Kanetsuna, T., Smith, P., & Morita, Y. (2006, November). Coping with bullying at school: Children's recommended strategies and attitudes to school-based interventions in England and Japan. *Aggressive Behavior, 32,* 570–580.

Kantrowitz, B., & Wingert, P. (1999, May 10). How well do you know your kid? (teenagers need adult attention). *Newsweek, 133*(19), 36.

Kao, G. (2000). Psychological well-being and educational achievement among immigrant youth. In D. J. Hernandez (Ed.), *Children of immigrants: Health, adjustment, and public assistance.* Washington, DC: National Academy Press.

Kao, G., & Tienda, M. (1995). Optimism and achievement: The educational performance of immigrant youth. *Social Science Quarterly, 76,* 1–19.

Kao, G., & Vaquera, E. (2006, February). The salience of racial and ethnic identification in friendship choices among Hispanic adolescents. *Hispanic Journal of Behavioral Sciences, 28,* 23–47.

Kaplan, H., & Dove, H. (1987). Infant development among the Ache of Eastern Paraguay. *Developmental Psychology, 23,* 190–198.

Kaplan, R. M., Sallis, J. F., Jr., & Patterson, T. L. (1993). *Health and human behavior.* Age specific breast cancer annual incidence. New York: McGraw-Hill.

Kaplan, S., Heiligenstein, J., West, S., Busner, J., Harder, D., Dittmann, R., Casat, C., & Wernicke, J. F. (2004). Efficacy and safety of atomoxetine in childhood attention-deficit/hyperactivity disorder with comorbid oppositional defiant disorder. *Journal of Attention Disorders, 8,* 45–52.

Karney, B. R., & Bradbury, T. N. (1995). The longitudinal course of marital quality and stability: A review of theory, method, and research. *Psychological Bulletin, 118,* 3–34.

Karney, B. R., & Bradbury, T. N. (2005). Contextual influences on marriage. *Current Directions in Psychological Science, 14,* 171–174.

Karpov, Y. V., & Haywood, H. C. (1998). Two ways to elaborate Vygotsky's concept of mediation: Implications for instruction. *American Psychologist, 53,* 27–36.

Kart, C. S. (1990). *The realities of aging* (3rd ed.). Boston: Allyn & Bacon.

Kartman, L. L. (1991). Life review: One aspect of making meaningful music for the elderly. *Activities, Adaptations, and Aging, 15,* 42–45.

Kartrowitz, E. J., & Evans, G. W. (2004). The relation between the ratio of children per activity area and off-task behavior and type of play in day care centers. *Environment & Behavior, 36,* 541–557.

Kaslow, F. W. (2001). Families and family psychology at the millennium: Intersecting crossroads. *American Psychologist, 56,* 37–44.

Kasser, T., & Sharma, Y. S. (1999). Reproductive freedom, educational equality, and females' preference for resource-acquisition characteristics in mates. *Psychological Science, 10,* 374–377.

Kastenbaum, R. (1999). Dying and bereavement. In J. C. Cavanaugh & S. K. Whitbourne (Eds.), *Gerontology: An interdisciplinary perspective.* New York: Oxford University Press.

Kastenbaum, R. J. (1992). *The psychology of death.* New York: Springer-Verlag.

Katchadourian, H. A. (1987). *Biological aspects of human sexuality* (3rd ed.). New York: Holt, Rinehart & Winston.

Kate, N. T. (1998, March). How many children? *American Demographics,* p. 35.

Kates, N., Grieff, B., & Hagen, D. (1990). *The psychosocial impact of job loss.* Washington, DC: American Psychiatric Press.

Katnrowitz, B., & Springen, K. (2005, May 16.) A peaceful adolescence. *Newsweek International Edition,* pp. 50–52.

Kato, K., & Pedersen, N. L. (2005). Personality and coping: A study of twins reared apart and twins reared together. *Behavior Genetics, 35,* 147–158.

Katrowitz, B., & Wingert, P. (1990, Winter/Spring). Step by step. *Newsweek Special Edition,* 24–34.

Katz, D. L. (2001). Behavior modification in primary care: The Pressure System Model. *Preventive Medicine: An International Devoted to Practice & Theory, 32,* 66–72.

Katz, L. G. (1989, December). Beginners' ethics. *Parents,* p. 213.

Katz, S., & Marshall, B. (2003). New sex for old: Lifestyle, consumerism, and the ethics of aging well. *Journal of Aging Studies, 17,* 3–16.

Kauffman, J. M. (1993). How we might achieve the radical reform of special education. *Exceptional Children, 60,* 6–16.

Kaufman, J. C., Kaufman, A. S., Kaufman-Singer, J., & Kaufman, N. L. (2005). The Kaufman Assessment Battery for Children—Second Edition and the Kaufman Adolescent and Adult Intelligence Test. In D. P. Flanagan & P. L. Harrison (Eds.), *Contemporary intellectual assessment: Theories, tests, and issues.* New York, Guilford Press.

Kaufman, M. T. (1992, November 28). Teaching compassion in theater of death. *The New York Times,* p. B7.

Kaufmann, D., Gesten, E., Santa Lucia, R. C., Salcedo, O., Rendina-Gobioff, G., & Gadd, R. (2000). The relationship between parenting style and children's adjustment: The parents' perspective. *Journal of Child & Family Studies, 9,* 231–245.

Kavale, K. (2002). Mainstreaming to full inclusion: From orthogenesis to pathogenesis of an idea. *International Journal of Disability, Development & Education, 49,* 201–214.

Kavale, K. A., & Forness, S. R. (2000, Sep.–Oct.). History, rhetoric, and reality: Analysis of the inclusion debate. *Rase: Remedial & Special Education, 21,* 279–296.

Kaye, W. H., Devlin, B., Barbarich, N., Bulik, C. M., Thornton, L., Badanu, S. A., Fichter, M. M., Halmi, K. A., Kaplan, A. S., Strober, M., Woodside, D. B., Bergen, A. W., Crow, S., Mitchell, J., Rotondo, A. Mauri, M., Cassano, G., Keel, P., Plotnicov, K., Pollice, C., Klump, K. L., Lilenfeld, L. R., Ganjei, J. K., Quadflieg, N., Berrettini, W. H., & Kaye, W. H. (2004). Genetic analysis of bulimia nervosa: Methods and sample description. *Journal of Eating Disorders, 35,* 556–570.

Kayton, A., (2007). Newborn screening: A literature review. *Neonatal Network, 26,* 85–95.

Kazdin, A. E., & Benjet, C. (2003). Spanking children: Evidence and issues. *Current Directions in Psychological Science, 12,* 99–103.

Kazura, K. (2000). Fathers' qualitative and quantitative involvement: An investigation of attachment, play, and social interactions. *Journal of Men's Studies, 9,* 41–57.

Keating, D. (1980). Thinking processes in adolescence. In J. Adelson (Ed.), *Handbook of adolescent psychology.* New York: Wiley.

Keating, D. (1990). Adolescent thinking. In S. S. Feldman & G. R. Elliott (Eds.), *At the threshold.* Cambridge, MA: Harvard University Press.

Keating, D. P., & Clark, L. V. (1980). Development of physical and social reasoning in adolescence. *Developmental Psychology, 16,* 23–30.

Kecskes, I., & Papp, T. (2000). *Foreign language and mother tongue.* Mahwah, NJ: Erlbaum.

Kedziora-Kornatowski, K., Szewczyk-Golec, K. Czuczejko, J., van Marke de Lumen, K., Pawluk, H., Motyl, J., Karasek, M., & Kedziora, J. (2007). Effect of melatonin on the oxidative stress in erythrocytes of healthy young and elderly subjects. *Journal of Pineal Research, 42,* 153–158.

Keefer, B. L., Kraus, R. F., Parker, B. L., Elliotst, R., et al. (1991). A state university collaboration program: Residents' perspectives. Annual Meeting of the American Psychiataric Association (1990, New York, New York). *Hospital and Community Psychiatry, 42* 62–66.

Keel, P. K., Leon, G. R., & Fulkerson, J. A. (2001). Vulnerability to eating disorders in childhood and adolescence. In R. E. Ingram & J. M. Price (Eds.), *Vulnerability to psychopathology: Risk across the lifespan.* New York, NY: Guilford Press.

Keller, H., Voelker, S., & Yovsi, R. D. (2005). Conceptions of parenting in different cultural communities: The case of West African Nso and northern German women. *Social Development, 14,* 158–180.

Keller, H., Yovsi, R., Borke, J., Kärtner, J., Henning, J., & Papaligoura, Z. (2004). Developmental consequences of early parenting experiences: Self-recognition and self-regulation in three cultural communities. *Child Development, 75,* 1745–1760.

Kellett, J. M. (2000). Older adult sexuality. In L. T. Szuchman & F. Muscarella et al. (Eds.), *Psychological perspectives on human sexuality.* New York: Wiley.

Kellman, P., & Arterberry, M. (2006). Infant visual perception. In W. Damon & R. M. Lerner (Eds.), *Handbook of child psychology: Vol. 2, Cognition, perception, and language* (6th ed.). New York: John Wiley & Sons Inc.

Kelly, G. (2001). *Sexuality today: A human perspective.* (7th ed.) New York: McGraw-Hill.

Kemper, R. L., & Vernooy, A. R. (1994). Metalinguistic awareness in first graders: A qualitative perspective. *Journal of Psycholinguistic Research, 22,* 41–57.

Kennell, J. H. (2002). On becoming a family: Bonding and the changing patterns in baby and family behavior. In J. Gomes-Pedro & J. K. Nugent (Eds.), *The infant and family in the twenty-first century*. New York: Brunner-Routledge.

Kenrick, D. T., Keefe, R. C., Bryna, A., Barr, A., & Brown, S. (1995). Age preferences and mate choice among homosexuals and heterosexuals: A case for modular psychological mechanisms. *Journal of Personality and Social Psychology, 69*, 1166–1172.

Kerner, M., & Aboud, F. E. (1998). The importance of friendship qualities and reciprocity in a multi-racial school. *The Canadian Journal of Research in Early Childhood Education, 7*, 117–125.

Kibria, N. (2003). *Becoming Asian American: Second-generation Chinese and Korean American identities*. Baltimore, MD: Johns Hopkins University Press.

Kidwell, J. S., Dunyam, R. M., Bacho, R. A., Pastorino, E., & Portes, P. R. (1995). Adolescent identity exploration: A test of Erikson's theory of transitional crisis. *Adolescence, 30*, 785–793.

Kiecolt, K. J., & Fossett, M. A. (1997). The effects of mate availability on marriage among black Americans: A contextual analysis. In R. J. Taylor, J. S. Jackson, & L. M. Chatters (Eds.), *Family life in black America* (pp. 63–78). Thousand Oaks, CA: Sage.

Killen, M., & Hart, D. (Eds.). (1995). *Morality in everyday life: Developmental perspectives*. New York: Cambridge University Press.

Kilner, J. M., Friston, J. J., & Frith, C. D. (2007). Predictive coding: An account of the mirror neuron system. *Cognitive Processes, 33*, 88–997.

Kim, J. (1995, January). You cannot know how much freedom you have here. *Money*, 133.

Kim, J., & Cicchetti, D. (2003). Social self-efficacy and behavior problems in maltreated children. *Journal of Clinical Child & Adolescent Psychology, 32*, 106–117.

Kim, J-S., Lee, E-H. (2003). Cultural and noncultural predictors of health outcomes in Korean daughter and daughter-in-law caregivers. *Public Health Nursing, 20*, 111–119.

Kim, K., & Smith, P. K. (1999). Family relations in early childhood and reproductive development. *Journal of Reproductive & Infant Psychology, 17*, 133–148.

Kim, S., & Park, H. (2006, January). Five years after the launch of Viagra in Korea: Changes in perceptions of erectile dysfunction treatment by physicians, patients, and the patients' spouses. *Journal of Sexual Medicine, 3*, 132–137.

Kim, U., Triandis, H. C., Kagitçibais, Ç., Choi, S., & Yoon, G. (Eds.). (1994). *Individualism and collectivism: Theory, method, and applications*. Thousand Oaks, CA: Sage.

Kim, Y., Choi, J. Y., Lee, K. M., Park, S. K., Ahn, S. H., Noh, D. Y., Hong, Y. C., Kang, D., & Yoo, K. Y. (2007). Dose-dependent protective effect of breast-feeding against breast cancer among never-lactated women in Korea. *European Journal of Cancer Prevention, 16*, 124–129.

Kim, Y., & Stevens, J. H. (1987). The socialization of prosocial behavior in children. *Childhood Education, 63*, 200–206.

Kimball, J. W. (1983). *Biology* (5th ed.). Reading, MA: Addison-Wesley.

Kim-Cohen, J. (2007). Resilience and developmental psychopathology. *Child and Adolescent Psychiatric Clinics of North America, 16*, 271–283.

Kimm, S. Y., (2003). Nature versus nurture in childhood obesity: A familiar old conundrum. *American Journal of Clinical Nutrition, 78*, 1051–1052.

Kimm, S. Y., Glynn, N. W., Kriska, A. M., Barton, B. A., Kronsberg, S. S., Daniels, S. R., Crawford, P. B., Sabry,

Z. I., & Liu, K. (2002). Decline in physical activity in black girls and white girls during adolescence. *New England Journal of Medicine, 347*, 709–715.

Kimmel, D., & Sang, B. (2003). Lesbians and gay men in midlife. In L. Garnets & D. Kimmel (Eds.), *Psychological perspectives on lesbian, gay, and bisexual experiences*. New York: Columbia University Press.

Kincl, L., Dietrich, K., & Bhattacharya, A. (2006, October). Injury trends for adolescents with early childhood lead exposure. *Journal of Adolescent Health, 39*, 604–606.

King, K. (2003). Racism or sexism? Attributional ambiguity and simultaneous memberships in multiple oppressed groups. *Journal of Applied Social Psychology, 33*, 223–247.

Kinney, H. C., Randall, L. L., Sleeper, L. A., Willinger, M., Beliveau, R. A., Zec, N., Rava, L. A., Dominici, L., Iyasu, S., Randall, B., Habbe, D., Wilson, H., Mandell, F., McClain, M., & Welty, T. K. (2003). Serotonergic brainstem abnormalities in Northern Plains Indians with the sudden infant death syndrome. *Journal of Neuropathology and Experimental Neurology, 62*, 1178–1191.

Kinsey, A. C., Pomeroy, W. B., & Martin, C. E. (1948). *Sexual behavior in the human male*. Philadelphia: Saunders.

Kirby, J. (2006, May). From single-parent families to stepfamilies: Is the transition associated with adolescent alcohol initiation? *Journal of Family Issues, 27*, 685–711.

Kirchengast, S., & Hartmann, B. (2003). Impact of maternal age and maternal-somatic characteristics on newborn size. *American Journal of Human Biology, 15*, 220–228.

Kisilevsky, B. S., Hains, S. M. J., Xing Xie, K. L., Huang, H., Ye, H. H., & Zhang, Z., & Wang, Z. (2003). Effects of experience on fetal voice recognition. *Psychological Science, 14*, 220–224.

Kitchener, R. F. (1996). The nature of the social for Piaget and Vygotsky. *Human Development, 39*, 243–249.

Kitterod, R., & Pettersen, S. (2006, September). Making up for mothers' employed working hours? Housework and childcare among Norwegian fathers? *Work, Employment and Society, 20*, 473–492.

Kitzmann, K., Gaylord, N., & Holt, A. (2003). Child witnesses to domestic violence: A meta-analytic review. *Journal of Consulting & Clinical Psychology, 71*, 339–352.

Klaczynski, P. A. (2004). A dua-process model of adolescent development: Implications for decision making, reasoning, and identity. In R. V. Kail (Ed.), *Advances in child development and behavior, Vol. 32*. San Diego, CA: Elsevier Academic Press.

Kleespies, P. (2004). The wish to die: Assisted suicide and voluntary euthanasia. In P. Kleespies (Ed.), *Life and death decisions: Psychological and ethical considerations in end-of-life care*. Washington, DC: American Psychological Association.

Klier, C. M., Muzik, M., Dervic, K., Mossaheb, N., Benesch, T., Ulm, B., & Zeller, M. (2007). The role of estrogen and progesterone in depression after birth. *Journal of Psychiatric Research, 41*, 273–279.

Kluger, J. (2006, July 10). The new science of siblings. *Time*, 47–55.

Knafo, A., & Plomin, R. (2006). Parental discipline and affection and children's prosocial behavior: Genetic and environmental links. *Journal of Personality and Social Psychology, 90*, 147–164.

Knafo, A., & Schwartz, S. H. (2003). Parenting and accuracy of perception of parental values by adolescents. *Child Development, 73*, 595–611.

Knaus, W. A., Conners, A. F., Dawson, N. V., Desbiens, N. A., Fulkerson, W. J., Jr., Goldman, L., Lynn, J., & Oye, R. K. (1995, November 22). A controlled trial to improve care for seriously ill hospitalized patients. The study to understand prognoses and preferences for outcomes and risks of treatments (SUPPORT). *Journal of the American Medical Association, 273*, 1591–1598.

Knickmeyer, R., & Baron-Cohen, S. (2006, December). Fetal testosterone and sex differences. *Early Human Development, 82*, 755–760.

Knight, K. (1994, March). Back to basics. *Essence*, 122–138.

Knutson, J. F., & Lansing, C. R. (1990). The relationship between communication problems and psychological difficulties in persons with profound acquired hearing loss. *Journal of Speech and Hearing Disorders, 55*, 656–664.

Kochanska, G. (1997). Mutually responsive orientation between mothers and their young children: Implications for early socialization. *Child Development, 68*, 94–112.

Kochanska, G. (1998). Mother–child relationship, child fearfulness, and emerging attachment: A short-term longitudinal study. *Developmental Psychology, 34*, 480–490.

Kochanska, G. (2002). Mutually responsive orientation between mothers and their young children: A context for the early development of conscience. *Current Directions in Psychological Science, 11*, 191–195.

Kochanska, G., & Aksan, N. (2004). Development of mutual responsiveness between parents and their young children. *Child Development, 75*, 1657–1676.

Kodl, M., & Mermelstein, R. (2004). Beyond modeling: Parenting practices, parental smoking history, and adolescent cigarette smoking. *Addictive Behaviors, 29*, 17–32.

Koenig, A., Cicchetti, D., & Rogosch, F. (2004). Moral development: The association between maltreatment and young children's prosocial behaviors and moral transgressions. *Social Development, 13*, 97–106.

Koenig, L. B., McGue, M., Krueger, R. F., & Bouchard, Jr., T. J. (2005). Genetic and environmental influences on religiousness: Findings for retrospective and current religiousness ratings. *Journal of Personality, 73*, 471–488.

Koh, A., & Ross, L. (2006). Mental health issues: A comparison of lesbian, bisexual and heterosexual women. *Journal of Homosexuality, 51*, 33–57.

Kohlberg, L. (1966). A cognitive-developmental anaylsis of children's sex-role concepts and attitudes. In E. E. Maccoby (Ed.), *The development of sex differences*. Stanford, CA: Stanford University Press.

Kohlberg, L. (1984). *The psychology of moral development: Essays on moral development* (Vol. 2). San Francisco: Harper & Row.

Kohn, A. (2006). *The homework myth: Why our kids get too much of a bad thing*. Cambridge, MA: Da Capo Press.

Koivisto, M., & Revonsuo, A. (2003). Object recognition in the cerebral hemispheres as revealed by visual field experiments. *Laterality: Asymmetries of Body, Brain & Cognition, 8*, 135–153.

Kolata, G. (2004, May 11). The heart's desire. *The New York Times*, p. D1.

König, R. (2005). Introduction: Plasticity, learning, and cognition. In R. König, P. Heil, E. Budinger, & H. Scheich (Eds.), *Auditory cortex: A synthesis of human and animal research*. Mahwah, NJ: Lawrence Erlbaum Associates.

Koopmans, S., & Kooijman, A. (2006, November). Presbyopia correction and accommodative intraocular lenses. *Gerontechnology, 5*, 222–230.

Koroukian, S. M., Trisel, B., & Rimm, A. A. (1998). Estimating the proportion of unnecessary cesarean sections in Ohio using birth certificate data. *Journal of Clinical Epidemiology, 51*, 1327–1334.

Koska, J., Ksinantova, L., Sebokova, E., Kvetnansky, R., Klimes, I., Chrousos, G., & Pacak, K. (2002). Endocrine regulation of subcutaneous fat metabolism during cold exposure in humans. *Annals of the New York Academy of Science, 967*, 500–505.

Kosmala, K., & Kloszewska, I. (2004). The burden of providing care for Alzheimer's disease patients in Poland. *International Journal of Geriatric Psychiatry, 19*, 191–193.

Koss, M. P., Goodman, L. A., Browne, A., Fitzgerald, L. F., Keita, G. P., & Russo, N. F. (1993). *No safe haven: Violence against women, at home, at work, and in the community.* Final report of the American Psychological Association Women's Programs Office Task Force on Violence Against Women. Washington, DC: American Psychological Association.

Kotre, J., & Hall, E. (1990). *Seasons of life.* Boston: Little, Brown.

Kozulin, A., (2004). Vygotsky's theory in the classroom: Introduction. *European Journal of Psychology of Education, 19*, 3–7.

Kraemer, B., Noll, T., Delsignore, A., Milos, G., Schnyder, U., & Hepp, U. (2006). Finger length ratio (2D:4D) and dimensions of sexual orientation. *Neuropsychobiology, 53*, 210–214.

Krähenbühl, S., & Blades, M. (2006, May). The effect of question repetition within interviews on young children's eyewitness recall. *Journal of Experimental Child Psychology, 94*, 57–67.

Kramer, A. F., Erickson, K. I., & Colcombe, S. J. (2006). Exercise, cognition, and the aging brain. *Journal of Applied Physiology, 101*, 1237–1242.

Kramer, L., Perozynski, L., & Chung, T. (1999). Parental responses to sibling conflict: The effects of development and parent gender. *Child Development, 70*, 1401–1414.

Kramer, M. S. (2003a). Food supplementation during pregnancy and functional outcomes. *Journal of Health, Population and Nutrition, 21*, 81–82.

Kramer, M. S. (2003b). The epidemiology of adverse pregnancy outcomes: An overview. *Journal of Nutrition, 133*, 1592S–1596S.

Krantz, S. G. (1999). Conformal mappings. *American Scientist, 87*, 436.

Krause, N., & Borawski-Clark, E. (1994). Clarifying the functions of social support in later life. *Research on Aging, 16*, 251–279.

Kreitlow, B., & Kreitlow, D. (1997). *Creative planning for the second half of life.* Duluth, MN: Whole Person Associates.

Krishnamoorthy, J. S., Hart, C., & Jelalian, E, (2006). The epidemic of childhood obesity: Review of research and implications for public policy. *Social Policy Report, 19*, 3–19.

Kroger, J. (2000). *Identity development: Adolescence through adulthood.* Thousand Oaks, CA: Sage.

Kroger, J. (2006). *Identity development: Adolescence through adulthood.* Thousand Oaks, CA: Sage Publications.

Krojgaard, P. (2005). Infants' search for hidden persons. *International Journal of Behavioral Development, 29*, 70–79.

Kronenfeld, J. J. (2002). *Health care policy: Issues and trends.* New York: Praeger.

Kronholz, J. (2003, August, 19). Trying to close the stubborn learning gap. *The Wall Street Journal,* pp. B1, B5.

Kronholz, J. (2003, September 2). Head Start program gets low grade. *The Wall Street Journal,* p A4.

Krout, J. A. (1988). Rural versus urban differences in elderly parents' contact with their children. *Gerontologist, 28*, 198–203.

Krueger, G. (2006, September). Meaning-making in the aftermath of sudden infant death syndrome. *Nursing Inquiry, 13*, 163–171.

Krueger, J., & Heckhausen, J. (1993). Personality development across the adult life span: Subjective conceptions vs. cross-sectional contrasts. *Journals of Gerontology, 48*, 100–108.

Kübler-Ross, E. (1969). *On death and dying.* New York: Macmillan.

Kübler-Ross, E. (Ed.). (1975). *Death: The final stage of growth.* Englewood Cliffs, NJ: Prentice-Hall.

Kübler-Ross, E. (1982). *Working it through.* New York: Macmillan.

Kuczynski, L., & Kochanska, G. (1990). Development of children's noncompliance strategies from toddlerhood to age 5. *Developmental Psychology, 26*, 398–408.

Kuhl, P. (2006). *A new view of language acquisition. Language and linguistics in context: Readings and applications for teachers.* Mahwah, NJ: Lawrence Erlbaum.

Kuhl, P., Tsao, F.-M., & Liu, H.-M. (2003). Foreign-language experience in infancy: Effects of short-term exposure and social interaction on phonetic learning. *Proceedings of the National Academy of Sciences, 100*, 9096–9101.

Kuhl, P. K., Andruski, J. E., Chistovich, I. A., Chistovich, L. A., Kozhevnikova, E. V., Ryskina, V. L., Stolyarova, E. I., Sundberg, U., & Lacerda, F. (1997, August 1). Cross-language analysis of phonetic units in language addressed to infants. *Science, 277*, 684–686.

Kuhn, D. (2000). Metacognitive devleopment. *Current Directions in Psychological Science, 9*, 178–181.

Kuhn, D., Garcia-Mila, M., Zohar, A., & Andersen, C. (1995). Strategies of knowledge acquisition. With commentary by S. H. White, D. Klahr, & S. M. Carver, and a reply by D. Kuhn. *Monographs of the Society for Research in Child Development, 60*, 122–137.

Kunkel, D., Wilcox, B. L., Cantor, J., Palmer, E., Linn, S., & Dowrick, P. (2004, February 20). *Report of the APA task force on advertising and children.* Washington, DC: American Psychological Association.

Kunzmann, U., & Baltes, P. (2005). *The psychology of wisdom: Theoretical and empirical challenges.* New York: Cambridge University Press.

Kupersmidt, J. B., & Dodge, K. A. (Eds.). (2004). *Children's peer relations: From development to intervention.* Washington, DC: American Psychological Association.

Kurdek, L. (2002). Predicting the timing of separation and marital satisfaction: An eight-year prospective longitudinal study. *Journal of Marriage & Family, 64*, 163–179.

Kurdek, L. (2003a). Differences between gay and lesbian cohabiting couples. *Journal of Social & Personal Relationships, 20*, 411–436.

Kurdek, L. (2003b). Negative representations of the self/spouse and marital distress. *Personal Relationships, 10*, 511–534.

Kurdek, L. (2006, May). Differences between partners from heterosexual, gay, and lesbian cohabiting couples. *Journal of Marriage and Family, 68*, 509–528.

Kurdek, L. A. (1993). The allocation of household labor in gay, lesbian, and heterosexual married children. *Journal of Social Issues, 49*, 127–139.

Kurdek, L. A. (1999). The nature and predictors of the trajectory of change in marital quality for husbands and wives over the first 10 years of marriage. *Developmental Psychology, 35*, 1283–1296.

Kurtines, W. M., & Gewirtz, J. L. (1987). *Moral development through social interaction.* New York: Wiley.

Kwant, P. B., Finocchiaro, T., Forster, F., Reul, H., Rau, G., Morshuis, M., El Banayosi, A., Korfer, R., Schmitz-Rode, T., & Steinseifer, U. (2007). The MiniACcor: Constructive redesign of an implantable total artificial heart, initial laboratory testing and further steps. *International Journal of Artificial Organs, 30*, 345–351.

La Leche League International. (2003). *Breastfeeding around the world.* Schaumburg, IL: La Leche League International.

Laas, I. (2006). Self-actualization and society: A new application for an old theory. *Journal of Humanistic Psychology, 46*, 77–91.

Labouvie-Vief, G. (1980). Beyond formal operations: Uses and limits of pure logic in life-span development. *Human Development, 23*, 141–161.

Labouvie-Vief, G. (1986). Modes of knowledge and the organization of development. In M. L. Commons, L. Kohlberg, F. Richards, & J. Sinnott (Eds.), *Beyond formal operations 3: Models and methods in the study of adult and adolescent thought.* New York: Praeger.

Labouvie-Vief, G. (1990). Modes of knowledge and the organization of development. In M. L. Commons, C. Armon, L. Kohlberg, F. A. Richards, T. A. Grotzer, & J. Sinnott (Eds.), *Adult development (Vol. 2). Models and methods in the study of adolescent thought.* New York: Praeger.

Labouvie-Vief, G. (2006). Emerging structures of adult thought. In J. J. Arnett & J. L. Tanner (Eds.), *Emerging adults in America: Coming of age in the 21st century.* Washington, DC: American Psychological Association.

Lacerda, F., von Hofsten, C., & Heimann, M. (2001). *Emerging cognitive abilities in early infancy.* Mahwah, NJ: Lawrence Erlbaum Associates.

Lachmann, T., Berti, S., Kujala, T., & Schroger, E. (2005). Diagnostic subgroups of developmental dyslexia have different deficits in neural processing of tones and phonemes. *International Journal of Psychophysiology, 56*, 105–120.

Lackey, C. (2003). Violent family heritage, the transition to adulthood, and later partner violence. *Journal of Family Issues, 24*, 74–98.

Ladd, G., & Petry, N. (2002). Disordered gambling among university-based medical and dental patients: A focus on Internet gambling. *Psychology of Addictive Behaviors, 16*, 76–79.

Ladd, G. W. (1983). Social networks of popular, average and rejected children in social settings. *Merrill-Palmer Quarterly, 29*, 282–307.

Laditka, S., Laditka, J., & Probst, J. (2006). Racial and ethnic disparities in potentially avoidable delivery complications among pregnant Medicaid beneficiaries in South Carolina. *Maternal & Child Health Journal, 10*, 339–350.

Laflamme, D., Pomerleau, A., & Malcuit, G. (2002). A comparison of fathers' and mothers' involvement in childcare and stimulation behaviors during free-play with their infants at 9 and 15 months. *Sex Roles, 47,* 507–518.

LaFromboise, T., Coleman, H. L., & Gerton, J. (1993). Psychological impact of biculturalism: Evidence and theory. *Psychological Bulletin, 114,* 395–412.

Lafuente, M. J., Grifol, R., Segarra, J., & Soriano, J. (1997). Effects of the Firstart method of prenatal stimulation on psychomotor development: The first six months. *Pre- & PeriNatal Psychology, 11,* 151–162.

Lahiri, D. K., Maloney, B., Basha, M. R., Ge, Y. W., & Zawia, N. H. (2007). How and when environmental agents and dietary factors affect the course of Alzheimer's disease: The "LEARn" model (latent early-life associated regulation) may explain the triggering of AD. *Current Alzheimer Research, 4,* 219–228.

Lam, V., & Leman, P. (2003). The influence of gender and ethnicity on children's inferences about toy choice. *Social Development, 12,* 269–287.

Lamaze, F. (1970). *Painless childbirth: The Lamaze method.* Chicago: Regnery.

Lambert, W. E., & Peal, E. (1972). The relation of bilingualism to intelligence. In A. S. Dil (Ed.), *Language, psychology, and culture* (3rd ed.). New York: Wiley.

Lamberts, S. W. J., van den Beld, A. W., & van der Lely, A-J. (1997, October 17). The endocrinology of aging. *Science, 278,* 419–424.

Lamm, B., & Keller, H. (2007). Understanding cultural models of parenting: The role of intracultural variation and response style. *Journal of Cross-Cultural Psychology, 38,* 50–57.

Lamm, H., & Wiesmann, U. (1997). Subjective attributes of attraction: How people characterize their liking, their love, and their being in love. *Personal Relationships, 4,* 271–284.

Lamont, J. A. (1997). Sexuality. In D. E. Stewart & G. E. Robinson (Eds.), *A clinician's guide to menopause. Clinical practice* (pp. 63–75). Washington, DC: Health Press International.

Lamorey, S., Robinson, B. E., & Rowland, B. H. (1998). *Latchkey kids: Unlocking doors for children and their families.* Newbury Park, CA: Sage.

Lanctot, K. L., Herrmann, N., & Mazzotta, P. (2001). Role of serotonin in the behavioral and psychological symptoms of dementia. *Journal of Neuropsychiatry & Clinical Neurosciences, 13,* 5–21.

Landrine, H., & Klonoff, E. A. (1994). Cultural diversity in causal attributions for illness: The role of the supernatural. *Journal of Behavior Medicine, 17,* 181–193.

Landy, F., & Conte, J. M. (2004). *Work in the 21st century.* New York: McGraw-Hill.

Lane, W. K. (1976, November). The relationship between personality and differential academic achievement within a group of highly gifted and high achieving children. *Dissertation Abstracts International, 37(5-A),* 2746.

Langer, E., & Janis, I. (1979). *The psychology of control.* Beverly Hills, CA: Sage.

Langford, P. E. (1995). *Approaches to the development of moral reasoning.* Hillsdale, NJ: Erlbaum.

Lansford, J. E., Chang, L, Dodge, K. A., Malone, P. S., Oburu, P., Palmérus, K., Bacchini, D., Pastorelli, C., Bombi, A. S., Zelli, A., Tapanya, S., Chaudhary, N., Deater-Deckard, K., Manke, B., & Quinn, N. (2005). Physical discipline and children's adjustment: Cultural normativeness as a moderator. *Child Development, 76,* 1234–1246.

Lansford, J. E., & Parker, J. G. (1999). Children's interactions in triads: Behavioral profiles and effects of gender and patterns of friendships among members. *Developmental Psychology, 35,* 80–93.

Larson, R. W., Clore, G. L., & Wood, G. A. (1999). The emotions of romantic relationships: Do they wreak havoc on adolescents? In W. Furman, B. B. Brown, & C. Feiring (Eds.), *The development of romantic relationships in adolescence.* New York: Cambridge University Press.

Larson, R. W., Richards, M. H., Moneta, G., Holmbeck, G., & Duckett, E. (1996). Changes in adolescents' daily interactions with their families from ages 10 to 18: Disengagement and transformation. *Developmental Psychology, 32,* 744–754.

Laskas, J. (2006, December 17). Dancing with the plumber. *Washington Post Magazine,* W35. Retrieved March 3, 2007 from LexisNexis Academic.

Lau, I., Lee, S., & Chiu, C. (2004). Language, cognition, and reality: Constructing shared meanings through communication. In M. Schaller & C. Crandall (Eds.), *The psychological foundations of culture.* Mahwah, NJ: Lawrence Erlbaum Associates.

Lau, S., & Kwok, L. K. (2000). Relationship of family environment to adolescents' depression and self-concept. *Social Behavior & Personality, 28,* 41–50.

Lauer, J. C., & Lauer, R. H. (1999). *How to survive and thrive in an empty nest.* Oakland, CA: New Harbinger Publications.

Laugharne, J., Janca, A., & Widiger, T. (2007). Post-traumatic stress disorder and terrorism: 5 years after 9/11. *Current Opinion in Psychiatry, 20,* 36–41.

Laumann, E. O., Paik, A., & Rosen, R. C. (1999). Sexual dysfunction in the United States: Prevalence and predictors. *Journal of the American Medical Association, 281,* 537–544.

Laursen, B., Hartup, W. W., & Koplas, A. L. (1996). Towards understanding peer conflict. *Merrill-Palmer Quarterly, 42,* 76–102.

Lauter, J. L. (1998). Neuroimaging and the trimodal brain: Applications for developmental communication neuroscience. *Phoniatrica et Logopaedica, 50,* 118–145.

Lavelli, M., & Fogel, A. (2005). Developmental changes in the relationship between the infant's attention and emotion during early face-to-face communication: The 2-month transition. *Developmental Psychology [serial online], 41,* 265–280.

Lavers-Preston, C., & Sonuga-Barke, E. (2003). An intergenerational perspective on parent–child relationships: The reciprocal effects of tri-generational grandparent–parent–child relationships. In R. Gupta & D. Parry-Gupta (Eds.), *Children and parents: Clinical issues for psychologists and psychiatrists.* London: Whurr Publishers, Ltd.

Lavzer, J. I., & Goodson, B. D., (2006). The "quality" of early care and education settings: Definitional and measurement issues. *Evaluation Review, 30,* 556–576.

Lawton, M. P. (2001). Emotion in later life. *Current Directions in Psychological Science, 10,* 120–123.

Lawton, M. P., Kleban, M. H., Moss, M., Rovine, M., & Glicksman, A. (1989). Measuring caregiving appraisal. *Journal of Gerontology: Psychological Sciences, 44,* 61–71.

Lazarus, R. S. (1968). Emotions and adaptations: Conceptual and empirical relations. In W. Arnold (Ed.), *Nebraska symposium on motivation.* Lincoln: University of Nebraska.

Lazarus, R. S. (1991). *Emotion and adaptation.* New York: Oxford University Press.

Lazarus, R. S., & Folkman, S. (1984). *Stress, appraisal, and coping.* New York: Springer.

Leaper, C. (2002). Parenting girls and boys. In M. Bornstein (Ed.), *Handbook of parenting: Vol. 1: Children and parenting.* Mahwah, NJ: Lawrence Erlbaum Associates.

Leaper, C., Anderson, K. J., & Sanders, P. (1998). Moderators of gender effects on parents' talk to their children: A meta-analysis. *Developmental Psychology, 34,* 3–27.

Leaper, C., & Smith, T. E. (2004). A meta-analytic review of gender variations in children's language use: Talkativeness, affiliative speech, and assertive speech. *Developmental Psychology, 40,* 993–1002.

Leary, W. E. (1996, November 20). U.S. rate of sexual diseases highest in developed world. *The New York Times,* p. C1.

Leathers, H. D., & Foster, P. (2004). *The world food problem: Tackling causes of undernutrition in the third world.* Boulder, CO: Lynne Rienner Publishers.

Leathers, S., and Kelley, M. (2000). Unintended pregnancy and depressive symptoms among first-time mothers and fathers. *American Journal of Orthopsychiatry, 70,* 523–531.

Leavitt, L. A., & Goldson, E. (1996). Introduction to special section: Biomedicine and developmental psychology: New areas of common ground. *Developmental Psychology, 32,* 387–389.

Lecours, A. R. (1982). Correlates of developmental behavior in brain maturation. In T. Bever (Ed.), *Regressions in mental development.* Hillsdale, NJ: Erlbaum.

Lee, B. H., Schofer, J. L., & Koppelman, F. S. (2005). Bicycle safety helmet legislation and bicycle-related nonfatal injuries in California. *Accidental Analysis and Prevention, 37,* 93–102.

Lee, K., & Homer, B. (1999). Children as folk psychologists: The developing understanding of the mind. In A. Slater & D. Muir (Eds.), *The Blackwell reader in developmental psychology.* Malden, England: Blackwell.

Lee, M., Vernon-Feagans, L., & Vazquez, A. (2003). The influence of family environment and child temperament on work/family role strain for mothers and fathers. *Infant & Child Development, 12,* 421–439.

Lee, R. M. (2005). Resilience against discrimination: Ethnic identity and other-group orientation as protective factors for Korean Americans. *Journal of Counseling Psychology, 52,* 36–44.

Leenaars, A. A., & Shneidman, E. S. (Eds.). (1999). *Lives and deaths: Selections from the works of Edwin S. Shneidman.* New York: Bruuner-Routledge.

Lefkowitz, E. S., Sigman, M., & Kit-fong Au, T. (2000). Helping mothers discuss sexuality and AIDS with adolescents. *Child Development, 71,* 1383–1394.

Legerstee, M., Anderson, D., & Schaffer, A. (1998). Five- and eight-month-old infants recognize their faces and voices as familiar and social stimuli. *Child Development, 69,* 37–50.

Lehman, D., Chiu, C., & Schaller, M. (2004). Psychology and culture. *Annual Review of Psychology, 55,* 689–714.

Lehr, U., Seiler, E., & Thomae, H. (2000). Aging in a cross-cultural perspective. In A. L. Comunian, & U. P. Gielen (Eds.), *International perspectives on human development.* Lengerich, Germany: Pabst Science Publishers.

Lemonick, M. D. (2000, October 30). Teens before their time. *Time, 67,* 68–74.

Leonard, C. M., Lombardino, L. J., Mercado, L. R., Browd, S. R., Breier, J. I., & Agee, O. F. (1996). Cerebral asymmetry and cognitive development in children: A magnetic resonance imaging study. *Psychological Science, 7,* 89–95.

Leonard, T. (2005, March 22). Need parenting help? Call your coach. *The Daily Telegraph (London),* p. 15.

Lepore, S. J., Palsane, M. N., & Evans, G. W. (1991). Daily hassles and chronic strains: A hierarchy of stressors? *Social Science and Medicine, 33,* 1029–1036.

Lerner, J. W. (2002). *Learning disabilities: Theories, diagnosis, and teaching strategies.* Boston: Houghton Mifflin.

Lerner, R. M., Fisher, C. B., & Weinberg, R. A. (2000). Toward a science for and of the people: Promoting civil society through the application of developmental science. *Child Development, 71,* 11–20.

Lerner, R. M., Theokas, C., & Jelicic, H. (2005). Youth as active agents in their own positive development: A developmental systems perspective. In W. Greve, K. Rothermund, & D. Wentura, *Adaptive self: Personal continuity and intentional self-development.* Ashland, OH: Hogrefe & Huber Publishers.

Lesko, A., & Corpus, J. (2006, January). Discounting the difficult: How high math-identified women respond to stereotype threat. *Sex Roles, 54,* 113–125.

Leslie, C. (1991, February 11). Classrooms of Babel. *Newsweek,* 56–57.

Lesner, S. (2003). Candidacy and management of assistive listening devices: Special needs of the elderly. *International Journal of Audiology, 42,* 2S68–2S76.

Lester, D. (1996). Psychological issues in euthanasia, suicide, and assisted suicide. *Journal of Social Issues, 52,* 51–62.

Lester, D. (2006, December). Sexual orientation and suicidal behavior. *Psychological Reports, 99,* 923–924.

Leung, C., Pe-Pua, R., & Karnilowicz, W. (2006, January). Psychological adaptation and autonomy among adolescents in Australia: A comparison of Anglo-Celtic and three Asian groups. *International Journal of Intercultural Relations, 30,* 99–118.

Leung, K. (2005). Special issue: Cross-cultural variations in distributive justice perception. *Journal of Cross-Cultural Psychology, 36,* 6–8.

Levano, K. J., Cunningham, F. G., Nelson, S., Roark, M., Williams, M. L., Guzick, D., Dowling, S., Rosenfeld, C. R., & Buckley, A. (1986). A prospective comparison of selective and universal electronic fetal monitoring in 34,995 pregnancies. *New England Journal of Medicine, 315,* 615–619.

LeVay, S., & Valente, S. M. (2003). *Human sexuality.* Sunderland, MA: Sinauer Associates.

Levenson, R. W., Carstensen, L. L., & Gottman, J. M. (1993). Long-term marriage: Age, gender, and satisfaction. *Psychology and Aging, 8,* 301–313.

Levick, S. E. (2004). *Clone being: Exploring the psychological and social dimensions.* Lanham, MD: Rowman & Littlefield.

Levine, R. (1994). *Child care and culture.* Cambridge: Cambridge University Press.

Levine, R. (1997a, November). The pace of life in 31 countries. *American Demographics,* 20–29.

Levine, R. (1997b). A *geography of time: The temporal misadventures of a social psychologist, or how every culture keeps time just a little bit differently.* New York: HarperCollins.

Levine, R. V. (1993, February). Is love a luxury? *American Demographics,* 29–37.

Levine, S. C., Huttenlocher, J., Taylor, A., & Langrock, A. (1999). Early sex differences in spatial skill. *Developmental Psychology, 35,* 940–949.

Levinson, D. (1992). *The seasons of a woman's life.* New York: Knopf.

Levinson, D. J. (1986). A conception of adult development. *American Psychologist, 41,* 3–13.

Levy, B. L., & Langer, E. (1994). Aging free from negative stereotypes: Successful memory in China and among the American deaf. *Journal of Personality and Social Psychology, 66,* 989–997.

Levy, B. R., (2003). Mind matters: Cognitive and physical effects of aging self-stereotypes. *Journal of Gerontology: Series B: Psychological Sciences and Social Sciences, 58B,* P203–P211.

Levy, B. R., Slade, M. D., & Kasl, S. V. (2002). Longitudinal benefit of positive self-perceptions of aging on functioning health. *Journal of Gerontology: Psychological Sciences, 57,* 166–195.

Levy, B. R., Slade, M. D., Kunkel, S. R., & Kasl, S. V. (2004). Longevity increased by positive self-perceptions of aging. *Journal of Personality and Social Psychology, 83,* 261–270.

Levy-Shiff, R. (1994). Individual and contextual correlates of marital change across the transition to parenthood. *Developmental Psychology, 30,* 591–601.

Lewin, T. (1995, May 11). Women are becoming equal providers: Half of working women bring home half the household income. *The New York Times,* p. A14.

Lewin, T. (2003, December 22). For more people in their 20s and 30s, going home is easier because they never left. *The New York Times,* p. A27.

Lewin, T. (2003, October 29). A growing number of video viewers watch from crib. *The New York Times,* pp. A1, A22.

Lewin, T. (2005, December 15). See baby touch a screen: But does baby get it? *The New York Times,* p. A1.

Lewis, B., Legato, M., & Fisch, H. (2006). Medical implications of the male biological clock. *JAMA: Journal of the American Medical Association, 296,* 2369–2371.

Lewis, C., & Lamb, M. (2003). Fathers' influences on children's development: The evidence from two-parent families. *European Journal of Psychology of Education, 18,* 211–228.

Lewis, C., & Mitchell, P. (Eds.). (1994). *Children's early understanding of mind: Origins and development.* Hillsdale, NJ: Erlbaum.

Lewis, C. S. (1958). *The allegory of love: A study in medieval traditions.* New York: Oxford University Press.

Lewis, C. S. (1985). A grief observed. In E. S. Shneidman (Ed.), *Death: Current perspectives* (3rd ed.). Palo Alto, CA: Mayfield.

Lewis, M., Feiring, C., & Rosenthal, S. (2000). Attachment over time. *Child Development, 71,* 707–720.

Lewis, M., & Ramsay, D. (2004). Development of self-recognition, personal pronoun use, and pretend play during the 2nd year. *Child Development, 75,* 1821–1831.

Lewis, R., Freneau, P., & Roberts, C. (1979). Fathers and the postparental transition. *Family Coordinator, 28,* 514–520.

Lewis, T. E., & Phillipsen, L. C. (1998). Interactions on an elementary school playground: Variations by age, gender, race, group size, and playground area. *Child Study Journal, 28,* 309–320.

Lewkowicz, D. (2002). Heterogeneity and heterochrony in the development of intersensory perception. *Cognitive Brain Research, 14,* 41–63.

Li, C., DiGiuseppe, R., & Froh, J. (2006, September). The roles of sex, gender, and coping in adolescent depression. *Adolescence, 41,* 409–415.

Li, G. R., & Zhu, X. D. (2007). Development of the functionally total artificial heart using an artery pump. *ASAIO Journal, 53,* 288–291.

Li, J., Laursen, T. M., Precht, D. H., Olsen, J., & Mortensen, P. B. (2005). Hospitalization for mental illness among parents after the death of a child. *New England Journal of Medicine, 352,* 1190–1196.

Li, N. P., Bailey, J. M., Kenrick, D. T., & Linsenmeier, J. A. W. (2002). The necessities and luxuries of mate preferences: Testing the tradeoffs. *Journal of Personality and Social Psychology, 82,* 947–955.

Li, S. (2003). Biocultural orchestration of developmental plasticity across levels: The interplay of biology and culture in shaping the mind and behavior across the life span. *Psychological Bulletin, 129,* 171–194.

Li, Y. F., Langholz, B., Salam, M. T., & Gilliland, F. D. (2005). Maternal and grandmaternal smoking patterns are associated with early childhood asthma. *Chest, 127,* 1232–1241.

Liao, S. (2005). The ethics of using genetic engineering for sex selection. *Journal of Medical Ethics, 31,* 116–118.

Libert, S., Zwiener, J., Chu, X., Vanvoorhies, W., Roman, G., & Pletcher, S. D. (2007, February 23). Regulation of Drosophila life span by olfaction and food-derived odors. *Science, 315,* 1133–1137.

Lickliter, R., & Bahrick, L. E. (2000). The development of infant intersensory perception: Advantages of a comparative convergent-operations approach. *Psychological Bulletin, 126,* 260-280.

Lidz, J., & Gleitman, L. R. (2004). Yes, we still need Universal Grammar: Reply. *Cognition, 94,* 85–93.

Light, L. L. (2000). Memory changes in adulthood. In S. H. Qualls & N. Abeles et al. (Eds.), *Psychology and the aging revolution: How we adapt to longer life* (pp. 73–97). Washington, DC: American Psychological Association.

Lillard, A. (1998). Ethnopsychologies: Cultural variations in theories of mind. *Psychological Bulletin, 123,* 3–32.

Lillard, A., & Else-Quest, N. (2006). Evaluating Montessori education. *Science, 313,* 1893–1894.

Lillard, L. A., & Waite, L. J. (1995). 'Til death do us part: Marital disruption and mortality. *American Journal of Sociology, 100,* 1131–1156.

Lindemann, B. T., & Kadue, D. D. (2003). *Age discrimination in employment law.* Washington, DC: BNA Books.

Lindsay, A., Sussner, K., Kim, J., & Gortmaker, S. (2006). The role of parents in preventing childhood obesity. *The Future of Children, 16,* 169–186.

Lindsey, B. W., & Tropepe, V. (2006). A comparative framework for understanding the biological principles of adult neurogenesis. *Progressive Neurobiology, 80,* 281–307.

Lindsey, E., & Colwell, M. (2003). Preschoolers' emotional competence: Links to pretend and physical play. *Child Study Journal, 33,* 39–52.

Lindstrom, H., Fritsch, T., Petot, G., Smyth, K., Chen, C., Debanne, S., et al. (2005, July). The relationships between television viewing in midlife and the development of Alzheimer's disease in a case-control study. *Brain and Cognition, 58,* 157–165.

Linn, M. C. (1997, September 19). Finding patterns in international assessments. *Science, 277,* 1743.

Lino, Mark. 2001. *Expenditures on children by families, 2000 annual report.* Washington, DC: U.S. Department of Agriculture, Center for Nutrition Policy and Promotion. Miscellaneous Publication No. 1528-2000.

Lippa, R. A. (2003). Are 2D:4D finger-length rations related to sexual orientation? Yes for men, no for women. *Journal of Personality and Social Psychology, 85,* 179–188.

Lipsett, L. (2003). Crib death: A biobehavioral phenomenon? *Current Directions in Psychological Science, 12,* 164–170.

Lipsitt, L. P. (1986a). Toward understanding the hedonic nature of infancy. In L. P. Lipsitt & J. H. Cantor (Eds.), *Experimental child psychologist: Essays and experiments in honor of Charles C. Spiker* (pp. 97–109). Hillsdale, NJ: Erlbaum.

Liskin, L. (1985, Nov.–Dec.). Youth in the 1980s: Social and health concerns: 4. *Population Reports, 85.*

Litovsky, R. Y., & Ashmead, D. H. (1997). Development of binaural and spatial hearing in infants and children. In R. H. Gilkey & T. R. Andersen (Eds.), *Binaural and spatial hearing in real and virtual environments* (pp. 571–592). Mahwah, NJ: Erlbaum.

Litrownik, A., Newton, R., & Hunter, W. (2003). Exposure to family violence in young at-risk children: A longitudinal look at the effects of victimization and witnessed physical and psychological aggression. *Journal of Family Violence, 18,* 59–73.

Little, T., Miyashita, T., & Karasawa, M. (2003). The links among action-control beliefs, intellective skill, and school performance in Japanese, US, and German school children. *International Journal of Behavioral Development, 27,* 41–48.

Little, T. D., & Lopez, D. F., (1997). Regularities in the development of children's causality beliefs about school performance across six sociocultural contexts. *Developmental Psychology, 33,* 165–175.

Litzinger, S., & Gordon, K. (2005, October). Exploring relationships among communication, sexual satisfaction, and marital satisfaction. *Journal of Sex & Marital Therapy, 31,* 409–424.

Liu, H., Kuhl, P., & Tsao, F. (2003). An association between mothers' speech clarity and infants' speech discrimination skills. *Developmental Science, 6,* F1–F10.

Livson, N., & Peskin, H. (1980). Perspectives on adolescence from longitudinal research. In J. Adelson (Ed.), *Handbook of adolescent psychology.* New York: Wiley.

Lobo, R. A., Beliske, S., Creasman, W. T., Frankel, N. R., Goodman, N. F., Hall, J. E., Ivey, S. L., Kingsberg, S., Langer, R., Lehman, R., McArthur, D. B., Montgomery-Rice, V., Notelovitz, M., Packing, G. S., Rebar, R. W., Rousseau, M., Schenken, R. S., Schneider, D. L., Sherif, K., & Wysocki, S. (2006). Should symptomatic menopausal women be offered hormone therapy? *Medscape General Medicine, 8,* 40.

Lock, R. D. (1992). *Taking charge of your career direction* (2nd ed.). Pacific Grove, CA: Brooks/Cole.

Loeb, S., Fuller, B., Kagan, S. L., & Carrol, B. (2004). Child care in poor communities: Early learning effects of type, quality and stability. *Child Development, 75,* 47–65.

Loehlin, J. C., Neiderhiser, J. M., & Reiss, D. (2005). Genetic and environmental components of adolescent adjustment and parental behavior: A multivariate analysis. *Child Development, 76,* 1104–1115.

Loftus, E. F. (2003, November). Make-believe memories. *American Psychologist,* 867–873.

Loftus, E. F. (2006). Memories of things unseen. *Current Directions in Psychological Science, 13,* 145–147.

Loftus, E. F., & Bernstein, D. M. (2005). Rich false memories: The royal road to success. In A. F. Healy, *Experimental cognitive psychology and its applications.* Washington, DC: American Psychological Association.

London, K., Bruck, M., & Ceci, S. J. (2005). Disclosure of child sexual abuse: What does the research tell us about the ways that children tell? *Psychology, Public Policy, & Law, 11,* 194–226.

Lonetto, R. (1980). *Children's conception of death.* New York: Springer.

Long, T., & Long, L. (1983). *Latchkey children.* New York: Penguin.

Lorenz, K. (1957). Companionship in bird life. In C. Scholler (Ed.), *Instinctive behavior.* New York: International Universities Press.

Lorenz, K. (1966). *On aggression.* New York: Harcourt Brace Jovanovich.

Lorenz, K. (1974). *Civilized man's eight deadly sins.* New York: Harcourt Brace Jovanovich.

Lorenz, K. Z. (1965). *Evolution and the modification of behavior.* Chicago: University of Chicago Press.

Lourenco, O., & Machado, A. (1996). In defense of Piaget's theory: A reply to 10 common criticisms. *Psychological Review, 103,* 143–164.

Love, J. M., Harrison, L., & Sagi-Schwaratz, A. (2003). Child care quality matters: How conclusions may vary with context. *Child Development, 74,* 1021–1033.

Love, J. M., Harrison, L., Sagi-Schwartz, A., van Ijzendoorn, M. H., Ross, C., Ungerer, J. A., Raikes, H., Brady-Smith, C., Boller, K., Brooks-Gunn, J., Constantine, J., Kisker, E. E., Paulsell, D., & Chazan-Cohen, R. (2003). Child care quality matters: How conclusions may vary with context. *Child Development, 74,* 1021–1033.

Lowe, M. R., & Timko, C. A. (2004). What a difference a diet makes: Towards an understanding of differences between restrained dieters and restrained nondieters. *Eating Behaviors, 5,* 199–208.

Lowrey, G. H. (1986). *Growth and development of children* (8th ed.). Chicago: Year Book Medical Publishers.

Lowton, K., & Higginson, I. (2003). Managing bereavement in the classroom: A conspiracy of silence? *Death Studies, 27,* 717–741.

Lu, M. C., Prentice, J., Yu, S. M., Inkelas, M., Lange, L. O., & Halfon, N. (2003). Childbirth education classes: Sociodemographic disparities in attendance and the association of attendance with breastfeeding initiation. *Maternal Child Health, 7,* 87–93.

Lu, L. (2006). The transition to parenthood: Stress, resources, and gender differences in a Chinese society. *Journal of Community Psychology, 34,* 471–488.

Lu, T., Pan, Y., Lap. S-Y., Li, C., Kohane, I., Chang, J., & Yankner, B. A. (2004, June 9). Gene regulation and DNA damage in the aging human brain. *Nature,* 1038.

Lu, X. (2001). Bicultural identity development and Chinese community formation: An ethnographic study of Chinese schools in Chicago. *Howard Journal of Communications, 12,* 203–220.

Lubinski, D. (2004). Introduction to the special section on cognitive abilities: 100 years after Spearman's (1904) "'General Intelligence,' objectively determined and measured." *Journal of Personality and Social Psychology, 86,* 96–111.

Lubinski, D., & Benbow, C. P. (2001). Choosing excellence. *American Psychologist, 56,* 76–77.

Lucas, R. E. (2005). Time does not heal all wounds: A longitudinal study of reaction and adaptation to divorce. *Psychological Science, 16,* 945–951.

Lucas, S. R., & Berends, M. (2002). Sociodemographic diversity, correlated achievement, and de facto tracking. *Sociology of Education, 75,* 328–349.

Lundberg, U. (2006, July). Stress, subjective and objective health. *International Journal of Social Welfare, 15,* S41–S48.

Luo, L. (2006). The transition to parenthood: Stress, resources, and gender differences in a Chinese society. *Journal of Community Psychology, 34,* 471–488.

Luthar, S. S., Cicchetti, D., & Becker, B. (2000). The construct of resilience: A critical evaluation and guidelines for future work. *Child Development, 71,* 543–562.

Lyall, S. (2004, February 15). In Europe, lovers now propose: Marry me, a little. *The New York Times,* p. D2.

Lye, T. C., Piguet, O., Grayson, D. A., Creasey, H., Ridley, L. J., Bennett, H. P., & Broe, G. A. (2004). Hippocampal size and memory function in the ninth and tenth decades of life: The Sydney Older Persons Study. *Journal of Neurology, Neurosurgery, and Psychiatry, 75,* 548–554.

Lykken, D., Bouchard, T., McGue, M., & Tellegen, A. (1993a). Heritability of interests: A twin study. *Journal of Applied Psychology, 78,* 649–661.

Lykken, D. T., McGue, M., Tellegen, A., & Bouchard, T. J., Jr. (1993b). Emergenesis: Genetic traits that may not run in families. *American Psychologist, 47,* 1565–1577.

Lymberis, S. C., Parhar, P. K., Katsoulakis, E., & Formenti, S. C. (2004). Pharmacogenomics and breast cancer. *Pharmacogenomics, 5,* 31–55.

Lynam, D. R. (1996). Early identification of chronic offenders: Who is the fledgling psychopath? *Psychological Bulletin, 120,* 209–234.

Lynch, M. E., Coles, C. D., & Corely, T. (2003). Examining delinquency in adolescents: Risk factors. *Journal of Studies on Alcohol, 64,* 678–686.

Lynn J., Teno, J. M., Phillips, R. S., Wu, A. W., Desbiens, N., Harrold J., Claessens, M. T., Wenger, N., Kreling, B., & Connors, A. F., Jr. (1997). Perceptions by family members of the dying experience of older and seriously ill patients. SUPPORT Investigators. Study to Understand Prognoses and Preferences for Outcomes and Risks of Treatments [see comments]. *Annals of Internal Medicine, 126,* 164–165.

Lynne, S., Graber, J., Nichols, T., Brooks-Gunn, J., & Botvin, G. (2007, February). Links between pubertal timing, peer influences, and externalizing behaviors among urban students followed through middle school. *Journal of Adolescent Health, 40,* 35–44.

Lyon, M. E., Benoit, M., O'Donnell, R. M., Getson, P. R., Silber, T., & Walsh, T. (2000). Assessing African American adolescents' risk for suicide attempts: Attachment theory. *Adolescence, 35,* 121–134.

Lyons, M. J., Bar, J. L., & Kremen, W. S. (2002). Nicotine and familial vulnerability to schizophrenia: A discordant twin study. *Journal of Abnormal Psychology, 111,* 687–693.

Lyons, T. H. (2007). Attachment theory and reactive attachment disorder: Theoretical perspectives and treatment implications. *Journal of Child and Adolescent Psychiatric Nursing, 20,* 27–40.

Ma, H., Bernstein, L., Pike, M. C., & Ursin, G. (2006). Reproductive factors and breast cancer risk according to joint estrogen and progesterone receptor status: A meta-analysis of epidemiological studies. *Breast Cancer Research, 8,* R43.

Mabbott, D. J., Noseworthy, M., Bouffet, E., Laughlin, S., & Rockel, C. (2006). White matter growth as a mechanism of cognitive development in children. *Neuroimaging, 15,* 936–946.

Maccoby, E. B. (1999). *The two sexes : Growing up apart, coming together.* New York: Belknap.

Maccoby, E. E. (1980). *Social development: Psychological growth and the parent–child relationship.* New York: Harcourt, Brace, Jovanovich.

Maccoby, E. E., & Lewis, C. C. (2003). Less day care or different day care? *Child Development, 74,* 1069–1075.

MacDonald, G. (2007, January 25). Montessori looks back—and ahead: As name marks 100 years, movement is taking stock. *USA Today,* p. 9D.

MacDonald, S., Hultsch, D., & Dixon, R. (2003). Performance variability is related to change in cognition: Evidence from the Victoria Longitudinal Study. *Psychology & Aging, 18,* 510–523.

MacDonald, W. (2003). The impact of job demands and workload stress and fatigue. *Australian Psychologist, 38,* 102–117.

MacDorman, M. F., Martin, J. A., Mathews, T. J., Hoyert, D. L., & Ventura, S. J. (2005). Explaining the 2001–02 infant mortality increase: Data from the linked birth/infant death data set. *National Vital Statistics Report, 53,* 1–22.

Macionis, J. J. (2001). *Sociology.* Upper Saddle River, NJ: Prentice Hall.

Mackenzie, K., & Peters, M. (2000). Handedness, hand roles, and hand injuries at work. *Journal of Safety Research, 31,* 221–227.

Mackey, M. C. (1990). Women's preparation for the childbirth experience. *Maternal-Child Nursing Journal, 19,* 143–173.

MacPhee, D., Kreutzer, J. C., & Fritz, J. J. (1994). Infusing a diversity perspective into human development courses. *Child Development, 65,* 699–715.

Maddi, S. R., (2006). Hardiness: The courage to grow from stresses. *Journal of Positive Psychology, 1,* 160–168.

Maddi, S. R., Harvey, R. H., Khoshaba, D. M., Lu, J. L., Persico, M., & Brow, M. (2006). The personality construct of hardiness, III: Relationships with repression, innovativeness, authoritarianism, and performance. *Journal of Personality, 74,* 575–598.

Maddox, G. L., & Campbell, R. T. (1985). Scope, concepts, and methods in the study of aging. In R. H. Binstock & E. Shanas (Eds.), *Handbook of aging and the social sciences* (2nd ed.). New York: Van Nostrand Reinhold.

Magai, C., & McFadden, S. H. (Eds.). (1996). *Handbook of emotion, adult development, and aging.* New York: Academic Press.

Mahgoub, N., & Lantz, M. (2006, December). When older adults suffer the loss of a child. *Psychiatric Annals, 36,* 877–880.

Makino, M., Hashizume, M., Tsuboi, K., Yasushi, M., & Dennerstein, L. (2006, September). Comparative study of attitudes to eating between male and female students in the People's Republic of China. *Eating and Weight Disorders, 11,* 111–117.

Maller, S. (2003). Best practices in detecting bias in nonverbal tests. In R. McCallum (Ed.), *Handbook of nonverbal assessment.* New York: Kluwer Academic/Plenum Publishers.

Mandel, D. R., Jusczyk, P. W., & Pisoni, D. B. (1995). Infants' recognition of the sound patterns of their own names. *Psychological Science, 6,* 314–317.

Mangan, P. A. (1997, November). *Time perception.* Paper presented at the annual meeting of the Society for Neuroscience, New Orleans.

Mangweth, B., Hausmann, A., & Walch, T. (2004). Body fat perception in eating-disordered men. *International Journal of Eating Disorders, 35,* 102–108.

Manlove, J., Franzetta, K., McKinney, K., Romano-Papillo, A., & Terry-Humen, E.(2004). *No time to waste: Programs to reduce teen pregnancy among middle school-aged youth.* Washington, DC: National Campaign to Prevent Teen Pregnancy.

Mann, C. C. (2005, March 18). Provocative study says obesity may reduce U.S. life expectancy. *Science, 307,* 1716–1717.

Manning, M., & Hoyme, H. (2007). Fetal alcohol spectrum disorders: A practical clinical approach to diagnosis. *Neuroscience & Biobehavioral Reviews, 31,* 230–238.

Manning, W., Giordano, P., & Longmore, M. (2006, September). Hooking up: The relationship contexts of "nonrelationship" sex. *Journal of Adolescent Research, 21,* 459–483.

Manstead, A. S. R. (1997). Situations, belongingness, attitudes, and culture: Four lessons learned from social psychology. In C. McGarty & S. A. Haslam et al. (Eds.), *The message of social psychology: Perspectives on mind in society.* Oxford, England: Blackwell Publishers, Inc.

Mao, A., Burnham, M. M., Goodlin-Jones, B. L., Gaylor, E. E., & Anders, T. F. (2004). A comparison of the sleep-wake patterns of cosleeping and solitary-sleeping infants. *Child Psychiatry and Human Development, 35,* 95–105.

Marchant, M., Young, K. R., & West, R. P. (2004). The effects of parental teaching on compliance behavior of children. *Psychology in the Schools, 41,* 337–350.

Marcia, J. E. (1980). Identity in adolescence. In J. Adelson (Ed.), *Handbook of adolescent psychology.* New York: Wiley

Marcovitch, S., Zelazo, P., & Schmuckler, M. (2003). The effect of the number of A trials on performance on the A-not-B task. *Infancy, 3,* 519–529.

Marcus, A. D. (2004, February 3). The new math on when to have kids. *The Wall Street Journal,* pp. D1, D4.

Marczinski, C., Milliken, B., and Nelson, S. (2003). Aging and repetition effects: Separate specific and nonspecific influences. *Psychology & Aging, 18,* 780–790.

Markus, H. R., & Kitayama, S. (1991). Culture and the self: Implications for cognition, emotion, and motivation. *Psychological Review, 98,* 224–253.

Marlier, L., Schaal, B., & Soussignan, R. (1998). Neonatal responsiveness to the odor of amniotic and lacteal fluids: A test of perinatal chemosensory continuity. *Child Development, 69,* 611–623.

Marmar, C. R., Neylan, T. C., & Schoenfeld, F. B. (2002). New directions in the pharmacotherapy of posttraumatic stress disorder. *Psychiatric Quarterly, 73,* 259–270.

Marsh, H., & Hau, K. (2004). Explaining paradoxical relations between academic self-concepts and achievements: Cross-cultural generalizability of the internal/external frame of reference predictions across 26 countries. *Journal of Educational Psychology, 96,* 56–67.

Marsh, H., Ellis, L., & Craven, R. (2002). How do preschool children feel about themselves? Unraveling measurement and multidimensional self-concept structure. *Developmental Psychology, 38,* 376–393.

Marsh, H. E., Craven, R., & Debus, R. (1998). Structure, stability, and development of young children's self-concepts: A multicohort-multioccasion study. *Child Development, 69,* 1030–1053.

Marsh, H. W., & Ayotte, V. (2003). Do multiple dimensions of self-concept become more differentiated with age? The differential distinctiveness hypothesis. *International Review of Education, 49,* 463.

Marsh, H. W., & Hau, K. T. (2003). Big-fish-little-pond effect on academic self-concept. *American Psychologist, 58,* 364–376.

Marshall, E. (2000, November 17). Planned Ritalin trial for tots heads into uncharted waters. *Science, 290,* 1280–1282.

Martikainen, P., & Valkonen, T. (1996). Mortality after the death of a spouse: Rates and causes of death in a large Finnish cohort. *American Journal of Public Health, 86,* 1087–1093.

Martin, C., & Fabes, R. (2001). The stability and consequences of young children's same-sex peer interactions. *Developmental Psychology, 37,* 431–446.

Martin, C. L. (1993). New directions for investigating children's gender knowledge. *Developmental Review, 13,* 184–204.

Martin, C. L. (2000). Cognitive theories of gender development. In T. Eckes & H. M. Trautner et al. (Eds.), *The developmental social psychology of gender.* Mahwah, NJ: Erlbaum.

Martin, C. L., & Ruble, D. (2004). Children's search for gender cues: Cognitive perspectives on gender development. *Current Directions in Psychological Science, 13,* 67–70.

Martin, C. L., Ruble, D. N., & Szkrybalo, J. (2002). Cognitive theories of early gender development. *Psychological Bulletin, 128,* 903–933.

Martin, J., & D'Augelli, A. (2003). How lonely are gay and lesbian youth? *Psychological Reports, 93,* 486.

Martin, J. A., Hamilton, B. E., Sutton, P. D., Ventura, S. J., Menacker, F., & Munson, M. L. (2005). Births: Final data for 2003. *National Vital Statistics Reports, 54,* Table J, p. 21.

Martin, P., Martin, D., & Martin, M. (2001). Adolescent premarital sexual activity, cohabitation, and attitudes toward marriage. *Adolescence, 36,* 601–609.

Martin, S., Li, Y., Casanueva, C., Harris-Britt, A., Kupper, L., & Cloutier, S. (2006). Intimate partner violence and women's depression before and during pregnancy. *Violence Against Women, 12,* 221–239.

Martin, W., & Freitas, M. (2002). Mean mortality among Brazilian left- and right-handers: Modification or selective elimination. *Laterality, 7,* 31–44.

Martins, S. S., Storr, C. L., Ialongo, N. S., & Chilcoat, H. D. (2007). Mental health and gambling in urban female adolescents. *Journal of Adolescent Health, 40,* 463–465.

Masataka, N. (1996). Perception of motherese in a signed language by 6-month-old deaf infants. *Developmental Psychology, 32,* 874–879.

Masataka, N. (1998). Perception of motherese in Japanese sign language by 6-month-old hearing infants. *Developmental Psychology, 34,* 241–246.

Masataka, N. (2000). The role of modality and input in the earliest stage of language acquisition: Studies of Japanese sign language. In C. Chamerlain & J. P. Morford (Eds.), *Language acquisition by eye.* Mahwah, NJ: Lawrence Erlbaum Associates.

Masataka, N. (2006). Preference for consonance over dissonance by hearing newborns of deaf parents and of hearing parents. *Developmental Science, 9,* 46–50.

Mash, E. J., & Barkley, R. A., (Eds.), (2003). *Child psychopathology* (2nd ed.). New York: Guilford Press.

Masling, J. M., & Bornstein, R. F. (Eds.). (1996). *Psychoanalytic perspectives on developmental psychology.* Washington, DC: American Psychological Association.

Maslow, A. H. (1970). *Motivation and personality* (2nd ed.). New York: Harper & Row.

Masters, W. H., Johnson, V., & Kolodny, R. C. (1982). *Human sexuality.* Boston: Little, Brown.

Matlin, M. (2003). From menarche to menopause: Misconceptions about women's reproductive lives. *Psychology Science, 45,* 106–122.

Matlin, M. M. (1987). *The psychology of women*. New York: Holt.

Maton, K. I., Schellenbach, C. J., Leadbeater, B. J., & Solarz, A. L. (Eds.). (2004). *Investing in children, youth, families and communities*. Washington, DC: American Psychological Association.

Matsumoto, A. (1999). *Sexual differentiation of the brain*. Boca Raton, FL: CRC Press.

Matsumoto, D., & Yoo, S. H. (2006). Toward a new generation of cross-cultural research. *Perspectives on Psychological Science, 1*, 234–250.

Matthews, K. A. (1982). Psychological perspectives on the Type A behavior pattern. *Psychological Bulletin, 91*, 293–323.

Matthews, K. A., Wing, R. R., Kuller, L. H., Meilahn, E. N., & Owens, J. F. (2000). Menopause as a turning point in midlife. In S. B. Manuck, & R. Jennings et al. (Eds.), *Behavior, health, and aging*. Mahwah, NJ: Erlbaum.

Mattson, S., Calarco, K., & Lang, A. (2006). Focused and shifting attention in children with heavy prenatal alcohol exposure. *Neuropsychology, 20*, 361–369.

Matusov, E., & Hayes, R. (2000). Sociocultural critique of Piaget and Vygotsky. *New Ideas in Psychology, 18*, 215–239.

Mauritzson, U., & Saeljoe, R. (2001). Adult questions and children's responses: Coordination of perspectives in studies of children's theories of other minds. *Scandinavian Journal of Educational Research, 45*, 213–231.

Maxwell, L. (2007, March). Competency in child care settings: The role of the physical environment. *Environment and Behavior, 39*, 229–245.

Mayer, J. D. (2001). Emotion, intelligence, and emotional intelligence. In J. P. Forgas (Ed.), *Handbook of affect and social cognition*. Mahwah, NJ: Erlbaum.

Mayer, J. D., Salovey, P., & Caruso, D. R. (2000). Emotional intelligence as zeitgeist, as personality, and as a mental ability. In R. Bar-On, J. D. A. Parker, & D. A. James (Eds.), *The handbook of emotional intelligence: Theory, development, assessment, and application at home, school, and in the workplace*. San Francisco, CA: Jossey-Bass.

Mayer, J. D., Salovey, P., & Caruso, D. R. (2004). Emotional intelligence: Theory, findings, and implications. *Psychological Inquiry, 15*, 197–215.

Mayes, L. C., & Lombroso, P. J. (2003). Genetics of childhood disorders: L.V. prenatal drug exposure. *Journal of the American Academy of Child and Adolescent Psychiatry, 42*, 1258–1261.

Mayo Clinic. (2000, March). Age-related macular degeneration: Who gets it and what you can do about it. *Women's Healthsource, 4*, 1–2.

Mayseless, O. (1996). Attachment patterns and their outcomes. *Human Development, 39*, 206–223.

McAdams, D., & Logan, R. (2004). What is generativity? In E. de St. Aubin & D. McAdams (Eds.), *Generative society: Caring for future generations* (pp. 15–31). Washington, DC: American Psychological Association.

McAlister, A., & Peterson, C. (2006, November). Mental playmates: Siblings, executive functioning and theory of mind. *British Journal of Developmental Psychology, 24*, 733–751.

McArdle, E. F. (2002). New York's Do-Not-Resuscitate law: Groundbreaking protection of patient autonomy or a physician's right to make medical futility determinations? *DePaul Journal of Health Care Law, 8*, 55–82.

McAuley, E., Kramer, A. F., & Colcombe, S. J. (2004). Cardiovascular fitness and neurocognitive function in older adults: A brief review. *Brain Behavior Immunology, 18*, 214–220.

McAuliffe, S. P., & Knowlton, B. J. (2001). Hemispheric differences in object identification. *Brain & Cognition, 45*, 119–128.

McCall, R. B. (1979). *Infants*. Cambridge, MA: Harvard University Press.

McCarthy, M. J. (1994, November 8). Hunger among elderly surges: Meal programs just can't keep up. *The Wall Street Journal*, pp. A1, A11.

McCartney, M. (2006, March 11). Mind gains: We are living longer but will we be able to keep our minds active enough to enjoy it? *Financial Times* (London, England), p. 1. Retrieved March 4, 2007 from LexisNexis Academic.

McCarty, M., & Ashmead, D. H. (1999). Visual control of reaching and grasping in infants. *Developmental Psychology, 35*, 620–631.

McCaul, K. D., Ployhart, R. E., Hinsz, V. B., & McCaul, H. S. (1995). Appraisals of a consistent versus a similar politician: Voter preferences and intuitive judgments. *Journal of Personality and Social Psychology, 68*, 292–299.

McCauley, K. M. (2007). Modifying women's risk for cardiovascular disease. *Journal of Obstetric and Gynecological Neonatal Nursing, 36*, 116–124.

McClement, S. E., Chochinov, H. M., Hack, T. F., Kristjanson, L. J., & Harlos, M. (2004). Dignity-conserving care: Application of research findings to practice. *International Journal of Palliative Nursing, 10*, 173–179.

McCloskey, L. A., & Bailey, J. A. (2000). The intergenerational transmission of risk for child sexual abuse. *Journal of Interpersonal Violence, 15*, 1019–1035.

McCrae, R., & Costa, P. (2003). *Personality in adulthood: A five-factor theory perspective* (2nd ed.). New York: Guilford Press.

McCrae, R. R., & Costa, P. T., Jr. (1990). *Personality in adulthood*. New York: Guilford.

McCrae, R. R., Costa, P. T., Jr., Ostendorf, F., Angleitner, A., Hebíková, M., Avia, M. D., Sanz, J., Sánchez-Bernardos, M. L., Kusdil, M. E., Woodfield, R., Saunders, P. R., & Smith, P. B. (2000). Nature over nurture: Temperament, personality, and life span development. *Journal of Personality and Social Psychology, 78*, 173–186.

McCrink, K., & Wynn, K. (2004). Large-number addition and subtraction by 9-month-old infants. *Psychological Science, 15*, 776–782.

McCullough, M. E., Tsang, J., & Brion, S. (2003). Personality traits in adolescence as predictors of religiousness in early maturity: Findings from the Terman longitudinal study. *Personality & Social Psychology Bulletin, 29*, 980–991.

McCutcheon-Rosegg, S., Ingraham, E., & Bradley, R. A. (1996). *Natural childbirth the Bradley way: Revised edition*. New York: Plume Books.

McDaniel, A., & Coleman, M. (2003). Women's experiences of midlife divorce following long-term marriage. *Journal of Divorce & Remarriage, 38*, 103–128.

McDonald, K. A. (1999, June 25). Studies of women's health produce a wealth of knowledge on the biology of gender differences. *Chronicle of Higher Education, 45*, pp. A19, A22.

McDonald, L., & Stuart-Hamilton, I. (2003). Egocentrism in older adults: Piaget's three mountains task revisited. *Educational Gerontology, 29*, 417–425.

McDonald, M. A., Sigman, M., Espinosa, M. P., & Neumann, C. G. (1994). Impact of a temporary food shortage on children and their mothers. *Child Development, 65*, 404–415.

McDonnell, L. M. (2004). *Politics, persuasion, and educational testing*. Cambridge, MA: Harvard University Press.

McDonough, L. (2002). Basic-level nouns: First learned but misunderstood. *Journal of Child Language, 29*, 357–377.

McElwain, N., & Booth-LaForce, C. (2006, June). Maternal sensitivity to infant distress and nondistress as predictors of infant–mother attachment security. *Journal of Family Psychology, 20*, 247–255.

McGee, G., Caplan, A., & Malhotra, R. (Eds.). (2004). *The human cloning debate*. Berkeley, CA: Hills Books.

McGlone, M., & Aronson, J. (2006, September). Stereotype threat, identity salience, and spatial reasoning. *Journal of Applied Developmental Psychology, 27*, 486–493.

McGlone, M., Aronson, J., & Kobrynowicz, D. (2006, December). Stereotype threat and the gender gap in political knowledge. *Psychology of Women Quarterly, 30*, 392–398.

McGough, R. (2003, May 20). MRIs take a look at reading minds. *The Wall Street Journal*, p. D8.

McGovern, M., & Barry, M. M. (2000). Death education: Knowledge, attitudes, and perspectives of Irish parents and teachers. *Death Studies, 24*, 325–333.

McGreal, D., Evans, B. J., & Burrows, G. D. (1997). Gender differences in coping following loss of a child through miscarriage or stillbirth: A pilot study. *Stress Medicine, 13*, 159–165.

McGrew, K. S. (2005). The Cattell-Horn-Carroll theory of cognitive abilities: Past, present, and future. In D. P. Flanagan & P. L. Harrison (Eds.), *Contemporary intellectual assessment: Theories, tests, and issues*. New York, Guilford Press.

McGuffin, P., Riley, B., & Plomin, R. (2001, February 16.) Toward behavioral genomics. *Science, 291*, 1232–1233.

McGuinness, D. (1972). Hearing: Individual differences in perceiving. *Perception, 1*, 465–473.

McGuire, S., McHale, S., & Updegraff, K. (1996). Children's perceptions of the sibling relationships in middle childhood: Connections within and between family relationships. *Personal Relationships, 3*, 229–239.

McHale, J. P., & Rotman, T. (2007). Is seeing believing? Expectant parents' outlooks on coparenting and later coparenting solidarity. *Infant Behavior & Development, 30*, 63–81.

McHale, S., Dariotis, J., & Kauh, T. (2003). Social development and social relationships in middle childhood. In R. Lerner & M. Easterbrooks (Eds.), *Handbook of psychology: Developmental psychology, Vol. 6*. New York: John Wiley & Sons, Inc.

McHale, S. M., Kim, J-Y., & Whiteman, S. D. (2006). Sibling relationships in childhood and adolescence. In P. Noller & J. A. Feeney (Eds.), *Close relationships: Functions, forms and processes*. Hove, England: Psychology Press/Taylor & Francis.

McHale, S. M., Shanahan, L., Updegraff, K. A., Crouter, A. C., & Booth, A. (2004). Developmental and individual differences in girls' sex-typed activities in middle childhood and adolescence. *Child Development, 75*, 1575–1593.

McKee, K., Wilson, F., Chung, M., Hinchliff, S., Goudie, F., Elford, H., et al. (2005, November). Reminiscence, regrets and activity in older people in residential care: Associations with psychological health. *British Journal of Clinical Psychology, 44*, 543–561.

McKenna, J. J. (1983). Primate aggression and evolution: An overview of sociobiological and anthropological perspectives. *Bulletin of the American Academy of Psychiatry and the Law, 11*, 105–130.

McKenzie, R. B. (1997). Orphanage alumni: How they have done and how they evaluate their experience. *Child & Youth Care Forum, 26*, 87–111.

McLoyd, V. C., Cauce, A. M., Takeuchi, D., & Wilson, L. (2000). Marital processes and parental socialization in families of color: A decade review of research. *Journal of Marriage and Family, 62,* 1070–1093.

McMillian, M. (2003–2004). Is No Child Left Behind "wise schooling" for African American male students? *High School Journal, 87,* [Special issue: From the simplicity of convention toward the complexity found in human interaction: Teaching learning and administration in high school during the 21st century], 25–33.

McNulty, J. K., & Karney, B. R. (2004). Positive expectations in the early years of marriage: Should couples expect the best or brace for the worst? *Journal of Personality and Social Psychology, 86,* 729–743.

McVittie, C., McKinlay, A., & Widdicombe, S. (2003). Committed to (un)equal opportunities?: "New ageism" and the older worker. *British Journal of Social Psychology, 42,* 595–612.

McWhirter, D. P., Sanders, S., & Reinisch, J. M. (1990). *Homosexuality, heterosexuality: Concepts of sexual orientation.* New York: Oxford University Press.

McWhirter, L., Young, V., & Majury, Y. (1983). Belfast children's awareness of violent death. *British Journal of Psychology, 22,* 81–92.

Mead, M. (1942). *Environment and education, a symposium held in connection with the fiftieth anniversary celebration of the Univeristy of Chicago.* Chicago: University of Chicago.

Meadows, B. (2005, March 14). The Web: The bully's new playground. *People,* 152–155.

Mealey, L. (2000). *Sex differences: Developmental and evolutionary strategies.* Orlando, FL: Academic Press.

Medeiros, R., Prediger, R. D., Passos, G. F., Pandolfo, P., Duarte, F. S., Franco, J. L., Dafre, A. L., Di Giunta, G., Figueiredo, C. P., Takahashi, R. N., Campos, M. M., & Calixto, J. B. (2007). Connecting TNF-alpha signaling pathways to iNOS expression in a mouse model of Alzheimer's disease: Relevance for the behavioral and synaptic deficits induced by amyloid beta protein. *Journal of Neuroscience, 16,* 5394–5404.

Medina, J. J. (1996). *The clock of ages: Why we age—How we age—Winding back the clock.* New York: Cambridge University Press.

Mednick, S. A. (1963). Research creativity in psychology graduate students. *Journal of Consulting Psychology, 27,* 265–266.

Meece, J. L., & Kurtz-Costes, B. (2001). Introduction: The schooling of ethnic minority children and youth. *Educational Psychologist, 36,* 1–7.

Meeus, W. (1996). Studies on identity development in adolescence: An overview of research and some new data. *Journal of Youth & Adolescence, 25,* 569–598.

Meeus, W. (2003). Parental and peer support, identity development and psychological well-being in adolescence. *Psychology: The Journal of the Hellenic Psychological Society, 10,* 192–201.

Mehran, K. (1997). Interferences in the move from adolescence to adulthood: The development of the male. In M. Laufer (Ed.), *Adolescent breakdown and beyond* (pp. 17–25). London, England: Karnac Books.

Meier, A., Bukusi, E., & Cohen, C. (2006). Independent association of hygiene, socioeconomic status, and circumcision with reduced risk of HIV infection among Kenyan men. *Journal of Acquired Immune Deficiency Syndromes, 43,* 117–118.

Meijer, A. M., & van den Wittenboer, G. L. H. (2007). Contribution of infants' sleep and crying to marital relationship of first-time parent couples in the first year after childbirth. *Journal of Family Psychology, 21,* 49–57.

Meisels, S. J., & Plunkett, J. W. (1988). Developmental consequences of preterm birth: Are there long-term deficits? In P. B. Baltes, D. L. Featherman, & R. M. Lerner (Eds.), *Lifespan development and behavior* (Vol. 9). Hillsdale, NJ: Erlbaum.

Meister, H., & von Wedel, H. (2003). Demands on hearing aid features—special signal processing for elderly users? *International Journal of Audiology, 42,* 2S58–2S62.

Meltzoff, A. (2002). Elements of a developmental theory of imitation. In A. Meltzoff & W. Prinz (Eds.), *The imitative mind: Development, evolution, and brain bases* (pp. 19–41). New York: Cambridge University Press.

Meltzoff, A. N. (1981). Imitation, intermodal coordination and representation in early infancy. In G. Butterworth (Ed.), *Infancy and epistemology.* Brighton: Harvester Press.

Meltzoff, A. N., & Moore, M. K. (1977). Imitation of facial and manual gestures by human neonates. *Science, 198,* 75–78.

Meltzoff, A. N., & Moore, M. K. (1989). Imitation in newborn infants: Exploring the range of gestures imitated and the underlying mechanisms. *Developmental Psychology, 25(6),* 954–962.

Meltzoff, A. N., & Moore, M. K. (1994). Imitation, memory, and the representation of persons. *Infant Behavior and Development, 17,* 83–99.

Meltzoff, A. N., & Moore, M. K. (1999). Persons and representation: Why infant imitation is important for theories of human development. In J. Nadel & G. Butterworth et al. (Eds.), *Imitation in infancy. Cambridge studies in cognitive perceptual development.* New York: Cambridge University Press.

Meltzoff, A., & Moore, M. (2002). Imitation, memory, and the representation of persons. *Infant Behavior & Development, 25,* 39–61.

Mendoza, C. (2006, September). Inside today's classrooms: Teacher voices on No Child Left Behind and the education of gifted children. *Roeper Review, 29,* 28–31.

Menella, J. (2000, June). The psychology of eating. Paper presented at the annual meeting of the American Psychological Society, Miami, FL.

Mennella, J., Kennedy, J., & Beauchamp, G. (2006). Vegetable acceptance by infants: Effect of formula flavors. *Early Human Development, 82,* 463–468.

Mercer, J. R. (1973). *Labeling the mentally retarded.* Berkeley: University of California Press.

Meredith H. V. (1971). Growth in body size: A compendium of findings on contemporary children living in different parts of the world. *Child Development & Behavior, 6,* 153–238.

Merewood, A. (2006). Race, ethnicity, and breastfeeding. *Pediatrics, 118,* 1742–1743.

Merill, D. M. (1997). *Caring for elderly parents: Juggling work, family, and caregiving in middle and working class families.* Wesport, CT: Auburn House/Greenwood Publishing Group.

Meritesacker, B., Bade, U., & Haverkock, A. (2004). Predicting maternal reactivity/sensitivity: The role of infant emotionality, maternal depressiveness/anxiety, and social support. *Infant Mental Health Journal, 25,* 47–61.

Mervis, J. (2004, June 11). Meager evaluations make it hard to find out what works. *Science, 304,* 1583.

Messer, S. B., & McWilliams, N. (2003). The impact of Sigmund Freud and *The Interpretation of Dreams.* In R. J. Sternberg (Ed.), *The anatomy of impact: What makes the great works of psychology great* (pp. 71–88). Washington, DC: American Psychological Association.

Messinger, D. (2002). Positive and negative infant facial expressions and emotions. *Current Directions in Psychological Science, 11,* 1–6.

MetLife Mature Market Institute. (2007). *The MetLife Market Survey of Nursing Home & Home Care Costs 2006.* Westport, CT: Author.

Meyer, M., Wolf, D., & Himes, C. (2006, March). Declining eligibility for social security spouse and widow benefits in the United States? *Research on Aging, 28,* 240–260.

Meyer-Bahlburg, H. F. L., Ehrhardt, A. A., Rosen, L. R., Gruen, R. S., Veridiano, N. P., Vann, F. H., & Neuwalder, H. F. (1995). Prenatal estrogens and the development of homosexual orientation. *Developmental Psychology, 31,* 12–21.

Meyers, R. H. (2004). Huntington's disease genetics. *NeuroRx, 2,* 255–262.

Miao, X., & Wang, W. (2003). A century of Chinese developmental psychology. *International Journal of Psychology, 38,* 258–273.

Michael, R. T., Gagnon, J. H., Laumann, E. O., & Kolata, G. (1994). *Sex in America: A definitive survey.* Boston: Little, Brown.

Michaels, M. (2006). Factors that contribute to stepfamily success: A qualitative analysis. *Journal of Divorce & Remarriage, 44,* 53–66.

Michel, G. L. (1981). Right-handedness: A consequence of infant supine head-orientation preference? *Science, 212,* 685–687.

Midlarsky, E., & Bryan, J. H. (1972). Affect expressions and children's imitative altruism. *Journal of Experimental Research in Personality, 6,* 195–203.

Miehl, N. J. (2005). Shaken baby syndrome. *Journal of Forensic Nursing, 1,* 111–117.

Mikhail, B. (2000). Prenatal care utilization among low-income African American women. *Journal of Community Health Nursing, 17,* 235–246.

Mikulincer, M., & Shaver, P. R. (2005). Attachment security, compassion, and altruism. *Current Directions in Psychological Science, 14,* 34–38.

Mikulincer, M., & Shaver, P. R., (2007). *Attachment in adulthood: Structure, dynamics, and change.* New York: Guilford Press.

Miles, M., Holditch-Davis, D., Schwartz, T., & Scher, M. (2007). Depressive symptoms in mothers of prematurely born infants. *Journal of Developmental & Behavioral Pediatrics, 28,* 36–44.

Miles, R., Cowan, F., Glover, V., Stevenson, J., & Modi, N. (2006). A controlled trial of skin-to-skin contact in extremely preterm infants. *Early Human Development, 2(7),* 447–455.

Miller, A. B. (1991). Is routine mammography screening appropriate for women 40–49 years of age? *American Journal of Preventive Medicine, 7,* 55–62.

Miller, E. M., (1998). Evidence from opposite-sex twins for the effects of prenatal sex hormones. In L. Ellis & L. Ebertz (Eds.), *Males, females, and behavior: Toward biological understanding.* Westport, CT: Praeger Publishers/Greenwood Publishing Group.

Miller, G., & Cohen, S. (2001). Psychological interventions and the immune system: A meta-analytic review and critique. *Health Psychology, 20,* 47–63.

Miller, J. L., & Eimas, P. D. (1995). Speech perception: From signal to word. *Annual Review of Psychology, 46,* 467–492.

Miller, P. A., & Jansen op de Haar, M. A. (1997). Emotional, cognitive, behavioral, and temperament characteristics of high-empathy children. *Motivation and Emotion, 21,* 109–125.

Miller, P. H., & Seier, W. L. (1994). *Strategy utilization deficiencies in children: When, where, and why.* San Diego, CA: Academic Press.

Miller-Perrin, C. L., & Perrin, R. D. (1999). *Child maltreatment: An introduction.* Thousand Oaks, CA: Sage.

Mills, E., & Siegfried, N. (2006). Cautious optimism for new HIV/AIDS prevention strategies. *Lancet, 368,* 1236–1236.

Mills, J. L. (1999). Cocaine, smoking, and spontaneous abortion. *New England Journal of Medicine, 340,* 380–381.

Mimura, K., Kimoto, T., & Okada, M. (2003). Synapse efficiency diverges due to synaptic pruning following overgrowth. *Phys Rev E Stat Nonlinear Soft Matter Physics, 68,* 124–131.

Minaker, K. L., & Frishman, R. (1995, October). Love gone wrong. *Harvard Health Letter,* pp. 9–12.

Minorities in Higher Education. (1990). *Report on minorities in higher education.* Washington, DC: Minorities in Higher Education.

Mishra, R. C. (1997). Cognition and cognitive development. In J. W. Berry, P. R. Dasen, & T. S. Saraswathi (Eds.), *Handbook of cross-cultural psychology, Vol. 2: Basic processes and human development* (2nd ed., pp. 143–175). Boston, MA: Allyn & Bacon.

Misra, D. P., Astone, N., & Lynch, C. D. (2005). Maternal smoking and birth weight: Interaction with parity and mother's own in utero exposure to smoking. *Epidemiology, 16,* 288–293.

Mistry, J., & Saraswathi, T. (2003). The cultural context of child development. In R. Lerner & M. Easterbrooks (Eds.), *Handbook of psychology: Developmental psychology,* (Vol. 6, pp. 267–291). New York: John Wiley & Sons, Inc.

Mitchell, B. A. (2006). *The boomerang age: Transitions to adulthood in families.* New Brunswick, NJ: Aldine-Transaction.

Mitchell, D., Haan, M., & Steinberg, F. (2003). Body composition in the elderly: The influence of nutritional factors and physical activity. *Journal of Nutrition, Health & Aging, 7,* 130–139.

Mitchell, K., Wolak, J., & Finkelhor, D. (2007, February). Trends in youth reports of sexual solicitations, harassment and unwanted exposure to pornography on the Internet. *Journal of Adolescent Health, 40,* 116–126.

Mitchell, S. (2002). *American generations: Who they are, how they live, what they think.* Ithaca, NY: New Strategists Publications.

Mittendorf, R., Williams, M. A., Berkey, C. S., & Cotter, R. F. (1990). The length of uncomplicated human gestation. *Obstetrics and Gynecology, 75,* 73–78.

Miyamoto, R. H., Hishinuma, E. S., Nishimura, S. T., Nahulu, L. B., Andrade, N. N., & Goebert, D. A. (2000). Variation in self-esteem among adolescents in an Asian/Pacific-Islander sample. *Personality & Individual Differences, 29,* 13–25.

Mizuno, K., & Ueda, A. (2002). Antenatal olfactory learning influences infant feeding. *Early Human Development, 76,* 83–90.

Mizuno, K., & Ueda, A. (2004). Antenatal olfactory learning influences infant feeding. *Early Human Development, 76,* 83–90.

Modern Language Association (2005). *Language map.* www.mla.org/census_map.2005.

Moldin, S. O., & Gottesman, I. I. (1997). Genes, experience, and chance in schizophrenia—positioning for the 21st century. *Schizophrenia Bulletin, 23,* 547–561.

Molfese, V. J., & Acheson, S. (1997). Infant and preschool mental and verbal abilities: How are infant scores related to preschool scores? *International Journal of Behavioral Development, 20,* 595–607.

Mondloch, C. J., Lewis, T. L., Budreau, D. R., Maurer, D., Dannemiller, J. L., Stephens, B. R., & Kleiner-Gathercoal, K. A. (1999). Face perception during early infancy. *Psychological Science, 10,* 419–422.

Money, J., & Ehrhardt, A. A. (1972). *Man and woman, boy and girl: The differentiation and dimorphism of gender identity from conception to maturity.* Baltimore: Johns Hopkins University Press.

Mongan, M. F. (2005). *HypnoBirthing: The Mongan method: A natural approach to a safe, easier, more comfortable birthing* (3rd Ed.). Deerfield Beach, FL: Health Communications, Inc.

Montague, D., & Walker-Andrews, A. (2002). Mothers, fathers, and infants: The role of person familiarity and parental involvement in infants' perception of emotion expressions. *Child Development, 73,* 1339–1352.

Montemayor, R., Adams, G. R., & Gulotta, T. P. (Eds.). (1994). *Personal relationships during adolescence.* Newbury Park, CA: Sage.

Montessori, M. (1964). *The Montessori method.* New York: Schocken.

Montgomery-Downs, H., & Thomas, E. B. (1998). Biological and behavioral correlates of quiet sleep respiration rates in infants. *Physiology and Behavior, 64,* 637–643.

Moon, C. (2002). Learning in early infancy. *Advances in Neonatal Care, 2,* 81–83.

Moore, K. L. (1974). *Before we are born: Basic embryology and birth defects.* Philadelphia: Saunders.

Moore, K. L., & Persaud, T. V. N. (2003). *Before we were born* (6th ed.). Philadelphia, PA: Saunders, pg. 36.

Moore, L., Gao, D., & Bradlee, M. (2003). Does early physical activity predict body fat change throughout childhood? *Preventive Medicine: An International Journal Devoted to Practice & Theory, 37,* 10–17.

Moores, D. F. (2004). No Child Left Behind: The good, the bad, and the ugly. *American Annals of the Deaf, 148,* 347–348.

Morales, J. R., & Guerra, N. F. (2006). Effects of multiple context and cumulative stress on urban children's adjustment in elementary school. *Child Development, 77,* 907–923.

Morange, M. (2002). *The misunderstood gene.* Cambridge, MA: Harvard University Press.

Morelli, G. A., Rogoff, B., Oppenheim, D., & Goldsmith, D. (1992). Cultural variation in infants' sleeping arrangements: Questions of independence [Special section: Cross-cultural studies of development]. *Developmental Psychology, 28,* 604–613.

Moreton, C. (2007, January 14). World's first test-tube baby Louise Brown has child of her own. *The Independent.*

Morfei, M. Z., Hooker, K., Carpenter, J., Blakeley, E. & Mix, C. (2004). Agentic and communal generative behavior in four areas of adult life: Implications for psychological well-being. *Journal of Adult Development, 11,* 55–58.

Morice, A. (1998, February 27–28). Future moms, please note: Benefits vary. *The Wall Street Journal,* p. 15.

Morris, L. B. (March 21, 2001). For elderly, relief for emotional ills can be elusive. *The New York Times,* p. A6.

Morris, P., & Fritz, C. (2006, October). How to improve your memory. *The Psychologist, 19,* 608–611.

Morrongiello, B., & Hogg, K. (2004). Mothers' reactions to children misbehaving in ways that can lead to

injury: Implications for gender differences in children's risk taking and injuries. *Sex Roles, 50,* 103–118.

Morrongiello, B., Corbett, M., McCourt, M., & Johnston, N. (2006, July). Understanding unintentional injury-risk in young children I. The nature and scope of caregiver supervision of children at home. *Journal of Pediatric Psychology, 31,* 529–539.

Morrongiello, B., Midgett, C., & Stanton, K. (2000). Gender biases in children's appraisals of injury risk and other children's risk-taking behaviors. *Journal of Experimental Child Psychology, 77,* 317–336.

Morrongiello, B. A. (1997). Children's perspectives on injury and close call experiences: Sex differences in injury-outcome process. *Journal of Pediatric Psychology, 22,* 499–512.

Morry, M. (2007, February). The attraction-similarity hypothesis among cross-sex friends: Relationship satisfaction, perceived similarities, and self-serving perceptions. *Journal of Social and Personal Relationships, 24,* 117–138.

Morse, R. M., & Flavin, D. K. (1992). The definition of alcoholism. *Journal of the American Medical Association, 268,* 1012–1014.

Moshman, D., Glover, J. A., & Bruning, R. H. (1987). *Developmental psychology.* Boston: Little, Brown.

Moss, M. (1997, March 31). Golden years? For one 73-year-old, punching time clock isn't a labor of love. *The Wall Street Journal,* pp. A1, A8.

Motschnig, R., & Nykl, L. (2003). Toward a cognitive-emotional model of Rogers's person-centered approach. *Journal of Humanistic Psychology, 43,* 8–45.

Moyad, M. A. (2004). Preventing male osteoporosis: Prevalence, risks, diagnosis and imaging tests. *Urological Clinics of North America, 31,* 321–330.

Moyer, M. S. (1992). Sibling relationships among older adults. *Generations, 16,* 55–58.

Mueller, E., & Vandell, D. (1979). Infant–infant interactions. In J. Osofsky (Ed.), *Handbook of infant development.* New York: Wiley.

Mueller, M., Wilhelm, B., & Elder, G. (2002). Variations in grandparenting. *Research on Aging, 24,* 360–388.

Muhuri, P. K., MacDorman, M. F., & Ezzati-Rice, T. M. (2004). Racial differences in leading causes of infant death in the United States. *Paediatric and Perinatal Epidemiology, 18,* 51–60.

Mumme, D., & Fernald, A. (2003). The infant as onlooker: Learning from emotional reactions observed in a television scenario. *Child Development, 74,* 221–237.

Munzar, P., Cami, J., & Farré, M. (2003). Mechanisms of drug addiction I. *New England Journal of Medicine, 349,* 2365–2365.

Murdock, T. B., & Bolch, M. B. (2005). Risk and protective factors for poor school adjustment in lesbian, gay, and bisexual (LGB) high school youth: Variable and person-centered analyses. *Psychology in the Schools, 42,* 159–172.

Murguia, A., Peterson, R. A., & Zea, M. C. (1997, August). Cultural health beliefs. Paper presented at the annual meeting of the American Psychological Association, Toronto, Canada.

Murphy, B., & Eisenberg, N. (2002). An integrative examination of peer conflict: Children's reported goals, emotions, and behaviors. *Social Development, 11,* 534–557.

Murphy, S., Johnson, L., & Wu, L. (2003). Bereaved parents' outcomes 4 to 60 months after their children's death by accident, suicide, or homicide: A comparative study demonstrating differences. *Death Studies, 27,* 39–61.

Murray, J. A., Terry, D. J., Vance, J. C., Battistutta, D., & Connolly, Y. (2000). Effects of a program of intervention on parental distress following infant death. *Death Studies, 4*, 275–305.

Murray, L., Cooper, P., Creswell, C., Schofield, E., & Sack, C. (2007, January). The effects of maternal social phobia on mother–infant interactions and infant social responsiveness. *Journal of Child Psychology and Psychiatry, 48*, 45–52.

Murray, S., Bellavia, G., & Rose, P. (2003). Once hurt, twice hurtful: How perceived regard regulates daily marital interactions. *Journal of Personality & Social Psychology, 84*, 126–147.

Murray-Close, D., Ostrov, J., & Crick, N. (2007, December). A short-term longitudinal study of growth of relational aggression during middle childhood: Associations with gender, friendship intimacy, and internalizing problems. *Development and Psychopathology, 19*, 187–203.

Murstein, B. I. (1976). *Who will marry whom? Theories and research in marital choice*. New York: Springer.

Murstein, B. I. (1986). *Paths to marriage*. Beverly Hills, CA: Sage.

Murstein, B. I. (1987). A clarification and extension of the SVR theory of dyadic pairing. *Journal of Marriage and the Family, 49*, 929–933.

Mutrie, N. (1997). The therapeutic effects of exercise on the self. In K. R. Fox (Ed.), *The physical self: From motivation to well being* (pp. 287–314). Champaign, IL: Human Kinetics.

Myers, B. J., Dawson, K. S., & Britt, G. C. (2003). Prenatal cocaine exposure and infant performance on the Brazelton Neonatal Behavioral Assessment Scale. *Substance use & abuse, 38*, 2065–2096.

Myers, D. (2000). *A quiet world: Living with hearing loss*. New Haven: Yale University Press.

Myers, N. A., Clifton, R. K., & Clarkson, M. G. (1987). When they were very young: Almost-threes remember two years ago. *Infant Behavior and Development, 10*, 123–132.

Myers, R. H. (2004). Huntington's disease genetics. *NeuroRx, 1*, 255–262.

Myklebust, B. M., & Gottlieb, G. L. (1993). Development of the stretch reflex in the newborn: Reciprocal excitation and reflex irradiation. *Child Development, 64*, 1036–1045.

Myrtek, M. (2007). *Type A behavior and hostility as independent risk factors for coronary heart disease*. Washington, DC: American Psychological Association.

NAACP Education Department. (2003). *NAACP call for action in education*. Baltimore, MD: NAACP.

Nadal, K. (2004). Filipino American identity development model. *Journal of Multicultural Counseling & Development, 32*, 45–62.

Nadeau, L., Boivin, M., Tessier, R., Lefebvre, F. & Robaey, P. (2001). Mediators of behavioral problems in 7-year-old children born after 24 to 28 weeks of gestation. *Journal of Developmental & Behavioral Pediatrics, 22*, 1–10.

Nagda, B. R. A., Gurin, P., & Johnson, S. M. (2005). Living, doing and thinking diversity: How does precollege diversity experience affect first-year students' engagement with college diversity? In R. S. Feldman (Ed.), *Improving the first year of college: Research and practice*. Mahwah, NJ: Lawrence Erlbaum.

Nagy, E. (2006). From imitation to conversation: The first dialogues with human neonates. *Infant and Child Development, 15*, 223–232.

Nagy, E. (2006). From imitation to conversation: The first dialogues with human neonates. *Infant and Child Development, 15*, 223.

Nagy, M. (1948). The child's theories concerning death. *Journal of Genetic Psychology, 73*, 3–27.

Nahmiash, D. (2006). *Abuse and neglect of older adults: What do we know about it and how can we identify it?* Westport, CT: Praeger Publishers/Greenwood Publishing Group.

Naik, G. (2002, November 22). The grim mission of a Swiss group: Visitor's suicides. *The Wall Street Journal*, pp. A1, A6.

Naik, G. (2004, March 10). Unlikely way to cut hospital costs: Comfort the dying. *The Wall Street Journal*, pp. A1, A12.

Nakagawa, M., Lamb, M. E., & Miyaki, K. (1992). Antecedents and correlates of the Strange Situation behavior of Japanese infants. *Journal of Cross-Cultural Psychology, 23*, 300–310.

Nakamura, M., Kyo, S., Kanaya, T., Yatabe, N., Maida, Y., Tanaka, M., Ishida, Y., Fujii, C., Kondo, T., Inoue, M., & Mukaida, N. (2004). hTERT-promoter-based tumor-specific expression of MCP-1 effectively sensitizes cervical cancer cells to a low dose of cisplatin. *Cancer Gene Therapy, 2*, 1–7.

Nam, C. B., & Boyd, M. (2004). Occupational status in 2000: Over a century of census-based measurement. *Population Research and Policy Review, 23*, 327–358.

Nanda, S., & Konnur, N. (2006, October). Adolescent drug & alcohol use in the 21st century. *Psychiatric Annals, 36*, 706–712.

Nangle, D. W., & Erdley, C. A. (Eds). (2001). *The role of friendship in psychological adjustment*. San Francisco: Jossey-Bass.

Nathanson, A., Wilson, B., & McGee, J. (2002). Counteracting the effects of female stereotypes on television via active mediation. *Journal of Communication, 52*, 922–937.

Nation, M., & Heflinger, C. (2006). Risk factors for serious alcohol and drug use: The role of psychosocial variables in predicting the frequency of substance use among adolescents. *American Journal of Drug and Alcohol Abuse, 32*, 415–433.

National Association for the Education of Young Children. (2005). Position statements of the NAEYC. Available online at http://www.naeyc.org/about/positions.asp#where.

National Center for Children in Poverty. (2005). *Basic facts about low-income children in the United States*. New York: National Center for Children in Poverty.

National Center for Educational Statistics. (2002). *Dropout rates in the United States: 2000*. Washington, DC: NCES.

National Center for Educational Statistics (2003). *Public high school dropouts and completers from the common core of data: school year 2000–01 statistical analysis report*. Washington, DC: NCES.

National Center for Health Statistics. (1994). *Division of vital statistics*. Washington, DC: Public Health Service.

National Center for Health Statistics. (2000). *Health United States, 2000 with adolescent health chartbook*. Hyattsville, MD.

National Center for Health Statistics. (2001). *Division of vital statistics*. Washington, DC: Public Health Service.

National Center for Health Statistics. (2003). *Division of vital statistics*. Washington, DC: Public Health Service.

National Center for Health Statistics. (2004). *SIDS death rate: 1980–2000*. Washington, DC: National Center for Health Statistics.

National Center for Health Statistics. (2006). National Hospital Discharge Survey: 2004 annual summary with detailed diagnosis and procedure data. *Vital and Health Statistics, 13*(162).

National Center for Health Statistics (Infant and Child Health Studies Branch). (1997). *Survival rates of infants*. Washington, DC: National Center for Health Statistics.

National Clearinghouse on Child Abuse and Neglect Information. (2004). *Child maltreatment 2002: Summary of key findings/National Clearinghouse on Child Abuse and Neglect Information*. Washington, DC: Author.

National Highway Traffic Safety Administration. (1994). *Age-related incidence of traffic accidents*. Washington, DC: National Highway Traffic Safety Administration.

National Institute of Aging. (2004, May 31). Sexuality in later life. Available online at http://www.niapublications.org/engagepages/sexuality.asp.

National Institute of Child Health and Human Development (NICHD). (1999). Child care and mother–child interaction in the first 3 years of life. *Developmental Psychology, 35*, 1399–1413.

National Institute of Child Health and Human Development Early Child Care Research Network, (2003). Does amount of time spent in child care predict socioemotional adjustment during the transition to kindergarten? *Child Development, 74*, 976–1005.

National Institute of Child Health and Human Development Early Child Care Research Network, & Duncan, G. J. (2003). Modeling the impacts of child care quality on child care quality on children's preschool cognitive development. *Child Development, 74*, 1454–1475.

National Institutes of Health. (2006, December 13) Adult male circumcision significantly reduces risk of acquiring HIV. NIH news release. Retrieved January 7, 2006 from http://www.nih.gov/news/pr/dec2006/niaid-13.htm.

National Research Council. (1997). *Racial and ethnic differences in the health of older Americans*. New York: Author.

National Safety Council. (1989). *Accident facts: 1989 edition*. Chicago: National Safety Council.

National Science Foundation (NSF), Division of Science Resources Statistics. (2002). *Women, minorities, and persons with disabilities in science and engineering: 2002*. Arlington, VA: National Science Foundation.

National Sleep Foundation. (2002). *Americans favor later high school start times, according to National Sleep Foundation Poll*. Washington, DC: National Sleep Foundation.

Navarro, M. (2006, May 25). Families add 3rd generation to households. *The New York Times*, pp. A1, A22.

Nawaz, S., Griffiths, P., & Tappin, D. (2002). Parent-administered modified dry-bed training for childhood nocturnal enuresis: Evidence for superiority over urine-alarm conditioning when delivery factors are controlled. *Behavioral Interventions, 17*, 247–260.

Nazzi, T., & Bertoncini, J. (2003). Before and after the vocabulary spurt: Two modes of word acquisition? *Developmental Science, 6*, 136–142.

NCADC (National Coalition Against Domestic Violence). (2003). *Poll finds domestic violence is women's main concern*. Denver, Colorado: Author.

NCPYP (National Campaign to Prevent Youth Pregnancy). (2003). *14 and younger: The sexual behavior of young adolescents*. Washington, D.C.: Author.

Needleman, H. L., & Bellinger, D. (Eds.). (1994). *Prenatal exposure to toxicants: Developmental consequences.* Baltimore: Johns Hopkins University Press.

Needleman, H. L., Riess, J. A., Tobin, M. J., Biesecker, G. E., & Greenhouse, J. B. (1996, February 7). Bone lead levels and delinquent behavior. *Journal of the American Medical Association, 2755,* 363–369.

Negy, C., Shreve, T., & Jensen, B. (2003). Ethnic identity, self-esteem, and ethnocentrism: A study of social identity versus multicultural theory of development. *Cultural Diversity & Ethnic Minority Psychology, 9,* 333–344.

Neher, A. (1991). Maslow's theory of motivation: A critique. *Journal of Humanistic Psychology, 31,* 89–112.

Neisser, U. (2004). Memory development: New questions and old. *Developmental Review, 24,* 154–158.

Nelson, C. A. (1987). The recognition of facial expressions in the first two years of life: Mechanisms of development. *Child Development, 58,* 889–909.

Nelson, C. A., & Bosquet, M. (2000). Neurobiology of fetal and infant development: Implications for infant mental health. In C. H. Zeanah, Jr. (Ed.), *Handbook of infant mental health* (2nd ed.). New York: Guilford Press.

Nelson, D. A., Hart, C. H., Yang, C., Olsen, J. A., & Jin, S. (2006). Aversive parenting in China: Associations with child physical and relational aggression. *Child Development, 77,* 554–572.

Nelson, K. (1996). *Language in cognitive development: Emergence of the mediated mind.* New York: Cambridge University Press.

Nelson, K., & Fivush, R. (2004). The emergence of autobiographical memory: A social cultural developmental theory. *Psychological Review, 111,* 486–511.

Nelson, L., Badger, S., & Wu, B. (2004). The influence of culture in emerging adulthood: Perspectives of Chinese college students. *International Journal of Behavioral Development, 28,* 26–36.

Nelson, L. D., Scheibel, K. E., & Ringman, J. M. (2007). An experimental approach to detecting dementia in Down syndrome: A paradigm for Alzheimer's disease. *Brain and Cognition, 64,* 92–103.

Nelson, L. J., & Cooper, J. (1997). Gender differences in children's reactions to success and failure with computers. *Computers in Human Behavior, 13,* 247–267.

Nelson, T. (2004). *Ageism: Stereotyping and prejudice against older persons.* Cambridge, MA: MIT Press.

Nelson, T., & Wechsler, H. (2003). School spirits: Alcohol and collegiate sports fans. *Addictive Behaviors, 28,* 1–11.

Nelson, T. O. (1994). Metacognition. In V. S. Ramachandran (Ed.), *Encyclopedia of human behavior* (Vol. 3). San Diego: Academic Press.

Nemeth, C. (1992). Minority dissent as a stimulant to group performance. In S. Worchel, W. Wood, & J. Simpson (Eds.), *Group processes and productivity.* Newbury Park, CA: Sage Publications.

Nesheim, S., Henderson, S., Lindsay, M., Zuberi, J., Grimes, V., Buehler, J., Lindegren, M. L., & Bulterys, M. (2004). *Prenatal HIV testing and antiretroviral prophylasix at an urban hospital—Atlanta, Georgia, 1997–2000.* Atlanta, GA: Centers for Disease Control.

Ness, J., Aronow, W., & Beck, G. (2006). Menopausal symptoms after cessation of hormone replacement therapy. *Maturitas, 53,* 356–361.

Ness, R. B., Grisso, J. A., Hirschinger, N., Markovic, N., Shaw, L. M., Day, N. L., & Kline, J. (1999). Cocaine and tobacco use and the risk of spontaneous abortion. *New England Journal of Medicine, 340,* 333–339.

Nettelbeck, T., & Rabbitt, P. M. (1992). Aging, cognitive performance, and mental speed. *Intelligence, 16,* 189–205.

Neugarten, B. L. (1972). Personality and the aging process. *The Gerontologist, 12,* 9–15.

Neugarten, B. L. (1977). Personality and aging. In J. E. Birren & K. W. Schaie (Eds.), *Handbook for the psychology of aging.* New York: Van Nostrand Reinhold.

Newbart, D. (2006, October 8). Record freshman diversity at U. of C.: 1 in 4 students black, Hispanic or from abroad. *Chicago Sun Times,* p. A09. Retrieved February 21, 2007 from LexisNexis Academic.

Newcomb, A. F., & Bagwell, C. L. (1995). Children's friendship relations: A meta-analytic review. *Psychological Bulletin, 117,* 306–347.

Newcombe, N., Drummey, A. B., & Lie, E. (1995). Children's memory for early experience. *Journal of Experimental Child Psychology, 59,* 337–342.

Newman, R., & Hussain, I. (2006). Changes in preference for infant-directed speech in low and moderate noise by 4.5- to 13-month-olds. *Infancy, 10,* 61–76.

Newston, R. L., & Keith, P. M. (1997). Single women later in life. In J. M. Coyle (Ed.), *Handbook on women and aging* (pp. 385–399). Westport, CT: Greenwood Press.

Newton, K., Reed, S., LaCroix, A., Grothaus, L., Ehrlich, K., & Guiltinan, J. (2006). Treatment of vasomotor symptoms of menopause with black cohosh, multibotanicals, soy, hormone therapy, or placebo. *Annals of Internal Medicine, 145,* 869–879.

Ng, S. (2002). Will families support their elders? Answers from across cultures. In T. Nelson (Ed.), *Ageism: Stereotyping and prejudice against older persons.* Cambridge, MA: The MIT Press.

Nguyen, L., & Frye, D. (1999). Children's theory of mind: Understanding of desire, belief and emotion with social referents. *Social Development, 8,* 70–92.

NIAAA (National Institute on Alcohol Abuse and Alcoholism). (1990). *Alcohol and health.* Washington, DC: U.S. Government Printing Office.

NICHD Early Child Care Research Network. (1997). The effects of infant child care on infant-mother attachment security: Results of the NICHD study of early child care. *Child Development, 68,* 860–879.

NICHD Early Child Care Research Network. (2000). The relation of child care to cognitive and language development. *Child Development, 71,* 960–980.

NICHD Early Child Care Research Network. (2001a). Child care and children's peer interaction at 24 and 36 months: The NICHD study of early child care. *Child Development, 72,* 1478–1500.

NICHD Early Child Care Research Network. (2001b). Child-care and family predictors of preschool attachment and stability from infancy. *Development psychology, 37,* 847–862.

NICHD Early Child Care Research Network. (2003a). Does quality of child care affect child outcomes at age 41/2? *Developmental Psychology, 39,* 451–469.

NICHD Early Child Care Research Network. (2003b). Families matter—even for kids in child care. *Journal of Developmental and Behavioral Pediatrics, 24,* 58–62.

NICHD Early Child Care Research Network. (2005). *Child care and child development: Results from the NICHD study of early child care and youth development.* New York: Guilford Press.

NICHD Early Child Care Research Network. (2006a). *Child care and child development: Results from the NICHD study of early child care and youth development.* New York: Guilford Press.

NICHD Early Child Care Research Network. (2006b). *The NICHD Study of Early Child Care and Youth Development (SECCYD): Findings for children up to age 4 1/2 years.* (Figure 5, p. 20). Washington, DC: National Institute of Child Health and Human Development.

Niederhofer, H. (2004). A longitudinal study: Some preliminary results of association of prenatal maternal stress and fetal movements, temperament factors in early childhood and behavior at age 2 years. *Psychological Reports, 95,* 767–770.

Nielsen, M., Dissanayake, C., & Kashima, Y. (2003). A longitudinal investigation of self–other discrimination and the emergence of minor self-recognition. *Infant Behavior & Development, 26,* 213–226.

Nieto, S. (2005). Public education in the twentieth century and beyond: high hopes, broken promises, and an uncertain future. *Harvard Educational Review, 75,* 43–65.

Nigg, J. T. (2001). Is ADHD a disinhibatory disorder? *Psychological Bulletin, 127,* 571–598.

Nihart, M. A. (1993). Growth and development of the brain. *Journal of Child and Adolescent Psychiatric and Mental Health Nursing, 6,* 39–40.

Nilsson, L. (2003). Memory function in normal aging. *Acta Neurologica Scandinavica, 107,* 7–13.

Nilsson, L. G., Bäckman, L., Erngrund, K., Nyberg, L., et al. (1997). The Betula prospective cohort study: Memory, health, and aging. *Aging Neuropsychology & Cognition, 4,* 1–32.

Nimrod, G., & Adoni, H. (2006, July). Leisure-styles and life satisfaction among recent retirees in Israel. *Ageing & Society, 26,* 607–630.

Niparko, J. K. (2004). Speech, language, and reading skills after early cochlear implantation. *JAMA: Journal of the American Medical Association, 291,* 2378–2380.

Nisbett, R. (1994, October 31). Blue genes. *New Republic, 211,* 15.

Nobuyuki, I. (1997). Simple reaction times and timing of serial reactions of middle-aged and old men. *Perceptual & Motor Skills, 84,* 219–225.

Nockels, R., & Oakeshott, P. (1999). Awareness among young women of sexually transmitted chlamydia infection. *Family Practice, 16,* 94.

Nolen-Hoeksema, S. (2001). Ruminative coping and adjustment to bereavement. In M. Stroebe & R. Hansson (Eds.), *Handbook of bereavement research: Consequences, coping, and care.* Washington, DC: American Psychological Association.

Nolen-Hoeksema, S. (2003). *Women who think too much: How to break free of overthinking and reclaim your life.* New York: Henry Holt.

Nolen-Hoeksema, S., & Davis, C. (2002). Positive responses to loss: Perceiving benefits and growth. In C. Snyder & S. Lopez (Eds.), *Handbook of positive psychology.* London: Oxford University Press.

Nolen-Hoeksema, S., & Larson, J. (1999). *Coping with loss.* Mahwah, NJ: Erlbaum.

Noller, P., Feeney, J. A., & Ward, C. M. (1997). Determinants of marital quality: A partial test of Lewis and Spanier's model. *Journal of Family Studies, 3,* 226–251.

Noonan, D. (2003, September 22). When safety is the name of the game. *Newsweek,* 64–66.

Noonan, D. (2003, September 29). High on testosterone. *Newsweek,* 50–52.

Nordin, S., Razani, L., & Markison, S. (2003). Age-associated increases in intensity discrimination for taste. *Experimental Aging Research, 29,* 371–381.

Norlander, T., Von Schedvin, H., & Archer, T. (2005). Thriving as a function of affective personality: Relation to personality factors, coping strategies and stress. *Anxiety, Stress & Coping: An International Journal, 18*, 105–116.

Norman, R. M. G., Malla, A. K. (2001). Family history of schizophrenia and the relationship of stress to symptoms: Preliminary findings. *Australian & New Zealand Journal of Psychiatry, 35*, 217–223.

Nossiter, A. (1995, September 5). Asthma common and on rise in the crowded South Bronx. *The New York Times*, pp. A1, B2.

Notaro, P., Gelman, S., & Zimmerman, M. (2002). Biases in reasoning about the consequences of psychogenic bodily reactions: Domain boundaries in cognitive development. *Merrill-Palmer Quarterly, 48*, 427–449.

Nowak, C. A. (1977). Does youthfulness equal attractiveness? In L. E. Troll, J. Israel, & K. Israel (Eds.), *Looking ahead*. Englewood, Cliffs, NJ: Prentice-Hall.

Nowak, M. A., Komarova, N. L., & Niyogi, P. (2001, January 5). Evolution of universal grammar. *Science, 291*, 114–116.

NPD Group. (2004). The reality of children's diet. Port Washington, NY: NPD Group.

Nuttman-Shwartz, O. (2007). Is there life without work? *International Journal of Aging & Human Development, 64*, 129–147.

Nugent, J. K., Lester, B. M., & Brazelton, T. B. (Eds.). (1989). *The cultural context of infancy, Vol. 1: Biology, culture, and infant development*. Norwood, NJ: Ablex.

Nyiti, R. M. (1982). The validity of "culture differences explanations" for cross-cultural variation in the rate of Piagetian cognitive development. In D. Wagner & H. Stevenson (Eds.), *Cultural perspectives on child development*. New York: Freeman.

Nylen, K., Moran, T., Franklin, C., & O'Hara, M. (2006). Maternal depression: A review of relevant treatment approaches for mothers and infants. *Infant Mental Health Journal, 27*, 327–343.

O'Connor, M., & Whaley, S. (2006). Health care provider advice and risk factors associated with alcohol consumption following pregnancy recognition. *Journal of Studies on Alcohol, 67*, 22–31.

O'Connor, P. (1994). Very close parent/child relationships: The perspective of the elderly person. *Journal of Cross-Cultural Gerontology, 9*, 53–76.

O'Dea, J., & Wilson, R. (2006). Socio-cognitive and nutritional factors associated with body mass index in children and adolescents: Possibilities for childhood obesity prevention. *Health Education Research, 21*, 796–805.

O'Grady, W., & Aitchison, J. (2005). *How children learn language*. New York: Cambridge University Press.

O'Hara, R., Schroder, C., Bloss, C., Bailey, A., Alyeshmerni, A., Mumenthaler, M., Friedman, L., & Yesavage, J. (2005). Hormone replacement therapy and longitudinal cognitive performance in postmenopausal women. *American Journal of Geriatric Psychiatry, 13*, 1107–1110.

O'Hare, W. (1997, September). *American Demographics*, 50–56.

O'Leary, S. G. (1995). Parental discipline mistakes. *Current Directions in Psychological Science, 4*, 11–13.

O'Toole, M. L., Sawicki, M. A., & Artal, R. (2003). Structured diet and physical activity prevent postpartum weight retention. *Journal of Women's Health, 12*, 991–998.

Oashi, O. (2003). A review on the psychological interventions for the modification of Type A behavior pattern. *Japanese Journal of Counseling Science, 36*, 175–186.

Oblinger, D. G., & Rush, S. C. (1997). *The learning revolution: The challenge of information technology in the academy*. Bolton, MA: Anker Publishing Co.

Ochsner Clinic Foundation. (2003). *Adult preventive health care screening recommendations*. New Orleans, LA: Ochsner Clinic Foundation.

Ocorr, K., Reeves, N. L., Wessells, R. J., Fink, M., Chen, H. S., Akasaka, T., Yasuda, S., Metzger, J. M., Giles, W., Posakony, J. W., Bodmer, R. (2007). KCNQ potassium channel mutations cause cardiac arrhythmias in Drosophila that mimic the effects of aging. *Proceedings of the National Academy of Sciences, 104*, 3943–3948.

OECD (Organization for Economic Cooperation and Development). (1998). *Education at a glance: OECD indicators, 1998*. Paris: Author.

OECD. (2005). Education at a glance: OECD indicators, 1998. Paris: Organization for Economic Cooperation and Development.

Ogbu, J. (1992). Understanding cultural diversity and learning. *Educational Researcher, 21*, 5–14.

Ogbu, J. U. (1988). Black education: A cultural-ecological perspective. In H. P. McAdoo (Ed.), *Black families*. Beverly Hills, CA: Sage.

Ogden, C. L., Kuczmarski, R. J., Flegal, K. M., Mei, Z., Guo, S., Wei, R., Grummer-Strawn, L. M., Curtin, L. R., Roche, A. F., & Johnson, C. L. (2002). Centers for Disease Control and Prevention 2000 growth charts for the United States: Improvements to the 1977 National Center for Health Statistics Version. *Pediatrics, 109*, 45–60.

Ogilvy-Stuart, A. L., & Gleeson, H. (2004). Cancer risk following growth hormone use in childhood: Implications for current practice. *Drug Safety, 27*, 369–382.

Okie, S. (2005). *Winning the war against childhood obesity*. Washington, DC: Joseph Henry Publications.

Olivardia, R., & Pope, H. (2002). Body image disturbance in childhood and adolescence. In D. Castle & K. Phillips (Eds.), *Disorders of body image*. Petersfield, England: Wrightson Biomedical Publishing.

Oliver, M. B., & Hyde, J. S. (1993). Gender differences in sexuality: A meta-analysis. *Psychological Bulletin, 114*, 29–51.

Oller, D. K., Eilers, R. E., Urbano, R., & Cobo-Lewis, A. B. (1997). Development of precursors to speech in infants exposed to two languages. *Journal of Child Language, 24*, 407–425.

Olshansky, S. J., Passaro, D. J., Hershow, R. C., Layden, J., Carnes, B. A., Brody, J., Hayflick, L., Butler, R. N., Allison, D. B., & Ludwig, D. S. (2005, March 17). Special report: A potential decline in life expectancy in the United States in the 21st century. *The New England Journal of Medicine, 352*, 1138–1145.

Olson, E. (2006, April 27). You're in labor, and getting sleeeepy. *New York Times*, p. C2.

Olson, S. (2003). *Mapping human history: Genes, race, and our common origins*. New York: Mariner Books.

Onishi, K., & Baillargeon, R. (2005). Do 15-month-old infants understand false beliefs? *Science, 308*, 255–258.

Orbuch, T. L., House, J. S., Mero, R. P., & Webster, P. S. (1996). Marital quality over the life course. *Social Psychology Quarterly, 59*, 162–171.

Oretti, R. G., Harris, B., & Lazarus, J. H. (2003). Is there an association between life events, postnatal depression and thyroid dysfunction in thyroid antibody positive women? *International Journal of Social Psychiatry, 49*, 70–76.

Ormont, L. R. (2001). Developing emotional insulation (1994. In L. B. Fugeri, *The technique of group treatment: The collected papers of Louis R. Ormont*. Madison, CT: Psychosocial Press.

Ornstein, P. A., & Elischberger, H. B. (2004). Studies of suggestibility: Some observations and suggestions, *Applied Cognitive Psychology, 18* [Special issue: Individual and developmental differences in suggestibility], 1129–1141.

Ortiz, S. O., & Dynda, A. M. (2005). Use of intelligence tests with culturally and linguistically diverse populations. In D. P. Flanagan & P. L. Harrison (Eds.), *Contemporary intellectual assessment: Theories, tests, and issues*. New York, Guilford Press.

Osofsky, J. (2003). Prevalence of children's exposure to domestic violence and child maltreatment: Implications for prevention and intervention. *Clinical Child & Family Psychology Review, 6*, 161–170.

Osofsky, J. D. (1995b). The effects of exposure to violence on young children. *American Psychologist, 50*, 782–788.

Ostrov, J., Gentile, D., & Crick, N. (2006, November). Media exposure, aggression and prosocial behavior during early childhood: A longitudinal study. *Social Development, 15*, 612–627.

Ouwehand, C., de Ridder, D. T., & Bensing, J. M. (2007). A review of successful aging models: Proposing proactive coping as an important additional strategy. *Clinical Psychology Review, 43*, 101–116.

Owen, J. E., Klapow, J. C., Roth, D. L., Nabell, L., & Tucker, D. C. (2004). Improving the effectiveness of adjuvant psychological treatment for women with breast cancer. The feasibility of providing online support. *Psycho-Oncology, 13*, 281–292.

Owsley, C., Stalvey, B., & Phillips, J. (2003). The efficacy of an educational intervention in promoting self-regulation among high-risk older drivers. *Accident Analysis & Prevention, 35*, 393–400.

Oxford, M., Gilchrist, L., Gillmore, M., & Lohr, M. (2006, July). Predicting variation in the life course of adolescent mothers as they enter adulthood. *Journal of Adolescent Health, 39*, 20–26.

Oyserman, D., Kemmelmeier, M., Fryberg, S., Brosh, H., & Hart-Johnson, T. (2003). Racial ethnic self-schemas. *Social Psychology Quarterly, 66*, 333–347.

Ozawa, M., & Yoon, H. (2003). Economic impact of marital disruption on children. *Children & Youth Services Review, 25*, 611–632.

Pachter, L. M., & Weller, S. C. (1993). Acculturation and compliance with medical therapy. *Journal of Development and Behavior Pediatrics, 14*, 163–168.

Pagani, L. S.. Remblay, R. E., Nagain, D., Zoccolillo, M., Vitaro, F., & McDuff, P. (2004). Risk factor models for adolescent verbal and physical aggression toward mothers. *International Journal of Behavioral Development, 28*, 528–537.

Paige, R. (2006, December). No Child Left Behind: The ongoing movement for public education reform. *Harvard Educational Review, 76*, 461–473.

Paikoff, R. L., & Brooks-Gunn, J. (1990). Physiological processes: What role do they play during the transition to adolescence? In R. Montemayor, G. R. Adams, & T. P. Gulotta (Eds.), *From childhood to adolescence: A transitional period?* Newbury Park, CA: Sage.

Paisley, T. S., Joy, E. A., & Price, R. J., Jr. (2003). Exercise during pregnancy: A practical approach. *Current Sports Medicine Reports, 2*, 325–330.

Pajkrt, E., Weisz, B., Firth, H. V., & Chitty, L. S. (2004). Fetal cardiac anomalies and genetic syndromes. *Prenatal Diagnosis, 24*, 1104–1115.

Pajulo, M., Helenius, H., & MaYes, L. (2006, May). Prenatal views of baby and parenthood: Association with sociodemographic and pregnancy factors. *Infant Mental Health Journal, 27*, 229–250.

Palan, P. R., Connell, K., Ramirez, E. Inegbenijie, C., Gavara, R. Y., Ouseph, J. A., & Mikhail, M. S. (2005). Effects of menopause and hormone replacement therapy on serum levels of coenzyme Q10 and other lipid-soluble antioxidants. *Biofactors, 25,* 61–66.

Palfai, T., Halperin, S., & Hoyer, W. (2003). Age inequalities in recognition memory: Effects of stimulus presentation time and list repetitions. *Aging, Neuropsychology, & Cognition, 10,* 134–140.

Palincsar, A.S., A.L. Brown, and J.C. Campione. 1993. First-grade dialogues for knowledge acquisition and use. *Contexts for Learning: Sociocultural Dynamics in Children's Development,* E. Forman, N. Minick, and C.A. Stone, eds. New York: Oxford University Press.

Palincsar, A. S., & Klenk, L. (1992). Fostering literacy learning in supportive contexts. *Journal of Learning Disabilities, 25,* 211–225, 229.

Palmore, E. (1975). *The honorable elders: A cross-cultural analysis of aging in Japan.* Durham, NC: Duke University Press.

Palmore, E. B. (1988). *The facts on aging quiz.* New York: Springer.

Palmore, E. B. (1992). Knowledge about aging: What we know and need to know. *Gerontologist, 32,* 149–150.

Palmore, E. B. (1999). *Ageism: Negative and Positive.* New York: Springer Publishing Co.

Paneth, N. S. (1995). The problem of low birth weight. *The Future of Children, 5,* 19–34.

Papousek, H., & Papousek, M. (1991). Innate and cultural guidance of infants' integrative competencies: China, the United States, and Germany. In M. H. Borstein (Ed.), *Cultural approaches to parenting.* Hillsdale, NJ: Erlbaum.

Pappano, L. (1994, November 27). The new old generation. *The Boston Globe Magazine,* 18–38.

Paquette, D., Carbonneau, R., & Dubeau, D. (2003). Prevalence of father–child rough-and-tumble play and physical aggression in preschool children. *European Journal of Psychology of Education, 18,* 171–189.

Paris, J. (1999). *Nature and nurture in psychiatry: A predisposition–stress model of mental disorders.* Washington, DC: American Psychiatric Press.

Park, K. A., Lay, K., & Ramsay, L. (1993). Individual differences and developmental changes in preschoolers' friendships. *Developmental Psychology, 29,* 264–270.

Parke, R., Simpkins, S., & McDowell, D. (2002). Relative contributions of families and peers to children's social development. In P. Smith & C. Hart (Eds.), *Blackwell handbook of childhood social development.* Malden, MA: Blackwell Publishers.

Parke, R. D. (1996). *New fatherhood.* Cambridge, MA: Harvard University Press.

Parke, R.D. (2004). Development in the family. *Annual Review of Psychology, 55,* 365–399.

Parker, J., Summerfeldt, L., & Hogan, M. (2004). Emotional intelligence and academic success: Examining the transition from high school to university. *Personality & Individual Differences, 36,* 163–172.

Parker, S., & Langer, J. (Eds.). (2005). *Biology and knowledge revisited: From neurogenesis to psychogenesis.* Mahwah, NJ: Lawrence Erlbaum Associates.

Parker, S. T. (2005). Piaget's legacy in cognitive constructivism, niche construction, and phenotype development and evolution. In S. T. Parker & J. Langer (Eds.), *Biology and knowledge revisited: From neurogenesis to psychogenesis.* Mahwah, NJ: Lawrence Erlbaum Associates.

Parker-Pope, T. (2003, December 9). How to give your child a longer life. *The Wall Street Journal,* pp. R1, R3.

Parker-Pope, T. (2003, October 21). The case for hormone therapy. *The Wall Street Journal,* pp. R1, R3.

Parker-Pope, T. (2004, May 4). When your spouse makes you sick: Research probes toll of marital stress. *The Wall Street Journal,* p. D1.

Parkes, C. M. (1997). Normal and abnormal responses to stress—a developmental approach. In D. Black, M. Newman, J. Harris-Hendricks, & G. Mezey (Eds.), *Psychological trauma: A developmental approach* (pp. 10–18). London, England: Gaskell/Royal College of Psychiatrists.

Parks, C., Sanna, L., & Posey, D. (2003). Retrospection in social dilemmas: How thinking about the past affects future cooperation. *Journal of Personality & Social Psychology, 84,* 988–996.

Parks, C. A. (1998). Lesbian parenthood: A review of the literature. *American Journal of Orthopsychiatry, 68,* 376–389.

Parlee, M. B. (1979, October). The friendship bond. *Psychology Today, 13,* 43–45.

Parmalee, A. H., Jr., & Sigman, M. D. (1983). Prenatal brain development and behavior. In P. H. Mussen (Ed.), *Handbook of child psychology* (Vol. 2, 4th ed.). New York: Wiley.

Parnell, T. F., & Day, D. O. (Eds.). (1998). *Munchausen by proxy syndrome: Misunderstood child abuse.* Thousand Oaks, CA: Sage.

Parten, M. B. (1932). Social participation among preschool children. *Journal of Abnormal and Social Psychology, 27,* 243–269.

Pascalis, O., de Haan, M., & Nelson, C. A. (2002). Is face processing species-specific during the first year of life? *Science, 296,* 1321–1323.

Pascoe, J. M. (1993). Social support during labor and duration of labor: A community-based study. *Public Health Nursing, 10,* 97–99.

Pasqualotto, F. F., Lucon, A. M., Sobreiro, B. P., Pasqualotto, E. B., & Arap, S. (2005). Effects of medical therapy, alcohol, smoking, and endocrine disruptors on male infertility. *Revista do Hospital das Clinicas, 59,* 375–382.

Patchin, J., & Hinduja, S. (2006, April). Bullies move beyond the schoolyard: A preliminary look at cyberbullying. *Youth Violence and Juvenile Justice, 4,* 148–169.

Patenaude, A., F., Guttmacher, A. E., & Collins, F. S. (2002). Genetic testing and psychology: New roles, new responsibilities. *American Psychologist, 57,* 271–282.

Paterson, D. S., Trachtenberg, F. L., Thompson, E. G., Belliveau, R. A., Beggs, A. H., Darnall, R., Chadwick, A. E., Krous, H. F., & Kinney, H. C. (2006). Multiple serotonergic brainstem abnormalities in sudden infant death syndrome. *JAMA: Journal of the American Medical Association, 296,* 2124–2132.

Patterson, C. (2003). Children of lesbian and gay parents. In L. Garnets & D. Kimmel (Eds.), *Psychological perspectives on lesbian, gay, and bisexual experiences* (2nd ed.). New York: Columbia University Press.

Patterson, C. (2006, October). Children of lesbian and gay parents. *Current Directions in Psychological Science, 15,* 241–244.

Patterson, C. J. (1992). Children of lesbian and gay parents. *Child Development, 63,* 1025–1042.

Patterson, C. J. (1994). Lesbian and gay families. *Current Directions in Psychological Science, 3,* 62–64.

Patterson, C. J. (1995). Families of the baby boom: Parents' division of labor and children's adjustment, [Special issue: Sexual orientation and human development] *Developmental Psychology, 31,* 115–123.

Patterson, C. J. (2002). Lesbian and gay parenthood. In M. Bornstein (Ed.), *Handbook of parenting.* Mahwah, NJ: Erlbaum.

Patterson, C., & Friel, L.V. (2000). Sexual orientation and fertility. In G. R. Bentley & N. Mascie-Taylor (Eds.), *Infertility in the modern world: Biosocial perspectives.* Cambridge, UK: Cambridge University Press.

Paul, P. (2006, January 16). Want a brainier baby? *Time, 167*(3), 104.

Paulesu, E., Démonet, J. F., Fazio, F., McCrory, E., Chanoine, V., Brunswick, N., Cappa, S. F., Cossu, G., Habib, M., Frith, C. D., & Frith, U. (2001, March 16). Dyslexia: Cultural diversity and biological unity. *Science, 291,* 2165–2167.

Pauli-Pott, U., Mertesacker, B., & Bade, U. (2003). Parental perceptions and infant temperament development. *Infant Behavior & Development, 26,* 27–48.

Pavis, S., Cunningham-Burley, S., & Amos, A. (1997). Alcohol consumption and young people: Exploring meaning and social context. *Health Education Research, 12,* 311–322.

Pavlov, I. P. (1927). *Conditioned reflexes.* London: Oxford University Press.

Paxton, S. J., Schutz, H. K., Wertheim, E. H., & Muir, S. L. (1999). Friendship clique and peer influences on body image concerns, dietary restraint, extreme weight-loss behaviors, and binge eating in adolescent girls. *Journal of Abnormal Psychology, 108,* 255–266.

Pear, R. (2000, March 19). Proposal to curb the use of drugs to calm the young. *The New York Times,* p. 1.

Pearlman, D., Zierler, S., Meersman, S., Kim, H., Viner-Brown, S., & Caron, C. (2006, February). Race disparities in childhood asthma: Does where you live matter? *Journal of the National Medical Association, 98,* 239–247.

Peck, R. C. (1968). Psychological developments in the second half of life. In B. L. Neugarten (Ed.), *Middle age and aging.* Chicago: University of Chicago Press.

Peck, S. (2003). Measuring sensitivity moment-by-moment: A microanalytic look at the transmission of attachment. *Attachment & Human Development, 5,* 38–63.

Peirano, P., Algarin, C., & Uauy, R. (2003). Sleep-wake states and their regulatory mechanisms throughout early human development. *Journal of Pediatrics, 143,* Supplement, S70–S79.

Pelham, B., & Hetts, J. (2001). Underworked and overpaid: Elevated entitlement in men's self-pay. *Journal of Experimental Social Psychology, 37,* 93–103.

Peltonen, L., & McKusick, V. A. (2001, February 16). Dissecting the human disease in the postgenomic era. *Science, 291,* 1224–1229.

Peltzer, K., & Pengpid, S. (2006). Sexuality of 16- to 17-year-old South Africans in the context of HIV/AIDS. *Social Behavior and Personality, 34,* 239–256.

Penninx, B., Guralnik, J. M., Ferrucci, L., Simonsick, E. M., Deeg, D., & Wallace, R. B. (1998). Depressive symptoms and physical decline in community-dwelling older persons. *Journal of the American Medical Association, 279,* 1720–1726.

Pennisi, E. (2000, May 19). And the gene number is . . . ? *Science, 288,* 1146–1147.

People Weekly. (2000, May 8). Giant steps. p. 117.

Pereira, A. C., Huddleston, D. E., Brickman, A. M., Sosunov, A. A., Hen, R., McKhann, G. M., Sloan, R., Gage, F. H., Brown, T. R., & Small, S. A. (2007). An in vivo correlate of exercise-induced neurogenesis in the adult dentate gyrus. *Proceedings of the National Academy of Sciences, 104*, 5638–5643.

Pereira-Smith, O., Smith, J., et al. (1988, August). Paper presented at the annual meeting of the International Genetics Congress, Toronto, Canada.

Peritto, L. A., Holowka, S., & Sergio, L. E. (2004). Baby hands that move to the rhythm of language: Hearing babies acquiring sign languages babble silently on the hands. *Cognition, 93*, 43–73.

Perlmann, J., & Waters, M. (Eds). (2002). *The new race question: How the census counts multiracial individuals.* New York: Russell Sage Foundation.

Perlmann, R. Y., & Gleason, J. B. (1990, July). Patterns of prohibition in mothers' speech to children. Paper presented at the Fifth International Congress for the Study of Child Language, Budapest, Hungary.

Perner, J., & Ruffman, T. (2005). Infants' insight into the mind: How deep? *Science, 308*, 214–216.

Perozzi, J. A., & Sanchez, M. C. (1992). The effect of instruction in L1 on receptive acquisition of L2 for bilingual children with language delay. *Language, Speech, and Hearing Services in Schools, 23*, 348–352.

Perreault, A., Fothergill-Bourbonnais, F., & Fiset, V. (2004). The experience of family members caring for a dying loved one. *International Journal of Palliative Nursing, 10*, 133–143.

Perrine, N. E., & Aloise-Young, P. A. (2004). The role of self-monitoring in adolescents' susceptibility to passive peer pressure. *Personality & Individual Differences, 37*, 1701–1716.

Perry, T., Steele, C., & Hilliar, A., III. (2003). *Promoting high achievement among African-American students.* Boston: Beacon Press.

Perry, W. G. (1970). *Forms of intellectual and ethical development in the college years.* New York: Holt.

Persson, A., & Musher-Eizenman, D. R. (2003). The impact of a prejudice-prevention television program on young children's ideas about race. *Early Childhood Research Quarterly, 18*, 530–546.

Persson, G. E. B. (2005). Developmental perspectives on prosocial and aggressive motives in preschoolers' peer interactions. *International Journal of Behavioral Development, 29*, 80–91.

Pérusse, D., Dionne, G., Saysset, V. Zoccolillo, M., Tarabulsy, G. M., Tremblay, N., & Tremblay, R. E. (2005). The genetic-environmental etiology of parents' perceptions and self-assessed behaviours toward their 5-month-old infants in a large twin and singleton sample. *Journal of Child Psychology and Psychiatry, 46*, 612–630.

Peters, A. (2003). Isolation or inclusion: Creating safe spaces for lesbian and gay youth. *Families in Society, 84*, 331–337.

Petersen, A. (2000). A longitudinal investigation of adolescents' changing perceptions of pubertal timing. *Developmental Psychology 36*, 37–43.

Peterson, A. C. (1988, September). Those gangly years. *Psychology Today*, 28–34.

Peterson, B. (2006, June). Generativity and successful parenting: An analysis of young adult outcomes. *Journal of Personality, 74*, 847–869.

Peterson, C., & Park, N. (2007). Explanatory style and emotion regulation. In J. J. Gross (Ed.), *Handbook of emotion regulation.* New York: Guilford Press.

Peterson, C., & Roberts, C. (2003). Like mother, like daughter: Similarities in narrative style. *Developmental Psychology, 39*, 551–562.

Peterson, D. M., Marcia, J. E., & Carependale, J. I. (2004). Identity: Does thinking make it so? In C. Lightfood, C. Lalonde, & M. Chandler, *Changing conceptions of psychological life.* Mahwah, NJ: Lawrence Erlbaum Associates.

Peterson, M., & Wilson, J. F. (2004). Work stress in America. *International Journal of Stress Management, 11*, 91–113.

Peterson, R. A., & Brown, S. P. (2005). On the use of beta coefficients in meta-analysis. *Journal of Applied Psychology, 90*, 175–181.

Petit, G., & Dodge, K. A. (2003). Violent children: Bridging development, intervention, and public policy. *Developmental Psychology, Special Issues: Violent Children, 39*, 187–188.

Petitto, L. A., Holowka, S., & Sergio, L. E. (2004). Baby hands that move to the rhythm of language: Hearing babies acquiring sign languages babble silently on the hands. *Cognition, 93*, 43–73.

Petrou, S. (2006). Preterm birth—What are the relevant economic issues? *Early Human Development, 82*(2), 75–76.

Pettingale, K. W., Morris, T., Greer, S., & Haybittle, J. L. (1985). Mental attitudes to cancer: An additional prognostic factor. *Lancet, 310*, 750.

Pettit, G. S., Bates, J. E., & Dodge, K. A. (1997). Supportive parenting, ecological context, and children's adjustment: A seven-year longitudinal study. *Child Development, 68*, 908–923.

Pfeiffer, S. I. (2001). Emotional intelligence: Popular but elusive construct. *Roeper Review, 23*, 138–142.

Phelan, P., Yu, H. C., & Davidson, A. L. (1994). Navigating the psychosocial pressures of adolescence: The voices and experiences of high school youth. *American Educational Research Journal, 31*, 415–447.

Philippot, P. & Feldman, R.S. (Eds.). (2004). *The Regulation of Emotion.* Mahwah, NJ: Erlbaum.

Phillips, D. (1992, September). Death postponement and birthday celebrations. *Psychosomatic Medicine, 26*, 12–18.

Phillips, D. A., Voran, M., Kisker, E., Howes, C., & Whitebook, M. (1994). Child care for children in poverty: Opportunity or inequity? *Child Development, 65*, 472–492.

Phillips, D. A., & Zimmerman, M. (1990). The developmental course of perceived competence and incompetence among competent children. In R. Sternberg & J. Kolligian (Eds.), *Competence considered.* New Haven, CT: Yale University Press.

Phillips, S., King, S., & DuBois, L. (1978). Spontaneous activities of female versus male newborns. *Child Development, 49*, 590–597.

Phillips-Silver, J., & Trainor, L. J. (2005, June 3). Feeling the beat: Movement influences infant rhythm perception. *Science, 308*, 1430.

Phillipson, S. (2006, October). Cultural variability in parent and child achievement attributions: A study from Hong Kong. *Educational Psychology, 26*, 625–642.

Phinney, J. S., Ferguson, D. L., & Tate, J. D. (1997). Intergroup attitudes among ethnic minority adolescents: A causal model. *Child Development, 68*, 955–969.

Phinney, J., Lochner, B., & Murphy, R. (1990). Ethnic identity development and psychological adjustment in adolescence. In A. Stiffman & L. Davis (Eds.), *Advances in adolescent mental health. Vol. 5. Ethnic issues.* Greenwich, CT: JAI Press.

Phinnye, J. S. (2005). Ethnic identity in late modern times: A response to Rattansi and Phoenix. *Identity, 5*, 187–194.

Piaget, J. (1932). *The moral judgment of the child.* New York: Harcourt, Brace & World.

Piaget, J. (1952). *The origins of intelligence in children.* New York: International Universities Press.

Piaget, J. (1954). *The construction of reality in the child* (Margaret Cook, Trans.). New York: Basic Books.

Piaget, J. (1962). *Play, dreams and imitation in childhood.* New York: Norton.

Piaget, J. (1983). Piaget's theory. In W. Kessen (Ed.), P. H. Mussen (Series Ed.), *Handbook of child psychology: Vol 1. History, theory, and methods* (pp. 103–128). New York: Wiley.

Piaget, J., & Inhelder, B. (1958). *The growth of logical thinking from childhood to adolescence* (A. Parsons & S. Seagrin, Trans.). New York: Basic Books.

Piaget, J., Inhelder, B., & Szeminska, A. (1960). *The child's conception of geometry.* New York: Basic Books. (Original work published 1948)

Picavet, H. S., & Hoeymans, N. (2004). Health related quality of life in multiple musculoskeletal diseases: SF-36 and EQ-5D in the DMC3 study. *Annals of the Rheumatic Diseases, 63*, 723–729.

Pinker, S. (1994). *The language instinct.* New York: William Morrow.

Pinker, S. (2005). So how does the mind work? *Mind & Language, 20*, 1–24.

Pipp, S., Easterbrooks, M., & Brown, S. R. (1993). Attachment status and complexity of infants' self- and other-knowledge when tested with mother and father. *Social Development, 2*, 1–14.

Pitts, D. G. (1982). The effects of aging upon selected visual functions. In R. Sekuler, D. Kline, & K. Dismukes (Eds.), *Aging and human visual function.* New York: Alan R. Liss.

Plomin, R. (1994a). *Genetics and experience: The interplay between nature and nurture.* Newbury Park, CA: Sage.

Plomin, R. (1994b). Nature, nurture, and social development. *Social Development, 3*, 37–53.

Plomin, R. (2005). Finding genes in child psychology and psychiatry: When are we going to be there? *Journal of Child Psychology and Psychiatry, 46*, 1030–1038.

Plomin, R., & Caspi, A. (1998). DNA and personality. *European Journal of Personality, 12*, 387–407.

Plomin, R., & McClearn, G. E. (Eds.). (1993). *Nature, nurture, and psychology.* Washington, DC: American Psychological Association.

Plomin, R., & McGuffin, P. (2003). Psychopathology in the postgenomic era. *Review of Psychology, 54*, 205–228.

Plomin, R., & Rutter, M. (1998). Child development, molecular genetics, and what to do with genes once they are found. *Child Development, 69*, 1223–1242.

Plonczynski, D. J., & Plonczynski, K. J. (2007). Hormone therapy in perimenopausal and postmenopausal women: Examining the evidence on cardiovascular disease risks. *Journal of Gerontological Nursing, 33*, 48–55.

Plosker, G., & Keam, S. (2006). Bimatoprost: A pharmacoeconomic review of its use in open-angle glaucoma and ocular hypertension. *PharmacoEconomics, 24*, 297–314.

Poest, C. A., Williams, J. R., Witt, D. D., & Atwood, M. E. (1990). Challenge me to move: Large muscle development in young children. *Young Children, 45*, 4–10.

Polansky, E. (1976). Take him home, Mrs. Smith. *Healthright, 2*(2).

Polivka, B. (2006, January). Needs assessment and intervention strategies to reduce lead-poisoning risk among low-income Ohio toddlers. *Public Health Nursing, 23*, 52–58.

Polivy, J., & Herman, C. (2002). If at first you don't succeed: False hopes of self-change. *American Psychologist, 57*, 677–689.

Polkinghorne, D. E. (2005). Language and meaning: Data collection in qualitative research. *Journal of Counseling Psychology, 52*, [Special issue: Knowledge in context: Qualitative methods in counseling psychology research], 137–145.

Pollack, W. (1999). *Real boys: Rescuing our sons from the myths of boyhood.* Owl Books.

Pollack, W., Shuster, T., & Trelease, J. (2001). *Real boys' voices.* Penguin.

Pollak, S., Holt, L., & Wismer Fries, A. (2004). Hemispheric asymmetries in children's perception of nonlinguistic human affective sounds. *Developmental Science, 7*, 10–18.

Pollitt, E., Golub, M., Gorman, K., Grantham McGregor, S., Levitsky, D., Schürch, B., Strupp, B., & Wachs, T. (1996). A reconceptualization of the effects of undernutrition on children's biological, psychosocial, and behavioral development. *Social Policy Report, 10*, 1–22.

Pomares, C. G., Schirrer, J., & Abadie, V. (2002). Analysis of the olfactory capacity of healthy children before language acquisition. *Journal of Developmental Behavior and Pediatrics, 23*, 203–207.

Ponton, L. E. (2001). *The sex lives of teenagers: Revealing the secret world of adolescent boys and girls.* New York: Penguin Putnam.

Poon, H. F., Calabrese, V., Scapagnini, G., & Butterfield, D. A. (2004). Free radicals and brain aging. *Clinical Geriatric Medicine, 20*, 329–359.

Population Council Report. (1995, May 30). The decay of families is global, studies says. *The New York Times*, p. A5.

Porath, A. J., & Fried, P. A. (2005). Effects of prenatal cigarette and marijuana exposure on drug use among offspring. *Neurotoxicological Teratology, 27*, 267–277.

Porges, S. W., Lipsitt, & Lewis P. (1993). Neonatal responsivity to gustatory stimulation: The gustatory-vagal hypothesis. *Infant Behavior & Development, 16*, 487–494.

Porter, E., & Walsh, M. (2005, February 9). Retirement becomes a rest stop as pensions and benefits shrink. *The New York Times*, p. A1.

Porter, R. H., Balogh, R. D., & Malkin, J. W. (1988). Olfactory influences on mother–infant interactions. In C. Rovee-Collier & L. Lipsitt (Eds.), *Advances in infancy research* (Vol. 5). Norwood, NJ: Ablex.

Portes, A., & Rumbaut, R. (2001). *Legacies: The story of the immigrant second generation.* Los Angeles: University of California Press.

Porzelius, L. K., Dinsmore, B. D., & Staffelbach, D. (2001). Eating disorders. In M. Hersen & V. B. Van Hasselt (Eds.), *Advanced abnormal psychology* (2nd ed.). New York: Kluwer Academic/Plenum Publishers.

Posthuma, D., & de Geus, E. (2006, August). Progress in the molecular-genetic study of intelligence. *Current Directions in Psychological Science, 15*, 151–155.

Poulain, M., Doucet, M., Major, G., Drapeau, V., Séries, F., Boulet, L., et al. (2006, April). The effect of obesity on chronic respiratory diseases: Pathophysiology and therapeutic strategies. *Canadian Medical Association Journal, 174*, 1293–1299.

Poulin-Dubois, D. (1999). Infants' distinction between animate and inanimate objects: the origins of naive psychology. In P. Rochat, *Early social cognition.* Hillsdale, NJ: Lawrence Erlbaum Associates.

Poulin-Dubois, D., Serbin, L., & Eichstedt, J. (2002). Men don't put on make-up: Toddlers' knowledge of the gender stereotyping of household activities. *Social Development, 11*, 166–181.

Poulin-Dubois, D., Serbin, L. A., Kenyon, B., & Derbyshire, A. (1994). Infants' intermodal knowledge about gender. *Developmental Psychology, 30*, 436–442.

Poulton, R., & Caspi, A. (2005). Commentary: How does socioeconomic disadvantage during childhood damage health in adulthood? Testing psychosocial pathways. *International Journal of Epidemiology, 23*, 51–55.

Powell, G. F., Brasel, J. A., & Blizzard, R. M. (1967). Emotional deprivation and growth retardation simulating idiopathic hypopituitarism: I. Clinical evaluation of the syndrome. *New England Journal of Medicine, 276*, 1272–1278.

Powell, M. B., Thomson, D. M., & Ceci, S. J. (2003). Children's memory of recurring events: Is the first event always the best remembered? *Applied Cognitive Psychology, 17*, 127–146.

Powell, R. (2004, June 19). Colleges construct housing for elderly: Retiree students move to campus. *The Washington Post*, p. F13.

Power, T. G. (1999). *Play and exploration in children and animals.* Mahwah, NJ: Erlbaum.

Prater, L. (2002). African American families: Equal partners in general and special education. In F. Obiakor & A. Ford (Eds.), *Creating successful learning environments for African American learners with exceptionalities.* Thousand Oaks, CA: Corwin Press, Inc.

Pratt, H., Phillips, E., & Greydanus, D. (2003). Eating disorders in the adolescent population: Future directions. *Journal of Adolescent Research, 18*, 297–317.

Pratt, M. W., Danso, H. A., Arnold, M. L., Norris, J. E., & Filyer, R. (2001). Adult generativity and the socialization of adolescents: Relations to mothers' and fathers' parenting beliefs, styles, and practices. *Journal of Personality, 69*, 89–120.

Prechtl, H. F. R. (1982). Regressions and transformations during neurological development. In T. G. Bever (Ed.), *Regressions in mental development.* Hillsdale, NJ: Erlbaum.

Prentice, A., Schoenmakers, I., Laskey, M. A., de Bono, S., Ginty, F., & Goldberg, G. R. (2006). Nutrition and bone growth and development. *Proceedings of the Nutritional Society, 65*, 348–360.

Prescott, C., & Gottesman, I. (1993). Genetically mediated vulnerability to schizophrenia. *Psychiatric Clinics of North America, 16*, 245–267.

Prescott, C. A., Caldwell, C. B., Carey, G., Vogler, G. P., Trumbetta, S. L., & Gottesman, I. I. (2005). The Washington University Twin Study of alcoholism. *American Journal of Medical Genetics, B, Neuropsychiatric Genetics, 31*.

Pressley, M. (1987). Are keyword method effects limited to slow presentation rates? An empirically based reply to Hall and Fuson (1986). *Journal of Educational Psychology, 79*, 333–335.

Pressley, M., & Levin, J. R. (1983). *Cognitive strategy research: Psychological foundations.* New York: Springer-Verlag.

Pressley, M., & Schneider, W. (1997). *Introduction to memory development during childhood and adolescence.* Mahwah, NJ: Lawrence Erlbaum.

Pressley, M., & VanMeter, P. (1993). Memory strategies: Natural development and use following instruction. In R. Pasnak & M. L. Howe (Eds.), *Emerging themes in cognitive development* (Vol. II). New York: Springer-Verlag.

Prezbindowski, A. K., & Lederberg, A. R. (2003). Vocabulary assessment of deaf and hard-of-hearing children from infancy through the preschool years. *Journal of Deaf Studies and Deaf Education, 8*, 383–400.

Price, D. W., & Goodman, G. S. (1990). Visiting the wizard: Children's memory for a recurring event. *Child Development, 61*, 664–680.

Price, R., & Gottesman, I. (1991). Body fat in identical twins reared apart: Roles for genes and environment. *Behavior Genetics, 21*, 1–7.

Prigerson, H. (2003). Costs to society of family caregiving for patients with end-stage Alzheimer's disease. *New England Journal of Medicine, 349*, 1891–1892.

Prigerson, H. G., Frank, E., Kasl, S. V., et al. (1995). Complicated grief and bereavement-related depression as distinct disorders: Preliminary empirical validation in elderly bereaved spouses. *American Journal of Psychiatry, 152*, 22–30.

PRIMEDIA/Roper National Youth Survey. (1999). *Adolescents' view of society's ills.* Storrs, CT: Roper Center for Public Opinion Research.

PRIMEDIA/Roper (1998). *Adolescents' view of society's ills.* Storrs, CT: Roper Center for Public Opinion Research.

Prince, M. (2000, November 13). How technology has changed the way we have babies. *The Wall Street Journal*, pp. R4, R13.

Prince, R. L., Smith, M., Dick, I. M., Price, R. I., Webb, P. G., Henderson, N. K., & Harris, M. M. (1991). Prevention of postmenopausal osteoporosis. A comparative study of exercise, calcium supplementation, and hormone replacement therapy. *New England Journal of Medicine, 325*, 1189–1195.

Probert, B. (2004). "I just couldn't fit in": Gender and unequal outcomes in academic careers. *Gender, Work & Organization, 12*, 50–72.

Principe, G. F., & Ceci, S. J. (2002). 'I saw it with my own ears': The effects of peer conversations on preschoolers' reports of nonexperienced events. *Journal of Experimental Child Psychology, 83*, 1–25.

Pronin, E., Steele, C., & Ross, L. (2004). Identity bifurcation in response to stereotype threat: Women and mathematics. *Journal of Experimental Social Psychology, 40*, 152–168.

Proper, K., Cerin, E., & Owen, N. (2006, April). Neighborhood and individual socio-economic variations in the contribution of occupational physical activity to total physical activity. *Journal of Physical Activity & Health, 3*, 179–190.

Propper, C., & Moore, G. (2006, December). The influence of parenting on infant emotionality: A multilevel psychobiological perspective. *Developmental Review, 26*, 427–460.

Pruchno, R., & Rosenbaum, J. (2003). Social relationships in adulthood and old age. In R. Lerner & M. Easterbrooks (Eds.), *Handbook of psychology: Developmental psychology, Vol. 6.* New York: John Wiley & Sons, Inc.

Puchalski, M., & Hummel, P. (2002). The reality of neonatal pain. *Advances in Neonatal Care, 2*, 245–247.

Puntambekar, S., & Hübscher, R. (2005). Tools for scaffolding students in a complex learning environment: What have we gained and what have we missed? *Educational Psychologist, 40*, 1–12.

Purdy, M. (1995, November 6). A kind of sexual revolution. *The New York Times,* pp. B1, B6.

Putney, N. M., & Bengtson, V. L. (2001). Families, intergenerational relationships and kinkeeping in midlife. In M. E. Lachman, (Ed.), *Handbook of midlife development.* Hoboken, NJ: John Wiley & Sons.

Putterman, E., & Linden, W. (2004). Appearance versus health: Does the reason for dieting affect dieting behavior? *Journal of Behavioral Medicine, 27,* 185–204.

Pyryt, M. C., & Mendaglio, S. (1994). The multidimensional self-concept: A comparison of gifted and average-ability adolescents. *Journal for the Education of the Gifted, 17,* 299–305.

Pyszczynski, T., Solomon, S., & Greenberg, J. (2003). *In the wake of 9/11: The psychology of terror.* Washington, DC: American Psychological Association.

Qian, Z-C, & Lichter, D. T. (2007). Social boundary and marital assimilation: Evaluating trends in racial and ethnic intermarriage. *American Sociological Review, 72,* 68–94.

Quade, R. (1994, July 10). Day care brightens young and old. *The New York Times,* p. B8.

Quartz, S. R. (2003). Toward a developmental evolutionary psychology: Genes, development, and the evolution of human cognitive architecture. In S. J. Scher & F. Rauscher (Eds.), *Evolutionary psychology: Alternative approaches.* Dordrecht, Netherlands: Kluwer Academic Publishers.

Quatromoni, P., Pencina, M., Cobain, M., Jacques, P., & D'Agostino, R. (2006, August). Dietary quality predicts adult weight gain: Findings from the Framingham Offspring Study. *Obesity, 14,* 1383–1391.

Quinn, J. B. (1993, April 5). What's for dinner, Mom? *Newsweek,* 68.

Quinn, M. (1990, January 29). Don't aim that pack at us. *Time,* 60.

Quinnan, E. J. (1997). Connection and autonomy in the lives of elderly male celibates: Degrees of disengagement. *Journal of Aging Studies, 11,* 115–130.

Quintana, S. (2004). Race, ethnicity, and culture in child development. *Child Development, 75,* v–vi.

Raag, T. (2003). Racism, gender identities and young children: Social relations in a multi-ethnic, inner-city primary school. *Archives of Sexual Behavior, 32,* 392–393.

Rabain-Jamin, J., & Sabeau-Jouannet, E. (1997). Maternal speech to 4-month-old infants in two cultures: Wolof and French. *International Journal of Behavioral Development, 20,* 425–451.

Rabin, R. (2006, June 13). Breast-feed or else. *The New York Times,* p. D1.

Rabkin, J., Remien, R., & Wilson, C. (1994). *Good doctors, good patients: Partners in HIV treatment.* New York: NCM Publishers.

Raeburn, P. (2004, October 1). Too immature for the death penalty? *The New York Times Magazine,* 26–29.

Raeff, C. (2004). Within-culture complexities: Multifaceted and interrelated autonomy and connectedness characteristics in late adolescent selves. In M. E. Mascolo & J. Li (Eds.), *Culture and developing selves: Beyond dichotomization.* San Francisco, CA: Jossey-Bass.

Rahman, Q., & Wilson, G. (2003). Born gay? The psychobiology of human sexual orientation. *Personality & Individual Differences, 34,* 1337–1382.

Raikes, H., Pan, B. A., Luze, G., Tamis-Le Monda, C. S., Brooks-Gunn, J., Constantine, J., Tarullo, L. B., Raikes, H. A., & Rodriguez, E. (2006). Mother-child book reading in low-income families: Correlations and outcomes during the first three years of life. *Child Development,* 954–953.

Raikkonen, K., Keskivaara, P., Keltikangas, J. L., & Butzow, E. (1995). Psychophysiological arousal related to Type A components in adolescent boys. *Scandinavian Journal of Psychology, 36,* 142–152.

Rakison, D., & Oakes, L. (2003). *Early category and concept development: Making sense of the blooming, buzzing confusion.* London: Oxford University Press.

Raman, L., & Winer, G. (2002). Children's and adults' understanding of illness: Evidence in support of a co-existence model. *Genetic, Social, & General Psychology Monographs, 128,* 325–355.

Ramey, C. T., & Ramey, S. L. (1998). Early intervention and early experience. *American Psychologist, 53,* 109–120.

Ramsey-Rennels, J. L., & Langlois, J. H. (2006). Infants' differential processing of female and male faces. *Current Directions in Psychological Science, 15,* 59–62.

Ranade, V. (1993). Nutritional recommendations for children and adolescents. *International Journal of Clinical Pharmacology, Therapy, and Toxicology, 31,* 285–290.

Randahl, G. J. (1991). A typological analysis of the relations between measured vocational interests and abilities. *Journal of Vocational Behavior, 38,* 333–350.

Rando, T. A. (1993). *Treatment of complicated mourning.* Champaign, IL: Research Press.

Rank, M. R., & Hirschl, T. A. (1999). Estimating the proportion of Americans ever experiencing poverty during their elderly years. *Journals of Gerontology Series B-Psychological Science and Social Sciences, 54,* S184–S193.

Rankin, B. (2004). The importance of intentional socialization among children in small groups: A conversation with Loris Malaguzzi. *Early Childhood Education Journal, 32,* 81–85.

Rankin, J., Lane, D., & Gibbons, F. (2004). Adolescent self-consciousness: Longitudinal age changes and gender differences in two cohorts. *Journal of Research on Adolescence, 14,* 1–21.

Ransjö-Arvidson, A. B., Matthiesen, A. S., Lilja, G., Nissen, E., Widström, A. M., & Unväs-Moberg. (2001). Maternal analgesia during labor disturbs newborn behavior: Effects on breastfeeding, temperature, and crying. *Birth, 28,* 5–12.

Ransom, R. L., Sutch, R., & Williamson, S. H. (1991). Retirement: Past and present. In A. H. Munnell (Ed.), *Retirement and public policy: Proceedings of the Second Conference of the National Academy of Social Insurance,* Washington, DC. Dubuque, IA: Kendall/Hunt.

Rao, V. (1997). Wife-beating in rural South India: A qualitative and econometric analysis. *Social Science & Medicine, 44,* 1169–1180.

Rapkin, B. D., & Fischer, K. (1992). Personal goals of older adults: Issues in assessment and prediction. *Psychology and Aging, 7,* 127–137.

Rapp, M., Krampe, R., & Balles, P. (2006, January). Adaptive task prioritization in aging: Selective resource allocation to postural control is preserved in Alzheimer disease. *American Journal of Geriatric Psychiatry, 14,* 52–61.

Raskauskas, J., & Stoltz, A. D. (2007). Involvement in traditional and electronic bullying among adolescents. *Developmental Psychology, 43,* 564–575.

Ratanachu-Ek, S. (2003). Effects of multivitamin and folic acid supplementation in malnourished children. *Journal of the Medical Association of Thailand, 4,* 86–91.

Rattner, A., & Nathans, J. (2006, November). Macular degeneration: Recent advances and therapeutic opportunities. *Nature Reviews Neuroscience, 7,* 860–872.

Rattan, S. I. S., Kristensen, P., & Clark, B. F. C. (Eds.) (2006). *Understanding and modulating aging.* Malden, MA: Blackwell Publishing on behalf of the New York Academy of Sciences, 2006.

Raudsepp, L., & Liblik, R. (2002). Relationship of perceived and actual motor competence in children. *Perception and Motor Skills, 94,* 1059–1070.

Ray, O. (2004). How the mind hurts and heals the body. *American Psychologist, 59,* 29–40.

Rayner, K., Foorman, B. R., Perfetti, C. A., Pesetsky, D., & Seidenberg, M. S. (2002, March). How should reading be taught? *Scientific American,* 85–91.

Raz, N., Rodrigue, K., Kennedy, K., & Acker, J. (2007, March). Vascular health and longitudinal changes in brain and cognition in middle-aged and older adults. *Neuropsychology, 21,* 149–157.

Reddy, L. A., & Pfeiffer, S. I. (1997). Effectiveness of treatment of foster care with children and adolescents: A review of outcome studies. *Journal of the American Academy of Child & Adolescent Psychiatry, 36,* 381–588.

Reddy, V. (1999). Prelinguistic communication. In M. Barrett (Ed,), *The development of language* (pp. 25–50). Philadelphia: Psychology Press.

Redshaw, M. E. (1997). Mothers of babies requiring special care: Attitudes and experiences. *Journal of Reproductive & Infant Psychology, 15,* 109–120.

Ree, M., & Carretta, T. (2002). g2K. *Human Performance, 15,* 3–24.

Rees, A. (2003). How homophobia hurts children: Nurturing diversity at home, at school, and in the community. *Sex Roles, 49,* 555–556.

Reese, E., & Cox, A. (1999). Quality of adult book reading affects children's emergent literacy. *Developmental Psychology, 35,* 20–28.

Reid, M., Miller, W., & Kerr, B. (2004). Sex-based glass ceilings in U.S. state-level bureaucracies, 1987–1997. *Administration & Society, 36,* 377–405.

Reifman, A. (2000). Revisiting *The Bell Curve. Psycoloquy,* 11.

Reiner, W. G., & Gearhart, J. P. (2004). Discordant sexual identity in some genetic males with cloacal exstrophy assigned to female sex at birth. *The New England Journal of Medicine, 350,* 333–341.

Reis, H. T., Collins, W. A., & Berscheid, E. (2000). The relationship context of human behavior and development. *Psychological Bulletin, 126,* 844–872.

Reis, S., & Renzulli, J. (2004). Current research on the social and emotional development of gifted and talented students: Good news and future possibilities. *Psychology in the Schools, 41,* 119–130.

Reiss, M. J. (1984). Human sociobiology. *Zygon Journal of Religion and Science, 19,* 117–140.

Reissland, N., & Shepherd, J. (2006, March). The effect of maternal depressed mood on infant emotional reaction in a surprise-eliciting situation. *Infant Mental Health Journal, 27,* 173–187.

Renner, L., & Slack, K. (2006, June). Intimate partner violence and child maltreatment: Understanding intra- and intergenerational connections. *Child Abuse & Neglect, 30,* 599–617.

Reschly, D. J. (1996). Identification and assessment of students with disabilities. *The Future of Children, 6,* 40–53.

Rescorla, L., Alley, A., & Christine, J. (2001). Word frequencies in toddlers' lexicons. *Journal of Speech, Language, & Hearing Research, 44,* 598–609.

Resnick, B. (2000). A seven step approach to starting an exercise program for older adults. *Patient Education & Counseling, 39,* 243–252.

Resnick, M. D., Bearman, P. S., Blum, R. W., Bauman, K. E., Harris, M. R., Jones, L., Tabor, J., Beuhring, T., Sieving, R., Shew, M., Ireland, M., Bearinger, L. H., & Udry, J. R. (1997). Protecting adolescents from harm: Findings from the National Longitudinal Study on Adolescent Health. *Journal of the American Medical Association, 278*, 823–832.

Resta R., Biesecker, B. B., Bennett, R. L., Blum, S., Estabrooks. H. S., Strecker, M. N., Williams J. L. (2006). A new definition of genetic counseling: National Society of Genetic Counselors' Task Force Report. *Journal of Genetic Counseling, 15*, 77–83.

Reuters Health eLine. (2002, June 26). Baby's injuring points to danger of kids imitating television. *Reuters Health eLine.*

Reutzel, D., Fawson, P., Smith J. (2006). Words to Go!: Evaluating a first-grade parent involvement program for "making" words at home. *Reading Research and Instruction* [serial online], *45*, 119–159.

Reyna, V. F. (1997). Conceptions of memory development with implications for reasoning and decision making. In R. Vasta (Ed.), *Annals of child development: A research annual* (Vol. 12, pp. 87–118). London, England: Jessica Kingsley Publishers.

Reyna, V. F., & Farley, F. (2006). Risk and rationality in adolescent decision making. *Psychological Science in the Public Interest, 7*, 1–44.

Rhoades, G., Stanley, S., & Markman, H. (2006, December). Pre-engagement cohabitation and gender asymmetry in marital commitment. *Journal of Family Psychology, 20*, 553–560.

Rholes, W., Simpson, J., Tran, S., Martin, A., & Friedman, M. (2007, March). Attachment and information seeking in romantic relationships. *Personality and Social Psychology Bulletin, 33*, 422–438.

Rhule, D. (2005). Take care to do no harm: Harmful interventions for youth problem behavior. *Professional Psychology: Research and Practice, 36*, 618–625.

Ricciardelli, L., & McCabe, M. (2003). Sociocultural and individual influences on muscle gain and weight loss strategies among adolescent boys and girls. *Psychology in the Schools, 40*, 209–224.

Ricciardelli, L. A., & McCabe, M. P. (2004). A biopsychosocial model of disordered eating and the pursuit of muscularity in adolescent boys. *Psychological Bulletin, 130*, 179–205.

Rice, F. P. (1999). *Intimate relationships, marriages, & families* (4th ed.). Mountain View, CA: Mayfield.

Rice, M. L., Huston, A. C., Truglio, R., & Wright, J. (1990). Words from "Sesame Street": Learning vocabulary while viewing. *Developmental Psychology, 26*,(3) 421–428.

Richards, H. D., Bear, G. G., Stewart, A. L., & Norman, A. D. (1992). Moral reasoning and classroom conduct: Evidence of a curvilinear relationship. *Merrill-Palmer Quarterly, 38*, 176–190.

Richards, M. H., Crowe, P. A., Larson, R., & Swarr, A. (1998). Developmental patterns and gender differences in the experience of peer companianship during adolescence. *Child Development, 69*, 154–163.

Richards, M. H., & Duckett, E. (1994). The relationship of maternal employment to early adolescent daily experience with and without parents. *Child Development, 65*, 225–236.

Richards, M. P. M. (1996). The childhood environment and the development of sexuality. In C. J. K. Henry & S. J. Ulijaszek (Eds.), *Long-term consequences of early environment: Growth, development and the lifespan developmental perspective.* Cambridge, England: Cambridge University Press.

Richards, R., Kinney, D. K., Benet, M., & Merzel, A. P. C. (1990). Assessing everyday creativity: Characteristics of the lifetime creativity scales and validation with three large samples. *Journal of Personality and Social Psychology, 54*, 476–485.

Richardson, G. A., Ryan, C., & Willford, J. (2002). Prenatal alcohol and marijuana exposure: Effects on neuropsychological outcomes at 10 years. *Neurotoxicology and Teratology, 24* [Special Issue], 311–320.

Richardson, K., & Norgate, S. (2007). A critical analysis of IQ studies of adopted children. *Human Development, 49*, 319–335.

Rideout V., Vandewater, E., & Wartella, E. (2003). *Zero to Six: Electronic media in the lives of infants, toddlers, and preschoolers.* Menlo Park, CA: Kaiser Family Foundation.

Riebe, D., Burbank, P., & Garber, C. (2002). Setting the stage for active older adults. In P. Burbank & D. Riebe (Eds.), *Promoting exercise and behavior change in older adults: Interventions with the transtheoretical mode.* New York: Springer Publishing Co.

Rigby, K., & Bagshaw, D. (2003). Prospects of adolescent students collaborating with teachers in addressing issues of bullying and conflict in schools. *Educational Psychology, 23*, 535–546.

Riley, L., & Bowen, C. (2005, January). The sandwich generation: Challenges and coping strategies of multigenerational families. *The Family Journal, 13*, 52–58.

Rimer, B. K., Meissner, H., Breen, N., Legler, J. & Coyne, C. A. (2001). Social and behavioral interventions to increase breast cancer screening. In N. Schneiderman & M. A. Speers et al. (Eds.), *Integrating behavioral and social sciences with public health.* Washington, DC: American Psychological Association.

Rinaldi, C. (2002). Social conflict abilities of children identified as sociable, aggressive, and isolated: Developmental implications for children at-risk for impaired peer relations. *Developmental Disabilities Bulletin, 30*, 77–94.

Ripple, C., & Zigler, E. (2003). Research, policy, and the federal role in prevention initiatives for children. *American Psychologist, 58*, 482–490.

Ripple, C. H., Gilliam, W. S., Chanana, N., & Zigler, E. (1999). Will fifty cooks spoil the broth? The debate over entrusting Head Start to the states. *American Psychologist, 54*, 327–343.

Ritchie, L. (2003). Adult day care: Northern perspectives. *Public Health Nursing, 20*, 120–131.

Ritzen, E. M. (2003). Early puberty: What is normal and when is treatment indicated? *Hormone Research, 60*, Supplement, 31–34.

Rivera-Gaziola, M., Silva-Pereyra, & J., Kuhl, P. K. (2005). Brain potentials to native and non-native speech contrasts in 7- and 11-month-old American infants. *Developmental Science, 8*, 162–172.

Robb, A., & Dadson, M. (2002). Eating disorders in males. *Child & Adolescent Psychiatric Clinics of North America, 11*, 399–418.

Robergeau, K., Joseph, J., & Silber, T. (2006, December). Hospitalization of children and adolescents for eating disorders in the state of New York. *Journal of Adolescent Health, 39*, 806–810.

Roberto, K. A. (1987). Exchange and equity in friendships. In R. G. Admas & R. Blieszner (Eds.), *Older adult friendships: Structure and process.* Newbury Park, CA: Sage.

Roberts, B., Helson, R., & Klohnen, E. (2002). Personality development and growth in women across 30 years: Three perspectives. *Journal of Personality, 70*, 79–102.

Roberts, B. W., Walton, K. E., & Viechtbauer, W. (2006). Patterns of mean-level change in personality traits across the life course: A meta-analysis of longitudinal studies. *Psychological Bulletin, 132*, 1–25.

Roberts, R. E., Phinney, J. S., Masse, L. C., Chen, Y. R., Roberts, C. R., & Romero, A. (1999). The structure of ethnic identity of young adolescents from diverse ethnocultural groups. *Journal of Early Adolescence, 19*, 301–322.

Roberts, S. (2006, Ocotber 15). It's official: To be married means to be outnumbered. *The New York Times*, p. 22.

Roberts, S. (2007, January 16). 51% of women are now living without spouse. *The New York Times*, p. A1.

Robins, R. W., & Trzesniewski, K. H. (2005). Self-esteem development across the lifespan. *Current Directions in Psychological Science, 14*, 158–162.

Robinson, A. & Stark, D. R. (2005). *Advocates in action.* Washington, DC: National Association for the Education of Young Children.

Robinson, A. J., & Pascalis, O. (2004). Development of flexible visual recognition memory in human infants. *Developmental Science, 7*, 527–533.

Robinson, G. (2002). Cross-cultural perspectives on menopause. In A. Hunter & C. Forden (Eds.), *Readings in the psychology of gender: Exploring our differences and commonalities.* Needham Heights, MA: Allyn & Bacon.

Robinson, G. E. (2004, April 16). Beyond nature and nurture. *Science, 304*, 397–399.

Robinson, J. P., & Bianchi, S. (1997, December). The children's hours. *American Demographics*, 20–23.

Robinson, J. P., & Godbey, G. (1997). *Time for life: The surprising ways Americans use their time.* College Park: Pennsylvania State University Press.

Robinson, N. M., Zigler, E., & Gallagher, J. J. (2000). Two tails of the normal curve: Similarities and differences in the study of mental retardation and giftedness. *American Psychologist, 55*, 1413–1421.

Rochat, P. (2004). Emerging co-awareness. In G. Bremner & A. Slater (Eds.), *Theories of infant development.* Malden, MA: Blackwell Publishers.

Roche, T. (2000, November 13). The crisis of foster care. *Time*, 74–82.

Roecke, C., & Cherry, K. (2002). Death at the end of the 20th century: Individual processes and developmental tasks in old age. *International Journal of Aging & Human Development, 54*, 315–333.

Roelofs, J., Meesters, C., Ter Huurne, M., Bamelis, L., & Muris, P. (2006, June). On the links between attachment style, parental rearing behaviors, and internalizing and externalizing problems in non-clinical children. *Journal of Child and Family Studies, 15*, 331–344.

Roffwarg, H. P., Muzio, J. N., & Dement, W. C. (1966). Ontogenic development of the human sleep–dream cycle. *Science, 152*, 604–619.

Rogers, C. R. (1971). A theory of personality in S. Maddi (Ed.), *Perspectives on personality.* Boston: Little Brown.

Rogers, S., & Willams, J. (2006). *Imitation and the social mind: Autism and typical development.* Guilford Press.

Roggeveen, A. B., Prime, D. J., & Ward, L. M. (2007). Lateralized readiness potentials reveal motor slowing in the aging brain. *Journal of Gerontology, B, Psychological Science and Social Science, 62*, P78–P84.

Rogoff, B. (1995). *Observing sociocultural activity on three planes: Participatory appropriation, guided participation, and apprenticeship.* New York: Cambridge University Press.

Rogoff, B., & Chavajay, P. (1995). What's become of research on the cultural basis of cognitive development? *American Psychologist, 50*, 859–877.

Rolls, E. (2000). Memory systems in the brain. *Annual Review of Psychology, 51*, 599–630.

Romaine, S. (1994). *Bilingualism* (2nd ed.). London: Blackwell.

Romero, A., & Roberts, R. (2003). The impact of multiple dimensions of ethnic identity on discrimination and adolescents' self-esteem. *Journal of Applied Social Psychology, 33*, 2288–2305.

Ron, P. (2006). Care giving offspring to aging parents: How it affects their marital relations, parenthood, and mental health. *Illness, Crisis, & Loss, 14*, 1–21.

Rönkä, A., & Pulkkinen, L. (1995). Accumulation of problems in social functioning in young adulthood: A developmental approach. *Journal of Personality and Social Psychology, 69*, 381–391.

Roopnarine, J. (1992). Father–child play in India. In K. MacDonald (Ed.), *Parent–child play*. Albany: State University of New York Press.

Roopnarine, J. (2002). *Conceptual, social-cognitive, and contextual issues in the fields of play*. Westport, CT: Ablex Publishing.

Roopnarine, J. L., Johnson, J. E., & Hooper, F. H. (Eds.). (1994). *Children's play in diverse cultures*. Albany: State University of New York Press.

Ropar, D., Mitchell, P., & Ackroyd, K. (2003). Do children with autism find it difficult to offer alternative interpretations to ambiguous figures? *British Journal of Developmental Psychology, 21*, 387–395.

Roper Starch Worldwide. (1997, August). Romantic resurgence. *American Demographics*, p. 35.

Rose, A. J. (2002). Co-rumination in the friendships of girls and boys. *Child Development, 73*, 1830–1843.

Rose, A. J., & Asher, S. R. (1999). Children's goals and strategies in response to conflicts within a friendship. *Developmental Psychology, 35*, 69–79.

Rose, R. J., Viken, R. J., Dick, D.M., Bates, J. E., Pulkkinen, L., & Kaprio, J. (2003). It *does* take a village: Nonfamilial environments and children's behavior. *Psychological Science, 14*, 273–278.

Rose, S., Jankowski, J., & Feldman, J. (2002). Speed of processing and face recognition at 7 and 12 months. *Infancy, 3*, 435–455.

Rose, S. A., & Feldman, J. F. (1997). Memory and speed: Their role in the relation of infant information processing to later IQ. *Child Development, 68*, 630–641.

Rose, S., Feldman, J., & Jankowski, J. (1999). Visual and auditory temporal processing, cross-modal transfer, and reading. *Journal of Learning Disabilities, 32*, 256–266.

Rose, S. A., Feldman, J. F., & Jankowski, J. J. (2004). Dimensions of cognition in infancy. *Intelligence, 32*, 245–262.

Rose, S. A., Feldman, J. F., Wallace, I. F., & McCarton, C. (1991). Information processing at 1 year: Relation to birth status and developmental outcome during the first 5 years. *Developmental Psychology, 27*, 723–737.

Rosen, K. S., & Burke, P. B. (1999). Multiple attachment relationships within families: Mothers and fathers with two young children. *Developmental Psychology, 35*, 436–444.

Rosenblatt, P. C. (1988). Grief: The social context of private feelings. *Journal of Social Issues, 44*, 67–78.

Rosenblatt, P. C. (2001). A social constructionist perspective on cultural differences in grief. In M. S. Stroebe, R. O. Hansson, W. Stroebe, & H. Schut (Eds.), *Handbook of bereavement research: Consequences, coping, and care*. Washington, DC: American Psychological Association Press.

Rosenblatt, P. C. & Wallace, B. R. (2005). *African American grief*. New York: Brunner-Routledge.

Rosenfeld, B., Krivo, S., Breitbart, W., & Chochinov, H. M. (2000). Suicide, assisted suicide, and euthanasia in the terminally ill. In H. M. Chochinov & W. Breitbart (Eds.), *Handbook of psychiatry in palliative medicine*. New York: Oxford University Press.

Rosenstein, D., & Oster, H. (1988). Differential facial responses to four basic tastes in newborns. *Child Development, 59*, 1555–1568.

Rosenthal, H., & Crisp, R. (2006, April). Reducing stereotype threat by blurring intergroup boundaries. *Personality and Social Psychology Bulletin, 32*, 501–511.

Rosenthal, R. (1994). Interpersonal expectancy effects: A 30–year perspective. *Current Directions in Psychological Science, 3*, 176–179.

Rosenthal, R. (2002). The Pygmalion effect and its mediating mechanisms. In J. Aronson (Ed.), *Improving academic achievement: Impact of psychological factors on education*. San Diego: Academic Press.

Rosenthal, R., & Jacobson, L. (1968). *Pygmalion in the classroom: Teacher expectation and pupils' intellectual development*. New York: Holt, Rinehart & Winston.

Ross, C. E., Microwsky, J., & Goldsteen, K. (1991). The impact of the family on health. In A. Booth (Ed.), *Contemporary families*. Minneapolis, MN: National Council on Family Relations.

Ross, M., & Wilson, A. E. (2003). Autobiographical memory and conceptions of self: Getting better all the time. *Current Directions in Psychological Science, 12*, 66–69.

Rossman, I. (1977). Anatomic and body composition changes with aging. In C. E. Finch & L. Hayflick (Eds.), *Handbook of the biology of aging*. New York: Van Nostrand Reinhold.

Rossouw, J. E. (2006). Implications of recent clinical trials of postmenopausal hormone therapy for management of cardiovascular disease. *Annals of the New York Academy of Sciences, 1089*, 444–453.

Rossouw, J. E., Prentice, R. L., Manson, J. E., Wu, L., Barad, D., Barnabei, V. M., Ko, M., LaCroix, A. Z., Margolis, K. L., & Stefanick, M. L. (2007). Postmenopausal hormone therapy and risk of cardiovascular disease by age and years since menopause. *Journal of the American Medical Association, 297*, 1465–1477.

Rotenberg, K. J., & Morrison, J. (1993). Loneliness and college achievement: Do loneliness scale scores predict college drop-out? *Psychological Reports, 73*, 1283–1288.

Roth, D., Slone, M., & Dar, R. (2000). Which way cognitive development? An evaluation of the Piagetian and the domain-specific research programs. *Theory & Psychology, 10*, 353–373.

Rothbart, M., & Derryberry, D. (2002). Temperament in children. In C. von Hofsten & L. Backman (Eds.), *Psychology at the turn of the millennium, vol. 2: Social, developmental, and clinical perspectives*. Florence, KY: Taylor & Frances/Routledge.

Rothbart, M. K., Ahadi, S. A., & Evans, D. E. (2000). Temperament and personality: Origins and outcomes. *Journal of Personality and Social Psychology, 78*, 122–135.

Rothbart, M. K., & Bates, J. E. (1998). Temperament. In N. Eisenberg (Ed.), *Handbook of child psychology: Vol. 3. Social, emotional, and personality development* (5th ed.) New York: Wiley.

Rothbaum, F., Rosen, K., & Ujiie, T. (2002). Family systems theory, attachment theory and culture. *Family Process, 41*, 328–350.

Rothbaum, F., Weisz, J., Pott, M., Miyake, K., & Morelli, G. (2000). Attachment and culture: Security in the United States and Japan. *American Psychologist, 55*, 1093–1104.

Rovee-Collier, C. (1993). The capacity for long-term memory in infancy. *Current Directions in Psychological Science, 2*, 130–135.

Rovee-Collier, C. (1999). The development of infant memory. *Current Directions in Psychological Science, 8*, 80–85.

Rovee-Collier, C., Hayne, H., & Colombo, M. (2001). *The development of implicit and explicit memory*. Philadelphia, PA: John Benjamins.

Row, J. W. & Kahn, R. L. (2000). *Breaking Down the Myths of Aging. Successful Aging*. New York: Dell Publications.

Rowe, D. C. (1994). *The effects of nurture on individual natures*. New York: Guilford Press.

Rowe, J. W., & Kahn, R. L. (1998). *Successful aging*. New York: Pantheon.

Rubenstein, A. J., Kalakanis, L., & Langlois, J. H. (1999). Infant preferences for attractive faces: A cognitive explanation. *Developmental Psychology, 35*, 848–855.

Rubin, D., & Greenberg, D. (2003). The role of narrative in recollection: A view from cognitive psychology and neuropsychology. In G. Fireman & T. McVay (Eds.), *Narrative and consciousness: Literature, psychology, and the brain*. London: Oxford University Press.

Rubin, D. C. (1986). *Autobiographical memory*. Cambridge, England: Cambridge University Press.

Rubin, D. C. (2000). Autobiographical memory and aging. In C. D. Park & N. Schwarz et al. (Eds.), *Cognitive aging: A primer*. Philadelphia: Psychology Press/Taylor & Francis.

Rubin, K. H., & Chung, O. B. (Eds.) (2006). *Parenting beliefs, behaviors, and parent-child relations: A cross-cultural perspective*. New York: Psychology Press.

Rubin, K. H., Fein, G., & Vandenberg, B. (1983). In E. M. Hetherington (Ed.), *Handbook of child psychology. Vol. 4. Socialization, personality and social development* (pp. 693–774). New York: Wiley.

Ruda, M. A., Ling, Q-D., Hohmann, A. G., Peng, Y. B., & Tachibana, T. (2000, July 28). Altered nociceptive neuronal circuits after neonatal peripheral inflammation. *Science, 289*, 628–630.

Rudy, D., & Grusec, J. (2006, March). Authoritarian parenting in individualist and collectivist groups: Associations with maternal emotion and cognition and children's self-esteem. *Journal of Family Psychology, 20*, 68–78.

Ruff, H. A. (1989). The infant's use of visual and haptic information in the perception and recognition of objects. *Canadian Journal of Psychology, 43*, 302–319.

Ruffman, T., Slade, L., & Redman, J. (2005). Young infants' expectations about hidden objects. *Cognition [serial online], 97*, B35–B43.

Rule, B. G., & Ferguson, T. J. (1986). The effects of media violence on attitudes, emotions and cognitions. *Journal of Social Issues, 42*, 29–50.

Rupp, D., Vodanovich, S., & Credé, M. (2006, June). Age bias in the workplace: The impact of ageism and causal attributions. *Journal of Applied Social Psychology, 36*, 1337–1364.

Russell, G., & Radojevic, M. (1992). The changing role of fathers? Current understandings and future directions for research and practice [Special section: Australian Regional Meeting: Attachment and the relationship the infant and caregivers]. *Infant Mental Health Journal, 13*, 296–311.

Russell, S., & Consolacion, T. (2003). Adolescent romance and emotional health in the United States: Beyond binaries. *Journal of Clinical Child & Adolescent Psychology, 32,* 499–508.

Russon, A. E., & Waite, B. E. (1991). Patterns of dominance and imitation in an infant peer group. *Ethology & Sociobiology, 12,* 55–73.

Rust, J., Golombok, S., Hines, M., Johnston, K., & Golding, J.; ALSPAC Study Team. (2000). The role of brothers and sisters in the gender development of preschool children. *Journal of Experimental Child Psychology, 77,* 292–303.

Rutter, M. (2003). Commentary: Causal processes leading to antisocial behavior. *Developmental Psychology, 39,* 372–378.

Rutter, M. (2006). *Genes and behavior: Nature-nurture interplay explained.* New York: Blackwell Publishing.

Ryan, B. P. (2001). Programmed *therapy for stuttering in children and adults 2nd ed.* Springfield, IL: Charles C. Thomas.

Ryan, C., & Rivers, I. (2003). Lesbian, gay, bisexual and transgender youth: Victimization and its correlates in the USA and UK. *Culture, Health & Sexuality, 5,* 103–119.

Ryan, J. J., Sattler, J. M., & Lopez, S. J. (2000). Age effects on Wechsler Adult Intelligence Scale-III subtests. *Archives of Clinical Neuropsychology, 15,* 311–317.

Ryan, K. E., & Ryan, A. M. (2005). Psychological process underlying stereotype threat and standardized math test performance. *Educational Psychologist, 40,* 53–63.

Rycek, R. F., Stuhr, S. L., McDermott, J., Benker, J., & Swartz, M. D. (1998). Adolescent egocentrism and cognitive functioning during late adolescence. *Adolescence, 33,* 745–749.

Ryff, C. D., & Singer, B. (2003). Flourishing under fire: Resilience as a prototype of challenged thriving. In C. L. Keyes & J. Haidt (Eds.), *Flourishing: Positive psychology and the life well-lived,* (pp. 15–36). Washington, DC: American Psychological Association.

Sachs, J. (2006, April 1). Will your child be fat? *Parenting, 20,* 112. Retrieved January 23, 2007 from LexisNexis Academic.

Sack, K. (1999, March 21). Older students bring new life to campuses. *The New York Times,* p. WH8.

Sacks, M. H. (1993). Exercise for stress control. In D. Goleman & J. Gurin (Eds.), *Mind–body medicine.* Yonkers, NY: Consumer Reports Books.

Saczynski, J., Willis, S., & Schaie, K. (2002). Strategy use in reasoning training with older adults. *Aging, Neuropsychology, & Cognition, 9,* 48–60.

Sadker, D., & Sadker, M. (2005). *Teachers, schools, and society.* New York: McGraw-Hill.

Sadker, M., & Sadker, D. (1994). *Failing at fairness: How America's schools cheat girls.* New York: Scribner's.

Saffran, J., Werker, J., & Werner, L. (2006). The infant's auditory world: Hearing, speech, and the beginnings of language. In W. Damon & R. M. Lerner (Eds.), Handbook of child psychology: Vol. 2, Cognition, perception, and language (6th ed.). New York: John Wiley & Sons Inc.

Sagrestano, L. M., McCormick, S. H., Paikoff, R. L., & Holmbeck, G. N. (1999). Pubertal development and parent–child conflict in low-income, urban, African American adolescents. *Journal of Research on Adolescence, 9,* 85–107.

Sallis, J., & Glanz, K. (2006, March). The role of built environments in physical activity, eating, and obesity in childhood. *The Future of Children, 16,* 89–108.

Salovey, P., & Pizarro, D. (2003). The value of emotional intelligence. In R. Sternberg & J. Lautrey (Eds.), *Models of intelligence: International perspectives.* Washington, DC: American Psychological Association.

Salthouse, T. A. (1989). Age-related changes in basic cognitive processes. In APA Master Lectures, *The adult years: Continuity and change.* Washington, DC: American Psychological Association.

Salthouse, T. A. (1990). Cognitive competence and expertise in aging. In J. E. Birren & W. K. Schaie, et al. (Eds.), *Handbook of the psychology of aging* (3rd ed.). San Diego, CA: Academic Press.

Salthouse, T. A. (1993). Speed mediation of adult age differences in cognition. *Developmental Psychology, 29,* 722–738.

Salthouse, T. A. (1994a). Aging associations: Influence of speed on adult age differences in associative learning. *Journal of Experimental Psychology: Learning, Memory, and Cognition, 20,* 1486–1503.

Salthouse, T. A. (1994b). The aging of working memory. *Neuropsychology, 8,* 535–543.

Salthouse, T. A. (2006). Mental exercise and mental aging: Evaluating the validity of the "Use it or lose it" hypothesis. *Perspectives on Psychological Science, 1,* 68–87.

Salthouse, T. A., Atkinson, T. M., & Berish, D. E. (2003). Executive functioning as a potential mediator of age-related cognitive decline in normal adults. *Journal of Experimental Psychology, General, 132,* 566–594.

Samet, J. H., Memarini, D. M., & Malling, H. V. (2004, May 14). Do airborne particles induce heritable mutations? *Science, 304,* 971.

Samuels, C. A. (2005). Special educators discuss NCLB effect at national meeting. *Education Week, 24,* 12.

Samuelsson, I., & Johansson, E. (2006, January). Play and learning—inseparable dimensions in preschool practice. *Early Child Development and Care, 176,* 47–65.

Sandberg, D. E., & Voss, L. D. (2002). The psychosocial consequences of short stature: A review of the evidence. *Best Practice and Research Clinical Endocrinology and Metabolism, 16,* 449–463.

Sanderson, C. A., & Cantor, N. (1995). Social dating goals in late adolescence: Implications for safer sexual activity. *Journal of Personality and Social Psychology, 68,* 1121–1134.

Sandis, E. (2000). The aging and their families: A cross-national review. In A. L. Comunian & U. P. Gielen (Eds.), *International perspectives on human development.* Lengerich, Germany: Pabst Science Publishers.

Sandler, B. (1994, January 31). First denial, then a near-suicidal plea: "Mom, I need your help." *People Weekly,* 56–58.

Sandoval, J., Frisby, Cl L., Geisinger, K. F., Scheuneman, J. D., & Grenier, J. R. (Eds.). (1998). *Test interpretation and diversity: Achieving equity in assessment.* Washington, DC: APA Books.

Sang, B., Miao, X., & Deng, C. (2002). The development of gifted and nongifted young children in metamemory knowledge. *Psychological Science (China), 25,* 406–409, 424.

Sangree, W. H. (1989). Age and power: Life-course trajectories and age structuring of power relations in East and West Africa. In D. I. Kertzer & K. W. Schaie (Eds.), *Age structuring in comparative perspective.* Hillsdale, NJ: Erlbaum.

Sanoff, A. P., & Minerbrook, S. (1993, April 19). Race on campus. *U.S. News and World Report,* pp. 52–64.

Sapolsky, R. (2005, December). Sick of poverty. *Scientific American,* 93–99.

Sargent, J. D., Tanski, S. E., & Gibson, J. (2007). Exposure to movie smoking among U.S. adolescents aged 10 to 14 years: A population estimate. *Pediatrics, 119,* 1167–1176.

Sarrel, P. M. (2000). Effects of hormone replacement therapy on sexual psychophysiology and behavior in postmenopause. *Journal of Womens Health & Gender-Based Medicine, 9,* (Suppl. 1), S-25–S-32.

Sasser-Coen, J. R. (1993). Qualitative changes in creativity in the second half of life: A life-span developmental perspective. *Journal of Creative Behavior, 27,* 18–27.

Satel, S. (2004, May 25). Antidepressants: Two countries, two views. *The New York Times,* p. H2.

Saunders, J., Davis, L., & Williams, T. (2004). Gender differences in self-perceptions and academic outcomes: A study of African American high school students. *Journal of Youth & Adolescence, 33,* 81–90.

Savin-Williams, R. (2003). Lesbian, gay, and bisexual youths' relationships with their parents. In L. Garnets & D. Kimme (Eds.), *Psychological perspectives on lesbian, gay, and bisexual experiences* (2nd ed). New York: Columbia University Press.

Savin-Williams, R., & Demo, D. (1983). Situational and transituational determinants of adolescent self-feelings. *Journal of Personality and Social Psychology, 44,* 824–833.

Savin-Williams, R., & Ream, G. (2003). Suicide attempts among sexual-minority male youth. *Journal of Clinical Child & Adolescent Psychology, 32,* 509–522.

Savin-Williams, R. C. (2003). Are adolescent same-sex romantic relationships on our radar screen? In P. Florsheim (Eds.), *Adolescent romantic relations and sexual behavior: Theory, research, and practical implications.* Mahwah, NJ: Lawrence Erlbaum.

Savin-Williams, R. C., & Berndt, T. J. (1990). Friendship and peer relations. In S. Feldman & G. Elliott (Eds.), *At the threshold: The developing adolescent.* Cambridge, MA: Harvard University Press.

Sawatzky, J., & Naimark, B. (2002). Physical activity and cardiovascular health in aging women: A health-promotion perspective. *Journal of Aging & Physical Activity, 10,* 396–412.

Sax, et al. (2004). *The American freshman: National norms for fall 2004.* Los Angeles: Higher Education Research Institute, UCLA.

Sax, L. (2005, March 2). The promise and peril of single-sex public education. *Education Week, 24,* 48–51.

Sax, L., & Kautz, K. J. (2003). Who first suggests the diagnosis of attention-deficit/hyperactivity disorder? *Annals of Family Medicine, 1,* 171–174.

Sax, L. J., Astin, A. W., Korn, W. S., & Mahoney, K. M. (2000). *The American freshman: National norms for Fall 2000.* Los Angeles: UCLA Higher Education Research Institute.

Saywitz, K. J., & Nathanson, R. (1993). Children's testimony and their perceptions of stress in and out of the courtroom. *Child Abuse & Neglect, 17,* 613–622.

Scarr, S. (1993). Biological and cultural diversity: The legacy of Darwin for development. *Child Development, 64,* 1333–1353.

Scarr, S. (1998). American child care today. *American Psychologist, 53,* 95–108.

Scarr, S., & Carter-Saltzman, L. (1982). Genetics and intelligence. In R. J. Sternberg (Ed.), *Handbook of human intelligence* (pp. 792–896). Cambridge, England: Cambridge University Press.

Schachter, E. P. (2005). Erikson meets the postmodern: Can classic identity theory rise to the challenge? *Identity, 5*, 137–160.

Schaefer, R. T., & Lamm, R. P. (1992). *Sociology* (4th ed.). New York: McGraw-Hill.

Schaeffer, C., Petras, H., & Ialongo, N. (2003). Modeling growth in boys' aggressive behavior across elementary school: Links to later criminal involvement, conduct disorder, and antisocial personality disorder. *Developmental Psychology, 39*, 1020–1035.

Schaie, K. W. (1977–1978). Toward a stage of adult theory of adult cognitive development. *Journal of Aging and Human Development, 8*, 129–138.

Schaie, K. W. (1991). Developmental designs revisited. In S. H. Cohen & H. W. Reese (Eds.), *Life-span developmental psychology: Methodological innovations*. Hillsdale, NJ: Erlbaum.

Schaie, K. W. (1993). The Seattle longitudinal studies of adult intelligence. *Current Directions in Psychological Science, 2*, 171–175.

Schaie, K. W. (1994). The course of adult intellectual development. *American Psychologist, 49*, 304–313.

Schaie, K. W., & Willis, S. L. (1993). Age difference patterns of psychometric intelligence in adulthood: Generalizability within and across ability domains. *Psychology and Aging, 8*, 44–55.

Schaie, K. W., & Zanjani, F. A. K. (2006). Intellectual development across adulthood. In C. Hoare, *Handbook of adult development and learning*. New York: Oxford University Press.

Schaller, M., & Crandall, C. S. (Eds.) (2004). *The psychological foundations of culture*. Mahwah, NJ: Lawrence Erlbaum Associates.

Scharfe, E. (2000). Development of emotional expression, understanding, and regulation in infants and young children. In R. Bar-On & J. Parker (Eds.), *The handbook of emotional intelligence: Theory, development, assessment, and application at home, school, and in the workplace*. San Francisco: Jossey-Bass/Pfeiffer.

Scharrer, E., Kim, D., Lin, K., & Liu, Z. (2006). Working hard or hardly working? Gender, humor, and the performance of domestic chores in television commercials. *Mass Communication and Society, 9*, 215–238.

Schatz, M. (1994). *A toddler's life*. New York: Oxford University Press.

Schechter, T., Finkelstein, Y., & Koren, G. (2005). Pregnant "DES daughters" and their offspring. *Canadian Family Physician, 51*, 493–494.

Schellenberg, E. G., & Trehub, S. E. (1996). Natural musical intervals: Evidence from infant listeners. *Psychological Science, 7*, 272–277.

Schemo, D. J. (2001, December 5). U.S. students prove middling on 32-nation test. *The New York Times*, p. A21.

Schemo, D. J. (2003, November 13). Students' scores rise in math, not in reading. *The New York Times*, p. A2.

Schemo, D. J. (2004, March 2). Schools, facing tight budgets, leave gifted programs behind. *The New York Times*, pp. A1, A18.

Scher, S. J., & Rauscher, F. (Eds.). (2003). *Evolutionary psychology: Alternative approaches*. Dordrecht, Netherlands: Kluwer Academic Publishers.

Scherer, M. (2004). Contrasting inclusive with exclusive education. In M. Scherer (Ed.), *Connecting to learn: Educational and assistive technology for people with disabilities*. Washington, DC: American Psychological Association.

Scherf, K. S., Sweeney, J. A., & Luna, B. (2006). Brain basis of developmental change in visuospatial working memory. *Journal of Cognitive Neuroscience, 18*, 1045–1058.

Schieber, F., Sugar, J. A., & McDowd, J. M. (1992). Behavioral sciences and aging. In J. E. Birren, B. R. Sloan, G. D. Cohen, N. R. Hooyman, & B. D. Lebowitz, *Handbook of mental health and aging (2nd ed.)*. San Diego, CA: Academic Press, 1992.

Schieman, S., McBrier, D. B., & van Gundy, K. (2003). Home-to-work conflict, work qualities, and emotional distress. *Sociological Forum, 18*, 137–164.

Schiffer, A., Pavan, A., Pedersen, S., Gremigni, P., Sommaruga, M., & Denollet, J. (2006, March). Type D personality and cardiovascular disease: Evidence and clinical implications. *Minerva Psichiatrica, 47*(1), 79–87.

Schiffer, A. A., Pedersen, S. S., Widdershoven, J. W., Hendriks, E. H., Winter, J. B., & Denollet, J. (2005). The distressed (type D) personality is independently associated with impaired health status and increased depressive symptoms in chronic heart failure. *European Journal of Cardiovascular Prevention and Rehabilitation, 12*, 341–346.

Schiller, J. S., & Bernadel, L. (2004). Summary health statistics for the U.S. population: National Health Interview Survey, 2002. *Vital Health Statistics, 10*, 1–110.

Schkade, D. A., & Kahneman, D. (1998). Does living in California make people happy? A focusing illusion on judgments of life satisfaction. *Psychological Science, 9*, 340–346.

Schlegel, A., & Barry, H., III. (1991). *Adolescence: An anthropological inquiry*. New York: The Free Press.

Schlossberg, N. (2004). *Retire smart, retire happy: Finding your true path in life*. Washington, DC: American Psychological Association.

Schmalz, D., & Kerstetter, D. (2006). Girlie girls and manly men: Chidren's stigma consciousness of gender in sports and physical activities. *Journal of Leisure Research, 38*, 536–557.

Schmidt, M., Pekow, P., Freedson, P., Markenson, G., & Chasan-Taber, L. (2006). Physical activity patterns during pregnancy in a diverse population of women. *Journal of Women's Health, 15*, 909–918.

Schmidt, P. J., & Rubinow, D. R. (1991). Menopause-related affective disorders: A justification for further study. *American Journal of Psychiatry, 148*, 844–852.

Schmitt, E. (2001, March 13). For 7 million people in census, one race category isn't enough. *The New York Times*, pp. A1, A14.

Schneider, B. (1997). Psychoacoustics and aging: Implications for everyday listening. *Journal of Speech-Language Pathology & Audiology, 21*, 111– 124.

Schneider, B. A., Atkinson, L., & Tardif, C. (2001). Child–parent attachment and children's peer relations: A quantitative review. *Developmental Psychology, 37*, 86–100.

Schneider, W., & Pressley, M. (1989). *Memory between two and twenty*. New York: Springer-Verlag.

Schnur, E., & Belanger, S. (2000). What works in Head Start. In M. P. Kluger & G. Alexander et al. (Eds.), *What works in child welfare*. Washington, DC: Child Welfare League of America.

Schoppe-Sullivan, S., Diener, M., Mangelsdorf, S., Brown, G., McHale, J., & Frosch, C. (2006, July). Attachment and sensitivity in family context: The roles of parent and infant gender. *Infant and Child Development, 15*, 367–385.

Schoppe-Sullivan, S., Mangelsdorf, S., Brown, G., & Sokolowski, M. (2007, February). Goodness-of-fit in family context: Infant temperament, marital quality, and early coparenting behavior. *Infant Behavior & Development, 30*, 82–96.

Schore, A. (2003). *Affect regulation and the repair of the self*. New York: W. W. Norton.

Schreiber, G. B., Robins, M., Striegel-Moore, R., Obarzanek, M., Morrison, J. A., & Wright, D. J. (1996). Weight modification efforts reported by black and white preadolescent girls: National Heart, Lung, and Blood Institute Growth and Health Study. *Pediatrics, 98*, 63–70.

Schulman, M. (1991). *The passionate mind: Bringing up an intelligent and creative child*. New York: Free Press.

Schulman, M., & Mekler, E. (1994). *Bringing up a moral child: A new approach for teaching your child to be kind, just, and responsible*. Reading, MA: Addison-Wesley.

Schultz, A. H. (1969). *The life of primates*. New York: Universe.

Schultz, R., & Curnow, C. (1988). Peak performance and age among superathletes: Track and field, swimming, baseball, tennis, and golf. *Journal of Gerontology, 43*, P113–P120.

Schulz, R. (Ed.). (2000). *Handbook on dementia caregiving: Evidence-based interventions for family caregivers*. New York: Springer Publishing.

Schulz, R., & Aderman, D. (1976). How medical staff copes with dying patients. *Omega, 7*, 11–21.

Schuster, C. S., & Ashburn, S. S. (1986). *The process of human development* (2nd. ed.). Boston: Little, Brown.

Schutt, R. K. (2001). *Investigating the social world: The process and practice of research*. Thousand Oaks, CA: Sage.

Schutz, H., Paxton, S., & Wertheim, E. (2002). Investigation of body comparison among adolescent girls. *Journal of Applied Social Psychology, 32*, 1906–1937.

Schwartz, C. E., Wright, C. L., Shin, L. M., Kagan, J., & Rauch, S. L. (2003, June 20). Inhibited and uninhibited infants "grown up": Adult amygdalar response to novelty. *Science, 300*, 1952–1953.

Schwartz, D., Dodge, K. A., Pettit, G. S., & Bates, J. E. (1997). The early socialization of aggressive victims of bullying. *Child Development, 68*, 665–675.

Schwartz, I. M. (1999). Sexual activity prior to coital interaction: A comparison between males and females. *Archives of Sexual Behavior, 28*, 63–69.

Schwartz, M. (2006, June 11). The hold-'em holdup. *The New York Times Magazine*, 52–58.

Schweinhart, L. J., Barnes, H. V., & Weikart, D. P. (1993). *Significant benefits: The High/Scope Perry Preschool Study through age 27 (Monographs of the High/Scope Educational Research Foundation, No. 10)*. Ypsilanti, MI: High/Scope Press.

Schwenkhagen, A. (2007). Hormonal changes in menopause and implications on sexual health. *The Journal of Sexual Medicine, 4*, Supplement, 220–226.

Scopesi, A., Zanobini, M., & Carossino, P. (1997). Childbirth in different cultures: Psychophysical reactions of women delivering in U.S., German, French, and Italian hospitals. *Journal of Reproductive & Infant Psychology, 15*, 9–30.

Scrimsher, S., & Tudge, J. (2003). The teaching/learning relationship in the first years of school: Some revolutionary implications of Vygotsky's theory. *Early Education and Development, 14* [Special issue], 293–312.

Scruggs, T. E., & Mastropieri, M. A. (1994). Successful mainstreaming in elementary science classes: A qualitative study of three reputational cases. *American Educational Research Journal, 31*, 785–811.

Sears, R. R. (1977). Sources of life satisfaction of the Terman gifted men. *American Psychologist, 32*, 119–129.

Sedikides, C., Gaertner, L., & Toguchi, Y. (2003). Pan-cultural self-enhancement. *Journal of Personality and Social Psychology, 84*, 60–79.

SEER. (2005). Surveillance, Epidemiology, and End Results Program (SEER) Program. (www.seer.cancer.gov) SEER*Stat Database: Incidence—SEER 9 Regs Public-Use, Nov 2004 Sub (1973–2002), National Cancer Institute, DCCPS, Surveillance Research Program, Cancer Statistics Branch, released April 2005, based on the November 2004 submission.

Segal, B. M., & Stewart, J. C. (1996). Substance use and abuse in adolescence: An overview. *Child Psychiatry & Human Development, 26,* 193–210.

Segal, J., & Segal, Z. (1992, September). No more couch potatoes. *Parents,* p. 235.

Segal, N. L. (1993). Twin, sibling, and adoption methods: Tests of evolutionary hypotheses. *American Psychologist, 48,* 943–956.

Segal, N. L. (2000). Virtual twins: New findings on within-family environmental influences on intelligence. *Journal of Educational Psychology, 92,* 188–194.

Segall, M. H., Dasen, P. R., Berry, J. W., & Poortinga, Y. H. (1990). *Human behavior in global perspective.* Boston: Allyn & Bacon.

Segalowitz, S. J., & Rapin I. (Eds.). (2003). *Child neuropsychology, Part I.* Amsterdam, The Netherlands: Elsevier Science.

Seidman, S. (2003). The aging male: Androgens, erectile dysfunction, and depression. *Journal of Clinical Psychiatry, 64,* 31–37.

Seidman, S. N., & Rieder, R. O. (1994). A review of sexual behavior in the United States. *American Journal of Psychiatry, 151,* 330–341.

Seifer, R., Schiller, M., & Sameroff, A. J. (1996). Attachment, maternal sensitivity, and infant temperament during the first year of life. *Developmental Psychology, 32,* 12–25.

Selig, S., Tomlinson, T., & Hickey, T. (1991). Ethical dimensions of intergenerational reciprocity: Implications for practice. *Gerontologist, 31,* 624–630.

Seligman, L. (1995). *Promoting a fighting spirit: Psychotherapy for cancer patients, survivors, and their families.* San Francisco: Jossey-Bass.

Semerci, Ç. (2006). The opinions of medicine faculty students regarding cheating in relation to Kohlberg's moral development concept. *Social Behavior and Personality, 34,* 41–50.

Sener, A., Terzioglu, R., & Karabulut, E. (2007, January). Life satisfaction and leisure activities during men's retirement: A Turkish sample. *Aging & Mental Health, 11,* 30–36.

Senghas, A., Kita, S., & Özyürek, A. (2004, September 17). Children creating core properties of language: Evidence from an emerging sign language in Nicaragua. *Science, 305,* 1779–1782.

Seppa, N. (1997, February). Wisdom: A quality that may defy age. *APA Monitor,* pp. 1, 9.

Serbin, L., & Karp, J. (2004). The intergenerational transfer of psychosocial risk: Mediators of vulnerability and resilience. *Annual Review of Psychology, 55,* 333–363.

Serbin, L., Poulin-Dubois, D., & Colburne, K. (2001). Gender stereotyping in infancy: Visual preferences for and knowledge of gender-stereotyped toys in the second year. *International Journal of Behavioral Development, 25,* 7–15.

Serbin, L., Poulin-Dubois, D., & Eichstedt, J. (2002). Infants' response to gender-inconsistent events. *Infancy, 3,* 531–542.

Serbin, L. A., Poulin-Dubois, D., Colburne, K. A., Sen, M. G., & Eichstedt, J. A. (2001). Gender stereotyping in infancy: Visual preferences for and knowledge of gender-stereotyped toys in the second year. *International Journal of Behavioral Development, 25,* 7–15.

Servin, A., Nordenström, A., Larsson, A., & Bohlin, G. (2003). Prenatal adrogens and gender-typed behavior: A study of girls with mild and severe forms of congenital adrenal hyperplasia. *Developmental Psychology, 39,* 440–450.

Sesser, S. (1993, September 13). Opium war redux. *The New Yorker,* 78–89.

Settersten, R. (2002). Social sources of meaning in later life. In R. Weiss & S. Bass (Eds.), *Challenges of the third age: Meaning and purpose in later life.* London: Oxford University Press.

Seven, R. (2006, November 26). The road taken. *The Seattle Times Pacific Northwest Sunday Magazine,* p. 6.

Shafer, R. G. (1990, March 12). An anguished father recounts the battle he lost—trying to rescue a teenage son from drugs. *People Weekly,* 81–83.

Shapiro, A. F., Gottman, J. M., & Carrère, S. (2000). The baby and the marriage: Identifying factors that buffer against decline in marital satisfaction after the first baby arrives. *Journal of Family Psychology, 14,* 124–130.

Shapiro, L. (1997, Spring/Summer). Beyond an apple a day. *Newsweek Special Issue,* 52–56.

Sharf, R. S. (1992). *Applying career development theory to counseling.* Pacific Grove, CA: Brooks/Cole.

Shaunessy, E., Suldo, S., Hardesty, R., & Shaffer, E. (2006, December). School functioning and psychological well-being of international baccalaureate and general education students: A preliminary examination. *Journal of Secondary Gifted Education, 17,* 76–89.

Shavelson, R., Hubner, J. J., & Stanton, J. C. (1976). Self-concept: Validation of construct interpretations. *Review of Educational Research, 46,* 407–441.

Shaver, P. (1994, August). Attachment and care giving in adult romantic relationships. Invited address presented at the annual meeting of the American Psychological Association, Los Angeles.

Shaver, P. R., Hazan, C., & Bradshaw, D. (1988). Love as attachment: The integration of three behavioral systems. In R. J. Sternberg & M. L. Barnes (Eds.), *The psychology of love* (pp. 68–99). New Haven, CT: Yale University Press.

Shaw, D. S., Winslow, E. B., & Flanagan, C. (1999). A prospective study of the effects of marital status and family relations on young children's adjustment among African American and European American families. *Child Development, 70,* 742–755.

Shaw, M. L. (2003). Creativity and whole language. In J. Houtz, *The educational psychology of creativity.* Cresskill, NJ: Hampton Press.

Shaywitz, B. A., Shaywitz, S. E., Blachman, B. A., Pugh, K. R., Fulbright, R. K. Skudlarski, P., Mencl, W. E., Constable, R. T., Holahan, J. M., Marchione, K. E., Fletcher, J. M., Lyon, G. R., Gore, J. C. (2004). Development of left occipitotemporal systems for skilled reading in children after a phonologically-based intervention. *Biological Psychiatry, 55,* 926–933.

Shaywitz, S. (2004). *Overcoming dyslexia: A new and complete science-based program for reading problems at any level.* New York: Vintage.

Shaywitz, S. E., Shaywitz, B. A., Pugh, K. R., Fulbright, R. K., Skudlarski, P., Mencl, W. E., Constable, R. T., Naftolin, F., Palter, S. F., Marchione, K. E., Katz, L., Shankweiler, D. P., Fletcher, J. M., Lacadie, C., Keltz, M., & Gore, J. C. (1999). Effect of estrogen on brain activation patterns in postmenopausal women during working memory tasks. *Journal of the American Medical Association, 281,* 1197–1202.

Shea, J. (2006, September). Cross-cultural comparison of women's midlife symptom-reporting: A China study. *Culture, Medicine and Psychiatry, 30,* 331–362.

Shea, J. D. (1985). Studies of cognitive development in Papua, New Guinea. *International Journal of Psychology, 20,* 33–61.

Shea, K. M., Wilcox, A. J., & Little, R. E. (1998). Postterm delivery: A challenge for epidemiologic research. *Epidemiology, 9,* 199–204.

Shealy, C. N. (1995). From Boys Town to Oliver Twist: Separating fact from fiction in welfare reform and out-of-home placement of children and youth. *American Psychologist, 50,* 565–580.

Sheets, R. H., & Hollins, E. R. (1999). *Racial and ethnic identity in school practices.* Mahwah, NJ: Lawrence Erlbaum.

Sheldon, K. M., Elliot, A. J., Kim, Y., & Kasser, T. (2001). What is satisfying about satisfying events? Testing 10 candidate psychological needs. *Journal of Personality and Social Psychology, 80,* 325–339.

Sheldon, K. M., Joiner, T. E., Jr., & Pettit, J. W. (2003). Reconciling humanistic ideals and scientific clinical practice. *Clinical Psychology, 10,* 302–315.

Sheldon, S., & Wilkinson, S. (2004). Should selecting saviour siblings be banned? *Journal of Medical Ethics, 30,* 533–537.

Shellenbarger, S. (2003, January 9). Yes, that weird daycare center could scar your child, researchers say. *The Wall Street Journal,* p. D1.

Shenkin, S. D., Starr, J. M., & Deary, I. J. (2004). Birth weight and cognitive ability in childhood: A systematic review. *Psychological Bulletin, 130,* 989–1013.

Sheridan, C., & Radmacher, S. (2003). Significance of psychosocial factors to health and disease. In L. Schein & H. Bernard (Eds.), *Psychosocial treatment for medical conditions: Principles and techniques.* New York: Brunner-Routledge.

Sherman, E. (1991). *Reminiscence and the self in old age.* New York: Springer.

Sherwin, B. B. (1991). The psychoendocrinology of aging and female sexuality. *Annual Review of Sex Research, 2,* 181–198.

Shi, L. (2003). Facilitating constructive parent–child play: Family therapy with young children. *Journal of Family Psychotherapy, 14,* 19–31.

Shimizu, M., & Pelham, B. (2004). The unconscious cost of good fortune: Implicit and explicit self-esteem, positive life events, and health. *Health Psychology, 23,* 101–105.

Shin, H. B., & Bruno. R. (2003). *Language use and English speaking ability: 2000.* Washington, DC: U. S. Census Bureau.

Shiner, R., Masten, A., & Roberts, J. (2003). Childhood personality foreshadows adult personality and life outcomes two decades later. *Journal of Personality, 71,* 1145–1170.

Shiono, P. H., & Behrman, R. E. (1995). Low birth weight: Analysis and recommendations. *The Future of Children, 5,* 4–18.

Shonk, S. M., & Cicchetti, D. (2001). Maltreatment, competency deficits, and risk for academic and behavioral maladjustment. *Developmental Psychology, 37,* 3–17.

Shor, R. (2006, May). Physical punishment as perceived by parents in Russia: Implications for professionals involved in the care of children. *Early Child Development and Care, 176,* 429–439.

Short, L. (2007, February). Lesbian mothers living well in the context of heterosexism and discrimination: Resources, strategies and legislative change. *Feminism & Psychology, 17,* 57–74.

Shrum, W., Cheek, N., Jr., & Hunter, S. M. (1988). Friendship in school: Gender and racial homophily. *Sociology of Education, 61,* 227–239.

Shulman, S., & Ben-Artzi, E. (2003). Age-related differences in the transition from adolescence to adulthood and links with family relationships. *Journal of Adult Development, 10,* 217–226.

Shurkin, J. N. (1992). *Terman's kids: The groundbreaking study of how the gifted grow up.* Boston: Little, Brown.

Shweder, R. A. (1998). *Welcome to middle age!: (And other cultural fictions).* New York: Oxford University Press.

Shweder, R. A. (2003). *Why do men barbecue?: Recipes for cultural psychology.* Cambridge, MA: Harvard University Press.

Siegal, M. (1997). *Knowing children: Experiments in conversation and cognition* (2nd ed.). Hove, England: Psychology Press/Erlbaum, Taylor & Francis.

Siegel, L. S. (1989). A reconceptualization of prediction from infant test scores. In M. H. Bornstein & N. A. Krasnegor (Eds.), *Stability and continuity in mental development: Behavioral and biological perspectives.* Hillsdale, NJ: Erlbaum.

Siegler, R. (2003). Thinking and intelligence. In M. Bornstein & L. Davidson (Eds.), *Well-being: Positive development across the life course* (pp. 311-320). Mahwah, NJ: Lawrence Erlbaum Associates.

Siegler, R. S. (1994). Cognitive variability: A key to understanding cognitive development. *Current Directions in Psychological Science, 3,* 1–5.

Siegler, R. S. (1995). How does change occur?: A microgentic study of number conservation. *Cognitive Psychology, 28,* 225–273.

Siegler, R. S. (1998). *Children's thinking* (3rd ed.). Upper Saddle River, NJ: Prentice Hall.

Siegler, R. S., & Ellis, S. (1996). Piaget on childhood. *Psychological Science, 7,* 211–215.

Siegler, R. S., & Richards, D. (1982). The development of intelligence. In R. Sternberg (Ed.), *Handbook of human intelligence.* London: Cambridge University Press.

Sierra, F. (2006, June). Is (your cellular response to) stress killing you? *Journals of Gerontology: Series A: Biological Sciences and Medical Sciences, 61,* 557–561.

Sigman, M. (1995). Nutrition and child development: More food for thought. *Current Directions in Psychological Science, 4,* 52–55.

Sigman, M., Cohen, S. E., & Beckwith, L. (1997). Why does infant attention predict adolescent intelligence? *Infant Behavior & Development, 20,* 133–140.

Sigman, M., Cohen, S., & Beckwith, L. (2000). Why does infant attention predict adolescent intelligence? In D. Muir & A. Slater (Eds.), *Infant development: The essential readings* (pp. 239–253). Malden, MA: Blackwell Publishers.

Silbereisen, R., Peterson, A., Albrecht, H., & Krache, B. (1989). Maturational timing and the development of problem behavior: Longitudinal studies in adolescence. *Journal of Early Adolescence, 9,* 247.

Silverstein, L. B., & Auerbach, C. F. (1999). Deconstructing the essential father. *American Psychologist, 54,* 397–407.

Silverthorn, P., & Frick, P. J. (1999). Developmental pathways to antisocial behavior: The delayed-onset pathway in girls. *Developmental & Psychopathology, 11,* 101–126.

Simcock, G., & Hayne, H. (2002). Breaking the barrier? Children fail to translate their preverbal memories into language. *Psychological Science, 13,* 225–231.

Simmons, R. (2002). *Odd girl out: The hidden culture of aggression in girls.* Orlando, FL: Harcourt.

Simmons, R., & Blyth, D. (1987). *Moving into adolescence.* New York: Aldine de Gruyter.

Simons, L., & Conger, R. (2007, February). Linking mother–father differences in parenting to a typology of family parenting styles and adolescent outcomes. *Journal of Family Issues, 28,* 212–241.

Simons, S. H., van Dijk, M., Anand, K. S., Roofthooft, D., van Lingen, R. A., & Tibboel. D. (2003). Do we still hurt newborn babies? A prospective study of procedural pain and analgesia in neonates. *Archives of Pediatrics and Adolescence, 157,* 1058–1064.

Simonton, D. K. (1989). The swan-song phenomenon: Last-works effects for 172 classical composers. *Psychology and Aging, 4,* 42–47.

Simonton, D. K. (1997). Creative productivity: A predictive and explanatory model of career trajectories and landmarks. *Psychological Review, 104,* 66–89.

Simpkins, S., Parke, R., Flyr, M., & Wild, M. (2006, November). Similarities in children's and early adolescents' perceptions of friendship qualities across development, gender, and friendship qualities. *Journal of Early Adolescence, 26,* 491–508.

Simpson, J., Collins, W., Tran, S., & Haydon, K. (2007, February). Attachment and the experience and expression of emotions in romantic relationships: A developmental perspective. *Journal of Personality and Social Psychology, 92,* 355–367.

Simpson, J. A. (1990). Influence of attachment styles on romantic relationships. *Journal of Personality & Social Psychology, 59,* 971–980.

Simpson, J. M., Thompson, J. F., & Ellwood, D. A. (2006). Intrapartum epidural analgesia and breastfeeding: A prospective cohort study. *International Breastfeeding Journal, 11,* 1–24.

Simpson, R., & Otten, K. (2005). Structuring behavior management strategies and building social competence. In D. Zager (Ed.), *Autism spectrum disorders: Identification, education, and treatment* (3rd ed.). Mahwah, NJ: Lawrence Erlbaum Associates.

Simson, S., Wilson, L., & Harlow-Rosentraub, K. (2006). *Civic engagement and lifelong learning institutes: Current status and future directions.* New York: Haworth Press.

Simson, S. P., Wilson, L. B., & Harlow-Rosentraub, K. (2006). Civic engagement and lifelong learning institutes: Current status and future directions. In L. Wilson & S. P. Simson (Eds.), *Civic engagement and the baby boomer generation: Research, policy, and practice perspectives.* New York: Haworth Press.

Sinclair, D. A., & Guarente, L. (2006). Unlocking the secrets of longevity genes. *Scientific American, 294,* 48–51, 54–57.

Singer, D. G., & Singer, J. L. (Eds.). (2000). *Handbook of children and the media.* Thousand Oaks, CA: Sage.

Singer, L. T., Arendt, R., Minnes, S., Farkas, K., & Salvator, A. (2000). Neurobehavioral outcomes of cocaine-exposed infants. *Neurotoxicology & Teratology, 22,* 653–666.

Singer, M. S., Stacey, B. G., & Lange, C. (1993). The relative utility of expectancy-value theory and social cognitive theory in predicting psychology student course goals and career aspirations. *Journal of Social Behavior and Personality, 8,* 703–714.

Singh, G. K., & Yu, S. M. (1995). Infant mortality in the United States: Trends, differentials, and projections 1950 through 2010. *The American Journal of Public Health, 85,* 957–964.

Singleton, L. C., & Asher, S. R. (1979). Racial integration and children's peer preferences. *Child Development, 50,* 936–941.

Sinnott, J. D. (1997). Developmental models of midlife and aging in women: Metaphors for transcendence and for individuality in community. In J. Coyle (Ed.), *Handbook on women and aging* (pp. 149–163). Westport, CT: Greenwood.

Sinnott, J. D. (1998a). Career paths and creative lives: A theoretical perspective on late-life potential. In C. Adams-Price (Ed.), *Creativity and successful aging: Theoretical and empirical approaches.* New York: Springer.

Sinnott, J. D. (1998b). *The development of logic in adulthood: Postformal thought and its applications.* New York: Plenum.

Sirois, B., & Burg, M. (2003). Negative emotion and coronary heart disease: A review. *Behavior Modification, 27,* 83–102.

Skinner, B. F. (1957). *Verbal behavior.* New York: Appleton-Century-Crofts.

Skinner, B. F. (1975). The steep and thorny road to a science of behavior. *American Psychologist, 30,* 42–49.

Skinner, J., Carruth, B., Wendy, B., & Ziegler, P. (2002). Children's food preferences: A longitudinal analysis. *Journal of the American Dietetic Association, 102,* 1638–1647.

Skinner, J. D., Ziegler, P., Pac, S., & Devaney, B. (2004). Meal and snack patterns of infants and toddlers. *Journal of the American Dietary Association, 104,* S65–S70.

Skipper, J. K., & Nass, G. (1966). Dating behavior: A framework of analysis and an illustration. *Journal of Marriage and the Family, 28,* 412–420.

Skowronski, J., Walker, W., & Betz, A. (2003). Ordering our world: An examination of time in autobiographical memory. *Memory, 11,* 247–260.

Slater, A., & Johnson, S. P. (1998). Visual sensory and perceptual abilities of the newborn: Beyond the blooming, buzzing confusion. In F. Simion, G. Butterworth et al. (Eds.), *The development of sensory, motor and cognitive capacities in early infancy: From perception to cognition.* Hove, England: Psychology Press/Erlbaum (UK) Taylor & Francis.

Slater, A., Mattock, A., & Brown, E. (1990). Size constancy at birth: Newborn infants' responses to retinal and real size. *Journal of Experimental Child Psychology, 49,* 314–322.

Slater, M., Henry, K., & Swaim, R. (2003). Violent media content and aggressiveness in adolescents: A downward spiral model. *Communication Research, 30,* 713–736.

Slavin, R. E. (1995). Enhancing intergroup relations in schools: Cooperative learning and other strategies. In W. D. Hawley & A. W. Jackson (Eds.), *Toward a common destiny: Improving race and ethnic relations in America.* San Francisco: Jossey-Bass.

Sleek, S. (1997, June). Can "emotional intelligence" be taught in today's schools? *APA Monitor,* p. 25.

Sliwinski, M., Buschke, H., Kuslansky, G., & Senior, G. (1994). Proportional slowing and addition speed in old and young adults. *Psychology and Aging, 9,* 72–80.

Sliwinski, M., Stawski, R., Hall, C., Katz, M., Verghese, J., & Lipton, R. (2006). Distinguishing preterminal and terminal cognitive decline. *European Psychologist, 11,* 172–181.

Small, B. J., & Bäckman, L. (1999). Time to death and cognitive performance. *Current Directions in Psychological Science, 8,* 168–172.

Small, G. W., Mazziotta, J. C., Collins, M. T., et al. (1995). Apolipoprotein E. type 4 allele and cerebral glucose metabolism in relatives at risk for familial Alzheimer's disease. *Journal of the American Medical Association, 273*, 942–947.

Smedley, A., & Smedley, B. D. (2005). Race as biology is fiction, racism as a social problem is real: Anthropological and historical perspectives on the social Construction of race. *American Psychologist, 60*, 16–26.

Smedley, B. D., & Syme, S. L. (Eds.). (2000). *Promoting health: Intervention strategies from social and behavioral research.* Washington, DC: National Academy of Sciences.

Smetana, J., Daddis, C., & Chuang, S. (2003). "Clean your room!" A longitudinal investigation of adolescent–parent conflict and conflict resolution in middle-class African American families. *Journal of Adolescent Research, 18*, 631–650.

Smetana, J., Yau, J., & Hanson, S. (1991). Conflict resolution in families with adolescents. *Journal of Research on Adolescence, 1*, 189–206.

Smetana, J. G. (1995). Parenting styles and conceptions of parental authority during adolescence. *Child Development 66*, 299–316.

Smetana, J. G. (2005). Adolescent-parent conflict: Resistance and subversion as developmental process. In L. Nucci (Ed.), *Conflict, contradiction, and contrarian elements in moral development and education.* Mahwah, NJ: Lawrence Erlbaum Associates.

Smith, G. C., et al. (2003). Interpregnancy interval and risk of preterm birth and neonatal death. *British Medical Journal, 327*, 313–316.

Smith, J. (2005, April 7). Coaches help mom, dad see "big picture" in parenting. *The Oregonian*, 8.

Smith, P. K. (1995). Grandparenthood. In M. H. Bornstein (Ed.), *Handbook of parenting.* Hillsdale, NJ: Erlbaum.

Smith, P. K., & Drew, L. M. (2002). Grandparenthood. In M. Bornstein (Ed.), *Handbook of parenting.* Mahwah, NJ: Erlbaum.

Smith, P. K., Pepler, D., & Rigby, K., (Eds.). (2004). *Bullying in schools: How successful can interventions be?* New York: Cambridge University Press.

Smith, R. (1999, March). The timing of birth. *Scientific American*, 68–75.

Smith, R. J., Bale, J. F., Jr., & White, K. R. (2005, March 2). Sensorineural hearing loss in children. *Lancet, 365*, 879–890.

Smith, S., Quandt, S., Arcury, T., Wetmore, L., Bell, R., & Vitolins, M. (2006, January). Aging and eating in the rural, southern United States: Beliefs about salt and its effect on health. *Social Science & Medicine, 62*, 189–198.

Smuts, A. B., & Hagen, J. W. (1985). History of the family and of child development: Introduction to Part 1. *Monographs of the Society for Research in Child Development, 50* (4–5, Serial No. 211).

Snarey, J. R. (1995). In a communitarian voice: The sociological expansion of Kohlbergian theory, research, and practice. In W. M. Kurtines & J. L. Gerwirtz (Eds.), *Moral development: An introduction.* Boston: Allyn & Bacon.

Snow, R. (1969). Unfinished Pygmalion. *Contemporary Psychology, 14*, 197–199.

Snowdon, D. A., Kemper, S. J., Mortimer, J. A., Greiner, L. H., Wekstein, D. R., & Markesbery, W. R. (1996, February 21). Linguistic ability in early life and cognitive function and Alzheimer's disease in late life: Findings from the nun study. *Journal of the American Medical Association, 275*, 528–532.

Snyder, H. M. (2002). *Juvenile arrests 2000.* Washington, DC: National Center for Juvenile Justice.

Snyder, J., Cramer, A., & Afrank, J. (2005). The contributions of ineffective discipline and parental hostile attributions of child misbehavior to the development of conduct problems at home and school. *Developmental Psychology, 41*, 30–41.

Snyder, M. (1974). The self-monitoring of expressive behavior. *Journal of Personality and Social Psychology, 30*, 526–537.

Soken, N. H., & Pick, A .D. (1999). Infants' perception of dynamic affective expressions: Do infants distinguish specific expressions? *Child Development, 70*, 1275–1282.

Solantaus, T., Leinonen, J., & Punamäki, R-L. (2004). Children's mental health in times of economic recession: Replication and extension of the family economic stress model in Finland. *Developmental Psychology, 40*, 412–429.

Soldo, B.J. (1996). Cross-pressures on middle-aged adults: A broader view. *Journal of Gerontology: Psychological Sciences and Social Sciences, 51B*, 271–273.

Solomon, A. (1995, May 22). A death of one's own. *New Yorker*, 54–69.

Solomon, W., Richards, M., Huppert, F. A., Brayne, C., & Morgan, K. (1998). Divorce, current marital status and well-being in an elderly population. *International Journal of Law, Policy and the Family, 12*, 323–344.

Somerset, W., Newport, D., Ragan, K., & Stowe, Z. (2006). Depressive disorders in women: From menarche to beyond the menopause. In L. M. Keyes & S. H. Goodman (Eds.), *Women and depression: A handbook for the social, behavioral, and biomedical sciences.* New York: Cambridge University Press.

Sontag, S. (1979). The double standard of aging. In J. H. Williams (Ed.), *Psychology of women: Selected readings.* New York: Norton.

Sophian, C., Garyantes, D., & Chang, C. (1997). When three is less than two: Early developments in children's understanding of fractional quantities. *Developmental Psychology, 33*, 731–744.

Sorensen, K. (1992). Physical and mental development of adolescent males with Klinefelter syndrome. *Hormone Research, 37*(Suppl. 3), 55–61.

Sorensen, T., Nielsen, G., Andersen, P., & Teasdale, T. (1988). Genetic and environmental influences on premature death in adult adoptees. *New England Journal of Medicine, 318*, 727–732.

Sotiriou, A., & Zafiropoulou, M. (2003). Changes of children's self-concept during transition from kindergarten to primary school. *Psychology: The Journal of the Hellenic Psychological Society, 10*, 96–118.

Sotos, J. F. (1997). Overgrowth: Section IV: Genetic disorders associated with overgrowth. *Clinical Pediatrics, 36*, 37–49.

Sousa, D. L. (2005). *How the brain learns to read.* Thousand Oaks, CA: Corwin Press.

Soussignan, R., Schaal, B., Marlier, L., & Jiang, T. (1997). Facial and autonomic responses to biological and artificial olfactory stimuli in human neonates: Re-examining early hedonic discrimination of odors. *Physiology and Behavior, 62*, 745–758.

Sowell E. R., Peterson, B. S., Thompson, P. M., Welcome, S. E., Henkenius, A. L., & Toga, A.W. (2003). Mapping cortical change across the human life span. *Nature Neuroscience, 6*, 309–315.

Sowell, E. R., Thompson, P. M., Holmes, C. J., Jerrigan, T. L., & Toga, A. W. (1999). In vivo evidence for post-adolescent brain maturation in frontal and striatal regions. *Nature Neuroscience, 10*, 859–861.

Sowell, E. R., Thompson, P. M., Tessner, K. D., & Toga, A. W. (2001). Mapping continued brain growth and gray matter density reduction in dorsal frontal cortex: Inverse relationships during postadolescent brain maturation. *Journal of Neuroscience, 21*, 8819–8829.

Spear, L. P. (2002). The adolescent brain and the college drinker: Biological basis of propensity to use and misuse alcohol. *Journal of Studies on Alcohol*, [Special issue: College drinking, what it is, and what to do about it: Review of the state of the science], Suppl. 14, 71–81.

Spear, P. D. (1993). Neural bases of visual deficits during aging. *Vision Research, 33*, 2589–2609.

Spearman, C. (1927). *The abilities of man.* London: Macmillan.

Spector, H. (2005, February 6). Awaiting a cancer cure: Mother's last hope is experimental gene therapy for her son. *Cleveland Plain Dealer*, p. A1.

Spelke, E. (1987). The development of intermodal perception. In P. Salapatek & L. Cohen (Eds.), *Handbook of infant perception* (Vol. 2). Orlando, FL: Academic Press.

Spence, S. H. (1997). Sex and relationships. In W. K. Halford & H. J. Markman (Eds.), *Clinical handbook of marriage and couples interventions* (pp. 73–105). Chichester, England: Wiley.

Spencer, M. B. (1991). Identity, minority development of. In R. M. Lerner, A. C. Petersen, & J. Brooks-Gunn (Eds.), *Encyclopedia of adolescence* (Vol. 1). New York: Garland.

Spencer, S. J., Fein, S., Zanna, M. P., & Olson, J. M. (Eds.) (2003). *Motivated social perception: The Ontario Symposium*, (Vol. 9). Mahwah, NJ: Erlbaum.

Spiegel, D. (1993). Social support: How friends, family, and groups can help. In D. Goleman & J. Gurin (Eds.), *Mind-body medicine.* Yonkers, NY: Consumer Reports Books.

Spiegel, D. (1996). Dissociative disorders. In R. E. Hales & S. C. Yudofsky (Eds.), *The American Psychiatric Press synopsis of psychiatry.* Washington, DC: American Psychiatric Press.

Spiegel, D., & Giese-Davis, J. (2003). Depression and cancer: Mechanisms and disease progression. *Biological Psychiatry, 54*, 269–282.

Spielman, D. A., & Staub, E. (2003). Reducing boys' aggression: Learning to fulfill basic needs constructively. In E. Staub (Ed.), *The psychology of good and evil.* Cambridge, England: Cambridge University Press.

Spira, A., Bajos, N., Bejin, A., & Beltzer, N. (1992). AIDS and sexual behavior in France. *Nature, 360*, 407–409.

Spraggins, R. E. (2003). *Women and men in the United States: March 2002.* Washington, DC: U.S. Department of Commerce.

Sprecher, S., Sullivan, Q., & Hatfield, E. (1994). Mate selection preferences: Gender differences examined in a national sample. *Journal of Personality and Social Psychology, 66*, 1074–1080.

Springer, S. P., & Deutsch, G. (1989). *Left brain, right brain* (3rd ed.). New York: Freeman.

Squatriglia, C. (2007, February 16). Ted Soulis—charitable painter, businessman. *San Francisco Chronicle*, p. B7.

Squire, L. R., & Knowlton, B. J. (1995). Memory, hippocampus, and brain systems. In M. S. Gazzaniga, *Cognitive neurosciences.* Cambridge, MA: The MIT Press.

Srivastava, S., John, O., & Gosling, S. D. (2003). Development of personality in early and middle adulthood: Set like plaster or persistent change? *Journal of Personality & Social Psychology, 84*, 1041–1053.

Sroufe, L. A. (1994). Pathways to adaptation and maladaptation: Psychopathology as developmental deviation. In D. Cicchetti (Ed.), *Developmental psychopathology: Past, present, and future.* Hillsdale, NJ: Erlbaum.

Sroufe, L. A. (1996). *Emotional development: The organization of emotional life in the early years.* New York: Oxford University Press.

Stacy, A. W., Sussman, S., Dent, C. W., Burton, D., et al. (1992). Moderators of peer social influence in adolescent smoking. *Personality & Social Psychology Bulletin, 18,* 163–172.

Stanjek, K. (1978). Das Uberreichen von Gaben: Funktion und Entwicklung in den ersten Lebensjahren. *Zeitschrift fur Entwicklungpsychologie und Pedagogische Psychologie, 10,* 103–113

Staudinger, U. M., & Baltes, P. B. (1996). Interactive minds: A facilitative setting for wisdom-related performance? *Journal of Personality and Social Psychology, 71,* 746–762.

Staudinger, U. M., & Leipold, B. (2003). The assessment of wisdom-related performance. In C. R. Snyder (Ed.), *Positive psychological assessment: A handbook of models and measures.* Washington, DC: American Psychological Association.

Staunton, H. (2005). Mammalian sleep. *Naturwissenschaften, 35,* 15.

Staus, M. A., Gelles, R. J., & Steinmetz, S. K. (2003). Spare the rod? In M. Silberman (Ed.), *Violence and society: A reader.* Upper Saddle River, NJ: Prentice Hall.

Stearns, E., & Glennie, E. (2006, September). When and why dropouts leave high school. *Youth & Society, 38,* 29–57.

Stedman, L. C. (1997). International achievement differences: An assessment of a new perspective. *Educational Researcher, 26,* 4–15.

Steele, C. (2003). Through the back door to theory. *Psychological Inquiry, 14,* 314–317.

Steele, C. M. (1997). A threat in the air: How stereotypes shape intellectual identity and performance. *American Psychologist, 52,* 613–629.

Steele, C. M., & Aronson, J. (1995). Stereotype threat and the intellectual test performance of African Americans. *Journal of Personality and Social Psychology, 69,* 797–811.

Steers, R. M., & Porter, L. W. (1991). *Motivation and work behavior* (5th ed.). New York: McGraw-Hill.

Stein, J. A., Lu, M. C., & Gelberg, L. (2000). Severity of homelessness and adverse birth outcomes. *Health Psychology, 19,* 524–534.

Stein, J. H., & Reiser, L. W. (1994). A study of white middle-class adolescent boys' responses to "semenarche" (the first ejaculation). *Journal of Youth and Adolescence, 23,* 373–384.

Stein, M. T., Kennell, J. H., & Fulcher, A. (2003). Benefits of a doula present at the birth of a child. *Journal of Developmental and Behavioral Pediatrics, 24,* 195–198.

Stein, Z., Susser, M., Saenger, G., & Marolla, F. (1975). *Famine and human development: The Dutch hunger winter of 1944–1945.* New York: Oxford University Press.

Steinberg, J. (1997, January 2). Turning words into meaning. *The New York Times,* pp. B1–B2.

Steinberg, L. (1993). *Adolescence.* New York: McGraw-Hill.

Steinberg, L., Dornbusch, S., & Brown, B. B. (1992). Ethnic differences in adolescent achievement: An ecological perspective. *American Psychologist, 47,* 723–729.

Steinberg, L., Lamborn, S. D., Darling, N., Mounts, N. S., & Dornbusch, S. M. (1994). Over-time changes in adjustment and competence among adolescents from authoritative, authoritarian, indulgent, and neglectful families. *Child Development, 65,* 754–770.

Steinberg, L., & Silverberg, S. (1986). The vicissitudes of autonomy in early adolescence. *Child Development, 57,* 841–851.

Steinberg, L. D., & Scott, S. S. (2003). Less guilty by reason of adolescence: Developmental immaturity, diminished responsibility, and the juvenile death penalty. *American Psychologist, 58,* 1009–1018.

Steiner, J. E. (1979). Human facial expressions in response to taste and smell stimulation. *Advances in Child Development and Behavior, 13,* 257.

Steinert, S., Shay, J. W., & Wright, W. E. (2000). Transient expression of human telomerase extends the life span of normal human fibroblasts. *Biochemical & Biophysical Research Communications, 273,* 1095–1098.

Steinhausen, H. C., & Spohr, H. L. (1998). Long-term outcome of children with fetal alcohol syndrome: Psychopathology, behavior, and intelligence. *Alcoholism, Clinical & Experimental Research, 22,* 334–338.

Stenberg, G. (2003). Effects of maternal inattentiveness on infant social referencing. *Infant & Child Development, 12,* 399–419.

Stephens, C., Pachana, N., & Bristow, V. (2006). The effect of hormone replacement therapy on mood and everyday memory in younger and mid-life women. *Psychology, Health & Medicine, 11,* 461–469.

Steri, A. O., & Spelke, E. S. (1988). Haptic perception of objects in infancy. *Cognitive Psychology, 20,* 1–23.

Stern, G. (1994, November, 30). Going back to college has special meaning for Mrs. McAlpin. *The Wall Street Journal,* p. A1.

Sternberg, J. (2005). The triarchic theory of successful intelligence. In D. P. Flanagan & P. L. Harrison (Eds.), *Contemporary Intellectual Assessment: Theories, Tests, and Issues.* New York: Guilford Press.

Sternberg, R. (2003a). A broad view of intelligence: The theory of successful intelligence. *Consulting Psychology Journal: Practice & Research, 55,* 139–154.

Sternberg, R. (2003b). Our research program validating the triarchic theory of successful intelligence: Reply to Gottfredson. *Intelligence, 31,* 399–413.

Sternberg, R. (2007, January). A systems model of leadership: WICS. *American Psychologist, 62,* 34–42.

Sternberg, R. J. (1982). Reasoning, problems solving, and intelligence. In R. J. Sternberg (Ed.), *Handbook of human intelligence* (pp. 225–307). Cambridge, England: Cambridge University Press.

Sternberg, R. J. (1985). *Beyond IQ: A triarchic theory of human intelligence.* New York: Cambridge University Press.

Sternberg, R. J. (1986). Triangular theory of love. *Psychological Review, 93,* 119–135.

Sternberg, R. J. (1987). Liking versus loving: A comparative evaluation of theories. *Psychological Bulletin, 102,* 331–345.

Sternberg, R. J. (1988). Triangulating love. In R. J. Sternberg & M. J. Barnes (Eds.), *The psychology of love.* New Haven, CT: Yale University Press.

Sternberg, R. J. (1990). *Metaphors of mind: Conceptions of the nature of intelligence.* Cambridge, England: Cambridge University Press.

Sternberg, R. J. (1991). Theory-based testing of intellectual abilities: Rationale for the Sternberg triarchic abilities test. In H. A. H. Rowe (Ed.), *Intelligence:*

Reconceptualization and measurement. Hillsdale, NJ: Erlbaum.

Sternberg, R. J. (1995). For whom the bell curve tolls: A review of *The Bell Curve. Psychological Science, 6,* 257–261.

Sternberg, R. J. (2005). The triarchic theory of successful intelligence. In D. P. Flanagan & P. L. Harrison (Eds.), *Contemporary intellectual assessment: Theories, tests, and issues.* New York, Guilford Press.

Sternberg, R. J. (2006). Intelligence. In K. Pawlik, & G. d'Ydewalle, *Psychological concepts: An international historical perspective.* Hove, England: Psychology Press/Taylor & Francis.

Sternberg, R. J., Conway, B. E., Ketron, J. L., & Bernstein, M. (1981). Peoples' conceptions of intelligence. *Journal of Personality and Social Psychology, 41,* 37–55.

Sternberg, R. J., & Grigorenko, E. L. (Eds.). (2002). *The general factor of intelligence: How general is it?* Mahwah, NJ: Lawrence Erlbaum.

Sternberg, R. J., Kaufman, J. C., & Pretz, J. E. (2002). *The creativity conundrum: A propulsion model of creative contributions.* Philadelphia, PA: Psychology Press.

Sternberg, R. J., & Lubart, T. I. (1992). Buy low and sell high: An investment approach to creativity. *Current Directions in Psychological Science, 1,* 1–5.

Sternberg, R. J., & The Rainbow Project Collaborators. (2006). The Rainbow Project: Enhancing the SAT through assessments of analytical, practical, and creative skills. *Intelligence, 34.*

Sternberg, R. J., Wagner, R. K., Williams, W. M., & Horvath, J. A. (1997). Testing common sense. In D. Russ-Eft, H. Preskill, & C. Sleezer (Eds.), *Human resource development review: Research and implications* (pp. 102–132). Thousand Oaks, CA: Sage.

Sterns, H. L., Barrett, G. V., & Alexander, R. A. (1985). Accidents and the aging individual. In J. E. Birren & K. W. Schaie (Eds.), *Handbook of the psychology of aging* (2nd ed.). New York: Van Nostrand Reinhold.

Stevens, J., Cai, J., Evenson, K. R., & Thomas, R. (2002). Fitness and fatness as predictors of mortality from all causes and from cardiovascular disease in men and women in the lipid research clinics study. *American Journal of Epidemiology, 156,* 832–841.

Stevens, N., Martina, C., & Westerhof, G. (2006, August). Meeting the need to belong: Predicting effects of a friendship enrichment program for older women. *The Gerontologist, 46,* 495–502.

Stevens-Ratchford, R. G. (1993). The effect of life review reminiscence activities on depression and self-esteem in older adults. *American Journal of Occupational Therapy, 47,* 413–420.

Stevenson, H. W., Chen, C., & Lee, S. Y. (1992). A comparison of the parent–child relationship in Japan and the United States. In L. L. Roopnarine & D. B. Carter (Eds.), *Parent-child socialization in diverse cultures.* Norwood, NJ: Ablex.

Stevenson, H. W., & Lee, S. (1996). The academic achievement of Chinese students. In M. H. Bond (Ed.), *Handbook of Chinese psychology.* London: Oxford University Press.

Stevenson, H. W., Lee, S., & Mu, X. (2000). Successful achievement in mathematics: China and the United States. In C. F. M. van Lieshout & P. G. Heymans (Eds.), *Developing talent across the life span.* Philadelphia, PA: Psychology Press.

Stevenson, M., Henderson, T., & Baugh, E. (2007, February). Vital defenses: Social support appraisals of black grandmothers parenting grandchildren. *Journal of Family Issues, 28,* 182–211.

Stewart, A. J., Copeland, A. P., Chester, N. L., Mallery, J. E., & Barenbaum, N. B. (1997). *Separating together: How divorce transforms families.* New York: Guilford Press.

Stewart, A. J., & Ostrove, J. M. (1998). Women's personality in middle age: Gender, history, and midcourse corrections. *American Psychologist, 53,* 1185–1194.

Stewart, A. J., & Vandewater, E. A. (1999). "If I had it to do over again . . .": Midlife review, midcourse corrections, and women's well-being in midlife. *Journal of Personality and Social Psychology, 76,* 270–283.

Stewart, M., Scherer, J., & Lehman, M. (2003). Perceived effects of high frequency hearing loss in a farming population. *Journal of the American Academy of Audiology, 14,* 100–108.

Stice, E. (2003). Puberty and body image. In C. Hayward (Ed.), *Gender differences at puberty.* New York: Cambridge University Press.

Stice, E., Presnell, K., & Bearman, K. (2001). Relation of early menarche to depression, eating disorders, substance abuse, and comorbid psychopathology among adolescent girls. *Developmental Psychology, 37,* 608–619.

Stice, E., & Shaw, H. (2004). Eating disorder prevention programs: A meta-analytic review. *Psychological Bulletin, 130,* 206–227.

Stitch, S. (2006, December 4). Going it alone. *Time,* p. F3.

Stockdale, M. S., & Crosby, F. J. (2004). *Psychology and management of workplace diversity.* Malden, MA: Blackwell Publishers.

Stolberg, S. G. (1998, April 3). Rise in smoking by young blacks erodes a success story in health. *The New York Times,* p. A1.

Stone, C. (2003). Counselors as advocates for gay, lesbian, and bisexual youth: A call for equity and action. *Journal of Multicultural Counseling & Development, 31,* 143–155.

Storfer, M. (1990). *Intelligence and giftedness: The contributions of heredity and early environment.* San Francisco: Jossey-Bass.

Strauch, B. (1997, August 10). Use of antidepression medicine for young patients has soared. *The New York Times,* pp. A1, A24.

Straus, M. A., & Gelles, R. J. (Eds.). (1990). *Physical violence in American families.* New Brunswick, NJ: Transaction.

Straus, M. A., Gelles, R. J., & Steinmetz, S. K. (2003). The marriage license as a hitting license. In M. Silberman (Eds.), *Violence and society: A reader.* Upper Saddle River, NJ: Prentice Hall.

Straus, M. A., & McCord, J. (1998). Do physically punished children become violent adults? In S. Nolen-Hoeksema (Ed.), *Clashing views on abnormal psychology: A Taking Sides custom reader* (pp. 130–155). Guilford, CT: Dushkin/McGraw-Hill.

Straus, M. A., Sugarman, D. B., & Giles-Sims, J. (1997). Spanking by parents and subsequent antisocial behavior of children. *Archives of Pediatrics and Adolescent Medicine, 151,* 761–767.

Straus, M. A., & Yodanis, C. L. (1996). Corporal punishment in adolescence and physical assaults on spouses in later life: What accounts for the link? *Journal of Marriage and the Family, 58,* 825–841.

Streissguth, A. (1997). *Fetal alcohol syndrome: A guide for families and communities.* Baltimore, MD: Paul H. Brookes.

Strelau, J. (1998). *Temperament: A psychological perspective.* New York: Plenum Publishers.

Strength, J. (1999). Grieving the loss of a child. *Journal of Psychology & Christianity, 18,* 338–353.

Striano, T., & Vaish, A. (2006, November). Seven- to 9-month-old infants use facial expressions to interpret others' actions. *British Journal of Developmental Psychology, 24,* 753–760.

Stroebe, M. S., Stroebe, W., & Hansson, R. O. (Eds.). (1993). *Handbook of bereavement: Theory, research, and intervention.* Cambridge, England: Cambridge University Press.

Stroh, L., K., Langlands, C. L., & Simpson, P. A. (2004). Shattering the glass ceiling in the new millennium. In M. S. Stockdale & F. J. Crosby (Eds.), *Psychology and management of workplace diversity.* Malden, MA: Blackwell Publishers.

Strube, M. (Ed.). (1990). Type A behavior. *Journal of Social Behavior and Personality, 5* [Special issue].

Stutzer, A., & Frey, B. (2006, April). Does marriage make people happy, or do happy people get married? *The Journal of Socio-Economics, 35,* 326–347.

Sugarman, S. (1988). *Piaget's construction of the child's reality.* Cambridge, England: Cambridge University Press.

Suinn, R. M. (2001). The terrible twos—Anger and anxiety: Hazardous to your health. *American Psychologist, 56,* 27–36.

Suitor, J. J., Minyard, S. A., & Carter, R. S. (2001). "Did you see what I saw?" Gender differences in perceptions of avenues to prestige among adolescents. *Sociological Inquiry, 71,* 437–454.

Sullivan, M., & Lewis, M. (2003). Contextual determinants of anger and other negative expressions in young infants. *Developmental Psychology, 39,* 693–705.

Suls, J., & Wallston, K. (2003). *Social psychological foundations of health and illness.* Malden, MA: Blackwell Publishers.

Suls, J., & Wills, T. A. (Eds.). (1991). *Social comparison: Contemporary theory and research.* Hillsdale, NJ: Erlbaum.

Summers, J., Schallert, D., & Ritter, P. (2003). The role of social comparison in students' perceptions of ability: An enriched view of academic motivation in middle school students. *Contemporary Educational Psychology, 28,* 510–523.

Sun, J., & Nathans, J. (2001, October). The challenge of macular degeneration. *Scientific American,* 69–75.

Sundin, O., Ohman, A., Palm, T., & Strom, G. (1995). Cardiovascular reactivity, Type A behavior, and coronary heart disease: Comparisons between myocardial infarction patients and controls during laboratory-induced stress. *Psychophysiology, 32,* 28–35.

Super, C. M. (1976). Environmental effects on motor development: A case of African infant precocity. *Developmental Medicine and Child Neurology, 18,* 561–576.

Super, C. M., & Harkness, S. (1982). The infant's niche in rural Kenya and metropolitan America. In L. Adler (Ed.), *Issues in cross-cultural research.* New York: Academic Press.

Suresh, I. S., Rattan, P. K., & Clark, B.F.C. (Eds.). (2006). *Understanding and modulating aging.* Malden, MA: Blackwell Publishing on behalf of the New York Academy of Sciences.

Suro, R. (1999, November). Mixed doubles. *American Demographics,* 57–62.

Sussman, S. K., & Sussman, M. B. (Eds.). (1991). *Families: Intergenerational and generational connections.* Binghamton, NY: Haworth.

Sutherland, R., Pipe, M., & Schick, K. (2003). Knowing in advance: The impact of prior event information on memory and event knowledge. *Journal of Experimental Child Psychology, 84,* 244–263.

Sutton, J. (2002). Cognitive conceptions of language and the development of autobiographical memory. *Language & Communication, 22,* 375–390.

Suzuki, L., & Aronson, J. (2005). The cultural malleability of intelligence and its impact on the racial/ethnic hierarchy. *Psychology, Public Policy, and Law, 11,* 320–327.

Swain, J. (2004). Is placement in the least restrictive environment a restricted debate? *PsycCRITIQUES,* pp. 23–30.

Swanson, H., Saez, L., & Gerber, M. (2004). Literacy and cognitive functioning in bilingual and nonbilingual children at or not at risk for reading disabilities. *Journal of Educational Psychology, 96,* 3–18.

Swanson, L. A., Leonard, L. B., & Gandour, J. (1992). Vowel duration in mothers' speech to young children. *Journal of Speech and Hearing Research, 35,* 617–625.

Swiatek, M. (2002). Social coping among gifted elementary school students. *Journal for the Education of the Gifted, 26,* 65–86.

Sy, T., Tram, S., & O'Hara, L. (2006, June). Relation of employee and manager emotional intelligence to job satisfaction and performance. *Journal of Vocational Behavior, 68,* 461–473.

Szaflarski, J., Holland, S., Schmithorst, V., & Byars, A. (2006, March). fMRI study of language lateralization in children and adults. *Human Brain Mapping, 27,* 202–212.

Taddio, A., Shah, V., & Gilbert-MacLeod, C. (2002). Conditioning and hyperalgesia in newborns exposed to repeated heel lances. *Journal of the American Medical Association, 288,* 857–861.

Taga, K., Markey, C., & Friedman, H. (2006, June). A longitudinal investigation of associations between boys' pubertal timing and adult behavioral health and well-being. *Journal of Youth and Adolescence, 35,* 401–411.

Tajfel, H. (1982). *Social identity and intergroup relations.* London: Cambridge University Press.

Takahashi, K. (1986). Examining the Strange Situation procedure with Japanese mothers and 12-month-old infants. *Developmental Psychology, 22,* 265–270.

Takala, M. (2006, November). The effects of reciprocal teaching on reading comprehension in mainstream and special (SLI) education. *Scandinavian Journal of Educational Research, 50,* 559–576.

Tallandini, M., & Scalembra, C. (2006). Kangaroo mother care and mother–premature infant dyadic interaction. *Infant Mental Health Journal, 27,* 251–275.

Tamis-LeMonda, C. S., & Bornstein, M. H. (1993). Antecedents of exploratory competence at one year. *Infant Behavior and Development, 16,* 423–439.

Tamis-LeMonda, C. S., & Cabrera, N. (1999). Perspectives on father involvement: Research and policy. *Social Policy Report, 13,* 1–31.

Tamis-LeMonda, C. S., & Cabrera, N. (2002). *Handbook of father involvement: Multidisciplinary perspectives.* Mahwah, NJ: Lawrence Erlbaum Associates.

Tan, H., Wen, S. W., Mark, W., Fung, K. F., Demissie, K., & Rhoads, G. G. (2004). The association between fetal sex and preterm birth in twin pregnancies. *Obstetrics and Gynecology, 103,* 327–332.

Tang, C., Wu, M., Liu, J., Lin, H., & Hsu, C. (2006). Delayed parenthood and the risk of cesarean delivery—Is paternal age an independent risk factor? *Birth: Issues in Perinatal Care, 33*, 18–26.

Tang, W. R., Aaronson, L. S., & Forbes, S. A. (2004). Quality of life in hospice patients with terminal illness. *Western Journal of Nursing Research, 26*, 113–128.

Tangney, J., & Dearing, R. (2002). Gender differences in morality. In R. Bornstein & J. Masling (Eds.), *The psychodynamics of gender and gender role*. Washington, DC: American Psychological Association.

Tangri, S., Thomas, V., & Mednick, M. (2003). Predictors of satisfaction among college-educated African American women in midlife. *Journal of Adult Development, 10*, 113–125.

Tannen, D. (1991). *You just don't understand*. New York: Ballantine.

Tanner, E., & Finn-Stevenson, M. (2002). Nutrition and brain development: Social policy implications. *American Journal of Orthopsychiatry, 72*, 182–193.

Tanner, J. (1972). Sequence, tempo, and individual variation in growth and development of boys and girls aged twelve to sixteen. In J. Kagan & R. Coles (Eds.), *Twelve to sixteen: Early adolescence*. New York: Norton.

Tanner, J. M. (1978). *Education and physical growth* (2nd ed.). New York: International Universities Press.

Tappan, M. (2006, March). Moral functioning as mediated action. *Journal of Moral Education, 35*, 1–18.

Tappan, M. B. (1997). Language, culture and moral development: A Vygotskian perspective. *Developmental Review, 17*, 199–212.

Tardif, T. (1996). Nouns are not always learned before verbs: Evidence from Mandarin speakers' early vocabularies. *Developmental Psychology, 32*, 492–504.

Tardif, T., Wellman, H. M., & Cheung, K. M. (2004). False belief understanding in Cantonese-speaking children. *Journal of Child Language, 31*, 779–800.

Taris, T., van Horn, J., & Schaufeli, W. (2004). Inequity, burnout and psychological withdrawal among teachers: A dynamic exchange model. *Anxiety, Stress & Coping: An International Journal, 17*, 103–122.

Tartamella, L., Herscher, E., & Woolston, C. (2005). *Generation extra large: Rescuing our children from the epidemic of obesity*. New York: Basic.

Task Force on Sudden Infant Death Syndrome (2005). The changing concept of sudden infant death syndrome: Diagnostic coding shifts, controversies regarding the sleeping environment, and new variables to consider in reducing risk. *Pediatrics, 105*, 650–656.

Tasker, F. L., & Golombok, S. (1997). *Growing up in a lesbian family: Effects on child development*. New York: Guilford Press.

Tatum, B. (2007). *Can we talk about race?: And other conversations in an era of school resegregation*. Boston: Beacon Press.

Tauriac, J., & Scruggs, N. (2006, January). Elder abuse among African Americans. *Educational Gerontology, 32*, 37–48.

Taveras, E., Sandora, T., Shih, M., Ross-Degnan, D., Goldmann, D., & Gillman, M. (2006, November). The association of television and video viewing with fast food intake by preschool-age children. *Obesity, 14*, 2034–2041.

Taylor, D. M. (2002). *The quest for identity: From minority groups to Generation Xers*. Westport, CT: Praeger Publishers/Greenwood Publishing.

Taylor, H. G., Klein, N., Minich, N. M., & Hack, M. (2000). Middle-school-age outcomes in children with very low birthweight. *Child Development, 71*, 1495–1511.

Taylor, R. J., Chatters, L. M., Tucker, M. B., & Lewis, E. (1991). Developments in research on black families. In A. Booth (Ed.), *Contemporary families*. Minneapolis, MN: National Council on Family Relations.

Taylor, S. E. (1991). *Health psychology* (2nd ed.). New York: McGraw-Hill.

Teerikangas, O. M., Aronen, E. T., Martin, R. P., & Huttunen, M. O. (1998). Effects of infant temperament and early intervention on the psychiatric symptoms of adolescents. *Journal of the American Academy of Child & Adolescent Psychiatry, 37*, 1070–1076.

Teicher, M. H., Anderson, S. L., Polcari, A., Anderson, C. M., & Navalta, C. P. (2002). Developmental neurobiology of childhood stress and trauma. *Psychiatric Clinics of North America, 25*, 397–426.

Teicher, M. H., Anderson, S. L., Polcari, A., Anderson, C. M., Navalta, C. P., & Kim, D. M. (2003). The neurobiological consequences of early stress and childhood maltreatment. *Neuroscience and Biobehavioral Review, 27*, 33–44.

Tellegen, A., Lykken, D. T., Bouchard, T. J., Jr., Wilcox, K. J., Segal, N. L., & Rich, S. (1988). Personality similarity in twins reared apart and together. *Journal of Personality and Social Psychology, 54*, 1031–1039.

Tenenbaum, H., & Leaper, C. (2003). Parent-child conversations about science: The socialization of gender inequities? *Developmental Psychology, 39*, 34–47.

Tenenbaum, H. R., & Leaper, C. (1998). Gender effects on Mexican-descent parents' questions and scaffolding during toy play: A sequential analysis. *First Language, 18*, 129–147.

Terman, D. L., Larner, M. B., Stevenson, C. S., & Behrman, R. E. (1996). Special education for students with disabilities: Analysis and recommendations. *The Future of Children, 6*, 4–24.

Terman, L. M., & Oden, M. H. (1959). *The gifted group at mid-life: Thirty-five years follow-up of the superior child*. Standord, CA: Standord University Press.

Termin, N. T., & Izard, C. E. (1988). Infants' responses to their mothers' expressions of joy and sadness. *Developmental Psychology, 24, 223*–229.

Terracciano, A., Costa, P., & McCrae, R. (2006, August). Personality plasticity after age 30. *Personality and Social Psychology Bulletin, 32*, 999–1009.

Terry, D. (2000, August, 11). U.S. child poverty rate fell as economy grew, but is above 1979 level. *The New York Times*, p. A10.

Tessor, A., Felson, R. B., & Suls, J. M. (Eds.). (2000). *Psychological perspectives on self and identity*. Washington, DC: American Psychological Association.

Teutsch, C. (2003). Patient–doctor communication. *Medical Clinics of North America, 87*, 1115–1147.

The Boston Globe. (2004, April 26). Oregon's vital experiment. *Boston Globe*, p. A12.

The Endocrine Society. (2001, March 1). *The Endocrine Society and Lawson Wilkins Pediatric Endocrine Society call for further research to define precocious puberty*. Bethesda, MD: The Endocrine Society.

The World Factbook. (2007, April 17). Estimates of infant mortality. Retrieved April 20, 2007 from https://www.cia.gov/cia/publications/factbook/rankorder/2091rank.html.

Thelen, E. (2002). Motor development as foundation and future of developmental psychology. In W. W. Hartup, W. Willard, & R. K. Silbereisen (Eds.), *Growing points in developmental science: An introduction*. Philadelphia, PA: Psychology Press.

Thelen, E., & Bates, E. (2003). Connectionism and dynamic systems: Are they really different? *Developmental Science, 6*, 378–391.

Thelen, E., & Smith, L. (2006). *Dynamic systems theories. Handbook of child psychology. Vol. 1, Theoretical models of human development* (6th ed.). New York: John Wiley & Sons Inc.

Thiessen, E. D., Hill, E. A., & Saffran, J. R. (2005). Infant-directed speech facilitates word segmentation. *Infancy, 7*, 53–71.

Thoman, E. B., & Whitney, M. P. (1989). Sleep states of infants monitored in the home: Individual differences, developmental trends, and origins of diurnal cyclicity. *Infant Behavior and Development, 12*, 59–75.

Thoman, E. B., & Whitney, M. P. (1990). Behavioral states in infants: Individual differences and individual analyses. In J. Colombo & J. Fagen (Eds.), *Individual differences in infancy: Reliability, stability, prediction* (pp. 113–136). Hillsdale, NJ: Erlbaum.

Thomas, A., & Chess, S. (1977). *Temperament and development*. New York: Brunner-Mazel.

Thomas, A., & Chess, S. (1980). *The dynamics of psychological development*. New York: Brunner-Mazel.

Thomas, A., Chess, S., & Birch, H. G. (1968). *Temperament and behavior disorders in children*. New York: New York University Press.

Thomas, P. (1994, September 6). Washington's infant mortality rate, more than twice the U.S. average, reflects urban woes. *The Wall Street Journal*, p. A14.

Thomas, P., & Fenech, M. (2007). A review of genome mutation and Alzheimer's disease. *Mutagenesis, 22*, 15–33.

Thomas, P., Lalloué, F., Preux, P., Hazif-Thomas, C., Pariel, S., Inscale, R., et al. (2006, January). Dementia patients caregivers quality of life: The PIXEL study. *International Journal of Geriatric Psychiatry, 21*, 50–56.

Thomas, R. M. (2001). *Recent human development theories*. Thousand Oaks, CA: Sage.

Thomas, S. (2006, December). From the editor—the phenomenon of cyberbullying. *Issues in Mental Health Nursing, 27*, 1015–1016.

Thompson, C., & Prottas, D. (2006, January). Relationships among organizational family support, job autonomy, perceived control, and employee well-being. *Journal of Occupational Health Psychology, 11*, 100–118.

Thompson, P. (1993). "I don't feel old": The significance of the search for meaning in later life. *International Journal of Geriatric Psychiatry, 8*, 685–692.

Thompson, R., Easterbrooks, M., & Padilla-Walker, L. (2003). Social and emotional development in infancy. In R. Lerner & M. Easterbrooks (Eds.), *Handbook of psychology: Developmental psychology, Vol. 6* (pp. 91–112). New York: John Wiley & Sons, Inc.

Thompson, R. A., & Limber, S. P. (1990). Social anxiety in infancy: Stranger and separation reactions. In H. Leitenberg (Ed.), *Handbook of social and evaluation anxiety*. New York: Plenum.

Thompson, R. A., & Nelson, C. A. (2001). Developmental science and the media. *American Psychologist, 56*, 5–15.

Thoms, K. M., Kuschal, C., & Emmert, S., (2007). Lessons learned from DNA repair defective syndromes. *Experimental Dermatology, 16*, 532–544.

Thomson, J. A., Ampofo-Boateng, K., Lee, D. N., Grieve, R., Pitcairn, T. K., & Demetre, J. D. (1998). The effectiveness of parents in promoting the development of road crossing skills in young children. *British Journal of Educational Psychology, 68*, 475–491.

Thordstein, M., Löfgren, N., Flisberg, A., Lindecrantz, K., & Kjellmer, I. (2006). Sex differences in electrocortical activity in human neonates. *Neuroreport: For Rapid Communication of Neuroscience Research 17*, 1165–1168.

Thornberry, T. P., & Krohn, M. D. (1997). Peers, drug use, and delinquency. In D. M. Stoff, J. Breiling, & J. D. Maser (Eds.), *Handbook of antisocial behavior* (pp. 218–233). New York: Wiley.

Thorne, B. (1986). Girls and boys together, but mostly apart. In W. W. Hartup & Z. Rubin (Eds.), *Relationships and development* (pp. 167–184). Hillsdale, NJ: Erlbaum.

Thornton, J. (2002). Myths of aging or ageist stereotypes. *Educational Gerontology, 28*, 301–312.

Thornton, J. (2004). Life-span learning: A developmental perspective. *International Journal of Aging & Human Development, 57*, 55–76.

Thorsheim, H. I., & Roberts, B. B. (1990). *Reminiscing together: Ways to help us keep mentally fit as we grow older.* Minneapolis: CompCare Publishers.

Thorson, J. A., Powell, F., Abdel-Khalek, A. M., & Beshai, J. A. (1997). Constructions of religiosity and death anxiety in two cultures: The United States and Kuwait. *Journal of Psychology and Theology, 25*, 374–383.

Thurlow, M. L., Lazarus, S. S., & Thompson, S. J. (2005). State policies on assessment participation and accommodations for students with disabilities. *Journal of Special Education, 38*, 232–240.

Time. (1980, September 8). People section.

Tincoff, R., & Jusczyk, P. W. (1999). Some beginnings of word comprehension in 6-month-olds. *Psychological Science, 10*, 172–175.

Ting, Y. (1997). Determinants of job satisfaction of federal government employees. *Public Personnel Management, 26*, 313–334.

Tinsley, B., Lees, N., & Sumartojo, E. (2004). Child and adolescent HIV risk: Familial and cultural perspectives. *Journal of Family Psychology, 18*, 208–224.

Tisserand, D., & Jolles, J. (2003). On the involvement of prefrontal networks in cognitive ageing. *Cortex, 39*, 1107–1128.

Tobin, J. J., Wu, D. Y. H., & Davidson, D. H. (1989). *Preschool in three cultures: Japan, China, and the United States.* New Haven, CT: Yale University Press.

Toga, A. W., & Thompson, P. M. (2003). Temporal dynamics of brain anatomy. *Annual Review of Biomedical Engineering, 5*, 119–145.

Toga, A. W., Thompson, P. M., & Sowell, E. R. Mapping brain maturation. *Trends in Neuroscience, 29*, 148–159.

Tolan, P. H., & Dodge, K. A. (2005). Children's mental health as a primary care and concern: A system for comprehensive support and service. *American Psychologist, 60*, 601–614.

Tolchinsky, L. (2003). *The cradle of culture and what children know about writing and numbers before being taught.* Mahwah, NJ: Lawrence Erlbaum Associates.

Tomblin, J. B., Hammer, C. S., & Zhang, X. (1998). The association of prenatal tobacco use and SLI. *International Journal of Language and Communication Disorders, 33*, 357–368.

Tomlinson-Keasey, C. (1985). *Child development: Psychological, sociological, and biological factors.* Homewood, IL: Dorsey.

Tongsong, T., Iamthongin, A., Wanapirak, C., Piyamongkol, W., Sirichotiyakul, S., Boonyanurak, P., Tatiyapornkul, T., & Neelasri, C. (2005). Accuracy of fetal heart-rate variability interpretation by obstetricians using the criteria of the National Institute of Child Health and Human Development compared with computer-aided interpretation. *Journal of Obstetric and Gynaecological Research, 31*, 68–71.

Topolnicki, D. M. (1995, January). The real immigrant story: Making it big in America. *Money,* 129–138.

Torvaldsen, S., Roberts, C. L, Simpson, J. M., Thompson, J. F., & Ellwood, D. A. (2006). Intrapartum epidural analgesia and breastfeeding: A prospective cohort study. *International Breastfeeding Journal, 24*, 1–24.

Toschke, A. M., Grote, V., Koletzko, B., & von Kries, R. (2004). Identifying children at high risk for overweight at school entry by weight gain during the first 2 years. *Archives of Pediatric Adolescence, 158*, 449–452.

Townsend, A., Noelker, L., Deimling, G., & Bass, D. (1989). Longitudinal impact of interhousehold caregiving on adult children's mental health. *Psychology and Aging, 4*, 393–401.

Towse, J., & Cowan, N. (2005). Working memory and its relevance for cognitive development. In W. Schneider, R. Schumann-Hengsteler, & B. Sodian (Eds.), *Young children's cognitive development: Interrelationships among executive functioning, working memory, verbal ability, and theory of mind.* Mahwah, NJ: Lawrence Erlbaum Associates.

Tracy, J., Shaver, P., & Albino, A. (2003). Attachment styles and adolescent sexuality. In P. Florsheim (Ed.), *Adolescent romantic relations and sexual behavior: Theory, research, and practical implications.* Mahwah, NJ: Lawrence Erlbaum Associates.

Trainor, L., & Desjardins, R. (2002). Pitch characteristics of infant-directed speech affect infants' ability to discriminate vowels. *Psychonomic Bulletin & Review, 9*, 335–340.

Trainor, L. J., Austin, C. M., & Desjardins, R. N. (2000). Is infant-directed speech prosody a result of the vocal expression of emotion? *Psychological Science, 11*, 188–195.

Trautwein, U., Lüdtke, O., Kastens, C., & Köller, O. (2006). Effort on homework in grades 5–9: Development, motivational antecedents, and the association with effort on classwork. *Child Development, 77*, 1094–1111.

Treas, J., & Bengston, V. L. (1987). The family in later years. In M. B. Sussman & S. K. Steinmetz (Eds.), *Handbook of marriage and the family.* New York: Plenum.

Treasure, J., & Tiller, J. (1993). The aetiology of eating disorders: Its biological basis. *International Review of Psychiatry, 5*, 23–31.

Trehub, S. E., (2003). The developmental origins of musicality. *Nature Neuroscience, 6*, 669–673.

Triandis, H. C. (1994). *Culture and social behavior.* New York: McGraw-Hill.

Trickett, P. K., Kurtz, D. A., & Pizzigati, K. (2004). Resilient outcomes in abused and neglected children: Bases for strengths-based intervention and prevention policies. In K. I. Maton & C. J. Schellenbach (Eds.), *Investing in children, youth, families and communities: Strength-based research and policy.* Washington, DC: American Psychological Association.

Trippet, S. E. (1991). Being aware: The relationship between health and social support among older women. *Journal of Women and Aging, 3*, 69–80.

Troll, L. E. (1985). *Early and middle adulthood* (2nd ed.). Monterey, CA: Brooks/Cole.

Tronick, E. (2003). Emotions and emotional communication in infants. In J. Raphael-Leff (Ed.), *Parent–infant psychodynamics: Wild things, mirrors and ghosts* (pp. 35–53). London: Whurr Publishers, Ltd.

Tronick, E. Z. (1995). Touch in mother–infant interactions. In T. M. Field (Ed.), *Touch in early development.* Hillsdale, NJ: Erlbaum.

Tropp, L. (2003). The psychological impact of prejudice: Implications for intergroup contact. *Group Processes & Intergroup Relations, 6*, 131–149.

Tropp, L., & Wright, S. (2003). Evaluations and perceptions of self, ingroup, and outgroup: Comparisons between Mexican-American and European-American children. *Self & Identity, 2*, 203–221.

Trotter, A. (2004, December 1). Web searches often overwhelm young researchers. *Education Week, 24*, 8.

Trzesniewski, K. H., Donnellan, M. B., & Robins, R. W. (2003). Stability of self-esteem across the life span. *Journal of Personality and Social Psychology, 84*, 205–220.

Tsao, F.-M., Liu, H-M., & Kuhl, P. K. (2004). Speech perception in infancy predicts language development in the second year of life: A longitudinal study. *Child Development, 75*, 1067–1084.

Tse, T., & Howie, L. (2005, September). Adult day groups: Addressing older people's needs for activity and companionship. *Australasian Journal on Ageing, 24*, 134–140.

Tucker, M. B., & Mitchell-Kernan, C. (Eds.). (1995). *The decline in marriage among African Americans: Causes, consequences, and policy implications.* New York: Russell Sage.

Tudge, J., & Scrimsher, S. (2003). Lev S. Vygotsky on education: A cultural-historical, interpersonal, and individual approach to development. In B. Zimmerman, (Ed.), *Educational psychology: A century of contributions.* Mahwah, NJ: Lawrence Erlbaum Associates.

Tulving, E., & Thompson, D. M. (1973). Encoding specificity and retrieval processes in episodic memory. *Psychological Review, 80*, 352–373.

Turati, C., Cassia, V. M., Simion, F., & Leo, I. (2006). Newborns' face recognition: Role of inner and outer facial features. *Child Development, 77*, 297–311.

Turkheimer, E., Haley, A., Waldreon, M., D'Onofrio, B., & Gottesman, I. I. (2003). Socioeconomic status modifies heritability of IQ in young children. *Psychological Science, 14*, 623–628.

Turner, J. C., & Onorato, R. S. (1999). Social identity, personality, and the self-concept: A self-categorizing perspective. In T. R. Tyler & R. M. Kramer (Eds.), et al. *The psychology of the social self. Applied social research.* Mahwah, NJ: Lawrence Erlbaum Associates.

Turner, J. S., & Helms, D. B. (1994). *Contemporary adulthood* (5th ed.). Forth Worth, TX: Harcourt Brace.

Turner-Bowker, D. M. (1996). Gender stereotyped descriptors in children's picture books: Does "Curious Jane" exist in the literature? *Sex Roles, 35*, 461–488.

Twenge, J. M., & Campbell, W. K. (2001). Age and birth cohort differences in self-esteem: A cross-temporal meta-analysis. *Personality and Social Psychology Review, 5*, 321–344.

Twenge, J. M., & Crocker, J. (2002). Race and self-esteem: Meta-analyses comparing whites, blacks, Hispanics, Asians, and American Indians and comment on Gray-Little and Hafdahl (2000). *Psychological Bulletin, 128*, 371–408.

Twomey, J. (2006). Issues in genetic testing of children. *MCN: The American Journal of Maternal/Child Nursing, 31*, 156–163.

Tyre, P. (2004, January 19). In a race against time. *Newsweek,* 62–66.

Tyre, P. (2006, September 11). The new first grade: Too much too soon? *Newsweek,* 34–44.

Tyre, P., & McGinn, D. (2003, May 12). She works, he doesn't. *Newsweek,* 45–52.

Tyre, P., & Scelfo, J. (2003, September 22). Helping kids get fit. *Newsweek,* 60–62.

Ubell, E. (1996, September 15). Are you at risk? *Parade Magazine,* 20–21.

Uchikoshi, Y. (2006). Early reading in bilingual kindergartners: Can educational television help? *Scientific Studies of Reading, 10,* 89–120.

Uhlenberg, P., Cooney, T., & Boyd, R. (1990). Divorce for women after midlife. *Journal of Gerontology, 45(1),* S3–S11.

Umana-Taylor, A., & Fine, M. (2004). Examining ethnic identity among Mexican-origin adolescents living in the United States. *Hispanic Journal of Behavioral Sciences, 26,* 36–59.

Umana-Taylor, A., Diveri, M., & Fine, M. (2002). Ethnic identity and self-esteem among Latino adolescents: Distinctions among Latino populations. *Journal of Adolescent Research, 17,* 303–327.

Umberson, D., Williams, K., Powers, D., Chen, M., & Campbell, A. (2005). As good as it gets? A life course perspective on marital quality. *Social Forces, 81,* 493–511.

UNC Center for Civil Rights. (2005, January 7). The socioeconomic compositions of the public schools: A crucial consideration in student assignment policy. Chapel Hill: The University of North Carolina at Chapel Hill.

Underwood, M. (2003). *Social aggression among girls.* New York: Guilford Press.

Underwood, M. (2005). Introduction to the special section: Deception and observation. *Ethics & Behavior, 15,* 233–234.

Unger, R., & Crawford, M. (1992). *Women and gender: A feminist psychology* (2nd ed.). New York: McGraw-Hill.

Unger, R. K. (Ed.). (2001). *Handbook of the psychology of women and gender.* New York: John Wiley & Sons.

UNAIDS & World Health Organization. (2006). *AIDS epidemic update.* Paris: World Health Organization.

UNESCO. (2006). *Compendium of statistics on illiteracy.* Paris: Author.

United Nations. (1990). *Declaration of the world summit for children.* New York: Author.

United Nations. (2002). *Building a society for all ages.* New York: United Nations.

United Nations. (2004). *Hunger and the world's children.* New York: Author.

United Nations Children's Fund. (2005). *Childhood under threat.* New York: United Nations.

United Nations Population Division. (2002). *World population ageing: 1950–2050.* New York: United Nations.

United Nations World Food Programme. (2004). Retrieved. March 1, 2004, from http://www.wfp.org.

UNICEF. (2005). *The state of the world's children.* New York: The United Nations Children's Fund U.S. Bureau of the Census. (2006). Women's earnings as a percentage of men's earnings: 1960-2005. Historical Income Tables-People. Table P-40. Washington, DC: U.S. Bureau of the Census.

University of Akron. (2006). *A longitudinal evaluation of the new curricula for the D.A.R.E. middle (7th grade) and high school (9th grade) programs: Take charge of your life.* Akron, OH: University of Akron.

Updegraff, K. A., Helms, H. M., McHale, S. M., Crouter, A. C., Thayer, S. M., & Sales, L. H. (2004). Who's the boss? Patterns of perceived control in adolescents' friendship. *Journal of Youth & Adolescence, 33,* 403–420.

Updegraff, K., McHale, S., & Crouter, A. (2000). Adolescents' sex-typed friendship experiences: Does having a sister versus a brother matter? *Child Development, 71,* 1597–1610.

Updegraff, K. A., McHale, S. M., Whiteman, S. D., Thayer, S. M., & Crouter, A. C. (2006). The nature and correlates of Mexican-American adolescents' time with parents and peers. *Child Development, 77,* 1470–1486.

Urberg, K., Luo, Q., & Pilgrim, C. (2003). A two-stage model of peer influence in adolescent substance use: Individual and relationship-specific differences in susceptibility to influence. *Addictive Behaviors, 28,* 1243–1256.

Urberg, K. A. (1982). The development of the concepts of masculinity and femininity in young children. *Sex Roles, 8,* 659–668.

Urquidi, V., Tarin, D., & Goodison, S. (2000). Role of telomerase in cell senescence and oncogenesis. *Annual Review of Medicine, 51,* 65–79.

U.S. Census Bureau. (2003). *Population reports.* Washington, DC: GPO.

USDHHS (U.S. Department of Health and Human Services). (1990). *Health United States 1989* (DHHS Publication No. PHS 90–1232). Washington, DC: U.S. Government Printing Office.

U.S. Census Bureau. (1996). *Poverty by educational attainment.* Washington, DC: Author.

U.S. Census Bureau. (2000). The condition of education. *Current Population Surveys, October 2000.* Washington, DC: Author.

U.S. Department of Education. (2005). 2003–04 National Postsecondary Student Aid Study (NPSAS:04), unpublished tabulations. Washington, DC: U.S. Department of Education.

U.S. Department of Health and Human Services, Administration on Children Youth and Families. (2007). *Child Maltreatment 2005. Washington, DC: I.s. Government Printing Office.*

U.S. Bureau of the Census. (2001). *Living arrangements of children.* Washington, DC: Author.

U.S. Bureau of the Census. (2002). *Statistical abstract of the United States (122nd ed.).* Washington, DC: U.S. Government Printing Office.

U.S. Bureau of the Census. (2004). *Current population survey, 2004 annual social and economic supplement.* Washington, DC: Author.

U.S. Bureau of the Census. (2005). *Current population survey.* Washington, DC: Author.

U.S. Advisory Board on Child Abuse and Neglect. (1995). *A nation's shame: Fatal child abuse and neglect in the United States.* Washington, DC: Superintendent of Documents.

U.S. Bureau of Labor Statistics. (2003). *Wages earned by women.* Washington, DC: U.S Bureau of Labor Statistics.

U.S. Bureau of the Census. (1998). *Statistical abstract of the United States (118th ed.).* Washington, DC: U.S. Government Printing Office.

Uylings, H. (2006). Development of the human cortex and the concept of "critical" or "sensitive" periods. *Language Learning, 56,* 59–90.

Vaillancourt, T., & Hymel, S. (2006, July). Aggression and social status: The moderating roles of sex and peer-valued characteristics. *Aggressive Behavior, 32,* 396–408.

Vaillant, G. E. (1977). *Adaptation to life.* Boston: Little, Brown.

Vaillant, G. E., & Vaillant, C. O. (1981). Natural history of male psychological health, X: Work as a predictor of positive mental health. *The American Journal of Psychiatry, 138,* 1433–1440.

Vaillant, G. E., & Vaillant, C. O. (1990). Natural history of male psychological health, XII: A 45-year study of predictors of successful aging. *American Journal of Psychiatry, 147(1),* 31–37.

Vaish, A., & Striano, T. (2004). Is visual reference necessary? Contributions of facial versus vocal cues in 12-month-olds' social referencing behavior. *Developmental Science, 7,* 261–269.

Vajragupta, O., Monthakantirat, O., Wongkrajang, Y., Watanabe, H., & Peungvicha, P. (2000). Chroman amide 12P inhibition of lipid peroxidation and protection against learning and memory impairment. *Life Sciences, 67,* 1725–1734.

Valiente, C., Eisenberg, N., & Fabes, R. A. (2004). Prediction of children's empathy-related responding from their effortful control and parents' expressivity. *Developmental Psychology, 40,* 911–926.

Van Balen, F. (2005). The choice for sons or daughters. *Journal of Psychosomatic Obstetrics & Gynecology, 26,* 229–320.

Van de Graaf, K. (2000). *Human anatomy,* (5th ed., p. 339). Boston: McGraw-Hill.

van den Hoonaard, D. K. (1994). Paradise lost: Widowhood in a Florida retirement community. *Journal of Aging Studies, 8,* 121–132.

van der Mark, I., van ijzendoorn, M., & Bakermans-Kranenburg, M. (2002). Development of empathy in girls during the second year of life: Associations with parenting, attachment, and temperament. *Social Development, 11,* 451–468.

van Honk, J., Schutter, D. L., Hermans, E. J., & Putman, P. (2004). Testosterone, cortisol, dominance, and submission: Biologically prepared motivation, no psychological mechanisms involved. *Behavioral & Brain Sciences, 27,* 160–161.

van Kleeck, A., & Stahl, S. (2003). *On reading books to children: Parents and teachers.* Mahwah, NJ: Lawrence Erlbaum Associates.

Van Manen, S., & Pietromonaco, P. (1993). *Acquaintance and consistency influence memory from interpersonal information.* Unpublished manuscript, University of Massachusetts, Amherst.

Van Mark, K., & Wynn, K. (2006). Six-month-old infants use analog magnitudes to represent duration. *Developmental Science, 9,* F41–F49.

Van Schoiack-Edstrom, L., Frey, K. S., & Beland, K. (2002). Changing adolescents' attitudes about relational and physical aggression. *School Psychology Review, 31,* 201–216.

Van Tassel-Baska, J., Olszewski-Kubilius, P., & Kulieke, M. (1994). A study of self-concept and social support in advantaged and disadvantaged seventh and eighth grade gifted students. *Roeper Review, 16,* 186–191.

van Wormer, K., & McKinney, R. (2003). What schools can do to help gay/lesbian/bisexual youth: A harm reduction approach. *Adolescence, 38,* 409–420.

van't Spijker, A., & ten Kroode, H. F. (1997). Psychological aspects of genetic counseling: A review of the experience with Huntington's disease. *Patient Education and Counseling, 32,* 33–40.

Vandell, D. L. (2000). Parents, peer groups, and other socializing influences. *Developmental Psychology, 36,* 699–710.

Vandell, D. L. (2004). Early child care: The known and the unknown. *Merrill-Palmer Quarterly, 50,* [Special issue: The maturing of human developmental sciences: Appraising past, present, and prospective agendas], 387–414.

Vandell, D. L., Burchinal, M. R., Belsky, J., Owen, M. T., Friedman, S. L., Clarke-Stewart, A., McCartney, K., & Weinraub, M. (2005). Early child care and children's development in the primary grades: Follow-up results from the NICHD Study of Early Child Care. Paper presented at the biennial meeting of the Society for Research in Child Development, Atlanta, GA.

Vandell, D. L., & Pierce, K. M. (2003). Child care quality and children's success at school. In A. Reynolds & M. Wang (Eds.), *Early childhood learning: programs for a new century* (pp. 115–139). New York: Child Welfare League.

Vandell, D. L., Shumow, L., & Posner, J. (2005). After-school programs for low-income children: Differences in program quality. In J. L. Mahoney, R. W. Larson, & J. S. Ecccles, *Organized activities as contexts of development: Extracurricular activities, after-school and community programs.* Mahwah, NJ: Lawrence Erlbaum Associates.

Vandello, J., & Cohen, D. (2003). Male honor and female fidelity: Implicit cultural scripts that perpetuate domestic violence. *Journal of Personality & Social Psychology, 84,* 997–1010.

Vanderburg, R. (2006, October). Reviewing research on teaching writing based on Vygotsky's theories: What we can learn. *Reading & Writing Quarterly: Overcoming Learning Difficulties, 22,* 375–393.

VanLaningham, J., Johnson, D., & Amato, P. (2001). Marital happiness, marital duration, and the U-shaped curve: Evidence from a five-wave panel study. *Social Forces, 78,* 1313–1341.

Vartanian, L. R. (2000). Revisiting the imaginary audience and personal fable constructs of adolescent egocentrism: A conceptual review. *Adolescence, 35,* 639–646.

Vaughn, V., McKay, R. J., & Behrman, R. (1979). *Nelson textbook of pediatrics* (11th ed.). Philadelphia: Saunders.

Vecchiotti, S. (2003). Kindergarten: An overlooked educational policy priority. *Social Policy Report,* 3–19.

Vedantam, S. (2004, April 23). Antidepressants called unsafe for children: Four medications singled out in analysis of many studies. *The Washington Post,* p. A03.

Vedantam, S. (2006, December 20). Short mental workouts may slow decline of aging minds, study finds. *The Washington Post,* p. A1.

Veevers, J. E., & Mitchell, B. A. (1998). Intergenerational exchanges and perceptions of support within "boomerang kid" family environments. *International Journal of Aging & Human Development, 46,* 91–108.

Vellutino, F. R. (1991). Introduction to three studies on reading acquisition: Convergent findings on theoretical foundations of code-oriented versus whole-language approaches to reading instruction. *Journal of Educational Psychology, 83,* 437–443.

Veneziano, R. (2003).The importance of paternal warmth. *Cross-Cultural Research: The Journal of Comparative Social Science, 37,* 265–281.

Veras, R. P., & Mattos, L. C. (2007). Audiology and aging: Literature review and current horizons. *Revista Brasileira de Otorrinolaringologia, 73,* 88–128.

Vereijken, C. M., Riksen-Walraven, J. M., & Kondo-Ikemura, K. (1997). Maternal sensitivity and infant attachment security in Japan: A longitudinal study. *International Journal of Behavioral Development, 21,* 35–49.

Verkerk, G., Pop, V., & Van Son, M, (2003). Prediction of depression in the postpartum period: A longitudinal follow-up study in high-risk and low-risk women. *Journal of Affective Disorders, 77,* 159–166.

Veras, R. P., & Mattos, L. C. (2007). Audiology and aging: Literature review and current horizons. *Revista Brasileira de Otorrinolaringologia (English Edition), 73,* 122–128.

Verkuyten, M. (2003). Positive and negative self-esteem among ethnic minority early adolescents: Social and cultural sources and threats. *Journal of Youth & Adolescence, 32,* 267–277.

Vernon, J. A. (1990). Media stereotyping: A comparison of the way elderly women and men are portrayed on prime-time television. *Journal of Women and Aging, 2,* 55–68.

Vidaver, R. M. et al. (2000). Women subjects in NIH-funded clinical research literature: Lack of progress in both representation and analysis by sex. *Journal of Women's Health, Gender-Based Medicine, 9,* 495–504.

Vilette, B. (2002). Do young children grasp the inverse relationship between addition and subtraction? Evidence against early arithmetic. *Cognitive Development, 17,* 1365–1383.

Vilhjalmsson, R., & Kristjansdottir, G. (2003). Gender differences in physical activity in older children and adolescents: The central role of organized sport. *Social Science Medicine, 56,* 363–374.

Villarosa, L. (2003, December 23). More teenagers say no to sex, and experts are sure why. *The New York Times,* p. D6.

Vincent, J. A., Phillipson, C. R., & Downs, M. (2006). *The futures of old age.* Thousand Oaks, CA: Sage Publications.

Vitaliano, P. P., Dougherty, C. M., & Siegler, I. C. (1994). Biopsychosocial risks for cardiovascular disease in spouse caregivers of persons with Alzheimer's disease. In R. P. Abeles, H. C. Gift, & M. G. Ory (Eds.), *Aging and quality of life.* New York: Springer.

Vitaro, F., & Pelletier, D. (1991). Assessment of children's social problem-solving skills in hypothetical and actual conflict situations. *Journal of Abnormal Child Psychology, 19,* 505–518.

Vizmanos, B., & Marti-Henneberg, C. (2000). Puberty begins with a characteristic subcutaneous body fat mass in each sex. *European Journal of Clinical Nutrition, 54,* 203–206.

Vohs, K. D., & Heatherton, T. (2004). Ego threats elicits different social comparison process among high and low self-esteem people: Implications for interpersonal perceptions. *Social Cognition, 22,* 168–191.

Volkow, N. D., Wang, G. J., Fowler, J. S., Logan, J., Gerasimov, M., Maynard, I., Ding, Y. S., Gatley, S. J., Gifford, A., & Granceschi, D. (2001). Therapeutic doses of oral methylphenidate significantly increase extracellular dopamine in the human brain. *Journal of Neuroscience, 21,* 1–5.

Volling, B. L., & Belsky, J. (1992). The contribution of mother–child and father–child relationships to the quality of sibling interaction: A longitudinal study. *Child Development, 63,* 1209–1222.

Vondra, J., Shaw, D., Swearingen, L., Cohen, M., & Owens, E. (1999). Early relationship quality from home to school: A longitudinal study. *Early Education and Development, 10,* 163–190.

Votruba-Drzal, E., Coley, R. L., & Chase-Lansdale, L. (2004). Child care and low-income children's development: Direct and moderated effects. *Child Development, 75,* 396–312.

Vyas, S. (2004). Exploring bicultural identities of Asian high school students through the analytic window of a literature club. *Journal of Adolescent & Adult Literacy, 48,* 12–18.

Vygotsky, L. S. (1926/1997). *Educational psychology.* Delray Beach, FL: St. Lucie Press.

Vygotsky, L. S. (1979). *Mind in society: The development of higher mental processes.* Cambridge, MA: Harvard University Press. (Original works published 1930, 1933, and 1935)

Wachs, T. (2002). Nutritional deficiencies as a biological context for development. In W. Hartup, W. Silbereisen, & K. Rainer (Eds.), *Growing points in developmental science: An introduction.* Philadelphia, PA: Psychology Press.

Wachs, T. D. (1992). *The nature of nurture.* Newbury Park, CA: Sage.

Wachs, T. D. (1993). The nature–nurture gap: What we have here is a failure to collaborate. In R. Plomin & G. E. McClearn (Eds.), *Nature, nurture, and psychology.* Washington, DC: American Psychological Association.

Wachs, T. D. (1996). Known and potential processes underlying developmental trajectories in childhood and adolescence. *Developmental Psychology, 32,* 796–801.

Wade, N. (2001, October 4). Researchers say gene is linked to language. *The New York Times,* p. A1.

Wagner, H. J., Bollard, C. M., Vigouroux, S., Huls, M. H., Anderson, R., Prentice, H. G., Brenner, M. K., Heslop, H. E., & Rooney, C. M. (2004). A strategy for treatment of Epstein-Barr virus-positive Hodgkin's disease by targeting interleukin 12 to the tumor environment using tumor antigen-specific T Cells. *Cancer Gene Therapy, 2,* 81–91.

Wagner, R. K., & Sternberg, R. J. (1985). Alternate conceptions of intelligence and their implications for education. *Review of Educational Research, 54,* 179–223.

Wahlin, T. (2007). To know or not to know: A review of behaviour and suicidal ideation in preclinical Huntington's disease. *Patient Education and Counseling, 65,* 279–287.

Wainwright, J. L., Russell, S. T., & Pattterson, C. J. (2004). Psychosocial adjustment, school outcomes, and romantic relationships of adolescents with same-sex parents. *Child Development, 75,* 1886–1898.

Waite, S. J., Bromfield, C., & McShane, S. (2005). Successful for whom? A methodology to evaluate and inform inclusive activity in schools. *European Journal of Special Needs Education, 20,* 71–88.

Wakefield, M., Reid, Y., & Roberts, L. (1998). Smoking and smoking cessation among men whose partners are pregnant: A qualitative study. Social Science & Medicine, 47, 657–664.

Wakschlag, L. S., Leventhal, B. L., Pine, D. S., Pickett, K. E., & Carter, A. S. (2006). Elucidating early mechanisms of developmental psychopathology: The case of prenatal smoking and disruptive behavior. *Child Development, 77,* 893–906.

Walcott, D., Pratt, H., & Patel, D. (2003). Adolescents and eating disorders: Gender, racial, ethnic, sociocultural and socioeconomic issues. *Journal of Adolescent Research, 18,* 223–243.

Waldfogel, J. (2001). International policies toward parental leave and child care. *Caring for Infants and Toddlers, 11,* 99–111.

Waldholz, M. (2003, December 3). Genetic testing hits the doctor's office: New screens can predict odds of getting 1,004 diseases; getting pre-emptive surgery. *The Wall Street Journal,* p. B1.

Walker, J., Anstey, K., & Lord, S. (2006, May). Psychological distress and visual functioning in relation to vision-related disability in older individuals with cataracts. *British Journal of Health Psychology, 11,* 303–317.

Walker, L. E. (1999). Psychology and domestic violence around the world. *American Psychologist, 54,* 21–29.

Walker, N. C., & O'Brien, B. (1999). The relationship between method of pain management during labor and birth outcomes. *Clinical Nursing Research, 8,* 119–134.

Walker-Andrews, A. S. (1997). Infants' perception of expressive behaviors: Differentiation of multimodal information. *Psychological Bulletin, 121,* 437–456.

Wallerstein, J., & Resnikoff, D. (2005). Parental divorce and developmental progression: An inquiry into their relationship. In L. Gunsberg & P. Hymowitz, *A handbook of divorce and custody: Forensic, developmental, and clinical perspectives.* Hillsdale, NJ: Analytic Press, Inc.

Wallerstein, J. S., Lewis, J. M., & Blakeslee, S. (2000). *The unexpected legacy of divorce.* New York: Hyperion.

Wallis, C. (1994, July 18). Life in overdrive. *Time,* 42–50.

Wals, M., & Verhulst, F. (2005). Child and adolescent antecedents of adult mood disorders. *Current Opinion in Psychiatry, 18,* 15–19.

Walster, H. E., & Walster, G. W. (1978). *Love.* Reading, MA: Addison-Wesley.

Walter, A. (1997). The evolutionary psychology of mate selection in Morocco: A multivariate analysis. *Human Nature, 8,* 113–137.

Walters, E., & Gardner, H. (1986). The theory of multiple intelligences: Some issues and answers. In R. J. Sternberg & R. K. Wagner (Eds.), *Practical intelligence.* New York: Cambridge University Press.

Wang, M. (2007). Profiling retirees in the retirement transition and adjustment process: Examining the longitudinal change patterns of retirees' psychological wellbeing. *Journal of Applied Psychology, 92,* 455–474.

Wang, M. C., Peverly, S. T., & Catalano, R. (1987). Integrating special needs students in regular classes: Programming, implementation, and policy issues. *Advances in Special Education, 6,* 119–149.

Wang, M. C., Reynolds, M. C., & Walberg, H. J. (Eds.). (1996). *Handbook of special and remedial education: Research and practice* (2nd ed.). New York: Pergamon Press.

Wang, Q. (2001). Culture effects on adults' earliest childhood recollection and self-description: Implication for the relation between memory and the self. *Journal of Personality and Social Psychology, 81,* 220–233.

Wang, Q. (2004). The emergence of cultural self-constructs: Autobiographical memory and self-description in European American and Chinese children. *Developmental Psychology, 40,* 3–15.

Wang, Q. (2006). Culture and the development of self-knowledge. *Current Directions in Psychological Science, 15,* 182–187.

Wang, S., & Tamis-LeMonda, C. (2003). Do child-rearing values in Taiwan and the United States reflect cultural values of collectivism and individualism? *Journal of Cross-Cultural Psychology, 34,* 629–642.

Wang, S-H., Baillargeon, R., & Paterson, S. (2005). Detecting continuity violations in infancy: A new account and new evidence from covering and tube events. *Cognition, 95,* 129–173.

Wannamethee, S. G., Shaper, A. G., Walker, M., & Ebrahim, S. (1998). Lifestyle and 15-year survival free of heart attack, stroke, and diabetes in middle-aged British men. *Archives of Internal Medicine, 158,* 2433–2440.

Ward, R. A. (1984). *The aging experience: An introduction to social gerontology* (2nd ed.). New York: Harper & Row.

Wardle, J., Guthrie, C., & Sanderson, S. (2001). Food and activity preferences in children of lean and obese parents. *International Journal of Obesity & Related Metabolic Disorders, 25,* 971–977.

Warnock, F., & Sandrin, D. (2004). Comprehensive description of newborn distress behavior in response to acute pain (newborn male circumcision). *Pain, 107,* 242–255.

Warren, J. R., Lee, J. C., & Cataldi, E. F. (2004). Teenage employment and high school completion. In D. Conley & K. Albright (Eds.), *After the bell—family background, public policy, and educational success.* London: Routledge.

Warshak, R. A. (2000). Remarriage as a trigger of parental alienation syndrome. *American Journal of Family Therapy, 28,* 229–241.

Wartella, E., Caplovitz, A., & Lee, J. (2004). From Baby Einstein to LeapFrog, from Dooms to the Sims, from instant messaging to Internet chat rooms: Public interest in the role of interactive media in children's lives. *Social Policy Report, 18(4),* 7–8.

Warwick, P., & Maloch, B. (2003). Scaffolding speech and writing in the primary classroom: A consideration of work with literature and science pupil groups in the USA and UK. *Reading: Literacy & Language, 37,* 54–63.

Wass, H. (2004). A perspective on the current state of death education. *Death Studies, 28,* 289–308.

Wasserman, G., Factor-Litvak, P., & Liu, X. (2003). The relationship between blood lead, bone lead and child intelligence. *Child Neuropsychology, 9,* 22–34.

Wasserman, J. D., & Tulsky, D. S. (2005). The history of intelligence assessment. In D. P. Flanagan & P. L. Harrison (Eds.), *Contemporary intellectual assessment: Theories, tests, and issues.* New York, Guilford Press.

Waterhouse, J. M., & DeCoursey, P. J. (2004). Human circadian organization. In J. C. Dunlap & J. J. Loros, (Eds.), *Chronobiology: Biological timekeeping.* Sunderland, MA: Sinauer Associates.

Waterland, R. A., & Jirtle, R. L. (2004). Early nutrition, epigenetic changes at transposons and imprinted genes, and enhanced susceptibility to adult chronic diseases. *Nutrition,* 63–68.

Waters, E., Merrick, S., Treboux, D., Crowell, J., & Albersheim, L. (2000). Attachment security in infancy and early adulthood: A twenty-year longitudinal study. *Child Development, 71,* 684–689.

Waters, L., & Moore, K. (2002). Predicting self-esteem during unemployment: The effect of gender financial deprivation, alternate roles and social support. *Journal of Employment Counseling, 39,* 171–189.

Watkins, D., Dong, Q., & Xia, Y. (1997). Age and gender differences in the self-esteem of Chinese children. *Journal of Social Psychology, 137,* 374–379.

Watson, J. B. (1925). *Behaviorism.* New York: Norton.

Watson, J. B., & Rayner, R. (1920). Conditioned, emotional reactions. *Journal of Experimental Psychology, 3,* 1–14.

Watson, J. K. (2000). Theory of mind and pretend play in family context (false belief). *Dissertation Abstracts International: Section B: The Sciences & Engineering, 60,* 3599.

Watts-English, T., Fortson, B. L., Gibler, N., Hooper, S. R., & De Bellis, M. D. (2006). The psychobiologic of maltreatment in childhood. *Journal of Social Issues, 62,* 717–736.

Wayment, H., & Vierthaler, J. (2002). Attachment style and bereavement reactions. *Journal of Loss & Trauma, 7,* 129–149.

Weaver, A., & Dobson, P. (2004). Home and dry—some toilet training tips to give parents. *Journal of Family Care, 14,* 64, 66.

Webb, R. M., Lubinski, D., & Benbow, C. P. (2002). Mathematically facile adolescents with math/science aspirations: New perspectives on their educational and vocational development. *Journal of Educational Psychology, 94,* 785–794.

Weber, B. (2005, February 25.) From sidelines or in the rink, goalies are targets, even at 8. *New York Times,* p. B1, B8.

Weber, B. A., Roberts, B. L., Resnick, M., Deimling, G., Zauszniewski, J. A., Musil, C., & Yarandi, H. N. (2004). The effect of dyadic intervention on self-efficacy, social support and depression for men with prostate cancer. *Psycho-Oncology, 13,* 47–60.

Webster, J., & Haight, B. (2002). *Critical advances in reminiscence work: From theory to application.* New York: Springer Publishing Co.

Webster, R. A., Hunter, M., & Keats, J. A. (1994). Peer and parental influences on adolescents' substance use: A path analysis. *International Journal of the Addictions, 29,* 647–657.

Wechsler, D. (1975). Intelligence defined and undefined. *American Psychologist, 30,* 135–139.

Wechsler, H., Issac, R., Grodstein, L., & Sellers, M. (2000). *College binge drinking in the 1990s: A continuing problem: Results of the Harvard School of Public Health 1999 College Health Alcohol Study.* Cambridge, MA: Harvard University.

Wechsler, H., Lee, J. E., Kuo, M., Seibring, M., Nelson, T. F., & Lee, H. (2002). Trends in college binge drinking during a period of increased prevention efforts: Findings from 4 Harvard School of Public Health college alcohol study surveys, 1993–2001.

Wechsler, H., & Nelson, T. F. (2001). Binge drinking and the American college student: What's five drinks. *Psychology of Addictive Behaviors, 15,* 287–291.

Weed, K., Ryan, E. B., & Day, J. (1990). Metamemory and attributions as mediators of strategy use and recall. *Journal of Educational Psychology, 82,* 849–855.

Wegienka, G., Havstad, S., & Kelsey, J. (2006). Menopausal hormone therapy in a health maintenance organization before and after Women's Health Initiative hormone trials termination. *Journal of Women's Health, 15,* 369–378.

Wei, J., Hadjiiski, L. M., Sahiner, B., Chan, H. P., Ge, J., Roubidoux, M. A., Helvie, M. A., Zhour, C., Wu, Y. T., Paramagul, C., & Zhang, Y. (2007). Computer-aided detection systems for breast masses: Comparison of performances on full-field digital mammograms and digitized screen-film mammograms. *Academy of Radiology, 14,* 659–669.

Weichold, K., Silbereisen, R., & Schmitt-Rodermund, E. (2003). Short-term and long-term consequences of early versus late physical maturation in adolescents. In C. Hayward (Ed.), *Gender differences at puberty.* New York: Cambridge University Press.

Weigel, D., Martin, S., Bennett, K. (2006). Contributions of the home literacy environment to preschool-aged children's emerging literacy and language skills. *Early Child Development and Care [serial online], 176,* 357–378.

Weinberg, M. K., & Tronick, E. Z. (1996a). Beyond the face: An empirical study of infant affective configurations of facial, vocal, gestural, and regulatory behaviors. *Child Development, 67,* 905–914.

Weinberg, R. A. (2004). The infant and the family in the twenty-first century. *Journal of the American Academy of Child & Adolescent Psychiatry, 43,* 115–116.

Weinberger, D. R. (2001, March 10). A brain too young for good judgment. *The New York Times*, p. D1.

Weiner, B. (1985). *Human motivation*. New York: Springer-Verlag.

Weiner, B. (1994). Integrating social and personal theories of achievement striving. *Review of Educational Research, 64*, 557–573.

Weinfield, N. S., Sroufe, L. A., & Egeland, B. (2000). Attachment from infancy to early adulthood in a high-risk sample: Continuity, discontinuity, and their correlates. *Child Development, 71*, 695–702.

Weinstock, H., Berman, S., & Cates, W., Jr. (2004). Sexually transmitted diseases among American youth: Incidence and prevalence estimates, 2000. *Perspectives on Sexual and Reproductive Health, 36*, 182–191.

Weiss, J., Cen, S., Schuster, D., Unger, J., Johnson, C., Mouttapa, M., et al. (2006, June). Longitudinal effects of pro-tobacco and anti-tobacco messages on adolescent smoking susceptibility. *Nicotine & Tobacco Research, 8*, 455–465.

Weiss, M. R., Ebbeck, V., & Horn. T. S. (1997). Children's self-perceptions and sources of physical competence information: A cluster analysis. *Journal of Sport & Exercise Psychology, 19*, 52–70.

Weiss, R. (2003, September 2). Genes' sway over IQ may vary with class. *The Washington Post*, p. A1.

Weiss, R., & Raz, I. (2006, July). Focus on childhood fitness, not just fatness. *Lancet, 368*, 261–262.

Weisz, A., & Black, B. (2002). Gender and moral reasoning: African American youth respond to dating dilemmas. *Journal of Human Behavior in the Social Environment, 5*, 35–52.

Weitzman, E., Nelson, T., & Wechsler, H. (2003). Taking up binge drinking in college: The influences of person, social group, and environment. *Journal of Adolescent Health, 32*, 26–35.

Wellman, H., Fang, F., Liu, D., Zhu, L., & Liu, G. (2006, December). Scaling of theory-of-mind understandings in Chinese children. *Psychological Science, 17*, 1075–1081.

Wellman, H. M., & Gelman, S. A. (1992). Cognitive development: Foundational theories of core domains. *Annual Review of Psychology, 43*, 337–375.

Werker, J. F., Pons, F., Dietrich, C., Kajikawa, S., Fais, L., & Amano, S. (2007). Infant-directed speech supports phonetic category learning in English and Japanese. *Cognition, 103*, 147–162.

Werner, E. E. (1972). Infants around the world: Cross-cultural studies of psychomotor development from birth to two years. *Journal of Cross-Cultural Psychology, 3*, 111–134.

Werner, E. E. (1995). Resilience in development. *Current Directions in Psychological Science, 4*, 81–85.

Werner, E. E. (2005). What can we learn about resilience from large-scale longitudinal studies? In S. Goldstein, & R. B. Brooks, *Handbook of resilience in children*. New York: Kluwer Academic/Plenum Publishers.

Werner, L. A., & Marean, G. C. (1996). *Human auditory development*. Boulder, CO: Westview Press.

Werner, N. E., & Crick, N. R. (2004). Maladaptive peer relationships and the development of relational and physical aggression during middle childhood. *Social Development, 13*, 495–514.

Wertsch, J. V. (1999). The zone of proximal development: Some conceptual issues. In P. Lloyd & C. Fernyhough (Eds.), *Lev Vygotsky: Critical assessments, Vol. 3: The zone of proximal development*. New York: Routledge.

West, J. R., & Blake, C. A. (2005). Fetal alcohol syndrome: An assessment of the field. *Experimental Biology and Medicine, 230*, 354–356.

Westerhausen, R., Kreuder, F., Sequeira Sdos, S., Walter, C., Woerner, W., Wittling, R. A., Schweiger, E., & Wittling, W. (2004). Effects of handedness and gender on macro- and microstructure of the corpus callosum and its subregions: A combined high-resolution and diffusion-tensor MRI study. *Brain Research and Cognitive Brain Research, 21*, 418–426.

Westermann, G., Mareschal, D., Johnson, M. H., Sirois, S., Spratling, M. W., & Thomas, M. S. (2007). Neuroconstructivism. *Developmental Science, 10*, 75–83.

Wethington, E., Cooper, H., & Holmes, C. S. (1997). Turning points in midlife. In I. H. Gotlib & B. Wheaton (Eds.), *Stress and adversity over the life course: Trajectories and turning points* (pp. 215–231). New York: Cambridge University Press.

Wexler, B. (2006). *Brain and culture: Neurobiology, ideology, and social change*. Cambridge, MA: MIT Press.

Whalen, C. K., Jamner, L. D., Henker, B., Delfino, R. J., & Lozano, J. M. (2002). The ADHD spectrum and everyday life: Experience sampling of adolescent moods, activities, smoking, and drinking. *Child Development, 73*, 209–227.

Whalen, J., & Begley, S. (2005, March 30). In England, girls are closing the gap with boys in math. *The Wall Street Journal*, p. A1.

Whaley, B. B., & Parker, R. G. (2000). Expressing the experience of communicative disability: Metaphors of persons who stutter. *Communication Reports, 13*, 115–125.

Wheeldon, L. R. (1999). *Aspects of language production*. Philadelphia: Psychology Press.

Wheeler, G. (1998, March 13). The wake-up call we dare not ignore. *Science, 279*, 1611.

Wheeler, S., & Austin, J. (2001). The impact of early pregnancy loss. *American Journal of Maternal/Child Nursing, 26*, 154–159.

Whelan, T., & Lally, C. (2002). Paternal commitment and father's quality of life. *Journal of Family Studies, 8*, 181–196.

Whitaker, B. (2004, March 29). Employee of the century. *CBS Evening News*.

Whitaker, R. C., Wright, J. A., Pepe, M. S., Seidel, K. D., & Dietz, W. H. (1997, September 25). Predicting obesity in young adulthood from childhood and parental obesity. *The New England Journal of Medicine, 337*, 869–873.

Whitbourne, S., Jacobo, M., & Munoz-Ruiz, M. (1996). Adversity in the elderly. In R. S. Feldman (Ed.), *The psychology of adversity*. Amherst: University of Massachusetts Press.

Whitbourne, S. K. (1996). *The aging individual: Physical and psychological perspectives*. New York: Springer.

Whitbourne, S. K. (2001). *Adult development and aging: Biopsychosocial perspectives*. New York: Wiley.

Whitbourne, S. K., & Sneed, J. R. (2004). The paradox of well-being, identity processes, and stereotype threat: Ageism and its potential relationships to the self in later life. In T. Nelson (Ed.), *Ageism: Stereotyping and prejudice against older persons*. Cambridge, MA: MIT Press.

Whitbourne, S. K., & Wills, K. (1993). Psychological issues in institutional care of the aged. In S. B. Goldsmith (Ed.), *Long-term care*. Gaithersburg, MD: Aspen.

Whitbourne, S. K., Zuschlag, M. K., Elliot, L. B., & Waterman, A. S. (1992). Psychosocial development in adulthood: A 22-year sequential study. *Journal of Personality and Social Psychology, 63*, 260–271.

White, N. (2003). Changing conceptions: Young people's views of partnering and parenting. *Journal of Sociology, 39*, 149–164.

Whitehurst, G. J., & Fischel, J. E. (2000). Reading and language impairments in conditions of poverty. In D. V. M. Bishop & L. B. Leonard (Eds.), *Speech and language impairments in children: Causes, characteristics, intervention and outcome*. Philadelphia: Psychology Press/Taylor & Francis.

Whiting, B. B., & Edwards, C. P. (1988). *Children of different worlds: The formation of social behavior*. Cambridge, MA: Harvard University Press.

Wickelgren, W. A. (1999). Webs, cell assemblies, and chunking in neural nets: Introduction. *Canadian Journal of Experimental Psychology, 53*, 118–131.

Widom, C. S. (2000). Motivation and mechanisms in the "cycle of violence" In D. J. Hansen (Ed.), *Nebraska Symposium on Motivation Vol. 46, 1998: Motivation and child maltreatment* (Current theory and research in motivation series). Lincoln, NE: University of Nebraska Press.

Wielgosz, A. T., & Nolan, R. P. (2000). Biobehavioral factors in the context of ischemic cardiovascular disease. *Journal of Psychosomatic Research, 48*, 339–345.

Wiggins, M., & Uwaydat, S. (2006, January). Age-related macular degeneration: Options for earlier detection and improved treatment. *The Journal of Family Practice, 55*, 22–27.

Wilcox, A., Skjaerven, R., Buekens, P., & Kiely, J. (1995, March 1). Birth weight and perinatal mortality: A comparison of the United States and Norway. *Journal of the American Medical Association, 273*, 709–711.

Wilcox, H. C., Conner, K. R., & Caine, E. D. (2004). Association of alcohol and drug use disorders and completed suicide: An empirical review of cohort studies. *Drug & Alcohol Dependence, 76* [Special issue: Drug abuse and suicidal behavior], S11–S19.

Wilcox, M. D. (1992). Boomerang kids. *Kiplinger's Personal Finance Magazine, 46*, 83–86.

Wilcox, S., Castro, C. M., & King, A. C. (2006). Outcome expectations and physical activity participation in two samples of older women. *Journal of Health Psychology, 11*, 65–77.

Wilcox, S., Everson, K., Aragaki, A., Wassertheil-Smoller, S., Moulton, C., & Loevinger, B. (2003). The effects of widowhood on physical and mental health, health behaviors, and health outcomes: The Women's Health Initiative. *Health Psychology, 22*, 513–522.

Wilcox, T., Woods, R., Chapa, C., & McCurry, S. (2007). Multisensory exploration and object individuation in infancy. *Developmental Psychology, 43*, 479–495.

Wildberger, S. (2003, August). So you're having a baby. *Washingtonian*, 85–86, 88–90.

Wiley, T. L., Nondahl, D. M., Cruickshanks, K. J., & Tweed, T. S. (2005). Five-year changes in middle ear function for older adults. *Journal of the American Academy of Audiology, 16*, 129–139.

Williams, J., & Binnie, L. (2002). Children's concept of illness: An intervention to improve knowledge. *British Journal of Health Psychology, 7*, 129–148.

Williams, J. M., & Currie, C. (2000). Self-esteem and physical development in early adolescence: Pubertal timing and body image. *Journal of Early Adolescence, 20*, 129–149.

Williams, K., & Dunne-Bryant, A. (2006, December). Divorce and adult psychological well-being: Clarifying the role of gender and child age. *Journal of Marriage and Family, 68*, 1178–1196.

Williams, R., Barefoot, J., & Schneiderman, N. (2003). Psychosocial risk factors for cardiovascular disease: More than one culprit at work. *JAMA: Journal of the American Medical Association, 290*, 2190–2192.

Willie, C., & Reddick, R. (2003). *A new look at black families* (5th ed.). Walnut Creek, CA: AltaMira Press.

Willis, S. (1996). Everyday problem solving. In J. E. Birren, K. W. Schaie, R. P. Abeles, M.Gatz, & T. A. Salthouse (Eds.), *Handbook of the psychology of aging* (4th ed.). San Diego: Academic Press.

Willis, S., Tennstedt, S., Marsiske, M., Ball, K., Elias, J., Koepke, K., Morris, J., Rebok, G., Unverzagt, F., Stoddard, A., & Wright, E. (2006). Long-term effects of cognitive training on everyday functional outcomes in older adults. *Journal of the American Medical Association, 296*, 2805–2814.

Willis, S. L. (1985). Educational psychology of the older adult learner. In J. E. Birren & K. W. Schaie (Eds.), *Handbook of the psychology of aging* (2nd ed.). New York: Van Nostrand Reinhold.

Willis, S. L., & Nesselroade, C. S. (1990). Long-term effects of fluid ability training in old-old age. *Developmental Psychology, 26*, 905–910.

Willott, J., Chisolm, T., & Lister, J. (2001). Modulation of presbycusis: Current state and future directions. *Audiology & Neuro-Otology, 6*, 231–249.

Wills, T., Resko, J., & Ainette, M. (2004). Smoking onset in adolescence: A person-centered analysis with time-varying predictors. *Health Psychology, 23*, 158–167.

Wilson, B. et al. (2002). Violence in children's television programming: Assessing the risks. *Journal of Communication, 52*, 5–35.

Wilson, M. N. (1989). Child development in the context of the black extended family. *American Psychologist, 44*, 380–385.

Wilson, R. (2004, December 3). Where the elite teach, it's still a man's world. *Chronicle of Higher Education, 51*, A8.

Wilson, R., Beck, T., Bienias, J., & Bennett, D. (2007, February). Terminal cognitive decline: Accelerated loss of cognition in the last years of life. *Psychosomatic Medicine, 69*, 131–137.

Wilson, R., Beckett, L., & Bienias, J. (2003). Terminal decline in cognitive function. *Neurology, 60*, 1782–1787.

Wilson, R. S. (1983). The Louisville twin study: Developmental synchronies in behavior. *Child Development, 54*, 298–316.

Wimmer, H., & Gschaider, A. (2000). Children's understanding of belief: Why is it important to understand what happened? In P. Mitchell & K. J. Riggs (Eds.), *Children's reasoning and the mind*. Hove, England: Psychology Press/Taylor & Francis.

Windle, M. (1994). A study of friendship characteristics and problem behaviors among middle adolescents. *Child Development, 65*, 1764–1777.

Wineburg, S. S. (1987). The self-fulfillment of the self-fulfilling prophecy. *Educational Researcher, 16*, 28–37.

Wines, M. (2006, August 24). Africa adds to miserable ranks for child workers. *New York Times.*, p.D1.

Winger, G., & Woods, J. H. (2004). *A handbook on drug and alcohol abuse: The biomedical aspects.* Oxford, England: Oxford University Press.

Wingert, P., & Brant, M. (2005, August 15). Reading your baby's mind. *Newsweek*, 32.

Wingert, P., & Kantrowitz, B. (1997, October 27). Why Andy couldn't read (bright children who are also learning disabled). *Newsweek, 130*, 56.

Wingert, P., & Katrowitz, B. (2002, October 7). Young and depressed. *Newsweek*, 53–61.

Wingert, P., & Kantrowitz, B. (2007, January 15). The new prime time. *Newsweek*, p. 38.

Wingfield, A., Tun, P. A., McCoy, S. L. (2005). Hearing loss in older adulthood: What it is and how it interacts with cognitive performance. *Current Directions in Psychological Science, 14*, 144–147.

Wink, P., & Dillon, M. (2003). Religiousness, spirituality, and psychosocial functioning in late adulthood: Findings from a longitudinal study. *Psychology & Aging, 18*, 916–924.

Winn, R. L., & Newton, N. (1982). Sexuality in aging: A study of 106 cultures. *Archives of Sexual Behavior, 11*, 283–298.

Winner, E. (1997). *Gifted children: Myths and realities.* New York: Basic Books.

Winner, E. (2000). The origins and ends of giftedness. *American Psychologist, 55*, 159–169.

Winsler, A. (2003). Introduction to special issue: Vygotskian perspectives in early childhood education. *Early Education and Development, 14, [Special Issue]*, 253–269.

Winsler, A., De Leon, J. R., & Wallace, B. A. (2003). Private speech in preschool children: Developmental stability and change, across-task consistency, and relations with classroom behavior. *Journal of Child Language, 30*, 583–608.

Winsler, A., Feder, M., Way, E., & Manfra, L. (2006, July). Maternal beliefs concerning young children's private speech. *Infant and Child Development, 15*, 403–420.

Winstead, B. A., & Sanchez, J. (2005). Gender and psychopathology. In J. Maddux (Ed.), *Psychopathology: Foundations for a contemporary understanding.* Mahwah, NJ: Lawrence Erlbaum Associates.

Winterich, J. (2003). Sex, menopause, and culture: Sexual orientation and the meaning of menopause for women's sex lives. *Gender & Society, 17*, 627–642.

Winters, K. C., Stinchfield, R. D., & Botzet, A. (2005). Pathways fo youth gambling problem severity. *Psychology of Addictive Behaviors, 19*, 104–107.

Wisborg, K., Kesmodel, U., Bech, B. H., Hedegaard, M., & Henriksen, T. B. (2003). Maternal consumption of coffee during pregnancy and stillbirth and infant death in first year of life: Prospective study. *British Medical Journal, 326*, 420.

Wise, L., Adams-Campbell, L., Palmer, J., & Rosenberg, L. (2006, August). Leisure time physical activity in relation to depressive symptoms in the Black Women's Health Study. *Annals of Behavioral Medicine, 32*, 68–76.

Witelson, S. (1989, March). Sex differences. Paper presented at the annual meeting of the New York Academy of Science, New York.

Witt, S. D. (1997). Parental influence on children's socialization to gender roles. *Adolescence, 32*, 253–259.

Woelfle, J. F., Harz, K., & Roth, C. (2007). Modulation of circulating IGF-I and IGFBP-3 levels by hormonal regulators of energy homeostasis in obese children. *Experimental and Clinical Endocrinology Diabetes, 115*, 17–23.

Woike, B., & Matic, D. (2004). Cognitive complexity in response to traumatic experiences. *Journal of Personality, 72*, 633–657.

Wolfe, M. S. (2006, May). Shutting down Alzheimer's. *Scientific American*, 73–79.

Wolfe, W. (2007, February 24). Late life love: Older couples find that love comes when they aren't looking for it and share the stories of their late-in-life romance. *The Star Tribune* (Minneapolis, MN), p. 1E.

Wolfson, C., Handfield-Jones, R., Glass, K. C., McClaran, J., et al. (1993). Adult children's perceptions of their responsibility to provide care for dependent elderly parents. *Gerontologist, 33*, 315–323.

Wolinsky, F., Wyrwich, K., & Babu, A. (2003). Age, aging, and the sense of control among older adults: A longitudinal reconsideration. *Journals of Gerontology: Series B: Psychological Sciences & Social Sciences, 58B*, S212–S220.

Wong, C. A., Scavone, B. M., Peaceman, A. M., McCarthy, R. J., Sullivan, J. T., Diaz, N. T., Yaghmour, E., Marcus, R. L., Sherwani, S. S., Sproviero, M. T., Yilmaz, M., Patel, R., Robles, C., & Grouper, S. (2005, February 17). The risk of cesarean delivery with neuraxial analgesia given early versus late in labor. *New England Journal of Medicine, 352*, 655–665.

Wood, R. (1997). Trends in multiple births, 1938–1995. *Population Trends*, 87, 29–35.

Woolf, A., & Lesperance, L. (2003, September 22). What should we worry about? *Newsweek*, 72.

Woolfolk, A. E. (1993). *Educational psychology* (5th ed.). Boston: Allyn & Bacon.

World Bank. (2003). *Global development finance 2003—Striving for stability in development finance.* Washington, DC: Author.

World Bank. (2004). *World development indicators 2004 (WDI).* Washington, DC: Author.

World Conference on Education for All. (1990, April). *World declaration on education for all and framework for action to meet basic learning needs,* (Preamble, p. 1). New York: Author.

World Health Organization. (1999). *Death rates from coronary heart disease.* Geneva: Author.

Worobey, J., & Bajda, V. M. (1989). Temperament ratings at 2 weeks, 2 months, and 1 year: Differential stability of activity and emotionality. *Developmental Psychology, 25*, 257–263.

Worrell, F., Szarko, J., & Gabelko, N. (2001). Multi-year persistence of nontraditional students in an academic talent development program. *Journal of Secondary Gifted Education, 12*, 80–89.

Wortman, C., & Silver, R. C. (1989). The myths of coping with loss. *Journal of Consulting and Clinical Psychology, 57*, 349–357.

Wortman, C. B., & Silver, R. C. (1990). Successful mastery of bereavement and widowhood: A life-course perspective. In P. B. Baltes & M. M. Baltes (Eds.), *Successful aging: Perspectives from the behavioral sciences.* Cambridge, England: Cambridge University Press.

Wright, J. C., Huston, A. C., Murphy, K. C., St. Peters, M., Piñon, M., Scantlin, R., & Kotler, J. (2001). *Child Development, 72*, 1347–1366.

Wright, J. C., Huston, A. C., Reitz, A. L., & Piemyat, S. (1994). Young children's perceptions of television reality: Determinants and developmental differences. *Developmental Psychology, 30*, 229–239.

Wright, J. C., Huston, A. C., Truglio, R., Fitch, M., Smith, E., & Piemyat, S. (1995). Occupational portrayals on television: Children's role schemata, career aspirations, and perceptions of reality. *Child Development, 66*, 1706–1718.

Wright, R. (1995, March 13). The biology of violence. *New Yorker*, pp. 68–77.

Wright, S. C., & Taylor, D. M. (1995). Identity and the language of the classroom: Investigation of the impact of heritage versus second language instruction on personal and collective self-esteem. *Journal of Educational Psychology, 87*, 241–252.

Wrosch, C., Bauer, I., & Scheier, M. (2005, December). Regret and quality of life across the adult life span: The influence of disengagement and available future goals. *Psychology and Aging, 20*, 657–670.

Wu, C., Zhou, D., & Chen, W. (2003). A nested case-control study of Alzheimer's disease in Linxian, northern China. *Chinese Mental Health Journal, 17*, 84–88.

Wu, P., Robinson, C., & Yang, C. (2002). Similarities and differences in mothers' parenting of preschoolers in China and the United States. *International Journal of Behavioral Development, 26,* 481–491.

Wyer, R. (2004). The cognitive organization and use of general knowledge. In J. Jost & M. Banaji (Eds.), *Perspectivism in social psychology: The yin and yang of scientific progress.* Washington, DC: American Psychological Association.

Wynn, K. (1992, August 27). Addition and subtraction by human infants. *Nature, 358,* 749–750.

Wynn, K. (1995). Infants possess a system of numerical knowledge. *Current Directions in Psychological Science, 4,* 172–177.

Wynn, K. (2000). Findings of addition and subtraction in infants are robust and consistent: Reply to Wakeley, Rivera, and Langer. *Child Development, 71,* 1535–1536.

Xiaohe, X., & Whyte, M. K. (1990). Love matches and arranged marriages: A Chinese replication. *Journal of Marriage and the Family, 52,* 709–722.

Yan, S., & Rettig, K. D. (2004). Korean American mothers' experiences in facilitating academic success for their adolescents. *Marriage & Family Review, 36,* 53–74.

Yan, Z., & Fischer, K. (2002). Always under construction: Dynamic variations in adult cognitive microdevelopment. *Human Development, 45,* 141–160.

Yang, C. D. (2006). *The infinite gift: How children learn and unlearn the languages of the world.* New York: Scribner.

Yang, R., & Blodgett, B. (2000). Effects of race and adolescent decision-making on status attainment and self-esteem. *Journal of Ethnic & Cultural Diversity in Social Work, 9,* 135–153.

Yang, S., & Rettig, K. D. (2004). Korean-American mothers' experiences in facilitating academic success for their adolescents. *Marriage & Family Review, 36,* 53–74.

Yankee Group. (2001). *Teenage online activities.* Boston: Author.

Yardley, J. (2001, July 2). Child-death case in Texas raises penalty questions. *The New York Times,* p. A1.

Yarrow, L. (1992, November). Giving birth: 72,000 moms tell all. *Parents, 148,* 159.

Yarrow, M. R., Scott, P. M., & Waxler, C. Z. (1973). Learning concern for others. *Developmental Psychology, 8,* 240–260.

Ybarra, M. L., & Mitchell, K. J., (2004). Online aggressor/targets, aggressors, and targets: A comparison of associated youth characteristics. *Journal of Child Psychology and Psychiatry, 45,* 1308–1316.

Yell, M. L. (1995). The least restrictive environment mandate and the courts: Judicial activism or judicial restraint? *Exceptional Children, 61,* 578–581.

Yelland, G. W., Pollard, J., & Mercuri, A. (1993). The metalinguistic benefits of limited contact with a second language. *Applied Psycholinguistics, 14,* 423–444.

Yerkes, R. M. (1923). *A point scale for measuring mental ability. A 1923 revision.* Baltimore, MD: Warwick & York.

Yildiz, O. (2007). Vascular smooth muscle and endothelial functions in aging. *Annals of the New York Academy of Sciences, 1100,* 353–360.

Yinger, J. (Ed.). (2004). *Helping children left behind: State aid and the pursuit of educational equity.* Cambridge, MA: MIT Press.

Yip, T., Sellers, R. M., & Seaton, E. K. (2006). African American racial identity across the lifespan: Identity status, identity content, and depressive symptoms. *Child Development, 77,* 1504–1517.

Yoshinaga-Itano, C. (2003). From screening to early identification and intervention: Discovering predictors to successful outcomes for children with significant hearing loss. *Journal of Deaf Studies & Deaf Education, 8,* 11–30.

Young, H., & Ferguson, L. (1979). Developmental changes through adolescence in the spontaneous nomination of reference groups as a function of decision context. *Journal of Youth and Adolescence, 8,* 239–252.

Young, S., Rhee, S., Stallings, M., Corley, R., & Hewitt, J. (2006, July). Genetic and environmental vulnerabilities underlying adolescent substance use and problem use: General or specific? *Behavior Genetics, 36,* 603–615.

Youniss, J., & Haynie, D. L. (1992). Friendship in adolescence. *Journal of Developmental and Behavioral Pediatrics, 13,* 59–66.

Yuill, N., & Perner, J. (1988). Intentionality and knowledge in children's judgments of actor's responsibility and recipient's emotional reaction. *Developmental Psychology, 24,* 358–365.

Zafeiriou, D. I. (2004). Primitive reflexes and postural reactions in the neurodevelopmental examination. *Pediatric Neurology, 31,* 1–8.

Zahn-Waxler, C., & Radke-Yarrow, M. (1990). The origins of empathic concern. *Motivation and Emotion, 14,* 107–130.

Zahn-Waxler, C., Robinson, J. L., & Emde, R. N. (1992). The development of empathy in twins. *Developmental Psychology, 28,* 1038–1047.

Zalenski, R., & Raspa, R. (2006). Maslow's hierarchy of needs: A framework for achieving human potential in hospice. *Journal of Palliative Medicine, 9,* 1120–1127.

Zalsman, G., Oquendo, M., Greenhill, L., Goldberg, P., Kamali, M., Martin, A., et al. (2006, October). Neurobiology of depression in children and adolescents. *Child and Adolescent Psychiatric Clinics of North America, 15,* 843–868.

Zampi, C., Fagioli, I., & Salzarulo, P. (2002). Time course of EEG background activity level before spontaneous awakening in infants. *Journal of Sleep Research, 11,* 283–287.

Zarit, S. H., & Reid, J. D. (1994). Family caregiving and the older family. In C. B. Fisher & R. M. Lerner (Eds.), *Applied developmental psychology.* New York: McGraw-Hill.

Zauszniewski, J. A., & Martin, M. H. (1999). Developmental task achievement and learned resourcefulness in healthy older adults. *Archives of Psychiatric Nursing, 13,* 41–47.

Zeedyk, M., & Heimann, M. (2006). Imitation and socio-emotional processes: Implications for communicative development and interventions. *Infant and Child Development, 15,* 219–222.

Zeidner, M., Matthews, G., & Roberts, R. D. (2004). Emotional intelligence in the workplace: A critical review. *Applied Psychology: An International Review, 53,* 371–399.

Zelazo, N., Zelazo, P. R., Cohen, K., & Zelazo, P. D. (1993). Specificity of practice effects on elementary neuromotor patterns. *Developmental Psychology, 29,* 686–691.

Zelazo, P. D., Muller, U., Frye, D., & Marcovitch, S. (2003). The development of executive function in early childhood. *Monographs of the Society for Research in Child Development, 68* 103–122.

Zelazo, P. R. (1998). McGraw and the development of unaided walking. *Developmental Review, 18,* 449–471.

Zellner, D., Loaiza, S., Gonzalez, Z., Pita, J., Morales, J., Pecora, D., et al. (2006, April). Food selection changes under stress. *Physiology & Behavior, 87,* 789–793.

Zeman, J., Cassano, M., Perry-Parrish, C., & Stegall, S. (2006, April). Emotion regulation in children and adolescents. *Journal of Developmental & Behavioral Pediatrics, 27,* 155–168.

Zernike, K., & Petersen, M. (2001, August 19). Schools' backing of behavior drugs comes under fire. *The New York Times,* pp. 1, 28.

Zettergren, P. (2003). School adjustment in adolescence for previously rejected, average and popular children. *British Journal of Educational Psychology, 73,* 207–221.

Zhang, Y., Proenca, R., Maffel, M., Barone, M., Leopold, L., & Friedman, J. M. (1994). Positional cloning of the mouse obese gene and its human homologue. *Nature, 372,* 425–432.

Zhe, C., & Siegler, R. S. (2000). Across the great divide: Bridging the gap between understanding of toddlers' and older children's thinking. *Monographs of the Society for Research in Child Development, 65,* (2, Serial No. 261).

Zhou, B. F., Stamler, J., Dennis, B., Moag-Stahlberg, A., Okuda, N., Robertson, C., Zhao, L., Chan, Q., Elliot, P., INTERMAP Research Group. (2003). Nutrient intakes of middle-aged men and women in China, Japan, United Kingdom, and United States in the late 1990s: The INTERMAP study. *Journal of Human Hypertension, 17,* 623–630.

Zhu, J., & Weiss, L. (2005). The Wechsler Scales. In D. P. Flanagan & P. L. Harrison (Eds.), *Contemporary intellectual assessment: Theories, tests, and issues.* New York, Guilford Press.

Zhul, J. L., Madsen, K. M., Vestergaard, M., Basso, O., & Olsen, J. (2005). Paternal age and preterm birth. *Epidemiology, 16,* 259–262.

Zigler, E., & Gilman, E. (1998). The legacy of Jean Piaget. In G. A. Kimble, M. Wertheimer et al. (Eds.), *Portraits of pioneers in psychology, (Vol. 3).* Mahwah, NJ: American Psychological Association.

Zigler, E., and Styfco, S. J. (2004). Moving Head Start to the states: One experiment too many. *Applied Developmental Science, 8,* 51–55.

Zigler, E. F., & Finn-Stevenson, M. (1995). The child care crisis: Implications for the growth and development of the nation's children. *Journal of Social Issues, 51,* 215–231.

Zimmer, C. (2003, May 16). How the mind reads other minds. *Science, 300,* 1079–1080.

Zimmer-Gembeck, M. J., & Collins, W. A. (2003). Autonomy development during adolescence. In G. R. Adams, & M. D. Berzonsky, *Blackwell handbook of adolescence.* Malden, MA: Blackwell Publishing.

Zirkel, S., & Cantor, N. (2004). 50 years after *Brown v. Board of Education*: The promise and challenge of multicultural education. *Journal of Social Issues, 60,* 1–15.

Zito, J. (2002). Five burning questions. *Journal of Developmental & Behavioral Pediatrics, 23,* S23–S30.

Zito, J. M., Safer, D. J., dosReis, S., Gardner, J. F., Boles, M., & Lynch, F. (2000). Trends in prescribing of psychotropic medications to preschoolers. *Journal of the American Medical Association, 283,* 1025–1030.

Ziv, M., & Frye, D. (2003). The relation between desire and false belief in children's theory of mind: No satisfaction? *Developmental Psychology, 39,* 859–876.

Zuckerman, M. (2003). Biological bases of personality. In T. Millon, & M. J. Lerner, (Eds.), *Handbook of psychology: Personality and social psychology, (Vol. 5).* New York: John Wiley & Sons.

Glossary

abstract modeling   the process in which modeling paves the way for the development of more general rules and principles. (Ch. 8)

acceleration   special programs that allow gifted students to move ahead at their own pace, even if this means skipping to higher grade levels. (Ch. 9)

accommodation   changes in existing ways of thinking that occur in response to encounters with new stimuli or events. (Ch. 5)

achieving stage   the point reached by young adults in which intelligence is applied to specific situations involving the attainment of long-term goals regarding careers, family, and societal contributions. (Ch. 13)

acquisitive stage   according to Schaie, the first stage of cognitive development, encompassing all of childhood and adolescence, in which the main developmental task is to acquire information. (Ch. 13)

activity theory   the theory suggesting that successful aging occurs when people maintain the interests, activities, and social interactions with which they were involved during middle age. (Ch. 18)

addictive drugs   drugs that produce a biological or psychological dependence in users, leading to increasingly powerful cravings for them. (Ch. 11)

adolescence   the developmental stage that lies between childhood and adulthood. (Ch. 11)

adolescent egocentrism   a state of self-absorption in which the world is viewed from one's own point of view. (Ch. 11)

adult day-care facilities   a facility in which elderly individuals receive care only during the day, but spend nights and weekends in their own homes. (Ch. 18)

affordances   options that a given situation or stimulus provides. (Ch. 4)

age stratification theories   the view that an unequal distribution of economic resources, power, and privilege exists among people at different stages of the life course. (Ch. 18)

ageism   prejudice and discrimination directed at older people. (Ch. 17)

agentic professions   occupations that are associated with getting things accomplished. (Ch. 14)

aggression   intentional injury or harm to another person. (Ch. 8)

Ainsworth Strange Situation   a sequence of staged episodes that illustrates the strength of attachment between a child and (typically) his or her mother. (Ch. 6)

alcoholics   persons with alcohol problems who have learned to depend on alcohol and are unable to control their drinking. (Ch. 11)

Alzheimer's disease   a progressive brain disorder that produces loss of memory and confusion. (Ch. 17)

ambivalent attachment pattern   a style of attachment in which children display a combination of positive and negative reactions to their mothers; they show great distress when the mother leaves, but upon her return they may simultaneously seek close contact but also hit and kick her. (Ch. 6)

amniocentesis   the process of identifying genetic defects by examining a small sample of fetal cells drawn by a needle inserted into the amniotic fluid surrounding the unborn fetus. (Ch. 2)

androgynous   a state in which gender roles encompass characteristics thought typical of both sexes. (Ch. 8)

anorexia nervosa   a severe eating disorder in which individuals refuse to eat, while denying that their behavior and appearance, which may become skeletal, are out of the ordinary. (Ch. 11)

anoxia   a restriction of oxygen to the baby, lasting a few minutes during the birth process, that can produce brain damage. (Ch. 3)

Apgar scale   a standard measurement system that looks for a variety of indications of good health in newborns. (Ch. 3)

applied research   research meant to provide practical solutions to immediate problems. (Ch. 1)

artificial insemination   a process of fertilization in which a man's sperm is placed directly into a woman's vagina by a physician. (Ch. 2)

assimilation   the process in which people understand an experience in terms of their current stage of cognitive development and way of thinking. (Ch. 5)

associative play   play in which two or more children actually interact with one another by sharing or borrowing toys or materials, although they do not do the same thing. (Ch. 8)

asthma   a chronic condition characterized by periodic attacks of wheezing, coughing, and shortness of breath. (Ch. 9)

attachment   the positive emotional bond that develops between a child and a particular individual. (Ch. 6)

attention deficit hyperactivity disorder (ADHD)   a learning disability marked by inattention, impulsiveness, a low tolerance for frustration, and generally a great deal of inappropriate activity. (Ch. 9)

attributions   people's explanations for the reasons behind their behavior. (Ch. 10)

auditory impairment   a special need that involves the loss of hearing or some aspect of hearing. (Ch. 9)

authoritarian parents   parents who are controlling, punitive, rigid, and cold, and whose word is law. (Ch.8)

authoritative parents   parents who are firm, setting clear and consistent limits, but who try to reason with their children, giving explanations for why they should behave in a particular way. (Ch. 8)

autobiographical memory   memory of particular events from one's own life. (Ch. 7)

autonomy   having independence and a sense of control over one's life. (Ch. 12)

autonomy-versus-shame-and-doubt stage   the period during which, according to Erikson, toddlers (aged 18 months to 3 years) develop independence and autonomy if they are allowed the freedom to explore, or shame and self-doubt if they are restricted and overprotected. (Ch. 6)

avoidant attachment pattern   a style of attachment in which children do not seek proximity to the mother; after the mother has left, they seem to avoid her when she returns as if they are angered by her behavior. (Ch. 6)

babbling   making speechlike but meaningless sounds. (Ch. 5)

Bayley Scales of Infant Development   a measure that evaluates an infant's development from 2 to 42 months. (Ch. 5)

behavior modification   a formal technique for promoting the frequency of desirable behaviors and decreasing the incidence of unwanted ones. (Ch. 1)

behavioral genetics   the study of the effects of heredity on behavior and Psychological Characteristics. (Ch. 2)

behavioral perspective   the approach suggesting that the keys to understanding development are observable behavior and outside stimuli in the environment. (Ch. 1)

bereavement   acknowledgment of the objective fact that one has experienced a death. (Ch. 19)

bicultural identity   Maintaining one's original cultural identity while integrating oneself into the dominant culture. (Ch. 9)

bilingualism   the use of more than one language. (Ch. 9)

bioecological approach   the perspective suggesting that different levels of the environment simultaneously influence individuals. (Ch. 1)

blended families   a remarried couple that has at least one stepchild living with them. (Ch. 10)

body transcendence versus body preoccupation   a period in which people must learn to cope with and move beyond changes in physical capabilities as a result of aging. (Ch. 18)

bonding close physical and emotional contact between parent and child during the period immediately following birth, argued by some to affect later relationship strength. (Ch. 3)

boomerang children young adults who return, after leaving home for some period, to live in the homes of their middle-aged parents. (Ch. 16)

brain death a diagnosis of death based on the cessation of all signs of brain activity, as measured by electrical brain waves. (Ch. 19)

Brazelton Neonatal Behavioral Assessment Scale (NBAS) a measure designed to determine infants' neurological and behavioral responses to their environment. (Ch. 4)

bulimia an eating disorder characterized by binges on large quantities of food, followed by purges of the food through vomiting or the use of laxatives. (Ch. 11)

burnout a situation that occurs when highly trained professionals experience dissatisfaction, disillusionment, frustration, and weariness from their jobs. (Ch. 16)

career consolidation a stage that is entered between the ages of 20 and 40, when young adults become centered on their careers. (Ch. 14)

case studies studies that involve extensive, in-depth interviews with a particular individual or small group of individuals. (Ch. 1)

centration the process of concentrating on one limited aspect of a stimulus and ignoring other aspects. (Ch. 7)

cephalocaudal principle the principle that growth follows a pattern that begins with the head and upper body parts and then proceeds down to the rest of the body. (Ch. 4)

cerebral cortex the upper layer of the brain. (Ch. 4)

Cesarean delivery a birth in which the baby is surgically removed from the uterus, rather than traveling through the birth canal. (Ch. 3)

chorionic villus sampling (CVS) a test used to find genetic defects that involves taking samples of hairlike material that surrounds the embryo. (Ch. 2)

chromosomes rod-shaped portions of DNA that are organized in 23 pairs. (Ch. 2)

chronological (or physical) age the actual age of the child taking the intelligence test. (Ch. 9)

classical conditioning a type of learning in which an organism responds in a particular way to a neutral stimulus that normally does not bring about that type of response. (Ch. 1)

cliques groups of from 2 to 12 people whose members have frequent social interactions with one another. (Ch. 12)

cognitive development development involving the ways that growth and change in intellectual capabilities influence a person's behavior. (Ch. 1)

cognitive neuroscience approaches approaches that examine cognitive development through the lens of brain processes. (Ch. 1)

cognitive perspective the approach that focuses on the processes that allow people to know, understand, and think about the world. (Ch. 1)

cohabitation couples living together without being married. (Ch. 14)

cohort a group of people born at around the same time in the same place. (Ch. 1)

collectivistic orientation a philosophy that promotes the notion of interdependence. (Ch. 8)

communal professions occupations that are associated with relationships. (Ch. 14)

companionate love the strong affection for those with whom our lives are deeply involved. (Ch. 14)

concrete operational stage the period of cognitive development between 7 and 12 years of age, which is characterized by the active, and appropriate, use of logic. (Ch. 9)

conservation the knowledge that quantity is unrelated to the arrangement and physical appearance of objects. (Ch. 7)

constructive play play in which children manipulate objects to produce or build something. (Ch. 8)

contextual perspective the theory that considers the relationship between individuals and their physical, cognitive, personality, and social worlds. (Ch. 1)

continuing-care community a community that offers an environment in which all the residents are of retirement age or older and need various levels of care. (Ch. 18)

continuity theory the theory suggesting that people need to maintain their desired level of involvement in society in order to maximize their sense of well-being and self-esteem. (Ch. 18)

continuous change gradual development in which achievements at one level build on those of previous levels. (Ch. 1)

controversial adolescents children who are liked by some peers and disliked by others. (Ch. 12)

cooperative play play in which children genuinely interact with one another, taking turns, playing games, or devising contests. (Ch. 8)

coping the effort to control, reduce, or learn to tolerate the threats that lead to stress. (Ch. 13)

coregulation a period in which parents and children jointly control children's behavior. (Ch. 10)

correlational research research that seeks to identify whether an association or relationship between two factors exists. (Ch. 1)

creativity the combination of responses or ideas in novel ways. (Ch. 13)

critical period a specific time during development when a particular event has its greatest consequences and the presence of certain kinds of environmental stimuli is necessary for development to proceed normally. (Ch. 1)

cross-sectional research research in which people of different ages are compared at the same point in time. (Ch. 1)

crowds larger groups than cliques, composed of individuals who share particular characteristics but who may not interact with one another. (Ch. 12)

crystallized intelligence the accumulation of information, skills, and strategies that people have learned through experience and that they can apply in problem-solving situations. (Ch. 9)

cultural assimilation model the model that fostered the view of American society as the proverbial melting pot. (Ch. 9)

cycle of violence hypothesis the theory that abuse and neglect of children leads them to be predisposed to abusiveness as adults. (Ch. 16)

cycle of violence hypothesis the theory that the abuse and neglect that children suffer predispose them as adults to abuse and neglect their own children. (Ch. 8)

decentering the ability to take multiple aspects of a situation into account. (Ch. 9)

decision/commitment component the third aspect of love that embodies both the initial cognition that one loves another person and the longer-term determination to maintain that love. (Ch. 14)

defensive coping coping that involves unconscious strategies that distort or deny the true nature of a situation. (Ch. 13)

deffered imitation an act in which a person who is no longer present is imitated by children who have witnessed a similar act. (Ch.)

dementia the most common mental disorder of the elderly, it covers several diseases, each of which includes serious memory loss accompanied by declines in other mental functioning. (Ch. 17)

dependent variable the variable that researchers measure in an experiment and expect to change as a result of the experimental manipulation. (Ch. 1)

developmental quotient an overall developmental score that relates to performance in four domains: motor skills, language use, adaptive behavior, and personal-social. (Ch. 5)

developmentally appropriate educational practice education that is based on both typical development and the unique characteristics of a given child. (Ch. 7)

difficult babies babies who have negative moods and are slow to adapt to new situations; when confronted with a new situation, they tend to withdraw. (Ch. 6)

discontinuous change development that occurs in distinct steps or stages, with each stage bringing about behavior that is assumed to be qualitatively different from behavior at earlier stages. (Ch. 1)

disengagement theory the period in late adulthood that marks a gradual withdrawal from the world on physical, psychological, and social levels. (Ch. 18)

disorganized-disoriented attachment pattern a style of attachment in which children show inconsistent, often contradictory behavior, such as approaching the mother when she returns but not looking at her; they may be the least securely attached children of all. (Ch. 6)

dizygotic twins twins who are produced when two separate ova are fertilized by two separate sperm at roughly the same time. (Ch. 2)

DNA (deoxyribonucleic acid) molecules   the substance that genes are composed of that determines the nature of every cell in the body and how it will function. (Ch. 2)

dominance hierarchy   rankings that represent the relative social power of those in a group. (Ch. 10)

dominant trait   the one trait that is expressed when two competing traits are present. (Ch. 2)

Down syndrome   a disorder produced by the presence of an extra chromosome on the 21st pair; once referred to as mongolism. (Ch. 2)

dynamic systems theory   a theory of how motor skills develop and are coordinated. (Ch. 4)

easy babies   babies who have a positive disposition; their body functions operate regularly, and they are adaptable. (Ch. 6)

ego transcendence versus ego preoccupation   the period in which elderly people must come to grips with their coming death. (Ch. 18)

egocentric thought   thinking that does not take into account the viewpoints of others. (Ch. 7)

ego-integrity-versus-despair stage   Erikson's final stage of life, characterized by a process of looking back over one's life, evaluating it, and coming to terms with it. (Ch. 18)

elder abuse   the physical or psychological mistreatment or neglect of elderly individuals. (Ch. 18)

embryonic stage   the period from 2 to 8 weeks following fertilization during which significant growth occurs in the major organs and body systems. (Ch. 2)

emotional intelligence   the set of skills that underlies the accurate assessment, evaluation, expression, and regulation of emotions. (Ch. 10)

emotional self-regulation   the capability to adjust emotions to a desired state and level of intensity. (Ch. 10)

empathy   an emotional response that corresponds to the feelings of another person. (Ch. 6)

empty nest syndrome   the experience that relates to parents' feelings of unhappiness, worry, loneliness, and depression resulting from their children's departure from home. (Ch. 16)

enrichment   an approach through which students are kept at grade level but are enrolled in special programs and given individual activities to allow greater depth of study on a given topic. (Ch. 9)

episiotomy   an incision sometimes made to increase the size of the opening of the vagina to allow the baby to pass. (Ch. 3)

Erikson's theory of psychosocial development   the theory that considers how individuals come to understand themselves and the meaning of others'—and their own—behavior. (Ch. 6)

euthanasia   the practice of assisting people who are terminally ill to die more quickly. (Ch. 19)

evolutionary perspective   the theory that seeks to identify behavior that is a result of our genetic inheritance from our ancestors. (Ch. 1)

executive stage   the period in middle adulthood when people take a broader perspective than earlier, including concerns about the world. (Ch. 13)

experiment   a process in which an investigator, called an experimenter, devises two different experiences for participants. (Ch. 1)

experimental research   research designed to discover causal relationships between various factors. (Ch. 1)

expertise   the acquisition of skill or knowledge in a particular area. (Ch. 15)

expressive style   a style of language use in which language is used primarily to express feelings and needs about oneself and others. (Ch. 5)

extrinsic motivation   motivation that drives people to obtain tangible rewards, such as money and prestige. (Ch. 14)

fantasy period   according to Ginzberg, the period, lasting until about age 11, when career choices are made, and discarded, without regard to skills, abilities, or available job opportunities. (Ch. 14)

fast mapping   instances in which new words are associated with their meaning after only a brief encounter. (Ch. 7)

female climacteric   the period that marks the transition from being able to bear children to being unable to do so. (Ch. 15)

fertilization   the process by which a sperm and an ovum—the male and female gametes, respectively—join to form a single new cell. (Ch. 2)

fetal alcohol effects (FAE)   a condition in which children display some, although not all, of the problems of fetal alcohol syndrome due to the mother's consumption of alcohol during pregnancy. (Ch. 2)

fetal alcohol syndrome (FAS)   a disorder caused by the pregnant mother consuming substantial quantities of alcohol during pregnancy, potentially resulting in mental retardation and delayed growth in the child. (Ch. 2)

fetal monitor   a device that measures the baby's heartbeat during labor. (Ch. 3)

fetal stage   the stage that begins at about 8 weeks after conception and continues until birth. (Ch. 2)

fetus   a developing child, from 8 weeks after conception until birth. (Ch. 2)

field study   a research investigation carried out in a naturally occurring setting. (Ch. 1)

first-year adjustment reaction   a cluster of psychological symptoms, including loneliness, anxiety, withdrawal, and depression, relating to the college experience suffered by first-year college students. (Ch. 13)

fluid intelligence   intelligence that reflects information processing capabilities, reasoning, and memory. (Ch. 9)

formal operational period   the stage at which people develop the ability to think abstractly. (Ch. 11)

fragile X syndrome   a disorder produced by injury to a gene on the X chromosome, producing mild to moderate mental retardation. (Ch. 2)

functional death   the absence of a heartbeat and breathing. (Ch. 19)

functional play   play that involves simple, repetitive activities typical of 3-year-olds. (Ch. 8)

gender   the sense of being male or female. (Ch. 6)

gender constancy   the belief that people are permanently males or females, depending on fixed, unchangeable biological factors. (Ch. 8)

gender identity   the perception of oneself as male or female. (Ch. 8)

gender schema   a cognitive framework that organizes information relevant to gender. (Ch. 8)

generalized slowing hypothesis   the theory that processing in all parts of the nervous system, including the brain, is less efficient. (Ch. 17)

generation gap   a divide between parents and adolescents in attitudes, values, aspirations, and world views. (Ch. 12)

generativity-versus-stagnation   stage according to Erikson, the stage during middle adulthood in which people consider their contributions to family and society. (Ch. 16)

genes   the basic unit of genetic information. (Ch. 2)

genetic counseling   the discipline that focuses on helping people deal with issues relating to inherited disorders. (Ch. 2)

genetic programming theories of aging   theories that suggest that our body's DNA genetic code contains a built-in time limit for the reproduction of human cells. (Ch. 17)

genotype   the underlying combination of genetic material present (but not outwardly visible) in an organism. (Ch. 2)

germinal stage   the first—and shortest—stage of the prenatal period, which takes place during the first 2 weeks following conception. (Ch. 2)

gerontologists   specialists who study aging. (Ch. 17)

gifted and talented   children who show evidence of high performance capability in areas such as intellectual, creative, artistic, leadership capacity, or specific academic fields. (Ch. 9)

glaucoma   a condition in which pressure in the fluid of the eye increases, either because the fluid cannot drain properly or because too much fluid is produced. (Ch. 15)

goodness-of-fit   the notion that development is dependent on the degree of match between children's temperament and the nature and demands of the environment in which they are being raised. (Ch. 6)

grammar   the system of rules that determines how our thoughts can be expressed. (Ch. 7)

grief   the emotional response to one's loss. (Ch. 19)

habituation   the decrease in the response to a stimulus that occurs after repeated presentations of the same stimulus. (Ch. 3)

handedness   the preference of using one hand over another. (Ch. 7)

hardiness   a personality characteristic associated with a lower rate of stress-related illness. (Ch. 13)

heterozygous   inheriting from parents different forms of a gene for a given trait. (Ch. 2)

holophrases   one-word utterances that stand for a whole phrase, whose meaning depends on the particular context in which they are used. (Ch. 5)

home care   an alternative to hospitalization in which dying people stay in their homes and receive treatment from their families and visiting medical staff. (Ch. 19)

homogamy   the tendency to marry someone who is similar in age, race, education, religion, and other basic demographic characteristics. (Ch. 14)

homozygous   inheriting from parents similar genes for a given trait. (Ch. 2)

hospice care   care provided for the dying in institutions devoted to those who are terminally ill. (Ch. 19)

humanistic perspective   the theory contending that people have a natural capacity to make decisions about their lives and control their behavior. (Ch. 1)

hypothesis   a prediction stated in a way that permits it to be tested. (Ch. 1)

identification   the process in which children attempt to be similar to their same-sex parent, incorporating the parent's attitudes and values. (Ch. 8)

identity achievement   the status of adolescents who commit to a particular identity following a period of crisis during which they consider various alternatives. (Ch. 12)

identity diffusion   the status of adolescents who consider various identity alternatives, but never commit to one or never even consider identity options in any conscious way. (Ch. 12)

identity foreclosure   the status of adolescents in this category neither explore nor commit to considering various alternatives. (Ch. 12)

identity-versus-identity-confusion stage   the period during which teenagers seek to determine what is unique and distinctive about themselves. (Ch. 12)

imaginary audience   an adolescent's belief that his or her own behavior is a primary focus of others' attentions and concerns. (Ch. 11)

in vitro fertilization (IVF)   a procedure in which a woman's ova are removed from her ovaries, and a man's sperm are used to fertilize the ova in a laboratory. (Ch. 2)

independent variable   the variable that researchers manipulate in an experiment. (Ch. 1)

individualistic orientation   a philosophy that emphasizes personal identity and the uniqueness of the individual. (Ch. 8)

industry-versus-inferiority stage   the period from age 6 to 12 characterized by a focus on efforts to attain competence in meeting the challenges presented by parents, peers, school, and the other complexities of the modern world. (Ch. 10)

infant mortality   death within the first year of life. (Ch. 3)

infant-directed speech   a type of speech directed toward infants; characterized by short, simple sentences. (Ch. 5)

infantile amnesia   the lack of memory for experiences that occurred prior to 3 years of age. (Ch. 5)

infertility   the inability to conceive after 12 to 18 months of trying to become pregnant. (Ch. 2)

information processing approaches   models that seek to identify the ways individuals take in, use, and store information. (Ch. 1)

information-processing perspective   the model that seeks to identify the way that individuals take in, use, and store information. (Ch. 11)

initiative-versus-guilt stage   according to Erikson, the period during which children aged 3 to 6 years experience conflict between independence of action and the sometimes negative results of that action. (Ch. 8)

institutionalism   a psychological state in which people in nursing homes develop apathy, indifference, and a lack of caring about themselves. (Ch. 18)

instrumental aggression   aggression motivated by the desire to obtain a concrete goal. (Ch. 8)

intelligence   the capacity to understand the world, think with rationality, and use resources effectively when faced with challenges. (Ch. 9)

intelligence quotient (or IQ score)   a measure of intelligence that takes into account a student's mental *and* chronological age. (Ch. 9)

intimacy component   the component of love that encompasses feelings of closeness, affection, and connectedness. (Ch. 14)

intimacy-versus-isolation stage   according to Erikson, the period of postadolescence into the early 30s that focuses on developing close relationships with others. (Ch. 14)

intrinsic motivation   motivation that causes people to work for their own enjoyment, not for the rewards work may bring. (Ch. 14)

intuitive thought   thinking that reflects preschoolers' use of primitive reasoning and their avid acquisition of knowledge about the world. (Ch. 7)

Kaufman Assessment Battery for Children, Second Edition (KABC-II)   an intelligence test that measures children's ability to integrate different stimuli simultaneously and step-by-step thinking. (Ch. 9)

Klinefelter's syndrome   a disorder resulting from the presence of an extra X chromosome that produces underdeveloped genitals, extreme height, and enlarged breasts. (Ch. 2)

labeling theory of passionate love   the theory that individuals experience romantic love when two events occur together: intense physiological arousal and situational cues suggesting that the arousal is due to love. (Ch. 14)

laboratory study   a research investigation conducted in a controlled setting explicitly designed to hold events constant. (Ch. 1)

language   the systematic, meaningful arrangement of symbols, which provides the basis for communication. (Ch. 5)

language-acquisition device (LAD)   a neural system of the brain hypothesized to permit understanding of language. (Ch. 5)

lateralization   the process in which certain cognitive functions are located more in one hemisphere of the brain than in the other. (Ch. 7)

learning disabilities   difficulties in the acquisition and use of listening, speaking, reading, writing, reasoning, or mathematical abilities. (Ch. 9)

learning theory approach   the theory that language acquisition follows the basic laws of reinforcement and conditioning. (Ch. 5)

least restrictive environment   the setting that is most similar to that of children without special needs. (Ch. 9)

life events models   the approach to personality development that is based on the timing of particular events in an adult's life rather than on age per se. (Ch. 16)

life expectancy   the average age of death for members of a population. (Ch. 17)

life review   the point in life in which people examine and evaluate their lives. (Ch. 18)

lifespan development   the field of study that examines patterns of growth, change, and stability in behavior that occur throughout the entire life span. (Ch. 1)

living wills   legal documents designating what medical treatments people want or do not want if they cannot express their wishes. (Ch. 19)

longitudinal research   research in which the behavior of one or more participants in a study is measured as they age. (Ch. 1)

low-birthweight infants   infants who weigh less than 2,500 grams (around 5 1/2 pounds) at birth. (Ch. 3)

mainstreaming   an educational approach in which exceptional children are integrated to the extent possible into the traditional educational system and are provided with a broad range of educational alternatives. (Ch. 9)

male climacteric   the period of physical and psychological change relating to the male reproductive system that occurs during late middle age. (Ch. 15)

marriage gradient   the tendency for men to marry women who are slightly younger, smaller, and lower in status, and women to marry men who are slightly older, larger, and higher in status. (Ch. 14)

masturbation   sexual self-stimulation. (Ch. 12)

maturation   the predetermined unfolding of genetic information. (Ch. 1)

memory   the process by which information is initially recorded, stored, and retrieved. (Ch. 5)

menarche   the onset of menstruation. (Ch. 11)

menopause   the cessation of menstruation. (Ch. 15)

mental age   the typical intelligence level found for people at a given chronological age. (Ch. 9)

mental representation   an internal image of a past event or object. (Ch.)

mental retardation   a significantly subaverage level of intellectual functioning that occurs with related limitations in two or more skill areas. (Ch. 9)

metacognition   the knowledge that people have about their own thinking processes, and their ability to monitor their cognition. (Ch. 11)

metalinguistic awareness   an understanding of one's own use of language. (Ch. 9)

metamemory   an understanding about the processes that underlie memory, which emerges and improves during middle childhood. (Ch. 9)

midlife crisis   a stage of uncertainty and indecision brought about by the realization that life is finite. (Ch. 16)

mild retardation   retardation in which IQ scores fall in the range of 50 or 55 to 70. (Ch. 9)

mnemonics   formal strategies for organizing material in ways that make it more likely to be remembered. (Ch. 15)

moderate retardation   retardation in which IQ scores range from around 35 or 40 to 50 or 55. (Ch. 9)

monozygotic twins   twins who are genetically identical. (Ch. 2)

moral development   the changes in people's sense of justice and of what is right and wrong, and in their behavior related to moral issues. (Ch. 8)

moratorium   the status of adolescents who may have explored various identity alternatives to some degree, but have not yet committed themselves. (Ch. 12)

multicultural education   a form of education in which the goal is to help minority students develop competence in the culture of the majority group while maintaining positive group identities that build on their original cultures. (Ch. 9)

multifactorial transmission   the determination of traits by a combination of both genetic and environmental factors in which a genotype provides a range within which a phenotype may be expressed. (Ch. 2)

multimodal approach to perception   the approach that considers how information that is collected by various individual sensory systems is integrated and coordinated. (Ch. 4)

mutual regulation model   the model in which infants and parents learn to communicate emotional states to one another and to respond appropriately. (Ch. 6)

myelin   a fatty substance that helps insulate neurons and speeds the transmission of nerve impulses. (Ch. 4)

nativist approach   the theory that a genetically determined, innate mechanism directs language development. (Ch. 5)

naturalistic observation   a type of correlational study in which some naturally occurring behavior is observed without intervention in the situation. (Ch. 1)

neglected adolescents   children who receive relatively little attention from their peers in the form of either positive or negative interactions. (Ch. 12)

neonates   the term used for newborns. (Ch. 3)

neuron   the basic nerve cell of the nervous system. (Ch. 4)

nonorganic failure to thrive   a disorder in which infants stop growing due to a lack of stimulation and attention as the result of inadequate parenting. (Ch. 4)

normative-crisis models   the approach to personality development that is based on fairly universal stages tied to a sequence of age-related crises. (Ch. 16)

norms   the average performance of a large sample of children of a given age. (Ch. 4)

obesity   body weight more than 20% higher than the average weight for a person of a given age and height. (Ch. 7)

object permanence   the realization that people and objects exist even when they cannot be seen. (Ch. 5)

onlooker play   action in which children simply watch others at play, but do not actually participate themselves. (Ch. 8)

operant conditioning   a form of learning in which a voluntary response is strengthened or weakened, depending on its association with positive or negative consequences. (Ch. 1)

operations   organized, formal, logical mental processes. (Ch. 7)

osteoporosis   a condition in which the bones become brittle, fragile, and thin, often brought about by a lack of calcium in the diet. (Ch. 15)

overextension   the overly broad use of words, overgeneralizing their meaning. (Ch. 5)

parallel play   action in which children play with similar toys, in a similar manner, but do not interact with each other. (Ch. 8)

passion component   the component of love that comprises the motivational drives relating to sex, physical closeness, and romance. (Ch. 14)

passionate (or romantic) love   a state of powerful absorption in someone. (Ch. 14)

peer pressure   the influence of one's peers to conform to their behavior and attitudes. (Ch. 12)

perception   the sorting out, interpretation, analysis, and integration of stimuli involving the sense organs and brain. (Ch. 4)

peripheral slowing hypothesis   the theory that suggests that overall processing speed declines in the peripheral nervous system with increasing age. (Ch. 17)

permissive parents   parents who provide lax and inconsistent feedback and require little of their children. (Ch. 8)

personal fables   the view held by some adolescents that what happens to them is unique, exceptional, and shared by no one else. (Ch. 11)

personality   the sum total of the enduring characteristics that differentiate one individual from another. (Ch. 6)

personality development   development involving the ways that the enduring characteristics that differentiate one person from another change over the life span. (Ch. 1)

phenotype   an observable trait; the trait that actually is seen. (Ch. 2)

physical development   development involving the body's physical makeup, including the brain, nervous system, muscles, and senses, and the need for food, drink, and sleep. (Ch. 1)

placenta   a conduit between the mother and fetus, providing nourishment and oxygen via the umbilical cord. (Ch. 2)

plasticity   the degree to which a developing structure or behavior is modifiable due to experience. (Ch. 4)

pluralistic society model   the concept that American society is made up of diverse, coequal cultural groups that should preserve their individual cultural features. (Ch. 9)

polygenic inheritance   inheritance in which a combination of multiple gene pairs is responsible for the production of a particular trait. (Ch. 2)

postformal thought   thinking that acknowledges that adult predicaments must sometimes be solved in relativistic terms. (Ch. 13)

postmature infants   infants still unborn 2 weeks after the mother's due date. (Ch. 3)

practical intelligence   according to Sternberg, intelligence that is learned primarily by observing others and modeling their behavior. (Ch. 13)

pragmatics   the aspect of language that relates to communicating effectively and appropriately with others. (Ch. 7)

preoperational stage   according to Piaget, the stage from approximately age 2 to age 7 in which children's use of symbolic thinking grows, mental reasoning emerges, and the use of concepts increases. (Ch. 7)

presbycusis   loss of the ability to hear sounds of high frequency. (Ch. 15)

presbyopia   a nearly universal change in eyesight during middle adulthood that results in some loss of near vision. (Ch. 15)

preterm infants   infants who are born prior to 38 weeks after conception (also known as premature infants). (Ch. 3)

primary aging   aging that involves universal and irreversible changes that, due to genetic programming, occur as people get older. (Ch. 17)

primary appraisal the assessment of an event to determine whether its implications are positive, negative, or neutral. (Ch. 13)

primary sex characteristics characteristics associated with the development of the organs and structures of the body that directly relate to reproduction. (Ch. 11)

principle of hierarchical integration the principle that simple skills typically develop separately and independently but are later integrated into more complex skills. (Ch. 4)

principle of the independence of systems the principle that different body systems grow at different rates. (Ch. 4)

private speech speech by children that is spoken and directed to themselves. (Ch. 7)

profound retardation retardation in which IQ scores fall below 20 or 25. (Ch. 9)

prosocial behavior helping behavior that benefits others. (Ch. 8)

proximodistal principle the principle that development proceeds from the center of the body outward. (Ch. 4)

psychoanalytic theory the theory proposed by Freud that suggests that unconscious forces act to determine personality and behavior. (Ch. 1)

psychodynamic perspective the approach stating that behavior is motivated by inner forces, memories, and conflicts that are generally beyond people's awareness and control. (Ch. 1)

psychological maltreatment abuse that occurs when parents or other caregivers harm children's behavioral, cognitive, emotional, or physical functioning. (Ch. 8)

psychoneuroimmunology (PNI) the study of the relationship among the brain, the immune system, and psychological factors. (Ch. 13)

psychophysiological methods research that focuses on the relationship between physiological processes and behavior. (Ch. 1)

psychosexual development according to Freud, a series of stages that children pass through in which pleasure, or gratification, is focused on a particular biological function and body part. (Ch. 1)

psychosocial development the approach that encompasses changes in our interactions with and understandings of one another, as well as in our knowledge and understanding of ourselves as members of society. (Ch. 1)

psychosomatic disorders medical problems caused by the interaction of psychological, emotional, and physical difficulties. (Ch. 13)

puberty the period during which the sexual organs mature. (Ch. 11)

race dissonance the phenomenon in which minority children indicate preferences for majority values or people. (Ch. 8)

rapid eye movement (REM) sleep the period of sleep that is found in older children and adults and is associated with dreaming. (Ch. 4)

realistic period the third stage of Ginzberg's theory, which occurs in early adulthood, when people begin to explore specific career options, either through actual experience on the job or through training for a profession, and then narrow their choices and make a commitment. (Ch. 14)

recessive trait a trait within an organism that is present, but is not expressed. (Ch. 2)

reciprocal socialization a process in which infants' behaviors invite further responses from parents and other caregivers, which in turn bring about further responses from the infants. (Ch. 6)

redefinition of self versus preoccupation with work role the theory that those in old age must redefine themselves in ways that do not relate to their work-roles or occupations. (Ch. 18)

reference groups groups of people with whom one compares oneself. (Ch. 12)

referential style a style of language use in which language is used primarily to label objects. (Ch. 5)

reflexes unlearned, organized, involuntary responses that occur automatically in the presence of certain stimuli. (Ch. 3)

reintegrative stage the period of late adulthood during which the focus is on tasks that have personal meaning. (Ch. 13)

rejected adolescents children who are actively disliked, and whose peers may react to them in an obviously negative manner. (Ch. 12)

relational aggression nonphysical aggression that is intended to hurt another person's psychological well-being. (Ch. 8)

resilience the ability to overcome circumstances that place a child at high risk for psychological or physical damage. (Ch. 8)

responsible stage the stage where the major concerns of middle-aged adults relate to their personal situations, including protecting and nourishing their spouses, families, and careers. (Ch. 13)

rhythms repetitive, cyclical patterns of behavior. (Ch. 4)

sample the group of participants chosen for the experiment. (Ch. 1)

sandwich generation couples who in middle adulthood must fulfill the needs of both their children and their aging parents. (Ch. 16)

scaffolding the support for learning and problem solving that encourages independence and growth. (Ch. 7)

schemas organized bodies of information stored in memory. (Ch. 15)

scheme an organized pattern of sensorimotor functioning. (Ch. 5)

scientific method the process of posing and answering questions using careful, controlled techniques that include systematic, orderly observation and the collection of data. (Ch. 1)

scripts broad representations in memory of events and the order in which they occur. (Ch. 7)

secondary aging changes in physical and cognitive functioning that are due to illness, health habits, and other individual differences, but which are not due to increased age itself and are not inevitable. (Ch. 17)

secondary appraisal the assessment of whether one's coping abilities and resources are adequate to overcome the harm, threat, or challenge posed by the potential stressor. (Ch. 13)

secondary sex characteristics the visible signs of sexual maturity that do not directly involve the sex organs. (Ch. 11)

secular trend a pattern of change occurring over several generations. (Ch. 11)

secure attachment pattern a style of attachment in which children use the mother as a kind of home base and are at ease when she is present; when she leaves, they become upset and go to her as soon as she returns. (Ch. 6)

selective optimization the process by which people concentrate on selected skills areas to compensate for losses in other areas. (Ch. 15)

self-awareness knowledge of oneself. (Ch. 6)

self-care children children who let themselves into their homes after school and wait alone until their caretakers return from work; previously known as *latchkey children*. (Ch. 10)

self-concept a person's identity, or set of beliefs about what one is like as an individual. (Ch. 8)

self-esteem an individual's overall and specific positive and negative self-evaluation. (Ch. 10)

senescence the natural physical decline brought about by aging. (Ch. 13)

sensation the physical stimulation of the sense organs. (Ch. 11)

sensitive period a specific, but limited, time, usually early in an organism's life, during which the organism is particularly susceptible to environmental influences relating to some particular facet of development. (Ch. 4)

sensorimotor stage (of cognitive development) Piaget's initial major stage of cognitive development, which can be broken down into six substages. (Ch. 5)

separation anxiety the distress displayed by infants when a customary care provider departs. (Ch. 6)

sequential studies research in which researchers examine a number of different age groups over several points in time. (Ch. 1)

severe retardation retardation in which IQ scores range from around 20 or 25 to 35 or 40. (Ch. 9)

sex cleavage sex segregation in which boys interact primarily with boys and girls primarily with girls. (Ch. 12)

sexually transmitted infection (STI) a infection that is spread through sexual contact. (Ch. 11)

sickle-cell anemia a blood disorder that gets its name from the shape of the red blood cells in those who have it. (Ch. 2)

skilled-nursing facilities a facility that provides full-time nursing care for people who have chronic illnesses or are recovering from a temporary medical condition. (Ch. 18)

slow-to-warm babies babies who are inactive, showing relatively calm reactions to their environment; their moods are generally negative, and they withdraw from new situations, adapting slowly. (Ch. 6)

small-for-gestational-age infants infants who, because of delayed fetal growth, weigh 90% (or less) of the average weight of infants of the same gestational age. (Ch. 3)

social clock the culturally-determined psychological timepiece providing a sense of whether we have reached the major benchmarks of life at the appropriate time in comparison to our peers. (Ch. 14)

social-cognitive learning theory learning by observing the behavior of another person, called a model. (Ch. 1)

social comparison the desire to evaluate one's own behavior, abilities, expertise, and opinions by comparing them to those of others. (Ch. 10)

social competence the collection of social skills that permits individuals to perform successfully in social settings. (Ch. 10)

social development the way in which individuals' interactions with others and their social relationships grow, change, and remain stable over the course of life. (Ch. 1)

social problem-solving the use of strategies for solving social conflicts in ways that are satisfactory both to oneself and to others. (Ch. 10)

social referencing the intentional search for information about others' feelings to help explain the meaning of uncertain circumstances and events. (Ch. 6)

social smile smiling in response to other individuals. (Ch. 6)

social speech speech directed toward another person and meant to be understood by that person. (Ch. 7)

social support assistance and comfort supplied by another person or a network of caring, interested people. (Ch. 18)

socialized delinquents adolescent delinquents who know and subscribe to the norms of society and who are fairly normal psychologically. (Ch. 12)

sociocultural theory the approach that emphasizes how cognitive development proceeds as a result of social interactions between members of a culture. (Ch. 1)

speech impairment speech that deviates so much from the speech of others that it calls attention to itself, interferes with communication, or produces maladjustment in the speaker. (Ch. 9)

Stanford-Binet Intelligence Scales, Fifth Edition (SB5) a test that consists of a series of items that vary according to the age of the person being tested. (Ch. 9)

state the degree of awareness an infant displays to both internal and external stimulation. (Ch. 4)

states of arousal different degrees of sleep and wakefulness through which newborns cycle, ranging from deep sleep to great agitation. (Ch. 3)

status the evaluation of a role or person by other relevant members of a group or society. (Ch. 10)

stereotype threat obstacles to performance that come from awareness of the stereotypes held by society about academic abilities. (Ch. 13)

stillbirth the delivery of a child who is not alive, occurring in less than 1 delivery in 100. (Ch. 3)

stimulus-value-role (SVR) theory the theory that relationships proceed in a fixed order of three stages: stimulus, value, and role. (Ch. 14)

stranger anxiety the caution and wariness displayed by infants when encountering an unfamiliar person. (Ch. 6)

stress the physical and emotional response to events that threaten or challenge us. (Ch. 13)

stuttering substantial disruption in the rhythm and fluency of speech; the most common speech impairment. (Ch. 9)

sudden infant death syndrome (SIDS) the unexplained death of a seemingly healthy baby. (Ch. 4, 19)

survey research a type of study where a group of people chosen to represent some larger population are asked questions about their attitudes, behavior, or thinking on a given topic. (Ch. 1)

synapse the gap at the connection between neurons, through which neurons chemically communicate with one another. (Ch. 4)

synaptic pruning the elimination of neurons as the result of nonuse or lack of stimulation. (Ch. 4)

syntax the way in which an individual combines words and phrases to form sentences. (Ch. 7)

Tay-Sachs disease a disorder that produces blindness and muscle degeneration prior to death; there is no treatment. (Ch. 2)

teacher expectancy effect the cycle of behavior in which a teacher transmits an expectation about a child and thereby actually brings about the expected behavior. (Ch. 10)

telegraphic speech speech in which words not critical to the message are left out. (Ch. 5)

temperament patterns of arousal and emotionality that represent consistent and enduring characteristics in an individual. (Ch. 6)

tentative period the second stage of Ginzberg's theory, which spans adolescence, when people begin to think in pragmatic terms about the requirements of various jobs and how their own abilities might fit with them. (Ch. 2)

teratogen a factor that produces a birth defect. (Ch. 2)

thanatologists people who study death and dying. (Ch. 19)

theoretical research research designed specifically to test some developmental explanation and expand scientific knowledge. (Ch. 1)

theories explanations and predictions concerning phenomena of interest, providing a framework for understanding the relationships among an organized set of facts or principles. (Ch. 1)

theory of mind knowledge and beliefs about how the mind works and how it affects behavior. (Ch. 6)

transformation the process in which one state is changed into another. (Ch. 7)

triarchic theory of intelligence a model that states that intelligence consists of three aspects of information processing: the componential element, the experiential element, and the contextual element. (Ch. 9)

triarchic theory of intelligence Sternberg's theory that intelligence is made up of three major components: componential, experiential, and contextual. (Ch. 13)

trust-versus-mistrust stage according to Erikson, the period during which infants develop a sense of trust or mistrust, largely depending on how well their needs are met by their caregivers. (Ch. 6)

Type A behavior pattern behavior characterized by competitiveness, impatience, and a tendency toward frustration and hostility. (Ch. 15)

Type B behavior pattern behavior characterized by noncompetitiveness, patience, and a lack of aggression. (Ch. 15)

ultrasound sonography a process in which high-frequency sound waves scan the mother's womb to produce an image of the unborn baby, whose size and shape can then be assessed. (Ch. 2)

underextension the overly restrictive use of words; common among children just mastering spoken language. (Ch. 5)

undersocialized delinquents adolescent delinquents who are raised with little discipline or with harsh, uncaring parental supervision. (Ch. 12)

uninvolved parents parents who show almost no interest in their children and indifferent, rejecting behavior. (Ch. 8)

universal grammar Noam Chomsky's theory that all the world's languages share a similar underlying structure. (Ch. 5)

very-low-birthweight infants infants who weigh less than 1,250 grams (around 2.25 pounds) or, regardless of weight, have been in the womb less than 30 weeks. (Ch. 3)

visual impairment a difficulty in seeing that may include blindness or partial sightedness. (Ch. 9)

wear-and-tear theories the theory that the mechanical functions of the body simply wear out with age. (Ch. 17)

Wechsler Intelligence Scale for Children—Fourth Edition (WISC-IV) a test for children that provides separate measures of verbal and performance (or nonverbal) skills, as well as a total score. (Ch. 9)

wisdom expert knowledge in the practical aspects of life. (Ch. 18)

X-linked genes genes that are considered recessive and located only on the X chromosome. (Ch. 2)

zone of proximal development (ZPD) according to Vygotsky, the level at which a child can *almost,* but not fully, perform a task independently, but can do so with the assistance of someone more competent. (Ch. 7)

zygote the new cell formed by the process of fertilization. (Ch. 2)

Credits

Photographs

Chapter 1 Page 2 Walter Hodges, Corbis/Bettman; p. 3 AP Wide World Photos; p. 5 Stephen Cannerelli/Syracuse Newspapers, The Image Works; p. 8 The Image Works; p. 15 Corbis/Bettmann; p. 15 Corbis/Bettmann; p. 17 Courtesy of the Library of Congress; p. 18 Getty Images Inc./Hulton Archive Photos; p. 19 Robert Voets/CBS Photo Archive, Getty Images, Inc.; p. 25 (right) David Grossman, The Image Works; p. 25 Laura Dwight, The Stock Connection; p. 27 Nina Leen/Time Life Pictures/Getty Images; p. 29 (top, left) David Young-Wolff, PhotoEdit Inc.; p. 29 (top, right) Michael Newman, PhotoEdit Inc.; p. 29 (bottom, left) Angelo Cavalli, AGE Fotostock America, Inc.; p. 29 (bottom, right) Robert Brenner, PhotoEdit, Inc.; p. 31 Bob Daemmrich, PhotoEdit Inc.; p. 35 PhotoEdit; p. 38 Elizabeth Crews, Elizabeth Crews Photography

Chapter 2 Page 46 Stockphoto.com/Black Star; p. 47 Yoav Levy, Phototake NYC; p. 50 (top, left) Don W. Fawcett, Photo Researchers, Inc.; p. 50 (top, right) L. Willatt, E. Anglian Regional Genetics Service/Science Photo Library, Photo Researchers, Inc.; p. 50 (bottom, right) Peter Menzel, Stock Boston; p. 53 Alfred Pasieka, Science Photo Library; p. 55 Bill Longcore, Photo Researchers, Inc.; p. 57 Yoav Levy, Phototake NYC; p. 62 © The New Yorker Collection 2003 Michael Shaw from cartoonbank.com. All Rights Reserved; p. 65 (top) Christopher Brown/Stock Boston, Inc., Jupiter Images/FoodPix/Creatas/BrandX/Banana Stock/PictureQuest; p. 65 (bottom) Ellen Senisi; p. 67 Tibor Hirsch, Photo Researchers, Inc.; p. 69 Will Hart; p. 71 (bottom) Dr. Yorgos Nikas/Photo Researchers, Inc; p. 72 Bradley R. Smith, Ph.D.; p. 73 (bottom) Janes Stevenson, Photo Researchers, Inc.; p. 74 Photo Researchers, Inc.; p. 75 © The New Yorker Collection 1998 William Hamilton from cartoonbank.com. All Rights Reserved; p. 79 Chris Harvey, Getty Images Inc./Stone Allstock

Chapter 3 Page 88 Albert Normandin, Masterfile Corporation; p. 85 AP Wide World Photos; p. 86 Fountain Group, Getty Images/Digital Vision; p. 89 Owen Franken, Corbis/Bettmann; p. 90 (top, left) Corbis/NY; p. 90 (top, right) Joe McDonald, Corbis/NY; p. 90 Peter Byron, Photo Researchers, Inc.; p. 91 Purestock, Alamy Images, Royalty Free; p. 93 Charles Gupton, Corbis NY; p. 95 Ansell Horn, Phototake NYC; p. 99 Courtesy of Diana Hegger. Photo by Hank Hegger; p. 100 Saturn Stills, Photo Researchers, Inc.; p. 103 Robert Holmes, Corbis/NY; p. 106 (top) David Young-Wolff, PhotoEdit Inc.; p. 106 (bottom) Laura Dwight, Laura Dwight Photography; p. 110 Laura Dwight, Jupiter Images/FoodPix/Creatas/Brand X/Banana Stock/PictureQuest

Chapter 4 Page 122 Laura Dwight, Laura Dwight Photography; p. 115 Bob Daemmrich, The Image Works; p. 123 (top, left) Corbis/Comstock Images Royalty Free; p. 123 (top, right) Comstock Images; p. 123 (bottom, right) Peter Cade, Getty Images Inc./Stone Allstock; p. 124 Ed Bock, Corbis/Stock Market; p. 128 (top) Laura Elliott, Comstock Images; p. 128 (second from top) L.J. Weinstein, Woodfin Camp & Associates.; p. 128 (second from bottom) Petit Format, Photo Researchers, Inc.; p. 128 (bottom) Laura Dwight, Laura Dwight Photography; p. 132 Steve Outram, The Stock Connection; p. 133 AP Wide World Photos; p. 136 (top left) Ian Hooton © Dorling Kindersley; p. 136 (top right) PhotoDisc/Getty Images; p. 136 (bottom) © The New Yorker Collection 1996 Mike Twohy from cartoonbank.com. All Rights Reserved.; p. 138 © Ellen B. Senisi; p. 139 Lawrence Migdale, Stock Boston; p. 140 Mark Richards/PhotoEdit/Courtesy of Joe Campos & Rosanne Kermoian; p. 141 (top) Charles A. Nelson III, Ph.D.; (bottom) Laura Dwight, Laura Dwight Photography; p. 142 Owen Franken, Corbis/Bettmann; p. 144 Fotopic, Omni-Photo Communications, Inc.

Chapter 5 Page 148: Jupiterimages; p. 149 Spike, Getty Images Inc./Stone Allstock; p. 150 Bill Anderson, Photo Researchers, Inc.; p. 151 David Young-Wolff, PhotoEdit Inc.; p. 154 Laura Dwight, PhotoEdit Inc; p. 156 Owen Franken, Stock Boston; p. 157 Irven DeVore, Anthro-Photo File; p. 158 Donna Day, Getty Images Inc./Stone Allstock; p. 160 David Sanders, Arizona Daily Star; p. 162 Getty Images, Inc./Image 100 Royalty Free; p. 168 The Image Works; p. 170 Laura-Ann Petitto, McGill University; p. 171 Myrleen Ferguson Cate, PhotoEdit Inc.; p. 174 (left)

Laura Dwight Photography; p. 174 (center) Giacomo Pirozzi, Panos Pictures; p. 174 (right) Earl & Nazima Kowall, Corbis NY; p. 177 Susanna Price © Dorling Kindersley

Chapter 6 Page 180 Dan Lim, Masterfile Organization; p. 181 Jo Foord © Dorling Kindersley; p. 183 Courtesy Dr. Carroll Izard; p. 186 Gary Conner, Jupiter Images/FoodPix/Creatas/BrandX/Banana Stock/PictureQuest; p. 188 Laura Dwight Photography; p. 190 Fredrik D. Bodin, Stock Boston; p. 191 (top) Harlow Primate Laboratory/University of Wisconsin; p. 191 (bottom) Mary Ainsworth, University of Virginia. Photo by Daniel Grogan; p. 193 William Hamilton/Johns Hopkins University; p. 194 Rob Wilke, Creative Eye/MIRA.com; p. 195 Keith Brofsky, Jupiter Images/Picture Quest/Royalty Free; p. 196 © Larry Williams/CORBIS; p. 200 Ellen Senisi; p. 203 George Goodwin, George Goodwin Photography; p. 204 Getty Images/Stockbyte; p. 206 Krista Greco, Merrill Education

Chapter 7 Page 210 Rommel, Masterfile Corporation; p. 211 Arnold Gold/New Haven Register, The Image Works; p. 214 Jeff Greenberg, PhotoEdit Inc.; p. 215 Dominic Rouse, Getty Images Inc./Image Bank; p. 216 G. Degrazia, Custom Medical Stock Photo, Inc.; p. 217 Courtesy Marcus E. Raichle, M.D., Washington University Medical Center, from research based on S. E. Petersen et al., Positron emission tomographic studies of the cortical anatomy of single-word processing. *Nature* 331:585–589 (1988); p. 219 (left) Charles Gupton, Stock Boston; p. 219 (right) Skjold Photographs; p. 220 Geoff Manasse, Getty Images, Inc./Photodisc; p. 225 Laura Dwight, Laura Dwight Photography; p. 230 Ann Purcell, Photo Researchers, Inc.; p. 262 © NovostiSovfoto

Chapter 8 Page 262 Bob Daemmrich, The Image Works; p. 251 Lawrence Migdale/Pix; p. 252 The Image Works; p. 255 (top) Laura Dwight, Laura Dwight Photography; p. 255 (bottom) Ursula Markus, Photo Researchers, Inc; p. 256 (top) Corbis RF; p. 56 (bottom) Michael Newman, PhotoEdit Inc.; p. 259 J. Greenberg, The Image Works; p. 260 Laura Dwight, Laura Dwight Photography; p. 261 Jeff Greenberg, PhotoEdit Inc.; p. 262 ©The New Yorker Collection 2002 Bruce Eric Kaplan from cartoonbank.com. All Rights Reserved.; p. 266 (top) Tony Freeman, PhotoEdit Inc.; p. 266 (bottom) Jose Luis Pelaez, CORBIS/NY; p. 268 AP Wide World Photos; p. 269 AP Wide World Photos; p. 273 Corbis Royalty Free; p. 275 Ellen Senisi, The Image Works; p. 276 Catherine Ursillo, Photo Researchers, Inc.; p. 278 (top) Albert Bandura, D. Ross & S.A. Ross, Imitation of film-mediated aggressive models. *Journal of Abnormal and Social Psychology*, 66, 1963, p. 8; p. 278 (bottom) Rick Kopstein

Chapter 9 Page 284 Rommel, Masterfile Corporation; p. 285 © Ellen Senisi; p. 287 (top) Jeff Greenberg, The Image Works; p. 287 (bottom) Sam Kittner Photography; p. 288 Ken Heyman, Woodfin Camp & Associates; p. 289 © The New Yorker Collection 2003 Christopher Weyant from cartoonbank.com. All Rights Reserved; p. 290 Mark Richards, PhotoEdit Inc.; p. 291 Barbara Stitzer, PhotoEdit Inc.; p. 292 Lester Sloan, Woodfin Camp & Associates; p. 295 Rex Interstock, The Stock Connection; p. 297 Jose Asel, Aurora & Quanta Productions Inc; p. 300 Richard T. Nowitz, CORBIS/NY; p. 301 Lawrence Migdale/Pix; p. 304 Michael Newman, PhotoEdit Inc.; p. 306 B. Daemmrich, The Image Works; p. 309 (top) Earl & Nazima Kowall, CORBIS/NY; p. 309 (bottom) Bob Daemmrich, Stock Boston; p. 313 Elizabeth Crews/ Elizabeth Crews Photography; p. 316 David Young-Wolff, PhotoEdit Inc.; p. 319 David Turnley, Corbis/Bettman; p. 321 Bob Daemmrich, The Image Works; p. 322 Kevin R. Morris, CORBIS/ NY; p. 323 Richard Hutchings, Photo Researchers, Inc.;

Chapter 10 Page 348 Jim Craigmyle, Masterfile Corporation; page 330: Brand X Pictures/Jupiterimages; p. 331 Anne Ackermann, Getty Images, Inc.; p. 333 Arthur Tilley, Getty Images, Inc./Taxi; p. 335 Robert Houser, Comstock Images; p. 336 Robert Brenner, PhotoEdit Inc.; p. 338 Richard Lord, The Image Works; p. 341 Syracuse Newspapers/Randi Anglin. The Image Works; p. 343 Ellen Senisi; p. 346 Bob Daemmrich, Stock Boston; p. 348 Richard Hutchings, PhotoEdit Inc.; p. 350 Peter Byron, PhotoEdit Inc.; p. 354 Comstock Royalty Free Division; p. 355 Donna Day, Getty Images, Inc./Photodisc; p. 357 Getty Images, Inc./ Photodisc; p. 359 (left) Corbis/Bettmann; p. 359 (right) Melchior DiGiacomo, Boys Town; p. 363

DOONESBURY © G.B. Trudeau. Reprinted with permission of UNIVERSAL PRESS SYNDICATE. All rights reserved. p. 364 Lawrence Migdale, Lawrence Migdale/Pix

Chapter 11   Page 370 Photodisc/Getty Images; p. 371 David Young-Wolff, PhotoEdit Inc.; p. 374 (left) Ellen Senisi, The Image Works; p. 374 (right) Ellen Senisi, The Image Works; p. 377 Jeff Greenberg, Omni-Photo Communications, Inc.; p. 378 Bob Daemmrich, The Image Works; p. 380 (top) Express Newspapers, Getty Images, Inc./Liaison; p. 380 The Image Works; p. 384 Kevin Radford, SuperStock, Inc.; p. 386 AP Wide World Photos; p. 388 © Miguel Fairbanks; p. 389 ©The New Yorker Collection 1999 Roz Chast from cartoonbank.com. All Rights Reserved; p. 392 © Michael Newman, PhotoEdit; p. 395 Tom & Dee Ann McCarthy, CORBIS/NY; p. 397 Michael Newman, PhotoEdit Inc.; p. 400 Roger Mastroianni

Chapter 12   Page 406 Tony Freeman, PhotoEdit; p. 407 David Young-Wolff, PhotoEdit Inc.; p. 409 Will Hart, PhotoEdit Inc.; p. 410 Doonesbury © 1997 G.B. Trudeau. Reprinted with permission of Universal Press Syndicate. All Rights Reserved; p. 411 Cleve Bryant, PhotoEdit Inc.; p. 414 Marilyn Humphries, The Image Works; p. 416 Peter Byron, PhotoEdit Inc.; p. 417 PhotoEdit Inc.; p. 418 Mary Kate Denny, PhotoEdit Inc.; p. 420 PhotoEdit Inc.; p. 422 Peter Turnley, CORBIS/NY; p. 424 Buccina Studios, Getty Images, Inc./Photodisc; p. 426 Bob Daemmrich, Stock Boston; p. 428 Ron Chapple, Getty Images, Inc./Taxi; p. 430 (top) Michael Newman, PhotoEdit Inc.; p. 430 (bottom) Dana White, PhotoEdit Inc.; p. 436 (top) Paula Lerner, Woodfin Camp & Associates; p. 436 (bottom) Evan Johnson

Chapter 13   Page 440 Jonathan Daniel, Getty Images; p. 441 B. Daemmrich, The Image Works; p. 443 Christopher Bissell, Getty Images Inc./Stone Allstock; p. 444 (top) Topham, The Image Works; p. 444 (bottom) AP Wide World Photos; p. 445 Jeff Widener, Corbis/Sygma; p. 447 Dennis MacDonald, PhotoEdit Inc.; p. 448 Dana Summers, Tribune Media Services TMS Reprints; p. 449 Anthony Magnacca, Merrill Education; p. 450 AP Wide World Photos; p. 451 (left) Bob Daemmrich, The Image Works; p. 451 (right) John Eastcott/Yva Momatiuk, Woodfin Camp & Associates; p. 453 Drew Crawford, The Image Works; p. 456 Mark Gamba, CORBIS/NY; p. 459 Robin Nelson, PhotoEdit Inc.; p. 462 Eastcott-Momatiuk, The Image Works; p. 464 Geri Engberg, Geri Engberg Photography; p. 465 Vicki Silbert, The Image Works; p. 467 Michael Newman, PhotoEdit Inc.; p. 470 Jeff Greenberg, PhotoEdit Inc.; p. 471 David Butow/CORBIS SABA

Chapter 14   Page 476 © powietrzynski/Alamy; p. 477 Rob Kinmonth; p. 480 Altrendo Images, Getty Images/Creative Express; p. 481 Jeff Greenberg, The Image Works; p. 484 Haruki Sato/HAGA, The Image Works; p. 486 China Tourism Press. Liu, Yang/Getty Images Inc./Image Bank; p. 489 Brian Yarvin, The Image Works; p. 490 A. Ramey, PhotoEdit Inc.; p. 492 B. Bachmann, The Image Worksp. 494 Comstock Images; p. 497 Photolibrary.com; p. 498 (top) Mark Richards, PhotoEdit Inc.; p. 501 Annie Griffiths Belt,CORBIS/NY; p. 502 Susan Van Etten, PhotoEdit Inc.; p. 504 Rhoda Sidney, The Image Works

Chapter 15   Page 510 © Benelux/zefa/Corbis; p. 511 Ethan Hill; p. 514 Lon C. Diehl, PhotoEdit Inc.; p. 515 A. Ramey, PhotoEdit Inc.; p. 516 Jim Cummins, Getty Images, Inc./Taxi; p. 518 © Doranne Jacobson/International Images; p. 521 Antonia Reeve, Photo Researchers, Inc.; p. 524 (left) Phil Banko, Getty Images Inc./Stone Allstock; p. 524 (right) George Goodwin, George Goodwin Photography; p.526 Ariel Skelley, Masterfile Corporation; p. 527 Ebby May, Getty Images Inc./Stone Allstock; p. 530 Adam Smith, SuperStock, Inc.; p. 532 Zephyr Picture, Photolibrary.com.; p. 534 Rhoda Sidney, PhotoEdit Inc.; p. 535 Robert Brenner, PhotoEdit Inc.; p. 536 Copyright © Spencer Grant/Photo Edit. All rights reserved

Chapter 16   Page 540 © Janine Wiedel Photolibrary/Alamy; p. 542 Deborah Van Kirk; p. 545 Hughes Martin, CORBIS/NY; p. 547 Michael J. Doolittle, The Image Works; p. 553 Michael Newman, PhotoEdit Inc.; p. 554 Flip Chalfant, Flip Chalfant Photography; p. 555 © The New Yorker Collection 2005 Barbara Smaller from cartoonbank.com. All Rights Reserved ; p. 556 Richard Lord, The Image Works; p. 557 Michael Newman, PhotoEdit Inc.; p. 561 L.D. Gordon, Getty Images Inc./Image Bank; p. 562 David Young-Wolff, PhotoEdit Inc.; p. 564 Penny Woli

Chapter 17   Page 570 Amwell, Getty Images Inc./Stone Allstock; p. 571 Michelle Gabel, The Image Works; p. 574 Nancy Brown, CORBIS/NY; p. 575 Yoav Levy, Phototake NYC; p. 576 (left) Kevin Dodge, Masterfile Corporation; p. 576 (right) Caroline Wood, Getty Images Inc./Stone Allstock; p. 577 Courtesy: D.L. Rosene, M.B. Moss,

Z.G. Lai and R.J. Killiany, Boston University School of Medicine; p. 579 Paul Parker, Photo Researchers, Inc; p. 581 p. 582 Russ Kinne, Comstock Images; p. 583 David Young-Wolff, PhotoEdit Inc.; p. 584 (top) George Musil, Visuals Unlimited; p. 587 Mark Richards, PhotoEdit Inc.; p. 592 Liba Taylor, Robert Harding World Imagery; p. 595 Marcel Yva Malherbe, The Image Works; p. 596 Max Ferguson (Contemporary Artist), Private Collection/The Bridgeman Art Library

Chapter 18   Page 602 Comstock Royalty Free Division; p. 603 Margaret Salmon and Dean Wiand; p. 607 R. Sydney, The Image Works; p. 608 Lawrence Migdale/Pix; p. 610 Richard Hutchings, PhotoEdit Inc.; p. 612 (left) Nathan Benn, Woodfin Camp & Associates; p. 612 (right) Lawrence Migdale/Pix; p. 616 E. Crews, The Image Works; p. 619 (left) Comstock Images; p. 621 Photolibrary.com; p. 626 Rhoda Sidney; p. 629 Novastock, The Stock Connection

Chapter 19   Page 636 Miles Ertman, Masterfile Corporation; p. 637 Tim Brown, Getty Images Inc./Stone Allstock; p. 640 Sean Cayton, The Image Works; p. 641 Paul Rezendes, Positive Images; p. 646 A. Ramey, PhotoEdit Inc.; p. 649 Mark Richards, PhotoEdit Inc.; p. 655 Markus Dlouhy/Das Fotoarchiv, Peter Arnold, Inc; p. 657 Azerud, Corbis/Sygma

Figures and Tables

Chapter 1   Figure 1-1: Figure courtesy of Eric Courchesne, Director of the Autism Center of Excellence, Department of Neurosciences, UCSD; Figure 1-2: From J. Kopp & J.B. Krakow *Child Development in the social context.* © 1982 by Addison Wesley Publishing Co., Inc. Reprinted by permission of Pearson Education.

Chapter 2   Figure 2-2: From Martin, J. A., & Park, M. M. (1999, September 14) Trends in twin and triplet births: 1980–1997. National Vital Statistics Reports, 47, 1–17. Washington, DC: Centers for Disease Control, National Center for Health Statistics; Figure 2-5: From J. W. Kimball, *Biology* (5th ed.). Copyright © 1984. Reprinted by permission of the McGraw-Hill Companies; Figure 2-6: From International Genome Sequencing Consortium. (2001); Figure 2-9: From T. J. Bouchard & M. McGue (1981). Familial studies of intelligence: A review. Science, 264, 1700–1701. Reprinted with permission of Dr. Matt McGue and Dr. Thomas Bouchard; Figure 2-10: From A. Tellegen et al. (1988). Personality similarity in twins reared apart and together. Journal of Personality and Social Psychology, 54, 1031–1039. Copyright © 1988 The American Psychological Association. Adapted with permission; Figure 2-11: From *Schizophrenia Genesis: The Origins of Madness* by Irving I. Gottesman. © 1999 by W.H. Freeman & Company. Used by permission; Figure 2-14: From Reproductive Medicine Associates of New Jersey, 2002; Figure 2-15: Reprinted from Moore, K. L. Before we are born: Basic embryology and birth defects (Philadelphia: Saunders, 1998), p. 96, with permission from Elsevier; Table 2-1: Reprinted with permission from McGuffin, P., Riley, B., & Plomin, R. (2001, Feb 16). Toward behavioral genomics, *Science, 291*, 1232–1249; Table 2-3: From Human Genome Project, 1998, as seen at: http://www.ornl.gov/sci/techresources/ Human_Genome/medicine/genetest.shtml; Table 2-4: Copyright © 1993 by the American Psychological Association. Adapted with permission.

Chapter 3   Figure 3-2: Adapted from Finkelstein, D. L., Harper, D. A., & Rosenthal, G. E. (1998). Does length of hospital stay during labor and delivery influence patient satisfaction? Results from a regional study. *American Journal of Managed Care, 4*, 1701–1708; Figure 3-4: Adapted from Infant and Child Health Studies Branch. (1997). Survival rates of infants. Washington, DC: National Center for Health Statistics Table 3-1: From Apgar, V. A proposal for a new method of evaluation in the newborn infant, *Current Research in Anesthesia and Analgesia, 32*, 1953, p. 260. Reprinted by permission; Table 3-2: Reprinted with permission from Preventing low birthweight. Copyright 1985 by the National Academy of Sciences. Courtesy of the National Academy Press, Washington, DC; Table 3-3: From Kamerman, S. B., Maternity to parental leave policies: Women's health, employment, and child and family well-being. *The Journal of American Women's Medical Association*, 55, Table 1 (Spring 2000), and from Kamerman, S. B., Parental leave policies. *Social Policy Report*, 14 (2000), Table 1.0; Table 3-6: From Eckerman, C. O., & Oehler, J. M. (1992). Very low birthweight newborns and parents as early social partners. In Friedman, S. L., & Sigman, M. B., The psychological development of low birthweight children. Norwood, NJ: Ablex. Reprinted by permission of the author.

Chapter 4   Figure 4-1: From Cratty, B. J. (1979). Perceptual and motor development in infants and children. (3rd Ed.) All rights reserved. Reprinted by permission of Allyn & Bacon; Figure 4-3: From Bornstein, M. H., & Lamb, M. E. (Eds.). (1992). *Developmental psychology: An advanced textbook.* p. 135. Hillsdale, NJ: Erlbaum; Figure 4-4: From Human anatomy, 5th edition, by K. Van De Graaff, p. 339. Copyright © 2000 by The McGraw-Hill Companies; Figure 4-5: From The postnatal development of the human cerebral cortex, Vol I–VIII by Jesse Le Roy Conel, Cambridge, Mass.: Harvard University Press, Copyright © 1939, 1975 by the President and Fellows of Harvard College; Figure 4-6: Adapted from Roffwarg, H. P., Muzio, J. N., & Dement, W. C. (1966). Ontogenic development of the human sleep–dream cycle. *Science, 152,* 604–619; Figure 4-7: Adapted from American SIDS Institute, based on data from the Center for Disease Control and the National Center for Health Statistics, 2004; Figure 4-8: Adapted from Frankenburg, W. K., Dodds, J., Archer, P., Shapiro, H., & Bresnick, B. (1992). The Denver II: A major revision and restandardization of the Denver Developmental Screening Test. Pediatrics, 89, 91–97; Figure 4-9: From UNICEF, The state of the world's children, 2005; Figure 4-10: From National Center for Children in Poverty at the Joseph L. Mailman School of Public Health of Columbia University. Analysis based on U.S. Bureau of the Census 2000 Current Population Survey; Figure 4-11: From LaLeche League International (2003). Breastfeeding around the world. Schaumburg, IL; Figure 4-13: Adaption used with permission of Alexander Semenoick. Original appeared in Fantz, R. L. (May, 1961). The origin of form perception. Scientific American, p. 72; Figure 4-14: From Pascalis, O., de Haan, M., & Nelson, C. A. (2002). Is face processing species-specific during the first year of life? Science, 296, p. 1322; Figure 4-15: Reproduced with permission from Pediatrics, Vol. 77, Page 657, Copyright 1986; Table 4-2: Adapted from Thoman, E. B., & Whitney, M. P. (1990). Behavioral states in infants: Individual differences and individual analyses. In J. Colombo & J. Fagen (Eds.), Individual differences in infancy: Reliability, Stability, Prediction. Hillsdale, NJ: Erlbaum; Table 4-4: Reproduced with permission from Pediatrics, Vol 89, Pages 91–97, 1992

Chapter 5   Figure 5-7: Photo Courtesy of G. Dehaene-Lambertz INSERM/CEA; Table 5-3: Bayley Scales of Infant Development. Copyright © 1969 by Harcourt Assessment, Inc. Reproduced with permission. All rights reserved. "Bayley Scales of Infant Development" is a trademark of Harcourt Assessment, registered in the United States of America and/or other jurisdictions; Table 5-4: Adapted from Benedict, H., "Early Lexical Development: Comprehension and Production," Journal of Child Language, 6, 1979, 183–200; Table 5-5: From Brown, R., & Fraser, C. (1963). The acquisition of syntax. In C. N. Cofer and B. Musgrave (Eds.), Verbal behavior and learning: Problems and processes. New York: McGraw-Hill

Chapter 6   Figure 6-3: From Infancy: Its place in human development by Jerome Kagan, Richard B. Kearsley, and Philip R. Zelazo, p. 107, Cambridge, Mass.: Harvard University Press, Copyright © 1978 by the President and Fellows of Harvard University College; Figure 6-5: Adapted from Bell, S. M., & Ainsworth, M. D. (1972). Infant crying and maternal responsiveness. Child Development, 43, 1171–1190. © The Society for Research in Development, Inc.; Figure 6-6: From National Center for Health Statistics (HRSA), Child Health USA, 2002

Chapter 7   Figure 7-1: From the National Center for Health Statistics in collaboration with the National Center for Chronic Disease Prevention and Health Promotion, 2000; Figure 7-2: From Zito, J. M., Safer, D. J., dosReis, S., Gardner, J. F., Boles, M., & Lynch F. (2000). Trends in prescribing of psychotropic medications to preschoolers. Journal of the American Medical Association, 283, 1025–1030; Figure 7-3: From Needleman, H. L., Riess, J. A., Tobin, M. J., Biesecker, G. E., & Greenhouse, J. B. (1996, February 7). Bone lead levels and delinquent behavior. Journal of the American Medical Association, 275, 363–369; Figure 7-5: From Fischer, K. W., & Rose, S. P. (1995). Concurrent cycles in the dynamic development of brain and behavior. Newsletter of the Society for Research in Child Development, p. 16. The Society for Research in Child Development, Inc. © The Society for Research in Child Development, Inc.; Figure 7-11: Adapted from Berko, J., The child's learning of English morphology, Word, 14 (1958), pp. 150–177; Figure 7-12: From Hart, B., & Risley, T. R., Meaningful differences in the everyday experience of young American children. Baltimore, MD: Paul H. Brookes Publishing, 1995. Reprinted by permission; Figure 7-13: From Rideout, V. J., Foehr, U. G., Roberts, D. F., & Brodie, M. (1999, November). Kids and media at the new millennium. A Kaiser Family Foundation Report. Washington, DC: Henry J. Kaiser Family Foundation; Figure 7-15: From Tobin, J. J., Wu, D. Y. H., & Davidson, D. D., Preschool in three cultures: Japan, China,

and the United States (New Haven: Yale University Press, 1989). Reprinted by permission of the publisher; Table 7-1: Reprinted by permission of the McGraw-Hill Companies, Inc.; Table 7-3: From Pinker, S. The language Instinct (New York: William Morrow, 1994

Chapter 8   Figure 8-1: Adapted from Farver, J. M., Kim, Y. K., & Lee, Y. (1995). Cultural differences in Korean- and Anglo-American preschooler's interaction and play behaviors. Child Development, 66, 1088–1099. © The Society for Research in Child Development, Inc.; Figure 8-3: From Scientific American, March 2002, p. 71; Figure 8-5: Used with permission of the Center for Media and Public Affairs, Washington, DC;

Chapter 9   Figure 9-1: From Barrett, D. E. , & Radke-Yarrow, M. R. (1985). Effects of nutritional supplementation on children's responses to novel, frustrating, and competitive situations. American Journal of Clinical Nutrition, 42, 102–120; Figure 9-2: From The National Center for Health Statistics, 2001; Figure 9-3: USDA; Figure 9-4: From Cratty, B. J. (1979). Perceptual and motor development in infants and children. P. 222 (2nd ed.) Englewood Cliffs, MJ: Prentice Hall; Figure 9-5: From Centers for Disease Control, 1999; Figure 9-6: From U.S. Surgeon General, 2000; Figure 9-8: From Dasen, P., Ngini, L., & Lavallee, M. (1979). Cross-cultural training studies of concrete operations. In L. H. Eckenberger, W. J. Lonner, & Y. H. Poortinga (Eds.), Cross-cultural contributions to psychology. Amsterdam: Swets & Zeilinger; Figure 9-9: From Modern Language Association, www.mla.org/census_map, 2005; U.S. Bureau of the Census, 2000; Figure 9-10: © UNESCO 2006. Reproduced by permission of UNESCO; Figure 9-11B: Biological Psychiatry; Figure 9-12: U.S. Bureau of the Census, 2000; Figure 9-13: Reprinted with the permission of Cambridge University Press; Figure 9-14: From Walters, E., & Gardner, H. (1986). The theory of multiple intelligences: Some issues and answers. In R.J. Sternberg & R.K. Wagner (Eds.) Practical Intelligence. Cambridge, England: Cambridge University Press; Table 9-1: Based on Challe, J. S. (1979). The great debate: Ten years later with a modest proposal for reading stages. In L. B. Resnick & P. A. Weaver, (Eds.). Theory and practice of early reading. Hillsdale, NJ: Lawrence Erlbaum Associates

Chapter 10   Figure 10-1: From R. Shavelson, J. J. Hubner, & J. C. Stanton, (1976). Self-concept: validation of construct interpretations. Review of Educational Research, 46, 407–441; Figure 10-3: Based on Dodge, K. A. (1985). A social information processing model of social competence in children. In M. Perlmutter (Ed.), Minnesota Symposia on Child Psychology (Vol 18), 77–126. Hillsdale, NJ: Erlbaum; Figure 10-4: From Hofferth, S., & Sandberg, J. F. (2001). How American children spend their time. Journal of Marriage and the Family, 63, 295–308; Figure 10-5: U.S. Bureau of the Census, 2004; Figure 10-6: Adapted from Stevenson, H. W., & Lee, S. (1990). Contexts of achievement: A study of American, Chinese, and Japanese children. Monographs of the Society for Research in Child Development, No. 221, 55, Nos. 1–2. © The Society for Research in Child Development, Inc.; Cartoon: Doonesbury, United Press Syndicate, Gary Trudeau; Table 10-3: Adapted from Zarbatany, L., Haratmann, D. P., & Rankin, B. D. (1990). The psychological functions of preadolescent peer activities. Child Development. 61, 1067–1080. © The Society for Research in Child Development, Inc.

Chapter 11   Figure 11-1: Adapted from Cratty, B.J., Perceptual and motor development in infants and children, 3rd ed. Prentice-Hall, 1986; Figure 11-2: Adapted from Eveleth, P., & Tanner, J., Worldwide Variation in Human Growth (New York: Cambridge University Press, 1976); Figure 11-3: Adapted from Tanner, J.M., Education and physical growth, 2nd ed. New York: International Universities Press; Figure 11-4: From Kimm et al., (2002). Decline in physical activity in black girls and white girls during adolescence. New England Journal of Medicine, 347; Figure 11-5: Sowell et al., Nature Neuroscience, Vol. 2, No. 10, Oct. 1999, p. 859

Chapter 12   Figure 12-1: From U.S. Bureau of the Census, 2000. Washington, DC. Increase in Bicultural Identity; Figure 12-2: From Boehm & Campbell, 1995. Adolescent Difficulties; Figure 12-3: From Steinberg, L., & Silverberg, S. B. (1986). The vicissitudes of autonomy in early adolescence. Child Development, 57, 841–851. © The Society for Research in Child Development, Inc.; Figure 12-4: Adapted from Table 3, pg. 1035. Fulgini, A. J., Tseng, V., & Lam, M. (1999). Attitudes toward family obligations among American adolescents with Asian, Latin American, and European backgrounds. Child Development, 70, 1030–1044. © The Society for Research in Child Development, Inc.; Figure 12-6: From Larson et al. (1996). Changes in adolescents' daily interactions with their families from ages 10–18: Disengagement and transformation. *Developmental Psychology, 32,* 744–745; Figure 12-8: From Newsweek.

Kantrowitz, B., & Wingert, P. How well do you know your kid? (teenagers need adult attention). © 1999 Newsweek, Inc. All rights reserved. Reprinted by permission; Table 12-1: From Childhood and society by Erik H. Erikson. Copyright 1950. © 1963 by W. W. Norton & Company, Inc., renewed © 1978, 1991 by Erik H. Erikson. Reprinted by permission of W. W. Norton & Company; Table 12-2: From Marcia, J.E. (1980). "Identity in Adolescence." In J. Adelson (Ed.) Handbook of Adolescent Psychology. New York: Wiley

Chapter 13 Figure 13-1: From Blair et al. "Physical fitness and all-cause mortality: A prospective study of healthy men and women." Journal of the American Medical Association, 262 (1989). pp. 2395–2401; Figure 13-2: From Fingerhut, L. A., & Kleinman, J. C. International and interstate comparisons of homicide among young males. Journal of the American Medical Association, 263, (1990), pp. 3292–3295; Figure 13-4: Adapted from Kaplan, R. M., Sallis, J. F., Jr., & Patterson, T. L. Health and human behavior. New York: McGraw, 1993. Reprinted courtesy of Dr. R. M. Kaplan; Figure 13-5: Adapted from Schaie, K. W. (1977–1978). Toward a stage of adult theory of adult cognitive development. International Journal of Aging and Human Development, 8, 129–138. Copyright © 1978 Baywood Publishing Co.; Figure 13-6: Used with permission of Dr. Robert J. Sternberg; Figure 13-7: From R. J. Sternberg & R. K. Wagner. (1993). The g-ocentric view of intelligence and job performance is wrong. Current Directions in Psychological Science, 2, 1–5; Figure 13-8: From Journal of Gerontology by Dennis, W. Copyright 1966 by Gerontological Society of America. Reproduced with permission of Gerontological Society of America in the format Textbook via Copyright Clearance Center; Figure 13-9: From National Center for Education Statistics, 2004. The condition of education 2004; 13-11: From Benton et al., 2003. College Problems; Table 13-1: From Cohen, S., Kamarck, T., & Mermelstein, R. (1983). "A global measure of perceived stress." Journal of Health and Social Behavior, 24, 385–396; Table 13-2: From Dr. Herbert Benson, New England Deaconess Hospital, Behavioral Medicine Division. Used with permission of Dr. Herbert Benson

Chapter 14 Figure 14-1: Adapted from National Opinion Research Center. (1998). Race and friends. Chicago, IL: General Social Survey; Figure 14-2: From Murstein, B. I. (1987). "A clarification and extension of the SVR theory of dyadic pairing." Journal of Marriage and the Family, 49, 929–933; Figure 14-3: From Sternberg, R.J. (1986). "Triangular theory of love" Psycological Review, 93, 11-135; Figure 14-4: From Janda, L. H., & Klenke-Hamel, K. E. (1980). Human sexuality. New York: Van Nostrand; Figure 14-5: Based upon data from William H. Grey, Milken Institute, reported in Suro, R. (Nov. 1999). "Mixed Doubles." American Demographics, 57–62; Figure 14-6: U. S. Bureau of the Census. (2001); Figure 14-7: From U. S. Bureau of the Census. (2001);Figure 14-9: From Kurdek, L.A. (1999). "The nature and predictors of the trajectory of change in marital quality for husbands and wives over the first ten years of marriage." Developmental Psychology, 35, 1283-1296; Figure 14-10: Adapted from Googans, B. & Burden, D. (1987). Vulnerability of working parents: Balancing work and home roles. Social Work, 32, 295–300; Figure 14-11: U.S. Bureau of the Census, 2006; Table 14-1: From Colarusso, C.A., & Neimiroff, R.A. Adult Development in Psychodyamic Theory and Practice (New York: Plenum Publishing, 1981); Table 14-3: From Buss, D. M. et al. (1990). "International preferences in selecting mates: A study of 37 cultures." Journal of Cross-Cultural Psychology, 21, 5–47

Chapter 15 Figure 15-1: Adapted from Pitts, D. G. (1982). The effects of aging upon selected visual functions. In R. Sekuler, D. Kline, & K. Dismukes (Eds.), Aging and human visual function. New York: Alan R. Liss; Figure 15-2: From DiGiovanna, A. G. (1994). Human aging: Biological perspectives. New York: McGraw-Hill; Figure 15-3: Adapted from Michael, R.T., Gagnon, J.H., Laumann, E.O., & Kolata, G. (1994). Sex in America: A Definitive survey. Boston: Little, Brown; Figure 15-4: From USA Weekend. (1997, August 22–24). "Fears Among Adults."P. 5; Figure 15-5: From U.S. Bureau of the Census, 1990b; Figure 15-6: Adapted from Baum, A. (1994). Behavioral, biological, and environmental interactions in disease processes. In S. Blumenthal, K. Matthews, & S. Weiss (eds.). New research frontiers in behavioral medicine: Proceedings of the National Conference. NIH Publications, Washington, DC; Figure 15-7: From World Health Organization. (1999). Death rates from coronary heart disease. Geneva: World Health Organization; Figure 15-8: Adapted from Kaplan, R. M., Sallis, J. F., Jr., & Figure 15-9: Adapted from Pettingale, K. W., Morris, T., Greer, S., & Haybittle, J. L. (1985). Mental attitudes to cancer: An additional prognostic factor. Lancet, 310, 750; Figure 15-10: From Schaie, W. (1985). Longitudinal studies of adult psychological development. New York: Guilford Press; Table 15-1: Adapted from Ochsner Clinic Foundation, 2003

Chapter 16 Figure 16-1: From The John D. and Catherine T. MacArthur Foundation Research Network on Successful Midlife Development, 1999; Figure 16-2: Adapted from Costa et al., 1986. The stability of personality, p. 148; Figure 16-4: From Walker, L. (1984). The battered woman syndrome. New York: Springer; Figure 16-5: From Monthly Labor Review, November, 2001, p. 6; Table 16-1: From Gould, R.L., & Gould, M.D. (1978). Transformations. New York: Simon & Schuster; Table 16-2: Adapted from Levine, R. (1997). A geography of time: The temporal misadventures of a social psychologist, or how every culture keeps time just a little bit differently. New York: Basic Books, 1997. [ISBN 0465028926]

Chapter 17 Figure 17-1: From U. S. Bureau of Census, 2000; Figure 17-2: From United Nations Population Division. 2002. World population ageing: 1950–2050. New York; Figure 17-3: From Whitbourne, S.(2001). Adult development and aging: Biophysical perspectives. New Yourk: Whiley; Figure 17-5: From National Highway Traffic Safety Administration. (1994); Figure 17-6: AARP Bulletin, 2005, p. 34; Figure 17-8: Adapted from Wannamethee, S. G., Shaper, A. G., Walker, M., & Ebrahim, S. (1998). Lifestyle and 15-year survival free of heart attack, stroke, and diabetes in middle-aged British men. Archives of Internal Medicine, 158, pp. 2433–2440. Reprinted by permission of the publisher; Figure 17-9: AARP/Maturity Sexuality Study, 1999; Figure 17-10: From U.S. Bureau of the Census, 1997; Figure 17-11: From Anderson, R. N. (2001). United States life tables, 1998. National Vital Statistics Reports, vol. 48, no. 18. Hyattsville, MD: National Center for Health Statistics; Figure 17-12: From Schaie, K.W. (1994). "The course of adult intellectual development." p. 307. American Psychologist, 49, 304–313; Table 17-1: From Palmore, E.B. (1982). The facts on aging quiz. New York: Springer.

Chapter 18 Figure 18-1: From Baltes, P. B., & Baltes, M. M. (1990). Psychological perspectives on successful aging: The model of selective optimization with compensation. In P. B. Baltes & M. M. Baltes (Eds.), Successful aging: Perspectives from the behavioral sciences. Cambridge, England: Cambridge University Press. Copyright 1990. Reprinted with permission of Cambridge University Press; Figure 18-4: From Heinemann, G. D., & Evans, P. L. (1990). "Widowhood: Loss, change, and adaptation," in T. H. Brubaker (Ed.), Family relationships in later life. Newbury Park, CA: Sage.; Figure 18-5: From Federal Interagency Forum On Aging-Related Statistics. (2000). Older Americans 2000: Key indicators of Well-Being (Older Americans). Washington, DC: National Institute on Aging; Table 18-1: From Atchley, R. C. (1982). "Retirement: Leaving the world of work," Annals of the American Academy of Political and Social Science, 464, 120–131

Chapter 19 Figure 19-1: From Hayward, M., Crimmins, E., & Saito, Y. (1997). "Cause of death and active life expectancy in the older population of the United States, Journal of Aging and Health, 122–131; Figure 19-4: From J. Lynn et al. (1997). Perceptions by family members of the dying experience of older and seriously ill patients. Annals of Internal Medicine, 126, 164–165; Table 19-1: From W.A. Knaus et al. (1995, November 22). "A controlled trial to improve care for seriously ill hospitalized patients. The study to understand prognoses and preferences for outcomes and risks of treatments (SUPPORT)." Journal of the American Medical Association, 273, 1591–1598.

Name Index

Abeare, C., 217
Aboud, F.E., 349
Abramson, L.Y., 417
Abril, 311
Abushaikha, 93
Achenbach, T.A., 151
Acheson, S., 164
Achter, J.A., 327
Ackerman, B.P., 182
Acocella, J., 14
Adams Hillard, P.J., 79
Adams, C., 107, 203, 255
Adams, C.R., 409, 425
Adamson, L., 186
Adelman, Kathy, 563
Ader, R., 451
Aderman, P.K., 648
Adler, P., 347
Adolph. K.E., 144
Adoni, 621
Afifi, T., 355
Afrank, 265
Aguiar, A., 157
Ahmed, E., 347
Ahn, W., 189
Ainsworth, Mary, 185, 191, 193, 197
Aitchison, 169, 170, 237
Aitken, R.J., 70
Akmajian, A., 168
Aksan, 186, 197
Akshoomoff, N., 22
Albers, L.L., 93, 100
Albino, A., 489
Albrecht, G.L., 449
Alderfer, C., 322
Aldwin, C., 462, 576
Ales, K.L., 78
Alexander, R.A., 107
Alfonso, V.C., 319
Alisky, J.M., 584
Allen, L., 76
Alley, A., 168
Allhusen, V., 243
Allison, C.A., 61
Allison, D.B., 290, 411
Aloise-Young, P., 430
Altholz, S., 296
Alvarez-Leon, E.E., 513
Amato, P., 355, 552
Amitai, Y., 81
Ammerman, R.T., 268
Amos, A., 391
Amsterlaw, J., 189, 263
An, J., 543
Anand, K.J., 142
Anders, T., 124
Anderson, B.L., 166, 176
Anderson, C., 166
Anderson, D., 279, 620
Andres-Pueyo, 32
Andrews, K., 262
Angus, J., 573
Ani, C., 133
Anisfield, M., 110

Annunziato, R., 447
Ansberry, C., 624
Anstey, 579
Antill, J.K., 492
Antonio, A., 466
Antonucci, T.C., 554, 563, 629
Antshel, K., 446
Apostoleris, N.H., 348
Apperley, I., 305
Apter, A., 371
Arai, 632
Archer, J., 411
Arcus, D., 61, 66, 202
Arenson, 418
Aries, P., 14
Arlotti, J.B., 136
Arnett, J.J., 423, 424, 478
Arnold, R.M., 166
Aronson, E., 472
Arredondo, 265
Arsenault, L., 69, 96
Artal, P., 81, 514
Arterberry, M., 186
Arts, 535
Asch, D.A., 652
Asendorpf, J.B., 188
Ashburn, S.S., 216
Asher, S.R., 346, 349
Ashmead, D.H., 141, 144
Ashwin, 217
Aslin, R.N., 139
Astington, 263
Atkinson, L., 192, 532
Auerbach, C.F., 194
Augustyn, Peggy, 241
Aviezer, O., 192
Avis, N., 516, 518
Avlund, K., 629
Axia, G., 142
Axinn, 433
Aydt, H., 255
Aylward, G.P., 164
Ayotte, V., 332
Azuma, S.D., 78

Babad, E., 363
Bacchus, L., 81
Bachman, J.G., 389
Bade, U., 202
Badger, S., 424
Baer, J.S., 80
Bagwell, C.L., 343
Bahna, 298
Bahrick, L.E., 144
Bailey, J.A., 558
Bailey, J.M., 63, 73
Baillargeon, R., 157, 228, 379
Baines, C.J., 528
Baird, A., 263
Bajda, V.M., 200
Bajor, J., 614
Baker, T., 393
Bakker, 561

Balaban, M.T., 121
Bale, 295
Ball, K., 562
Ball, M., 579
Ball, S., 241
Ballen, 92
Baltes, Margaret, 12, 534, 595, 611, 614
Baltes, Paul, 534
Bamaca, M., 314
Bamshad, M.J., 9
Bandura, Albert, 19, 28, 274, 275, 277
Banich, M.T., 217
Barinaga, 12
Barker, E., 307, 416
Barnett, R.C., 496, 497, 543
Baron-Cohen, S., 73, 217, 256
Barr, H.M., 80
Barr, R.A., 161
Barrett, D.E., 288
Barry, H., 424
Bass, 359
Bates, E., 130, 172, 266, 559
Bathurst, K., 353
Batty, 136
Baudinniere, P., 188
Bauer, P.J., 162
Bauman, K.E., 427
Baumeister, R.E., 333
Baumgart, 121
Baumring, Diana, 264
Bayley, Nancy, 164, 531
Beach, B.A., 33
Beal, Carole, 305, 348
Beals, K., 490
Bearce, 161
Beardslee, W.R., 294
Bearman, P.S., 416
Becerra, R.M., 557
Beck, M., 518, 598
Becker, B., 271
Becker, G., 369, 616
Becker, J.B., 429
Beckman, M., 376
Beckwith, L., 164, 165
Beehr, 621
Behne, 175
Behrends, 428
Behrman, R.E., 50, 214
Beilin, H., 25, 301
Belanger, S., 245
Belcher, J.R., 356
Belgrad, S.L., 305
Belkin, L., 50
Bell, J.P., 436, 576
Bell, R., 197
Bellagamba, 188
Bellavia, G., 494
Bellezza, F.S., 537
Bellinger, D., 76
Belluck, P., 266, 267
Belmaker, R.H., 65
Belsky, J., 193, 194
Ben-Zeev, T., 472

Benbow, C.P., 256, 327
Benedict, H., 168
Benenson, J.F., 348
Bengston, V.L., 556, 629
Benini, F., 142
Benjamin, J., 65
Benjuya, N., 578
Bennett, A., 68
Bennett, P., 176
Benoit, D., 194
Benson, 183
Benson, Herbert, 454
Benton, E., 468
Berenbaum, S.A., 73, 256
Berendes, H., 78
Bergen, H., 417
Berko, J., 236
Berkowitz, L., 446
Bernal, M.E., 254
Bernard, J., 487, 488
Berndt, T.J., 342, 425, 433
Berrick, J.D., 358
Berry, A., 301
Berscheid, Ellen, 483, 513
Bertin, E., 186
Bertoncini, J., 170
Bewley, 81
Beyene, Y., 616
Bianchi, S.M., 240, 555
Bigelow, A., 186
Binnie, 214
Bionna, R., 454
Birch, H.G., 202, 290
Bird, G., 554
Birkelund, E., 523
Birlouez-Aragon, I., 589, 591
Bishop, D.V.M., 296, 345, 426
Bjorklund, D.F., 26, 110, 301, 302
Black, M.M., 120, 164, 423
Blades, 231
Blake, J., 169, 325
Blakemore, S., 255
Blakeslee, S., 160
Blank, M., 233
Blennow, K., 584
Blieszner, R., 556
Blizzard, R.M., 287
Blodgett, B., 411
Bloom, L., 169, 537
Blount, B.G., 175
Blumenthal, S., 269
Blumstein, D.L., 625
Blundon, J., 260
Blustein, D.L., 411
Blythe, D., 372
Bober, S., 260
Bogatz, G.A., *241*
Bolger, N., 490
Bolmeijer, E., 608
Bologh, R.D., 142
Bolton, P., 65
Bonichini, S., 142
Bonke, B., 58
Bookheimer, S.Y., 584

Bookstein, F.L., 76
Booth, C., 194
Booth, W., 506
Booth-LaForce, 193
Bor, W., 280
Borawski-Clark, E., 628
Borden, M.E., 241
Borland, M.V., 332
Bornstein, R.F., 77, 165, 170, 186, 239, 261, 379
Bos, H., 296
Boshuizen, 535
Bosquet, M., 72
Bouchard, T.J., 63, 64, 65, 266
Boulton, M.J., 348
Bowen, D.J., 555
Bowen, G.L., 385
Bowen, N.K., 385
Bower, B., 221
Bower, T.G.R., 151
Bowers, K.E., 575
Bowlby, John, 197
Boyatzis, C.J., 255
Boyd, G.M., 392
Boyd, R., 552
Boyle, 304
Boysson-Bardies, B., 169
Bracey, J., 314
Bracken, B., 326, 333
Bradbury, T.N., 551
Bradlee, M., 290
Bradley, R.H., 92, 197, 239
Brainerd, C., 301
Braithwaite, V., 347
Brandon, T., 393
Branje, S.J.T., 351
Brant, M., 293
Branum, A., 97
Brasel, J.A., 287
Brassard, M.R., 269
Brazelton, T. Berry, 131
Brecher, M., 587
Bredekamp, S., 245
Breedlove, G., 92
Breheny, M., 518
Brehm, S.S., 324, 490
Bremner, J.D., 270
Brennan, K.A., 490
Brent, D.A., 236
Bridges, J.S., 203
Briere, J.N., 267
Britt, 79
Brockington, I.F., 639
Brody, N., 64
Bromberger, J.T., 563
Bronfenbrenner, Urie, 23, 28
Bronstein, P., 195
Brook, U., 372
Brooks, J., 185
Brooks-Gunn, J., 37, 245, 322, 372
Brown, A.L., 79
Brown, B.B., 253, 288
Brown, J.D., 409
Brown, J.L., 304, 319, 326
Brown, Louise, 3, 4
Brown, R., 171, 194
Brown, W.M., 425, 426
Browne, B.A., 257
Browne, K., 557, 559
Brownell, C., 261
Brownell, H., 611
Brownlee, S., 289
Brubaker, T., 632
Bruck, M., 230, 231
Brueggemann, I., 91

Bruno, R., 306
Brutsaert, 526
Bryan, J., 274
Bryant, J., 240
Bryant, J.A., 240, 644
Buchanan, C.M., 369
Buchman, D.
Budd, K., 587
Bugg, J., 532
Buitelaar, J., 78
Bukowski, W.M., 426
Bumpus, L., 422
Bunch, K., 262
Burbank, P., 575
Burd, L., 79, 325
Burdjalov, V.F., 121
Burgess, R.L., 426
Burnham, M.M., 122
Burns, D.M., 586
Burock, D., 339
Burrows, G.D., 101
Burt, V.L., 586
Bushman, B.J., 279, 392
Buss, A.H., 26, 27
Buss, David, 486, 553, 555
Buss, K.A., 184
Bussey, K., 274
Butcher, 290
Butler, K.G., 296
Butterworth, G., 157

C., 492
Cabrera, N., 194, 241
Cadinu, M.R., 262
Cain, B.S., 516, 518
Caine, 417
Calarco, 80
Caldera, Y.M., 203
Caldwell, B.M., 197
Calhoun, F., 79
Callister, L.C., 88
Calvert, S.L., 257
Camarota, S.A., 563
Cameron, P., 557
Camfield, 480
Cami, J., 391
Campbell, A., 241
Campbell, F., 243, 255, 333
Campione, 304
Campos, J.J., 139, 143, 187
Camras, L.A., 184
Canals, J., 131
Candy, J., 255
Canfield, R., 165
Cannon, T.D., 68
Cantor, N., 433
Carbonneau, R., 195
Cardala, E.B., 136
Cardman, M., 384
Carey, K., 473
Carmichael, M.
Carpendale, J.J.M., 413
Carper, 22
Carr, C.N., 391
Carrere, S., 493, 498
Carroll, D., 597
Carswell, H., 260
Cartensen, L.L., 551, 613
Carter-Saltzman, L., 65
Caruso, 365, 460
Carvajal, F., 186
Carver, C.S., 529
Carver, L., 186, 187
Cascalho, M., 591

Case, R., 21, 228, 231
Casper, L.M., 492, 555
Caspi, A., 65, 69, 199
Catalano, R., 323
Catell, A., 319
Cath, S., 356
Cauce, A.M., 358
Caughlin, J., 494
Cavallini, A., 139
Ceci, S.J., 230, 231
Chadwick, A., 259
Chaiklen, S., 233
Chall, J., 310
Chamberlain, P., 359
Champion, 275
Chan, C.G., 409
Chang, C., 228
Chao, R.K., 421
Chapman, J., 59, 275
Chase-Lansdale, 243
Chasnoff, I.J., 78
Chassin, L., 393
Cheek, N., 427
Chen, C., 319, 424, 584
Cherlin, A., 554, 556
Cherney, I., 203
Cherry, K.E., 597
Chess, Stella, 202
Cheung, 263
Chien, S., 106
Chisolm, T., 515, 579
Chiu, C., 301
Chomsky, Noam, 173
Choy, 81
Christakis, 166
Christine, J., 168
Christophersen, E.R., 19
Chronis, A., 298
Chuang, S., 423
Chung, S.A., 497, 588, 590
Cicchetti, D., 120, 263, 269, 270, 271, 294, 416
Cirulli, F., 120
Claes, M., 266
Clark, E., 195
Clark, K.B., 379
Clark, R., 90, 218, 236, 535, 588
Clarke-Stewart, K., 243
Clarkson, M.G., 161
Claxton, L.J., 129
Claes, M., 266
Cliff, D., 566
Clifton, R., 141, 161
Clinton, J.F., 495
Clore, G.L., 433
Clubb, P.A., 230
Cnattingius, S., 78
Cobbe, E., 609
Cohen, J., 409, 449, 451, 557
Cohen, L., 165, 294
Cohen, S., 34, 107, 158, 164
Cohn, R.M., 609
Coie, 280
Cokley, K., 385
Colburn, 166
Colburne, K.A., 203
Colcombe, S.J., 578
Cole, M., 76, 170, 192, 195
Coleman, M., 554
Colen, C., 436
Coley, R.L., 243
Colino, S., 214
Collett, B.R., 265
Collins, F.S., 58
Collins, W.A., 75, 422, 433, 490

Colom, J.M., 32
Colpin, 75
Coltrane, S., 203, 255
Colwell, 260, 261
Compton, R., 217
Comunian, A.L., 610
Condit, V., 373
Condry & Condry, 203
Condry, J., 203, 271
Condry, S., 271
Conger, 265
Conklin, H.M., 53
Conn, V.S., 515
Connell-Carrick, 220
Conner, 417
Connor, R., 562, 563
Consolacion, T., 435
Continelli, L., 541
Cook, A.S., 642
Coon, V.S., 584
Cooney, T., 543, 552
Coons, S., 123
Cooper, R.P., 311
Cooperstock, M.S., 97
Copple, C., 245
Corballis, M.C., 217
Corcoran, J., 436
Cordes, 229
Cordon, I.M., 162
Corliss, S., 584
Corpus, 472
Corr, D., 649
Corsaro, W., 255
Costa, Paul, 544, 547, 548, 605
Costello, E., 132
Costigan, A.T., 75
Cottrell, 136
Courage, M.L., 161
Courchesne, E., 22
Couture, G., 269
Couzin, J., 76
Cowan, C.P., 491
Cowan, N., 302
Cowgill, D.O., 574
Cowley, G., 583
Cox, A., 246
Cox, C., 559
Crane, E., 55
Cratty, B., 219, 291
Craven, R., 253
Crawford, D., 203, 494
Crawford, M., 503
Crews, D., 17
Crick, N.R., 276, 279, 280
Crimmins, E., 642
Crisp, A., 472
Critser, G., 372
Crockett, L.J., 430
Crohan, 563
Cronkite, 444
Crouter, A.C., 422, 430
Crowley, B., 449, 554
Crowley, K., 232
Cructhley, A., 307
Cruz, N., 298
Cuddy, 573
Cuijpers, 608
Culbertson, J.L., 164
Culver, V., 655
Cummings, E., 276, 612
Cunningham, J.D., 492
Cunningham-Burley, S., 391
Curtis, J., 271, 469
Cynader, M., 120
Cyr, M., 496

Daddis, C., 423
Dahl, E., 523
Dainton, M., 356
Daly, T., 323
Danhauer, S., 584
Daniels, M., 65, 235, 319
Dar, R., 157
Dare, W.N., 81
Dariotis, J., 347
Darling, 434
Darnton, N., 496
Darwin, Charles, 26, 28, 183
Dasen, P.R., 157, 301
Davey, M., 271, 587
Davidov, 314
Davidson, A.L., 430, 434, 560
Davidson, R.J., 184, 263
Davis, Emory, 131
Davis, L., 411, 489
Davis-Kean, P.E., 333
Dawson, B., 186
Dawson, G., 79
Day, D.O., 267, 303, 495
de Anda, D., 557
De Bourdeaudhuij, 373
De Clercq, 382
De Gelder, B., 144
de Jesus Moreno, M., 584
de Koeyer, 188
De Leon, J.R., 238
de Rosnay, 187
De Roten, Y., 229
de St. Aubin, McAdams, E., 17
de Vries, M.W., 656
Deakin, M.B., 490
Dearing, R., 341
Deaux, K., 501, 563
Decarrie, T.G., 157
DeCasper, Anthony, 73, 109, 111, 141
Decety, 275
deChateau, P., 89
Deforche, 373
DeFrain, J., 639
DeGasperi, 578
Degnen, 609
deHaan, 140
Dehaene-Lambertz, 173
Dejin-Karlsson, E., 80
Dekovic, M., 266
DeLamater, 433, 434, 435
DeLisi, 22, 53
Dell, D.L., 518
DeLoache, J., 195
Delva, 444
DeMarini, 55
DeMeersman, 525
Demers, R.A., 168
Demetriou, A., 21
Demir, A., 561
Demo, D., 411
Deng, C., 303
Denizet-Lewis, B., 433
Dennis, T.A., 195, 460
Dennison, 134
Denny, F.W., 375
Denollet, 526
DePaulo, B., 499
Dernetz, V., 193
Derryberry, D., 200
deSchipper, E., 206
Desmarais, S., 469
Desoete, A., 382
Deurenberg, P., 287
Deurenberg-Yap, M., 287
Deutsch, G., 216

Deveny, K., 255
deVilliers, J.G., 237
DeVita, 492
Devlin, B., 65
DeVries, M.W., 103
deVries, R., 202, 224
DeWitt, P.M., 553
Diamond, L., 435, 490
Dick, D.M., 53, 68
Diego, 143
Diener, E., 480, 548, 549
Dieter, J., 143
Dietz, W., 133, 289
DiGiovanna, A.G., 514, 515, 516, 592
DiLalla, L.F., 164
Dildy, G.A., 78
Dilworth-Bart, J., 216
DiMatteo, M.R., 93
Dimick, K.M., 391
Dimino, 324
DiPietro, J.A., 73, 75, 78
DiPrete, 465
Dishion, T., 423
Dissanayake, C., 188
Dittman, 620
Dixon, R., 174, 557, 595, 611
Dmietrieva, 424
Dobson, K.S., 107
Dodge, Kenneth, 266, 280, 294, 346, 426, 558
Doka, K.J., 632, 649
Doman & Doman, 176
Donat, 312
Dondi, M., 107
Dong, Q., 410
Donlan, C., 229
Donnellan, M.B., 409
Donnerstein, E., 279
Doress, P.B., 625
Dorn, L., 372
Dornbusch, S.M., 427, 431
Dorofaeff, 375
Dortch, S., 465
Dougherty, C.M., 626
Doussard-Roosevelt, J.A., 96
Doyle, R., 97, 492, 553
Drapeau, M., 229
Dreman, S., 493
Drew, L.M., 357
Drews, S., 80
Driedger, Sharon, 527
Dromi, E., 170
Druzin, M.L., 78
Dryfoos, J.G., 424
Dubeau, D., 195
DuBois, D.L., 203, 427
Dubois, L., 173
DuBreuil, S.C., 162
Duckett, E., 353
Duenwald, M., 75
Dukes, R., 411
Dulitzki, M., 99
Duncan, G.J., 101, 133, 216, 322
Dunne-Bryant, 553
Durbin, J., 625
Durkin, K., 255
Dutton, D.G., 559
Dweck, C., 253, 361
Dyer, C.B., 261, 632
Dyson, A.H., 33

Eagly, A.H., 487, 503
Easterbrooks, M., 193, 194

Eastman, Q., 125
Eaton, M.J., 203, 218, 219
Ebstein, R.P., 65
Eccles, J.S., 369
Ecenbarger, W., 393
Eckerman, C.O., 110
Edelman, S., 528
Edison, S.C., 161
Edwards, C.P., 25, 255
Egan, S.K., 347
Egeland, B., 192
Ehrensaft, M., 557
Ehrhardt, A.A., 256
Eichstedt, J., 204, 255
Eigsti, I., 270
Eimas, P.D., 141
Einbinder, S.D., 133
Eisbach, 263
Eisenberg, N., 266, 274, 275, 276
Eitel, B.J., 513
Elder, G.H., 409, 556, 578
Eley, T.C., 26, 53, 65, 416
Elkind, David, 379, 382, 641
Elliot, E., 302
Ellis, L., 221, 253
Ellis, S., 301
Ellison, S., 516
Else-Quest, N.M., 90, 246
Emde, R.N., 189
Emery, R.E., 557
Emmert, 588
Emslie, G.J., 294
Endo, S., 198
Engh, T., 221
England, 465
Englund, M.M., 175, 429
Ennett, S.Y., 427
Enns, L.R., 203
Enright, 552, 553
Ensenauer, 57
Epperson, S.E., 470
Erber, J.T., 535, 574
Erdley, C.A., 342
Erickson, Erik, 578
Erikson, Erik, 17, 28, 252
Eslea, M., 347
Espelage, D.L., 347
Espenschade, A., 291
Estabrook, P.A., 444
Estell, D., 345, 426
Ethier, L., 269
Evans, B.J., 101, 278, 451
Evans, D.E., 268
Everson, M., 559
Eyer, D., 89

Fabes, R.A., 255, 275
Factor-Litvak, P., 216
Fainsilber-Katz, L., 493
Faith, M.S., 61, 290
Falk, P.J., 498
Fane, 79
Fangman, 103
Farah, 239
Farhi, P., 279
Farley, 383
Farmer, T., 345, 426, 429
Farre, M., 391
Farver, J.M., 278
Faulkner, G., 444
Favez, N., 229
Fawson, 177
Fayers, 395
Feeney, J.A., 490, 551

Fein, G., 260
Feiring, C., 192
Feldhusen, J.E., 38
Feldman, R., 164, 165, 202, 276, 323, 345, 364, 421
Feldman, R.S., 8, 97
Feldstein, S., 193
Felson, R.B., 253
Felten, D., 451
Fennema, E., 472
Fenson, L., 236
Ferguson, L., 428, 430
Ferguson, T.J., 240
Fernald, Anne, 107, 133, 140, 170, 172, 187, 189
Ferrario, S., 584
Festinger, Leon, 332
Fetterman, D.M., 33
Fiatarone, M.S.A., 575, 577
Field, T.M., 90, 97, 98, 110, 143, 196, 198, 214
Fields-Meyer, T., 408, 492
Figley, C.R., 551
Finch, C.S., 588, 589
Fincham, F.D., 494
Findlen, B., 559
Fine, M., 355, 416
Fingerhut, L.A., 446, 523
Finkbeiner, A.K., 101
Finkelstein, D.L., 79, 93
Finn-Stevenson, M., 132, 133, 243
Fisch, 74
Fischel, J.E., 239
Fischer, C., 21, 157, 217
Fiske, Susan, 536, 573
Fitch, W., 173
Fitneva, S.A., 231
Fitzgerald, L.E., 263
Fivush, R., 229, 230
Flanagan, C., 319
Flavell, John, 189, 301
Flavin, D.K., 391
Fletcher, A.C., 263, 431
Flom, 144, 203
Flor, D., 422
Flynn, E., 263
Fogel, A., 156, 188
Fogg, 465
Fok, 98
Foote, 79
Ford, D., 416
Forman, M., 78
Forness, 324
Forrester, M., 188
Fothergill-Bourbonnais, F., 653
Fowers, B.J., 9, 26, 314
Fozard, J.L., 578
Fraenkel, P., 543
Fraley, R.C., 190
Frank, L., 288
Frankel, S., 59, 587
Fransen, M., 56
Frazier, L.M., 74
Fredriksen, B., 375
Freedman, A.M., 128, 516
Freeman, E., 518
Freiberg, P., 396
French, S., 449
Freneau, P., 555
Freud, Sigmund, 15, 17, 28, 276
Frey, K.S., 493
Frick, J., 186
Frick, P.J., 430, 431
Fried, P.A., 79, 80
Friederici, 186

Friedland, 584
Friedman, D., 395
Friedman, S., 371
Friend, R.M., 361
Frietas, 221
Frishman, R.G., 588
Friston, 198
Frith, 198
Fritz, G., 220, 537
Froh, 416
Frosch, D.L., 278
Fry, C.L., 609
Frye, D., 263
Fuchs, D., 323
Fuchs, L.S., 323
Fugate, W.N., 543
Fuligni, A.J., 375, 421
Funk, J., 279
Furman, W., 423, 433
Furstenberg, F.F., 492, 556

Gabbay, S., 516
Gabelko, N., 327
Gable, S., 290
Gaertner, L., 480
Gagnon, S.G., 164
Galambos, N., 416
Galbraith, K.M., 652
Gallagher, J.J., 326, 386
Gallagher, L., 68
Gallistel, C.R., 160
GamaSosa, 578
Gandour, J., 175
Ganger, J., 236
Ganong, L., 554
Gao, D., 290
Garber, C., 575
Garcia-Moreno, C., 557
Gardner, H., 319, 469
Garland, J.E., 294
Garnett, L.R., 575, 577
Garrison, M., 166
Garry, 162
Garyantes, 228
Gatz, 583
Gauldren, M.E., 78
Gault, 311
Gauthier, Y., 189
Gauvain, M., 379
Gavin, L.A., 423, 586
Gawande, A., 579
Gaylord, 268
Gazmarian, J.A., 81
Gazzinga, M.S., 216
Gearhart, 73
Gee, H., 53
Gelfand, M.M., 587
Gelles, R.J., 268
Gelman, D., 160
Gelman, R., 189, 214, 228, 229, 255,
    379, 381
Genovese, J., 21
Gentile, 279
Gerber, M.S., 120, 307, 499
Geronimus, 436
Gerrish, C.J., 136
Gershoff, E., 266
Gersten, R., 324
Gesell, Arnold, 163, 164
Gesser, G., 643
Ghimire, 433
Giammattei, J., 290
Giarusso, 624
Gibbons, 425

Gibbs, N., 74, 77, 78
Gielen, 610
Giese-Davis, 529
Gifford-Smith, M., 342
Gijselaers, 535
Gilbert, 241, 417
Giles, 307
Giles-Sims, 266, 269
Gillespie, N.A., 65
Gilley, 584
Gillies, 304
Gilligan, Carol, 340
Gilliland, A.L., 81
Gillmore, 437
Gilmer, 576
Gilstrap, 231
Ginzberg, E., 501
Giordana, S., 373
Giordano, 433
Glanz, 290
Glasgow, K.L., 361
Gleason, J.B., 176, 490
Gleeson, 288
Gleitman, L., 170, 173
Glick, P., 468, 470
Glover, 203
Gluhoski, V., 657
Godbey, 566
Goetz, A., 26
Gohlke, 288
Goldberg, A.E., 88, 173
Goldfarb, Z., 94
Goldman, R., 294
Goldsmith, L.T., 34, 184, 416
Goldson, D.B., 70
Goldsteen, 553
Goldstein, A.P., 280
Goldston, D.B., 417
Goleman, D., 181, 551
Golensky, 296
Golinkoff, R.M., 189
Golombok, S., 75, 256, 357, 436
Goode, E., 220, 294
Goodison, 590
Goodlin-Jones, B.L., 124
Goodman, J.C., 141, 229, 230, 231, 620
Goodson, 243
Goodwin, M.H., 348
Goold, S.D., 643, 650
Gopnik, A., 177
Gordon, B.N., 551
Gosling, 547
Goswami, U., 231
Gottesman, I.I., 55, 64, 68
Gottfredson, G.D., 502
Gottfried, A.W., 353
Gottlieb, G.L., 26, 120, 195
Gottman, John M., 493, 498, 551, 558
Gould, Roger, 544
Goyette-Ewing, 354
Graddol, D., 306
Graham, E., 420
Graham, S., 9, 88, 361
Granic, I., 423
Grant, V.J., 626
Grantham, Y., 416
Grantham-McGregor, S., 133
Gratch, G., 156
Gray-Little, B., 335, 411
Green, F.L., 189
Green, M.H., 505
Greenberger, 424
Greenfield, P.M., 8, 379
Greenway, C., 304
Greenwood, P.W., 289, 470

Greer, M., 620
Gregory, S., 132, 434
Greydanus, D., 373
Grieff, B., 562
Griffith, D.R., 78
Griffiths, P., 220
Grigel, F., 492
Grigorenko, E., 288, 317
Groome, L.J., 76, 121, 122
Groopman, J., 58
Gross, P.A., 96, 555
Grossman, K.E., 186, 190
Grunbaum, J.A., 416, 417
Grundy, J.F., 555
Grusec, J.E., 19, 273, 274
Grych, B., 195
Gschaider, A., 263
Guarente, L., 591
Guasti, M.T., 237
Guerrero, A., 385
Guerrini, I., 76
Gulota, T.P., 409, 425
Gunnar, M.R., 187
Gunnarsdottir, I., 134
Gupta, U., 53, 483
Gurewitsch, 75
Guricci, 287
Gurin, P., 466
Gurling, 76
Gutek, G.L., 242
Guterl, F., 17
Guthrie, G., 290
Guttmacher, A.E., 58
Guttman, J., 537
Guzsman, R., 311
Gyurcsik, N.C., 444
Gyurke, J., 164

Haan, N., 462
Haas, A.P., 418
Hack, M., 97
Hafdahl, A.R., 411
Hagen, R., 266, 562
Hahn, C.S., 75
Haight, B., 8
Haines, J., 373
Haith, M.H., 139, 143
Hales, K.A., 100
Halford, G.S., 262, 302
Hall, E., 254, 291, 562
Hall, R.G., 287
Hallahn, D.P., 298
Halliday, M.K.A., 171
Halpern, L.E., 124
Hammer, C.S., 80
Hamon, 433
Hane, A., 193
Hankin, B.L., 417
Hanson, R., 68, 193, 626
Hansson, R.O., 628
Happe, F.G.E., 611
Hardway, 375
Hardy, 193
Harlow, Harry, 191
Harlow-Rosentraub, 598
Harmon, A., 386
Harnish, R.M., 168
Harrell, J.S., 393, 610
Harrington, R., 465
Harris, C.M., 436
Harris, J., 65, 156
Harris, J.R., 259, 498, 586
Harrison, 374
Harrist, A., 196

Hart, B., 32, 238, 266, 269, 339
Harter, S., 409
Hartmann, B., 78
Hartshorne, T.S., 628
Hartup, W.W., 346, 482
Harvey, E., 205
Harvey, M., 353, 354
Harway, M., 557
Harwood, R.L., 196, 266
Haskett, M., 271
Haslam, C., 80
Haslett, A., 484
Hatfield, E., 486
Hattery, A., 503
Hau, 331
Haugaard, J.J., 268
Hauser, M., 173
Hay, D., 104, 259
Hayden, T., 50
Hayes, C.W., 26
Hayflick, L., 588
Haynie, D.L., 425
Hays-Thomas, R., 574
Hayslip, B., 449, 554, 626, 649
Hayward, M., 642
Haywood, H.C., 304
Hazan, C., 489
Healy, P., 417
Hecht, M.L., 483
Hegger, Diana, 99
Heimann, M., 110, 229
Heiser, S., 571
Helenius, H., 80, 495
Helms, D.B., 9
Helson, R., 480, 543
Hemesath, K., 545
Hencke, R.W., 157
Hendin, 418
Hendrick, C., 483
Hendrick, S., 483
Hendrie, H.C., 584
Henretta, 555
Henry, J., 279, 430, 612
Herman, C., 447
Hermann, N., 584
Hernandez-Reif, M., 143, 186
Hernstein, Richard J., 65, 322
Heron, G., 114
Herscher, 290
Hershey, 200
Hertenstein, M.J., 143, 187
Herterelendy, F., 87
Hertz-Pannier, 173
Hessling, R., 583
Hetherington, E.M., 554
Hetts, 469
Heubusch, K., 554
Heuven, 561
Hewitt, J.K., 270
Hewlett, B., 195
Hewstone, M., 349
Heymen, J.D., 269
Hietala, 68, J.
Higgins, D., 269
Highley, J.R., 217
Hightower, J.R.R., 416
Hill, R.D., 175, 203
Hillman, J., 587
Hines, M., 79, 256
Hinojisa, T., 221
Hirsch, B.J., 427
Hirsch, H.V., 120
Hirsh-Pasek, K., 171
Hirshberg, L., 187
Hitlin, 409

Hitt, J., 520
Hjelmstedt, A., 75
Ho, B., 556
Hobart, C., 492
Hobdy, J., 449, 554
Hoelterk, L.F., 433
Hoeymans, N., 576
Hofer, M.A., 190
Hofferth, S.L., 354
Hogg, K., 215
Hohmann-Marriott, B., 492
Holahan, C.J., 614
Holden, C., 266
Holland, J.C., 254, 502, 529
Hollenstein, T., 423
Hollich, G.J., 170
Hollins, E.R., 254
Holmes, C.S., 574
Holowaka, S., 169
Holt, A., 268
Holtzman, 58
Holyrod, R., 355
Holzman, L., 303
Homer, B., 189
Honey, J.L., 104
Hong, 242
Hooper, F.H., 261
Hooven, C., 493
Hopkins, B., 132
Hopkins-Golightly, T., 89
Horiuchi, S., 589
Hornik, R., 187
Horowitz, A., 579
Horwath, C.C., 586
Houts, R.M., 220, 494
Howard, A., 392
Howe, J., 315, 326
Howe, M.L., 161, 162
Howsen, M., 332
Hoyme, 325
Huang, J., 431
Hubbs-Tait, 216
Hubscher, 233
Hudson, J.A., 231
Huesmann, L.R., 279
Hughes, F.P., 136
Huizink, A., 78, 79
Hultsch, D., 515
Hummel, 142
Humphrey, 230, 260
Humphrey, R., 365
Hunt, E., 30, 125, 434
Hunter, G.R., 268, 427, 435
Huppe, M., 496
Huston, A., 493, 494
Hutchinson, A., 217
Hutton, P.H., 14
Hyde, J.S., 90, 102, 256, 433, 434, 435, 472, 496, 543, 587
Hyssaelae, L., 80

Iacono, W.G., 53
Ialongo, N., 276
Iannotti, R.J., 276
Iglesias, J., 119, 186
Iida, M., 490
Ingersoll, Thoman, 121
Ingoldsby, 433
Ingraham, 92
Ingram, 591
Inhelder, B, 225, 378
Inoue, 562
Insel, P.M., 447
Inzlicht, M., 472

Irizarry, 196
Ironson, 529
Isaksen, S.G., 461
Isay, R.A., 436
Isbell, 470
ith et al, 97
Izard, C.E., 182, 183, 184

Jackson, H., 275
Jackson, L.A., 469
Jacobo, M., 578
Jacobson, L., 362, 558
Jacques, H., 416
Jang, 65
Jankowski, J., 165
Jansen, Mary, 275
Janssens, J.M.A.M., 266
Jayawant, S., 120
Jayawardena, K., 632
Jazwinski, S.M., 588
Jelicic, 331
Jeng, S.
Jenks, J., 279
Jernigan, 9
Ji, G., 352
Ji-liang, S., 629
Jiao, S., 352
Jimenez, J., 311
Jing, Q., 352
Jirtle, 63
Joe, S., 417
Johannes, C., 57, 516, 518
Johannson, 260
John, O., 547
Johnson, D., 61, 80, 119, 172, 261, 290, 435, 466, 552, 587, 653
Johnson, Primas, J.L., 103
Johnston, D., 389
Jolles, J., 577
Jones, A., 23
Jones, H.E., 79
Jones, L.C., 298
Jones, S., 110
Jones-Harden, B., 358
Jongudomkarn, D., 480
Joseph, H., 61
Jost, H., 64
Joy, M., 81
Jurimae, T., 291
Jusczyk, P.W., 141, 168

Kacapyr, E., 565
Kadue, D.D., 620
Kagan, J., 61, 66, 67, 185, 188, 199
Kahan, 186
Kahana-Kalman, R., 186
Kahn, A., 395, 526, 581, 583, 622
Kahneman, D., 549
Kail, R., 156, 157, 302, 381
Kaiser, L.L., 76
Kalakanis, L., 140
Kalb, C., 75, 214, 294
Kalsi, M., 514
Kaltiala-Heino, R., 347, 368, 371
Kaneda, H., 580
Kantrowitz, B., 260, 408, 416, 519
Kao, G., 349
Kaplan, H., 41, 132, 297, 454
Kaplanski, J., 578
Kaprio, 68
Karabulut, 621
Karlson, H., 269
Karney, B.R., 495, 551

Karnilowicz, 421
Karp, J., 558
Karpov, Y.V., 304
Kart, C.S., 577
Kashima, Y., 188
Kaslow, F.W., 550
Kasser, T., 487
Kassner, C.T., 653
Kastenbaum, R., 640, 643, 644, 645, 648
Kates, N., 562
Katz, D.L., 19
Kauffman, J.M., 298, 323
Kaufman, R.J., 256, 266, 317, 462
Kauh, T., 347
Kautz, K.J., 297
Kavale, K.A., 324
Kayton, A., 94
Kazura, K., 195
Keam, 514
Kearsley, R., 185
Keating, D., 377, 379
Kecskes, I., 307
Kedizora-Kornatowska, K., 591
Kelber, S.T., 495
Keller, 188, 497
Kellett, J.M., 587
Kelley, M., 495
Kellogg, J.W., 434
Kelly, J., 194
Kelly-Vance, L., 203
Kemper, R.L., 305
Kendall, A., 586
Kennedy, Rose, 391
Kenrick, D.T., 490
Kerstetter, 203
Kevorkian, Dr. Jack, 650
Kibria, N., 433
Kidman, A.D., 528
Kidwell, J.S., 412
Kiel, 184
Kiesner, J., 262
Killen, M., 339
Kilner, 198
Kim, J., 271, 274, 421, 520, 564
Kimoto, T., 119
King, A., 203
Kinney, 76
Kinsey, A.C., 435
Kirchengast, S., 78
Kisilevsky, B., 111, 141
Kit-fong Au, T., 396
Kita, 169
Kitterod, 496
Kitzmann, K., 268
Klebanov, P.K., 322
Kleepsies, P., 652
Kleinman, J.C., 446
Kless, S.J., 347
Klier, C.M., 104
Klohnen, E., 543
Kloszewska, I., 584
Klute, 426
Knafo, A., 422
Knap, N.F., 422
Knaus, W.A., 650
Knickmeyer, 73, 256
Knight, K., 90, 254
Knowlton, B.J., 216
Kobrynowicz, 472
Kochanska, G., 186, 193, 196, 197, 204
Koenig, A., 65, 270
Koh, 436
Kohlberg, Lawrence, 258, 337, 338, 339, 340

Kohn, A., 311
Koivisto, M., 216
Kolata, G., 74, 287
Kolodny, R.C., 587
Komarova, N.L., 173
Konrad, 190
Kooijman, 514
Koopmans, 514
Koppleman, 293
Koren, 79
Koroukian, A.M., 100
Koska, J., 287
Kosmala, K., 584
Koss, M.P., 559
Kotch, J., 559
Kotre, J., 562
Kozulin, A., 233
Kraemer, B., 436
Krahenbuhl, S., 231
Kramer, A.F., 578
Krcmar, 382
Kreuger, J., 125
Krietlow, B., 622
Krietlow, D., 622
Kristensen, 588
Kristjansdottir, G., 291
Kroger, J., 414
Krohn, M.D., 431
Krojgaard, 157
Kronenfeld, 103
Kronholz, 245
Krowitz, A., 139
Kubilius, 411
Kubler-Ross, Elisabeth, 646, 648
Kuczynski, L.E., 204, 273
Kuebli, J., 230
Kuhl, P.K., 166, 169, 175, 176, 177
Kuhn, D., 302
Kulieke, M., 411
Kunkel, D., 240
Kupersmidt, J.B., 426
Kurdek, L., 490, 494, 498
Kurtz, D.A., 271
Kurtz-Costes, B., 385
Kuschal, 588
Kwant, 591
Kwok, L.K., 416

Laas, I., 23
Labouvie-Vief, Gisela, 379, 456, 457
Lacerda, F., 229
Lacharite, C., 269
Lachmann, T., 296
Lackey, C., 557
Lacourse, E., 266
Ladd, G., 431
Laditka, S., 103
Laflamme, D., 203, 498
Lahiri, D.K., 584
Lally, 195
Lam, M., 255
Lam, V., 421
Lamaze, Dr. Fernand, 91
Lamb, M., 194, 195
Lambert, R., 307
Lamberts, S.W. Jr., 577
Lamkin, 537
Lamm, H., 449, 497
Lamon, S.J., 472
Lamprecht, 333
Lanctot, K.L., 584
Landau, B., 170
Landrine, H., 446
Lane, D., 34, 425

Lang, A.A., 80
Langer, E., 139
Langford, P.E., 273
Langlois, J.H., 140
Lansford, J.E., 269, 348
Larkey, L.K., 483
Larsen, S.E., 91
Larson, J., 423, 433
Larsson, 256
Lau, I., 301
Lau, S., 416
Laumann, E.O., 516
Laumann-Billings, L., 557
Laursen, B., 346
Lauter, J.L., 72
Lavallee, M., 301
Lavelli, M., 156
Lavzer, 243
Lawrence, 80
Lay, 260
Leadbeater, B., 416
Leadbeater, B.J., 271
Leader, J., 657
Leaper, C., 176, 203, 257
Leathers, S., 495
Leavitt, L.A., 70
Lee, A.M., 189, 291, 293, 301, 444, 591
Lees, N., 396
Lefkowitz, E.S., 396
Legato, 74
Legerstee, M., 188, 198
Lehman, D., 140
Leipold, H., 12
Leman, P., 255
Lemonick, M.D., 369
Leon, G.R., 255
Leonard, C.M., 175, 216, 267
Leonard, L.B., 296
Lepore, S.J., 451
Lerner, R.M., 36, 296, 332
Lesko, 472
Lesner, S., 580
Lesperance, 293
Lester, D., 436
Leung, K., 421
Levano, K.J., 100
LeVay, S., 436
Levenson, R.W., 551
LeVine, 176
Levine, R., 486, 566
Levinson, Daniel, 544, 606–607
Levy, B.L., 586
Levy-Shiff, 498
Lewin, T., 503, 555
Lewis, C.C., 74, 142, 182
Lewis, J.M., 347, 484, 529
Lewis, T., 185, 188, 192, 194, 243
Lewkowicz, D., 144
Leyens, Jacques-Philippe, 35
Li, S., 26, 53, 416, 465, 487, 640
Li-qing, Z., 629
Liang, H., 416
Liao, S., 50, 632
Libert, S., 590
Liblik, R., 291
Lichter, 487
Lickliter, R., 144
Lidz, J., 173
Light, L.L., 597
Lillard, A., 246, 263, 492
Limber, 185
Lindemann, B.T., 620
Linden, W., 447
Lindsey, E., 260, 261, 577
Lindstrom, H., 566

Linn, A., 361
Lino, M., 495
Lippa, R.A., 436
Lipsitt, Lewis P., 109, 125, 127, 142
Liskin, L., 435
Lister, J., 515, 570
Litovsky, R.Y., 141
Litrownik, A., 268
Litzinger, S., 551
Liu, H., 166, 169, 175, 518
Livson, N., 371
Lloyd, B., 298
Lluis-Font, 32
Lobo, R.A., 519
Lochner, B., 411
Lock, R.D., 561
Loeb, S., 205
Loehlin, J.C., 267
Loftus, E.F., 162, 231
Logan, R., 543
Lombroso, P.J., 79
London, B., 339
Lonetto, R., 641
Longmore, 433
Lopez, M.F., 466
Lord, 579
Lorenz, Konrad, 26, 28, 89, 190, 276, 277
Love, J.M., 205, 243
Lowe, M.R., 447
Lowrey, G.H., 216
Lowton, K., 644
Lu, M.C., 91, 314, 498, 533
Lubart, T.I., 462
Lubinski, D., 256, 319, 327
Lucas, R., 428, 549
Lucas, S.R., 480
Lund, R., 629
Lundberg, U., 449
Luthar, S.S., 271, 429
Lutz, S., 290
Lynam, D.R., 431
Lynch, M.E., 80
Lyon, G.R, 417
Lyons, N.P., 68

Mabbott, D.J., 217
Maccoby, E.B., 205, 243
Maccoby, Eleanor, 264
MacDonald, S., 246, 506, 515
MacDorman, M.F., 100, 102
Macionis, J.J., 553, 609
Mackenzie, T.D., 221
Mackey, M.C., 91, 495
MacPhee, D., 9
MacWhinney, B., 173
Maddox, G.L., 614
Mahgoub, N., 640
Maital, S., 170
MaKuc, D.M., 523
Malatesta, C., 184
Malcuitt, G., 203, 498
Malkin, J.W., 142
Malla, A.K., 68
Malling, 55
Mallis, M., 255
Mallon, G.P., 435
Mancini, J.A., 556
Mandel, D.R., 141
Mangan, P.A., 579
Manlove, J., 437
Mann, C.C., 289, 418
Manning, M., 325, 433
Manstead, A.S.R., 481

Mao, A., 122
Marcia, James, 413–414
Marcovitch, S., 156
Marcus, Cyril, 417
Marczinski, C., 515
Marean, G.C., 140
Markey, 371
Markison, S., 580
Marlier, L., 107
Marmer, C.R., 294
Marschark, M., 296
Marsh, H.E., 253, 331, 332
Marshall, E., 298
Marston, P.J., 483
Marti-Henneberg, C., 368
Martin, C.E., 81, 176, 203, 221, 255, 257, 258, 264, 417, 431, 435, 492
Martin, C.L., 492
Martinez, R., 411
Marx, S., 294
Masataka, N., 141, 170, 171, 175
Mascher, 9
Mash, E.J., 416
Masling, J.M., 15
Maslow, Abraham, 23, 28
Masten, A.S., 199
Masteron, Carrie, 612
Masters, W.H., 587
Mastropieri, M.A., 323
Masunaga, H., 598
Matic, 462
Matlin, M., 176
Maton, K.I., 37, 271
Matsumoto, A., 9, 217
Matthews, K.A., 460, 518, 563
Mattison, M.A., 591
Mattos, 515
Mattson, M., 80, 591
Matula, K., 164
Matusov, E., 26
Mauritzson, U., 262
Maxwell, 243
Mayberry, R.I., 263
Mayer, J.D., 365, 460
Mayes, L.C., 79, 495
Mayseless, O., 192
Mazzota, P., 584
McAdams, D.P., 543
McAlister, A., 263
McAuliffe, S.P., 216
McBrier, D.B., 505
McCabe, M., 269, 410
McCall, R.B., 124
McCann, J., 584
McCarthy, M.J., 586
McCarty, M., 144
McCauley, K.M., 519
McClelland, D.C., 317
McCloskey, L.A., 558
McCord, J., 269
McCoy, 580
McCrae, R., 61, 200, 202, 544, 547, 548, 605
McCrink, K., 160
McCullough, M.E., 38
McCutcheon-Rosegg, S., 92
McDonald, K.A., 21, 523
McDonnell, L.M., 312
McDonough, L., 172
McElwain, N., 193
McGee, J., 257
McGlone, M., 472
McGough, R., 296
McGovern, M., 644
McGreal, D., 101, 639

McGrew, K.S., 319
McGue, M., 64
McGuiness, D., 443
McHale, S., 347, 351, 422
McKay, R.J., 50
McKenna, J.J., 277
McKinlay, A., 574
McKinney, R., 436
McKusick, V.A., 54
McLoyd, V.C., 357
McNulty, J.K., 495
McVittie, C., 574
McWhirter, L., 435
Mead, Margaret, 313
Mealey, L., 204
Medeiros, R., 584
Medina, J.J., 575
Mednick, S.A., 460
Meece, J.L., 385
Meertens, 56
Meeus, W., 414
Mehran, K., 370
Meijer, A.M., 497
Meisels, S.J., 96
Meister, H., 580
Melinder, 231
Meltzoff, Andrew, 110, 157, 177, 198
Melville, K., 554
Melzer, L., 578
Mendaglio, S., 409
Mendel, Gregor, 50
Mendoza, C., 326
Menlove, F.L., 19
Mennella, J., 136
Mercer, J.R., 322
Mercuri, A., 307
Meredith, H.V., 287
Meritesacker, B.B., 202
Merrill, D.M., 556
Mertz, M.E., 632
Mervis, J., 37
Mesle, F., 589
Messer, S.B., 17
Messinger, D., 186
Meyer-Bahlburg, H.F.L., 436
Mezey, 81
Miao, X., 303, 352
Michael, R.T., 434, 435, 516
Michaels, M., 554
Michel, G.L., 57, 221
Michnick-Golinkoff, R., 171
Microwsky, J., 553
Midalrsky, E., 274
Miehl, N.J., 120
Mikhail, B., 103
Mikulincer, M., 192, 489
Miles, R., 90, 96
Miller, A.B., 79, 196, 231, 266
Miller, B., 275, 545
Miller-Perrin, C.L., 269
Milliken, B., 515
Mills, J.L., 80
Mimura, K., 119
Minerbrook, S., 427
Mishra, R.S., 301
Mistry, J., 157
Mitchell, B.A., 543, 555
Mitchell-Kernan, C., 492
Mittendorf, R., 87
Miyaki, K., 195
Mizuno, K., 142
Moane, G., 480
Moffitt, T.E., 69
Moise-Titus, J., 279
Moldin, S.O., 55

Molfese, V.J., 164
Monaco, 173
Mondloch, C.J., 140
Moneta, 261
Money, J., 256
Montague, D., 186
Montemayor, R., 409, 425
Montessori, M., 246
Moon, C., 109
Moore, K., 61, 198, 202, 216, 290
Moos, R.H., 444
Morange, M., 13, 319
Morelli, G., 8
Moreton, 3
Morfei, M.Z., 554
Morice, A., 103
Morikawa, H., 172
Morris, T., 55, 499, 537
Morrison, J.H., 473
Morrongiello, B., 215
Morse, R.M., 391
Moss, M., 621
Motschnig, R., 22
Moyad, M.A., 576
Mueller, N., 556
Muhuri, P.K., 125
Mulder, E., 78, 79
Mumme, Donna, 187, 189
Muniz-Ruiz, M., 578
Munzar, P., 391
Murdock, M.C., 436, 461
Murguia, A., 446
Murphy, B., 411
Murray, B., 65, 494
Murray, Charles, 322
Murray, J.A., 101
Murray-Close, D., 276
Musher-Eizenman, 279
Mutrie, N., 444
Myers, D., 58, 79, 586
Myers, Nancy, 161
Myklebust, B.M., 127

Nadal, K., 416
Nadeau, L., 96
Nagda, B.R.A., 466
Nagle, R.J., 164
Nagy, E., 110, 157
Nahmiash, D., 632
Naik, G., 652
Naimark, 586
Nakagawa, M., 195
Nanda, S., 389
Nangle, D.W., 342
Nass, G., 433
Nathans, J., 579
Nathanson, A., 257
Navarro, M., 556, 616
Nawaz, S., 220
Nazzi, T., 170
Neale, J.M., 361
Needleman, H.L., 76
Negy, C., 336
Neher, A., 23
Neiderhiser, 267
Neisser, U., 161
Nelson, C.A., 72, 140, 172, 186, 203, 229,
       361, 374, 382, 424, 468, 574, 584
Nesheim, 78
Ness, R.B., 80
Neubauer, 534
Neugarten, Bernice, 607
Neumark-Sztainer, 373
Newcomb, A.F., 343, 426

Newman, R., 111
Newsom, C.A., 296, 616
Newton, R., 268, 587
Neylan, T.C., 294
Ngini, L., 301
Nguyen, L., 255, 263
Nicholas, C.D., 217
Niederhoffer, H., 73
Nielsen, M., 188
Nieto, S., 313
Nigg, J.T., 297
Nihart, M.A., 216
Nilsson, L., 595
Nimrod, G., 621
Nisbett, R., 322
Niyogi, P., 173
Nobuyuki, I., 515
Nockels, R., 395
Noels, K., 307
Nolen-Hoeksema, S., 417
Noller, P., 551
Noonan, D., 520
Nordenstroem, 256
Nordin, S., 580
Norgate, 63
Norman, R.M.G., 68
Norton, 434
Notaro, P., 214
Nowak, C.A., 173
Nugent, B., 132, 255
Nusbaum, H.C., 141
Nuttman-Schwartz, 620
Nuysse, 121
Nylen, K., 104

O'Connor, M.J., 65, 81
O'Grady, W., 169, 170, 171, 237
O'Malley, C., 263, 444
O'Toole, M.E., 81
Oakes, L., 151
Oakshott, P., 395
Oblinger, 387
Ocorr, K., 590
Oden, M., 531
Ogbu, J., 361, 386
Ogilvy-Stuart, A.L., 288
Ogle, 591
Oishi, S., 480, 549
Okada, M., 119
Okamoto, Y., 231
Okie, 298
Olivarda, 371
Oliver, M.B., 433
Oller, D.K., 169
Olson, C., 9, 586
Olszewski, P., 411
Oltjenbruns, K.A., 642
Onorato, R.S., 336
op de Haar, 275
Oretti, R.G., 103
Orford, J., 562
Osofsky, J., 268, 278
Oster, H., 142
Ostrov, J., 276, 279
Ostrove, J., 544
Owen, J.E., 529
Owsley, C., 579
Oxford, M., 437
Oyserman, D., 314
Ozyurek, 169

Pachter, L.M., 446
Padilla-Walker, L., 193

Paige, R., 311
Paik, A., 516
Paikoff, R.L., 372
Paisley, T.S., 81
Pajulo, M., 495
Palan, P.R., 519
Palincsar, A.S., 304
Palladino, D.E., 411
Palsane, M.N., 451
Panagiotides, H., 186
Paneth, N.S., 97, 101
Papousek, H., 175
Papousek, M., 175
Papp, T., 307
Paquette, D., 195
Paris, J., 68
Park, R.D., 260, 597
Parke, R., 194, 203
Parker, J.G., 194, 296, 348
Parkes, C.M., 449
Parlee, M.B., 482
Parmelee, A.H., Jr., 124
Parnell, T.F., 267
Parten, Mildres, 260
Pascalis, O., 140, 165
Pasqualotto, F.F., 74
Patenaude, A.F., 58
Paterson, C., 125, 157
Patterson, S., 454, 498
Patz, R.J., 268
Paulesu, E., 296
Pauli-Pott, U., 202
Pavis, S., 391
Pavlov, Ivan, 107
Paxton, S.J., 425
Payne, A., 259
Pe-Pua, 421
Peal, W., 307
Pear, R., 214
Peck, Robert, 194
Pederson, N., 63
Pelham, 449, 469
Pelletier, D., 346
Peltonen, L., 53
Peltzer, K., 435
Pempek, 166
Pengpid, 435
Pennington, J., 294
Penninx, B., 583
Peplau, L.A., 490
Peretz, J.E., 462
Perlmann, J., 9, 176
Perner, J., 274
Perozzi, J.A., 307
Perrinne, N.E., 430
Perry, Willian, 347, 457
Persson, A., 276, 279
Peskin, H., 371
Peters, M., 221
Peterson, A.C., 176, 263, 269, 298,
       413, 543
Peterson, R., 446
Petit, G., 280
Petitto, L.A., 169
Petras, H., 276
Petrou, S., 97
Petry, 431
Pettersen, 496
Pettingale, K.W., 529
Pettit, G., 266
Peverly, S.T., 323
Phelan, P., 430
Phillippot, P., 276, 345

Phillips, D., 203, 537, 579
Phillips-Silver, J., 141
Phillipsen, L.C., 347
Phinney, J.S., 411, 428
Phipps, M.G., 436
Piaget, Jean, 28, 150, 225, 273, 378
Picavet, H.S., 576
Pick, A.D., 186
Pietromonaco, P., 289, 536
Pillai, A.L., 436
Pinker, S., 236, 237
Pipe, S.M., 230
Pipp, S., 194
Pisoni, D.B., 141
Pitts, D.G., 514
Pizzigati, K., 271
Platsidou, M., 21
Platt, 591
Plomin, R., 26, 32, 53, 56, 61, 65, 325, 416
Plonczynski, D.J., 519
Plosker, G., 514
Podolski, C., 279
Poest, C.A., 218
Polivka, B., 216
Polivy, J., 447
Polkinghorne, D.E., 34
Pollack, W., 410
Pollak, S., 216
Pollard, J., 307
Pollitt, E., 133, 288
Pomares, C.G., 141
Pomerlau, O.F., 498
Pomeroy, W.B., 435
Ponirakis, 372
Poon, H.F., 589
Porath, 79
Porges, S.W., 142
Porter, L.W., 142, 620
Posner, 243
Poulain, M., 293
Poulin, M., 203
Poulin-Dubois, D., 204, 255
Poulton, R., 69
Powell, R., 231, 287
Power, T.G., 260
Pratt, H., 373, 543
Prechtl, H.F.R., 128
Prescott, C., 68, 141
Presnell, 416
Pressley, M., 303, 381
Prezbindowski, A.K., 33
Price, D.W., 64, 81, 229
Prigerson, H., 584
Prime, 515
Prince, M., 97, 513
Prohaska, T., 364
Propper, C., 61, 202
Pruchno, R., 628
Pruzek, 134
Puchalski, M., 142
Pufall, P., 301
Pulkkinen, L., 431
Pungello, E.P., 241
Puntambekar, S., 233
Purdy, M., 587
Putney, N.M., 556
Putterman, E., 447
Pyryt, M.C., 409

Qian, Z-C, 487
Quartz, S.R., 27
Quatromoni, P., 447
Quinn, J.B., 555
Quinnan, E.J., 612

Raag, T., 255
Rabain-Jamin, J., 175
Rabkin, J., 641
Radke-Yarrow, M., 275
Radmacher, S., 529
Radojevic, M., 194
Radwan, 319
Raeff, C., 421
Raggi, 298
Rahman, Q., 436
Rakison, D., 151
Raman, L., 214
Ramani, 261
Ramey, C.T., 241
Ramey, S.L., 239
Ramsay, D.S., 188, 260
Ramsey-Rennels, J.L., 140
Ranade, V., 214
Rankin, B., 242, 425
Ransjo-Arvidson, A.B., 93
Ratanachu-Ek, S., 133
Rattner, A., 579
Raudsepp, L., 291
Rautava, P., 80
Ray, O., 449
Rayner, R., 312
Raz, S., 290, 577
Razani, L., 580
Rebok, G.W., 579
Reddy, V., 169
Redman, 157
Redshaw, M.E., 90
Reese, E., 246
Reeve, H.K., 573
Reider, R.O., 434
Reiner, W.G., 73
Reinisch, J.M., 435
Reinke, 57
Reis, H.T., 26
Reis, S., 326
Reiss, M.J., 267, 277
Reker, G.T., 643
Remein, R., 641
Renzulli, J., 326
Reschly, D.J., 322
Rescorla, L., 168
Resnick, G., 192, 423, 586
Ressner, J., 639
Resta, R., 56
Reutzel, R., 177
Revonsuo, A., 216
Reyna, V.F., 158, 383
Reynolds, M.C., 323
Rhoades, G., 492
Rholes, W., 490
Rhule, D., 37
Ricciardelli, L.A., 410
Rice, F.P., 241, 481
Richards, M.H., 303, 353, 426
Richardson, A., 63, 417
Richardson, G.A., 79
Rideout, V.J., 166, 240,
    279, 290
Riebe, D., 575
Riley, B., 555
Rime, B., 202
Rimpela, M., 368
Rinaldi, C, 346
Ripple, C.H., 216, 245
Risley, T.R., 238
Ritzen, E.M., 369
Rivers, I., 436
Roberts, B., 176, 199, 370, 416, 492,
    499, 555
Robins, R., 409

Robinson, D.L., 63, 165, 189, 240, 245,
    305, 326, 566
Rochat, P., 186, 188
Roche, T., 358
Rockney, R., 220
Roeder, K., 65
Roelofs, J., 194
Roeyers, H., 382
Roffwarg, H.P., 124
Rogers, Carl, 22, 28
Rogers, Williams, 110
Roggeveen, A.B., 515
Rogish, F., 270
Rogoff, B., 21, 157
Romaine, S., 307
Roman-Vinas, 513
Ronka, A., 431
Roopnarine, J., 195, 260, 261
Rose, A.J., 164, 165, 217, 346, 494
Rose, R.J., 53, 68
Rosen, K., 194, 196, 276, 516
Rosenblatt, Eli, 656
Rosenman, R.H., 526
Rosenstein, D., 142
Rosenthal, G.E., 192, 362, 363, 421,
    472, 629
Ross, C.E., 229, 277, 436, 553
Rossouw, J.E., 519
Rotenberg, K.J., 473
Roth, D., 157
Roth, W.T., 447
Rothbart, M.K., 200
Rothbaum, F., 196, 422
Rothberg, S.T., 535, 574
Rovee-Collier, Carolyn, 161
Rovine, M., 193
Rowan, G.T., 254
Rowe, D.C., 63, 581, 622
Rubenstein, A.J., 140
Rubin, D., 260, 426, 497
Rubinow, D.R., 518
Ruble, D., 203, 257, 258
Ruff, H.A., 143
Ruffman, T., 157
Rule, B.G., 240
Rush, 387
Russell, D., 194, 435, 583
Rust, J., 256, 257
Rutter, M., 13, 53, 56, 430
Ryan, C., 436, 532
Ryan, E.B., 303
Rycek, R.F., 382

Saar, M., 291
Sabeau-Jouannet, E., 175
Sacks, K., 454
Sadker, D., 468, 470
Sadker, M., 468
Saeljoe, R., 262
Saez, L., 307
Saffran, J., 141, 175
Sage, 357
Sagi, A., 192
Sagrestano, L.M., 423
Saito, Y., 642
Sales, B.D., 40
Sallis, J.F., 290, 454
Salovey, P., 365, 460
Salthouse, Timothy, 443, 533, 536, 578
Sameroff, A.J., 202
Sammel, H., 518
Sampson, P.D., 80
Samuelson, I., 260
Sanchez, M.C., 307, 417

Sandberg, D.E., 287, 354
Sanders, P., 176
Sanders, S., 435
Sanderson, S., 290, 433
Sandis, E., 573
Sandoval, J., 322
Sandrin, D., 142
Sang, B., 303
Sangree, W.H., 609
Sanoff, A.P., 427
Santini, D.L., 78
Saraswathi, T., 157
Sarrel, P.M., 519
Sasser-Coen, J.R., 461
Sattler, J.M., 532
Saults, J., 302
Saunders, J., 411
Savage-Rumbaugh, E.S., 173
Savin-Williams, R., 411, 433, 490
Sawatzky, 586
Sawicki, M.A., 81
Sax, L., 297
Scadden, L., 498
Scarr, S., 65, 243
Scelfo, J., 298
Schaefer, C., 260, 449
Schaffer, C., 276
Schaie, K. Warner, 457–458, 532, 533,
    594, 595
Scharfe, E., 182
Scharrer, E., 257
Schatz, M., 156
Schaufeli, W., 561
Schecter, 79
Scheiber, F., 579
Scheier, M.F., 529
Schellenbach, C., 271
Schellenberg, E.G., 140
Schemo, D.J., 312, 325, 384, 385
Scher, S.J., 27
Scherer, M., 140, 323
Schick, K., 230
Schieber, F., 536
Schieman, S., 505
Schiffer, A.A., 526
Schiller, J.S., 202
Schirrer, 141
Schkade, D.A., 549
Schlegel, A., 424
Schlossberg, Nancy, 620
Schmalz, D., 203
Schmidt, M., 81, 518
Schmitt, E., 415
Schmitt-Rodermund, E., 371
Schmuckler, 156
Schneider, E.L., 381, 515
Schneiderman, E., 529
Schnieder, 192
Schnur, E., 245
Schoenfeld, F.B., 294
Schofer, 293
Schoppe-Sullivan, S.J., 194, 202
Schore, A., 184
Schrander-Stumpl, 56
Schrieber, G.B., 289
Schuetze, 79
Schulman, P., 177
Schultz, R., 411
Schulz, R., 584, 648
Schuster, C.S., 216
Schutt, R.K., 31
Schutz, H., 425
Schwartz, C.E., 422, 433
Schwenkhagen, A., 517, 519
Sciaraffa, M.A., 203

Scopesi, A., 88
Scott, Mary, 275, 375
Scrimsher, S., 232, 235
Scruggs, T.E., 323
Sears, R.R., 326
Seaton, 481
Sedikides, C., 480
Segal & Segal, 298
Segal, B.M., 63
Segal, J., 298
Segal, Z., 298
Seidman, S.N., 434, 588
Seier, W.L., 231
Seifer, R., 202
Seligman, L., 529
Sellers, 481
Semerci, C., 339
Sener, A., 621
Senghas, A., 169
Serbin, L.A., 203, 204, 255, 558
Serra-Majem, 513
Servin, A., 256
Sesser, S., 393
Settersten, R., 613
Shackelford, 26
Shaffer, R.G., 433
Shapiro, L., 214, 231, 498
Sharf, R.S., 562
Sharma, Y.S., 487
Shaunessy, E., 326
Shaver, P., 192, 489, 490
Shaw, D.S., 312
Shay, J.W., 590
Shaywitz, S.E., 296
Shea, J.D., 98, 379, 518
Sheets, R.H., 254
Sheldon, K.M., 23, 59, 479, 480
Shen, Y.-C., 497
Sheppard, A., 355
Sheridan, C., 529
Sheu, C., 221
Shields, 359
Shimizu, M., 449
Shin, H.B., 306
Shiner, R., 199
Shiono, P.H., 96
Shirley, L., 255
Shonk, S.M., 270
Shopper, M., 356
Shreve, 336
Shrum, W., 427
Shumow, 243
Shurkin, J.N., 326
Shuster, 410
Shute, N., 93
Sieber, J.E., 40
Siegel, M., 164
Siegler, I.C., 156
Siegler, Robert S., 158, 229, 231, 626
Sierra, F., 589
Sigman, M.D., 133, 164, 165, 396
Silbereisen, R., 371
Silliman, E.R., 296
Silver, R.C., 626
Silverstein, L.B., 194
Silverthorn, P., 430
Simmons, R, 372
Simons, M., 142, 265
Simonton, D.K., 461
Simpson, J.A., 192, 490
Simson, S.P., 598
Sinclair, D.A., 591
Singer, D.G., 79
Singh, G.K., 385, 483
Sinnott, J., 457, 458

Sippola, L.K., 426
Six, L.S., 537
Skinner, B.F., 19, 28, 173, 1332
Skipper, J.K., 433
Slade, M.D., 157
Slater, A., 106, 279
Slavin, R.E., 304
Slep, A., 269
Sliwinski, M., 443
Slone, M., 157
Small, B.J., 584
Smedley, B.D., 9, 527
Smetana, J., 421, 422, 423, 424
Smit, F., 608
Smith, A., 87
Smith, A.P., 130, 177
Smith, D., 580
Smith, E., 267, 271, 295
Smith, P.K., 357, 449, 451
Smuts, A.B., 266
Snarey, J.R., 339
Snidman, N., 61, 66
Snowdon, D.A., 584
Snyder, J., 265, 363
Soenen, 75
Soken, N.H., 186
Soldo, B.J., 556
Sontag, S., 64, 576
Sophian, C., 228
Sorensen, K., 64
Sosa, B.B., 231
Sotirou, A., 332
Sotos, J.F., 55
Sousa, 312
Soussignan, R., 142, 184
Sowell, E.R., 443
Spearman, C., 319
Spelke, E.S., 165
Spence, S.H., 513, 551
Spencer, M.B., 296, 427
Spiegel, D., 529
Spieker, D., 194
Spira, A., 435
Spitzer, 121
Spohr, H.L., 79
Spratt, 193
Sprecher, S., 486
Springen, K., 408
Springer, K., 216
Squatriglia, C., 637
Squire, S., 162
Srivastava, S., 543, 547, 548
Sroufe, L.A., 183, 184, 192, 263
Stahl, S.M., 246
Stalvey, B., 579
Stanhope, R., 288
Stanjek, K., 275
Stanley, J.C., 492
Stanton, J.C., 215
Stark, 245
State, 53
Staub, 274
Staunton, 123
Stedman, L.C., 384, 385
Steele, C., 472
Steffen, V.J., 503
Stein, J.A., 92, 98
Steinberg, J.H., 285, 375, 430
Steinberg,, L., 423
Steiner, J.E., 141, 142
Steinert, S., 590
Steinhausen, H.C., 79
Steinmetz, S.K., 269
Stephens, C., 518
Stern, G., 534

Sternberg, J., 315, 317, 483, 484
Sternberg, R., 319, 321, 459, 462
Stevens, N., 274, 482
Stevens-Ratchford, R.G., 608
Stewart, A.J., 140, 544, 545, 552
Stice, E., 372, 416
Stolberg, S.G., 101, 393
Stone, C., 436
Storfer, M., 65
Stratton, 134
Strauch, B., 294
Straus, M.A., 268, 269, 557
Streissguth, A., 80
Strelau, J., 202
Striano, T., 186, 187
Stroebe, W., 640
Stuart-Hamilton, I., 21
Stutzer, A., 493
Styfco, S.J., 206, 245
Sugarman, D.B., 269, 379
Suinn, R.M., 451
Suitor, J.J., 429
Sullivan, M., 161, 182, 469, 486
Suls, J., 253
Sumartojo, E., 396
Sun, J., 579
Super, C.M., 124, 132
Suro, R., 487
Susman, E.J., 372
Sussman, M.B., 616
Sussman, S.K., 616
Sutherland, R., 230
Sutton, J., 229
Svejda, M., 187
Swaim, R., 279, 449
Swanson, H., 307
Swanson, L.A., 175
Swiatek, M., 327
Syme, S.L., 527
Szaflarski, J., 217
Szarko, J., 327
Szeminska, A., 225
Szkrybalo, J., 203, 258
Szuchman, L.T., 535, 574

Taga, K., 371
Takala, M., 304
Tallandini, M., 97
Tamis-LeMonda, C., 165, 194, 241, 266
Tan, H., 97
Tang, W.R., 99
Tangney, J., 341
Tannen, D., 176
Tanner, E., 132, 133
Tanzi, R.E., 588
Tappin, D., 220
Tardiff, C., 192, 263
Tardiff, T., 170
Tarin, D., 590
Taris, T., 561
Tartamella, L., 290
Tasker, F.L., 436
Tate, D.C., 428
Tatum, B., 336
Taveras, E., 290
Taylor, D.M., 97, 193, 255, 307, 314, 357, 586
Taylor, Shelley, 450, 536
Teerikangas, O.M., 202
Teicher, M.H., 270
Tellegen, Auke, 65
ten Kroode, H.F., 57
Tenenbaum, H.R., 176
Tepper, L., 372

Terman, Oden, 38, 326
Terry, D., 102
Terziglu, 621
Tessier, R., 589, 591
Tessor, A., 253
Teutsch, C., 647
Tharp, R.G., 232
Thelen, Esther, 121, 130
Theokas, 331
Thiessen, E., 175
Thoman, Whitney, 122
Thomas, A., 15, 202, 575
Thompson, R.A., 185, 193, 374, 443
Thordstein, M., 121
Thornberry, T.P., 431
Thornton, J., 456, 573
Thorsdottir, I., 134
Thorsheim, H.I., 608
Tincoff, R., 168
Ting, Y., 506
TInsley, B., 396
Tisserand, D., 577
Toga, A.W., 374, 443
Toguchi, Y., 480
Tolchinsky, L., 8
Tomblin, J.B., 80
Tongsong, T., 73
Topolnicki, D.M., 563
Toschke, A.M., 134
Toth, A.L., 416
Tracy, J., 489
Trainor, L.J., 111, 141, 176
Trautwein, U., 311
Trehub, S.E., 140, 141
Trelease, J., 410
Tremblay, R.E., 276
Trickett, P.K., 271
Trippet, S.E., 562
Troll, L.E., 513
Tronick, E.Z., 41, 197
Tropp, L., 336, 428
Trotter, A., 387
Trzesniewski, K.H., 333, 409
Tsao, F.-M., 166, 169, 175
Tseng, V., 421
Tucker, M., 492
Tudge, J., 232, 235
Turati, C., 140
Turkheimer, E., 322
Turner, J.C., 498
Turner-Bowker, D.M., 257
Twenge, J.M., 333
Twomey, J., 57
Tyre, P., 298, 311
Tyrrell, D.A., 449

Uauy, R., 121
Uhlenberg, P., 552, 624
Ulusoy, M., 561
Umana-Taylor, A., 314, 416
Umberson, D., 552
Underwood, M., 40, 276
Unger, R.K., 203, 410, 502
Updegraff, K.A., 409, 422
Urquidi, V., 590
Uwaydat, 579
Uylings, H., 12

Vaccaro, 187
Vaillant, George, 500, 501, 543
Vaillant, T., 501
Vaish, A., 186, 187

Vajragupta, O., 589, 591
Valente, S.M., 436
Van Balen, F., 50
van den Beld, A.W., 577
van den Wittenboer, 497
van der Lely, A.J., 577
van der Mark, I., 189
van Earp, T.G.M., 68
van Gundy, K., 505
van Hofsten, 229
van Horn, J., 561
van Kleeck, A., 246
Van Manen, S., 536
Van Meter, 303
Van tassel-Baska, J., 411
van Wormer, K., 436
van't Spijker, A., 57
Vandell, D.J., 205, 243
Vandenberg, L.R., 260
Vanderburg, 234
Vanderwater, E.A., 240, 279, 290, 545
VanLaningham, J., 552
vanMarle, 160
Vanmechelen, E., 584
Vargha-Khadem, 162
Vartanian, 383
Vaughn, V., 50, 296
Vazquez, 497
Vedantam, S., 294, 596
Veevers, 555
Vellutino, F.R., 311
Veneziano, R., 194
Veras, 515
Vereijken, C.M., 195
Verhulst, 164, 294
Verkerk, G., 104
Verkuyten, M., 411
Vernon, J.A., 65, 574
Vernooy, A.R., 305
Verny, T.R., 81
Vidaver, R.M., 524
Vierthaler, J., 640
Vilette, B., 228
Villarosa, L., 436, 495
Vinovakis, 245
Vitaliano, P.P., 584, 626
Vitaro, F., 346
Vizmanos, B., 368
Volkow, N.D., 297
Volling, B.L., 194
von Wedel, H., 580
Voss, L.D., 287
Votruba-Drzal, E., 243
Vyas, S., 314
Vygotsky, Lev, 25, 26, 28, 232, 261, 303, 319

Wachs, T., 61, 288
Wade, N., 173
Wahler, J., 516
Wahlin, T., 58
Waite, B.E., 492
Wakefield, M., 81
Wakschalg, L.S., 80
Walberg, H.J., 323
Walcott, D., 373
Walden, T.A., 110
Waldfogel, J., 102
Walker, L.E., 557, 579
Walker, N.C., 93
Walker-Andrews, A.S., 186
Wallace, I.F., 238
Walster, E., 483, 513
Walter, A., 446, 487

Wang, S., 157, 229, 253, 266, 323, 352, 620
Ward, C.M., 515, 551
Wardle, J., 290
Warin, J., 258
Warkentin, V., 188
Warnock, F., 142
Warren, J.R., 79
Warshak, R.A., 554
Wartella, E.A., 166, 240, 279, 290
Wass, H., 644
Wasserman, G., 216
Waterhouse, J.M., 121
Waterland, R.A., 63
Waterman, A., 411
Waters, E., 190, 192
Watkinson, B., 80, 410
Watson, J., 107
Watson, John B., 18, 28, 263
Watts-English, T., 270
Waugh, E., 196
Waxler, C.Z., 275
Weaver, A., 554
Webb, R.M., 327
Webster, J., 608
Wechsler, H., 315, 391
Weed, K., 303
Wei, J., 528
Weichold, K., 371
Weigel, D., 177
Weinberg, M.K., 90, 104, 436
Weinberger, D.R., 375
Weiner, Bernard, 359
Weinfield, N.S., 192
Weiss, A.S., 290, 321
Weissman, D., 217
Weitzman, E., 391
Wellman, H.M., 263, 381
Werker, 141
Werker, J.F., 175

Werner, E.E., 140, 271, 276
Wertheim, E.H., 425
Wertsch, J.V., 235
West, S., 325
Westemann, 217
Westerhausen, R., 256
Wethington, E., 545
Wexler, B., 12
Whalen, C.K., 297
Whaley, B.B., 81, 296
Wheeldon, L.R., 236
Wheeler, G., 361
Whelan, T., 195
Whitaker, B., 289
Whitbourne, S.K., 17, 574, 578, 590, 614
White, B.L., 233, 263, 295, 495
Whitehurst, G.J., 239
Whiting, B.B., 255
Whitman, R., 217
Whyte, M.K., 484
Widdiecombe, S., 574
Widstrom, 75
Wiesman, 483
Wiggins, 579
Wilcox, A., 101, 144, 417, 525, 555
Wildberger, S., 77
Wiley, 514
Wilhelm, B., 556
Wilkinson, 59
Williams, B., 214, 553
Willis, S., 535, 596
Willis, Sherry, 467
Willott, J., 515, 570
Wilson, J.F., 229, 257, 436, 514
Wilson, L.B., 641
Wimmer, H., 263
Windle, M., 431
Winer, G., 214
Wines, M., 14
Winger, G., 76

Wingert, P., 416, 519
Wingfield, A., 580
Wink, P., 543
Winn, R.L., 587
Winner, E., 611
Winsler, A., 25, 234, 238
Winstead, B.A., 417
Winterich, J., 518
Wisborg, K., 81
Wismer Fries, A., 216
Witelson, S., 217
Witt, S.D., 257
Woike, B., 462
Wolfe, W., 584, 586, 603
Wong, P.T., 643
Wood, D., 50, 263, 421, 433, 487
Woods, A.M., 76
Woolf, A., 293
Woolston, 290
Worell, F., 370
Worobey, J., 200
Worrell, F., 327
Wortman, C.B., 626, 657
Wright, J.C., 40, 240, 257, 307, 314, 590
Wu, B., 424
Wu, C., 584
Wyer, R., 381
Wynn, Karen, 160, 228

Xia, Y., 410
Xiaohe, X., 484

Yan, G., 21, 6298
Yang, R., 174
Yardley, J., 103
Yarnell, J., 587
Yarrow, L., 275
Yell, M.L., 323

Yelland, G.W., 307
Yildiz, 577
Yinger, J., 312
Yip, T., 481
Yodanis, C.L., 557
Yoshinaga-Itaano, C., 295
Young, H., 430
Young, V., 591
Youniss, J., 425
Yu, A.P., 218, 219
Yu, H.C., 430
Yuill, N., 274

Zafeiriou, D.I., 128
Zafiropoulou, M., 332
Zahn-Waxler, C., 189, 195, 275, 276
Zalenski, R., 23
Zalsman, G., 416
Zampi, C., 124124
Zauszniewski, J.A., 17
Zea, Maria, 446
Zeedyk, M., 110
Zeidner, M., 460
Zelazo, Philip R., 127, 156, 185, 302
Zeman, J., 276
Zernike, K., 298
Zerwas, 261
Zettergren, 429
Zhang, Y., 80, 289, 421
Zhe, C., 231
Zhou,D., 276, 525, 584
Zhu, J., 97, 317
Zigler, E.F., 206, 216, 243, 245, 326
Zimmerman, M.A., 191, 214
Zion, C., 468
Zito, J., 214
Ziv, M., 263
Zotti, A., 584
Zuckerman, M., 65

Subject Index

Abortion, 75, 76
Abstract modeling, 275
Accommodation, 151
Achieving stage, 458
Acquisitive stage, 458
Active life spans, 586
Activity theory, 613
Acute battering incident, 558
Addictive drugs, 389, 391
Adolescence
  acquired immunodeficiency
    syndrome (AIDS), 394
  addictive drugs, 389, 391
  adolescent egocentrism, 382
  alcohol use, 391–392
  alcoholics, 391
  anorexia nervosa, 373–374
  autonomy, quest for, 420–422
  bicultural identity, 415
  body image, 370
  bulimia, 373–374
  cliques, 425
  cognitive growth, 374–376
  controversial adolescents, 428
  crowds, 425
  cultural assimilation model, 415
  dating, 432–433
  depression and suicide, 416–419
  dropping out of school, 387–388
  early maturation, 370–371
  ethnic and racial differences, 385
  false consensus effect, 391
  formal operational stage, 378
  gender relations, 426–427
  generation gap, 422–425
  identify, focus on, 408–409
  identity achievement, 414
  identity diffusion, 414
  identity foreclosure, 414
  identity formation, 411–413
  identity, race, and ethnicity,
    415–416
  identity-*versus*-identity-confusion
    stage, 411
  illegal drug use, 389
  imaginary audience, 382
  information processing
    perspective, 381–382
  Internet, and the, 386–387
  juvenile delinquency, 430–431
  late maturation, 371–372
  Marcia's approach to identity
    development, 413–414
  masturbation, 433–434
  menarche, 368
  metacognition, 381
  moratorium, 414
  neglected adolescents, 428
  obesity, 372
  online gambling, 431
  parents, conflicts with, 423–424
  peer pressure, 429–430
  peers, relationships with, 425–427
  permissiveness with affection, 435
  personal fables, 383
  physical maturation, 366–367
  Piagetian approaches, 378–381

  pluralistic society model, 415
  popularity and rejection, 428–429
  primary sex characteristics, 369
  psychological moratorium,
    412–413
  puberty, 367–370
  race segregation, 427–428
  reference groups, 425
  rejected adolescents, 428
  relationships, impact of changing,
    420–42
  school performance, 383–384
  secondary sex characteristics, 369
  secular trend, 369
  self-concept, 409
  self-esteem, 409–410
  sex cleavage, 426
  sexual orientation, 435–436
  sexual relationships, 433–435
  sexually transmitted infections,
    394–399
  sleep deprivation, 375
  smoking, and, 393
  social comparison, 425–427
  socialized delinquents, 431
  societal pressures and reliance on
    friends and peers, 412
  socioeconomic status and school
    performance, 385
  spermarche, 369
  teenage pregnancies, 436–437
  undersocialized delinquents, 430
Adolescent egocentrism, 382
Adult day-care facilities, 617
Adulthood
  attachment styles and romantic
    relationships, 489–490
  choosing a partner, 485–489
  combinations of love, 484
  decision/commitment component,
    484
  developmental tasks, 478
  Erikson's view of young adulthood,
    481
  falling in love, 482–483
  filtering models, 487–488
  gay and lesbian relationships,
    490–491
  homogamy, 487
  intimacy component, 484
  intimacy-*versus*-isolation stage, 481
  labeling theory of passionate love,
    483
  marriage gradient, 487
  parenthood, transition to, 497–498
  passion component, 484
  passionate and compassionate love,
    483–484
  relationships, course of, 491–500
  social clocks of, 480–481
  spouse, seeking a, 485–486
  Sternberg's Triangular Theory, 484
  stimulus-value-role theory,
    482–483
Affordances, 144
Age of viability, 97
Age ranges, role of, 6

Age stratification theories, 609–610
Age-graded influences, 10
Age-related macular degeneration
  (AMD), 579
Ageism, 573
Agentic professions, 503
Aggression, 276
  cognitive approaches to, 279–280
  emotional self-regulation, 276
  instrumental aggression, 276
  relational aggression, 276
  roots of, 276–277
  social learning approaches,
    277–278
  television viewing, and, 278–279
Aging, 573–574
AIDS (Acquired immunodeficiency
  syndrome), 78, 394
Ainsworth Strange Situation, 191
Alcohol use, 391–392
Alcoholics, 391
Alleles, 51
Alzheimer's disease, 583–585
Ambivalent attachment pattern, 192
Amniocentesis, 56, 57
Anal stage, 16
Androgen, 204, 256
Androgynous, 258
Anesthesia and pain-reducing drugs,
  use of, 93
Anorexia nervosa, 373–374
Anoxia, 88
Apgar scale, 88, 89
Applied research, 36
Appraisal of theory, 156–157, 228
Artificial insemination, 74
Assimilation, 20, 151
Assisted suicide, 650, 652
Associative play, 260, 261
Asthma, 292–293
Attachment, 190–191
  across cultures, 195
  styles and romantic relationships,
    489–490
Attention deficit hyperactivity
  disorder (ADHD), 297–298
Attributions, 359, 360
Auditory impairments, 295–296
Auditory perception, 140–141
Authoritarian parents, 264
Authoritative parents, 264–265
Autism, 22, 263
Autobiographical memory, 229–230,
  597
Automatization, 159
Autonomous cooperation stage, 273
Autonomy, quest for, 420–422
Autonomy-*versus*-shame-and-doubt
  stage, 200
Autostimulation, 124
Avoidant attachment pattern, 192
Axon, 118

Babbling, 169
Babinski reflex, 127
Back-to-sleep guideline, 125

Bayley Scales of Infant Development,
  163, 164
Behavior modification, 19
Behavioral genetics, 53
Behavioral perspective, 18, 19–20, 28
Behavioral states, 122
Bell Curve controversy, 322–323
Benevolent sexism, 470
Bereavement, 656
Bicultural identity, 314, 415
Bilingualism, 306–307
Binet's test, 315–316
Binocular vision, 139
Bioecological approach, 25
Biological approach, 23–24
Birthing procedures, alternative,
  91–92
Blended families, living in, 356–357
Body image, 370
Body transcendence *versus* body
  perception, 605–606
Bonding, 89, 90
Boomerang children, 555
Bradley Method, 91
Brain cell decline, 577
Brain death, 639
Brain growth, 217–218
Brain waves, 121
Braxton-Hicks contractions, 87
Breastfeeding *versus* bottle-feeding,
  135–137
Breech position, 99
Broca's area, 169
Bulimia, 373–374
Bullying, 347
Burnout, 561–562

Cancer, threat of, 527–530
Capacities, 18
Careers
  agentic professions, 503
  burnout, 561–562
  career consolidation, 500–501
  choosing a, 506
  communal professions, 503
  extrinsic motivation, 504
  fantasy period, 501
  gender and career choices, 502–504
  Ginzberg's Career Choice Theory,
    501–502
  Holland's Personality Type
    Theory, 502
  immigrants, role of, 564–565
  intrinsic motivation, 504
  midlife, jobs at, 561
  realistic period, 501
  satisfaction on the job, 505
  status, 504
  switching careers, 563
  tentative period, 501
  unemployment, 562
Case studies, 34–35
Castration anxiety, 256
Cataracts, 579
Centration, 224
Cephalocaudal principle, 117

Cerebellum, 218
Cerebral cortex, 120, 218
Cervix, 87
Cesarean delivery, 99–100
Chemotherapy, 527
Chicken pox, 78
Child abuse
    cycle of violence hypothesis, 269
    physical abuse, 267–269
    psychological maltreatment,
        269–270
    resilience, 270–271
    warning signs, 268
Child-care centers, 242
Child-rearing practices, cultural
        differences in, 266–267
Childbirth
    age of viability, 97
    anesthesia and pain-reducing drugs,
        use of, 93
    breech position, 99
    cesarean delivery, 99–100
    complications, 95–104
    dual spinal-epidural, 93
    epidural anesthesia, 93
    fetal monitors, 99
    infant mortality, 100, 101
    labor, 94
    leave polices, 102
    low-birthweight infants, 96, 98
    newborn medical screening, 94
    pain, 92–93
    postdelivery hospital stay, 93
    postmature infants, 98
    postpartum depression, 103–104
    preterm infants, 95–97
    race and infant mortality, 101
    respiratory distress syndrome
        (RDS), 96
    small-for-gestational-age infants, 96
    stillbirth, 100
    transverse position, 99
    very-low-birthweight infants, 97
    walking epidural, 93
Childbirth attendants, 92
Chlamydia, 395
Chorionic villus sampling (CVS),
        56, 57
Chromosomes, 48
Chronological (or physical) age, 316
Chronosystem, 24
Cilia, 514
Circular reaction, 153
Circumcision, 108
Classical conditioning, 18, 107–109
Cliques, 425
Cluster suicide, 417
Code-based approaches to reading, 311
Cognitive development, 6, 7, 456–462,
        593–599
    autobiographical memory, 229–230
    automatization, 159
    Bayley Scales of Infant
        Development, 163, 164
    brain growth and, 217–218
    cognitive neuroscience of
        memory, 162
    concepts, understanding of, 159–160
    cross-modal transference, 165
    developmental quotient, 163
    developmental scales, 163–164
    duration of memories, 161–162
    encoding, 159
    explicit memory, 162

forensic developmental psychology,
        230–231
    individual differences in
        intelligence, 162–167
    infant intelligence, 163
    infantile amnesia, 161
    information processing approaches,
        158, 228–232
    memory during infancy, 160–161
    multimodal approach to
        perception, 165
    myelin, 218
    preschoolers' understanding of
        numbers, 228–229
    qualitative changes, 165
    quantitative changes, 165
    retrieval, 159
    scaffolding, 233
    scripts, 230
    visual-recognition memory,
        164–165
    visual-recognition memory
        measurement, 163
    Vygotsky's view, 232–235
    zone of proximal development
        (ZPD), 233–234
Cognitive growth, 374–376
Cognitive neuroscience approaches, 22
Cognitive neuroscience of
        memory, 162
Cognitive perspective, 20, 28
Cohabitation, 492
Cohort, 9–10, 38
Cohort effects, 531, 594
Collectivism, 25
Collectivistic orientation, 253
College education
    changing college student, 466–467
    demographics of, 464–465
    dropping out of school, 473
    first-year adjustment reaction,
        467–468
    gender and college performance,
        468–470, 471
    gender gap in college attendance,
        465
    maturation reform, 467
    role of, 463–364
    stereotype threat and
        disidentification with school,
        470–472
Communal professions, 503
Comprehension, linguistic, 168
Computer safety, 293
Computerized axial tomography
        (CAT) scan, 34
Concepts, understanding of, 159–160
Concrete operational stage, 300
Conservation, 225
Constructive play, 260, 261
Contact comfort, 191
Contextual element of intelligence, 319
Contextual perspective, 23–24, 28
Continuing-care communities, 616
Continuity theory, 614
Continuos change, 11
Control group, 34
Controversial adolescents, 428
Conventional morality, 338, 339
Cooperative learning, 304
Cooperative play, 260, 261
Coregulation, 351
Correlation coefficient, 32–33
Correlational research, 31

Correlational studies, 31–32
Corticotropin-releasing hormone
        (CRH), 86
Creativity, role of, 461–462
Critical periods, 11–12
Cross-modal transference, 165
Cross-race friendships, 349
Cross-sectional research, 38–39
Crystallized intelligence, 319, 532
Cultural assimilation model, 313, 415
Cultural patterns of growth, 287
Cycle of violence hypothesis,
        269, 558–559

Dating, 432–433
Death
    adolescence, in, 641
    assisted suicide, 650, 652
    bereavement, 656
    brain death, 639
    conceptions, differing, 643–644
    definition, 638–639
    DNR, 649–650
    durable power of attorney, 650
    education programs, 644–655
    euthanasia, 650, 652
    functional death, 638–639
    funerals and mourning, 655–656
    grief, 656, 657
    health-care proxy, 650
    home care, 653
    hospice care, 653
    infancy and childhood, death in,
        639–640
    late adulthood, in, 642–643
    living wills, 650, 651
    middle adulthood, in, 642
    miscarriage, 639
    process of, 646–648
    sudden infant death syndrome
        (SIDS), 639–640
    thanatologists, 644
    voluntary active euthanasia, 652
    young adulthood, in, 641–642
Decentering, 300
Decision/commitment
        component, 484
Decoding others' facial and vocal
        expressions, 186
Dementia, 583
Dendrites, 118
Dependent variable, 35
Depression and suicide, 416–419
DES (diethylsyilbestrol), 79
Developmental change, 37–38
Developmental diversity, 8–9
Developmental quotient, 163
Developmental scales, 163–164
Developmentally appropriate
        educational practice, 245–246
Deviation IQ scores, 317
Diaries, 34
Difficult babies, 201
Discontinuous change, 11
Disengagement theory, 612–613
Disorganized-disoriented attachment
        pattern, 192
Divorce, 354–355, 552–553
Dizygotoc twins, 49
DNA (deoxyribonucleic acid)
        molecules, 48
DNA-based gene tests, 58
DNR, 649–650

Dominance hierarchy, 348
Dominant trait, 51
Doulas, 92
Down syndrome, 55, 324
Dual spinal-epidural, 93
Dual-earner couples, 496–497
Dualistic thinking, 457
Durable power of attorney, 650
Duration of memories, 161–162

Early adulthood
    cognitive development, 456–462
    college, 463–473
    creativity, role of, 461–462
    intellectual growth, 456
    intelligence, 459–462
    life events and cognitive
        development, 462
    motor functioning, 443–444
    nutrition, role of, 447
    obesity, 447
    Perry's approach to postformal
        thinking, 457
    physical development, 442–443
    physical disabilities, 449
    postformal thought, 456–457
    Schaie's stages of development,
        457–458
    senescence, 443
    stress, and, 449, 450
Early childhood education
    child-care centers, 242
    developmentally appropriate
        educational practice, 245–246
    effectiveness of, 243
    family child-care centers, 242
    Head Start, 245
    international comparison, 244
    Montessori approach, 246
    preschools, 242
    purpose of, 244
    quality of, 243
    role of, 242
    school child care, 243
Early marital conflict, 494–495
Early maturation, 370–371
Easy babies, 201
Ectoderm, 72
Education programs, 644–655
Effective parenting skills, 264–265
Ego transcendence versus ego
        preoccupation, 606
Ego-integrity-versus-despair stage, 605
Egocentric thought, 226–227
Elder abuse, 632
Electroencephalogram (EEG), 34, 121
Embryonic stage, 72
Embryoscopy, 57
Emotional intelligence, 364–366, 460
Emotional self-regulation, 276
Emotions in infancy, 182–184
Empathy, 189, 275
Empty nest syndrome, 554–555
Encoding, 159, 302
Endoderm, 72
Enrichment, 327
Environmental influences, 65–66
Epidural anesthesia, 93
Episiotomy, 87–88
Erectile dysfunction, 520
Erikson's Stage of Generativity versus
        Stagnation, 543
Erikson's theory, 412, 413

Erikson's theory of psychosocial development, 200
Erikson's view of young adulthood, 481
Ethgender, 411
Ethnography, 33
Ethology, 26
Euthanasia, 650, 652
Evolutionary perspective, 26, 27, 28
Executive stage, 458
Exercise, benefits of, 516
Exosystem, 23
Expectation effects, 362–363
Experiencing emotions, 184
Experiential element of intelligence, 319
Experiment, 34–35
Experimental group, 34
Experimental research, 31
Expertise, development of, 534–535
Explicit memory, 162
Expressive style, 172
Extrinsic motivation, 504
Extroversion, 65

False consensus effect, 391
False labor, 87
Familial retardation, 324
Family child-care centers, 242
Family lives, 264
Family relationships, role of, 629–632
Family size, 496
Fantasy period, 501
Fast mapping, 236
Fathers and attachment, 194
Fathers and the prenatal environment, 80–81
Female climacteric, 517
Fertility rate, 496
Fertilization, 70–71
Fetal alcohol effects (FAE), 80
Fetal alcohol syndrome (FAS), 79, 324
Fetal blood sampling, 57
Fetal monitors, 99
Fetal stage, 72–73
Fetus, 72
Field study, 36
Filtering models, 487–488
First words, 170
First-trimester screen, 56
First-year adjustment reaction, 467–468
Fixation, 17
Fluid intelligence, 319, 532
Forensic developmental psychology, 230–231
Formal operational stage, 378
Fragile X syndrome, 55
Free will, 22
Friendships, development of, 259–260
Full inclusion, 324
Functional death, 638–639
Functional magnetic resonance imaging (fMRI) scan, 34
Functional play, 260, 261
Functionality, 227
Funerals and mourning, 655–656

Gamete intrafallopian transfer (GIFT), 74
Gardner's eight intelligences, 320
Gay and lesbian relationships, 357, 490–491, 498–499

Gender
  androgynous, 258
  approaches to gender development, 258
  career choices, and, 502–504
  cognitive approaches, 257–258
  college performance, and, 468–470, 471
  definition, 203
  differences, gender, 203
  gender constancy, 258
  gender identity, 257
  gender schema, 257
  roles, gender, 203–204
  social learning approaches, 257
Gender constancy, 258
Gender differences, 176
Gender gap in college attendance, 465
Gender identity, 254–259, 257
Gender relations, 426–427
Gender schema, 257
Generalized slowing hypothesis, 578
Generation gap, 422–425
Generativity *versus* stagnation stage, 17
Genes, 48
Genetic counseling, 56–57
Genetic programming theories of aging, 588
Genetics
  alleles, 51
  amniocentesis, 56, 57
  behavioral genetics, 53
  chorionic villus sampling (CVS), 56, 57
  chromosomes, 48
  dizygotic twins, 49
  DNA (deoxyribonucleic acid) molecules, 48
  DNA-based gene tests, 58
  dominant trait, 51
  Down syndrome, 55
  embryoscopy, 57
  environmental influences, 65–66
  fetal blood sampling, 57
  first-trimester screen, 56
  Fragile X syndrome, 55
  genes, 48
  genetic counseling, 56–57
  genotype, 51
  germ line therapy, 59
  heterozygous, 51
  homozygous, 51
  influence on the environment, 69
  inhaled air and genetic mutations, 54
  inherited and genetic disorders, 54–56
  karotype, 56
  Klinefelter's syndrome, 55
  meiosis, 49
  mitosis, 49
  monozygotic twins, 49
  multiple births, 49–50
  ovum, 48
  phenotype, 51
  phenylketonuria (PKU), 51
  polygenic inheritance, 52
  polygenic traits, 52
  preimplantation genetic diagnosis (PGD), 59
  prenatal testing, 56
  psychological disorders, 68–69
  reaction range, 52
  recessive trait, 51

  sex of a child, establishing, 50
  sickle-cell anemia, 55
  sonoembryology, 57
  sonogram, 57
  spontaneous mutation, 55
  Tay-Sachs disease, 55
  transmission of genetic information, 51–52
  Turner syndrome, 55
  ultrasound sonography, 56, 57
  x-linked genes, 52
  zygote, 48
Genital herpes, 395
Genital stage, 16
Genotype, 51
Germ line therapy, 59
Germinal stage, 71–72
Gifted and talented, 325–326
Ginzberg's Career Choice Theory, 501–502
Glaucoma, 514, 579
Gonorrhea, 395
Goodness-of-fit, 202
Gould's Transformation in adult development, 544
Grammar, 237
Grandparent, becoming a, 556–557
Grief, 656, 657
Group care, 357–358

Habituation, 109
Hair cells, 514
Happiness, components of, 479–480
Head Start, 245
Health-care proxy, 650
Hearing, 514–515
Height, changes in, 513–514
Hemispheres, 73
Hemophilia, 52, 53
Heredity and environment, interaction of, 60–62
Heteronomous morality, 273
Heterozygous, 51
Hierarchical integration, principle of, 118
History-graded influences, 10
Holland's Personality Type Theory, 502
Holophrases, 170
Home care, 653
Home environment, role of the, 351–359
Homogamy, 487
Homozygous, 51
Hormone therapy, 519
Hormones, use of, 287–288
Hospice care, 653
Human papilloma virus (HPV), 395
Humanistic perspective, 22–23, 28
Husband-coached childbirth, 91
Hypertension, 580
Hypnobirthing, 92
Hypothesis, 30
Hyssaelae, 80

Identification, 256
Identify, focus on, 408–409
Identity, 227
Identity achievement, 414
Identity diffusion, 414
Identity foreclosure, 414
Identity formation, 411–413
Identity, race, and ethnicity, 415–416

Identity-*versus*-identity-confusion stage, 411
Illegal drug use, 389
Imaginary audience, 382
Immigrants, role of, 564–565
Imprint, 89
In vitro fertilization (IVF), 3, 74
Incipient cooperation stage, 273
Independence of systems, principle of, 118
Independent variable, 35
Individual differences in intelligence, 162–167
Individual differences, role of, 6, 8
Individualism, 25
Individualistic orientation, 253
Industry-*versus*-inferiority stage, 331
Infancy and childhood, death in, 639–640
Infancy, life cycles of
  autostimulation, 124
  behavioral states, 122
  rhythms, 121
  sleep, 121–124
Infant intelligence, 163
Infant mortality, 100, 101
Infant-directed speech, 173, 174–175
Infant-infant interaction, 198
Infantile amnesia, 161
Infants
  child care, and, 205–206
  choosing an infant care provider, 206–207
Infertility, 74–75
Information processing approaches, 21–22, 158, 228–232, 302–303
Information processing perspective, 381–382
Inhaled air and genetic mutations, 54
Inherited and genetic disorders, 54–56
Initiative-*versus*-guilt-stage, 253
Injuries, 214–215
Institutionalism, 617
Instrumental aggression, 276
Intellectual development, 299–308, 314–315
  centration, 224
  conservation, 225
  egocentric thought, 226–227
  functionality, 227
  identity, 227
  intuitive thought, emergence of, 227
  language and thought, relation between, 224
  operations, 223
  Piaget's stage of preoperational thinking, 223–224
  preoperational stage, 223
  transformation, 225–226
Intellectual growth, 456
Intelligence, 64–65, 459–462, 531–532
Intelligence quotient (IQ score), 316–317, 321
Intelligence testing, 315
Interactional synchrony, 193
Interactionist approaches, 173–174
Internal aging, 576–577
International comparison, 244
Internet, 386–387
Intimacy component, 484
Intimacy-*versus*-isolation stage, 481
Intonation, 305
Intraocular lens implants, 579

Intrinsic motivation, 504
Intuitive thought, emergence of, 227
Isovaleric acidemia (IVA), 47

Juvenile delinquency, 430–431

Karotype, 56
Kaufman Assessment Battery for
    Children, Second Edition
    (KABC-II), 317
Klinefelter's syndrome, 55

**Labeling theory of passionate love,
    483**
Labor, 86–88, 94
Laboratory study, 36
Lamaze birthing techniques, 91
Language
    babbling, 169
    Broca's area, 169
    comprehension, linguistic, 168
    expressive style, 172
    fast mapping, 236
    first words, 170
    gender differences, 176
    grammar, 237
    holophrases, 170
    infant-directed speech, 173, 174–175
    interactionist approaches, 173–174
    language, definition of, 167
    language-acquisition device
        (LAD), 173
    learning theory approach, 172–173
    morphemes, 168
    nativist approach, 173
    overextension, 172
    phonology, 168
    poverty and language development,
        238–239
    pragmatics, 238
    prelinguistic communication, 169
    private speech, 237
    production, linguistic, 168
    referential style, 172
    roots of, 167
    semantics, 168
    sentences, 170–171
    sign language, 170
    social speech, 238
    speech capabilities, 237
    syntax, 236
    telegraphic speech, 171, 172
    underextension, 172
    universal grammar, 173
Language-acquisition device
    (LAD), 173
Lanugo, 89
Latchkey children, 354
Late adulthood
    activity theory, 613
    adult day-care facilities, 617
    age stratification theories, 609–610
    ageism, 573
    aging, 573–574
    alzheimer's disease, 583–585
    autobiographical memory, 597
    body transcendence versus body
        perception, 605–606
    brain cell decline, 577
    caring for an aging spouse, 625–626
    cognitive development, 593–599

continuing-care communities, 616
continuity theory, 614
culture, impact of, 609–610
death of a spouse, 626–628
dementia, 583
disengagement theory, 612–613
ego-integrity-versus-despair
    stage, 605
ego transcendence versus ego
    preoccupation, 606
elder abuse, 632
family relationships, role of,
    629–632
financial issue, 618–619
generalized slowing hypothesis, 578
genetic programming theories of
    aging, 588
health and wellness, 581–587
hearing, and, 579–580
institutionalism, 617
intelligence in older people, 593–595
internal aging, 576–577
learning in later life, 598
Levinson's Final Season: The Winter
    of Life, 606–607
life expectancy, 589–590
life review, 607–608
living arrangements, 616–617
marriage, 624–628
memory, 595–598
memory changes, 597–598
myths of aging, 575
Neugarten's study, 607
osteoporosis, 576
Peck's Developmental tasks,
    605–606
peripheral slowing hypothesis, 578
personality continuity and change,
    604–608
physical development, 572
physical transitions, 574–578
plasticity, 595
postponing aging, 590–591
primary aging, 575
reaction time, slowing, 578
redefinition of self versus
    preoccupation with work
    role, 605
relationships, 623–624
secondary aging, 575
selective optimization, 614
sexuality, 587–588
skilled-nursing facilities, 617
social networks, importance of,
    628–629
social support, importance of, 629
taste and smell, 580
telomere therapy, 590
vision, and, 579
wear-and-tear theories of aging,
    588–589
wisdom, role of, 610–611
work and retirement, 619–622
Late maturation, 371–372
Lateralization, 216–217
Lead poisoning, 215–216
Learning disabilities, 296
Learning in later life, 598
Learning theory approach, 172–173
Least restrictive environment, 323
Leave polices, 102
Leisure time, 565–566
Levinson's Final Season: The Winter of
    Life, 606–607

Life events and cognitive
    development, 462
Life events models, 543
Life expectancy, 589–590, 590–593
Life review, 607–608
Lifespan approach, 11
Lifespan development, 4
    approaches to, 7
    definition, 5
Living arrangements, 616–617
Living wills, 650, 651
Long-term memory, 535
Longitudinal studies, 37–38, 38
Loving contrition stage, 558
Low-birthweight infants, 96, 98

Macrosystem, 23, 24
Macula, 579
Mainstreaming, 324
Male climacteric, 518–519
Marcia's approach to identity
    development, 413–414
Marriage, 624–628
    components of a successful
        marriage, 493
    dual-earner couples, 496–497
    early marital conflict, 494–495
    family size, 496
    fertility rate, 496
    replacement level, 496
Marriage gradient, 487
Masturbation, 433–434
Maturation, 13
Maturation reform, 467
Maximally Discriminative Facial
    Movement Coding System
    (MAX), 183
Meconium, 106
Meiosis, 49
Memory, 302, 595–598
Memory changes, 597–598
Memory during infancy, 160–161
Memory schemas, 536
Memory, role of, 535–536
Menarche, 368
Menopause, 516–517
Mental representation, 156
Mental retardation, 324–325
Mesosystem, 23
Metacognition, 381
Metal age, 316
Metalinguistic awareness, 305–306
Metamemory, 303
Microsystem, 23
Middle adulthood
    cancer, threat of, 527–530
    cohort effects, 531
    competence in, 533–534
    coronary heart disease, 525–526
    crystallized intelligence, 532
    ethnic and gender diffferences, 523
    expertise, development of,
        534–535
    fluid intelligence, 532
    intelligence, role of, 531–532
    memory, role of, 535–536
    polyphasic activities, 525
    preventative screening
        recommendations, 522
    selective optimization, 534
    socioeconomic status, role of, 523
    stress in, 524–525
    type A behavior pattern, 525

type B behavior pattern, 526
wellness and illness, 521–523
Middle childhood years
    academic success and failure, 359–362
    accidents, 293
    asthma, 292–293
    attention deficit hyperactivity
        disorder (ADHD), 297–298
    bilingualism, 306–307
    Binet's test, 315–316
    blended families, living in, 356–357
    bullying, 347
    chronological (or physical) age, 316
    computer safety, 293
    concrete operational stage, 300
    coregulation, 351
    cross-race friendships, 349
    crystallized intelligence, 319
    cultural patterns of growth, 287
    decentering, 300
    deviation IQ scores, 317
    divorce, impact of, 354–355
    dominance hierarchy, 348
    emotional intelligence, 364–366
    expectation effects, 362–363
    fluid intelligence, 319
    friendships, building, 342–347
    gay and lesbian parents, families
        with, 357
    group care, 357–358
    health, 292
    height and weight changes, 287
    home environment, role of the,
        351–359
    hormones, use of, 287–288
    information processing approaches,
        302–303
    intellectual development, 299–308,
        314–315
    intelligence quotient (IQ score),
        316–317
    intelligence testing, 315
    Kaufman Assessment Battery for
        Children, Second Edition
        (KABC-II), 317
    language development, 304–306
    latchkey children, 354
    metal age, 316
    metalinguistic awareness, 305–306
    motor development, 291–292
    multigenerational families, 356
    nutrition, 288
    obesity, 289–290
    physical development, 286–291
    Piagetian approach to cognitive
        development, 300–301
    poverty and family life, 357
    psychological disorders, 294
    race and family life, 357–358
    reading skills, development of,
        310–312
    reversibility, 300
    schooling, 308–310
    self-child care, 353–354
    self-fulfilling prophecy, 362
    sex segregation, 347–348
    single-parent families, 355–356
    social competence, 345–347
    social problem-solving, 345–346
    special needs children, 295–296
    stages of friendships, 343–344
    Stanford-Binet Intelligence Scales,
        Fifth Edition (SB), 317
    status, 343–344344

teacher expectancy effect, 362
triarchic theory of intelligence, 319
Vygotsky's approach to cognitive development and classroom instruction, 303–304
Wechsler Intelligence Scale for Children-Revised (WISC-IV), 316, 317, 318
Midlife crisis, 544, 545
Midlife transition, 544
Midlife, jobs at, 561
Midwife, 92
Mild retardation, 325
Mirror neurons, 198
Miscarriage, 75, 639
Mitosis, 49
Mnemonics, 536
Moderate retardation, 325
Monozygotic twins, 49
Montessori approach, 246
Moral development
    abstract modeling, 275
    autonomous cooperation stage, 273
    definition, 273
    empathy, 275
    heteronomous morality, 273
    incipient cooperation stage, 273
    models, 274
    Piaget's view, 273–274
    prosocial behavior, 274
    reasoning, moral, 274
    social learning approaches, 274
Moratorium, 414
Morphemes, 168
Mothers and attachment, 193–194
Motor development, 291–292
Motor functioning, 443–444
Multicultural education, 313
Multifactorial transmission, 61
Multigenerational families, 356
Multimodal approach to perception, 143–144, 165
Multiple births, 49–50
Mumps, 78
Mutual regulation model, 196–197
Myelin, 119, 218, 292
Myths of aging, 575

Nativist approach, 173
Naturalistic observation, 33–34, 35
Nature (genetic factors), 11, 12–13
Neglected adolescents, 428
Neo-Piagetian theory, 21
Neonatal jaundice, 106
Neonates, 86
Nervous system
    axon, 118
    cerebral cortex, 120
    components, 118
    dendrites, 118
    environmental influences, 120
    myelin, 119
    neurons, 118
    neurotransmitters, 118
    plasticity, 120
    sensitive period, 120
    shaken baby syndrome, 120
    synapses, 118
    synaptic pruning, 119–120
Neugarten's study, 607
Neurons, 72, 118
Neuroticism, 65
Neurotransmitters, 118
New York Longitudinal Study, 201

Newborn medical screening, 94
Newborns
    circumcision, 108
    classical conditioning, 107–109
    habituation, 109
    neonatal jaundice, 106
    operant conditioning, 109
    orienting response, 109
    physical competence, 105–106
    reflexes, 106
    sensory capabilities, 106–107
    social competence, 110–111
    states of arousal, 110–111
    swallowing reflex, 106
Non-normative life events, 10
Nonhuman animal studies, 62
Nonverbal coding, 182
Nonverbal decoding, 186
Normative-crisis models, 542–543
Nurture (environmental factors), 11, 12–13
Nutrition, 288
Nutrition, role of, 447

Obesity, 214, 289–290, 372, 447
Object permanence, 154–155
Obstetricians, 92
Oedipal conflict, 256, 275
Online gambling, 431
Onlooker play, 260
Operant conditioning, 18, 19, 109
Operations, 223
Optimization of the prenatal environment, 81
Oral stage, 16
Orienting response, 109
Osteoporosis, 444, 513, 576
Overextension, 172
Ovum, 48

Pace of life, worldwide, 567
Pain, 92–93
Pain and touch, sensitivity to, 142–143
Parallel play, 260, 261
Parent coaching, 267
Parenthood, 495–497, 497–498
Partial sightedness, 295
Particular periods, focus on, 11, 12
Pascalis, 140, 165
Passionate and compassionate love, 483–484
Peck's Developmental tasks, 605–606
Peer pressure, 429–430
Peers, relationships with, 425–427
Penis envy, 256
Perception, 138
Perimenopause, 517
Peripheral slowing hypothesis, 578
Permissive parents, 264
Permissiveness with affection, 435
Perry's approach to postformal thinking, 457
Personal fables, 383, 641
Personality continuity and change, 604–608
Personality development, 6, 7
    autonomy-versus-shame-and-doubt stage, 200
    definition, 199
    difficult babies, 201
    easy babies, 201
    Erikson's Stage of Generativity versus Stagnation, 543

Erikson's theory of psychosocial development, 200
    goodness-of-fit, 202
    Gould's Transformation in adult development, 544
    inhibition to the unfamiliar, 202
    life events models, 543
    midlife crisis, 544, 545
    midlife transition, 544
    New York Longitudinal Study, 201
    normative-crisis models, 542–543
    seasons of life theory, 544
    slow-to-warm babies, 201
    stability versus change, 547–549
    temperament, 200–202
    trust-versus-mistrust stage, 200
Persons of the opposite sex sharing living quarters (POSSLQS), 492
Phallic stage, 16, 256
Phenotype, 51
Phenylketonuria (PKU), 51
Phonemes, 305
Phonological recoding, 310
Phonology, 168
Physical abuse, 267–269
Physical competence, 105–106
Physical development, 6, 7, 442–443, 572
    body shape and structure, 213
    breastfeeding versus bottle-feeding, 135–137
    health and illness, 214
    height and weight, differences in, 213
    obesity, 214
Physical disabilities, 449
Physical growth
    cephalocaudal principle, 117
    hierarchical integration, principle of, 118
    independence of systems, principle of, 118
    infants, in, 116
    principles, 117
    proximodistal principle, 117
Physical maturation, 366–367
Physical traits, 63–64
Physical transitions, 512–513, 574–578
Piaget's stage of preoperational thinking, 223–224
Piaget's Theory of cognitive development, 20–21, 273–274, 300–301, 378–381
    accommodation, 151
    appraisal of theory, 156–157, 228
    assimilation, 151
    circular reaction, 153
    mental representation, 156
    object permanence, 154–155
    schemes, 151
    sensorimotor stage, 152–156
    substage 1: simple reflexes, 153
    substage 2: First habits and primary circular reactions, 153
    substage 3: Secondary circular reactions, 153
    substage 4: Coordination of secondary circular reactions, 154
    substage 5: Tertiary circular reaction, 155
    substage 6: Beginnings of thought, 156
    summation, 150
Placenta, 72
Plasticity, 120, 595

Pleasure principle, 15
Pluralistic society model, 314, 415
Polygenic inheritance, 52
Polygenic traits, 52
Polyphasic activities, 525
Popularity and rejection, 428–429
Postconventional morality, 338, 339
Postdelivery hospital stay, 93
Postformal thought, 456–457
Postmature infants, 98
Postpartum depression, 103–104
Postponing aging, 590–591
Potty training, 219–220
Poverty
    and family life, 357
    and language development, 238–239
Practical intelligence, 460
Pragmatics, 238, 305
Preconventional morality, 338
Preimplantation genetic diagnosis (PGD), 59
Prelinguistic communication, 169
Prenatal growth and development
    age of mother, 77–78
    alcohol use and tobacco, 79–80
    drug use by mother, 78
    ectoderm, 72
    embryonic stage, 72
    endoderm, 72
    fathers and the prenatal environment, 80–81
    fertilization, 70–71
    fetal alcohol effects (FAE), 80
    fetal alcohol syndrome (FAS), 79
    fetal stage, 72–73
    fetus, 72
    germinal stage, 71–72
    health of the mother, 78
    hemispheres, 73
    mother's diet, role of, 76–77
    mother's prenatal support, 78
    neurons, 72
    optimization of the prenatal environment, 81
    placenta, 72
    teratogen, 76
    umbilical cord, 72
Prenatal testing, 56
Preoperational stage, 223
Presbycusis, 514
Presbyopia, 514
Preschool years
    aggression and violence, 275–280
    associative play, 260, 261
    constructive play, 260, 261
    cooperative play, 260, 261
    effective parenting skills, 264–265
    family lives, 264
    friendships, development of, 259–260
    functional play, 260, 261
    injuries, 214–215
    onlooker play, 260
    parallel play, 260, 261
    theory of mind, 262–263
Preterm infants, 95–97
Preventative screening recommendations, 522
Primary aging, 575
Primary sex characteristics, 369
Private speech, 237
Production, linguistic, 168
Profound retardation, 325
Prosocial behavior, 274
Prostrate gland, 519

Proximodistal principle, 117
Psychoanalytic theory, 15–16
Psychodynamic perspective, 15, 17, 28
Psychological disorders, 68–69, 294
Psychological maltreatment, 269–270
Psychological moratorium, 412–413
Psychoneuroimmunologists, 524
Psychoneuroimmunology (PNI), 449
Psychophysiological methods, 34
Psychosexual development, 16
Psychosocial development, 17, 252–253
Psychosomatic disorders, 451
Puberty, 367–370
Punishment, 19

Qualitative changes, 165
Quantitative changes, 165

Race
    and family life, 357–358
    and infant mortality, 101
Race dissonance, 254
Race segregation, 427–428
Radiation therapy, 527
Random assignment, 35
Reaction range, 52
Reaction time, 515–516
Reaction time, 578
Reactive attachment disorder, 192–193
Reading skills, development of,
    310–312
Realistic period, 501
Reasoning, moral, 274
Recessive trait, 51
Reciprocal socialization, 197
Reciprocal teaching, 304
Reciprocal transaction, 25
Redefinition of self *versus*
    preoccupation with work
    role, 605
Reference groups, 425
Referential style, 172
Reflexes, 106
Reinforcement, 19
Reintegrative stage, 458
Rejected adolescents, 428
Relatedness and behavior, contrasting,
    62–63
Relational aggression, 276
Relationships, 623–624
    impact of changing, 420–42
    marriage, 550–551
Remarriage, 553–554
Replacement level, 496
Research setting, choosing, 36
Resemblances, family, 63–64
Resilience, 270–271
Respiratory distress syndrome
    (RDS), 96
Responsible stage, 458
Retrieval, 159
Reversibility, 300
Rhythms, 121
Roots of, 167

Sample, 36
Sandwich generation, 555
Satisfaction on the job, 505
Scaffolding, 233
Schaie's stages of development,
    457–458
Schemes, 151

School child care, 243
School performance, 383–384
Scientific method, 30
Scripts, 230
Seasons of life theory, 544
Secondary aging, 445, 575
Secondary sex characteristics, 369
Secure attachment pattern, 191
Selective optimization, 534, 614
Self, development of, 187–188
    collectivistic orientation, 253
    individualistic orientation, 253
    initiative-*versus*-guilt-stage, 253
    psychosocial development, 252–253
    race dissonance, 254
    self-concept, 253
Self-actualization, 22
Self-awareness, 188
Self-child care, 353–354
Self-concept, 253, 409
Self-esteem, 334–336, 409–410
    gender differences, 410
    socioeconomic status and race
        differences, 410–411
Self-fulfilling prophecy, 362
Self-understanding, shift in, 332
Semantics, 168
Senescence, 443
Sensation, 138
Senses, development of
    affordances, 144
    auditory perception, 140–141
    binocular vision, 139
    multimodal approach to perception,
        143–144
    pain and touch, sensitivity to,
        142–143
    perception, 138
    sensation, 138
    smell and taste, 141–142
    sound localization, 140
    visual cliff experiment, 139
    visual perception, 138–140
Sensitive period, 11, 12, 120
Sensorimotor stage, 152–156
Sensory capabilities, 106–107
Sensory memory, 535
Sentences, 170–171
Separation anxiety, 185
Sequence, 186
Sequential studies, 39
Sesame Street, 241
Severe retardation, 325
Sex cleavage, 426
Sex in middle adulthood
    erectile dysfunction, 520
    female climacteric, 517
    hormone therapy, 519
    male climacteric, 518–519
    menopause, 516–517
    perimenopause, 517
    prostrate gland, 519
Sex of a child, establishing, 50
Sex segregation, 347–348
Sexual orientation, 435–436
Sexual relationships, 433–435
Sexuality, 587–588
Sexually transmitted infections,
    394–399
Shaken baby syndrome, 120
Short-term memory, 535
Sickle-cell anemia, 55
Sign language, 170
Single-parent families, 355–356
Skilled-nursing facilities, 617

Sleep, 121–124
Sleep deprivation, 375
Slow-to-warm babies, 201
Slowing down, 515–516
Small-for-gestational-age infants, 96
Smell and taste, 141–142
Smiling, 185–186
Smoking, 393
Sociability
    Ainsworth Strange Situation, 191
    ambivalent attachment pattern, 192
    attachment across cultures, 195
    avoidant attachment pattern, 192
    contact comfort, 191
    decoding others' facial and vocal
        expressions, 186
    disorganized-disoriented
        attachment pattern, 192
    emotions in infancy, 182–184
    experiencing emotions, 184
    fathers and attachment, 194
    infant-infant interaction, 198
    interactional synchrony, 193
    Maximally Discriminative Facial
        Movement Coding System
        (MAX), 183
    mothers and attachment, 193–194
    mutual regulation model, 196–197
    nonverbal coding, 182
    nonverbal decoding, 186
    reactive attachment disorder, 192–193
    reciprocal socialization, 197
    secure attachment pattern, 191
    separation anxiety, 185
    sequence, 186
    smiling, 185–186
    social referencing, 186–187
    social smile, 185
    stranger anxiety, 184–185
Social clocks, 480–481
Social comparison, 332–333, 425–427
Social competence, 110–111, 345–347
Social construction, 6
Social development, 6, 7
Social learning approaches, 257, 274,
    277–278
Social networks, importance of,
    628–629
Social problem-solving, 345–346
Social reality, 332
Social referencing, 186–187
Social smile, 185
Social speech, 238
Social support, importance of, 629
Social world, developing with others
    in a, 9–10
Social-cognitive learning theory, 19
Socialized delinquents, 431
Sociobiologists, 277
Sociocultural theory, 25, 26
Sociocultural-graded influences, 10
Socioeconomic status, role of, 385,
    410–411, 523
Solid foods, introduction to, 137
Sonoembryology, 57
Sonogram, 57
Sound localization, 140, 514
Special needs children, 295–296
Speech capabilities, 237
Speech impairment, 296
Spermarche, 369
Spontaneous mutation, 55
Spousal abuse
    acute battering incident, 558
    coping with spousal abuse, 559

    cultural roots, 559–560
    cycle of violence hypothesis,
        558–559
    hidden epidemic, as a, 557–558
    loving contrition stage, 558
    prevalence of, 557–558
    tension building stage, 558
Spouse, seeking a, 485–486
Stability *versus* change, 547–549
Stanford-Binet Intelligence Scales,
    Fifth Edition (SB), 317
States of arousal, 110–111
Status, 343–344344, 504
Stereotype threat and disidentification
    with school, 470–472
Sternberg's Triangular Theory, 484
Stillbirth, 100
Stimulus-value-role theory, 482–483
Stranger anxiety, 184–185
Stress, 449, 452, 524–525
    coping style, 453
    coping with, 454
    defensive coping, 453
    emotion-focused coping, 452
    hardiness, 453
    primary appraisal, 450
    resilience, and, 454
    secondary appraisal, 450
    social support, 452
Stuttering, 296
Substage 1: simple reflexes, 153
Substage 2: First habits and primary
    circular reactions, 153
Substage 3: Secondary circular
    reactions, 153
Substage 4: Coordination of secondary
    circular reactions, 154
Substage 5: Tertiary circular
    reaction, 155
Substage 6: Beginnings of thought, 156
Sudden infant death syndrome (SIDS),
    124–125, 639–640
Superego, 15
Supportive parenting, 266
Surrogate mother, 74
Survey research, 34
Swallowing reflex, 106
Switching careers, 563
Synapses, 118
Synaptic pruning, 119–120
Syntax, 236
Syphilis, 78, 395

Taste and smell, 580
Tay-Sachs disease, 55
Teacher expectancy effect, 362
Teenage pregnancies, 436–437
Telegraphic speech, 171, 172
Television, role of, 239–241
Telomere therapy, 590
Temperament, 60, 200–202
Tension building stage, 558
Tentative period, 501
Teratogen, 76
Terminal decline, 643
Thalidomode, 78
Thanatologists, 644
Theoretical research, 36
Theory of mind, 189, 262–263
Transformation, 225–226
Transmission of genetic information,
    51–52
Transverse position, 99
Treatment group, 34

Triarchic theory of intelligence, 319, 459
Trichomoniasis, 395
Trust-*versus*-mistrust stage, 200
Turner syndrome, 55
Type A behavior pattern, 525
Type B behavior pattern, 526

Ultrasound sonography, 56, 57
Umbilical cord, 72
Underextension, 172
Undersocialized delinquents, 430
Unemployment, 562

Uninvolved parents, 265
Universal grammar, 173

Vernix, 89
Very-low-birthweight infants, 97
Vision, 514
Visual acuity, 514
Visual cliff experiment, 139
Visual impairment, 295
Visual perception, 138–140
Visual-recognition memory, 164–165
Visual-recognition memory measurement, 163
Voluntary active euthanasia, 652

Vygotsky's approach to cognitive development and classroom instruction, 303–304
Vygotsky's view, 232–235

Walking epidural, 93
Wear-and-tear theories of aging, 588–589
Wechsler Intelligence Scale for Children-Revised (WISC-IV), 316, 317, 318
Weight, changes in weight, 513
Wellness and illness, 521–523

Whole-language approaches to reading, 313
Wisdom, role of, 610–611
Work and retirement, 619–622
Working memory, 302, 535

X-linked genes, 52

Zone of proximal development (ZPD), 233–234, 303
Zygote, 48
Zygote intrafallopian transfer (ZIFT), 74

	ADOLESCENCE (12 to 20 years)	YOUNG ADULTHOOD (20 to 40 years)
PHYSICAL DEVELOPMENT		
	• Girls begin the adolescent growth spurt around age 10, boys around age 12. • Girls reach puberty around age 11 or 12, boys around age 13 or 14. • Primary sexual characteristics develop (affecting the reproductive organs), as do secondary sexual characteristics (pubic and underarm hair in both sexes, breasts in girls, deep voices in boys).	• Physical capabilities peak in 20s, including strength, senses, coordination, and reaction time. • Growth is mostly complete, although some organs, including the brain, continue to grow. • For many young adults, obesity becomes a threat for the first time, as body fat increases. • Stress can become a significant health threat. • In the mid-30s, disease replaces accidents as the leading cause of death.
COGNITIVE DEVELOPMENT	• Abstract thought prevails. Adolescents use formal logic to consider problems in the abstract. • Relative, not absolute, thinking is typical. • Verbal, mathematical, and spatial skills improve. • Adolescents are able to think hypothetically, divide attention, and monitor thought through metacognition. • Egocentrism develops, with a sense that one is always being observed. Self-consciousness and introspection are typical. • A sense of invulnerability can lead adolescents to ignore danger.	• As world experience increases, thought becomes more flexible and subjective, geared to adept problem solving. • Intelligence is applied to long-term goals involving career, family, and society. • Significant life events of young adulthood may shape cognitive development.
SOCIAL/ PERSONALITY DEVELOPMENT	• Self-concept becomes organized and accurate and reflects others' perceptions. Self-esteem grows differentiated. • Defining identity is a key task. Peer relationships provide social comparison and help define acceptable roles. Popularity issues become acute; peer pressure can enforce conformity. • Adolescents' quest for autonomy can bring conflict with parents as family roles are renegotiated. • Sexuality assumes importance in identity formation. Dating begins.	• Forming intimate relationships becomes highly important. Commitment may be partly determined by the attachment style developed in infancy. • Marriage and children bring developmental changes, often stressful. Divorce may result, with new stresses. • Identity is largely defined in terms of work, as young adults consolidate their careers.
THEORIES & THEORISTS		
Jean Piaget	Formal operations stage	
Erik Erikson	Identity-versus-confusion stage	Intimacy-versus-isolation stage
Sigmund Freud	Genital stage	
Lawrence Kohlberg	Postconventional morality level may be reached	